Road to Victory

ROAD TO VICTORY

WINSTON S. CHURCHILL
1941–1945

by
Martin Gilbert

HEINEMANN : LONDON

William Heinemann Ltd
10 Upper Grosvenor Street, London W1X 9PA

LONDON   MELBOURNE   TORONTO

JOHANNESBURG   AUCKLAND

434 29186 2
First published 1986
© 1986 C & T Publications Ltd

Printed and bound in Great Britain by
Richard Clay (The Chaucer Press) Ltd
Bungay, Suffolk

Contents

Maps

between pages 1354 and 1371

Illustrations

Front Jacket

1 Crossing the Rhine, 25 March 1945 (*Imperial War Museum*)

Section 1

2 Washington, December 1941, on the White House lawn (*Imperial War Museum*).

3 Addressing a Joint Session of Congress, Boxing Day, 1941 (*Imperial War Museum*).

4 Above the Atlantic, 14 January 1942 (*Keystone Press Agency*).

5 With Maisky and Molotov, 26 May 1942 (*Camera Press*).

6 On Soviet soil for the first time, 13 August 1942 (*Broadwater Collection, Churchill College, Cambridge*).

7 In Casablanca, with his son Randolph, January 1943 (*Imperial War Museum*).

8 With Roosevelt at Casablanca, January 1943 (*Joan Bright Astley Albums*).

9 Churchill's team, Casablanca (*Joan Bright Astley Albums*).

10 Roosevelt's team, Casablanca (*Joan Bright Astley Albums*).

11 In the cockpit of his 'Commando' (*Imperial War Museum*).

12 With President Inönü of Turkey, 31 January 1943 (*Broadwater Collection*).

13 In the Roman amphitheatre at Carthage, 1 June 1943 (*Imperial War Museum*).

14 With General Marshall and General Eisenhower, Algiers, 3 June 1943 (*Imperial War Museum*).

Section 2

15 With his daughter Mary, Quebec, August 1943 (*Imperial War Museum*).

Dedicated to
Ilana Kholmiansky,
her husband Michael,
her son Maxim,
her brother-in-law Alexander,
and to all their friends, and mine,
with affection and hope

Preface

THIS volume covers Churchill's life from the Japanese attack on British, Dutch and American possessions in the Far East in December 1941 to the defeat of Germany in Europe in May 1945. The story told here is based principally on two sets of unpublished material: Churchill's own private papers, put at my disposal by the Churchill Trustees, and the papers of the Prime Minister's Office and Ministry of Defence, available for public research at the Public Record Office, Kew. Also at Kew are the records of the War Cabinet and its principal Committees, including the Chiefs of Staff Committee, which were involved with Churchill in the day by day making of British war policy.

The story of the wartime conferences, a main area of Churchill's efforts, is told whenever possible from transcripts of the meetings prepared at the time. Most of these transcripts are likewise in the Public Record Office, Kew, as are the papers of the Foreign Office, the War Office, the Air Ministry, the Admiralty and other Government departments on whose documents I have drawn. Among other sets of papers available at Kew are those of two of Churchill's closest colleagues of the war years, the Secretary of State for Foreign Affairs, Anthony Eden, and the head of Churchill's Defence Staff, General Sir Hastings Ismay.

As with each of the earlier volumes of this biography I am grateful to Her Majesty The Queen, who graciously gave me permission to seek guidance on various points from the Royal Archives, and to make use of the letters which her father sent to Churchill on many occasions during the war. For help in answering my various queries relating to the Royal Archives I should like to thank Sir Robin Mackworth-Young, Librarian, Windsor Castle, his successor Oliver Everett, and the other members of the staff of the Royal Archives for their courtesy over many years.

I am grateful to Her Majesty Queen Elizabeth The Queen Mother for permission to reproduce an extract from one of her letters to Churchill; and to Sir Martin Gilliat for his help on an historical matter relating to Her Majesty. I am also grateful to His Royal Highness the Duke of Kent for the text of several letters which Churchill sent to his mother, and for his help in answering my queries concerning them.

I am grateful to the editor of *The Times*, for allowing me to make two appeals for recollections and materials through his letter columns, the first in 1968 and the second in 1983; and to the late Roy Plomley, for encouraging me to make a similar appeal on Desert Island Discs. The response to both the appeals was substantial, bringing me information about several episodes which would otherwise have remained unknown.

Churchill's grandson, Winston S. Churchill MP, has also made material available to me, including his grandfather's wartime photograph albums.

In the decade before I began work on this biography, I was fortunate to have several conversations with three men who were in close contact with Churchill during the years of this volume: Field Marshal Viscount Alanbrooke, Lord Beaverbrook, and Viscount Chandos.

In the late autumn of 1968, following Randolph Churchill's death, I was asked to continue the work which he had taken up to the outbreak of the First World War. In doing so, I was fortunate to be able to make use of an interview which he had conducted, a year earlier, with John Bevan, who, from 1942 to 1945, was head of the London Controlling Section, responsible for the British strategic deception plans, as well as for the cover plans for Churchill's journeys.

Since October 1968, when I began the preliminary work collecting material for this volume, I was able to talk to many of Churchill's colleagues and contemporaries who had worked with him during the war years. All those to whom I spoke were most generous of their time and recollections, as well as providing me with a considerable amount of historical material in the form of diaries, letters and documents. In the last months of 1968, in 1969 and 1970, I was fortunate to have a number of talks with Field Marshal Montgomery of Alamein, Field Marshal Alexander of Tunis, Lord Casey, Air Marshal Sir Richard Peirse, and, during a visit to Ankara in the summer of 1969, with Ismet Inönü, the former President of the Turkish Republic. I was later to have several talks with the Earl of Avon, who guided me to one essential archival source. Earl Mountbatten of Burma gave me many vivid memories at a luncheon in London on 15 January 1975.

I am also grateful to Marshal of the Royal Air Force Sir Arthur Harris, for his help both in 1969 and again in 1984, a few months before his death; and to W. Averell Harriman for his kindness in discussing with me in detail his recollections of Churchill and Stalin during the Moscow meetings of August 1942 and October 1944.

During the course of my researches, Churchill's daughter, Sarah, Lady Audley, gave me graphic accounts of her own wartime recollections of travels with her father, as did his daughter Lady Soames, who also made available to me material from her own and her mother's archives, and has always been most encouraging to me in my task.

Four members of Churchill's wartime Private Office have been exceptionally helpful in providing me with personal recollections, with documents from their private archives, and with comments and guidelines. In this regard, I cannot thank sufficiently Sir John Martin, Churchill's Principal Private Secretary during the years covered by this volume, who also read the typescript; Sir John Peck, who answered innumerable queries; Christopher Dodds, who gave me his recollections of work in the Private Office in the summer of 1944, and Sir John Colville, who not only gave me considerable help in answering my queries, but made available to me his private diary of the war years, which was then unpublished.

Another member of Churchill's Private Office staff who has given me help over many years was Patrick Kinna, who frequently accompanied Churchill overseas, and provided me with his recollections of each of these journeys. Similar help was given to me by Sir Richard Pim, head of Churchill's Map Room, who gave me access to his own unpublished recollections, and was always willing to try to answer every query.

From Churchill's Defence Office, I have received continual help and encouragement from Lieutenant-General Sir Ian Jacob, who read my typescript, had many important comments, and made available to me his diary and notes of several of the wartime conferences at which he was present.

Churchill's secretaries of the war years have likewise been generous of their time and recollections. With this, as with previous volumes, Kathleen Hill recalled many episodes of working with Churchill, and answered my queries. Elizabeth Nel gave me access to her wartime letters home, shared her recollections with me, and extended her hospitality to me in distant Port Elizabeth. Marian Walker Spicer let me see her personal diary of the war years, and also answered my many questions, as did Lady Onslow. From General Ismay's staff, Joan Bright Astley provided me with valuable material and important memories of several wartime conferences. As with previous volumes, Grace Hamblin has been ever willing to help with points of detail and recollections, and made available to me her wartime letters of her visit to Russia with Clementine Churchill.

As with the two previous volumes, I have been considerably helped by Sir William Deakin, who has discussed with me many of the controversial episodes in these pages, both from his personal recollections, and from the perspective of one who was the first to study in detail the voluminous files of Churchill's wartime premiership.

For help on all aspects of Signals Intelligence, I am grateful to Edward Thomas, who has unfailingly answered my questions, and who read the typescript with an eagle eye. I am also deeply indebted to Sir David Hunt for his thorough scrutiny of the text, and for his many important suggestions.

On military, naval and air matters, I have been guided once more by Dr Christopher Dowling, Keeper of the Department of Education and Publications, Imperial War Museum, who has not only answered many queries himself, but has guided me to others with expert knowledge elsewhere.

This volume, and the last, was read in proof by John Cruesemann, to whose scrutiny I am much indebted, as also to Elisabeth Barker, for her many helpful comments and suggestions, the last of which she had sent me only a few days before her death. I am also grateful to Janet Bord for her most thorough scrutiny of the text in its final stage. The maps were drawn for this volume by Terry Bicknell. In preparing the index, I was helped by Natalie Gilbert and Jane Steiner.

No historian of British policy in the Second World War can work without the documents available for research at the Public Record Office, Kew. My own indebtedness to the Keeper of the Public Record Office, G. H. Martin, and to his staff, particularly those of the Search Rooms and the Stacks, is immense. I am also grateful to Elizabeth Forbes, of the Cabinet Office Historical Section, and to the Staff at Hepburn House.

Many people sent me accounts of their meetings with Churchill during the war, or of episodes at which he was present and which they witnessed. I greatly appreciate their willingness to help me and, in many instances, to talk to me or to correspond on points of detail. For this help, I should like to thank the Rt Hon. Julian Amery, Douglas Baird-Murray, Lady Jane Bethell, Commander Kenneth Cohen, J. H. Colegrave, George Davy, Sir Reginald Dorman Smith, Brenda M. Duncan, Lord Duncan Sandys, Colonel Peter Dunphie, Paul Falla, Alistair Forbes, Sir Laurence Grafftey-Smith, Admiral Sir Guy Grantham, Dr Adam Gray, Christopher Harland, C. W. Hill, Vice-Admiral Sir Cecil Hughes Hallett, Wing-Commander Sir Archibald James, F. Cyril James, Professor R. V. Jones, Anita Leslie,

Maurice Lush, Denis Kelly, John J. McCloy, Sir Donald MacDougall, Doris Miles, Sir Guy Millard, Sir Charles Mott-Radclyffe, Squadron-Leader Vernon Noble, Sir Michael Perrin, Sir Walter Pretyman, Dorothy Pugh, Professor R. J. V. Pulvertaft, George Rance, Sir Patrick Reilly, Sir Frank Roberts, Robert Robertson, Robin Sanderson, Julian Sandys QC, Lord Segal of Wytham, Iris R. Spiers, John Stewart, S. C. Stratton, Ian Todd, Donald Wiedenmayer, Sir Edgar Williams and Alan W. Wright.

It would have been impossible to prepare such a substantial amount of material for publication without the help and guidance of many experts, archivists and custodians of archives, all of whom have been exceptionally generous of their time in answering my many queries over many years. I am most grateful for the assistance given by the 2nd Viscount Alanbrooke; Eversley Belfield; M. A. Bennett, Buyer, Harrods; Robert Browder; A. Butterworth; Alan Campbell-Johnson; Jeremy Carver; Ned Chase; Percy Cohen; Lady Coleridge; Miss H. Collyer, Acting Divisional Nursing Officer, St Bartholomew's Hospital; Tom Dalby; the Duke of Devonshire; Piers Dixon; M. D. Drury, Historic Buildings Representative for South East, The National Trust; Dr Michael Dunnill; Robert Edmonds; C. R. Ferriroli, National Book League; Abram Games; Richard Gott; Bruce Gray; G. V. Hamilton, Managing Director, Fortnum & Mason plc; Dr Philip Hanson; C. W. Harrison, Archivist, London Borough of Lewisham; A. D. K. Hawkyard, Archivist, Harrow School; Dr Roger Highfield; K. Holdsworth; Roger T. Jones; Kathleen Kelly; Robert Lacey; Richard Lamb; Dr Hugh L'Etang; S. K. Lewer; Julian Lewis; Norman Longmate; Major G. H. van Loo; Professor Richard Lovell; Professor Arthur Marder; Brigadier P. W. Mead; P. R. Melton, Naval Historical Branch, Ministry of Defence; Patricia J. Methven, Archivist, King's College, London; Lord Moyne; K. Murphy, Archivist, The *Guardian*; Jan Nowak; Garrison Norton; Miss Dorothy Osmond; Sylvia Owide, Secretary to Garry H. Weston, Fortnum & Mason plc; Sir Michael Palliser; James Parton; the Rt Hon. J. Enoch Powell; David Preiskel; Robert Price; Steve Race; Captain Stephen Roskill; Lady Rowan; Professor Oleg Rzheshevsky; Suzanne Savery, Curator of Research Materials, Fort Lauderdale Historical Society; A. D. H. Simonsz, Counsellor for Press and Cultural Affairs, Royal Netherlands Embassy; Dr Harold Smith; A. W. Spence; Andrzej Suchcitz, Assistant Keeper of Archives, the Polish Institute and Sikorski Museum; Bickham Sweet-Escott; Lord Trenchard; Eleanor Vallis, Archives Assistant, the Library, Nuffield College, Oxford; Aenid de Vine Hunt; Tony Whittome, Hutchinson Publishing Group Limited; Marjorie Wolf; and Dr Ronald W. Zweig.

Beginning in the summer of 1980, the material in the Churchill papers on which the first draft of this book was based was photocopied and sorted, first by William Sturge, and later by Larry Arnn and Taffy Sassoon. In the latter phases of the work, I was also helped in this task by Joshua Layish and Penina Stone. When this volume was in its first draft, in the late autumn of 1985, John Ramster helped me to resolve many of the final queries. I am also grateful to my former history master at Highgate School, Alan W. Palmer, and to W. Roger Smith of William Heinemann Ltd, for help on many points of detail.

For undertaking the typing of my manuscript, and then of the first draft of the typescript, a total of more than a million words, I am grateful to Sue Rampton, without whose patience and energy the task could not possibly have been completed so swiftly. She was assisted, in the mechanical sense, by the Research Machines 380Z computer, which transformed her work, as she transformed mine. In the final phase of work on the typescript, I was helped by the considerable effort and perseverance of Brenda Harry.

I am once again grateful to the Warden and Fellows of Merton College, Oxford, for their patience and consideration towards a colleague whose work has forced him for more than seventeen years, to be more noticeable by his absence than by his participation, and for their generosity in giving me substantial photocopying facilities.

It would not have been possible to complete the considerable research involved, first in tracking down and then sorting and sifting the mass of material for the war years, had it not been for the considerable generosity of several individuals and institutions, who during the period when this volume was in preparation, provided essential resources. I am particularly grateful in this regard to Professor Harry Jaffa, and to Carlton and Eileen Appleby; to F. Bartlett Watt, Professor D. McCormack Smyth and the Churchill Society for the Advancement of Parliamentary Democracy; to Robert Hastings; and to the Rockefeller Foundation, which awarded me one of its annual Fellowships.

At the end of the day, for this volume as for its predecessors, my principal thanks must go to my wife Susie, who for more than fourteen years has given so much of her time, her energy and her skill to ensure that no aspect of the work should fall below the standards she has sought to set. If the reader of these pages emerges content, it is in large measure due to her efforts, and to her determination that the story should be told as accurately and honestly as possible.

Merton College,   Martin Gilbert
Oxford
25 October 1985

1

'Extraordinary Changes'

IMMEDIATELY he heard of the Japanese attack on Pearl Harbour on 7 December 1941, Churchill made plans to travel to Washington to see President Roosevelt. His intention was to leave London on December 10, embarking at the Clyde on the following morning. The fullest cypher staff should be taken, he minuted to the head of his Defence Office, General Ismay, on December 8, adding that arrangements should be made 'for keeping informed both ends, especially in regard to Libyan telegrams'.[1]

These Libyan telegrams, sent daily from General Auchinleck, told of the continuing success of the Western Desert offensive, codename 'Crusader', which had been launched on November 18, and was intended not only to drive the German and Italian forces from Libya, but also, by forcing the Germans to keep an embattled military force in the Western Desert, to offer the Red Army a measure of relief on the eastern front. 'Last night Tobruk garrison advanced westward and made good progress,' Auchinleck telegraphed to Churchill on December 8.[2]

During December 8 Churchill also telephoned Anthony Eden, who was then in Scotland on his way to Russia, to propose that Eden should continue to Russia, while he, Churchill, set off across the Atlantic. 'I demurred,' Eden later recalled, 'saying that I did not see how we could both be away at once. He said we could. The emphasis of the war had shifted, what now mattered was the intentions of our two great allies. We must each go to one of them.'[3]

Eden sought to dissuade Churchill from leaving so soon. 'I still rather wish,' he telegraphed on December 9, 'that you could postpone a fortnight till my return.'[4] But at the War Cabinet on December 8,

[1] 'Most Secret', 'Only to be handled in a box', 8 December 1941: Premier papers, 3/458/3.
[2] 'Susan' No. 1643, 8 December 1941: Premier papers, 3/290/1. Auchinleck was the Commander-in-Chief, Middle East, the Eighth Army being commanded by General Ritchie.
[3] The Earl of Avon, *The Eden Memoirs, The Reckoning*, London 1965, page 285.
[4] Telegram of 9 December 1941, unnumbered sent 7.31 p.m.: Churchill papers, 20/46.

Churchill had obtained his colleagues' approval for his visit to Roosevelt, and he at once wrote to the King, explaining that 'The whole plan of Anglo-American defence and attack has to be concerted in the light of reality. We have also to be careful,' Churchill added, 'that our share of munitions and other aid which we are receiving from the United States does not suffer more than is, I fear, inevitable.' [1]

In a telegram to Roosevelt on December 9, Churchill explained the purpose of his proposed visit: to review 'the whole war plan', and to discuss the problems of production and distribution, problems which were causing him 'concern', and which he felt 'can best be settled on the highest executive level'. For this reason, he would take Lord Beaverbrook with him: Beaverbrook who, as Minister of Supply, was aware of the weaknesses in America's existing production schedules. Churchill ended his telegram to Roosevelt: 'It would also be a very great pleasure to me to meet you again, and the sooner the better.' [2]

In response to Churchill's suggestion, Roosevelt told the British Ambassador to Washington, Lord Halifax, that 'on security grounds' as regards Churchill's return voyage, he did not 'at all like the idea' of Churchill's visit. He would prefer a meeting in Bermuda, 'which would be secret' and would 'save' Churchill's time. The first possible date for a meeting, Roosevelt added, would be January 7. [3] 'We do not think there is any serious danger about the return journey,' Churchill replied. 'There is however great danger in our not having a full discussion on the highest level about the extreme gravity of the naval position, as well as upon all the production and allocation issues involved.' He had hoped, Churchill added, 'to start tomorrow night', but would now postpone his sailing until he received details of the rendezvous from Roosevelt. 'I never felt so sure about final victory,' Churchill added, 'but only concerted action will achieve it.' [4]

Further messages from Roosevelt fixed the date of their meeting for just before Christmas, and in Washington as Churchill had wished. Before leaving, he opposed a suggestion at the War Cabinet that Britain should urge Stalin to declare war on Japan. In view of 'the enormous service' which Russia was giving 'by hammering the German Army on her Western front', he told his colleagues on December 10, he did not wish to ask Russia to declare war on Japan: to do so, he explained, 'would make it impossible for Russia to bring

---

[1] Letter of 8 December 1941, 'Most Secret': Royal Archives.
[2] Prime Minister's Personal Telegram, T.947, 'Private and Personal', 9 December 1941, 'Most Secret', Foreign Office No. 6812 to Washington: Premier papers, 3/458/5.
[3] Telegram No. 5695 of 9 December 1941: Churchill papers, 20/46.
[4] Prime Minister's Personal Telegram, T.962, 'Secret', 10 December 1941: Premier papers, 3/458/5.

divisions from Siberia which might be of incalculable value on her western front'. Churchill also pointed out that, as a result of Japan's attack on British possessions in the Far East, 'he could not now offer the Russians' the ten squadrons of aircraft promised for their southern front.[1] In view of the 'evident strong wish of the United States, China and I expect Australia', Churchill told Eden, 'that Russia should come in against Japan, you should not do anything to discourage a favourable movement if Stalin feels strong enough to do so'. 'All I meant,' Churchill went on to explain, 'was that we should not put undue pressure upon him considering how little we have been able to contribute.'[2]

The telegrams from Auchinleck continued to bring Churchill encouraging news. 'Consider tide turned' was the message on December 9.[3] This was followed by a second telegram that day, from Advanced Headquarters, Eighth Army: 'We made good progress yesterday, though enemy is still fighting stubborn delaying action.'[4] On December 10 Auchinleck informed Churchill: 'Enemy is apparently in full retreat but his remaining tanks are still covering his withdrawal. El Adem is in our hands; South African and Indian troops joined hands with British troops from Tobruk, and I think it is now permissible to claim that siege of Tobruk has been raised.'[5] On December 11 Auchinleck telegraphed in triumph: 'We are pressing our pursuit vigorously.'[6]

On December 11 Germany and Italy declared war on the United States. By this declaration, Hitler and Mussolini brought the United States into the war in Europe. On the Moscow front, the Red Army had halted the German advance. In North Africa, British troops continued to drive the Germans and Italians westward across the Libyan desert. During December 11 Churchill gave the House of Commons a survey of the war, broadcast that same night, and using, as he later wrote, 'the coldest form of factual narration'.[7] Of the slow progress of General Auchinleck's advance in the western desert since November 18, Churchill commented: 'Victory is traditionally elusive. Accidents happen. Mistakes are made. Sometimes right things turn out wrong and wrong things turn out right. War is very difficult, especially to those who are taking part in it or conducting it.'

[1] War Cabinet No. 126 of 1941, 10 December 1941, 6 p.m.: Cabinet papers, 65/24.
[2] Prime Minister's Personal Telegram, T.976, 'Haughty' No. 23, 12 December 1941: Churchill papers, 20/46.
[3] 'Susan' No. 1644, 9 December 1941: Premier papers, 3/290/1.
[4] 'Susan' No. 1646, 7 p.m., 10 December 1941: Premier papers, 3/290/1.
[5] 'Susan' No. 1646, 7 p.m., 10 December 1941: Premier papers, 3/290/1.
[6] CS/346, 11 December 1941: Premier papers, 3/290/1.
[7] Winston S. Churchill, *The Second World War*, volume 3, London 1950, page 552.

Churchill was confident, however, that Auchinleck would, in the end, destroy the entire German and Italian armed forces in Cyrenaica, as he had set out to do, sustained, as he was, by 'an absolutely unrelenting spirit of the offensive', not only in his generals, 'but in the troops and in every man'.

At sea, the loss of British merchant shipping had been substantially reduced, and a 'great recovery' was in progress in Britain's shipping capacity. 'These,' Churchill said, 'are the foundations upon which we live and carry forward our cause.' In the east, there had been a 'striking change'. Moscow, Leningrad and the oilfields of Baku had all remained under Soviet control, as the Russian armies had resisted the onslaught with 'glorious steadfastness and energy', halted the German advance, and forced the German armies back, 'inspired by the feeling of advance after long retreat and of vengeance after monstrous injury'.

A week earlier, Churchill pointed out, 'the three great spheres' of Libya, the Atlantic and Russia 'would almost have covered the scene of war with which we were concerned'. Since then, Japan had attacked Britain and the United States. 'I know that I speak for the United States as well as for Britain,' he continued, 'when I say that we would all rather perish than be conquered. And on this basis, putting it at its worst, there are quite a lot of us to be killed.' [1]

The widening of the war, so frightening a prospect for those countries not previously closely engaged in it, such as Australia, was for Churchill a miracle of deliverance from more than two years of British isolation, weakness, and omnipresent danger of defeat. The accession of the United States as a 'full war partner', he telegraphed to John Curtin, the Prime Minister of Australia, on December 12, 'makes amends for all and makes the end certain'. [2] 'We have no longer any need to strike attitudes to win United States' sympathy,' he wrote to Attlee that same day, in opposing a reduction in food rations in Britain, 'we are all in it together, and they are eating better meals than we are.' To reduce the ration at such a moment 'would savour of panic'. Britain's position had 'immeasurably improved' by the 'full involvement' of the United States. [3]

American preoccupation with Japan would also clearly affect the promised supplies to Russia: indeed, in the immediate aftermath of Pearl Harbour, all such supplies had been halted. 'I hope to loosen this up,' Churchill had informed Eden on the eve of his departure, adding:

[1] *Hansard*, 11 December 1941, columns 1686–97.
[2] Prime Minister's Personal Telegram, T.974, 12 December 1941: Churchill papers, 20/49.
[3] Prime Minister's Personal Minute, M.109a/1, 12 December 1941: Churchill papers, 20/36.

'Am just off.'[1] 'God speed to your journey from us all,' was Eden's message from Murmansk.[2]

Churchill left London by night train on the evening of December 12, accompanied by Lord Beaverbrook. Churchill asked his daughter Mary, a Lance Bombardier in the ATS, to travel north with him. Also on the train was Kathleen Hill, Churchill's secretary and stenographer for the previous five years.

As Churchill travelled, he worked his way through his boxes, dictating to Mrs Hill, and contemplating many different aspects of the war. Commenting on a note from his Parliamentary Private Secretary, Colonel Harvie-Watt, that his broadcast was thought by Members of Parliament to have been 'ill-advised', as he had appeared 'very tired', Churchill replied: 'Yes. Well, who forces me? & why am I not allowed a gramophone record of a statement in the House?': a reference to Parliament's refusal, since he had become Prime Minister in May 1940, to allow his House of Commons speeches to be recorded and then re-broadcast.[3] Replying to a suggestion from the Viceroy of India that negotiations should be opened with the Indian nationalists, on the basis of their demands for 'real power', Churchill minuted: 'Personally, I would rather accord India independence than that we should have to keep an army there to hold down the fighting races for the benefit of the Hindu priesthood and caucus.'[4]

Churchill's principal thoughts during the journey were, however, on the question of future war strategy, and on how most effectively to involve the United States in the Mediterranean and European war. In a minute to Sir Dudley Pound, who was in an adjoining compartment, Churchill expressed his hopes for an American military landing at Casablanca, to 'decide the action of French North Africa', and detach it from Vichy France.[5] To his friend, Field Marshal Smuts, the Prime Minister of South Africa, Churchill wrote of his hopes to 'procure' assistance from Roosevelt for a 'forward policy' in French North Africa, and also in West Africa, but, he cautioned Smuts, 'they may well be too much preoccupied with the war with Japan'.[6]

The war with Japan was also a feature of Churchill's own changing

[1] Prime Minister's Personal Telegram, T.972, 'Personal and Most Secret', 12 December 1941: Churchill papers, 20/46

[2] 'Hectic' No. 6, 'Most Secret', 'Personal', 13 December 1941: Churchill papers, 20/46.

[3] 'Report by Parliamentary Private Secretary', 12 December 1941, and marginal annotations: Harvie-Watt papers.

[4] Prime Minister's Personal Minute, M 1103/1 (to Leo Amery and Sir Edward Bridges), 13 December 1941: Churchill papers, 20/36.

[5] Prime Minister's Personal Minute, M(A)2, 'Secret', 13 December 1941: Churchill papers, 20/36. 'A' referred to 'Arcadia', the codeword for the Washington visit.

[6] Prime Minister's Personal Telegram, T.973, 'Most Secret', Dominions Office No. 1368, 12 December 1941: Churchill papers, 20/46.

perspective. On December 11 he had asked the Chiefs of Staff Committee if the 18th Division, then rounding the Cape on its way to the Middle East, could be diverted to Burma. The Chiefs of Staff agreed to this, subject to the necessary recommendation of the Joint Planning Staff.[1] Two days later, on December 12, Churchill informed General Auchinleck that the 18th Division would be diverted to Bombay, required there 'by grievous need of strengthening long-starved India and enabling a stronger resistance to be made to Japanese advance against Burma and down Malay peninsula'. Meanwhile, Auchinleck's command was to be extended eastwards to include Iraq and Persia 'thus giving local unity of command', Churchill explained, 'in event of Turkish and Caucasus danger reviving'. General Wavell, who had formerly covered these areas from India, 'must now look east', and would be given command of the Burma front. In addition to the 18th Division, Wavell would receive the four fighter squadrons which were also rounding the Cape, intended for the Caucasus.

'I am glad things are going well in your grand campaign,' Churchill ended. 'Try increasingly to mention names of regiments about which enemy is already informed. It gives so much satisfaction here.'[2]

In a telegram to Wavell, announcing the reinforcements which were on their way to him, Churchill noted that the Russian victories and Auchinleck's Libyan advance 'have for the time being relieved danger of German irruption into Syrian-Iraq-Persian theatre'. Wavell should 'marry' the new forces at his disposal as he thought best and 'work them into the Eastern fighting front to the highest advantage'.[3]

Churchill's train reached Gourock, on the Clyde, on the morning of December 13. In a telephone call from Gourock, Churchill warned General Ismay 'in the strongest terms', as Ismay reported to the Chiefs of Staff Committee that morning, of the need to send towards the Far East, as fast as it could be done, 'everything that was fit for the battle', including if possible 'at least' six squadrons of bombers. There was however, Churchill added, 'no question' of taking anything away from Auchinleck's advance 'until the victory had been won'.[4]

From Gourock, Churchill was taken by boat to the *Duke of York*,

[1] Chiefs of Staff Committee No. 417 of 1941, 11 December 1941: Cabinet papers, 79/16. Churchill was not present at this meeting, at which Admiral of the Fleet Sir Dudley Pound took the chair. The three others present were Air Chief Marshal Sir Charles Portal, General Sir Alan Brooke (who felt that the 18th Division might be needed to support Turkey, 'whose position was of even greater importance than before') and Major General Sir Hastings Ismay.
[2] 'Susan' No. 146, Prime Minister's Personal Telegram, T.977, 'Private', 12 December 1941: Premier papers, 3/290/1, telegram No. 200.
[3] Telegram No. 57503, 'Private', 12 December 1941: Premier papers, 3/290/1, telegram No. 201.
[4] Chiefs of Staff Committee No. 421 of 1941, 10.30 a.m., 13 December 1941: Cabinet papers,

sister ship of the *Prince of Wales* which had been sunk off Malaya three days earlier. 'Every day on board,' wrote Colonel Jacob, 'brings home the bitterness of that blow.' [1]

Churchill dictated his messages while on board the battleship to Patrick Kinna, who had accompanied him on the first visit to Roosevelt in August. [2] In these messages, Churchill reiterated his confidence in the outcome of the war. 'Entry of the United States as a full partner seems to me decisive on final result,' he telegraphed on December 14 to Alfred Duff Cooper, Britain's Minister resident in Singapore. Churchill also told Duff Cooper that the 18th Division, 'now rounding Cape', as well as four fighter squadrons and some anti-aircraft and anti-tank guns, were being diverted from Egypt to the Far East. As to the air re-inforcements for which Duff Cooper had asked, 'Libyan battle goes well,' Churchill pointed out, 'but till we have a definite decision I cannot withdraw anything from there.' Arrangements were being made however, he added, 'to transfer four to six Bomber Squadrons to your theatre at earliest possible moment thereafter'. [3]

On the following day, Churchill turned his attention to the future of Singapore itself. 'Beware,' he minuted for the Chiefs of Staff Committee on December 15, 'lest troops required for ultimate defence Singapore Island and fortress are not used up or cut off in Malay peninsula. Nothing compares in importance with the fortress,' and he went on to ask: 'Are you sure we shall have enough troops for the prolonged defence?' The Chiefs of Staff might consider, Churchill wrote, moving the 9th Australian Division from Palestine to Singapore, and he ended his minute: 'Report action.' [4]

While on board ship, and amid violent gales, Churchill learned of the continuing success of the Russian counter-attacks launched at Tula on December 1, at Taganrog on December 2 and at Tikhvin on December 8. 'It is impossible,' Churchill telegraphed to Stalin, 'to describe the relief with which I have heard each successive day of the wonderful victories on the Russian front. I never felt so sure of

---

79/16. General Brooke was in the Chair. The others present were Vice-Admiral H. R. Moore (Vice-Chief of the Naval Staff), Air Chief Marshal Sir Wilfrid Freeman (Vice-Chief of the Air Staff), and Ismay.

[1] 'Operation "Arcadia", Washington Conference, December 1941': Jacob papers.

[2] The Member of Parliament Charles Mott-Radclyffe later recalled: 'One of the most remarkable characters on the Prime Minister's Staff was his shorthand-writer Patrick Kinna, who shadowed him everywhere, taking down almost every sentence uttered from some discreet place of vantage, within hearing but out of sight. He would then disappear and type out the memorandum or the draft telegram.' (Sir Charles Mott-Radclyffe, *Foreign Body in the Eye*, London 1975, page 132.)

[3] Prime Minister's Personal Telegram, T.996, 'Lanca', No. 53, 'Personal and Secret', 14 December 1941: Churchill papers, 20/46.

[4] 'Grey' No. 8, 15 December 1941: Churchill papers, 20/50.

the outcome of the war.'¹ Eden delivered this message to Stalin in Moscow, reporting to Churchill on December 17: 'I am sure that he is entirely with us against Hitler.' Eden added that Stalin 'was much pleased with your message'.²

In the Far East, Japanese forces were pressing down the Malay Peninsula, invading Penang on December 17, and seizing intact a large number of small craft which were soon to enable a series of Japanese amphibian attacks further down the coast. 'The House is very depressed about Malaya,' Harold Nicolson noted that day, 'and fears that Singapore may fall. The Tories are angry with Winston, and are in fact in a bad mood.'³ Events in the Far East, Clement Attlee wrote to Churchill three days later, 'have rather disturbed public, press and MPs, most of whom seem to have been oblivious of danger of which we have been conscious for months'.⁴

The Far East situation worsened daily. On December 17 Japanese forces had landed in North Borneo, Dutch forces having previously withdrawn, destroying the oil-fields as they left. On the night of December 18 Japanese forces on the Chinese mainland effected a landing on the island of Hong Kong. In Malaya, isolated British units, sent to defend the northern regions of the Peninsula, were forced into retreat. On December 17 Duff Cooper had telegraphed to Churchill from Singapore 'we cannot hope to hold the greater part of Malaya', and he added: 'We cannot afford to fritter away our small resources.' The 'greatest danger', Duff Cooper warned, 'is that of our force being exhausted in a series of separate campaigns, e.g. the command reserve is already engaged in the North West'.⁵

On December 18 the British forces in Kedah had been forced to evacuate. Urged to do so by Duff Cooper in Singapore, and with the support of General Dill on board the *Duke of York*, on December 19 Churchill ordered the British forces in Malaya to concentrate on the defence of Johore 'for the purpose of holding Singapore': 'nothing', he minuted to Ismay that same day 'must compete with maximum defence of Singapore'.⁶

'How calm we all are,' Clementine Churchill wrote to her husband

¹ Prime Minister's Personal Telegram, T.1013, 'Most Secret and Immediate', 'Grey' No. 3, 15 December 1941: Churchill papers, 20/47.
² 'Hectic' No. 15, 'Personal and Most Secret', 17 December 1941: Churchill papers, 20/47.
³ Harold Nicolson diary, 17 December 1941: Nigel Nicolson (editor), *Harold Nicolson, Diaries and Letters 1939–1945*, London 1967, page 198.
⁴ Letter of 20 December 1941, copy, Attlee papers.
⁵ 'Duchy' No. 76, 'Most Secret and Personal', Singapore, 17 December 1941: Churchill papers, 20/47.
⁶ 'Grey' No. 22, 19 December 1941: Churchill papers, 20/50.

that same December 19. 'Hong Kong threatened immediately, Singapore ultimately? perhaps not so ultimately, Borneo invaded— Burma? to say nothing of the blows to America in the Pacific.' Her letter ended: 'Well my beloved Winston. May God keep you and inspire you to make good plans with the President. It's a horrible world at present, Europe over-run by the Nazi hogs and the Far East by yellow Japanese lice.'[1]

In Cyrenaica, Auchinleck's forces continued their steady advance. 'Our troops are in full pursuit and have already made considerable progress,' Auchinleck had telegraphed on December 17, 'while our armoured forces and mobile field columns are moving against enemy lines of retreat.'[2] 'Pursuit of retreating enemy continued throughout yesterday,' Auchinleck reported on the morning of December 18, 'being pressed relentlessly by our forces, which advanced 30 miles.'[3] An hour later he telegraphed again: 'Our bombers and fighters harassing enemy retreating columns continuously.'[4] A further telegram from Auchinleck on December 19 reported yet further successes: 'Our Air forces are making very heavy attacks on enemy and find excellent targets. There are signs of considerable enemy disorganization.'[5]

'Please continue,' Churchill telegraphed to Auchinleck on December 19, 'to send me your admirable accounts, which will help me in convincing American doubters of the wisdom of our Middle Eastern campaign.'[6]

For three days, the *Duke of York* went ahead of its escort, and he had 'thought it better', Churchill explained to Attlee, to maintain wireless silence.[7] As the battleship proceeded westward through storms and heavy seas, out of contact with London, Churchill dictated his thoughts on the future conduct of the war in a series of memoranda, the first of which, 'The Atlantic Front', was dictated on December 16, 'The Pacific Front' on December 17 and '1943' on December 18.

It was essential, Churchill stressed in 'The Atlantic Front', for Britain and the United States to send Russia the supplies they had promised 'without fail and punctually'. In this way alone, he wrote, 'shall we

---

[1] Letter of 18 December 1941: Mary Soames, *Clementine Churchill*, London 1979, page 311.
[2] 'Susan' No. 1657, 17 December 1941: Premier papers, 3/290/1.
[3] 'Susan' No. 1657, Cairo, 10 a.m., 18 December 1941: Premier papers, 3/290/1.
[4] 'Susan' No. 1660, Cairo, 11 a.m., 18 December 1941: Premier papers, 3/290/1.
[5] 'Susan' No. 1662, Cairo, 6 p.m., 19 December 1941: Premier papers, 3/290/1.
[6] Prime Minister's Personal Telegram, T.1043, 'Grey' No. 25, 19 December 1941: Churchill papers, 20/49.
[7] 'Grey' No. 24, sent 4.47 p.m., 19 December 1941: Premier papers, 3/458/6.

hold our influence over Stalin and be able to weave the mighty Russian effort into the general texture of the war'. This was the priority: but Russian successes might drive the Germans to attack Turkey and move southward. That threat was sufficient for Britain to make 'every effort' to encourage Turkey 'to resist a German inroad'. Efforts should also be made 'to win over French North Africa', offering the Vichy Government in France a choice—'a blessing or a cursing'.[1] The blessing would be an offer by Britain and the United States 'to re-establish France as a Great Power with her territories undiminished', except for Syria and the frontier zone of Spanish Morocco.

This offer to 're-establish' France would be backed, Churchill explained, by the 'active aid' of a British and United States Expeditionary Force, landing on the Atlantic seaboard of Morocco, and in Algeria and Tunisia, assisted by the advance of 'Acrobat' forces from the east. Such a campaign, Churchill wrote, 'must be fought in 1942'. As to General de Gaulle, he wrote, 'Through no particular fault of his own, he has not been of any important help to us. Indeed, his Movement has created new antagonisms in French minds.' British and American obligations to de Gaulle should be redefined, 'so as to make those obligations more closely dependent upon the eventual effort by him and the French nation to rehabilitate themselves'. If, Churchill explained, the Vichy Government 'were to act as we desire about French North Africa, the United States and Great Britain must labour to bring about a reconciliation between the Free French (de Gaullists) and those other Frenchmen who will have taken up arms once more against Germany. If, on the other hand, Vichy resists in collaboration with Germany and we have to fight our war into French North and West Africa, then the de Gaullists' Movement will be of value and must be aided and used to the full.'

Churchill's memorandum of December 16 also proposed the despatch of United States troops to Northern Ireland; their presence being known to Germany, and their 'actual numbers' magnified, would serve 'as a powerful additional deterrent against an attempt at invasion by Germany'. American bomber squadrons could also 'come into action' from the British Isles against Germany: the arrival in Britain of, 'say', twenty American bomber squadrons 'would be the most direct and effective reply to the Declaration of War by Germany upon the United States'.[2]

[1] 'Behold, I set before you this day a blessing and a curse,' (Deuteronomy, chapter 11, verse 26). 'And it shall come to pass, when the Lord thy God hath brought thee in unto the land whither thou goest to possess it, that thou shalt put the blessing upon mount Gerizim, and the curse upon mount Ebal' (Deuteronomy, chapter 11, verse 29).

[2] 'Part 1—The Atlantic Front', 16 December 1941, Defence Committee Memorandum 'Secret', No. 12 of 1942, 1 February 1942: Churchill papers, 4/235.

Churchill's memorandum of December 17, 'The Pacific Front', envisaged Singapore Island and fortress resisting the Japanese attacks 'for at least six months', although the naval base 'would not be usable' by either side. If the United States were to recover 'major sea control' in the Pacific Japan's armies in the Malay Peninsula, Indo-China, Siam and Burma would be 'immediately imperilled'. All would depend upon the commissioning, possibly by May 1942, of the two new American 16-inch-gun battleships. Meanwhile, as much 'interim offensive action' as possible would have to be devised by American, British and Dutch naval units, using 'every conceivable means'. It was difficult to say, Churchill concluded, how much injury Britain and America would have to suffer before naval supremacy was regained, how strongly the Japanese would fortify themselves in their new positions, 'and whether the Philippines and Singapore can hold out so long'.[1]

Churchill's third memorandum, '1943', dictated on December 18, envisaged that in the year 1943 British and American expeditions would be sent to recover 'places lost' to the Japanese, that Britain would be 'intact and more strongly prepared against invasion than ever before', and that the whole west and north African shores, from Dakar to the Suez Canal, and the whole Levant coast to the Turkish frontier, 'would be in Anglo-American hands'. A 'footing' might even have been established by 1943 in Sicily and Italy, 'with reactions inside Italy which might be highly favourable'. The war could only be ended, however, through one of two developments. The first was 'the defeat in Europe of the German armies'; the second, 'internal convulsions in Germany produced by the unfavourable course of the war, economic privations and the Allied bombing offensive'. But although a German 'internal collapse' was always possible, 'we must not count on this'. Plans must proceed upon the assumption that German army and airforce resistance to the allies would continue 'at its present level', assisted by 'increasingly numerous' U-boat flotillas. It was therefore necessary 'to prepare for the liberation of the captive countries of Western and Southern Europe by the landing, at suitable points, of British and American armies strong enough to enable the conquered populations to revolt'.

Churchill envisaged 'adequate and suitably equipped' Allied forces landing in 'several of the following countries', Norway, Denmark, Holland, Belgium, the French Channel coast and the French Atlantic coast, as well as Italy, 'and possibly the Balkans'. Following those Allied landings, the German garrisons 'would prove insufficient to cope both with the strength of the liberating forces and the fury of the revolting peoples'. Churchill went on to warn:

[1] 'Part II—The Pacific Front', 17 December 1941, Defence Committee Memorandum, 'Secret', No. 12 of 1942, 1 February 1942: Churchill papers, 4/235.

We must face here the usual clash between short-term and long-term projects. War is a constant struggle and must be waged from day to day. It is only with some difficulty and within limits that provision can be made for the future. Experience shows that forecasts are usually falsified and preparations always in arrear. Nevertheless, there must be a design and theme for bringing the war to a victorious end in a reasonable period. All the more is this necessary when under modern conditions no large-scale offensive operation can be launched without the preparation of elaborate technical apparatus.

Churchill envisaged 'the summer of 1943' as the date for the Anglo-American liberation of Europe. Plans should be made for all the landings he had mentioned, with 'three or four' picked out for the actual landings, as late as possible, 'so as to profit by the turn of events and make sure of secrecy'. These plans should be based upon armoured and mechanized forces capable of disembarking 'not at ports but on beaches'. By maintaining command of the seas, and ensuring 'superior air power', the allies 'might hope', Churchill wrote, 'to win the war at the end of 1943 or 1944', and he ended: 'There might be advantage in declaring now our intention of sending armies of liberation into Europe in 1943. This would give hope to the subjugated peoples and prevent any truck between them and the German invaders. The setting and keeping in movement along our courses of the minds of so many scores of millions of men is in itself a potent atmospheric influence.' [1]

Churchill's fourth and final ship-board memorandum was dictated on December 20. Entitled 'Notes on the Pacific', it reiterated his view that Britain and America, whom he now referred to as 'the Allies', must expect to be deprived 'one by one' of their possessions and strong-points in the Pacific, and that the Japanese would establish themselves 'fairly easily in one after the other, mopping up local garrisons'. But he argued that the resources of Japan were 'a wasting factor', already overstrained by the long and 'wasteful' war in China, and that it was therefore 'right and necessary to fight them at every point where we have a fair chance to keep them burning and extended'. Allied sea and air power must be built up until it made possible bombing raids on Japan itself. 'The burning of Japanese cities by incendiary bombs,' he wrote, 'will bring home in a most effective way to the people of Japan the dangers of the course to which they have committed themselves and nothing is more likely to cramp the reinforcing of their overseas adventures.' Russia, even if not at war with Japan, might still be willing, Churchill reflected, to allow Allied aircraft 'to refuel in Siberia before and after bombing Japan'.

[1] 'Part III—1943', 18 December 1941, 'Most Secret', Defence Committee Memorandum No. 12 of 1942, 1 February 1942: Churchill papers, 4/235.

Churchill saw no reason to 'fear', as he expressed it, that the war in the Pacific would absorb 'an unduly large proportion of United States' forces'. The danger would be if the United States decided to create, for the reconquest of the Pacific and the defeat of Japan, a vast army of ten million men which, 'for at least two years while it was training', would absorb all the available American supplies 'and stand idle defending the American continent'. For this reason, the Americans should be encouraged and helped 'to regain their naval power in the Pacific'.[1] As Churchill saw it, such an emphasis would leave the main United States forces and supplies available for the European landings of 1943, and the liberation of Europe.

Thus Churchill's focus, as he approached the American continent, was for the creation of a European front, and a massive American commitment to it, within a year and a half.

With Churchill presiding, the Chiefs of Staff Committee met on board the *Duke of York* on the morning of December 18. Also present were the Minister of Supply, Lord Beaverbrook, two of the Chiefs of Staff, Admiral Pound and Sir Charles Portal, and Field Marshal Sir John Dill. Three days earlier, Pound, Portal and Dill had sent Churchill a memorandum, suggesting that when the British delegation reached Washington they should ask for a Joint 'Staff Conference', between the President, Churchill, and the Chiefs of Staff of the two countries, in order to reach agreement on general lines 'as to how we are going to fight the war together', and to issue a directive for the future strategical discussions to take place between the Chiefs of Staff. A machinery would also have to be agreed upon, 'for establishing permanent Joint Staff collaboration between the two countries and between other Allies, as necessary, e.g. the Russians, the Chinese and the Dutch'.[2]

In approving this suggestion at the morning meeting on December 18, Churchill 'thought it important', as the minutes of the meeting noted, 'to put before the peoples of both the British Empire and the United States the mass invasion of the Continent of Europe as the goal for 1943'. Churchill then set out what he saw as the 'three phases' of the war to come:

'(i)   Closing the ring.
(ii) Liberating the populations.
(iii) Final assault on the German citadel.'[3]

[1] 'Part IV, Notes on the Pacific', 20 December 1941, Defence Committee Memorandum No. 12 of 1942, 1 February 1942: Churchill papers, 4/235.
[2] 'Secret', undated, submitted to Churchill on 15 December 1941: Premier papers, 3/458/7.
[3] 'CR' 8, 'Record of a Meeting of the Chiefs of Staff held on 18th December 1941 at 11 a.m.', 18 December 1941: Premier papers, 3/458/2.

Churchill again presided over a shipboard meeting of the Chiefs of Staff on the following day, when he set out the six 'main points' which he felt should be put forward in conference with the Americans. The first point was that a 'concerted effort' should be made by Britain and the United States 'to re-establish our Naval position in the Pacific as soon as possible' and to recapture those British and American possessions in the Far East 'which may in the meanwhile fall into enemy hands'.

Dudley Pound, in commenting on this suggestion, warned that unless Britain and America were to obtain 'capital ship superiority' in the Far East, 'we should soon find ourselves in a state of inferiority due to constant attrition'. Churchill did not disagree, but he stressed that the war against Japan 'would loom large in American eyes', and that in presenting the Americans with Britain's views on joint strategy 'we should have to be careful not to give the impression that we were concentrating exclusively on our problems and ignoring those of America'.

Churchill's other points for discussion with the Americans, on which there was no dissent, were the despatch of a United States force to Northern Ireland 'to enable us to release trained British troops' for overseas, the bombing of Germany by United States squadrons based on the United Kingdom, the United States 'to take the lead in occupying North Africa' by preparing an expeditionary force 'of say 25,000 men to be augmented by a force totalling up to 150,000 men during the next six months', the United States to leave 'the largest number of destroyers possible in the Atlantic', and United States help to Britain both to build 'improvised aircraft carriers' and to provide the aircraft needed for them.[1]

Patrick Kinna, the shorthand writer who accompanied Churchill on the *Duke of York*, later recalled how 'U-boats were constantly reported in our vicinity and I think the possibility of naval action privately excited the Prime Minister'. Kinna added:

I well remember one morning when I was taking dictation from WSC in his cabin, feeling none too well because of the very rough seas, my feelings being aggravated by the PM's cigar-smoke, I could hear some matelots whistling and I knew only too well from experience that the PM could not bear whistling at any time. I hoped he couldn't hear it—but he did! Suddenly

<hr/>

[1] 'CR' 10, 'Record of Staff Conference held on 19th December 1941 at 12.30 p.m.', 19 December 1941: Premier papers, 3/458/2.

he angrily told me to go and tell those sailors to stop whistling. I had a shrewd idea what they would say to me! However, I hastily left his cabin, not knowing quite what to do. I think I said a few hurried prayers and the whistling miraculously ceased. I returned to continue taking dictation, the Prime Minister obviously believing that I had quietened the ship's company![1]

On December 20 there was further news from Auchinleck. A Royal Air Force raid on Benghazi had caused 'great damage and much confusion'. At the same time, a Long Range Desert Group patrol had destroyed twenty-two aircraft on the ground and destroyed four petrol stores west of Sirte. 'Our advance into the heart of Cyrenaica continues,' Auchinleck added, 'and the relentless attack of the RAF on the enemy's retreating forces, coupled with continued pressure of our forward columns, has kept him on the run all day.'[2] The British 'problem', Auchinleck telegraphed on the following day, 'is to get strong enough forces forward' to 'destroy or envelop' the enemy forces in and around Benghazi itself, 'and to maintain them when they get there'.[3]

While still on board the *Duke of York*, Churchill learnt from Anthony Eden the details of Stalin's demand for secret assurances on the postwar Soviet frontiers. Under Stalin's plan, Britain and the United States would agree at once that the Baltic States, parts of Finland, and parts of Roumania would be incorporated into the Soviet Union after the war. 'Stalin, I believe, sincerely wants military agreements,' Eden telegraphed to Churchill on December 21, 'but he will not sign until we recognize his frontiers, and we must expect badgering on this issue.' Eden added: 'Meanwhile our position and that of America is completely safeguarded.'[4] Stalin's 'demands about Finland, Baltic States and Roumania', Churchill telegraphed to Attlee on December 21, 'are directly contrary to the first, second and third articles of the Atlantic Charter, to which Stalin has subscribed'. There could be 'no question' whatever, Churchill stressed, of making any such territorial arrangement, 'secret or public, direct or implied, without prior agreement with the United States'. Frontier questions could only be resolved 'at the Peace Conference when we have won the war'.[5]

The 'mere desire' to have a published agreement with Russia,

[1] Patrick Kinna recollections: letter to the author, 10 October 1984.
[2] 'Susan' No. 1663, Cairo, 6 a.m., 20 December 1941: Premier papers, 3/290/1.
[3] 'Susan' No. 1664, Cairo, 9 a.m., 21 December 1941: Premier papers, 3/290/1.
[4] 'Hectic' No. 38, 21 December 1941: Churchill papers, 20/47.
[5] 'Grey' No. 26, 20 December 1941: Premier papers, 3/399.

Churchill told Attlee on December 20, 'should never lead us into making wrongful promises', nor should Eden be 'downhearted' if he had to leave Moscow 'without any flourish of trumpets'. The Russians, Churchill added, 'have got to go on fighting for their lives anyway, and are dependent upon us for very large supplies which we have most painfully gathered, and which we shall faithfully deliver'.[1]

In a telegram to Eden that same day, Churchill continued: 'Naturally you will not be rough with Stalin,' but he went on to reiterate that there could be no 'secret and special pacts' without the United States, and that to approach Roosevelt with Stalin's territorial proposals would be 'to court a blank refusal' and might lead to 'lasting trouble on both sides'.

In this telegram to Eden, Churchill set out his own thoughts of what the post-war settlement might be. The war since June 1941 had shown the 'particular danger' threatening Leningrad, then besieged by German forces. The 'first object' of the Peace Conference would be 'for prevention of any new outbreak by Germany'. The separation of Prussia from South Germany, as well as the 'actual definition' of Prussia itself, would be 'one of the greatest issues to be decided'. But, Churchill wrote, 'all this lies in a future which is uncertain and probably remote. We have to win the war by a hard and prolonged struggle.' To raise such issues publicly now, he feared, 'would only be to rally all Germans round Hitler'.[2]

When, two weeks later, Eden, anxious to obtain an Anglo-Soviet treaty which might help to keep the Russians fighting, raised the possibility of recognizing Russia's 1941 frontiers, Churchill telegraphed: 'Perhaps you have not seen my "Grey" 26 to the Lord Privy Seal. We have never recognised the 1941 frontiers of Russia except *de facto*. They were acquired by acts of aggression in shameful collusion with Hitler. The transfer of the peoples of the Baltic States to Soviet Russia against their will would be contrary to all the principles for which we are fighting this war and would dishonour our cause. This also applies to Bessarabia and to Northern Bukovina and in a lesser degree to Finland which I gather it is not intended wholly to subjugate and absorb.'

Russia could, Churchill told Eden, 'upon strategical grounds make a case for the approaches to Leningrad which the Finns have utilized to attack her. There are islands in the Baltic which may be essential to the safety of Russia. Strategical security may be invoked at certain

[1] 'Grey' No. 26, 20 December 1941: Premier papers, 3/399.

[2] 'Grey' No. 28 ('Haughty' No. 85), Prime Minister's Personal Telegram, T.1047, 'Personal and Secret', 20 December 1941: Churchill papers, 20/47. The separation of Prussia from South Germany was to remain Churchill's aim until the end of the war. It disregarded the fact that many of the most extreme Nazis were South Germans, and some of the most dedicated and daring anti-Nazis were Prussians.

points on the frontiers of Bukovina or Bessarabia. In these cases the population would have to be offered evacuation and compensation if they desired it. In all other cases transference of territory must be regulated after the war is over by freely and fairly conducted plebiscites.' Churchill added: 'In any case there can be no question of settling frontiers until the Peace Conference. I know President Roosevelt holds this view as strongly as I do and he has several times expressed his pleasure to me at the firm line we took at Moscow. I could not be an advocate for a British Cabinet bent on such a course.'

Churchill's rebuke to Eden continued: 'You suggest that "the acid test of our sincerity" depends upon our recognising the acquisition of these territories by the Soviet Union irrespective of the wishes of their peoples. I, on the contrary, regard our sincerity involved in the maintenance of the principles of the Atlantic Charter, to which Stalin has subscribed. On this also we depend for our association with the USA.'[1]

It was clear to Churchill that Stalin's demand for frontier changes would involve 'the forcible transfer of large populations against their will into the Communist sphere'. Such a transfer, he explained to the Australian Prime Minister, John Curtin, was clearly forbidden by the Atlantic Charter, 'and by attempting it we should only vitiate the fundamental principles of freedom which are the main impulse of our Cause'.

There was to be no 'bargain' with Stalin, Churchill told Curtin.[2] There could be no incivility either: on December 20, the day on which Churchill urged Eden not to enter into any territorial discussions, he sent Stalin 'sincere good wishes for your birthday', and expressed his hope that future anniversaries 'will enable you to bring to Russia victory, peace and safety after so much storm'.[3] Stalin was sixty-two years old on December 21. In reply to the birthday greetings, he sent Churchill and the British Army 'my sincere congratulations in connection with your recent victories in Libya'.[4] At his birthday banquet in the Kremlin, as Eden reported to Churchill, 'we drank your health and some others. Stalin spoke very warmly of you.'[5]

[1] 'Grey' No. 261, 7 January 1942: Premier papers, 3/399/6, folios 87–8.
[2] 'Grey' No. 109. Prime Minister's Personal Telegram, T.1072, 'Winch' No. 12 to Australia, 'Personal and Most Secret', 25 December 1941: Premier papers, 3/399/6, folio 86.
[3] 'Grey' No. 44, Prime Minister's Personal Telegram, T.1048, 20 December 1941: Churchill papers, 20/49.
[4] 'Following for Prime Minister from M. Stalin, received through Soviet Embassy, London', 'Taut' No. 240, 'Most Secret', Churchill papers, 20/47.
[5] 'Hectic' No. 38, 21 December 1941: Churchill papers, 20/47.

On Sunday December 21 the *Duke of York* reached United States territorial waters. On his last day on board ship, Churchill dictated a letter to his wife, setting out an account of his voyage:

My darling,

Yesterday, Saturday, finished the longest week I have lived since the war began. We have had almost unceasing gales. For a long time going round the Bloody Foreland in the worst part of the U-boat and Focke-Wulf areas we could not make more than six knots unless we threw off our destroyer escort. For 36 hours we were within 5 or 600 miles of Brest, with its bomber squadrons, and it was very fortunate that no Focke Wulf spotted us through the gaps in the clouds. Three days ago we left our destroyers behind as they could not keep up in the rough sea, and in half an hour we hope to meet the American destroyer escort just North of Bermuda. The weather has again turned so rough that we shall no doubt leave them behind too and press on, but even so we now speak of Tuesday afternoon as the likely time for reaching Annapolis. If this is realised, the voyage will have taken ten days, which is a big slice in times like these.

I am very well and have not suffered from seasickness at all, though I took two doses of Mothersill the first day. These ships literally cannot go more than 17 or 18 knots in a really heavy sea. No-one is allowed on deck, and we have two men with broken arms and legs.

I have a lovely cabin in the bridge structure as well as my apartments aft. These latter are unusable owing to the noise and vibration. Here it is cool and quiet and daylight. I spend the greater part of the day in bed, getting up for lunch, going to bed immediately afterwards to sleep and then up again for dinner. I manage to get a great deal of sleep and have also done a great deal of work in my waking hours. We have been very well supplied with official telegrams and secret news. We have 27 cypherers on board for this service alone, and all my telegrams from Auchinleck and others are coming through, but of general news one knows but little except what the wireless says, and oddly enough we have got practically nothing from the United States wireless. I do not, therefore, know the situation I shall find on arrival. I feel I ought to go to Canada while I am over this side, but I do not quite know when or how I shall come back. I shall certainly stay long enough to do all that has to be done, having come all this way at so much trouble and expense.

We make a very friendly party at meal times, and everyone is now accustomed to the motion. The great stand-by is the cinema. Every night we have a film. I have seen some very good ones. The one last night, 'Blood and Sand', about bull-fighters, is the best we have seen so far. The cinema is a wonderful form of entertainment, and takes the mind away from other things.

About these other things. The worst that has happened is the collapse of the resistance of Hong Kong; although one knew it was a forlorn outpost, we expected that they would hold out on the fortified island for a good many weeks, possibly for several months, but now they seem on the verge of surrender after only a fortnight's struggle. Not very good news has also come in from Malaya. Owing to our loss of the command of the sea, the Japanese have an unlimited power of reinforcement, and our people are retreating under orders to defend the Southern tip and the vital Fortress of Singapore. I have given a good many instructions to move men, guns and aircraft in this direction.

We must expect to suffer heavily in this war with Japan, and it is no use the critics saying 'Why were we not prepared?' when everything we had was already fully engaged. The entry of the United States into the war is worth all the losses sustained in the East many times over. Still these losses are very painful to endure and will be very hard to repair.

On the other hand there is good news. We made a fine kill of U-boats round Gibraltar, about seven altogether in a week. This is a record. There has never been such a massacre, and it should douch the spirits of the survivors when they get home to see how many of their companion vessels have been sent to the bottom. But the best of all is Auchinleck's continuous victorious advance. Before the end of the year he will be at Benghazi and well on the road farther West. No doubt there will still be pockets of resistance to mop up, but there is every hope that the whole armed force of the enemy, which amounted to 100,000 Italians and 50,000 Huns, will be dead or captured. That, at any rate, would be a clean job, and gives relief as well as encouragement at an anxious juncture. It is very important for the Americans that we should have proofs that our soldiers can fight a modern war and beat the Germans on even terms, or even at odds, for that is what they have done. This lends weight to our counsels and requests.

I had been hoping till an hour ago to dine with the President tomorrow, Monday, night—and this is not yet impossible—but it is still blowing hard and from my porthole I can see, every minute, tremendous seas pouring over the bows of the ship, while down below can be heard the crash of them striking the sides. We are running obliquely across the waves and sometimes the ship rolls very heavily. However, once you get used to the motion, you don't care a damn.

You can imagine how anxious I am to arrive and put myself in relation to the fuller news and find out what is the American outlook and what they propose to do. Long and not free from risk as the voyage has been, I am glad I did not try to fly, although they make you fine stories of how you can cover the Atlantic in 12 or 14 hours. In the Winter time this is very rare. There are all kinds of difficulties and dangers, and sometimes you are kept waiting 6, 8 or 10 days for favourable weather, so that the tortoise may still beat the hare. Everything is being kept open for the return journey, as I, particularly, do not wish to make up my mind; nor does anyone know how it will be accomplished. As soon as I get established in the White House I will ring you up on the trans-Atlantic cable. I wish particularly to know the length of your stockings, so that I can bring you a few pairs to take the edge off Oliver Lyttelton's coupons.

I had a telegram from Randolph asking for a message for his paper 'Parade'. You should ask Brendan to show you one of these. It is quite a fine publication, and I have sent them a Christmastide greeting.

They seem to have kept Anthony's visit to Russia very secret up to the present, but I suppose it will be out at the same time as mine, i.e. tomorrow or the day after. I look forward so much to talking to you over the telephone, but we shall have to be careful as, of course, it is not secret.

I have read two books, 'Brown on Resolution' and 'Forty Centuries Look Down'. You would like both of them, particularly the opening part of 'Brown on Resolution', which is a charming love story most attractively told.[1] The other is a very good account of Napoleon's relations with Josephine, and his excursions of various kinds to and in Egypt. I will bring them both back for you.

I am frightfully fed up with the idea of an extra day being tacked on to all these others, but one had to accept the inevitable. Being in a ship in such weather as this is like being in a prison, with the extra chance of being drowned.[2] Nevertheless, it is perhaps a good thing to stand away from the canvas from time to time and take a full view of the picture. I find it has clarified my ideas, although for the first few days one was numb and dull and stupid. That process may have proved restful and preparatory for the busy days that are to come. . . .[3]

On his last day on the *Duke of York*, Churchill studied the comments of the Chiefs of Staff on his three memoranda. They were particularly concerned lest the bombing of Germany be allowed to take second place to the landing of large Allied forces on the Continent, before a 'greatly predominant' British bomber force had been used 'for a considerable period against the heart of Germany'. The date of 'late 1943 or early 1944' was the one they envisaged as more feasible for the 'liberating' operation of which Churchill had written, and which he had envisaged in the summer of 1943. For the Chiefs of Staff, 'the realisation of the bomber programme' in 1943 should be the predominant British aim, with 'less emphasis' put on the landing operations in that year.[4] The Chiefs of Staff also concluded, in a separate memorandum on the war in the Pacific, that 'Until we have disposed of Germany and Italy we must accept the fact that the Japanese will be able to run wild in the Western Pacific'.[5]

In his reply, sent to the Chiefs of Staff on December 21, Churchill

---

[1] *Brown on Resolution* by C. S. Forester (1899–1966) was published in 1929. It is a story of individual courage and resistance, set in the First World War.

[2] A reference to Dr Johnson's remark: 'No man will be a sailor who has contrivance enough to get himself into jail; for being in a ship is being in a jail, with the chance of being drowned.' (*Journal of a Tour to the Hebrides*, 3rd edition, page 126, 31 August 1773.)

[3] 'At sea' (letter written on 21 December 1941): Spencer-Churchill papers.

[4] 'Note on the Sequence of events in the Offensive against Germany', undated: Premier papers, 3/499/2. The covering note, date 20 December 1941, was signed by Pound, Dill and Portal.

[5] 'Note on the development of operations against Japan', undated: Premier papers, 3/499/2.

suggested that it was 'imprudent' to adopt this attitude towards Japan. 'The Americans may take this view themselves,' he noted. 'But they may equally well hold that they must try their utmost to fight Japan.' As to 'disposing' of Germany and Italy, this was 'easy to write', but on the question of how it was to be done, the 'only answer' offered by the Chiefs of Staff in their paper was, Churchill pointed out, 'by bombing German cities and towns'. Yet night air bombing of German 'civilian populations and industries' had, he wrote, 'fallen far short of expectations'. To reduce Germany 'to submission' by air bombing alone might take two, three or four years. There was certainly 'no guarantee' that it would not take so long. 'No attempt is to be made at large scale landings on the Continent,' Churchill reflected on the Chiefs of Staff paper, 'until Germany is reduced to very great weakness by night air bombing.'

Even if night air bombing were 'a certain method of subduing Germany', Churchill wrote, 'the force of events will compel a much more complex strategy upon us'.

All thoughts about 1943 were, Churchill wrote, 'highly speculative'. But unless there were 'some forecast and looking ahead' the preparations necessary for action 'will not be undertaken, and we shall be in the same position in 1943 as we are now'. Churchill added: 'It may well be that an effort by us and the Americans prepared for 1943 would not in fact come off until 1944, but if we do not begin making plans now it will never come off.'

Churchill's note ended:

The negative in our counsels in the present time is as 10:1. There is, therefore no need to fear any excess of venturesome offensive action for 1943 at this stage. I cannot, however, agree that all talk of this must be postponed until Germany has been so weakened by night air-bombing as not to be able to offer any effective resistance to liberating armies. When we consider the immense length of coastline which Hitler has to defend and the choice we have where to hit him, and that he will have to maintain a major Russian front; that he will be fighting us in the Mediterranean basin: that his Air Force is far weaker than the British, Russian and American Air Forces put together: that his people will have a bad winter and may be upset by the slaughter in Russia and the entry of the United States, I think there is a good chance of our being able to make four or five simultaneous Anglo-American landings on the Continent in the summer of 1943.

Most people outside our very limited circle would be horrified at the idea that all offensive action must be postponed till even later years; in fact, I am sure they would not put up with it. Still less will they do so if all the time Japan is 'running wild' in the East Indies and Northern Australia. I hope, therefore, that we shall speak with confidence and decision upon the liberating offensive of 1943, and that we shall ask for the vessels and tackle and tanks to be prepared on this basis, and that we shall hold out to the captive populations the hope of relief.

'If things go badly,' Churchill added, 'nothing would be easier than to delay and play for safety as we are so often accused of doing.'[1]

[1] 'Most Secret', 21 December 1941: Premier papers, 3/499/2.

2
Three Weeks in The New World

O N 22 December 1941 after ten days on board ship, Churchill landed at Hampton Roads, and flew from there to Washington. 'There was the President waiting in his car,' he later recalled. 'I clasped his strong hand with comfort and pleasure.'

For three weeks, Churchill was Roosevelt's guest at the White House. Each evening, Churchill later recalled, 'I wheeled him in his chair from the drawing room to the lift as a mark of respect, and thinking also of Sir Walter Raleigh spreading his cloak before Queen Elizabeth.'[1] After several days at the White House Churchill wrote to his wife: 'I have not had a minute since I got here to tell you about it. All is very good indeed, and my plans are going through. The Americans are magnificent in their breadth of view.'[2]

At their first meeting, at the White House on the evening of December 22, Roosevelt had been accompanied by Cordell Hull, Sumner Welles and Harry Hopkins, while Churchill took with him Beaverbrook and Lord Halifax. There was 'general agreement', as Halifax's notes recorded, 'that if Hitler was held in Russia he must try something else', and that his most probable line of advance would be through Spain and Portugal, 'en route to North Africa'. British success in Libya, and the prospect of 'joining hands' with the French in North Africa, was thought to be 'another reason to make Hitler want if he could to get hold of Morocco as quickly as possible'. Those present at the meeting were agreed, as Halifax recorded, 'that it was vital to forestall the Germans in North West Africa and in the Atlantic islands'.

---

[1] Winston S. Churchill, *The Second World War*, volume 3, London 1950, page 588.
[2] 'White House' (undated postscript to letter of 21 December 1941): Spencer-Churchill papers.

The discussion then turned to the need 'to have all plans made' for a joint landing in North Africa, 'with or without invitation'. Churchill emphasized 'the immense psychological effect' likely to be produced both in France and among French troops in North Africa 'by the association of the United States with the undertaking'.

In reply, Roosevelt said that he was 'anxious that American land forces should give their support as quickly as possible wherever they could be most helpful, and favoured the idea of a plan to move into North Africa being prepared for either event, i.e. invitation or no invitation'.

Roosevelt then offered to send three or four United States divisions to Northern Ireland, to relieve the British troops there, an offer which Churchill 'warmly welcomed'. It was not thought, Halifax's note continued, 'that this need conflict with the preparation of a United States force for North Africa'.[1]

In a report to the War Cabinet on the following day, Churchill gave a survey of this first discussion. Concern for a possible German move into French North Africa, he reported, had led to agreement on the need for an American approach to Vichy France, 'saying that this was the final chance for them to reconsider their positions and come out on the side that was pledged to the restoration of France'. In North Africa itself, it was felt that Weygand might be approached, in view of America's 'willingness to send a force to North Africa'. Meanwhile, in view of the possibility of 'smooth promises' of no value from Pétain and Weygand, it was agreed that it would be 'desirable to have all plans made for going into North Africa, with or without invitation'.

Churchill then gave an account of the fighting in Libya, 'by which', he noted, 'the President and other Americans were clearly much impressed and cheered'.

The first night's discussion included the possibility of the British Dominions 'and all other Allies' being a party to discussions of war strategy. 'The general conclusion,' Churchill reported, 'was that it was important to bring them all in, but not to establish any permanent body that would limit the action or capacity to take prompt decision of United States, Great Britain and Russia.'[2]

During Churchill's three weeks in Washington, twelve meetings were held between the British and American Chiefs of Staff. These meetings soon dispelled his fears of an American 'Asia-first' strategy. At the first meeting, on December 22, General Marshall and Admiral

---

[1] 'Most Secret', 'Record of Conversation, December 22nd 1941, White House, Washington', 23 December 1941: Premier papers, 3/458/7.
[2] 'Grey' No. 73, 24 December 1941: Churchill papers, 20/50.

Stark, for the United States, reiterated the American-British Staff Conversations conclusion of February 1941, that the Atlantic and European theatre of war was the 'decisive one', and stated that notwithstanding Japan's entry into the war, 'our view remains that Germany is still the key to victory'. The note ended: 'Once Germany is defeated, the collapse of Italy and the defeat of Japan must follow.'[1]

On December 22, as these discussions proceeded, Japanese troops landed on the Philippines. Three days later, Hong Kong finally surrendered after a seventeen-day siege. Speaking to the Dominion representatives at the White House at noon on December 23, Churchill reflected that Britain had nevertheless avoided 'the worst possible situation', whereby Japan would have made war on Britain alone, and America remained out of the war. 'On balance,' he commented, 'we could not be dissatisfied with the turn of events.' Now that the Russians were 'fighting back magnificently', and the 'powerful assistance' of the United States was assured, 'we could therefore look to the future with hope and confidence'.[2]

At four o'clock that afternoon, Roosevelt introduced Churchill to a press conference of American journalists and broadcasters. In the crowded room he could not be seen even when he stood up. When he climbed on to his chair 'so that they could see him better', the American record of the Conference noted, 'loud and spontaneous cheers and applause rang through the room'.

In answer to a question about Australian anxiety about Singapore, Churchill replied: 'We are going to do our utmost to defend Singapore and its approaches until the situation becomes so favourable to us that the general offensive in the Pacific can be resumed.' Was not Singapore 'the key to the whole situation out there', Churchill was asked. 'The key to the whole situation,' he replied, 'is the resolute manner in which the British and American Democracies are going to throw themselves into the conflict.'

Pressed to say how long it would take to 'lick these boys', Churchill replied: 'If we manage it well, it will only take half as long as if we manage it badly.'[3]

[1] General George C. Marshall and Admiral Harold R. Stark 'Summation' of 22 December 1941: W. Averell Harriman and Elie Abel, *Special Envoy to Churchill and Stalin, 1941–1946*, London 1976, page 117.

[2] Washington War Conference, 1st Meeting, 12 noon, 23 December 1941: Premier papers, 3/458/4. The Dominions Representatives present were R. W. Close (Union of South Africa), Major R. G. Casey (Australia), Leighton McCarthy (Canada) and F. Langstone (New Zealand). On 19 March 1942 Casey was appointed Britain's Minister Resident in the Middle East, with a place in the War Cabinet (until December 1943).

[3] 'Confidential', 'Press Conference No. 794', 'Executive Office of the President', 4 p.m., 23 December 1941: Premier papers, 4/71/2.

Immediately after the press conference, at the first full meeting of the British and United States representatives at the White House, Churchill spoke of what a 'great comfort' it was to find 'so much agreement on fundamentals between the two Governments, particularly at a moment of great emergency when the United States had recently been subjected to violent surprise attack'. He was glad, he said, that American troops were to go to Ireland, and 'emphatically' welcomed the idea of American bombing squadrons operating from the United Kingdom. 'They would not only add powerfully to the weight of attack on Germany,' Churchill told the Conference, 'but they could also make their presence felt over France by dropping leaflets and bombing the French invasion ports.' [1]

During December 23 Churchill telephoned his wife from the White House. 'He might have been speaking from the next room,' Clementine Churchill wrote to her daughter Mary on the following day. 'But it was not *very* satisfactory as it was a public line and we were both warned by the Censors breaking in that we were being listened to!' [2]

From Auchinleck came two telegrams on December 24. The first, sent that morning, reported that 'We were advancing all yesterday and pressure on enemy from air and ground were continuous'. From the 'most secret source', Auchinleck added, 'it appears that enemy can no longer use Benghazi'. [3] This news had come to Auchinleck direct from the Government Code and Cypher School at Bletchley. An Enigma decrypt of December 21 had shown the German Panzer forces intended to hold Benghazi only for one more day. [4]

On the afternoon of December 24, Auchinleck telegraphed again. 'Royal Dragoons occupied Benghazi this morning. The Army of the Nile sends you hearty greetings for Christmas.' [5]

Churchill and Roosevelt met again at six o'clock on the evening of December 24, to discuss the need to reinforce Singapore. At Churchill's request, Roosevelt agreed to allow a British Brigade Group embarked in the United States transport *Mount Vernon* for Colombo, to be allowed to proceed to Singapore. [6] To the Australian representative in Washington, Major Casey, Churchill explained that, with the capture of Benghazi, the time had come when Auchinleck could

---

[1] Washington War Conference, 2nd Meeting, 5 p.m., 23 December 1941: Cabinet papers, 99/17.

[2] Letter of 23 December 1941: Mary Soames, *Clementine Churchill*, London 1979, page 311.

[3] 'Susan' No. 1669, Cairo, 8 a.m., 24 December 1941: Premier papers, 3/290/1.

[4] MK 1140 of 21 December 1941: F. H. Hinsley and others, *British Intelligence in the Second World War*, volume 2, London 1981, page 314.

[5] 'Susan' No. 1670, 'Personal', Cairo, 4 p.m., 24 December 1941: Premier papers, 3/290/1.

[6] 'Most Secret' (Note by Brigadier Hollis), 24 December 1941: Premier papers, 3/458/7.

he asked whether he could spare some Hurricane squadrons to move eastward. It might even be possible, Churchill told Casey, to spare a regiment of American M.3 light tanks from the Middle East.[1]

That evening, Christmas Eve, Churchill and Roosevelt stood on a White House balcony as the lights of the White House Christmas tree were turned on. Tens of thousands watched from the lawns and open spaces as the lights came on, and Churchill spoke of how, although far from his family, 'yet I cannot truthfully say that I feel far from home'. His remarks continued:

Whether it be the ties of blood on my mother's side, or the friendships I have developed here over many years of active life, or the commanding sentiment of comradeship in the common cause of great peoples who speak the same language, who kneel at the same altars, and, to a very large extent, pursue the same ideals, I cannot feel myself a stranger here in the centre and at the summit of the United States. I feel a sense of unity and fraternal association which, added to the kindliness of your welcome, convinces me that I have a right to sit at your fireside and share your Christmas joys.

After speaking of what a 'strange Christmas Eve' it was, with war 'raging and roaring over all the lands and seas', Churchill continued:

Let the children have their night of fun and laughter. Let the gifts of Father Christmas delight their play. Let us grown-ups share to the full in their unstinted pleasures before we turn again to the stern task and the formidable years that lie before us, resolved that, by our sacrifice and daring, these same children shall not be robbed of their inheritance or denied their right to live in a free and decent world.[2]

That night Churchill dined at the White House. One of the Americans present, Percy Chubb, later recalled how amid the relaxed atmosphere of an informal gathering:

The conversation was dominated by the President and the Prime Minister, discussing, of all things, the Boer War. Churchill was subdued and looked tired. After all, he had just arrived across the Atlantic and had faced a press conference on his arrival that day. In contrast, the President was in a buoyant mood and kept needling Churchill for having been on the wrong side in the Boer War. (FDR had been part of an informal group of Boer sympathizers at Harvard.) When he felt crowded too far, Churchill would take a puff of his cigar and counterattack with a verbal sally and then settle back again into his chair.

The conversation then got round to the question of the food supply we were shipping to England—'too many powdered eggs' said Churchill, 'the only good thing you can make with them is Spotted Dick'.

[1] Washington War Conference, 3rd Meeting, 6 p.m., 24 December 1941: Cabinet papers, 99/17.
[2] Franklin D. Roosevelt archive, Franklin D. Roosevelt Library, Hyde Park (New York State).

'Nonsense' said FDR, 'You can do as much with a powdered egg as with a real egg.' I opened my mouth for the only time all evening to ask how you could fry a powdered egg. . . .

During the evening, Roosevelt spoke of his unhappy childhood, and of how his ambition at Harvard had not been fulfilled. 'When I hear a man say that his childhood was the happiest time of his life,' Churchill commented, 'I think, "my friend, you have had a pretty poor life".'[1]

Patrick Kinna, who worked at the White House throughout Churchill's visit, later recalled:

One morning the Prime Minister wanted to dictate while he was in his bath—not a minute could be wasted—He kept submerging in the bath and when he 'surfaced' he would dictate a few more words or sentences. Eventually he got out of the bath when his devoted valet, Sawyers, draped an enormous bath-towel around him. He walked into his adjoining bedroom, followed by me, notebook in hand, and continued to dictate while pacing up and down the enormous room. Eventually the towel fell to the ground but, quite unconcerned, he continued pacing the room dictating all the time.

Suddenly President Roosevelt entered the bedroom and saw the British Prime Minister completely naked walking around the room dictating to me. WSC never being lost for words said 'You see, Mr President, I have nothing to conceal from you. . . .'[2]

On Christmas Day Churchill went to church with the President, 'surrounded', Colonel Jacob noted in his diary, 'by bevies of G-men, armed with Tommy-guns and revolvers'. But church 'was immediately followed by a meeting'.[3]

At the meeting, means of defending Singapore were discussed. After the meeting Churchill telegraphed to Auchinleck, asking him to release four squadrons of fighter aircraft and an armoured brigade with a hundred American tanks for the Far East: 'a hard request', he admitted, but the Allies were 'desperately short' of aircraft and tanks 'in the new theatre which the Japanese attack has opened'. For his part, Roosevelt had agreed, Churchill told Auchinleck, that American squadrons would 'come over to attack Germany from the British Isles', as well as offering, in North Africa, 'to put such a screw on Vichy or on French North Africa as will give us the best chance of bringing them out on our side'; failing that, 'some highly-trained American divisions may be thrown into the scale' in North Africa. 'All our

---

[1] 'Dining with FDR and Winston Churchill': note communicated to the author by Percy Chubb, New Jersey, 1962.

[2] Patrick Kinna recollections: letter to the author, 10 October 1984.

[3] 'Operation "Arcadia", Washington Conference, December 1941', diary of Lieutenant-Colonel E. I. C. Jacob.

success in the West,' Churchill cautioned Auchinleck, 'would be nullified by the fall of Singapore.' [1]

To the Australian Prime Minister, John Curtin, Churchill was able to report, after his meeting with the President, 'that should the Philippines fall', Roosevelt was agreeable to diverting United States troops and aeroplanes to Singapore. The President was also willing, Churchill added, 'to send substantial United States forces to Australia, where the Americans are anxious to establish important bases for the war against Japan'. [2] This telegram was also sent on December 25.

That night Churchill dined with Roosevelt at the White House. One of the American guests, Garrison Norton, later recalled how, after dinner, during the film 'Oliver Twist', when the reel had to be changed, 'Churchill rose rapidly and excused himself with the words: "I must go and do some homework." He then disappeared, leaving Roosevelt and his family at the film.' [3]

The 'homework' was Churchill's speech to the Senate and House of Representatives. 'I cannot help reflecting,' he told them on December 26, 'that if my father had been American and my mother British, instead of the other way round, I might have got here on my own. In that case, this would not have been the first time you would have heard my voice.' At this, there was much laughter, and later a great shout of approval when he said, of the Japanese, 'what sort of a people do they think we are?' But there was less applause when he declared: 'If we had kept together after the last war, if we had taken common measures for our safety, this renewal of the curse need never have fallen upon us.' And there was silence when, in the last moments of his speech, he declared: 'Five or six years ago it would have been easy, without shedding a drop of blood, for the United States and Great Britain to have insisted on the fulfilment of the disarmament clauses of the treaties which Germany signed after the Great War.' At that time too, he said, 'there would have been the opportunity for assuring to Germany those raw materials which we declared in the Atlantic Charter should not be denied to any nation, victor or vanquished. That chance has passed. It is gone. Prodigious hammer-strokes have been needed to bring us together again. . . .'

At the end of his speech, Churchill expressed his hope and faith, 'sure and inviolate, that in the days to come the British and American peoples will for their own safety and for the good of all walk together

[1] 'Grey' No. 103, Prime Minister's Personal Telegram, T.1071, 25 December 1941: Churchill papers, 20/47.

[2] 'Grey' No. 109, Prime Minister's Personal Telegram, T.1072, 'Personal and Most Secret', 25 December 1941: Churchill papers, 20/47.

[3] Garrison Norton (former Under Secretary of the Navy), in conversation with the author, 27 December 1964.

side by side in majesty, in justice, and in peace'.[1] 'There was a great scene at the end,' Sir Charles Wilson noted in his diary. 'The Senators and Congressmen stood cheering and waving their papers till he went out.'[2] 'I thought your Washington speech the best you have ever done,' Randolph Churchill wrote to his father from Cairo, 'particularly the delivery, which was wonderfully confident and clear'.[3]

On the afternoon of December 26 Churchill and Roosevelt discussed the need to find adequate shipping for the movement of American troops to Northern Ireland and Iceland. They also discussed the shipping needs involved in accepting an invitation 'to enter French North Africa' if such an invitation were given, and for the movement of reinforcements by sea to the Middle East and the Far East. 'We now found ourselves,' Churchill commented, 'in the not unusual position of wishing to do three separate things, and not quite having the resources to carry them out.' But, recalling the 'vast efforts' that had been made in 1918 to transport two million American troops across the Atlantic to France, 'he would be very unwilling to accept the idea that in present conditions we could not find the shipping to convey the comparatively small forces involved in these different movements'.[4]

That same evening, at a meeting of the British Chiefs of Staff, Churchill said that his mind was 'moving in the direction' of an Anglo-American agreement based on three points: Germany to be recognized as 'the main enemy', the general direction of the Pacific war to be done from Washington, and the general direction of operations in the 'Atlantic and European theatre' to be done from London. He was about to discuss this with General Marshall.[5]

That night, as Churchill lay in bed at the White House, it was so hot that he decided to open the bedroom window. 'It was very stiff,' he told his doctor on the following morning. 'I had to use considerable force and I noticed all at once that I was short of breath. I had a dull pain over my heart. It went down my left arm. It didn't last very long, but it has never happened before. What is it? Is my heart all right?'

Sir Charles Wilson put his stethoscope to Churchill's chest, noting in his diary later that day:

---

[1] Speech of 26 December 1941, broadcast live from Washington: Churchill papers, 9/153.
[2] Diary entry for 26 December 1941: Lord Moran, *Winston Churchill, The Struggle for Survival, 1940–65*, London 1966, page 15.
[3] Letter of 6 January 1942: Churchill papers, 1/369.
[4] Washington War Conference, 4th Meeting, 4.30 p.m., 26 December 1941: Cabinet papers, 99/17.
[5] 'CR' 19, Chiefs of Staff Committee, 7 p.m., 26 December 1941: Premier papers, 3/458/2.

There was not much to be found when I examined his heart. Indeed, the time I spent listening to his chest was given to some quick thinking. I knew that when I took the stethoscope out of my ears he would ask me pointed questions, and I had no doubt that whether the electro-cardiograph showed evidence of a coronary thrombosis or not, his symptoms were those of coronary insufficiency.

The textbook treatment for this is at least six weeks in bed. That would mean publishing to the world—and the American newspapers would see to this—that the PM was an invalid with a crippled heart and a doubtful future. And this at a moment when America has just come into the war, and there is no one but Winston to take her by the hand.

I felt that the effect of announcing that the PM had had a heart attack could only be disastrous. I knew, too, the consequences of one of his imaginative temperament of the feeling that his heart was affected. His work would suffer. On the other hand, if I did nothing and he had another and severer attack— perhaps a fatal seizure—the world would undoubtedly say that I had killed him through not insisting on rest. These thoughts went racing through my head while I was listening to his heart. I took my stethoscope out of my ears. Then I replaced it and listened again. Right or wrong, it seemed plain that I must sit tight on what had happened, whatever the consequences.

'Well,' he asked, looking full at me, 'is my heart all right?'

'There is nothing serious,' I answered. 'You have been overdoing things.'

'Now, Charles, you're not going to tell me to rest. I can't. I won't. Nobody else can do this job. I must. What actually happened when I opened the window?' he demanded. 'My idea is that I strained one of my chest muscles. I used great force. I don't believe it was my heart at all.'

He waited for me to answer.

'Your circulation was a bit sluggish. It is nothing serious. You needn't rest in the sense of lying up, but you mustn't do more than you can help in the way of exertion for a little while.'

There was a knock at the door. It was Harry Hopkins. I slipped away. I went and sat in a corner of the secretaries' room, picking up a newspaper, so that they would not talk to me. I began to think things out more deliberately. I did not like it, but I determined to tell no one.[1]

Churchill's angina pectoris of 26 December 1941 was to remain a secret for twenty-four years, until, immediately after his death, the doctor published his diary, including this entry. But it did not prevent the Conference from continuing with its urgent work. Nor did it prevent Churchill from seeing General Marshall on the morning of December 27, to discuss the question of a Supreme Commander of all Allied forces in the Far East.

At ten o'clock that evening, December 27, at a Staff Conference

[1] Sir Charles Wilson (later Lord Moran), diary entry, 27 December 1941: Moran, *op. cit.*, pages 16–17. Dr Michael Dunnill writes: 'The description that Moran gives is fairly typical of an attack of angina pectoris. This is caused by a deficiency of blood supply to the heart muscle

held at the White House, Churchill told Halifax, Pound, Dill and Portal of General Marshall's views, 'in strict confidence', that he 'most strongly desired' the Supreme Command to be given to General Wavell. When Churchill had suggested that same day, in a meeting with Roosevelt, that the Americans might like to appoint their own commander, it was Roosevelt who, as Churchill told the Conference, had been 'most insistent' that there was 'no American officer suitable for the post'.

Pound, Dill and Portal each opposed Marshall's suggestions, being 'very apprehensive' of the effect on American public opinion if the command was given to a British officer 'and the course of the campaign in that theatre proved unfavourable to British interests'. Churchill, however, argued that Britain 'ought not to shirk the responsibility offered to us', although it would he felt be 'sounder' to give an American Admiral 'command of all the Naval forces', and to instruct him 'to co-operate with General Wavell'.[1]

On the morning of December 28 Churchill and Roosevelt spent five hours together receiving representatives, as Churchill reported to Attlee, of the other Allied Powers, the 'friendly Powers' and the British Dominions, and making 'heartening statements' to them. At the same time, Churchill told Attlee, 'we are making great exertions to find shipping necessary for the various troop movements required'.[2] Churchill also had a further meeting with Roosevelt about the Far Eastern Command, after which he reported to the British representatives Roosevelt's insistence that Wavell should be supreme Commander. There would be an American Second-in-Command and, at the same time, an American Admiral. It was important to emphasize, commented Air Marshal Harris, of the Joint Staff Mission in Washington, that Wavell was the American choice. The Americans had been 'very bitter at times', Harris explained, 'in blaming the British when things went wrong'.

Churchill then asked his advisers to work out proposals for a 'Joint

---

due to narrowing of the coronary arteries, that is the arteries supplying the heart muscle, by atheroma. This pain is typically in the chest but radiates down the left arm and is brought on by excessive effort such as the use of considerable force to open the window. If the patient persists in the effort, shortness of breath due to failure of the left ventricle and consequent waterlogging of the lungs often occurs and I see that Churchill said that he was in fact short of breath.' Dr Dunnill adds: 'The symptoms described should have acted as a warning that the Prime Minister's heart was not a hundred per cent fit but a great many people have attacks of angina pectoris like this and live for many years. In fact the course adopted by Moran on this occasion was quite correct. To have ordered bed rest for six weeks would not have been good therapy as there is no evidence that this does the patient any good and only tends to make them neurotic.' (Letter to the author, 15 October 1984.)

[1] 'CR' 22, 10 p.m., 27 December 1941: Cabinet papers, 99/17.
[2] 'Grey' No. 141, 'Winch' No. 14, 28 December 1941: Churchill papers, 20/50.

Body' to provide the machinery whereby the Prime Minister and President, 'acting in consultation', could exercise 'control' over the Supreme Commander-in-Chief.[1]

On the afternoon of December 28 Churchill left Washington by train for Ottawa, travelling in Roosevelt's private railroad car. During the journey, he dictated telegrams to the Australian and New Zealand Prime Ministers about the decision to set up a unified South-Western Pacific Command. General Wavell was to be the Supreme Commander, with an American officer as his Deputy. His orders would come from 'an appropriate joint body', responsible to Churchill as British Minister of Defence and Roosevelt as Commander-in-Chief of all United States forces.[2]

'The President and the American staffs regard this decision as of the utmost urgency,' Churchill explained to John Curtin on December 29. 'The decision has come from them.'[3] Reporting the decision to Attlee, Churchill commented: 'I have not attempted to argue the case for or against our accepting this broadminded and selfless American proposal, of merits of which as a war winner I have become convinced. Action is urgent. . . .'[4]

Churchill reached Ottawa on the morning of December 29. 'We drove to Government House through streets banked with snow,' Sir Charles Wilson noted in his diary. 'After a hot bath, Winston seemed his usual self.' The Prime Minister then lunched with the Canadian War Cabinet. In the evening, there was dinner and a reception at Government House. In his spare moments, Churchill worked on his speech to the Canadian Parliament. 'So far,' the doctor noted, 'nothing untoward has happened,' and he added:

Whenever we are alone, he keeps asking me to take his pulse. I get out of it somehow, but once, when I found him lifting something heavy, I did expostulate. At this he broke out:

'Now, Charles, you are making me heart-minded. I shall soon think of nothing else. I couldn't do my work if I kept thinking of my heart.'

The next time he asked me to take his pulse I refused point-blank.

'You're all right. Forget your damned heart.'

He won't get through his speech tomorrow if this goes on.[5]

[1] 'CR' 23, 12.30 p.m., 28 December 1941: Cabinet papers, 99/17. Wavell took up his Command on 15 January 1942. In March 1942 Harris returned to Britain to become Commander-in-Chief, Bomber Command.

[2] 'Grey' No. 148, Prime Minister's Personal Telegram T.1081, 28 December 1941: Churchill papers, 20/49.

[3] 'Grey' No. 156, 'Winch' No. 13, Prime Minister's Personal Telegram, T.1078, 29 December 1941: Churchill papers, 20/47.

[4] 'Grey' No. 148, Prime Minister's Personal Telegram, T.1081, 28 December 1941: Churchill papers, 20/49.

[5] Diary entry for 29 December 1941: Moran op. cit., page 18.

Churchill's speech to the Canadian Parliament, delivered on December 30, surveyed the war in all its phases, praising Canada's contribution from the first days. Speaking of the peoples of the British Empire, he said, 'We have not journeyed all this way across the centuries, across the oceans, across the mountains, across the prairies, because we are made of sugar candy.' Neither the length of the struggle, 'nor any form of severity it may assume, shall make us weary or shall make us quit'. In 1940, when he had warned the French Government 'that Britain would fight on alone whatever they did, their Generals told their Prime Minister and his divided Cabinet: "In three weeks England will have her neck wrung like a chicken." ' [1] Churchill paused, and then burst out: 'Some chicken! Some neck!'

On the morning of December 31 Churchill gave a press conference at Government House, Ottawa. 'Do you think Singapore can hold on?' he was asked. 'I sure do,' he replied.

During the Ottawa press conference, Churchill was also asked about Yugoslavia. 'They are fighting with the greatest vigour and on quite a large scale,' he replied, 'and we don't hear very much of what is going on there. It is all very terrible. Guerilla warfare and the most frightful atrocities by the Germans and Italians, and every kind of torture.' Churchill added, of the fighting behind the German lines in Yugoslavia: 'The people manage to keep the flag of freedom flying.' [2]

Had he had any 'peace feelers' from the Axis, Churchill was asked. 'We have had none at all,' he replied, 'but then I really think they must be hard pressed for materials of all kinds, and would not want to waste the paper and ink.' [3]

While in Ottawa, Churchill learned of the worsening situation in Malaya. 'If Malay Peninsula has been starved for sake of Libya and Russia,' he telegraphed to Attlee, 'no one is more responsible than I, and I would do exactly the same again.' [4] That night, he returned by train to Washington, and to further talks with Roosevelt. 'For the first time,' noted Sir Charles Wilson, 'I have seen Winston content to listen. You could almost feel the importance he attaches to bringing the

[1] Speech of 30 December 1941: Churchill papers, 9/153.
[2] This was a reference, though Churchill did not say so, to the forces under General Mihailović, who, as the Yugoslav Legation in London informed Churchill on 9 April 1942, had, for more than nine months, 'been leading a fight in Yugoslavia against enormous odds', and who, in April 1942, requested from Britain 'an up-to-date submarine' and a British Bomber Squadron or Flight of long range aircraft to act as a liaison force. Churchill's comment, as on so many requests for action, was: 'what can be done?'. (Note of 9 April 1942, and 'Annex': Chiefs of Staff Committee No. 215 of 1942, 10 April 1942: Cabinet papers, 80/36.)
[3] 'Summary of Press Interview with the Rt Hon Winston Churchill', 11 a.m., 31 December 1941: Premier papers, 4/71/2.
[4] 'Grey' No. 172, 30 December 1941: Churchill papers, 20/50.

President along with him, and in that good cause he has become a very model of restraint and self-discipline; it is surely a new Winston who is sitting there quite silent. And when he does say anything it is always something likely to fall pleasantly on the President's ear.' [1]

From London, Clementine Churchill had written of her own thoughts that Christmas, 'trying to picture and realize the drama in which you are playing the principal—or rather it seems—the only part', and she added: 'I pray that when you leave, the fervour you have aroused may not die down but will consolidate into practical and far-reaching action.' [2]

Having returned to Washington on January 1, Churchill agreed to Roosevelt's draft declaration by the Allied and Associated Powers, to be known henceforth, at Roosevelt's suggestion, as the 'United Nations': a phrase which appeared, as Churchill pointed out to the President, in Byron's poem *Childe Harold's Pilgrimage*.[3] 'The Declaration could not by itself win battles,' Churchill later reflected, 'but it set forth who we were and what we were fighting for.'[4] The declaration pledged all signatories to employ their 'full resources, military or economic' against Germany, Japan and their allies, to co-operate with each other, and 'not to make a separate armistice or peace with the enemies'. Complete victory, they declared, was essential 'to defend life, liberty, independence, and religious freedom, and to preserve human rights and justice in their own lands as well as in other lands. . . .' Twenty-six nations signed the Declaration, headed by the United States, Britain and the Soviet Union, and including several nations then under Nazi rule: Belgium, Czechoslovakia, Luxembourg, Holland, Norway, Poland and Yugoslavia.

On Friday January 2 Churchill and Roosevelt presided jointly over a meeting on Supply, to work out the scale of United States war production for 1942, and the increased scales for 1943. Two further meetings took place on January 3, with Beaverbrook as Britain's principal negotiator. As a result of these discussions, the 1942 programme represented an increase of up to 70%, on the figures fixed three weeks earlier, when America had come into the war. Most important, the planned 12,750 operational aircraft were increased to 45,000, as were the planned 15,450 tanks, while the 262,000 machine guns planned for 1942 were increased to 500,000. At the same time, the 1943 production of operational aircraft was fixed at 100,000 and

---

[1] Diary entry, 31 December 1941, Moran *op. cit.*, pages 19–20.
[2] Letter of 29 December 1941: Spencer-Churchill papers.
[3] The Allied and Associated Powers had first been called the 'United Nations' at the St James's Palace meeting in London in June 1941.
[4] Winston S. Churchill, *The Second World War*, volume 3, London 1950, page 605.

tanks at 75,000. All other weapons of war were to be increased in similar proportions. The forthcoming American budget, Churchill told Attlee, 'will contain necessary financial provisions', and he added: 'Max has been magnificent and Hopkins a godsend. Hope you will be pleased with immense resultant increase in programme.' [1]

Churchill remained at the White House for two more days. On January 3 he rebuked Stalin for an article which had been published in *Pravda* on the last day of 1941, critical of the Americans. It was assumed, Churchill wrote, 'that such articles have the approval of the Russian Government', and he added: 'I feel you will allow me to point out to you the very great danger which might be caused here by a continuance of such criticism.' Churchill went on to remind Stalin that 'from the very first day of the Nazi attack upon you, I have laboured to get all possible support for Soviet Russia in the United States, and therefore I must venture to send you this most private and entirely friendly comment'. [2] In reply, Stalin stated that the article 'had no official character whatever', nor was it directed 'to any other purpose but the common interests of our countries in the struggle against aggression'. [3]

To Attlee, Churchill sent an account of the atmosphere at the White House. 'We live here as a big family,' he telegraphed on January 3, 'in the greatest intimacy and informality, and I have formed the very highest regard and admiration for the President. His breadth of view, resolution and his loyalty to the common cause are beyond all praise.' Churchill added: 'There is not the slightest sign here of excitement or worry about the opening misfortunes, which are taken as a matter of course and to be retrieved by the marshalling of overwhelming forces of every kind. There will, of course, be a row in public presently.' [4]

On January 5 Churchill left Washington by air for Florida, accompanied only by his doctor, Sir Charles Wilson, his Principal Private Secretary, John Martin, and his ADC, 'Tommy' Thompson. There, in a secluded bungalow at Pompano, not far from Miami, and on the edge of the beach, he worked, rested and swam. The reason for going to Florida, Colonel Jacob noted, was Churchill's worry 'that his continued presence in the White House might be irksome and liable

---

[1] 'Grey' No. 230, 4 January 1942: Cabinet papers, 120/29.
[2] 'Grey' No. 203, Prime Minister's Personal Telegram, T.12/2, 3 January 1942: Churchill papers, 20/132.
[3] Telegram received by Churchill on 9 January 1942: Churchill papers, 20/68.
[4] 'Grey' No. 202: Cabinet papers, 120/29.

to cause suspicion in the minds of the officials in the Services, and the members of the Cabinet, who might think he was trying to establish too intimate a connection with the President'.[1] It was also, as Churchill himself later recalled, because 'my American friends thought that I was looking tired and ought to have a rest'.[2] 'Am resting in south,' Churchill telegraphed to Attlee on January 7, 'on Charles Wilson's advice for a few days after rather a strenuous time.'[3]

The weather in Florida, noted the doctor, 'is balmy after the bitter cold of Ottawa—oranges and pineapples grow here. And the blue ocean is so warm that Winston basks half-submerged in the water like a hippopotamus in a swamp.'[4] In a letter home, John Martin also described the Florida visit:

It wasn't always sunny or warm, though on our first morning I had to buy some exotic clothes because my ordinary ones were much too hot; but the sea was always hot and we had marvellous bathing, sometimes in surf against which it was hardly possible to stand upright. We were closely guarded by Secret Service men and, though the Press soon scented our presence, we were not molested in any way. The story was put about that a Mr Lobb, an invalid requiring quiet, was staying in the house and, to explain my un-transatlantic accents when answering the phone, I was his English butler.[5]

During Churchill's five days in Florida, a daily courier, and at least once, two couriers in a single day, flew down with papers and telegrams. For further information Churchill could telephone to his Private Office in Washington, 'and indeed', Colonel Jacob noted, 'he quite frequently did so'.[6] 'More bathing, mixed with some work,' John Martin noted in his diary on January 7.[7] The work was considerable: memoranda and telegrams about the extent and nature of Wavell's command in the Pacific, the need to reinforce Britain's naval and air position in the Mediterranean with a consequent 'relaxation' of the bomber offensive against Germany, opposition to further constitutional change in India 'at a moment when enemy is upon the frontier'; reassurances and encouragement to New Zealand, worries about whether 'anything can be done to protect Singapore', and a reiteration of his opposition to pledging the Baltic States to the Soviet Union.[8] 'I

---

[1] 'Operation "Arcadia", Washington Conference, December 1941': pages 38–9.
[2] Winston S. Churchill, *The Second World War*, volume 3, London 1950, page 612.
[3] 'Grey' No. 250, 7 January 1942: Churchill papers, 20/50.
[4] Diary entry for 5 January 1942: Moran, *op. cit.*, pages 20–21.
[5] Letter of 11 January 1942: Martin papers.
[6] 'Operation "Arcadia", Washington Conference, December 1941': page 39.
[7] John Martin diary, 7 January 1942: Martin papers.
[8] 'Grey' No. 258 and 'Grey' No. 275 (Wavell's Command); 'Grey' No. 256 (Mediterranean); 'Grey' No. 255 (India); 'Grey' No. 262 (New Zealand); 'Grey' No. 277 (Singapore): Cabinet papers, 120/29.

could not be an advocate for a British Cabinet bent on such a course,'
he informed Eden on January 8. 'No one can foresee,' he added, 'how
the balance of power will lie or where the winning armies will stand
at the end of the war. It seems probable however that the United
States and the British Empire, far from being exhausted, will be the
most powerful armed and economic bloc the world has ever seen, and
that the Soviet Union will need our aid for reconstruction far more
than we shall then need theirs.'[1]

While in Florida, Churchill rewrote his four mid-Atlantic surveys
of the future of the war in the light of the Washington decisions.
In this revised survey, he envisaged 'large offensive operations'
being possible in Europe by the summer of 1943, and reiterated that
it was 'right to assign primacy to the war against Germany'. The
Washington discussions had in all matters of strategic priority
and supply, taken the British view. Now, in this final memorandum, Churchill suggested that the United States should plan to send
troops to Persia, which, 'if the Russian southern front is beaten
in (which may well happen), could be sent north, on to Russian
soil, to protect the oilfields of the Caspian and the frontiers of
India'.[2]

On January 10, after lunching with Consuelo Balsan at Fort Lauderdale, Churchill left Florida by train for Washington. Consuelo,
formerly Duchess of Marlborough, had been a friend for more than
forty years. In the years before the outbreak of war in 1939, Churchill
had often painted at her château in northern France. Announcing his
return to Roosevelt, but having been warned to be very careful about
talking on the telephone, Churchill told the President: 'I mustn't tell
you on the open line how we shall be travelling, but we shall be
coming by puff puff.'[3]

As Churchill's train travelled northward to Washington, Japanese
forces made their first assault on the Dutch East Indies, while continuing their rapid descent through the Malay Peninsula. In North
Africa, seven of the eight German and Italian divisions which had
been engaged in Cyrenaica succeeded in withdrawing westward, to a
strong defensive position on the eastern border of Tripolitania. This
move by Rommel cast in jeopardy Churchill's plans for operation

---

[1] 'Grey' No. 261, 8 January 1942: Cabinet papers, 120/29.

[2] 'Palm Beach, Florida', undated, Roosevelt Library Map Room: Warren F. Kimball (editor),
Churchill and Roosevelt, The Complete Correspondence, volume 1, 'Alliance Emerging', Princeton, New
Jersey, 1984, document C-153X, pages 314–23. There is a copy of these notes, as sent to the
British Chiefs of Staff Committee and Defence Committee, in Premier papers, 3/499/1, folios 28–
48.

[3] 'Notes' by John Martin: Martin papers.

'Acrobat', the clearance of Tripoli. 'I am sure you and your armies did all in human power,' he telegraphed to Auchinleck from Washington on January 11, 'but we must face facts as they are. . . .'[1] When Auchinleck replied that he was still pushing on with his advance, Churchill telegraphed his pleasure at this news, which he would show to Roosevelt 'today', January 13, and he added: 'Will support you whatever the result.'[2]

Churchill and Roosevelt prepared to resume their 'Arcadia' discussions. 'I am emphasizing in my talks here,' Churchill telegraphed to Stalin on January 11, 'the extreme importance of making punctual deliveries to Russia of the promised quotas.'[3] On January 12 Churchill and Roosevelt again presided jointly at a meeting of the Combined Chiefs of Staff. The need to reinforce the Americans in the Far East, General Marshall explained, meant that the number of American troops which could go to Northern Ireland would have to be reduced from 16,000 to 4,100, and the number to go to Iceland from 8,000 to 2,500. Churchill agreed to this proposal, pointing out that any 'uninterrupted success' by the Japanese 'might have widespread repercussions'.[4]

The Washington War Conference was over. In its report, it was noted that Roosevelt 'set great store' in organizing operation 'Super-Gymnast', a combined Anglo-American landing in North Africa, for which Britain and the United States would both contribute 90,000 troops, together with 'a considerable air force'.[5] In addition, Roosevelt told Churchill privately that, in the event of a Japanese advance towards Australia, 50,000 United States troops would be sent for Australia's defence.[6]

The Washington War Conference also decided to set up a Combined Chiefs of Staff to determine and recommend 'the broad programme of requirements based on strategic policy', to establish a Combined Raw Materials Board for the 'planned and expeditious' utilization of the raw material resources of the United Nations for the prosecution of the war, and to form a 'common pool' of the entire munitions resources of Britain and the United States 'about which the

[1] 'Grey' No. 295, Prime Minister's Personal Telegram, T.41/2, 11 January 1942: Churchill papers, 20/88.

[2] 'Grey' No. 322, Prime Minister's Personal Telegram, T.53/2, 13 January 1942: Churchill papers, 20/68.

[3] 'Grey' No. 297, Prime Minister's Personal Telegram, T.45/2, 11 January 1942: Churchill papers, 20/132.

[4] Washington War Conference, 9th Meeting, 5.45 a.m., 12 January 1942: Cabinet papers, 99/17.

[5] 'Most Secret', Washington War Conference Memorandum No. 17, 'The Washington War Conference (Military Subjects)', 20 January 1942: Cabinet papers, 99/17.

[6] Winston S. Churchill, *The Second World War*, volume 3, London 1950, page 624.

fullest information will be exchanged' and advice given as to consignments. The note on this munitions agreement ended: 'Any differences arising, which it is expected will be rare, will be resolved by the President and the Prime Minister in agreement.'

Also established as a result of the Washington War Conference was an Anglo-American Shipping Adjustment Board, whereby the shipping resources of Britain and America 'will be deemed to be pooled'.[1] The most important decision of all, from the British perspective, was the agreement, as the United States and British Chiefs of Staff expressed it, that 'only the minimum of forces necessary for safeguarding of vital interests in other theatres should be diverted from operations against Germany'.[2]

As news reached Washington each hour of the deteriorating situation in Malaya, Churchill sought to encourage John Curtin, the Australian Prime Minister. Malaya itself, Churchill felt, was lost. 'I do not see how anyone could expect Malaya to be defended,' he told Curtin, 'once the Japanese obtained command of the sea and whilst we are fighting for our lives against Germany and Italy.' The only 'vital point' was the fortress of Singapore and its 'essential hinterland'. So far, Churchill told Curtin, 'the Japanese have only had two white battalions and a few gunners against them, the rest being Indian soldiers'. He was confident that Singapore could be defended, and supported Wavell's hope 'that a counter-stroke will be possible in February'. As to criticism of the decision to give the United States the naval command of the Australian and New Zealand area of the Pacific, despite the almost negligible United States naval force in that area, Dudley Pound was of the opinion, Churchill told Curtin, 'and I agree with him, that the advantage of persuading the United States to undertake the responsibilities for this area as a part of their main Pacific Command, outweighs such criticism'.[3]

That same day, Churchill's confidence in the ability of Singapore to resist a direct assault was shaken when he read a report from the Colonial Secretary, Lord Moyne, on the lack of defences in the city. 'This is a shocking tale,' he telegraphed from Washington, 'and everybody seems to blame. Why did not Duff Cooper report the lack

[1] Washington War Conference, Memorandum No. 17, Annexes VI, VII and VIII: Cabinet papers, 99/17.
[2] Washington War Conference, Memorandum No. 17, Annex 1, 'American and British Strategy', 'Memorandum by the United States and British Chiefs of Staffs', 14 January 1942: Cabinet papers, 99/17.
[3] 'Grey' No. 307, Prime Minister's Personal Telegram, T.50/12, 13 January 1942: Churchill papers, 20/68.

of preparations and provision of gas-masks, steel hats etc, for civil population? These elements of deficiency must have been known to him before war broke out.'[1]

'Battle for Singapore will be close run thing,' Wavell telegraphed to Churchill from his new headquarters in Batavia, in the Dutch East Indies, as Churchill was preparing to leave Washington, 'and we shall need luck in getting in convoys safely and up to time.'[2]

That same day there was a momentary cause for hope when it was learned, as Churchill telegraphed to John Curtin, that the 'vital convoy' including the American transport ship *Mount Vernon*, had reached Singapore 'safely and punctually' with 9,000 troops, including an anti-tank regiment with fifty guns, and fifty Hurricane fighters.[3] But Churchill continued to worry about the city's ability to resist a direct assault. 'What are the defences and obstructions on the landward side?' he asked Wavell by telegram on January 14, just before leaving Washington, and he went on to ask: 'Are you sure you can dominate with Fortress cannon any attempt to plant siege batteries?'[4]

On January 14 Churchill left Washington for London, flying from Norfolk, Virginia to Bermuda in a Boeing flying boat. At the start of the four hour journey the Captain, Kelly Rogers, invited him to visit the control deck. Rogers' own account described the sequel:

When he entered the control deck the Prime Minister was smoking a cigar. There is no danger therefrom. He did, however, ask if it was safe to strike a match when his cigar went out while he was sitting at the controls. I assured him it was quite safe and that smoking could safely be indulged in anywhere throughout the aircraft. His questions concerning the operation of the controls and general behaviour of the aircraft made it quite clear that he would like to handle her himself. I invited him to do so and he responded immediately.

I disengaged the automatic pilot and whispered an instruction in Captain Shakespeare's ear, who was on watch at the time in the co-pilot's seat, to apply only such corrections to the controls as would be necessary if the aircraft got beyond the Prime Minister's control. No major correction was necessary, and in fact the Prime Minister asked if he could make a couple of slightly banked turns, which he did with considerable success; he was at the controls

[1] 'Grey' No. 311, 13 January 1942: Cabinet papers, 120/29.
[2] Telegram 00040, 'Taut' No. 528, 14 January 1942: Churchill papers, 20/68.
[3] Prime Minister's Personal Telegram, T.55/2A, 14 January 1942: Churchill papers, 20/68.
[4] 'Grey' No. 341, Prime Minister's Personal Telegram, T.62/2, 14 January 1942: Churchill papers, 20/88.

about twenty minutes altogether and afterwards described to me the difference between this aircraft and the one he had flown as long ago as 1913.[1]

At Bermuda, the *Duke of York* was ready to take Churchill, Pound, Portal and Beaverbrook back to England. But with the worsening situation in Malaya uppermost in his mind, Churchill persuaded them to continue their return journey by the same flying boat that had brought them to Bermuda. Leaving Bermuda on January 16, the flying boat flew through the night, eastward across the Atlantic. 'During the night,' Captain Rogers later wrote, 'the Prime Minister and Lord Beaverbrook again visited the control deck. The aircraft was riding through a brilliantly starlit sky, with the outline of the cloud tops just visible below, and both the Prime Minister and Lord Beaverbrook surprised me by saying that they envied me my job.'[2]

As dawn broke, the flying boat deviated slightly southward approaching within five or six minutes' flying time of German-occupied France, and the German anti-aircraft batteries in Brest. 'We are going to turn north at once,' Portal informed Churchill, the moment the error was discovered.

The flying boat flew towards Plymouth. There a British radar watcher reported a 'hostile bomber' flying in from the direction of Brest. Six Hurricanes were ordered into the air to shoot down the intruder. Fortunately, as Churchill later commented, 'they failed in their mission'.[3]

While still in Washington, Churchill had made a further effort to persuade the War Cabinet to allow his speeches in the House of Commons to be recorded. If his speech on his return could be recorded, he had telegraphed to Attlee on January 11, it would avoid 'the burden of my having to deliver the speech again on the 9 o'clock broadcast'. If not successful, the experiment 'need not be repeated'.[4] Churchill's request was discussed by the War Cabinet on January 12, when, as the official minutes recorded, 'the wisdom of recording the Prime Minister's statement in the House was doubted'. One problem was the difficulty of dealing with possible interruptions. The other was the difficulty, once this initial concession had been made, 'to refuse the

[1] 'Article by Capt. Kelly Rogers', issued to the Press on 23 January 1942: Premier papers, 4/71/2, folios 648–50.
[2] 'Article by Capt. Kelly Rogers', issued to the Press on 23 January 1942: Premier papers, 4/71/2, folio 651.
[3] Winston S. Churchill, *The Second World War*, volume 3, London 1950, page 629. The flight had taken 17 hours and 55 minutes. The distance covered was 3,365 miles.
[4] 'Grey' No. 291, 11 January 1942: Cabinet papers, 120/29.

request that other speeches should be broadcast'. The broadcasting of proceedings in Parliament generally 'was strongly deprecated'. To avoid the strain of making a Parliamentary statement and a broadcast on the same day, the Ministers felt that 'there was no real reason' why the broadcast should not be delayed 'until some days after his return'.[1]

Shortly before ten in the morning of January 17, Churchill landed at Plymouth, after a flight of nearly eighteen hours. That evening, at six o'clock, he reported to the War Cabinet on his visit to Washington. 'The United States Administration,' he told his colleagues, 'were tackling war problems with the greatest vigour, and were clearly resolved not to be diverted from using all the resources of their country to the utmost to crush Hitler, our major enemy.' Joint boards and committees would be set up to deal with raw materials, munitions, assignments, and shipping. The idea, 'underlying' these bodies, Churchill explained, 'was that the resources of Great Britain and the United States were regarded as a common pool to be used for the prosecution of the war'.[2]

Churchill then gave a summary of the position of Roosevelt, and of the American administration:

An Olympian calm had obtained at the White House. It was perhaps rather isolated. The President had no adequate link between his will and executive action. There was no such organisation as the Secretariat of the Cabinet or of the Chiefs of Staff Committee. When the President saw the Ministerial heads of the Fighting Services, who were really little more than Private Secretaries and responsible to him only, meetings were quite informal. Although Mr Harry Hopkins lacked experience of military matters, his instincts were fundamentally sound, and he played a great part in helping the President to give effect to his policies.

The Prime Minister thought that there was little risk of the Americans abandoning the conventional principles of war. They were not above learning from us, provided that we did not set out to teach them.

The State Department, Churchill added, 'were apt to be somewhat jumpy', but he wanted his colleagues to know that Roosevelt's last words to him, on leaving, had been: 'Trust me to the bitter end.'[3]

Churchill also gave an account of the Washington War Conference

[1] War Cabinet No. 4 of 1942, 12 January 1942: Cabinet papers, 65/25.
[2] War Cabinet No. 8 of 1942, 17 January 1942: Cabinet papers, 65/25.
[3] 'Other Points Touched on in Discussion', War Cabinet No. 8 of 1942, 17 January 1942: Cabinet papers, 65/25.

to the King, who recorded in his diary that the Prime Minister 'was now confident of ultimate victory, as the United States of America were starting on a full output of men and material'. Britain and America, Churchill told the King, 'were now "married" after many months of "walking out" '.[1]

---

[1] King George VI, diary, 19 January 1942: John W. Wheeler-Bennett, *King George VI, His Life and Reign*, London 1958, page 535.

3

The Fall of Singapore

ON the day of Churchill's return to Britain from the United
States, General Auchinleck's forces captured Halfaya, and with
it more than 5,000 German and Italian troops. 'Hearty congratulations,' Churchill telegraphed, 'on another brilliant and timely success.'[1] That night General Brooke, the Chief of the Imperial General
Staff, dined at No. 10 Annexe with Churchill, his wife, and his
daughter Mary. 'A very pleasant quiet homely dinner,' he noted in
his diary. 'He could not have been nicer. After dinner went to his
study where I remained with him until midnight discussing the possibilities of Singapore island holding out. Also drew his attention to the
dangers of Rangoon.'[2] On the following day, the Japanese captured
the port and airbase of Tavoy, in south Burma, less than 250 miles
south-east of Rangoon.

Across the North Sea and Arctic Ocean, British aid to Russia proceeded under convoy to Archangel and Murmansk. On 17 January
1942 one of the escorting destroyers, HMS *Matabele*, was torpedoed
and sunk, with the loss of 247 officers and men. But when, on the
following day, Churchill learned that aircraft supplies to Russia had
fallen, by 45 aircraft, behind the amount promised, he minuted to Sir
Archibald Sinclair, the Secretary of State for Air: 'It seems a very
great pity to fall short in Russian deliveries by these comparatively
small quantities which cannot affect your main problem here. I must
emphasize that exact and punctual deliveries to Russia are of the
utmost importance, as this is all we can do to help them.'[3]

While he had been in Washington, Churchill had envisaged that
'fortress' Singapore would be able to hold off a Japanese attack for as

[1] Prime Minister's Personal Telegram, T.67/2, 17 January 1942: Churchill papers,
20/88.
[2] Brooke diary, 17 January 1942: Arthur Bryant, *The Turn of the Tide 1939–1943*, London
1957, page 298.
[3] Prime Minister's Personal Minute, M.2/2, 18 January 1942: Churchill papers, 20/67.

long as two months. But on January 19 he learned from Wavell, in answer to his question of January 14, that there were no permanent defensive fortifications on the landward side of the naval base or the city. All its defences had been constructed, Wavell telegraphed, 'entirely to meet seaward attack'. Many of the fortress guns 'can only fire sea-wards'. In addition, part of the garrison had already been sent northward to Johore, to meet the Japanese forces there, while many of the remaining troops, he wrote, were 'of doubtful value'. Wavell added: 'I am sorry to give you depressing picture but I do not want you to have false picture of island fortress.' [1]

The source of Wavell's report was an officer whom Wavell had sent to Singapore to plan the island's defence. When he read it, Churchill was 'staggered', as he wrote to the Chiefs of Staff Committee. It had never occurred to him or to Dill, with whom he had discussed the matter on the way to Washington, 'that the gorge of the fortress of Singapore with its splendid moat half-a-mile to a mile wide was not entirely fortified against an attack from the northward'. His minute continued:

What is the use of having an island for a fortress if it is not to be made into a citadel? To construct a line of detached works with searchlights and cross-fire combined with immense wiring and obstruction of the swamp areas and to provide the proper ammunition to enable the fortress guns to dominate enemy batteries planted in Johore, was an elementary peace-time provision which it is incredible did not exist in a fortress which has been twenty years building. If this was so, how much more should the necessary field works have been constructed during the two and a half years of the present war? How is it that not one of you pointed this out to me at any time when these matters have been under discussion? More especially should this have been done because in my various minutes extending over the last two years I have repeatedly shown that I relied upon this defence of Singapore Island against a formal siege, and have never relied upon the Kra Isthmus plan.

In England, Churchill pointed out, it had been found necessary to protect 'the gorges' of all forts against a landing raid from the rear. The Portsdown Hill forts at Portsmouth showed 'the principles which have long prevailed'.

There was, Churchill added, another case in connection with the Malay Peninsula 'where you all seem to have been misinformed' by the Joint Planning Staff and the Joint Intelligence Committee: this was on the 'state of the terrain' between Singora and Johore. As Churchill explained, 'I was repeatedly informed at the time of the Japanese landing that owing to the season of the year the ground was so water-logged that there could be no question of an advance

[1] Telegram No. 00118, 'Private and Most Secret', 19 January 1942: Churchill papers, 20/68.

southward in force until the spring. Pray look this up and find out who and what was the foundation of this opinion, so violently falsified by events.' It was, Churchill added, 'most disquieting to me that such frightful ignorance of the conditions should have prevailed'.

Merely to have seaward batteries at Singapore, Churchill went on, and no fixed defences or forts to protect their rear, 'is not to be excused on any grounds'. By such 'neglect', the whole security of the Singapore fortress 'has been at the mercy of 10,000 men breaking across the Straits in small boats', and he went on to 'warn' that such an eventuality 'will be one of the greatest scandals that could possibly be exposed'.

Despite this dismal and dangerous situation, Churchill still hoped that something might be done. 'Let a plan be made at once to do the best possible,' he instructed the Chiefs of Staff, and he then set out a ten-point plan, including the mining and obstructing of the likely landing grounds, the construction of field works and strong points with field artillery and machine-gun crossfire, the construction of defence works by the 'entire male population', up to the limit of the picks and shovels available and the planting of field batteries at each end of the Straits 'carefully masked and with searchlights, so as to destroy any enemy boat that may seek to enter the Straits'.

Not only must the defence of Singapore Island be maintained 'by every means', Churchill added, 'but the whole Island must be fought for until every single Unit and every single strong point has been separately destroyed'. The city of Singapore must be converted into a citadel 'and defended to the death'. No surrender could be contemplated, 'and the Commander, Staffs and principal Officers are expected to perish at their posts'.[1]

After the War Cabinet that evening, Sir Alexander Cadogan noted in his diary: 'PM seems prepared for worst in Malaya but not hopeless yet.'[2]

Churchill's ten-point plan for the last-minute defence of Singapore was discussed by the Chiefs of Staff, who sent on its practical suggestions, though not the instruction to 'perish at their posts', to Wavell.[3] But at the same time, in a personal message to Wavell on the night of January 19, Churchill pointed out that since Wavell had become Supreme Commander of the allied nations in the south-western Pacific, 'I cannot of course send you any instructions.' He could of

---

[1] Prime Minister's Personal Minute, D.4/2, 'Most Secret', 19 January 1942: Churchill papers, 20/67.
[2] Cadogan diary, 19 January 1942: David Dilks (editor), *The Diaries of Sir Alexander Cadogan, OM, 1938–1945*, London 1971.
[3] Telegram No. 65356, 20 January 1942: Churchill papers, 20/68.

course continue to correspond with Wavell 'whenever I have suggestions to make or questions to ask'; and this, he felt, would be 'especially
the case' when the local defence of a fortress like Singapore was
involved. 'I want to make it absolutely clear,' Churchill explained,
'that I expect every inch of ground to be defended, every scrap of
material or defences to be blown to pieces to prevent capture by the
enemy and no question of surrender to be entertained until after protracted fighting among the ruins of Singapore City.'[1]

In preparation for a meeting of the Chiefs of Staff Committee on
the morning of January 21, Churchill, having read a further telegram
from Wavell which gave little hope of a prolonged defence, suggested
to the Chiefs of Staff that they should consider, and ask Wavell,
whether it might not be best to abandon the indefensible Singapore.
At the same time as abandoning Singapore, they should demolish its
naval and military installations so as to render the harbour virtually
useless to the Japanese, and order the troops and aircraft then on
their way to Singapore to go instead to the defence of Burma. 'We
may,' Churchill wrote, 'by muddling things and hesitating to take an
ugly decision, lose both Singapore and the Burma Road.' The decision
would obviously depend upon how long the defence of Singapore
could be maintained. 'If it is only for a few weeks,' he wrote, 'it is
certainly not worth losing all our reinforcements and aircraft.'[2]

No decision was reached by the Chiefs of Staff that morning, nor,
that same evening, by the Chiefs of Staff Committee, over which
Churchill presided. Churchill's own mind, as he later wrote, 'was not
made up. I leaned upon my friends and counsellors. We all suffered
extremely at this time.'[3]

'If Singapore could only hold out for another three or four weeks,'
Churchill asked Pound, Portal, Brooke and Ismay, 'was it not only
throwing good money after bad to send more reinforcements there;
should not they be sent to Burma?' He could not 'overemphasize', he
added, 'the importance of keeping open the Burma Road'. If the
Chinese 'failed to continue the fight', the road might only be 'the first
step' to an Asia united under the Japanese.

He was in favour of sending reinforcements to Singapore, Churchill
told the Chiefs of Staff, only if there was 'a reasonable chance of the
fortress holding'.[4]

[1] Prime Minister's Personal Telegram T.82/2, 'Personal and Secret', despatched 4.30 a.m., 20
January 1942: Churchill papers, 20/68.
[2] Prime Minister's Personal Minute, D.6/2, 'Most Secret', 21 January 1942: Churchill papers,
20/67.
[3] Winston S. Churchill, *The Second World War*, volume 4, London 1951, page 49.
[4] Chiefs of Staff Committee No. 4 (Operations) of 1942, 6 p.m., 21 January 1942: Cabinet
papers, 79/56.

During January 21 the Chiefs of Staff telegraphed to General Percival, in command of Singapore, to ensure 'should the worst come to the worst', that nothing which could possibly be of any use to the Japanese should be omitted 'from the general scorched-earth schemes'. At the Defence Committee which met that evening, Churchill stressed that 'we could not now consider Singapore as a fortress'. If the battles in Johore 'went against us', it was possible that a 'prolonged defence of Singapore' could not be made. Taking 'the widest view', he felt that Burma 'was more important than Singapore', and should be reinforced: but this was primarily a matter for Wavell, as Supreme Commander, to decide. Meanwhile, the 'immediate issue', he said, was to give 'highest priority' to the battle of Johore and the defence of Singapore island.[1]

Eden, who was present at this meeting of the Defence Committee as were Lord Beaverbrook and A. V. Alexander, noted in his diary:

After meeting, Max and I and Alexander had drinks with Winston. We spoke of Australia and domestic situation. Max and I urged patience with former and understanding of seriousness of latter if news from Malaya continued to deteriorate, as it probably would. Winston was tired and depressed, for him. His cold is heavy on him. He was inclined to be fatalistic about the House, maintained that bulk of Tories hated him, that he had done all he could and would be only too happy to yield to another, that Malaya, Australian Government's intransigence and 'nagging' in House was more than any man could be expected to endure. I urged reforms in Whips' Office and organization of pro Government speakers. Max backed me in latter, citing example of last war. But Winston would not be interested, arguing that Ll.G was young and therefore right to insure against future, but that he was sixty-seven.[2]

Churchill's minute of January 21, in which he had first mooted the possible abandonment of Singapore, was a secret communication to the three Chiefs of Staff, and to General Ismay, his representative on the Defence Committee. Inadvertently, a copy was shown to Australia's representative with the War Cabinet, Sir Earle Page, who communicated its contents to John Curtin.[3] On Saturday January 24 Curtin telegraphed to Churchill that the evacuation of Malaya and Singapore 'would be regarded here and elsewhere as an inexcusable

[1] Defence Committee No. 4 of 1942, 21 January 1942: Cabinet papers, 69/4.
[2] Eden diary, 21 January 1942: Eden memoirs, *The Reckoning*, *op. cit.*, page 318. In December 1916 (when he became Prime Minister), Lloyd George had been fifty-three years old.
[3] Sir Earle Page had served as Deputy Prime Minister of Australia from 1934 to 1939 (and was briefly Prime Minister in April 1939). In 1941 and 1942 he was Special Australian Envoy to the British War Cabinet, before returning to Australia as a member of the Australian War Cabinet.

betrayal'.[1] That weekend, at Chequers, Churchill was preparing a speech in answer to criticisms in the House of Commons of the rapid Japanese advance towards Singapore: the debate was fixed for Tuesday, January 27. While at Chequers, Churchill learned from his Parliamentary Private Secretary, Colonel Harvie Watt, that the Parliamentary Labour Party had voted by 'a considerable majority' not to allow Churchill to broadcast his speech direct.[2] During the weekend, news reached Churchill from North Africa of a substantial German advance: the first serious setback to Britain's desert strategy since Auchinleck had launched the 'Crusader' offensive more than two months earlier.

'PM getting worked up for speech in House next Tuesday,' John Martin noted in his diary on January 23, and on the following day: 'PM working on speech.'[3] As he worked, he learned from the 8th Army of the imminent evacuation of Benghazi, and was 'much disturbed'. 'I had certainly never been led to suppose that such a situation could arise,' he telegraphed to Auchinleck on January 25, fearing that the news foreshadowed 'the failure of "Crusader" and the ruin of "Acrobat" '—the plan to advance as far as Tunis.[4]

Churchill returned to London from Chequers after lunch on Monday, January 26. That evening, at a meeting of the War Cabinet, he assured Sir Earle Page that the decision reached by the Defence Committee on January 21 had been 'that the Battle of Johore and the defence of Singapore Island should be given the highest priority', and he pointed out that Wavell's instructions were 'that the battle should be fought out, if need be, in the ruins of Singapore'.[5]

That day Churchill was still 'absorbed' in his speech, as he telegraphed to Field Marshal Dill.[6] He was determined, also, that the vote should be one of Confidence in the Coalition. His wife Clementine, his daughter Diana, and his brother Jack were among those who went to hear him. 'It is because things have gone badly,' Churchill declared, 'and worse is to come, that I demand a Vote of Confidence.'[7]

Churchill spoke for nearly two hours. 'One can actually feel the wind of opposition dropping sentence by sentence,' Harold Nicolson

---

[1] 'Mr Curtin to Prime Minister', despatched 5 a.m., 24 January 1942, received 12.5 a.m., 'Johcu' No. 21, 'Most Secret', 24 January 1942: Churchill papers, 20/69.

[2] 'Parliamentary Private Secretary's Report, 23 January 1942' (initialled by Churchill on 25 January 1942): Harvie Watt papers.

[3] John Martin, diary entries for 23 and 24 January 1942: Martin papers.

[4] Prime Minister's Personal Telegram, T.116/2, 25 January 1942: Churchill papers, 20/69.

[5] War Cabinet No. 11 of 1942, Minute 3, Confidential Annex, 25 January 1942, 6 p.m.: Cabinet papers, 65/29.

[6] Prime Minister's Personal Telegram, T.119/2, 26 January 1942: Churchill papers, 20/69.

[7] Hansard, 27 January 1942, columns 591–619.

noted in his diary, 'and by the time he finishes it is clear that there is really no opposition at all—only a certain uneasiness.'[1] The debate continued for two more days. But for Churchill it was overshadowed by the news from North Africa, which continued to give cause for alarm. 'I am most anxious,' he telegraphed to Auchinleck on January 28, 'to hear further from you about defeat of our armour by inferior enemy numbers. This cuts very deep.'[2] But there was an element of hope on January 28, when Enigma intercepts revealed Rommel's intentions to clear the area up to Benghazi, and then to withdraw to a waiting line.[3]

On January 29 Churchill wound up the three-day debate. His speech, noted Henry Channon, 'was conciliatory, tactful—and, finally successful'. Its theme was expressed in a single sentence. 'I submit to the House,' he said, 'that the main strategic and political decision to aid Russia, to deliver an offensive in Libya and to accept a consequential state of weakness in the then peaceful theatre of the Far East, was sound, and will be found to have played a useful part in the general course of the War, and that this is in no wise invalidated by the unexpected naval misfortunes and the heavy forfeits which we have paid, and shall have to pay in the Far East.' 'For this Vote of Confidence,' he added, 'on that I rest.'

Churchill spoke for forty-two minutes, holding 'the vast audience enthralled'.[4] 'In no way,' he ended, 'have I mitigated the sense of danger and impending misfortunes—of a minor character and of a severe character—which still hang over us. But at the same time I avow my confidence, never stronger than at this moment, that we shall bring this conflict to an end in a manner agreeable to the interests of our country, and in a manner agreeable to the future of the world.'[5]

The vote was 464 in support of the Government and one against. The lone opponent was James Maxton, of the Independent Labour Party. As the vote was taken, Churchill left with his wife; 'arm-in-arm and beaming', Harold Nicolson noted in his diary, 'they push through the crowds in the Central Lobby'. On the ticker-tape, 'ticking imperturbably', the news was of German claims to have entered Benghazi, and Japanese claims to have reached to within eighteen miles

[1] Harold Nicolson, diary entry for 27 January 1942: Nigel Nicolson (editor), *op. cit.*, page 207.

[2] Prime Minister's Personal Telegram, T.129/2, 28 January 1942: Churchill papers, 20/88.

[3] Prime Minister's Personal Telegram, T.129/2, 28 January 1942: Churchill papers, 20/88. Churchill's reference in this telegram to Enigma as 'the most secret stuff' was changed in his memoirs to 'the information'. As late as 1963, this telegram, referring as it did to Enigma, was withdrawn from the Churchill papers on the grounds of 'national security'.

[4] Henry Channon diary, 29 January 1942: Robert Rhodes James (editor), *Chips, the Diaries of Sir Henry Channon*, London 1967, page 319.

[5] *Hansard*, 29 January 1942, column 1017.

of Singapore.[1] Both claims were true. That same day, the Government at last made public the sinking of the battleship *Barham*, with the loss of 500 lives, the previous December.[2]

In a Most Secret cypher telegram sent from Singapore to London on January 27, Wavell had reported seven British aircraft destroyed on the ground, and a further thirteen damaged, during a Japanese air attack. Reading this telegram, Churchill minuted to Portal: 'This sort of thing will finish us—unless it can be stopped.'[3]

'I agree that these losses are deplorable,' Portal minuted in reply, 'but I am afraid they are inevitable where, as in Singapore, our fighters have no forward aerodromes from which to operate, and in consequence there is no depth to the defence.' To protect the bombers from the danger of such attacks, Portal explained, Wavell was withdrawing them, and his maintenance and base units, to Sumatra and Java. 'From there,' Portal added, 'he intends to direct them, as much as possible, against Japanese aerodromes in Malaya in order to reduce the scale of air attack on Singapore,' where only the fighters would continue to operate.[4]

On the following morning, reading details in the *Daily Express* of troop movements on Singapore Island, Churchill took up the question of the army's censorship in Singapore. 'They seem to give everything away about themselves in the blandest manner,' he minuted. 'After all, they are defending a fortress and not conducting a Buchmanite revival.'[5]

January 30 was Roosevelt's sixtieth birthday. 'Many happy returns of the day,' Churchill telegraphed, 'and may your next birthday see us a long lap forward on our road.'[6] Roosevelt's reply, sent that same

[1] Harold Nicolson diary, 29 January 1942: Nigel Nicolson (editor), *op. cit.*, page 208. On 2 February 1942 Lord Beaverbrook wrote to Harry Hopkins: 'Churchill has had many experiences in a life full of colour but came up against a new situation on his return from Washington. Some ten or fifteen of his followers set themselves up as authorities on the Far East and on Singapore in particular. They had two or three good days of popularity and then they were required to present their case to public opinion. A most extraordinary reaction set in and by the weekend Churchill had been established in authority and power exceeding all that had gone before.' (Quoted in A. J. P. Taylor, *Beaverbrook*, London 1972, pages 506–7.)

[2] The announcement of the sinking of the *Barham* had been kept secret because the Admiralty knew, from the Enigma decrypts, that the U-boat commander did not realize that his target had been sunk (Hinsley and others, *British Intelligence in the Second World War*, volume 2, London 1981, pages 328–9).

[3] Minute of 28 January 1942: Air Ministry papers, 19/557.

[4] 'Secret', 29 January 1942: Air Ministry papers, 19/557.

[5] Prime Minister's Personal Minute (to the Secretary of State for War and the Minister of Information), M.17/2, 'Action this Day', 30 January 1942: Churchill papers, 20/67.

[6] Prime Minister's Personal Telegram T.137/2, 30 January 1942: Churchill papers, 20/59.

day, gave Churchill 'great pleasure'; as Charles Wilson recorded. 'It is fun,' the President telegraphed, 'to be in the same decade with you.' [1]

'The Americans are very broadminded,' Churchill telegraphed to Wavell on February 7, 'but if they think they are being squeezed out by what they call Britishers you will get the contrary reactions in a vehement form.' [2] Within three weeks, Churchill was to inform Roosevelt that British Intelligence had, before Pearl Harbour, been able to read some of the American diplomatic telegrams. 'From the moment we became allies,' Churchill added, 'I gave instructions that this work should cease.' He was now anxious to warn Roosevelt of the danger of 'our enemies' being able to read these same messages. [3]

On the afternoon of February 9 news reached the Cabinet that the Japanese had managed to penetrate five miles into Singapore Island. [4] The fortress was now both breached and besieged. In India, pressure had mounted for an immediate promise of Dominion Status once the war was over. In China, Chiang-Kai-shek had offered to co-ordinate his own war strategy with Britain, in a joint effort to halt the Japanese onslaught.

Churchill now contemplated yet another distant journey, by air to India, to meet Chiang-Kai-shek there. He also wanted, as Eden's Private Secretary, Oliver Harvey, noted in his diary, 'to consult with Indian leaders as to formation of an Assembly to work out a constitution for after the war'. Churchill had first proposed this journey four days earlier, at a meeting of the Cabinet at which India had been a central item on the agenda. The idea of Churchill going to India, Sir Alexander Cadogan noted in his diary, was 'brilliantly imaginative and bold and was generally welcomed!' [5]

On his return from India, Churchill intended to stop in Cairo, 'and', as Oliver Harvey noted in his diary, 'clear up the mess there (as to which he is very worried)'. But there was a 'complication' as far as this journey was concerned: 'the doctors', Harvey added, 'have told him that his heart is not too good and he needs rest'. Harvey also learned from Eden that Churchill had 'confessed that he did feel his heart a bit—he had tried to dance a little the other night but found he quickly lost his breath!'.

[1] Sir Charles Wilson, diary entry for 30 January 1942: Moran, *op. cit.*, pages 25–8.
[2] Prime Minister's Personal Telegram, T.192/3, 7 February 1942: Churchill papers, 20/69.
[3] Letter of 25 February 1942: Churchill papers, 20/52.
[4] Sir Alexander Cadogan, diary entry for 9 February 1942: David Dilks (editor), *The Diaries of Sir Alexander Cadogan OM 1938–1945*, London 1971, pages 432–3.
[5] Sir Alexander Cadogan, diary entry for 5 February 1942: David Dilks (editor), *op. cit.*, page 432.

In discussing Churchill's planned visit to India, Eden and Harvey agreed that Churchill 'was the only person who could do it all. But for his heart there could be no question he was the right one to go.' Harvey added: 'What a decision to take, and how gallant of the old boy himself! But his age and more especially his way of life must begin to tell on him. He had beer, 3 ports and 3 brandies for lunch today, and has done it for years.'[1] On the following day, with Churchill's health much in mind, Harvey told Eden 'he must be prepared to take over'. Harvey added: 'I think he is.'[2]

By midnight on February 9 the Japanese had widened their bridgehead on Singapore Island. The idea of abandoning Singapore was now itself abandoned. 'There must at this stage be no thought of saving the troops or sparing the population,' Churchill telegraphed to Wavell. 'The battle must be fought to the bitter end at all costs.' Commanders and senior officers, he added, 'should die with their troops'. Churchill relied upon Wavell to show 'no mercy to weakness in any form'. With the Russians and Americans fighting as they were, 'the whole reputation of our country and our race is involved'.[3] In reply, however, Wavell warned Churchill: 'Morale of some troops is not good, and none is as high as I should like to see.' The conditions and the ground were 'difficult for defence', and the 'chief troubles' were lack of sufficient training in some of the reinforcing troops 'and inferiority complex which bold and skilful Japanese tactics and their command of the air have caused'.[4]

On February 10 the Pacific War Council held its first meeting, in London, with Churchill in the Chair, and with Dutch, Australian and New Zealand representatives present. London, and Washington were to be the places of decision. The Council, Churchill explained, would not deal with 'the detailed conduct of the war', for which purpose Wavell had been appointed Supreme Commander, but would 'review the broad fundamental policies which should be followed in the war against Japan'. It was important, Churchill added, 'that the machine should not be clogged with details and that control should rest in the fewest possible hands'.[5]

From hour to hour, Churchill received the news of the relentless Japanese advance on Singapore Island. 'The battle must be fought to the bitter end,' he telegraphed to Roosevelt on February 11,

[1] Harvey diary, 9 February 1942: John Harvey (editor), *The War Diaries of Oliver Harvey*, London 1978, pages 92–3.

[2] Harvey diary, 10 February 1942: *op. cit.*, pages 93–4.

[3] Prime Minister's Personal Telegram, T.206/2, 'Clear the Line', despatched at 1.30 a.m., 10 February 1942: Churchill papers, 20/70.

[4] 'Most Secret', received 1.05 p.m., 11 February 1942: Churchill papers, 20/70.

[5] Pacific War Council, 1st Meeting, 6 p.m., 10 February 1942: Cabinet papers, 99/26.

'regardless of consequences to the city or its inhabitants.'[1] That same day, Oliver Harvey noted that Churchill was not going to India 'because of Singapore. He feels he must be here when it falls.'[2]

As well as the pressures which arose because the war was going so badly, Churchill was involved in an ominous dispute between two of his Ministers, Ernest Bevin and Lord Beaverbrook. Bevin, as Minister of Labour, insisted that the powers of the Minister for Production were not to include control over the labour force. Churchill worked hard to resolve the differences between the two men. 'I have lavished my time and strength during the last week,' he wrote to Beaverbrook on February 10, 'in trying to make arrangements which are satisfactory to you and to the public interest and to allay the anxieties of the departments with whom you will be brought in contact. I can do no more.'[3]

Churchill had now to reconstruct his Government, to maintain the balance of parties, and to put the best man available in the post to be changed. On February 11 he saw Sir Stafford Cripps, to whom he repeated his offer of the Ministry of Supply. But Cripps refused to accept this office, unless he were also made a member of the War Cabinet. That same day, Churchill saw his friend of forty years, Violet Bonham Carter. For the first time in their long friendship, she told Harold Nicolson, 'she had found him depressed. He was querulous about criticism, unhappy at Cripps not consenting to take office, worried by the absence of alternative Ministers whom he could invite to join the Government. But underneath it all was a dreadful fear, she felt, that our soldiers are not as good fighters as their fathers were. "In 1915," said Winston, "our men fought on even when they had only one shell left and were under a fierce barrage. Now they cannot resist dive-bombers. We have so many men in Singapore, so many men— they should have done better." '[4]

There was a further apparent blow for Churchill on February 12: a pinprick as far as the global war was concerned, but a major vexation for the British public. Two German battle cruisers, *Scharnhorst* and *Gneisenau*, and the cruiser *Prinz Eugen*, slipped out of Brest harbour—

---

[1] Prime Minister's Personal Telegram, T.209/2, Former Naval Person to President No. 27 (this numbered series had begun with No. 25 on 7 February 1942), 11 February 1942: Churchill papers, 20/70.
[2] Oliver Harvey, diary, 11 February 1942: John Harvey (editor), *op. cit.*, page 94.
[3] Letter of 10 February 1942: Churchill papers, 20/53.
[4] Harold Nicolson, diary, 12 February 1942: Nigel Nicolson (editor), *Harold Nicolson, Diaries and Letters, 1939–1945*, London 1967, page 211.

over which Churchill had so nearly flown on his way back from Washington—and sailed up the Channel in broad daylight, passing the Dover batteries and reaching the North Sea.[1] This 'Channel Dash' was a feather in the cap for the Germans. The British, who lost all six Swordfish aircraft and four Hampden bombers from the air forces sent to intercept the warships, were cast down. 'The country is more upset about the escape of the German battleships than about Singapore,' Henry Channon noted in his diary on February 13. The *Daily Mail* had published an anti-Government, anti-Churchill leader, the first of the war. 'Everyone is in a rage against the Prime Minister,' Channon wrote, and he added that Churchill, 'angered by the *Daily Mail* leader, is in a defiant, truculent mood.'[2] That morning, the three German warships reached the safety of German ports. 'Another blow,' Cadogan noted in his diary. 'Poor Winston must be in a state.'[3]

That day, Churchill's secretary, Elizabeth Layton, wrote to her mother of the 'dreadful battle in the Channel over the German battleships'. Her letter continued: 'I had to go into the Cabinet Room at about 3 p.m. for dictation. He was striding up and down, all on edge. He dictated four telegrams like a whirlwind, and then phoned this and phoned that. I wondered if I should go, and once did slip out, but was recalled. Did another telegram, he marched up and down, talking to himself, a mass of compressed energy. Presently he sat down opposite me and said, "There's a bloody great battle going on out there." I said, "Do you think we might get them?" He said, "Don't know. We winged 'em but they aren't dead yet." '[4]

Unknown to the *Daily Mail*, Channon, Cadogan, Elizabeth Layton or the British public, Enigma decrypts revealed that each of the three German ships had been damaged during the dash. 'This,' Churchill informed Roosevelt, 'will keep them out of mischief for at least six months, during which both our Navies will receive important accessions of strength.'[5] Churchill prefaced the information of the damage to the ships with the words 'as you may have learned from most secret sources'. The battle cruisers had run on to the mines which had been laid on the previous day, and on the day of the dash itself, on the basis of Enigma indications, requiring last minute interpretation, of the positions through which the ships were likely to proceed. *Scharnhorst*

[1] Although the weather had been clear in the Channel in the forenoon, it deteriorated during the afternoon; by the time the three German ships had reached the Dutch coast there was fog.
[2] Henry Channon, diary, 13 February 1942: Robert Rhodes James (editor), *Chips, The Diaries of Sir Henry Channon*, London 1967, page 321.
[3] Cadogan diary, 13 February 1942: David Dilks (editor), *op. cit.*, page 433.
[4] Letter of 16 February 1942: Nel papers.
[5] Prime Minister's Personal Telegram, T.241/2, 'Former Naval Person to President' No. 29, 'Personal and Secret', 16 February 1942: Churchill papers, 20/70.

did not reappear for twelve months. *Gneisenau*, further damaged while in Kiel during a raid by Bomber Command, was put out of action for the rest of the war.[1]

On the morning of February 14 Churchill received a telegram from Wavell, to say that, in Singapore, General Percival had reported Japanese troops 'close to town' and his own troops 'incapable of further counter-attack'.[2] In his reply, with which General Brooke concurred, Churchill gave Wavell the authority to instruct Percival to surrender. 'You are of course sole judge,' Churchill telegraphed, 'of the moment when no further result can be gained at Singapore, and should instruct Percival accordingly.'[3]

On February 15 at seven o'clock in the evening Singapore time, midday in Britain, the British and Dominion troops in Singapore surrendered unconditionally to the Japanese. That night, from Chequers, Churchill broadcast to the nation. A former Private Secretary, Jock Colville, who was then in Pretoria, the South African capital, noted in his diary: 'Outside in Church Street I heard a familiar voice coming from the wireless in a small cafe. It was Winston announcing the fall of Singapore. The nature of his words and the unaccustomed speech and emotion with which he spoke convinced me that he was sorely pressed by critics and opponents at home. All the majesty of his oratory was there, but also a new note of appeal lacking the usual confidence of support.'[4]

During his broadcast, Churchill stressed the wider aspects of the war, seeking to answer his question, 'Are we up or down?' The United States with its 'vast resources' was an Ally. The British Commonwealth and the United States were in the war 'all together, however long it lasts, till death or victory'. He could not believe that there was 'any other fact in the whole world which can compare with that. That is what I have dreamed of, aimed at and worked for, and now it had come to pass.' The Russian armies, too, had not been defeated—'they

[1] F. H. Hinsley and others, *British Intelligence in the Second World War*, volume 2, London 1981, pages 179–88.

[2] Telegram No. 01161, 'Most Immediate', despatched 8.50 a.m., received 10.40 a.m., 14 February 1942: Churchill papers, 20/70.

[3] Prime Minister's Personal Telegram, T.231/2, 'Most Immediate', 'Personal and Private': Churchill papers, 20/70.

[4] John Colville diary, February 1942: Colville papers. This, and all subsequent entries from Colville's diary are taken from the original transcripts made available to me by Sir John Colville, and subsequently published by him in *The Fringes of Power: Downing Street Diaries 1939–1955*, London 1985. All historians of Churchill's wartime Premiership are in Colville's debt. In Stalin's secretariat, it seems, 'it was forbidden under pain of death to keep a diary'. (Information conveyed to the author in the House of the Soviet Army, Moscow, 12 August 1985.)

have not been torn to pieces'—nor had the Russian people been conquered or destroyed. It was the advance of the Russian armies that 'for the first time' had, Churchill declared, 'broken the Hitler legend'. But the obstacles for Britain were severe:

We have only just been able to keep our heads above water at home; only by a narrow margin have we brought in the food and the supplies; only by so little have we held our own in the Nile Valley and the Middle East. The Mediterranean is closed, and all our transports have to go round the Cape of Good Hope, each ship making only three voyages in the year.

Not a ship, not an aeroplane, not a tank, not an anti-tank gun or an anti-aircraft gun has stood idle. Everything we have has been deployed either against the cnemy or awaiting his attack. We are struggling hard in the Libyan Desert, where perhaps another serious battle will soon be fought. We have to provide for the safety and order of liberated Abyssinia, of conquered Eritrea, of Palestine, of liberated Syria, and redeemed Iraq, and of our new ally, Persia.

A ceaseless stream of ships, men, and materials has flowed from this country for a year and a half, in order to build up and sustain our armies in the Middle East, which guard those vast regions on either side of the Nile Valley. We had to do our best to give substantial aid to Russia. We gave it her in her darkest hour, and we must not fail in our undertaking now.

'How then,' Churchill asked, 'in this posture, gripped and held and battered as we were, could we have provided for the safety of the Far East against such an avalanche of fire and steel as has been hurled upon us by Japan? Always, my friends, this thought overhung our minds.'

For the time being, 'many misfortunes, severe torturing losses, remorseless and gnawing anxieties lie before us'. But the only real danger, the only crime, would be 'a weakening in our purpose and therefore in our unity—that is the mortal crime'. Whoever was guilty of that crime, or of bringing it about in others, 'it were better for him that a millstone were hanged about his neck and he were cast into the sea'.

As in June 1940 with the fall of France, so once more, in February 1942, with the fall of Singapore, Churchill sought to draw strength, unity and faith in victory from the disaster. His broadcast ended:

I speak to you all under the shadow of a heavy and far-reaching military defeat. It is a British and Imperial defeat. Singapore has fallen. All the Malay Peninsula has been overrun. Other dangers gather about us out there, and none of the dangers which we have hitherto successfully withstood at home and in the East are in any way diminished.

This, therefore, is one of those moments when the British race and nation can show their quality and their genius. This is one of those moments when it can draw from the heart of misfortune the vital impulses of victory. Here is the moment to display that calm and poise combined with grim determination which not so long ago brought us out of the very jaws of death. Here is another occasion to show—as so often in our long story—that we can meet reverses with dignity and with renewed accessions of strength.

We must remember that we are no longer alone. We are in the midst of a great company. Three-quarters of the human race are now moving with us. The whole future of mankind may depend upon our action and upon our conduct. So far we have not failed. We shall not fail now. Let us move forward steadfastly together into the storm and through the storm.[1]

At the time of the evacuation of Dunkirk, Churchill had rallied the nation. Now, with the fall of Singapore, he seemed unable to turn the tide of depression. 'I fear a slump in public opinion which will deprive Winston of his legend,' Harold Nicolson noted in his diary on February 16. 'His broadcast last night was not liked. The country is too nervous and irritable to be fobbed off with fine phrases. Yet what else could he have said?'[2]

[1] Broadcast of 15 February 1942: Churchill papers, 9/157.
[2] Harold Nicolson diary, 16 February 1942: Nigel Nicolson (editor), *op. cit.*, page 211.

4

'Nothing but disaster to show'

I N the aftermath of the fall of Singapore, the Japanese prepared to consolidate and extend their power throughout the Far East and Pacific regions. 'Now that Singapore has fallen,' Churchill telegraphed to Reginald Dorman Smith, the Governor of Burma, on 16 February 1942, 'more weight will assuredly be put into the attack upon you.' [1] That same day, General Auchinleck telegraphed to Churchill from North Africa: 'We all realize situation consequent on fall of Singapore and you may rely on us to hang on and do our bit to help you through to victory.' [2]

At a meeting of the Defence Committee on the evening of February 16, it was decided not to send 'inadequate' forces to the forward areas, or to try to defend the Dutch East Indies, but to concentrate on the defence of Burma, Ceylon and Australia: such, Cadogan noted, was the 'general consensus'. [3] 'It seems to me,' Churchill telegraphed to Roosevelt on February 17, 'that the most vital point at the moment is Rangoon, alone assuring contact with China.'

On February 17, hoping to assuage Parliamentary distress at the loss of Singapore, and at the 'Channel dash' of the three German warships, Churchill made a statement in the House of Commons. While the three German warships had been sheltering in Brest, he pointed out, 3,299 bomber sorties had been made upon them from Britain, involving the loss of 247 lives, and 43 aircraft. The decision that the ships should return to Germany had been made on account of this continual air pressure. Why the 'dash' had not been detected, he did not know: he had set up a secret inquiry to try to find out. [4] He

---

[1] Telegram No. 73, Prime Minister's Personal Telegram, T. 243/2, 16 February. 1942: Churchill papers, 20/70.

[2] Telegram CS/737, 'Most Secret': 16 February 1942: Churchill papers, 20/70.

[3] Cadogan diary, 16 February 1942: David Dilks (editor), *op. cit.*, page 434.

[4] The Board of Enquiry into the escape of the ships, the Bucknill Enquiry, revealed a series of misjudgements, and breakdowns in apparatus, followed by delay in reporting and acting on

could, however, now reveal that the two battle cruisers 'have received damage in their passage which will keep them out of action for some time to come'. As to the loss of Singapore, 'it would ill become the dignity of the Government or the House', Churchill said, 'and would render poor service to the Alliance of which we are part, if we were drawn into agitated or excited recriminations at a time when all our minds are oppressed with a sense of tragedy and with the sorrow of so lamentable a misfortune'.

Several members of Parliament expressed their dissatisfaction at Churchill's attitude: 'the public outside are immensely disturbed', declared a leading Liberal MP, Sir Percy Harris, in seeking a full-scale Debate on the fall of Singapore. But Churchill replied that 'a Debate held today in excitement, and pierced with charges and counter-charges' exchanged at a moment 'of great anxiety and distress', would only contribute towards what he called the 'rattling' process which he saw going on in the Press and elsewhere, 'which tends to give a feeling of insecurity . . .'.[1]

Churchill's statement, and even more his answer, went badly. 'It started all right,' according to Harold Nicolson, who noted in his diary: 'but when people asked questions, he became irritable and rather reckless. He spoke about "anger" and "panic" which infuriated people and will, I fear, be broadcast throughout the world by our enemies.'[2]

At Churchill's weekly luncheon with the King that day, the King recorded in his diary that the Prime Minister was 'very angry about all this, and compares it to hunting the tiger with angry wasps about him'.[3] Visiting Churchill that afternoon, Brooke found him 'in a dejected mood'. He was 'just back', Churchill told Brooke, 'from dealing with a troublesome House'. Brooke's own comment, in his diary, was: 'I am afraid he is in for a lot more trouble.'[4]

That evening, at 10 Downing Street, at the second meeting of the Pacific War Council, Churchill spoke of the 'grievous blow' of the loss of Singapore, and the prospect of 'further reverses' in the Far East. Of the twelve divisions which the Allies had been able to 'muster' in the Pacific, four had 'vanished' with the loss of Singapore and two were 'locked up' in Luzon, in the Philippines. The Japanese had twenty-

---

radar plots of the ships by coastal radar stations (Command Paper 6775, cited in F. H. Hinsley and others, *British Intelligence in the Second World War*, London 1981, pages 184–8).

[1] *Hansard*, 17 February 1942, columns 1671–87.
[2] Harold Nicolson diary, 17 February 1942: Nigel Nicolson (editor), *op. cit.*, page 212.
[3] King George VI, diary, 17 February 1942: John W. Wheeler-Bennett, *King George VI, op. cit.*, page 537.
[4] Brooke diary, 17 February 1942: Bryant, *op. cit.*, volume 1, page 307.

four divisions, as well as naval and air superiority, giving them the
initiative, 'which they were ready, at all times, to seize with boldness
and skill'. Their troops were better trained and equipped to fight in
tropical vegetation, through swamps, and on surf-ridden beaches.
'They moved quicker and ate less than our men.'

Nevertheless, after listening to a Dutch appeal that a 'stubborn
resistance' should be offered in Java, Churchill told the Pacific War
Council: 'Any question of abandoning Java without a fight was unthinkable. All forces in the island of whatever nationality should resist to
the end. There should be no withdrawal and no surrender.'[1]

On the morning of February 18 Churchill went, as usual, to the
Map Room in No. 10 Annexe, where Captain Pim showed him the
latest ship and troop positions. On this occasion, Pim later recalled:

I found the Prime Minister very much depressed and from what he said it
was obvious that he felt the irksomeness of having to put up with criticism as
soon as events went badly—circumstances which he had prophesied when he
spoke of tears and blood many months before. He said he was tired of it all
and hinted that he was very seriously thinking of handing over his responsibilities to other shoulders. My reply was, and I remember the words,
'But, my God, sir, you cannot do that.'

He then said he wondered what were the views of the ordinary citizen, did
they also accept the views of the Press or were they prepared to support him in
bad days as well as fair. I gave it as my view that the loudest shouts, certainly in
Parliament, came from those who saw the possibility of a re-shuffle and hoped
to be in the running for some greater or smaller Government position. . . .[2]

Churchill had good reason to be depressed: in a telegram on February 18, reflecting on the fall of Malaya and Singapore, Wavell told
Churchill of the 'lack of real fighting spirit' among the troops, not
only in Malaya, but also 'so far' in Burma. Wavell added: 'Neither
British, Australians or Indians have shown any real toughness of mind
or body,' although the Australians had fought well in Johore. The
conditions of fighting, Wavell concluded, were 'admittedly difficult',
but they 'should not have been insuperable'.[3]

There was no way that Churchill could answer his critics by giving them an account of Wavell's secret report. Instead, he had to
be patient, and as impervious as he could be to the 'view of the
Press'. That same day, as the Japanese continued their advance into
Burma, Brooke noted in his diary: 'If the Army cannot fight better

[1] Pacific War Council, No. 2, 6 p.m., 17 February 1942: Cabinet papers, 99/26. The two
Dutch representatives were Dr P. S. Gerbrandy (Prime Minister of the Netherlands Government) and E. Michiels Van Verduynen (Netherlands Minister to the Court of St James).
[2] Recollections of Captain Pim (later Captain Sir Richard Pim, KBE, Kt): Pim papers.
[3] Telegram No. 01531, 18 February 1942: Churchill papers, 20/70.

than it is doing at the present we shall deserve to lose our Empire'.[1]

In the week following the fall of Singapore, Churchill was still under considerable pressure to reconstruct the Government. 'You are being looked upon as a faithful friend of Ministers who have outlived their usefulness,' Brendan Bracken wrote to him on February 17, forwarding a letter from Beaverbrook proposing a four-man War Cabinet, consisting only of Churchill, Bevin—'the strongest man in the present Cabinet' Eden 'the most popular member of the Cabinet'—and Attlee.[2] On February 19 the changes were announced. The War Cabinet was reduced from nine to seven members. Five of the seven were unchanged: Churchill, Attlee, Anderson, Eden, and Bevin. Churchill retained the Ministry of Defence but gave up the leadership of the House of Commons to Sir Stafford Cripps, who entered the War Cabinet as Lord Privy Seal. Attlee became Deputy Prime Minister and Dominions Secretary. Oliver Lyttelton was brought back from Cairo to enter the War Cabinet as Minister of State with general supervision over production. Ernest Bevin, John Anderson and Anthony Eden retained their old positions. Kingsley Wood ceased to be a member of the War Cabinet but remained Chancellor of the Exchequer. Lord Beaverbrook and Arthur Greenwood resigned from the War Cabinet, Lord Moyne from the Government. 'This really is a large sweep,' the editor of the The Times noted in his diary, 'capable of re-invigorating the conduct of the war and public confidence.'[3]

Beaverbrook's resignation saddened Churchill considerably. Here was one of the few men whose company and zeal he found stimulating at both the personal and the political level. But Beaverbrook, whose asthma, intensified by his frenetic pace of work, had long been a cause of personal distress, propelling him to resign, now had the added reasons of having opposed Attlee as Deputy Prime Minister, and having wanted Eden, not Cripps, to lead the House of Commons. Shortly afterwards, Churchill told W. P. Crozier, the editor of the *Manchester Guardian*, in regard to Beaverbrook's resignation:

He needn't have gone. He could have had any one of three or four offices if he had liked to stop. He could have gone back to the Ministry of Aircraft Production if he had chosen. I didn't want him to go. He was good for me!

[1] Brooke diary, 18 February 1942: Bryant, *op. cit.*, volume 1, page 311.
[2] Letter of 17 February 1942, and covering note (undated): Churchill papers, 20/52.
[3] Barrington-Ward diary, 19 February 1942: Donald McLachlan, *In the Chair, Barrington Ward of 'The Times', 1927–1948*, London, 1971, page 192.

Any number of times, if things were going badly, he would encourage me saying, 'Look at all the things on your side. Look what you've accomplished. Be of good courage!' and he put courage and pep into me.[1]

In his letter of resignation, Beaverbrook told Churchill: 'everything that has been done by me has been due to your holding me up', and he added: 'I owe my reputation to you. The confidence of the public really comes from you. And my courage was sustained by you.' As for Churchill, Beaverbrook added: 'In leaving, then, I send this letter of gratitude & devotion to the leader of the nation, the saviour of our people, & the symbol of resistance in the free world.'[2]

Churchill replied on the following day:

My dear Max,

Thank you for all you say in yr splendid letter wh is a vy gt comfort & encouragement to me.

We have lived & fought side by side through terrible days, & I am sure our comradeship & public work will undergo no break. All I want you to do now is to recover yr strength & poise, so as to be able to come to my aid when I shall vy greatly need you.

Yr work during the crisis at M.A.P. in 1940 played a decisive part in our salvation. You shaped the Russian policy upon munitions wh is all we can do for them. The figures of the Ministry of Supplies speak for themselves. You are one of our few fighting men of genius.

I am always yr affectionate friend,

W[3]

On the day of his Cabinet changes, Churchill's confidence was boosted by a telegram from Roosevelt. The fall of Singapore, wrote the President, 'gives the well-known back seat driver a field day but no matter how serious our setbacks have been, and I do not for a moment underrate them, we must constantly look forward to the next moves that need to be made to hit the enemy'. Roosevelt added:

I hope you will be of good heart in these trying weeks because I am very sure that you have the great confidence of the masses of the British people. I want you to know that I think of you often and I know you will not hesitate to ask me if there is anything you think I can do. When I speak on the radio next Monday evening I shall say a word about those people who treat the episode in the Channel as a defeat. . . .[4]

'I am most deeply grateful to you for your warm-hearted telegram,'

[1] Quoted in A. J. P. Taylor, *Beaverbrook*, London 1972, page 517.

[2] Letter of 26 February 1942: Churchill papers, 20/52.

[3] Letter of 27 February 1942: A. J. P. Taylor, *Beaverbrook*, London 1972, page 518; copy in Churchill papers, 2/440.

[4] 'Secret and Personal', President to Prime Minister No. 106 (At Churchill's suggestion Roosevelt had begun numbering his telegrams from No. 100): Churchill papers, 20/70.

Churchill replied. 'The pressure here has never been dangerous and I have used it to effect wholesome changes and accessions. You may take it everything is now solid.' Churchill added: 'I do not like these days of personal stress and I have found it difficult to keep my eye on the ball. We are however in the fullest accord in all main things.' He was looking forward to Roosevelt 'rubbing it in' about the 'easement' in the Atlantic as a result of the flight of the German warships from Brest, 'but of course', he warned, with his eye still on the Enigma decrypts, 'we cannot dwell too much upon the damage they sustained'.

Churchill's message to Roosevelt also contained the sentence: 'Democracy has to prove that it can provide a granite foundation for war against tyranny.'[1] As he sent this message the focus of British concern was turned to Burma. Churchill and Roosevelt had already agreed that the main defence of Australia would fall upon the United States. But the Australian Government had refused to allow a division of Australian troops who were then returning from the Middle East to be diverted to Rangoon. Yet these troops, Churchill telegraphed to John Curtin on February 20, were 'the only force that can reach Rangoon in time to prevent its loss and the severance of communication with China'. Churchill added: 'There is nothing else in the world that can fill the gap.'[2]

Churchill then asked Roosevelt for a message which he could add to this 'very strong cable' to Australia.[3] Roosevelt responded at once. 'I hope,' he replied, in a telegram which Churchill sent on at once to John Curtin, 'you can persuade Australian Government to allow proposed temporary diversion of their leading Australian Division to Burma. I think this of utmost importance.' Roosevelt's message ended: 'Tell them I am speeding additional troops as well as planes to Australia and that my estimate of the situation there is highly optimisitic and by no means dark.'[4]

Roosevelt's appeal was in vain. So too was a second appeal from the President two days later.[5] Once more, the Australian Government refused to divert their troops. 'Looking back on the event,' Brooke later wrote, 'I still feel that the arrival of this Division in Rangoon at

---

[1] Prime Minister's Personal Telegram, No. T.257/2, No. 30 to Roosevelt, 'Personal and Secret', 20 February 1942: Churchill papers, 20/70.

[2] Prime Minister's Personal Telegram, T.265/2, No. 233 to Australia, 20 February 1942: Churchill papers, 20/88.

[3] Prime Minister's Personal Telegram, T.266/2, No. 31 to Roosevelt, 20 February 1942: Churchill papers, 20/88.

[4] Telegram No. 107 from Roosevelt to Churchill; No. 235 to Australia, Prime Minister's Personal Telegram, T.267/2, 'Most Secret and Personal', 21 February 1942: Churchill papers, 20/70.

[5] Joint Staff Mission, Washington, No. 65, 23 February 1942: Churchill papers, 20/70.

that time might well have restored the situation and saved Burma.'[1] But Churchill understood the Australian decision. 'As was perhaps natural,' he had told the Chiefs of Staff Committee on February 20, 'they were much concerned with the immediate defence of Australia, and further appeals were most unlikely to affect their decision.'[2]

On February 22 there were further Government changes: six Cabinet Ministers and nine Under-Secretaries of State were replaced. Among the newcomers was Sir James Grigg as Secretary of State for War. 'After nearly two years of strain and struggle,' Churchill told the House of Commons on February 24, 'it was right and necessary that a Government called into being in the crash of the Battle of France should undergo both change and reinvigoration'. As to the recent public discussion of whether he should give up his post of Minister of Defence, Churchill told the House that, 'However tempting it might be to some when much trouble lies ahead to step aside adroitly and put someone else up to take the blows, the heavy and repeated blows, which are coming, I do not intend to adopt that cowardly course. . .'. A few moments later Churchill declared:

The House and the nation must face the blunt and brutal fact that if, having entered a war, yourself ill-prepared, you are struggling for life with two well-armed countries, one of them possessing the most powerful military machine in the world, and then, at the moment when you are in full grapple, a third major antagonist with far larger military forces than you possess suddenly springs upon your comparatively undefended back, obviously your task is heavy and your immediate experiences will be disagreeable.

Churchill told the House of Commons that if they were to look forward 'across the considerable period of immediate punishment' through which Britain would have to make its way in consequence of 'the sudden onslaught of Japan', and recognize the extent to which Britain's position had been 'enormously improved' by the 'wonderful strength and power' of Russia, and the accession of the United States 'with its measureless resources' to the common cause, they would see the prospect of ultimate victory.[3]

To the King, at their Tuesday luncheon that day, Churchill confided his hidden fear, that, as the King noted in his diary, 'Burma,

[1] Field Marshal Lord Alanbrooke, 'Notes on My Life', volume 5, page 361: Bryant, *op. cit.*, volume 1, page 311.
[2] Chiefs of Staff Committee No. 6 (Operations) of 1942, 1 p.m., 20 February 1942: Cabinet papers, 79/56.
[3] *Hansard*, 24 February 1942, columns 36–48.

Ceylon, Calcutta and Madras in India and part of Australia may fall into enemy hands.'[1]

The war in Burma was going badly, its future made even more bleak by the Australian refusal to send a division to Rangoon. 'We have made every appeal,' Churchill telegraphed to the Governor of Burma, 'reinforced by President, but Australian Government absolutely refuses'. Churchill's final exhortation: 'Fight on'.[2]

With Burma at their mercy, the Japanese moved first against the Dutch on Java. Dutch, British, American and Australian naval units joined the battle, under a Dutch admiral. 'Every day gained is precious,' Churchill telegraphed to Air Vice-Marshal Maltby, in Java, on February 26, 'and I know that you will do everything humanly possibly to prolong the battle'.[3]

The battle for Java was an unequal and hopeless struggle. 'Papa is at a very low ebb,' Mary Churchill noted in her diary on February 27, after lunching with her father and mother at 10 Downing Street. 'He is not too well physically,' she added, 'and he is worn down by the continuous crushing pressure of events. . . .'[4]

On February 28 Japanese forces invaded Java, sustained in their assault by both naval and air superiority: the inexorable result of Pearl Harbour. The British naval losses off Java were considerable. As the Japanese drove forward, the destroyer *Jupiter* struck a mine laid earlier that same day by the Dutch, and sank with heavy loss of life. Three other Royal Navy destroyers, *Electra*, *Encounter* and *Stronghold*, were sunk in action. The heavy cruiser *Exeter*, one of the victors of the Battle of the River Plate in December 1939, was sunk by an overwhelming superiority of Japanese naval gunfire, aircraft, and torpedoes. Also sunk were an Australian, an American, and two Dutch cruisers.[5] On shore, the Dutch surrendered on March 8, when 5,000 British and American airmen, and 8,000 British and Australian troops, were taken prisoner. Amid such a disaster, the important and successful British air, sea and army raid on the German radar station at Bruneval, near Le Havre, was small consolation, revealing as it did that in some respects German radar was more advanced than the British.[6]

[1] King George VI, diary 24 February 1942: John W. Wheeler-Bennett, *King George VI, op. cit.*, page 598.
[2] Prime Minister's Personal Telegram, T.293/2, 'Personal and Secret', 25 February 1942: Churchill papers, 20/70.
[3] Prime Minister's Personal Telegram, T.302/2, 26 February 1942: Churchill papers, 20/88.
[4] Mary Churchill, diary 27 February 1942: Mary Soames, *Clementine Churchill, op. cit.*, page 314.
[5] *Perth* (Australian), *Houston* (United States), *Java* and *de Ruyter* (Dutch).
[6] F. H. Hinsley and others, *British Intelligence in the Second World War*, volume 2, London 1981, page 249. During the raid the British captured the receiver, the amplifier, the pulse generator, the transmitter, the aerial element and, together with one of the operators himself, full details of the operating method.

'These are as you say days of anguish for Winston,' Clementine Churchill wrote to her sister Nellie Romilly on February 28, 'so full of strength & yet so impotent to stem this terrible tide in the Far East.'[1]

As Java fell, Churchill focused his attention on the defence of Ceylon, and of the naval base at Trincomalee. 'Let me have list and time-table of the naval re-inforcements,' he minuted to the Chiefs of Staff Commitee on February 28, 'and the building up of our fleet in the Indian Ocean during March, April, and May.'[2] To Admiral Sir Herbert Richmond, who was worried about the future of Ceylon, Churchill replied the same day: 'I can assure you that you are not alone in your anxiety about Trincomalee. We are fully aware of the covetous eyes which the enemy must be casting at Ceylon.'[3]

'We seem to lose a new bit of the Empire almost every day,' General Brooke wrote despondently to a friend, 'and are faced with one nightmare situation after another. This process does not make Cabinet Ministers any more attractive. But Winston is a marvel; I can't imagine how he sticks it.'[4] There was further concern on February 28, when Churchill read of Auchinleck's proposal to take no forward action against Rommel until June. 'This is intolerable,' he wrote to Eden, 'and will be judged so by Stalin, Roosevelt, and everybody else.'[5]

Another worry which grew in intensity as February turned to March was the successful U-boat campaign in American waters. This had already led Churchill to fear a German landing on the Bahamas, to seize the Governor-General, the Duke of Windsor. 'What about the danger of a landing party kidnapping him one night?', he had minuted on February 24.[6] 'The Germans would be very glad to get hold of the Duke and use him for their own purposes,' he explained four days later. 'In my opinion,' he added, 'continued protection against an attack by 50 men *during darkness* should be provided. Very considerable issues are involved.'[7]

At the end of January 1942 the U-boats, which had hitherto used the same Enigma as other ships and authorities both in German home waters and in the Atlantic, acquired their own form of Enigma machine, unique to them. Suddenly, the U-boat's most secret signals, which had been so carefully monitored at Bletchley since the summer of 1941, became unreadable once more, and were to remain a secret

[1] Letter of 28 February 1942: Mary Soames, *Clementine Churchill, op. cit.*, page 314.
[2] Prime Minister's Personal Minute, D.35/2, 28 February 1942: Churchill papers, 20/67.
[3] Letter of 28 February 1942: Churchill papers, 20/59.
[4] Undated: Bryant, *op. cit.*, volume 1, page 335.
[5] Prime Minister's Personal Minute, M.59/2, 28 February 1942: Churchill papers, 20/67.
[6] Minute dated 24 February 1942, to the Colonial Secretary: Churchill papers 20/63.
[7] Prime Minister's Personal Minute, M.56/2, 28 February 1942: Churchill papers, 20/63.

for nearly a year, followed by a further six months irregularities and delays in decrypting. This development, coming at a time when the U-boat fleet was rapidly increasing in size, coincided with a move of the U-boats to what Churchill called 'American Waters': in the Atlantic west of the 40th Meridian, and in the Caribbean. The U-boat successes there during the next six months were largely responsible for an alarmingly sharp rise in the monthly rate of Allied merchant ship losses, especially of tankers. When, in the late summer of 1942, the U-boats turned once more against the Atlantic convoys, these losses were to reach unprecedented levels.[1]

Churchill's doctor, Charles Wilson, who had no knowledge of the reasons behind the suddenly increased sinkings, noted in his diary:

I have been finding out that wherever he goes he carries in his head the monthly figures of all sinkings, though he never talks about them. He is always careful to consume his own smoke; nothing he says could discourage anyone. When I say the PM never talks, I am not quite accurate. There are times—this does not happen very often—when I fancy I serve as a safety-valve. Occasionally, too, I may pick up by chance a stray hint of what is going on in his head.

One day when things at sea were at their worst, I happened to go to the Map-room. There I found the PM. He was standing with his back to me, staring at the huge chart with the little black beetles representing German submarines. 'Terrible,' he muttered. I was about to retreat when he whipped round and brushed past me with his head down. I am not sure he saw me. He knows that we may lose the war at sea in a few months and that he can do nothing about it.

'I wish to God,' Wilson added, 'I could put out the fires that seem to be consuming him.'[2]

Not only 'fires' but ill-health was affecting Churchill's demeanour and sapping his strength. On March 2 Anthony Eden and Sir Alexander Cadogan agreed 'that for the last fortnight there has been no direction of the war. War Cabinet doesn't function—there hasn't been a meeting of Defence Committee.' Cadogan added: 'There's no hand on the wheel. (Probably due to P.M's health.)' Both Brendan Bracken and Stafford Cripps had urged that Eden should be 'Deputy Defence Minister'.[3]

That week Mary Churchill noted in her diary that her father was 'saddened—appalled by events' and, on another occasion, 'he is desperately taxed'.[4]

[1] F. H. Hinsley and others, *British Intelligence in the Second World War*, volume 2, London 1981, pages 228–33, 547–56, and Appendix 19, pages 747–52.
[2] Sir Charles Wilson diary, undated: Moran, *op. cit.*, page 32.
[3] Sir Alexander Cadogan, diary, 2 March 1942: David Dilks (editor), *op. cit.*, page 438.
[4] Diary entries: Lady Soames papers.

Churchill continued to fulfil a punishing work schedule. On March 3, as well as studying the official and secret papers of the day, and dictating several minutes and telegrams, he had a meeting with the Chancellor of the Exchequer at 10, a Cabinet meeting to discuss Indian constitutional reform at 12, luncheon with the King to report on the war situation, an interview with the Mexican Ambassador at 3, short meetings with each of the new Under Secretaries of State at 6, and Lord Beaverbrook to dine at 8.30: Beaverbrook whom, after his recent resignation, Churchill was still keen to bring back into the Government.[1] Then, at 10 that same evening, there was a meeting of the Defence Committee to discuss equipment failures and weaknesses in the Western Desert, aid to the Yugoslavs in their fight behind German lines, and a possible attack on *Tirpitz*, which was then at Trondheim. *Tirpitz* was 'the most important vessel in the naval situation today', Churchill told his colleagues, 'and her elimination would profoundly affect the course of the war'.[2]

The attack on *Tirpitz*, when examined by the naval experts, proved impossible; instead, on April 27, in an attempt to put *Tirpitz* out of action by air attack, Bomber Command mounted a raid on Trondheim. The German Enigma message reporting on the raid, and decrypted at Bletchley, while describing the attack itself as 'most courageous', reported however that there had been no damage to the ship, smoke having provided her with the best possible protection.[3]

Six months later, in a daring raid planned by SOE, a Norwegian naval officer, Leif Larsen, sailed from SOE's Shetland base with a newly developed one-man submarine, code name 'Chariot', in an attempt to sink the *Tirpitz*. Larsen managed to reach a point from where his attack could have succeeded, but lost his 'Chariots' in an unlucky squall.[4]

These setbacks were in the future: in March 1942 Churchill could only worry about the power of *Tirpitz* to do harm. On March 3, the day on which he had warned the Defence Committee of the danger,

[1] Prime Minister's Engagement Card, Tuesday 3 March 1942. On India, Oliver Harvey noted in his diary on the following day, 'the Cabinet are about to take an immense step, an offer of complete independence like a Dominion after the war. This idea originated with the PM himself who cut across the obstructionism of the Viceroy and the India Office ...' (Harvey diary, 3 March 1942: John Harvey, editor, *op. cit.*, pages 104–5.) Three days later, Harvey noted: 'It was Winston who originated the idea of an imaginative appeal to India on the broadcast' (Harvey diary, 6 March 1942: *op. cit.*, pages 105–6).

[2] Defence Committee No. 7 of 1942, 10 p.m., 2 March 1942: Cabinet papers, 69/4. The Ministers present were Churchill, Attlee, Eden, Lyttelton, A. V. Alexander, Sir James Grigg and Sir Archibald Sinclair. Also present were the three Service chiefs, Sir Dudley Pound, Sir Charles Portal and Sir Alan Brooke, and General Ismay.

[3] Signal 0011 of 29 April 1942: F. H. Hinsley and others, *British Intelligence in the Second World War*, volume 2, London 1981, page 212.

[4] Leif Larsen sailed from the Shetlands on 26 October 1942.

Lord Beaverbrook wrote of Churchill, to a friend: 'The Prime Minister is an austere man, who works night and day. It is said that he drinks. But this is not true. I drink every day, or have in the past taken more to drink every day than the Prime Minister—yet I am known as an abstemious man. I do not know a fault of his life, save only a too strong devotion to his friends.' Beaverbrook added: 'His home life is excellent. His relationship with Mrs Churchill might be told in story form as an example of a life-time of domestic content.'[1]

'Poor old PM in a sour mood and a bad way,' Sir Alexander Cadogan noted in his diary on March 4.[2] Nearly three months had passed since Pearl Harbour. 'When I reflect how I have longed and prayed for the entry of the United States into the war,' Churchill telegraphed to Roosevelt on March 5, 'I find it difficult to realize how gravely our British affairs have deteriorated since December 7. We have suffered the greatest disaster in our history at Singapore, and other misfortunes will come thick and fast upon us. Your great power will only become effective gradually because of the vast distances and the shortage of ships.'[3]

Over Europe, no such shortage of aircraft seemed to inhibit action. But when Sir Charles Portal proposed, on March 5, to renew the daylight 'Circus' operations over France, 'with the object of inducing German fighters to accept combat with our own fighter forces', Churchill's was the voice of caution. 'You are terribly short of fighter aircraft,' he minuted three days later. 'But it pays to lose plane for plane. If you consider Circus losses will come within that statement it wd be worthwhile. But beware of the future.'[4]

To help him plan that future, Churchill decided to enlist the help of the Commodore, Combined Operations, Lord Louis Mountbatten, proposing, in a letter to Sir Dudley Pound on March 5, that Mountbatten should become a full member of the Chiefs of Staff Committee. 'I want him to exercise influence upon the war as a whole,' Churchill explained: 'upon future planning in its broadest sense; upon the concert of the three Arms and their relations to the main strategy; upon Combined Operations in the largest sense, not

[1] Letter of 3 March 1942, to Mrs Inge: Beaverbrook papers.
[2] Sir Alexander Cadogan diary, 4 March 1942: David Dilks (editor), *op. cit.*, page 440.
[3] Prime Minister's Personal Telegram No. T.323/2, Churchill to Roosevelt No. 37, 5 March 1942: Churchill papers, 20/71.
[4] Minutes of 5 and 8 March 1942: Premier papers, 3/11/3, folio 73. Churchill's warning was not fanciful: 'Circus' losses to planes and pilots alike were at a higher rate than in the Battle of Britain.

only those specific Operations which his own organization will execute.' Churchill added: 'I am quite prepared to proceed step by step, and see how we get on.' [1] On the following day, Churchill informed the Chiefs of Staff Committee that henceforth Mountbatten's title would be 'Chief of Combined Operations', and that he would have 'full and equal membership' of their Committee, with the acting rank of Vice-Admiral. At the same time, General Brooke succeeded Pound as Chairman of the Committee. 'No publicity,' Churchill added, 'will be given at present to any of these changes.' [2]

'He has been very tired,' Averell Harriman wrote, of Churchill, in a letter to Roosevelt on March 6, 'but is better in the last day or two. I believe he will come back with renewed strength, particularly when the tone of the war improves.' The fall of Singapore, Harriman noted, had shaken Churchill 'to such an extent' that he had been unable to stand up to the bewildered British public 'with his old vigor'. But the Government would not fall, despite assertions to that effect by 'a number of astute people'. There was 'no other man in sight', Harriman wrote, 'to give the British the leadership Churchill does'. [3]

At midnight on March 6 the British Commander in Burma, General Alexander, gave orders for Rangoon to be abandoned, and for the troop convoys still on their way to the city to be turned back. This further blow to Britain's position in the Far East opened up a threat both to Ceylon and to India. At this moment of danger, Churchill felt unable to resist continuing pressure from the Foreign Office, eager to clear the way for an Anglo-Soviet treaty, to give Stalin assurances about the post-war Soviet frontier. With the renewal of a German offensive on Russia imminent, Churchill was fully aware of the importance for the western Allies of Stalin retaining confidence in their intentions. The continuous aid to Russia, and future military diversions to help Russia, seemed an essential factor in Russia's own ability to continue the war, and in her willingness to do so as an Ally.

In the first week of March Churchill suggested to Eden that he, Churchill, should go to meet Stalin himself. He would go to the Persian capital, Teheran, or even to Russia, to the Caspian port of Astrakhan, 'clearing up Cairo on the way', as Oliver Harvey noted in his diary on March 6. Beaverbrook, who had visited Stalin in Moscow in August 1941, would go with him.

Harvey commented on Churchill's plan to go to Russia: 'This from a man afflicted with heart who may collapse at any minute.

[1] Letter of 5 March 1942: Churchill papers, 20/53.
[2] Prime Minister's Personal Minute, D.49/2, 6 March 1942: Churchill papers, 20/67.
[3] Letter of 6 March 1942: W. Averell Harriman and Elie Abel, *Special Envoy to Churchill and Stalin, 1941–1946*, London 1976, pages 126–7.

What courage and what gallantry, but is it the way to do things?'[1]

To help Russia, every avenue was to be explored. 'We *are* going to study the possibility of a "second front" in West!' Sir Alexander Cadogan wrote in his diary on March 7, noting that Churchill had just sent 'a good telegram' to Stalin about maintaining British military aid quotas to Russia.[2]

The American Ambassador in London, Gilbert Winant, who had returned briefly to Washington, explained to Roosevelt what Churchill called the 'Foreign Office view' of the need to accede to Stalin's demand, and on March 7 Churchill telegraphed to the President:

The increasing gravity of the war has led me to feel that the principles of the Atlantic Charter ought not to be construed so as to deny Russia the frontiers she occupied when Germany attacked her. This was the basis on which Russia acceded to the Charter, and I expect that a severe process of liquidating hostile elements in the Baltic States, etc., was employed by the Russians when they took these regions at the beginning of the war. I hope therefore that you will be able to give us a free hand to sign the treaty which Stalin desires as soon as possible. Everything portends an immense renewal of the German invasion of Russia in the spring, and there is very little we can do to help the only country that is heavily engaged with the German armies.

'The weight of the war is very heavy now,' Churchill added, 'and I must expect it to get steadily worse for some time to come.'[3] Roosevelt and the State Department declined, however, to proceed as Stalin wished, and the Treaty, in the form demanded by Stalin, never came to pass. 'This may be a critical period,' Roosevelt telegraphed to Churchill on March 8, 'but remember always it is not as bad as some you have so well survived before.'[4]

On March 7, at Churchill's request, Roosevelt sent the Prime Minister a long survey of American plans. 'I am becoming more and more interested,' Roosevelt wrote, 'in the establishment of a new front this summer on the European continent, certainly for air and raids.' For the Americans, 'from the point of view of shipping and supplies', this would be 'infinitely easier' than any other theatre of war, 'because of a maximuum distance of about three thousand miles'. Although losses would 'doubtless be great', as Roosevelt expressed it, they would be 'compensated for by at least equal German losses and by compelling Germans to divert large forces of all kinds from Russian fronts'.

The flaw in these plans was the Japanese threat to so many scattered

---

[1] Oliver Harvey diary, 6 March 1942: John Harvey (editor), *op. cit.*, pages 105–6.

[2] Sir Alexander Cadogan diary, 7 March 1942: *op. cit.*, pages 440–1.

[3] Prime Minister's Personal Telegram, T.340/2, Churchill to Roosevelt No. 40, 'Personal and Secret', 7 March 1942: Churchill papers: 20/71.

[4] President to Prime Minister, No. 113, 8 March 1942: Churchill papers, 20/71.

Far Eastern territories, from India to Australia. For America to give Britain the requested aid in these war zones, Roosevelt informed Churchill in this same message, would result in America's contribution to the 1942 air offensive against Germany being 'somewhat curtailed', and any American contribution to land operations in 1942 on the continent of Europe being 'materially reduced'. America's ship-building programme was already at 'about the maximum that could be obtained'. Shipping currently available could transport about 130,000 men; by June 1943 it would be possible to transport a total of 170,000 and by December 1943 a total of 270,000. Neglecting losses, Roosevelt noted, 'the total troop carrying capacity of US vessels by June 1944 will be 400,000 men'.[1] Thus, in the very documents in which there was a discussion of a 'second front' for 1942, there was a reference to June 1944, the precise date of the actual second front, and to the shipping realities on which that date in 1944 was ultimately to depend. Meanwhile, one of the main targets of Britain's spring bombing offensive over western Germany would, Churchill reported to Roosevelt on March 20, be the bombing of U-boat construction yards and bases. 'All is in readiness for this,' Churchill reported, 'including a vastly improved method of finding our way to the target, first tried at Essen a fortnight ago.' Britain was also studying plans for an attack by long-range aircraft upon U-boats coming from Bordeaux to the Caribbean. 'It is a question of competing claims,' Churchill added.[2]

Every aspect of war policy was thrashed out in the long and often daily telegrams between Churchill and Roosevelt, and in the telegrams which Churchill also exchanged on vital matters with Harry Hopkins. In one such telegram to Hopkins, after appealing for 'drastic action' to provide additional American escort warships in the Atlantic, Churchill wrote: 'I am enormously relieved by the splendid telegrams I have had from the President on the largest issues. It is most comforting to feel we are in such complete agreement on war outlook.' Churchill's telegram to Hopkins ended with 'personal greetings' for Admiral King, General Marshall and General Arnold, and the message: 'Happy days will come again.'[3]

A military intelligence report a day later, on March 13, gave Churchill cause for hope. Its details of Japanese troop movements, Churchill minuted to the Chiefs of Staff, made it appear 'very unlikely that an immediate full scale invasion of Australia could take place'. If

[1] President to Prime Minister, No. 113, received 8 March 1942: Churchill papers, 20/71.

[2] Prime Minister's Personal Telegram, T.425/2, Prime Minister to President, No. 53, 'Personal and Secret', 20 March 1942: Churchill papers, 20/72.

[3] Prime Minister's Personal telegram, T.367/2, 'Personal and Secret', 12 March 1942: Churchill papers, 20/71.

the Ceylon situation were to become 'solid for us', Churchill added, the Japanese would be more likely to 'turn northwards upon China'.[1]

The fate of Russia now began to dominate Churchill's thinking, as it had done in the summer of 1941. Intelligence information of the most secret sort made it clear, as Churchill had indicated to Roosevelt on March 7, that the Germans were preparing a major offensive, and that Hitler's declaration in Berlin on March 15, assuring his listeners that Russia was about to be 'annihilatingly defeated' was not mere rhetoric.[2] In his telegram to Stalin, received on March 12, Churchill reported that he had given 'express directions' that British supplies to Russia 'shall not in any way be interrupted or delayed', and that with the improvement in the weather Britain was resuming its heavy air offensive on Germany 'both by day and night'.[3]

This bombing offensive was indeed planned to be of substantial benefit to Russia, despite Churchill's own doubts at to its effectiveness. 'You need not argue the value of bombing Germany,' he minuted to Sir Archibald Sinclair and Sir Charles Portal on March 13, 'because I have my own opinion about that, namely, that it is not decisive, but better than doing nothing, and indeed is a formidable method of injuring the enemy'. The Archbishop of Canterbury, Churchill added, had spoken to him for half an hour at luncheon on March 12 'on the failure of high-level bombing'.[4]

To Sir John Dill, in Washington, Churchill wrote on March 14 about 'taking the weight off Russia during the summer by the heaviest air offensive against Germany which can be produced, having regard to other calls on our air power. . . .'[5] This policy received, on March 15, Stalin's own 'appreciation' on behalf of the Soviet Government.[5] The same day, in a telegram to General Auchinleck, Churchill ex-

[1] Prime Minister's Personal Directive, D.54/2, 'Most Secret', 13 March 1942: Churchill papers, 20/67.

[2] Adolf Hitler's speech of 15 March 1942 (the third anniversary of the German occupation of Prague).

[3] Prime Minister's Personal Telegram, T.352/2, 9 March 1942: Churchill papers, 20/132. On 14 February 1942 Bomber Command had approved a policy of bombing population centres. Raids on Essen, Cologne (March 13), Lübeck (March 28) and Hamburg (April 8 9 and April 17–18), were part of the new policy. In retaliation, the Germans launched a series of 'Baedeker' raids on towns of historic interest: Exeter (April 23–4, April 24–5 and April 25–6), Bath (April 25–6 and April 26–7), Norwich (April 27–8 and April 28–9) and York (April 28–9) in which 938 British civilians were killed. On April 27 Churchill had told the War Cabinet 'that Department should do all they could to ensure that disproportionate publicity was not given to these raids. Our attacks on Germany were inflicting much greater damage; and it was important to avoid giving the impression that the Germans were making full reprisal.' (War Cabinet No. 53 of 1942, 5.30 p.m., 27 April 1942: Cabinet papers, 65/26.)

[4] Prime Minister's Personal Minute, M.93/2, 'Secret and Private', 13 March 1942: Churchill papers, 20/67.

[5] Prime Minister's Personal Telegram, T.384/2, 14 March 1942: Churchill papers, 20/88.

[6] Telegram of 15 March 1942: Churchill papers, 20/132.

pressed his 'deepest anxiety' at the lack of any planned offensive action in the Western Desert before July, the date which Auchinleck had set. 'A heavy German counterstroke upon the Russians must be expected soon,' Churchill warned, 'and it will be thought intolerable that the 635,000 men on your ration strength should remain unengaged preparing for another set-piece battle in July.'[1] But if, Churchill added in a second telegram to Auchinleck on the following day, 'it is decided that you must stand on the defensive until July', then it would be necessary to consider the transfer of fifteen air squadrons from the Western Desert 'to sustain the Russian left wing in the Caucasus'.[2]

With Russia's danger and Auchinleck's delay uppermost in his mind, Churchill again proposed a journey to both Cairo and Russia. In Cairo, Oliver Harvey noted in his diary on March 17, the Prime Minister would 'clear up the military situation'. He would then go on 'and meet Stalin at somewhere like Baku'. Churchill had put this proposal to the Soviet Ambassador, Ivan Maisky, on the previous day, and asked Maisky, 'if he thought Stalin would come to meet him'. Maisky replied that 'he was sure he would'. Harvey again commented: 'But what courage!'[3]

In a further effort to help Russia, Churchill decided to send Lord Beaverbrook to Washington, as his personal emissary, seeking American support for Stalin's territorial demands. The crux of Churchill's worry had been set out in a telegram to Roosevelt on March 5. Protecting Egypt and Palestine from a German attack through Syria, the 'Levant-Caspian' front, depended, Churchill wrote, 'entirely upon Russia, who will be formidably attacked in the spring'.[4]

Telegraphing direct to Stalin on March 20, Churchill reported that Beaverbrook was on his way to Washington to help 'smooth out' the question of a treaty on Russia's post-war frontiers. He added a formal assurance that if, as Maisky had reported, the Germans did indeed decide to use poison gas on the Russian front, 'His Majesty's Government will treat any use of this weapon of poison gas against Russia exactly as if it was directed against ourselves.' There was in Britain an 'immense store' of gas bombs, Churchill told Stalin, which 'I have been building up'. These bombs were for discharge from aircraft, 'and we shall not hesitate to use these over all suitable objectives in Western Germany from the moment that your armies and people are assaulted in this way.'[5]

[1] Prime Minister's Personal Telegram, T.383/2, 15 March 1942: Churchill papers, 20/88.
[2] Prime Minister's Personal Telegram, T.393/2, 16 March 1942: Chuurchill papers, 20/88.
[3] Oliver Harvey diary, 17 March 1942: John Harvey (editor), *op. cit.*, pages 109–10.
[4] Prime Minister's Personal Telegram, T.442/2, 22 March 1942: Churchill papers, 20/88.
[5] Prime Minister's Personal Telegram, T.431/2, 'Personal and Secret', 20 March 1942: Churchill papers, 20/72. The offer to retaliate with poison gas on Germany, if Germany used it against Russia, had been discussed and approved by the Defence Committee of the War Cabinet

Replying to Churchill's offer, Stalin expressed his 'gratitude' for the promise of retaliation. He also offered, if Britain wished it, 'to issue an analogous warning to Germany, in consideration of the possibility of a German gas attack on England'. His telegram ended: 'The Soviet Government would be most grateful if the British Government could help the USSR to obtain from England certain chemical means of defence, which it now lacks, and also certain materials for use in chemical counter-attack, in case of a German chemical attack on the USSR. If there is no objection on your side, I could send a specialist in these matters to England in the near future.'[1]

Helping Russia was one of the most urgent points discussed at Chequers on the night of March 20 by Churchill, Pound and Portal, at a conference on Britain's six most urgent naval and air dispositions. These six were the defence of Ceylon, the capture of Madagascar, the defence of the coast of Egypt and Libya against invasion 'now that we have no battle fleet', air patrols in Home waters and the Bay of Biscay, increased 'security against invasion across the Channel', and the bombing offensive against Germany. This latter, Churchill minuted to the Chiefs of Staff Committee on March 21, 'is our main effort, and at present, apart from munitions, our sole means of helping Russia'.[2]

At a meeting of the Chiefs of Staff Committee on March 25, General Brooke expressed himself as 'strongly opposed' to the despatch of an 'air contingent' to Russia to help against the expected German offensive, as this would entail withdrawing fighter aircraft from the Middle East 'during the critical summer months'. Churchill was disappointed with the view. 'We might soon receive indications,' he said, 'that the weight of the German air offensive in the Mediterranean theatre was about to be transferred to the Russian front.' He would 'liked to have seen' a British air contingent operating side by side with the Russians' during the spring campaign in the East. But he 'fully appreciated' Brooke's arguments.[3]

Events in the Far East continued to turn against the Allies. On March 23 the Japanese occupied the Andaman Islands, in the Bay of

---

on 18 March 1942 (Defence Committee No. 8 of 1942: Cabinet paper, 69/4). Before agreeing to retaliation, Churchill had told the Defence Committee, 'we would have to ensure that our own preparations to meet gas attack were in good working order'.

[1] Telegram No. 6 from Moscow, 30 March 1942; Churchill papers, 20/73.

[2] Prime Minister's Personal Minute, D.61/2, 'Most Secret', 21 March 1942: Churchill papers, 20/67.

[3] Chiefs of Staff Committee No. 13 (Operations) of 142, 25 March 1942: Cabinet papers, 79/56.

Bengal. In China, a renewed Japanese attack led within six weeks to the loss of the Burma road link between India and China. In Burma itself, following the capture of Rangoon, British troops and Burmese refugees were driven back towards the Indian border. There, General Alexander, who had commanded the British forces throughout their long retreat, held the line against an invasion of India. From Stafford Cripps, who had just reached India to negotiate on behalf of the War Cabinet with the Indian National Congress, Churchill learned on March 25 of the considerable efforts being made to defend India. The officer in charge of road and rail developments in the border areas, General Wood, had, Cripps reported, 'given me an excellent impression of drive and determination'. Cripps added: 'All officers and ranks are working night and day, fully impressed by urgency of task.'[1]

Summing up the war in Europe and the Far East, Churchill told the Conservative Party Central Council on March 26 that, in the previous twelve months, 'we have had an almost unbroken series of military misfortunes. We were driven out of Cyrenaica, and have now only partly re-established ourselves there. We were driven out of Greece and Crete.' Turning to the Far East, Churchill spoke of the 'new and formidable antagonist', telling the assembled Conservatives: 'Hong Kong has fallen; the Malay Peninsula and the possessions of the brave Dutch in the East Indies have been overrun. Singapore has been the scene of the greatest disaster to British arms which our history records. The Allied squadrons in the Netherlands East Indies have been virtually destroyed in the action off Java. Burma is invaded; Rangoon has fallen; very hard fighting is proceeding in Upper Burma. Australia is threatened: India is threatened.' Added to the worsening turn in the Battle of the Atlantic, it was, Churchill confessed, 'a melancholy tale', but one 'which I do not fear to tell or to face. . . .'

The 'grand alliance' of nearly thirty States and Nations, Churchill told the assembled Conservatives, could not have come into existence but for Britain's resistance in 1940. It had now only to march on together 'until tyranny is trampled down'.[2]

In the early hours of March 28, British naval units, Special Service troops, and aircraft of Coastal and Bomber Command, carried out a raid on the dry dock and harbour installations of the Atlantic coast port and naval fortress of St Nazaire. A Royal Navy destroyer, HMS

---

[1] 'Personal and Secret', unnumbered, sent and received 25 March 1942: Churchill papers, 20/72.

[2] Speech of 26 March 1942, Caxton Hall, London: Churchill papers, 9/157.

Campbelltown, the former USS *Buchanan*, with bows specially stiffened, and filled with five tons of delayed-action high explosives, forced her way through the double torpedo baffle at the entrance to the lock and rammed the centre of the lock gate. Special Service troops then landed, and set about the work of demolition. Several dock installations, including the lock pumping station, and the dry dock operating gear, were destroyed. The Germans counter-attacked in force. The operation, Churchill was told on the morning of March 29, 'was successful but costly'. Many Germans had been killed by their own fire at very close range. The lock pumping station had been demolished.[1] Four Victoria Crosses were won during the attack.

Four hundred Germans had been killed in the raid on St Nazaire. The dry dock, which might have provided asylum for the *Tirpitz*, remained unusable until the end of the war. This was the third operation under the control of Admiral Mountbatten since his appointment as Chief of Combined Operations.[2] 'We were executing a number of raids on the enemy-occupied coastline from Norway to the Bay of Biscay,' Brooke told General Marshall ten days later, 'in order to force on the enemy a feeling of insecurity and uncertainty.'[3]

In an effort to increase Allied activity against Germany in the west, Churchill and Roosevelt now tried to expedite the arrival of the first United States bomber groups to England. 'Never was there so much good work to be done and so few to do it,' he telegraphed to the President on March 29. 'We must not let our summer air attacks on Germany decline into a second-rate affair. Everything is ready for your people here, and there are targets of all kinds, from easy to hard, to work up in contact with the enemy.' Even a hundred American heavy bombers working from Britain before the end of May 'would lift our air offensive to the proper scale', as well as releasing six British air squadrons for patrol work over the Bay of Biscay.

At Roosevelt's own urging, Churchill pointed out, 'we are emphasizing bombing attacks on U-boat nests'; to this end, 250 bombers had struck at Lübeck on the previous night, March 28. 'Results are

---

[1] 'News Received from Upper War Room, Admiralty, 9 a.m. on Sunday, 29.3.42', 29 March 1942: Premier papers, 3/376.

[2] The first of Mountbatten's raids had been against German shipping and factories on the island of Vaagsö, off the western coast of Norway. The second had been the capture of a German radar installation at Bruneval, in northern France.

[3] Chiefs of Staff Committee No. 112 of 1942, 9 April 1942: Cabinet papers, 79/56.

said to be best ever.'[1] But it was still on relief to Russia that Churchill's thoughts were most focused. 'After dinner,' General Brooke noted in his diary on March 30, 'had to go round to see PM at 10.30 p.m. Was kept up till 1 a.m. discussing possibilities of some form of offensive in northern France to assist Russia in the event of German attack being successful, as it probably will be.' The 'universal cry' to start a second front, Brooke added, was going to be 'hard to contend with, and yet what can we do with some ten Divisions against the German masses. Unfortunately the country fails to realize the situation we are in.'[2]

Press criticisms of the Government for the war setbacks, demands for a second front to help Russia, and an outburst of criticism from the Australian Prime Minister, John Curtin, harking back to the British attempt to help Greece in April 1941, all contributed to Churchill's sense of frustration and outrage. 'A small section of the foreign or overseas correspondents,' he had telegraphed to Curtin on March 23, 'make a speciality of decrying the British war effort to America and Australia.' As a result of this, the critical responses from America and Australia were telegraphed back to Britain 'and given prominence by all who wish to rock the boat'. In this way, 'we are all got into a mood where we claw each other instead of the enemy'. Churchill's telegram ended: 'We cannot afford this indulgence. The war is not fought to amuse the newspapers, but to save the peoples.'[3]

'Much harm has been done to the country this winter,' Churchill wrote to Lord Trenchard on March 30, 'by writers and speakers who had dwelt only on our 15 per cent shortcomings so that people have forgotten the 85 per cent solid achievement.'[4] The same day, Churchill lunched with the editor of *The Times*, Robin Barrington-Ward. He had no complaint, he said, about the 'sober, reasoned criticism' of *The Times* or the *Manchester Guardian*, it was the campaign in the *Daily Mirror*, *Daily Mail* and *Daily Herald*, which were 'calculated to undermine the Army', to which he was opposed. Barrington-Ward's account of the lunch—his first with Churchill since immediately after Pearl Harbour—continued:

Winston said 'I am an old man' (he didn't sound it), 'not like Lloyd George coming out of the last war at 56 or so. I may be 70 before this war ends.' (This was taking refuge in the view that reconstruction would be for someone else to take up in the future. He cannot see what the assurance, and in some measure the accomplishment, of it means to public confidence and

---

[1] Prime Minister's Personal Telegram, T.493/2, Churchill to Roosevelt No. 60, 'Personal and Secret', 29 March 1942: Churchill papers, 20/72.

[2] Brooke diary, 30 March 1942: Bryant, *op. cit.*, volume 1, page 371.

[3] Prime Minister's Personal Telegram, T.459/2, 23 March 1942: Churchill papers, 20/88.

[4] Letter of 30 March 1942: Churchill papers, 20/53.

war energy *now*.) 'No man has had to bear such disasters as I have.' I said the nation had taken them very well.

Far from storming he bore my candour and listened most patiently. Not quite as fit and sparkling as at our last lunch. A very impressive person with strong limitations. His utter absence of pomposity is engaging. He was wearing his one-piece 'siren suit'. Ate heartily.[1]

Churchill did not underestimate the reasons for Parliamentary and Press unease. 'Our position here has always been quite solid,' he telegraphed to Roosevelt on April 1, 'but naturally with nothing but disaster to show for all one's work, people were restive in Parliament and the Press,' and he added: 'I find it very difficult to get over Singapore, but I hope we shall redeem it ere long.'[2]

---

[1] Barrington-Ward diary, 30 March 1942: Donald McLachlan, *In the Chair: Barrington-Ward of 'The Times'*, London 1971, pages 194–5.

[2] Prime Minister's Personal Telegram, T.519, Churchill to Roosevelt No. 62, 'Personal and Secret', 'No distribution', 1 April 1942: Churchill papers, 20/73.

5
Towards a Second Front

BY April 1942 Britain's military resources were fully stretched, not only by Rommel's success in North Africa and Japan's continuing advance through Burma—where Mandalay was bombed on April 3 with the loss of two thousand lives—but also by the uncertainty as to where the next blow might fall. In the Mediterranean, it was Malta which had come under the ferocious air attack of more than six hundred German and Italian aircraft. In the Far East, both India and Australia seemed equally likely targets for Japan's next strike.

'Speaking as one amateur to another,' Churchill telegraphed to Roosevelt on April 1, 'my feeling is that the wisest stroke for Japan would be to press on through Burma northwards into China and try to make a job of that. They may disturb India, but I doubt its serious invasion.' Britain was sending forty to fifty thousand men a month to the East: as they rounded the Cape of Good Hope they could be diverted wherever emergency called them, to Suez, to Basra, to Bombay, to Ceylon or to Australia.

In this telegram Churchill told Roosevelt that he had given Australia's Prime Minister a pledge that if Australia were 'seriously invaded' by six or eight Japanese divisions, 'Britain will come to his aid.'[1] One way of making the Japanese 'anxious for their numerous conquests', and thus preventing them 'scraping together troops for further large excursions', would be American Commando raids, of which Roosevelt had spoken to Churchill in Washington.

'All now depends,' Churchill warned, 'upon the vast Russo-German

---

[1] In a telegram to the Australian representative in Washington on that same day, April 1, Churchill wrote: 'We must be careful not to direct our limited reserves to theatres where there will be no fighting. No one knows yet whether Japanese will strike at Australia or India or, even more likely, South China. They have enough for a considerable operation in any one of these directions but surely not in all of them at once. I am by no means convinced that Australia is the chosen target. Once the enemy shows his hand decisions can be made.' (Telegram No. 2106, 1 April 1942, 'Personal and Most Strictly Secret': Churchill papers, 20/73.)

struggle.' Britain was doing all she could to help, but would have 'to fight every convoy through to Murmansk'. Stalin was 'pleased' with Britain's deliveries, which were due to go up 50 per cent after June, although this would be difficult to achieve in view of the 'new war' in the Far East, and also of shipping shortages.

Churchill ended his telegram of April 1: 'I am personally extremely well, though I have felt the weight of the war rather more since I got back than before.' Perhaps, he added, 'when the weather gets better I may propose myself for a week-end with you and flip over. We have so much to settle that would go easily in talk.'[1]

Earlier that day, Churchill had appealed to Roosevelt for help over Malta, for the American aircraft carrier *Wasp* to transport fifty British Spitfires for which no other carrier was available. Such help, Churchill wrote, would give Britain 'a chance of inflicting a very severe and possibly decisive check on enemy'.[2]

Roosevelt agreed.[3] He also sent Churchill, on April 2, a cryptic message about 'a plan which I hope Russia will greet with enthusiasm'. To explain the plan, he was sending both Harry Hopkins and General Marshall to see Churchill. The plan not only depended upon 'complete co-operation' between Britain and the United States, but, Roosevelt added, 'I would like to be able to label it the plan of the United Nations.'[4] 'Delighted Harry and Marshall are coming,' Churchill replied later that same day. 'Looking forward to their arrival and the sooner the better.'[5]

On April 3, Good Friday, Roosevelt wrote a covering letter for his two emissaries:

Dear Winston,

What Harry & Geo Marshall will tell you all about has my heart & mind in it. Your people & mine demand the establishment of a front to draw off pressure on the Russians, & these peoples are wise enough to see that the Russians are to-day killing more Germans & destroying more equipment than you & I put together. Even if full success is not attained, the big objective will be.

Go to it! Syria & Egypt will be made more secure, even if the Germans find out about our plans.

---

[1] Prime Minister's Personal Telegram, T.519/2, Prime Minister to President No. 62, 1 April 1942, 'Personal and Secret', 'No Distribution': Churchill papers, 20/73.

[2] Prime Minister's Personal Telegram, T.510/2, Prime Minister to President No. 61, 'Personal and Secret', 1 April 1942: Churchill papers, 20/73.

[3] President to Prime Minister, No. 130, 'Personal and Secret', received 3 April 1942: Churchill papers, 20/73.

[4] President to Prime Minister, No. 129, 2 April 1942: Churchill papers, 20/73.

[5] Prime Minister's Personal Telegram, T.524/2, Prime Minister to President No. 63, 'Personal and Secret', 2 April 1942: Churchill papers, 20/73.

Best of luck—*make* Harry go to bed early & let him obey Dr Fulton, USN, whom I am sending with him as super nurse with full authority.

As ever,
FDR [1]

In a series of minutes at the beginning of April, Churchill explored every avenue of war production, with a view to future offensive action by British troops. The question whether to manufacture a thousand new tanks, or manufacture only five hundred and 'rework' five hundred, had to be resolved.[2] There was a proposal to be considered for creating an Order of Merit for industrial achievement.[3] There was the need 'to increase the airborne forces to the utmost limit as soon as possible', including preparation of a scheme for converting all bombers, 'as they fall obsolete', to troop-carrying purposes.[4] There was the search for a policy to ensure the 'maximum new production' of artillery.[5]

Determined to see a successful bomber offensive by the end of 1942, Churchill pressed for plans to be made by the Air Ministry 'to make sure that the maximum weight of the best type of bombs is dropped on the German cities by the aircraft placed at their disposal'. Crews must be practised in the use of the new 'blind bombing' apparatus. Navigators must master new methods of navigation 'to get them within twelve and fifteen miles of the target', before the blind bombing equipment came into play. In order to prevent the bombers being immobilized by bad weather, preparations had to be made for 'adequate runways', homing devices, fog-clearing gear on the aerodromes, and de-icing and blind-landing equipment on the planes.[6]

On April 4 Japanese naval forces, which had earlier entered the Indian Ocean, were reported steering towards Ceylon. Among them were five aircraft carriers. That morning, severe air attacks were delivered on the harbours of Colombo and Trincomalee. In the ensuing air battle, twenty-one Japanese and nineteen British aircraft were shot down, and both the armed merchant cruiser *Hector* and the destroyer *Tenedos* were sunk. At sea, the cruisers *Dorsetshire* and *Cornwall*, which had left harbour for safety before the attack, were sunk by Japanese aircraft, and more than five hundred men were drowned. On April 5,

---

[1] 'The White House, Washington, April 3, 11 p.m.': Churchill papers, 20/52.
[2] Prime Minister's Personal Minute, M.121/2, 'Secret', 3 April 1942: Churchill papers, 20/67.
[3] Prime Minister's Personal Minute, M.122/2, 3 April 1942: Churchill papers, 20/67.
[4] Prime Minister's Personal Minute, D.79/2, 7 April 1942: Churchill papers, 20/67.
[5] Prime Minister's Personal Minute, M.128/2, 7 April 1942: Churchill papers, 20/67.
[6] Prime Minister's Personal Minute, M.138/2 (to Sir Archibald Sinclair), 'Secret', 14 April 1942: Churchill papers, 20/67.

in a second air attack on Trincomalee, the aircraft carrier *Hermes* and the destroyer *Vampire* were sunk, with the loss of over three hundred lives.

The port of Calcutta had already been cleared, in case of a Japanese attack on Bengal. But the defence preparations put into effect for Ceylon had been effective, and Colombo was not to go the way of Singapore. 'Ceylon news seems good,' Churchill telegraphed on April 5 to Sir Stafford Cripps—who was then in New Delhi—'and it is lucky we did not withdraw fighter forces.' [1] This was a reference to pressure from the Government of India to have the fighters in Ceylon transferred to India.

For the moment, Ceylon was saved from invasion; but in the Pacific, Japanese forces landed in the Solomon Islands on April 6. In the Indian Ocean, that same day, Japanese bombs fell on India for the first time, on two ports in the Madras Presidency. [2] Churchill and his advisers could not tell if the Japanese ships involved were there as 'a mere demonstration', as Churchill telegraphed to Roosevelt on April 7, or a prelude 'to an invasion in force' of Ceylon. If invasion was their plan, Churchill warned, 'our naval forces are not strong enough to oppose this'. There were five, 'possibly six' Japanese battleships, and five aircraft-carriers, believed to be in the Indian Ocean. 'We cannot of course make head against this force,' Churchill wrote, 'especially if it is concentrated.' The situation was therefore one 'of grave anxiety'.

To 'compel' the Japanese forces to withdraw from the Indian Ocean, Churchill suggested some action by the United States Pacific Fleet, 'as you must now be decidedly superior to the enemy forces in the Pacific'. [3] Answering criticisms in the House of Commons six days later, that there had not been sufficient foresight in British policy, Churchill declared: 'an immense amount of study and discussion preceded these lamentable events, but study and discussion are not in themselves sufficient to prepare against attack by a superior force of the enemy.' [4]

Hopkins and Marshall reached London on April 8, when they gave Churchill the 'plan' to which Roosevelt had referred in his cryptic message six days earlier. The plan was a United States Joint Staff memorandum on future operations in western Europe, the area 'favoured as the theatre in which to stage the first major offen-

[1] Prime Minister's Personal Telegram, T.537/2, 5 April 1942: Churchill papers, 20/73.
[2] The ports were Coconada and Vizagapatam.
[3] Prime Minister's Personal Telegram, T.547/2, Prime Minister to President, No. 65, 7 April 1942: Churchill papers, 20/73.
[4] *Hansard*, 13 April 1942: columns 41–9.

sive by the United States and Great Britain'. Only in western Europe, the memorandum stated, could their combined land and air resources be fully developed, 'and the maximum support given to Russia'.

The decision to launch this offensive should be made '*at once*', because of the 'immense preparations' required. Forty-eight divisions were to participate, thirty American and eighteen British. Also required were 5,800 combat aircraft: 3,250 Americans and 2,550 British. The American forces involved could be brought over by 1 April 1943, 'but only if 60 per cent of the lift is carried by non-US ships'. Using only American ships, 'the date of the assault must be postponed to the late summer of 1943'.

Roosevelt's 'plan' envisaged an assault on 'selected beaches' between Le Havre and Boulogne, carried out by a first wave of at least six divisions, and 'nourished' at the rate of at least 100,000 men a week. Their objective would be Antwerp. Since 'invasion on this scale' could not take place for a year, a plan should also be prepared for earlier action on a smaller scale, 'by such forces as may be available from time to time', either to take advantage of a 'sudden German disintegration' or ' "as a sacrifice" to avert an imminent collapse of Russian resistance'.

As only five American divisions could be despatched for any such 'immediate' action in the autumn of 1942, 'the chief burden', the plan explained, 'would fall on the UK'. For example, on 15 September 1942 the United States could provide half the number of troops required, but only 700 of the 5,700 combat aircraft needed.[1] No wonder Clementine Churchill described her husband as 'bearing not only the burden of his own country but for the moment of an unprepared America. . . .'[2]

On the afternoon of April 8, Hopkins and Marshall unfolded the 'plan' to Churchill, who expressed himself favourably disposed to it. That night, Hopkins and Marshall were Churchill's guests at dinner. The 'plan' was not discussed. The talk ranged over the American Civil War and the First World War. Only Brooke broached the subject of their mission, sufficiently, as Hopkins noted, 'to indicate that he had a great many misgivings.'[3]

On the second day of Hopkins' and Marshall's London mission, the American forces on the Bataan Peninsula in the Philippines surren-

---

[1] 'Operations in Western Europe' 'Secret': Churchill papers, 20/52.

[2] In a letter to Churchill, urging him to dissuade their son from leaving the Staff in Cairo to join a parachute unit (letter of 11 April 1942: Mary Soames, *Clementine Churchill*, *op. cit.*, page 315).

[3] Brooke diary, 8 April 1942: Bryant, *op. cit.*, volume 1, page 352.

dered to the Japanese, and 35,000 American troops were taken prisoner. That morning, Marshall outlined the 'plan' to the Chiefs of Staff Committee. If the Russian situation developed 'unfavourably', Marshall told the British Chiefs of Staff, 'we might have to stage an "Emergency Operation" on the Continent to help them'. It was equally likely, he said, that a 'break in German morale might occur'. If, at the same time, the Germans 'failed' in their 1942 offensive against Russia, 'we ought', Marshall argued, 'to be prepared to exploit the consequences'.

Brooke, Mountbatten and Portal then each explained to Marshall the problems, and indeed the impossibility of a major European landing in 1942. A force landed in 1942 'to relieve the Russians' could not exceed 'some 7 divisions and 2 armoured divisions'. This force would not be 'strong enough', Brooke stated, 'to maintain a bridgehead against the scale of attack which the Germans could bring against it, and it was unlikely that we could extricate the forces if the Germans made a really determined effort to drive us out'. Mountbatten warned that it would be 'extremely difficult', given the small size of the ports on the French coast, 'to maintain a force over open beaches' and Portal noted, from the point of view of fighter support of the land forces, 'that we could not afford more casualties than might result from one or two months fighting'.[1]

Brooke commented in his dairy, of the two and a half American divisions available for northern Europe in September 1942: 'no very great contribution!'[2]

On April 10, in Philadelphia, Maxim Litvinoff, Soviet Ambassador to the United States and a former Soviet Foreign Minister, called publicly for the opening of a 'Second Front' as soon as possible. That same day, in London, King George VI wrote to Churchill: 'I have asked Mr Hopkins & General Marshall to lunch with me on Wednesday. . . .' That same Wednesday, when Churchill was to lunch with the King at 10 Downing Street, Hopkins and Marshall were also invited. 'I am sure we shall appreciate their presence,' the King wrote to Churchill, '& it will be a compliment to them.'[3]

As talk proceeded in London for a possible second front in 1942, talks broke down in Delhi on the proposals which Sir Stafford Cripps had taken to India, on behalf of Churchill and the Cabinet, for Indian self-government after the war. The All-India Congress Committee, unwilling to wait until after the war, had demanded a National Government 'immediately'. In reporting this to Churchill on Friday,

[1] Chiefs of Staff Committee No. 112 of 1942, 9 April 1942: Cabinet papers, 79/56.
[2] Brooke diary, 9 April 1942: Bryant, *op. cit.*, volume 1, page 354.
[3] 'Buckingham Palace, April 10th 1942': Churchill papers, 20/52.

April 10, Cripps commented: 'There is clearly no hope of agreement and I shall start home on Sunday.'[1] 'Even though your hopes have not been fulfilled,' Churchill replied, 'you have rendered a very important service to the common cause and the foundations have been laid for the future progress of the peoples of India.'[2] 'We are not depressed,' Cripps replied, 'though sad at the result,' and he added: 'Now we must get on with the job of defending India.'[3]

On April 10, before leaving for Chequers, Churchill discussed the American second front plan with Eden. Churchill's fear, Eden noted in his diary, was that the General Staff would say 'yes' to the plan, 'and make this a pretext for doing less elsewhere'.[4] That night Hopkins and Marshall dined at Chequers with the three Chiefs of Staff. 'We were kept up till 2 a.m.,' Brooke noted in his diary, 'doing a world survey but little useful work.'[5]

Discussion on the proposed second front continued at Chequers throughout April 11. On April 12 Churchill sent Roosevelt his personal assessment of the American plan: 'your masterly document', he called it. 'I am in entire agreement in principle with all you propose,' Churchill wrote, 'and so are the Chiefs of Staff.' The proposals for the 'interim operation' in 1942 'met the difficulties and uncertainties in an absolutely sound manner'. If, Churchill added, 'as our experts believe, we can carry this whole plan through successfully, it will be one of the grand events in all the history of the war'.[6]

There was a serious dispute on April 12 between Churchill and Roosevelt: not the second front, but India, was the cause. In a private letter to Churchill, Roosevelt urged that Cripps should remain in India until a 'Nationalist Government' could be set up, on the understanding that 'following the termination of a period of trial and error they would be enabled then to determine upon their own form of constitution. . . .'[7]

This message reached Churchill when he was talking to Hopkins at

---

[1] Telegram No. 984-S, 10 April 1942: Churchill papers, 20/73.

[2] Prime Minister's Personal Telegram, T.556, 11 April 1942: Churchill papers, 20/73.

[3] Telegram No. 988 S, 11 April 1942: Churchill papers, 20/73.

[4] Eden diary, 10 April 1942: Eden memoirs, *The Reckoning, op. cit.*, page 325.

[5] Brooke diary, 10 April 1942: Bryant, *op. cit.*, volume 1, page 354.

[6] Prime Minister's Personal Telegram. T.561/2, Prime Minister to President No. 68, 'Personal and Secret', 'No distribution', 'Sent only to Mr Eden (personal)', 12 April 1942: Churchill papers, 20/73.

[7] Telegram dated 11 April 1942, received 12 April 1942, 'no distribution': Churchill papers, 20/73.

3 a.m. in the early hours of April 12. Hopkins at once tried to telephone Churchill's answer to Roosevelt, but, 'owing to atmospherics', as Churchill explained later that morning, 'he could not get through'. Churchill added:

You know the weight which I attach to everything you say to me, but I did not feel I could take responsibility for the defence of India if everything had again to be thrown into the melting-pot at this critical juncture. That, I am sure, would be the view of Cabinet and of Parliament. As your telegram was addressed to Former Naval Person I am keeping it as purely private, and I do not propose to bring it before the Cabinet officially unless you tell me you wish this done. Anything like a serious difference between you and me would break my heart, and would surely deeply injure both our countries at the height of this terrible struggle.[1]

On the morning of April 14 Marshall again attended a meeting of the Chiefs of Staff, when he expressed the view that 'within the next three or four months we were very likely to find ourselves in the position when we were forced to take action on the Continent'. This, he explained, 'might be either because we might not be able to hold back while the Russians were being driven back or borne down, or because a favourable opportunity had presented itself'. Whatever forces had to be sent to India or the Middle East, Marshall added, he thought it 'essential that our main project, i.e. operations on the Continent, should not be reduced to the status of a "residuary legatee" for whom nothing was left.'

One problem, replied Mountbatten, was the availability of landing-craft. By 1943 'the position would have greatly improved'. If Britain were 'forced this year to undertake an operation on the Continent', Brooke warned, 'it could only be on a small scale'.[2]

That evening, Hopkins saw Churchill at 6.30 and dined with him at 8.30.[3] Both Hopkins and Marshall were then present, at 10.30 p.m., at a meeting of the Defence Committee at 10 Downing Street. Churchill opened the meeting by saying that the Defence Committee had met to consider the 'momentous proposal' which Hopkins and Marshall had brought over, and which had now been 'fully discussed and examined by the Staffs'. He had 'no hesitation', as the minutes of the meeting recorded, 'in cordially accepting the plan. The conception underlying it accorded with the classic principles of war—namely, concentration against the main enemy. One broad reservation must however be made—it was essential to carry on the defence of India

[1] Prime Minister's Personal Telegram, T.561/2, Prime Minister to President No. 68, 'Personal and Secret', 12 April 1942: Churchill papers, 20/88.
[2] Chiefs of Staff Committee No. 118 of 1942, 14 April 1942: Cabinet papers, 79/56.
[3] Prime Minister's Engagement Card, Tuesday 14 April 1942.

and the Middle East. We could not possibly face the loss of an army of 600,000 men and the whole man-power of India. Furthermore, Australia and the island bases connecting that country with the United States must not be allowed to fall.' This meant, he explained, 'that we could not entirely lay aside everything in the furtherance of the main object proposed by General Marshall.'

Marshall then spoke of how the proposals for a second front in Europe constituted a 'definite aim'. Given this aim, the Americans had already begun to transform their war programmes: the production programme of landing craft, for example, had been stepped up 'two or three times'. He felt certain 'that all other difficulties that might arise would dissolve in like manner'. As for the non-European war zones, careful calculations 'had been made as to the requirements elsewhere, such as the holding of "important points" in Australia and the South West Pacific', and he had arranged 'to provide what was required'. He did not want, Marshall added, 'to divert further forces to these places'.

Brooke, who spoke after Marshall, said that while the Chiefs of Staff 'welcomed the idea of an offensive in Europe', it was necessary to take measures 'to prevent a collapse in the Indian Ocean'. For this purpose, Britain would need American assistance. Churchill, speaking after Brooke, confirmed that 'for the next two or three months', Britain would be unable 'to cope unaided' with Japanese naval strength in the Indian Ocean.

Harry Hopkins then gave his view of the plan. 'The American nation,' he said, 'was eager to join in the fight alongside the British.' It was true that each country would be fighting 'for its own interests'. But each wished to fight alongside the other. The decision to proceed with a second front in Europe in 1943 was 'one of the most momentous which had ever been faced'. On it, Hopkins said, 'depended the preservation of all that democracy held dear'. The decision, once taken, could not be reversed. If adopted, the share of the United States 'would constitute their major effort'.

Clement Attlee welcomed the American plan. Hitherto, he said, 'we had been hanging on to the best of our ability and with few resources'. Now the time had come to take the initiative. Anthony Eden then gave his support to what he called 'the great picture of two English speaking countries setting out for the redemption of Europe'. The publicity involved, he added, 'would show our own public that we were not permanently wedded to the defensive'.

Summing up the discussion, Churchill noted that there was 'complete unanimity on the framework. The two nations would march ahead in a noble brotherhood of arms.' But as the plan could be 'fatally compromised' by Japanese action in the Indian Ocean, he would send Roosevelt a request for Britain's 'vital requirements' there. As to the European plan, 'full preparations could now start and we could go ahead with the utmost resolution'. It would gradually become known, Churchill added, 'that the English speaking peoples were resolved on a great campaign for the liberation of Europe': perhaps even a public announcement should eventually be made. He could assure Hopkins and Marshall 'that nothing would be left undone on the part of the British Government and people which could contribute to the success of the great enterprise on which they were about to embark'.[1]

To Roosevelt, Hopkins telegraphed that 'not only agreement in principle, but a real meeting of minds' would, he believed, be achieved.[2] Marshall commented, however, that most of the participants held 'reservations regarding this and that', and added that 'great firmness' would be needed to avoid 'further dispersions'.[3] But Churchill's perspective was of the war in being: where the possible imminent German threat to Russia had to be balanced by the equally imminent Japanese threat to India. On April 14 Churchill sent Cripps, who was then in Cairo, an Air Ministry note which had Churchill's full support. 'Despite great importance of bombing Germany as means of weakening German offensive against Russia,' the note read, 'this has not been allowed to influence reinforcements of India.'[4] On the following day, April 15, Churchill appealed direct to Roosevelt for some American heavy bombers to be sent to India. Churchill explained: 'There are at present about fourteen, and fifty more are authorised. But none of these was able to attack the Japanese naval forces last week. We have taken everything from Libya which is possible without ruining all prospects of a renewed offensive. We are sending every suitable aircraft to the East which can be efficiently serviced out there, but without your aid this will not be sufficient. Might I press you, Mr President, to procure the necessary decisions?'[5]

Roosevelt responded at once, noting that 46 heavy and medium bombers, as well as 50 fighters, were already on their way to India for

---

[1] Defence Committee No. 10 of 1942, 14 April 1942: Cabinet papers, 69/4.

[2] Telegram of 13 April 1942: Robert E. Sherwood, *The White House Papers of Harry L. Hopkins*, volume 2, London 1949, page 539.

[3] On his return to the United States, however, Marshall wrote to Churchill: 'These discussions resulted in our laying a firm foundation for a full measure of cooperation without the interminable delays and usual misunderstanding common to such joint enterprises' (Letter of 28 April 1942: Churchill papers, 20/58).

[4] Air Ministry note, enclosed in Prime Minister's Personal Telegram, T.568/2, 'Personal and Most Secret', 14 April 1942: Churchill papers, 20/73.

[5] Prime Minister's Personal Telegram, T.570/2, Prime Minister to President No. 69, 'Personal and Secret', 15 April 1942: Churchill papers, 20/73.

use under Wavell's command.[1] On Roosevelt's suggestion, this bomber force was to be provided with a further 34 heavy and medium bomber aircraft from America's British allocations.[2]

The urgency of aid to India did not deflect Churchill, however, from the need for action to support Russia: that too was a part of the delicate balance of priorities. When, on April 16, Clement Attlee proposed the transfer of Bomber Command to India and the Middle East, Churchill replied: 'It is no use flying out squadrons which sit helpless and useless when they arrive. We have built up a great plan here for bombing Germany, which is the only way in our power of helping Russia.' Churchill added: 'One has to be sure that we do not ruin our punch here without getting any proportionate advantage elsewhere.'[3]

On April 17 Churchill sent Roosevelt his conclusions on the American plan 'against the main enemy'. It was acceptable, subject to 'one broad qualification', that a proportion of the combined resources of the two countries should 'for the moment' be set aside to halt the Japanese advance. On this need, Marshall had felt 'confident', Churchill reported, 'that we could together provide what was necessary for the Indian Ocean and other theatres, and yet go right ahead with your main project'. Joint plans and preparations for 1943 were to start 'at once'. But Britain, Churchill warned, 'might however feel compelled to act this year'. Roosevelt had envisaged September as the earliest possible date for European operations in 1942. Churchill felt that 'things may easily come to a head before then'. His telegram continued:

Marshall explained that you had been reluctant to press for an enterprise that was fraught with such grave risks and dire consequences until you could make a substantial air contribution; but he left us in no doubt that, if it were found necessary to act earlier, you, Mr President, would earnestly wish to throw in every available scrap of human and material resources.

We are proceeding with plans and preparations on that basis. Broadly speaking, our agreed programme is a crescendo of activity on the Continent, starting with an ever-increasing air offensive both by night and day and more frequent and large-scale raids, in which United States troops will take part.[4]

On April 18 the first American bombers struck at Tokyo, Kobe,

[1] Prime Minister's Personal Telegram, T.589/2 (to General Wavell), 'Personal and Secret', 18 April 1942: Churchill papers, 20/73.
[2] Note by Portal, enclosed in Prime Minister's Personal Telegram T.592/2, Prime Minister to President, No. 72, 'Personal and Secret', 19 April 1942: Churchill papers, 20/73.
[3] Prime Minister's Personal Minute, M.139/2, 16 April 1942: Churchill papers, 20/67.
[4] Prime Minister's Personal Telegram, T.586/2, Prime Minister to President No. 70, 'Secret and Personal', 17 April 1942: Churchill papers, 20/73.

Yokohama and Nagoya.[1] That same day, a German submarine, surfacing in the West Indies, shelled oil installations on the Dutch island of Curaçao. In the Mediterranean, Malta was under such severe bombardment that only two months' bread supplies were left. Churchill urged Roosevelt to authorize the aircraft carrier *Wasp* to make a second dash to Malta with air reinforcements. 'Without this aid,' he telegraphed, 'I fear Malta will be pounded to bits.' Meanwhile, he pointed out, 'its defence is wearing out the enemy's Air Force and effectively aiding Russia'.[2]

'I am pleased to say,' Roosevelt replied on April 25, 'that *Wasp* is to be made available for the second trip with Spitfires for Malta.'[3]

Roosevelt was also 'delighted', as he telegraphed to Churchill on April 22, with 'the agreement which was reached between you and your military advisers and Marshall and Hopkins'. This move, he believed, 'will be very disheartening to Hitler, and may well be the wedge by which his downfall will be accomplished'. Whatever might be their 'mutual difficulties', Roosevelt added, 'I am frank to say that I feel better about the war than at any time in the past two years.'[4]

While at Chequers, Churchill prepared for a speech to the House of Commons in Secret Session. 'I had to cope with morning duty,' Elizabeth Layton wrote to her parents, 'speech (10,000 words), then a really fearful scramble in the middle of the afternoon when he actually came striding through into our office to dictate an additional paragraph, which he has never done before, and then on and on with speech till it was ready for next day.'[5]

On April 23, at the Secret Session, Churchill stressed the setbacks which had occurred since the previous December. 'Not only have we failed to stem the advance of the new enemy,' he said, 'but we have had to weaken seriously the hopeful operations we were carrying on against the old.' Nor could he 'encourage the House to expect good news' from the Burma war zone. 'The best that can be hoped for,' he said, 'is that the retreat will be as slow as possible. . . .' But the war with Japan was 'the lesser war'. It was against Germany and Italy that 'the major war' was being fought. In the Atlantic, mainly off the coast of North America, where shipping was unescorted, more Allied

---

[1] This news was not released by the United States War Department until 10 May 1942.

[2] Prime Minister's Personal Telegram, T.617/2, Prime Minister to President No. 76, 'Personal and Secret', 24 April 1942: Churchill papers, 20/74.

[3] President to Prime Minister, No. 140, 'Personal and Secret', 25 April 1942, 'Scrambled to Chequers, 7.30 a.m., 25 April 1942': Churchill papers, 20/74.

[4] President to Prime Minister, No. 139, 'Priority', 'Secret and Personal', received 9.58 p.m., 22 April 1942: Churchill papers, 20/74.

[5] Letter of 16 April 1942: Nel papers.

tonnage had been sunk in less than sixty days, than in the last five months of the Battle of the Atlantic before America came into the war. In North Africa, 'a decisive victory' had just been missed: 'By what narrow margins, chances and accidents was the balance tipped against us no man can compute.' But it was in Europe 'that the immediate main clash impends'—the new German offensive against Russia— and to help Russia 'there is nothing that we would not do'.

Munitions were being sent to Russia, Churchill told the House, 'to the utmost extent which our shipping can carry'. Britain was convoying to Russia not only her own contribution, but also that of the United States. The *Tirpitz*, *Scheer* and *Hipper* lay in Trondheim fiord, a constant danger. 'Traps' of U-boats lay in wait for the convoys. 'It is a grim and bitter effort amid fearful gales and ceaseless perils,' Churchill declared, 'but if it be in human power we will carry our tanks, our aircraft, and all the other essential supplies to our heroic ally in her sublime struggle.' When the German armies attacked, 'bleeding copiously upon a two-thousand mile front in the East', the British bombing offensive which would be 'on their back in the German homeland', had, in fact, already begun. 'Half a dozen German cities have already received the full measure that they meted out to Coventry. Another thirty or more are on the list.'

The war would not be ended, Churchill told the House, by defeating Japan, but 'only through the defeat in Europe of the German armies', or a German internal collapse. This latter could not be counted on. 'We have, therefore, to prepare for the liberation of the captive countries of western and southern Europe by the landing at suitable points, successively or simultaneously, of British and American armies strong enough to enable the conquered populations to revolt.' This was not the first time Churchill had expressed this view. But he did so now after finding 'that these simple but classical conceptions of war' were shared, 'earnestly and spontaneously', by the Government and 'dominant forces' in the United States. The visit of Hopkins and Marshall was, he said, 'to concert with us the largest and swiftest measures of this offensive character'. The liberation of the continent of Europe by equal numbers of British and American troops 'is the main war plan of our two nations'.

For Churchill the invasion of occupied Europe had always been the one definite road to victory. 'The timing, the scale, the method, the direction of this supreme undertaking,' he told the House, 'must remain unknown and unknowable till the hour strikes and the blow falls.' [1]

---

[1] Secret Session, House of Commons, 23 April 1942: Winston S. Churchill, *Secret Session Speeches*, London 1946, pages 46–75. The notes and typescript of this speech are in the Churchill papers, 9/155.

Churchill's speech had lasted for an hour and fifty minutes. It 'opened the eyes of the House so much', he wrote to his son, who was then in Cairo, 'to the vast panorama of the war and its many grievous dangers, that the debate utterly collapsed. . . .'[1]

When Eden went to see Churchill on the day after the Secret Session, the Prime Minister had just woken up from his afternoon sleep. 'He was in tearing spirits,' Eden noted in his diary. 'Said he could not remember where he was on waking, he had had such deep sleep and he was striding about his room in vest and drawers with cigar in his mouth, whisky and soda at his side and calling for Nellie to produce his socks! We spoke of Government and I urged him to bring as many of Cabinet into his plans as he could. He agreed though arguing this must slow up machine. However Cripps, Oliver and I, he thought pretty powerful with himself.'[2]

Eden and Churchill discussed a telegram just received from Stalin, informing Churchill that the Soviet Foreign Minister, Vyacheslav Molotov, was on his way to London. Molotov's mission was twofold, to bring to London a draft Anglo-Soviet Treaty, and to exchange views with the British Government 'on the question of opening a second front in Europe'.[3]

While Churchill awaited Molotov's visit, the final preparations went ahead for Operation 'Ironclad', the aim of which, as Churchill explained to the War Cabinet on April 24, was 'to prevent our being forestalled by the Japanese in the occupation of Madagascar'.

An hour before the War Cabinet met to discuss 'Ironclad', Churchill had presided at a meeting of the Chiefs of Staff Committee. At that meeting, Brooke raised the possibility of a hostile Vichy reaction to the operation, fearing, as he told the Committee, that the British force might be forestalled by the Japanese, as a result of a Vichy invitation to Japan, or even by direct French opposition, bringing about 'such counter action on the part of the French as would make our last position worse than the first'. Replying to Brooke, Eden argued that as Vichy France would be 'reluctant to break' with the United States, no such invitation to Japan, or direct French action, would take place. He therefore advised that 'Ironclad' should proceed. 'It was, of course, a much easier course to do nothing,' Churchill commented. 'If the enterprise were abandoned, we should not have to take any risks. But having informed the President and General Smuts that we intended

---

[1] 'Personal', 2 May 1942: Churchill papers, 1/369.

[2] Eden diary, 24 April 1942: Eden memoirs, *The Reckoning, op. cit.*, page 326. Nellie was the parlourmaid who sometimes stood in for Churchill's valet Sawyers.

[3] Prime Minister's Personal Telegram, T.608/2, 22 April 1942: Premier papers, 3/403. To maintain secrecy, in the preliminary correspondence Molotov was referred to as 'Mr Cocktail'.

to carry out the operation at an early date, if we now reversed the decision and the Japanese walked into the Island, our inaction would take a deal of explaining away.'

Churchill added that if Vichy were to react 'badly' to the occupation of Madagascar, Roosevelt might prefer, having kept clear of the operation at its inception, 'to bring the full weight of American pressure on the French as a deterrent'.[1]

The force needed for 'Ironclad' had turned the Cape, and was in the Indian Ocean, Churchill told the War Cabinet when it met at noon, and he added that the United States Government had been informed of the operation, 'but preferred not to be openly associated with it'.

It would be possible to land on Madagascar, and to seize the island from its Vichy rulers. But, Portal warned the War Cabinet, Britain did not have sufficient forces 'to make ourselves so strong in the Island that we could hold it, whatever forces Japan might send against it'. The hope was that Japan 'might well hesitate before sending a large force to attack Madagascar, more especially in view of the very long distance involved'.[2]

Five days later, Roosevelt sent Churchill the text of his speech for that night, in which he gave 'Ironclad' his support with the words: 'The United Nations will take measures if necessary to prevent the use of French territory in any part of the world for military purposes by the Axis powers.' Roosevelt added: 'The good people of France will readily understand that such action is essential for the United Nations to prevent assistance to the armies or navies or air forces of Germany, Italy and Japan.'[3] 'Most grateful for your telegram about "Ironclad",' Churchill replied, 'for which all goes forward. Also for allowing *Wasp* to have another good sting.'[4]

---

[1] Chiefs of Staff Committee No. 29 (Operations) of 1942, 11 a.m., 24 April 1942: Cabinet papers, 79/56.

[2] War Cabinet No. 52 of 1942, Confidential Annex, 24 April 1942: Cabinet papers, 65/30.

[3] President to Prime Minister, No. 142, 29 April 1942: Churchill papers, 20/74.

[4] Prime Minister's Personal Telegram, T.653/2, Prime Minister to President No. 82, 'Personal and Secret': Churchill papers, 20/74. British fighter planes, flown from the United States carrier *Wasp* to Malta, were playing a major part in protecting the island base.

6

'We shall drive on to the end'

BRITAIN had now been at war with Germany for thirty-two months; the Soviet Union for nearly ten months; America for five months. In this new situation of the wider war, one of Britain's most onerous commitments remained the convoying of war supplies to Russia. Churchill had spoken about this 'grim and bitter effort' in his Secret Session speech on 23 April 1942. Ten days before that, he had told the War Cabinet that he 'thought it was important that we should make the Russian Government realise the extent of the risks which were being run, and the efforts which were being made in maintaining the northern supply route to Russia'.[1] One such convoy, PQ13, had left Iceland for Russia on April 1. Attacked by German aircraft and destroyers, five out of her nineteen ships were sunk, and the principal escort vessel, the cruiser *Trinidad*, badly crippled by torpedoes. On the next convoy, heavy pack-ice north of Iceland forced fourteen of the twenty-three ships to return. One of the remainder proceeding to Russia was sunk. Only eight reached their destination. On April 26 Churchill had warned Harry Hopkins by telegram of 'the serious convoy situation', and of a serious backlog of supplies which could not be convoyed. Churchill added that Britain was asking the Russians to help 'with increased measures of protection' for the convoys.[2]

Reading this message, Roosevelt telegraphed to Churchill on April 27 that he was 'greatly disturbed', not only by what he called 'the political repercussions in Russia, but even more the fact that our supplies will not reach them promptly'. To have these supplies blocked, 'except for the most compelling reasons', seemed to Roosevelt 'a serious mistake'. Were any word to reach Stalin that American

---

[1] War Cabinet No. 47 of 1942, 13 April 1942: Cabinet papers, 65/26.
[2] Prime Minister's Personal Telegram, T.634/2, 'Personal and Secret', 26 April 1942: Churchill papers, 20/74.

supplies were stopping 'for any reason', it would, Roosevelt warned, 'have a most unfortunate effect'.[1]

Replying by telegram on April 28, Churchill explained that, 'with the best will in the world', the cycle of convoys to Russia 'cannot be more than three in two months'. One convoy, limited to twenty-five merchant ships, had just sailed: this was PQ15. In view of Roosevelt's concern, Britain would consider increasing future convoys to 'as many as 35' ships. But Roosevelt had to realize that the voyage of each of these convoys 'entails major fleet operations'. The agreements with Russia called for 150,000 tons of supplies a month. Were each ship in the convoys to carry 6,000 tons of cargo, this quota could be fulfilled. Hitherto, however, Churchill explained to Roosevelt, the ships had been carrying 'about half this tonnage'. One solution would be to load 'priority goods' into a much smaller number of ships. 'We are at our utmost strain,' Churchill ended, 'for convoy escorts.'[2] But in reply, Roosevelt was emphatic that Britain should recognize 'the urgent necessity of getting off one more convoy in May in order to break the log-jam of ships already loaded or being loaded for Russia'. Any schemes involving further delays 'would leave impossible and very disquieting impression in Russia', Roosevelt warned.[3] But Churchill could make no drastic changes in an already dangerous policy. 'With very great respect,' he telegraphed to the President in reply, 'what you suggest is beyond our power to fulfil.' Churchill then set out for Roosevelt the scale of convoy problems. On the current convoy there had been an attack by hostile destroyers. The attack had been beaten off. But one British destroyer had been damaged. The cruiser *Edinburgh*, 'one of our best', had been badly damaged by U-boats, and was being towed into Murmansk where the *Trinidad*, damaged on the previous convoy, 'is still penned'. The *Tirpitz* was still undamaged in Trondheim harbour, despite several 'desperate attacks' on her by British aircraft. 'I beg you,' Churchill added, 'not to press us beyond our judgement in this operation, which we have studied most intently, and of which we have not yet been able to measure the full strain. I can assure you, Mr President, we are absolutely extended, and I could not press the Admiralty further.'[4]

Roosevelt agreed to submit the matter to discussion between Dudley Pound and Admiral King; having read their exchange of telegrams, he informed Churchill that he now felt that it was 'essential for us'—

---

[1] President to Prime Minister, No. 141, 'Priority', 27 April 1942: Churchill papers, 20/74.

[2] Prime Minister's Personal Telegram, T.645/2, Prime Minister to President, No. 80, 'Personal and Secret', 28 April 1942: Churchill papers, 20/74.

[3] President to Prime Minister, No. 143, 30 April 1942: Churchill papers, 20/74.

[4] Prime Minister's Personal Telegram, T.670/2, Prime Minister to President, No. 85, 'Personal and Secret', 2 May 1942: Churchill papers, 20/74.

the Americans—'to acquiesce in your views'. He also proposed pressing the Russians to reduce their munitions requirements 'to absolute essentials' on the grounds that 'preparations for "Bolero" will require all possible munitions and shipping'.[1] Bolero was the codename just given to the build-up of forces for the impending 'second front' operations in western Europe.

On April 27 Churchill was present when the War Cabinet heard for the first time of the problems confronting the manufacture of Tank Landing Craft. These LSTs, as they were known, Landing Ships, Tanks, to differentiate them from LSI, Landing Ships, Infantry, were to prove the decisive factor in each subsequent strategic plan involving amphibious landings. The War Cabinet were warned: 'The latest specifications for Tank-Landing Craft would mean that it would take materially longer to build the large numbers required.'[2]

After the disasters and worries of January, February and March, Churchill's spirits were picking up. 'Luncheon with Winston alone,' Anthony Eden noted in his diary on April 27. 'He was in better form than I have known him for ages. We spoke of painting and pictures, the light on the Horse Guards, the right tactics in politics and so forth.'[3]

At a time of stress in September 1941, Churchill had left London briefly to go down for a few hours to his beloved Chartwell. He did so again that week, during the long and difficult controversy with Roosevelt over the Russian convoys. 'I went to Chartwell last week,' Churchill told Randolph in a letter on May 2, 'and found Spring there in all its beauty. The goose I called the naval aide-de-camp and the male black swan have both fallen victims to the fox. The Yellow Cat however made me sensible of his continuing friendship, although I had not been there for eight months.'[4]

On April 22 the ships needed for the Madagascar landing were assembled at Durban, including the battleship *Ramillies* and the aircraft carrier *Illustrious*. Churchill followed the preparations from day to day, minuting to the Chiefs of Staff Committee on April 30:

Too much stress should not be laid on 'gaining control of the whole island'. It is 900 miles long, and all that really matters are the two or three principal

---

[1] President to Prime Minister, No. 145, 'Secret and Personal', 3 May 1942, Churchill papers, 20/74.
[2] War Cabinet No. 53 of 1942, 27 April 1942: Cabinet papers, 65/26.
[3] Eden diary, 27 April 1942: Eden memoirs, *The Reckoning*, *op. cit.*, page 326.
[4] 'Personal', 2 May 1942: Churchill papers, 1/369.

centres, and above all Diego Suarez. We are not setting out to subjugate Madagascar, but rather to establish ourselves in key positions to deny it to a far-flung Japanese attack. A principal object must be to get our best troops forward to India and Ceylon at the earliest moment, replacing them with garrison battalions from East or West Africa. Getting this place is meant to be a help and not a new burden.

The 'true defence' of Madagascar, Churchill added, was the Eastern Fleet, based upon Colombo.[1] After liberation, he telegraphed to Roosevelt, 'the territory will remain French', and Madagascar receive 'all the economic benefit' accorded to those French territories 'which have already joined the United Nations'.[2]

On Friday, May 1, Churchill went to Chequers for the weekend. Three Americans, the American Ambassador, Gilbert Winant, his wife, and Admiral Stark, were the only guests that night. On Saturday, May 2, Lord Cherwell, Sarah Churchill and Sir Edward Bridges came to dine and sleep. The duty Secretary was John Peck.[3] That Saturday Churchill dictated a letter to Robert Graves, saying how much he had enjoyed *Sergeant Lamb of the Ninth* and *Proceed Sergeant Lamb.* 'I have read very few books during this war,' Churchill wrote, 'in fact I think only six or seven altogether. I find sometimes a book dwells with me for several months, and I read a chapter or two at a time.' He had 'greatly enjoyed' these two books, 'as indeed I have all your pictures of the past which you have a wonderful gift of recalling'. Also, Churchill added, 'I am a great lover of narrative, in which art you excel.'[4]

While at Chequers on the evening of May 1, Churchill set out for the Chiefs of Staff Committee his thoughts on an alternative to a 'medium' cross-channel attack in 1942. The new concept was operation 'Jupiter', a British amphibious landing in northern Norway. 'High political and strategic importance must be attached thereto,' Churchill explained. 'It may be all that we have to offer the Russians.'

In the north of Norway, about seventy German bombers and a hundred fighters, based on two airports, and protected by about 10,000 or 12,000 'effective fighting men', were taking 'a heavy toll of our convoys'. If Britain could gain possession of these two airfields,

---

[1] Prime Minister's Personal Minute, D.90/2, 'Secret', 30 April 1942: Churchill papers, 20/67.
[2] Prime Minister's Personal Telegram, T.667/2, Prime Minister to President, No. 84, 'Personal and Most Secret', 1 May 1942: Churchill papers, 20/74.
[3] 'Chequers, List of Guests for Week-end, Friday 1.5.42': Chequers Visitors' Book.
[4] Letter of 2 May 1942: Churchill papers, 20/53.

Churchill wrote, and could establish its own military force there, on a similar scale, 'not only would the Northern sea route to Russia be kept open, but we should have set up a second front on a small scale from which it would be most difficult to eject us. If the going was good we could advance gradually southward, unrolling the Nazi map of Europe from the top.'[1]

As always, Clementine Churchill was the hostess at the Chequers weekend, ensuring, amid the pressures and disruptions of war, an atmosphere of calm and comfort, giving the pleasant illusion of normal times. Since October 1941 she herself had been working to the limits of her strength in raising funds for the Russian Red Cross, through her Red Cross Aid to Russia Fund. In all, as a result of her organizing work, meetings and speeches, she was to raise medical supplies and clothing valued at four million pounds: the first million by January 1942. In February 1942, the England-Wales football match had raised £12,500 for the fund, at that time the largest sum ever raised for charity by a single sporting event.[2]

On May 2, during the Chequers weekend, Churchill sent his son Randolph a letter of political and private news. 'The depression following Singapore,' he confided, 'has been replaced by an undue optimism, which I am of course keeping in proper bounds.' Churchill also sent Randolph some news of his three sisters, of his mother, of his wife Pamela, and of his eighteen-month-old son Winston:

Mary has become a Sergeant, and is much counted on in her Battery. She tells me that she has written to you. Your Mother has been suffering from tiredness as a result of her Russian Fund and other activities. She has had a sore throat, which is now better.

Pamela seems very well, and is a great treasure and blessing to us all. Winston was in the pink when I saw him last. He has not so far grown old enough to commit the various forms of indiscretion which he would be expected to inherit from his forebears. Sarah and Diana are both well and lively, and send their love.[3]

That weekend at Chequers, Churchill learned of the Japanese capture of Mandalay. He at once gave orders for Reginald Dorman Smith, the Governor of Burma, to return by air to India.[4] That same

---

[1] Prime Minister's Personal Minute, D.91/2, 1 May 1942: Churchill papers, 20/67.
[2] Mary Soames, *Clementine Churchill*, op. cit., page 324.
[3] Letter of 2 May 1942: Churchill papers, 20/53.
[4] Prime Minister's Personal Telegram, T.675/2, 3 May 1942: Churchill papers, 20/88.

day, he informed Wavell that there was now 'no sense' in Alexander remaining in command of a force reduced to little more than a brigade. 'He is needed for very important business,' Churchill explained. 'Whenever you consider that his command has fallen to the level of a division or less, and that no important military advantage can be gained by his retention of it, you should order him to return to India by air, leaving him no options.' This is what had been done to General Gort before Dunkirk.[1]

Gort was not only on Churchill's mind in regard to a British withdrawal. On May 4, as the German and Italian air bombardment of Malta continued to gain in intensity, he telegraphed to Gort, who was then Governor of Gibraltar: 'You should proceed forthwith to Malta and assume command as Governor, Commander-in-Chief and Supreme Commander in the island.' Churchill added: 'Every effort must be made to prolong the resistance of the fortress to the utmost limit. We recognize you are taking over a most anxious and dangerous situation at a late stage. We are sure that you are the man to save the fortress and we shall strive hard to sustain you.'[2]

By the time Gort arrived in Malta, its fighter strength had been reduced to six serviceable aircraft.[3] Two days later, sixty Spitfires reached the island under escort of Roosevelt's *Wasp*. 'Many thanks to you all for timely help. Who said a wasp couldn't sting twice?' Churchill telegraphed to the ship's company.[4] That night, Rome Radio broadcast that thirty-seven German and Italian aircraft had failed to return. Only three Spitfires had been shot down, and only one pilot lost.[5]

'For the moment the strain on Malta seems to have lessened,' Churchill telegraphed to Wavell on May 5, 'and Hitler has had to shift both a fighter and a bomber group eastward for his offensive against Russia. He is even more strained in the air than we are at sea. . . .'[6]

The danger to Malta remained, however. There was a 'grave peril' to the island owing to shortages of supplies, Churchill telegraphed to

[1] Prime Minister's Personal Telegram, T.671/2, 3 May 1942: Churchill papers, 20/88.
[2] Prime Minister's Personal Telegram, T.683/2, 4 May 1942: Churchill papers, 20/74.
[3] J. R. Colville, *Man of Valour, The Life of Field-Marshal the Viscount Gort*, London 1972, page 247.
[4] Prime Minister's Personal Telegram, T.710/2, 10 May 1942: Churchill papers, 20/75. The *Wasp*, transferred to the Pacific, was sunk by Japanese torpedoes on 15 September 1942. 'Happily,' Churchill noted in his war memoirs, 'her gallant crew were saved. They had been a link in our chain of causation.'
[5] Lord James Douglas-Hamilton, *The Air Battle for Malta: The Diaries of a Fighter Pilot*, Edinburgh 1981, page 95.
[6] Prime Minister's Personal Telegram, T.687/2 'most Secret', 5 May 1942: Churchill papers, 20/74.

Auchinleck that same day, 'and it is essential to make sure that food and ammunition reach them during the June dark period at latest'. A 'successful offensive in Libya', Churchill added, 'would be the most certain method of securing this'.[1]

The date of Auchinleck's new offensive was discussed by the War Cabinet on May 8. Auchinleck had given June 15 as the date before which an offensive 'would not be justified'.

Churchill had already pointed out to Auchinleck, on April 26, that the General's assessment, made on April 25, of the number of German tanks in eastern Cyrenaica, '265 runners plus 45 in workshops', was at variance with the 'special information' which had been sent to him on April 21, that there were 'only 161 German tanks serviceable in the forward areas'.[2] Later 'most secret' information, however, as Churchill telegraphed to Auchinleck on April 30, 'confirms your estimate', while another telegram told of reinforcements, completing 12,000 men, which would reach Rommel by the end of May.[3]

Not only the growing strength of Rommel's army, but also his intention to attack the British Forces before they attacked him, were becoming clear through a series of decrypts. One such decrypt, on May 2, was decisive, revealing as it did that the basic measurement used by the Panzer Army's Quartermaster General in his fuel calculations, would be raised substantially by June 1, and that Rommel would then have enough fuel for thirty-eight days' operations.[4] On May 4, Military Intelligence concluded, from this and other pointers, that Rommel would launch an offensive early in June.[5] Brooke presented this information to the War Cabinet on May 8.

During this War Cabinet of May 8, Brooke expressed his surprise that Auchinleck had not taken into account in fixing the day 'the possibility of upsetting the Axis plans by timing his offensive so as to take advantage of the offensive contemplated by General Rommel'.

Churchill asked each Minister his view 'individually'. There was a 'general consensus of opinion', the minutes recorded, that the advantage to be gained by postponing the offensive until June 15 'were

[1] Prime Minister's Personal Telegram, T.691/2, 'Personal and Secret', 5 May 1942: Churchill papers, 20/74.

[2] Prime Minister's Personal Telegram, T.632/2, 26 April 1942: Churchill papers, 20/88. On 30 July 1963, when the Enigma was still secret, this telegram was removed from the Churchill papers and deposited in the Cabinet Office.

[3] Prime Minister's Personal Telegram, T.656/2, 30 April 1942: Churchill papers, 20/88. This telegram was likewise removed from the Churchill papers on 30 July 1963, and deposited in the Cabinet Office, in order to protect the Enigma secret.

[4] CX/MSS/945/T12, of 2 May 1942: Hinsley and others, op. cit., volume 2, London 1981, page 361.

[5] Military Intelligence Summary of 4 May 1942: Hinsley and others, op. cit., volume 2, London 1981, page 362.

more than offset by the disadvantages of delay until that date'; and the needs of Malta were again given 'great importance'. Churchill, in summing up the discussion, commented 'that battles were not won by arithmetical calculations of the strength of the opposing forces'. At the same time, he said, it should be made clear to Auchinleck 'that the War Cabinet were prepared to assume full responsibility for the consequences if an attack took place and were not successful'.[1]

A few hours after this meeting Churchill reported to Auchinleck the view of the Chiefs of Staff, the War Cabinet and the Defence Committee that the loss of Malta would be 'a disaster of the first magnitude' to the British Empire, 'and probably fatal in the long run to the defence of the Nile Valley'. For this reason, and 'in spite of the risks', Auchinleck should attack the enemy 'and fight a major battle', if possible during May, 'and the sooner the better'. In this, Churchill added, 'you will no doubt have regard to the fact that the enemy himself may be planning to attack you early in June, and is trying to be ready by then'.[2]

On May 4, in the Coral Sea, a Japanese invasion fleet on its way to the Solomon Islands had been intercepted, and in a three-day battle was savagely mauled, less than five hundred miles from Australia.[3] The same day, Japanese forces landed on Corregidor, forcing the garrison to surrender. On May 5 a combined military and naval force landed on Madagascar: Operation 'Ironclad' had begun. 'Powerful British forces,' Churchill told the Pacific War Council that evening, 'had attacked Madagascar that morning. First reports received were satisfactory and stated that the opposition was slight.' It would be difficult for the Japanese to establish air bases on Madagascar now, 'as they would be unaware of our strength, and the Island was a great distance from Singapore'.[4]

Two days later, the French naval and military commanders surrendered, and a British Admiral entered Diego Suarez harbour.[5]

---

[1] War Cabinet No. 59 of 1942, 8 May 1942: Cabinet papers, 65/30.

[2] Prime Minister's Personal Telegram, T.702/2, 'Personal and Secret', 8 May 1942: Churchill papers, 20/75. To hide all references, however oblique, to the Enigma intercepts of German messages, the last eight words of this telegram were omitted in the version published in Churchill's war memoirs (volume 4, London 1951, page 275).

[3] The Japanese lost seven major warships, the Americans lost 1 aircraft carrier, 1 destroyer and 1 tanker.

[4] Pacific War Council, 11th Meeting, 6 p.m., 5 May 1942: Cabinet papers, 99/26.

[5] The Admiral was Rear-Admiral Syfret. The British military force was commanded by Major-General Sturges. On 9 May 1942 Churchill sent them and their troops a telegram of congratulations 'upon the swift and resolute way in which your difficult and hazardous operation was carried through' (Prime Minister's Personal Minute, T.706/2, 9 May 1942: Churchill papers, 20/75).

These operations, Churchill told the House of Commons on May 7, 'which were not without risks of various kinds, have been carried out with great dash and vigour'. The French had also fought 'with great gallantry and discipline'. Churchill added: 'We grieve that bloodshed has occurred between the troops of our two countries whose peoples at heart are united against the common foe.'[1]

Admiral Syfret, who had been Churchill's Naval Secretary at the Admiralty, and was a personal friend, wanted to move south from Diego Suarez, to capture the rest of Madagascar. His request was put to Churchill by the First Lord of the Admiralty and the First Sea Lord. But Churchill wanted the troops used in 'Ironclad' to proceed 'almost immediately' to India.[2] 'I cannot see,' Churchill minuted to A. V. Alexander and Pound on May 15, 'why the fact we have a garrison and an Air Force in Diego Suarez makes Madagascar "an additional commitment". Most people would think it would be a deterrent requiring a considerable Japanese expedition. Nothing could be more foolish than to squander our resources. . . .'[3] It was also essential, in Churchill's view, to put at Wavell's disposal in India sufficient forces to enable Wavell to contemplate as soon as possible, 'offensive schemes' against the Japanese, 'particularly', as he explained to Wavell, 'by attacking Rangoon by an amphibious operation'. Such an operation would give Chiang-Kai-shek some encouragement 'to hold out' against the Japanese in China, especially if it were also to disrupt Japanese communications through Burma.[4]

Three days later, in a minute for the Chiefs of Staff, Churchill elaborated his ideas of a 'general amphibious British air and land offensive' against Burma as 'the aim we set before ourselves for the autumn and winter of 1942'. For this, landing-craft must be 'prepared locally and a proportion sent from home', and British and American air reinforcements 'gathered to the utmost limit permissible by other needs'. All such offensive plans were dependent, however, 'upon the fortunes of war in Libya, in the Caucasus, and in Australia', but in each sphere it must be assumed 'that the course of events is not unfavourable to us'.[5]

*   *   *

[1] *Hansard*, 7 May 1942, column 1433.

[2] Prime Minister's Personal Telegram (to Admiral Syfret), T.728/2, 'Most Immediate', 15 May 1942: Churchill papers, 20/75.

[3] Prime Minister's Personal Minute, N.186/2, 'Secret', 15 May 1942: Churchill papers, 20/67.

[4] Prime Minister's Personal Telegram (to General Wavell), T.729/2, 'Most secret', 15 May 1942: Churchill papers, 20/75.

[5] Prime Minister's Personal Minute, D.102/2, 'Most Secret', 18 May 1942: Churchill papers, 20/67.

Molotov's imminent arrival in Britain, and the Anglo-Soviet Treaty which he wished to sign, was discussed by the War Cabinet on May 7. Sir Alexander Cadogan, who was present, noted in his diary that Churchill 'evidently hopes the Treaty is off the map', telling his colleagues: 'We must remember that this is a *bad* thing. We oughtn't to do it, and I shan't be sorry if we don't.'[1] Meanwhile, Stalin had appealed to Churchill to take 'all possible measures' to ensure the arrival of war materials on some ninety ships 'bottled up at present in Iceland or in the approaches from America to Iceland'. This material was needed in May, being 'extremely important for our front'.[2] On May 8 the Germans launched a brief prelude to their impending new offensive, attacking the Kerch peninsula. On the following day Churchill replied to Stalin: 'We are resolved to fight our way through to you with the maximum amount of war materials.' The pressure of the *Tirpitz* at Trondheim made the passage of every convoy 'a serious fleet operation'. Nevertheless, 'we shall continue to do our utmost'.

'I am sure you will not mind my being quite frank,' Churchill added, and went on to list some of the help which the Soviet's own naval and air forces could give to the convoys, including provision of long range fighters to cover the convoys 'for that part of the voyage when they are approaching your coasts', and anti-submarine patrols by Soviet aircraft and surface vessels.[3]

May 10 marked the completion of the second year of Churchill's premiership. That night he broadcast to the British people, live, from the Cabinet War Room. He recalled, first, the time when France had fallen and Britain was alone. 'It fell to me in those days,' he said, 'to express the sentiments and resolves of the British nation in that supreme crisis of its life. That was to me an honour far beyond any dreams and ambitions I had ever nursed, and it is one that cannot be taken away.'

In his broadcast, Churchill spoke of the war in Russia, and of how the Russians 'like us, resolved never to give in'. Under 'their warrior chief, Stalin', they fought from the first day 'till tonight' with 'unflinching vigour'. As for Hitler, he forgot the Russian winter: 'We all

[1] Cadogan diary, 7 May 1942: David Dilks (editor), *op. cit.*, pages 450–1.
[2] 'Personal and Secret', Kremlin, 6 May 1942: Premier papers, 3/403.
[3] Prime Minister's Personal Telegram, T.707/2, 'Personal and Most Secret', 9 May 1942: Churchill papers, 20/75.

heard about it at school, but he forgot it.' Churchill paused, then added: 'I have never made such a bad mistake as that.'

Churchill then told his listeners of the British pledge to treat any 'unprovoked' German use of poison gas against Russia 'exactly as if it were used against ourselves', and to use Britain's 'great and growing' air superiority 'to carry gas warfare on the largest possible scale far and wide against military objectives in Germany'. It was therefore for Hitler to choose 'whether he wishes to add this additional horror to aerial warfare'.[1]

Churchill then spoke of Madagascar and Malta, the one now held in trust 'for that gallant France which we have known and marched with', the other being defended against unknown perils. He also spoke of Japan, confronted by the far greater power, 'actual and potential' of the United States. 'I am not prone to make predictions,' he said, 'but I have no doubt tonight that the British and American sea power will grip and hold the Japanese; and that overwhelming air power, covering vigorous military operations, will lay them low.' Churchill's broadcast ended:

Therefore tonight I give you a message of good cheer. You deserve it, and the facts endorse it. But be it good cheer or be it bad cheer will make no difference to us; we shall drive on to the end, and do our duty, win or die. God helping us, we can do no other.[2]

Churchill had intended to say something in his broadcast about the criticisms of his war leadership which had grown since the fall of Singapore. At the last moment he deleted the passage which he had prepared. It read:

Everyone feels safer now, and in consequence the weaker brethren become more vocal. Our critics are not slow to dwell upon the misfortunes and reverses which we have sustained, and I am certainly not going to pretend that there have not been many mistakes and shortcomings. In particular I am much blamed by a group of ex-ministers for my general conduct of the war. They would like very much to reduce my power of direction and initiative.

Though I have to strive with dictators, I am not, I am glad to say, a dictator myself. I am only your servant. I have tried to be your faithful servant but at any moment, acting through the House of Commons, you can dismiss

---

[1] He did not. When a Member of Parliament, J. J. Tinker, wrote to Churchill about the possibility that Hitler might prefer gas bombs to high explosive bombs over German cities, because of the lesser damage done by gas, Churchill noted in the margin of Tinker's letter: 'You may be sure we shall give them what they like least—but we cannot fail in our comradeship to Russia' (Letter of 12 May 1942: Churchill papers, 20/61).

[2] Broadcast of 10 May 1942: BBC Written Archive Centre. On May 15 Harry Hopkins telegraphed to Churchill: 'I thought your last Sunday's speech was one of the best you have yet delivered' (Telegram of 15 May 1942: Churchill papers, 20/75).

me to private life. There is one thing, however, which I hope you will not do; I hope you will never ask me or any successor you may choose to bear the burden of responsibility in times like these without reasonable authority and the means of taking decisions.[1]

On May 14 Churchill left London by night train for Yorkshire, where he spent two days visiting bomber stations, army units and armaments factories.[2] On May 15 he spoke from the steps of Leeds Town Hall, telling the crowd: 'We have reached a period in the war when it would be premature to say that we have topped the ridge, but now we see the ridge ahead.'[3] Elizabeth Layton, who was among those accompanying Churchill on this journey, wrote to her mother in Canada: 'He was given a staggering welcome, and was *so* touched and pleased with it all.' Miss Layton added: 'There is no doubt about it at all; people regard him, one and all, as *their* PM, and I don't believe there will ever be anyone quite like him. He appeals to the masses as well as to the brains and "élite". And he sure deserves it; he is just as warm-hearted and one might even say lovable as he could possibly be.'[4]

[1] 'Broadcast Speech, 10.5.42, (*Not Used*)': Churchill papers, 9/157.
[2] 'Programme 14–16 May 1942', 'Secret': Nel papers.
[3] Speech of 16 May 1942, Leeds: Churchill papers, 9/158.
[4] Letter of 16 May 1942: Nel papers.

7

War on Many Fronts

ON 12 May 1942 the Red Army launched an offensive against
the Germans south of Kharkov, seeking to upset the timetable
of Germany's own impending attack. The attack itself did not achieve
any permanent recovery of Soviet territory, but it did force the Germans to delay their own planned onslaught. On May 13, in explaining
to Churchill why Soviet air cover could not be provided for the Arctic
convoys, Stalin noted that 'our air forces in their vast majority are
engaged at the battle-front'.[1]

On May 15, at a meeting of the Chiefs of Staff Committee, Dudley
Pound urged that Stalin 'be asked to forgo the supplies temporarily
until the melting of the ice gave a more reasonable chance of transporting them safely to Northern Russia', and spoke of a six weeks'
delay.[2] This was also the advice of all three Chiefs of Staff, in a minute
to Churchill on the following day.[3] Churchill, who had not been present at the meeting of May 15, replied to the Chiefs of Staff on May
17:

Not only Premier Stalin but President Roosevelt will object very much to
our desisting from running the convoys now. The Russians are in heavy
action, and will expect us to run the risk and pay the price entailed by our
contribution. The United States ships are queueing up. My own feeling,
mingled with much anxiety, is that the convoy ought to sail on the 18th. The
operation is justified, if a half gets through. Failure on our part to make the
attempt would weaken our influence with both our major Allies. There are
always the uncertainties of weather and luck, which may aid us. I share your
misgivings, but I feel it is a matter of duty.[4]

[1] 'Message from M. Stalin to Mr Churchill', 13 May 1942: Premier papers, 3/403.
[2] Chiefs of Staff Committee No. 151 of 1942, 15 May 1942: Cabinet papers, 79/21.
[3] Minute of 15 May 1942 (signed by Brooke, Pound and Portal), 'Annex', Chiefs of Staff
Committee No. 152 of 1942, 16 May 1942: Cabinet papers, 79/21.
[4] Prime Minister's Personal Minute, D.100/2, 'Most Secret', 17 May 1942: Churchill papers,
20/67.

At a meeting of the War Cabinet on May 18 Churchill noted that the May and June convoys would sail for six to seven days within range of German bombers based in Norway. Of the hundred bombers available to the Germans, sixty were long range. Only in July would it be possible for the convoys to take a more northerly route, outside the bomber range. Lives and cargoes would be saved if the May and June convoys were cancelled. Nevertheless, Churchill told the War Cabinet, it was 'our duty to fight these convoys through whatever the cost. The Russians were engaged in a life and death struggle against our common enemy. There was little we could do to help them, except by maintaining the flow of supplies by this northern route.' Churchill added that in the April convoy, 22 out of 25 ships had got through, 'in spite of our apprehensions; and this time we might again do better than we feared'.

The War Cabinet reached the following decisions: the May convoy, 'due to leave that night', should sail as arranged; Stalin should be informed that orders had been given for it to sail 'notwithstanding the additional risk to which it would be subject'; Stalin should be 'strongly urged' to send heavy bombers to attack the aerodromes in Norway from which the German aircraft were operating; and the sailing of the June convoy should be decided by the War Cabinet 'in the light of the losses sustained by the May convoy'.[1]

In a telegram to Stalin on May 19, Churchill warned of the dangers to the May convoy, and urged a Soviet bomber attack on the German aerodromes in Norway. 'If luck is not with us,' he warned, 'and the convoy suffers very severe losses, the only course left to us may be to hold up further convoys until we get more sea room when the ice recedes to the northward in July.'[2]

On May 20 Vyacheslav Molotov reached London. Discussions on the Anglo-Soviet Treaty began on the following morning, when he told Churchill 'that he must have as a minimum the Russian frontiers as at the time of Hitler's aggression on Russia in June 1941'. This would mean British recognition of the post-war incorporation in the Soviet Union of eastern Poland, which Russia had annexed under the Nazi-Soviet Pact of August 1939. The demand was rejected, as was Russia's claim for the eastern regions of Roumania. Molotov had made it clear, Churchill told the War Cabinet that afternoon, that the Soviet Union 'would not be able to make any concession' between the Soviet and British view.[3]

On the morning of May 22, Molotov pressed Churchill for a 'second

[1] War Cabinet No. 64 of 1942, 18 May 1942, Confidential Annex: Cabinet papers, 65/30.
[2] Prime Minister's Personal Telegram, T.743/2, 'Personal and Most Secret', 19 May 1942: Churchill papers, 20/75.
[3] War Cabinet No. 65 of 1942, 21 May 1942, 5.30 p.m.: Cabinet papers, 65/26.

front' in Europe capable of drawing off at least forty German divisions from the eastern front, and of doing so during the forthcoming German offensive. In reply, Churchill explained that the 'inescapable consequence' of German air mastery of western Europe was 'that large portions of the Continental coastline were denied to us as places for disembarkation'. But plans were being studied, Churchill said, and preparations made, for possible landings in the Pas de Calais, the Cherbourg 'tip', and part of the Brest area.

During the course of their discussion on May 22, Molotov asked Churchill what Britain's 'position and attitude' would be if the Soviet Army failed to hold out during 1942. Churchill replied that if 'contrary to expectation' the Soviet armies were defeated, and 'the worst came to the worst', then:

... we should fight on, and, with the help of the United States, hope to build up overwhelming air superiority, which in the course of the next eighteen months or two years would enable us to put down a devastating weight of air attack on the German cities and industries. We should moreover maintain the blockade and make landings on the Continent against an increasingly enfeebled opposition. Ultimately the power of Great Britain and the United States would prevail.

Churchill went on to tell Molotov that it 'should not be overlooked' that after the fall of France 'Great Britain had stood alone for a whole year with but a handful of ill-equipped troops between her and Hitler's victorious and numerous divisions. But what a tragedy for mankind would be this prolongation of the war, and how earnest was the hope for Russian victory, and how ardent the desire that we should take our share in conquering the evil foe.' It was the 'dearest wish' of the British nation and Army, Churchill added, 'to come to grips with the enemy at the earliest possible moment and so to aid the gallant fight of the Russian Army and people'.[1]

On May 23 Churchill informed Stalin of Molotov's reception: 'We have given him a full and true account of our plans and resources.' As regards the proposed Anglo-Soviet Treaty, Churchill added, 'he will explain to you the difficulties, which are mainly that we cannot go back on our previous undertakings to Poland, and have to take account of our own and American opinion'.[2]

[1] '22 May 1942, 11 a.m., Operations on the Continent, 1942–43': transcript enclosed in Prime Minister's Personal Telegram, T.776/2, 28 May 1942: Churchill papers, 20/88.

[2] Prime Minister's Personal Telegram, T.754/2, 23 May 1942: Premier papers, 3/399/6, folio 89. A week later, Churchill telegraphed to Roosevelt: 'I must tell you that we received invaluable help from Winant during our Russian negotiations. He made the Russians understand, as no one else could do, how injurious to good relations between us three, must have been the American reaction to the old treaty.' (Prime Minister's Personal Telegram, T.821/2, Prime Minister to President No. 99, 4 June 1942: Premier papers, 3/399/6, folio 91.)

The negotiations for an Anglo-Soviet Treaty were concluded on May 26. To Churchill's relief, they contained no territorial provisions on Poland or the Baltic States.[1] Much of the credit for this belonged to Eden. The War Cabinet, Churchill said, were 'greatly indebted to the Foreign Secretary for his skilful handling of the negotiations and for the very satisfactory result which had been achieved'.[2] 'Now that we have bound ourselves to be Allies and friends for twenty years,' Churchill telegraphed to Stalin on May 27, 'I take occasion to send you my sincere good wishes and to assure you of the confidence that I feel that victory will be ours.'[3]

On the day of the signature of the Anglo-Soviet Treaty, Churchill had studied a note prepared by Combined Operations on the design of piers for use on the beaches of northern France. Two types of piers were possible: rigid 'scaffolding' piers and floating 'pontoon' piers. Each would have to be about a mile in length, and forty foot high at the seaward end, to link the beach with ships of twenty foot draught. All floating piers, the Combined Operations memorandum warned, 'suffer from the disadvantage of having to be securely moored with heavy anchors'.[4]

Churchill was no stranger to this problem: in 1917, as Minister of Munitions in Lloyd George's Government, he had put forward a plan to establish an artificial harbour in the Heligoland Bight.[5] He now minuted to Mountbatten, about the piers: 'They *must* float up and down on the tide. The anchor problem must be mastered. The ships must have a side flap cut in them and a drawbridge long enough to overreach the moorings of the piers. Let me have the solution worked out. Don't argue the matter. The difficulties will argue for themselves.'[6]

On May 27, at Churchill's request, the Chiefs of Staff Committee discussed yet again the possibility of a landing on the Continent in August or September 1942. The training of the assault forces, reported Vice Admiral Ramsay, 'was being seriously interfered with by the shortage of landing craft'. This shortage was created, he explained, 'by present raiding policy'. But Brooke, replying, pointed out that these raids, under Mountbatten's command, were 'part of our

[1] Text of Political and Military Treaties: Cabinet papers, 66/24. Churchill had been faced both by Roosevelt's rejection of any territorial pledges to Stalin and by strong Conservative and Catholic opposition in Britain. Instead of an agreement on post-war frontiers, Stalin accepted the idea, proposed by Sir Alexander Cadogan, of a pledge of post-war cooperation under a Treaty lasting twenty years.
[2] War Cabinet No. 67 of 1942, 26 May 1942, Confidential Annex: Cabinet papers, 65/30.
[3] Prime Minister's Personal Telegram, T.762/2, 27 May 1942: Premier papers, 3/399/6, folio 90.
[4] 'Piers for Use on Beaches', undated: Churchill Archives Trust.
[5] Letter from A. K. Cocks, a member of the planning staff for the cross-Channel landing.
[6] Manuscript note dated 26 May 1942: Churchill Archives Trust.

"Second Front" campaign'.[1] The 1942 landings were only intended to take place, General Paget added, 'if there was a distinct crack in German morale', but Portal pointed out, as he had done on a number of previous occasions, that a 'deterioration of the situation on the eastern front might make it essential to undertake an operation in the west, even at heavy cost to ourselves, and it would be prudent to prepare for such an eventuality'.[2]

The Chiefs of Staff Committee met that same evening, May 27, with Churchill in the Chair, to answer his question: 'what operations could we launch in western Europe on the assumption that heavy fighting continued throughout the summer on the Russian front but that no decision was in sight'. With the landing craft at present available, replied General Paget, 'we could not put ashore more than 4,300 men, together with 160 tanks, in the first flight'. This small assaulting force, he added, 'would have the greatest difficulty in establishing a bridgehead wide enough to permit the disembarkation of supporting forces without serious interference from the coast defence guns'. It would probably require a further three weeks, added Lord Mountbatten, to put ashore 'a force equivalent to six divisions (132,000 men)'. In ten months' time, however, by March 1943, the landing-craft situation 'would have improved to such an extent as to enable 100,000 men and 18,000 vehicles to be landed on the initial assault', which could be made 'on a very wide front, thereby increasing the prospects of tactical surprise'.

Churchill said he was 'not prepared to accept the view' that it would take as long as three weeks to put six divisions ashore, and wanted Mountbatten to consider improving on this timetable by examining 'the use of floating piers and other forms of landing devices'. But he agreed that it would be 'looking for trouble' to try to force a bridgehead on the narrow frontage 'which was imposed upon us by our limited number of armoured assault craft'. Churchill added:

The fact that we had made a gallant but fruitless attempt to open a second front in this area would be no consolation to the Russians. An assault in this area would probably cause a patriot uprising in the north of France and failure on our part would result in terrible consequences to our French

[1] Five simultaneous raids were being planned against the Cap Griz Nez to Le Touquet area of the Channel coast: operation 'Turnscrew' to capture or kill German military personnel at Ambleteuse; 'Roughshod' to destroy the German military headquarters at Wimereux; 'Earthquake' to immobilize German gun batteries at Equihen; 'Busybody' to capture or kill German military personnel at Hardelot; and 'Dearborn' to capture and bring back to Britain the new German radar equipment installed at St Cecily, together with its personnel. (Defence Ministry papers, 2/346.)

[2] Chiefs of Staff Committee No. 162 of 1942, 10.30 a.m., 27 May 1942: Cabinet papers, 79/56. General Sir Bernard Paget was Commander-in-Chief, Home Forces.

supporters. In view of the military arguments which had been put forward, he was not prepared to give way to popular clamour for the opening of a second front in Europe in these circumstances.

Churchill did not intend, however, to leave the matter there. The time had come, he believed, to examine the possibility of an operation in Northern Norway, 'with the object of securing the airfields from which the enemy air forces were harassing our Russian convoys'. He suggested a force of one or two divisions should be embarked as if it were a convoy, and then turn south from the convoy course to land in the vicinity of the German airfields. A second convoy could bring a supporting force. 'This operation,' Churchill suggested, 'might well be the prelude to the rolling-up of the German forces in Norway.'

This project, said Pound, was already being examined.[1] 'All we could do,' Brooke told the Chiefs of Staff Committee on June 1, 'if things went badly for the Russians', was some 'desperate venture' such as an operation designed to capture and hold Boulogne 'for a week or two', with the intention of 'bringing on a large air battle'.[2] This was operation 'Imperator', for which Mountbatten and the Ministry of War Transport were now asked to work out the shipping needs.[3] The War Cabinet's Joint Intelligence Sub-Committee warned that same day, June 1, that between August and October it might be 'touch and go' on the eastern front 'which adversary collapses first'.[3]

Aware through the Enigma decrypts of German messages of Rommel's imminent attack in the Western Desert, Churchill had hoped to encourage Auchinleck to strike first. But Auchinleck had felt unable to do so. 'Of course, we realize that success cannot be guaranteed,' Churchill had telegraphed to Auchinleck on May 21. 'There are no safe battles. But whether this one arises from an enemy attack and your forestalling or manoeuvring counter-stroke, or whether it has to be undertaken by you on its own, we have full confidence in you and your glorious army, and whatever happens, we will sustain you by every means in our power.'[4]

On the night of May 26, Rommel struck. 'This may be the biggest

---

[1] Chiefs of Staff Committee No. 46 (Operations) of 1942, 5.30 p.m., 27 May 1942: Cabinet papers, 79/56.

[2] Chiefs of Staff Committee No. 166 of 1942, 1 June 1942: Cabinet papers, 79/56. Also considered as possible objectives for 'Imperator' were Abbeville and Amiens.

[3] 'The possible Course of the Russian Campaign and its Implications', Joint Intelligence Sub-Committee Paper No. 200 (Final) of 1942, 'Secret', 1 June 1942: Cabinet papers, 79/21.

[4] Prime Minister's Personal Telegram, T.747/2, 21 May 1942: Churchill papers, 20/88.

encounter we have ever fought,' Churchill telegraphed to Roosevelt after the first details of the battle had reached him. At the same time, he reported on the progress of the May convoy to Russia. Of the thirty-five ships, five had already been sunk or forced to turn back. For this reason, Churchill explained, he had asked the Chiefs of Staff to study a possible landing in northern Norway, 'the occupation of which seems necessary to ensure the flow of our supplies next year to Russia'.[1] Four days later, the War Cabinet decided to postpone the June convoy by ten days to a fortnight. The Admiralty, Churchill told his colleagues, 'should have the necessary latitude in this matter'.[2]

That same day, Churchill asked the Chiefs of Staff to give detailed consideration to the northern Norway operation, 'Jupiter', as an alternative to an invasion of western Europe that autumn, pointing out that it would not only keep open the northern sea route to Russia, but would constitute 'a second front on a small scale from which it would be most difficult to eject us'. If the 'going was good', he added, 'we could advance gradually southward, unrolling the Nazi map of Europe from the top'. All that had to be done was 'to oust the enemy from the airfields and destroy their garrisons'.[3]

On the night of May 30 more than a thousand British bombers raided Cologne, the first '1,000 bomber' raid of the war. Thirty-nine aircraft were lost, and 1,455 tons of bombs were dropped. 'I hope you were pleased with our mass air attack on Cologne,' Churchill telegraphed to Roosevelt. 'There is plenty more to come. . . .'[4] Of the dangers to Russia, as well as those to China with which Roosevelt was also much concerned, Churchill commented: 'It is often easier to see dangers gathering than to have the power to ward them off, and very often they don't happen.' As to the 'Sledgehammer' operation against the coast of France, Lord Louis Mountbatten was on his way to Washington and would explain 'some of the practical difficulties as we see them here'. Churchill added: 'We are still working at it and trying to make plans to overcome them. All preparations should go forward with the utmost speed. . . .'[5]

Roosevelt himself was becoming aware of the perilous Russian

---

[1] Prime Minister's Personal Telegram, T.772, Prime Minister to President No. 91, 27 May 1942: Churchill papers, 20/75.

[2] War Cabinet No. 70 of 1942, 1 June 1942: Cabinet papers, 65/30.

[3] Prime Minister's Personal Minute, D.106/2, 'Most Secret', 1 June 1942: Churchill papers, 20/67.

[4] That same night, June 1, 1,036 British bombers raided Essen and the Ruhr. Thirty-five were lost.

[5] Prime Minister's Personal Telegram, T.800/2, Prime Minister to President, No. 96, 'Personal and Secret', 1 June 1942: Churchill papers, 20/75,

situation. On June 1, after talks with Molotov in Washington, he reported to Churchill: 'I have a very strong feeling that the Russian position is precarious and may grow steadily worse during the coming weeks.' He was therefore anxious that 'Bolero'—the codename for the build-up of American troops and supplies in the United Kingdom in preparation for a cross-Channel landing, 'proceed to definite action beginning in 1942'. Nor, because of weather conditions, could such action be delayed until the end of 1942. This would give Molotov's mission 'some real results'.[1] But, Churchill confided to the Chiefs of Staff four days later, 'I do not think there is much doing on the French coast this year.'[2]

Churchill's hopes for a Norwegian attack were also dampened, after operation 'Jupiter' had been examined by the Joint Planning Staff. On June 5 the Joint Planners concluded that Britain 'could not capture and hold the Northern Norway air bases', because of the inability to provide adequate defence for the shipping that would have to be left in the fiords, and because, having captured the aerodromes, itself 'a hazardous operation', the chances of being able to hold them throughout the winter were 'so slight as to be unacceptable'.[3]

Three days later, at a meeting of the Chiefs of Staff Committee, Churchill stressed that, as it was 'extremely improbable' that the 'Sledge-hammer' landings across the Channel would 'come off', the Northern Norway plan 'should be very carefully studied'. But the Chiefs of Staff were again 'doubtful' as the minutes of the meeting recorded, that 'Jupiter' was practicable, 'as at present conceived'. It was however being 'carefully studied'.[4]

As part of the strategy to help Russia, Churchill had approved operation 'Jackpot', the seizure of the island of Spitzbergen. Were the Germans to occupy Spitzbergen, Churchill minuted to the Chiefs of Staff on June 6, an 'additional impediment' might then be placed on convoys to Russia. 'Surely,' he added, 'it at least doubles the range of the German aircraft, which can be refuelled at their base at Spitzbergen and sally out with good radius against us the further our route lies to the north.'[5]

---

[1] President to Prime Minister, 'Secret', 1 June 1942: Churchill papers, 20/75.
[2] Prime Minister's Personal Minute, D.110/2, 'Secret', 5 June 1942: Churchill papers, 20/67. The Normandy landings took place two years and one day after Churchill wrote this minute.
[3] 'Operation Jupiter', 'Report by the Joint Planning Staff', War Cabinet Paper No. 574 of 1942, 'Most Secret', 5 June 1942: Cabinet papers, 79/21.
[4] Chiefs of Staff Committee No. 51 (Operations) of 1942, 8 June 1942: Cabinet papers, 79/56.
[5] Prime Minister's Personal Minute, D.111/2A, 'Most Secret', 6 June 1942: Churchill papers, 20/67.

On June 7 the Chiefs of Staff cancelled the Spitzbergen plan. Their reason, Churchill told Eden, was Admiral Tovey's 'extreme reluctance to continue Russian convoys'. Churchill told Eden: 'The politicians are much abused, but they get little help or inspiration from their Service advisers.' This, Eden commented, 'can hardly be denied'.[1]

In a minute to the Chiefs of Staff Committee on June 8, Churchill set out his opposition to the proposed 'tip and run' landing in France, codename 'Imperator'. 'Certainly it would not help Russia,' he wrote, 'if we launched such an enterprise, no doubt with world publicity, and came out a few days later with heavy losses.' Even the more substantial landing in France, the 'Sledgehammer' plan for the autumn of 1942, should not be attempted 'unless the Germans are demoralized by ill-success against Russia'. It should be recognized, Churchill warned, 'that, if Russia is in dire straits, it would not help her or us to come a nasty cropper on our own'.

Plans for 'Sledgehammer' should go forward, Churchill ended, but the launching of 'Sledgehammer' should be dependent 'not on a Russian failure, but on a Russian success, and consequent proved German demoralization in the West'.[2]

At a meeting of the Chiefs of Staff Committee to discuss this minute, it was agreed that plans for 'Sledgehammer' should be 'completed and kept ready', but that no decision should be taken to mount the operation 'until the course of the Russian battle became clearer'. As for 'Imperator', the Boulogne landing, this, said Churchill, appeared from a military point of view to be 'unsound and unprofitable'. It was therefore agreed that 'Imperator' should be cancelled.[3]

Each night, at midnight, Churchill was sent the next day's newspapers by special courier from Fleet Street. He would often read them before going to bed. On the following morning, if time and work allowed, he would read them again. From this reading would arise many questions to Ministers, and even to proprietors.

Churchill's scrutiny of the Press included material sent to him regularly by the American division of the Ministry of Information. It was on reading their report of a *Time* magazine article which referred to 'oft-burned, defensive-minded Britain', that he wrote to Brendan

---

[1] Eden diary, 7 June 1942: Eden memoirs, *The Reckoning*, *op. cit.*, page 331.

[2] Prime Minister's Personal Minute, D.116/2, 'Most Secret', 8 June 1942: Churchill papers, 20/67.

[3] Chiefs of Staff Committee No. 51 (Operations) of 1942, 8 June 1942: Cabinet papers, 79/56.

Bracken: 'This vicious rag should have no special facilities here.' [1]

As well as reading the daily newspapers, Churchill made it his task to read through each morning a mass of Foreign Office telegrams. In one of these, he read a protest from Sir Horace Seymour, the British Minister to China, about an 'unhelpful' article in the *New Statesman* on British policy in India. [2] This prompted him to protest to Bracken: 'Pray stop any repetition of any *New Statesman* comments outside this country till you have been personally consulted on the text of each message.' Churchill added: 'You can recur to me at any hour of the night or day.' [3]

On June 4, in the Pacific, a powerful Japanese sea and air force sought to capture Midway Island, stepping stone to Pearl Harbor. In a savage battle, all four Japanese aircraft carriers were sunk. The American aircraft carrier *Yorktown* was also destroyed. But the Japanese thrust for Midway had failed. [4] 'The business in the Pacific is going well,' Roosevelt had telegraphed to Churchill on the morning of June 7, 'and I am sure we are inflicting some very severe losses on the Jap Fleet.' [5] That same day, as Rommel pressed forward his attack in Libya, Churchill telephoned Eden. 'We were both depressed,' Eden noted in his diary, 'by extent to which Rommel appears able to retain offensive.' Churchill told Eden: 'I fear that we have not very good generals.' [6] 'We know we have had heavy losses,' Auchinleck telegraphed to Churchill on the following day, 'but so has the enemy, and so far he has little to show for it strategically.' [7]

On June 9, Churchill informed Auchinleck that, unless Australia was to be threatened by a Japanese invasion 'within the next few days', two fresh Divisions, the 8th Armoured Division and the 44th Division, the one at the Cape, the other nearing Freetown, would both be sent to him. 'We feel,' Churchill added, 'that with this rapidly

---

[1] Minute of 7 June 1942: Premier papers, 4/26/8, folio 796. On being told by Bracken that *Time* was owned by Henry Luce, Churchill noted: 'surely some protest should be made to him. He was well treated over here. I took some trouble with him myself.' (Minute of 10 June 1942: Premier papers, 4/26/8, folio 795.)

[2] Telegram No. 1442 from Chungking, 22 October 1942: Premier papers, 4/26/8, folio 792.

[3] Prime Minister's Personal Minute, M.479/2, 24 October 1942: Premier papers, 4/26/8, folio 791.

[4] This American success had been made possible by the decrypting of Japanese naval signals, a decrypting in which British and American Intelligence had worked together (F. H. Hinsley and others, *British Intelligence in the Second World War*, volume 3, Part 1, London 1983, page 269).

[5] President to Prime Minister, No. 155, 7 June 1942: Churchill papers, 20/76.

[6] Eden diary, 7 June 1942: Eden memoirs, *The Reckoning*, *op. cit.*, page 331.

[7] Telegram of 8 June 1942: Churchill papers, 20/89.

approaching reserve behind you, you will be able to act with greater freedom in using your existing resources.' [1]

On the morning of June 9, Molotov returned to England, and went straight to Chequers. To the alarm of the British policy-makers, he had brought with him a Soviet-American draft communiqué 'with regards to the urgent task of creating a second front in Europe in 1942'. As Anthony Eden noted: 'We were not consulted about this wording and could not have agreed to it, with its implication of a definite pledge.' That night, at dinner in London, Churchill explained to his Soviet guest the 'problems' of a second front in 1942. 'I think that this did much good,' Eden noted in his diary. 'At least it helped to increase confidence.' [2]

Molotov met Churchill again in the early evening of June 10, when Churchill gave him an aide-mémoire, drafted by the Chiefs of Staff, explaining that, because of the problem of landing-craft, it was not yet possible to say whether a Continental landing was feasible in 1942, and that Britain could therefore 'give no promise'. But, the aide-mémoire continued, 'provided that it appears sound and sensible', Britain would 'not hesitate' to put into effect the landing on the Continent planned for August or September. Meanwhile, supplies of aircraft, tanks and other war equipment would continue to be sent to Russia 'to the best of our ability', both by the Persian route and by 'the hazardous Northern route'.

In the air, the aide-mémoire pointed out, Britain was already 'containing in the various theatres of war about one half of the German fighter strength and one third of their bomber strength'. In order to force the Germans to make further withdrawals from their air strength in the east, 'we shall continue our bombing of German towns and industry, and also our day bomber and fighter offensive over Occupied France'.

The Germans would also be kept 'fighting hard' in Libya, the aide-mémoire noted, in a paragraph added at Churchill's suggestion to the final draft, and it went on to point out that eleven Axis divisions, including two German armoured divisions and one German motorized division, were being held down in Libya. A further thirty-three German divisions were being forced to remain in western Europe, and would not be transferred to the eastern front, as a result of the policy

---

[1] Prime Minister's Personal Telegram, T.842/2, 'Most Secret and Personal', 9 June 1942: Churchill papers, 20/76.

[2] Eden diary, 9 June 1942: Eden memoirs, *The Reckoning*, op. cit., page 330.

of raids against 'selected points on the Continent'. These raids would increase 'in size and scope' during the summer, keeping the Germans 'constantly on the alert, never knowing at what point the next attack may come'.

At Churchill's suggestion, there was also a paragraph in the aide-mémoire about the way in which, 'for the last four months', Malta had contained 'considerable air forces' in Sicily. 'At one time they had over four hundred first-line aircraft pounding the Island,' the aide-mémoire noted, and it went on to state that Britain would continue to send large fighter reinforcements 'to keep the air battle going there'.

Britain was also prepared, Molotov was told, to send a force of four fighter and two fighter-bomber squadrons to Murmansk, 'with a view to releasing Russian air forces for operations on other parts of the Russian front'. The aide-mémoire concluded:

Finally, the most important of all, we are concentrating our maximum effort on the organization and preparation of a large scale invasion of the Continent of Europe by British and American forces in 1943. We are setting no limit to the scope and objectives of this campaign, which will be carried out in the first instance by over a million men, British and American, with air forces of appropriate strength. [1]

At the farewell meeting to Molotov at 10 Downing Street, Sir Alexander Cadogan noted in his diary: 'PM in quite good form—and his rompers!' [2] Oliver Harvey added: 'PM very firm on limitations of what was possible for us this year: he would not authorize any large-scale operation which didn't offer fair prospect of success, since a failure would not help Russia either.' Harvey added: 'Roosevelt had calmly told Molotov he would be prepared to contemplate a sacrifice of 120,000 men if necessary—*our* men. PM said he would not hear of it.' [3]

Molotov flew back to Russia on the night of June 10. On the following morning, in the Prime Minister's room in the House of Commons, the War Cabinet heard from Churchill of the different plans to carry on the war in Europe, and to carry the war to Europe. There would 'shortly' be a 'butcher and bolt' raid across the Channel, lasting twenty-four hours and employing some six to seven thousand men: codename 'Rutter'. The largest operation, 'Sledgehammer', which would employ six divisions, 'was only considered to be practicable if German morale had started to crack'. It would take two months to assemble the shipping needed for such a force, and September was, from the point of view of weather conditions, the last month in which it could be carried out. It had been explained to

---

[1] 'Aide-Mémoire', 10 June 1942: Cabinet papers, 120/684.
[2] Cadogan diary, 10 June 1942: David Dilks (editor), *op. cit.*, page 457.
[3] Harvey diary, 10 June 1942: John Harvey (editor), *op. cit.*, pages 131–2.

Molotov, Churchill added, 'that a landing on the Continent this year which was doomed to failure, and resulted in another Dunkirk with considerable slaughter, would do nothing to help the Russians and would, moreover, prejudice the larger scale operations planned for 1943'.

Churchill emphasized that in his talk with Molotov he had not committed Britain 'in any way' to do 'Sledgehammer'. He then explained that he had opposed the large-scale cross-Channel raid planned to follow 'Rutter', and to lead to a three-or four-day temporary occupation of Amiens or Abbeville. This was operation 'Imperator', aimed at forcing the Germans to an air battle over the Occupied zone 'in which we might subject the German Air Force to considerable wastage'. Operation 'Imperator' was now dead.

A fourth operation, codename 'Round-Up', was one of 'grand conception', involving, as Churchill explained, 'no less than one million American troops', as well as twenty-one British divisions to land in Europe in 1943. April 1943 was the date mentioned, but, Churchill commented, 'it was unlikely that the American forces would be trained in time'. May 1943, he felt, was a more realistic date, especially as far as the availability of landing-craft was concerned.

Churchill then spoke of the possible northern Norway operation, codename 'Jupiter'. If there were to be no cross-Channel attack in 1942, he said, then 'Jupiter' should still be considered. 'A firm foothold in Norway,' he said, 'would immensely increase the security of our Russian Convoys and would open the highway to the south and enable us to start to unroll Hitler's map of Europe from the top.' The occupation of Spitzbergen, however, was not considered by the Chiefs of Staff to be essential for the protection of the Russian convoys. This operation, 'Jackpot,' would not therefore go ahead.[1]

Reflecting further upon 'Jupiter', Churchill told the Chiefs of Staff two days later that a northern Norway expedition would also be a 'convenient prelude and accompaniment' to the plans for a cross-Channel landing in 1943, the substantial 'Roundup'. The 'distraction' caused by 'Jupiter' to German military movements, Churchill added, 'would far exceed the employment of our own resources'. If the Germans in France were not 'sufficiently demoralized' later in 1942 for 'Sledgehammer' to go ahead, then 'Jupiter' should be tried: not western France, but northern Norway, would be the European operation for 1942, and could be carried out, Churchill suggested, by some 25,000 troops 'of high quality'.[2]

Turning to the Far East, Churchill telegraphed to Wavell on June 12

[1] War Cabinet No. 73 of 1942, 11 June 1942, Confidential Annex, Cabinet papers, 65/30.
[2] 'Jupiter', note enclosed with Prime Minister's Personal Directive, D.119/2, 13 June 1942: Churchill papers, 20/67.

to urge that preparations go forward for the capture of Rangoon and Moulmein in Burma, 'and, thereafter, striking at Bangkok'. For this, Churchill explained, 'we should first have to fight our way along the coast amphibiously from Chittagong via Akyab, and at the right time launch an overseas expedition of forty or fifty thousand of our best British troops with suitable armour across the northern part of the Bay of Bengal'. Such an attack, Churchill added, 'would be seizing the initiative and making the enemy conform, instead of being, through no fault of your own, like clay in the hands of the potter. It would be war on a large scale. . . .' For such a plan, Churchill told Wavell, 'I could leave you Alexander.' But no such plan would be possible if the Russian southern front was 'beaten in' and Germany overran the Caucasus, 'or if Auchinleck were beaten back by Rommel'.[1]

That same day, Rommel's forces drove forward to within fifteen miles of Tobruk. 'Your decision to fight it out to the end,' Churchill telegraphed to Auchinleck, 'most cordially endorsed. We shall sustain you whatever the result.' He added: 'Retreat would be fatal. This is a business not only of armour but of will power. God bless you all.'[2]

At Chequers, on Friday, June 12, Lord Louis Mountbatten, who had just returned from Washington, was among the overnight guests. As they talked that night, it became clear to Churchill that, with so many competing war plans, and a growing problem of the allocation of United States aircraft in the different war zones, it would be sensible to visit Roosevelt once more. He was also worried about the second front. It would be impossible, Churchill telegraphed to Roosevelt on June 13, to deal by correspondence 'with all the many difficult points outstanding'. For this reason, 'I feel it is my duty to come to see you.' He would bring with him General Brooke, 'whom you have not yet met', and Ismay. Clementine Churchill—'Colonel White'—would not be able to come, however, feeling that 'she had better stay here on account of her Russian fund'.

In telling the President about his imminent journey, Churchill also congratulated Roosevelt on the Midway battle, which had 'very decidedly altered the balance of the naval war'.[3]

The King's permission was sought. Only by 'another personal visit to

[1] Prime Minister's Personal Telegram, T.862/2, 'Secret and Personal', 12 June 1942: Churchill papers, 20/76.
[2] Prime Minister's Personal Telegram, T.870/2, 'Personal and Most Secret', 13 June 1942: Churchill papers, 20/76.
[3] Prime Minister's Personal Telegram, T.864/2, Prime Minister to President, No. 101, 'Personal and Secret', 13 June 1942: Churchill papers, 20/76.

Washington', John Martin wrote to Sir Alexander Hardinge on June 13, 'can he settle all the many difficult points outstanding between ourselves and the Americans on the highest level, which cannot satisfactorily be dealt with by correspondence'.[1] That night Churchill telegraphed General Brooke to tell him of the impending Washington visit. 'He considered Roosevelt was getting a little off the rails,' Brooke noted in his diary, 'and some good talks as regards Western Front were required.'[2]

Churchill planned to leave London on June 18. As he waited, Rommel's forces continued to beat back those of Auchinleck. The Malta convoys were also in disarray: of six supply ships which had entered the Mediterranean on the night of June 12, only two reached Malta, while of eleven which sailed to Malta from the eastern Mediterranean, not a single one could pass the Italian naval force which had blocked its path. Among the escort ships, one cruiser and four destroyers were sunk, and a second cruiser put out of action.[3] At this critical moment, in India, Gandhi announced his intention of launching a 'Quit India' movement, based upon complete non-cooperation with the British, and with the demand for immediate independence. 'If Gandhi tries to start a really hostile movement against us in this crisis,' Churchill minuted on June 14, 'I am of opinion that he should be arrested, and that both British and United States opinion would support such a step. If he likes to starve himself to death,' Churchill added, 'we cannot help that.'[4] The 'chief threat to India at the moment', Wavell warned Churchill that same day, 'is raids on shipping in Bay of Bengal which I can do little to prevent and which would do much harm material and moral'. The air force in India, Wavell added, was not only 'quite inadequate' for the task of an offensive against Burma, as Churchill had wished, but was inadequate 'even for defence of India against seaborne attack'. It was 'deficient', Wavell stressed, 'in numbers, in reserves, in range, in hitting power and in training'.[5]

*   *   *

[1] 'Most Secret', 13 June 1942: Premier papers, 3/459, folios 106–7. 'As on former occasions,' Hardinge replied, 'I shall be very glad when he is safely back in this country!' ('Most Secret', 14 June 1942: Premier papers, 3/459, folio 105.)

[2] Brooke diary, 13 June 1942: Bryant, op. cit., volume 1, page 397.

[3] The destroyers, all sunk on 15 June 1942, were Airedale, Bedouin, Hasty and Nestor. On June 16 the cruiser Hermione and the destroyer Oakley (on loan to the Polish navy and renamed Kujawiak) were sunk, the Hermione torpedoed in the eastern Mediterranean, the Kujawiak sunk by a mine off Malta. On June 12, the day of the sailing of the convoys, the destroyer Grove had been torpedoed in the eastern Mediterranean. The cruiser put out of action was Liverpool.

[4] Prime Minister's Personal Minute (to the Secretary of State for India), M.250/2, 'Secret', 14 June 1942: Churchill papers, 20/67.

[5] Telegram No. 14299/C, 'Secret and Personal', 14 June 1942: Churchill papers, 20/76,

The news from the Western Desert worsened throughout June 14. 'A Sunday disturbed by many calls from the PM,' General Brooke noted in his diary, 'who was much disturbed at bad turn taken by operation in Middle East. Rommel certainly seems to be getting the better of Ritchie and is out-generalling him.'[1] On June 15 Auchinleck telegraphed to Churchill that General Ritchie had been ordered 'not to allow his forces to be invested in Tobruk'. At the War Cabinet that day, it was felt that this could mean, if the need arose, that Ritchie might give up Tobruk, leaving only a garrison there. This garrison, Churchill telegraphed that same day, should contain as many troops 'as are necessary to hold the place for certain'.

In preparation for his second visit to Washington, Churchill set out for the Chiefs of Staff his concept of operation 'Round-Up', the cross-Channel invasion planned for 1943. At least six 'heavy disembarkations' should be attempted at the first wave. 'The enemy cannot be ready everywhere.' A second wave of landings 'nourishes the landings effected, and presses where the going is good'. Meanwhile, operation 'Jupiter' in northern Norway would be in progress already. There would also be landings, or feints, planned for Denmark, Holland, Belgium, at the Pas de Calais 'where the major air battle will be fought', on the Cotentin Peninsula, at Brest, at St Nazaire and at the mouth of the Gironde.

In the first wave, 'at least' ten armoured brigades would go ashore. 'These brigades must accept very high risks in their task of pressing on deeply inland, rousing the populations, deranging the enemy's communications, and spreading the fighting over the widest possible areas.' Behind the 'confusion and disorder' created by this first wave, the second wave would be launched. Within a week, not less than 400,000 men 'should be ashore and busy'. The moment any port was gained, and open, the third wave should go in, comprising not less than 300,000 men with their artillery. If after two weeks, Churchill wrote, '700,000 men are ashore, if air supremacy has been gained, if the enemy is in considerable confusion, and if we hold at least four workable ports, we shall have got our claws well into the job'. The phase of 'sudden violence irrespective of losses' being over, the campaign would then follow the 'normal and conventional lines of organization and supply'. Only in such a 'scale and spirit', Churchill ended, could the landings be undertaken 'with good prospects of success'.[2]

On June 15, at the last meeting of the Chiefs of Staff Committee

[1] Brooke diary, 14 June 1942: Bryant, *op. cit.*, volume 1, page 397.
[2] 'Operation "Round-Up"', 'Most Secret', attached to Prime Minister's Personal Minute, D.121/2, 15 June 1942: Churchill papers, 20/67.

before his departure for Washington, Churchill remarked that 'while subscribing to the principle that the bulk of our resources should be concentrated against Germany', it would be 'a mistake to neglect the Far Eastern theatre altogether'. A 'small diversion' of assault shipping and air forces to the Far East 'might pay a handsome dividend,' he said, 'by keeping China in the war and by engaging Japanese forces in a process of attrition'. Such a diversion would also enable the British forces in India to be 'actively engaged with the enemy'. In reply, Dudley Pound stressed that Britain could not afford large-scale offensive operations against the Japanese from Australia and Fiji, such as the Americans had proposed, 'until Germany was beaten and that threat to our sea power eliminated'. The plan to reopen the Burma road to China, operation 'Anakim', would however continue to be studied by the Joint Planning Staff, although, as Brooke explained, it was only a 'feasible operation if the Japanese were at the time actively engaged elsewhere'.[1]

On June 15 Churchill received a message from his former Party leader, Prime Minister and political adversary, Stanley Baldwin. 'If you ever have a chance of a chat with Winston,' Baldwin told a friend, 'tell him he has all my affection, support and sympathy in his tremendous task.'[2] On the following day, in a letter to the King, Churchill advised that Anthony Eden should be entrusted to form a government in the event of Churchill's death on his trans-Atlantic journey, which was to be entirely by air. Eden possessed, Churchill wrote to the King, 'the resolution, experience and capacity which these grievous times require'.[3]

---

[1] Chiefs of Staff Committee No. 52 (Operations) of 1942, 15 June 1942: Cabinet papers, 79/56.

[2] Harvie Watt to Churchill, 15 June 1942. The friend was Lord Winterton. Churchill marked the message, 'Mrs C to see': Churchill papers, 20/55.

[3] Letter of 16 June 1942: Churchill papers, 20/52.

8

June 1942,
Return to Washington

AT midday on 17 June 1942, Churchill left London by train for Stranraer, on the first stage of his journey to Washington. It was to be his third meeting with Roosevelt in ten months. At Stranraer, a motor boat took Churchill to the flying boat, the same Boeing Clipper which had brought him back from Bermuda in January. 'Huge flying-boat,' General Brooke noted in his diary, 'beautifully fitted up with bunks to sleep in, dining-saloon, steward's office, lavatories etc.'[1]

The flight across the Atlantic took twenty-six and a half hours. The start had been timed for after dark, to avoid the danger of meeting a German Focke-Wolf plane which, as Brooke later recalled, 'was apt to cruise over the Western Approaches'.[2] Churchill was accompanied on this journey by his doctor Sir Charles Wilson, whose 'advice', John Martin had informed Churchill on the previous day, 'is clear, that there would be a real risk in undertaking such a journey without a medical attendant'.[3] Also with Churchill were the head of his Defence Office, General Ismay, his Principal Private Secretary, John Martin, and his aide-de-camp, 'Tommy' Thompson, as well as General Brooke and Brigadier Stewart, Director of Plans at the War Office.

'PM in tremendous form', Brooke noted in his diary on the morning of June 18, 'and enjoying himself like a schoolboy', as the Boeing Clipper flew over an Atlantic convoy of some thirty-five ships.[4] General Ismay later recalled:

---

[1] Brooke diary, 17 June 1942: Bryant, *op. cit.*, volume 1, page 399.
[2] Brooke recollections: Bryant, *op. cit.*, volume 1, page 400.
[3] Note of 16 June 1942: Premier papers, 3/459, folios 109–10.
[4] Brooke diary, 18 June 1942: Bryant, *op. cit.*, volume 1, page 400. On landing at the Anacostia Naval Air Station on the Potomac, Churchill had been met by Roosevelt's naval aide, Captain Macrae, Lord Halifax, Oliver Lyttelton, Sir John Dill and General Marshall.

When we were about four hours from Washington, the Prime Minister looked at his watch. 'It is nearly eight o'clock, Tommy. Where's dinner?' Tommy explained that he was engaged to dine at the British Embassy, and that it was only about 4.30 p.m. according to sun time. The Prime Minister retorted that he didn't go by sun time. 'I go by tummy time, and I want my dinner.' He had it—and so did we all—and a very good dinner it was! We landed on the Potomac River three or fours hours later, and assembled at the British Embassy in time for a second meal.[1]

After spending the night of June 18 at the British Embassy in Washington, Churchill flew by United States Navy plane to New Hackensack airfield near Hyde Park, Roosevelt's home on the Hudson River north of New York City. As Churchill travelled on this last stage of his journey, Japanese forces in China, more than 100,000 strong, launched their overland invasion of Fukien Province, while in North Africa, Rommel ordered two columns of tanks forward towards the Egyptian frontier.

The flight to New Hackensack took Churchill over Philadelphia and New York, 'where the skyscrapers', as John Martin noted, 'reduced to the size of cardboard models, made a rather beautiful panorama'.[2] Roosevelt awaited Churchill at New Hackensack airfield, 'and saw us make', Churchill later recalled, 'the roughest bump landing I have ever experienced'. Churchill's account continued:

He welcomed me with great cordiality, and, driving the car himself, took me to the majestic bluffs over the Hudson River on which Hyde Park, his family home, stands. The President drove me all over the estate, showing me its splendid views.

In this drive I had some thoughtful moments. Mr Roosevelt's infirmity prevented him from using his feet on the brake, clutch, or accelerator. An ingenious arrangement enabled him to do everything with his arms, which were amazingly strong and muscular. He invited me to feel his biceps, saying that a famous prize-fighter had envied them. This was reassuring; but I confess that when on several occasions the car poised and backed on the grass verges of the precipices over the Hudson I hoped the mechanical devices and brakes would show no defects.

All the time we talked business, and though I was careful not to take his attention off the driving we made more progress than we might have done in formal conference.[3]

A decision had to be reached about the Second Front. In a note which he gave Roosevelt later that day, Churchill stressed: 'No responsible British military authority has so far been able to make a

[1] *The Memoirs of General Lord Ismay*, London 1960, page 250.
[2] Letter of 26–7 June 1942: Martin papers.
[3] Winston S. Churchill, *The Second World War*, volume 4, London 1951, pages 338–9.

plan for September 1942 which had any chance of success unless the Germans became utterly demoralized,' of which, Churchill added, 'there is no likelihood'. Were there a plan for September 1942 which offered 'a reasonable prospect of success' in Europe, the British Government would 'cordially welcome it', but if no attack in France was possible that year on a substantial scale, 'ought we not to be preparing', Churchill asked, 'some other operation' by which the Allies could gain 'positions of advantage', and which, directly or indirectly, could take 'some of the weight off Russia'? In this setting, Churchill wrote, the operation against French North-West Africa 'should be studied'.[1]

That night Churchill and Roosevelt travelled by Presidential train to Washington. Reaching the White House shortly after nine in the morning, Churchill went to the same room in which he had stayed in January. There he had breakfast, glanced at the newspapers, and read official telegrams for an hour, before going, with Ismay, to the President's study. As Churchill and Roosevelt talked, a pink piece of paper was brought in and handed to Roosevelt. It was a telegraphic message. Roosevelt read it, and then, without a word, passed it to Churchill. The message read: 'Tobruk has surrendered, with twenty-five thousand men taken prisoners.'[2]

Churchill did not believe that the news could be true, and asked Ismay to telephone to London. Ismay left the room to make the telephone call, returning in a few minutes with a second message, which had just reached Washington from Admiral Harwood, Com-mander-in-Chief of the British naval forces in the Mediterranean. The message began: 'Tobruk has fallen . . .'.[3]

'This was one of the heaviest blows I can recall during the war,' Churchill later wrote. At Singapore, 85,000 men had surrendered 'to inferior numbers'. At Tobruk, 25,000 men were now reported to have surrendered 'to perhaps one-half of their numbers'. It soon emerged that the number which had surrendered at Tobruk was even larger than first reported: in all, 33,000. Harwood's telegram had continued: '. . . situation deteriorated so much that there is a possibility of heavy air attack on Alexandria in near future. . . .'[4]

It was, Churchill later recalled, 'a bitter moment', and he added: 'Defeat is one thing; disgrace is another.'[5] For a moment or two,

---

[1] 'Secret', 20 June 1942: Cabinet papers, 99/20, folio 24.
[2] Winston S. Churchill, *The Second World War*, volume 4, London 1951, page 343.
[3] Telegram No. 698, 1209 C, 21 June 1942, War Cabinet No. 78 of 1942, 21 June 1942: Cabinet papers, 65/30.
[4] Telegram No. 698, 1209 C, 21 June 1942, War Cabinet No. 78 of 1942, 21 June 1942: Cabinet papers, 65/30.
[5] Winston S. Churchill, *The Second World War*, volume 4, London 1951, page 343.

Ismay later recalled, 'no one spoke'. The silence was then broken by Roosevelt, who asked only, 'What can we do to help?'[1]

Throughout that morning, Churchill and Roosevelt discussed future military strategy, with Marshall, Brooke, Hopkins and Ismay in attendance. The principal conclusion which they reached was that plans and preparations for 'Bolero', the build-up of United States forces in Britain with a view to a cross-Channel operation in 1943 'on as large a scale as possible', were to be pushed forward 'with all speed and energy'. They felt, however, that it was 'essential' that the United States and Britain 'be prepared to act offensively in 1942'.

The second set of conclusions concerned what form that 1942 offensive action should take. The preference of both leaders was for operations 'in France or the Low Countries'. Such operations, if they could be launched successfully in 1942, would 'yield greater political and strategic gains than operations in any other theatre'. Plans and preparations for a cross-Channel operation in 1942 were therefore 'to be pressed forward with all possible speed, energy and ingenuity', and the 'most resolute efforts' made to overcome 'the obvious dangers and difficulties of the enterprise'.

If a 'sound and sensible plan' could be contrived for a cross-Channel operation in 1942, the two leaders and their military advisers decided, 'we should not hesitate to give effect to it'. If, on the other hand, detailed examination were to show that 'despite all efforts', success in a 1942 cross-Channel operation 'is improbable', then the British and Americans 'must be ready with an alternative'.[2]

The alternative proposed was a landing in French North Africa, operation 'Gymnast'. The possibilities of such a landing would be explored 'completely in all details as soon as possible'. The troops needed for a North African landing in 1942 would 'in the main' be found from 'Bolero' units which had not yet left the United States. The Combined Chiefs of Staff would also consider the possibility of operations in Norway, or in the Iberian peninsula, for the autumn and winter of 1942. Such were the military conclusions of the Washington conference.[3]

On the afternoon of June 21, two senior American officers came to Churchill's room. They had just spent some time with Roosevelt, discussing the 1943 cross-Channel landings. Those officers were General Eisenhower and General Mark Clark. 'I was immediately impressed,'

---

[1] *The Memoirs of General The Lord Ismay*, London 1960, page 255.

[2] War Cabinet Paper No. 278 of 1942 (also Chiefs of Staff Paper No. 195, Operations, of 1942), 'Most Secret', 2 July 1942: Churchill papers, 4/277.

[3] Note by General Ismay: Winston S. Churchill, *The Second World War*, volume 4, London 1951, pages 344–5.

Churchill later wrote, 'by these remarkable but hitherto unknown men.'[1] Four days later, Eisenhower was appointed commander of all United States forces in the European theatre.

At 9.30 on the evening of June 21, Churchill, Roosevelt and their advisers discussed the need for greater preventive measures against German submarines off the east coast of the United States.[2] During the discussion, Ismay wrote to Churchill nine years later, 'you successfully pressed King to start the convoy system'.[3] Two hours later Churchill and Roosevelt met again. The discussion centred around what the minutes described as 'the deterioration of the situation in the Middle East and the possibility of sending large numbers of American troops, starting with the Second Armoured Division which had been specially trained in desert warfare to that theatre as soon as possible'. This idea was General Marshall's. The Second Armoured Division had done its training in the deserts of California. It was agreed that Churchill, with Roosevelt's 'full approval', should inform Auchinleck that he might expect a reinforcement 'of a highly trained American Armoured division equipped with Sherman or Lee tanks during August'.[4]

In a telegram dictated later that night, Churchill informed Auchinleck that it had been agreed that the armoured division would leave for Suez on July 5. 'Here in Washington,' he reported, 'the President is deeply moved by what has occurred and he and other high United States Authorities show themselves disposed to lend the utmost help.'

'I earnestly hope,' Churchill told Auchinleck, that on the Sollum frontier line 'stern resistance' would be made, as 'special intelligence'—a reference to the Enigma decrypts—'has shown stresses which enemy has undergone'. He was 'naturally disconcerted', Churchill added, by Auchinleck's decision to withdraw to Matruh, which 'may well put us back to where we were eighteen months ago and leave all the work of that period to be done over again'.

Churchill was certain, he told Auchinleck, that the defence of the Nile Delta could be 'effectively maintained'. He hoped no one would be 'unduly impressed by the spectacular blows which the enemy has struck at us'. He was sure, he wrote, 'that with your perseverance and resolution and continued readiness to run risks, the situation can be

---

[1] Winston S. Churchill, *The Second World War*, volume 4, London 1951, pages 345–6.

[2] Roosevelt's advisers at this meeting were Admiral King, General Marshall and Lieutenant-General Arnold; Churchill was accompanied by Field Marshal Dill, General Brooke, Admiral Little, Major General Ismay and Commodore Patterson (Cabinet papers, 99/20, folio 30).

[3] General Ismay, 'Notes on Mr Churchill's Visit to Washington in June, 1942 (Tobruk time)', notes written in 1947 for Churchill's war memoirs: Churchill papers, 4/274.

[4] 'Notes of a meeting held at the White House at 11.30 p.m. on Sunday, June 21st, between the President and the Prime Minister', 'Most Secret': Cabinet papers, 99/20, folio 33.

restored, especially in view of the large reinforcements approaching'. These included the 8th Armoured Division and the 49th Division. Churchill's telegram ended:

The main thing now is for you to inspire all your forces with an intense will to recover and strive not to accept the freak decisions produced by Rommel's handful of heavy armour. Make sure that all your manpower plays a full part in these critical days. His Majesty's Government is quite ready to share your responsibilities in making the most active and daring defence.[1]

The American newspapers of June 22 reported not only the fall of Tobruk but also the 'impending fall' of Churchill's Government. Churchill saw these reports while lunching that day with Roosevelt and Hopkins. That night he telephoned Eden—it was then five in the morning, British time—to ask about 'the position at home'. Eden was able at once to put Churchill's mind at rest. 'I told him that I had heard not one word of this. Of course there was much grief.' But nothing had happened 'to shake us'.[2]

On the morning of June 23, Churchill, Roosevelt and their naval advisers discussed the 'very urgent' need for extra escort vessels.[3] 'It was argued,' noted the minutes, 'that one merchant vessel saved was worth two merchant vessels building, plus the value of the cargo and the lives of the crew.' But it was also argued that any additional escort vessels ordered now 'would cut into the output of merchant vessels which would come into service in the vital important period between the autumn of 1942 and the summer of 1943', whereas the new escort vessels would not be ready until after then. The governing factor was steel plate. Part of the delay in the availability of steel plate, pointed out Admiral King, was caused 'by the demands of "Bolero" '. Escort vessels, argued Admiral Little, were the only way of defeating the submarine campaign, the success of which 'depended upon the morale of the submarine crews', and he added: 'the battle could never be won merely by renewing and expanding the Merchant Fleet'.

Churchill and Roosevelt accepted Admiral Little's advice. It was agreed that the 'first essential', in Admiral King's phrase, was to accelerate the production of escort vessels, but without cutting down on the production of those merchant vessels which would come into service during the 'critical' period.[4]

---

[1] 'Googly' No. 13, sent at 6.31 a.m., 22 June 1943: Cabinet papers, 99/20, folios 35–6.
[2] Eden recollections: Eden memoirs, *The Reckoning*, op. cit., page 331.
[3] Roosevelt was accompanied at this meeting by Harry Hopkins, Averell Harriman, Lou Douglas and four Admirals, King, Land, Vickery and Farber. Churchill was accompanied by Sir Arthur Salter, Colonel Jacob and Admirals Little and Dorling.
[4] 'Minutes of a meeting held at the White House at 11.45 a.m. on Tuesday, June 23rd, 1942', 'Most Secret': Cabinet papers, 99/20, folios 49–50.

On the afternoon of June 23, Churchill, Roosevelt and their advisers discussed the further reinforcement of the Middle East by sending United States air forces then in India.[1] In a memorandum from Marshall which Churchill at once telegraphed to Attlee in London and to Auchinleck in the Western Desert, the Americans announced that all available American heavy bombers in India, about ten, had been 'ordered to Cairo immediately', while a complete pursuit group of eighty P-40 planes was to be loaded at Quonsett, Rhode Island, in four days' time 'for immediate departure' for West Africa and the Cairo air ferry route. A light bombardment squadron intended for China, and then in Florida, would leave on the following day 'to receive formal orders at Omdurman'. A medium bombardment group of fifty-seven B-25s, then in California, would fly east on the following day 'to pick up new equipment for immediate departure for Cairo'. A further thirty-six new planes would be sent off by squadrons 'as rapidly as equipped'.[2] A further forty United States fighter bombers were then at Basra, on their way to Russia. Churchill asked if they too could be sent to Egypt, subject to Stalin's approval.[3]

That evening, Churchill left Washington by train for Camp Jackson in South Carolina. There on the morning of June 24, in the presence of the Secretary for War, Henry Stimson, Churchill saw a battalion of American troops doing a parachute drop. 'I had never seen a thousand men leap into the air at once,' he later recalled.[4] That afternoon, after lunching with Stimson and Marshall in the train, Churchill watched a brigade of young soldiers at a field firing exercise using live ammunition. 'The troops were obviously green,' Ismay later recalled, 'and in reply to a question by the Prime Minister, I ventured the opinion that it would be murder to pit them against continental soldiery. Churchill agreed that they were still immature, but added that they were magnificent material who would soon train on.'[5] In conversation with the American Generals, Churchill later wrote, 'I consistently pressed my view that it takes two years or more to make a soldier.'[6]

To his hosts at Camp Jackson, Henry Stimson and General Mar-

---

[1] Those present at this discussion, which began at 2.45, were Roosevelt, Harry Hopkins, Marshall and Arnold, Churchill, Brooke and Ismay (Cabinet papers, 99/20, folio 52).

[2] 'Googly' No. 25, 'Secret', 24 June 1942: Churchill papers, 20/86.

[3] On 7 July 1942 Roosevelt telegraphed to Churchill: 'Have just had word from Stalin that he has no objection to transfer of 40 A-20s from Basra to Egypt. Instructions have gone forward to transfer planes at once' (Prime Minister's Personal Telegram, T.968/2, Prime Minister to President No. 161, 7 July 1942: Churchill papers, 20/77).

[4] Winston S. Churchill, *The Second World War*, volume 4, London 1951, page 347. There were, in fact, just over 600 parachutists. ('Inspection Program, Camp Jackson, South Carolina': Cabinet papers, 99/20, folio 56.)

[5] *The Memoirs of General The Lord Ismay*, London 1960, page 256.

[6] Winston S. Churchill, *The Second World War*, volume 4, London 1951, page 347.

shall, Churchill wrote a letter of thanks for the 'instructive day' which they had allowed him to spend with their troops, and he added: 'I have had considerable experience of such inspections and I can say that I have never been more impressed than I was with the bearing of the men whom I saw. The undemonstrative, therefore grim, determination which was everywhere manifest not only in the seasoned troops but in the newly-drafted, bodes ill for our enemies.'[1]

Camp Jackson was home to 60,000 American troops, several thousand of whom were involved in the day's events. 'We both enjoyed the opportunity to "display our wares",' Stimson telegraphed to Churchill on his and Marshall's behalf three days later, 'and we are delighted that you are pleased. My regret is that all of our troops could not have had the great inspiration of your presence and interest in their efforts in our common cause.'[2]

After his day at Camp Jackson, Churchill flew back to Washington, where he dined at the British Embassy. On the following day, June 25, he met the Dominion and Indian representatives in Washington and attended a meeting of the Pacific War Council. He also spoke to the Embassy Staff, many of whom were unhappy, as Brenda Duncan, a cypher clerk, later recalled, 'at being there in safety with all that was happening to our country, and at being separated from our loved ones'. Churchill understood their unhappiness, making them feel, Brenda Duncan recalled, that they were doing 'a worthwhile job and that he was proud of us all. He put new heart in us.'[3]

That same day, in London, a motion was placed in the Order Paper of the House of Commons, that 'this House, while paying tribute to the heroism and endurance of the Armed Forces of the Crown in circumstances of exceptional difficulty, has no confidence in the central direction of the war'. Later that day, in telegraphing to Auchinleck about the imminent American reinforcements, Churchill commented: 'Do not have the slightest anxiety about course of affairs at home. Whatever views I may have about how the battle was fought, or whether it should have been fought a good deal earlier, you have my entire confidence, and I share your responsibilities to the full.'[4]

In his telegram of June 25, Churchill spoke of the defence of Egypt,

---

[1] Letter of 25 June 1942 ('My dear Stimson'): Churchill papers, 20/53.

[2] Telegram forwarded by General Eisenhower on 27 June 1942: Premier papers, 4/71/3, folio 833. On 25 June 1942 Auchinleck had taken over Command of the Eighth Army.

[3] Brenda Duncan, recollections: letter to the author, 20 January 1982.

[4] 'Googly' No. 27, Prime Minister's Personal Telegram, T.913/2, 'Personal', 25 June 1942: Cabinet papers, 120/34. General Ismay, writing eighteen years later, asked: 'Would many Prime Ministers, facing a vote of Censure, have been so considerate, loyal and generous to the commander whose defeat had caused this political storm?' (*The Memoirs of General The Lord Ismay*, London 1960, page 257.)

noting that Auchinleck had 700,000 men on his ration strength in the Middle East. 'Every fit male,' Churchill wrote, 'should be made to fight and die for victory,' and he added: 'You are in the same kind of situation as we should be if England were invaded, and the same intense drastic spirit should reign.' [1]

On the morning of June 25 it had become clear in Washington that the Second Armoured Division would not be able to go to the Middle East. The shipping of this division from the United States, Churchill telegraphed to Auchinleck later that day, 'presents very grave difficulties' and would involve 'serious interference' with the next two Cape of Good Hope convoys. Marshall had therefore proposed, and Brooke had considered 'even more attractive' from Auchinleck's point of view, the despatch of three hundred Sherman tanks and one hundred self-propelled 105-millimetre gun howitzers. These, Churchill added, would be sent from the United States to the Middle East 'as an urgent move'. [2] To accelerate the despatch of this vital reinforcement 'as a rush move', Brooke explained to Churchill, two sea trains would be used, 'taken from the Havana sugar traffic', with a speed of fifteen and thirteen knots respectively. [3]

On the night of June 25, Churchill left the United States by Flying Boat from Baltimore; as he said goodbye to Harry Hopkins, he remarked: 'Now for England, home, and—a beautiful row.' [4]

[1] 'Googly' No. 27, Prime Minister's Personal Telegram, T.913/2, 'Personal', 25 June 1942: Cabinet papers, 120/34.

[2] 'Googly' No. 31, Prime Minister's Personal Telegram, T.915/2, 25 June 1942: Churchill papers, 20/77.

[3] 'Most Secret', 25 June 1942: Cabinet papers, 99/20, folio 63.

[4] The Memoirs of General The Lord Ismay, London 1960, page 257.

9

'Torch': 'A turning-point in the whole war'

AS Churchill's Boeing Clipper flew eastward, touching down briefly in Newfoundland in the early hours of 27 June 1942 for refuelling, Rommel's forces crossed the Egyptian frontier and advanced nearly fifty miles inside Egypt. At five o'clock that morning the Clipper touched down in Stranraer harbour. Elizabeth Layton, who was waiting in the special train, wrote to her parents of how, 'Presently he came, looking just his usual cheerful self, followed by a small knot of Officers—what might be described as a gaggle of generals. I was on the phone in the office; he came marching into the carriage and said, "Hullo, how are you, is everything all right?" ' [1] The news as Churchill boarded the train was that the Government had lost a by-election at Maldon. [2]

Reaching London that afternoon, Churchill was met at Euston Station by his wife and the members of the War Cabinet. Then, at five-thirty that afternoon, he gave the War Cabinet an account of his American journey. Despite 'the defeat of our forces in the Middle East', he said, and perhaps even more due to rumours of its effect on the political situation in Britain, the attitude of the American administration had been 'very staunch'. [3]

Churchill spent Sunday June 28 at Chequers, with his wife and a small, mostly family gathering. Each of his three daughters, Mary, Sarah and Diana, was present. So too was Lord Cherwell. [4] His son

[1] Elizabeth Layton, letter of 27 June 1942: Nel papers. Churchill's special train had the codename 'Dives'.

[2] On 25 June 1942, following the death of Sir E. A. Ruggles-Brise, Conservative Member of Parliament for Maldon, Essex, since 1924, the official Conservative candidate, R. J. Hunt, received only 6,226 votes, as against 12,219 votes cast for Tom Driberg, the Independent Labour candidate.

[3] War Cabinet No. 82 of 1942, 27 June 1942: Cabinet papers, 65/26.

[4] Also at Chequers were Oliver Lyttelton, Sir Sholto Douglas and Air Marshal Harris ('Guests for Sunday, 28th June': Chequers Lists).

Randolph was in North Africa, recovering from an injury incurred when a jeep in which he was travelling crashed during a Commando raid behind German lines. The doctor who attended him in Alexandria, Samuel Segal, later recalled his patient's two broken lower ribs and 'a great deal of pain'.[1] Randolph had, in fact, dislocated a vertebra, and had to remain in hospital for a month.[2] 'It is very disappointing that we failed to achieve anything,' Randolph wrote to his father from hospital. 'On the other hand, it has filled us with confidence for future operations of a similar kind.'[3]

That Sunday, Churchill telegraphed to Auchinleck, who had just taken direct operational command of the forces in the field: 'Do not vex yourself with anything but the battle. Fight it out wherever it flows. Nothing matters but destroying the enemy's armed and armoured force.' Churchill added: 'A strong stream of reinforcements is approaching. We are sure you are going to win in the end.'[4]

In a telegram direct to Churchill on June 28, General Marshall reported from Washington that not only would the 100 howitzers and 300 tanks be ready for despatch in two weeks' time, but that the tanks would include 'British type radio and compass', as well as tools, spare parts and water cans.[5]

On June 29, while still at Chequers, Churchill prepared his speech on the Vote of Censure. He also found time to write to his doctor, Sir Charles Wilson, who had accompanied him to the United States. 'I was almost sorry,' Churchill wrote, 'not to be able to provide you with some work. But your presence kept the marauders away.'[6]

*   *   *

[1] Lord Segal of Wytham, recollections: letter to the author, 17 January 1982. In 1942 Samuel Segal was Chief Medical Officer, 201 Group, Royal Air Force. In 1945 he was one of two Labour candidates in the General Election, who defeated Randolph and his fellow Conservative, Julian Amery, at Preston.

[2] Of the others involved in the crash, Arthur Merton, the *Daily Telegraph* war correspondent, died in hospital in Alexandria; Fitzroy Maclean was knocked out, did not regain consciousness for three days, and had a fractured collar bone, broken arm and head injuries; Corporal Rose fractured his arm; and David Stirling cracked a bone in his wrist (Brian Roberts, *Randolph: A Study of Churchill's Son*, London 1984, page 225).

[3] 'Secret and Personal', 24 June 1942: Churchill papers, 4/276.

[4] Prime Minister's Personal Telegram, T.923/2, 'Secret and Personal', 28 June 1942: Churchill papers, 20/77.

[5] Telegram of 28 June 1942, 'Secret': Churchill papers, 20/77. The three hundred Sherman tanks, the engines of which were not yet fitted, were sent in convoy from the United States, sailing around the Cape of Good Hope to the Suez Canal. The three hundred engines followed in a second ship. But that ship, while off Bermuda, was sunk by a German submarine. Without even troubling Churchill, Roosevelt and Marshall at once ordered a further supply of Sherman engines to be sent in a fast ship, to overtake the Suez-bound convoy.

[6] Letter of 29 June 1942: Churchill papers, 20/53.

Churchill now prepared himself for a German assault on Cairo. With Auchinleck in the forward zone, responsibility for the defence of the Egyptian capital fell principally upon the new Minister Resident in the Middle East, Richard Casey, the former Australian Minister in the United States. 'While Auchinleck fights at the front,' Churchill telegraphed to Casey on June 30, 'you should insist upon the mobilization for battle of all the rearward services. Everybody in uniform must fight exactly like they would if Kent or Sussex were invaded.' Churchill added, to this Australian whom he had first met on the western front in 1916: 'Tank hunting parties with sticky bombs and bombards, defence to the death of every fortified area or strong building, making every post a winning post and every ditch a last ditch. This is the spirit you have got to inculcate. No general evacuation, no playing for safety. Egypt must be held at all costs.' [1]

On July 1 German forces reached El Alamein, 130 miles inside Egypt, less than 40 miles from Alexandria, and only 80 miles from Cairo. That same day, in the Crimea, the Germans captured the town, fort and harbour of Sebastopol. These twin setbacks for the Allied cause coincided with the first day of the Vote of Censure debate in the House of Commons. The Vote was moved by a Conservative MP, Sir John Wardlaw-Milne, who held the attention of the House until, in a moment of apparent aberration, he proposed that the Duke of Gloucester should be made Commander-in-Chief. 'The House roared with disrespectful laughter,' Henry Channon noted in his diary, 'and I at once saw Winston's face light up, as if a lamp had been lit within him and he smiled genially. He knew now that he was saved, and poor Wardlaw-Milne never quite regained the hearing of the House.' [2]

Wardlaw-Milne had urged that Churchill be replaced by a more effective war leader, arguing that the Prime Minister was interfering, and interfering disastrously, in the military, naval and air effort. But a second anti-Government speaker, Admiral of the Fleet Sir Roger Keyes, argued the reverse, that Churchill was not doing enough and was allowing himself to be swayed and overruled by the bad judgement of the military, naval and air chiefs. According to Keyes, Churchill 'could never be induced to override the advice of the Chiefs of Staff Committee, or to undertake any enterprise, unless they were prepared to share fully with him in the responsibility'. This was hardly the case which Wardlaw-Milne had striven to make, nor was Keyes'

[1] Prime Minister's Personal Telegram, T.932/2, 'Personal and Secret', 30 June 1942: Churchill papers, 20/77.
[2] Channon diary, 1 July 1942: Robert Rhodes James (editor), Chips, op. cit., page 334.

call at the end of his speech: 'We look to the Prime Minister to put his house in order, and to rally the country once again for its immense task.'

As Keyes sat down, a Labour Member rose to point out that the No Confidence motion was directed 'against the central direction of the war'. If the motion were carried, 'the Prime Minister has to go'. Yet Keyes 'is appealing to us to keep the Prime Minister there'. Keyes rose again. 'It would,' he said, 'be a deplorable disaster if the Prime Minister had to go.' [1]

Such opposition as existed was clearly in disarray.

That night, John Martin was 'up late', as he noted in his diary, 'in connection with preparation of PM's speech' on the following day.[2] Two secretaries, Elizabeth Layton and Jo Sturdee, were also up late that night, working until 5.30 a.m. to take down, and then to type out, nearly 9,000 words.

On the following day, July 2, the debate resumed. Churchill worked in his room at the House, finishing his speech. Elizabeth Layton, who was again called upon to type it, wrote home:

Well, it really was quite an exciting day down at the House. I couldn't help wondering if we all shouldn't be out of jobs before nightfall. I went on duty at 1.30—and we were in such a state of nerves that every time the phone rang I jumped perceptibly and Mr Martin fair snatched it off. I had to go in for a while and he was eating his lunch (I remember that the peas wouldn't stay on the fork and he was annoyed); he was in a state of nerves unusual for him, though I must say he is usually a bit worked up before a speech. It is a terrific effort to make one of these hour-and-a-half deliveries. Presently he turned on a really sweet smile and asked me to wait outside (he is always nice to us when he is worked up), so I sat and sat, and sometimes took phone messages, and often the bell rang and Mr Martin or Mr Rowan hurried in.[3]

The second day of the debate was opened by Aneurin Bevan. 'The Prime Minister,' he said, 'wins debate after debate and loses battle after battle. The country is beginning to say that he fights debates like a war and the war like a debate.' According to Bevan, the strategy of the war was wrong, and the 'wrong weapons' were being produced. In addition, the army was 'ridden by class prejudice'. It was 'badly led'.

In summing up against the Government, a former Secretary of State

[1] *Hansard*, 1 July 1942.
[2] John Martin diary, 1 July 1942: Martin papers.
[3] Elizabeth Layton, letter of 14 July 1942: Nel papers. Leslie Rowan was a Private Secretary to Churchill from 1941 to 1945, then (at Potsdam), his Principal Private Secretary. He kept no diary. Jock Colville, who did, later wrote of Rowan: 'Of the brightest intelligence, he was serious of purpose but possessed a rollicking sense of fun.' (John Colville, *The Fringes of Power, Downing Street Diaries 1939–1955*, London 1985, page 764.)

for War, Leslie Hore-Belisha, asked the House of Commons how it could place reliance 'in judgements that have so repeatedly turned out to be misguided', and he referred back to the loss of Crete in the summer of 1941, as well as to the fall of Singapore and the defeat in Libya.

While Hore-Belisha had been speaking, Churchill was still putting the finishing touches to his speech. 'Mr Hore-Belisha got up at three,' noted Elizabeth Layton, 'and we kept getting messages to say that HE ought to be in the Chamber. However, HE was only about five minutes late, and I felt I should say a little prayer for him as he went off.'[1]

Churchill, following Hore-Belisha, defended his record and that of his administration, accepting responsibility 'for everything that has happened', and went on to explain the system of decision making:

Under the present arrangement the three Chiefs of Staff, sitting almost continuously together, carry on the war from day to day, assisted not only by the machinery of the great departments which serve them, but by the Combined General Staff, in making their decisions effective through the Navy, Army, and Air Forces over which they exercise direct operational control. I supervise their activities, whether as Prime Minister or Minister of Defence. I work myself under the supervision and control of the War Cabinet, to whom all important matters are referred, and whom I have to carry with me in all major decisions. Nearly all my work has been done in writing, and a complete record exists of all the directions I have given, the inquiries I have made, and the telegrams I have drafted. I shall be perfectly content to be judged by them.[2]

Churchill asked 'no favours' he said, either for himself or for the Government. He had undertaken the office of Prime Minister and Minister of Defence 'after defending my predecessor to the best of my ability', at a time when the life of the empire 'hung upon a thread', and he added: 'I am your servant, and you have the right to dismiss me when you please. What you have no right to do is to ask me to bear responsibilities without the power of effective action. . . .' Churchill ended:

---

[1] Elizabeth Layton, letter of 14 July 1942: Nel papers.

[2] Three weeks later Churchill telegraphed to General Smuts, in South Africa: 'All decisions are taken by the War Cabinet on the advice of the Chiefs of Staff's Committee, with both of which bodies I live in the closest association. Complete unity prevails inside this circle. This unity extends to the larger War Cabinet circle, which includes Dominions and Indian representatives and various additional Ministers of Cabinet rank, but, of course, it is not possible to initiate all war plans in so numerous a gathering. I can well believe there is fretfulness outside these two concentric circles. We are never likely to run short of volunteers for the higher direction of the war. However, the political situation, both Party and Parliamentary, is quite solid, and, of course, it is well known that I would not continue to bear the responsibility without the modest directing powers I possess.' (Prime Minister's Personal Telegram, T.1036/2, 25 July 1942: Churchill papers, 20/88.)

All over the world, throughout the United States, as I can testify, in Russia, far away in China, and throughout every subjugated country, all our friends are waiting to know whether there is a strong, solid Government in Britain and whether its national leadership is to be challenged or not.

Every vote counts. If those who have assailed us are reduced to contemptible proportions and their Vote of Censure on the National Government is converted to a vote of censure upon its authors, make no mistake, a cheer will go up from every friend of Britain and every faithful servant of our cause, and the knell of disappointment will ring in the ears of the tyrants we are striving to overthrow.[1]

'Exactly at 5 he finished,' noted Elizabeth Layton, and she added: 'the Debate closed at 5, and he didn't want to finish a moment before time, so no one else would be able to cap his remarks!'[2]

The House voted, defeating the motion of No Confidence by 475 votes to 25. 'Good for you,' Roosevelt telegraphed that same day.[3] 'Action of House of Commons today delighted me,' Harry Hopkins telegraphed from Washington, adding: 'These have been some of the bad days. No doubt there will be others. Those who run for cover with every reverse, the timid and the faint of heart, will have no part in winning the war.' Hopkins ended: 'I know you are of good heart, for your military defeats and ours, and our certain victories to come, will be shared together. More power to you.'[4]

Hopkins' telegram gave Churchill much pleasure. 'Thank you so much my friend,' he replied. 'I knew you and the President would be glad of this domestic victory. I hope one day I shall have something more solid to report.'[5]

At half past five that afternoon, Churchill was back at Downing Street, where he received a young officer just returned from Cairo, Julian Amery, the son of the Secretary of State for India, Leo Amery. The tale which the young man had to tell was of low morale in Cairo, and of troops, especially from the armoured units, who had 'lost confidence in the Command'. Amery later recalled how: 'I went on to say that, as far as I could judge, Auchinleck was doing all in his power to save the situation. But one extra thing could still be done to influence the outcome. This was to give a boost to the Army's morale;

---

[1] 'Central Direction of the War', *Hansard*, 2 July 1942, columns 527–610. Those voting against the Government included Aneurin Bevan (who had seconded the No Confidence motion), Leslie Hore-Belisha, Admiral of the Fleet Sir Roger Keyes, James Maxton and Sidney Silverman.

[2] Elizabeth Layton, letter of 14 July 1942: Nel papers.

[3] President to Prime Minister, No. 160, Washington, 2 July 1942: Churchill papers, 20/77.

[4] Telegram No. 0129, Washington, 2 July 1942: Churchill papers, 20/77.

[5] Prime Minister's Personal Telegram, T.943/2, 3 July 1942: Churchill papers, 20/77.

and the only way of doing this that I could see was for Churchill to go to Egypt himself.' Churchill then asked: 'What should I do out there to improve morale?' 'Your presence among the troops in the battle area would be enough. It would have an electric effect,' Amery replied. 'You mean just go round and talk to them.' 'Yes, to the officers and to the men.'[1]

That night Churchill dined with his brother Jack, and Anthony Eden.[2] There was much discussion of the war situation, 'the problems of the army, its Trade Union outlook, paucity of tanks etc'. Eden added: 'Winston said repeatedly we had not done as well as we should, "I am ashamed," etc.' When Churchill suggested that he fly at once to Cairo, Eden said he did not like the idea, as Churchill would not be able to help, and would be 'in the way'. 'You mean like a great blue-bottle buzzing over a huge cowpat?' Churchill asked. That, said Eden, was exactly what he meant. Brendan Bracken, who appeared at that moment, likewise opposed Churchill's journey, on the grounds of risk. 'W would not have it,' Eden noted. 'Anyway,' Churchill told Eden, 'he had made his testament in my favour before he went to the United States and he was not indispensable.'[3]

In Cairo there was a feeling of imminent invasion. Should Egypt be overrun, Churchill told the War Cabinet at noon on July 3, 'the enemy should be fought ruthlessly and with Russian methods applied'.[4] That night Brooke found Churchill 'in one of his unpleasant moods, going back over old ground and asking where the 750,000 men in the Middle East were, what they were doing, and why they were not fighting'. In Churchill's mind, Singapore and Tobruk were to be followed by Cairo. Afterwards, Brooke noted, 'with that astounding charm of his, he came up to me and said to me, "I am sorry, Brookie, if I had to be unpleasant about Auchinleck and the Middle East." '[5]

The June convoy to Russia, PQ17, with 200,000 tons of war material, had sailed from Iceland for Archangel on June 27. The convoy consisted of thirty-four merchant ships, and twenty-one escort vessels including six destroyers and two submarines. Also in support were two British and two American cruisers: the first joint Anglo-American escort, and three further destroyers. On the morning of

---

[1] Julian Amery, *Approach March, a venture in autobiography*, London 1973, pages 308–9.
[2] Eden was later to marry Jack Churchill's daughter, Clarissa.
[3] Eden diary, 2 July 1942: Eden memoirs, *The Reckoning*, op. cit., page 332.
[4] War Cabinet No. 85 of 1942, 3 July 1942, Confidential Annex: Cabinet papers, 65/31.
[5] Brooke diary, 3 July 1942: Bryant, op. cit., volume 1, page 419.

July 4 a merchant ship was sunk by torpedoes fired from a German aircraft. That evening, three more of the merchantmen were torpedoed by German aircraft. Then, believing that the *Tirpitz*, which had left Trondheim more than twenty-four hours earlier, was about to attack, Dudley Pound ordered the escort force to withdraw immediately 'at high speed', and the convoy 'to disperse and proceed to Russian ports'. Those signals were timed at 9.11 p.m. and 9.23 p.m. At 9.35 p.m. a third signal was sent from the Admiralty: 'Convoy is to scatter.'

The knowledge that two American cruisers were at risk, as well as the British, may, Churchill later reflected, 'have disturbed the poise' with which Pound was 'accustomed to deal with these heart-breaking decisions'. Churchill had not been consulted. 'Indeed,' he later wrote, 'so strictly was the secret of these orders being sent on the First Sea Lord's authority being guarded by the Admiralty that it was not until after the war that I learned these facts.'[1]

The Germans did indeed send *Tirpitz* to attack the convoy. But they recalled her as soon as they established that the convoy was coming under heavy and successful attack from aircraft and submarines. Without its escort, the scattered convoy was at the mercy of these attackers. In particular, air attacks from the German bases in north Norway took a heavy toll of the unprotected merchant ships. If the convoy and its escort had continued as a formed body they would have been better protected against air and submarine attack, but they would probably then have been attacked by *Tirpitz* and her squadron, including other major warships. Losses might well in that case have been even heavier. As it was, of the thirty-four merchant vessels which had left Iceland, twenty-three were sunk, fourteen of them American. Only eleven ships, six of them American, two British, two Russian and one Panamanian, reached Archangel. Of the 200,000 tons of war materials which had left Iceland, only 70,000 tons were delivered. Churchill on learning of the loss, gave immediate instructions that all Red Cross supplies to Russia should in future be distributed 'in at least six ships of any one convoy'.[2] The disaster to PQ17 also made Churchill keener on the proposed British landing in northern Norway, to seize the German air bases there. 'We are having frightful difficulties about the Russian convoys,' he telegraphed to Roosevelt when the extent of the PQ17 disaster was known. 'All the more necessary to try to clear the way and maintain contact with Russia.'[3]

*   *   *

[1] Winston S. Churchill, *The Second World War*, volume 4, London 1951, pages 235–6.

[2] Prime Minister's Personal Minute, M.276/2 (to the Minister of War Transport), 'Action this Day', 7 July 1942: Churchill papers, 20/67.

[3] Prime Minister's Personal Telegram, T.967/2, Prime Minister to President, No. 107, 'Personal and Secret', 8 July 1942: Churchill papers, 20/77.

The time had now come, Churchill believed, to tell first Roosevelt and then Stalin, that the 1942 landings in France, operation 'Sledge-hammer', would not take place. 'No responsible British General, Admiral or Air Marshal,' he noted for the Chiefs of Staff on July 5, was prepared to recommend it 'as a desirable or even as a practicable operation in 1942'. Confirmation of additional American landing-craft had not been obtained, nor could the three American divisions required reach Britain in time to be trained 'for the special amphibious work required'. Additionally, if 'Sledgehammer' went ahead in September 1942, it would interrupt the training of troops, and put at risk many of the landing-craft required for the far larger 'Round-Up' operation planned for 1943. 'It may therefore be said,' Churchill con-cluded, 'that premature action in 1942, while probably ending in dis-aster, would decisively injure the prospects of well-organized, large-scale action in 1943.' In 1942, the 'urgency', both military and political, was for the northern Norway plan, operation 'Jupiter'. 'Our whole power to help Russia in any effectual manner this year,' Churchill wrote, 'depends upon our driving the enemy aircraft from the northern airfields of Norway.' [1]

At the Chiefs of Staff Committee on July 6, at which Churchill presided, 'it was unanimously agreed', as the minutes recorded, 'that Operation "Sledgehammer" offered no hope of success and would merely ruin all prospects of "Round-Up" in 1943'. On the following day, when Churchill reported to the War Cabinet that his advisers were in harmony on this question, the War Cabinet agreed that a cross-Channel attack in 1942 was 'out of the question', as it might put back the landings of 1943 'for two or three months'. Churchill also urged that a detailed examination of the northern Norway expedition, operation 'Jupiter', should go ahead. It offered 'such attractive possi-bilities from so many points of view', Churchill explained, 'that it seemed desirable that no effort should be spared to work out a prac-ticable plan'. [2] But with every decision which Churchill, the Chiefs of Staff and the War Cabinet now reached, there was the need to con-vince the Americans. This was both a burden and a necessity: 'As America is now our great strategic reserve for the final blows,' General Smuts telegraphed to Churchill on July 7, 'much of your time will have to be devoted wisely to guiding Washington in its war effort and not letting vital war direction slip out of our hands.' Smuts added: 'I think your service in this respect can now be at least as great as your

---

[1] Prime Minister's Personal Minute, D.125/2, 'Most Secret', 5 July 1942: Churchill papers, 20/17.
[2] War Cabinet No. 87 of 1942, 7 July 1942, Confidential Annex: Cabinet papers, 65/31.

Empire war service. Your contacts with Roosevelt are now a most valuable war asset. . . .' [1]

In a telegram to Roosevelt on July 8, Churchill stressed that 'Gymnast', the Americans' own planned landing in French North Africa, was 'by far the best chance for effecting relief to the Russian front in 1942'. This, Churchill added, 'has all along been in harmony with your ideas. In fact it is your commanding idea. Here is the true Second Front of 1942.'

The War Cabinet and the Defence Committee both agreed, Churchill told Roosevelt, that the landing in French North Africa was 'the safest and most fruitful stroke that can be delivered this autumn', and one which Britain would aid 'in every way', either by the transfer of 'American or British' landing forces from the United Kingdom, or with landing craft and shipping. 'You can if you choose,' Churchill added, 'put the punch in partly from here and the rest direct across the Atlantic.' [2] In a second telegram that day, Churchill suggested to Roosevelt that General Marshall should command 'maximum "Bolero" ', the cross-Channel build-up of American forces in Britain. 'We shall sustain him,' Churchill wrote, 'to the last inch.' [3]

At the War Cabinet on July 7, there was another discussion about the northern Norway expedition. Dudley Pound pointed out that, according to a 'most intensive study' by the Chiefs of Staff, 'Jupiter' would depend for its success upon a British air striking force being established at the Russian port of Murmansk. But 'in view of our recent experiences with the PQ convoys, it was by no means certain that this could be done'. In addition, to control all German airfields between Petsamo and Narvik 'by separate simultaneous operations' would entail 'operations on a large scale'. [4] On July 8 Churchill entrusted the planning of 'Jupiter' to a Canadian officer, General McNaughton, minuting to the Chiefs of Staff: 'The decision whether or not to adopt the plan will be reserved.' [5]

Not only Churchill, but also Eden, was upset by the Chiefs of Staff opposition to 'Jupiter'. 'Chiefs of Staff have no ideas and oppose everything,' Sir Alexander Cadogan noted in his diary on July 8, after a talk with Eden, while Churchill had said, as Eden reported:

---

[1] Telegram No. 1211, 'Most Secret and Personal', received 8 a.m., 7 July 1942: Churchill papers, 20/77.

[2] Prime Minister's Personal Telegram, T.967/2, Prime Minister to President, No. 107, 'Personal and Secret', 8 June 1942: Churchill papers, 20/77.

[3] Prime Minister's Personal Telegram, T.971/2, Prime Minister to President No. 108, 'Personal and Secret', 8 July 1942: Churchill papers, 20/88.

[4] War Cabinet No. 87 of 1942, 7 July 1942, Confidential Annex: Cabinet papers, 65/31.

[5] Prime Minister's Personal Minute, M.278/2, 8 July 1942: Churchill papers, 20/67.

'We'd better put an advertisement in the papers, asking for ideas.'[1]

Fears that the Germans might push on to Cairo were slightly lessened in the second week of July, as reinforcements to Auchinleck raised the size of his army to 'about double Rommel in men', as Churchill reported to the Australian and New Zealand Prime Ministers on July 11, sending them also details of the American tank and air reinforcements to Egypt, and of Stalin's willingness to send three divisions of 'partly-equipped Poles' as well as to release the forty American fighter bombers then on their way to Russia. 'All ideas of evacuation have been repressed,' Churchill wrote, 'the intention being to fight for every yard of ground to the end.' Such a situation would not however, in his view, arise.[2] That same day he instructed Sir Charles Portal to authorize 'heavy and continuous bombing on the largest scale' against Benghazi and Tobruk, so that the Germans were denied the use of them 'as supply ports'.[3]

From Cairo, Auchinleck pressed for more troops to be sent to his 'northern' theatre, to block any possible advance by the Germans through Turkey or Persia, into Palestine and Syria. 'The only way in which a sufficient army can be gathered in the northern theatre,' Churchill telegraphed on July 12, 'is by your defeating or destroying General Rommel and driving him at least to a safe distance.' If Auchinleck were to fail in defeating or destroying Rommel, 'then there is no possibility of a transference to the north, and we shall continue to be entirely dependent on the Russian front holding'.[4] From Auchinleck, however, came news of a delay in any renewed offensive, owing to the 'bad condition' of the British 'Valentine' tanks when in action on July 11.[5] 'Severe measures must be taken,' Churchill minuted on July 13, 'against the delinquents.'[6]

---

[1] Cadogan diary, 8 July 1942: David Dilks (editor), op. cit., page 461.

[2] Prime Minister's Personal Telegram, T.989/2 (to John Curtin and Peter Fraser), 11 July 1942: Churchill papers, 20/88. The details of Russian aid began: 'To show you what a good comrade Premier Stalin is proving himself. . . .'

[3] Prime Minister's Personal Minute, M.283/2, 11 July 1942: Churchill papers, 20/67.

[4] Prime Minister's Personal Telegram, T.986/2, 'Personal', 12 July 1942: Churchill papers, 20/77.

[5] Telegram No. 2274, 12 July 1942.

[6] Prime Minister's Personal Minute, M.285/2 (to the Secretary of State for War), 13 July 1942, 'Secret': Churchill papers, 20/67. On the following day General Auchinleck telegraphed to Churchill: 'General condition of these tanks was better than those received earlier this year, but the performance of the engines was below standard. Some higher gears could not be engaged. In a number of cases the cylinder head gaskets were blowing. All engines required tuning and adjustments to steering gear had to be carried out. In most cases clutch withdrawal levers required adjustment. All 2-pounder guns required buffer piston clearances checked. This is a

The flow of American aid to Auchinleck promised to prove crucial in preventing any German incursion into the Nile Delta. Noting this, Churchill felt the need to show Roosevelt that Britain was not entirely a debtor. 'I feel anxiety about the negative attitude we are adopting towards Admiral King and the American operations in the Pacific,' Churchill minuted on July 13 to A. V. Alexander and Dudley Pound. 'I promised we would assist by making diversions in any way possible, but of course I did not commit us to any particular operation. We must now show a helpful attitude.' Admiral Somerville had two 'first-class carriers', as well as *Warspite*. 'He has been doing nothing for several months,' Churchill commented, 'and we cannot really keep this fleet idle indefinitely.' [1]

At a meeting of the Defence Committee on the evening of July 13 it was decided, on the recommendation of the Chiefs of Staff, that the losses in convoy PQ17 made it necessary to cancel not only the July convoy, but those for August and September as well. [2] 'If half had got through we would have persevered,' Churchill explained to Roosevelt, 'but with only about a quarter arriving the operation is not good enough.' But of nearly six hundred tanks in PQ17, five hundred had been lost. 'This cannot help anybody but the enemy.'

Churchill also told Roosevelt, that in a single week, nearly 400,000 tons of shipping had been lost, including the Russian convoy, 'a rate unexampled in either this war or the last, and, if maintained, evidently beyond all existing replacement plans'. [3]

Churchill had now to tell Stalin not only that PQ18 was cancelled, but also that no further Arctic convoys would sail that summer—after which Archangel would be ice-bound and inaccessible. On the night of July 14 he dined with the Soviet Ambassador, Ivan Maisky, and was joined after dinner by Eden. Maisky had already told Eden of

---

Middle East modification which must be done in United Kingdom. They were not marked, so checking had to be done. Approximately 160 items of tank fittings were deficient of which 120 were important, such as towing shackle, armament components, periscope components, power traverse control boxes. Some of these items may have been pilfered in transit.' (Telegram of 14 July 1942: Churchill papers, 20/89.)

[1] Prime Minister's Personal Minute, 290/2, 13 July 1942: Churchill papers, 20/67. Vice-Admiral Sir James Somerville had retired from the Royal Navy in 1939, but returned to the Admiralty on the outbreak of war. From 1942 to 1944 he served as Commander-in-Chief, Eastern Fleet, with the rank of Admiral. In 1944 he was appointed head of the British Admiralty Delegation, Washington.

[2] 'After a brief discussion, the Committee agreed to recommend that convoys should not be sent to Northern Russia in present circumstances' (Chiefs of Staff Committee No. 205 of 1942, 13 July 1942: Cabinet papers, 79/22. Those present were Brooke, Pound, Portal and Ismay.)

[3] Prime Minister's Personal Telegram, T.998/2, Prime Minister to President, No. 113, 'Personal and Secret', 14 July 1942: Churchill papers, 20/77.

'very grave' reports from the Russian front.[1] In an attempt to limit the convoy ban to PQ17 alone, Churchill suggested to Pound and A. V. Alexander that the Admiralty examine the following plan: assuming 'all goes well' in Malta, he wrote, send to the Arctic the two most modern aircraft carriers of the Mediterranean Fleet, *Indomitable* and *Victorious*, as well as the older carriers *Argus* and *Eagle*, 'at least' five of the auxiliary aircraft carriers, all the Dido class cruisers and at least twenty-five destroyers. This armada should then proceed to Archangel 'keeping southward, not hugging the ice, but seeking the clearest weather, and thus fight it out with the enemy'. If the supply ships could be moved in convoy 'under an umbrella of at least 100 fighter aircraft'—from the aircraft carriers—'we ought to be able to fight our way through and out again, and if a Fleet action results, so much the better'.[2]

Neither Pound nor A. V. Alexander were prepared to accept such a plan. Churchill at once telegraphed to Stalin with the news of the cancellation of the remaining convoys for 1942, and setting out the dangers not only to Britain, but also to the planned second front, if the convoy system were to lead to a clash between British and German naval forces. As Churchill explained:

If one or two of our very few most powerful battleships were to be lost or even seriously damaged while *Tirpitz* and her consorts, soon to be joined by *Scharnhorst*, remained in action, the whole command of the Atlantic would be lost. Besides affecting the food supplies by which we live, our war effort would be crippled; and above all the great convoys of American troops across the ocean, rising presently to as many as 80,000 in a month, would be prevented, and the building up of a really strong second front in 1943 rendered impossible.

Churchill went on to inform Stalin that his naval advisers were 'unable to hold out any hopes that convoys attempting to make the passage in perpetual daylight would fare any better, even if as well, as PQ17'. To attempt to send any further convoys to Russia that summer 'could bring no benefit to you and would only involve grievous injury to our common cause'.

Although PQ18 was cancelled, Britain was prepared to despatch some of its ships 'immediately' to the Persian Gulf. The Soviet authorities in London would be consulted as to which priority cargoes should go by this route. By October it would be possible to send 75,000 tons of supplies a month on the trans-Persia route. Meanwhile, Britain was asking the United States for further rolling stock and trucks to increase that tonnage still further, possibly to as high as 100,000 tons for

[1] Eden memoirs, *The Reckoning*, op. cit., page 336.
[2] Prime Minister's Personal Minute, M.294/2, 'Secret', 'Action this Day', 15 July 1942: Churchill papers, 20/67.

October. This was 30,000 tons higher than the amount which had reached Russia on PQ17.

Churchill now returned to his 'Jupiter' plan, asking Stalin to study the possibility of a joint Anglo-Soviet expedition to northern Norway, to 'drive the enemy out' of the airfields there.[1] If, in North Africa, Rommel were beaten back by the autumn, Britain 'might be able to send powerful air forces' to operate on the left, or southern flank, of the Russian front line. The three divisions of Polish troops then in Russia, which Stalin had offered to join their fellow-Polish soldiers then in Palestine, would prevent any diminution of the preparations 'now going forward on a vast scale for the Anglo-American mass invasion of the Continent'. The early preparations for a second front had already led the Germans to withdraw two heavy bomber groups from South Russia to France. 'Believe me,' Churchill ended, 'there is nothing that is useful and sensible that we and the Americans will not do to help you in your grand struggle. The President and I are ceaselessly searching for means to overcome the extraordinary difficulties which geography, salt water and the enemy's air power interpose.'[2]

Stalin still believed, however, that the principal help to Russia lay in an almost immediate Anglo-American landing in northern Europe. But Churchill and his Chiefs of Staff were convinced that such a landing could not take place until 1943. On July 16 General Marshall, Admiral King and Harry Hopkins flew from Washington to London to finalize the competing claims of the North African landings planned for later in 1942, and the major Cross-Channel invasion of 1943. Before the three Americans left Washington, the head of the British Joint Staff Mission in Washington, Field Marshal Dill, telegraphed to Churchill after a talk with Marshall, to warn the Prime Minister that Marshall's 'first love' for action was still the Pacific, and that the General was convinced that Churchill too did not want Europe, but the 'Gymnast' plans for an American landing in North Africa to have priority. Marshall was also convinced, Dill wrote, that there had been 'no real drive' behind the preparations for a cross-Channel landing in 1943. In addition, Dill warned, there were also 'highly placed Americans who do not believe that anything better than a stalemate with Germany is possible'. Dill's telegram ended:

---

[1] On 18 July 1943 Ivan Maisky told Sir Alexander Cadogan that the Soviet army was 'too busy' elsewhere to be able to participate in the northern Norway operation. 'That rather exonerates us!' Cadogan noted in his diary (Cadogan diary, 18 July 1943: David Dilks, editor, *op. cit.*, page 463).

[2] Prime Minister's Personal Telegram, T.1000/2, 'Personal, Most Secret', 14 July 1942: Churchill papers, 20/88. The words 'my comrade, and friend', after the words 'Believe me', were dictated by Churchill, but omitted in the version of this telegram as finally sent (Prime Minister's Personal Telegram, T.1020/2, 17 July 1942: Churchill papers, 20/78).

May I suggest with all respect that you must convince your visitors that you are determined to beat the Germans, that you will strike them on the continent of Europe at the earliest possible moment even on a limited scale, and that anything which detracts from this main effort will receive no support from you at all?

Marshall believes that your first love is 'Gymnast', just as his is 'Bolero', and that with the smallest provocation you always revert to your old love. Unless you can convince him of your unswerving devotion to 'Bolero' everything points to a complete reversal of our present agreed strategy and the withdrawal of America to a war of her own in the Pacific, leaving us with limited American assistance to make out as best we can against Germany.[1]

Roosevelt's instructions to Hopkins, Marshall and King were that they should reach 'immediate agreement' with the British on 'joint operational plans' for 1942 and 1943. His premise, Roosevelt wrote, was that Germany should be defeated before Japan. 'Defeat of Germany,' he told his three emissaries, 'means the defeat of Japan, probably without firing a shot or losing a life.'[2]

On July 16 the Joint Intelligence Committee, in a paper for the Chiefs of Staff Committee, calculated, on the basis of its precise knowledge of German military strength on the eastern front, that even if Germany did not eliminate Russia in the autumn of 1942 she could and would withdraw 'sufficient land forces' from the eastern front to be able to count on resisting 'any Allied landing in Europe'. At the same time, the Joint Intelligence Committee warned, there was always the danger that the Germans themselves might occupy French North Africa, thus greatly increasing the threat to Allied shipping. If Russia were still fighting at the end of 1942, the Joint Intelligence Committee's report added, and if the Allies 'copied the German policy and occupied neutral territory', the Mediterranean would be Germany's Achilles heel.[3]

On the eve of the visit of Hopkins, Marshall and King, all indications, strategic, political and Intelligence, as seen in London, pointed to a landing in French North Africa as against a cross-Channel landing, as the more propitious battle zone for the coming nine months.

On the evening of July 18, Churchill and the Chiefs of Staff Committee met at Chequers to consider the imminent American visit, and to examine once more the British arguments in favour of 'Gymnast' as against 'Sledgehammer'. At this meeting were Churchill, Pound,

[1] Joint Staff Mission Telegram, JSM 300, 'Personal', 15 July 1942: Churchill papers, 20/78.
[2] 'Instructions for London Conference, July 1942', 16 July 1942: Robert E. Sherwood, *The White House Papers of Harry L. Hopkins*, London 1949, volume 2, pages 603–5.
[3] Joint Intelligence Committee Report No. 265 of 1942, 16 July 1942: Cabinet papers, 121/412.

Portal, Brooke, Mountbatten and Ismay. Lord Cherwell was also present, although not a member of the Committee. They concluded once again that the Americans must be persuaded that the 'only feasible proposition' for 1942 'appeared to be' an American landing in French North Africa. This operation 'would in effect be the right wing of our Second Front'. If necessary, British troops could participate in the 'more easterly' landings, as could British naval units.

The fate of Russia remained high on the British agenda. At the Chequers meeting of July 18, it was also agreed that 'if things went very badly on the Russian southern flank', serious consideration would have to be given to asking the Americans to send forces to the Levant-Caspian front. It was 'to be remembered', however, as the minutes recorded, that the transportation of a single division to the Levant-Caspian front would involve the same amount of shipping as for three divisions for 'Bolero'.[1]

On July 19 General Marshall and Admiral King began their discussions with the American military representatives in London, of whom Eisenhower was the senior. That same day, Hopkins went to Chequers, where, as he telegraphed to Roosevelt, he found Churchill 'pretty restless and quite unhappy that we did not go to see him in the first place'.[2] Three days later, on July 22, in the Cabinet room at 10 Downing Street, the three Americans argued before Churchill and the British Chiefs of Staff in favour of a bridgehead to be held on the Cherbourg peninsula. 'Without "Sledgehammer",' Marshall warned, 'we were faced with a defensive attitude in the European theatre.'[3]

On July 22 Churchill and his Chiefs of Staff turned to the War Cabinet for support against the Americans. The Chiefs of Staff were opposed to 'Sledgehammer', Brooke explained, because Cherbourg lay 'on the fringe of the area over which fighters could operate from this country'. 'I had no trouble in convincing the Cabinet,' he noted in his diary that night.[4] After Brooke had spoken, Mountbatten gave the War Cabinet his reasons, as Chief of Combined Operations, for opposing the attack on Cherbourg. Such an operation, he argued, would not really help Russia 'since we could not bring our strong Air Force fully to bear against the enemy's Air Force in this area'. Dudley Pound then spoke in favour of the North Africa plan.

As the meeting came to an end, Churchill asked each member of the War Cabinet to give his view about the Cherbourg operation.

[1] Chiefs of Staff Committee No. 75 (Operations) of 1942, 10.30 p.m., 18 July 1942: Cabinet papers, 79/56.
[2] Robert E. Sherwood, *The White House Papers of Harry L. Hopkins*, volume 2, London 1949, page 609.
[3] Combined Staff Conference, 22 July 1942: Cabinet papers, 99/190.
[4] Brooke diary, 22 July 1942: Bryant, *op. cit.*, volume 1, page 425.

The official minutes of the meeting recorded that all the members of the War Cabinet 'expressed themselves in favour of making it clear that we did not agree to operation "Sledgehammer" being carried out in 1942', and favoured an operation on the North African coast.[1]

Confronted by this unanimity of War Cabinet, Chiefs of Staff and Prime Minister, the three Americans reported back to Roosevelt for instructions. The British unanimity, and the strength of argument that lay behind it, was decisive; two days later, Marshall reported to Brooke that the Americans had accepted the British position. 'Sledgehammer' was dead. 'Gymnast', enlarged to 'Mohican', and now re-named 'Torch', was alive. The joint Anglo-American war effort to help Russia, and to form a second front in 1942, would not be against northern Europe, but against North Africa. 'A very trying week,' Brooke noted in his diary that night, 'but it is satisfactory to feel that we have got just what we wanted out of US Chiefs.'[2]

Churchill had telegraphed these decisions to Stalin on July 14; Stalin's reply was sent on July 23. 'First,' Stalin declared, 'the British Government refuses to continue the sending of war materials to the Soviet Union via the Northern route. Second, in spite of the agreed communiqué concerning the urgent tasks of creating a second front in 1942, the British Government postpones this matter until 1943.' The Soviet naval experts, Stalin added, considered the arguments used to end the northern convoys 'wholly unconvincing', believing 'that with goodwill and readiness to fulfil the contracted obligations these convoys could be regularly undertaken and heavy losses could be inflicted on the enemy'. As to convoy PQ17, Stalin told Churchill, 'our experts found it also difficult to understand and to explain the order given by the Admiralty that the escorting vessels of the PQ17 should return whereas the cargo boats should disperse and try to reach the Soviet ports one by one without any protection at all. Of course, I do not think that regular convoys to the Soviet Northern ports could be effected without risk or losses.'

Not only the fact of the recall of PQ17, but even more its timing, caused Stalin to protest. 'I never expected,' he wrote, 'that the British Government will stop despatch of war materials to us just at the very

[1] War Cabinet No. 94 of 1942, 22 July 1942, Confidential Annex: Cabinet papers, 65/31. The North African operation was here given the codename 'Mohican', described by General Brooke as 'a more powerful and extended version' of operation 'Gymnast'. The members of the War Cabinet (all of whom were present on this occasion) were: Churchill, Attlee, Cripps, Anderson, Eden, Lyttelton, Bevin and Lord Halifax (who, as Ambassador to the United States, was a member of the War Cabinet and, being in London, was present at this decisive meeting). The others present, but not members of the War Cabinet, were A. V. Alexander, Sir James Grigg, Sir Archibald Sinclair, Brooke, Pound, Portal and Mountbatten.

[2] Brooke diary, 24 July 1942: Bryant, *op. cit.*, volume 1, page 428.

moment when the Soviet Union, in view of the serious situation on the Soviet–German front, requires these materials more than ever. It is obvious that the transport via Persian Gulf could in no way compensate for the cessation of convoys to the Northern ports.'

Stalin's telegram of July 23 ended with a statement that, with regard to the 'creating of a second front in Europe, I am afraid it is not being treated with the seriousness it deserves. Taking fully into account the present position on the Soviet–German front, I must state in the most emphatic manner that the Soviet government cannot acquiesce in the postponement of a second front in Europe until 1943.' [1]

The decisions which had been reached, Churchill telegraphed to Smuts on July 25, represented 'complete unity between soldiers and statesmen and our two countries'. [2] This 'complete unity' could not hide, however, a continuing American dislike of the decision to give up a cross-Channel landing in 1942. On July 24 Churchill asked Eden to see Gilbert Winant, whom Eden found 'very critical of us for not starting up second front'. Eden noted in his diary: 'I reminded him that his people did not suggest anything before October which would be useless for Russia and even then scale could not be enough, on American plan, to affect Eastern front. He had no arguments, but was obstinate and said we should ask Americans for what we wanted by given date and put it up to them. I told him I saw no use in this since we both knew American contribution must be of the smallest this year. I have never seen Winant so put out. He dislikes "Gymnast".' [3]

On July 24 Hopkins, Marshall and King went with Churchill to Greenwich. John Martin, who accompanied them, described the evening in a letter home:

I have never seen so many Admirals. Their Lordships gave us an excellent dinner, after which we went to the young officers' gun-room, where the PM toasted Admiral (Jackie) Fisher's grandson who was one of them and happened to be celebrating his 21st birthday. Alexander, the First Lord, then sat down at the piano and for about an hour thumped out I should think every song in the Students' Song Book and conducted community singing with great gusto. The room was crowded with sub-lieutenants, admirals and Wrens (who have a training course for officers at Greenwich), all singing at the tops of their voices (not excluding the PM), the most cheerful party I have seen for a long time. Altogether a memorable evening, which the Americans obviously enjoyed enormously. It ended with Auld Lang Syne and the two National Anthems. [4]

[1] Telegram sent on 23 July 1942: Premier papers, 3/463.
[2] Prime Minister's Personal Telegram, T. 1036/2, 'Most Secret and Personal', 25 July 1942: Churchill papers, 20/78.
[3] Eden diary, 24 July 1942: Eden memoirs, *The Reckoning, op. cit.*, page 337.
[4] Letter of 26 July 1942: Martin papers.

On Saturday, July 25, Marshall, Hopkins and King were Churchill's guests at Chequers. 'Besides reaching complete agreement on action,' Churchill telegraphed to Roosevelt two days later, 'relations of cordial intimacy and comradeship have been cemented between our high officers.' Churchill doubted however if success would have been achieved without Hopkins's 'invaluable aid'.[1] In reply, Roosevelt expressed his own happiness at the 'successful meeting of minds', and he added: 'I cannot help feeling that the past week represented a turning-point in the whole war and that now we are on our way shoulder to shoulder.'[2]

Among those who met Churchill in July 1942 was the Director of Military Operations, General Kennedy. 'Ring me up at any time if you have any news, or would like to give me a fresh appreciation,' Churchill had told Kennedy after a meeting on July 17, and he added: 'I am on the scrambler all night.' Returning to the War Office, Kennedy wrote in his diary:

Winston certainly inspires confidence. I do admire the unhurried way in which he gets through such a colossal amount of work, and yet never seems otherwise than at leisure. He was particularly genial and good-humoured today. I can well understand how those around him become devoted to him—and dominated by him. I remember Dudley Pound once saying, 'You cannot help loving that man,' and I can quite see the truth of this sentiment. There is one thing that Winston's enemies and critics must admit—he has only one interest in life at this moment, and that is to win the war. Every waking moment is devoted to that. He lives his peculiar life, indoors, and rarely going out. Yet this seems to suit him well, and he shows little sign of wear and tear, and he looks in better health than some of the other politicians who work less than he does. Of course he has not the worry of departmental life, with its constant interruptions and distractions, and he can arrange his routine as he wishes. It is an extraordinary *tour de force* all the same.[3]

---

[1] Prime Minister's Personal Telegram, T.1044/2, Prime Minister to President, No. 123, 'Personal and Most Secret', 27 July 1942: Churchill papers, 20/78.

[2] Telegram of 28 July 1942, 'Secret': Churchill papers, 20/78.

[3] Bernard Fergusson (editor), *The Business of War, The War Narrative of Major-General Sir John Kennedy*, London 1957, pages 225–6.

10

Cairo, August 1942:
'Singleness of aim'

T HE decision to give priority in 1942 to a joint Anglo-American landing in French North Africa put all other plans into abeyance. Yet Churchill was concerned that these other aspects of war policy and planning should not be too ruthlessly eclipsed. An offensive in Burma, codename 'Anakim', which Wavell was to undertake, 'should not be turned down or hamstrung', Churchill warned the Chiefs of Staff on 27 July 1942. Only the 'very gravest reasons' should prevent Wavell from being sent the landing craft which had been used in the Madagascar landings.[1] Even the Russian convoy for September might be re-considered, Churchill wrote, if the losses to PQ17 turned out not to be as severe as at first feared.[2] In a paper for the War Cabinet on July 21, Churchill had argued that 'renewed, intense efforts' should be made by the Allies to develop during the winter and onwards 'ever growing, ever more accurate and ever more far-ranging Bomber attacks on Germany'. In this way alone, he believed, could Britain prepare the conditions which would be favourable 'to the major military operations on which we are involved'.[3]

This major operation remained, in Churchill's mind, the cross-Channel landing, second in timing, but not in importance, to the North African landings now being planned for October 1942. The 'Bolero' process, Churchill told Roosevelt, in reference to the transfer to Britain of American troops for an eventual cross-Channel landing, 'will continue at full blast', subject only to any 'necessary impingement' made upon it by the North African arrangements.

[1] Prime Minister's Personal Minute, D.138/2, 26 July 1942: Churchill papers, 20/67.
[2] Prime Minister's Personal Minute, M.318/2 (for the Chiefs of Staff Committee), 'Most Secret', 27 July 1942: Churchill papers, 20/67.
[3] 'A Review of the War Position', War Cabinet paper No. 311 of 1942, 'Most Secret', 21 July 1942: Premier papers, 3/499/3.

The success of the North African landings, now codenamed 'Torch', depended, Churchill telegraphed to Roosevelt, on 'secrecy and speed'. Secrecy, he added, 'can only be maintained by deception'. As part of this deception Churchill would be 'running' the no longer operative northern Norway plan, operation 'Jupiter', and would 'work up' the discarded Cherbourg operation, 'Sledgehammer', 'with the utmost vigour'. These two deceptions would cover all troop movements in the United Kingdom. Roosevelt's own troop movements, Churchill suggested, should be explained to all those outside 'the secret circles' as intended for Suez or Basra, 'thus explaining tropical kit'. As a further deception, the Canadian Army in Britain would be 'fitted for Arctic service'.[1]

It was Stalin's reaction to the abandonment of the Cherbourg landing which was now of concern to both Churchill and Roosevelt. 'We have got always to bear in mind the personality of our ally,' Roosevelt telegraphed to Churchill on July 29, 'and the very difficult and dangerous situation that confronts him. No one can be expected to approach the war from a world point of view whose country has been invaded. I think we should try to put ourselves in his place.' Stalin should be told 'quite specifically', Roosevelt added, 'that we have determined upon a course of action in 1942', even without giving him any details of where that operation would be.[2]

Churchill had already decided to go to Cairo, together with Brooke, to examine the possibility of a change of command, and on July 29 he told the Cabinet of his proposed visit. 'Mr Attlee nodded his head,' noted Eden. 'Nobody else said much, except Mr Bevin, who approved. I thought that they were all as surprised as I and only learnt afterwards that some of them were not. I asked whether the doctor approved, but I was also troubled by the risks of the journey, though it was clearly useless to speak to the Prime Minister about these; they would only whet his appetite.'[3]

On July 30 Eden showed Churchill a telegram from Sir Archibald Clark Kerr, the British Ambassador in Moscow, stressing 'the immense advantages' of an early meeting between Churchill and Stalin. 'Although Molotov professes to have passed on faithfully to the Soviet Government all that was said to him in London and given him in writing,' Clark Kerr reported, 'it now looks as if he had to some

---

[1] Prime Minister's Personal Telegram, T.1044/2, Prime Minister to President, No. 123, 'Personal and Most Secret', 27 July 1942: Churchill papers, 20/78. Only two copies of this telegram were made, one for General Ismay and the Chiefs of Staff, the other for the King.

[2] President to Prime Minister, No. 171, 'Personal and Most Secret', 29 July 1942: Churchill papers, 20/78.

[3] Eden memoirs, The Reckoning, op. cit., page 338.

extent failed to interpret to Stalin the mind of the Prime Minister.'[1]
'Took the telegram round to Winston,' Eden noted in his diary, 'and
he jumped at it.'[2]

In sending this telegram to Eden, Cadogan had noted: 'I should
attach enormous importance to a Stalin–Churchill meeting.' The
moment 'may well come', Cadogan warned, 'when the Russians are
no longer attracted by "jam tomorrow". We may have to put our
cards on the table.'[3]

Churchill now proposed going on from Egypt to Russia. 'I am
starting for Cairo forthwith,' he telegraphed to Stalin on July 30. 'I
have serious business there, as you may imagine. From there I will, if
you desire it, fix a convenient date for our meeting. . . .' Meanwhile,
'preliminary arrangements' were being made for another 'large
convoy' to Archangel.[4] This convoy, Churchill told Roosevelt later
that day, would sail on about September 4, with forty ships.[5]

The plans for Churchill's departure to Cairo and Moscow, and
the many telegrams connected with it, were prepared in utmost
secrecy. Among those who were closest to those secrets were the
secretaries who worked with Churchill day and night: Kathleen
Hill, Elizabeth Layton and Jo Sturdee. It was Elizabeth Layton who
set down, in a letter home, the mood of the preparations in their
earliest stages:

> I was on early duty, and he was in bed, and he dictated in shorthand a
> two or three page telegram. Presently Anthony came in. I fidgeted around,
> longing to go, because it makes you feel very awkward when they start talking
> about their colleagues or opposite numbers in other lands, and so forth. But
> twice lately I've been told, 'Come back—what are you sneaking out for? I'll
> tell you when to go.' So presently he said, 'Now read that, and then she'll
> read you my answer.'
> I surreptitiously scanned the outlines and put in the commas and the full-
> stops hastily, and wrote 'a' or 'the' above the dots because I never remember
> to differentiate. Then he said, 'Now Miss Layton, read to the Foreign Secre-
> tary. And don't gabble—read slowly—and don't whisper—read out loud.' So
> I started off, trying to go slow, and as loud as I thought suitable.

[1] Telegram No. 1082 from Moscow, sent 28 July 1942, received 29 July 1942, 'Personal and
Most Secret' (Sir Archibald Clark Kerr to Sir Alexander Cadogan): Premier papers, 3/76A/1,
folio 17.

[2] Eden diary, 30 July 1942: Eden memoirs, *The Reckoning, op. cit.*, page 338.

[3] Minute of 29 July 1942: Premier papers, 3/76A/1, folios 14–16.

[4] Prime Minister's Personal Telegram, T.1062/2, 30 July 1942: Churchill papers, 20/88.

[5] Prime Minister's Personal Telegram, T.1064/2, 'Personal and Most Secret', 30 July 1942:
Premier papers, 3/76A/1.

In a few seconds: 'No, No; *much* louder—he wants to be able to hear it; and *much* slower. Come on now, Miss Layton, *come on.*' So I took a deep breath and fairly bawled it at him, about one word a minute.

I looked at The Boss, and there was a very definite twinkle, so I sort of grinned back. He really does make you laugh at times. But you have no idea how silly your own voice sounds at such times, and you long to race through it all and rush out. However, Anthony was twinkling too, and I couldn't help but feel amused . . . that night I had about seven terribly exciting telegrams to do—exciting because they were so secret!

'Of course,' Elizabeth Layton noted, of the Russian visit, 'we all felt very upset at his going. It seems such a risk—but then he wouldn't go if the stakes involved weren't worth it. And I feel quite positive that he knows when is the psychological moment to strike, and therefore it must be now. I admire his courage and determination more than I could ever tell you.' [1]

'But what energy and gallantry of the old gentleman, setting off at 65 across Africa in the heat of mid-summer!' noted Oliver Harvey when Eden told him of Churchill's imminent journey.[2] In the War Cabinet, Eden commented that, against the advantages of such a visit must be put 'the risks to the Prime Minister's health which such a journey would involve'. To this, Churchill replied that he believed it was his duty to go, and that the risk to health 'should not be over-stressed'. He felt 'confident of his fitness to undertake the journey', would take his medical adviser with him, and would take 'all due precautions'. He would meet Stalin at Astrakhan, on the Caspian Sea, or 'such other place as would suit Stalin'. He would give Stalin an account 'of our discussions with the United States authorities and of our plans for 1942'. General Brooke would go with him.[3]

On July 31 Churchill suggested to Stalin a meeting at Astrakhan or in the Caucasus, 'or similar convenient meeting place'. In his telegram Churchill added: 'We could then survey the war together and take decisions hand in hand,' while he would tell Stalin of the plans he had made with Roosevelt 'for offensive action in 1942'.[4] On receiving this telegram, Stalin formally invited Churchill to the Soviet Union. The most suitable meeting place, he telegraphed later that same day, would be Moscow, as neither he, the members of his Government nor the senior members of the Soviet General Staff could leave the capital

---

[1] Elizabeth Layton, letter of 3 August 1942: Nel papers.

[2] Harvey diary, 30 July 1942: John Harvey (editor), *op. cit.*, page 145. In fact, Churchill was only four months short of his sixty-eighth birthday.

[3] War Cabinet No. 100 of 1942, 30 July 1942, Confidential Annex: Cabinet papers, 65/27.

[4] Prime Minister's Personal Telegram, T.1062/2, 'Absolutely Secret' ('Handed to Monsieur Maisky by PM for despatch'), 31 July 1942: Premier papers, 3/76A/1.

at such a moment of 'intense struggle' on the eastern front.[1] 'I will certainly come to Moscow to meet you,' Churchill replied.[2] Moscow was nearly eight hundred miles further for Churchill to fly than Astrakhan, which he had suggested.

On July 31, with the 'true' second front constantly in mind, Churchill proposed to Roosevelt that General Marshall should be the Supreme Commander of the eventual cross-Channel landing, with, 'in the meanwhile', Eisenhower acting as his deputy in London, and General Alexander—who had just extricated the British forces from Burma—as Task Force Commander to work 'with and under' Eisenhower.

Churchill went on to explain to Roosevelt that both Eisenhower and Alexander would also work at the North Africa landings, enabling Eisenhower 'to draw for "Torch" the necessary forces with the least injury to "Bolero" and "Round-Up"'.[3] In this way, the cross-Channel landing, still envisaged for 1943, would retain its primacy in the hierarchy of planning and command.

On the night of July 31 Churchill and his wife had to drive to Farnborough where, shortly before midnight, Churchill was tested for high altitude flying. Put into what was known as the 'Chamber' he, and Sir Alexander Cadogan who was to go with him, were given oxygen masks and 'taken up' to the equivalent of 15,000 feet. There they were kept for a quarter of an hour, with a little extra oxygen to help them. When the test was over, Cadogan noted in his diary: 'PM complained of pain, but we discovered that was due to clumsy adjustment of his oxygen mask.' Throughout the experiment, Clementine Churchill had looked at Churchill through a port-hole. Afterwards his blood pressure was taken. All was judged well for the flight on the following night.[4]

On the afternoon of July 31, a telegram from Auchinleck gave added urgency to the Cairo stage of Churchill's journey. After a conference on the previous day with his Corps Commanders, Auchinleck reported,

[1] 'Absolutely Secret', Kremlin, 31 July 1942: Premier papers, 3/76A/1, folio 7.

[2] Prime Minister's Personal Telegram, T.1082/2, 'Absolutely Secret', 1 August 1942: Premier papers, 3/76A/1, folio 6.

[3] Prime Minister's Personal Telegram, T.1066/2, 'Absolutely Secret', 31 July 1942: Churchill papers, 20/78.

[4] Cadogan diary, 31 July 1942: David Dilks (editor), op. cit., page 465. The test had been conducted by Roland Winfield, himself a former pilot, who later recalled Churchill's remark about the 'damnable muzzle', and the work through the night to design a special mask which would enable Churchill to take oxygen and to smoke a cigar at the same time. (Roland Winfield, The Sky Belongs to Them, London 1976, page 69.) Winfield was senior service officer at the Royal Air Force Physiology Laboratory at Farnborough.

it was 'reluctantly' concluded that owing to lack of resources, and Rommel's effective consolidation of his position, it was 'not feasible to renew our efforts to break enemy front or turn his southern flank'. There could certainly be no new British offensive until mid-September.[1] This 'depressing account', as Churchill described it to the War Cabinet on August 1, had made him feel that 'the time had now been reached when General Auchinleck could once more concern himself with the duties of Commander-in-Chief, Middle East, some other General being appointed to command the Eighth Army'.[2] To assist him in his deliberations, Churchill had asked Field Marshal Smuts to meet him in Cairo. At noon on August 1 Churchill lunched with his brother Jack, Eden, Beaverbrook and Bracken, the last two wanting to accompany him to Moscow. But after a talk with Eden, Churchill decided to go to Moscow with only Brooke and Cadogan.[3] That afternoon he received a handwritten message from King George VI, from Windsor Castle:

My dear Prime Minister,

I must send you one line before you leave to wish you bon voyage & a safe return.

I know from what you have so often told me, that you have long planned this journey to find out for yourself the reason for the many difficulties & delays in the Middle East.

I feel that your visit East will be even more epoch-making than those you have paid to the West, not that I would wish to belittle the latter in any way, but because of two people with whom you will make personal contact, Smuts & Stalin. Two great men in their own spheres, utterly different in character, but with a single aim to win this war. You have this same aim & what could be better than that you should meet them at this moment. The results of your deliberations may be the turning point of the war, knowing what powerful forces are coming to help from the West.

You & I know what this country has done, is doing & will continue to do towards the winning of the war. Your journey will not be too easy physically, so I pray you to take great care of yourself, though I know you have already taken steps to ensure this.

I shall follow your journey with the greatest interest & shall be more than delighted when you are safely home again.

As I have told you before, your Welfare means a great deal not only to the United Nations, but to me personally. With my very best wishes to you on your new venture,

Believe me

Your very sincere and grateful friend

George R.I.[4]

---

[1] Telegram No. 30295, 'Most Secret', 31 July 1942.

[2] War Cabinet No. 101 of 1942, 1 August 1942, Confidential Annex: Cabinet papers, 65/31.

[3] Eden recollections: Eden memoirs, *The Reckoning*, *op. cit.*, page 338.

[4] 'Windsor Castle, August 1st 1942': Churchill papers, 20/52.

To this letter Churchill replied, also by hand, that same day:

Sir,

I am deeply touched by Yr Majesty's most kind & gracious letter. Always Sir you are vy good to me. I wish indeed that it had been in my power to bring about earlier & more decisive success. But the ultimate result is sure.

I trust indeed and pray that this journey of mine will be fruitful. Only my conviction that it is my duty has led me to it. I am shocked by Auchinleck's latest wire (about remaining on the Defensive till the middle of September). How strong will the enemy be by then! In Russia too the materials for a joyous meeting are meagre indeed. Still I may perhaps make the situation less edged.

I am looking forward to meeting my old friend Smuts again. His wisdom & his courage will be a comfort in these serious days that lie ahead.

I hope Yr Majesty will have some rest & peace at Balmoral, & once more expressing my grateful thanks for all the kindness & friendship with which I have been honoured,

I remain,

Yr Majesty's faithful & devoted servant,

Winston S. Churchill.[1]

At 8.30 that evening Churchill and his wife left Downing Street. As he got into his car, 'he looked up and smiled', Elizabeth Layton wrote home, 'and made the V sign—not at the Secretaries or his Minister but at *me*! And then they drove off. I was completely overcome.'[2]

Shortly before midnight on Saturday August 1, as Churchill waited with his wife at Lyneham airport, a message was telephoned to him from London. It was a telegram from Field Marshal Dill in Washington, stating that in 'the American mind', an offensive in Europe in 1943 was 'excluded' by the acceptance of a North Africa landing in 1942. 'Torch' in 1942 would make the cross-Channel 'Round-Up' impossible in 1943.

This American support enabled Churchill to approach Stalin with greater confidence, although his task was clearly going to be an exceptionally difficult one. Not only was there to be no limited second front in Europe in 1942 at Christmas, but the more substantial second front envisaged in Europe in 1943 would probably be postponed until 1944. Dill ended his telegram: 'May what you are at have the success which courage and imagination deserve.'[3]

Churchill and his wife said goodbye to each other at Lyneham airport. The aircraft in which he was to fly was not the comfortable

[1] Letter of 1 August 1942: Royal Archives.
[2] Elizabeth Layton, letter of 3 August 1942: Nel papers.
[3] Joint Staff Mission Telegram, JSM 332, 'Personal', 1 August 1942: Churchill papers, 20/78. Churchill authorized copies of this telegram to be sent to the King, Eden and Attlee.

Boeing Clipper, but an unheated four engine bomber, an American Liberator, named 'Commando'. There were no beds, as on the Clipper, but two shelves, on which one could lie down, and a copious supply of blankets. Churchill took one shelf, and his doctor the other.

'It was both dramatic & mysterious,' Clementine Churchill wrote three days later, 'standing in the dark on that aerodrome while your monster bomber throbbing, roaring & flashing blue light taxied away into the blackness. It seemed a long time taking off. Finally we saw its huge dim shape air borne against the row of "glim" lights. . . .' Her letter continued:

I think much of you my Darling & pray that you may be able to penetrate & then solve the problem of the Middle East stultification or frustration or what is it?

This first part of your journey is less dramatic & sensational than your visit to the Ogre in his Den; but I should imagine it may be more fruitful in results.[1]

Churchill and Cadogan reached Gibraltar at dawn: Brooke had flown out earlier. After a day in Gibraltar, they flew on overnight to Egypt. Churchill later recalled:

It was my practice on these journeys to sit in the co-pilot's seat before sunrise, and when I reached it on this morning of August 4 there in the pale, glimmering dawn the endless winding silver ribbon of the Nile stretched joyously before us. Often had I seen the day break on the Nile. In war and peace I had traversed by land or water almost its whole length, except the 'Dongola Loop', from Lake Victoria to the sea. Never had the glint of daylight on its waters been so welcome to me.

Now for a short spell I became 'the man on the spot'. Instead of sitting at home waiting for the news from the front I could send it myself. This was exhilarating.[2]

On reaching Cairo, Churchill's doctor had been worried, briefly, about the Prime Minister's pulse. But there were no further health problems. 'The Embassy is hot and steamy,' the doctor noted in his diary, 'but the PM's bedroom is air-conditioned, and anyway he does not feel extremes of heat and cold like other people.' Wilson added: 'He is in great heart. No longer is he compelled to deal with great

---

[1] Letter of 4 August 1942: Spencer-Churchill papers.
[2] Winston S. Churchill, *The Second World War*, volume 4, London 1951, page 412. Among those on the flight was Roland Winfield, responsible for the oxygen equipment. 'I produced the mask which we had modified for him at Farnborough,' Winfield later recalled, 'and a most impressive sight it was—the Prime Minister sitting there, wearing the green nose-piece and green chin-rest, puffing away at the cigar sticking out of the middle of it. He looked exactly as though he was in a Christmas party disguise.' (Roland Winfield, *The Sky Belongs To Them*, London 1976, page 69.)

events by correspondence; he is "the man on-the-spot". Twice he has said this to me. A great feeling of elation stokes the marvellous machine, which seems quite impervious to fatigue.'[1]

Churchill spent his first morning in Cairo with the Minister Resident, Richard Casey, and then with Air Chief Marshal Tedder. In the early afternoon he saw Smuts, and in the late afternoon Auchinleck. On August 5 he saw General Wavell, who had flown from India, and in the evening held a meeting of all the principle commanders, as well as Casey. Much of the discussion was about the command; Churchill had asked Smuts to come to Cairo from South Africa in order to help him in the decision. It was Auchinleck who urged Churchill to see his Chief of Staff, General Corbett, from whom Churchill learned, as he later recalled, 'that Auchinleck was anxious to lay down the command of the Eighth Army at the earliest moment and return to his wider sphere in Cairo'.

Churchill's first instinct was to offer the Middle East command to Brooke, and he did so. 'I know that no man would fill it better,' Churchill later wrote, and he added: 'He thought it over, and had a long talk the next morning with General Smuts. Finally he replied that he had been CIGS for only eight months, he believed he had my full confidence, and the Staff machine was working very smoothly. Another change at this moment might cause a temporary dislocation at this critical time.'[2]

During his discussions, Churchill also saw Colonel Davy, Auchinleck's Director of Military Operations. 'He just quietly grilled me,' Davy later recalled. 'He wanted a lot of detailed information and in his characteristic fashion he asked questions which cut at right-angles across one's normal method of assessing military strength. At school I had been fairly quick at mental arithmetic and it stood me in good stead at this interview. How many tanks have we? How many cannon have we? How many bayonets have we?' Churchill then asked Davy about the state of training of divisions not in the Eighth Army and their dates of readiness; the reserves of mines and ammunition, 'and a vast number of administrative details', for more than two hours. There was no aspect of the preparations about which Churchill did not want to know. 'Having pumped me on statistics and the tactical and strategical situation in the desert,' Davy added, 'he threw a tactful fly over me on personalities. I gave it merely a sniff, as I did not wish to be disloyal to the Auk . . .'[3]

'The PM hates the idea of removing one of his commanders,'

---

[1] Sir Charles Wilson diary, 4 August 1942: Moran, *op. cit.*, pages 49–50.
[2] Winston S. Churchill, *The Second World War*, volume 4, London 1951, page 413.
[3] Brigadier G. M. O. Davy, typescript: Letter to the author, 14 February 1982.

Charles Wilson noted in his diary on August 4, Churchill's second day in Cairo.[1] Two days later, Churchill had made up his mind: Auchinleck must leave the Eighth Army. 'Exactly what I have always told him from the start,' Brooke noted in his diary. As Auchinleck's replacement in the field, Churchill looked with favour on General Gott, whom Brooke, while admiring as a 'brilliant commander', feared was 'very tired'.[2] General Alexander would replace Auchinleck in his other post as Commander-in-Chief. 'My colleagues were delighted,' Eden later recalled, 'but none more than I.'[3]

There were other matters to be discussed in addition to that of the commands. On August 4, Brooke and Churchill gave a survey of the second front discussion to Smuts, and to Richard Casey, recently appointed Minister of State in the Middle East. Also present during this survey were the three local Commanders-in-Chief, General Auchinleck, Air Chief Marshal Tedder and Admiral Harwood, together with General Wavell, who had come specially to Cairo from India. Brooke warned that if the Germans, having reached the Caucasus, were able to develop a 'serious threat' to the Persian Gulf, it might be necessary to consider whether to abandon Egypt and the North African campaign altogether, 'and concentrate on the defence of the Persian Gulf'. The Chiefs of Staff had come to this view, Brooke explained, because of a report from the Oil Control Board in which it was stated 'that the loss of Abadan and Bahrein would probably lead to a 20% cut in our various fields of activity'.[4]

Speaking after Brooke, Churchill reported on the visit of Hopkins, Marshall and King to London, and on the decision not to seek a bridgehead on the Cherbourg Peninsula that autumn. 'The arguments against it were overwhelming,' he said. 'The size of the forces which could be landed were insignificant compared with the strength which the Germans could mass against the landing during the winter, if not earlier.' The resources which would have had to be 'used up' could have included the special landing craft required 'for the training and organization of the much larger forces which could be employed next Spring'. The smaller operation would 'hamstring' the larger. As to the alternative of operations in North Africa, 'designed to gain possession of the whole coast from Casablanca to Tunis', a plan which had 'always appealed strongly' to Roosevelt, this had led to unanimous agreement, with plans and preparations to proceed 'with the utmost speed and energy'.

[1] Sir Charles Wilson diary, 4 August 1942: Moran, *op. cit.*, pages 49–50.
[2] Brooke diary, 3 August 1942: Bryant, *op. cit.*, volume 1, page 438.
[3] Eden memoirs, *The Reckoning, op. cit.*, page 338.
[4] Chiefs of Staff Paper No. 352 of 1942, 4 August 1942: Cabinet papers, 80/37.

It remained, Churchill said, for him to give Stalin 'an account of our plans'. Stalin would 'undoubtedly dislike the idea of there being no Second Front in Europe this year', but it would be necessary 'to convince him of the great advantages which would accrue to the common cause from a success in North Africa'. If the Germans 'attempted to meet us there', Churchill explained, 'they could only do it with forces withdrawn from the Russian front', while the Anglo-American threat to north-west Europe would remain. 'We should be carrying out a flanking movement to the main battle.'

He intended while in Moscow, Churchill added, to find out what forces the Russians had available for the defence of the Caucasus, 'and thus to estimate the extent of the danger which might arise on that flank this year'.[1]

On August 5 Churchill flew from Cairo to inspect the Eighth Army in its positions at Alamein. When he was about to board the Dakota for the flight to the desert, Brooke's Military Assistant, Colonel Peter Dunphie, later recalled, he asked if he could smoke on the aircraft. 'An anxious RAF officer,' Dunphie noted, 'said with some hesitation that he would go and see whether the auxiliary tanks were full or not, but Churchill continued: "I enjoy a cigar but not at the risk of being incinerated." '[2]

Having inspected the Eighth Army positions at Alamein with General Gott, Churchill asked Gott to drive with him to the airfield which was to be his next stop, in order to assure himself that Gott was not as tired out as Brooke had suggested. 'He inspired me at once with a feeling of confidence,' Churchill wrote three weeks later, 'and although he said he would be all the better for a few months' leave, I accepted his statement that he was feeling capable of going on, in view of the imminence of renewed battle as it then seemed.'[3] Brooke, however, in a further talk with Gott, was convinced, as he later recalled, that Gott was too tired to continue, and that General Montgomery was 'far better qualified' for the command.[4]

On August 6, after a further day in conference, first with Brooke and then with Smuts, Churchill telegraphed to Attlee with details of the new commands. Alexander would be Commander-in-Chief, Near East Command, comprising Egypt, Palestine and Syria, with its centre

[1] 'Most Secret', 'Minutes of a Meeting held in the British Embassy, Cairo, at 1800 hours on Thursday, 4th August 1942', 4 August 1942: Premier papers, 3/76A/12, folios 119–32.

[2] Colonel Peter Dunphie, recollections: letter to the author, 24 March 1982. That afternoon, when Dunphie asked Churchill if he would like a cup of tea, Churchill replied: 'Young man, I have long made it a rule of my life never to drink non-alcoholic drinks between meals. I would like a large whisky and soda.'

[3] Letter of 29 August 1942 (to Mrs Gott): Churchill papers, 20/54.

[4] Brooke recollections: Bryant, *op. cit.*, volume 1, page 443.

in Cairo. Gott would command the Eighth Army, under Alexander. Montgomery would succeed Alexander in command of the British forces landing in French North Africa in October as part of operation 'Torch'. This decision was sent to London, to be approved by the War Cabinet. 'I have no doubt,' Churchill explained, 'the changes will impart a new and vigorous impulse to the Army and restore confidence in the Command, which I regret does not exist at the present time.' Churchill's telegram continued: 'Here I must emphasise the need of a new start and vehement action to animate the whole of this vast but baffled and somewhat unhinged organisation.'[1]

'A decision has now become most urgent,' Churchill telegraphed to Attlee on the following day, 'since Alexander has already started and Auchinleck has, of course, no inkling of what is in prospect.' Churchill added: 'I must apprise him tomorrow.'[2]

Churchill spent August 7 visiting the 51st Highland Division, which had just landed in Egypt. He then returned to the British Embassy for dinner. After dinner, as he was going up the stairs to his room, he passed Colonel Jacob, who said to him: 'This is bad about Gott.' 'What has happened?' Churchill asked. 'He was shot down this afternoon flying into Cairo,' Jacob replied.[3] Gott had been killed flying on the same route that Churchill had taken, unescorted, two days earlier.[4]

Gott was dead; that same evening Churchill, Smuts and Brooke discussed, as Brooke noted in his diary, 'how the matter should be settled'. Brooke pressed for Montgomery to replace Gott. Churchill, Brooke noted, was 'rather in favour' of General Maitland Wilson. But Smuts also advocated Montgomery, and Churchill deferred to their advice.[5] That same night, in London, the War Cabinet was meeting to deal with the matters following upon Gott's appointment.

The 'general feeling', the minutes recorded, was that the War Cabinet 'did not favour' Churchill's proposal to create two commands, the Near East Command for Egypt, Syria and Palestine, and a Middle East Command for Iraq and Persia. Nevertheless, the minutes added, 'the case against the re-organisation was neither so strong nor so clear-cut that they could properly oppose the views of those on the spot'.[6]

As the War Cabinet discussion continued, a private secretary

---

[1] 'Reflex' No. 27, 8.15 p.m., 6 August 1942: Cabinet papers, 120/66.

[2] 'Reflex' No. 35, 7 August 1942: Cabinet papers, 120/66.

[3] Winston S. Churchill, *The Second World War*, volume 4, London 1951, page 418.

[4] Brooke recollections: Bryant, *op. cit.*, volume 1, page 449.

[5] Brooke diary, 7 August 1942: Bryant, *op. cit.*, volume 1, page 449.

[6] War Cabinet No. 108 of 1942, 11.15 p.m., 7 August 1942, Confidential Annex: Cabinet papers, 65/31.

entered the Cabinet room 'white faced', as Eden later recalled, and with the words: 'I fear that this is bad news.'[1] In his hand was a telegram from Churchill to Attlee announcing Gott's death. This telegram was followed shortly afterwards by a second one, in which Churchill informed Attlee that Brooke 'decisively recommends Montgomery for Eighth Army. Smuts and I feel this post must be filled at once. Pray send him by special plane at earliest moment.'[2]

On August 8 Colonel Jacob flew to Auchinleck's headquarters, bringing with him a letter from Churchill. The letter informed Auchinleck that he was to be replaced by Alexander, and offered a new 'Middle East Command' comprising Iraq and Persia, with his headquarters in Basra or Baghdad.[3] Three months later, in conversation with a number of Members of Parliament, including Harold Nicolson, Churchill spoke of Auchinleck's dismissal from Cairo. Nicolson noted in his diary:

He tells us at length how he decided to remove Auchinleck and how he broke the news to him. 'It was a terrible thing to have to do. He took it like a gentleman. But it was a terrible thing. It is difficult to remove a bad General at the height of a campaign: it is atrocious to remove a good General. We must use Auchinleck again. We cannot afford to lose such a man from the fighting line.'[4]

To the War Cabinet, Churchill had telegraphed on August 7, that he could not advise that Auchinleck 'should be ruined and cast aside as unfit to render any further service'. If he agreed to accept the Iraq–Persia command, Churchill added, 'he will in no way have lost confidence in himself, but, on the contrary, will address himself to his new task with single-minded vigour'.[5]

On August 8 Churchill inspected four armoured brigades. None of them, he discovered, had yet received their Sherman tanks. In Cairo he made enquiries, discovering that the tanks were not expected until September 5, five days later than the date on which they had originally been expected. 'In view of the immense importance of beating Rommel as a prelude to "Torch",' Churchill telegraphed to Dudley Pound on August 9, 'I beg you will make a renewed effort to regain

---

[1] Eden recollection: Eden memoirs, *The Reckoning, op. cit.*, page 338.
[2] War Cabinet No. 108 of 7 August 1942, 11.15 p.m., Confidential Annex: Cabinet papers, 65/31.
[3] 'Most Secret and Personal', 8 August 1942: Churchill papers, 20/54.
[4] Harold Nicolson diary, 6 November 1942: Nigel Nicolson (editor), *op. cit.*, page 259.
[5] 'Reflex' No. 35, 7 August 1942: Cabinet papers, 120/66.

the lost five days, all of which can be used.' To Sinclair and Portal, Churchill telegraphed that same day for 'a proportion, if only a small one, of the very latest types of fighter aircraft', for which both Tedder and Air Vice-Marshal Coningham had asked him, and which Coningham had declared he could make 'desert-worthy'.[1]

On August 9 Churchill spoke to the Staff of the British Embassy. For some of the women, it was their third consecutive summer in the heat of Cairo without a break. Others had been evacuated to Cairo from ports in Greece and the Balkans. Many of the men had been anxious to join the Army or the Air Force, but had not been allowed to because they could not be replaced by equally qualified persons. Churchill told them how much their work at the Embassy was valued. To hear this from him, wrote Michael Wright to Leslie Rowan, was 'heartening and envigorating, to an extent which even he may not realize'.[2] All had appreciated 'most deeply' his thoughtfulness 'in sparing for them time from more important preoccupations'.[3]

It was during August 9 that Churchill dictated a letter to his wife:

My darling,

I have been so busy at anxious work since I arrived nearly a week ago that I have not found a moment to write. I told Ismay to keep you informed by my telegrams of all that I am doing. Martin or he should show you anything I send that is of any personal interest. It was absolutely necessary that I should come here. This splendid army, about double as strong as the enemy, is baffled and bewildered by its defeats.

Rommel is living almost entirely on transport, and food and fuel captured from us. He is living from hand to mouth; his army's life hangs on a thread, but meanwhile a kind of apathy and exhaustion of the mind rather than the body has stolen over our troops which only new strong hands, and above all the gleam of victory can dispel. I went to the front on Wednesday; saw the Alamein and Ruweisat positions and was everywhere greeted with rapture by the troops who of course are scattered about an immense area to avoid air attack.

I drove all day with Auchinleck, Ramsden, Gott and Coningham (RAF). I had long talks with Tedder and his Admiral, with the Minister of State, with Smuts and Brooke continually. We have all been seeing separately the necessary people and collected opinions from all useful quarters. We had no doubt whatever of the changes which I forecast in my Cabinet telegram.

[1] Telegrams of 9 August 1942: Winston S. Churchill, *The Second World War*, volume 4, London 1951, Appendix C, page 787. Air Vice-Marshal Coningham (known as 'Mary') worked with the Eighth Army in North Africa, where, in February 1943, he formed the 1st Tactical Air Force. In 1944 he commanded the 2nd Tactical Air Force in southern England/Northern Europe. He was killed in 1948 while travelling in a passenger aircraft which crashed in the Atlantic.

[2] Letter of 9 August 1942: Premier papers, 4/71/4, folio 1011. Michael Wright was First Secretary in the British Embassy, Cairo.

[3] 'I was struck again in the desert,' Michael Wright wrote to Churchill on October 7, 'and am constantly impressed here in Cairo, with the tonic effect of your visit.' (Letter of 7 October 1942: Premier papers, 4/71/4, folios 1021–2.)

They were necessary to victory and am very glad that except in the matter of calling the Middle East the Near East they have been endorsed by the Cabinet. Smuts was magnificent in counsel. We could work together with the utmost ease. He fortified me where I am inclined to be tender-hearted, namely in using severe measures against people I like.

All was then set on Thursday. I had had a long drive alone with Gott and without making him any offer or suggestion I convinced myself of his high ability, charming simple personality and that he was in no way tired, as was alleged. One knows at once when one can make friends. Imagine my grief when even while the Cabinet was sitting I had to telegraph that he had been killed.

He was killed flying in to have a bath and a restful night in Cairo. Although a Corps Commander he just took his place in the ordinary flying-bus, a Bombay. He was flying from Burg El Arab where I had landed the day before, when almost over the airfield where the Air Force gave me a most delicious feast of Cairo delicacies he was caught by six enemy 109's which were coming to raid this very airfield. They were driven off and scattered but two of them pounced on this helpless machine and shot it down in flames. Out of 18 there were 3 survivors. This seems to me to be very grim, and even sinister considering that I had brought all concerned to realise that he should immediately be given Command of the Eighth Army. Air Marshal Coningham who was coming in to dine at the Embassy could have brought him in his faster plane, but did not know of his intention. Here one sees the hand of fate.

I had thought that Alexander with his grand capacities for war and Gott with his desert prowess and his hold on the troops would have made an ideal combination. However, the order must ever be 'carry on'. In Montgomery, who should be here on Tuesday we have a highly competent, daring and energetic soldier, well-acquainted with desert warfare. If he is disagreeable to those about him he is also disagreeable to the enemy. I am confident that the new arrangement will work well.

Some of the figures whom Auchinleck had got around him were very _____ [1]. He was about to hand over the Eighth Army to General Corbett, entirely unfitted to command a Division in a back area. He has made a continuous succession of bad choices, each of whom has had to be removed after a disaster and of those that were left I am making a thorough clearance. I am seeing myself all the men who will be appointed to the Corps and chief posts. There are some very fine fellows in the field. Lumsden has recovered from his wound. McCreery, another tank General, sent out from the War Office to advise on all tank affairs, but completely ignored by Auchinleck, has all the qualities of leadership and battle. He looks like Lawrence but rather taller, in fact a good deal taller. But I will not trouble you with this.

Yesterday I spent six hours with the four armoured brigades that are all preparing and are a magnificent well-trained resolute body of men thirsting for action, but with only a few tanks to train on. I told them (in seven speeches) how the President had given me Shermans; how the Navy were

[1] Gap in the original dictated letter, as sent.

bringing them as fast as possible and how in a few weeks they would be the most powerful and best equipped armoured force of its size in the world. At one place they nearly all came from Oldham.[1] They showed the greatest enthusiasm.

I intend to see every important unit in this army, both back and front and make them feel the vast consequences which depend upon them and the superb honour which may be theirs. The more I study the situation on the spot the more sure I am that a decisive victory can be won if only the leadership is equal to the opportunity.

Here were live in Capuan luxury. The weather is delightful. My host and hostess are charming; the food pre-war. My rooms are air-cooled. The wonderful air of the desert with its fierce sunshine and cool breeze invigorates me so much that I do not seem to need as much sleep as usual. Of course however I sleep in instalments which is most refreshing.

Jacqueline is most agreeable and the baby, with whom I have been ———[2] is a fat preter-naturally solemn child as may well be said by the seriousness of its surroundings.[3] I have had all Randolph's friends to lunch with me: David Stirling, who strolled in from behind the German lines, a tall, slim, dandified figure, recalling Don Juan 'he was the mildest mannered man that ever scuttled ship or cut a throat'.[4]

Kellett, MP, the young Lords Lansdowne and Cadogan, both very nice boys.[5] Now Russians have arrived and de Gaulle, but Smuts I am sorry to say has gone. He has promised to come to England in September to stay at least a month so I shall convene a formal session of the Imperial War Cabinet then.

I found Tom Mitford yesterday with the Armoured Brigade and will get him in to dinner when I return from this new adventure.[6]

I start at midnight Monday and have a bath at Teheran and should reach Moscow (DV) before dark on Tuesday. This is much shorter than I had imagined. I am not looking forward to this part of my mission because I bear so little in my hand, and sympathise so much with those to whom I go.

I informed General Auchinleck by letter yesterday of the decisions taken. He is coming to see me here in a few minutes and I must close this letter without even having had time to read it through.

Before signing this letter, Churchill added, in the margin, about General Gott's death: 'You should write to his wife. I am writing too,' and then, in a final paragraph in his own hand: 'Both your darling

---

[1] Churchill's first Constituency (1900–1905).

[2] Gap in the original dictated letter, as sent.

[3] Sir Miles Lampson (later Lord Killearn), Churchill's host, was married to Jacqueline Castellani. Their son Victor Miles George Aldous Lampson had been born on 9 September 1941.

[4] Byron, Don Juan, Canto III, stanza 41.

[5] Edward Orlando Kellett, born May 1902, Conservative MP for Aston, 1939, Lieutenant Colonel, 1940, killed in action, March 1943: the 7th Marquess of Lansdowne, born in January 1917, killed in action in Italy in August 1944; the 7th Earl Cadogan, born in 1914, served throughout the Second World War, first in North Africa and then in Italy.

[6] Clementine Churchill's cousin, brother of the 'Mitford sisters', killed in action in 1945.

letters have arrived. Do send something by every plane that leaves. You may show any parts of this you think suitable to Attlee, Anthony, and others in our secrets. But the fewer the better. Tender love my dearest. This should reach you in 48 hours. I hope then to be in Moscow. As always, your ever loving husband. W.' [1]

On August 10, Churchill's last day in Cairo, he gave Alexander a directive on his task as Commander in Chief of all British forces in the Middle East. The directive read:

1. Your prime and main duty will be to take or destroy at the earliest opportunity the German-Italian Army commanded by Field-Marshal Rommel, together with all its supplies and establishments in Egypt and Libya.

'2. You will discharge or cause to be discharged such other duties as pertain to your Command, without prejudice to the task described in paragraph 1, which must be considered paramount in His Majesty's interests.' [2]

'I am sure,' Churchill explained to Ismay, 'that simplicity of task and singleness of aim are imperative now.' [3]

In preparation for his meeting with Stalin, Churchill was concerned to maintain future convoys to Russia. 'It is indispensable to run further PQs after September,' he telegraphed to Attlee on August 10. 'I shall be asked about this and I must know. I cannot believe Admiralty resources will not admit of this as well as "Torch".' The reply, Churchill added, should be sent to him in Moscow. [4] Churchill had also sought Roosevelt's permission to allow Averell Harriman to accompany him to Moscow. 'I feel things would be easier if we all seemed to be together,' Churchill had telegraphed on August 5, and he added: 'I have a somewhat raw job.' [5]

Roosevelt at once approved of Harriman's journey. 'Averell has just arrived,' Churchill telegraphed on August 8, 'and we shall be off soon on our further quest.' [6]

Shortly after midnight on August 10, Churchill flew eastwards to

---

[1] Letter of 9 August 1942: Spencer-Churchill papers.

[2] 'Most Secret', British Embassy, Cairo, 10 August 1942. This instruction, which was hand-written by Churchill, was later given by Churchill to the King. It is now in the Royal Archives at Windsor.

[3] Minute of 10 August 1942: Winston S. Churchill, *The Second World War*, volume 4, London 1951, page 424.

[4] 'Reflex' No. 68, 10 August 1942: Churchill papers, 20/87.

[5] 'Reflex' No. 11, 'Most Secret', 5 August 1942: Premier papers, 3/76A/3, folio 7.

[6] 'Reflex' No. 41, 'Most Secret and Personal', 8 August 1942: Premier papers, 3/76A/11, folio 59.

Teheran, a journey of 1,300 miles. 'I expect he will get killed in a crash next,' Oliver Harvey noted in his diary, reflecting on the death of General Gott.[1] Churchill himself, on learning from the pilot that the Liberator would fly at 9,000 feet, looked at the map, saw several mountains of 10,000 and 11,000 feet on the route, and asked him to go up to 12,000 feet, which he did. Using their oxygen tubes, crew and passengers crossed the mountains without incident, but reached Teheran too late in the morning to continue immediately, as had been planned, northwards to the Soviet Union. Instead, Churchill lunched with the Shah, who, Churchill reported to Eden, 'expounded the principles of the allied cause with the greatest vigour and explained why he was convinced that the interests of Persia lay wholly with Britain and the United States'.[2]

That afternoon, Churchill sent a message by what was feared to be an insecure telegraphic line, to 'Mrs Green', to say that 'Mr Green' was resting in a 'delightful Persian garden'. That same day Clementine Churchill replied. 'I am glad you are having a short respite from trouble and anxiety.'[3]

Later that afternoon, in conference with Averell Harriman and several senior British and American railway officials, Churchill listened to Harriman's proposal to give the United States full responsibility for the working of the newly completed Trans-Persia railway, by which Allied supplies were about to travel from the Gulf ports to southern Russia.[4]

While Churchill was in Teheran, news reached him of an air and submarine attack on a convoy which was taking supplies from Gibraltar to Malta. This was operation 'Pedestal'. One escort ship had been sunk, the aircraft carrier *Eagle*.

Early on the morning of August 12, Churchill left Teheran in the Liberator bomber, flying north-west across Persia, then north across the Soviet border and north-east across the Caspian Sea, crossing the mouth of the Volga river and then flying north-west again, partly along the Volga, towards Moscow. To the west of the flight path, German forces were pushing the Russians back into the Caucasus, and towards the Volga itself.

The flight was a long and at times a bumpy one. During it, as Churchill later recalled, 'I pondered on my mission to this sullen, sinister Bolshevik State I had once tried so hard to strangle at its birth, and which, until Hitler appeared, I had regarded as the mortal

[1] Harvey diary, 10 August 1942: John Harvey (editor), *op. cit.*, pages 148–9.
[2] 'Reflex' No. 67, 'Most Secret', 12 August 1942: Churchill papers, 20/87.
[3] Letter of 12 August 1942: Spencer-Churchill papers.
[4] This was agreed to on Churchill's return to Cairo. The proposal emanated from Roosevelt.

foe of civilised freedom. What was it my duty to say to them now?' To take to Moscow the message that there was to be no second front in Europe in 1942, Churchill added, 'was like carrying a large lump of ice to the North Pole'.[1]

11

Moscow, August 1942:
'The ogre in his den'

A T 5 o'clock on the afternoon of Wednesday, 12 August 1942, Churchill's Liberator landed at Moscow, after a ten and a half hour flight. Both Molotov and the Chief of the Soviet General Staff, Marshal Shaposhnikov, were at the airport to welcome him.

Churchill's first duty on Soviet soil was to inspect a Red Army guard of honour, and then, together with Averell Harriman, to take a march past. A microphone was then produced, and Churchill was asked to speak a few words. The sound recordist missed the first sentence, but caught the second. 'And we are determined,' Churchill was saying, 'that we will continue, hand in hand, whatever our sufferings, whatever our toils, we will continue hand in hand, like comrades and brothers until every vestige of the Nazi régime has been beaten into the ground, until the memory only of it remains as an example and a warning for a future time.' [1]

Churchill was then driven to the villa put at his disposal outside the capital, State Villa No. 7. Churchill later recalled:

Everything was prepared with totalitarian lavishness. There was placed at my disposal, as aide-de-camp, an enormous, splendid-looking officer (I believe of a princely family under the Czarist régime), who also acted as our host and was a model of courtesy and attention. A number of veteran servants in white jackets and beaming smiles waited on every wish or movement of the guests. A long table in the dining-room and various sideboards were laden with every delicacy and stimulant that supreme power can command. I was conducted through a spacious reception room to a bedroom and bathroom of almost equal size. Blazing, almost dazzling, electric lights displayed the spotless cleanliness. The hot and cold water gushed.

I longed for a hot bath after the length and the heat of the journey. All was instantly prepared.

[1] 'Moscow, August 1942', 'Commentary': Premier papers, 4/71/4, folios 952–5.

After 'all necessary immersions and ablutions', Churchill added, we were regaled in the dining-room with every form of choice food and liquor, including of course caviare and vodka, but with many other dishes and wines from France and Germany far beyond our mood or consuming powers.'[1]

At seven o'clock that night, twelve hours after having left Teheran, Churchill was driven from State Villa No. 7 to the Kremlin, half an hour's drive away. He was accompanied only by his interpreter, Major Dunlop, Sir Archibald Clark Kerr and Averell Harriman, as the plane bringing General Brooke, Air Chief Marshal Tedder, Sir Alexander Cadogan and General Wavell and Colonel Jacob to Moscow had been forced to return to Teheran with engine failure shortly after take-off.

'The first two hours,' Churchill telegraphed on the following morning to Attlee and the War Cabinet, 'were bleak and sombre.'[2] Stalin began the discussion by stating that the news from the eastern front 'was not good' and that the Germans were making 'a tremendous effort to get to Baku and Stalingrad'. He did not know, he said, how the Germans had been able to gather together 'so many troops and tanks and so many Hungarian, Italian and Roumanian divisions'. He was sure 'that they had drained the whole of Europe of troops'.

Although the position in Moscow was 'sound', Stalin told Churchill, nevertheless 'he could not guarantee in advance that the Russians would be able to withstand a German attack'. In the south, the Red Army 'had been unable to stop the German offensive'.

When Churchill commented that he did not think the Germans were 'strong enough in the air' to make a fresh offensive either at Voronezh or in the north, Stalin—'looking very grave' as the minutes of the meeting recorded—replied 'that, in view of the length of the front, it was quite possible for Hitler to detach twenty divisions and create a strong attacking force—twenty divisions and two to three Panzer divisions would be quite enough'. Considering 'what Hitler had', Stalin added, 'it would not be difficult for him to detail such a force'.

Churchill then said that he supposed that what Stalin 'wanted him to come to' was the question of the second front, to which Stalin replied, 'this was as the Prime Minister wished'. The minutes of the meeting continued with Churchill's words:

The Prime Minister said that he wished to speak frankly and would like to invite complete frankness from Stalin. He would not have come to Moscow unless he had felt sure that he would be able to discuss realities. When M. Molotov had come to London he had told him that we were trying to make

---

[1] Winston S. Churchill, *The Second World War*, volume 4, London 1951, pages 428–9.
[2] 'Reflex' No. 85, 13 August 1942: Premier papers, 3/76A/11, folios 52–7.

plans for a diversion in France. He had also made it clear to M. Molotov that he could make no promises about 1942, and he had given M. Molotov a memorandum to this effect. Since then an exhaustive Anglo-American examination of the problem had been carried out.

Churchill then told Stalin that, as a result of this examination:

The British and American Governments did not feel themselves able to undertake a major operation in September, which was the only month in which the weather was to be counted upon. That was to say, an operation which would have the effect of bringing German infantry and tank divisions back from the Russian front. But, as M. Stalin knew, the British and American Governments were preparing for a very great operation in 1943. For this purpose a million American troops were now scheduled to reach the United Kingdom at their point of assembly in the Spring of 1943, making an expeditionary force of 27 divisions, to which the British Government were prepared to add 21 divisions. Nearly half of this force would be armoured.

'So far', Churchill explained, only two and a half American divisions had reached the United Kingdom, but the 'big transportation' would take place in October, November and December of 1942. Churchill was 'well aware', he said, 'that this plan offered no help to Russia in 1942'. It was even possible, Churchill added, that when the Anglo-American plan for 1943 was ready, 'the Germans would have a stronger army in the west than they now had'. At this point, as the minutes note, 'Stalin's face crumpled up into a frown'.

Churchill then spoke of Britain's 'good reasons' against an attack on the French coast in 1942, telling Stalin:

We had only enough landing craft for an assault landing on a fortified coast—enough to throw ashore six divisions and maintain them. If it were successful, more divisions might be sent, but the limiting factor was landing craft, which were now being built in very large numbers in the United Kingdom and especially in the United States.

He could say that for one division which could be carried this year it would be possible next year to carry eight or ten times as many. He had studied in detail two particular operations: something could be done in September with a small force at the Pas de Calais or on the stretch between Dunkirk and Dieppe. Such an operation would have for its object the drawing of the enemy air arm into an intense struggle. But we had not transport enough for forces capable of making any penetration which would be deep enough to be of help.

The Pas de Calais had this very great advantage, that we could dominate it from the air, and probably a very heavy battle would follow with the enemy. On the other hand, the enemy knew all about it and there was no doubt that, in this sector, he could now bring a larger land force against us than we could transport this year. Therefore, having regard to this and the tremendous tides in the Straits of Dover which had a rise and fall as much as 30 feet, all landing operations were of the greatest difficulty.

One advantage would be to bring about an air battle, but it seemed almost certain that this advantage would be brought by the total defeat and destruction of the expeditionary force. Thus, the enemy would have a triumph and we would have a disaster, which would be of no good to anyone.

Furthermore, in order to make this attack on the Pas de Calais this year, we should have to interrupt the training of a large mass of troops for the great operation of 1943, to take away key men, and to use up large numbers of landing craft and other apparatus which we were preparing for 1943. On these and other grounds, therefore, we did not think it would be wise to make any attempt on the Pas de Calais.

Stalin, 'who had begun', as the minutes noted, 'to look very glum', seemed 'unconvinced' and asked if it were possible to attack any other part of the French coast. The minutes recorded the ensuing discussion:

The Prime Minister then showed him a map which indicated the difficulties of making an air umbrella over the North French coast. Over the Pas de Calais it was possible to make a 60 percent effort and over Cherbourg 20 percent, and so on, down to 5 percent over the tip of Brittany.

M. Stalin did not seem to understand and asked some questions about the range of fighter planes. Could not they, for instance, come and go all the time?

The Prime Minister explained that they could indeed come and go, but in these circumstances they could not fight, and he added that an air umbrella to be effective had to be kept up.

M. Stalin then suggested that the Channel Islands should be captured.

The Prime Minister replied that he too had thought of that and he and the Americans had been considering the question of deep-water harbours which had obvious advantages. These lay in the region where we could give the minimum of air cover, whereas, while we could put up an air umbrella over the Pas de Calais, it only had shallow harbours.

M. Stalin then suggested a demonstration on the Pas de Calais and a landing at Cherbourg.

The Prime Minister replied that this had been considered, but he regarded it as a waste of seed-corn. We would be on the defensive. It would be a running sore for us and not for the enemy. It would do more harm to us than to him, because it would eat into all the forces destined for the big attack next year.

M. Stalin said that there was not a single German division in France of any value.

The Prime Minister contested this and said that he knew that there were in France 25 German divisions, nine of which were of the first line.

M. Stalin replied that his information was otherwise and that, in any case, the German divisions in France were of only two regiments apiece.

The Prime Minister said that he had exact information about the number and character of these divisions.

M. Stalin expressed doubts and repeated his statement that the German divisions had been reduced to two regiments apiece and that their artillery could be dealt with from the air. After all, this was a war.

The Prime Minister said that war was war but not folly, and it would be folly to invite a disaster which would help nobody.

Churchill added that he had brought Brooke and Wavell with him so that the military points could be explained in detail to the Russian General Staff. There was 'such a point', Churchill commented, 'beyond which statesmen could not carry discussions of this kind'. The minutes of the meeting continued:

M. Stalin (whose glumness had by now much increased) said that, as he understood it, we were unable to create a second front with any large force and unable even to land six divisions.

The Prime Minister said that this was so. We could land six divisions, but the landing of them would be more harmful than helpful and he was prepared to explain this in detail.

M. Stalin asked if he was to take it that the Prime Minister considered any attempt of this kind unwise.

The Prime Minister replied that this was so, for it would greatly injure the big operation planned for next year. He went on to say that he feared the news he brought was not good news, but he could assure M. Stalin that if, by throwing in 150,000 to 200,000 men we could render him aid by drawing away from the Russian front appreciable German forces, we would not shrink from this course on the grounds of loss. But if it drew no men away and spoiled the prospects for 1943, it would be a great error.

M. Stalin (who had become restless) said that his view about war was different. A man who was not prepared to take risks could not win a war.

When Churchill spoke of the lack of landing craft, Stalin said 'that shipping was not the point'. The troops could be sent by air: the British 'should not be so afraid of the Germans' and tended 'to over-estimate their strength'. Stalin added: 'Why were we so afraid of the Germans? He could not understand. He had some little time ago landed from the air a brigade of 2,500 men in the Dorogobuzh area. They had fought the Germans for four months and, when their work was done, they came home again by air. His experience showed that troops must be blooded in battle. If you did not blood your troops you had no idea what their value was.'

Churchill replied by a reference to 1940, asking Stalin whether he 'had ever asked himself why Hitler did not come to England in 1940, when we had only 20,000 trained troops, 200 guns and 50 tanks; and when Hitler had everything he needed: landing craft, barges, tanks, guns, planes, &c. He did not come. If he had come, he (the Prime Minister) would not be here to tell the tale. The fact was that Hitler was afraid of the operation.'

The discussion continued:

M. Stalin said that this was no analogy. The landing of Hitler in England would have been resisted by the people, whereas in the case of a British landing in France the people would be on the side of the British.

The Prime Minister said that it was all the more important, therefore, not to expose the people of France, by a withdrawal, to the vengeance of Hitler and to waste them when they would be needed in the big operations in 1943.

M. Stalin (who looked glummer still) said that if we could not make a landing in France this year he was not entitled to demand it or to insist upon it, but he was bound to say that he did not agree with Mr Churchill's arguments.

The Prime Minister thanked him, and said he hoped Stalin would allow the Generals to go into details.

M. Stalin agreed, and said that of course the military experts must be consulted, but it was not for them to decide, it was for Mr Churchill and himself to decide.

The Prime Minister agreed.

Churchill now came to what he hoped would be a turning point in the discussion. Bringing out a map of Southern Europe, the Mediterranean and North Africa, he asked Stalin: 'What was a second front?' 'Was it only a landing on a fortified coast opposite England? Or could it take the form of some other great operations which might be useful to the common cause? Suppose we did this or that at Cherbourg or the Pas de Calais'—and here Churchill pointed to a map which he had drawn himself—'that would not engage a great force of the enemy. If we could hold the enemy at this point or that and at the same time attack elsewhere, for instance, in the Loire, the Gironde or the Scheldt, this was full of promise and success. This was indeed what had been planned for 1943. This was in fact a general picture of next year's big operation.'

Stalin's reponse was brief: he 'feared that it was not practicable'. Churchill agreed that 'it would indeed be difficult to land a million men, but that we should have to persevere and to try'.

The talk turned to the bombing of Germany. The present bombing of the German 'centres of industry', Churchill told Stalin, 'was nothing to what would be done in six months, or even in three months' time'.[1]

[1] A month later, Churchill telegraphed to Stalin from London: 'I thought you might like to know the weight of bombs dropped by the Royal Air Force on Germany since 1st July this year. The total amount from 1st July to 6th September was 11,500 tons. The tonnage dropped on the

Stalin agreed that 'this bombing was of tremendous importance', telling Churchill: 'Some military experts were inclined to underrate its effects, but he did not. It was not only German industry that should be bombed, but the population too. This was the only way of breaking German morale. In six months from now the situation might be quite different. The Germans might be on the Volga and able to withdraw from Russia sixty divisions.'

Now, Stalin told Churchill, Germany had 'almost nothing in the west'. Their 'whole forces', he insisted, 'were engaged in Russia'. Churchill disagreed. There were 'nine good divisions' in the German forces in western Europe, 'of which three were armoured'.

Churchill did not say so, but this information came from Enigma: from the Germans' own most secret military messages. Not knowing of Churchill's source, Stalin belittled the information. The Germans, he said, 'were very good at giving false information to Allied agents. They were swindlers and blackmailers and they were masters of the trick of muddling up divisions.'

Churchill then returned to the bombing of Germany. As regards the German civil population, he said, 'we looked upon its morale as a military target. We sought no mercy and we would show no mercy'; to which Stalin replied 'that that was the only way'. The minutes of the meeting continued:

The Prime Minister said that we hoped to shatter twenty German cities as we had shattered Cologne, Lübeck, Düsseldorf, and so on. More and more aeroplanes and bigger and bigger bombs. M. Stalin had heard of 2-ton bombs. We had now begun to use 4-ton bombs, and this would be continued throughout the winter. If need be, as the war went on, we hoped to shatter almost every dwelling in almost every German city. (These words had a very stimulating effect upon the meeting, and thenceforward the atmosphere became progressively more cordial.)

M. Stalin smiled and said that would not be bad.

The Prime Minister replied that it would be better still.

M. Stalin suggested that the four-ton bombs should be dropped with parachutes, otherwise they dug themselves into the ground.

With the atmosphere now somewhat improved, Churchill reverted to the question of a second front in 1942, 'which', he said, 'was what

---

more important targets was Duisburg 2,500 tons, Düsseldorf 1,250 tons, Saarbrucken 1,150 tons, Bremen and Hamburg 1,000 tons each, Osnabruck 700 tons, Kassel, Wilhelmshaven, Mainz, Frankfurt, all about 500 tons; Nuremberg received 300 tons and there were many other lesser tonnages. Included in the bombs dropped were six 8,000-lb bombs and 1,400 4,000-lb bombs. We have found that by using these with instantaneous fuses the bombs do not break up but explode most effectively, so that parachutes are not required' (Prime Minister's Personal Telegram, T.1215/2, No. 213 to Moscow, 'Personal and Secret', 12 September 1942: Churchill papers, 20/80).

he had come for'. He did not think that France 'was the only place
for such an operation', he told Stalin. 'There were other places, and
we and the Americans had decided upon another operation, which he
was authorized by the American President to impart to Stalin secretly.
He would now proceed to do so.' At this, as the minutes noted, 'M.
Stalin sat up and grinned.'

Before Churchill could speak of the secret, Stalin remarked, teas-
ingly, that he 'hoped that nothing about it would appear in the British
press'. There then followed a brief moment of badinage:

> The Prime Minister replied that he wished he could control the British
> press as M. Stalin controlled the Soviet press.
>
> M. Stalin said that Mr Churchill had quite enough powers to exercise
> control whenever he wished to.

Churchill then gave Stalin an outline of the 'Torch' landings. 'The
operation,' he said, 'consisted of the seizing of the North Coast of
French Africa—the whole of it.'

Stalin, as the minutes recorded, 'showed great interest'. Churchill
went on to give him the details. 'Two hundred and fifty thousand
men had been set aside for this purpose,' he explained, '7 divisions of
American troops and 5 divisions of British troops. The operation would
be on that basis, as 7 was to 5. The troops would be landed at Casablanca, Oran, Algiers and, if possible, Bizerta.'

The 'Torch' operation, Churchill added, had been planned for October 'because it was not thought that Hitler would be able to move troops
from the Pas de Calais in time to stop it'. Surely, Stalin asked, while it
would be difficult to find political reasons to justify an attack on North
Africa, it would be 'much easier to justify a landing in France'. But to
this Churchill answered 'that he could justify a landing in North Africa'
and he went on to describe the 'military advantages' of freeing the
Mediterranean 'whence still another front could be opened'. In September, Churchill told Stalin, 'we must win in Egypt', and in October in
North Africa, 'all the time holding the enemy in Northern France'. 'If
we could end the year in possession of North Africa,' Churchill added,
'we could threaten the belly of Hitler's Europe.'

'Stalin's interest quickened,' the minutes recorded. Churchill went
on to tell him that the North African landings 'should be considered
in conjunction with the 1943 operation'. That, Churchill said, was
what Britain and the United States 'had decided to do'.

Churchill then asked Averell Harriman to speak. 'The President,'
said Harriman, 'was in full agreement with the Prime Minister on the
decisions reached. He was pressing for as early a date as possible for
"Torch".' Churchill, who, the minutes noted, 'had meanwhile drawn

a picture of a crocodile', explained to Stalin with the help of the picture 'how it was our intention to attack the soft belly of the crocodile as we attacked its hard snout'.

Harriman, continuing, told Stalin that 'in spite of the fact' that Roosevelt had 'serious preoccupations' in the Pacific, 'his eyes were turned upon the European theatre of war as of primary concern'. Roosevelt would support the war in Europe, Harriman added, 'to the limit of the resources at his disposal'.

Stalin now made his first comment about 'Torch', telling Churchill: 'May God help this enterprise to succeed.' The minutes of the meeting added: 'His interest was now at a high pitch.'

Churchill now told Stalin that with 'Torch' 'we wanted to take the strain off the Russians' and he added:

If we attempted that in Northern France we should meet with a rebuff. If we tried in North Africa we had a good chance of victory and then we could help in Europe. If we could get North Africa, Hitler would have to bring his air force back or otherwise we would destroy his allies, even, for instance, Italy, and make a landing. The operation would have an important influence on Turkey and on the whole of Southern Europe, and all he was afraid of was that we might be forestalled. If North Africa were won this year we could make a deadly attack upon Hitler next year.

Churchill now turned to the question of the Russian southern flank, telling Stalin that he and Roosevelt 'had been turning over in their minds the question of helping in the defence of the Caspian Sea and the Caucasus'. Nothing definite had been decided, 'but he and the President thought that if we could put a powerful Anglo-American air force into Northern Persia that would help both us and the Russians. The Caucasian mountains and the neutrality of Turkey, Churchill stressed, were matters of material importance to us in that they shielded the oil of Abadan, the loss of which would threaten our whole position in India and the Middle East.'

At this point, as the minutes noted, 'M. Stalin's interest flagged a little.' There could, Churchill said, be no 'definite proposal' for Anglo-American help from Northern Persia until Britain had won the battle in Egypt.

Churchill now spoke of the deception needed in preparing 'Torch', if it were to succeed, telling Stalin:

Clever people have been talking on the lines of 'Torch' for some time past. Our aim was to pretend that we were going to strike at the Pas de Calais. Every day the Germans could for themselves see preparations which suggested this. It was of the utmost importance that nothing should be said or done to indicate that we were not going to attack Hitler in France.

At the present moment there were 350 German bombers waiting to resist our landing when it came. Hitler would remove these for work elsewhere if he had the least idea we were not going to make a landing.

Churchill went on to tell Stalin that he proposed, 'this month', if the weather were favourable, 'to make a raid on France on a large scale in order to seek information and to test the German resistance. We might lose as many as 10,000 men on this operation, which would be no more than a reconnaissance. Another means of confusing the Germans would be a sham attack on Norway. No attack would be made, but we were going on pretending that we were aiming at it. Several divisions, indeed, were being fitted out with Arctic equipment in order to suggest to the Germans that our intentions lay towards Norway.'

'By this time,' the minutes noted, 'M. Stalin was very cheerful.' Was 'Torch' aimed 'against the Germans?' he asked. It was against 'Germany's weakest ally', Churchill replied. 'It would probably result in the German seizure of unoccupied France, but he did not care whether they threw Pétain into the sea or not.'

Churchill then told Stalin of the welcome which the Americans might expect in North Africa if they said on arrival 'We come to liberate France'. At this point Stalin's interest, as the minutes noted, 'was again at high pitch'. It was important to show that this operation was being undertaken 'in the interests of France', Stalin commented, 'Otherwise the French might think that it was being undertaken by the Americans in their own interest.' It would be made clear from the beginning, Churchill assured him, 'that it was the first step in the deliverance of France'.

The minutes of the meeting continued:

M. Stalin at this point seemed suddenly to grasp the strategic advantages of 'Torch'. He saw four outstanding advantages:—
(1) It would take the enemy in the rear.
(2) It would make the Germans and French fight each other.
(3) It would put Italy out of action.
(4) It would keep the Spaniards neutral.

It was a 'good scheme', Stalin added, 'but he would like to see it put on a sounder political basis'. When Harriman said that Roosevelt was 'not afraid of the political aspects' of 'Torch' and Churchill said he was not afraid of them either, Stalin, as the minutes recorded, 'seemed satisfied'. The meeting then 'gathered round a globe', on which Churchill 'explained to M. Stalin the immense advantages of clearing the enemy out of the Mediterranean', after which Harriman pointed out 'how much the present long hauls round the Cape would be shortened'.

It was 10.40 p.m. Churchill's first meeting with Stalin was at an end. It had lasted three hours and forty minutes.[1]

As this first meeting ended, Churchill told Stalin that he would hold himself at Stalin's disposal 'should he wish to see me again'. In reply, Stalin said that it was the Russian custom 'that the visitor should state his wishes'. Churchill added, in his telegram to Attlee: 'He knows the worst, and we parted in an atmosphere of goodwill.'[2]

In his conversation with Stalin, Churchill had made no mention of the Arctic convoys. But he was certain, as he telegraphed to Attlee on the morning of August 13, that 'only the plainest and most realistic dealing is helpful'. For this reason he hoped that, despite the sinking of the aircraft carrier *Eagle* in the Mediterranean, 'you ought at least to be able to send sixty ships in the September PQ'. Churchill added: 'Please reassure me about this. I must have something to say.'[3]

On the morning of Thursday August 13 German troops in the Caucasus reached the town of Mineralniye Vody. In the Mediterranean, the 'Pedestal' convoy continued to suffer from intense air and submarine attack, and three further escort ships were sunk, the anti-aircraft ship *Cairo*, the cruiser *Manchester* and the destroyer *Foresight*, as well as eight merchant ships and six aircraft.[4]

That morning, Thursday, August 13, Churchill returned to the Kremlin to see Molotov, and to explain to him 'more clearly and fully' the character of the various operations: the abandoned 'Sledgehammer'; 'Round-up' for the Channel Coast, and 'Bolero', the build-up of substantial American forces in Britain for an eventual cross-Channel assault; 'Torch', imminent against French North Africa; and 'Jupiter', the possible joint Anglo-Soviet landing in northern Norway. Churchill sent an account of their conversation to Attlee and the War Cabinet. 'I pointed out,' he reported, 'how injurious to the common cause it would be if, owing to recriminations about dropping "Sledgehammer", we were forced to argue publicly against such enterprises. I also explained more fully the political setting of "Torch". He listened affably but contributed nothing.'[5]

During this discussion, Molotov commented that there was 'no abso-

[1] 'Meeting at the Kremlin on Wednesday, August 12, 1942, at 7 p.m.', 12 August 1942: Premier papers, 3/76A/12, folios 100–118. Subsequently printed for the Cabinet as War Cabinet Paper No. 373 of 1942, 23 August 1942, Cabinet papers, 127/23.

[2] 'Reflex' No. 85, 13 August 1942: Cabinet papers, 120/66.

[3] 'Reflex' No. 81, 13 August 1942: Cabinet papers, 120/66.

[4] The American tanker *Ohio*, first attacked north of Cape Bon on August 12, succeeded in reaching Malta after three days of continuous air bombardment, but on arrival, was declared a 'total loss' (*British Merchant Vessels Lost or Damaged by Enemy Action During Second World War, 3rd September 1939 to 2nd September 1945*, London 1947, page 39).

[5] 'Reflex' No. 93, sent at 1.30 p.m., 14 August 1942: Cabinet papers, 120/66.

lute certainty' about the 'Torch' operation taking place. Churchill assured him, however, that preparations 'were proceeding with all possible speed, and the latest date for it to take place was 80 days hence, but 60 days was a possibility'.

The situation on the eastern front, Molotov stressed, 'was far worse than in May or June'. The Russians, he added, 'were anxious something should be done to relieve the pressure on this side'.[1]

The aeroplane bringing Brooke, Wavell, Cadogan, Tedder and Jacob from Teheran reached Moscow at five in the afternoon of August 13. Six hours later they joined Churchill for his second meeting with Stalin. 'Then,' Churchill reported to Attlee and the War Cabinet, 'there began a most unpleasant discussion.' It began with Stalin handing Churchill a document protesting against the British decision not to launch a cross-Channel attack in 1942: a decision which, in the words of the Soviet document, 'inflicts a mortal blow to the whole of Soviet public opinion', and which 'complicates the situation of the Red Army at the front and prejudices the plan of the Soviet Command'. The 'most favourable' conditions existed for the creation of a second front in Europe in 1942, 'inasmuch as almost all the forces of the German army, and the best forces to boot have been withdrawn to the Eastern front, leaving in Europe an inconsiderable amount of forces and these of inferior quality'.[2]

Not only was a second front in 1942 'possible', Stalin's aide-mémoire asserted, it should also be 'effective'. 'I was however unfortunately unsuccessful,' Stalin ended, 'in convincing Mr Prime Minister of Great Britain there, while Mr Harriman, the representative of the President of the USA, fully supported Mr Prime Minister in the negotiations held in Moscow.'[3]

The 'atmosphere of goodwill' of the Wednesday night meeting had disappeared. In its place, Clark Kerr told Eden, 'the Prime Minister found the atmosphere cold and clouded'.[4] Churchill listened while Stalin's aide-mémoire was translated to him. He would, he said, answer it in writing, but that Stalin must understand 'we have made up our minds upon the course to be pursued and that reproaches were vain'.[5]

[1] 'Interview of Prime Minister with M. Molotov on August 13th at 12 a.m.': Premier papers, 3/67A/12, folios 97–9.

[2] 'Reflex' No. 93, Prime Minister's Personal Telegram, T.1112/2, 14 August 1942: Premier papers, 3/76A/9.

[3] 'Most Secret', 'Aide-Mémoire' (Translation), 13 August 1942: Premier papers, 3/76A/11, folios 39–40. The original МЕМОРАНДУМ, signed by Stalin, note by Leslie Rowan, 'Handed to PM by M. Stalin at meeting of 13.8.42' is in Premier papers, 3/76A/11, folios 42–3.

[4] Telegram No. 84 from Moscow to the Foreign Office, 'Most Secret', 16 August 1942: Premier papers, 3/76A/11, folio 16.

[5] 'Reflex' No. 93, Prime Minister's Personal Telegram, T.1112/2, 14 August 1942: Premier papers, 3/76A/9.

Churchill then re-iterated his arguments against a cross-Channel landing in 1942. 'It would be no help to Russia,' he said, 'if the United Nations were to do something that would lead simply to disaster involving them in profitless loss.' When Harriman declared, in support of Churchill, that 'the President was prepared for any sacrifice which offered a reasonable prospect of success', Stalin replied that 'if, as he assumed, Mr Harriman was speaking of the "Torch" project, this operation did not concern the Soviet directly'.

As far as the second front was concerned, Stalin continued, 'there was a difference of view as to the importance of the Russian front'. This front, in Stalin's view, 'was of first-rate importance, while he understood the British and American Governments held it to be only of secondary importance'. Hearing these words, Churchill 'protested that this was not the case'.

Stalin then spoke of the British and American supplies to Russia, those already received and those promised for the future. The Soviet Government, he said, 'had obtained little from United States and Great Britain. He did not wish to make a complaint, but felt bound to state the fact.'[1]

Averell Harriman later recalled how, to Churchill's surprise, Stalin then attacked him 'in the most vicious way'. Referring to the scattering of the escort of convoy PQ17, Stalin told Churchill: 'This is the first time in history the British Navy has ever turned tail and fled from the battle. You British are afraid of fighting. You should not think the Germans are supermen. You will have to fight sooner or later. You cannot win a war without fighting.'

Stalin was 'really insulting', Harriman recalled, and while the Soviet leader was still speaking, Harriman, remembering his own visit to Moscow a year earlier with Lord Beaverbrook, passed Churchill a note: 'Don't take this too seriously—this is the way he behaved last year.' But the 'violence of Stalin's attack was stunning to the British Prime Minister, who had come so far for this discussion, and who had done so much for the Allied cause for nearly three years'.[2]

In his report to Attlee, Churchill gave the following account of the conversation with Stalin after he had received Stalin's aide-mémoire:

Thereafter we argued for about two hours, during which he said a great many disagreeable things, especially about our being too much afraid of fighting the Germans, and if we tried it like the Russians we should find it not so bad, that we had broken our promise about 'Sledgehammer', that we had

---

[1] 'Minutes of a Meeting held in the Kremlin, Moscow, on Thursday, August 13th, 1942, at 11.15 p.m.', 13 August 1942: Premier papers, 3/76A/12, folios 81–90.

[2] Averell Harriman recollections: in conversation with the author, London, 18 July 1973.

failed in delivering the supplies promised to Russia and only sent remnants after we had taken all we needed for ourselves. Apparently these complaints were addressed as much to the United States as to Britain.[1]

Another witness of this confrontation between Stalin and Churchill was Colonel Jacob who, some ten minutes after the meeting had started, was summoned into the room in order, at Churchill's request, to take a record of what was being said:

I found things were not going too well. The Prime Minister's scheme had evidently miscarried, and a desultory argument about the possibility of a second front and similar matters, was proceeding. Stalin appeared quite at home, and made his remarks in a very low, gentle, voice, with an occasional gesture of the right hand, and never looked the Prime Minister in the face. The interpreting was done from Russian into English by Pavlov, and from English into Russian by Dunlop—an unfortunate arrangement. I naturally could not judge whether Dunlop was speaking good Russian, but Pavlov's English was crude in the extreme. Stalin was coming out with all kinds of insulting remarks, but one could not really tell whether they were being faithfully put across by Pavlov, because his vocabulary was limited.

After a time, during which Stalin was suggesting that we were not prepared to operate on the Continent because we were frightened of the Germans, the Prime Minister made an impassioned speech, in which he said that the object of his visit was to try to establish real comradeship between himself and Stalin, and in which he expressed his disappointment that Stalin should apparently not believe the sincerity of his statements, and distrust his motives.[2]

Averell Harriman listened mesmerized as Churchill answered Stalin in what, Harriman later reflected, was 'the most brilliant' of Churchill's wartime utterances. As Harriman recalled:

He described what the British had done in the year they had stood alone, what they had achieved. But he forgot that to have anything interpreted accurately you had to say a few words, and then let them be interpreted. Winston went on and on. At one point the interpreter got so enthralled by Winston's speech that he put his pencil down.

When Winston finished, the interpreter translated. But as he tried to translate, Winston kept on pushing him: 'Did you tell him this?' 'Did you tell him that?' The interpreter stumbled along. Winston got angrier and angrier: 'Have you told him this? Have you made that clear?' Stalin began to laugh and then he said—not having heard a half of what Winston had wanted to be interpreted: 'Your words are not important, what is vital is the spirit.'[3]

Before Dunlop translated Churchill's speech, Jacob noted that, 'the Prime Minister told him to repeat it in English, to make certain that

[1] 'Reflex' No. 93, Prime Minister's Personal Telegram, T.1112/2, 14 August 1042: Premier papers, 3/76A/9.
[2] Jacob notes: Jacob papers.
[3] Averell Harriman recollections: in conversation with the author, London, 18 July 1973.

he had got it right. This Dunlop began to do, but it was soon clear that he had not got it correctly. This disconcerted the Prime Minister, and he asked me to tell Dunlop what it was he had really said.'[1]

Jacob now told Dunlop what Churchill had been saying, and Dunlop at last translated an accurate version into Russian. In his reply, Churchill informed Attlee, 'I repulsed all his contentions squarely but without taunts of any kind. I suppose he is not used to being contradicted repeatedly but he did not become at all angry or even animated. On one occasion I said, "I pardon that remark only on account of the bravery of the Russian troops."'

After some time, Stalin told Churchill that he could carry the argument no further: he 'must accept' the British and American decision that there would be no cross-Channel invasion in 1942.[2] But, Stalin added, Russia would fight on 'whatever' Britain and America did.[3] Then, 'abruptly', as Churchill reported, Stalin invited him to dine with him that night. Churchill's account to Attlee continued:

Accepting the invitation, I said I would leave by plane at dawn the next morning i.e. 15th. Joe seemed somewhat concerned at this and asked could I not stay longer. I said, certainly, if there was any good to be done, and that I would wait one more day anyhow. I then exclaimed there was no ring of comradeship in his attitude. I had travelled far to establish good working relations. We had done our utmost to help Russia and would continue to do so. We had been left entirely alone for a year against Germany and Italy. Now that the three great Nations were allied, victory was certain provided we did not fall apart, and so forth. I was somewhat animated in this passage and before it could be translated he made the remark that he liked the temperament (or spirit?) of my utterance. Thereafter the talk began again in a somewhat less tense atmosphere.

He plunged into a long discussion of two Russian trench mortars firing rockets which he declared were devastating in their effects and which he offered to demonstrate to our experts if they could wait.[4] He said he would let us have all information about them, but should there not be something in return. Should there not be an agreement to exchange information of inventions. I said that we would give them everything without any bargaining except only those devices which, if carried in aeroplanes over the enemy lines and shot down would make our bombing of Germany more difficult. He accepted this. He also agreed that his Military authorities should meet our Generals and this was arranged for three o'clock this afternoon. I said they would require at least 4 hours to go fully into the various technical questions involved in 'Sledgehammer', 'Round-Up', 'Torch'. He observed at one

[1] Jacob notes: Jacob papers.
[2] 'Reflex' No. 93, Prime Minister's Personal Telegram, T.1112/2, 14 August 1942: Premier papers, 3/76A/9.
[3] Harriman recollections: in conversation with the author, London, 18 July 1973.
[4] This was the Katyusha rocket.

moment that 'Torch' was militarily correct but that the political side required more delicacy, i.e. more careful handling.

From time to time he returned to 'Sledgehammer', grumbling about it. When he said our promise had not been kept, I replied 'I repudiate that statement. Every promise has been kept.' And I pointed to the aide-mémoire I gave Molotov. He made a sort of apology saying that he was expressing his sincere and honest opinions, that there was no mistrust between us but only a difference of view.

At one point in the discussion, Churchill thanked Stalin for allowing the forty American Boston bombers then on their way to Russia to be diverted to Cairo. At that remark, Stalin 'made a half-disdainful gesture', telling Churchill: 'They were American planes. When I give you Russian planes you may thank me.' By this he did not mean to disparage the American planes, Churchill told Attlee, 'but said he counted on his own strength'.[1] Churchill's report of the conversation continued:

Finally I asked about the Caucasus. Was he going to defend the mountain chain, and with how many divisions. At this he sent for a relief model and with apparent frankness and knowledge explained the strength of this barrier, for which he said 25 divisions were available. He pointed to the various passes and said they would be defended. I asked were they fortified and he said yes certainly. The Russian front line which the enemy had not yet reached is north of the main range. He said they would have to hold out for two months when the snow would make the mountains impassable. He expressed himself quite confident of his ability to do this, and also recounted in detail the strength of the Black Sea Fleet which was already at Batum. He expressed, however, suspicion of Turkish intentions and indicated that he did not trust them not to attack him in the rear. If they did he would smash them.

All this part of the talk was easier, but when Harriman asked about the plans for bringing American aircraft across Siberia, to which the Russians have only recently consented after long American pressing, he replied, curtly, 'Wars are not won with plans.' Harriman backed me up throughout and we neither of us yielded an inch nor spoke a bitter word.

It was arranged that Cadogan and Molotov should meet today to draw up a communiqué and to discuss publicity. Stalin assented to this with a short laugh, remarking that they were the two who had drawn up the Anglo-American-Russian communiqué issued in London.

He made his salute and held out his hand to me on leaving and I took it.

'In the public interest,' Churchill informed Attlee, 'I shall go to the dinner. . . .'

On the morning of Friday, August 14, Churchill and his advisers

[1] Stalin told Churchill that his aircraft production was 1,800 a month plus 600 training aircraft. On 7 October 1942 Churchill learned that Roosevelt had given instructions for the production in the United States in 1943 of 100,000 combat aircraft, or more than 8,300 a month (Dill to Churchill, 2342, Z/7, 7 October 1942: Churchill papers, 20/81).

discussed the explanation of Stalin's 'performance' on the Thursday night, and the 'transformation from the good ground we have reached the night before'. Churchill reported the explanation he had reached when he telegraphed to Attlee during August 14:

I think the most probable is that his Council or Commissars did not take the news I brought as well as he did. They perhaps have more power than we suppose and less knowledge. And that he was putting himself on the record for future purposes and for their benefit and also letting off steam for his own. Cadogan says a similar hardening up followed the opening of the Eden interview at Christmas, and Harriman says that this technique was also used at the beginning of the Beaverbrook mission.

It is my considered opinion that in his heart so far as he has one Stalin knows we are right and that six divisions on 'Sledgehammer' would do him no good this year. Moreover I am certain that this sure-footed and quick military judgment makes him a strong supporter of 'Torch'. I think it not impossible that he will make amends. In that hope I persevere. Anyhow I am sure it was better to have it out this way than any other. There was never at any time the slightest suggestion of their not fighting on and I think myself that Stalin has good confidence that he will win.

'I make great allowances,' Churchill ended his report of August 14, 'for the stresses through which they are passing.'[1]

As well as discussing the reason for Stalin's switch of mood, Churchill and his advisers also prepared an answer to Stalin's aide-mémoire. In this reply, Churchill stated at the outset: 'The best front in 1942 and the only large-scale operation possible from the Atlantic is "Torch". If this can be effected in October it will give more aid to Russia than any other plan.' It also 'prepares the way' for 1943. But a cross-Channel attack on Cherbourg and the Channel Islands 'would be a hazardous and futile operation', which in the opinion of all British naval, military and air authorities 'could only end in disaster'. Even if the landing itself took place successfully, 'it would not bring a single division back from Russia', and would serve far more as 'a running sore for us than for the enemy', using up 'wastefully and wantonly the key men and the landing craft required for real action in 1943'. That, the British aide-mémoire stated, 'is our settled view'. If desired, General Brooke could go into the details with the Russian commanders.

No promise had been broken by Britain or the United States, Churchill reiterated. In his aide-mémoire given to Molotov on 10 June 1942 it was distinctly stated: 'We can, therefore, give no promises.' This aide-mémoire of June 1942 had followed upon 'lengthy conversations' in which 'the very small chance' of a cross-Channel

---

[1] 'Reflex' No. 93, 'Personal and Secret', 14 August 1942: repeated as Prime Minister's Personal Telegram T.1112/2 of 15 August 1942 to President Roosevelt: Premier papers, 3/76A/9.

landing in 1942 had been made 'abundantly clear'. Nor could Britain admit that the conversations with Molotov about the second front, 'safeguarded as they were by reservations both oral and written, formed any ground for altering the strategic plans of the Russian High Command'.

Churchill's aide-mémoire also contained the warning which he had given verbally to Stalin. Pointing out that 'all the talk' about an Anglo-American invasion of France in 1942 had 'misled the enemy' and held large air forces and considerable military forces on the French Channel coast, Churchill continued:

It would be injurious to all common interests, especially Russian interests, if any public controversy arose in which it would be necessary for the British Government to unfold to the nation the crushing argument which they conceive themselves to possess against 'Sledgehammer'. Widespread discouragement would be caused to the Russian armies, who have been buoyed up on this subject, and the enemy would be free to withdraw further forces from the West. The wisest course is to use 'Sledgehammer' as a blind for 'Torch', and proclaim 'Torch' when it begins as the second front. This is what we ourselves mean to do.

'We reaffirm our resolve,' Churchill's aide-mémoire ended, 'to aid our Russian Allies by every practicable means.'[1]

In support of the British position, Averell Harriman wrote to Stalin that same day, to 'reaffirm' Churchill's statement 'that no promise has been broken regarding the Second Front'.[2] Sir Alexander Cadogan, who handed the British aide-mémoire to Molotov in the early afternoon of August 14, told Molotov that Churchill 'felt puzzled and much disheartened'.[3]

At noon on August 14 General Brooke went to see Churchill at State Villa No. 7, 'and found him', he noted in his diary, 'with a headache'. He was 'not very pleased' with the result of his meeting with Stalin, and was also 'rather depressed at results of last convoy to Malta. . . .'[4]

Brooke stayed at Churchill's villa for lunch. Among the other guests was the American Ambassador to Moscow, William H. Standley. The American influence in these discussions, though not direct, was considerable. That day, in Washington, General Eisenhower was handed the outline plan for 'Torch'. The aim of the first American amphi-

---

[1] Aide-Mémoire of 14 August 1942, enclosed in 'Reflex' No. 93: Premier papers, 3/76A/12.

[2] Letter dated 14 August 1942, enclosed in 'Reflex' No. 101, 15 August 1942: Churchill papers, 20/87.

[3] Telegram No. 84, Moscow to the Foreign Office (from Sir Archibald Clark Kerr), 'Most Secret', 16 August 1942: Premier papers, 3/76A/11, folio 16.

[4] Brooke diary, 14 August 1942: Bryant, op cit., volume 1, page 462.

bious landing of the war, as the Directive of August 14 made clear, was to come ashore at various points inside the Mediterranean on its southern shore: simultaneous landings at two of the principle Mediterranean ports of French North Africa, Oran and Algiers.[1]

After lunch on August 14 Churchill took his usual rest, as he would have done in London, while Brooke went off to see the mortar demonstration which Stalin had promised. At nine o'clock in the evening, Churchill returned to the Kremlin, for his third meeting with Stalin. Colonel Jacob, who was present, noted in his diary:

Immediately we arrived, the party moved into dinner, headed by Stalin dressed, as usual, in his little lilac-coloured tunic, buttoned up to the neck, his cotton trousers stuffed into long boots. He has rather a shambling walk, and it was extraordinary to see this little peasant, who would not have looked at all out of place in a country lane with a pickaxe over his shoulder, calmly sitting down to a banquet in these magnificent halls.

Harriman was on Stalin's left. There must have been about one hundred people present, including all the leading Generals not actually engaged at the front, and various Commissars, with a good sprinkling of Americans. We had barely sat down, before Molotov sprang to his feet and proposed the Prime Minister's health in a very short speech. Pavlov translated the speech, and then we drank the toast. The Prime Minister replied, and proposed Stalin's health. Stalin then proposed the President's health, linking with it that of Mr Harriman: and so it went on.

Every five minutes throughout the dinner we were drinking somebody's health. The interesting thing on this occasion was that a large number of the toasts were proposed by Stalin, who toasted all his Generals and Admirals in turn, starting with Voroshilov, Shaposhnikov, the Chiefs of Staff, Voronov, the Commander of their Artillery, and proceeding through the chief airmen, the chief Admirals and so on.

Each time he proposed a health, Stalin made a speech of three or four sentences, and then wandered round the table, clinking glasses with the men whose health he had proposed, and cracking jokes with Molotov and others, all in the most informal and self-possessed manner. Meanwhile, the Prime Minister was left rather high and dry, with no-one to talk to; and one could see that this was not the kind of party which appealed to him at all.[2]

On the following morning, Churchill telegraphed to Attlee:

The dinner passed off in a very friendly atmosphere and the usual Russian ceremonies. Wavell made an excellent speech in Russian. I proposed Stalin's health and Alexander Cadogan proposed death and damnation to the Germans. Though I sat on Stalin's right, I got no opportunity of talking

---

[1] Jacob diary: Jacob papers.
[2] Jacob diary: Jacob papers.

about serious things. Pavlov, the little interpreter, was a very poor substitute for Maisky.[1]

What little talk there was on serious matters concerned the possibility of sending British and American air squadrons to help in the defence of the Caucasus. Churchill proposed sending twenty squadrons to Russia 'after Rommel had been defeated in North Africa', or as many as forty squadrons with American participation. 'That would be a great help,' was Stalin's reply.[2]

Out of Churchill's hearing, Stalin renewed his complaints of the previous night about Britain. As Harriman reported to Roosevelt:

Stalin told me the British Navy had lost its initiative. There was no good reason to stop the convoys. The British Armies didn't fight either at Singapore, etc. The US Navy fought with more courage and so did the Army at Bataan.

The British Air Force was good, he admitted. He showed little respect for the British military effort but much hope in that of the U.S.[3]

Harriman later recalled how, during the dinner on August 14, Stalin told his guests a long story about a prewar visit to Moscow by Lady Astor and George Bernard Shaw. During the visit, Lady Astor had proposed to Stalin to invite Lloyd George to visit the Soviet Union. Stalin had 'demurred', recalling that Lloyd George had been Prime Minister during the period of Western intervention against the Bolsheviks. 'It was Churchill who misled him,' Lady Astor had told Stalin, whereupon the Soviet leader had replied, according to his own account, that he preferred an 'outright enemy' like Churchill to a pretended friend like Lloyd George. 'Well, Churchill is finished,' Lady Astor had said, but Stalin had disagreed. 'If a great crisis comes,' he recalled saying, 'the English people might turn to the old war horse.'

Churchill then told Stalin that there was 'much truth' in what Lady Astor had said about him. 'You know,' he admitted, 'I was not friendly to you after the last war. Have you forgiven me?' To which Stalin replied, 'All that is in the past. It is not for me to forgive. It is for God to forgive.'[4]

The banquet had already lasted for nearly four hours when Stalin took Churchill into an adjoining room for coffee and liqueurs. 'The Prime Minister perked up a bit,' Colonel Jacob noted, when photographs were taken of him sitting with Stalin on sofas.'[5] As Churchill telegraphed to Attlee:

---

[1] 'Reflex No. 110', 15 August 1942: Cabinet papers, 120/67.
[2] Harriman recollections: Abel and Harriman, *op. cit.*, page 161.
[3] Harriman to Roosevelt: Abel and Harriman, *op. cit.*, page 161.
[4] Harriman recollections: Abel and Harriman, *op. cit.*, page 161.
[5] Jacob diary: Jacob papers.

Stalin and I were photographed together, also with Harriman. Stalin made quite a long speech proposing the quote Intelligence Service unquote in the course of which he made a curious reference to the Dardanelles in 1915, saying that the British had won and the Germans and Turks were already retreating but we did not know because intelligence was faulty. This picture, though inaccurate, was evidently meant to be complimentary to me.[1]

Stalin then suggested that Churchill might like to see a film. At this, Colonel Jacob noted, 'he threw his hand in and came away'.[2] He had left when he did, Churchill telegraphed to Attlee on the following morning, 'As I was afraid we should be drawn into a lengthy film and was fatigued.' His report continued:

When I said good-bye to Stalin he said that any differences that existed were only of method. I said we would try to remove even those differences by deeds. After a cordial handshake I then took my departure and got some way down the crowded room but he hurried after me and accompanied me an immense distance through corridors and staircases to the front door where we again shook hands.[3]

This walk and handshake were, as Colonel Jacob noted, 'a most unusual occurrence'.[4] To Harriman, who stayed behind for a few more minutes, Stalin explained that walking Churchill to the door 'was a courtesy he owed to a man four years older than himself'.[5] 'This long walk,' Clark Kerr telegraphed to Eden, 'or rather trot, for he had to be brisk in order to keep pace with Mr Churchill, is, I understand, without precedent in the history of the Soviet Kremlin in so far as we have impinged upon it.'[6]

At nine o'clock on the morning of Saturday August 15 Churchill sent for Colonel Jacob, to discuss with him Wednesday night's stormy meeting with Stalin, 'and forming', Jacob noted, 'second thoughts about what took place'. Churchill told Jacob that 'perhaps he had been unduly depressed and that Stalin had perhaps not meant to be as insulting as he had first thought'.

Jacob suggested to Churchill 'that he certainly ought to have another meeting with Stalin alone', and that as so much turned on the

---

[1] 'Reflex' No. 110, 15 August 1942: Cabinet papers, 120/67.
[2] Jacob diary: Jacob papers.
[3] 'Reflex' No. 110, 15 August 1942: Cabinet papers, 120/67.
[4] Jacob diary: Jacob papers.
[5] Harriman recollection: Abel and Harriman, op. cit., page 161.
[6] Telegram No. 84, Moscow to Foreign Office, 'Most Secret', 16 August 1942: Premier papers, 3/76A/11, folios 16-17.

efficiency of the interpreters, 'we should fit him out' with one of the members of the British Military Mission to Moscow, whom Jacob knew to be bilingual: Major A. H. Birse. Churchill agreed. Later that morning, as the evening meeting with Stalin was being arranged, Birse acted as interpreter for Brooke and Wavell, at their meeting with Marshal Voroshilov, Marshal Shaposhnikov and General Voronov. At this meeting the British Generals explained, as Churchill had promised Stalin they would, why a cross-Channel landing in 1942 was impossible. Voroshilov and Shaposhnikov, who replied, 'showed only too clearly', Colonel Jacob noted, 'how totally unable the Russians are to appreciate the nature of large scale operations across the sea'. The Russians then refused to answer any questions on the situation in the Caucasus, Voroshilov stating that they were 'only authorized to discuss the Second Front'.[1]

The meeting came to an end with the Russians 'reaffirming', as Colonel Jacob telegraphed to General Hollis, 'their unshakeable belief that the second front in 1942 was the decisive move which could be made, but resigned to its absence'. The final proceedings, Jacob added, were 'decidedly cordial'.[2]

The meeting over, Colonel Jacob returned to State Villa No. 7 to report to Churchill on what had occurred. The Russians, meanwhile, agreed to a further meeting of generals to discuss the Caucasus, which began at 6.30, when Voroshilov stated his 'complete confidence in the ability of the Russians to hold the region'. After a discussion on possible Anglo-American air support in the Caucasus, all of which, Voroshilov explained, was 'subject to Stalin's approval', the Soviet Marshal then said he wanted to make a statement 'off the record'. This, Jacob noted, 'turned out to be a final plea in favour of the Second Front'. If the British and Americans could act in Europe in 1942, Voroshilov declared, 'the defeat of the Germans would be assured'.[3]

By the time Jacob had returned to State Villa No. 7 to report on these talks to Churchill, the Prime Minister had left for his meeting with Stalin, set for seven o'clock. He was accompanied by Major Birse, the new interpreter. During the drive into Moscow, Birse later recalled, 'Mr Churchill asked me how long I had been in Russia and when I replied that I was born in St Petersburg, educated there and had spent altogether thirty years in the country, he seemed reassured. He said he had had rather difficult meetings with Stalin, but he was determined to have another attempt to get closer to him.' Churchill

---

[1] Jacob diary: Jacob papers.
[2] 'Reflex' No. 109, 'Most Secret', 16 August 1942: Premier papers, 3/76A/11, folio 21.
[3] Jacob diary: Jacob papers.

then asked Birse 'whether the Russian people were any happier under the Soviet regime. I replied, I thought they were hardly any happier, but on the other hand each citizen had at least a better chance in life. I pointed out that there was no freedom as we understood that word and that the NKVD were all-powerful.'

Shortly before seven, Churchill's car entered one of the Kremlin gates and 'drove on', Birse recalled, 'past the Palace, the meeting place of the Supreme Soviet, past the giant bell at the foot of a tall belfry, through the Kremlin square and to the entrance leading to the Government offices', where Stalin and other members of the Soviet Government had their private offices. 'We were led up the stairs by Stalin's bodyguard and ushered into Stalin's presence.' Birse added: 'He received us in his large Conference Room. There was a long table covered with a green cloth down one side of the room and his own writing desk at the end facing the door. Three or four large windows gave a view of the Moskva River, with the British Embassy on the opposite bank. On the walls of the room were portraits of Lenin and Marx. The furniture was stiff and lacked comfort, but the good lighting, light panelling on the walls and green cloth on the table lent an air of brightness.' [1]

Stalin was standing beside the writing table, looking glum and sulky I thought, and there was no smile of greeting on his face. He was a short stocky figure. His dark hair grew stiffly upwards from a low forehead. He had a thick moustache. His sallow complexion and oriental cast of features revealed his Caucasian origin. He was dressed in a khaki tunic, with his breeches thrust into a pair of black high boots. As he shook Churchill's hand, his eyes turned to the ground and he did not look into his guest's face.

I was introduced as the new interpreter. I felt a soft, limp hand in mine, with no welcoming pressure—only a quick look at my face. He then waved us to the head of the conference table, and we took our seats—four of us, for Stalin had Pavlov, his own interpreter, with him.

I had my scribbling pad with me, with two or three sharpened pencils which I always carried in my pocket, and I set these out in front of me, ready to begin. Churchill spoke slowly and clearly, and I found no difficulty either in writing my notes or in putting them across in Russian. His remarks were prefaced by a kind of suppressed murmur, as if he were trying out the richness of his words while on their way from brain to tongue, as if he were repeating them to himself, testing them, discarding the inappropriate, and choosing precisely the right expression. I could almost hear them travelling from the depths of his being to burst into life.

---

[1] 'Notes on the Meetings of the Big Three', sent by Major Birse to Churchill on 12 June 1947: Churchill papers, 4/391A.

Major Birse's account continued:

At first Stalin hardly even looked up, seemingly absorbed in doodling, but once or twice during my translation he looked at me, the first time with no expression at all, but later something like a look of approval seemed to emerge, like the sun breaking through the dark clouds. When he spoke, in answer to some of Churchill's questions, until I had become accustomed to his voice, I found it difficult to follow what he said, on account of his low voice and unfamiliar Georgian accent. It was as if a native of the remote Highlands of Scotland were speaking English. His Russian was perfectly correct, simple and with no flourishes, but it sounded foreign until one's ear got used to it. . . .

Although 'ostensibly only a farewell visit', Birse commented, it 'assumed a sombre tone with Stalin's inevitable references to a Second Front'. Birse added:

Churchill gradually brought the talk round to more congenial subjects, such as the defence of the Caucasus, the proposed landings in North Africa, and the northern convoys. After the talk had been proceeding for nearly an hour, with Pavlov putting Stalin's words into English and me scribbling and interpreting Churchill into Russian, my chief turned to me and asked:
'Are you getting me across all right?'
I replied that I thought I was, whereupon he said:
'I think you are doing very well.'
By this time Stalin's face had lighted up and he had permitted himself an occasional smile.

It was Churchill who opened the proceedings by thanking Stalin, as Birse's notes recorded, 'for all his courtesy and hospitality'. Churchill told the Soviet leader:

I realised that what I had to say about the opening of a second front would be very painful to our Russian friends and so I thought it would be my duty to come myself to see you, Premier Stalin—that it would be more friendly and a proof of my sincere feelings if I came myself—rather than communicate through our Ambassador or by an exchange of telegrams.

I asked for plain speaking and I should like to say that I have no feeling in my heart about anything that has been said, though naturally we have not agreed on all points. I hope that nothing stands between us. I came here, apart from direct business, with the earnest wish for a personal understanding. That was also the wish of the President of the USA and I hope he feels that progress has been made. I received a nice message from the President this morning.[1]

The message from Roosevelt was then read out by Stalin's inter-

[1] 'Record of the Prime Minister's Meeting with Mr Stalin at the Kremlin at 7 p.m. on the 15th August 1942', notes made by Major Birse during the meeting, 15 August 1942: Premier papers, 3/76A/12, folios 30–4.

preter, Pavlov, and translated by Pavlov into Russian. 'Mr Stalin's understanding of our difficulties,' Roosevelt had telegraphed, 'and his cordiality, have made me very happy. I only wish that I might be with you both, as that would complete the party.' The telegram ended: 'Give Mr Stalin my warmest regards and keep me in touch with developments.'[1]

Stalin then answered Churchill's opening remarks:

If I were asked to give an appreciation of events, e.g. the visit of Mr Churchill, I would say that this personal exchange of views has been of the most importance. The fact that we have met is of very great value. We have got to know each other and we have understood one another. Obviously there are differences between us, but differences are in the nature of things. The fact that the meeting has taken place, that personal contact has been established, means that the ground has been prepared for future agreement. All that is very valuable.

'I am inclined,' Stalin added, 'to look upon things with optimism.'

Churchill then produced a paper giving the scheduled arrivals of American troops in Britain. Out of the total shown, of a million troops, 'about 85,000 have landed in the UK so far'. He was 'not entitled', Churchill explained, 'to give you this paper, although I am sure that the President would like me to do so. However, I would like you to look at it.'

Churchill handed Stalin the paper, which Stalin examined and then returned. 'Mr Stalin expressed satisfaction,' Birse noted, 'but suggested that the arrivals might be behind the schedule through sinkings in the Atlantic.' But Churchill was able to assure Stalin that there had been 'hardly any losses' of troop transports, all of which were escorted in convoy. The discussion then turned to 'Torch':

The Prime Minister went on to say that he was most pleased at Mr Stalin's very swift appreciation of the military significance of 'Torch', though he quite recognises that it affects Russia only indirectly. He was pleased to note Mr Stalin's judgment in seizing on the four advantages which he had mentioned. Mr Stalin asked if the Prime Minister thought it would succeed.

The Prime Minister replied that he had very great hopes of its success in October and that it would create much difficulty for Hitler and Vichy. The defenders are very half-hearted and it should not be a difficult task for the British and American troops who will be employed there.

Mr Stalin remarked that the indirect effect on Russia will be very great. It will be a blow to the Axis Powers. He asked if he might put a few questions. If the operation succeeds, the South of France must also be occupied? Were we prepared to do so?

The Prime Minister replied that of course what we wanted to do was to

[1] President to Prime Minister, No. 179, 'Secret'; Premier papers, 3/76A/11, folio 26.

put this army into France and Italy. That would mean a frontal and a flank attack.

Success in North Africa, Churchill explained, would probably force the Germans to occupy the Vichy coast, as well as Sicily and Italy. But at the same time, she could not remove her aircraft and troops 'from the French coast opposite England'. Then, as Churchill explained:

In order to make Germany anxious about an attack from across the Channel, there will be a more serious raid in August, although the weather might upset it. It will be a reconnaissance in force. Some 8,000 men with 50 tanks will be landed. They will stay a night and a day, kill as many Germans as possible and take prisoners. They will then withdraw.

That is a reconnaissance in force. It can be compared to a bath which you feel with your hand to see if the water is hot. But of course such operations depend on the weather. The air must be fairly clear to enable fighter protection to be given and the sea not too rough to enable the men to be landed. As we intend to withdraw immediately after the operation, I am having leaflets prepared which will tell the French to stay in their houses, to prevent reprisals as at St Nazaire.

The object is to get information and to create the impression of an invasion. Most important, I hope it will call forth a big air battle.

Stalin asked whether, after this cross-Channel raid, the Germans would not broadcast the 'failure of a British attempt at invasion'. They would 'certainly say that', Churchill replied, 'but if we take prisoners and kill many Germans', he added, 'then we too can say something about it'. If 'Torch' succeeded, said Stalin, then 'everybody will understand'.[1]

The discussion then turned to the Eastern front. 'We had an agreeable conversation,' Churchill telegraphed to Attlee on the following day, in the course of which Stalin 'gave me full account of the Russian position which seemed very encouraging. He certainly speaks with great confidence of being able to hold out until the winter.'[2]

During this part of their talk, Churchill asked Stalin particularly whether the Red Army would be able to hold the Caucasus mountain passes, and also prevent the Germans reaching the Caspian, taking the oilfields round Baku, with all that meant, and then driving southwards through Turkey or Persia. In reply, Stalin spread out the map, and then said with quiet confidence: 'We shall stop them. They will not cross the mountains.' Stalin added: 'There are rumours that the Turks will attack us in Turkestan. If they do I shall be able to

---

[1] 'Record of the Prime Minister's Meeting with Mr Stalin at the Kremlin at 7 p.m. on the 15th August 1942', notes made by Major Birse during the meeting, 15 August 1942: Premier papers, 3/76A/12, folios 30–4.

[2] 'Reflex' No. 112, 16 August 1942: Premier papers, 3/76A/11, folios 13–15.

deal with them as well.' Churchill then told Stalin there was no danger of this. 'The Turks meant to keep out, and would certainly not quarrel with England.' [1]

On the previous day, Stalin had told Churchill that twenty-five Red Army Divisions would be assigned to the defence of the Caucasus mountain line, and the Black Sea and Caspian shore lines at either end of the mountains. The two ports, Batum on the Black Sea and Baku on the Caspian, could both be held, in Stalin's view, until the winter snows 'greatly improve their position'. Brooke, who had flown over the eastern Caucasus and seen only minimal defences, was sceptical of this Soviet confidence. But now, in their private conversation, Stalin told Churchill 'other solid reasons for his confidence' including, as Churchill telegraphed on the following day to Attlee, 'a counter offensive on a great scale, but as he asked me to keep this specially secret, I will not refer to it further here'.

Churchill's 'own feeling', he told Attlee, was that it was 'an even chance' that the Caucasus would hold, although Brooke 'will not go as far as this.' [2]

At one point during the discussion about the Eastern front, Churchill told Stalin 'that we were prepared to send squadrons of the RAF to assist in the defence of Caucasia'. These squadrons, Stalin replied, 'would be very valuable'. Stalin also told Churchill that he had received his warning about the German intention to attack, a warning which Churchill had sent in April 1941, about the location and movement of German divisions intended for the invasion of Russia. He had 'never doubted it', Stalin replied, 'but he wanted to gain time, six months, but it was impossible'.

As the discussion came to an end Churchill said that he 'sincerely hoped for cordiality and friendliness between them in the future'. Churchill added: 'We have no antagonistic interests.' Stalin, as Birse noted, 'quite agreed', whereupon Churchill replied 'that we must work night and day for victory'. [3]

Churchill and Stalin had been talking for more than an hour. Meanwhile, at State Villa No. 7, the commander of the Polish forces, General Anders, was waiting to dine with the British Prime Minister, to discuss the employment of his Polish troops in the Middle East. 'When I got up to leave,' Churchill reported to Attlee, Stalin 'asked when was the next time he was going to see me. I said I was leaving at dawn. He

[1] Winston S. Churchill, *The Second World War*, volume 4, London 1951, page 445.

[2] 'Reflex' No. 134, 17 August 1942: Cabinet papers, 120/67.

[3] 'Record of the Prime Minister's Meeting with Mr Stalin at the Kremlin at 7 p.m. on the 15th August 1942', notes made by Major Birse during the meeting, 15 August 1942: Premier papers, 3/76A/12, folios 30–4.

then said "why do you not come over to my apartment in the Kremlin and have some drinks?".'[1] Then, as Churchill later recalled:

I said that I was in principle always in favour of such a policy. So he led the way through many passages and rooms till we came out into a roadway still within the Kremlin, and in a couple of hundred yards gained the apartment where he lived. He showed me his own rooms, which were of moderate size, simple, dignified, and four in number—a dining-room, working room, bedroom, and a large bathroom.

Presently there appeared, first a very aged housekeeper and later a handsome red-haired girl, who kissed her father dutifully. He looked at me with a twinkle in his eye, as if, so I thought, to convey, 'You see, even we Bolsheviks have family life.' Stalin's daughter started laying the table, and in a short time the housekeeper appeared with a few dishes. Meanwhile Stalin had been uncorking various bottles, which began to make an imposing array. Then he said, 'Why should we not have Molotov? He is worrying about the communiqué. We could settle it here. There is one thing about Molotov—he can drink.'

I then realised that there was to be a dinner. I had planned to dine at State Villa Number Seven, where General Anders, the Polish commander, was awaiting me, but I told my new and excellent interpreter, Major Birse, to telephone that I should not be back till after midnight. Presently Molotov arrived. We sat down, and, with two interpreters, were five in number. Major Birse has lived twenty years in Moscow, and got on very well with the Marshal, with whom he for some time kept up a running conversation, in which I could not share.

We actually sat at this table from 8.30 p.m. till 2.30 the next morning, which, with my previous interview, made a total of more than seven hours. The dinner was evidently improvised on the spur of the moment, but gradually more and more food arrived. We pecked and picked, as seemed to be the Russian fashion, at a long succession of choice dishes, and sipped a variety of excellent wines. Molotov assumed his most affable manner, and Stalin, to make things go, chaffed him unmercifully.

Presently we talked about the convoys to Russia. This led him to make a rough and rude remark about the almost total destruction of the Arctic convoy in July.

'Mr Stalin asks,' said Pavlov, with some hesitation, 'has the British Navy no sense of glory?' I answered, 'You must take it from me that what was done was right. I really do know a lot about the Navy and sea-war.' 'Meaning,' said Stalin, 'that I know nothing.' 'Russia is a land animal,' I said; 'the British are sea animals.' He fell silent and recovered his good-humour. I turned the talk on to Molotov. 'Was the Marshal aware that his Foreign Secretary on his recent visit to Washington had said he was determined to pay a visit to New York entirely by himself, and that the delay in his return was not due to any defect in the aeroplane, but because he was off on his own?'

[1] 'Reflex' No. 112, 16 August 1942: Premier papers, 3/76A/11, folios 11–15.

Although almost anything can be said in fun at a Russian dinner, Molotov looked rather serious at this. But Stalin's face lit with merriment as he said:

'It was not to New York he went. He went to Chicago, where the other gangsters live.'

Relations having thus been entirely restored, the talk ran on. I opened the question of a British landing in Norway with Russian support, and explained how, if we could take the North Cape in the winter and destroy the Germans there the path of the convoys would henceforward be open. This idea was always, as has been seen, one of my favourite plans. Stalin seemed much attracted by it, and, after talking of ways and means, we agreed we must do it if possible.[1]

As Major Birse recorded, it was Stalin who had 'proposed that an operation against Northern Norway should be undertaken, with the object of capturing the German bases there and at Petsamo'. To this, Churchill had 'immediately agreed, welcoming the suggestion warmly', and telling Stalin that he had 'always wished for such an operation'. Stalin then recalled that there had been a former plan of a similar nature, but that the respective General Staffs 'had not wished it'. Churchill 'agreed with Mr Stalin', as Birse noted, 'that representatives of the staff were sometimes too ponderous and slow', adding 'that he had recently dismissed five generals in the Middle East'.

As their discussion continued, Stalin asked Churchill for lorries instead of tanks. Russian tank production was 'satisfactory', he explained, but they were short of lorries 'and the demand was very great'. Stalin then explained how each Red Army Armoured Brigade 'had to be supplied with lorries to carry its lorry-borne infantry, how they were rapidly motorising infantry divisions, and what enormous requirements there were for lorries in the back areas'.

Stalin asked Churchill for 20,000 to 25,000 lorries a month; 'it was immaterial', he said, whether they came from Britain or the United States. Russia's own production, he said, was 2,000 lorries a month. 'Send us lorries instead of tanks,' Stalin asked, and went on to press for more aluminium, as 'Russia was very short'.

Churchill replied that he would go 'immediately' into the question of these supplies. A few moments later, the discussion turned to the bombing of Germany. As Birse recorded:

The Prime Minister said that our bombing of German towns would increase as soon as the nights lengthened. Mr Stalin said that the Russians intended to bomb Berlin very soon and also a number of other towns, like: Koenigsberg, Danzig, Tilsit, Memel. Mr Stalin several times emphasized the importance of air forces in this war.

[1] Winston S. Churchill, *The Second World War*, volume 4, London 1951, pages 446–7.

Stalin then asked for 'some figures' of British manpower. There were, Churchill replied, fifteen divisions in the Middle East, ten in India, and thirty in Britain, of which twenty were 'fully equipped'. Churchill added: 'We were pushing on with the equipment of the remainder.' The discussion then became more personal, recorded once more by Birse:

The Prime Minister said that if Mr Stalin was going to meet President Roosevelt and got as far as Iceland, he should come on to England; he would get a magnificent reception.

Mr Stalin replied that he would like to do so, but receptions were not so important at present; the chief thing was victory. He said he had been to England in 1907 to attend a Bolshevik conference, together with Lenin, Plekhanov, Gorky and others.

The Prime Minister asked whether Trotsky had been there.

Mr Stalin replied that he had, but he had gone away a disappointed man, not having been given any organisation to represent, such as the Army, which Trotsky had hoped for.

The talk now turned to Russia's pre-war Ambassador to London, and to the era of appeasement:

The Prime Minister said that Mr Maisky was a good Ambassador.

Mr Stalin agreed, but said that he might be better; he spoke too much and could not keep his tongue between his teeth.

The Prime Minister said that Mr Maisky had recently addressed a meeting of members of the House of Commons in one of the Committee Rooms, which was quite right and proper. The Axis wireless, however, described it as Mr. Maisky haranguing the House from the Strangers Gallery on the subject of Anglo-Soviet relations.

The Prime Minister said that early in 1938, before Prague and Munich, he had had a plan for a League of the three Great Democracies: Great Britain, USA and USSR, which between them could lead the world. There were no antagonistic interests between them.

Mr Stalin agreed and said that he had always hoped for something of that nature, only under Mr Chamberlain's government such a plan would have been impossible. He recalled the visit to Moscow of the British Delegations in 1939. No talks with them were possible. For instance, the British and French military chiefs were asked what forces they could put up against Germany in the West. The French replied eighty divisions, although he did not believe that they were fully equipped, and the British said three divisions. The French did not understand the value of tanks. Then the delegation asked what the Russians could put up on the Polish frontier.

Mr Stalin had the impression that the talks were insincere and only for the purpose of intimidating Hitler, with whom the Western Powers would later come to terms.

The Prime Minister pointed out that he had not been in the Government

for eleven years, but he had always warned it of the danger. He agreed that
the Delegations in 1939 had no weight behind them.

There was then a brief reference to Roosevelt:

The Prime Minister said, jokingly, that he thought the President of the
USA, when he met Mr Stalin, would probably want him to do something
about God! Mr Stalin appreciated the joke and replied that he personally
respected God and hoped that with God's help they would achieve victory.[1]

There were several other topics of conversation, recalled by Major
Birse. Churchill, he noted:

. . . made a reference to the Duke of Marlborough, who in his time—the
War of the Spanish Succession—had put an end to a menace to Europe's
freedom, a menace as great as Hitler's. He referred to Marlborough's genius
as a military leader, and to the brilliant victories he had won at Blenheim,
Ramillies and so forth.
A sly, mischievous look came over Stalin's face as he listened, and then, to
cap what Churchill had said, he remarked. 'I think England had a greater
general in Wellington, who defeated Napoleon, the greatest menace of all
time.'
He then proceeded to exhibit his knowledge of history by references to
Wellington's invasion of Spain (at that time a Second Front!) and the final
victory at Waterloo, quoting chapter and verse with regard to some of the
battles. I imagine that he had made a special study of the Napoleonic wars,
which in many respects paralleled the one then in progress.[2]

During their discussion Stalin asked Churchill why he had 'bombed
his Molotov' when Stalin had sent Molotov to Berlin in 1940. To this
Churchill replied 'that in war no advantages can ever be neglected'.
Stalin then said that Molotov was engaged in conversation with
Ribbentrop, who was saying that 'the British Empire was now
finished' and that the time had come to work out the partition of
those lands between Germany and Russia. 'At this moment,' Stalin recounted, 'the bombers arrived, and Ribbentrop decided to continue the
discussion in the dugout. When safely established underground
Ribbentrop continued saying that, as he had already mentioned, the
British Empire need no longer be taken account of. Molotov interrupted
at this point with the awkward question: "Then why are we down here
now?"' This, Major Birse recalled, had 'pleased Stalin very much' and
he told Churchill 'that his Molotov had a good sense of humour'.[3]
It was after midnight, but Sir Alexander Cadogan had not yet

[1] Major Birse's 'rough notes from memory of the conversation between the Prime Minister
and Mr Stalin at supper in Mr Stalin's private apartments at the Kremlin, on the night of 15th
to 16th August 1942': Premier papers, 3/76A/12, folios 35–7.
[2] A. H. Birse, *Memoirs of an Interpreter*, New York 1967, page 103.
[3] Quoted in Bryant, *op. cit.*, volume 1, page 472.

returned with the draft communiqué. Churchill and Stalin talked about the past, as Churchill later recalled:

'Tell me,' I asked, 'have the stresses of this war been as bad to you personally as carrying through the policy of the Collective Farms?'

This subject immediately roused the Marshal.

'Oh no,' he said, 'the Collective Farm policy was a terrible struggle.'

'I thought you would have found it bad,' said I, 'because you were not dealing with a few score thousands of aristocrats or big landowners, but with millions of small men.'

'Ten millions,' he said, holding up his hands. 'It was fearful. Four years it lasted. It was absolutely necessary for Russia, if we were to avoid periodic famines, to plough the land with tractors. We must mechanise our agriculture. When we gave tractors to the peasants they were all spoiled in a few months. Only Collective Farms with workshops could handle tractors. We took the greatest trouble to explain it to the peasants. It was no use arguing with them. After you have said all you can to a peasant he says he must go home and consult his wife, and he must consult his herder.' This last was a new expression to me in this connection.

'After he has talked it over with them he always answers that he does not want the Collective Farm and he would rather do without the tractors.'

'These were what you call Kulaks?'

'Yes,' he said, but he did not repeat the word. After a pause, 'It was all very bad and difficult—but necessary.'

'What happened?' I asked.

'Oh, well,' he said, 'many of them agreed to come in with us. Some of them were given land of their own to cultivate in the province of Tomsk or the province of Irkutsk or farther north, but the great bulk were very unpopular and were wiped out by their labourers.'

There was a considerable pause. Then, 'Not only have we vastly increased the food supply, but we have improved the quality of the grain beyond all measure. All kinds of grain used to be grown. Now no one is allowed to sow any but the standard Soviet grain from one end of our country to the other. If they do they are severely dealt with. This means another large increase in the food supply.'

I record as they come back to me these memories, and the strong impression I sustained at the moment of millions of men and women being blotted out or displaced for ever. A generation would no doubt come to whom their miseries were unknown, but it would be sure of having more to eat and bless Stalin's name. I did not repeat Burke's dictum, 'If I cannot have reform without injustice, I will not have reform.' With the World War going on all round us it seemed vain to moralise aloud.

At about one o'clock in the morning—it was now Sunday, August 16—Sir Alexander Cadogan returned to Stalin's rooms with the draft communiqué, in which the British and Soviet Governments expressed their determination to carry on the war 'with all their power and energy' until the complete destruction 'of Hitlerism and any similar tyranny' had been achieved. The two leaders also reaffirmed 'the existence of the close friendship and understanding' between the Soviet Union, Britain and the United States 'in entire accordance with the Allied relationship existing between them'.

The communiqué was almost ready. Then, as Churchill later recalled:

A considerable sucking-pig was brought to the table. Hitherto Stalin had only tasted the dishes, but now it was half-past one in the morning and around his usual dinner hour. He invited Cadogan to join him in the conflict, and when my friend excused himself our host fell upon the victim single-handed. After this had been achieved he went abruptly into the next room to receive the reports from all sectors of the front, which were delivered to him from 2 a.m. onwards. It was about twenty minutes before he returned, and by that time we had the communiqué agreed. Finally, at 2.30 a.m. I said I must go. I had half an hour to drive to the villa, and as long to drive back to the airport. I had a splitting headache, which for me was very unusual. I still had General Anders to see. I begged Molotov not to come and see me off at dawn, for he was clearly tired out. He looked at me reproachfully, as if to say, 'Do you really think I would fail to be there?' [1]

Churchill was pleased with this, his fourth talk with Stalin in four days. 'I had a very good interpreter,' he telegraphed to Attlee, 'and was able to talk much more easily. The greatest goodwill prevailed, and for the first time we got on to easy and friendly terms.' Churchill added: 'I feel that I have established a personal relationship which will be helpful.'

In his telegram to Attlee, Churchill stressed Stalin's support for the northern Norway landing, 'which he thinks essential in November or December'. Without it, Churchill told Attlee, 'I really do not see how we are going to be able to get through the supplies which will be needed to keep this tremendous fighting army equipped.' The Trans-Persian route was only working 'at half what we hoped'. As Stalin would also rather have lorries than tanks, 'of which he is making 2,000 a month', as well as aluminium, the northern convoys seemed essential. [2]

Churchill returned to State Villa No. 7. It was 3.15 in the morning. There, General Anders awaited him. General Brooke, who was also present, recalled Churchill's words: 'Ah! my poor Anders. I have been detained by M. Stalin and now I must fly off, but you come along to Cairo and we shall have a talk there.' Anders, who had already flown

---

[1] Winston S. Churchill, *The Second World War*, volume 4, London 1951, pages 447–9.
[2] 'Reflex' No. 112, 16 August 1942: Premier papers, 3/76A/11, folios 13–15.

from Tashkent to Moscow to see Churchill, now prepared to continue to Cairo 'as if', Brooke later recalled, 'it was in the next street'.[1]

After Anders had left, Colonel Jacob noted, 'the Prime Minister had a bath'. Then, while he was still dressing, Jacob went in to talk to him. Exhausted by his long evening, Churchill lay down on a sofa, giving Jacob, and the British Ambassador to Moscow, Sir Archibald Clark Kerr, an account of his conversation with Stalin. 'The Prime Minister was very tired,' Jacob noted, 'and lay talking with his eyes shut. Nevertheless, he was very satisfied with the way things had gone, and felt that his visit had turned out a great success.'[2]

As Churchill gave Jacob and Clark Kerr an account of his seven hours with Stalin, Molotov arrived at State Villa No. 7. It was 4.30 in the morning. In less than half an hour the Prime Minister had reached the airport: 'We started at 5.00 a.m.,' he informed Attlee, 'with full military ceremonies as dawn was breaking.'[3] As the band played the 'Internationale', 'God Save the King' and the 'Star Spangled Banner', Churchill stood to attention and saluted. 'Then a series of good-byes,' General Brooke noted in his diary, 'to Molotov, Shaposhnikov, Anders, etc. etc. Finally at 5.30 a.m. we took off in four Liberators and flew off in formation.'[4]

The confrontation with Stalin was over. 'On the whole,' Churchill telegraphed to Attlee, 'I am definitely encouraged by my visit to Moscow. I am sure that the disappointing news I brought could not have been imparted except by me personally without leading to really serious drifting apart.' Churchill's telegram ended:

It was my duty to go. Now they know the worst, and having made their protest are entirely friendly; this in spite of the fact that this is their most anxious and agonising time. Moreover M. Stalin is entirely convinced of the great advantages of Torch and I do trust that it is being driven forward with superhuman energy on both sides of the ocean.[5]

Reflecting on the talks between Churchill and Stalin, Molotov commented to Clark Kerr on August 20 that 'ultimately even their

---

[1] Brooke recollections: Bryant, *op. cit.*, volume 1, page 473.

[2] Jacob diary: Jacob papers, pages 56–7. On his return to London, Churchill wrote to the Secretary of State for War, Sir James Grigg, and to General Ismay: 'I am much impressed by the work and bearing of Colonel E. I. C. Jacob, RE. He showed marked ability and competence when he accompanied me during my recent visit to the Middle East and Moscow. I consider that the position which he holds and the duties which he discharges in my Defence Office should carry with them the rank of Brigadier, and I should be glad if arrangements could be made for Colonel Jacob to be promoted to that rank. I do not contemplate being able to release him from his present duties for other service' (Prime Minister's Personal Minute, M.365/2, 'Personal', 11 September 1942: Churchill papers, 20/67).

[3] 'Reflex' No. 112, 16 August 1942: Premier papers, 3/76A/11, folios 7–8.

[4] Brooke diary, 16 August 1942: Bryant, page 471.

[5] 'Reflex' No. 112, 16 August 1942: Premier papers, 3/76A/11, folios 7–8.

rough places had done good because their roughness came of frankness and sincerity—two things that were essential as a foundation of understanding'. 'When I said that Churchill had taken a liking to Stalin,' Clark Kerr replied, 'he said this had been fully reciprocated and that Stalin had been impressed by the Prime Minister's spirit and by his dynamic qualities.' Clark Kerr added: 'So far as I am able to judge I should say that this was true. Stalin is a lonely man and head and shoulders above those about him. It must therefore have been stimulating to meet a man of his own calibre.' [1]

'Congratulations on the successful outcome of your visit,' Attlee telegraphed to Churchill on August 17. 'We are greatly in your debt.' [2]

'After rounding of sundry dangerous corners,' Clark Kerr telegraphed to Eden, 'the Prime Minister's visit came, as I had hoped, to a happy end at 5 o'clock this morning, when he set out in fine fettle on his flight to Teheran.'

'For myself,' Clark Kerr added, 'I feel that the visit has been immensely worthwhile and that the Prime Minister is much to be congratulated upon the way in which, by sheer force of his personality, he has beaten down the barrier which seemed unshakeable and dispelled the long standing and tenacious suspicions which have clouded the judgement of Stalin. I am left with high hopes that the way has now been cleared of much that cluttered it up and that we may now look forward to the future with some confidence.' [3]

'As a bearer of unwelcome news,' King George VI telegraphed to Churchill on August 17, 'your task was a very disagreeable one, but I congratulate you heartily on the skill with which you have accomplished it.' The personal relationship 'which you have established with Stalin', the King added, 'should be valuable in the days to come, and your long journey has, I am sure, been well worthwhile. I hope that you are not too tired, and that you will be able to take things more easily now.' [4]

As Churchill flew from Moscow, southward across southern Russia and the Caspian sea, Soviet forces evacuated the Caucasian oil town of Maikop. Reaching Teheran, Churchill telegraphed to Stalin: 'I am very glad I came to Moscow: firstly because it was my duty to tell the tale; and, secondly, because I feel sure our contacts will play a helpful

---

[1] 'Tulip' No. 230 'to Sir Alexander Cadogan', 'Most Secret', 21 August 1942: Premier papers, 3/76A/10, folio 7.

[2] 'Tulip' No. 156, sent 11.10 a.m., 17 August 1942: Premier papers, 3/76A/11, folio 9.

[3] No. 84 from Moscow to the Foreign Office, 'Most Secret': Premier papers, 3/76A/11, folio 16.

[4] 'Tulip' No. 166, 'Most Secret', 17 August 1942: Premier papers, 3/76A/8, folio 2.

part in furthering our cause.' [1] Commenting on the Russian reaction to the news of no European landing in 1942, Churchill telegraphed to Roosevelt on August 17: 'In the upshot they have swallowed this bitter pill. Everything for us now turns on hastening "Torch" and defeating Rommel.' [2] Russia would not let the Western Allies down, or be knocked out of the war. 'There was never any suggestion about the Russians not fighting on,' Churchill telegraphed on August 27 to the Prime Ministers of Canada and Australia, 'and I think Stalin has good confidence that he will win.' [3]

With Washington, Cairo and Moscow behind him, Churchill could now see how the course of the war was set. The United States would work for the defeat of Hitler in Europe, with a cross-Channel landing as its principal means. First, however, Britain and the United States would fight together to drive the Germans from North Africa, and to establish Allied control from the Atlantic coast of Africa to the Suez Canal. Such help as could be given to Russia would continue to be sent, both by northern convoy and, increasingly, by the trans-Persia Caspian route. At Stalin's request the Anglo-American bombing of German cities would be intensified. But the timing of the 'Second Front' would be determined in London and Washington, not in Moscow. There would be no cross-Channel landing in 1942, nor until such time as Churchill, Roosevelt and their military advisers judged it to be a feasible operation of war. North Africa would be the focal point of Anglo-American efforts for the remaining four and a half months of 1942.

Churchill's task was to ensure that the Chiefs of Staff and the commanders in the field worked in harmony; that the essential war supplies flowed in the quantities needed to the areas which needed them; that all secondary operations agreed upon by the Chiefs of Staff were given the support they needed; and, above all, that in all matters of war policy, he and Roosevelt remained in the closest contact and accord. Such were the lessons and decisions of his long and tiring travels, which now, with those decisions behind them, continued in a new and invigorated way, and with a renewed sense of eventual, if not imminent, triumph over both Germany and Japan.

---

[1] Prime Minister's Personal Telegram, T.1115/2, 16 August 1942: Churchill papers, 20/132.
[2] Prime Minister's Personal Telegram, T.1116/2, 17 August 1942: Churchill papers, 20/88.
[3] Prime Minister's Personal Telegram, T.1138A/2, 'Most Secret and Personal', 27 August 1942: Churchill papers, 20/79.

12

Return to Cairo

AFTER spending the night at the British Embassy in Teheran, Churchill flew on the morning of 17 August 1942 from Teheran, across the mountains of Kurdistan, the Tigris, the Euphrates, the Dead Sea and the Sinai desert to Cairo, a flight of six hours. On reaching Cairo, he held talks with the new Commander-in-Chief of the Middle East Forces, General Alexander, and the new Commander of the Eighth Army, Lieutenant General Montgomery, about the coming offensive. Alexander, as Churchill reported to Attlee, 'has good hopes it will take place in September, but I cannot hurry the process beyond his judgement. He realizes the extreme urgency.' The new offensive against Rommel would be 'a decisive stroke', to be carried out before the Anglo-American landings in North Africa.[1]

After lunch at the British Embassy, and a rest, Churchill had various appointments, but, as Colonel Jacob noted, 'was not feeling at all well'. He then called for Sir Charles Wilson, who 'sent him home to bed'.[2]

While Churchill rested, recovering his strength after so long and tiring a series of journeys, news reached Cairo of an outbreak of violence in India. As a result of Gandhi's call on the British to 'Quit India', riots had broken out in Calcutta, whereupon Gandhi was placed under house arrest. 'My own conviction,' Churchill telegraphed to the Viceroy of India that evening, 'is that if this situation is handled with the poise and strength which the Government of India is showing under your guidance it will soon demonstrate the very slender hold which the Congress have both upon the Indian masses and upon the dominant forces in Indian life and society.'[3]

---

[1] 'Reflex' No. 134, 17 August 1942; Churchill papers, 20/87.
[2] Jacob diary, 17 August 1942; Jacob papers.
[3] 'Reflex' No. 136, Prime Minister's Personal Telegram, T.1121/2, 'Most Secret and Personal', 17 August 1942: Churchill papers, 20/79.

At a conference in Cairo on August 18, Churchill, Brooke, Wavell, Alexander, Tedder and others discussed a scheme, put forward by Brooke, for a Persia-Iraq military command, independent of the Middle East Command. 'PM is taken with my scheme,' Brooke noted in his diary, 'and meeting took to it too.'[1] It was clear from the most secret sources of British intelligence that Hitler had no immediate plan to deflect his forces in southern Russia southwards through the Caucasus to the oilfields of Iraq and Persia, and to the Persian Gulf. Yet such an advance, if it were to take place, 'far outweighed', as Brooke later reflected, 'anything that might be gained through the capture of Stalingrad'.[2] A separate command would ensure readiness against any such German move. The strategic study of the 'growing danger' to Persia and Iraq from the Caucasus 'is urgent', Churchill telegraphed to Attlee three days later.[3]

'I heard the PM singing in his bath this morning,' Churchill's doctor noted in his diary on August 19, 'and he was in high spirits when Alex arrived at the Embassy to drive him into the desert.'[4] That afternoon, quite recovered from the exertions of travel, Churchill drove with Alexander and Brooke to Montgomery's headquarters,130 miles from Cairo. Churchill later recalled:

As the shadows lengthened we reached Montgomery's headquarters at Burg-el-Arab. Here the afterwards famous caravan was drawn up amid the sand-dunes by the sparkling waves. The General gave me his own wagon, divided between office and bedroom. After our long drive we all had a delicious bathe. 'All the armies are bathing now at this hour all along the coast,' said Montgomery as we stood in our towels. He waved his arm to the westward. Three hundred yards away about a thousand of our men were disporting themselves on the beach.[5]

Churchill spent the night of August 19 in an ambulance which Montgomery had converted into a caravan. 'On the way to bed,' Brooke noted in his diary, 'PM took me down to the beach where he was transformed into a small boy wishing to dip his fingers into the sea. In the process he became very wet indeed.'[6]

While Churchill was in the desert on August 19, a force of 5,000 men, mostly Canadians, but with some British and American troops in support, had crossed the English Channel to land at Dieppe. The Dieppe raid took nine hours. Nearly a thousand of the attacking troops

[1] Brooke diary, 18 August 1942: Bryant, *op. cit.*, volume 1, page 476.

[2] Brooke recollections: Bryant, *op. cit.*, volume 1, page 477.

[3] 'Reflex' No. 176, 'Most Secret and Personal', 21 August 1942: Churchill papers, 20/87.

[4] Sir Charles Wilson diary, 19 August 1942: Moran, *op. cit.*, page 66.

[5] Winston S. Churchill, *The Second World War*, volume 4, London 1951, page 462.

[6] Brooke diary, 19 August 1942: Bryant, *op. cit.*, volume, 1, page 477.

were killed, and two thousand taken prisoner.[1] 'Morale of returning troops reported to be excellent,' Mountbatten telegraphed to Churchill on the following day, and he added: 'All I have seen are in great form.' The troops had been unable to capture the town before the planned time for withdrawal, Mountbatten reported, but all the evidence suggested that the Germans must have been 'rattled' by the attack, and its air support was 'faultless'. In the air battle, 96 German aircraft had been shot down. So had 98 British aircraft 'but', Mountbatten noted, '30 pilots are safe'.[2] The lessons learnt at Dieppe, Mountbatten told the War Cabinet, would be 'invaluable' in planning for the future cross-Channel invasion.[3] 'My general impression of "Jubilee",' Churchill telegraphed to the War Cabinet two days later, 'is that the results fully justified the heavy cost. The large scale air battle alone justified the raid.'[4]

Churchill's immediate sense of satisfaction was weakened when, in the months to come, he read the detailed reports of the Dieppe raid. 'Although for many reasons everyone was concerned to make this business look as good as possible,' he minuted to Ismay three months later, 'the time has now come when I must be informed more precisely about the military plans'; and he went on to ask: 'Who made them? Who approved them? What was General Montgomery's part in it? and General McNaughton's part? What is the opinion about the Canadian generals selected by General McNaughton? Did the General Staff check the plans? At what point was V.C.I.G.S. informed in C.I.G.S.'s absence?'[5] Churchill's minute continued:

At first sight it would appear to a layman very much out of accord with the accepted principles of war to attack the strongly fortified town front without first securing the cliffs on either side, and to use our tanks in frontal assault off the beaches by the Casino, &c., instead of landing them a few miles up the coast and entering the town from the back.[6]

In reply, Ismay pointed out that the outline plan had been started in Combined Operations headquarters during the early part of April 1942, that shortly afterwards Montgomery became the senior officer concerned with the raid, and that the outline plan was approved by the Chiefs of Staff Committee on 13 May 1942. The Vice Chief of the

---

[1] This was Operation 'Jubilee', formerly Operation 'Rutter'.

[2] 'Tulip' No. 222, 'Most Secret', 20 August 1942: Cabinet papers, 65/31. The British losses were later learned to have been 107 aircraft, with 37 pilots safe (War Cabinet No. 118 of 1942, 25 August 1942: Cabinet papers, 65/27).

[3] War Cabinet No. 115 of 1942, 20 August 1942, Confidential Annex: Cabinet papers, 65/31.

[4] 'Reflex' No. 177, 'Most Secret and Personal', 21 August 1942: Churchill papers, 20/87.

[5] The Vice-Chief of the Imperial General Staff (VCIGS) was General Sir Archibald Nye.

[6] Prime Minister's Personal Minute, D.224/2, 'Secret', 21 December 1942: Premier papers, 3/256, folio 8.

Imperial General Staff, Ismay added, 'was not specially informed of the Operation'. As to the frontal assault, it had been intended to attack the cliffs on either side thirty minutes before the attack on the town itself, but 'owing to the limitations of air photographs, the position was stronger than anticipated'. The German fire positions built into the cliffs had not been shown in the photographs. In addition, Ismay told Churchill, the Army representatives at a meeting on 25 April 1942 had 'pressed for a frontal assault'.[1]

Ironically, April 25 was the anniversary of the Gallipoli landings at Cape Helles and Anzac Cove. Churchill took his enquiry no further. Nine years later, reflecting on the Dieppe raid, Churchill wrote:

It was a costly but not unfruitful reconnaissance in force. Tactically it was a mine of experience. It shed revealing light on many shortcomings in our outlook. It taught us to build in good time various new types of craft and appliances for later use. We learnt again the value of powerful support by heavy naval guns in an opposed landing, and our bombardment technique, both marine and aerial, was thereafter improved. Above all it was shown that individual skill and gallantry without thorough organisation and combined training would not prevail, and that team work was the secret of success. This could only be provided by trained and organised amphibious formations. All these lessons were taken to heart.

Strategically, Churchill reflected, the Dieppe raid 'served to make the Germans more conscious of danger along the whole coast of Occupied France. This helped to hold troops and resources in the West, which did something to take the weight off Russia.'[2]

The question of immediate British air support for Russia in the Caucasus had been raised in Cairo, when Tedder expressed his fears that it would interfere with the air support needed for the North African landings in October. 'Everybody always finds it convenient,' Churchill telegraphed to Attlee, Eden, Ismay and Portal on August 19, 'to ease themselves at the expense of Russia, but grave issues depend upon preserving a good relationship with this tremendous army now under dire distress.' As Churchill had already explained, 'I have committed His Majesty's Government to this policy in my talks with Stalin, and I must ask the Cabinet for support.'[3]

On August 20, after a bathe in the sea before breakfast, Churchill visited Montgomery's forward positions at Alam Halfa, inspecting those areas across which it was already known, from the most secret

---

[1] 'Most Secret', 29 December 1942: Premier papers, 3/256, folios 3–7.
[2] Winston S. Churchill, *The Second World War*, volume 4, London 1951, page 459.
[3] 'Reflex' No. 159, 'Most Secret and Personal', 19 August 1942: Churchill papers, 20/87.

source of British intelligence, that Rommel's attack would come.[1] Nine years later, Churchill recalled how:

I was taken to the key point south-east of the Ruweisat Ridge. Here, amid the hard, rolling curves and creases of the desert, lay the mass of our armour, camouflaged, concealed, and dispersed, yet tactically concentrated. Here I met the young Brigadier Roberts, who at that time commanded the whole of our armoured force in this vital position. All our best tanks were under him. Montgomery explained to me the disposition of our artillery of all natures. Every crevice of the desert was packed with camouflaged concealed batteries. Three or four hundred guns would fire at the German armour before we hurled in our own.

Although of course no gatherings of troops could be allowed under the enemy's continuous air reconnaissance, I saw a great many soldiers that day, who greeted me with grins and cheers. I inspected my own regiment, the 4th Hussars, or as many of them as they dared to bring together—perhaps fifty or sixty—near the field cemetery, in which a number of their comrades had been newly buried. All this was moving, but with it all there grew a sense of the reviving ardour of the Army. Everybody said what a change there was since Montgomery had taken command. I could feel the truth of this with joy and comfort.[2]

At the end of the day, Montgomery produced a small notebook in which he asked Churchill to write a message. The message read: 'May the anniversary of Blenheim, which marks the opening of the new Command, bring to the Commander-in-Chief of the Eighth Army and his troops the fame and fortune they will surely deserve.'[3]

'There is no doubt,' Colonel Jacob noted in his diary after Churchill's return from Montgomery's headquarters, 'that the arrival of Alexander and Monty has already made a great difference to the atmosphere of the Army, and the Prime Minister feels very pleased about it all.'[4]

Recalling that day of travelling, inspections and conferences, Brooke later wrote:

The day had been a wonderful example of Winston's vitality. We had been called at 6 a.m. He had started the day with a bathe in the sea; we had then spent a very strenuous day touring the front. This had entailed motoring in clouds of sand, long walks between troops, addressing groups of troops, talks with officers, in fact, a non-stop tour of inspection. Return to camp with another bathe, contrary to his doctor's orders. He was rolled over by

---

[1] F. H. Hinsley and others, *British Intelligence in the Second World War*, volume 2, London 1981, pages 412–17.

[2] Winston S. Churchill, *The Second World War*, volume 4, London 1951, page 464.

[3] Field Marshal Bernard L. Montgomery, *Ten Chapters, 1942–1945*, London 1946, facsimile message of 20 August 1942.

[4] Jacob diary, 20 August 1942: Jacob papers.

the waves and came up upside down doing the 'V' sign with his legs! Then followed a drive to aerodrome, and, as soon as we had emplaned, he said, 'I am now going to sleep,' and pulled out a bit of black velvet or cloth from his pocket which he placed over his eyes. The effect was marvellous. He instantaneously went to sleep and never woke up till we had bumped half-way down the Heliopolis runway. Then followed a conference, dinner, after which he kept me up till 2 a.m. on the lawn outside the Embassy. On our way up to bed he said, 'Breakfast on the verandah at 8.30 as usual . . .' [1]

The conference had been set up to discuss the transfer of the running of the Trans-Persia railway from British to United States control, the effect of which was to release more than a thousand British railway personnel and troops for service elsewhere in the Middle East, including Iraq which might suddenly become vulnerable to a German attack if the Caucasus were to be overrun. At the dinner, Sir Alexander Cadogan wrote in a letter home, Churchill was 'in terrific form', and he described how:

He held forth the whole of dinner, ragging everyone. Sir Charles Wilson, his 'Personal Physician', is one of his principal butts. To Winston's delight, poor C.W. fell ill of the usual local tummy complaint, and Winston now goes about saying to everyone 'Sir Charles has been a terrible anxiety to us the whole time, but I hope we'll get him through!' Last night at dinner Winston held forth to the whole table on medicine, psychology & etc. (all Sir Charles' subjects) and worked himself up to a terrific disquisition. I suspect (and I inferred from Sir Charles' expression) that it was pretty good nonsense. And I think Winston must have had an inkling of that too, as he ended up 'My God! I do have to work hard to teach that chap his job!' [2]

On the morning of August 21 Churchill telegraphed to the War Cabinet on the setting up of a separate military command of Iraq and Persia. It had been his intention to give this command to Auchinleck, but Auchinleck had declined. He now decided to appoint General Sir Henry Maitland Wilson to the post, with his headquarters in Baghdad.

Having finished the draft telegram, Churchill gave it to Colonel Jacob 'to polish up' for scrutiny by Brooke. By midday, Brooke had accepted the scheme, which was then telegraphed to the War Cabinet. 'Before lunch,' Jacob noted in his diary, 'the Prime Minister saw all the senior Officers of GHQ and gave them a pep talk.' Late that same afternoon he discussed with Alexander's senior ordnance and intelligence officers the relative strengths of the Eighth Army and the

[1] Brooke recollections: Bryant, op. cit., page 480.
[2] Sir Alexander Cadogan, letter of 21 August 1942: David Dilks (editor), op. cit., pages 475–6.

Axis forces in the western desert. 'We then spent a happy couple of hours,' Jacob noted, 'at the good old pastime of whittling away the enemy's strength on paper. In the end the Prime Minister was satisfied that he had got a fair comparison of men, vehicles, weapons etc, and it was generally agreed that taking one thing and another into account, we were about fifty-fifty with the enemy in the Western Desert.' When Churchill asked General Macreery, Alexander's Chief of Staff, 'which armoured forces he would rather have, the enemy's or our own', Macreery 'stated definitely that he would rather have ours'.[1]

Later that evening, Churchill sent Attlee and the War Cabinet his reflections on all he had seen and heard in Cairo and in the desert. 'I am sure we were heading for disaster under the former régime,' he telegraphed. 'The army was reduced to bits and pieces and oppressed by a sense of bafflement and uncertainty. Apparently it was intended in face of heavy attack to retire eastward to the Delta. Many were looking over their shoulders to make sure of their seat in the lorry, and no plain plan of battle or dominating will-power had reached the units.' The change of command had altered all this in a matter of days. From what he himself could 'see of the troops and hear from their commanders', Churchill explained, 'a complete change of atmosphere has taken place. Alexander ordered Montgomery to prepare to take the offensive and meanwhile to hold all positions and Montgomery issued an invigorating directive to his commanders, of which I will circulate the text on my return. The highest alacrity and activity prevails. Positions are everywhere being strengthened, and extended forces are being sorted out and regrouped in solid units.' The roads were 'busy with the forward movement of troops, tanks, and guns'.

'I am satisfied,' Churchill's telegram ended, 'that we have lively, confident, resolute men in command, working together as an admirable team under leaders of the highest military quality. Everything has been done and is being done that is possible, and it is now my duty to return home, as I have no part to play in the battle which must be left to those in whom we place our trust.'[2]

The most secret source of British Intelligence had indicated that Rommel might launch his attack as early as August 25. Churchill therefore set in train that morning a series of urgent measures for the defence of Cairo and the Suez Canal. This defensive line was put under the command of General Maitland Wilson, already appointed to take over the responsibility of the newly formed Persia-Iraq

[1] Jacob diary, 21 August 1942: Jacob papers.
[2] 'Reflex' No. 177, 'Most Secret and Personal', 21 August 1942: Churchill papers, 20/87.

Command, but now deemed indispensable for the emergency of which so few people knew.

During August 22 Churchill also saw Lord Gort, who had flown from Malta to report on the progress of the siege, and General Anders, who had at last arrived from Moscow to discuss the plight of 60,000 Poles still in Russia, most of them in labour battalions. These Poles, refugees from the German attack of September 1939, had not been allowed to join the Polish forces which, having been formed in Russia, were at that very moment gathering in Palestine for service in the Western Desert. Churchill promised to help, and was to do so on his return to London. This meeting with General Anders was conducted in French, a language, Colonel Jacob noted, which 'the Prime Minister insists on talking whenever he gets the opportunity. He doesn't talk very fast, and he has not a very large vocabulary, nor can his accent be said to be exactly Parisian; nevertheless he manages to hold his own all right. . . .'[1]

Immediately after this meeting with Anders, Churchill received a telegram from the War Cabinet, to say that they were 'delighted' with his resolution of the Iraq-Persia command. 'This pleased the Prime Minister very much,' Colonel Jacob noted in his diary, 'and he marched up and down his bedroom, saying that he knew all along he had laid a very good egg that morning.'[2]

Having studied the most recent Enigma decrypts on August 22, Churchill, Brooke and Alexander discussed the implications of what they revealed: that Rommel's offensive might well begin in three days' time, and would certainly begin within a week. Later that day, talking to the Cairo Press corps, Churchill declared: 'There is one thing I would like to make absolutely clear. We are determined to fight for Egypt and the Nile Valley as if it were the soil of England itself.'[3]

During his talk to the journalists, Churchill spoke of his previous hostility to Communism, and the new found friendship with Russia. Churchill told the correspondents: 'When you are fighting for the biggest things in the world, when your comrade is fighting like a bear, you must let bygones be bygones. You must think of the needs of the present, and the chances of the future.' Asked by these Cairo journalists, all them war reporters for the Western Desert, 'What about a

[1] Jacob diary, 22 August 1942: Jacob papers. When reminded about the Polish request a month later, Churchill commented: 'Our relations with the Soviet are pretty bleak at present and I have not thought it opportune to make this request' (Prime Minister's Personal Telegram, T.1375/2, OZ 1664, 26 October 1942: Churchill papers, 20/81). Later, he was to do so, and to do so successfully.

[2] Jacob diary, 22 August 1942: Jacob papers.

[3] 'Talk given on the record by Mr Winston Churchill', 22 August 1942: Premier papers, 4/71/4, folio 1051.

second front?' Churchill replied: 'I thought you were the second front.'[1]

Churchill left Cairo by air for Gibraltar, where he spent the following morning. 'It was a great relief,' Brooke later recalled, 'to have succeeded in getting Winston away before Rommel's attack. I heaved a sigh of relief as I saw his plane take to the air.'[2]

'If disposal of all the Allied decorations were today placed by providence in my hands,' General Douglas MacArthur told the senior British intelligence officer at his headquarters in the Far East, 'my first act would be to award the Victoria Cross to Winston Churchill. No one of those who wear it deserves it more than he. A flight of 10,000 miles through hostile and foreign skies may be the duty of young pilots, but for a Statesman burdened with the world's cares, it is an act of inspiring gallantry and valour.'[3]

[1] 'Off the record' statement, 22 August 1942: Premier papers, 4/71/4, folios 1039–42.
[2] Brooke recollections: Bryant, op. cit., volume 1, page 484.
[3] 'C' to Churchill, C/503, 25 August 1942, 'Most Secret': Churchill papers, 20/58.

13

Fighting for 'Torch'

ON the evening of 24 August 1942, Clementine Churchill was waiting at Lyneham aerodrome, near Swindon, to welcome her husband. Waiting with her were Randolph Churchill, Portal and John Martin, who noted in a letter home: 'The PM seemed remarkably fit and fresh. . . .'[1] In the train back to London, during 'a much needed dinner', Sir Alexander Cadogan noted: 'PM in cracking form.'[2] 'I am not at all tired,' Churchill wrote to the King on the following day. 'We had a wonderful journey back, only twenty-six hours from Cairo, of which five were spent having a bath and a rest at Gibraltar.'[3]

There was to be no rest in London, where, two days after his return, Churchill learned of pressure from Washington to reduce the scale of the North Africa landings. In a memorandum sent to London by the Joint Services Mission, the United States Joint Chiefs of Staff had put forward a series of arguments, seeking to exclude Algiers from the area of operation, and restricting the landings to the Atlantic coast of Morocco. The American Chiefs were afraid that the American forces could be trapped inside the Mediterranean, either by the action of German submarines, or by Spanish intervention at Germany's urging closing the Straits of Gibraltar.[4] 'I have just now seen the new directive produced by your Chiefs of Staff,' Churchill telegraphed to Roosevelt just after nine o'clock on the evening of August 26.[5]

The two senior American officers in London, General Eisenhower and General Mark Clark, were both opposed to the curtailment now envisaged in Washington. Both were also as eager as Churchill for a

[1] Letter of 30 August 1942: Martin papers.
[2] Cadogan diary, 24 August 1942: David Dilks (editor), *op. cit.*, page 476.
[3] Letter of 25 August 1942: Churchill papers, 20/59.
[4] Joint Staff Mission telegram, JSM 365, 25 August 1942: Cabinet papers, 122/1582.
[5] Prime Minster's Personal Telegram, T.1134/2, Prime Minister to President, No. 138, 'Personal and Most Secret', 26 August 1942: Churchill papers, 20/79.

specific date to be set for the landings, something General Marshall had yet to do. Once a date was fixed, and Eisenhower given specific instructions as to the landing places, Churchill telegraphed to Roosevelt on August 27, 'endless objections, misgivings and well-meant improvements will fall back into their proper place, and action will emerge from what will otherwise be almost unending hummings and hawings'. If Roosevelt were to decide on date and place, Churchill added, it would give Eisenhower 'a chance which he has not now got'.

Churchill then set out for Roosevelt the difference between 'Torch' and the two cross-Channel schemes, the abandoned 'Sledgehammer' operation against Cherbourg and the 'Jubilee' raid on Dieppe. 'There,' he wrote, 'we were up against German efficiency and the steel-bound, fortified coasts of France. In "Torch" we have to face at the worst weak, divided opposition and an enormous choice of striking-points at which to land.' The risks and difficulties involved would be 'doubled by delay' and would 'far outstrip' any increase of forces which such a delay might obtain.

It was Churchill's opinion, he told Roosevelt, 'that you and I should lay down the political data and take this risk upon ourselves'. If the North African landings could take place in October—the date Churchill pressed for was October 14—the Germans would not have time to force their way through Spain. Such Vichy resistance in North Africa as existed would be overcome 'by the suddenness and scale of the attack'. Nor, in October, would Hitler, pinned in the Pas de Calais by concern about a cross-Channel invasion, have the forces available to overrun occupied France. Churchill's telegram continued: 'All these data may prove erroneous, in which case we shall have to settle down to hard slogging. For this we have already been prepared, but a bold, audacious bid for a bloodless victory at the outset may win a very great prize. Personally, I am prepared to take any amount of responsibility for running the political risks and being proved wrong about the political assumptions.'

Churchill ended his telegram: 'I feel that a note must be struck now of irrevocable decision and superhuman energy to execute it.' [1]

At a specially convened meeting of the Chiefs of Staff Committee on the morning of August 27, Brooke informed Churchill that the Chiefs of Staff 'were directly opposed to the American view.' It was 'essential' to include landings at Algiers and Oran, and if possible Philippeville and Bône, while 'something also should be done at Casablanca'.

Brooke asked Churchill if he would send a telegram on this subject

[1] Prime Minister's Personal Telegram, T.1132/2, Prime Minister to President, No. 136, 'Personal and Most Secret', 27 August 1942: Churchill papers, 20/79.

to Roosevelt, and this Churchill at once agreed to do. He then dictated a draft, whose views were found to be 'completely identical' with a draft prepared by the Chiefs of Staff.[1] 'We are all profoundly disconcerted,' Churchill's telegram began. 'It seems to me that the whole pith of the operation will be lost if we do not take Algiers as well as Oran on the first day.'

The American Staffs had asked to switch the main American effort to Casablanca, on the Atlantic coast. Such a 'complete change' in the plans, Churchill warned, 'would of course be fatal to the date and thus possibly to the whole plan'. In October, Hitler would not have the power to move into Unoccupied France, and into Spain. But in November, 'with every week that passes his power to bring pressure upon Vichy and Madrid Governments increases rapidly'. Churchill added:

I hope, Mr President, you will bear in mind the language I have held to Stalin, supported by Harriman with your full approval. If 'Torch' collapses or is cut down as is now proposed I should feel my position painfully affected. For all these reasons, I most earnestly beg that the memorandum may be reconsidered, and that the American Allied Commander-in-Chief may be permitted to go forward with the plans he has made, upon which we are all now working night and day. The Staffs are communicating similar views to their American colleagues.[2]

On Saturday, August 29, Churchill discussed 'Torch' at Chequers with Eden, Brooke and Eisenhower, 'rather inconclusively', as Oliver Harvey noted in his diary on the following day, 'as Roosevelt hasn't yet replied to PM's message asking that date of October 14 be fixed and that decision be taken to do Algiers and Oran, even if Casablanca be dropped'.[3]

During the meeting, Churchill remarked that as the necessary forces 'did not appear to be forthcoming from the United States of America, the conclusion was that there could be no "Torch"'.[4]

On August 30 Roosevelt telegraphed to Churchill that he had as yet come to no decision as to date and scale, save that Casablanca must remain an objective. 'I still would hope,' Roosevelt added, 'for October 14.'[5] But three days later, Eisenhower told Churchill that

[1] Chiefs of Staff No. 103 (Operations), 11 a.m., 27 August 1942: Cabinet papers, 79/57.

[2] Prime Minister's Personal Telegram, T.1138/2, Prime Minister to President No. 139, 'Personal and Secret', 27 August 1942: Churchill papers, 20/79.

[3] Harvey diary, 30 August 1942: John Harvey (editor), *op. cit.*, pages 153–4.

[4] Chiefs of Staff Committee No. 105 (Operations) of 1942, 29 August 1942: Cabinet papers, 79/57.

[5] President to Prime Minister, No. 180, 31 August 1942: Churchill papers, 20/90.

October 30 was the earliest possible date. Nor was it yet certain that Roosevelt would agree to reinstate the Algiers landing.

On the day after Churchill's return from Cairo, the King's brother, the Duke of Kent, was killed in an air crash. He was thirty-nine years old, and had been killed instantaneously when the aeroplane in which he was travelling to inspect RAF establishments in Iceland had crashed into a hillside in North-West Scotland, and burst into flames.

'The King is in the deepest sorrow,' Churchill wrote to another of the Duke of Kent's brothers, the Duke of Windsor, on August 27, 'and his grief is shared by the whole nation.'[1] To the Duchess of Kent, Churchill wrote on August 29:

It is with the deepest sorrow that I learnt the news of yr irreparable loss. The Duke of Kent had endeared himself to all by his charming nature & willingness to help & serve. His death in action & on duty deprives his countrymen of an honoured public figure. What it must mean to your Royal Highness & yr happy family I cannot find words to express. In this hard war such strokes of fate fall upon many homes; and all dwell under the shadow. From all these homes there flows to you today a tide of human sympathy & affection to which—though I know the uselessness of words—I wish to add my own feelings. May you be granted the strength to bear the sorrow is the only prayer that we can utter.[2]

During their discussions in Moscow, Churchill and Stalin had agreed that there should be 'the fullest possible interchange of information regarding warlike inventions between ourselves and the Russians', and both men had expressed their intention to sign a 'regular agreement' on the subject. Churchill instructed Cadogan to prepare a draft, which Cadogan then showed to Molotov. Both Governments, the draft read, 'hereby agree to furnish each other all information relating to devices already employed by them for the prosecution of the war, or which may henceforth be discovered or invented'.

[1] Letter of 27 August 1942: Churchill papers, 2/447.
[2] Letter of 29 August 1942: Archives of His Royal Highness the Duke of Kent. On 23 December 1942 Churchill wrote to the Duchess of Kent: 'I received with emotion the photograph of the late Duke of Kent wh yr Royal Highness so kindly sent me. I value it deeply & it will always remind me of his charming personality, & the many pleasant meetings we had. Once more thanking yr Royal Highness. Believe me with all sympathy & respect.' (Letter of 23 December 1942: Archives of His Royal Highness the Duke of Kent.)

Churchill had made it clear to Stalin, however, 'that there were certain items of equipment which it would be in the common interest of the Allies to keep secret from each other'.[1] The draft agreement therefore expressly stated that if either Government considered that 'in the common interest' there would be 'disadvantage' in giving such information in a particular case, they would 'indicate the reasons on which they base this view'.

This draft, elaborated to include 'any necessary specifications, plans etc. relating to weapons, devices or processes', became, on Churchill's instructions, the basic agreement with the Soviet Union 'for the fullest possible interchange of information regarding warlike inventions'.[2]

On August 28 the Germans broke through the Russian defences south-west of Stalingrad. That same day, contemplating the possibility that the Russians would lose the naval command of the Black Sea, Churchill suggested to the Chiefs of Staff sending 200 tanks to Turkey. This, he wrote, 'might make all the difference to the Turkish will-power to resist' once the Germans controlled the Black Sea. 'We must proceed,' he added, 'on the basis, which personally I adopt, that we trust Turkey. The whole Nile position would be greatly embarrassed if Turkey were forced to succumb.'[3]

During August, Montgomery had awaited Rommel's attack on his defensive position based on Alam Halfa. Throughout the month, Enigma decrypts revealed the extent to which fuel supply was Rommel's main problem, affecting both the date of the attack, and its scale. As a result of this knowledge, attacks on his Italian supply ships were intensified. On August 15 the freighter *Lerici* had been sunk by submarine, and two days later the freighter *Pilo*. Their sinking took place just when an Enigma decrypt revealed that the Panzer Army's fuel consumption had been exceeding intake since the beginning of the month. On August 21 the Royal Air Force torpedoed the tanker *Pozarica*, which was carrying fuel for the Italians. Here too, an Enigma decrypt revealed that as a result of this sinking the Italian fuel supply situation was 'likewise very strained'.

On August 24 an Enigma decrypt gave details of a fuel supply programme involving the despatch of twenty ships to North Africa

[1] 'Exchange of Information with the Russians', Chiefs of Staff Committee No. 283 of 1942, 8 October 1942: Cabinet papers, 79/23.

[2] Chiefs of Staff Committee No. 389 of 1942, 'Interchange of Information with the Russians', 29 August 1942: Cabinet papers, 80/37. The agreement was signed on 29 September 1942.

[3] Prime Minister's Personal Minute, D.143/2, Most Secret', 28 August 1942: Churchill papers, 20/67.

between August 25 and September 5. On the second day of this programme, the Royal Air Force was able seriously to disrupt it by bombing the Corinth Canal. On August 28 an Enigma decrypt gave details of the fuel cargoes of eight more ships, the first of which was to sail that same day. Decrypts now gave not only the cargoes, but also the time of sailing, and even, as not hitherto, the routes. Three of the eight ships, *Dielpi* with 2,200 tons of fuel for the German Air Force, *Istria* with 200 tons for the Italians, and *Camperio*, were sunk on August 27.

Rommel could wait no longer, and at four in the afternoon of August 30 decided to launch his attack that night, knowing that his troops had fuel for only four and a half days' fighting, instead of the fifteen days that he had hoped, and having sufficient ammunition for only four to six days.[1]

Rommel knew the risk he was taking with his desperate shortage of fuel. Churchill, reading the daily Enigma decrypts, also knew it. Late on August 30, the Enigma decrypts confirmed Rommel's fuel supply had been struck a further, irreparable blow, the torpedoing of *San Andrea*, whose cargo had already been reported by an earlier decrypt as a 'key factor' in the Panzer Army's fuel programme. Churchill could only await with confidence, and Rommel with apprehension, the outcome of the now unequal battle.

On the night of August 30, the attack on Alam Halfa began. 'Rommel has begun the attack for which we have been preparing,' Churchill telegraphed to both Roosevelt and Stalin early the following morning. 'An important battle may now be fought.'[2] For three days the battle was fought on the lines which Montgomery and his staff had envisaged, and for which they had planned. On September 2, beset by problems of fuel supply, Rommel was forced to withdraw. The roads to Cairo and Alexandria were intact.[3]

[1] F. H. Hinsley and others, *British Intelligence in the Second World War*, volume 2, London 1981, pages 419–21. Whilst intelligence about fuel supplies and the cargoes of the Panzer Army's supply shipping came principally from decrypts of Enigma messages, the routes, timings and other details came mainly from Bletchley Park's breaking of the Italian cypher, C 38m. It was chiefly decrypts of the latter which guided Allied aircraft and submarines in their successful attacks on these convoys.

[2] Prime Minister's Personal Telegram, T.1153/2, Prime Minister to President, No. 141, 'Personal and Secret', 31 August 1942: Churchill papers, 20/79; Prime Minister's Personal Telegram T.1154/2 Foreign Office No. 188 to Moscow, 'Personal and Secret', 31 August 1942: Churchill papers, 20/79.

[3] Montgomery's losses were 984 British troops, 405 New Zealanders, 257 Australians, 65 South Africans and 39 Indians. 'It was indeed an Empire battle,' Churchill later wrote, 'in which the Mother Country bore the brunt' (Winston S. Churchill, *The Second World War*, volume 4, London 1951, page 492).

Despite the victory at Alam Halfa, Roosevelt still hesitated to fix a date for the North African landings, or to include Algiers as the third landing place, simultaneously with Oran and Casablanca. To break the deadlock, Churchill contemplated a further visit to Washington. In some alarm, Charles Wilson approached Brooke on the morning of September 1, to warn 'that last time the PM was in Washington he had had trouble with his heart and that he thought it unwise for him to go'. Wilson asked Brooke to offer to go in Churchill's place.[1]

At eleven that morning the Chiefs of Staff met together with Churchill, Attlee, Eden and Lyttelton, and approved a telegram from Churchill to Roosevelt, stressing the need for a three-city landing, and an early date. The President was told that:

... in spite of the difficulties, it seems to us vital that Algiers should be occupied simultaneously with Casablanca and Oran. Here is the most friendly and hopeful spot where the political reaction would be most decisive throughout North Africa. To give up Algiers for the sake of the doubtfully practicable landing at Casablanca seems to us a very serious decision. If it led to the Germans forestalling us not only in Tunis but in Algiers, the results on balance would be lamentable throughout the Mediterranean.

Mr President, to sum up, 'Torch' like 'Gymnast' before it, has always been viewed as primarily a United States enterprise. We have accepted an American command and your leadership, and we will do our utmost to make a success of any plan on which you decide. We must, however, say quite plainly that we are sure that the best course is to persevere along the general lines so clearly set out in the agreed directive handed to General Eisenhower on the 14th August. . . .

'I am sure,' Churchill ended, 'that, if we both strip ourselves to the bone as you say, we would find sufficient naval cover and combat loadings for simultaneous attempts at Casablanca, Oran and Algiers.'[2]

Churchill was upset by this divergence of views with the United States. 'PM seemed dejected, tired and depressed,' Brooke noted in his diary when the meeting was over.[3] On the following day, after talking to Eden, Oliver Harvey noted in his diary: 'We hear PM's heart is bad again. Sir C. Wilson has said he really mustn't fly Atlantic again.'[4]

On September 3 Roosevelt accepted that the North African landings would take place at all three cities: Algiers, Oran and Casablanca. At Casablanca, 68,000 United States troops would land in the assault and follow up. At Oran, 45,000 United States troops would land, and at Algiers the assault would be carried out by 10,000

[1] Brooke diary, 1 September 1942: Bryant, op. cit., volume 1, page 493.
[2] Prime Minister's Personal Telegram, T.1161/2, Prime Minister to President, No. 142, 1 September 1942: Churchill papers, 20/79.
[3] Brooke diary, 1 September 1942: Bryant, op. cit., volume 1, page 493.
[4] Harvey diary, 2 September 1942: John Harvey (editor), op. cit., page 155.

United States troops, 'followed within the hour by British troops to make the landing secure'.[1]

Churchill's remaining concern, which Eisenhower and Brooke shared with him, was to obtain a cut in the numbers landing at Casablanca in order, as Brooke noted in his diary, to 'render Algiers possible'. To secure this reduction, Churchill was 'sending Eisenhower, Ramsay and Mountbatten to Washington'.[2] With Mountbatten, Churchill intended to send a letter to Harry Hopkins, in which, as drafted, he stated forthrightly: 'I am deeply perturbed by the way "Torch" is being knocked about, and above all at the needless delays which add so much to our joint troubles.' It was a powerful letter, setting out the history of the agreements of July and August which had been overturned in September. 'An amphibious operation like this,' he wrote, 'has to be fitted together like a jewelled bracelet; for each particular landing-place the right ships must be chosen, and these ships must be chosen in accordance with the needs of the particular work each landing party has to do.' Churchill's letter continued:

At any rate, all was going forward, and until a week ago there was no reason why we should not have made the date October 15. Then suddenly out of the blue arrived the shattering memorandum of the United States Chiefs of Staff, which altered the whole character and emphasis of the operation—discarding Algiers, the softest and most paying spot, and throwing all the major weight upon Casablanca and the Atlantic shore, which after prolonged study we think may be quite impossible on account of the surf for a sea landing, and which is certainly four to one against, even in October.

It seemed so easy, no doubt, to say, 'Abandon Algiers; switch around to Casablanca; find other troops for Oran,' but look at the effect this had on all the work which had been done. I have been a witness of the distresses into which your two brilliant officers have been thrown by the delays and by the changes in policy coming from the United States Chiefs of Staff. Indeed, Eisenhower's position has been a very painful one. On the one hand, below him British and American Staff Officers clamouring for decisions on a whole host of points of detail; on the other, the restriction of the rigid and at the same time changeable control from across the ocean.

What is the use of putting up an Allied Commander-in-Chief or Supreme Commander if he cannot have the slightest freedom in making his plan or deciding how, when, and where to apply his forces? We are prepared to take his decisions and to obey. Even if we do not agree we will obey, after having put the facts before you. We are only out to help him in every way to give effect to the President's great strategic conception. Now the whole matter has

[1] President to Prime Minister, No. 182, 'Most Secret', 3 September 1942: Churchill papers, 20/79.
[2] Brooke diary, 3 September 1942: Bryant, *op. cit.*, volume 1, page 493.

to go back across the Atlantic and completely new schemes are sent us. I do not see how a united command is possible if the Supreme Commander is not allowed to act.

'Frankly,' Churchill added, 'I do not understand what is at the back of all this. . . .'[1]

Churchill's letter was ready to be sent, and Mountbatten to take it, when a telegram from Roosevelt, reaching Churchill on September 5, accepted the British plan for a larger force to land at Algiers. Roosevelt added: 'I am directing all preparations to proceed.'[2]

Churchill was delighted, and appreciative. 'I have just had your telegram,' he replied, 'and it is evident that you too have skinned yourselves to the bone.'[3] Roosevelt now replied with a single word: 'Hurrah!'[4] To this Churchill replied with equal exuberance, in three words: 'Okay full blast.'[5]

The North Africa landings were to go ahead as originally conceived. On September 6 Churchill informed Stalin: 'Operation "Torch", though set back about three weeks beyond the earliest date I mentioned to you, is on, full blast'. So too was the next Arctic convoy, PQ18, whose forty merchant ships had already started from Iceland on the long haul to Bear Island and beyond. Churchill's telegram to Stalin ended: 'May God prosper all our undertakings.'[6] In one sphere his prayer was quickly answered: he had asked Stalin to provide additional long-range bomber cover east of Bear Island, and this, three days later, Stalin agreed to do.[7]

Stalin's interest in Britain's bombing efforts, and their effect on Russia's own struggle, prompted Churchill to ask Portal, on September 10, to make out, for Stalin, a list of German towns bombed since August 1, 'with the weight of bombs dropped on each and the number of aircraft used.'[8] Portal did so, beginning in July rather than August, 'since August was a month of bad weather'. On September 11 Churchill sent the information to Stalin: from July 1 to September 6 a total of 11,500 tons of bombs had been dropped on

[1] Draft letter, unsent: Winston S. Churchill, *The Second World War*, volume 4, London 1951, pages 483–5.
[2] President to Prime Minister, No. 183, 4 September 1942: Churchill papers, 20/79.
[3] Prime Minister's Personal Telegram, T.1181/2, Prime Minister to President No. 144, 'Personal and Most Secret', 5 September 1942: Churchill papers, 20/79.
[4] President to Prime Minister, No. 185, 5 September 1942: Churchill papers, 20/79.
[5] Prime Minister's Personal Telegram, T.1187/2, Prime Minister to President, No. 145, 'Personal and Secret', 6 September 1942: Churchill papers, 20/79.
[6] Prime Minister's Personal Telegram, T.1190/2, 'Personal and Secret', Foreign Office to Moscow No. 197, 'Most Immediate, Most Secret', 6 September 1942: Churchill papers, 20/79.
[7] Moscow to Foreign Office, No. 133, 'Personal and Secret', 9 September 1942: Churchill papers, 20/80.
[8] Prime Minister's Personal Minute, M.360/2, 10 September 1942: Air Ministry papers, 19/557.

Germany, the heaviest, 2,500 tons, on Duisburg. Six of the bombs were 8,000-pound bombs.[1]

On the Egyptian front, the Enigma decrypts continued to expose Rommel's fuel supply sailings, and fuel shortages. When one signal reported the sailing of a convoy from Italy to North Africa on September 6 Churchill minuted to Pound and Portal: 'This is evidently an occasion for a supreme effort, even at the risk of great sacrifices by the Navy and Air Force. Pray inform me tonight what action you are taking.'[2] The action ordered locally by the Royal Air Force was already in train: to attack the convoy, and three of its four merchant ships were sunk. 'You have no doubt followed the sinkings of Rommel's vital ships,' Churchill telegraphed to Alexander on September 6 'and know how small his margin is'.[3] Those ships were the ones bringing aviation fuel. 'I have good hopes about all the Egyptian fighting,' Churchill telegraphed to Roosevelt on September 7, 'and believe Rommel is hard pressed.'[4]

'My next trouble,' Brooke wrote in his diary on September 8, 'will now be to stop Winston from fussing Alex and Monty and egging them on to attack before they are ready.' Brooke added: 'It is a regular disease that he suffers from, this frightful impatience to get an attack launched.'[5] Churchill's session 'in the caravan by the sea', as he phrased it to Alexander in a short telegram on September 11, had done much to put his mind at ease, however, and his telegram was limited to three polite and gentle probing sentences. 'It would be a help to me,' Churchill wrote, 'to know about when you think it will come off. I know you will be thinking about general problems as well as your own. I had hoped to have heard from you before.'[6] 'Am pushing ahead as fast as possible with arrangements for offensive,' Alexander replied, adding that the battle of Alam Halfa had 'proved able generalship of Montgomery whose handling of situation was excellent. . . .' The battle had shown, however, the 'urgent need' of

---

[1] 'Personal and Secret', 11 September 1942: Air Ministry papers, 19/557. For the full report, see page 178 n.1.
[2] Boniface 1371, T.10, Prime Minister's Personal Minute, M.350/2, 6 September 1942: Churchill papers, 20/67.
[3] Prime Minister's Personal Telegram, T.1188/2, 'Private and Personal', OZ1189, 6 September 1942: Churchill papers, 20/79.
[4] Prime Minister's Personal Telegram, T.1194/2, 7 September 1942: Churchill papers, 20/88.
[5] Brooke diary, 8 September 1942: Bryant, *op. cit.*, volume 1, page 503.
[6] Prime Minister's Personal Telegram, T.1211/2, OZ1247, 'Personal', 11 September 1942: Churchill papers, 20/80.

further 'intensive training', especially for the Mobile Striking Force. [1]

The planned counter-attack in the Western Desert had been given the codename 'Lightfoot'. It, and 'Torch', now both moved forward with renewed cohesion of planning and purpose. On September 8 Churchill's guests at dinner were Generals Eisenhower and Mark Clark; their aim was to discuss the final date for the North Africa attack. 'November 8—sixty days from today,' was Eisenhower's answer to Churchill's question of when it could be launched. [2] 'This is a tragedy,' Churchill minuted to the Chiefs of Staff Committee on the following day, 'and every effort must be made to save at least ten days.' Can 'nothing be done', he asked, to accelerate the loading of ships in Britain: 'Time is our chief enemy now.'

Churchill was also worried about the security aspects of delay, and about security in general. Casablanca, he proposed, should henceforth be called Dunkirk, with Oran to be Calais and Algiers to be Boulogne. A small map should be made, he suggested, of the North African coast, with these French names substituted. 'Thereafter no one should use the guilty names in conversation.' [3] Two weeks later, Bizerta was also given a Channel port cover-name: Havre. [4]

The principal cover plan for 'Torch' was devised by Colonel Bevan, head of the London Controlling Section, a branch of the War Cabinet Offices with headquarters in the Central War Rooms. Bevan, whose deception schemes covered every wartime operation from mid-1942, as well as Churchill's own overseas travels, set the 'Cover' for the north African landings inside the Mediterranean, with Crete as the imagined objective. Studying this plan, Churchill felt it was 'well considered', but added: 'I have a great fear that with all the talk that is here and in the United States, the enemy will find out that we are going to North Africa.' [5]

The date of November 8 was to stand: each Tuesday Churchill gave a dinner at Downing Street for Eisenhower and Clark, to discuss the evolving plans. 'I was nearly always alone with them,' Churchill later wrote, 'and we talked all our affairs over, back and forth, as if we were all of one country.' [6] At Chequers, on Friday, September 12, Eisenhower and Clark were Churchill's guests at dinner, together with the Minister of War Transport, Lord Leathers, the Vice Chief of the

[1] CS, 1505, 'Personal and Most Secret', 12 September 1942: Churchill papers, 20/80.

[2] Winston S. Churchill, *The Second World War*, volume 4, London 1951, page 487.

[3] Prime Minister's Personal Minute, D.147/2, 'Most Secret', 9 September 1942: Cabinet papers, 79/57.

[4] Prime Minister's Personal Minute, D.163/2, to General Ismay, 25 September 1942: Churchill papers, 20/67.

[5] Prime Minister's Personal Minute, D.148/2, 'Most Secret', 11 September 1942: Churchill papers, 20/67.

[6] Winston S. Churchill, *The Second World War*, volume 4, London 1951, page 472.

Naval Staff, Admiral Moore, Pound, Brooke and Mountbatten, to discuss the naval schedules for Torch.[1] Admiral Moore later recalled:

We were late starting dinner, which did not end till about 10.30—then we all had to attend a movie (a regular Hollywood type)—then about 12.30 a.m. we started the meeting about 'Torch'. About 3.0 a.m. the PM said—'it's time you people went to bed, I am going to do my papers' and went into his small sanctum to do so! Luckily, knowing his habits, I was up by 8.0 and had the Admiralty on the telephone with latest information, and sure enough soon after 8.30 I was summoned to give him the news! We went on with the main meeting about 10.0 or so.[2]

The Staff Conference lasted until luncheon on the Saturday.[3] Churchill still hoped, as he had explained to Admiral Moore on the previous day, to 'scrape two days off the ten days allowed for loadings', making it possible to do 'Torch' on November 4. 'As for other reasons,' he explained, 'I should be content with November 8 as the firm, final date, there are four days to veer and haul upon.'[4] 'PM as usual trying to get the last ounce out of the naval forces . . .' Brooke noted in his diary when the Staff Conference was over.[5]

Churchill was disappointed that 'Torch' could not be accelerated by four days, but bowed to the conclusions of the Staff Conference that November 8 was the earliest possible date. He was also disappointed that the desert offensive, 'Lightfoot', was, as he phrased it to Brooke, 'to straggle over into October'. But here too he deferred to Alexander's judgement.[6]

On September 12 the Arctic convoy, PQ18, for which Stalin had agreed to provide air cover of 48 long-range bombers, 10 torpedo bombers and 200 fighters, reached the danger zone. Thirteen out of the forty merchant ships in the convoy were sunk by German air and submarine attack, but forty of the attacking aircraft were destroyed, for the loss of only four of the British naval fighter escort. Two U-boats were also sunk. Out of the seventy-five escorting warships, two were lost, the destroyer *Somali* which was sunk in tow after being damaged by German torpedoes, and the minesweeper *Leda*, torpedoed

[1] 'List of Guests at Chequers, Week-End 11–14 September 1942': Chequers Trust.

[2] Letter of 30 April 1966: I am grateful to the late Professor Arthur Marder for this document. Moore added: 'The PM liked working up to 2 or 3 in the morning—but he stopped in bed till 8 or 9 a.m. Then he sat up in bed—looking like a pink cherub, and went through his telegrams etc. If the news was good he bounced up and down like a small boy with joy—if the news was bad he would slowly slide down pulling up the sheet till his face was hardly visible, as though to keep out the bad news!'

[3] Prime Minister's Engagement Cards, entry for 12 September 1942.

[4] Prime Minister's Personal Minute, M.366/2, 'Most Secret', 11 September 1942: Churchill papers, 20/67.

[5] Brooke diary, 12 September 1942: Bryant, *op. cit.*, page 501.

[6] Prime Minister's Personal Minute (to General Brooke), M.371/2, 'Secret', 13 September 1942: Churchill papers, 20/67.

in the Greenland Sea. On September 13, in an attempted landing at Tobruk, part of Alexander's preparation for 'Lightfoot', the destroyer *Sikh* was sunk by the gunfire of the German shore batteries, and the destroyer *Zulu* by aircraft bombs, and the following day the anti-aircraft ship *Coventry* was sunk by dive bombers.

On September 14, amid news of these severe losses, Churchill received a disappointing telegram from Wavell about operation 'Anakim', the plan to strike back at the Japanese in Burma. An exceptionally heavy monsoon, and a 'heavy sick rate' from malaria, were among the reasons why hopes of 're-occupying Burma this winter' had been postponed, but, Wavell added, 'on the whole we have got through this difficult summer in good shape and ready to hit harder every succeeding round'.[1] 'You know I am trying to act offensively as soon as I can,' Wavell telegraphed three weeks later, 'but, at the moment, prospects are not too bright.' In Burma, Wavell reported, the Japanese were making 'aerodromes and air shelters' on a scale sufficient for 'several hundred aircraft'. For his part, Wavell could expect little naval support before 1943, as there was such a shortage of small craft as to 'make escort of my expedition rather precarious'.[2]

Churchill studied each report and forecast, commenting only when he felt that matters were getting out of hand. 'I deplore,' he noted on September 14, on a diplomatic telegram from the British Ambassador in Turkey, 'these lengthy bi-political discussions based on the suggestion "if we lose Egypt" and "if Russia collapses in the Caucasus".' These questions, he added, had evidently encouraged the Ambassador 'to spread himself in his usual length, and to give us a number of glimpses of the obvious'.[3]

On a personal note, Churchill's 83-year-old aunt, Lady Leslie, wrote to him from Ireland on September 14: 'I am all puffed up with pride at your great achievements, yes, puffed out like an old pouter pigeon.' Her letter ended: 'Jack Leslie and I are well, we march downhill serenely hand in hand, holding on to life to see the Allies victorious!'[4] 'Dearest Leonie,' Churchill replied to his aunt's greeting, 'I was so glad to see your vigorous and youthful handwriting again. It is a great pleasure to me to know that you follow my toils. It seems to me that the tide of destiny is moving steadily in our favour, though our voyage will be long and rough.'[5]

---

[1] 22546, C, 'Personal', 14 September 1942: Churchill papers, 20/80.

[2] 24583, C, 'Personal', 5 October 1942: Churchill papers, 20/80.

[3] Prime Minister's Personal Minute, M.374/2 (to Anthony Eden), 'Secret', 14 September 1942: Churchill papers, 20/67. The Ambassador was Sir Hughe Knatchbull-Hugessen.

[4] Letter of 14 September 1942: Churchill papers, 1/368. Leonie Leslie's younger son Norman had been killed in action on the western front in October 1914.

[5] Letter of 30 September 1942: Churchill papers, 1/368. Lady Leslie died on 21 August 1943. Sir John Leslie died on 25 January 1944.

14

'Ties . . . of self-preservation'

T HE final preparations for 'Torch' had been made. 'If you can make it from your end,' Churchill telegraphed to Roosevelt on 15 September 1942, 'we will make it from this,' and he added, of Britain's ability to contribute a powerful wireless transmitter for propaganda broadcasts into Vichy France, once 'Torch' had begun: 'We British will come in only as and when you judge expedient. This is an American enterprise in which we are your helpmeets.'[1]

Following his Moscow visit, Churchill was again eager to see the northern Norway landings fill the gap between the success of the north African landings and the launching of the cross-Channel attack. The sequence of military events, as he saw it, was thus 'Torch', 'Jupiter' and 'Round-up'. 'There were the strongest reasons,' he told the Chiefs of Staff on September 15, 'both political and strategic, for seizing Northern Norway and thus joining hands with our powerful Russian ally and enabling us to send munitions and help to her.' The strain on the Royal Navy and the Merchant Navy in continuing to run the PQ convoys was 'very great', Churchill declared. 'He would like to see a plan made for "Jupiter" to take place in January or February.' Churchill added: 'We could not contemplate a period of inactivity between "Torch" in late 1942 and "Round-up" in late 1943.'

Brooke was still worried about the manpower problems of finding the five divisions 'which would be necessary' for northern Norway, but Churchill pointed out that Stalin had only envisaged the use of two British divisions, and 'had promised the help of three Russian divisions'. The Chiefs of Staff, Churchill added, should consider 'as a matter of urgency', ways and means of launching 'Jupiter'. To this

---

[1] Prime Minister's Personal Telegram, T.1225/2, Prime Minister to President, No. 148, 'Personal and Most Secret', 15 September 1942: Churchill papers, 20/80. The wireless transmitter plan was given the codename 'Aspidistra'.

end, he would like to see staff conversations begin with the Russians 'as soon as possible'.[1]

'Torch by itself' Churchill informed the Chiefs of Staff on September 16, was 'no substitute' for the Second Front in Europe.[2]

Churchill now awaited news from the Western Desert. 'I do not wish to know either your plan or the exact date,' he telegraphed to Alexander on September 17, 'but I must know which week it falls in, otherwise I cannot form the necessary judgements affecting the general war.'[3] In reply, Alexander regretted that the launching of 'Lightfoot' would have to be postponed until October 23. Was the attempt on Tobruk, Churchill asked, 'related to this new retarded date or to an earlier one?' and he went on to stress that it was 'vital to influence French action in "Torch" by a victory in Egypt'. The date mentioned by Alexander, 'does not give sufficient time for impression to soak in'. He was 'greatly distressed to receive such bad news, for which I was not prepared, having regard to your strength compared with the enemy'.[4]

Alexander continued to make his plans according to his own date and design. On September 22 Churchill informed Roosevelt, however, that his, Churchill's, 'persisting anxiety' was not North Africa but Russia. With 'Torch' set for November 8, there were no naval escort vessels free for the next Arctic convoy, PQ19. For PQ18, a total of 77 escort vessels had been required, for 40 merchant ships, of which, nevertheless, 13 had been sunk. 'The time has therefore come,' Churchill wrote, 'to tell Stalin, first that there will be no more PQs till the end of the year, i.e. January.' This, Churchill added, 'is a formidable moment in Anglo-American-Soviet relations and you and I must be united in any statement made about convoys'. There would also be disappointment for Stalin in the unloading from PQ19 of 154 aircraft, assigned by the United States to Britain, and then assigned by Britain to Russia, but now urgently requested by General Marshall for the impending 'Torch'. Churchill had been obliged to give his personal authorization for these aircraft to be unloaded.[5]

---

[1] Chiefs of Staff Committee No. 263 of 1942, 15 September 1942: Cabinet papers, 29/57.

[2] Prime Minister's Personal Minute, D.154/2, 'Most Secret', 16 September 1942: Churchill papers, 20/67.

[3] Prime Minister's Personal Telegram, T.1230/7, 'Personal and Secret', OZ, 1288, 17 September 1942: Churchill papers, 20/80.

[4] Prime Minister's Personal Telegram, T.1237/2, 'Personal and Most Secret', OZ, 1317, 20 September 1942: Churchill papers, 20/80.

[5] Prime Minister's Personal Telegram, T.1280/2 (to Stalin), 30 September 1942: Churchill papers, 20/80.

To cushion Stalin's disappointment about the convoys, Churchill proposed to Roosevelt the start of staff conversations on 'Jupiter', the northern Norway plan. If Roosevelt were able 'to take an interest in this', Churchill wrote, 'it would be most helpful'. This 'new project' was necessary 'to break the blow' about the convoys. At the same time, plans should still go ahead whereby it would be possible to launch a cross-Channel invasion in 1943, and not wait until 1944.

If 'Lightfoot' and 'Torch' succeeded, and the Allies were to control the whole of the North African shore by the end of 1942, much shipping, now forced to make the long voyage around the Cape of Good Hope, would be liberated. 'This is our first great prize.' If the Russian need was 'sufficiently grave and their demands imperative', this shipping could be used towards 'Jupiter', instead, as Churchill told Roosevelt, 'of attacking the under-belly of the Axis by Sardinia, Sicily and even possibly Italy'. The option should be kept open, and 'proper Staff studies' put in train. 'I should be most grateful for your counsel on all this,' Churchill wrote.[1]

Among Churchill's worries was a sense that the Americans were allowing the plans for 'Torch' to overshadow the far more complex plans for 'Round-up'. At a Staff Conference on September 21, held at Chequers, Eisenhower gave details of the number of United States troops who could now be expected in the United Kingdom. 'They were now aiming at a ground force of 150,000,' Eisenhower told him, though the 'total target figure', including air forces, 'might reach 400,000.' When Mountbatten pointed out that there was a United States 'embargo' on the shipment of landing-craft and assault shipping from the United States, Admiral Sir John Cunningham explained that this was because the Americans 'did not intend to send more landing craft to this country than was sufficient for the troops available'.[2] Churchill then remarked that he had not realized 'the very considerable falling off' of the forces intended for the 'Bolero' preparatory measures, 'nor that "Round-up" had so far receded in the minds of the American

---

[1] Prime Minister's Personal Telegram, T.1242/2, Prime Minister to President, No. 151, 22 September 1942: Cabinet papers, 120/852.

[2] Admiral Sir John Cunningham was then Chief of Supplies and Transport at the Admiralty. On 5 October 1943 he succeeded his cousin, Admiral Sir Andrew Cunningham, as Commander-in-Chief, Mediterranean, following Sir Andrew Cunningham's appointment as First Sea Lord.

Chiefs of Staff'. As a result, Churchill warned, 'we might well find ourselves with too low a scale of forces in this country'.[1]

It was at this meeting that Eisenhower announced that the date of 'Torch' was finally fixed for November 8. 'Everything is being worked to this,' Churchill informed Roosevelt in his telegram on the following day.'[2] Alexander had already chosen October 23 for his own offensive. Churchill had now to wait, and curb his anxieties. During September 22 he wrote to Sir Stafford Cripps: 'I myself find waiting more trying than action.'[3] On the following day Brooke noted in his diary:

> After lunch PM sent for me to discuss a wire he wanted to send to Alexander. I tried to stop him and told him that he was only letting Alex see that he was losing confidence in him, which was a most disconcerting thing before a battle. He then started all his worst arguments about generals only thinking about themselves and their reputations and never attacking until matters were a certainty; of never being prepared to take any risks, etc. He said this delay would result in Rommel fortifying a belt twenty miles deep by forty miles broad; that we should never get through owing to a series of Maginot defences. I had a very unpleasant three-quarters of an hour. However, I succeeded in getting a very definite tempering down of the message.[4]

As sent, Churchill's telegram was conciliatory and encouraging. 'We are in your hands,' it began, 'and of course a victorious battle makes amends for much delay. Whatever happens, we shall back you up and see you through.'[5]

On September 24 the German forces surrounding Stalingrad seemed poised to break the city's last line of defences. In London, pressure grew to take some drastic action: one Conservative Member of Parliament, Eric Errington, suggested that in order to provide 'uplift to our people and the Russians', a number of British heavy bombers should be sent to bomb the Germans in front of Stalingrad 'even if it meant loss and failure to return'.[6] The northern Norway operation, one of the possible means of help to Russia, was, however, being criticized at that very moment by the Canadian Prime Minister,

---

[1] 'Staff Conference held at Chequers on Monday 21st September 1942': Cabinet papers, 79/87.

[2] Prime Minister's Personal Telegram, T.1242/2, Prime Minister to President No. 151, 'Personal and Most Secret', 22 September 1942: Churchill papers, 20/80.

[3] Letter of 22 September 1942: Churchill papers, 20/56.

[4] Brooke diary, 23 September 1942: Bryant, *op. cit.*, page 505.

[5] Prime Minster's Personal Telegram, T.1255/2, 23 September 1942: Churchill papers, 20/88.

[6] 'Confidential', 24 September 1942: Churchill papers, 20/57. To this letter, Portal submitted a draft reply which he thought might amuse Churchill 'at a moment when he is not too busy'.

Mackenzie King. Churchill explained to King, in a telegram on September 24: 'I am under dire necessity of convincing Premier Stalin of our resolve to help him to the utmost of our strength.'[1]

There was also the promise which Churchill had made to Stalin to examine the possibility of twenty Anglo-American air squadrons being sent to southern Russia. 'How soon,' Churchill telegraphed to Harry Hopkins, 'shall I hear about the plan of Anglo-American air aid to the Russian southern flank?'[2] This was Operation 'Velvet'. But even while Churchill was searching for means to help Russia, the Russians were making matters difficult. One incident, to which Eden drew Churchill's attention, was the closing down of the British Naval hospital for merchant seamen at Murmansk. On September 27 Churchill telegraphed to Molotov:

I should be glad if you would look into the matter personally yourself. Terrible cases of mutilation through frostbite are now arriving back here, and I have to consider constantly the morale of the merchant seamen, who have hitherto gone so willingly to man the merchant ships to Russia. The British hospital unit was sent simply to help, and implied no reflection on Russian arrangements under the pressure of air bombardment, etc. It is hard on men in hospital not to have nurses who speak their own language. At any rate, I hope you will give me some solid reason which I can give should the matter be raised in Parliament, as it very likely will be.[3]

Before Molotov could reply, Churchill learned from an Enigma decrypt of the German plan for naval action on the Caspian Sea, as soon as German troops had crossed the Caucasus. He at once decided to send this information about German intentions to Stalin. 'I have got the following information,' he wrote, 'from the same source that I used to warn you of the impending attack on Russia a year and a half ago. I believe this source to be absolutely trustworthy. Pray let this be for your own eye.' The information read:

The draft read, as if from Churchill to Errington: 'I think your idea is simply splendid. I can't think why the Air Staff had not thought of it before. I have told Air Marshal Harris to send 1,000 bombers tonight. As you say, it won't matter at all if they don't return—we've got plenty more where they came from. I have also instructed the First Sea Lord to send the Home Fleet to sail up the Volga and all our aircraft carriers to the Sea of Azov to bomb the German Lines of Communication in the Crimea. If that doesn't uplift our people and the Russians I don't know what will. Thank you so much for your most helpful suggestions. Do let me know if you think of any more.' ('Confidential', 29 September 1942: Churchill papers, 20/57.)

[1] Prime Minister's Personal Telegram, T.1257/2, 24 September 1942: Churchill papers, 20/88.

[2] Prime Minister's Personal Telegram, T.1260/2, 25 September 1942: Churchill papers, 20/80.

[3] Prime Minister's Personal Telegram, T.1267/2, No. 241 to Moscow, 'Personal and Private', 27 September 1942: Churchill papers, 20/80. In a negative reply five days later, Molotov referred to 'certain irregularities in the actions of the respective British naval authorities' (Moscow, 2 October 1942: Churchill papers, 20/80).

Germans have already appointed an Admiral to take charge of naval operations in the Caspian. They have selected Makhach-Kala as their main naval base. About twenty craft including Italian submarines, Italian torpedo boats and mine-sweepers are to be transported by rail from Mariupol to the Caspian as soon as they have got a line open. On account of the icing-up of the Sea of Azov the submarines will be loaded before the completion of the railway line.

'No doubt,' Churchill commented, 'you are already prepared for this kind of attack.' It seemed to him 'to make all the more important' the plan to reinforce the Soviet Air Force in the Caspian and the Caucasus theatre by twenty British and American squadrons. 'I have never stopped working at this,' Churchill added, 'since we were together and I hope in a week or so to have the final approval of the President and to be able to make you a definite joint offer.' [1]

On October 3 Stalin informed Churchill that the situation in the Stalingrad area had 'deteriorated', and pressed for 800 fighter aircraft a month, 500 from the United States and 300 from Britain, to improve the position on the Stalingrad front. [2] On October 5, the day that this telegram reached Churchill in London, Roosevelt approved Churchill's request that twenty Anglo-American air squadrons should be sent to the Caspian-Caucasus region, 'and that operation should not be contingent upon any other'. Roosevelt authorized Churchill to tell Stalin that plans for 'Velvet' would be activated 'without delay'. [3] The air forces sent to Russia under 'Velvet', Churchill explained to Stalin, would operate under the strategic control of the Soviet High Command, and would be 'available for combat early in the New Year'. [4] For his part, Churchill suggested to Roosevelt a 'desperate effort' to meet Stalin over the next Arctic convoy. [5] This took the form, as he explained to Roosevelt on October 7, of preparing ten merchant ships to sail individually and unescorted 'during the October dark'. [6] In the event, thirteen ships set off for Russia with war cargoes in October. Five arrived.

The German threat to the Caucasus continued. But in a telegram to Wavell on October 7, Churchill commented that he felt 'much more comfortable' about the Caucasus than he had done 'when we

[1] Prime Minister's Personal Telegram, T.1270/2, 'Most Secret and Personal', 30 September 1942: Churchill papers, 20/80.

[2] 'Personal and Secret', Kremlin, 3 October 1942: Churchill papers, 20/80.

[3] President to Prime Minister No. 189, received 6 October 1942 at 5.25 a.m.: Churchill papers, 20/80.

[4] Prime Minister's Personal Telegram, T.1314/2, 8 October 1942: Churchill papers, 20/132.

[5] Prime Minister's Personal Telegram, T.1296, Prime Minister to President, No. 157, 6 October 1942: Churchill papers, 20/80.

[6] Prime Minister's Personal Telegram, T.1300/2, Prime Minister to President, No. 139, 'Personal and Secret', 7 October 1942: Churchill papers, 20/80.

were all in Moscow now nearly two months ago'. 'Indeed,' Churchill added, 'it looks as if Hitler's campaign against Russia in 1942 will be a great disappointment to him.'[1] Churchill's comment was not mere speculation; daily decrypts showed that the German forces were facing a fierce opponent in southern Russia, and that there had been a setback in the German plans there. 'My latest information,' Churchill telegraphed to Stalin on October 8, 'shows that the German plans for sending shipping to the Caspian by rail have been suspended.'[2]

The impending North Africa offensive gave Churchill considerable cause for concern. After the 'unpleasant surprises' of the previous two years, he later wrote, 'it was difficult to banish anxiety', and he added: 'As I had been so lately over the very ground where the battle was to be fought, and had the picture of the creased and curving rocky desert, with its hidden batteries and tanks and our Army crouched for a counterspring, so vividly in my mind's eye, the whole scene was fiercely lighted.' Another reverse, Churchill reflected, 'would not only be disastrous in itself, but would damage British prestige and influence in the discussions we were having with our American Allies'.[3]

'If "Torch" fails,' Churchill told Eden on the night of October 1, 'then I'm done for and must go and hand over to one of you.'[4] Six days later, Eden was told by Beaverbrook that Churchill was 'bowed' and 'not the man he was'. Churchill's 'powers of recuperation', Eden replied, 'were very great and I was not worried'.[5]

Eden's instinct was right; those who were with Churchill at Chequers that weekend found no slackening of his powers, or of his charm. Setting off for Chequers on October 8, Elizabeth Layton noted:

I had to go in the car with him and it is a 2-hour journey to this place. The light was just fading, and most of the way it was 'Pull that blind down— that one up—now down again—put the light on—off—etc'. He really was *sweet*—he kept making odd little remarks like—'Frost will soon be here'. 'How fast do you think we are travelling'—to which I said 'About 50'—'Oh no, *much* more—at least 60'.

[1] Prime Minister's Personal Telegram, T.1305/2, OZ 1476, 'Personal', 7 October 1942: Churchill papers, 20/88.
[2] Prime Minister's Personal Telegram, T.1313/2, 8 October 1942: Churchill papers, 20/88. On 26 October 1942 Churchill told the War Cabinet: 'that on the 8th October he had sent a long telegram to M. Stalin'. This telegram had dealt with the arrangements for sending convoys to North Russia, and our and the American offer to send 20 squadrons to the Caucasus front. On the same day he had also sent a short telegram imparting to M. Stalin a piece of secret news. On the 13th he had received the answer 'Thank you', but he had not been able to ascertain to which of his two telegrams of 8th October this reply referred (War Cabinet No. of 1942, 26 October 1942: Cabinet papers, 65/32.)
[3] Winston S. Churchill, *The Second World War*, volume, 4, London 1951, page 489.
[4] Harvey diary, 2 October 1942: John Harvey (editor), *op. cit.*, pages 165–6.
[5] Eden diary, 8 October 1942: Eden memoirs, *The Reckoning*, *op. cit.*, page 343.

At Chequers itself, work continued as before. As Elizabeth Layton noted:

I did most of the Old Man's work, and all the mornings. He was simply *sweet* all the time—never barked once. Except when he had said for the 40th time one dinner-time 'now I must get up'. So finally I thought he was going to, and went to take the work he had done, out of his box. Immediately 'what are you putting your fingers in my box for? SIT DOWN', grumble grumble. So I sat, feeling (and I suppose looking) very crushed. A few minutes later 'Now you may take the things out of my box. And don't look so nervous—no one is going to bite you' with a grin. One time he came into the office and said 'I'm now going up to work. I'll have my box and Miss Layton'. . . .[1]

On October 9, while he was still at Chequers, Churchill learned that two Italian fuel ships on their way to North Africa, the *Unione* and the *Nino Bixio*, whose route and cargoes had been revealed by the Enigma decrypts, had been attacked and sunk by the Royal Air Force.[2] At the same time, a decrypted message from the German-Italian Army at Alamein revealed that food rations were at 'an unsurpassably low level', with motor transport and spares a cause of extreme anxiety, and fuel supplies strained.[3] 'You will no doubt have seen the recent highly satisfactory MK about enemy shortages and sicknesses,' Churchill telegraphed to Alexander on October 10.[4]

Alexander had seen signals containing a paraphrase of the Enigma decrypts. The substance was always the same as the German original, but the words had been paraphrased in the interests of security. Churchill had long felt that these paraphrases failed to convey the force of the original eavesdropped message.[5] 'I have given direction,' he telegraphed to Alexander on October 12, 'for more exactly textual MKs to be sent from now on. I trust you are getting all these yourself and taking all precautions.'[6]

[1] Elizabeth Layton, letter of 12 October 1942: Nel papers.

[2] Hinsley and others, *op. cit.*, volume 2, page 427. For health reasons, Rommel had already left North Africa, having handed over his command to General Stumme. It is probable that he would not have returned, but for Stumme's death in action on 23 October 1942.

[3] Boniface 1499, T.1 of October 1942 and T.12 of 9 October 1942: Hinsley and others, *op. cit.*, volume, 2 page 427.

[4] Prime Minister's Personal Telegram, T.1327/2, OZ 1509, 'Private', 'Most Secret', 10 October 1942: Churchill papers, 20/81. 'MK' was the prefix of the Bletchley special messages. When MK 9999 had been reached, a new series was begun. Each series was given a different digram, 'QT', 'VL', etc.

[5] One of those who read both the original decrypts and the paraphrases has commented: 'I'm afraid they were very palid paraphrases, reduced to officialese.' (A former Bletchley hand, in conversation with the author, 27 May 1985.) Hence Churchill's wish that Alexander should have something more vivid.

[6] Prime Minister's Personal Telegram, T.1334/2, OZ 1538, 'Most Secret and Private', 12 October 1942, Premier papers, 3/299/1, folio 264. A note by Desmond Morton on this telegram, to Churchill's Defence Registry, reads: 'This telegram is not be to be distributed. Will you please return this copy to me' (Churchill papers, 20/81).

At Stalingrad, the Soviet defences held, and slowly the Red Army began the actual encirclement of the besieging forces. Speaking at Edinburgh on October 12, Churchill spoke of Stalingrad's 'heroic defence'. He also contrasted the 'excitement and emotion of those great days when we stood alone and unaided against what seemed overwhelming odds', with the situation two years later, with Britain 'surrounded by a concourse of Governments and nations, all of us bound together in solemn unbreakable alliance, bound together by ties not only of honour but of self preservation.'[1]

Churchill was in Scotland to receive the Freedom of the City of Edinburgh, and to visit the Home Fleet. 'Your presence with us,' Admiral Tovey signalled on October 15, 'has been an encouragement and inspiration to all.'[2]

Returning to London, Churchill asked Harry Hopkins to help ensure that they should go together into the question of United States aircraft production for 1943 and 1944: 'as these matters are so deadly', he wrote, 'and there is such a danger of giving offence, I wanted greatly to go into it all with you while time remains and before large mass production is finally fixed'.[3] Concerned also to follow more closely the situation on the eastern front, Churchill asked for a daily report on the Russian weather conditions along the whole front. 'The best possible will do,' he told Ismay.[4]

Five days later, pressed by Eden to give his views on the post-war organization of the Four Great Powers, including Russia, he wrote: 'It sounds very simple to pick out these four Big Powers.[5] We cannot, however, tell what sort of a Russia and what kind of Russian demands we shall have to face.' Churchill added: 'It would be a measureless disaster if Russian barbarism overlaid the culture and independence of the ancient States of Europe.' What Churchill hoped for, he told Eden, was a 'United States of Europe', excluding Russia, in which 'the barriers between nations will be greatly minimized and unrestricted travel will be possible', guarded by an international police force one of whose tasks would be 'keeping Russia disarmed'. On the whole, Churchill did not approve of such speculations. 'It would be

[1] Speech of 12 October 1942, Edinburgh: Churchill papers, 9/158.
[2] 'Personal', Telegram No. 642, 15 October 1942: Churchill papers, 20/81.
[3] Prime Minister's Personal Telegram, T.1345/Z, Foreign Office to Washington No. 6389, 'Personal and Secret', 16 October 1942: Churchill papers, 20/81.
[4] Prime Minister's Personal Minute, D.174/2, 16 October 1942: Churchill papers, 20/67.
[5] The United States, the Soviet Union, Britain and China.

easy to dilate upon these themes,' he wrote. 'Unhappily the war has prior claims on your attention and on mine.'[1] This was Churchill's consistent view: two days earlier he had written to Eden: 'I hope these speculative studies will be entrusted mainly to those on whose hands time hangs heavy, and that we shall not overlook Mrs Glasse's Cookery Book recipe for jugged hare—"First catch your hare".'[2]

At a meeting of the Pacific War Council on October 21, Churchill surveyed the war in Europe and the Far East. He had 'no doubt', he told the Dominion representatives, including Field Marshal Smuts, 'that on balance we were today far better off', and he went on to list the hopeful signs as he saw them:

In Russia the Germans had suffered heavy losses; all Europe was seething with revolt; the United States were developing their vast strength; and at sea we were making great preparations to cope with the increasing U-boat menace. In the air our power and predominance was growing; that of the Japanese was shrinking both in quantity and quality, and the size of the German air force was contracting. Our capacity for the production of aircraft was already three times as great as that of the Axis.

Later in the meeting, talking of the Eastern front, Churchill pointed out that an 'unknown factor' in the German position was the power of Russia to strike back'.[3] As for Britain, Churchill told the Chiefs of Staff Committee on the following day, he was 'most anxious that there should be no slackening of the bomber effort during the rest of the year, but rather it should be built up'. The Germans were going to have 'a very trying winter', and it would 'ease their minds a great deal if they thought the bombing was easing off'.[4]

---

[1] Prime Minister's Personal Minute, M.474/2, 'Most Secret', 21 October 1942: Churchill papers, 20/67.

[2] Prime Minister's Personal Minute, M.461/2, 18 October 1942: Churchill papers, 20/67. Hanna Glasse was the author of a popular treatise on cookery, first published in 1747, in which the extravagance of French cooks was severely condemned. The proverb 'First catch your hare' is not found in her book, but (as the Dictionary of National Biography notes) 'her words "Take your hare when it is cased" may have suggested it'. The word 'cased' meant 'skinned'.

[3] Pacific War Council, 13th Meeting, 21 October 1942: Cabinet papers, 99/26.

[4] Chiefs of Staff Committee No. 297 of 1942, 22 October 1942: Cabinet papers, 79/23.

15

Towards Alamein, and beyond

I N the Western Desert, Alexander and Montgomery prepared for
the great offensive: British, Australian and other Commonwealth
troops being ready for the battle. 'Events are moving in our favour
both in North Africa and Vichy France,' Churchill telegraphed on 20
October 1942 to Alexander. 'Torch' was going forward 'steadily and
punctually'; but, he added, 'all our hopes are centred upon the battle
you and Montgomery are going to fight. It may well be the key to the
future.'[1] An Enigma decrypt that day revealed that in five days' time
the fuel stocks of the Panzer army would be down to four and a half
days' battle supply, and that only three days' worth of this fuel was
located between Tobruk and Alamein. This message, sent by Enigma
to Berlin from the Panzer Army headquarters, was, like all these most
secret signals, decrypted at Bletchley at virtually the same moment
that it was read in Berlin. The decrypt was then sent to Brigadier
Menzies in London, and from Menzies direct to Churchill, to the
Chiefs of Staff, and to Montgomery. This particular decrypt went on
to say that as a result of this fuel shortage, the Panzer army 'did not
possess the operational freedom of movement which was absolutely
essential in consideration of the fact that the British offensive can be
expected to start any day'.[2]

'The battle in Egypt began tonight at 8 p.m. . . .' With these words
Churchill announced to Roosevelt in a telegram on October 23 the
opening of the offensive on which so much depended.[3] 'The whole
force of the Army will be engaged,' Churchill added.[3] That same day,
General Stumme, Rommel's successor, was killed in action, and
Rommel was recalled to Egypt.

[1] Prime Minister's Personal Telegram, T.1354/2, OZ 1603, 20 October 1942: Churchill papers,
20/81.
[2] QT 4077 of 20 October 1942, CX/MSS/1562/T23: F. H. Hinsley and others, *British Intelligence in the Second World War*, volume 2, London 1981, page 427.
[3] Prime Minister's Personal Telegram, T.1363/2, Prime Minister to President, No. 170,
'Personal and Secret', 'Clear the Line', 23 October 1942: Churchill papers, 20/81.

On October 24, as Montgomery's forces sought to exploit their unprecedentedly heavy artillery bombardment of the German–Italian defences, Churchill inspected the coastal defences at Dover, before going to Chequers for the weekend. Two of his daughters, Sarah and Mary, were there, as were Lord Cherwell and Anthony Eden. The majority of the guests were Americans: President Roosevelt's wife Eleanor and their son Elliott, the American Ambassador, Gilbert Winant, and Harry Hopkins' soldier son Robert, who had accompanied Churchill to Dover.[1] While at Chequers, Churchill prepared a memorandum on the conduct of the war. In it he wrote of the preparations that had gone forward 'without ceasing' for the cross-Channel attack in 1943. It was the success of 'Lightfoot' and 'Torch', however, that 'will dictate our main action in 1943', when not only would a route be opened through the Mediterranean under air protection, 'but we shall also be in a position to attack the under-belly of the Axis at whatever may be the softest point, i.e. Sicily, Southern Italy or perhaps Sardinia; or again, if circumstances warrant, or as they may do, compel, the French Riviera or perhaps even, with Turkish aid, the Balkans'.

Until the summer of 1943, Churchill wrote, the war 'will be waged in the Mediterranean theatre', but it would still be necessary to continue 'at full blast' the build-up of American forces in preparation for a cross-Channel landing, and to persuade the Americans 'not to discard' that landing, 'albeit much retarded'. Churchill's order of priorities was, as he listed them, first, to preserve the United Kingdom and its communications; second, 'Lightfoot' and 'Torch' 'and their exploitation'; and third, the build-up of British and American forces in the United Kingdom, 'for a retarded but still paramount' cross-Channel landing.[2]

Churchill had learned from Mountbatten that Operation 'Jupiter', the attack on northern Norway, to free the Arctic convoys from German air attack, was 'not a practicable proposition' in the winter of '1942–43'. Even so, he minuted to Mountbatten and the Chiefs of Staff Committee on October 26, the snow ploughs needed for 'Jupiter' should be 'brought into existence at the earliest moment', in case the scheme were to prove 'just as desirable in 1943–44'. Churchill added: 'If we do not make the weapons now, we shall never even have an option open to us on future plans.'[3] Every opportunity should be

---

[1] 'List of Guests for Weekend October 24–26': Chequers Visitors Book. Churchill telegraphed to Harry Hopkins on October 24: 'Robert inspected Dover with me today and is coming to spend the weekend. He is a charming boy': Prime Minister's Personal Telegram, T.1365/2, 24 October 1942: Churchill papers, 20/81.

[2] 'Policy for the Conduct of the War', 'Most Secret', 24 October 1942: Churchill papers, 23/10.

[3] Prime Minister's Personal Minute, M.493/2, 'Most Secret', 26 October 1942: Churchill papers, 20/67.

taken to improve on the existing snow plough design, Churchill telegraphed to Roosevelt four days later, 'so that we shall be fully prepared to grasp our opportunity when it occurs, as certainly it will'.[1]

At the War Cabinet on October 26 it was learned that the Eighth Army had already taken nearly 1,500 prisoners in the Western Desert.[2] It was a day of danger, however, for Alexander's army, with several counter-attacks being planned against it by the 15th and 21st Panzer Divisions. But, as Alexander later informed Churchill, these counter-attacks 'were dispersed before starting by RAF bombing'. That night, a series of Allied advances 'along the whole front', had secured Kidney Ridge, 'a small but important spur in this featureless plain'.[3]

From Moscow had come five separate accusations in two days that, in the spring of 1941, Britain had intended using its unexpected visitor, Rudolf Hess, for a negotiated peace with Hitler. 'I should treat the Russians coolly,' Churchill minuted to Eden on the following day, 'not getting excited about the lies they tell, but going steadily on with our task.'[4] That task, as Churchill saw it, was in the Western Desert, and was going well. 'In Alexander and Montgomery,' he telegraphed to the Prime Ministers of Canada, Australia and New Zealand on October 27, 'we have Generals determined to fight the battle out to the very end.'[5] In answer to a public statement by Wendel Willkie, that the offensive in Egypt was due 'to pressure of public opinion', Churchill told Eden that he was prepared to invite Willkie to England, as 'I am anxious not to lose him entirely, but it was not necessary to "hurry this"' he added. 'We must let events speak. Words do not count now as much as they do in time of peace. What matters is action.'[6]

On October 27 the 15th and 21st Panzer Divisions counter-attacked five times, 'with all available tanks, German and Italian', as Alexander informed Churchill two weeks later. They 'gained no ground', however, 'and suffered heavy, and worse still, disproportionate casualties, for our tanks, fighting on the defensive, suffered but lightly'. When

---

[1] Prime Minister's Personal Telegram, T.1396/Z, Prime Minister to President, No. 177, 'Most Secret and Personal', 30 October 1942: Churchill papers, 20/81.

[2] Among the British dead was Peter Wood, second son of Lord Halifax, killed in action on 26 October 1942. By 2 November 1942, about 1,700 British and Allied troops had been killed.

[3] CS/1689, IZ 2128, 9 November 1942: Churchill papers, 20/82.

[4] Prime Minister's Personal Minute, M.494/Z, 'Most Secret', 27 October 1942: Churchill papers, 20/67.

[5] Prime Minister's Personal Telegrams, T.1381/Z and T.1386/Z, 'Personal and Most Secret', 27 October 1942: Churchill papers, 20/81.

[6] Prime Minister's Personal Minute, M.494/2, 'Most Secret', 27 October 1942: Churchill papers, 20/67.

Rommel attempted to concentrate his forces for the final counter-attack, Alexander added, 'the RAF once more intervened on a devastating scale. In two and a half hours bomber sorties dropped eighty tons of bombs in his concentration area, measuring three miles by two, and the enemy's attack was defeated before he could even complete his forming up. This was the last occasion on which the enemy attempted to take the initiative.' [1]

Alexander now paused in his offensive in order to regather his forces and reserves for a further assault. When details of the pause first reached Churchill, they came without any description of the previous day's battle. 'It is most necessary that the attack should be resumed before "Torch",' Churchill minuted to Brooke. 'A stand-still now will be proclaimed a defeat. We consider the matter most grave.' [2]

To Alexander, Churchill drafted a troubled telegram that day. 'We are glad the battle started well,' he began, 'and are sure that you intend to press it remorselessly to a finish. We have nothing to fear from a bataille d'usure.' The Enigma decrypts showed clearly, Churchill pointed out, that: 'The enemy is hard run for petrol and ammunition, and our air superiority weighs heavily upon him.' Churchill continued: 'We do not of course know what you have in mind and therefore were somewhat concerned to see that on the 27th the attack on Kidney Ridge by two battalions was the only substantial thrust. And now by your latest Sitrep most units appear to be coming back into reserve.' Churchill's draft ended: 'We should be grateful if you could tell us if you have any large-scale attacks impending because we feel that the intensity and scale of the battle will be hard for the enemy to bear.' [3]

It was Churchill's reading of the Enigma decrypts which made it clear to him how hard pressed the Germans were. But as soon as he realized that Alexander was pausing merely for an instant, in order to attack again, Churchill sent him a telegram of encouragement: 'We assure you that you will be supported whatever the cost,' he telegraphed on October 29, 'in all the measures which you are taking to shake the life out of Rommel's army and make this a fight to the finish.'

A series of decrypts of German messages had, as Churchill noted in

[1] CS/1689, IZ 2128, 9 November 1942: Churchill papers, 20/82.

[2] Prime Minister's Personal Minute, M.498/2, 28 October 1942: Churchill papers, 20/67.

[3] Draft telegram: Michael Howard, *Grand Strategy*, volume 4, August 1942–September 1943, London 1972, page 68. After Professor Howard had cited this telegram in the Official History it was located in Premier papers 3/299/1, folio 227, where a note states: 'Document draft letter from PM to Gen. Alexander dated 28.10.42 was extracted from this file and is now held in the Joint Intelligence Committee Secretariat in file 83/43/1'. This note is dated 28 January 1972, an example of the care with which, twenty-seven years after the end of the war, the Enigma secret was still being preserved.

this telegram to Alexander, enabled the Royal Air Force to pinpoint and to sink the 'vitally-needed tankers' bringing tank and aircraft fuel across the Mediterranean to the German and Italian forces. Further decrypts had revealed 'the conditions of intense strain and anxiety behind the enemy's front', giving the Defence Committee 'solid grounds for confidence in your final success'.[1]

The decrypts of German messages threw an extensive light on German military, naval and air movements. They did not reveal, however, other aspects of German policy, which were to become known in the West as a result of information smuggled out of Germany to neutral Switzerland. This information, which was sent on to London and published in the British newspapers, revealed the extent of the German slaughter of Jews on the eastern front, the murder by gas of Polish Jews in three special 'death' camps at Chelmno, Belzec and Treblinka, and of the deportation of Jews from France, Belgium and Holland to an 'unknown destination' in the East.[2] This information led to a public protest by Christians and Jews, meeting at the Albert Hall on October 29. In preparation for the meeting, Churchill wrote to the Archbishop of Canterbury:

I cannot refrain from sending, through you, to the audience which is assembling under your Chairmanship at the Albert Hall today to protest against Nazi atrocities inflicted on the Jews, the assurance of my warm sympathy with the objects of the meeting. The systematic cruelties to which the Jewish people—men, women, and children—have been exposed under the Nazi régime are amongst the most terrible events of history, and place an indelible stain upon all who perpetrate and instigate them. Free men and women denounce these vile crimes, and when this world struggle ends with the enthronement of human rights, racial persecution will be ended.[3]

'My thoughts are with you on this anniversary,' Churchill telegraphed to the Zionist leader, Dr Chaim Weizmann, for the anniversary of the Balfour Declaration, the British Government's First World War pledge of a Jewish National Home in Palestine. 'Better days will surely come,' Churchill added, 'for your suffering people and for the great cause for which you have fought so bravely.'[4]

*   *   *

[1] Prime Minister's Personal Telegram, T.1392/2, OZ 1700, 'Bigot', 'Most Secret', 29 October 1942: Churchill papers, 20/81. The six 'Boniface' decrypts mentioned by Churchill in his telegram to Alexander were QT/4474, QT/4592, QT/4599, QT/4642, QT/4644 and QT/4682.

[2] While the mass murder of Jews at Chelmno, Belzec and Treblinka (and later at Sobibor and Majdanek) was known and publicized in the west by the autumn of 1942, the location of Auschwitz remained the 'unknown destination' of the Jewish deportees until the early summer of 1944.

[3] Letter of 29 October 1942: Churchill papers, 20/54.

[4] Prime Minister's Personal Telegram, T.1394A/2, No. 6636 to Washington, 30 October 1942:

On October 30 Alexander telegraphed to Churchill and Brooke that, despite 'a lot of trouble and delay' caused by minefields and anti-tank guns, he and Montgomery were 'about to put in a large scale attack with infantry and tanks to break a way through for the Tenth Corps'.[1] Twenty-four hours later, Alexander telegraphed again: 'Enemy is fighting desperately, but we are hitting him hard and continuously, and boring into him without mercy. Have high hopes he will crack soon.'[2] That same day, Churchill sent Roosevelt a report which he had just received from Montgomery, of the 'great satisfaction' felt in the Western Desert with the Sherman tanks.[3]

As Alexander prepared to renew the offensive in the Western Desert, the final preparations went forward for the North Africa landings. On October 31 Churchill wrote to Roosevelt: 'I pray that this great American enterprise, in which I am your Lieutenant and in which we have the honour to play an important part, may be crowned by the success it deserves.'[4] The battle in Egypt, Churchill telegraphed to Roosevelt on the following day, 'is now rising to its climax and our hopes are higher than I dare to say'.[5]

At five o'clock on the morning of November 2, Alexander launched operation 'Supercharge'. The 'Enemy reacted at once,' he informed Churchill in his battle telegram a week later, 'by taking only action possible in the form of vicious armoured and infantry counter-attacks in which he lost heavily from our tanks and anti-tank guns.'[6]

The Axis forces were now poised to retreat. On the evening of November 2, Rommel sent an emergency situation report to the High Command of the German Armed Forces: his forces, he reported, were exhausted. 'The army,' he warned, 'will therefore no longer be in a position to prevent a further attempt by strong enemy tank formations to break through, which may be expected tonight or tomorrow.' On the other hand, Rommel told Berlin, an 'ordered' withdrawal of his troops was impossible in view of the lack of motor vehicles. Rommel added: 'The slight stocks of fuel do not allow for a movement to the rear over great distances.' On the 'one available road' his troops would

---

Churchill papers, 20/81. Dr Weizmann was then in New York. The 25th anniversary of the Balfour Declaration (issued when Churchill had been Minister of Munitions, fell on 2 November 1942). The message was not for publication.

[1] CS/1642, 'Private', 'Most Secret', 30 October 1942: Churchill papers, 20/81.

[2] CS/1594, 'Personal', 'Most Secret', 31 October 1942: Churchill papers, 20/82.

[3] Prime Minister's Personal Telegram, T.1403/2, Prime Minister to President, No. 179, 'Personal and Secret', 31 October 1942: Churchill papers, 20/82.

[4] 'Most Secret', 31 October 1942: Churchill papers, 20/54.

[5] Prime Minister's Personal Telegram, T.1410/2, Prime Minister to President, No. 181, 'Personal and Secret', 1 November 1942: Churchill papers, 20/82.

[6] CS/1689, IZ 2128, 9 November 1942: Churchill papers, 20/82.

certainly be attacked 'night and day' by the Royal Air Force. In this situation, 'the gradual annihilation of the army must be faced'.[1]

The decrypt of this message reached Churchill on the night of November 2, when a copy was also sent to Cairo for Alexander. Three other decrypts that same day testified to the imminence of a German retreat, and the exhaustion of the German army.[2] 'Presume you have read all the Boniface,' Churchill telegraphed to Alexander on November 4, 'including especially No. QT/5086 sent you night of 2nd.'[3]

All indications were that 'Lightfoot' and 'Torch' would both be victorious. On November 3 Churchill telegraphed to Roosevelt that General Giraud had decided to leave Vichy France for North Africa: a British submarine, under a United States captain, took him from the Riviera to Gibraltar.[4]

' "Torch" movements are proceeding with precision and so far amazing secrecy', Churchill telegraphed to Alexander on November 4. During the morning, Alexander was able to telegraph to Churchill in triumph:

After twelve days of heavy and violent fighting Eighth Army has inflicted a severe defeat on the enemy's German and Italian forces under Rommel's command in Egypt. The enemy's front has broken, and British armoured formations in strength have passed through and are operating in the enemy's rear areas. Such portions of the enemy's forces as can get away are in full retreat, and are being harassed by our armoured and mobile forces and by our Air Forces. Other enemy divisions are still in position, endeavouring to stave off defeat, and these are likely to be surrounded and cut off.

The RAF has throughout given support to the land battle, and are bombing the enemy's retreating columns incessantly.

Fighting continues.[5]

Churchill at once sent a copy of this telegram to Roosevelt. 'I feel sure,' he told the President, 'you will regard this as a good prelude to "Torch".'[6]

---

[1] QT/5086: Hinsley and others, *British Intelligence in the Second World War*, volume 2, page 448.

[2] QT/5032, 5039 and 5073: Hinsley and others, *British Intelligence in the Second World War*, volume 2, page 448.

[3] Prime Minister's Personal Telegram, T.1420/Z, OZ 1764, 4 November 1942: Churchill papers, 20/82.

[4] Prime Minister's Personal Telegram, T.1413/2, Prime Minister to President, No. 182, 'Personal and Secret', 3 November 1942: Churchill papers, 20/82. General Giraud was given the codename 'Kingpin'.

[5] CS/1647, IZ 2047, 9.50 a.m., 4 November 1942: Churchill papers, 20/82.

[6] Prime Minister's Personal Telegram, T.1423/2, Prime Minister to President, No. 184, 'Personal and Secret', 4 November 1942: Churchill papers, 20/82.

Churchill then telegraphed to Alexander, praising his progress and that of 'your brilliant lieutenant', Montgomery. Churchill added that if Alexander's 'reasonable hopes' were maintained, and a 'general retreat' was apparent, he proposed 'to ring the bells all over Britain for the first time this war'. Churchill added: 'Try to give me the moment to do this in the next few days. At least 20,000 prisoners would be necessary.' [1] That evening Churchill received a message from Casey, in Cairo, that 9,000 prisoners had been taken 'so far', including General Ritter von Thoma, commander of the German Africa Corps 'and a number of other senior German and Italian officers'. More than 260 German and Italian tanks had been captured or destroyed. Casey's message ended: '8th Army continues to advance'. [2]

On the eve of the North Africa landings, Churchill asked Roosevelt to be allowed to explain the plans to General de Gaulle, whom Roosevelt, with his hopes of Vichy defections to the Allies, had excluded from all knowledge of the plan. 'You will remember,' Churchill explained to the President on November 5, 'that I have exchanged letters with him of a solemn kind in 1940 recognizing him as the Leader of Free Frenchmen. I am confident his military honour can be trusted.'

Churchill told Roosevelt that he would explain to de Gaulle that 'Torch' was 'a United States enterprise and a United States secret'. As a 'consolation prize' for the exclusion of Free French forces in the landings, a member of de Gaulle's movement, General Le Gentilhomme, would be appointed Governor-General of recently conquered Madagascar. As for de Gaulle's relations with General Giraud, who was to be the senior French officer in the 'Torch' operation, 'I should think myself,' Churchill told Roosevelt, 'they will join forces politically, though under what conditions I cannot foresee.' [3]

Churchill had first met Giraud in 1937, during his visit to the Maginot Line, when he had listened entranced to Giraud's description of his adventures behind enemy lines as an escaped prisoner-of-war during the First World War. 'As fellow escapers,' Churchill later wrote, 'this gave us something in common.' [4] In April 1942, on learning that Giraud had again escaped from a German prison camp, and had returned to France, Churchill had telegraphed to Roosevelt: 'I am highly interested in the escape of General Giraud and his arrival at Vichy. This man might play a decisive part in bringing about

[1] Prime Minister's Personal Telegram, T.1424/2, OZ 1771, 'Bigot', 4 November 1942: Churchill papers, 20/82.

[2] MOS/55, 4 November 1942: Churchill papers, 20/82.

[3] Prime Minister's Personal Telegram, T.1435/2, Prime Minister to President, No. 185, 'Personal and Secret', 5 November 1942: Churchill papers, 20/82.

[4] Winston S. Churchill, *The Second World War*, volume 4, London 1951, page 544.

things of which you had hopes. Please tell me anything you know.' [1]

Giraud now waited at Gibraltar for 'Torch' to begin. Despite Churchill's wish to tell de Gaulle of the plan, Roosevelt had persuaded him not to give de Gaulle any information 'until subsequent to a successful landing'.[2] Churchill had therefore to restrict himself to a letter to de Gaulle about the Free French forces taking part in Montgomery's advance. 'The fruits of the victory have yet to be gathered,' he wrote, 'but they may well be abundant.' Churchill added: 'It will, I am sure, give you the same pleasure as it does me to see the Boche getting a taste of the medicine with which they have dosed others so mercilessly. Both your Fighting French Brigades are well forward in the hunt on the southern flank.' [3]

'We are not telling de Gaulle anything,' Churchill informed Casey, 'until "Torch" is lit.' [4] 'I am still sorry about de Gaulle,' he telegraphed to Roosevelt, adding: 'But we are ready to accept your view.' [5]

The success of the Eighth Army in the Western Desert had brought a new mood to Britain, after three years of war, setback, and surrender. It was as if Dunkirk, the Blitz, Singapore and Tobruk had been avenged. On November 5 Churchill received a handwritten letter from the King:

My dear Winston,

I must send you my warmest congratulations on the great Victory of the 8th Army in Egypt. I was overjoyed when I received the news and so was everybody else. In our many talks together over a long period I knew that the elimination of the Africa Corps, the threat to Egypt, was your *one* aim, the most important of all the many other operations with which you have had to deal.

When I look back and think of all the many arduous hours of work you have put in, and the many miles you have travelled, to bring this battle to such a successful conclusion you have every right to rejoice; while the rest of our people will one day be very thankful to you for what you have done. I cannot say more.

At last the Army has come into its own, as it is their victory primarily, ably helped by the forces of the air, and of those that work under the surface of the sea.

'I am so pleased,' the King ended, 'that everybody is taking this

---

[1] Telegram of 29 April 1942.

[2] President to Prime Minister, No. 207, 'Personal and Secret', 5 November 1942: Churchill papers, 20/82.

[3] 'Secret', 5 November 1942: Churchill papers, 20/54.

[4] Prime Minister's Personal Telegram, T.1444/2, 'Personal and Most Secret', OZ 1798, 6 November 1942: Churchill papers, 20/82.

[5] Prime Minister's Personal Telegram, T.1445/2, 6 November 1942: Churchill papers, 20/82.

victory in a quiet and thankful way, though their rejoicing is very deep and sincere.'[1]

From Churchill's aunt Leonie came 'a wave of love & congratulations' on November 6. 'We are all rejoicing,' she wrote, 'over the news from Libya. The tide is turning, and I like to think of how pleased you must be. Your visit to the desert is having good results.' General Alexander, she added, 'is not only very able, but also lucky'.[2] There was also a telegram for Churchill from General Marshall. 'Having been privileged,' he wrote, 'to witness your courage and resolution on the day of the fall of Tobruk, I am unable to express my full delight over the news from the Middle East and my admiration for the British Army.'[3] 'I am most grateful to you for your message,' Churchill replied. 'I was indeed touched at the time of Tobruk by the kindness and delicacy you all showed.'[4]

For the first time since he had become Prime Minister, Churchill received a spate of congratulations and praise, and outpouring of national rejoicing. 'You *have* pulled us through the dark tunnel into the light of dawn!' was how his cousin Clare Sheridan expressed it.[5]

The exuberance of victory was reflected in the messages exchanged between Churchill and Alexander. 'My regards to Montgomery,' Churchill telegraphed on the night of November 6. 'He has been magnificent. I wish I could have been with you both in these great days.'[6] That same night, Alexander telegraphed to Churchill from the Western Desert: 'Ring out the bells! Prisoners estimated at 20,000, tanks 350, guns 400, motor transport *several thousand*. Our advanced mobile forces are south of Mersa Matruh. 8th Army is advancing.'[7] Churchill at once sent on the facts of Alexander's message to Roosevelt, Stalin and Eisenhower, the latter then at Gibraltar in the last stages of preparation for 'Torch'.[8]

Churchill lunched on November 6 at 10 Downing Street. Among the guests was Harold Nicolson. In his diary Nicolson gave an account of the lunch, and of Churchill's account of the 'Battle of Egypt':

[1] Buckingham Palace, 5 November 1942: Churchill papers, 20/59.

[2] Letter of 6 November 1942: Churchill papers, 1/368.

[3] 'Personal', 7 November 1942: Churchill papers, 20/82.

[4] Prime Minister's Personal Telegram, T.1463/2, 'Personal', 8 November 1942: Churchill papers, 20/82.

[5] Letter of 8 November 1942: Churchill papers, 1/318.

[6] Prime Minister's Personal Telegram, T.1454/2, OZ 1808, 'Personal', 6 November 1942: Churchill papers, 20/82.

[7] No. 68827, 'Personal', 6 November 1942: Churchill papers, 20/82. Three days later, 25,000 prisoners had reached Alexandria (General Alexander to Churchill, 05/1689, 9 November 1942: Churchill papers, 20/82).

[8] The telegram to Roosevelt was Prime Minister's Personal Telegram, T.1450/2, Prime Minister to President, No. 187, 'Personal and Secret'; the telegram to Eisenhower was Gibraltar No. 92 and to Stalin, Foreign Office to Kuibyshev No. 1517: Churchill papers, 20/82.

'The enemy,' he says, 'were stuck to the Alamein position like limpets to a rock. We cut them out'—at that he makes a gesture of someone cutting a limpet off a rock with a knife—'we detached them utterly. And what happens to a limpet when it loses its rock. It dies a miserable death. Thirst comes to it—aching, inescapable thirst. I should not like our armies to be suffering what the Africa Corps will suffer in these days.' He does not think that Rommel will make much of a stand before Halfaya, or even there. 'The next days will show. There is more jam to come. Much more jam. And in places where some of you least expect.'

Brendan Bracken then comes in and Winston tells him to arrange for all the bells in England to be tolled on Sunday. Some hesitation was expressed by all of us. 'Not at all,' says Winston, 'not at all. We are not celebrating final victory. The war will still be long. When we have beaten Germany, it will take us two more years to beat Japan. Nor is that a bad thing. It will keep America and ourselves together while we are making peace in Europe. If I am still alive, I shall fling all we have into the Pacific.'[1]

On November 7 Churchill decided not to order the ringing of the church bells until after the 'Torch' landing, 'in case', as he telegraphed to Alexander, 'of some accident which would cause distress'.[2] That same day, with the forces of 'Torch' only twelve hours from their launching, Churchill wrote to the King:

I am deeply grateful to Your Majesty for the most kind and gracious letter with which I have been honoured. I shall always preserve it during the remaining years of my life, and it will remain as a record of the support and encouragement given by the Sovereign to his First Minister in good and dark days alike. No Minister in modern times, and I daresay in long past days, has received more help and comfort from the King, and this has brought us all thus far with broadening hopes and now I feel to brightening skies.

It is needless to me to assure Your Majesty of my devotion to Yourself and Family and to our ancient and cherished Monarchy—the true bulwark of British freedom against tyrannies of every kind; but I trust I may have the pleasure of feeling a sense of personal friendship which is very keen and lively in my heart and has grown strong in these hard times of war.

In a postscript, Churchill informed the King that 'Torch' 'goes on with the utmost precision'. Air attacks could be expected that morning on the fast convoy approaching Algiers, 'but our carriers should give them a good drubbing'.[3]

The 'Torch' landings took place in the early hours of Sunday November 8, at Algiers, Oran and Casablanca. Churchill's son Randolph was among the troops off Algiers. 'Well here we are,' he

[1] Harold Nicolson diary, 6 November 1942: Nigel Nicolson (editor), *op. cit.*, page 259.

[2] Prime Minister's Personal Telegram, T.1457/Z, OZ 1814, 7 November 1942: Churchill papers, 20/82.

[3] Letter of 7 November 1942: Churchill papers, 20/59.

wrote to his father at ten in the morning, 'safe and sound in the anchorage to the West of Algiers. Nearly everything has gone according to plan.' Despite numerous alarms during the journey, there had been 'no serious air attack'. Everyone was 'in tremendous heart, and all feel it is a real privilege to be taking part in these great events'. In addition, Randolph reported: 'All goes well between us and the Americans.'[1]

At luncheon on November 8, Churchill told de Gaulle of the scope and scale of 'Torch'. Eden, who was also present, told Oliver Harvey that 'the General was at his best. He said that it was necessary to think of France and we were right to choose Giraud for this.'[2]

'Algiers will probably be taken this evening,' Darlan telegraphed to his superiors in Vichy France at half past eleven that morning. An aircraft of the Fleet Air Arm, having seen friendly signals from the ground, had already landed at Blida Airfield, and anti-Vichy Frenchmen, including the local commander, had held the airfield until Allied troops arrived from the beaches. At Casablanca and Oran, as at Algiers, there was fierce fighting, and several setbacks, but everywhere the Allied forces succeeded in wresting the ports from Vichy control.

By nightfall on November 8 it was clear that the initial phase of 'Torch' had succeeded. 'Let me congratulate you,' Churchill telegraphed to General Marshall, 'on all the news so far received of the great events taking place in French North Africa,' and he added: 'We shall find the problems of success not less puzzling though more agreeable than those we have hitherto surmounted together.'[3]

For the moment, however, the atmosphere of success was all pervasive. 'Once he began to bark, then quickly stopped himself,' Elizabeth Layton noted of a dictation session on the weekend of the victory, 'and said "No, no; quite all right, *quite* all right. Tonight you may rejoice. Tonight there is sugar on the cake." '[4]

[1] 'Sunday 8 November 1942, 10.00 a.m.': Churchill papers, 1/369.
[2] Prime Minister's Personal Telegram, T.1463/2, 'Personal', 8 November 1942: Churchill papers, 20/82.
[3] Harvey diary, 8 November 1942: John Harvey (editor), *op. cit.*, pages 178–9.
[4] Elizabeth Layton, letter of 18 November 1942: Nel papers.

16
Planning for 1943

ON 9 November 1942 Churchill telegraphed to Oliver Lyttelton, who was in Washington on a supply mission, that as a result of the success of the North African landings 'an entirely new view must be taken of possibilities of attacking Hitler in 1943'.[1] What this new view was, he set out in detail in a paper for the Chiefs of Staff on November 9, provoked to do so by a Chiefs of Staff paper on future American–British strategy which wished to follow up 'Lightfoot' and 'Torch' by the occupation of Sicily and Sardinia.[2] Both Churchill and Eden were 'horrified at this', Oliver Harvey noted in his diary.[3] To accept the conquest of these two islands as 'the limit of our action', Churchill wrote in his detailed response, 'would be most regrettable'. It would typify 'a prevailing inhibition against facing the Germans anywhere except on the other side of salt water', courting the criticism 'Safety First'.

Churchill then set out his plan for 1943. The effort that year, he wrote, 'should clearly be a strong pinning down of the enemy in Northern France and the Low Countries by continuous preparations to invade, and a decisive attack on Italy or, better still, Southern France'. This should be combined with operations 'and other forms of pressure' to bring Turkey into the war, 'and operate over land with the Russians into the Balkans'.

Once French North Africa was 'comfortably and securely in Allied hands', Churchill argued, Britain and America 'must then go forward to the attack on Italy, with the object of preparing the way for a very large-scale offensive on the underbelly of the Axis in 1943'. Churchill ended his argument against limiting the Allied offensive in 1943 to the capture of Sicily and Sardinia with the question: 'Is it really to be supposed that the Russians will be content with our lying down like this during the whole of 1943, while Hitler had a third crack at them?'

[1] Prime Minister's Personal Telegram, T.1468/2, OZ 1832, 'Personal', 9 November 1942: Churchill papers, 20/82.
[2] Chiefs of Staff Paper No. 345 of 1945(O).
[3] Harvey diary, 10 November 1942: John Harvey (editor), *op. cit.*, pages 180–1.

and with his own answer, that however 'alarming' the prospect might seem, 'we must make an attempt to get on to the mainland and fight in the line against the enemy in 1943.'[1]

On November 10 Churchill spoke at the Lord Mayor's Luncheon at the Mansion House. 'I have never promised anything but blood, tears, toil, and sweat,' he said. 'Now, however, we have a new experience. We have victory—a remarkable and definite victory. The bright gleam has caught the helmets of our soldiers, and warmed and cheered all our hearts.' The Germans had received back again 'that measure of fire and steel which they have so often meted out to others'.

In speaking of the victory, Churchill sought to strike a balance between confidence and caution. 'Now this is not the end,' he warned. 'It is not even the beginning of the end. But it is, perhaps, the end of the beginning.'

The newspapers had described how, during Rommel's retreat, the coastal road 'crammed with fleeing German vehicles' had been under 'blasting attacks' from the Royal Air Force. Reading these reports, Churchill told his listeners, 'I could not but remember those roads of France and Flanders, crowded, not with fighting men, but with helpless refugees—women and children—fleeing with their pitiful barrows and household goods, upon whom such merciless havoc was wreaked. I have, I trust, a humane disposition, but I must say I could not help feeling that what was happening, however grievous, was only justice grimly reclaiming her rights.'

Britain had not entered the war 'for profit or expansion, but only for honour and to do our duty in defending the right'. This she would do. 'We mean to hold our own. I have not become the King's First Minister in order to preside over the liquidation of the British Empire.' For that task, if ever it were to be prescribed, 'someone else would have to be found', and, under democracy, 'I suppose the nation would have to be consulted.'[2] Britain's only aim in the war was to 'effect the liberation of the people of Europe from the pit of misery into which they have been cast by their own improvidence and by the brutal violence of the enemy'. Britain's victory in the Western Desert, and the American landings in North Africa, constituted 'a new bond between

---

[1] Prime Minister's Personal Minute, D.193/2, 'Most Secret', 9 November 1942: Churchill papers, 20/67.

[2] Eight days later, Churchill told the War Cabinet that in view of criticisms of British Colonial policy then current from the United States 'it might be a good plan that a full statement should be drawn up for publication on the development of the British Colonial Empire, vindicating our past and present policy, and indicating the probable trends of future policy'. (War Cabinet No. 154 of 1942, 18 November 1942: Cabinet papers, 65/28.)

the English-speaking peoples and a new hope for the whole world'.[1]

On this optimistic note Churchill's speech ended. Unknown to his listeners, he had learned three days earlier, from the Enigma decrypts, that the Germans, despite having occupied the town of Vladikavkaz, realized that they would not be able to reach the Caspian Sea or the oilfields of Baku. Instead, they would resort to air bombardment. 'You have no doubt realized,' Churchill had telegraphed to Stalin on November 7, 'that when Hitler despairs of taking Baku he will try to wreck it by air attack. Pray accept this from me.'[2] In contrast to the earlier lack of response, Stalin replied at once, from the Kremlin: 'Many thanks for your warnings concerning Baku. We are taking the necessary measures to combat the danger.'[3]

Four months had passed since the Vote of Censure in the House of Commons, and the charge that it was Churchill's method of war direction which was responsible for an unending series of defeats and setbacks. Yet, as Churchill explained to the House of Commons on November 11, 'before the Vote of Censure in the early days of July, all measures in our power had already been taken first to repel the enemy's further assault and, secondly, to take decisive offensive action against him. See then how silly it is for people to imagine that Governments can act on impulse or in immediate response to pressure in these large-scale offensives. There must be planning, design and forethought, and after that a long period of silence, which looks—I can quite understand it—to the ordinary spectator as if it were simply apathy or inertia, but which is in fact steady indispensable preparation for the blow.' Moreover, Churchill commented, 'you have first to get sufficient ascendancy even to prepare to strike such a blow'.

During his speech on November 11 Churchill added a personal note. 'I am certainly not one of those who need to be prodded,' he said. 'In fact, if anything, I am a prod,' and he added: 'My difficulties rather lie in finding the patience and self-restraint to wait through many anxious weeks for the results to be achieved.'[4]

Churchill's speech was met with much cheering. 'It was a creditable, indeed amazing, performance, for an overworked man of 68,' Henry Channon noted in his diary.[5] 'Altogether it has been a triumphant

---

[1] Speech of 10 November 1942, Mansion House, London: BBC Written Archive Centre.

[2] Prime Minister's Personal Telegram, T.1448/Z, 'Personal and Secret', No. 1516 to Kuibyshev, 'Immediate', 'Most Secret', 7 November 1942: Churchill papers, 20/82. Circulation of this telegram was limited to three of those who were aware of the Enigma decrypts, Eden, Ismay and Bridges.

[3] 'Personal', Kremlin, 10 November 1942: Churchill papers, 20/82.

[4] *Hansard*, 11 November 1942, columns 20–39.

[5] Channon diary, 11 November 1942: Robert Rhodes James (editor), *op. cit.*, page 341. Churchill was, in fact, still 67.

and most cheering week for the PM,' John Martin wrote home, and he added: 'a well-deserved triumph'.[1]

On November 11, German troops entered Unoccupied France. The days of the Vichy Government were almost over. In North Africa, the pace of Montgomery's victories was rapid. On November 13 the Eighth Army entered Tobruk. 'There is a long road still to tread,' Churchill telegraphed to the Emir Abdullah of Transjordan that same day, 'but the end is sure.'[2]

Roosevelt was as determined as Churchill to take advantage of the Allied victories in North Africa. In a telegram which reached Churchill on November 12, he set out the 'additional steps' which he felt should be taken 'when and if' the southern shore of the Mediterranean was under Allied control. These steps, Roosevelt hoped, would be discussed by Churchill and his Chiefs of Staff in London, and by Roosevelt himself and his Combined Staff in Washington. The 'possibilities' as Roosevelt set them out in his telegram to Churchill were a 'forward movement' directed against Sardinia, Sicily, Italy, Greece and other 'Balkan areas', and included 'the possibility of obtaining Turkish support for an attack through the Black Sea against Germany's flank'.[3]

Nothing pleased him more, Churchill replied to Roosevelt on the following day, 'than to read what you say about trying to bring Turkey in. Our minds have indeed moved together on this, as in so much else.'[4] Meanwhile, in an attempt to retain a military position in North Africa, and to frustrate any Allied advance across the Mediterranean, the Germans set up a bridgehead in Tunisia.

That weekend, at Chequers, Churchill invited his senior advisers to discuss future strategy: among those present during the weekend were Brooke, Pound, Portal, Ismay and Mountbatten, as well as Eden and Smuts.[5] 'You know how anxious we are,' Churchill telegraphed to Stalin on Friday November 13, 'to take off you some of the undue weight which you have steadfastly borne in these last hard months.'[6]

That Friday, in the Pacific, a naval battle began at the approaches

[1] Letter of 12 November 1942: Martin papers.

[2] Prime Minister's Personal Telegram, T.1490/2, 13 November 1942: Churchill papers, 20/82.

[3] President to Prime Minister, No. 210, 'Priority', 12 November 1942: Churchill papers, 20/82. Churchill sent copies to the King, Smuts, Attlee, Pound, Brooke, Bridges, Ismay and Eden.

[4] Prime Minister's Personal Telegram, T.1491/2, Prime Minister to President, No. 189, 'Personal and Secret', 13 November 1942: Churchill papers, 20/82.

[5] 'Guests for Weekend November 13–16, Revised List': Chequers Lists.

[6] Prime Minister's Personal Telegram, T.1492/2, 13 November 1942: Churchill papers, 20/88.

to Guadalcanal in the Solomon Islands, in which a Japanese expedition was forced to withdraw, after heavy losses.[1] On the Saturday,
Stalin telegraphed to Churchill about the battle in the Caucasus:
'Vladikavkaz is in our hands and, it seems to me, will remain in our
hands.'[2] At Chequers, Churchill minuted to Pound: 'I am most anxious to run a Russian convoy late in December,' and asking Pound to
approach the United States Navy for 'at least 20 or 25 destroyers' for
the convoy escorts. These destroyers, he noted, could easily be saved
from the 'excessive escorts' which the American navy was using for
their troop convoys in 'Torch'.[3] Roosevelt was unable to comply,
however, informing Churchill that destroyer losses and damage to
destroyers in the recent naval operations in the Pacific 'have been so
serious as to necessitate an immediate return of the destroyers
borrowed from the Pacific for "Torch" '. Roosevelt ended his telegram: 'I wish I could send you a more favourable answer.'[4]

While Churchill had been preparing for his conference on strategy
at Chequers, both Lyttelton and Halifax had telegraphed from the
United States to urge him to cross the Atlantic once more, in order to
discuss future strategy with Roosevelt in Washington. 'The PM
mercifully does not want to go,' Oliver Harvey noted in his diary on
November 14, 'and his doctor is dead against it.' Harvey added, of
the imminent strategic discussion: 'The Russian army having played
the allotted role of killing Germans, our Chiefs of Staff think by 1944
they could stage a general onslaught on the exhausted animal.'
Harvey added that both Churchill and Eden 'reject these foolish
military views, and must now decide what we can do next year which
the Chiefs of Staff can be made to accept'.[5]

In his telegram to Roosevelt on November 13, Churchill had expressed his own hopes for a 'rapid stocking-up of Turkey with British
and American arms, particularly tanks, flak and anti-tank guns' and
the gathering during the winter of a 'considerable' Allied army in
Syria.[6]

---

[1] The Japanese lost 2 battleships, 8 cruisers, 6 destroyers and 8 troop transports, with 4 cargo transports destroyed on the beaches. The American losses were limited to 2 cruisers. 'I am so glad to read about this splendid American naval victory in the Solomons,' Churchill telegraphed to Roosevelt on November 17. 'Pray accept my warmest congratulations and thanks' (Prime Minister's Personal Telegram, T.1517/2, Prime Minister to President No. 192, 'Personal and Secret', 17 November 1942: Churchill papers, 20/83).

[2] 'Personal and Secret', Kremlin, 14 November 1942: Churchill papers, 20/83.

[3] Prime Minister's Personal Minute, M.529/2, 'Secret', 14 November 1942: Churchill papers, 20/67.

[4] President to Prime Minister, No. 218, 'Personal and Most Secret', 19 November 1942: Churchill papers, 20/83.

[5] Harvey diary, 14 November 1942: John Harvey (editor), op. cit., pages 182–5.

[6] Prime Minister's Personal Telegram, T.1491/2, Prime Minister to President, No. 189, 'Personal and Secret', 13 November 1942: Churchill papers, 20/82.

On Sunday November 15, with the 'Torch' landings successfully carried out, church bells were indeed rung throughout Britain to celebrate the victory in Egypt. 'Many grim people say it is premature and "tempting Providence",' John Martin wrote home. 'As the PM said it is strange to describe "thanksgiving" as "tempting Providence"; but it is a poor heart that never rejoices and we can let ourselves go for once without forgetting all the difficulties and dangers still ahead.'[1] That Sunday Randolph Churchill wrote to his father from liberated Algiers: 'Alexander's victory seems to be complete. All here are thrilled by it. Well done!'[2]

By coincidence, shortly after writing these words, Randolph Churchill met in the lobby of an hotel the former French Foreign Minister, Pierre Flandin. Churchill and his son had known Flandin quite well before the war, and had visited him in his country home in France. Now Flandin was on a short visit to North Africa, where he had a farm at Philippeville. Randolph and Flandin talked together for about an hour and a half. Flandin intended to return to German-occupied Vichy France, to rejoin his children: 'he genuinely wishes to see the Germans beaten', Randolph reported. 'He says the internal situation of Italy is very weak. We ought to attack Europe through Italy and the Balkans.' It was 'vital that British and American troops should reach Vienna, Bucharest and Budapest before the Russians'.[3]

At Chequers on Sunday November 15, even as Randolph was talking to Flandin in the lobby of an hotel in Algiers, Churchill was discussing with his advisers the future strategy of the war. After lunch they were joined by Eisenhower's Chief of Staff, Brigadier-General Bedell Smith. The focus of the discussion was Roosevelt's telegram to Churchill of November 11, in which the President has asked for 'a survey of the possibilities including forward movement directed against Sardinia, Sicily, Italy, Greece and other Balkan areas and including the possibility of obtaining Turkish support for an attack through the Black Sea against Germany's flank'.[4]

Roosevelt's strategic plan was similar, if not identical, to Churchill's 'underbelly of the Axis' argument of November 9. It was discussed at Chequers on November 15, and again at a meeting of the Defence Committee on November 16. Churchill's support for it, and his elaboration of it, were set out in a note to the British Chiefs of Staff which he sent to Roosevelt on November 17. 'I endorse the above

[1] Letter of 12 November 1942: Martin papers.
[2] Letter of 15 November 1942, Algiers: Churchill papers, 1/369.
[3] Letter of 15 November 1942, Algiers: Churchill papers, 1/369. Two other points made by Flandin were that 'the Germans will very quickly fortify the Riviera' and that he did not mind 'if the Russians are first in Berlin'.
[4] President to Prime Minister, No. 210, 11 November 1942: Cabinet papers, 65/28.

conception by the President,' Churchill wrote. After conquering the African shore of the Mediterranean, the Allies, should, as he phrased it, 'strike at the under-belly of the Axis in effective strength and in the shortest time', using bases in North Africa. Long range bombers sent by the United States to North Africa, as well as American bombers already in the Middle East, could operate 'against Italian targets'. The bombing weight of British night air attacks 'should be brought to bear on Italy whenever the weather is more favourable than for bombing Germany'. Every endeavour should be made 'to make Italy feel the weight of the war'. Italian industrial centres should be attacked 'in an intense fashion', with every effort made to render them uninhabitable and 'to terrorize and paralyse the population'.

Once Tripoli and Tunis had fallen to the Allies, the 'immediate objective' for Allied attack was 'obviously' either Sardinia or Sicily. From either of these two islands, 'intensified' air attacks could be made continuously upon Naples, Rome and the naval bases of the Italian fleet, raising the war against Italy 'to an intense degree'.

Two other benefits of the success of 'Torch', Churchill believed, were that the trans-Atlantic convoys could be restored to standard strength, and the PQ convoys to Russia begin again in the latter part of December. Meanwhile a decision was needed 'within the next week' about whether Sardinia or Sicily were to be attacked next. Sicily, Churchill wrote, 'is by far the greater prize'.

Roosevelt's suggestion about Turkey was also 'of vital importance', Churchill wrote. A 'supreme and prolonged effort' should be made to bring Turkey into the war in the Spring of 1943. Allied troops could move to Turkey by rail and road from Syria. If the Russians could maintain themselves in the Caucasus, hold the Caspian and even make a 'counterstroke' against the Germans, British land and air forces stationed in Persia, Iraq and Syria in order to check a German advance towards the Persian Gulf would be free 'to assist the Turks'. A 'target date' for this 'should be April or May'. Beginning at once, Turkey should be equipped from both Egypt and the United States with tanks, anti-tank guns and anti-aircraft guns, 'and active construction of airfields must be undertaken'.

It would seem 'a great mistake', Churchill wrote, to attack Rhodes, and other Italian islands in the eastern Mediterranean, 'until we have got Turkey on our side'. With Turkey as an ally, and with a Russian advance towards Rostov-on-Don and the Black Sea, it would be possible to open the Dardanelles 'under heavy air protection' to the passage of supplies to Russian Black Sea ports, 'and to any naval assistance the Russians might require in the Black Sea'.[1]

[1] 'Note by the Minister of Defence to the Chiefs of Staff on Plans and Operations in the

Codenames were being allocated to each of the possible post-'Torch' operations. The first to get a name was the proposed attack on Sardinia. This had become operation 'Brimstone'. One of its problems was the naval support required. To help Russia, Churchill had ruled, as Dudley Pound told the Chiefs of Staff Committee on November 18, 'that the provision of Royal Navy escorts for the northern convoys, at the rate of three every two months, 'should have priority over other operations'. This meant, as Pound explained, that the Home Fleet destroyers 'would no longer be available' for operations in the Mediterranean. As a result, it would be difficult, 'if not impossible', to provide an adequate naval escort for 'Brimstone' from British resources.[1]

Four days later, Churchill minuted to Pound:

My hope was and is that if we can get hold of 'Brimstone' the same or equivalent follow-up convoys would sustain us there as would otherwise go to 'Torch'. I had thought of 'Brimstone', once it had been taken, as the same thing as 'Torch' only in a slightly different area. The rather taller flower grows off the same stem. You do not have to have a separate stem for every blossom.

We must go into this in detail. It is the troops already in or assigned to 'Torch' who will do 'Brimstone', and they will require no more supplies.[2]

On November 23 Churchill reiterated, in a minute to General Holmes, that the naval support for 'Brimstone' was not intended to be additional to the forces being used for 'Torch'. His aim was to make use of forces from 'Torch' when they could be 'diverted to other seaports not far away'. As Churchill saw it, these forces would serve a purpose far beyond the North African shore. As he told Holmes in his minute of November 23: 'I never meant the Anglo-American Army to be stuck in North Africa. It is a spring-board and not a sofa.'[3]

The success of 'Torch' was partly due to the chance presence in North Africa of Admiral Darlan, who was visiting his sick son, and who gave orders, as Eisenhower reported to Churchill, for the Vichy

Mediterranean, Middle East and Near East', 17 November 1942: Prime Minister's Personal Telegram, T.1525/2, Prime Minister to President, No. 195, 17 November 1942: Churchill papers, 20/83. War Cabinet No. 543 of 1942, 'Most Secret', 25 November 1942: Churchill papers, 23/10.

[1] Chiefs of Staff Committee No. 319 of 1942, 18 November 1942: Cabinet papers, 79/58.

[2] Prime Minister's Personal Minute, M.542/2, 22 November 1942, Annex II, Chiefs of Staff Committee No. 324 of 1942, 23 November 1942: Cabinet papers, 79/58.

[3] Prime Minister's Personal Minute, M.546/Z, 23 November 1942: Churchill papers, 20/67. General Holmes was Director of Movements, War Office.

forces in Morocco to stop their resistance to the Americans.[1] These orders were obeyed. On Eisenhower's advice, the Allies recognized Darlan's influence and status. But considering what Churchill described to Roosevelt as Darlan's 'odious record', including his orders to the French warships off Casablanca to attack the American landing force, Churchill urged that Darlan's ascendancy should be 'a temporary expedient, justifiable solely by the stress of battle'.[2] Roosevelt replied that he too had 'encountered the deep currents of feeling against Darlan,' and felt, as he told Churchill, 'I should act fast.'[3] He therefore issued a Press statement on November 18, using almost exactly Churchill's phrase, 'a temporary expedient, justified solely by the stress of battle'.[4]

On the evening of November 18, Churchill presided at the first meeting of the newly established Anti-U Boat Warfare Committee, charged with finding some means to meet the relentless challenge of German submarine successes. In October 1942, U-boats had sunk 29 Allied ships in convoy and 54 ships sailing independently. In November the figure rose to 39 ships in convoy, and 70 ships sailing independently. The total tonnage of Allied shipping lost that November to U-boat attack was 721,700 tons, the highest figure for any month of the war. The reason for the U-boat successes was the British inability to read the German Enigma key used in its U-boat communications. In December 1942 this key was broken: Pound informed the United States Chief of Naval Operations of this triumph on December 13. It came, he wrote, after 'months of strenuous endeavour'.[5] In January, the sinkings were to fall dramatically, as a result of successful evasive routing of the known and located dangers.

Successful Intelligence work in the west was paralleled by successful military endeavour in the east. On November 19 the Red Army began the encirclement of the German Sixth Army besieging Stalingrad.

---

[1] Telegram No. 527 (Eisenhower to Combined Chiefs of Staff), 'Most Secret', 14 November 1942: Cabinet papers, 65/28.

[2] Prime Minister's Personal Telegram, T.1519/2, Prime Minister to President, No. 193, 'Personal and Secret', 17 November 1942: Churchill papers, 20/83.

[3] President to Prime Minister, No. 213, 'Urgent, Personal and Secret', 18 November 1942: Churchill papers, 20/83.

[4] President to Prime Minister, No. 214, 'Personal and Urgent', 'Copy of Press release', Washington, 17 November 1942: Churchill papers, 20/83.

[5] Hinsley and others, *British Intelligence in the Second World War*, volume 2, London 1981, page 233. In December 1942 the Allied ships sunk by U-boat fell to 19 in convoy and 25 sailing individually. In January 1943 the figures had dropped to 15 and 18 respectively.

'The operations are developing not badly,' Stalin telegraphed to Churchill on November 20.[1] Three days later the German forces were encircled. Their commander, General von Paulus, proposed ending the siege and breaking out of the Russian ring. Hitler ordered him to stand and fight. Von Paulus obeyed, and his army was destroyed.[2]

The planning for the campaign of 1943 was in full progress in both London and Washington. Roosevelt and Churchill were in accord that their respective Staffs should examine in detail, and prepare plans for, the 'soft under-belly' campaigns against Sicily, Sardinia, Italy and the Balkans, with every effort made to bring in Turkey as an Ally, for an assault against the Germans in the region of Bulgaria. Churchill was still convinced, however, that the cross-Channel attack, codename 'Round-up', should be prepared for 1943. Without it, he minuted to the Chiefs of Staff Committee on November 18, solemn undertakings, and 'an immense amount of work', would both be undermined. 'We have, in fact,' Churchill warned, 'pulled in our horns to an almost extraordinary extent, and I cannot imagine what the Russians will say or do when they realise it.'

'My own position,' Churchill informed the Chiefs of Staff Committee, in his minute of November 18, 'is that I am still aiming at a "Round-up" retarded till August. I cannot give this up without a massive presentation of facts and figures which prove physical impossibility.'[3]

On November 24 Churchill was shown a letter from one of Eisenhower's deputies in London, Major General Russell P. Hartle, stating, as a matter not for discussion but already, so it seemed, decided, that, under a directive from the United States War Department, any construction 'in excess of the requirements for a force of 427,000' in the preparations for 'Bolero' must be accomplished 'entirely' by British labour and British materials, 'and that Lend-Lease materials cannot be furnished in these instances'.

In sending a copy of this directive to Roosevelt on November 25,

[1] Telegram of 20 November 1942. Kremlin, 'Personal and Secret': Churchill papers, 20/83. Churchill sent this telegram to Smuts who was then in Cairo on his way back to South Africa, with the covering note: 'I have received enclosed from Uncle Joe.' (Prime Minister's Personal Telegram, T.1554/2, 20 November 1942: Churchill papers, 20/88.)

[2] Von Paulus surrendered to the Russians on 2 February 1943, together with eight German Generals and 45,000 men. On 7 November 1943 Stalin described in a public broadcast how '146,700 dead Germans were picked up on the field and burned'.

[3] Prime Minister's Personal Minute, D.202/2, 'Most Secret', 'Action this Day', 18 November 1942: Churchill papers, 20/67.

Churchill noted that Britain had been preparing under 'Bolero' for the build-up of a cross-Channel force of 1,100,000 men. The War Department directive, he pointed out, was 'the first intimation we have had that this target is to be abandoned'.

It 'Bolero' were to be reduced as drastically as the War Department directive implied, it was clear, Churchill warned, that 'Round-up', the cross-Channel invasion itself, would have to be abandoned 'for ever'. This, Churchill warned Roosevelt, would be 'a most grievous decision'. His telegram continued:

All my talks with Stalin, in Averell's presence, were on the basis of a postponed 'Round-up', but never was it suggested that we should attempt no Second Front in Europe in 1943, or even 1944.

Surely, Mr President, this matter requires most profound consideration. I was deeply impressed with all General Marshall's arguments that only by 'Round-up' could the main forces be thrown into France and the Low Countries, and only in this area could the main strength of the British Metropolitan and United States Overseas Air Forces be brought into action. One of the arguments we used against 'Sledgehammer' was that it would eat up in 1942 the seed-corn needed for the much larger 'Round-up' in 1943. No doubt we have all been sanguine of our shipping resources, but that is a matter which time can correct. Only by the building up of a 'Round-up' force here as rapidly and regularly as other urgent demands on shipping allow can we have the means of coming to grips with the main strength of the enemy and liberating the European nations. It may well be that, try as we will, our strength will not reach the necessary levels in 1943. But if so it becomes all the more important to make sure we do not miss 1944.

A chance for a cross-Channel landing might even come in 1943, Churchill told Roosevelt. In the east, Stalin's offensive might reach Rostov-on-Don, 'which is his aim'. In the Mediterranean, the operations following on 'Torch' might 'drive Italy out of the war'. Widespread demoralization might then set in among the Germans, 'and we must be ready to profit by any opportunity which offers'. Churchill's telegram ended:

I do beg of you, Mr President, to let me know what has happened. At present we are completely puzzled by this information and the manner in which it has reached us. It seems to me absolutely necessary either that General Marshall and Admiral King with Harry should come over here or that I should come with my people to you.[1]

In his reply, Roosevelt sought to reassure Churchill that the build-up of troops in England, for an eventual cross-Channel landing, would continue, 'as rapidly', he telegraphed a few days later, 'as our shipping

[1] Prime Minister's Personal Telegram, T.1589/2, Prime Minister to President, No. 211, 'Personal and Secret', 24 November 1942: Churchill papers, 20/83.

and other resources permit', and that the United States had 'no intention of abandoning "Round-up".' [1] On the following day, however,
Mountbatten told the Chiefs of Staff Committee 'that although some
help was being received from the United States, very great difficulties
were being encountered in obtaining the personnel and equipment for
the maintenance and repair of landing craft'.[2] Within six weeks
Mountbatten had reported that, despite an agreement to the contrary,
'the Americans were putting the good engines into their own landing
craft and fitting ours with the unsatisfactory type'.[3]

Churchill's morning reading of the newspapers fuelled his quests
and queries. On November 21 he read in *The Times* that the Ministry
of Food had banned the exchange of rationed food. He wrote at once
to the Minister, Lord Woolton:

I hope it is not true that we are enforcing a whole set of vexatious regulations of this kind. It is absolutely contrary to logic and good sense that a
person may not give away or exchange his rations with someone who at the
moment he feels has a greater need. It strikes at neighbourliness and
friendship. I should be so sorry to see the great work you have done spoilt by
allowing these officials, whose interests are so deeply involved in magnifying
their functions and their numbers, to lead you to strike a false note.

'The matter must be brought before the Cabinet next week,' Churchill
added, 'unless you can reassure me.' [4]

On Sunday November 22 Churchill announced a number of
Ministerial changes. Sir Stafford Cripps was to leave the War Cabinet
to become Minister of Aircraft Production. Eden was to succeed
Cripps as Leader of the House of Commons, while Lord Cranborne
succeeded Cripps as Lord Privy Seal. Cranborne was himself succeeded at the Colonial Office by Oliver Stanley. The Home Secretary
and Minister for Home Security, Herbert Morrison, was to enter the
War Cabinet, joining his Labour colleagues Attlee and Bevin.

The scene that Sunday at Chequers was recorded by Elizabeth
Layton, who sent home a secretary's-eye view of the day's events:

It was without doubt the *most awful* day I've ever known. We had: Staff,

[1] President to Prime Minister, No. 222, 'Personal and Secret', 26 November 1942: Churchill papers, 20/83.
[2] Chiefs of Staff Committee No. 329 of 1942, 27 November 1942: Cabinet papers, 79/58.
[3] Chiefs of Staff Committee No. 8 of 1943, 8 January 1943: Cabinet papers, 79/88.
[4] Prime Minister's Personal Minute, M.539/2, 21 November 1942: Churchill papers, 20/67.

E. Bridges, Morrison, Brendan and various others. Mrs Hill was feeling awful and looked shocking—poor, poor thing, she is so brave and she won't give in. I honestly worked like a Trojan, and tried to save her all I could. At one stage in the afternoon they all conglomerated in the little office—I was typing like mad. He was sitting surrounded by the swarm, standing, sitting or perching on odd corners in the room. Staff was dictating to me on the machine, Brendan was on the phone to his office 'now hold on, get poised, just coming up. . . .' and as we finished our typing he grabbed it and hurled it over the phone to the press.[1]

On November 24 Churchill was able to inform Stalin that a convoy of over thirty ships would sail from Iceland on December 22. Because of 'Torch', he explained, the Germans had moved 'the bulk' of their aircraft from northern Norway to southern Europe. Churchill also told Stalin that efforts would be made to bring Turkey into the war by the spring of 1943. Not only would this enable Britain and America to 'open the shipping route to your left flank on the Black Sea', but would also enable them to bomb heavily from Turkish bases the Rumanian oilfields. A land move into Turkey would be additional to offensive action in the central Mediterranean, 'which will absorb our sea power and much of our Air power'. Once established in Tunisia with 'overpowering Air', Britain and America would be able to 'bring the war home to Mussolini and his Fascist gang with an intensity not yet possible'.[2] In Britain itself, a strong Anglo-American army and air force was being built up, the Germans were being 'pinned' in the Pas de Calais, and Britain and America 'are ready to take advantage of any favourable opportunity'. At the same time, 'our bombers will be blasting Germany with ever-increasing violence. Thus the halter will tighten upon the guilty doomed.'

The one 'limiting factor' in Anglo-American plans, Churchill explained, was the U-boat success in the Atlantic. 'You who have so much land,' he wrote, 'may find it hard to realize that we can only live and fight in proportion to our sea communications.'

Churchill ended his telegram with reference to the battle of Stalingrad. 'The glorious news of your offensive is streaming in,' he wrote.

---

[1] Elizabeth Layton, letter of 29 November 1942: Nel papers.

[2] In a memorandum for the War Cabinet entitled 'position of Italy', Churchill argued: 'If we increase the severity of our pressure upon Italy, the desire and indeed the imperative need of getting out of the war will come home to all the Italians, including the rank and file of the Fascist party.' If there was a revolution in Italy, and an Armistice Government came into power, it was 'at least arguable', Churchill wrote, 'that the German interests would be as well served by standing on the Brenner as by undertaking the detailed defence of Italy against the wishes of its people, and possibly of a provisional Government'. (War Cabinet Paper No. 546 of 1942, 'Most Secret', 25 November 1942: Churchill papers, 23/10.)

'We are watching it with breathless attention.'[1] Two days later he proposed to Roosevelt that the three leaders meet in January 1943 in Iceland. 'Our ships might lie in Hvalfjord,' he wrote, 'and we would place a suitable ship at Stalin's disposal wearing the Soviet flag *pro tem.*' Stalin had talked with 'some zest' in Moscow, Churchill recalled, 'of his desire to fly and of his confidence in the Russian machines'. Only at a 'meeting between principals', Churchill added, 'will real results be achieved'.[2] Roosevelt, however, ruled out any northern meeting place on account of what he later called the 'vile climate and icing on the wings', and suggested instead either 'an oasis south of Algiers', or Khartoum.[3]

Stalin welcomed the proposed efforts to bring Turkey into the war. 'This would be of great importance,' he telegraphed to Churchill on November 27, 'in order to accelerate the defeat of Hitler and his accomplices.' As to Britain and America having used Admiral Darlan in North Africa, Stalin's comment was to use a Russian proverb: 'even the devil himself and his grandma' should be used if the military need dictated it. Stalin's worry was the Second Front. When Churchill said that in the Pas de Calais Britain and America were ready to take advantage of any opportunity, 'I hope this does not mean,' he wrote, 'that you changed your mind with regard to your promise given in Moscow to establish a Second Front in Western Europe in the spring of 1943.'[4] Churchill had not changed his mind. 'I certainly think,' he minuted to the Chiefs of Staff Committee on November 29, 'we should make all plans to attack the French coast either in the Channel or in the Bay of Biscay, and that 12 July 1943 should be fixed as the target date.' Judging by conditions on the Russian front, Churchill wrote, 'it does not look as if Hitler will be able to bring back any large force from the east to the west. He has now to watch the southern coast of France as well.' The battles on the Russian front, he added, 'have already greatly modified and may fundamentally change the situation'.[5]

On the day of Stalin's telegram about Darlan and the devil, French naval officers in Toulon, acting on Darlan's orders, scuttled seventy-three French warships and naval craft to prevent them from being seized by the Germans.[6] 'From the flame and smoke of the explosions

---

[1] Prime Minister's Personal Telegram, T.1584/2, 24 November 1942: Churchill papers, 20/88.

[2] Prime Minister's Personal Telegram, T.1601/2, 26 November 1942: Churchill papers, 20/88.

[3] Brigadier E. I. C. Jacob, 'Operation "Symbol", Casablanca, December 1942, Preliminary Reconnaissance': Jacob papers. The 'vile climate and icing on the wings' reason is in Roosevelt's letter to Churchill of 14 December 1942.

[4] 'Personal and Secret', Kremlin, 27 November 1942: Churchill papers, 20/84.

[5] Prime Minister's Personal Minute, D.208/2, 'Most Secret', 'Action this Day', 29 November 1942: Churchill papers, 20/67.

[6] The scuttled ships included 1 battleship, 2 battle-cruisers, 7 cruisers, 29 destroyers and torpedo boats and 16 submarines.

at Toulon,' Churchill declared in a broadcast from Chequers on November 29, 'France will rise again.' [1]

November 30 was Churchill's sixty-eighth birthday. 'May Providence continue watching over you,' his aunt Leonie wrote from Ireland.[2] The year 1943, he had told his listeners on his eve of birthday broadcast, 'must be a stern and terrible year', but it would be met by Britain 'with a strong will, a bold heart and a good conscience'.[3] 'However much we may differ in outlook on certain matters,' Stafford Cripps wrote to Churchill that day, 'it has been a great joy to me to witness your tireless work for victory.' Cripps added: 'As you now enter upon a new year of effort you must be vastly and rightly stimulated by the result of all your hard and incessant work through the dark days of defeat and disappointment. May God guard and guide you in the days to come.'[4]

On Churchill's birthday it was work as usual, including a War Cabinet meeting at 5.30 in the afternoon and a Staff Conference at 10.30 in the evening. At the War Cabinet, Churchill read out Stalin's telegram of November 27, telling his colleagues that the changed military situation 'made it all the more incumbent upon us to start a Second Front in Europe' in 1943. 'Our present activities in the Mediterranean,' Churchill added, 'important though they were, could only be regarded as an inadequate contribution compared with the efforts Russia was making.'[5]

Churchill was excited by the news of Russia's successes in the Caucasus and at Stalingrad. The chances of a cross-Channel invasion succeeding, he telegraphed to Roosevelt on December 1, 'may be greatly improved by the present battles on the Russian front'. The whole question of 'Round-up' might be re-examined 'in the light of Russian victories'.[6]

These Russian victories owed much to the effect of 'Torch' in forcing the Germans to divert large numbers of aircraft from the Russian front to Tunisia, and further troops for the occupation of Vichy France.

---

[1] Broadcast, 29 November 1942: BBC Written Archives Centre.

[2] Letter of 26 November 1942: Churchill papers, 1/368.

[3] Broadcast, 29 November 1942: BBC Written Archives.

[4] Letter of 29 November 1942: Churchill papers, 20/56. Churchill also received birthday telegrams from the King and Queen, Smuts, Harry Hopkins (on his behalf and Roosevelt's), Eisenhower, Marshall, Arnold, Winant and Stimson.

[5] War Cabinet No. 162 of 1942, 30 November 1942: Cabinet papers, 65/28.

[6] Prime Minister's Personal Telegram, T.1633/2, Prime Minister to President, No. 216, 2 December 1942: Churchill papers, 20/84.

'Torch' had also brought about the removal from Norway of the entire force of German torpedo aircraft which had been attacking the Russian convoys. Transport aircraft, an essential component of the German eastern strategy, were likewise transferred in considerable numbers.

The transfer of these forces from Russia to Tunisia added several months to the Tunisian campaign, leading to sacrifices and delays being incurred by the western Allies which would have been substantially less had not the Germans drawn so fully and so rapidly on their forces in Russia. It was this diversionary effect of 'Torch' that led General Warlimont to describe the North African landings as 'decisive for the whole conduct of the war'.[1]

For the British and Americans, the German decision to fight in Tunisia also led to a major drain on Allied shipping, both as a result of the need to go on sending convoys to Tunisia itself, but also because all shipping for Egypt, the Middle East and India had to continue to use the far longer route around the Cape of Good Hope, a drain on time, fuel and man-power.

Even as 'Torch' made its contribution to the Russian land battle, Churchill remained alert to any weakening of British pledges to Russia. During his birthday he read of a proposal from the British Military Mission in Moscow to vary the plans being made for the twenty air squadrons promised for the Caucasus front. The Military Mission proposed sending the aircraft themselves, but not the British personnel to man them.[2] 'The object of the 20 squadrons,' Churchill minuted to Portal, 'was not merely to afford material support but to promote good relations between the Anglo-American and Russian air forces and troops through their fighting together in the same theatre. I do not therefore favour the whittling away of the 20 squadrons into an additional packet of aircraft and a lesser number of squadrons. We do not want to dismount our squadrons and then be reproached by the Russians for not doing more fighting ourselves.' If the battle being fought on the Russian southern front went well, Churchill added, 'even better destinations than the Southern Caucasus may be open to our 20 squadrons'.[3]

---

[1] G. A. Harrison, *Cross-Channel Attack* (the official United States Army history), Washington 1950, page 143. General Warlimont was Deputy to General Jodl in the Operations Staff of the German armed forces. Four hundred of the five hundred German aircraft sent to Tunisia were from the Russian front, as were some hundreds of transport aircraft which had to be taken away from their work supplying the German forces then surrounded at Stalingrad. As a result of this transfer, German bombers had to be sent to the eastern front for transport work, a move which led Hermann Goering to comment later: 'There died the core of the German bomber fleet.' ('The Rise and Fall of the German Air Force', 1948: Air Ministry papers, 41/33.)

[2] Churchill later learned that this proposal had been made by Soviet officials (Prime Minister's Personal Telegram, T.1684/2, Prime Minister to President No. 225, 'Most Secret and Personal', 8 December 1942: Churchill papers, 20/84).

[3] Prime Minister's Personal Minute, M.563/2, 30 November 1942: Churchill papers, 20/67.

At a meeting of the Chiefs of Staff Committee on the evening of November 30, Churchill spoke of the 'intense pressure' which was certain to come from the Russians 'for the launching of a Continental operation' in the summer of 1943. It 'now looked probable', he said, that North Africa would be in Anglo-American hands by the end of 1942, the Mediterranean open to Allied shipping by the end of April, and 'Brimstone', or 'such other follow-up operations' as were decided upon, completed by 'the end of June' 1943. The possibility was therefore 'opened', he told the Chiefs of Staff Committee, 'of our being in a position to launch "Round-up" in say August or September'. The Germans, 'already extended at so many points', would not know 'where the next main thrust would come'.

Churchill now gave the Chiefs of Staff Committee his view of where the 'Round-up' forces should strike. What he had in mind, he said, was 'a strong attack in the Pas de Calais area by a force of say ten divisions to bring on the air battle while the real re-entry was launched through the Bay of Biscay ports with adequate support by carrier-borne aircraft'.[1]

For ten days, Enigma decrypts had given precise details of the strong German reinforcements being sent to Tunisia, including several formations of high quality. On November 21 Brooke had sent Churchill an estimate, based on Enigma, that 7,000 German and 3,000 Italian troops had already arrived, with 50 tanks, and that a further 8,000 German and 7,000 Italian troops would be arriving shortly, with 80 more tanks, a total reinforcement of 25,000 men.[2]

On December 1 the German–Italian forces, counter-attacking west of Tunis with their reinforcements, forced a British brigade to retreat. The chances of a rapid advance to Tunis receded. Another setback was the Australian Government's decision to order the return of the 9th Australian Division to Australia; a decision, Churchill telegraphed to John Curtin, 'which we do not consider is in accordance with the general strategic interests of the United Nations'.[3]

Churchill was now seriously concerned as to whether the various operations proposed for the central Mediterranean might not set back the cross-Channel operation too far. He was feeling 'uncertain', he

[1] Chiefs of Staff Committee No. 191 (Operations) of 1942, 10.30 p.m., 30 November 1942: Cabinet papers, 79/58.

[2] Brooke's estimate was based upon Boniface CX/MSS/1698/T.32 and 1462: Hinsley and others, *British Intelligence in the Second World War*, op. cit., volume 2, page 501.

[3] Prime Minister's Personal Telegram, T.1631/2, 2 December 1942: Churchill papers, 20/88.

minuted to Brooke on December 1, about 'Brimstone', the assault on Sardinia. 'The price may be too heavy,' he wrote, 'and the delay too long. We cannot afford to waste the summer and our shipping in campaigning in "Brimstone". It may be that we should close down the Mediterranean activities by the end of June with a view to "Round-up" in August.' Britain could not possibly be 'content', he added, 'with locking up large forces in French North Africa and some subsequent "Brimstone" operations'.[1]

On December 3, in a 'most secret' paper about the prospects for a cross-Channel landing in force in 1943, Churchill pointed out the importance of the effect which Russia's military successes would have on the chances of such a landing being successful. 'Before the end of 1942,' he wrote, 'it may be possible for us to draw with certainty at least the conclusion that no important transfers of German troops can be made in 1943 from the Eastern to the Western theatre.' Not only had the German task of maintaining internal security in France been 'rendered more onerous' as a result of the occupation of the Vichy zone, but further German divisions would probably have to be found 'to hold down Italy against the menace of "Torch" and to garrison Sicily and perhaps Sardinia'. Behind German lines, the Yugoslav resistance was continuing, and German reinforcements might have to be sent to the Balkans—to Greece, Roumania and Bulgaria—on account both of the 'general situation' and the 'possible entry of Turkey against them, for which we are to work'.

Here then, Churchill pointed out, were new facts, none of which had been present when the cross-Channel landings had been discussed with the Americans in London five months earlier. The 'whole position must be completely re-surveyed', he believed, 'with the object of finding means for engaging United States and British armies directly on the continent'. For this purpose, he wrote, if Sardinian operations could be concluded 'by the beginning of June', the landing craft needed for the cross-Channel invasion could be back in Britain by the end of June. The month of July, he proposed, 'should be devoted to preparation and rehearsal'; the month of August, or 'if the weather is adverse' September, 'should be taken as the striking target'.

Churchill ended his paper of December 3 with a 'target schedule' which he set out in a chronological table:

End of 1942—
   Occupation of Tunisia and completion of 'Torch'.
   Entry of the British Eighth Army into Tripolitania.
   Resumption of PQ Convoys.

[1] Prime Minister's Personal Minute, M.569/Z, 'Most Secret', 1 December 1942: Churchill papers, 20/67.

End of January—

Capture of Tripoli and total clearance of North African shore from Axis Forces.

End of March—

Completion of any 'Brimstone' or similar operation.

Culmination of policy of bringing Turkey into the war and movement of the Tenth Army to the Turkish theatre.

End of June—

Completion of concentration in Great Britain of all landing-craft, whether from Mediterranean or United States.

Concentration of the Anglo-American Expeditionary Army in Great Britain.

Suspension of PQ Convoys.

End of July—

Completion of all preparations for 'Round-up' and assembly in United States of the 15 supporting Divisions.

August and September—

Action.

Churchill's proposal was circulated to the Chiefs of Staff Committee and the War Cabinet.[1]

If the forces needed for 'very large operations' on the Continent were not available for 1943, Churchill told a Staff Conference attended by Attlee and Eden on December 3, 'it looked as if we should be leaving the Russians to fight the German army alone once more'. Britain 'could not accept this position', Churchill added, 'and great efforts must be made to engage the enemy. The idea that all we need to do was to drop bombs on Germany was not enough.'

Speaking next, Portal explained that the American Chiefs of Staff were acting upon the assumption that the strategy for 1943 was for 'executing a defensive encircling move in North Africa, rather than an offensive move into the Continent', with the result that 'the US Chiefs of Staff had withdrawn great resources to the Pacific'.

Churchill was surprised to learn this. He had 'never accepted that idea', he said. He had 'always held to the idea of a great offensive in 1943, and had said as much in Moscow'.

Commenting on this, Brooke stated that 'the Prime Minister had not said that in Moscow in his presence'. While making 'full allowance', he said, for the favourable events which had taken place on the Russian front and elsewhere, 'he still felt that we could not reckon with any certainty on being able to enter the Continent from the United Kingdom in 1943 in sufficient strength to overcome German resistance'.

[1] 'Note by the Minister of Defence', Chiefs of Staff Committee paper No. 429 (O) of 1942, 'Most Secret', 3 December 1942: Churchill papers, 23/10.

Churchill suggested that the German strength in France was overrated. But Lord Leathers, the Minister of War Transport, reverting to the landing craft situation, so essential for a cross-Channel landing, pointed out, not only that 'the whole of the United States new construction was being taken for the Pacific', but that the Pacific theatre 'was absorbing so much' that the United States could not even provide their share of naval escorts for the next convoy to northern Russia.[1]

The question of limited resources and claimant priorities emerged a second time on December 3, when Churchill minuted to Sir Archibald Sinclair and Sir Charles Portal, who had proposed a substantial bombing offensive in Italy: 'The heat should be turned on Italy in the manner proposed by you at present, but Germany should not be entirely neglected.' Churchill added: 'I am looking forward to a big raid on Berlin this month if conditions are favourable.'[2]

To try to ensure that the cross-Channel invasion would take place in August or September 1943, Churchill pressed for a three-Power conference, for himself, Roosevelt and Stalin. Such a conference, he informed Roosevelt on December 3, was 'the only way of making a good plan for 1943. At present we have no plan for 1943 which is on the scale or up to the level of events.' Khartoum was at Roosevelt's 'disposal'. Marrakesh 'I can personally vouch for as regards accommodation, climate, and, barring any extraordinary lapse, weather.' As to timing, Churchill advised, 'the sooner the better. Every day counts'. All prospect of an attack in Europe in 1943 depended on an early decision.[3]

On December 3 Churchill telegraphed to Stalin, in support of the conference idea, and expressing the hope that Stalin would join him and Roosevelt 'somewhere' in North Africa. 'We must decide at the earliest moment the best way of attacking Germany in Europe with all possible force in 1943,' Churchill wrote. Such a decision could only be settled between the heads of Governments and States, 'with their high expert authorities at their side'. It was only by such a meeting, Churchill added, 'that the full burden of the war can be shared according to capacity and opportunity'.[4]

At such a Three Power conference, many disparate efforts could be

[1] Staff Conference, Chiefs of Staff Committee No. 192 (Operations) of 1942, 3 December 1942: Cabinet papers, 79/58.

[2] Prime Minister's Personal Minute, M.580/2, 3 December 1942: Premier papers, 3/14/3, folio 339.

[3] Prime Minister's Personal Telegram, T.1649/2, Prime Minister to President No. 219, 'Personal and Secret', 3 December 1942: Premier papers, 3/420/1, folios 21–2.

[4] Prime Minister's Personal Telegram, T.1648/2, 'Most Secret and Personal', 3 December 1942: Premier papers, 3/420/1, folio 23.

brought into harmony. Thus operation 'Velvet', the Anglo-American air force to be established in the Caucasus, 'might well', as Churchill informed Roosevelt that same day, 'be brought into the general scheme and should be decided at this Conference'. In the meanwhile, all preparations for 'Velvet' should go forward.[1] So too should the preparation of landing ships and landing craft needed for the cross-Channel invasion. Reading of the way in which the lessons of the Dieppe raid were being applied to developments in design and use of these craft, Churchill noted: 'If it is attempted to apply these high grade conditions to all movements from one shore to the other, the only result will be to render operations of this character utterly impossible.' Churchill's minute ended: 'The maxim "Nothing avails but perfection" may be spelt shorter, "Paralysis".'[2]

---

[1] Prime Minister's Personal Telegram, T.1651/Z, Prime Minister to President No. 220, 'Personal and Secret', 3 December 1942: Churchill papers, 20/84.

[2] Prime Minister's Personal Minute, D.211/2, 6 December 1942: Churchill papers, 20/67.

17
The Tunisian Disappointment

ON 6 December 1942 Stalin telegraphed to Churchill that, to his 'great regret', he would 'not be in a position to leave the Soviet Union' for the proposed Anglo-American-Soviet conference in January, as 'important military operations of our winter campaign are developing'. These operations, he added, 'will not be relaxed in January, probably to the contrary'. Stalin also told Churchill that he was 'waiting' for Churchill's reply about 'the establishment of the Second Front in Western Europe in the spring of 1943'.[1] This was a setback to Churchill's hopes for a clear plan, agreed upon by the three leaders, for a cross-Channel invasion in August or September 1943. Meanwhile, in North Africa, Admiral Darlan not only continued to serve the Allied cause, but persuaded the Vichy Governor-General of West Africa, Pierre Boisson, to declare for the Allies, bringing them at a stroke the use of the naval and air base at Dakar. Of Boisson, Eisenhower telegraphed, for Churchill: 'He lost a leg and his hearing to the Hun in 1918 and has no love for him whatsoever.'[2]

Reports from the former Vichy territories in North Africa showed, nevertheless, as Churchill telegraphed to Roosevelt on December 9, that French Fascist organizations 'continue their activities and victimise our former French sympathizers, some of whom have not yet been released from prison'.[3]

There was considerable Parliamentary dislike of Darlan's ascendancy in French North Africa, and of Eisenhower's support for the Admiral. 'In war,' Churchill told a Secret Session of the House of Commons on December 10, 'it is not always possible to have everything go exactly as one likes. In working with Allies it sometimes happens that they develop opinions of their own.' Since 1776, he

---

[1] 'Personal and Secret', 6 December 1942: Premier papers, 3/420/1, folio 20.
[2] Telegram No. 1553, 'Urgent', 'Most Secret', 9 December 1942: Churchill papers, 20/84.
[3] Prime Minister's Personal Telegram, T.1693/2, Prime Minister to President No. 227, 9 December 1942: Churchill papers, 20/84.

added, 'we have not been in the position of being able to decide the policy of the United States'.

Churchill spoke to a hostile House, which nursed deep suspicions against Vichy France. Yet this same Vichy France, he pointed out, had maintained for most of its life-span a legal and even 'fairly intimate' relationship with the United States, giving Britain 'a window on that courtyard which would not have otherwise existed'. Churchill then spoke of the French 'mentality' at a time when 'terrible defeat and ruin' had overtaken them:

I am not at all defending, still less eulogising, this French mentality. But it would be very foolish not to try to understand what is passing in other people's minds, and what are the secret springs of action to which they respond. The Almighty in His infinite wisdom did not see fit to create Frenchmen in the image of Englishmen.

In a State like France, which has experienced so many convulsions— Monarchy, Convention, Directory, Consulate, Empire, Monarchy, Empire, and finally Republic—there has grown up a principle founded on the *droit administratif* which undoubtedly governs the action of many French officers and officials in times of revolutions and change. It is a highly legalistic habit of mind, and it arises from a subconscious sense of national self-preservation against the dangers of sheer anarchy. For instance, any officer who obeys the command of his lawful superior or of one whom he believes to be his lawful superior is absolutely immune from subsequent punishment.

Much therefore turns in the minds of French officers upon whether there is a direct, unbroken chain of lawful command, and this is held by many Frenchmen to be more important than moral, national, or international considerations. From this point of view many Frenchmen who admire General de Gaulle and envy him in his role nevertheless regard him as a man who has rebelled against the authority of the French State, which in their prostration they conceive to be vested in the person of the antique defeatist who to them is the illustrious and venerable Marshal Pétain, the hero of Verdun and the sole hope of France.

Now all this may seem very absurd to our minds. But there is one point about it which is important to us. It is in accordance with orders and authority transmitted or declared to be transmitted by Marshal Pétain that the French troops in North-West Africa have pointed and fired their rifles against the Germans and Italians instead of continuing to point and fire their rifles against the British and Americans. I am sorry to have to mention a point like that, but it makes a lot of difference to a soldier whether a man fires his gun at him or at his enemy; and even the soldier's wife or father might have a feeling about it too. . . .

In the 'circumstances prevailing', Churchill told the Secret Session, he considered that Eisenhower was right to entrust Darlan with authority. Even if he was 'not quite right', Churchill added, 'I should have been very reluctant to hamper or to impede his action when so many lives and such vitally important issues hung in the balance.'

Churchill ended his speech with what he later recalled as 'some bitterness', telling the House of Commons:

I must say I think he is a poor creature with a jaundiced outlook and disorganised loyalties who in all this tremendous African episode, West and East alike, can find no point to excite his interest except the arrangements made between General Eisenhower and Admiral Darlan. The struggle for the Tunisian tip is now rising to its climax and the main battle impends. Another trial of strength is very near on the frontiers of Cyrenaica. Both these battles will be fought almost entirely by soldiers from this Island. The First and Eighth British Armies will be engaged to the full. I cannot take my thoughts away from them and their fortunes, and I expect that will be the feeling of the House of Commons.

Churchill then asked the House of Commons to treat 'with proper reprobation' what he described as 'that small, busy, and venomous band who harbour and endeavour to propagate unworthy and unfounded suspicions, and so to come forward unitedly with us in all the difficulties through which we are steadfastly and successfully making our way'.[1]

'I do not remember any speech,' Churchill later wrote, 'out of hundreds which I made, where I felt opinion change so palpably and decisively.'[2] This was also Churchill's view at the time. 'I have never seen the House so unanimous,' he telegraphed to Roosevelt, 'as it was today in Secret Session. I explained the whole story to them and they understood it as well as you and I do ourselves.'[3] 'Your speech,' wrote Colonel Harvie Watt, 'has been acclaimed as one of the best you have ever made in the House.'[4] Even Stalin seemed aware of the nature of the controversy, and wished to give his point of view. 'Eisenhower's policy with regard to Darlan, Boisson, Giraud and others is perfectly correct,' he telegraphed to Roosevelt a week after the House of Commons debate. 'I think it a great achievement that you succeeded in bringing Darlan and others into the waterway of the Allies fighting Hitler. Some time ago I made this known also to Mr Churchill.'[5]

Perhaps the most remarkable section of Churchill's Secret Session speech concerned, not Darlan but de Gaulle. Churchill's words were

---

[1] Secret Session, House of Commons, 10 December 1942: Winston S. Churchill, *Secret Session Speeches*, London 1946, pages 76–96.

[2] Winston S. Churchill, *The Second World War*, volume 4, London 1951, pages 573–6.

[3] Prime Minister's Personal Telegram, T.1696/2, Prime Minister to President, No. 228, 'Personal and Secret', 10 December 1942: Churchill papers, 20/84.

[4] 'Report by Parliamentary Private Secretary', 11 December 1942: Harvie Watt papers.

[5] 'Personal and Most Secret', 17 December 1942: Churchill papers, 20/85.

omitted from the edition of the Secret Session speeches published in 1946, and omitted also from the version of the speech published in the collected speeches of Winston Churchill twenty years later. This is what Churchill said:

I must now say a word about General de Gaulle. On behalf of His Majesty's Government I exchanged letters with him in 1940 recognising him as the Leader of all Free Frenchmen wherever they might be, who should rally to him, in support of the Allied cause. We have most scrupulously kept our engagements with him and have done everything in our power to help him. We finance his Movement. We have helped his operations. But we have never recognized him as representing France. We have never agreed that he and those associated with him, because they were right and brave at the moment of French surrender, have a monopoly on the future of France. I have lived myself for the last 35 years or more in a mental relationship and to a large extent in sympathy with an abstraction called France. I still do not think it is an illusion. I cannot feel that de Gaulle is France, still less that Darlan and Vichy are France. France is something greater, more complex, more formidable than any of these sectional manifestations.

I have tried to work as far as possible with General de Gaulle, making allowances for his many difficulties, for his temperament and for the limitations of his outlook. In order to sustain his Movement at the moment of the American occupation of French North Africa and to console him and his friends for their exclusion from the enterprise we agreed to his nominee, General Legentilhomme, being proclaimed as High Commissioner for Madagascar, although this adds somewhat to our difficulties in pacifying that large island, which oddly as it seems to us would much prefer Darlan. We are at the present time endeavouring to rally Jibuti to the Free French Movement. Therefore I consider that we have been in every respect faithful in the discharge of our obligations to de Gaulle, and we shall so continue to the end.

However now we are in Secret Session the House must not be led to believe that General de Gaulle is an unfaltering friend of Britain. On the contrary, I think he is one of those good Frenchmen who have a traditional antagonism engrained in French hearts by centuries of war against the English. On his way back from Syria in the summer of 1941 through the French Central and West African Colonies he left a trail of anglophobia behind him. On August 25, 1941, he gave an interview to the correspondent of the 'Chicago Daily News' at Brazzaville in which he suggested that England coveted the African colonies of France, and said: 'England is afraid of the French Fleet. What in effect England is carrying out is a war time deal with Hitler in which Vichy serves as a go-between.'

He explained that Vichy served Germany by keeping the French people in subjection and England by keeping the fleet out of German hands.

All this and much more was very ungrateful talk, but we have allowed no complaint of ours to appear in public.

Again this year in July General de Gaulle wished to visit Syria. He promised me before I agreed to facilitate his journey, which I was very well able to stop, that he would behave in a helpful and friendly manner, but no sooner did he get to Cairo than he adopted a most hectoring attitude and in Syria his whole object seemed to be to foment ill-will between the British military and Free French civil administrations and state the French claims to rule Syria at the highest, although it had been agreed that after the war, and as much as possible even during the war, the Syrians are to enjoy their independence.

I continue to maintain friendly personal relations with General de Gaulle and I help him as much as I possibly can. I feel bound to do this because he stood up against the Men of Bordeaux and their base surrender at a time when all resisting will-power had quitted France. All the same, I could not recommend you to base all your hopes and confidence upon him, and still less to assume at this stage that it is our duty to place, so far as we have the power, the destiny of France in his hands. Like the President in the telegram I have read, we seek to base ourselves on the will of the entire French nation rather than any sectional manifestations even the most worthy.[1]

'At the Secret Session yesterday on Darlan,' Oliver Harvey noted in his diary on December 11, 'I gather the PM put up a brilliant performance but nonetheless this left an unpleasant taste in the mouth for the attack it contained on General de Gaulle.'[2] 'I am sure,' King George VI wrote to Churchill after reading, and returning, Churchill's copy of the speech, 'the House now has a very clear idea of the political make-up of France.'[3]

Churchill spoke, in the second week of December, direct to General Giraud. It was a telephone conversation, and his Private Office, listening to the Prime Minister's side of the conversation, 'nearly collapsed laughing'. As Elizabeth Layton explained in a letter home:

He is not the least bit self-conscious about his French, and it is just as you have heard only worse. Well, speaking of a prospective broadcast by this Frenchman (who cannot speak a word of English) he was heard to say 'C'est le moment pour frapper le mot droit' (note 'droit') which sounded so peculiar. He went on and on most fluently, ending with (speaking of the enemy) 'ils crackeront'.[4]

In an attempt to resolve the North African dilemma, Churchill asked Roosevelt for the appointment of a British civilian administrator; a man whom Eisenhower might be expected to find sympathetic. 'For your personal information,' he telegraphed on December 12, 'I had Harold Macmillan in mind.'[5] Three weeks later, after

[1] Typescript of Secret Session speech of 10 December 1942: Churchill papers, 9/156.

[2] Harvey diary, 11 December 1942: John Harvey (editor), *op. cit.*, page 181.

[3] Letter of 30 December 1942, Buckingham Palace: Churchill papers, 20/59.

[4] Elizabeth Layton, letter of 13 December 1942: Nel papers.

[5] Prime Minister's Personal Telegram, T.1704/2, Prime Minister to President, No. 229, 'Personal and Most Secret', 12 December 1942: Churchill papers, 20/85.

several attempts by Roosevelt to reduce his area of authority, Macmillan was in Algiers to take up his appointment as Minister Resident at Allied Headquarters. 'He will be, I am sure, a help,' Churchill telegraphed to Roosevelt. 'He is animated by the friendliest feelings towards the United States, and his mother hails from Kentucky.'[1]

Churchill's hopes for a cross-Channel invasion in August or September 1943 depended upon the clearing-out of all German and Italian forces from Tunisia during the first month or so of the new year. Hitler's decision to reinforce Tunisia, and to hold it for as long as possible, was to destroy all chance of 'Round-up' in 1943. But this was not yet obvious in December 1942, when Churchill still hoped for a cross-Channel decision. As late as December 14 he was telling Pound that, 'personally', he would only choose the Sardinia and Sicily operations 'if I were satisfied after intense efforts that "Round-up" was impossible in 1943'.[2]

Still confident that the Axis could be driven out of Tunisia, Churchill nevertheless deprecated over-confidence, and had even issued a warning about this to Montgomery. 'It might be well,' Churchill telegraphed to Alexander, 'for you to give a friendly hint from me to General Montgomery about the disadvantages of his making confident statements that he will beat and out-wit Rommel before the impending battle has been fought. I hear a certain amount of unfavourable comment from those who have the highest admiration for Montgomery's military qualities. Will he not seem foolish if as is possible there is no battle at Agheila and Rommel slips away.'[3] This was indeed what happened: Rommel withdrew from his Agheila positions without serious interference.

'Tunisia not going well,' Cadogan noted after a War Cabinet on December 14, 'So PM on his usual (and to me well-founded) complaint that, out of about 110,000 men there, there are only about 10,000 fighting men.'[4]

Enigma decrypts in the third week of December, however, showed the effect of Allied attacks on the build-up of the Axis forces. 'Boniface

[1] Prime Minister's Personal Telegram, T.1759/2, Prime Minister to President, No. 242, 'Personal and Secret', 27 December 1942: Churchill papers, 20/85.
[2] Prime Minister's Personal Minute, M.607/2, 'Most Secret', 14 December 1942: Churchill papers, 20/67.
[3] Prime Minister's Personal Telegram, T.1699/2, 'Private and Most Secret', OZ 2187, 11 December 1942: Churchill papers, 20/84.
[4] Cadogan diary, 14 December 1942: David Dilks (editor), op. cit., page 499.

shows the hard straits of the enemy,' Churchill telegraphed to Eisenhower on December 16, 'the toll taken of his supplies by submarines
and surface ships, and especially the effect which our bombing is
having upon the congested ports.' Churchill added: 'It seems to me,
speaking of course as a layman, that it is wise to keep the enemy
bleeding and burning up his strength, even if we sustain equal losses.
Thus a larger animal crushes the life out of a weaker and never gives
him the chance to gather strength for a spring.'

Churchill told Eisenhower how he had 'much admired the way you
had pressed forward so vehemently to the East', and was sure this was
right 'whatever the immediate results might be'.[1] But by December
12 two German counter-attacks against Eisenhower's forces had
already destroyed any hope of an Allied offensive that month. When,
on December 24, Eisenhower's attack against the strongly defended
German defences north east of Medjez el-Bab had failed, after bitter
fighting, Eisenhower postponed the attempt to take Tunis because of
the continual rain, which had greatly hampered the assault.[2]

With Tunis firmly under Axis control, and Stalin unable to leave his
fighting forces, Churchill and Roosevelt made plans to meet in Casablanca. 'The sooner the better,' Churchill telegraphed to Roosevelt
on December 21. 'I am greatly relieved. It is the only thing to do.'[3]
The meeting, set for mid-January, was given the codename 'Symbol'.

Meanwhile, the future of a major cross-Channel operation in 1943
had reached a point of decision. On December 15 Sir Archibald Clark
Kerr, who had specially returned from Moscow, described to the
Chiefs of Staff the seriousness of Stalin's expectations of a second
front in 1943. The Soviet leader, Clark Kerr explained, 'was expecting
something formidable from us and the Americans early next year'.
While he had been 'temporarily consoled' by the 'unexpected success
and size' of 'Torch', he did not regard it as a second front. 'If he now

---

[1] Prime Minister's Personal Telegram, T.1714/2, No. 603 to Algiers, 'Private, Personal and
Secret', 16 December 1942: Churchill papers, 20/85.

[2] The British assault had also been hampered, according to General Anderson, because, as he
complained to Churchill, his tanks were 'ineffective compared to the Germans''. Churchill at
once took this complaint up with Sir James Grigg and General Brooke, minuting on December
23: 'It is the same story we had a year ago in the Gazala battle. You now say that the layout in
your paper attached is the best possible. It means that 89 obsolete 2-pounder tanks are to go
into action with the 11th Division, and only 80 6-pounders. I am not at all convinced that this is
right. The Armoured Divisions have already been reduced to a single brigade of tanks. Now this
brigade of tanks is to be further more than halved to accommodate the organisation of command.
Thus a British Armoured Division to go into action in February is only to have 80 effectively-
gunned tanks. This is an altogether inadmissible diminution of striking power, and I wish the
matter to be reviewed.' (Prime Minister's Personal Minute, M.635/2, 'Action this Day', 23
December 1942: Churchill papers, 20/67.)

[3] Prime Minister's Personal Telegram, T.1746/2, Prime Minister to President, No. 238,
'Personal and Most Secret', 21 December 1942: Churchill papers, 20/85.

failed to get what he expected,' Clark Kerr warned, 'he would probably turn very sour. Moreover, it was impossible to say whether, faced by the knowledge that there would be no second front, Russian morale would hold.'

In returning to Russia, Clark Kerr added, he would have to take back something 'very attractive' as an alternative to the second front, 'if he was to have any success'. But in dealing with Stalin, Clark Kerr told the Chiefs of Staff, 'nothing was impossible, and he did not exclude, under certain circumstances, the chance of his making a separate peace with Hitler'.

Brooke then asked Clark Kerr if Stalin would accept, for 1943, 'a limited operation, say with the object of capturing the Cherbourg Peninsula'. Clark Kerr did not think that this would be acceptable.

Stalin, he pointed out, had been promised 'a considerable operation involving a million men, and with this promise he had been kept quiet'. But Portal commented that it was 'probably time to say' that Britain and the United States 'could only get on to the Continent if the Russians beat the Germans', and that we could help the Russians in this task by 'relieving pressure' on them through 'the exploitation of "Torch", leading if possible to the elimination of Italy'.

Clark Kerr was distraught at such reasoning, feeling 'that we did not fully recognize the strain under which the Russians were now carrying on'. The Russians, he said, 'feared that we were building up a vast army which might one day turn round and compound with Germany against Russia'. He 'regretted to say' that there was in Britain 'a body of opinion which indirectly supported this Russian belief'. The information that there was not to be a second front in 1943 would be 'a bad shock for Stalin', and he, the Ambassador, 'could not say what the results would be, but they would be serious'.[1]

On the day after he had presented to the Chiefs of Staff this plea for a second front in 1943, Clark Kerr lunched with Churchill.[2] That evening, at a Staff Conference at which Churchill presided, Brooke submitted a memorandum from the Chiefs of Staff, warning that the rate and scale of the American build-up in Britain was inadequate to allow a successful cross-Channel landing in 1943. Brooke added that the 'magnificent' German rail routes in western Europe would allow the Germans rapidly to bring superior forces to confront the Allied troops who had been put ashore. It would be more sensible militarily, Brooke argued, and this was the Chiefs of Staff's formal recommendation, to hold 40 German divisions in north-west Europe 'by

[1] Chiefs of Staff Meeting No. 346 of 1942, 15 December 1942: Cabinet papers, 79/87.
[2] Churchill's Engagement Cards, entry for 16 December 1942. Eden and Casey were also present.

the threat of a cross-Channel operation', while at the same time taking military action in the Mediterranean to 'force Italy out of the war and perhaps enter the Balkans'.

This Mediterranean initiative, the Chiefs of Staff believed, 'would be better strategy, from the Russian point of view, than for us to stake everything on "Round-up" which could, at best, afford Russia no relief before August'. The 'defection of Italy' in itself, Brooke asserted, would lead to 'a vastly increased German commitment in holding down the Balkans, even if the Bulgarian, Rumanian and Hungarian divisions remained unaffected'.

The choice was now clear: a cross-Channel operation in 1943, as promised to Stalin, or a Mediterranean strategy as advised by the Chiefs of Staff. Eden, who with Churchill had listened to Brooke's presentation, said that although he had been hoping that it would be possible to do a 'large scale' cross-Channel operation in the summer of 1943, he had been 'convinced' by the Chiefs of Staff arguments and thought that their conclusions were 'sound'.

Churchill's preference, like Eden's, was for a cross-Channel landing in 1943, a landing, he argued, which 'was still the better strategy, if only adequate forces for a successful re-entry to the Continent could be assembled in this country'. This, according to the Chiefs of Staff figures, was clearly impossible. Churchill was therefore 'prepared to agree', he said, with their conclusion, but 'with the proviso' that they should re-examine the cross-Channel figures, with a view to making the cross-Channel landing possible. He was 'a little reluctant' to accept their figures, he said, 'until they had been confirmed in discussion with the Americans'. But unless the Americans 'could vastly improve' on their estimates of the number of troops and landing craft which they could assemble, 'he saw no alternative to the strategy recommended by the Chiefs of Staff'.[1]

Not British strategic concepts, but the American weakness, had destroyed all hopes for a second front in 1943, and switched the emphasis of planning and action to the Mediterranean.

Even on Christmas Day, Churchill did some dictation, though far less than usual. 'That morning he was in a grand temper,' Elizabeth Layton wrote home, 'and left us in peace most of the time and just sat up in bed reading a book and looking like a benevolent old cherub.

[1] Staff Conference, 6.15 p.m., 16 December 1942: Cabinet papers, 79/58. Those present were Churchill (in the Chair), Eden, Brooke, Pound, Portal, Mountbatten and Ismay.

(He only gets up before lunch if he has to!) I was glad to be the second to wish him a Happy Christmas (Sawyers the first).'[1]

Churchill spent Christmas 1942, the fourth Christmas of the war, at Chequers, surrounded by his family; his wife, his three daughters, his brother John, his daughter-in-law Pamela, and his grandson 'Baby Winston'.[2] On Christmas Eve, a telegram from General Alexander reported that, 'if the enemy stands' there could be no attack towards Tunisia 'before the end of January'.[3]

On Christmas Day, the Churchills and the Roosevelts exchanged greetings. 'Last year,' Churchill telegraphed, 'I passed a happy Christmas in your home and now I send my heartfelt wishes to you and all around you on this brighter day than we have yet seen. My wife joins with me in this message to you and Mrs Roosevelt.'[4] 'The Roosevelts send the Churchills warm personal Christmas greetings,' came the message that evening from across the Atlantic. 'The old team-work is grand.'[5]

On Christmas Day, while Churchill was at Chequers, news reached him that Admiral Darlan had been assassinated in Algiers. 'Darlan's murder,' he later wrote, 'however criminal, relieved the Allies of their embarrassment at working with him, and at the same time left them with all the advantages he had been able to bestow during the vital hours of the Allied landings.'[6] In Darlan's place as High Commissioner and Commander-in-Chief, Eisenhower at once put General Giraud, who had been the Allies' original choice. De Gaulle, in a further conversation with Churchill on December 27, agreed to work with Giraud, but added, as Churchill reported to the War Cabinet, that he regarded Giraud 'as qualified for a military rather than a political role'.[7] 'I must say,' Churchill telegraphed to Roosevelt on December 28, 'I strongly favour a meeting between de Gaulle and Giraud as soon as possible, before rivalries crystallize.'[8]

On the battle front, Alexander telegraphed to Churchill on Decem-

---

[1] Elizabeth Layton, letter of 8 January 1943: Nel papers.

[2] 'List of Guests for Christmas Weekend, 1942': Chequers Lists.

[3] CS/1779, 'Immediate', despatched 10.45 a.m., received 16.08 p.m., 24 December 1942: Churchill papers, 20/85.

[4] Prime Minister's Personal Telegram, T. 1752/2, Prime Minister to President, No. 241, 25 December 1942: Churchill papers, 20/85.

[5] President to Prime Minister, No. 244, 25 December 1942: Churchill papers, 20/59.

[6] Winston S. Churchill, The Second World War, volume 4, London 1951, page 578.

[7] War Cabinet No. 173 of 1942, 28 December 1942: Cabinet papers, 65/28.

[8] Prime Minister's Personal Telegram, T.1765/2, Prime Minister to President, No. 244, 'Personal and Secret', 28 December 1942: Churchill papers, 20/85.

ber 27 that he 'hoped to seize Tripoli by February 1st'.[1] Replying that same day, Churchill told Alexander: 'Reading Boniface, after discounting enemy's natural tendency to exaggerate his difficulties in order to procure better supplies. I cannot help hoping that you will find it possible to strike earlier than the date mentioned in paragraph 6.'[2] The date for the start of the offensive was January 14.

It was not Alexander however, but Eisenhower, whose timetable caused Churchill the greater concern. 'I am far from happy,' Churchill telegraphed to Alexander on December 28, 'about the First Army and the Americans. Eisenhower is reconciling himself to a two months delay, due allegedly to rainy weather, before making a main offensive against Tunis and Bizerta.' This delay would give the new German commander, General von Arnim, 'time to strengthen himself, albeit by a costly process'.[3]

The 'costly process' was the Allied ability, as a result of the Enigma decrypts, to intercept and sink a substantial number of von Arnim's supply ships. 'The warfare on the African coast,' Churchill telegraphed to Stalin on December 29, 'is very costly to the enemy on account of heavy losses in transit and at the ports. We shall do our utmost to finish it as quickly as possible.'[4]

As between operation 'Brimstone', the possible attack on Sardinia, whose difficulties the Americans had stressed, and the more complex operation 'Husky', the codename for an attack on Sicily, Churchill now felt that Sicily 'alone gives a worthwhile prize, even if we have to wait till May'. By waiting till May, he minuted to the Chiefs of Staff Committee, it would at least mean that escorts would be available to continue the Arctic convoys to Russia 'till the end of March'.[5] The December convoy had prospered 'beyond all expectation'. Churchill telegraphed to Stalin on December 29, and he had therefore arranged to send a full convoy of 'thirty or more ships' to Russia in January.[6]

*   *   *

[1] CS/1782, 'Most Immediate', 27 December 1942: Churchill papers, 20/85.

[2] Prime Minister's Personal Telegram, T.1761/2, 27 December 1942: Churchill papers, 20/88.

[3] Prime Minister's Personal Telegram, T.1763/2, OZ 2341, 'Most Secret' ('for you and Montgomery alone'), 28 December 1942: Churchill papers, 20/85. General Von Arnim, commanding the Fifth Panzer Army, had assumed command in Tunisia on 8 December 1942. He and Rommel commanded two independent armies (Rommel in Cyrenaica, von Arnim in Tunisia), except for the brief period between 23 February and 9 March 1943, when Rommel was Commander-in-Chief, Army Group Africa, and thus Axis Supreme Commander in North Africa.

[4] Prime Minister's Personal Telegram, T.1771/2, No. 429 to Moscow, 'Personal, Private and Most Secret', 29 December 1942: Churchill papers, 20/85.

[5] Prime Minister's Personal Minute, D.228/2, 'Action this Day', 'Most Secret', 27 December 1942: Churchill papers, 20/67.

[6] Prime Minister's Personal Telegram, No. T.1771/2, No. 429 to Moscow, 'Personal, Private and Most Secret', 29 December 1942: Churchill papers, 20/85.

Churchill now envisaged what he described to the Chiefs of Staff Committee as two 'combined and concurrent operations', one against western Europe, launched from Britain, and the second against southern Europe, launched from North Africa. Unless there were a cross-Channel operation, he minuted to the Chiefs of Staff Committee on December 28, the British and American air forces based in Britain would be 'limited to bombing only'. Britain's resources in 'small shipping' would not be utilized, and the weight of the British Home Army and of the American forces gathered in Britain 'will not count'. Thus, Churchill warned, 'we shall have failed to engage the enemy with our full strength, and may even fail to keep him pinned down in the West while we attack in the South'. If both attacks could be planned, it would be important to decide 'which theatre should be considered the major or the minor, and how the emphasis and priorities should be cast'.[1] 'My supreme object,' Churchill informed Stalin on the following day, 'is for the British and Americans to engage the enemy with the largest numbers in the shortest time.' The 'shipping stringency', he added, 'is most severe. I will inform you what passes.'[2]

When the Chiefs of Staff, in consultation with the Combined Operations Headquarters and the Joint Planning Staff, examined the possibilities for offensive action in 1943 they came, however, to a sombre conclusion. Britain's resources in assault shipping and landing craft would, they warned, be 'insufficient to mount more than one large-scale amphibious operation at a time'. Even if 'overriding priority' were given 'forthwith' to the cross-Channel build-up, at the cost of all overseas training and operations, 'the maximum of British manned craft which could be made available in August 1943 would not enable us to assault across the channel on a front exceeding six brigades at full operational strength with an immediate follow up to complete four divisions within 48 hours'. The Chiefs of Staff added: 'If, on the other hand, we decide to exploit our success in North Africa by successive amphibious operations in the Mediterranean we cannot, even at three months' notice, mount a cross channel operation in August 1943—to take advantage of any sudden deterioration in German military power—on a scale exceeding an initial assault on a front of five brigades at full operational strength with an immediate follow-up in landing craft to complete three divisions within 48 hours.'

Even if more landing craft could be produced, the Chiefs of Staff

[1] Prime Minister's Personal Minute, D.231/2, 28 December 1942: Churchill papers, 20/67; 'British Strategy in 1943, Note by the Minister of Defence', Chiefs of Staff Committee paper No. 485 (O) of 1942, 'Most Secret', 29 December 1942: Churchill papers, 23/10.

[2] Letter of 30 December 1942, 'Personal and Most Secret', War Cabinet paper No. 611 of 1942: Churchill papers, 23/10.

warned, 'we cannot man them since the Admiralty have neither the men nor the extra resources for training them. Our strategy in 1943 is therefore gravely hampered by lack of naval assault forces.' There was, in addition, 'a serious danger that our strategy in 1944 will be similarly hampered unless drastic action is taken early next year to solve the manning problem for assault craft'. The War Cabinet, the Chiefs of Staff ended, 'should be aware of the seriousness of the position'.[1]

The shipping needs of Britain, whether for the transport of food, weapons, or men, would have to be met mainly from the United States. On December 30 Churchill thanked Roosevelt for the promise which he had just made to Oliver Lyttelton in Washington, that Britain's 27 million ton import programme, as well as Britain's 'other essential needs', would be met by United States ships. 'This is an undertaking,' Churchill told the President, 'of the highest importance to these islands.' The whole of Britain's manpower requirements, Churchill added, 'is based upon striking the strongest blows we can in 1943. We will run the utmost risk for this; but unless our shipping resources are, in fact, replenished as you so kindly propose, I shall be forced immediately to reduce the British war effort in overseas theatres even though this involves prolongation of the war and leaves you a greater portion of the burden we are eager to share.'[2]

To make arrangements for his meeting with Roosevelt, Churchill had sent Brigadier Jacob to North Africa to consult with Generals Eisenhower and Bedell Smith. On December 30 Churchill was able to report to Roosevelt that Jacob, Eisenhower and Bedell Smith 'have found admirable accommodation'.[3] The conference was to take place near Casablanca. 'I propose later to visit your army,' Churchill telegraphed to Alexander on December 31. 'It is only a night's flight either way.' Churchill also sent a message for Montgomery: 'tell him,' he wrote, 'how splendid we all think his work has been. The supreme prize lies ahead.'[4]

The ending of Eisenhower's advance, and the steady pace of von Arnim's reinforcement, now caused Churchill considerable alarm. 'I am deeply concerned,' he telegraphed to Eisenhower on December 31, 'about the unfavourable turn in Tunisia, and our staffs take an even more serious view. The danger is on the seaward flank.' British

---

[1] 'Draft Report to War Cabinet', Chiefs of Staff Committee No. 4 (Operations) of 1943, 'Most Secret', 5 January 1943: Cabinet papers, 80/67.

[2] Letter of 30 December 1942, 'Personal and Most Secret', War Cabinet paper No. 611 of 1942: Churchill papers, 23/10.

[3] Prime Minister's Personal Telegram, T.1773/3, Prime Minister to President, No. 248, 'Most Secret and Personal', 30 December 1942: Churchill papers, 20/85.

[4] Prime Minister's Personal Telegram, T.1/3, OZ 2392, 'Most particularly Secret', dictated 31 December 1942, sent 1 January 1943: Churchill papers, 20/105.

troop and tank reinforcements were on their way, Churchill added, 'and we are pushing the 11th Armoured Division, which has been much more heavily armed, out to you as fast as is humanly possible. Nothing matters now but the battle in the Tunisian Tip.' [1]

Churchill had been disappointed that Tunisia had not been captured in the aftermath of Alamein, and before the Germans had been able to send over reinforcements. Already by January 1943 the German reinforcements made a total of 43,000 men, and were esti-mated at reaching 100,000 men by the beginning of March.[2] 'It was a near thing Anderson's Army Corps did not carry the Tunisian Tip at the first bound,' he telegraphed to Smuts on January 6. 'If our original plan had been followed out we should have had the whole place.' He was 'a little anxious about the forward troops during January as the communications are so bad', but, he added, 'the enemy is lacking in transport and weather impedes all movement. Although things have not gone as quietly as we hoped we have got the enemy fighting in a very expensive place for him.' [3]

At six o'clock on New Year's Eve Churchill summoned Sir James Grigg, Lord Leathers and General Brooke to discuss the trans-portation of a brigade of tanks from Britain as reinforcements for Eisenhower's command. 'A strenuous effort must be made,' he had told them that same day 'with full battle urgency, to have this brigade embarked complete in the convoy which leaves about the 17th January.' [4]

Learning of Churchill's visit to North Africa, Oliver Harvey noted in his diary on December 31: 'I hope he may clear it up, as he cleared up Cairo.' [5] At a meeting of the Chiefs of Staff Committee that evening, Churchill expressed his hope that it would be possible for the Royal Air Force to undertake 'two or three heavy raids' on Berlin during the first period of favourable weather in January. 'During the course of the raids,' he said, 'leaflets should be dropped warning the Germans that our attacks were reprisals for the per-secution of the Poles and the Jews.' [6]

*   *   *

[1] Prime Minister's Personal Telegram, T.1779/2, 'Personal and Secret', No. 977 to Algiers, 31 December 1942: Churchill papers, 20/85.

[2] Prime Minister's Personal Minute, D.2/3A, 'Action this Day', 4 January 1943: Churchill papers, 4/397A.

[3] Prime Minister's Personal Telegram, T.42/3, 'Personal and Secret for you alone', 6 January 1943: Churchill papers, 20/105.

[4] Prime Minister's Personal Minute, M.646/2, 'Secret', 'Action this Day', 31 December 1942: Churchill papers, 20/67.

[5] Harvey diary, 31 December 1942: John Harvey (editor), op. cit., page 206.

[6] Chiefs of Staff Committee No. 211 (Operations) of 1942, 6.30 p.m., 31 December 1942: Cabinet papers, 79/58.

Churchill's personal codename at the Casablanca conference was to be 'Air Commodore Frankland'.[1] Roosevelt was to be 'Admiral Q'.[2] If Casablanca were to become 'too public', Churchill told Roosevelt, the meeting place could be moved to Marrakech, 'one of the best places I had ever struck'.[3] As preparations went forward for the flight to North Africa, Churchill's daughter Mary noted in her diary, after a talk with her mother: 'We talked entirely of the family— & especially of Papa. It appears that he *might* get a coronary thrombosis—& it might be brought on by anything like a long &/or high flight. The question is whether he should be warned or not. Mummie thinks he should not—I agree with her. . . .'[4]

From General Alexander came details, on January 5, of his intended offensive, timed to begin in nine days' time and to reach Tripoli, 200 miles to the west, within ten days. On January 14, Alexander told Churchill, Montgomery would 'move forward in strength, and the military operations thus begun 'will continue intensively until Tripoli is reached'. Alexander warned, however, that a heavy gale on January 4 had caused 'extensive damage' to Allied ships and unloading facilities in Benghazi harbour: this might cause 'a few days postponement of forward move or restrict size of force'.[5] On the following day, however, Alexander was able to report to Churchill: 'No change in Montgomery's date.'[6]

Searching for a source of further reinforcements, not only for North Africa but for a possible Turkish front, Churchill asked the Chiefs of Staff Committee to examine the scale of Auchinleck's Tenth Army in Persia and Iraq. With the German army no longer able to push beyond the Caucasus, the Tenth Army 'can now be considered available in whole or in part for action in the Eastern Mediterranean or in Turkey'. In Egypt, the Eighth Army had also been able to cut back its scale of equipment, so much so, Churchill noted, that there were 'at least three divisions' worth of equipment going spare'. All stocks and equipment, Churchill wrote, 'must be examined in the light of these facts', one of which was that in or on its way to India there were 220,000 tons of ammunition, yet only 25,000 tons had been fired in

---

[1] Prime Minister's Personal Telegrams, T.14/3 and T.15/3, Prime Minister to President, Nos. 251 and 252, 'Most Secret and Personal', 2 January 1943: Churchill papers, 20/105.

[2] Prime Minister's Personal Telegram, T.21/3, 3 January 1943: Churchill papers, 4/394A.

[3] Prime Minister's Personal Telegram, T.43/3, Prime Minister to President, No. 255, 'Most Secret and Personal', 7 January 1943: Churchill papers, 20/105. Churchill had spent a month in Marrakech in January 1936.

[4] Mary Churchill diary, 3 January 1943: Mary Soames, page 330.

[5] CS/1790, 'Most Secret and Personal', 5 January 1943: Churchill papers, 20/105.

[6] CS/1793, 'Personal and Most Secret', 6 January 1943: Churchill papers, 20/105.

the Western Desert in the first month of the campaign that began at Alamein.[1]

As Alexander and Montgomery prepared for the drive towards Tripoli, Churchill drew the Chiefs of Staff Committee's attention to the most recent decrypts of German messages, from which he was 'pretty sure that the Germans in Tunisia are very short of transport and have not the necessary mobility for a large-scale deep-ranging thrust'. This being so, on noting 'in Boniface' von Arnim's anxiety about an attack in the southern sector, Churchill asked that the possibility of a southern operation should not be excluded, especially as it would force von Arnim to divert forces to the south, and thus give 'the relief we seek' in the northern sector.[2]

On January 9, Alexander sent Churchill the detailed plan of advance on Tripoli. The heavy bombing of Tripoli had already started, causing bottlenecks on the coastal road.[3] That same day, amidst the tensions of the Tunisian battle, Churchill was told of a complaint by Ivan Maisky, who insisted that Churchill had promised Stalin to send two Arctic convoys, each of thirty ships, to Russia in January and February. 'Monsieur Maisky is not telling the truth. . . .' Churchill minuted to Eden on January 9. The only promise he had made was for 'a full convoy of thirty or more ships' in January. 'I now understand,' Churchill added, 'that 20 ships only are to go on 17th January and 30 on 11th February.' This made 50 ships in all, including a February convoy for which Churchill had made no promise.

Churchill's minute continued: 'Maisky should be told that I am getting to the end of my tether with these repeated Russian naggings, and that it is not the slightest use trying to knock me about any more.' Britain's escort vessels all over the world were 'so attenuated', he wrote, 'that losses out of all proportion are falling upon the British Mercantile Marine'. The Russian convoys were absorbing escort vessels that would clearly have been of use elsewhere. Only that morning, Churchill noted, 'news has come in of six out of nine great tankers being sunk, full of oil and greatly needed, because we can only provide an escort of one destroyer and a few corvettes for this vital convoy'.[4] These sinkings were of an Atlantic convoy.[5] The January convoy to Russia, fully escorted, reached Archangel without

<hr/>

[1] Prime Minister's Personal Minute, D.3/3, 'Action this Day', 'Secret', 5 January 1942: Churchill papers, 4/397A.

[2] Prime Minister's Personal Minute, D.4/3, 5 January 1943: Cabinet papers, 79/88 (Chiefs of Staff Committee of 5 January 1943, Annex).

[3] CS/1802, 'Most Secret and Personal', 9 January 1943: Churchill papers, 20/105.

[4] Prime Minister's Personal Minute, M.20/3, 9 January 1943: Churchill papers, 4/397A.

[5] Sinkings in the first and second week of January included the tanker *British Vigilance* on January 3, the *Benalbanach* on January 7, the *Yorkwood* on January 8, the tanker *Oltenia II* on

loss. Yet if extra American destroyers could not be made available for escort duty, Churchill pointed out to Eden, the Atlantic convoys would be reduced to a thirty-six day cycle.

'The December convoy has now been fought through successfully,' Churchill telegraphed to Stalin on January 10, 'and you will have received details of the fine engagement fought by our light forces against heavy odds.' Nineteen ships would sail on January 17 and a 'full convoy' of twenty-eight to thirty on February 11. Since it was clear from the experience of the December convoy that the Germans meant 'to disrupt the passage of further convoys by surface forces', it would be necessary for Britain 'immediately to increase our escorts beyond the scale originally contemplated for January'. With the increased hours of daylight in the Arctic in the spring, a still further increase in escort would be necessary. The sailing of thirty merchant ships in March and after would therefore be 'dependent upon the Americans assisting in the escort vessels'. Lack of such assistance would delay the convoys.[1]

With Maisky's complaint still angering him, Churchill minuted that same day to Portal: 'What has happened to the 200 Spitfires we sent to Stalin round the Cape? Where have they got to now? We get no thanks for any of this, but it is interesting to know what has happened.'[2]

On the following day, January 11, Churchill sent his Private Office 'the following telegram is to be filled in and sent off at the earliest moment after the event. The best figures available will do.' The telegram read: 'Prime Minister to Premier Stalin, We dropped—tons of high explosive and—incendiaries on—last night.'[3]

As Churchill prepared to leave for Casablanca, he had to deal with an appeal from Chiang-Kai-shek, sent through President Roosevelt, for a British force of seven divisions 'to assist in the recapture of Burma'. This was operation 'Ravenous'. But 'I now learn,' the Chinese leader had told Roosevelt, 'that only three divisions are to be employed in limited operations' with the objective of capturing Akyab

---

January 8, the tanker *Empire Lytton* on January 9, the *William Wilberforce* on January 9, the tanker *British Dominion* on January 10, and *Ocean Vagabond* on January 10.

[1] Prime Minister's Personal Telegram, T.58/3, 'Most Secret and Personal', 10 January 1943: Churchill papers, 20/105.

[2] Prime Minister's Personal Minute, M.25/3, 'Secret', 10 January 1943: Churchill papers, 4/397A.

[3] 'Most Secret', 11 January 1943: Premier papers, 3/14/2, folio 103.

and the line of the Chindwin river. This was operation 'Cannibal'. 'Offensive action by the Chinese,' Roosevelt telegraphed to Churchill, 'and the timeliness of a thrust into Burma this spring are all important.' [1]

In reply, Churchill assured Roosevelt that he had been 'ardently pressing General Wavell to take the offensive to the utmost, but', he explained, 'as we have had to cut off his supplies of landing craft for the sake of "Torch" and future operations in the "Torch" area or elsewhere', it had not been possible to manage more than operation 'Cannibal', leaving 'Ravenous' till after the monsoon. Churchill added, in defence of Wavell: 'I am quite sure that he has been most anxious to bring the greatest force to bear on land upon the enemy and to press forward, but it is absolutely no use Chiang or Stillwell saying that men can be maintained at particular points in these mountainous and rain-sodden jungles when in effect we know that they cannot.' [2]

---

[1] President to Prime Minister, No. 254, 'Personal and Secret', 8 January 1943: Cabinet papers 79/25 (Annex II to Chiefs of Staff Committee of 9 January 1943).
[2] 'Personal and Secret', 9 January 1943: Cabinet papers, 79/25.

18
January 1943: Casablanca

ON the evening of 11 January 1943 Churchill was ready to leave for Casablanca, but bad winter weather forced him to postpone his departure until the following day. During the delay, he prepared a note about Government plans for the post-war world: unemployment and low wages to be abolished, education to be greatly improved and prolonged, 'great developments' to be undertaken in housing and health, but at the same time no increase in the cost of living, the Beveridge Plan of Social Insurance 'to abolish want', a guarantee that wartime savings would not lose their value. All these promises were for a time when the United States would be a strong competitor, and Britain's own foreign investments would have almost disappeared. 'The question steals across the mind,' Churchill wrote, 'whether we are not committing our 45 million people to tasks beyond their compass, and laying on them burdens beyond their capacity to bear.' The broad mass of the people, he noted, 'face the hardships of life undaunted, but they are liable to get very angry if they feel they have been gulled or cheated'.

It was because he did not want to deceive people 'by false hopes and airy visions of Utopia and El Dorado', Churchill explained, 'that I have refrained so far from making promises about the future. We must all do our best, and we shall do it much better if we are not hampered by a cloud of pledges and promises which arise out of the hopeful and genial side of man's nature and are not brought into relation with the hard facts of life.' [1]

A month later, after having read the Beveridge Report in detail, Churchill minuted to the War Cabinet: 'This approach to social security, bringing the magic of averages nearer to the rescue of the millions, constitutes an essential part of any post-war scheme of national betterment.' [2]

*   *   *

[1] 'Promises about post-war conditions', War Cabinet paper No. 18 of 1943, 'Secret', 12 January 1943: Churchill papers, 23/11.
[2] War Cabinet Paper No. 65 of 1943, 'Secret', 15 February 1943: Churchill papers, 23/11.

Churchill left England by air for Casablanca on the evening of January 12, in his Liberator bomber, the 'Commando', travelling with Portal, Sir Charles Wilson, Averell Harriman, John Martin, Inspector Thompson, 'Tommy' Thompson and Sawyers the valet. During the journey Churchill was woken up by the heat of a makeshift heating pipe, and feared that it might ignite the petrol fumes in the bomber. Waking up Portal, he managed to find the source of the heating, a special petrol heater, and have it turned off.[1]

Nine hours after take off, the Liberator landed at Medouina airport near Casablanca, where Churchill awaited the arrival of a second plane with Pound, Brooke and Ismay. Churchill then drove to the suburb of Anfa, where he was to stay at the Villa Mirador, known in the jargon of 'Anfa Camp' as 'Villa 3'. At noon on that first day of 'Symbol', General Marshall and General Mark Clark were his luncheon guests at the Villa Mirador.[2]

'Conditions most agreeable,' Churchill telegraphed to Attlee that evening. 'I wish I could say the same of the problems. I think at least a fortnight will be required.' Roosevelt—'Admiral Q'—was expected on the following day.[3] The setting of the Conference was ideal. 'Sunshine, oranges, eggs,' noted John Martin in his diary on January 14, the day of Roosevelt's arrival.[4] 'It gave me intense pleasure,' Churchill later wrote, 'to see my great colleague here on conquered or liberated territory which he and I had secured in spite of the advice given him by all his military experts.'[5]

The work of the conference began on the afternoon of January 13. The British Chiefs of Staff were guided by Field Marshal Dill, who, with his insight as head of Britain's Joint Staff Mission in Washington, advised 'on how best', as Brigadier Jacob noted, 'to tackle the Americans'. Although the Americans 'were honestly of the opinion that Germany was the primary enemy', Dill reported, 'they did not see how quite to deal with her, especially as they felt that there were great and urgent tasks to be done in Burma and the Pacific'.

The Chiefs of Staff's discussion with Dill was continued at six that evening with Churchill in the Villa Mirador. The 'essential' thing, Churchill told the Chiefs of Staff, was to make the attack on Sicily 'as cheap in resources as possible and to advance to the utmost the date on which it could be staged'. At the same time, he 'was of the opinion that the present situation demanded that somehow in 1943', not only

---

[1] Sir Charles Wilson, notes relating to 13 January 1943: Moran, *op. cit.*, pages 78–9.

[2] John Martin diary, 13 January 1943: Martin papers.

[3] 'Stratagem' No. 7, 'Hush, Most Secret', 10.15 p.m., 13 January 1943: Cabinet papers, 120/76.

[4] John Martin diary, 13 January 1943: Martin papers.

[5] Winston S. Churchill, *The Second World War*, volume 4, London 1951, page 605.

the Sicily landings, but also 'some kind' of cross-Channel 'Sledge-hammer' operation, and a Far Eastern 'Anakim', should be carried out in the autumn. 'Only in this way,' Churchill told the Chiefs of Staff, 'should we be taking our fair share of the burden of the war.' [1]

The Chiefs of Staff, Jacob wrote, 'were dismissed on this note', and the rest of the evening was given up 'to ice-breaking dinner parties'. Brooke and Portal dined with General Marshall, while Churchill 'had the sailors of both sides and Lord Leathers at his villa'. [2]

At a second meeting with the Chiefs of Staff at Casablanca, held on the morning of January 15, Churchill 'emphasised', as the minutes recorded, that some kind of cross-Channel 'Sledgehammer' operation would be necessary in 1943, 'in order to broaden the area of the fighting and to make use of the powerful Anglo-American forces remaining in the United Kingdom which could not be used elsewhere'. [3]

On January 15, Harold Macmillan, General Eisenhower, Air Marshal Tedder and General Alexander were among those who reached Casablanca. The 'easy, smiling grace of Alexander', Churchill later wrote, 'won all hearts. His outspoken confidence was contagious.' [4] Alexander brought news of an imminent breakthrough towards Tripoli. That same day, a telegram from Stalin to Churchill announced: 'We are finishing the liquidation of the group of the German troops surrounded near Stalingrad.' [5]

Not to allow Britain's contribution to the war effort to be overlooked, Churchill decided to send Stalin an account of the British air raids on Germany. But here there was a hitch. As Brigadier Jacob telegraphed to General Hollis on the morning of January 15: 'Lack of news is causing trouble. Aggravated by absence of any bags so far, and by lack of any local contact such as existed in previous visiting places'—these were Washington and Moscow. Jacob went on to suggest that Hollis, in his daily news telegrams to Casablanca, should not confine himself to the 'bare bones' of the Central War Room records, 'but send us such things as summary of main questions under considera-

---

[1] Chiefs of Staff (S), 1st Meeting, Casablanca, 4.30 p.m. (until 6 p.m.), 13 January 1943: Cabinet papers, 99/24.

[2] Jacob notes of 13 January 1943, Jacob typescript, page 35: Jacob papers.

[3] Chiefs of Staff Committee (S), 3rd Meeting, 10.30 a.m., 15 January 1943: Cabinet papers, 99/24.

[4] Winston S. Churchill, *The Second World War*, volume 4, London 1951, page 606.

[5] 'Personal and Most Secret', 15 January 1943: Churchill papers, 20/105.

tion by Cabinet, Chiefs of Staff etc., and any interesting political or Ministry of Information titbits'.[1]

'Reference attached telegram from Jacob,' Hollis minuted to John Peck, and to his own Ministry of Defence staff, 'I suppose we must pad out the daily news wire.' To this end, Major Carver of the Defence Staff was asked to prepare a summary of Chiefs of Staff business of the previous day, 'dull though it may be', Hollis noted, and 'leaving out of course the more obvious tripe'. Hollis added: 'We must try and cook up a meaty dish for tomorrow.'[2]

On January 17 Churchill was able to telegraph to Stalin: 'We dropped 142 tons of high explosives and 218 tons of incendiaries on Berlin last night.'[3] On January 18 he telegraphed again: 'In last night's raid we dropped 117 tons of high explosive and 211 tons of incendiary bombs on Berlin.'[4] This message, like the first, was sent from London, Churchill having telegraphed to Eden and Sinclair seven hours earlier: 'If second night's attack on Berlin was on an appreciable scale, you should send another telegram to Stalin from me with the new total of bombs dropped.'[5]

It was not only for news of Britain's air offensive that Churchill had agitated at the start of the Casablanca conference. The Enigma decrypts were another area of his intense concern. Before leaving London, he had asked Brigadier Menzies to 'repeat all really important messages to me textually'.[6] On January 18 he signalled to Menzies from Casablanca: 'Why have you not kept me properly supplied with news? Volume should be increased at least five-fold with important messages sent textually.'[7]

No special Enigma link, however, had been provided for Casablanca. As a result of Churchill's discontent, all future conferences were to be adequately provided with a Special Liaison Unit for this purpose. While at Casablanca, Churchill was able to receive Enigma decrypts, however, through the Admiralty's most secret channel, a morning telegram from Menzies, and an evening 'Sunset' telegram. The 'Sunset' series was material based upon Enigma decrypts. This material was prepared in the Naval Intelligence Department of the

[1] 'Stratagem' No. 16, 'Immediate', sent 11.30 a.m., 15 January 1943: Premier papers, 3/420/3, folio 61.

[2] 'Secret', 15 January 1943: Premier papers, 3/420/3, folio 59.

[3] Prime Minister's Personal Telegram, T.69/3, 'Most Immediate', 17 January 1943: Churchill papers, 20/105.

[4] Prime Minister's Personal Telegram, T.70/3, 'Most Immediate', Foreign Office No. 23 to Moscow, 7.10 p.m. 18 January 1943: Churchill papers, 20/105.

[5] 'Stratagem' No. 70, 'Most Secret and Personal', 12.11 a.m., 18 January 1943: Premier papers, 3/14/2, folio 91.

[6] Dir/C Archive, number 2031, 11 January 1943.

[7] 'Stratagem' No. 71, 18 January 1943: Cabinet papers, 120/76.

Admiralty, primarily for daily despatch to the British Admiralty Delegation in Washington.[1]

The first plenary meeting of the Casablanca Conference was held in the afternoon of January 15, with Eisenhower and Alexander giving details of their operations and plans. The 'opening of the Mediterranean', Churchill commented, 'would have its effect on the attitude of Turkey', while the British 10th Army, consisting of six divisions, which had been established in Persia with a view to meeting a German threat through the Caucasus, 'was now available to encourage and support the Turks'.[2] This was Churchill's first reference, at Casablanca, to his hopes of being able to persuade Turkey to enter the war.

The first decision reached by Churchill and Roosevelt at Casablanca was to invite General de Gaulle to fly out 'immediately' to meet General Giraud.[3] It was the hope of both Churchill and Roosevelt that de Gaulle would agree to recognize Giraud's authority in North Africa.

Each day at Casablanca the British Chiefs of Staff held at least one meeting alone, and two with their American counterparts, to discuss war strategy. Each evening they made their report to Churchill, who telegraphed their conclusions to Attlee and the War Cabinet. The American Army and Navy authorities, he reported in a detailed telegram on January 17, were 'very keen on more vigorous action in Burma to help China', culminating later in the year in a large-scale offensive against Burma, operation 'Anakim'.[4] General Marshall was also keen on this, Churchill noted, 'but otherwise' Marshall's emphasis 'seemed to lie' towards building up a cross-Channel invasion 'at the expense of the Mediterranean'.

Churchill then informed the War Cabinet that, in contrast to General Marshall, Roosevelt was 'strongly in favour of the Mediterranean being given prime place', and was 'increasingly inclined' to operation

[1] Details about the 'Sunset' series, as well as Dir/C 2031 and Stratagem No. 71, are in F. H. Hinsley and others, *British Intelligence in the Second World War*, volume 2, London 1981, page 4, note 6.

[2] 'Anfa', '1st Meeting', 'Minutes of Meeting held at Anfa Camp on Friday, January 15, 1943, at 17.30': Cabinet papers, 99/24 Roosevelt was accompanied at this meeting by two of his sons, Elliot and Franklin Jnr.

[3] 'Stratagem' No. 35 (Churchill to Attlee), 'Most Immediate', 16 January 1943: Cabinet papers, 65/37.

[4] The 'more vigorous action' in Burma was Operation 'Ravenous', for which Chiang-Kai-shek had also been pressing.

'Husky', against Sicily. Nothing definite had been settled however, between Churchill and Roosevelt, pending, as Churchill wrote, the results of further Staff conversations. As between Sicily and Sardinia, the Americans were 'increasingly' turning to Sicily, Churchill added, Admiral King having gone so far as to say that if it was decided to attack Sicily 'he would find the necessary escorts'.[1]

The problems of shipping were being discussed at Casablanca by the British Minister of War Transport, Lord Leathers, and Averell Harriman, with the expert assistance of General Somervell. One of their main problems was to ensure that, whatever land operations were decided upon, escort shipping was kept available for the trans-Atlantic and Arctic convoys. It was in the light of these oceanic supply needs that the attack on Sicily gained in attraction as the Casablanca talks continued: the troops were already in North Africa and would not need to be brought there across the Atlantic.[2]

The question of co-ordination of air command, and the evolution of an acceptable Anglo-American bombing policy, was undertaken, for Britain, by Portal and Tedder, and for the United States by Arnold and Eaker, the new commander of the United States Air Forces in the United Kingdom. There was also a military decision to reorganize the North African Command, in which the respective Chiefs of Staff were the main negotiators, with General Brooke, as Brigadier Jacob noted, 'often acting as go-between and general lubricator'.[3]

In his telegram to Attlee and the War Cabinet on January 17, Churchill had explained that the situation was being 'decisively changed by the victorious advance' of the Desert Army, and told his colleagues of the 'great impression' which Alexander had made on Roosevelt and all those present 'by his clear, precise, confident accounts of his progress and intentions'. In an attempt to ensure that the remaining North African campaigns were fought with a close harmony of interest and understanding, Churchill had brought Alexander and Eisenhower together, first alone with each other, and then with Brooke and Marshall. The result, he told the War Cabinet, had been 'a perfect understanding' between the two Commanders-in-Chief, 'and arrangements for visits when necessary'.[4]

Among the British team at Casablanca were the Joint Planners and Lord Mountbatten. They preferred an attack on Sardinia rather than Sicily, believing that the Sardinia operation could be carried out

[1] Stratagem No. 56, 'Hush Most Secret', 17 January 1943: Cabinet papers, 120/76.
[2] Abel and Harriman, op. cit., page 184.
[3] Brigadier E. I. C. Jacob, 'Operation "Symbol", Casablana, December 1942', typescript, page 49.
[4] 'Stratagem' No. 56, 'Hush Most Secret', 17 January 1943: Cabinet papers, 120/76.

three months earlier than Sicily. Harriman also had favoured the earlier, Sardinia, plan. Churchill however, strongly supported by Brooke, preferred Sicily, as being a more important objective. A landing in Sicily, the Joint Planners believed, could not even be started before August 30. But after Churchill and the Chiefs of Staff had studied all the available figures, they set, with Roosevelt's approval, the night of July 9 as the date of the first landings on Sicily. The landings in Sardinia, Churchill had always described as 'that piddling operation', Sicily as the only operation in the Mediterranean worth doing, 'the glittering prize'.[1]

While he was at Casablanca, Churchill's discontent with his Private and Defence Office communications continued. 'I am not satisfied,' he telegraphed to Hollis on January 18, 'with speed or volume of information you are sending. Note also that telegrams from war front should always bear date and hour of local origin. Pray endeavour to ensure earlier and fuller information from General Montgomery. You need not decode Sitreps etc. before sending them on here. We have to decode them ourselves anyway.' Other than a single official telegram from London, Churchill added, 'we still have no information on the first raid on Berlin other than that gathered from local newspapers. . . .'[2]

The telegram from London had reported that 201 bombers had taken part in the raid on Berlin and that only one, 'repeat one', had failed to return; that as a result of bad weather 'probably not more than' 140 of the bombers had dropped their bombs, 'but good fires are reported'; that the bombs had been dropped between 18,000 and 21,000 feet; that the German defences having been caught by surprise by the 'speed and direction of the attack', there had been only light anti-aircraft fire; and that night fighters and anti-aircraft guns in the United Kingdom 'are on the alert for retaliation'.[3]

At the second plenary meeting, held on the afternoon of January 18, Churchill told Roosevelt 'that he wished it made clear that if and

---

[1] Jacob notes, pages 43–4: Jacob papers.

[2] 'Stratagem' No. 69, 'Most Secret and Personal', 12.45 p.m., 18 January 1943; Cabinet papers, 120/76. It was in anticipation of a German reprisal raid that Churchill asked John Martin to telegraph that same day to his Private Office in London: 'Air Commodore Frankland wishes you to ensure that Mrs Frankland and the servants go down to the shelter in the event of air raid warning' ('Stratagem' No. 80, 'Hush Most Secret', sent at 6.55 p.m., received at 10.25 p.m., 18 January 1943: Cabinet papers, 120/76.)

[3] 'Telescope' No. 75, sent 12.36 a.m., received 4.35 p.m., 17 January 1943: Cabinet papers, 120/78.

when Hitler breaks down, all of the British resources and effort will be turned towards the defeat of Japan'. Not only were British interests involved, Churchill added, 'but her honour is engaged'. If it were thought 'well for the effect on the people of the United States of America, the British Government would enter into a treaty or convention with the United States government to this effect'. A formal agreement regarding British efforts against Japan, replied Roosevelt, was 'entirely unnecessary', but efforts should be made 'to obtain an engagement from Russia to concentrate on the defeat of Japan after Germany had been eliminated from the war'.

Turning once more to the question of Turkey, which was much on his mind, Churchill stated that 'the Turks might be "influenced" to enter the war by the successes of Russian troops on the north and those of the United States and the United Kingdom troops on the south. Since most of the troops involved in "reinforcing" Turkey would be British,' Churchill added, 'he asked that the British be allowed to play the Turkish hand, just as the United States is now handling the situation with reference to China.' Roosevelt, the minutes noted, 'concurred in this view', and went on to say that if the cross-Channel operation should be undertaken, 'he felt that it should be under British command'. In his view, Churchill replied, 'the command of operations should, as a general rule, be held by an officer of the nation which 'furnishes the majority of troops'.[1]

'It was a most satisfactory meeting,' Churchill telegraphed to Attlee and the War Cabinet. After five days of discussions, 'and a good deal of apparent disagreement', the Combined Chiefs of Staff 'are now I think unanimous in essentials about the conduct of the war in 1943'. The main decision was to re-affirm the principle 'that we must concentrate first on the defeat of Germany'. It was also agreed that the 'security of sea communications' was to be 'the first charge upon our combined resources'. A third decision was that preparations for the invasion of Sicily, operation 'Husky', 'are to go ahead at once with a view to carrying out the operation at the earliest moment possible'.

Also to go ahead 'towards the end of this year' was operation 'Anakim', Wavell's invasion of Burma, for which the Americans had undertaken 'to supply the lion's share of the assault shipping and landing craft', which would be American manned during the actual landing. In the Pacific, operations for the capture of Rabaul and the clearing of Japanese forces from New Guinea were to continue 'in order to retain the initiative and hold Japan'. Whether this offensive

[1] 'Anfa', '2nd Meeting', 'Minutes of meeting held at Anfa Camp on Monday, January 18, 1943, at 17.00': Cabinet papers, 99/24.

should subsequently be carried forward to Truk would be decided 'later in the year'.

In Europe, operation 'Bolero', the build-up of troops in Britain in preparation for a cross-Channel landing, was to go ahead 'as fast as our commitments allow', with a view to a limited landing 'of some sort'—operation 'Sledgehammer'—in 1943, or even operation 'Round-up', 'a return to the continent with all available forces' if Germany were to show 'definite signs of collapse'.

With this outline of operations, Churchill commented, 'Admiral Q and I were in complete agreement'.

In his telegram to Attlee, Churchill went on to explain how, during the second Plenary, he and Roosevelt had learned of American fears, expressed at the Combined Chiefs of Staff discussions, that Britain 'might pull out' once Germany were defeated, leaving America to fight alone in the Pacific. 'I thought it right,' Churchill told Attlee and the War Cabinet, 'to say in categorical terms that our interest and our honour were alike engaged and that the determination of British Parliament and people to devote their whole resources to the defeat of Japan once Germany had been brought to her knees was not in doubt.'

To resolve any doubts there might be about Britain remaining in the war to the end, 'we propose', Churchill informed the War Cabinet, to include in the statement issued at the end of the Conference 'a declaration of firm intention of the United States and the British Empire to continue the war relentlessly until we have brought about the "unconditional surrender" of Germany and Japan'. The omission of Italy from such a declaration was, he said, deliberate, and would be designed 'to encourage a break up there'. Churchill added that Roosevelt 'liked the idea' of such a declaration, which would, in Churchill's opinion, 'stimulate our friends in every country'.[1]

Churchill was worried, as he informed Attlee and the War Cabinet, that 'all our military operations taken together are on a very small scale compared to the mighty resources of Britain and the United States and still more to the gigantic effort of Russia'. Roosevelt, he was sure, shared this view, as Hopkins had spoken to Churchill on the subject on the previous day, saying in effect, 'It is all right, but it is not enough.' Making all allowances, Churchill added, 'for our tremendous efforts on the sea and in the air, I still feel this most strongly,

[1] The phrase 'unconditional surrender' appeared in one of the reports with which Roosevelt had been briefed before the conference; a State Department Sub-Committee report on security problems, which recommended the 'unconditional surrender' of the Axis armies. In giving this report to Roosevelt in December 1942, the United States Chiefs of Staff recommended that no armistice should be granted to Germany, Italy or Japan 'until they accepted unconditional surrender of their armed forces'.

and during the remaining days of the conference we must bend ourselves to the task of weighting our blows more heavily'.[1]

It was also proposed at this plenary session, and 'unanimously
agreed', as Churchill reported in a separate telegram to Attlee and
Eden, that General Alexander should become Eisenhower's deputy
Commander-in-Chief of the whole of North Africa. General Marshall
had proposed that any cross-Channel invasion 'which may be
undertaken this year' be under British command. The plenary session
accepted a further proposal, agreed upon in advance of the session by
Churchill and Roosevelt, that Britain should 'play the hand' in
Turkey, whether in supply of munitions or in diplomacy, with the
Americans 'taking the lead' in China and French North Africa.

Churchill ended his telegram to Attlee and Eden by asking: 'Is not
this the opportunity and the moment for me to get into direct touch
with the Turks?' and proposing to fly to Cyprus to meet the Turkish
Prime Minister, Ismet Inönü, while General Brooke would meet the
Turkish Commander-in-Chief. 'I can then go into the whole future
with them,' Churchill explained.[2]

Attlee and Eden took Churchill's proposal to the War Cabinet,
which urged him to return home. Even a visit to Cairo was not
thought well of. 'Your special trips have been recognized to be of
highest importance,' Attlee and Eden replied, 'but it is undeniable
that there is a feeling that you should not run these flying risks except
in cases of absolute necessity.' As to a meeting with the Turks, 'we
think it extremely doubtful', Attlee and Eden reported on behalf of
the War Cabinet, 'whether you would get anything substantial out of
them', especially before Britain had been able to 'clear North Africa'
and drive the Germans from Tunisia. . . . 'We do not want you to
court either a rebuff or a failure,' Attlee and Eden declared.[3] Churchill
was determined to go, however, and the War Cabinet deferred to his
further urgings that, if he did not go, 'a golden opportunity may be
lost'.[4]

The War Cabinet on January 20 also discussed the proposed announcement of 'unconditional surrender'. The only comment which they had
was to oppose the omission of Italy from the announcement. The
omission of Italy, the War Cabinet minutes recorded, 'was liable to be
misunderstood in, for example, the Balkans'. It 'was such a mistake',

[1] 'Stratagem' No. 98, 19 January 1943: Premier papers, 4/72/1, folios 148–9.
[2] 'Stratagem' No. 102, 'Personal and Most Secret', 19 January 1942: Cabinet papers,
120/76.
[3] 'Telescope' No. 182, 'Personal and Most Secret', 20 January 1943: Cabinet papers, 65/37.
[4] 'Stratagem' No. 144, 'Personal and Secret' (to Eden), 22 January 1943: Churchill papers,
20/127.

the minutes added, 'at any rate at this stage, to make any distinction between the three partners in the Axis'.[1] Eden and Attlee then telegraphed this decision to Churchill. 'The Cabinet were unanimously of opinion,' they wrote, 'that balance of advantage lay against excluding Italy, because of misgivings which would inevitably be caused in Turkey, in the Balkans, and elsewhere. Nor are we convinced that effect on Italians would be good. Knowledge of all rough stuff coming to them is surely more likely to have desired effect on Italian morale.'[2]

In the east, January 18 saw the capture by the Red Army of more than 50,000 German troops on the Voronezh front, and, in the north, the raising of the siege of Leningrad by the establishment of a ten mile wide corridor from the city to the Red Army front line. Stalin, having received Churchill's first message about British bombing raids, replied on January 19: 'I wish the British Air Force further successes, more particularly in bombing Berlin.'[3] But news that day of the loss of four out of the eighteen ships of the January convoy to Murmansk, codename 'JW 52', led Churchill to telegraph Eden of his concern. 'This will make our position with the Bear even worse than it is now,' he warned. 'I trust you will look into this yourself.'[4]

The secrecy of 'Symbol' was well kept. 'Everything is quiet,' Clementine Churchill wrote from London on January 14. 'So far at *this* end "the secret" is water-tight.'[5] Five days later the Prime Minister of Australia telegraphed from Canberra: 'Having learned that the President, Mrs Churchill and yourself are meeting in Washington....'[6]

At Casablanca, Averell Harriman noted that Churchill and Roosevelt 'are much pleased with meeting, although both are disappointed by slowness of new moves'. Harriman also noted that both General Marshall and Admiral King, the two senior American officers

---

[1] War Cabinet No. 12 of 1943, 5.30 p.m., 20 January 1943, Confidential Annex: Cabinet papers, 65/37.

[2] 'Telescope' No. 212, 21 January 1943: Cabinet papers, 120/79.

[3] 'Personal and Secret', Kremlin, 19 January 1943: Premier papers, 3/14/Z, folio 88.

[4] 'Stratagem' No. 100, 'Hush Most Secret', 19 January 1943: Cabinet papers, 120/76.

[5] Letter of 14 January 1943: Mary Soames, page 311.

[6] Telegram of 19 January 1943: Churchill papers, 20/05.

present, 'always try to blame British' for the postponement of the cross-Channel invasion. 'I got the feeling,' he added, 'they understand difficulties thoroughly, but now and later will put blame on British for no action.' [1]

At 12 o'clock on January 20, Churchill saw General Eaker.[2] Still to be resolved was whether the United States Air Force in Britain, which Eaker commanded, were to join the British night bombers over Germany, as Sir Arthur Harris wished, or, as the Americans preferred, to continue their still small-scale daylight raids. Eaker had flown out to Casablanca, at General Arnold's urgent request, specifically to present the American case. On the previous evening, and long into the night, he had prepared his arguments, helped by one of his aides, Captain James Parton. Many years later, Eaker recalled the sequel of his late night efforts:

Well, he said, 'General, your General Arnold tells me you're very unhappy about my request to your President that you discontinue your daylight bombing effort and join Marshal Harris and the RAF in the night effort.' I said, 'Yes, sir, I am. And I've set down here on a single page the reasons why I'm unhappy, and I have served long enough in England now to know that you will listen to both sides of any controversy before you make a decision.' So he sat down on the couch and took up this piece of paper, called me to sit beside him, and he started reading. And he read like some aged person, with his lips half audibly. And one of the reasons that I had set down on this memorandum—I'd said that if the British bombed by night and the Americans by day, bombing them thus around the clock will give the devils no rest. And it will prevent the nightwatchers from going to the factories in the daytime. There are a million men now standing on the West Wall to stop our tiny bomber offensive of 100 planes. If it were not for this, they could be marshalled into divisions and sent to the Eastern Front.

When the old man read this and got to the bombing around the clock, he repeated it. I heard him. He finished, and he said to me, 'I want you to know that I admire very much the effort you and your gallant crews are making, but I'm aware of your tragic losses, sometimes ten percent on a single raid.' He said, 'You know, my mother was an American, and it breaks my heart to see these tragic losses you're suffering. Marshal Harris tells me his average is less than two percent on a mission at night. That's the primary reason that I've suggested that you join the RAF.' But he said, 'You have not convinced me now that you are right, but you have convinced me you should have a further opportunity to prove your case. So when I see your President at lunch today, I shall say to him that I withdraw my objection

[1] Harriman notes: Abel and Harriman, pages 184–5. To prepare a definite plan for the cross-Channel landing, an Allied Inter-Service Staff was set up, to work in London under Lieutenant-General Frederick Morgan, who was appointed Chief of Staff, Supreme Allied Commander (known as COSSAC).

[2] Prime Minister's Engagement Cards, 20 January 1943.

and my request that you join the RAF in night bombing, and I shall suggest that you be allowed to continue for a time.'

'So I've always felt,' Eaker reflected, 'that it was the PM who saved our daylight bombing effort at that critical juncture.' [1]

On the evening of January 20, Roosevelt dined with Churchill at the Villa Mirador, and after dinner spent about fifteen minutes in Churchill's War Room, which Captain Pim had fitted out with maps of each theatre of the war. Also after dinner, 'a number of American negro troops', as Pim later recalled, 'sang Spirituals and other songs in the drawing-room. The repertoire included a solo of the "Londonderry Air" which, while in my view it was an inferior rendering of "Danny Boy", touched the Prime Minister deeply.' On the following morning, while still in bed, Churchill asked Pim to repeat the words of the song, 'so that his typist, sitting beside his bed, could record them and he would send them to Mrs Churchill'. [2]

Reporting on his dinner with Roosevelt, Churchill telegraphed to Eden: 'He is in great form and we have never been so close. He has gone today up the line to inspect his troops.'

Churchill also told Eden that he was 'sorry' that the War Cabinet did not wish him to visit Turkey. 'I think we may be losing a golden opportunity,' Churchill warned, and he went on to explain: 'I had not intended to extort any pledge but only to explain to them the ways in which we are now able to help them place themselves in a position of security.'

As to the invitation to de Gaulle to come to Casablanca, he could be told, Churchill added, 'that I had already arranged for him and General Giraud to have two separate villas side by side and they can meet each other alone, as often, and as long as they like'. [3]

At a meeting of the British Chiefs of Staff Committee at noon on January 21, Churchill commented that he had heard September mentioned as the date for the launching of the Sicily landing. 'This, of course, would be quite unacceptable,' he said. He would like to see the operation launched in May. 'It surely could not be necessary,' he asked, 'to train every single man taking part in the operation and he did not feel that sufficient ingenuity was being displayed in overcoming obstacles. It

---

[1] Ira C. Eaker, transcript: Randolph Churchill papers. (This transcript was sent to Randolph Churchill by Colonel Donald F. Martin, Department of the Air Force, Washington, for use in this biography.)

[2] Pim Recollections, typescript: Pim papers.

[3] 'Stratagem' No. 144, 'Personal and Secret', sent at 2.42 p.m. 21 January 1943: Cabinet papers, 120/76.

would be extremely unfortunate if the operation were delayed by us beyond the date at which the Americans would be ready.'

To Dill's suggestion that Sardinia should be attacked in May and Sicily in 'August or September', Churchill told the meeting that he 'feared that if we assaulted Sardinia we might get involved in a long campaign for the reduction of the island and might thus be prevented from securing the richer prize of Sicily. Russian convoys would also be stopped for a very long period.' [1]

On January 22, reluctantly, but at Churchill's repeated urging, de Gaulle arrived in Casablanca, and agreed to meet Giraud. He also saw Churchill, who reported to the War Cabinet on the following day:

I had a long talk with de Gaulle yesterday and told him plainly that there must be an arrangement, and it was the duty of any Frenchman who became an obstacle to French unity or to the relations between the various French sections and the two great allies, to efface himself and that certainly no individual would be allowed to obstruct the necessary forward march of the war, and that I should not hesitate to speak in public about these matters, much as I should regret to have to proclaim him as the obstacle. The President whom he saw after dinner was much more kindly and paternal. He reminded him about the American Civil War, where brother had fought against brother and yet had come together.

'De Gaulle did not make a bad impression,' Churchill added, 'though the President was somewhat concerned at the spiritual look which he sometimes had in his eyes. They parted on almost affectionate terms. We shall see what will come of the dual treatment today.' [2]

Sir Charles Wilson had been a witness to de Gaulle's departure from the Villa Mirador:

. . . the PM stood in the hall watching the Frenchman stalk down the garden path with his head in the air. Winston turned to us with a whimsical smile:

'His country has given up fighting, he himself is a refugee, and if we turn him down he's finished. Well, just look at him! Look at him!' he repeated. 'He might be Stalin, with 200 divisions behind his words. I was pretty rough with him. I made it quite plain that if he could not be more helpful we were done with him.'

'How,' I asked, 'did he like that?'

'Oh,' the PM replied, 'he hardly seemed interested. My advances and my threats met with no response.'

Harry Hopkins had told me of the President's quip that de Gaulle claimed to be the lineal descendant of Joan of Arc. I repeated this to the PM. He was not amused. It did not seem at all absurd to him.

[1] Chiefs of Staff (S), 10th Meeting, 12 noon, 21 January 1943: Cabinet papers, 99/24.
[2] 'Stratagem' No. 198, 'Hush Most Secret', 23 January 1943: Cabinet papers, 65/37.

France without an Army is not France. De Gaulle is the spirit of that Army. 'Perhaps,' he said sadly, 'the last survivor of a warrior race.'

If this Frenchman's arrogance, his defiance of everyone and everything, do at times get on the PM's nerves, there are days when he cannot withhold his admiration. He was in tears when he said: 'England's grievous offence in de Gaulle's eyes is that she has helped France. He cannot bear to think that she needed help. He will not relax his vigilance in guarding her honour for a single instant.'[1]

With de Gaulle's arrival in Casablanca, Churchill and Roosevelt had asked Harold Macmillan, and his American opposite number, Robert Murphy, to help work out an agreement between de Gaulle and Giraud 'for the prosecution of the war of liberation', based upon their existing spheres of jurisdiction.[2]

In a letter home, Harold Macmillan wrote of how, 'apart from chaff', he thought the negotiations between de Gaulle and Giraud, which eventually took place on January 23, and the handshake which the two men were persuaded to make in front of the cameras, would prove the beginning, 'though only just the beginning, of the loosening out of a very complicated situation between the various French peoples'. No fusing of Free French and Giraudists proved possible; but both men agreed to a communiqué that Frenchmen should unite to fight beside the Allies against the Axis.

In his letter home, Macmillan described Churchill's daily life at Casablanca:

The Emperor of the East's villa was guarded by marines, but otherwise things were fairly simple. His curious routine of spending the greater part of the day in bed and all the night up made it a little trying for his staff. I have never seen him in better form. He ate and drank enormously all the time, settled huge problems, played bagatelle and bezique by the hour, and generally enjoyed himself.

At the 'Emperor of the West' villa, Macmillan noted 'a lot of bezique, an enormous quantity of highballs, talk by the hour, and a general atmosphere of extraordinary goodwill'. If the Red Emperor had been there as well, he wrote, 'it would have made the thing perfect'. The meetings of 'the emperors and the staffs', Macmillan noted, took place at night, and he added: 'I thought the PM handled the situation with consummate skill.'[3]

[1] Sir Charles Wilson diary, 22 January 1943: Lord Moran, op. cit., pages 80–1.

[2] 'Stratagem' No. 54 (Churchill to Attlee, Eden and the War Cabinet), 'Hush Most Secret', 17 January 1943: Churchill papers, 20/127. General Giraud's jurisdiction (as of 17 January 1943) was of French North Africa, French West Africa, and Togoland. General de Gaulle's jurisdiction comprised French Equatorial Africa, Djibouti, Madagascar, Reunion Island and the Cameroons.

[3] Letter of 26 January 1943: Harold Macmillan, War Diaries, Politics and War in the Mediterranean, January 1943–May 1945, London 1984, page 9.

The third and final plenary session was held on the afternoon of January 23. Speaking of assistance to Russia, in relation to the other commitments of Britain and the United States, Roosevelt suggested retaining in the next round of supply negotiations the sentence in the Combined Chiefs of Staff report that 'supply to Russia will not be continued at prohibitive cost to the United Nations efforts'. But Churchill replied that aid to Russia 'must be pushed and no investment could pay a better dividend'. The United Nations, Churchill insisted, 'cannot let Russia down'.

In the discussion which followed, both Admiral King and General Marshall stressed the extent of the shipping losses to the northern convoys. 'Such losses,' Marshall warned, 'made it impossible for us to attack on other fronts and thus eliminate the possibility of forcing the Germans to withdraw ground and air troops from the Russian front.' It must be 'made certain', Marshall warned, that, by continuing the convoys to Russia, 'we do not hazard' the success of the Sicily landing. If 'passage of convoys on the northern route were prohibitive in cost', Churchill agreed, 'they must be stopped'. Whatever was decided, Churchill added, Stalin must be told 'the facts'. The convoys would be stopped 'if the losses are too great'.

Turning to the timing for the Sicily landings, Churchill pressed for the earliest possible date, telling the conference 'that he feared the gap of perhaps four months during the summer when no United States or British troops would be in contact with the Germans'. Roosevelt accepted this argument, commenting that such a gap 'might have a serious effect all over the world'.

In the discussion which followed, Churchill pressed for a June date for 'Husky', but, after Marshall had warned of the need to avoid any timing which would be 'at the expense of adequate preparation', it was agreed that the July date should stand, 'subject to an instruction that in the next three weeks, without prejudice to the July date, there should be an intense effort made to try and achieve the favourable June moon as the date of the operation'.[1]

The results of the eight days of discussions, 'almost continuously', of every facet of Anglo-American war policy had been, Churchill reported in his telegram that day to Attlee and the War Cabinet, 'from one point of view, very remarkable'. The priority of 'Hitler's extinction' as against Japan had been re-established. Priority had been secured for the Mediterranean over the cross-Channel assault that summer, without prejudice to the 'maximum' development of the build-up in Britain of the forces that would be needed for a cross-

[1] 'Anfa', '3rd Meeting', 'Minutes of Meeting held at Anfa Camp, on Saturday, January 23, 1943, at 1700': Cabinet papers, 99/24.

Channel invasion when it came. For the Mediterranean move, Sicily had been secured instead of Sardinia. In the Far East, 'important naval and landing craft help' had been secured for the assault on the Japanese in Burma, an assault 'on which the Americans are very keen'. It was agreed that Britain should play the 'Turkish hand'. Finally, changes in command had been agreed upon 'with the greatest cordiality', whereby Alexander would bc Eiscnhower's deputy, charged with 'plans and execution' of the capture of Sicily, with Tedder to command the whole Mediterranean theatre in the air. 'It now remains,' Churchill added, 'to add speed and weight to all our actions.' [1]

That day, the Eighth Army entered Tripoli.

The Casablanca conference ended on January 24. That morning, as Brigadier Jacob noted:

I was sent for by the Prime Minister at 9 a.m. I found him in bed in his room upstairs, with the windows tight shut, the heating full on, dictating and having breakfast by turns. A draft communiqué which the President had sent him over was the business in hand, and he was busy redrafting it. He wanted me to check it over, and see that all the names and titles were correct—'Wigs by Clarkson' was his expression for what he wanted filled in and checked. [2] The Prime Minister in bed in the mornings reminds me in an extraordinary way of my grandmother, who in her later years had the same rather slothful physical habits, and slow movements, combined with the extremely masterful brain demanding continual employment, and a constant stream of helpers, servants etc round her. She used to sit in bed having breakfast, while also writing a note to someone in the parish, ordering the meals for the day, telling me to get on my bicycle to fetch something from the butcher, and keeping her husband, who was aching to get on with his duties in the parish, hanging round for last injunctions.

The Prime Minister is much the same. Sawyers brings the breakfast; then Kinna is sent for to take something down; meanwhile the bell is rung for the Private Secretary on duty who is asked for news, and told to summon someone, say CIGS or Pug. Then it is the candle for lighting cigars that is wanted. Then someone must get Hopkins on the phone. All this while the

[1] 'Stratagem' No. 198, 'Hush, Most Secret', sent at 7.04 p.m., 23 January 1943: Cabinet papers, 120/76.
[2] Sir Ian Jacob writes: '"Wigs by Clarkson". This goes back to the early part of the century. At the theatre Clarkson's seemed to have a monopoly of headdresses, wigs etc, and in every programme there always appeared "Wigs by Clarkson". So, when Winston had approved the text of the communiqué at Casablanca, all he had to say was "Wigs by Clarkson", and I knew that he wanted the text in its setting cleaned up and the necessary ancillary remarks included.' (Sir Ian Jacob, letter to the author, 28 October 1984.)

Prime Minister is half sitting, half lying, in his bed, breathing rather ster-
torously, and surrounded by papers.

On this morning, there was none too much time to spare, as the communiqué had to be ready, and the PM dressed and round at villa No. 2 by
12.30 for the press conference. As soon as I had checked up the facts, and
Green and Kinna had retyped the communiqué, I was sent round to No. 2
to get Hopkins' agreement.[1]

With the Americans in agreement, Jacob returned to Churchill's
room. All was ready for the final act of operation 'Symbol', the Press
Conference, at which de Gaulle and Giraud were placed in chairs
alternating with Churchill and Roosevelt, and then asked to shake
hands as the photographers hastened to record the appearance of
unity. The two Frenchmen then departed, leaving Roosevelt and
Churchill to speak to the fifty newspapermen in outline about what
had been decided. It was Roosevelt who then read out a paragraph,
prepared for him, as a result of his discussion with Churchill on
January 18, about the need for some declaration of the resolve of
Britain and America to see the war through to the total defeat or
'unconditional surrender' of Germany and Japan, and also, despite
Churchill's reluctance, of Italy.

To the fifty newspapermen, Roosevelt spoke of 'the determination
that peace can come to the world only by the total elimination of
German and Japanese war power', an elimination which meant 'the
unconditional surrender by Germany, Italy and Japan'. This did not
mean 'the destruction of the population of Germany, Italy or Japan',
he said, but it did mean 'the destruction of the philosophies in those
countries which are based on conquest and the subjugation of other
people'.

Speaking after Roosevelt, Churchill spoke of the Eighth Army's
chase of Rommel from Alamein, 'where I last saw them', to Tripoli,
'and Rommel is still flying before them', he added. 'But I can give
you this assurance—everywhere that Mary went the lamb is sure to
go.' Churchill then appealed to the newspapermen in their presentation of the Conference to their readers:

Give them the picture of unity, thoroughness, and integrity of the political
chiefs. Give them that picture, and make them feel that there is some reason
behind all that is being done. Even when there is some delay there is design

---

[1] Jacob notes: Jacob typescript, pages 59–60. Patrick Kinna writes: 'Sergeant Geoffrey Green,
RAF, a tall, slim pleasant young man who was sometimes loaned to us by the Air Ministry for
very busy trips. Did not work personally for the PM (who as you know didn't accept new faces!)
but he was an excellent shorthand writer and typist and did work for senior people with us at
Conferences. I think he got on very well with in particular, Harry Hopkins.' (Letter to the
author, 8 October 1985.)

and purpose, and as the President has said, the unconquerable will to pursue this quality, until we have procured the unconditional surrender of the criminal forces who plunged the world into storm and ruin.[1]

Following the Press Conference, the journalists were given the text of the Unconditional Surrender Declaration, which read:

The President and the Prime Minister, after a complete survey of the world war situation, are more than ever determined that peace can come to the world only by a total elimination of German and Japanese war power. This involves the simple formula of placing the objective of this war in terms of an unconditional surrender by Germany, Italy and Japan. Unconditional surrender by them means a reasonable assurance of world peace for generations. Unconditional surrender means not the destruction of the German populace, nor of the Italian or Japanese populace, but does mean the destruction of a philosophy in Germany, Italy, and Japan which is based on the conquest and subjugation of other peoples.

It was 'false', Churchill wrote to Harry Hopkins two years later, to suggest that the demand for 'Unconditional Surrender' prolonged the war. 'Negotiation with Hitler was impossible,' he added. 'He was a maniac with supreme power to play his hand out to the end, which he did; and so did we.'[2]

When the Casablanca conference ended on January 24, Churchill drove with Roosevelt to Marrakech, a four-hour drive, to see again, and to show the President, the sunset tinting red the snow on the distant Atlas mountains, which he had seen, and been so moved by, six years earlier. Churchill's doctor was a witness to the scene at the Villa Taylor, that evening:

It was the hour when the sun was setting. To see the colours changing over the snow-capped mountains, Winston climbed on to the roof. It was so lovely that he insisted the President must see it. Two of his servants, by holding hands, made a chair with their arms, and in this fashion he was carried up the winding stairs to the roof-top, his paralysed legs dangling like the limbs of a ventriloquist's dummy, limp and flaccid. We stood gazing at the purple hills, where the light was changing every minute.

'It's the most lovely spot in the whole world,' the PM murmured.

When the President was carried back to his room, Wilson walked with Churchill in the garden of the villa, among the orange trees. 'I love these Americans,' he told his doctor. 'They behaved so generously.'

---

[1] Press Conference No. 875, Anfa Camp, French Morocco, 'Confidential', 12.15 p.m., 24 January 1943: Premier papers, 4/72/1, folios 172–82.

[2] Robert E. Sherwood, *The White House Papers of Harry L. Hopkins*, volume 2, London 1949, pages 692–3.

That night, at dinner, Roosevelt and Churchill made what the doctor described as 'affectionate little speeches to each other, and Winston sang'.[1] Averell Harriman, who was also present, recalled Roosevelt's talk of compulsory education, of fighting diseases through immunisation, and of birth control. 'Occasionally,' he noted, 'the PM interjected a pessimistic—and realistic—note. He doesn't like the new ideas but accepts them as inevitable.'[2]

Even as the dinner proceeded, the final conference documents were being drafted by Hopkins and Harriman, and brought in to Churchill and Roosevelt for their scrutiny and approval. The first was a letter, signed jointly by Roosevelt and Churchill, to be sent to their respective Chiefs of Staff. On the previous day the Combined Chiefs of Staff had presented Churchill and Roosevelt with their final report, in which they proposed the 'Husky' attack on Sicily to take place in July 1943, with a parallel suspension of the convoys to Russia on account of 'Husky's' shipping needs, the 'Anakim' attack on Burma to take place in November 1943; the destruction by air bombardment of the oil refineries at Ploesti in Rumania, and the build-up in Britain of fifteen Divisions of trained and equipped United States troops mounting in all to 384,000 men by 15 August 1943 and 938,000 men by 31 December 1943. This build-up was to enable the preparation of a raid to be launched from Britain against the northern coast of France during 1943 'with the primary object of provoking air battles and causing enemy losses'. As well as this limited attack, the Combined Chiefs of Staff also proposed preparing for an operation against the Cotentin Peninsula, set for 1 August 1943, aimed at 'seizing and holding a bridgehead and, if the state of German morale and resources permit, at vigorously exploiting successes'.[3] The Combined Chiefs of Staff also endorsed operation 'Pointblank', the joint Anglo-American strategic bombing offensive against Germany, aimed at disrupting German military and industrial production, and creating a decline in German morale, as a pre-requisite to a cross-Channel landing.

While 'cordially approving' these proposals, Churchill and Roosevelt, in a joint reply, stressed four points: the desirability of finding means of running the convoys to North Russia even through the period of the Sicily landings, the urgency of sending air reinforcements to the American forces in China and of finding personnel to make them fully operative, the importance of achieving a June landing in Sicily and the 'grave detriment to our interest which will be incurred by an

---

[1] Sir Charles Wilson, diary and recollections, 24 January 1943: Moran, *op. cit.*, page 82.
[2] Harriman notes: Abel and Harriman, *op. cit.*, page 191.
[3] Combined Chiefs of Staff Paper, No. 170/2, 'Final Report to the President and Prime Minister', 'Most Secret', 23 January 1943: Premier papers, 3/420/5, folios 12–23.

apparent suspension of activities during summer months', and, fourthly, the need to build up the United States striking force in Britain 'more quickly' so as to be able to 'profit by favourable August weather' for some form of cross-Channel attack, operation 'Sledge-hammer'.[1]

The second joint message agreed upon by Roosevelt and Churchill at Marrakech was a telegram to Stalin, setting out what had been decided at Casablanca: decisions and operations which, together with the 'powerful' Soviet offensive, 'may well bring Germany to her knees in 1943'.

Their 'main desire', Churchill and Roosevelt told Stalin, had been 'to divert strong German land and air forces from the Russian front and to send Russia the maximum flow of supplies'. No exertion would be spared to send Russia material assistance 'by every available route'. Once the Axis had been cleared out of North Africa, a large-scale amphibious operation would be launched in the Mediterranean, while, from the air bases set up in North Africa, Britain and the United States would launch 'an intensive bombardment of important Axis targets in southern Europe'. The allied bomber offensive against Germany from Britain would also be increased 'at a rapid rate'. As Churchill and Roosevelt explained:

We believe an increased tempo and weight of daylight and night attacks will lead to greatly increased material and morale damage in Germany and rapidly deplete German fighter strength. As you are aware, we are already containing more than half German air force in Western Europe and the Mediterranean. We have no doubt our intensified and diversified bombing offensive, together with the other operations which we are undertaking, will compel further withdrawals of German air and other forces from the Russian front.

Roosevelt and Churchill also explained to Stalin that they would concentrate on 'a strong American land and air force' in Britain which, combined with British forces, 'will prepare themselves to re-enter the continent of Europe as soon as practicable'. As the two leaders explained: 'These concentrations will certainly be known to our enemies, but they will not know where or when, or on what scale, we propose striking. They will therefore be compelled to divert both land and air forces to the shores of France, the Low Countries, Corsica, Sardinia, Sicily, the heel of Italy, Yugoslavia, Greece, Crete and the Dodecanese.'

This telegram from Roosevelt and Churchill to Stalin ended: 'Our ruling purpose is to bring to bear upon Germany and Italy the

[1] Note signed 'FDR, WSC', 25 January 1943: Premier papers, 3/420/5, folios 8–9.

maximum forces by land, sea and air which can be physically applied.'[1]

On receiving a copy of this telegram, the War Cabinet had sent Churchill several points of criticism. These were delivered to him in Marrakech, but answered from Cairo. As he informed his colleagues:

Stalin will be flattered by having attributed to him publicly the command of his victorious armies, never having been to Sandhurst or the Staff College. President has already imparted these points verbally to the journalists of the world for early release. I see also that in his general order to the Russian troops published this morning, he speaks of himself as 'Supreme Commander in Chief'.[2]

'Nothing in the world,' Churchill noted later that day, 'will be accepted by Stalin as an alternative to our placing 50 or 60 Divisions in France by the spring of this year. I think he will be disappointed and furious with the joint message. Therefore I thought it wise that the President and I should both stand together. After all our backs are broad.'[3]

There was also a sentence in the final communiqué to which the War Cabinet took exception, in which Churchill and Roosevelt declared, of the Casablanca conference, that 'nothing like this has ever occurred before'. 'It is a somewhat bombastic document,' noted Oliver Harvey, citing this phrase, 'and will give Stalin a wry smile and Goebbels a laugh.'[4] Churchill replied to criticism of this specific phrase: 'whereas most of the communiqué was the President's idea, this particular sentence was one of my own'. However, as the communiqué had been given to all the papers for release on the following day, 'and the President is thousands of miles away, I do not know what I can do'. Churchill added: 'It is perfectly true, though we might have left it for others to say so.'[5]

At 7.45 a.m. on the morning of January 25, Roosevelt left Marrakech to return to the United States. After Roosevelt had gone, Churchill brought out his paints, and, climbing the tower which he

---

[1] Prime Minister's Personal Telegram, T.74/3, 'Decypher Yourself', 'Most Immediate', 'Most Secret', Foreign Office London to British Embassy Moscow No. 35, 25 January 1943 (received in London as Stratagem No. 224 of 25 January 1943): Churchill papers, 20/105.

[2] 'Stratagem' No. 251, 'Most Secret', 26 January 1943: Premier papers, 4/72/1, folio 124.

[3] 'Stratagem' No. 255, 'Most Secret', 26 January 1943: Churchill papers, 20/127.

[4] Harvey diary, 26 January 1943: John Harvey (editor), op. cit., pages 213–14.

[5] 'Stratagem' No. 251, 'Most Secret', 26 January 1943: Churchill papers, 20/127.

climbed the night before with Roosevelt, 'gazed for a long time in silence at the Atlas mountains'. He seemed 'reluctant', wrote the doctor, 'to break the illusion of a holiday, which for a few hours had given him a chance to catch his breath'.[1]

At midday, Churchill telegraphed to his wife: 'We are here in a fairyland villa in Marrakech. Weather brilliant. Am going to paint a little this afternoon from roof of the same view of the pink gateway. My friend has gone. We motored here together yesterday 250 kilometres, being guarded by sentries all the way. They all admit I had not over-stated the beauty of this place.'[2]

That afternoon, Churchill painted a picture of the Atlas mountains from the tower of the Villa Taylor. It was the only picture which he painted during the whole war.

Churchill's hopes of going on from North Africa to Turkey had continued to be opposed in London. A telegram from the War Cabinet, reaching him on January 24, warned of the 'rebuff' which might result if Turkey, despite Churchill's personal advocacy, refused to come into the war.[3] 'Neither the President nor I are at all convinced by the arguments put forward,' Churchill had replied at once to Attlee. 'No one would wish to urge Turks to step outside their bounds, but mere occupation by us and use of Turkish aerodromes would give us the power to paralyse Ploesti oilfields with consequences judged by Chiefs of Staff to be of far reaching importance.' Beside this Churchill added, 'there could surely be no doubt that arrival of Turkey on Allied side in four or five months' time when the great operations on which we are resolved will be afoot, would be an invaluable makeweight to our war effort against our enemies'. Both Brooke and Roosevelt took this view, Churchill noted, Roosevelt agreeing with him that the rebuff 'if received, which is questionable, would not have any noticeable consequences. If, on the other hand, the Turks accept, it would surely not be in their interest to let this important contact with the winning side lapse into a failure. As to their pressing inordinate demands of munitions upon me and the President,' Churchill ended, 'I should naturally report these to you before agreeing with them.'[4]

---

[1] Sir Charles Wilson diary and recollections, 25 January 1943: Moran, *op. cit.*, pages 82–3.

[2] 'Stratagem' No. 238, 'Personal', 25 January 1943: Cabinet papers, 120/77.

[3] 'Telescope' No. 274, received at Casablanca, 24 January 1943: Cabinet papers, 120/79.

[4] 'Stratagem' No. 222, sent from Casablanca at 4.57 a.m., 25 January 1943: Cabinet papers, 120/77.

At a meeting of the War Cabinet at noon on January 25, it was agreed that, having regard to the 'strong views' expressed by both Churchill and Roosevelt, Churchill should be authorized to seek a meeting with Inönü.[1] From the Villa Taylor, Churchill replied that afternoon to Attlee and Eden:

I am most grateful to you for allowing me to try my plan. We may only get a snub, in which case it will be my fault, but I do not think it will do for me to wait for the Turkish answer. I think there is a shade of odds in favour of their coming. If they come, I think I can get things pushed on a bit. How difficult everything becomes once one cannot talk together!

'It is rather odd,' Churchill added, 'to think that this morning up to noon I had the option of either answering my questions tomorrow in the House of Commons or of meeting General Wilson in Cairo (D.V.).'[2]

On the evening of January 25, Churchill prepared to fly eastwards, as he had hoped, to Egypt. As a cover plan, hints were to be dropped that he was 'on his way' to Moscow.[3] 'We are just off over Atlas mountains which are gleaming with their sunlit snows,' Churchill telegraphed to Attlee and Eden at sunset on January 25. 'You can imagine how much I wish I were going to be with you tomorrow on the Bench but duty calls.'[4]

[1] War Cabinet No. 15 of 1943, 25 January 1943, Confidential Annex: Cabinet papers, 65/37.

[2] 'Stratagem' No. 235, 'Hush Most Secret', 25 January 1943: Churchill papers, 20/127.

[3] 'Stratagem' No. 201 (Sir Edward Bridges from John Martin), 9.04 p.m., 23 January 1943: Cabinet papers, 120/77.

[4] 'Stratagem' No. 243, 'Hush Most Secret', 25 January 1943: Churchill papers, 20/127.

19

'...it wouldn't be a bad moment to leave'

FLYING overnight from Casablanca, Churchill reached Cairo on the morning of January 26. 'We have now arrived here after a very comfortable journey,' he telegraphed to Attlee, Eden and the War Cabinet, 'and it is refreshing to feel that the enemy, who was almost at our gates, is now 1,500 miles away.'[1] It was, he wrote to the King, 'a very different state of affairs from what I left five months ago'.[2]

While in Cairo, on January 27, Churchill learned of further Russian successes in pushing the Germans back both from the Caucasus and Stalingrad. 'Pray accept my renewed expressions of admiration,' he telegraphed to Stalin, 'at the continued marvellous feats of the Soviet Armies.'[3] That same day he learned that President Inönü of Turkey would receive him near Adana, in western Turkey.

His object in going to Turkey, Churchill telegraphed to Smuts that same morning, 'will be to fit them up as well as possible with arms and to trust to the march of events to bring them in at the climax of the Mediterranean campaign'.[4]

Churchill was feeling confident that the combination of the Casablanca decisions, and the fact, as he told Smuts, that 'Montgomery is at Rommel's heels near the Tunisian border', was a turning point in the history of the war. While still in Cairo, he sent a personal message to all the Dominion Prime Ministers. The message ended:

Without wishing to indulge in any complacency, I cannot help feeling that things are quite definitely better than when I was last in Cairo, when the enemy was less than seventy miles away. If we should succeed in retaining

[1] 'Stratagem' No. 251, 'Most Secret', 26 January 1943: Churchill papers, 20/127.
[2] 'Stratagem' No. 259, 'Most Secret', 26 January 1943: Premier papers, 4/72/1, folio 81.
[3] 'Stratagem' No. 265, 'Most Secret and Personal', 27 January 1943: Churchill papers, 20/105.
[4] 'Stratagem' No. 273, 'Most Secret', 27 January 1943: Cabinet papers, 120/77.

the initiative in all theatres, as does not seem impossible, and if we can sincerely feel that we have brought every possible division or fighting unit of our forces into the closest and most continuous contact with the enemy from now on, we might well regard the world situation as by no means devoid of favourable features. Without the cohesion and unity of the entire British Empire and Commonwealth of Nations through periods of desperate peril and forlorn outlook, the freedom and decencies of civilized mankind might well have sunk for ever into the abyss.[1]

The atmosphere in Cairo was of relief and hope. It was also a time of relaxation. 'The PM had an enormous breakfast,' Brigadier Jacob noted on January 27, 'consisting of 2 eggs, ham and chicken, coffee, toast, butter and marmalade, two mangoes, and a glass of orange juice as well.'[2] Lying in his bed, in a gauze anti-mosquito net, Churchill read the papers that had arrived from Casablanca, and prepared for his Turkish visit. 'All well here,' he telegraphed to his wife, 'and much better than last time. Am also hopeful of the new adventure.'[3]

It was on January 27 that American heavy bombers, based in Britain, made their first major air raid on Germany, a daylight raid on the port of Wilhelmshaven. In the air battle during the raid, twenty-two German aircraft were shot down, for a loss of three American. 'It seems to me most important,' Churchill telegraphed to Sir Archibald Sinclair that same day, 'to keep on at the big city whenever the weather allows lest it be thought their feeble but vaunted reprisals have damped our ardour.'[4]

Churchill remained in Cairo for four days, lunching on January 28 with Captain Deakin, his former research assistant of the last three pre-war years, who was in Cairo with SOE. He also saw, that same evening, the head of SOE in the Middle East, Colonel Keble.[5]

Churchill's meetings with Deakin and Keble were to be decisive for British policy towards the resistance forces in German and Italian occupied Yugoslavia. As a result of what he learnt from Deakin and Keble, Churchill asked for a note to be prepared about the respective fighting abilities, regions and objectives of the Serb resistance leader General Mihailovic, whom Britain was currently supporting, and the

[1] 'Stratagem' No. 272, 'Most Secret', 27 January 1943: Churchill papers, 20/105.
[2] Jacob notes for 27 January 1943: Jacob papers.
[3] 'Stratagem' No. 271, 'Private', sent at 9 p.m., 27 January 1943: Cabinet papers, 120/77.
[4] 'Stratagem' No. 264, sent at 12.30 p.m., 27 January 1943: Cabinet papers, 120/77. The principal German reprisal raid had taken place in the London area on 20 January 1943. In all, 328 civilians were killed in Britain that January.
[5] Churchill Engagement Cards, 28 January 1943. SOE, Special Operations Executive, under the Ministerial control of Lord Selborne, was responsible for British operations throughout German-occupied Europe.

forces in Croatia and Slovenia under the command of the partisan leader Josip Broz Tito, which were receiving no outside help, and which the Germans were declaring to be Communist.

The report, which was completed in two days, noted that between February 1942 and January 1943 some twenty-five air sorties had been made over Yugoslavia, dropping stores, arms, explosives and personnel in areas under the control of General Mihailovic. A British Mission of four officers and three wireless operators had been established at Mihailovic's headquarters. The groups under Mihailovic, the note pointed out, were holding down three German and six Bulgarian divisions. But there were also, in the more northern regions of Croatia and Slovenia, 'other resisting elements' not under Mihailovic's command. These elements were led by students, schoolmasters and skilled workers 'who are politically extreme Left', but the rank and file, which was not racially confined to Croats and Slovenes, but contained many Serbs, were 'peasants, deserters from Italian and Croat armies, and refugees whose homes have been destroyed and who are not necessarily politically minded'. It was 'not accurate to adopt the German technique of branding the whole movement as "Communist"'.

Most important, the note pointed out that the activity of these Croat and Slovene partisan forces had 'proved sufficient' to tie down thirty divisions in areas 'vital' both to Italy's communications with the Balkans and to Germany's communications between her armies in Greece, her allies in Bulgaria and Rumania, and central Europe.

The 'evidence of recent months' was that Mihailovic had 'but slender contact' with these areas, and 'little prospect' of widening sufficiently the basis of support for his movement in those two regions. If resistance in Croatia and Slovenia was to be maintained, and 'raised to a level sufficiently effective to be of real military value to the Allied war effort', the note advised, 'aid must be organized independently of the existing programme regarding General Mihailovic'.

The note went on to point out that 'at the present time' no aid 'from any quarter' was reaching the Croat and Slovene partisans, but that if this situation continued, 'either the Russians or the Americans will, for different reasons, take a practical interest'. This would 'inevitably' lead to the weakening 'of the whole British position'. The prospect of two members of the United Nations backing 'mutually antagonistic groups' in Yugoslavia 'could only have lamentable consequences'.

The note went on to advise British aid to the 'other resisting elements' besides Mihailovic, and the despatch of British officers to both sides 'in a position to bring pressure to bear on either side by withholding supplies'. The words 'on either side' were underlined.

To send provisions and supplies to Croatia and Slovenia, as well as to Serbia, further aircraft would have to be allocated, over and above the existing single flight of four aircraft, and because of the greater distance to Croatia and Slovenia, Liberators alone would be effective: two extra flights of four Liberators each were suggested.[1]

Churchill, who accepted these arguments, subsequently showed the note to Eisenhower, whom he asked for help towards providing the extra Liberators.[2] The first two British officers to be parachuted into Tito's headquarters in German-occupied Yugoslavia were Churchill's former research assistant, Captain F. W. D. Deakin, and Captain William F. Stuart.

Concerned that the secrecy of his imminent journey to Turkey should be maintained, on January 29 Churchill telegraphed to Stalin: 'I should be obliged if you would not contradict any rumour you may hear that I am coming again to Moscow, because it is thought important my real movements, of which I have informed you, should be secret for a few days.'[3] Stalin willingly accepted his role as decoy.

While still in Cairo on January 29, Churchill dictated a lengthy statement of the British position, 'from which', as Brigadier Jacob noted, 'he intended to speak when he met President Inönü'. The paper reached the Joint Planning Staff 'bit by bit, hot from the typewriter, for the Commanders-in-Chief to check'. Brooke, Portal and Pound then made 'a few alterations', which Brooke took to Churchill.[4]

During the evening, Portal learned that one of the two Liberator bombers returning to England from Casablanca had crashed, and two members of the British delegation had been killed.[5] On Brooke's instructions, the news was kept from Churchill 'in view of tomorrow's journey'.[6] The second Liberator, with Pound, Mountbatten, Harriman and Ismay on board, had arrived without incident.

On the morning of January 30, Churchill himself flew by Liberator from Cairo to Adana. Operation 'Satrap' had begun. Sir Alexander Cadogan, who had flown out to Cairo to accompany Churchill to Turkey, noted that the Prime Minister's bomber, his favourite

---

[1] B1/2/1/134/78. 'Operations in Yugoslavia', 30 January 1943, Chiefs of Staff Paper No. 44 of 1943 of 11 February 1943, Annex: Cabinet papers, 80/39, folios 153–6.
[2] Chiefs of Staff Paper No. 44 of 1943, 'Support of Operations in Yugoslavia', 11 February 1943: Cabinet papers, 80/39, folio 152.
[3] 'Stratagem' No. 296, 'Most Secret', 29 January 1943: Cabinet papers, 120/77.
[4] Jacob notes for 29 January 1943: Jacob papers.
[5] Brigadier Dykes and Brigadier Stewart.
[6] Jacob notes for 29 January 1943: Jacob papers.

'Commando', 'has been made very comfortable, with a saloon with armchairs and windows'. Flying up the coast of Palestine and Syria, the Liberator landed at Adana after a four-hour flight. After lunching in a special train which had been set on a siding for the British delegation, Churchill was taken in this train 'over the flat, flooded country', as Cadogan noted in his diary, for about six miles, to a spot where, on a siding, they found Inönü's train awaiting them.[1] The two trains were then joined together. 'The PM met President Inönü when the two trains linked,' Brigadier Jacob noted. His account continued:

The latter was in a small saloon which formed part of his private coach. This contained a table in the middle and three or four deep armchairs covered with cherry-coloured silk. The two head men and the Ministers and the Ambassador sat themselves down in the armchairs and other smaller chairs round the edge, and then gradually more and more people were squeezed in. Marshal Chakmak was there, and our Generals were brought in and introduced. Then the more junior members of our party.

The PM was conducting proceedings in French, and made the necessary introductions. When my turn came, he said that I was the 'fils du Marechal Jacob', and then turning to Marshal Chakmak he said, 'Vous savez. Aux Indes.' Chakmak looked pretty blank of course, but bowed politely! All the time the Press were doing their best to insert themselves and to take photographs, till finally the saloon resembled the Black Hole of Calcutta. However, everything comes to an end at last, and the PM and the President decided that there should be a formal meeting of the two delegations forthwith.[2]

'We went along and were presented,' Cadogan noted in his diary, 'and then left PM and President alone together for half an hour. When I asked PM later what had happened, he said "Nothing".'[3]

On the previous day, in Cairo, Churchill had prepared for Inönü a substantial appraisal of the war situation. This he was now ready to read to the Turks. The plan was for him to read it out in English, with a member of the British Embassy in Ankara, Paul Falla, translating it into French for the benefit of the Turks. Paul Falla later recalled:

Churchill led off with a set piece reviewing Anglo-Turkish relations from before the 'terrible slash' (I think he called it) of 1914, and describing how the Allied forces were getting on. I was supposed to turn this into French as he went along (I mean by the 'consecutive' method), but (a) I was seated too far down the table (and many Turks are deaf) and (b) when I rendered '1500 miles' as '2500 kilometres' he thought I had got the figure wrong,

[1] Cadogan diary, 30 January 1943: David Dilks (editor), op. cit., page 508.
[2] Jacob notes for 30 January 1943: Jacob papers.
[3] Cadogan diary, 30 January 1943: David Dilks (editor), op. cit., page 509.

waved me aside and read from his typescript in Churchill-French (*moovay* 'to move' (troops) and so on).[1]

Churchill now proceeded to translate on the spot what he had written in his paper. As Brigadier Jacob noted:

This amounted to doing orally with no time for thought or preparation, a long Unseen into French, no small task.

The PM's French is fairly fluent, and he was rarely stuck for a word. But of course he could only make a perfectly literal translation, and his accent is almost pure English. The result was therefore completely intelligible to all the English present even if they had no knowledge of the language beyond what they learnt at school; but I feel sure the Turks could only have formed a very hazy idea of what the whole thing was about.

The PM waded resolutely on, and came out at the far end bloody but unbowed. It was really quite a tour de force, of an unusual kind! Peculiar though it all was, I do not think anyone felt like laughing. They couldn't help admiring his determination and self-possession. The Turks were much too polite to express any surprise or amusement.[2]

Churchill's paper stressed that if Germany, in search of a route to the oil of Iraq and Persia, were to attack Turkey, Britain and the United States could be relied upon to come to Turkey's aid, with troops, weapons and aircraft. Prudence, he argued, would lead Turkey to accept this aid even before the danger was imminent. More airfields could be prepared before the summer, and equipped with material, spare parts and field workshops. 'The nests must be made,' Churchill told Inönü, 'so that the birds can fly there at once. Unless the nests are ready, the birds cannot live and cannot strike. The work, which is really vital to the defence of Turkey, should be pushed forward with frantic energy, and British and American engineers and Air Force officers volunteer their services to any extent that may be needed.'

Churchill then set out the Allied hopes, based upon the decisions of the Casablanca conference, and he did so in as enticing a way as possible to show the Turks the merits of participation. 'Naturally,' he said, 'we cannot give details about the exact plans and dates, but our intention is to destroy Italy; shatter her entirely; beat her out of the war, both by terrific bombing from Tunis and from Great Britain and by heavy attacks over the sea, for which great preparations are required and are being made.' The 'breaking down' of Italy, Churchill

[1] Paul S. Falla, letter to the author, 29 October 1984 (Turkish national day). Falla added: 'I had not previously seen Churchill in the flesh. Later I was in the "office" carriage with cypher clerks, Mrs Sterndale-Bennett (the Minister's wife) typing like mad, and so on. WSC came through from the next carriage and of course we all stood up. He demurred with "I beg you" or the like, in quite a sincere and touching way. I was struck then by his pink, fluffy, almost babyish appearance.'

[2] Jacob notes for 30 January 1943: Jacob papers.

added, 'would lead to contact with the Western Balkans and with the highly hopeful resistance maintained both by General Mihailovic in Serbia and the Partisans in Croatia and Slovenia'. Churchill continued:

According to our expectations and reasonable hopes, we shall drive the enemy from the coasts of Africa into the sea before the summer, and perhaps much earlier. In the event the summer months will see in the Mediterranean the largest operations it is in the power of Great Britain and the United States to conduct. These operations, and above all the Italian attitude, will cause the very greatest agitation throughout the Balkans. The further advance of the Russian armies cannot be excluded. Operations across the Black Sea must be considered a possibility, with their superior fleet.

This would be a moment of danger for Germany. 'It is therefore in the summer,' Churchill told the Turks, 'that we must consider the crisis temperature will rise very high, and the need for Turkey to be secure will be paramount.'

Churchill told Inönü that the British and Americans 'are quite sure that we shall win'. That was why, he said, Roosevelt had called the Casablanca conference 'the "Unconditional Surrender Conference"'. Both nations were peaceful nations 'who had made very little preparation for the war. But we are now becoming warlike nations, with far greater resources of men and munitions than the Germans, Japanese and Italians can produce.'[1] Inönü replied that he had listened to Churchill's statement 'with great attention'. As to the help which might be accorded Turkey if she were attacked, he said, the 'whole matter was governed by political considerations, Turkey being at present neutral'. There was 'no suggestion', Churchill insisted, 'of asking Turkey to make any engagement'.[2]

The talks between Churchill and Inönü were resumed in the early evening. Cadogan was impressed by the way in which Churchill conducted them. The Turks, he felt, were 'very relieved to find that we aren't pressing them to do anything definite. Frightened, of course, of Russia, about which we gave them such reassurances as we could.'[3] Early in the discussion, when Inönü remarked that Turkey 'had not taken an active part in any way' in the war, Churchill interrupted to say that 'he made no reproach against Turkey for this'. Later, Churchill told Inönü that after the war 'the United States would be the strongest and most important nation', committed to a 'solid international structure', much stronger than the League of Nations had been, 'to disarm the oppressors and maintain international justice'.

[1] 'First Meeting (General)', 5.30 p.m., 30 January 1943: Premier papers, 3/446/3, Annex (1).
[2] 'First Meeting (General)', 5.30 p.m., 30 January 1943: Premier papers, 3/446/3.
[3] Cadogan diary, 30 January 1943: David Dilks (editor), op. cit., page 509.

Russia would be a part of this organization. But, he warned, 'Post-war Russia might not be the same as the Russia of former years; it might be even more imperialistic.' For that reason, Turkey's 'best protection' lay in an international arrangement, 'perhaps accompanied by special guarantees applying to her'.

Turkish action 'on our side', Churchill then asserted, 'would place her on the side of the Great Powers and would ensure that Turkey would find herself together with the United Kingdom and the United States'. This would furnish 'an absolute guarantee' that Russia would not act against Turkey. He, Churchill, 'would not be a friend of Russia if she imitated Germany'. If she did so, 'we should arrange the best possible combination against her, and he would not hesitate to say so to Stalin'.

At one point in the discussion it was the Turkish Prime Minister, Sukru Saracoglu, who took up the questioning. What 'line' would Britain take, he asked, if Russia adopted a policy 'out of harmony' with her relations with Britain. Churchill replied that he had seen Molotov and Stalin and his impression was 'that both desired a peaceful and friendly association with the United Kingdom and the United States'. In the economic sphere, Great Britain and the United States 'had much to give to Russia and they could help in the reparation of Russia's losses'.

'He could not see twenty years ahead,' Churchill told the Turkish Prime Minister, 'but we had, nevertheless, made a treaty for twenty years. He thought Russia would concentrate on reconstruction for the next ten years. There would probably be changes; communism had already been modified. He thought we should live in good relations with Russia and, if Great Britain and the United States acted together and maintained a strong air force, they should be able to ensure a period of stability. Russia might even gain by this. She possessed vast undeveloped areas, for instance, in Siberia.'

The minutes of the discussion continued:

M. Saracoglu noted that the Prime Minister had expressed the view that Russia would become imperialistic. This made it necessary for Turkey to be very prudent.

The Prime Minister remarked that there would be an international organization to secure peace and security which would be stronger than the League of Nations. He was not afraid of communism.

M. Saracoglu said that he looked for something more real. All Europe was full of Slavs and Communists. All the defeated countries would become Bolshevist and Slav if Germany was beaten.

The Prime Minister said that this might be possible but things did not always turn out as badly as was expected. But if they did so it was better that

Turkey should be strong and closely associated with the United Kingdom and the United States.

'All agreed,' the minutes noted, 'to the necessity of this.' [1]

That night there was what Cadogan described as a 'large and convivial dinner' in Inönü's coach. 'Went off quite well,' he noted. 'PM held forth to us for a bit afterwards in our saloon, but we got to bed soon after midnight. He's right not to press the Turks.' [2]

Churchill slept that night in his Turkish train. 'I arrived here yesterday, and have had long and most friendly exchanges of views,' he telegraphed to Attlee on the morning of January 31. Of the Turkish President, Prime Minister and Foreign Minister, Churchill commented: 'I found them excellent to deal with and am sure we can hope for good results.' [3] That morning, Churchill dictated a paper, which he called 'pensées matinales' about post-war security. Summoning Cadogan to read it, he told him that he proposed giving it to Inönü at their final meeting later that morning. 'I didn't see anything much wrong with it,' Cadogan noted, 'though we altered a few details. He was awfully proud of it.' [4]

At 11 o'clock that morning, Churchill had his third and final meeting with Inönü. At the meeting, Churchill 'emphasized', as the minutes recorded, 'that he was not asking Turkey to give any engagement, but it was as well to face these possibilities and to be prepared for all eventualities'. He would 'never ask Turkey to rush into a disaster', however, 'for that would be equally a disaster for ourselves'. [5]

While Churchill and Inönü were talking, the military members of the British delegation were talking to their Turkish opposite numbers. [6]

As a result of these talks, the Turkish military authorities agreed to give Britain a list of the naval, military and air equipment 'required by the Turkish forces', and would prepare a scheme for the 'reception, utilization and maintenance' of all 'modern equipment' Britain might send. A plan would also be prepared by British Staff officers, to be sent to Ankara 'forthwith' and in collaboration with the Turkish General Staff, 'for the movement and subsequent maintenance of British forces into Turkey in the event of Turkey being drawn into the

---

[1] 'Second Meeting (Political)', 30 January 1943: Premier papers, 3/446/3.
[2] Cadogan diary, 30 January 1943: David Dilks (editor), op. cit., page 509.
[3] 'Stratagem' No. 309, 'Most Secret', 31 January 1943: Cabinet papers, 120/77.
[4] Cadogan diary, 31 January 1943: David Dilks (editor), op. cit., pages 509-11.
[5] 'Fourth Meeting (Political)', 11.30 a.m., 31 January 1943: Premier papers, 3/446/3.
[6] 'Fifth Meeting (Military)', 11.45 a.m., 31 January 1943: Premier papers, 3/446/3. The British representatives included General Brooke, General Maitland Wilson, and General Alexander. The Turkish representations were headed by Marshal Chakmak, Chief of the Turkish General Staff.

war'. This plan would show 'for each month in 1943' the size and nature of these forces, and, when made, would be kept 'continually up to date'.[1]

'You must understand,' Churchill telegraphed to Attlee later that day, 'that I pursued a method of perfect trust and confidence, asking for no engagement but giving to the utmost in our power.' Inönü had told Churchill that he was 'in complete sympathy' with Britain. 'I find him a very agreeable man,' Churchill reported, 'and we made friends at once. Indeed, he was most warm and cordial in all his attitude and he and his ministers reiterated again and again that they longed for the victory of England.'

In his telegram to Attlee, Churchill stressed that when he had made it clear to the Turks 'that I did not wish them to enter the war in any circumstances which would lead to Turkish disaster, which would be our disaster too, but that when the circumstances are favourable I was sure it would be in the interests of Turkey to play her part', this was accepted 'with lively accord'. When Churchill asked the Turks if they would have trouble with the Germans over his visit, 'they said they did not care'.[2]

Churchill's 'morning thoughts' also met with Inönü's approval, asserting as they did that a new world organization would, after the war, embody the spirit, but lack the weaknesses, of the pre-war League of Nations. 'Great Britain,' Churchill asserted, 'will certainly do her utmost to organise coalition resistance to any act of aggression committed by any Power. . . .'[3] That afternoon Churchill was to fly in his Liberator from Adana to Cyprus. But, as Brigadier Jacob noted:

Just before lunch the PM caused a slight earth tremor by saying that he would not go to Cyprus, as he must get back to Cairo and do a lot of telegraphing to Roosevelt, Stalin and the War Cabinet, so as to give them the results of the meeting. We all then went in to lunch, it being already 1.30 and the train gradually began to move off to get back to Adana. The lunch was an occasion for further complimentary speeches and much back-slapping. Everyone announced themselves to be 'd'accord'. At 2.40 the PM came striding down the corridor announcing: 'Come on! We have only 5 minutes to spare if we are to reach Cairo before dark.' Everyone rushed for their baggage, and hurled themselves helter skelter into the waiting cars. . . .[4]

---

[1] 'Stratagem' C/5, 'Most Secret', 1 February 1943: Cabinet papers, 120/77.

[2] 'Stratagem' C/3, 'Most Secret', 31 January 1943: Churchill papers, 20/127. Churchill sent an identical telegram to Roosevelt, with the added opening sentence: 'I hope indeed you are safely returned and are not unduly tired.' ('Stratagem' C/Unnumbered, 1 February 1943: Cabinet papers, 120/77.)

[3] 'Stratagem' C/6, 'Most Secret', 1 February 1943: Churchill papers, 20/105.

[4] Jacob notes, 30 January 1943: Jacob papers.

On reaching the plane, Churchill told the pilot that they would be going to Cairo. 'Pilot said that was the first he had heard of it,' Cadogan noted in his diary, 'he thought we were bound for Cyprus. Before he could start up engines, PM changed again, and said we would go to Cyprus.' [1] Sir Charles Wilson recorded the sequel:

The engines roared, we began to move, and at that moment the pilot carelessly allowed the right wheel to leave the runway, whereupon the big tyre at once sank a foot into the mud. The engines raced, but nothing happened. We were bogged. The Turks looked sympathetic.

I was afraid that the PM might be upset by the delay, but when I looked round he was nowhere to be seen. I found him surrounded by Turks, who were all talking at once. Winston had taken charge in his best Sidney Street manner, and kept pointing to the wheel and gesticulating to the Turks. If only he could make them understand his plan.

Lorries with chains appeared, but all were of no avail. The Turks crept away. Spades were produced and men dug round the sunken wheel. The PM removed his hat and mopped his head. At last it was decided that we must change aeroplanes. [2]

It was four o'clock when Churchill's plane left Adana. An hour and a half later it landed in Nicosia, where Churchill was the guest of Sir Charles Wooley, the Governor of Cyprus. 'Tea on arrival,' Cadogan noted in his diary, 'and then Winston put me on to draft telegrams.' That night Cadogan discussed the telegrams with Churchill in his bedroom, 'and got to bed fairly early'. [3] The telegrams included a detailed account of the agreements reached at Adana, and a copy of Churchill's 'Morning Thoughts', given the more formal title, 'Note on Post War Security.' [4]

Churchill spent the night of January 31 in Cyprus, telling the island's notables at Government House on the following day that the United Nations would 'march forward from strength to strength until unconditional surrender is extorted from those who have laid the world in havoc and in ruins'. [5] That same day he spoke to the Fourth Hussars, the regiment of which he was Colonel in Chief, and now under Brigadier Moffatt's Command. 'Winston was grand,' Moffatt wrote to his wife, 'he radiated confidence and made a most stirring speech to the troops.' [6] Half a million British and American troops were in

---

[1] Cadogan diary, 31 January 1943: David Dilks (editor), *op. cit.*, pages 509–11.
[2] Sir Charles Wilson diary, 31 January 1943: Moran, *op. cit.*, pages 86–7.
[3] Cadogan diary, 31 January 1943: David Dilks (editor), *op. cit.*, pages 509–11.
[4] 'Stratagem' C/6, 'Most Secret', 1 February 1943: Cabinet papers, 120/77.
[5] Speech of 1 February 1943 (Cyprus): Churchill papers, 9/161.
[6] Letter from Brigadier J. Moffatt to his wife (in England): Churchill papers, 20/87. Moffatt's son had been killed in action, flying off Malta, in September 1942.

North Africa, Churchill told the assembled soldiers, 'and that is not all. They will soon be turning North, across the Mediterranean, carrying the war to a tense climax.'[1] In a telegram to General Barnes, his fellow officer of half a century earlier, Churchill reported that he had found their former regiment 'in fine fettle and up to full strength'.[2]

That afternoon Churchill returned to Cairo, where he learned of the surrender of the German Sixth Army at Stalingrad, part of a 'tremendous feat of arms', he told a Press Conference that evening, 'performed by our Russian Ally under the general command and direction of Premier Stalin, a great warrior, and a name which will rank with those most honoured and most lasting in the history of the Russian people'.[3]

Churchill spent the night of February 1 in Cairo. 'I hope to pay a surprise visit to Eisenhower's Headquarters for a few hours on my way home,' he telegraphed to Eden on February 1, on learning of the American decision to recognize General Giraud as the authority for all French interests in North Africa, 'and will go into the matter on the spot with those concerned'.[4] From Cairo, on February 1, Churchill took up a question which Stalin had asked Roosevelt in a recent telegram, about the 'slowing down' of the Allied operations in North Africa. 'So far as the British Eighth Army is concerned,' Churchill telegraphed to Stalin, 'we have since then taken Tripoli, and hope shortly to enter Tunisia in force and drive the enemy from the Mareth and Gabes positions. The clearing and restoring of the harbour at Tripoli is proceeding with all speed, but at present our line of communications runs to Benghazi, and part even to Cairo, 1,500 miles away.' The British First Army, Churchill added, 'reinforced by strong American forces, is bringing its supplies forward, and will attack in conjunction with the Eighth Army as soon as possible'. 'The wet weather was a serious factor,' as were also the communications, 'which, both by road and rail, are slender and 500 miles long.' However, Churchill stressed the hope 'that the enemy will be completely destroyed or driven from the African shore by the end of April, and perhaps earlier'.

His 'own estimate' of German strength, Churchill told Stalin, was that there were now 150,000 German and Italian troops in North Africa, of whom 'perhaps 40,000 only are fighting troops and weak in weapons'. This estimate, Churchill noted, 'is based on good

---

[1] Speech of 1 February 1943 (Cyprus): Churchill papers, 9/161.
[2] 'Stratagem' No. 328, 2 February 1943: Cabinet papers, 120/77.
[3] Speech of 1 February 1943 (Cairo): Churchill papers, 9/161.
[4] 'Stratagem' No. 323, 'Most Secret', 1 February 1943: Churchill papers, 20/127.

information', in fact, though he did not say so, the regular reading of the Panzer Army Africa's instructions and messages. 'The destruction of these German forces,' Churchill added, 'is our immediate aim.'

'Please accept my congratulations,' Churchill ended, 'on the surrender of Field Marshal Paulus and the end of the German Sixth Army. This is indeed a wonderful achievement.' [1] Eight German generals, and 45,000 troops, had been captured in two days. More than 146,000 Germans had been killed.

In this telegram to Stalin of February 1, Churchill also reported that the Turkish Government was 'of course, apprehensive of their position after the war in view of the great strength of the Soviet Republic'. Churchill added: 'I told them that in my experience the USSR had never broken an engagement or treaty; that the time for them to make a good arrangement was now, and that the safest place for Turkey was to have a seat with the victors, as a belligerent, at the peace table. All this I said in our common interest in accordance with our Alliance, and I hope you will approve.' [2] Eight days later, Churchill telegraphed to Inönü: 'I cannot conceal my desire for a warm renewal of friendship between Russia and Turkey similar to that achieved by Mustafa Kemal. Thus Turkey while increasing her own defences would stand between two victorious friends.' He was thinking 'not only of the war', Churchill explained, 'but of the post war period'. [3]

On January 30, Stalin had telegraphed to Roosevelt and Churchill, asking what had been decided at Casablanca. [4] 'I think he is entitled to more precise information,' Churchill informed Roosevelt from Cairo on February 2, 'and no-one can keep secrets better.' He should therefore be told, Churchill believed, of the plans to attack Italy across the central Mediterranean 'with the object of promoting an Italian collapse, and establishing contact with Yugoslavia'. The Anglo-American force would expect to meet with 'serious opposition' from German forces. 'If not, our task will be much easier.' This operation, involving 300,000 to 400,000 men, was intended to take place 'in July or earlier if possible'. Stalin should also be told of the Anglo-American plan 'for a heavy operation across the Channel' in August, for which between

[1] Prime Minister's Personal Telegram, T.92/3, 'Stratagem' No. 320 from Cairo, 1 February 1943, No. 54 from Foreign Office (London) to Moscow, 'Most Immediate', 2 February 1943: Cabinet papers, 120/714.

[2] Prime Minister's Personal Telegram, T.92/6, 'Stratagem' No. 320 from Cairo, 1 February 1943, No. 54 from Foreign Office to Moscow, 'Most Immediate', 2 February 1943: Cabinet papers, 120/714.

[3] Prime Minister's Personal Telegram, T.122/3, 'Personal and Secret', 9 February 1943: Cabinet papers, 120/714.

[4] 'Most Secret', 'Kremlin', 30 January 1943: Churchill papers, 20/105.

17 and 20 British and United States divisions would be available, of which 4 to 7 would be United States divisions. This operation would involve at least 850,000 men. The 'limiting factor' would be the number of assault landing craft available.

Churchill also wanted Stalin to know that, in accepting these conclusions of their Combined Chiefs of Staff, he and Roosevelt had 'enjoined upon them the need for the utmost speed and for reinforcing the attacks to the extreme limit that is humanly possible'.[1]

From Cairo, Churchill also exhorted Wavell to press ahead with plans for the reconquest of Burma, operation 'Anakim'. If the difficulties should prove insoluble, Churchill telegraphed, 'let it be only after the most intense effort in human power to overcome them'. 'Very great forces' had been gathered in India, Churchill added, 'and it would be a disaster if they were to stand idle at a time when the whole Empire must be in the closest contact with the enemy.'[2]

In reply, Wavell pointed out that 'the forces gathered' in India, as Churchill had called them, were 'not excessive for defence of country two thirds size of Europe which until lately had very real threat from East and possible threat from West besides internal danger', but that nevertheless he had 'every intention to use these forces offensively to maximum capacity'. It was because of cuts in shipping, necessary for operations elsewhere, that India, Wavell explained, 'is still short of much essential equipment'.[3]

Churchill, still travelling as 'Colonel Frankland', now made plans to visit Eisenhower, who was in Algiers with Admiral Sir Andrew Cunningham. 'I hope,' Churchill telegraphed to Eisenhower from Cairo, 'that the Admiral will be able to give our party bath and breakfast and that it will be agreeable to you if I lunch with you in a small circle.' His arrival should be kept secret. He would travel from the airfield to Cunningham's villa 'in a closed station wagon'.[4]

On the evening of February 2, Churchill dined at the British Embassy in Cairo. Cadogan, who was present, noted in his diary: 'Sat between Winston and Randolph. The latter a dreadful young man.

---

[1] Prime Minister's Personal Telegram, T.96/3, 'Stratagem' No. 331, 'Most Secret', 2 February 1943: Churchill papers, 20/105.
[2] Prime Minister's Personal Telegram, T.97/3, 'Stratagem' No. 335, 'Most Secret', 2 February 1943: Churchill papers, 20/105.
[3] CY/317, 'Most Secret and Personal', 4 February 1943: Churchill papers, 20/106.
[4] Prime Minister's Personal Telegram, T.98/3, 'Stratagem' No. 338, 'Personal and Most Secret', February 1943: Churchill papers, 20/105. Churchill's party was to consist of General Brooke, Sir Alexander Cadogan, Brigadier Jacob, Leslie Rowan (in place of John Martin), Sir Charles Wilson, Commander Thompson, Patrick Kinna, Sawyers the valet and a detective. Admiral Sir Andrew Cunningham, Commander-in-Chief, Mediterranean, was appointed First Sea Lord in October 1943, when he was succeeded in the Mediterranean by his cousin, Admiral Sir John Cunningham (formerly Chief of Supplies and Transport at the Admiralty, and Commander-in-Chief, Levant).

He has been an incubus on our party ever since Casablanca.' Cadogan added: 'Very silly of Winston to take him about. Father and son snapped at each other across me, which was disconcerting. However, we got Winston on to the Omdurman campaign, on which he held forth, at the dinner-table, till 11.30.'[1]

On the following morning, February 3, Churchill flew by Liberator from Cairo across the Western Desert to the airfield at Castel Benito, outside Tripoli, a flight of nearly six hours. From the airfield he was driven to Eighth Army headquarters. Brigadier Jacob, who followed with Patrick Kinna in a second Liberator, reached the camp in time to find Churchill 'in the middle of making an address to the officers and men of 8th Army HQ in a natural little amphitheatre'.[2] 'PM was in his element when he addressed the troops,' noted Charles Wilson. 'No one can do this sort of thing so well.'[3]

In his speech, Churchill pointed out that the Eighth Army had driven the German forces 'from pillar to post' more than 1,400 miles, a distance 'as far as from London to Moscow', and had altered the face of the war 'in a most remarkable way'. The 'days of your victories are by no means at an end', he declared. With the Eighth Army in the east, and the First British Army, and American and French forces within 30 or 40 miles of Bizerta and Tunis in the west, 'we may hope to achieve the final destruction or expulsion from the shores of Africa of every armed German or Italian'. Churchill ended his speech by telling the assembled soldiers and airmen: 'after the war when a man is asked what he did it will be quite sufficient for him to say, "I marched and fought with the Desert Army". And when history is written and all the facts are known, your feats will gleam and glow and will be a source of song and story long after we who are gathered here have passed away.'[4]

Churchill spent the night in one of Montgomery's three converted caravans. On the following morning, February 4, in an armoured car with Montgomery and General Leese, Commander of the Tenth Corps, he was driven into Tripoli. 'Great precaution had been taken,' noted Brigadier Jacob, 'and armed men stood on every knoll and by every homestead.' In Tripoli itself, the assembled British forces were amazed to see the Prime Minister in their midst. As his car came opposite each unit, Jacob noted, 'they removed headdresses and gave three cheers'.[5]

[1] Cadogan diary, 2 February 1943: David Dilks (editor), op. cit., page 511.
[2] Jacob notes for 3 February 1943: Jacob papers.
[3] Wilson diary and recollections, for 3 February 1943: Moran, op. cit., page 87.
[4] Speech of 3 February 1943, Eighth Army Headquarters: Churchill papers, 9/161.
[5] Jacob notes for 4 February 1943: Jacob papers.

In the main square of Tripoli, Churchill took the march past of the 51st Division. 'All around were the veterans of the Eighth Army,' Jacob noted, 'standing in the last city of Mussolini's Empire. No wonder the tears rolled down the Prime Minister's cheeks as he took the salute. . . .' It was an occasion, Jacob added, 'that made all the anxiety, the disappointments, the hardships and the setbacks of the Middle East campaign seem to be robbed of their sting. The bitter moment in the White House when Tobruk fell was swallowed up in the joy of the morning in Tripoli.'[1]

Churchill lunched that day at an army picnic provided by Montgomery. For a brief moment the war intruded, with puffs of shell burst high up in the sky as a German reconnaissance aircraft was seen and chased away. After lunch, Churchill was shown various captured German mines and other devices, and a British 'Scorpion' anti-mine vehicle, first used at Alamein.[2] Churchill was then driven on again to an open space where 8,000 men of the New Zealand Division were drawn up in six masses of company columns, at the head of which stood Lieutenant-General Sir Bernard Freyberg, their commander.

Churchill inspected, and then spoke to, the assembled New Zealanders, describing Freyberg, who had fought at Gallipoli, as the 'salamander of the British Empire'.[3] He then took the march past, in his Royal Air Force Commodore's uniform. 'We felt quite worried,' Jacob noted, 'about the possible effect of the heat on his unaccustomed spine, but he didn't seem unduly troubled, and took no harm.'[4]

In his speech to the New Zealand Division, Churchill spoke of how the victories over Rommel would long live in the annals of war, 'and will be studied minutely by other generations than our own', and he declared: 'The good cause will not be trampled down. Justice and freedom will reign among men.'[5]

[1] Jacob notes for 4 February 1943: Jacob papers.

[2] The 'Scorpion' consisted of a tank chassis with a motor mounted above one track, with an armoured cubby-hole for a man to sit in and drive the motor. The motor was so arranged as to drive a horizontal drum mounted on two strong arms which projected about ten feet in front of the tank chassis. Fixed to the drum were chains, so that when the drum revolved they flew out and beat the ground with a flail-like action, thus blowing up ahead of the tank any anti-tank mine that might be in its path, and thereby clearing a track through the minefield.

[3] In his book *Marlborough: His Life and Times*, volume 1, London 1933, page 443, Churchill wrote: 'At the council of war Lord Cutts, already an officer of proved daring, afterwards Marlborough's famous "Salamander", urged caution. He volunteered himself to go ashore with fifty grenadiers and test the severity of the fire.' Cutts was given the nickname Salamander because he could live in the hottest fire, like the legendary salamander described by Pliny in his Natural History. In 1916 Freyberg had won the Victoria Cross on the western front. Two years earlier, Churchill had obtained a commission for him in the newly formed Royal Naval Division.

[4] Jacob notes for 4 February 1943: Jacob papers.

[5] Speech of 4 February 1943 (to the New Zealand Division): Churchill papers, 9/161.

Returning to the aerodrome at Castel Benito, Churchill inspected a South African squadron, and various units of ground staff. Then, returning to Tripoli, he was taken, towards sunset, on a tour of the harbour, crowded with British motor launches and minesweepers, 'each little vessel', as Jacob noted, 'giving three cheers as we passed'.[1]

On the western Mole, Churchill watched while sappers worked at closing a large gap which had been blown through the Mole during the fighting. The re-opening of the port at Tripoli was to ensure that there would be no delay on supply grounds to the final offensive. 'First 2 big ships had been got in this morning,' Cadogan noted in his diary.[2]

General Robertson, the acting General Officer Commanding the Tripoli base, showed Churchill the harbour repair works in progress, but was 'very anxious to get him away soon', as Jacob noted, 'for fear of a dusk air raid. So we were rather hustled off.'[3] Churchill was then driven back to Eighth Army headquarters, where he slept for a while in one of the caravans, dined with Montgomery, and was then driven back to the airfield at Castel Benito.

It was after midnight. The flight on to Algiers being planned to begin at four in the morning, Churchill was to sleep that night in the stationary Liberator. As Jacob noted:

It wasn't long before the PM joined us, and after a drink all round, produced of course by Sawyers from the bowels of the bomb-bay, he decided to go to bed where Sir Charles had already preceded him. It was quite a business hoisting him into his perch and undressing him. At one stage I heard Sawyers say; 'You are sitting on your hot water bottle. That isn't at all a good idea.' To which the PM replied: 'Idea? It isn't an idea, it's a co-incidence.'[4]

At four o'clock on the morning of Friday, February 5, Churchill's Liberator left Castel Benito for the five-hour flight to Algiers. In Algiers, as a result of the murder of Admiral Darlan, security precautions were considerable. Later that morning Churchill telegraphed to Attlee:

---

[1] Jacob notes for 4 February 1943: Jacob papers.
[2] Cadogan diary, 4 February 1943: David Dilks (editor), op. cit., page 511.
[3] Jacob notes for 4 February 1943: Jacob papers. The repair work at Tripoli, away from which Churchill was somewhat brusquely hustled, did not go well. There were considerable delays in getting the port working, much anger about this in military circles, and an eventual enquiry.
[4] Jacob notes for 4 February 1943: Jacob papers.

2. On the White House lawn, Washington, December 1941: 'The Americans . . . were not above learning from us, providing we did not set out to teach them' (page 43)

3. Addressing a Joint Session of Congress, Washington, Boxing Day 1941: 'Prodigious hammer strokes have been needed to bring us together again' (page 29)

4. At the controls of the Boeing Flying Boat in which he returned across the Atlantic, 14 January 1942. The pilot recalled: 'The Prime Minister asked if he could make a couple of slightly banked turns, which he did with considerable success' (page 41)

5. With Ivan Maisky, Eden, Molotov, and (far right) Lieutenant-Commander 'Tommy' Thompson, London, 26 May 1942. Churchill later wrote, of Molotov: 'We gave him a full and true account of our plans and resources' (page 111)

6. At Moscow airport, 12 August 1942. Churchill told those who came to meet him: 'We will continue, hand in hand, whatever our sufferings, whatever our toils . . .' (page 173)

7. In Casablanca, January 1943. Left to right: Churchill's Principal Private secretary, John Martin, his naval Aide-de-Camp, Lieutenant-Commander C. R. ('Tommy') Thompson, his detective, Detective-Sergeant Walter Thompson, and his son Randolph. 'Conditions most agreeable,' Churchill told Clement Attlee, 'I wish I could say the same of the problems' (page 293)

8. With Roosevelt at Casablanca, January 1943, a few minutes before Roosevelt announced the Allied aim: the 'unconditional surrender' of Germany, Italy and Japan (page 309)

9. The British team at Casablanca, January 1943. Front row: Air Chief Marshal Sir Charles Portal, Admiral of the Fleet Sir Dudley Pound, Churchill, Field Marshal Sir John Dill and General Sir Alan Brooke. Back row, Lieutenant-Commander C. R. Thompson, Brigadier Dykes, General Alexander, John Martin, Lord Louis Mountbatten, General Ismay, Lord Leathers, Harold Macmillan, Leslie Rowan and Colonel Jacob

10. The United States team at Casablanca: front row, General Marshall, President Roosevelt and Admiral King. Back row, Harry Hopkins, General Arnold, General Somervell and Averell Harriman. Churchill described the American Chiefs of Staff as 'one of the stupidest strategic teams ever seen', but they were, he added, 'good fellows' (page 843)

11. Churchill in the cockpit of the specially converted Liberator bomber in which he flew from Cairo to Adana (Turkey), 30 January 1943

12. With President Ismet Inönü, 31 January 1943. 'I find him a very agreeable man,' Churchill told Attlee, 'and we made friends at once' (page 325)

13. In the Roman amphitheatre at Carthage, with General Anderson, 1 June 1943, just before Churchill addressed the assembled troops. Churchill later wrote 'I was speaking from where the cries of Christian virgins rent the air whilst roaring lions devoured them—and yet—I am no lion, and certainly not a virgin' (page 424)

14. Algiers, 3 June 1943. Discussing plans for the invasion of Sicily and the eventual capture of Rome (pages 424–5). Left to right: Anthony Eden, General Brooke, Air Chief Marshal Tedder, Admiral Sir Andrew Cunningham (behind Churchill), General Alexander, General Marshall, General Eisenhower and (far right) General Montgomery

We are here in Admiral's villa which is next door to General Eisenhower's. Both are surrounded by barbed wire and heavily guarded and patrolled. We came here by circuitous route in bullet-proof car. I do not propose leaving precincts. No one considers in these circumstances there is any danger provided precautions are taken.

I am planning flying direct from here to England as soon as thoroughly satisfactory weather conditions are established. I should be glad of a day's rest however, after very strenuous week. Yesterday I reviewed over 40,000 repeat 40,000 of our troops in Tripoli. The Italians were second to none in their enthusiasm. Also we got two 9,000 ton ships into harbour through gap.

Please do not worry about my personal safety, as I take the utmost care of myself and am very quick to see where danger lies. I hope to take my questions in the House on Tuesday. I must ask a few days' grace on my return before making a statement, which I expect to do on Thursday.[1]

Throughout the day, Churchill discussed the problems of French control over the newly liberated areas, first with Macmillan, Eisenhower and Cunningham, then with Macmillan and Murphy, and finally with Giraud. The result was that the American-negotiated predominance of Giraud as Civil and Military Commander-in-Chief, given by Roosevelt 'the right and duty of preserving all French interests in North Africa', was ended. It was replaced by a French War Committee and Economic High Command, on which the Giraudists and Gaullists obtained equal representation. Both were now to be given 'every facility' to bring about the union under one authority of all Frenchmen fighting against Germany. 'He had dealt with the matter,' Churchill later reported to the War Cabinet, 'on the basis of the principle of equality between Generals Giraud and de Gaulle.' He had also asked Giraud 'to restore the laws of the Republic, particularly those affecting the Jews. It was essential for the prosecution of the war in North Africa that we should have a tranquil countryside and unsabotaged communications.'[2]

The victories in North Africa had led General Alexander to inform Churchill, while he was still in Algiers: 'Sir, the orders you gave me on August 15th 1942 have been fulfilled. His Majesty's enemies together with their impedimenta have been completely eliminated from Egypt, Cyrenaica, Libya, and Tripolitania. I now await your further instructions.'[3]

That night Churchill dined with Admiral Cunningham, before driving, at midnight, to the airport. Boarding his 'Commando' once

---

[1] 'Stratagem' No. 353, 'Hush Most Secret', 5 February 1943: Cabinet papers, 120/77.
[2] War Cabinet No. 25 of 1943, 7 February 1943, Confidential Annex: Cabinet papers, 65/37.
[3] Text in Prime Minister's Personal Telegram No. T.113/3, Prime Minister to President, No. 262, 8 February 1943: Churchill papers, 20/106. Churchill gave the original of Alexander's telegram to King George VI; it is now in the Royal Archives at Windsor.

more, he waited for take-off, but because of magneto failure, the bomber would not start. For two and a half hours nothing could be done, and Churchill decided to return to Algiers for what was left of the night. Had the bomber taken off when it was ready, Churchill telegraphed to Eden on the following morning, it would have had to approach England in broad daylight, probably without escort. Jacob, who was present at the discussion as to whether or not to return, noted in his diary:

John Martin, who like all the rest of us was anxious to be off, especially as we were all dressed up, loaded and ready to take off, and who felt that a return to Algiers in the middle of the night would be most irritating for our hosts said:

'You will remember that last time you did the whole flight from Gibraltar in daylight. We are starting only one or two hours later than we intended to start, and we should in any case have done some of the end of the journey in daylight. Surely it would be best to go on.'

However, the PM saw a lovely opportunity of a longer stay in Algiers, in surroundings of which he highly approved. So he burst out on John's head: 'You know absolutely nothing whatever about it!' Randolph, who also expostulated somewhat, was also thoroughly bitten.

The PM then staggered to his feet, and before anyone could say anything further he left the aircraft and was off to Algiers in Admiral Cunningham's car, which fortunately had remained until we actually took off. There was nothing for it, so we all piled out, taking only essential luggage, and got into cars and followed the Prime Minister. All except Sir Charles, who being in bed and half asleep, decided to stay where he was.[1]

'It was obliging of the magneto to cut out before we started,' Churchill telegraphed to Eden, 'rather than later on.'[2]

Churchill spent all of February 6 at Algiers. During the day he saw both Noguès, who at the moment of the American landings in North Africa had been Governor-General of Morocco, and Peyrouton, then Vichy Ambassador to the Argentine, who had been brought by the Americans across the Atlantic to be Governor-General of Algeria. 'I told them,' Churchill later recalled, 'that if they marched with us, we would not concern ourselves with past differences.'[3]

For the rest of February 6 Churchill 'did nothing in particular', as Jacob noted in his diary, but spent the afternoon 'playing bezique with Randolph'. That evening he set off again for the airfield, and for the Liberator. 'Once more we settled ourselves in,' Jacob noted, 'and Sawyers produced the drinks. The PM sat opposite me, and it seemed

---

[1] Jacob notes for 5 February 1943: Jacob papers.
[2] 'Stratagem' No. 361, 'Hush Most Secret', 6 February 1943: Cabinet papers, 120/77.
[3] Winston S. Churchill, *The Second World War*, volume 4, London 1951, pages 647–8.

that his mind was thinking of crashes. He said to me: "It would be a pity to have to go out in the middle of such an interesting drama without seeing the end. But it wouldn't be a bad moment to leave. It is a straight run in now, and even the Cabinet could manage it!"' [1]

At eleven that night, the Liberator took off for England. Churchill, after a frantic search for the Quadrinox pills which he took to ensure sleep, slept through the night.

---

[1] Jacob notes for 6 February 1943: Jacob papers.

20

Temporary Setbacks

C HURCHILL had been away from England for nearly four weeks. As he was preparing to leave Algiers on the night of 5 February 1943, Clementine Churchill had written to him from Downing Street, to greet him on his return to Lyneham airfield in Wiltshire:

My Darling,

Welcome Home. The anxiety & tension has been severe. What an in-spiration was the visit to Turkey—and how glad I am you did not allow yourself to be deviated from that extra lap of your journey—

I'm thinking of you flying thro the tenebrous dark & pray you make a good land-fall.

Your loving & expectant Clemmie.[1]

On the following morning, Clementine learned that her husband's plane had been delayed. 'Thank God engine trouble discovered before you started,' she wrote again, to await his arrival on the morning of February 7. 'I shall come to station to meet you. Please let me get into train before you come out. I like to kiss my Bull-finch privately & not be photographed doing it!'[2]

Shortly after midnight in the early hours of Sunday, February 7, Churchill's Liberator flew from Algiers to Lyneham, a flight of eight and a half hours. At one o'clock he reached London. Awaiting him at Paddington were thirteen Ministers, including Attlee, Eden and Bevin. There was also a note that Averell Harriman had telephoned 'to say how glad he was to hear that you were safely back'.[3]

That Sunday evening Churchill presided over his first War Cabinet in four weeks, giving an account of his journey and impressions. The bearing of the troops he had seen two days earlier in Tripoli was, he said, 'magnificent, and their turn-out on parade truly remarkable in the circumstances'.[4]

[1] Letter of 5 February 1943: Spencer-Churchill papers.
[2] Postscript of 6 February 1943: Spencer-Churchill papers.
[3] Note by John Peck, 7 February 1943: Premier papers, 4/72/1, folio 87.
[4] War Cabinet No. 25 of 1943, 5.30 p.m., 7 February 1943, Confidential Annex: Cabinet papers, 65/37.

Churchill was already thinking about his next overseas journey. In a note to Portal suggesting some 'minor improvements' in the Lancaster bomber aircraft which was being prepared to replace the Liberator for his personal use, he added: 'it would be a wonderful thing if there could be a pressure chamber fitted, so that an old person like me could make a direct flight to Russia'.[1] His brief stay in Cyprus had also set off various thoughts in this regard. On February 10 he minuted to Eden, and to the Chiefs of Staff Committee: 'I am thinking about the possibility of another conference in about six or seven months, to which I hope it may be possible to persuade Stalin to come. Cyprus struck me as very suitable for this purpose, and I really think a camp should be constructed at Troodos, and also on the plan to hold the chief members of the kind of party we had at "Symbol".' A moderate expense in order to make temporary villas, Churchill added, would be justifiable. He ended: 'Look what a short distance it is for Stalin.'[2]

At noon on February 11 Churchill rose to give the House of Commons an account of his travels, and of the war situation. 'He has a slight cold,' Harold Nicolson noted in his diary, 'looks less well than he did on arrival, but is in tearing spirits.'[3] Churchill spoke for more than two hours. The 'dominating aim' of Anglo-American policy, he said, was 'to make the enemy burn and bleed in every way that is physically and reasonably possible, in the same way as he is being made to burn and bleed along the vast Russian front from the White Sea to the Black Sea'. It was to make the necessary plans for action that he had gone to Casablanca, and it was to ensure that no vestige of Nazi or Fascist power, or of the Japanese 'war-plotting machine', remained after the war that the conference had demanded 'the unconditional surrender of all our foes'. Justice had to be done 'upon the wicked and the guilty, and, within her proper bounds, justice must be stern and implacable'. There was now 'a complete plan of action', and a 'definite design'. Although there would surely be 'disappointments and failures', there was no longer any question 'of drifting or indecision, or being unable to form a scheme or waiting for something to turn up'. For good or for ill, 'We know exactly what it is that we wish to do. We have the united and agreed advice of our experts behind it, and there is nothing now to be done but to work these plans out in their detail and put them into execution one after the other.'[4]

[1] Prime Minister's Personal Minute, M.38/3, 'Secret', 9 February 1943: Churchill papers, 4/397A.
[2] Prime Minister's Personal Minute, M.43/3, 'Most Secret', 10 February 1943: Churchill papers, 4/397A.
[3] Nicolson diary, 11 February 1943: Nigel Nicolson (editor), *op. cit.*, page 279.
[4] Speech of 11 February 1943: *Hansard*, columns 1468–88.

On February 12 Churchill's 'slight cold' had worsened, and he had to spend the day in bed.[1] He was able to deal, however, with a few matters which he judged urgent. One was his wish to push ahead with closer contacts with the partisans in Yugoslavia. 'The number of enemy divisions being contained in these regions is most remarkable,' he minuted to Major Morton, adding that in Cairo he had 'appealed strongly' to the Chief of the American Air Staff, General Arnold, 'to give us eight more Liberators fitted for discharging paracargoes or agents'.[2]

In the second week of February, Churchill was concerned about 'the harm which is done' by criticisms in the *News Chronicle* of General Eisenhower, 'under whom we have agreed to serve'.[3] On the previous day Churchill had told the House of Commons: 'I appeal to all patriotic men on both sides of the Atlantic Ocean to stamp their feet on mischief-makers and sowers of tares, wherever they may be found, and let the great machines roll into battle under the best possible conditions for our success.'[4]

On February 13, while still in bed, Churchill reacted critically to a message from Eisenhower, suggesting that the Sicily invasion would have to be postponed from June to July.[5] A month's delay, he told Eisenhower, would be a 'disastrous hiatus'.[6] 'I think it is an awful thing,' Churchill telegraphed to Hopkins that same day, 'that in April, May and June, not a single American or British soldier will be killing a single German or Italian soldier while the Russians are chasing 185 divisions around.' Britain and America would be 'very much open to grievous reproach at the hands of Russia', he believed, 'if, considering how very small is the sphere on which we are acting, we impose these enormous delays'. There would not have been a North African landing at all, Churchill reminded Hopkins, 'if we had yielded to the fears of the professionals'.[7]

'We shall become a laughing stock,' Churchill repeated in a minute that same day to the Chiefs of Staff Committee, 'if, during the spring and early summer, no British and American soldiers are firing at any German and Italian soldiers.' Every effort should be made to try to

[1] John Martin diary, 12 February 1943: Martin papers.
[2] Prime Minister's Personal Minute, DM.2/3, 12 February 1943: Churchill papers, 4/397A.
[3] Prime Minister's Personal Minute, M.48/3 (to the Minister of Information), 12 February 1943: Churchill papers, 4/397A.
[4] *Hansard*, 11 February 1943.
[5] NAF No. 144 of 11 February 1943, to the Combined Chiefs of Staff: Cabinet papers, 105/139.
[6] Prime Minister's Personal Telegram, T. 155/3, 'Personal and Private, also Secret', 13 February 1943: Churchill papers, 20/106.
[7] Prime Minister's Personal Telegram, T.156/3, 'Personal and Most Secret', 13 February 1943: Churchill papers, 20/106.

reinstate the June date, 'so that if at the worst it fails, it does not fail through us or our side'.[1]

One reason for Churchill's sense of urgency was his knowledge of various proposals which had reached London from anti-Fascist groups in Italy. If the invasion of Sicily were to succeed, these groups could give a lead in negotiations to 'put Italy out of the war'. To Eden, Churchill minuted on February 13: 'I shall support such a movement to the utmost. I am not going to take the responsibility of carrying on this war a day longer than is necessary to achieve full victory.'[2]

As if to underline the contrast between the Anglo-American plans and the Russian reality, on February 14, while still confined to bed, Churchill received news that the Red Army had liberated Rostov-on-Don, driving the Germans from this major river, road and rail junction. This news, Churchill telegraphed to Stalin, 'leaves me without power to express to you the admiration and the gratitude which we feel to the Russian arms', and he added: 'My most earnest wish is to do more to aid you.'[3] That same day, in telling Alexander how the reading out of his reply to Churchill's original directive had aroused the utmost enthusiasm in the House of Commons on February 11, Churchill added that he had telegraphed privately to Eisenhower, 'stressing the importance to the common cause' of the June rather than the July date for the invasion of Sicily. 'The astounding victories on the Russian front,' Churchill commented, 'are changing the whole aspect of the war.'[4]

In Tunisia, on February 14, there was a potential setback for Eisenhower's plans for the conquest of Tunis, and the Sicily invasion, when the Germans succeeded in breaking through Eisenhower's lines. Even before the full extent of Rommel's success was known, however, Stalin telegraphed to Churchill with his disappointment at the timetable established at Casablanca: 'It is evident from your message,' Stalin wrote, 'that, contrary to your previous calculations, the end of operations in Tunis is expected in April instead of February. I hardly need to tell you how disappointing is such a delay.' Stalin added: 'Strong activity of the Anglo-American troops in North Africa is more than ever necessary at this moment, when the Soviet armies are

---

[1] Prime Minister's Personal Minute, D.14/3, 'Most Secret', 13 February 1943: Churchill papers, 4/397A.

[2] Prime Minister's Personal Minute, M.58/3, 'Most Secret', 13 February 1943: Churchill papers, 4/397A.

[3] Prime Minister's Personal Telegram, T.168/3, 'Personal and Secret', No. 84 from Foreign Office to Moscow, 14 February 1943: Churchill papers, 20/106.

[4] Prime Minister's Personal Telegram, T.169/3, 'Personal and Private', OZ 442, 14 February 1943: Churchill papers, 20/106.

still in a position to maintain their powerful general offensive. With simultaneous pressure on Hitler from our front and from your side we could achieve great results. Such a situation would create serious difficulties for Hitler and Mussolini. In this way the intended operations in Sicily and the Eastern Mediterranean could be expedited.'

Stalin went on to express his fear 'that it may happen that the Germans, after having a respite, which will enable them to re-muster their forces, may once more recover their strength'. His telegram ended on a positive note: 'Many thanks for your very warm congratulations on the liberation of Rostov. Our troops today captured Kharkov.' [1]

Stalin's telegram reached London as Churchill's cold took a turn for the worse. On the evening of February 16, Sir Charles Wilson diagnosed inflammation of the base of the lung. On the following day Dr Geoffrey Marshall of Guy's Hospital confirmed the diagnosis. Churchill had pneumonia. When he protested at being advised to rest, Dr Marshall replied that he called pneumonia 'the old man's friend'. 'Why?' Churchill asked. 'Because it takes them off so quietly,' Marshall replied. A compromise was reached. Churchill 'only to have the most important and interesting papers' sent to him, 'and to read a novel'. He chose *Moll Flanders*, about which, he later recalled, 'I had heard excellent accounts, but had not found time to test them.' [2]

For a week Churchill remained in bed 'in fever and discomfort'. Sometimes, he later recalled, he felt 'very ill'.[3] One piece of good news to reach Churchill on his sick bed was the Eighth Army's capture of Ben Gardane. 'Delighted you have got Ben Gardane at the exact date you predicted,' Churchill telegraphed to Montgomery. 'You were certainly right that Rommel is very sensitive about his right flank.' [4] On the following day Montgomery telegraphed in reply: 'Have today secured Medenine airfields and begin work on them tomorrow.' [5]

Much worried by the possibility of a month's postponement of the invasion of Sicily, on February 17 Churchill asked Roosevelt to read

---

[1] 'Personal and Most Secret', 16 February 1943: Churchill papers, 20/106.

[2] Winston S. Churchill, *The Second World War*, volume 4, London 1951, page 651. *Moll Flanders, The Fortunes and Misfortunes of the Famous*, a romance by Daniel Defoe, published in 1722, set both in Britain and in the American colonies.

[3] Winston S. Churchill, *The Second World War*, volume 4, London 1951, page 651.

[4] Prime Minister's Personal Telegram, T.181/3, OZ 461, 'Personal', 16 February 1943–Churchill papers, 20/106.

[5] Air Ministry Telegram No. 10957, Main Eighth Army U/2778, 17 February 1943: Churchill papers, 20/106.

the telegram from the British Chiefs of Staff and Mountbatten to their American counterparts, in which they wished to make it 'perfectly clear' that Britain would be ready in June. 'It would be a great pity,' Churchill commented, 'to lose a month if it could possibly be saved.'[1] But Eisenhower was adamant, and in a long and reasoned reply, stressed that, 'I am always burning with a desire to speed up the pace of winning.' Eisenhower added that, in clearing Rommel from Tunisia, 'we must be prepared for hard and bitter fighting and the end may not come as soon as we hope'.[2]

Churchill persevered, following up the British Chiefs of Staff paper with a telegram of his own to Hopkins. The result was a decision by the American Chiefs of Staff to support the British view, and to instruct Eisenhower to bring the Sicily landing forward to June. Eisenhower was also instructed to report by April 10 'what progress had been made'.[3]

No one had yet proposed a code name for the British operations against the Tunisian Tip. On February 17, from his sick bed, Churchill suggested 'Vulcan'.[4] That same day, he was alarmed to read two separate reports, a public statement by Admiral Cunningham about the success of Allied supplies now entering Tripoli harbour, and an Enigma decrypt, exhorting Rommel to bomb the port. Churchill at once urged the Chiefs of Staff Committee to send 'remonstrances' to Cunningham, adding:

He is the best fellow in the world, but he ought not to have said the passage marked in red, which is directly contrary to our policy of minimising the use of Tripoli harbour, and which is calculated to deprive Montgomery of the element of surprise expressing itself in an unexpectedly early attack with greater strength. On the advice of the Chiefs of Staff Committee I purposely lent myself to a very discouraging view of the Tripoli unloadings. But all this is undone. Boniface shows that this is Hitler's view.[5]

Churchill had cause for satisfaction that day however, when General Lindsell, Lieutenant General Administration, informed him of the successful discharge of cargoes at Tripoli harbour. 'Bravo,' Churchill telegraphed in reply on February 17. Henceforth, Lindsell sent Churchill daily reports and weekly summaries of the unloadings, first

---

[1] Prime Minister's Personal Telegram, T.184/3, Prime Minister to President, No. 268, 'Personal and Most Secret', 17 February 1943: Churchill papers, 20/106. The Chiefs of Staff's telegram was Chiefs of Staff (W) 473.

[2] Telegram No. 1375 from Algiers, 'Urgent, Secret', 17 February 1943: Churchill papers, 20/106.

[3] Churchill reported on this decision to King George VI in a letter on 22 February 1943: Churchill papers, 4/290.

[4] Prime Minister's Personal Minute, D.20/3, 17 February 1943: Churchill papers, 4/397A.

[5] Prime Minister's Personal Minute, D.22/3, 17 February 1943: Churchill papers, 4/397A.

from Tripoli, then from Tripoli, Benghazi, Sfax and Sousse. 'Tell them they are unloading history,' Churchill telegraphed to Lindsell a week later, and, in further telegrams each week thereafter: 'Magnificent,' 'Many congratulations,' 'Never mind setback,' 'Splendid! you have done your bit in the victory,' and, finally, 'Good. The results of your labours are apparent.'[1]

The German offensive against the Americans in Tunisia had continued. On February 18 it was learned in London that 170 American tanks had been lost, and several airfields captured. This setback, coupled with Eisenhower's own earlier doubts about the June date for operation 'Husky', led Churchill to propose, on February 19, a new approach to the invasion of Sicily. 'In view of the delaying attitude adopted by General Eisenhower towards "Husky",' he minuted on February 19, 'I wish a final Joint Planners Sub-Committee and the Chief of Combined Operations Department to work out a study of our doing it all alone by ourselves in June, and taking nothing from the United States except landing craft, escorts etc.'

Churchill's all-British invasion of Sicily was to be based upon the four British divisions already in Tunisia, with two more 'on the way or under orders', six from the Eighth Army, operating from Tripoli, and two more 'thrown in' from Persia, 'making a total of 14 divisions for an operation for which the requirements were set at $9\frac{1}{2}$'. Churchill's proposal continued:

There would be great advantages in having it all done by British troops, with the Americans giving us a hand at the landings, with the air force, &c. The Americans could then come in to the ports we had taken and go into action without having to go through the training for assault landings. Anyhow, let us see how this would work out. It would at least be a spur, in fact a tremendous spur, if we can make the offer.[2]

A further cause of friction with the United States, and a public one, was the American reaction to the arrest of Gandhi in India. Gandhi had been arrested, on the advice of the War Cabinet, while Churchill was in Cairo. Gandhi's arrest, and his detention at Poona, followed his call for an all-India campaign against participation in the war effort, and for the grant of immediate independence. On February 9, Gandhi had declared a three-week hunger strike. Churchill was

[1] Telegrams of 17 and 24 February 1943 (Prime Minister's Personal Telegram T.212/3), 8, (OZ 684) 14, (OZ 754) 22, (OZ 834) and 29 March 1943 (OZ 888) and 13 May 1943 ('Pencil' No. 67): Premier papers, 3/299/1.
[2] Prime Minister's Personal Minute, D.23/3 (for Chiefs of Staff Committee), 'Most Secret', 19 February 1943: Churchill papers, 4/397A.

sceptical of the genuineness of the hunger strike itself. 'I have heard,' he had telegraphed to the Viceroy, Lord Linlithgow, on February 13, 'that Gandhi usually has glucose in his water when doing his various fasting antics. Would it be possible to verify this?'[1] The answer was negative. 'I am told,' replied the Viceroy, 'that his present medical attendant tried to persuade him to take glucose yesterday and again today, and that he refused absolutely.'[2] When, on February 19, Churchill asked about the activities in New Delhi of Roosevelt's emissary, William Phillips, he was told by Leo Amery that 'both Linlithgow and Halifax have taken a firm line against the emissary intervening in a purely domestic Indian matter'. But, Amery added, 'I do hope you will make it quite clear to the President that his people must keep off the grass.'[3]

Two days later, on February 21, Churchill telegraphed to the Viceroy: 'It is a great comfort to me, as the Gandhi episode approaches its climax, to feel that we can count on your steadfast and unflinching action.'[4] That same day, Churchill urged Lord Halifax to make it clear to Cordell Hull 'and other contacts' in Washington, that the British Government 'will not in any circumstances alter the course it is pursuing about Gandhi', and that any American intervention would cause 'great embarrassment between the two Governments'. Halifax should 'make sure', Churchill asked, 'that you put the whole case before Harry Hopkins', and he added, 'You may be certain there will be no weakness here.'[5]

Gandhi 'is near dying', Oliver Harvey noted on February 22. 'The Government persists in refusing to release him. American opinion is disquieted.'[6]

As Gandhi lay fasting to the death in Poona, the focus of world attention, concern and controversy, Churchill lay ill in London, the extent of his illness a well kept secret. News that it was pneumonia had, however, reached Roosevelt and Hopkins. 'Do hope that you are feeling better,' Hopkins had telegraphed on February 18.[7] 'Thank you so much,' Churchill replied. 'Expect a week more of this sort of

---

[1] Prime Minister's Personal Telegram, T.157/3, 'Personal and Secret', 13 February 1943: Churchill papers, 20/106.

[2] 'Most Secret', 38548/C, 15 February 1943: Premier papers, 4/49/3, folio 531.

[3] Secretary of State's Minute, P.4/43, 19 February 1943: Premier papers, 4/49/3, folio 494.

[4] Prime Minister's Personal Telegram, T.203/3, 'Most Secret', 21 February 1943: Churchill papers, 20/107.

[5] Prime Minister's Personal Telegram, T.204/4, No. 1188 to Washington, 'Personal for Lord Halifax', 21 February 1943: Churchill papers, 20/107.

[6] Harvey diary, 22 February 1943: John Harvey (editor), *op. cit.*, pages 222–3.

[7] 'Most Secret', received at 9.50 a.m. on 19 February 1943: Churchill papers, 20/106.

thing but situation is pronounced under control.'[1] 'PM still has temperature of 101,' Sir Alexander Cadogan noted in his diary on February 19, explaining why Eden was having to postpone an intended visit to Washington.[2]

Rumours of the seriousness of Churchill's illness circulated widely in Whitehall. Churchill had asked Eden to postpone his visit for a week, Oliver Harvey noted, 'as owing to his cold he doesn't feel able to take on the extra work of Foreign Office and House of Commons'.[3] 'The PM's cold has developed into inflammation of the lung,' noted Marian Holmes, one of the Downing Street typing pool, and she added: 'Sir Charles Wilson and two nurses in attendance.'[4] 'Anxiety about the PM,' Marian Holmes added on the following day. 'He has pneumonia and his temperature was up last night. Thankfully it is down this morning.'[5]

'It was miserable having him ill,' Elizabeth Layton wrote to her parents, 'and knowing how he hated it. He was so sweet, too, anytime one had to go in; seemed quite glad to see one.'[6]

Churchill remained in bed at the Annexe, where he did his work, his study having been taken over by the two nurses who were brought to be with him at all times. One of those nurses, Doris Miles, later recalled how, during Churchill's treatment with sulphonamides, he 'demanded to know exactly how the drug worked'.

During his treatment, Churchill complained of head pains. 'I had to rub his head with oil of wintergreen,' Doris Miles recalled. 'This became something of a ritual every evening and he would sing an old music-hall song while I was doing it:

> "Wash me in the water
> Which you washed your dirty daughter in
> And I will be whiter
> Than the whitewash on the wall".'[7]

As Churchill lay in bed, Rommel's thrust against Eisenhower intensified. On February 20 German forces broke through the Kasserine Pass. Visiting London on the following day, Mary Churchill

---

[1] Prime Minister's Personal Telegram, T.198/3, 'Personal and Secret', 19 February 1943: Churchill papers, 20/106.

[2] Cadogan diary, 19 February 1943: David Dilks (editor), *op. cit.*, page 514.

[3] Harvey diary, 19 February 1943: John Harvey (editor), *op. cit.*, page 221.

[4] Marian Holmes diary, 20 February 1943: Marian Walker Spicer papers. Three days earlier Miss Holmes had been told that she would in future be working 'exclusively for the PM'. She began her new duties on 24 March 1943.

[5] Marian Holmes diary, 21 February 1943: Marian Walker Spicer papers.

[6] Elizabeth Layton, letter of 17 March 1943: Nel papers.

[7] Doris Miles, letter to the author, 14 January 1982. This song was popular among the soldiers on the western front in 1916, at the time when Churchill was commanding the 6th Royal Scots Fusiliers.

noted in her diary that her mother 'is not *seriously* worried about Papa—but he is pretty ill', and she added: 'I was shocked when I saw him. He looked so old & tired—lying back in bed.' [1]

Churchill had been too ill for his Tuesday lunch with the King on February 16. On Monday, February 22, he had to cancel the following day's lunch as well. 'PM's health is still stationary,' Oliver Harvey noted that day: 'He is taking no papers.' [2] During the day, Churchill received a three page handwritten letter from the King, in place of their Tuesday talk. 'I am very sorry to hear that you are ill,' the King wrote, 'and I hope that you will soon be well again. But do please take this opportunity for a rest. And I trust you will not forget that you have earned one after your last tour, and you must get back your strength for the strenuous coming months.' The King was much concerned, as was Churchill, by the American actions and hesitations in French North Africa, writing to his Prime Minister:

I do not feel at all happy about the present political situation in North Africa. I know we had to leave the political side of Torch to the Americans, while we were able to keep Spain and Portugal friendly during the time the operation was going on. Since then I feel the underhand dealings of Murphy with the French in North Africa, and his contacts with Vichy, have placed both America and this country in an invidious position. [3] I know we had to tread warily at the start, but is there nothing we can do now to strengthen Macmillan's and Alexander's hands in both the political and military sphere, to make the two French sides come together.

It looks as if the US Forces have had a sound defeat last week, which will not help them in French eyes, and as if we shall have to do all the fighting there. The state of affairs, according to the telegrams I have seen, looks as if it was deteriorating.

Now I hear that from the American point of view the date of Husky will have to be postponed to the later one, whereas we can plan for the earlier one, which will be an aggravation of our difficulties in preparing the operation.

This fact will throw out all our careful calculations for convoys and escorts, and will upset our import programme again. I should not think of bothering you with these questions at this moment, but I do feel worried about them, and I would like an assurance from you that they are being carefully watched.

[1] Mary Churchill diary, 21 February 1942: Mary Soames, *Clementine Churchill*, London 1979, page 332.

[2] Harvey diary, 22 February 1943: John Harvey (editor), *op. cit.*, pages 222–3.

[3] Robert Murphy had been the American Political Representative in Algiers during the Vichy period. In November 1942 he had been given the responsibility of telling Darlan about 'Torch', on the eve of the landings. He was a supporter of General Giraud, whose cause he had pressed at Casablanca.

The King's letter ended: 'I cannot discuss these vital matters with anyone but yourself.'[1]

Churchill was in bed with a temperature of 102° when the King's letter reached him. But he dictated his reply at once, and at length, the first part of his letter a strong defence of Anglo-American policy in North Africa, and the accommodation with the once reviled men of Vichy:

I do not feel seriously disturbed by the course of events in North Africa, either political or even military, although naturally there is much about both aspects which I would rather have different.

I have been reading all the key telegrams with attention up till two days ago, when I must admit I have fallen a little behind. I am sure however there is no question of Murphy being in with Vichy. What would he get out of that? His aim is to uphold Giraud and to procure a quiet, tranquil Government for the 16 million people living in French North Africa. In this way alone would he gain any credit. It is quite true that we have for this purpose and to safeguard our vital communications, to work with a mass of French officials who were appointed by Vichy; but without them I really do not know how the country could be governed. Even in Syria we have done this to some extent. I do not myself see any danger of these officials changing their sides or obstructing our operations. Their own bread and butter depends upon their good behaviour, and possibly their lives as well.

The irruption of de Gaulle or his agents into this field, especially if forcibly introduced by us, would cause nothing but trouble. De Gaulle is hostile to this country, and I put far more confidence in Giraud than in him. It is entirely his fault that a good arrangement was not made between the two French functions. The insolence with which he refused the President's invitation (and mine) to come and make a friendly settlement at Casablanca may be founded on stupidity rather than malice. Whatever the motive, the result has been the same, namely, to put him and his French National Committee practically out of court with the Americans. He now wishes to go on a tour round his dominions, *mes fiefs* as he calls them. I have vetoed this, as he would simply make mischief and spread Anglophobia wherever he went.

Churchill added that he could not see 'any future' for the Fighting French Movement while de Gaulle 'remains at their head'.

Churchill's letter then dealt with the King's unease about the delay in the invasion of Sicily:

As I told Your Majesty the last time we met, I tried all I could to bring the Operation 'Husky' forward to June. In this I was splendidly seconded

[1] Letter of 22 February 1942: Churchill papers, 20/92.

by the Chiefs of Staff and all concerned. General Eisenhower, however, expressed a decided opinion that a June operation would be 'unlikely to succeed', and was for July at the earliest. Our Chiefs of Staff therefore sent their paper to the Combined Chiefs of Staff in Washington, and I also telegraphed to Hopkins asking him to put this through, with the result that, according to my latest information, the Combined Chiefs of Staff— who are the supreme and official body through which command is exercised—have ordered General Eisenhower to prepare for the June operation with the utmost zeal, and to report to them by April 10 what progress has been made. Thus you see the American Chiefs of Staff took the same view as ours did, and, if I may say so, as I did. That is how the matter stands now.

The crisis with Eisenhower over the date of 'Husky' was now over. Churchill turned next, in his letter to the King, to the course of the battle in Tunisia. He was 'not at all satisfied', he wrote, 'with the way in which the 1st Army was handled by Anderson'. It had been 'much reduced to bits and pieces', being 'very much in the state in which Montgomery found the 8th Army when we got rid of Auchinleck'. 'However,' Churchill addded, 'I suspend judgement till we hear from Alexander.'

Churchill then dwelt upon the American reverses at the Kasserine Pass:

The 2nd American Army Corps sustained a heavy defeat, and apparently was deprived of about half its important weapons without inflicting any serious loss upon the enemy. The 'Boniface' used this expression: '. . . on account of the low fighting value of the enemy', and then proceeded to order further offensives.

However, the enemy make a great mistake if they think that all the troops we have there are in the same green state as our United States friends. We have about six of our finest infantry brigade groups and the 6th Armoured Division as well as a brigade of heavy Churchill tanks there. More are on the way. The supplies have come in better.

Churchill was confident of the outcome of a new battle, telling the King:

If the enemy heave themselves on in a general attack, I think they will find that the rest of the Army is not at all on the same level as those they overthrew so easily in the plains of Gafsa. In fact already the 1st Guards Brigade have come into action at Sbeitla, and have made the enemy feel that they have come up against bone at last. In order to make this new offensive, not foreseen in their original plan, the enemy have stripped the Mareth line pretty thin.

Montgomery, who has the whole picture before him and who has been receiving splendid daily deliveries in Tripoli harbour as well as from Benghazi sometimes reaching a total of 6,000 tons from the two ports together, will soon be able to bring the 10th Corps up, whose transport he has had to use to maintain himself so far and to build up reserves. I look forward to both the 10th and 30th Corps being in action in Tunisia by the middle of March, or it may be earlier. Nevertheless, matters may not wait so long, because if Montgomery feels the enemy is wilting on his front, he will certainly use his strength against them.

I suppose Your Majesty realises that these two Corps of the 8th Army, comprising together about 160,000 men, are perhaps the best troops in the world. Therefore I look confidently forward to their entry into action. More-over we have General Alexander under Eisenhower to concert and combine the entire movements. It may well be that the enemy is wasting strength on a false assumption that we are all as green as the Americans, and will give Montgomery an earlier chance.

Of the United States troops who had been worsted in battle, Churchill reassured the King: 'I need scarcely say that no word of mine is intended in disparagement of the Americans. They are brave but not seasoned troops, who will not hesitate to learn from defeat, and who will improve themselves by suffering until all their strongest martial qualities have come to the front.' Churchill added: 'What a providential thing it was that I perpetually pressed for General Eis-enhower to take the Command, as the defeat of the American Corps, if it had been under a British general, would have given our enemies in the United States a good chance to blaspheme.' 'Generally,' Churchill told the King, 'I feel we may await with reasonable con-fidence the development of the situation in North Africa, and I look forward to an improvement before too long.'

On the seventh and final page of his letter, Churchill referred to 'the old humbug Gandhi', whose hunger strike, he noted, 'is lasting much longer than we were assured was possible', so much so that 'one wonders whether his fast is *bona fide*'. Churchill had sent a private telegram to the Viceroy, he added, 'exhorting him to unflinching steadfastness'.

Churchill's final paragraph in his letter to the King was about himself. 'Although,' he wrote, 'I have been hampered by a high fever from reading all the telegrams, I think I have the picture truly in my mind, and I wish indeed that I could have given this account to Your Majesty verbally at luncheon. I send this instead.' [1]

Churchill's confidence in the outcome of the battle in North Africa had not been misplaced. On the afternoon of February 22, before the Eighth Army had made a move, Rommel sent out an order calling off his attack. This order was sent through signals which were decrypted,

[1] Letter of 22 February 1943: Churchill papers, 4/290.

and passed on to Montgomery. 'The battle in Tunisia is all right,' Churchill telegraphed to Stalin on February 24. 'The enemy have shot their bolt and will now be brought into the grip of the vice.' What the Russians were doing on the eastern front, he commented, 'is simply indescribable'.[1] That night, in a cinema room set up near his bedroom, Churchill watched a film which Stalin had sent him, of the surrender of von Paulus at Stalingrad.[2]

As Churchill suffered from his pneumonia, the aspect of the war which gave him the most cause for relief was the decision of the American Combined Chiefs to urge Eisenhower to speed up the June invasion of Sicily. On February 24 he telegraphed to Hopkins: 'Thank you so much for helping to get the target date for "Husky" settled for June. None of this recent fighting should affect it, though some will try to say so.' Churchill's own assessment of the recent fighting was a confident one. 'I think the Tunis battle is good,' he told Hopkins, 'and going to be better; and our men, British and American, are fighting like brothers, mingled together and side by side. A reward lies ahead of them all.' At Tripoli harbour, he noted, 6,300 tons of war supplies had been unloaded on the previous day, while at the same time Montgomery 'is sharpening his claws'.[3]

The unloading of supplies at Tripoli was, as Churchill knew, the key to any successful offensive against the Tunisian Tip. To Alexander, Churchill telegraphed on February 24, about the recent setbacks to the Americans, however, pointing out that the Enigma decrypts had given 'ample warning' of the attack, which ought to have been met by a tactical withdrawal. Of the villages which had been lost in the German advance, Churchill reflected: 'Nobody cared about these places, whose names had never been heard of till they were lost.' What mattered now was to return to the plan of attack. 'I am sure,' he told Alexander, 'you have in your hands now all the threads necessary to bring about a very fine event before the middle of April.' Churchill ended his telegram: 'How glad I am you are there. The unloadings at Tripoli are splendid. Please keep me informed.'[4]

*   *   *

[1] Prime Minister's Personal Telegram, T.213/3, 'Personal and Most Secret', No. 131 to Moscow, 24 February 1943: Cabinet papers, 120/858.

[2] Winston S. Churchill, *The Second World War*, volume 4, London 1951, page 661.

[3] Prime Minister's Personal Telegram, T.217/3, 'Personal and Secret', 24 February 1943: Churchill papers, 20/107.

[4] Prime Minister's Personal Telegram, T.215/3, 24 February 1943: Churchill papers, 4/394A.

Churchill's health was no longer causing concern to those closest to him: 'I can see for myself,' Clementine Churchill wrote to her daughter Mary on February 24, 'that he is better. His face looks quite different. He has lost that weary look.'[1] To Hopkins, Churchill telegraphed that same day: 'Am feeling definitely better now. So is Gandhi. Once he saw that his antics would have no effect he took a marked turn for the better. I am so glad you did not get drawn in.'[2] It had been said that Gandhi might easily die on the eleventh day of his fast. 'Now,' Churchill telegraphed to the Viceroy, 'at fifteenth day, bulletins look as if he might get through.' Surely, Churchill added, 'with all these Congress Hindu doctors round him, it is quite easy to slip glucose or other nourishment into his food'.[3]

On the sixteenth day of his hunger strike, Gandhi was still alive. 'I do not think Gandhi has the slightest intention of dying,' Churchill telegraphed that day to General Smuts, 'and I imagine he has been eating better meals than I have for the last week. It looks now highly probable that he will see his fast out. What fools we should have been to flinch before all this bluff and sob-stuff.'[4]

On the following day, Churchill telegraphed to the Viceroy: 'It now seems almost certain that the old rascal will emerge all the better from his so-called fast.' The 'weapon of ridicule', Churchill advised, 'so far as is compatible with the dignity of the Government of India, should certainly be employed'. Churchill told Linlithgow: 'Your own strong, cool, sagacious handling of the matter has given me the greatest confidence and satisfaction.'[5] That same day Linlithgow telegraphed to Churchill: 'I have long known Gandhi as the world's most successful humbug and have not the least doubt that his physical condition and the bulletins reporting it from day to day have been deliberately cooked so as to produce the maximum effect on public opinion.' Britain had won 'an important victory', Linlithgow believed, 'which will help to discredit a wicked system of blackmail and terror, and I am much obliged to you for your staunch support'.[6]

Gandhi ended his fast on March 3. Shortly afterwards, he was released from prison.[1]

*   *   *

[1] Letter of 24 February 1943: Mary Soames, op. cit., page 332.
[2] Prime Minister's Personal Telegram, T.217/3, 24 February 1942: Churchill papers, 4/397A.
[3] Prime Minister's Personal Telegram, T.216/3, 'Private and Personal', 24 February 1943: Churchill papers, 2/107.
[4] Prime Minister's Personal Telegram, T.228/3, No. 319 to Cape Town, 26 February 1943: Churchill papers, 20/107.
[5] Prime Minister's Personal Telegram, T.237/3, 'Personal and Secret', 27 February 1943: Premier papers, 4/49/3, folio 525.
[6] 'Most Secret', 40076/C, 27 February 1943: Premier papers, 4/49/3, folio 522.

On the evening of February 24, Churchill dictated a telegram to Harold Macmillan, in Algiers, approving a suggestion by Giraud that Pierre Flandin, a former French Prime Minister, should join his Council. There had already been newspaper opposition to Flandin's possible appointment. Churchill saw no reason, however, to challenge the appointment, telegraphing to Macmillan:

I am not opposed to the idea of Flandin being used in a small post. He is much the ablest Frenchman in North Africa. When he sent his telegram to Hitler congratulating him on Munich he sent one also to Chamberlain and Mussolini. I do not consider this fault decisive observing that Chamberlain himself was Prime Minister for eight months in the war.

When Flandin was taken into the Vichy Government he immediately had the idea of making a stand against the Germans and was of course crushed and sacked. He has rare ability and profound knowledge and also is a man of stuffing and character. I am not running him in anyway but if Giraud and others on the spot think he can help I can well believe they are right and anyhow see no reason for us to interfere.

'Pay no attention,' Churchill added, 'to the newspapers' clack and chatter.'[2]

This telegram caused some concern to Churchill's Principal Private Secretary, John Martin, who telephoned Eden to say that the Foreign Secretary might perhaps see this telegram before it was sent. On the following morning, Eden called on Churchill who, as he later recalled, 'looked flushed and clearly had a fever'. Eden's account continued:

After referring to one or two matters of business I then added, expecting no trouble: 'By the way, about that telegram you thought of sending last night to Algiers. . . .' 'Thought of sending? What do you mean? I sent it.' I replied: 'No, it hasn't gone yet. I wanted to talk to you about it first.'

---

[1] Churchill later telegraphed to the Viceroy of India: 'I assented to letting Gandhi out on the grounds of his grievous state of health. He seems to have recovered a good deal of political vitality since then. He is a thoroughly evil force, hostile to us in every fibre, largely in the hands of the native vested interests and frozen to his idea of the hand spinning-wheel and inefficient cultivation methods for the over-crowded population of India. I look forward to a day when it may be possible to come to an understanding with the real forces that control India and which, at any political settlement, will be allied with a marked improvement in the well-being of the masses, whom the reformers often forget, but who constitute for us a sacred duty.' (Prime Minister's Personal Telegram, T.1139/4, No. 480 to the Viceroy, circulation restricted to the King and Sir Edward Bridges, 'Personal and Secret', 27 May 1944: Churchill papers, 20/165.)

[2] Prime Minister's Personal Telegram, T.214/3, final draft, 24 February 1943: Churchill papers, 20/107. A year later, in a reference to Flandin's support of the Munich Agreement of 1938 and the policy of appeasement. Churchill minuted to Eden that Flandin was 'no more guilty' than Neville Chamberlain or Lord Halifax. (Prime Minister's Personal Minute, M.244/4, 4 March 1944: Premier papers, 3/182/3.)

Churchill gripped the counterpane with both hands and growled: 'By what right do you interfere with my private correspondence?' I said that the message I had been shown was not private correspondence. 'How did you know about it?' 'You know,' I answered, 'that the Foreign Secretary sees all important messages.' He retorted that he was not dead yet and would send any telegrams he chose.

As his temperature was clearly mounting by leaps and bounds I said, 'All right, we'll talk about it later,' and left, adjuring the private secretary on my way to send for his doctor, Sir Charles Wilson, and Mr Brendan Bracken and to ask them to persuade the Prime Minister not to send any more telegrams until his temperature was normal again.

I had no sooner reached the House of Commons than I was told that the Prime Minister wanted to speak to me on the telephone. I said I could not do so as I had to be in the Chamber and persisted in this refusal all day. At length, after the House rose I called in to see Mr Churchill, who was reclining benignly in bed with the telegram on the counterpane.

He asked after my day in the House and my son's progress in the Royal Air Force and other casual topics before at last he glanced at the telegram and added: 'Oh, by the way, you remember that message I intended to send? Perhaps we had better not send it.' He took it up and tore it through.

Eden later reflected on this incident, which was, he wrote, 'characteristic of Mr Churchill and of something very lovable in him'. First, Eden explained, 'the indignation sparked by fever, then reflection and a generous acceptance expressed without halftones or hesitation; these were the successive stages which endeared him to those whom he berated. There was nothing I could say that evening, but he knew how I felt and the deep affection that was unspoken.' [1]

On February 24, as the fighting on the eastern front reached a new intensity, the Germans had launched a counter-offensive in the Donets Basin. Three days later, the possibility that the Germans might use poison gas against the Russian forces became known to Churchill through a report from the British Military Mission in Moscow. He immediately minuted to Ismay, for the Chiefs of Staff Committee:

> In the event of the Germans using gas on the Russians, my declaration of last year of course stands. We shall retaliate by drenching the German cities with gas on the largest possible scale. We must expect their counter-measures. Is everything in readiness for this contingency both ways?
>
> It is quite possible that another warning like I gave last year might check

[1] Eden recollections: Eden memoirs, *The Reckoning*, *op. cit.*, page 367.

them off at the last minute, but we must be ready to strike and make good any threat we utter with the utmost promptitude and severity.[1]

The answer to Churchill's questions was provided by the Vice Chiefs of Staff. In Britain, they reported, 'we are prepared offensively and defensively for gas warfare and are in a position to retaliate by air on a very large scale'. In the Middle East, North Africa and India, however, 'although our troops are equipped defensively, we are hardly in a position to carry out gas warfare'. As to the American forces in Britain, they were 'not yet ready either offensively or defensively except for personal equipment'.[2]

The Americans regained control of the Kasserine pass on February 24. 'I was sure the Kasserine battle would turn out all right in the end,' Churchill telegraphed to Eisenhower two days later.[3] He was critical, however, of the British air commanders for what he described that same day to Portal as 'our total failure to build up air superiority in Tunisia', considering, he wrote, 'we have already assigned to this theatre 1,200 American first line aircraft, 500 British first line aircraft, the whole of the Middle East first line aircraft (about 1,000), all with their lavish tails of hundreds of thousands of men and squandering of our shipping'. The 'outstanding impression on my mind', Churchill added, 'of the four months since the landing, is of the failure and breakdown in the Allied air'.[4]

Portal replied with details of recent changes and plans, and expressing his confidence in Coningham and Tedder. Churchill had himself been pleased to see Coningham's influence 'in recent operations', he replied to Portal two days later, but he went on to tell the Chief of the Air Staff:

... here is the place where we want to fight the Hun and where the Hun has to fight us in the air, and every effort should be made by us, apart from the Americans, to bring the strongest forces constantly into action.

Are you watching all this yourself? Have you got a plan which all subordinates should be made to follow? At present I am afraid the word 'failure' must attach to the Allied air operations in Tunisia. The more I stand back from the picture and look at it, the more this stands out. I am counting on you to retrieve it now that you have the best men on the spot and in the right places.[5]

Amid the pressures and uncertainties of the Tunisian battle,

---

[1] Prime Minister's Personal Minute, D.27/3, 'Most Secret', 27 February 1943: Premier papers, 3/88/3, folio 321.

[2] Note of 19 April 1943: Premier papers, 3/88/3, folios 316–20.

[3] Prime Minister's Personal Telegram, T.224/3, No. 1895, 'Personal and Secret', 25 February 1943: Churchill papers, 20/107.

[4] Prime Minister's Personal Minute, M.74/3, 25 February 1943: Churchill papers, 4/397A.

[5] Prime Minister's Personal Minute, M.80/3, 27 February 1943: Churchill papers, 4/397A.

Churchill continued to keep Stalin informed of Britain's war effort in Europe. 'Last night,' he telegraphed to the Soviet leader on March 2, 'the Royal Air Force dropped over 700 tons of bombs on Berlin. Raid reported most successful. Out of 302 four-engined bombers we lost 19.' [1] In welcoming this news, Stalin replied: 'I regret that the Soviet Air Force, absorbed in the struggle against the Germans at the front, is not yet in a position to take part in the bombing of Berlin.' [2]

On Wednesday March 3, Churchill was well enough to go to Chequers. 'Papa is progressing very slowly,' Clementine Churchill wrote to their daughter Mary after a few days, 'but (I hope & believe) safely through his convalescence to his normal strong state of health.' [3] Doris Miles, one of the two nurses who had been with Churchill since his illness began, accompanied him to Chequers. There she later recalled, 'it was a question of making him do chest exercises, and giving him various medicines. I had to march into the dining room after dinner (all male) and present him with a red capsule on a large silver tray—I was then told: "The price of a good woman is above rubies".' Doris Miles added:

He prepared his speeches at Chequers, often in the bath (he was proud of being able to turn the taps off with his toes). He took immense pains with them, walking around in his bath towel, and going through them with Charles Wilson or Lord Cherwell.

I was very struck by his immense vigour and enthusiasm, his determination to get over his illness as quickly as possible. He told me that he ate and drank too much, (roast beef for breakfast) and took no exercise at all, but was much fitter than 'old so-and-so who is two years younger than me'.

He loved watching films, particularly newsreels, and was delighted if he featured in them: 'Look Pug, there we are!' He was very kind to me—interested to know that my husband was a Surgeon Lieutenant in a destroyer on the Russian convoys. . . . [4]

---

[1] Prime Minister's Personal Telegram, T.247/3, No. 164 to Moscow, 'Personal and Secret', 2 March 1943: Churchill papers, 20/107.

[2] 'Personal and Secret', Kremlin 3 March 1943: Premier papers, 3/14/2, folio 81. The British air raid on Berlin had one tragic repercussion in Britain. On the following day, after news of the Berlin raid had been announced over the radio, many Londoners expected a reprisal raid, and on the night of March 3, in anticipation of a raid that night, 600 people crowded into the underground shelter at Bethnal Green. When the alert was sounded, at least 900 more tried to enter the shelter. At that moment, anti-aircraft rockets, discharged from a battery a third of a mile away, caused panic, many of those at the shelter being afraid that the Germans were dropping parachute mines, as they had done in 1940. In the ensuing crush to enter the shelter, a woman fell, and others fell on top of her, pressed by at least 150 people still outside the shelter, desperate to enter it. In all, 173 people were killed: 27 men, 84 women and 62 children under sixteen. (Report prepared by Laurence R. Dunne, Command Paper 6583, January 1945: Premier papers, 4/40/15.)

[3] Letter of 26 February 1943: Mary Soames, *Clementine Churchill*, London 1979, page 333.

[4] Doris Miles, letter to the author, 14 January 1982.

On his second day at Chequers, Churchill read a minute by Ismay about a report which was being prepared, to show Britain's minimum shipping needs in all theatres. He replied, with particular reference to the material which Wavell still sought for the planned liberation of Burma:

All our operations are being spoiled by overloading and playing for safety as a certainty. The 'Anakim' demands are altogether excessive. An operation of war cannot be thought out like building a bridge; certainty is not demanded, and genius, improvisation and energy of mind must have their parts. I am far from satisfied with the way the Indian campaign is being conducted. The fatal lassitude of the Orient steals over all these Commanders. Similarly, 'Husky' is being run on the basis of altogether excessive demands.

Commanders should be made to feel that they have to make some personal contribution to victory if they are to get any honour out of it. Everywhere the British and Americans are overloading their operational plans with so many factors of safety that they are ceasing to be capable of making any form of aggressive war. For six or eight months to come Great Britain and the United States will be playing about with half a dozen German divisions. That is the position to which we are reduced, and which you should labour sedulously to correct.[1]

Throughout the war, Churchill had to try to strike a balance between excess of caution and wise restraint. In a telegram drafted to be sent to Stalin on March 4, signed by himself and Roosevelt jointly, Churchill addressed himself to the second front in Europe. It had not been abandoned, he wrote, as Stalin had protested in his telegram of February 16, but Stalin should realize that the Anglo-American plan for a cross-Channel landing was 'crippled for lack of shipping'. In case the Germans should 'weaken sufficiently', however, Britain and America were 'preparing to strike earlier than August', and plans, Churchill assured him, 'are kept alive from week to week'. The telegram ended, nevertheless, with a warning. If Germany did not weaken, Churchill insisted, 'a premature attack with insufficient forces would merely lead to a bloody repulse and a great triumph for the enemy'.[2]

The Chiefs of Staff wished to insert a paragraph into this telegram, asking for information about Russia's future operations. Churchill minuted: 'I feel so very conscious of the poor contribution the British and American armies are making in only engaging perhaps a dozen German divisions during the greater part of this year while Stalin is

---

[1] Prime Minister's Personal Minute, D.36/3, 'Most Secret', 3 March 1943: Churchill papers, 4/397A.
[2] Prime Minister's Personal Telegram, T.257/3, 'Personal and Most Secret', Prime Minister to President No. 271, 4 March 1943: Churchill papers, 20/107.

facing 185, that I should not be prepared myself to court the certain rebuff which would attend a request for information as to his plans.'[1]

Once more, Churchill also sent Stalin news of Britain's actual initiatives over Germany. 'The weather being unsuitable over Berlin,' he telegraphed on March 4, 'we cast about 800 tons with good results last night on Hamburg.' These were 'very heavy discharges', especially compressed 'into such short periods', and they would be increasing in both weight and frequency during the next few months. 'I expect the Nazi experiences will be very severe,' Churchill added, 'and make them less keen about war than they used to be.'[2]

Churchill was worried that Stalin's pressures might lead to an American change of emphasis in the decision to make Sicily the immediate Anglo-American priority. On March 4 he telegraphed to Field Marshal Dill, in Washington, in a telegram marked 'for your eyes alone', that Dill should 'on no account' give any encouragement to the postponement of the June date for 'Husky', the invasion of Sicily, for the sake of 'Bolero', the build-up of the cross-Channel forces in Britain.[3] The invasion of Sicily, he stressed to the Chiefs of Staff Committee, 'has supreme priority', although he hoped that the demands for it in terms of men and materials would be kept 'within the bounds of reason'. He was 'by no means convinced' that a successful cross-Channel attack, even the limited 'Sledgehammer' landing, could be successful in the conditions 'likely to prevail in August', the earliest date envisaged for 'Sledgehammer' when it had been discussed at Casablanca. 'Anyhow,' he wrote, Britain must not throw away the 'substance' of the Sicily invasion for 'this shadow' of a limited cross-Channel attack.[4]

On the following day, March 5, Dill reported back to Churchill that, after 'much opposition', the Americans had agreed to keep to the June date for Sicily. 'Delighted to know you are back at duty,' Dill added, 'and in fighting form.'[5] 'Tell General Marshall I am deeply grateful,' Churchill replied.[6]

On March 5, the Royal Air Force made its first mass air raid on the German industrial city of Essen, dropping 986 tons of bombs. These

[1] Prime Minister's Personal Minute, D.37/3, 'Most Secret', 4 March 1943: Churchill papers, 4/397A.

[2] Prime Minister's Personal Telegram, T.258/3, 'Most Secret and Personal', 4 March 1943: Churchill papers, 20/107.

[3] Prime Minister's Personal Telegram, T.260/3, OZ 647, 'Personal and Secret', 4 March 1943: Churchill papers, 20/107.

[4] Prime Minister's Personal Telegram, T.260/3, OZ 647, 'Personal and Secret', 4 March 1943: Churchill papers, 20/107.

[5] IZ 917, 'Personal and Secret', 5 March 1943: Churchill papers, 20/107.

[6] Prime Minister's Personal Telegram, T.275/3, OZ 680, 'Personal', 7 March 1943: Churchill papers, 20/107.

bombs had been dropped, Churchill informed Stalin, 'in an area of about two square miles'.[1]

In the Pacific, a Japanese invasion force on its way to New Guinea was intercepted by American naval and air forces in the Bismarck Sea, and all twenty-two ships in the force, ten warships and twelve troop transports, were sunk. Of the 150 Japanese aircraft involved, 102 were shot down. The American losses were only three fighters and a single bomber. 'Accept my warmest congratulations,' Churchill telegraphed to Roosevelt from Chequers on March 5, 'on your brilliant victory in the Pacific which fitly salutes the end of your first ten years.'[2]

Churchill was almost completely recovered from his pneumonia. 'I am much better,' he wrote to a friend on March 5, 'but I am staying in the country for a few days. Of course, I work wherever I am and however I am. That is what does me good.'[3]

Churchill remained at Chequers from March 3 to March 15. On March 7 he felt well enough to drive over to Ditchley Park, 'just him and me', noted Elizabeth Layton, 'panting along with pencil and notebook'. It was 'about an hour's drive', she added, 'and all the way there he spouted hard and I had an awful time trying to hear everything and get it all down—no joke you know, when the car goes swinging round a corner and your spare pencil falls on the floor and his papers (which you are holding) begin to slide off your knee, and his matches (which you are holding) rattle down beside you, and his spare cigar (which you are holding) makes a dive down behind you, and his box (which you are holding in position with your foot) slams shut and rushes across the floor of the car! It is a bit apt to put you off your outlines, but I managed it all right, thank heavens.'

At Ditchley, Churchill was greeted by Lady Diana Cooper who, Elizabeth Layton noted, 'threw her arms round his neck and shrieked "DARLING, how glad we are to see you" '.[4] Churchill stayed at Ditchley for lunch, returning to Chequers at about four o'clock that afternoon.

On March 8 King George VI drove to Chequers to lunch with Churchill, in place of their usual weekly lunch at Buckingham Palace.[5] 'The two of them talked hard in the room next to the office, and we could hear the two tongues wagging like mad! But I fear my boss still holds the floor!' When the King was ready to return to London,

[1] Prime Minister's Personal Telegram, T.267/3, No. 197 to Moscow, 'Personal and Secret', 6 March 1943: Churchill papers, 20/107.

[2] Prime Minister's Personal Telegram, T.262/3, Prime Minister to President, No. 272, 'Personal', 5 March 1943: Churchill papers, 20/107. Roosevelt had been inaugurated President for the first time on 5 March 1933.

[3] Letter of 5 March 1943 (to Viscount Camrose): Camrose papers.

[4] Elizabeth Layton, letter of 17 March 1943: Nel papers.

[5] John Martin diary, 8 March 1943: Martin papers.

Churchill '*would* go to the door', Elizabeth Layton added, 'in spite of instructions to the contrary, but suffered no setbacks'.

Remaining on duty throughout the twelve days at Chequers, Elizabeth Layton observed him in all his moods, writing to her parents when the convalescence was over:

> The more one is with him the more one gets to understand his funny little ways, and why he gets cross at this or that. One can anticipate his wants sometimes, and he always appreciates that. He likes one to know what kind of a smoke he wants, or when he wants a different pen passed to him. I think what he likes most is to be *quite* sure that you (one) won't say anything unless there is something to be said!!! There is nothing in the world he hates more than to waste one minute of his time! So even if you sit beside him for an hour and do nothing at all, you feel not altogether wasted as I think he likes to feel someone is there and that if he does want anything he won't have to wait for it.[1]

In August 1941 Churchill had written a note, the opening words of which were 'Renown awaits the Commander who first, in this war, restores the artillery to its prime importance upon the battlefield, from which it has been ousted by heavily armoured tanks'.[2] On 26 February 1943 Churchill had telegraphed to Montgomery, in Tunisia: 'I am sending you by the first sure hand some notes called "Renown Awaits" which you said you would like to see.' Churchill added, with a reference to the most recent Enigma decrypt: 'The Boniface which you have no doubt seen, discloses a deeply interesting prospect. If Rommel tries to chop up your spearheads in the next few days he may easily bring about an encounter battle on terms unexpected by him.' Churchill ended his telegram, as the prospect of a decisive battle in Tunisia loomed: 'I feel the greatest confidence in your genius and your Army, and all my thoughts are with you.'[3]

---

[1] Elizabeth Layton, letter of 17 March 1943: Nel papers.
[2] 'Secret', 'A Note by the Minister of Defence', printed on 30 August 1941: Cabinet papers, 120/10.
[3] Prime Minister's Personal Telegram, T.229/3, OZ 586, 'Personal and Secret', 26 February 1943: Churchill papers, 2/143.

21
Tunisia, 'The hunt is on'

FROM day to day, the Enigma decrypts continued to give Churchill a precise picture of German military intentions in Tunisia, enabling him to see, and to share with Alexander and Montgomery, each imminent German move. 'If Rommel tries to chop up your spearheads in the next few days,' he telegraphed to Montgomery on reading one such decrypt on 26 February 1943, 'he may easily bring about an encounter battle on terms unexpected by him.' Churchill added: 'I feel the greatest confidence in your genius and your Army, and all my thoughts are with you.'[1]

For several weeks, Montgomery had been preparing an offensive against the German-held Mareth Line, intending to launch his attack in the third week of March. The decrypted message to which Churchill referred in this telegram gave notice, however, that Rommel would attempt to forestall Montgomery's advance by an attack of his own. Having received the decrypt from 'C', Churchill had immediately asked for a sketch map both of the operations proposed in it, and of the units which Britain had 'to meet the impending blow'.[2] He could thus see, as Rommel could not, the situation on both sides of the front line.

On February 26, as Montgomery awaited this German offensive against his own positions, the commander of the 5th Panzer Army, General von Arnim, launched an attack in northern Tunisia. Alexander, forewarned by the Enigma decrypts as to the scale and timing of this thrust, was able to direct the Allied forces there in such a way as to inflict heavy losses on the Germans, both in men and tanks. After a week of intense fighting, von Arnim called off the attack, in

[1] Prime Minister's Personal Telegram, T.229/3, OZ 586, 'Personal and Secret', 26 February 1943: Churchill papers, 20/97.
[2] Prime Minister's Personal Minute, M.75/3, 'Secret' (to General Brooke and the Director of Military Intelligence), 26 February 1943: Churchill papers, 4/397A. The decrypt was CX/MSS/2177/T14.

which the Germans lost fifty tanks. Ironically, an Enigma decrypt on
February 28 revealed to 'C' and to Churchill that Rommel was
opposed to the 'intolerable dissipation of forces' that was resulting
from von Arnim's attack.[1]

On February 27, Alexander returned to his headquarters after three
days in the American and French front lines. 'Broadly speaking,' he
telegraphed to Churchill on the day of his return, 'Americans require
experience and French require arms.' He was sending the Americans
the best British officers available 'to give instruction in battle technique
and to help them train for war'. Alexander's telegram continued: 'The
repulse of the enemy in the south and re-establishment of former positions have put heart into Americans. I have ordered vigorous but in
meantime minor offensive action in south to regain initiative. I am
frankly shocked at whole situation as I found it.' He was, he explained,
'regrouping whole force into three parts,' the French under General
Anderson, the Americans under General Friedenhall, and the Eighth
Army under Montgomery.

Alexander's telegram contained a word of warning. 'Hate to disap-
point you,' he wrote, 'but final victory in North Africa is not (repeat
not) just around the corner. A very great deal requires to be done
both on land and in the air.'[2]

In studying the daily Enigma decrypts, and drawing his Commander's attention to particular aspects of them, Churchill was
always alert to the dangers of discovery. 'You will I am sure,' he
telegraphed to Montgomery on March 1, 'guard our precious secret
even, so far as possible, in your dispositions. Tell even your most
trusted commanders only the minimum necessary.'[3] One of the two
decrypts to which Churchill had drawn Montgomery's attention
that day showed that, at that point in the battle in northern Tunisia, one of von Arnim's units, the 21st Panzer Division, had 'only 47
serviceable tanks'.[4]

A single division at Medenine guarded Montgomery's supply lines
to the south and east of Mareth. As Medenine was twenty miles behind
the southern end of the Mareth Line, no extra troops seemed to be
needed there. On February 28, however, a further Enigma decrypt
revealed Rommel's intention to attack Medenine with three Panzer
divisions, thus encircling the British forces in front of the Mareth Line.
Further decrypts during the next three days gave the exact size of the

---

[1] CX/MSS/2190/T14: Hinsley and others, *op. cit.*, volume 2, page 594.
[2] Telegram MG 531, 'Personal and Most Secret', 27 February 1943: Churchill papers,
20/107.
[3] Prime Minister's Personal Telegram, T.245/3, 1 March 1943: Churchill papers, 4/396.
[4] No. VM 5207.

forces which Rommel was intending, within six or seven days, to throw into this battle: a total of 160 tanks and 200 guns. [1]

Montgomery responded at once to this unexpected challenge, which the Enigma decrypts had revealed, and which local radio intercepts and air intelligence had confirmed. Rushing up the New Zealand Division two hundred miles along the single tarmac road, 201 Guards Brigade, 400 tanks, 350 field guns and 470 anti-tank guns, Montgomery switched the balance of forces to Britain's favour. The Royal Air Force, too, alerted by Enigma, was able, just in time, to increase its forward strength, building it up to double that which was known to be available to Rommel.

Rommel, unaware that he had lost both the element of surprise and the superiority of armour, launched his attack against Medenine on the morning of March 6. In fierce fighting, the trap was sprung; of 140 German tanks committed to the battle, 52 were counted, derelict, on the battleground on the following day. Not a single British tank was lost. The German assault infantry, their protective shield itself assaulted, were pinned down and depressed by 'a devastating volume' of fierce and medium gunfire. At seven o'clock that evening, Rommel intervened personally, ordering 'an immediate cessation of the battle'. [2]

Rommel's decision to call off the battle of Medenine was decisive for the future course of the war. Had he succeeded in driving back the Eighth Army, which he might indeed have done without his Enigma messages being read, all the Anglo-American plans for 'Husky' could have been set back, and a landing on Sicily might even have proved impossible in 1943.

This success for Britain's most secret source came at a time of sudden fear that the secret was about to be exposed. Churchill's warning to Montgomery on March 1 about the security of Enigma had been a timely one. Eight days later, on March 9, the Enigma decrypts themselves revealed that the Germans were suspicious of Britain's impressive Intelligence, in regard to the strength, place and timing of Rommel's attack. Only later did it become clear that they still did not imagine that their Enigma machine cyphers were vulnerable. [3]

*   *   *

[1] The decrypts were VM 5007 of 0342 and VM 5207 of 1646, 28 February 1943: CX/MSS/2190/T14: F. H. Hinsley and others, *British Intelligence in the Second World War, Its Influence on Strategy and Operations*, vol 2, London 1981, pages 593–5.

[2] Major-General David Belchem, *All in the Day's March*, London 1978, page 147. Belchem was head of Montgomery's Operations Staff from 1943 to 1945.

[3] F. H. Hinsley and others, *British Intelligence in the Second World War*, volume 2, London 1981, page 596.

While still at Chequers, Churchill followed the course of the Tunisian battle from Alexander's reports. 'It is a great comfort to me,' he telegraphed on March 9, 'to feel your hand at work not only on the First Army front but in the whole combination.' He was glad to learn, also, of the success of the 'much-abused' Churchill tanks, 'for whose thick skins', he noted, 'I have some responsibility . . .'.[1] That same day, as he read of the air battles in North Africa, Churchill telegraphed to Eisenhower: 'Pray convey my compliments to crews of Mitchells, Lightnings and Fortresses on brilliant and fertile action.'[2]

On March 11, Churchill replied to the questions raised in Stalin's telegram of February 16, and to which Roosevelt had earlier replied, along the lines of Churchill's draft. 'I am now well enough to reply myself,' Churchill explained. The preparations for the invasion of Sicily were going ahead 'a month earlier than we had planned at Casablanca'. Plans were being investigated for possible operations against the Dodecanese, Crete and mainland Greece. The battle for Tunis was in progress, and would engage a quarter of a million Axis troops. There were also thirty German divisions in France and the Low Countries.

In Britain, Churchill told Stalin, a substantial invasion force was being gathered, including 27 United States divisions of between 40,000 and 50,000 men each, and 16 British divisions 'being prepared for a cross-Channel operation in August'.[3] The bomber offensive from the United Kingdom had been going 'steadily forward'. In February, more than 10,000 tons of bombs had been dropped on Germany. A further 4,000 tons had been dropped in the first ten days of March. As to the cross-Channel attack, as opposed to the 'operation' envisaged for August, Churchill told Stalin:

. . . it is the earnest wish of the President and myself that our troops should be in the general battle in Europe which you are fighting with such astounding prowess. But in order to sustain the operations in North Africa, the Pacific and India, and to carry supplies to Russia, the import programme into the United Kingdom has been cut to the bone and we have eaten, and

---

[1] Prime Minister's Personal Telegram, T.281/3, 'Most Secret', 9 March 1943: Churchill papers, 20/107.

[2] Prime Minister's Personal Telegram, T.285/3, 'Secret and Personal', No. 2034, 9 March 1943: Churchill papers, 20/107.

[3] Worried about having given Stalin details of United States military plans and arrangements, Churchill telegraphed to Stalin two days later, that this information about the size and scale of forces, and operational plans, 'should be considered as a separate message of a military operational character addressed to yourself as Marshal and Commander-in-Chief. Let these paragraphs be between you and me'. (Prime Minister's Personal Telegram, T.296/3, 'Personal and Most Secret', 13 March 1943: Churchill papers, 20/107.)

are eating, into reserves. However, in case the enemy should weaken sufficiently we are preparing to strike earlier than August, and plans are kept alive from week to week. If he does not weaken a premature attack with inferior and insufficient forces would merely lead to a bloody repulse, Nazi vengeance on the local population if they rose, and a great triumph for the enemy.

The cross-Channel situation, Churchill added, 'can only be judged nearer the time'. In making 'this declaration of our intentions there for your own personal information, I must not be understood to limit our freedom of decision'.[1]

Churchill was still at Chequers, where, on March 11, Eden reported him 'in good spirits, but thinner and older looking for his illness'.[2] 'Do take care of yourself and get really well,' Randolph Churchill wrote from North Africa on March 12.[3] That same day, at Chequers, the King of Greece was expected for lunch, and in good time the Chequers guard was lined up in front and prepared to give the royal salute. Elizabeth Layton noted the sequel:

My young friend John Corbould was the officer in charge—he had been there on the previous similar occasion and had felt rather inadequate, so was resolved to do the thing properly this time. They were all lined up half an hour before the arrival was due. We all waited anxiously, staring out of the window and fidgeting around. Presently, when the tension was getting almost unbearable, one of the police came rushing into the courtyard waving his hand—the signal. The guard drew itself up. John drew himself up. Just as the car came into the courtyard he barked, all in the approved style 'Guard—Royal Salute'.

We all craned from the office window. The guard crashed their guns. Sawyers, Him, etc. rushed to the front door. Out of the car stepped—Prof! Dear quiet mousy vegetarian Prof. who was staying the whole time with us and had just been out during the morning on business! Needless to say we all collapsed on the office floor and howled. It was quite interesting to see the King when he did come, but somehow much of the enthusiasm we had worked up had evaporated![4]

[1] Prime Minister's Personal Telegram, T.277/3, No. 214 to Moscow, 'Personal and Most Secret', 11 March 1943: Churchill papers, 20/107.

[2] Harvey diaries, 11 March 1943: John Harvey (editor), *op. cit.*, pages 227–8.

[3] Letter of 12 March 1943: Churchill papers, 1/375. On March 24 the Palestine Hebrew daily newspaper, *Davar*, reported that an 89-year-old Jewish woman, Leah Vitkind, was fasting because of a vow she had made to fast 'if she should live to hear that Mr Churchill had recovered from his illness'. Shown this press report, Churchill noted: 'Thank her & tell her to begin taking nourishment again.' (Undated note, John Martin papers.)

[4] Elizabeth Layton, letter of 17 March 1943: Nel papers.

Throughout his convalescence at Chequers, Churchill had continued to send Stalin details of Britain's bombing raids. 'From the bottom of my heart,' Stalin telegraphed on March 15, 'I welcome the British aviation striking hard against the German industrial centres.'[1] But Stalin's disappointment, not to say anger, at the delays in North Africa, was expressed that same day in outspoken words. At the height of the Red Army's fighting, in February and March, he telegraphed to Churchill, 'the weight of the Anglo-American offensive in North Africa has not only not increased, but there has been no development of the offensive at all, and the time limit for the operations set by yourself was extended'. Thirty-six German divisions had meanwhile been transferred from western Europe to the eastern front. In these circumstances, Stalin wrote, 'it is extremely important that the blow from the West should not be put off, that it should be struck in the spring or in the early summer'.[2]

Sending both Stalin's telegrams of March 15 to Eden, who was then in Washington, Churchill commented that they 'emphasize the feeling which has for some time been growing in my mind that there are two forces to be reckoned with in Russia: (a) Stalin himself, personally cordial to me. (b) Stalin in council, a grim thing behind him which we and he have both to reckon with.'[3]

For Britain, it was the continuing shipping losses in the Atlantic which were the focus of concern during the third week of March. These losses were discussed on March 16, the day after Churchill's return from Chequers, at the Defence Committee, and again on March 17, at a meeting of the Anti-U-boat Warfare Committee over which Churchill likewise presided. The presence of a German battle fleet in northern Norway made it impossible, the Defence Committee concluded, on the advice of the Naval Staff, to send the March convoy to Archangel.[4]

At the War Cabinet on March 18, Churchill reported severe losses in the Atlantic, with 'about 20 merchant ships having been sunk in the last two days'.[5] Britain's naval resources, he warned, 'were stretched to the uttermost, and the strength of the escorts to our Atlantic convoys was inadequate to meet the enemy's concentration of U-boats'.[6]

[1] 'Personal and Secret', Kremlin, 15 March 1943: Churchill papers, 20/108.
[2] 'Personal and Secret', Kremlin, 15 March 1943: Churchill papers, 20/108.
[3] Prime Minister's Personal Telegram, T.320/3, 'Personal and Most Secret', 18 March 1943: Churchill papers, 20/108.
[4] Convoy JW 54, due to sail on 27 March 1943. The German battle fleet consisted of *Tirpitz*, *Scharnhorst*, the cruiser *Lutzow*, and eight destroyers.
[5] It was learned later that day that 17 ships had been sunk. They were from the trans-Atlantic convoys HX 229 and SC 122.
[6] War Cabinet No. 42 of 1943, Confidential Annex, 18 March 1943, 'single copy, no circulation': Cabinet papers, 65/37.

In a telegram to Roosevelt on the evening of March 18, and with the approval of the War Cabinet, Churchill warned that the cancellation of the March convoy to north Russia 'will be a heavy blow to Stalin and his Government' and would 'certainly excite their grievous resentment'. The news should not therefore be broken to him on its own. 'I feel,' Churchill wrote, 'that it will be right and wise to place the picture before him as a whole, dark though it be.' The Atlantic convoy sinkings, Churchill added, were proof 'that our escorts are everywhere too thin'. The strain upon the British Navy, he warned, 'is becoming intolerable'.[1] A week later, Churchill told Stalin the bad news: the March convoy was not to sail. If one or two of Britain's most modern battleships were to be lost, Churchill explained, or even seriously damaged 'while *Tirpitz* and other large units of the German battle fleet remained in action, the whole command of the Atlantic would be jeopardized, with dire consequences to our common cause'. But although the thirty ships of the March convoy would not sail to north Russia, 'we are doing our utmost', Churchill told Stalin, 'to increase the flow of supplies by the Southern route'. The monthly figure of these supplies had already doubled in the previous six months. It was intended that the August figure would reach 240,000 tons. 'If this is achieved,' Churchill pointed out, 'the monthly delivery will have been increased eightfold in twelve months,' and would in some way 'offset both your disappointment and ours at the interruption of the Northern Convoys'.[2]

In his reply, Stalin stated: 'I understand this unexpected action as a catastrophic diminution of supplies of arms and raw materials to the USSR on the part of Great Britain and the United States of America,' as all other routes were limited in capacity. The ending of the northern convoy, he added, 'cannot fail to affect the position of the Soviet troops'.[3] Stalin made no further complaint. 'My own feeling,' Churchill telegraphed to the British Ambassador in Moscow, 'is that they took it like men.'[4] Stalin's reply, Churchill told the War Cabinet, 'was courageous and not unsatisfactory'.[5]

As was clear at the meeting of the Anti-U-Boat Warfare Committee

---

[1] Prime Minister's Personal Telegram, T.325/3, No. 1783 to Washington (for Eden and Halifax to send to the President), 18 March 1943: Churchill papers, 20/108.

[2] Prime Minister's Personal Telegram, T.364/3, 'Most Secret', 25 March 1943: Churchill papers, 20/108. After being approved by Roosevelt, this telegram was sent to Stalin five days later: Prime Minister's Personal Telegram, T.404/3, 'Personal and Most Secret', 30 March 1943: Churchill papers, 20/109.

[3] 'Personal and Secret', 2 April 1943: Churchill papers, 20/109.

[4] Prime Minister's Personal Telegram, T454/3, No. 345 to Moscow, 'Personal and Secret', 4 April 1943: Churchill papers, 20/109.

[5] War Cabinet No. 48 of 1943, 5 April 1943, Confidential Annex: Cabinet papers, 65/38.

on March 17, and from Churchill's telegram to Roosevelt on the following day, the third week of March marked the climax of the Atlantic war, and its biggest crisis. An Intelligence estimate at the beginning of the month had given a figure of sixty-six for the number of U-boats in the north Atlantic, a record number.[1] The sinkings, too, were rising precipitately: 42 ships in March compared with 26 in February.[2] On March 22 Portal warned that 'we can no longer rely on evading U-boat packs and, hence, we shall have to fight the convoys through them'.[3] The reason for the increased, and almost unbearable, shipping losses was, Portal told the Anti-U-Boat Warfare Committee eight days later, was 'failure of evasion' based on the Enigma decrypts'.[4]

The crisis, which had arisen from the problems of decrypting the new German naval Engima, was about to be resolved by an outstanding Intelligence success at Bletchley. On March 19 Brigadier Menzies informed Churchill that a further major setback to the solution of the U-boat Enigma decrypts, which had been resumed, though haltingly, in December 1942, had now been successfully overcome.[5] Within two months, the mortal danger was to have passed.

In the second week of March, Enigma decrypts of German dispositions in the Mediterranean disclosed that four merchant vessels and a tanker, whose cargoes were described by Kesselring as 'decisive for the future conduct of operations' in north Africa, would sail for Tunisia on March 12 and March 13, in two convoys. Alerted by this decrypt, British air and naval forces sank the tanker and two of the merchant ships. Unfortunately, before despatching the intercepting force, the British authorities failed to provide sufficient alternative sightings, so as to protect the Enigma source. An Enigma decrypt on March 14 made it clear that the suspicions of the German Air Force had been aroused, a breach of security being blamed for the loss of the vital cargoes. Churchill, reading this decrypt, minuted at once that the Enigma would be withheld unless it was 'used only on great occasions or when thoroughly camouflaged'.[6]

[1] Operational Intelligence Centre (Admiralty), SI No. 544 of 15 March 1943: Hinsley and others, *British Intelligence in the Second World War*, volume 2, London 1981, page 562.

[2] Michael Howard, *Grand Strategy*, volume 4, August 1942–August 1943, London 1972, page 310.

[3] AU No. 90 of 1943, 22 March 1943: Hinsley and others, *supra*, page 563.

[4] AU No. 103 of 1943, 30 March 1943: Hinsley and others, *supra*, page 563.

[5] Dir/C Archive, No. 2634, 19 March 1943: F. H. Hinsley and others, *British Intelligence in the Second World War*, volume 2, London 1981, page 750.

[6] Dir/C Archives, No. 2592: Hinsley and others, *British Intelligence in the Second World War*, volume 2, London 1981, page 647.

Fortunately for Britain, the Germans did not suspect that their Enigma secret was the cause of this apparent breach of their security. There was also a psychological aspect: 'while not minimizing seriousness of arousing enemy misgivings', Admiral Cunningham replied on March 15, 'I consider his statement comes as much from a desire to cover his failure in protecting the convoy as from real base of suspicion. He did the same thing,' Cunningham added, 'in excusing recent failures against 8 Army.' [1]

In Tunisia, following his victory over Rommel at Medenine, Montgomery had continued with his plans for an offensive against the main enemy defences in southern Tunisia, the Mareth Line. Rommel himself had left North Africa on March 9, having handed over command of the Army Group Africa to von Arnim. An Italian officer, General Messe, took over command of the Panzer Army Africa, which was renamed the 1st (Italian) Army. It was not until March 18 that an Enigma decrypt revealed that Rommel had gone. Montgomery's offensive, codename 'Pugilist', was to begin at ten o'clock in the evening of March 21. 'The stage is set,' he telegraphed to Churchill on the previous night, 'and you will receive confirmation when curtain goes up.' [2]

That night, as 'Pugilist' was about to begin, Churchill broadcast live from Chequers. He spoke of the post-war world, and plans for a fairer society in the aftermath of victory. But he also gave his 'earnest advice' to concentrate 'even more zealously upon the war effort, and if possible not to take your eye off the ball even for a moment'. Some time next year, 'but it may well be the year after', Britain might beat Hitler, by which, Churchill explained, 'I mean beat him and his powers of evil into death, dust and ashes.' Then would come the time for great social changes.

Churchill's vision of the post-war world was wide-ranging, echoing the concerns which he had felt when President of the Board of Trade before the First World War, and as Chancellor of the Exchequer between the wars. 'We must,' he said, 'establish on broad and solid foundations a National Health Service.' There would also have to be 'national compulsory insurance for all classes for all purposes from the cradle to the grave'. Educational opportunities would have to be extended and prolonged and 'fair competition' so extended that Britain would need to draw her leaders 'from every type of school and wearing every kind of tie'. Tradition, he said, may play its part, 'but

---

[1] CNS/2030, 15 March 1943: Hinsley and others, *British Intelligence in the Second World War*, volume 2, London 1981, page 647.

[2] MA/152, 'Personal', 'Most Secret', sent 11.05 p.m., 20 March 1943, received 1.05 a.m., 21 March 1943: Churchill papers, 20/108.

broader systems must now rule'. If State enterprise and free enterprise were both made to serve the national interests, 'and pull the national wagon side by side', then there would be no need 'to run into that horrible, devastating slump or into that squalid epoch of bickering and confusion which mocked and squandered the hard-won victory we gained a quarter of a century ago'.

As Churchill's broadcast was ending he told his listeners: 'I have just received a message from General Montgomery, that the Eighth Army are on the move and that he is satisfied with their progress,' and he added: 'Let us wish them God speed in their struggle, and let us bend all our efforts to the war and to the ever more vigorous prosecution of our supreme task.'[1]

Randolph Churchill wrote to his father from North Africa two days later that the conclusion of the broadcast, with the news of Montgomery's advance, was 'the most dramatic announcement I have heard on the wireless since the invasion of Holland and Belgium'.[2] 'We listened with deepest interest and pleasure to your masterly broadcast last night,' Field Marshal Smuts telegraphed from Cape Town. 'It is as timely as Montgomery's move, which I trust will now be pressed with unabated speed.'[3] In his telegram of March 21, Montgomery had informed Churchill that the New Zealand Corps had 'moved round enemy west flank, and at 13.00 hours to-day was fifteen miles southwest of El Hamma and is directed on Gabes. 30th Corps attacked enemy east flank last night and established a bridgehead through the main obstacles and minefields of Mareth position, and this bridgehead is being widened and success exploited.' Montgomery added: 'Enemy clearly intends to stand and fight, and I am preparing for a dog-fight battle in Mareth area, which may last several days. Action of New Zealand Corps in Gabes area may have a decisive effect on the battle.'[4]

On March 23, Churchill sent Stalin an account of Montgomery's continuing advance. 'We have about 70,000 Germans and 50,000 Italians inside the closing circle,' he wrote, 'but it is too soon to speculate on what will happen. You will be able yourself to judge from the map the possibilities that are open.'[5] In studying the report from the battle scene, Churchill was perturbed by one aspect of them, which he at once communicated by telegram to Alexander:

[1] Broadcast of 21 March 1943, broadcast live from Chequers: BBC Written Archive Centre.
[2] Letter of 24 March 1943: Churchill papers, 1/375.
[3] Telegram of 22 March 1943: Churchill papers, 20/108.
[4] 'Unnumbered message', 'Personal and Very Urgent', 1.30 p.m., 21 March 1943: Churchill papers, 20/108.
[5] Prime Minister's Personal Telegram, T.353/3, 'Personal, Secret and Operational', No. 280 to Moscow, 6 p.m., 23 March 1943: Churchill papers, 20/108.

... the proceedings on the First Army's sea flank do not seem at all satisfactory. We appear to be continually defeated in engagements of brigades
and battalions and the unit ascendancy of the Germans over our men seems
to be apparent. I sent you a telegram on this area after the evacuation of
Sedjenane and I shall be much obliged if you will at your convenience let me
know what is happening. Are our men being steadily outfought? If so why
cannot we bring superior numbers? Are you really so short of men that you
must use the precious paratroops as ordinary infantry? Or are you massing
for a counter-stroke elsewhere on the First Army front? [1]

Replying on the following day, Alexander explained that the 50th
Division had met 'very strong opposition', that 'great difficulties' had
been experienced in getting tanks and anti-tank guns across the Wadi
Zigzaou, and that 'strong enemy counter attacks' had pushed the
50th Division back across the Wadi at one point. An advance by the
51st Division, he added, had been stopped by minefields 'and accurate
fire'. As a result of this failure of the frontal attack Montgomery was
'not persevering with this right thrust at present', but, as Churchill
had surmised, was reinforcing elsewhere, to carry out an outflanking
move. As for the Germans, Alexander added, 'it is doubtful whether
they have the numbers to stand for long the hammering from artillery
and air which they are getting'. [2]

If Alexander were to need further troops, Churchill telegraphed on
March 24, the 56th British Infantry Division was arriving in Palestine
'and might be shipped to Tripoli'. There was also the 10th Indian
Infantry Division in Cyprus. 'No doubt you have full particulars. Let
me know if there is anything we can do.' [3] 'All good wishes,' Churchill
telegraphed five minutes later to Montgomery. 'We have every confidence you will pull it off.' [4]

In a telegram on March 26, Churchill learned from Montgomery
that the Germans were 'fighting desperately' but that he hoped to be
able to maintain the momentum of his operations 'and not have to
stop because of casualties'. Montgomery asked Churchill for reinforcements from Egypt, and also the 56th British Infantry Division
'sent up at once'. There would be no invasion of Sicily, he warned, 'if
we do not finish this business properly'. [5]

Churchill acted at once to give Montgomery the reinforcements for
which he had asked. 'Let me have a graph of the forward movement

[1] Prime Minister's Personal Telegram, T.354/3 War Office telegram No. 63259, 'Personal and
Secret', 6.35 p.m., 23 March 1943: Churchill papers, 20/108.
[2] MA/163, 'Personal and Most Secret', 24 March 1943: Churchill papers, 20/108.
[3] Prime Minister's Personal Telegram, T.359/3, 'Personal and Secret', OZ 849, 4.30 p.m., 24
March 1943: Churchill papers, 20/108.
[4] Prime Minister's Personal Telegram, T.360/3, 'Personal and Secret', OZ 850, 4.35 p.m., 24
March 1943: Churchill papers, 20/108.
[5] Telegram No. 26384, 'Most Secret', 26 March 1943: Churchill papers, 20/108.

of this Division by the fastest means from Palestine and thence by sea to Tripoli,' he minuted to Brooke about the 56th Division.[1]

On March 27 General Messe's forces prepared to withdraw from the Mareth Line. The Eighth Army was about to achieve its objective. 'I hope you will now be able to break and defeat the enemy and completely drive him out of Tunis,' Stalin telegraphed to Churchill from the Kremlin. 'I hope also,' he added, 'that the air offensive against Germany will go on inexorably increasing.'[2] That night, the Royal Air Force again raided Germany: 395 heavy bombers, as Churchill telegraphed to Stalin, 'flung 1050 tons on Berlin in 50 minutes. The sky was clear over the target and the raid was highly successful. This is the best Berlin has yet got. Our loss is 9 only.'[3]

From Montgomery, on March 28, Churchill received the signal of victory: 'After seven days of continuous and heavy fighting,' Montgomery telegraphed, 'Eighth Army has inflicted severe defeat on enemy.' Enemy resistance was 'disintegrating'. The Eighth Army was in possession of the whole Mareth Line defences.[4] 'Bravo!' Churchill replied. 'I was sure of it. Now the question is the cop.'

Churchill then sent Montgomery a summary of the most recent Enigma decrypts: General Messe's 164th Division 'has lost nearly all its vehicles and heavy weapons', that the 21st and 15th Panzer Divisions 'are regathering on heights south-east of El Hamma', and that the Italian Commander-in-Chief of the Mareth garrisons had asked the 15th Panzer Division to provide a battle group 'to cover his retreat' to a point 13 miles south-east of El Hamma and 13 miles south-west of Gabes. 'You should have received all this through other channels,' Churchill wrote, 'but to make sure I repeat it.'[5]

With this precious information from the enemy's own communications, Churchill telegraphed the details to Smuts that same day, with the preface: ' "Boniface" shows that. . . .' After giving Smuts the details, Churchill added: 'I cannot but be hopeful that we may put a cork in the Gafsa bottle-neck and that the Italian 20th and 21st Corps may be cut off.'[6]

[1] Prime Minister's Personal Minute, M.193/3, 26 March 1943: Churchill papers, 4/397A.
[2] 'Personal and Most Secret', Kremlin, 27 March 1943: Churchill papers, 20/108.
[3] Prime Minister's Personal Telegram, T.384/3, 'Personal and Secret', 28 March 1943: Premier papers, 3/14/2, folio 77.
[4] 'Personal and Most Secret', 11.30 a.m., 28 March 1943: Churchill papers, 20/108. Churchill at once sent a copy of this telegram to the King.
[5] Prime Minister's Personal Telegram, T.391/3, 28 March 1943: Churchill papers, 4/396.
[6] Prime Minister's Personal Telegram, T.392/3, 28 March 1943: Churchill papers, 4/396. This telegram is the first evidence the author has seen that General Smuts was aware of the Enigma secret. Presumably Churchill had informed him of it during their meeting in Cairo in August 1942.

Churchill had to monitor not only the course of the battle, but the relationship between the Allies who were fighting it. On March 28 he learned that Eisenhower had been 'rather hurt' that the King's message to the troops before the battle had not gone through Eisenhower, but through Alexander. Churchill wrote at once to the King's Private Secretary, taking 'fullest responsibility for the Channel used', and going on to explain and to advise:

There is no doubt that the situation had changed very rapidly in Tunisia. 'Torch', which was to be a preponderantly American operation, has now fallen into the practical control of Alexander, Cunningham, Tedder and Montgomery. This is not surprising considering we have twelve British divisions in action compared to three American, and have probably suffered five times the casualties. Nevertheless in view of the great importance of keeping things sweet and pleasant with our Allies and with Eisenhower, who is a good man, I am on the look-out for an opportunity of advising the King to send another message to General Eisenhower and all the troops under his command.

The opportunity for such a message, Churchill pointed out, 'might come if the battle takes a markedly favourable turn in the next few days'.[1]

Churchill's worry lest he had offended Eisenhower was expressed again in a telegram to Alexander three days later, when he reported that he was arranging 'at the first suitable opportunity' for the King to send Eisenhower a message of congratulations 'for all the Allied troops'. He had also referred to Eisenhower 'in a laudatory manner' in Parliament on the previous day.[2] Churchill's telegram continued:

I trust you will take every opportunity to remove any soreness that may exist in Eisenhower's mind, and give him the assurance that I and all at home wish to work whole-heartedly with him and that we recognize what a vital part he plays in keeping the whole show together. It is not unnatural that the American High Command should be disconcerted by the extraordinary changes wrought in the situation by the arrival on the scene of six British divisions from the Desert and two more from England, making our proportion of troops engaged four to one and I suppose our losses six or seven to one. This, together with our providing all the naval power inside the Mediterranean, has transformed 'Torch' from a primarily American operation into a preponderantly British one.

[1] 'Secret', 28 March 1943 (to Sir Alexander Hardinge): Churchill papers, 20/93.
[2] Churchill had told the House of Commons on 30 March 1943: 'The very fine, unceasing advance of the United States forces and the increasing activities on the French sector and on the Front of the British First Army, all play their part in the combinations of General Eisenhower, the Supreme Commander, and his Deputy, General Alexander.'

'All the more,' Churchill added, 'I and others at home must not fail at any time in the tact and consideration which the harmony of the common cause requires.' [1]

In the fourth week of March, Marian Holmes began work as one of the small team of secretaries who worked for Churchill in a rota system, from the 8.30 early morning duty until long after midnight, under the general supervision of Kathleen Hill. In her diary, Miss Holmes described that first encounter at No. 10 Annexe:

At last my initiation and baptism of fire. 11.30 p.m. Mr Rowan introduced me very firmly and said twice 'This is Miss Holmes.' The PM was so absorbed in the documents he was reading that he did not hear and did not even look up. He went straight in to dictating and I took it down on the silent typewriter. 'Here you are'—he still didn't look at me. I took the papers, he reached for more work from his despatch box and I made for the door. Loud voice 'Dammit, don't go. I've only just started.' He then looked up. 'I am so sorry. I thought it was Miss Layton. What is your name?' 'Miss Holmes' 'Miss Hope?' 'Miss Holmes' 'Oh'. He then carried on dictating directives and comments on various documents from his box, every so often glancing at me over his spectacles. 'That is all for the moment. You know you must never be frightened of me when I snap. I'm not snapping at you but thinking of the work.' This was said with a cherubic smile. When I took the work back to the PM, he said he wouldn't need me for the moment but to stay around. This was my first formal encounter working for him and I think I have been accepted. [2]

Marian Holmes had indeed been accepted and was to remain one of the inner secretarial circle until the end of the war.

On March 29, Churchill saw the Editor of *The Times*, Robin Barrington-Ward, for their third talk of the war. In his diary, the editor noted that Churchill showed no signs of his recent illness, describing him as 'pinky, fresh in colour, hardly a wrinkle, voice firm, all his usual animation and emphasis'. The two men talked for nearly an hour and a half. In politics, Churchill said, he had 'no axe to grind'. He would 'stand on his broadcast' of March 21, and 'the Tory Party would fight on that'. Churchill added: 'I shall come out of the war an old man. I shall be 70. I have nothing more to ask for.'

Speaking of Russia, Churchill told Barrington-Ward: 'I have wooed Joe Stalin as a man might woo a maid.' But he favoured confederations of smaller States once the war was won, telling Barrington-

---

[1] Prime Minister's Personal Telegram, T.423/3, OZ 914, 'Private and Most Secret', 31 March 1943: Churchill papers, 20/109.
[2] Marian Holmes diary, 24 March 1943: Marian Walker Spicer papers.

Ward: 'I do not want to be left alone in Europe with the Bear.'[1]

On March 30 Churchill learned from Eden, who was still in Washington, that Roosevelt 'was worried about difficulties which are being discovered' in the planning of the Sicily landings, 'and so', Churchill telegraphed to Harry Hopkins, 'am I'. Churchill suggested to Hopkins a meeting in North Africa in the latter part of April, between Hopkins and Marshall for the United States, and Brooke and Churchill for Britain, 'in order to survey and if possible clinch the business or, in the last resort, to explore alternatives.'

The suggestion that it might be necessary to give up the Sicily invasion was, Churchill felt, the result of 'heavy weather' being made by the American planners. 'At present,' he pointed out to Hopkins, 'there are only three weak Italian divisions there and no German.' At the same time, 'events are moving in Tunisia and the enemy is already preparing to evacuate Sfax and Sousse'.[2] To counter the American doubts, Churchill submitted his own hopes for 'Husky' for examination by the British Chiefs of Staff. The Tunisian Tip would be under Allied control by May 15 'at worst', he wrote, and the invasion of Sicily would have begun on July 10. At that date, the German and Italian troops in Sicily would total 70,000. The British and American total would be 135,000.

The capture of Sicily was, Churchill told the Chiefs of Staff, 'such a modest and even petty objective' for the Allied armies. It was 'only a stepping stone' which had to be followed up. If German forces were then brought down into Italy, the taking of Rome and Naples might be 'beyond our power'. Plans should therefore be ready in the Eastern Mediterranean, for an attack on the Dodecanese Islands.[3] But if the Germans did not come to Italy's aid, the Italians might 'crumble' and Italy be forced out of the war. 'We may become possessed of Sardinia without fighting. Corsica may be liberated.' All the available Allied forces could then be moved 'northwards into Italy' until they came in contact with the Germans on the Brenner Pass, or along the French Riviera. 'How far,' Churchill asked, 'have these possibilities been studied?'

[1] Barrington-Ward diary, 29 March 1943: McLachlan, *op. cit.*, page 205.

[2] Prime Minister's Personal Telegram, T.415/3, 'Personal and Most Secret', 30 March 1943: Churchill papers, 20/109.

[3] The largest of which was Rhodes. In seeking Turkish help in the attack on the Dodecanese, Churchill asked Eden: 'Can we offer them Rhodes as the price? (Prime Minister's Personal Minute, M.227/3, 'Most Secret', 4 April 1943: Churchill papers, 4/397A.) The codename for the attack on the Dodecanese was 'Handcuff'.

In this note to the Chiefs of Staff Committee, Churchill suggested that even if, after the conquest of Sicily, Italy remained in the war with German help, it would be worth trying to get 'a footing both on the toe and heel of Italy'. The possession of the Italian port of Taranto 'would confer great advantages upon us', enabling the Allies to get a footing on the Dalmatian coast, 'so that we can foment the insurgents of Albania and Yugoslavia by weapons, supplies and possibly Commandos'. There were, Churchill believed, 'great possibilities' in the Yugoslav theatre, including the possibility that the Yugoslav underground leader, General Mihailovic, 'in spite of his present naturally foxy attitude', would throw 'his whole weight' against the Italians, the moment the Allies were able to give him 'any effective help'.[1]

These ideas, Churchill informed Roosevelt three days later, were 'only intended as a channel for thought and planning'. To this end, he was sending it to the President, Hopkins and Marshall.[2] Meanwhile, Churchill had to watch closely over the relations between Eisenhower and Alexander. On April 3 Eisenhower had pressed Alexander for information about his plan of operations for Tunisia. 'There would be an awful row,' Churchill minuted to Brooke, 'if Eisenhower's message ever saw the light of day.' After the battle was over, Churchill told Brooke, 'I shall ask Alexander to keep his Chief more fully informed.' So much depended, he wrote, 'on going through the ceremonial processes'.[3]

Churchill was at Chequers for the weekend beginning April 2. 'We had good news about Tunisia,' Elizabeth Layton wrote to her parents, 'so the boss was in a grand temper, and really I've seldom had such fun! He was very nice to us all and treated us like human beings for once! Poor man, don't think I ever blame him for not doing so—it is so understandable.'

Churchill's good mood that weekend was much enjoyed. Elizabeth Layton noted:

One night, for instance, he did some dictation and then walked out saying 'Do that, then off to bed with you.' Then he came back into the office beaming all over his face, to say 'Miss Layton, you are the repository of the nation's secrets.' So I said, jokingly 'I won't tell, you know,' and he said, in like vein, 'I know you won't. I know you would rather die.' And so I would.

[1] Prime Minister's Personal Minute, D.66/3, 'Most Secret', 2 April 1943: Churchill papers, 4/397A.
[2] Prime Minister's Personal Telegram, T.459/3, Prime Minister to President, No. 279, 'Personal and Most Secret', 5 April 1943: Churchill papers, 20/109.
[3] Prime Minister's Personal Minute, M.238/3, 'Most Secret and Private', 6 April 1943: Churchill papers, 4/397A.

Churchill returned to London on April 5. Elizabeth Layton, who accompanied him, wrote to her parents:

He is so funny in the car; he may dictate, or he may just think for the whole hour, mumbling and grumbling away to himself; or he may be watching the various things we pass, suddenly making little ejaculations like 'Oh—look at the lambs,' or 'What kind of an aeroplane is that'—to which little reply is expected. I think he knows now that I have learnt not to waste his time by making any fool observations, which one might have felt oneself compelled to break the silence by doing. . . .[1]

Churchill reached London in time to lunch with Ambassador Winant.[2] That evening he awaited as patiently as he could the telegram from North Africa, for in the early hours of April 6 Montgomery had launched a further offensive in Tunisia, at Wadi Akarit. Five minutes before noon he telegraphed to Churchill: 'I delivered a heavy attack against enemy in Akarit position early this morning. I did two things not done by me before, in that I attacked centre of enemy position, and in the dark with no moon.' The attack had been delivered, Montgomery explained, by 'about three infantry divisions, supported by 450 guns, and enemy was surprised and overwhelmed and all objectives were captured'. Through the 'hole' created by this attack, he was sending the New Zealand Division and an armoured division, 'and this movement has now just begun at the time of sending you this'. His troops were 'in tremendous form'. The number of prisoners had been estimated at two thousand after only six hours' fighting, 'and many more are flowing in'.[3] Churchill at once passed on details of Montgomery's attack to Stalin. 'I know you like to hear any good news,' he commented. 'The hunt is on.'[4]

Churchill also sent Stalin on April 6 a detailed account of the continuing British and American air raids on Germany. On April 3, 900 tons of bombs had been dropped on the Krupp factories at Essen, and 'last night' 1,400 tons of bombs had been dropped on Kiel, 'one of the heaviest discharges we have ever made'. American daylight bombing had also gathered in intensity, with a raid on April 5 on the Renault tank assembly lines near Paris.[5] 'I must again emphasize,' Churchill's report ended, 'that our bombing of Germany will increase

[1] Elizabeth Layton, letter of 7 April 1943: Nel papers.

[2] Churchill Engagement Cards, 5 April 1943.

[3] 'Special Un-numbered Message', 'Most Secret', sent at 11.55 a.m., 6 April 1943: Cabinet papers, 118/86. These 'Special Un-numbered Messages', although sent by the Enigma channel, were not about Enigma matters. The channel was used for privacy.

[4] Prime Minister's Personal Telegram, T.465/3, 'Personal and Secret', 6 April 1943: Churchill papers, 20/109.

[5] In these three attacks, 4 American and 33 British bombers had been lost. The British raids had involved 348 heavy bombers on Essen and 507 on Kiel.

in scale month by month and that we are able to find the targets with much more certainty.'[1]

At the beginning of April, Churchill was shown the text of a protest by the new Commander-in-Chief of the Polish forces, General Anders, to Stalin, in which Anders castigated Russia's delay in allowing Polish refugee families in Russia to join their soldier-husbands, whom Stalin had already allowed to go to Persia, as part of a reconstituted Polish Army. In Anders's protests, Churchill minuted to Cadogan, 'we see all those elements of instability which have led to the ruin of Poland through so many centuries in spite of the individual qualities and virtues of the Poles'. Churchill added: 'General Anders is anxious to procure the release by the Russian Government of the unhappy families of his Polish troops, but he himself always expressed the most bitter sentiments against that Government which I have no doubt have been carried to them.' The Poles, Churchill pointed out, had 'no power to procure any releases from the Russian Government, and at the present time my influence is not supported by a sufficient military contribution to the common cause to make my representations effective. We have armed and are feeding and paying these Polish troops, and they now begin the usual Polish fissiparous and subversive agitation.'[2]

In an attempt to mitigate the blow to Russia of the cancellation of the March, April and May convoys, Churchill urged upon the Ministers concerned, and upon Portal, that every effort should be made to fly out through West Africa and Persia the aircraft that would have gone by the northern route. 'It is very important,' he minuted on April 6, 'that I should telegraph to Marshal Stalin that we are sending those, which are his anyway, with the utmost speed and by the shortest route.' The despatch of these aircraft—Airacobras and Hurricanes—was, Churchill added, 'of high importance and urgency'.[3]

To Stalin, Churchill pointed out that same day that once Bizerta and Tunis had been captured, store ships would be able to pass

---

[1] Prime Minister's Personal Telegram, T.460/3, 'Personal and Most Secret', 6 April 1943: Churchill papers, 20/109.

[2] Prime Minister's Personal Minute, M.244/3, 3 April 1943: Churchill papers, 4/397A.

[3] Prime Minister's Personal Minute, M.241/3, 'Action this Day', 6 April 1943: Cabinet papers, 79/60 (Chiefs of Staff Committee No. 71, Operations, of 1943, 9 April 1943, Annex 1). This minute was addressed to the Minister of Production (Sir Stafford Cripps), the Secretary of State for Air (Sir Archibald Sinclair), the Foreign Secretary (Anthony Eden) and the Chief of the Air Staff (Sir Charles Portal).

through the Mediterranean, 'thus shortening the voyage to Egypt and the Persian Gulf'. But he did not disguise from Stalin, any more than from himself, that much severe fighting was still to come in Tunisia. As he told Stalin:

Hitler, with his usual obstinacy, is sending the Hermann Goering and the 9th German Divisions into Tunisia, chiefly by air transport, in which at least 100 large machines are employed. The leading elements of both of these divisions have already arrived. Therefore we must expect a stubborn defence of the Tunisian tip by about a quarter of a million men, less any they lose on the way. Our forces have a good superiority both in numbers and equipment. We are taking a very heavy toll of all the ships that go across with fuel, ammunition, vehicles &c. When we have captured the southern airfields, we shall be able to bring very heavy constant air attack to bear upon the ports, and we are making every preparation to prevent a Dunkirk escape.[1]

A few days earlier, in a conversation in the House of Commons with Victor Cazalet, Churchill had talked about 'the Axis having a "Bumkirk" in Tunisia'. Cazalet added: 'He seems in great form and has thoroughly enjoyed being in the House for an hour or two each day, provided he is talking all the time. He cannot bear to sit on the bench for a minute without taking part in what is going on.'[2]

On April 7, at luncheon with the Spanish Ambassador, the Duke of Alba, Churchill had raised the question of the action of the Spanish Government in closing the Franco-Spanish frontier to Jewish refugees and escaped prisoners of war. In the account of the luncheon which he sent to the Foreign Office, Churchill pointed out that he had told the Ambassador, in connection with the refugees, 'that if his Government went to the length of preventing these unfortunate people seeking safety from the horrors of Nazi domination, and if they went farther and committed the offence of actually handing them back to the German authorities, that was a thing which would never be forgotten and would poison the relations between the Spanish and British peoples'.[3]

In sending this message to Sir Samuel Hoare in Madrid, the Foreign Office toned down the final phrase, deleting all reference to poison. Churchill's intervention was, nevertheless, successful: the border was

---

[1] Prime Minister's Personal Telegram, T.460/3, op. cit.

[2] Letter of 8 April 1943: Robert Rhodes James, Victor Cazalet, a Portrait, London 1976, page 283.

[3] Note dated 7 April 1943: Premier papers, 4/21/2, folio 335. Assuming that the Duke of Alba would send an account of the conversation to Madrid, and knowing that British Intelligence was reading the diplomatic traffic passing between the Spanish Embassy in London and the Foreign Ministry in Spain, Churchill minuted somewhat mischievously to Eden: 'I hope you will see in "Boniface" an account of my talk with Alba' (Prime Minister's Personal Minute, M.254/3, 'Secret', 11 April 1943: Premier papers, 4/21/2, folio 332).

opened once more, and hundreds of Jews, as well as British and American escaped prisoners-of-war, managed to find refuge, and safety, on Spanish soil.

On April 7, Montgomery's renewed offensive in Tunisia continued to be successful: 'Enemy in full retreat from Akarit position,' he telegraphed to Churchill that day. 'Prisoners taken yesterday now total 6,000. Am pursuing northwards.' [1] 'Enemy in full retreat northward, hotly pursued by Montgomery's armour,' Churchill telegraphed to Stalin as soon as Montgomery's message reached him, and he added: '6,000 prisoners in all.' [2]

Despite Montgomery's initial success, Churchill was nervous. 'Sometimes he is just as nervy and on edge as he could be,' Elizabeth Layton wrote to her parents on April 7, 'and barks at you for nothing at all; like this morning, for instance. He had had more good news (Montgomery's breakthrough at Akarit) and I was on duty and he was on edge, and I just couldn't seem to do anything right. I did my typing all right, but when asked to read it back I read too quickly.' Asked to ' "Just write this," ' Elizabeth Layton started writing in her shorthand book. 'No NO, WHY DON'T YOU USE YOUR MACHINE. . . .', Churchill exclaimed. 'At the end of the morning I felt as if I'd been run over by a steam-roller.' Miss Layton added, 'But he went to the House and delivered his bit about Montgomery, and was loudly cheered, and I watched it coming over the tape at 12.30 p.m. today, not many minutes after I'd typed it to his dictation (which is quite a little thrill).' [3]

That evening, Churchill learned from Alexander that United States troops had 'joined hands' with the Eighth Army. [4] A day of nervous anticipation was over.

Although Stalin was disappointed at the suspension of three convoys, he too rejoiced in the North African victories. 'I hope that this time,' he telegraphed to Churchill, 'the Anglo-American forces will finally defeat and destroy Rommel and other Hitler gangs in Tunis. It will be of the greatest importance for our common struggle.' The British bombing of Germany was likewise welcomed. 'Every blow

[1] MA/217 (Alexander to Churchill), 'Most Secret', 7 April 1943 (time of arrival, 1.22 p.m.): Churchill papers, 20/109.
[2] Prime Minister's Personal Telegram, T.472/3, 'Personal and Secret', 7 April 1943: Churchill papers, 20/109.
[3] Elizabeth Layton, letter of 7 April 1943: Nel papers.
[4] MA/222, 'Most Secret', 'Personal', 7 April 1943 (time of arrival, 8.40 p.m.): Churchill papers, 20/109.

delivered by your Air Force to the vital German centres,' Stalin added, 'evoked a most lively echo in the hearts of many millions throughout the width and breadth of our country.'[1]

On April 8 Churchill learned of further American hesitations over 'Husky'. In a telegram on the previous day, Eisenhower had warned that the presence of two German divisions on Sicily cast doubt on the ability of the Allies to invade the island successfully, and that both Alexander and Montgomery shared this view.[2] This was a 'most depressing telegram', Churchill telegraphed to Hopkins.[3]

'This statement,' Churchill minuted for the Chiefs of Staff Committee on April 8, 'contrasts oddly with the confidence which General Eisenhower showed about invading the Continent across the Channel, where he would have to meet a great many more than two German divisions.' Churchill's minute continued: 'If the presence of two German divisions is held to be decisive against any operations of an offensive or amphibious character open to the million men now in French North Africa, it is difficult to see how the war can be carried on. Months of preparation, sea power and air power in abundance, and yet two German divisions are sufficient to knock it all on the head. I do not think we can rest content with such doctrines.'

Churchill noted that in Eisenhower's original statement 'we were told that it was General Alexander and General Montgomery who shared Eisenhower's view'. Now it appeared that 'only General Alexander' shared them. 'I hope he may be allowed to speak for himself,' Churchill commented. 'I cannot believe that he has expressed himself in this crude fashion.' It was 'perfectly clear', Churchill warned, 'that the operations must either be entrusted to someone who believes in them, or abandoned', and he added:

I trust the Chiefs of Staff will not accept these pusillanimous and defeatist doctrines, from whomever they come. I propose to telegraph shortly to the President, because the adoption of such an attitude by our commanders would make us the laughing-stock of the world. Especially is this true when, side by side with it, we are urged to attack the French coast across the scour of the Channel.

Meanwhile it would seem that General Eisenhower should be asked what he means by 'two German divisions'. A German division consists of about 20,000 men. Does he mean divisions of that strength and of the standard German scale and equipment? On the other hand, the divisions which are fighting in North Africa at the moment are not perhaps more than 4,000 or 5,000 strong. We have the figures, for instance, for the 164th division.

[1] 'Personal and Most Secret', Kremlin, 7 April 1943: Churchill papers, 20/109.
[2] Telegram No. 2274, NAF/201, of 7 April 1943: Cabinet papers, 105/140.
[3] Prime Minister's Personal Telegram, T.484/3, 'Personal and Most Secret', 9 April 1943: Churchill papers, 20/109.

Similarly, we are told that the resistance may amount to eight divisions as against nine which we should employ. Again, the strength of the divisions is the point of substance. The three Italian divisions now in 'Husky' land are said to have no more than 8,000 combatants.

General Eisenhower should also be asked what alternatives he proposes, and what happens if two German divisions (strength unspecified) meet him at any of the other places he may propose.

Reflecting on the implications of Eisenhower's new-found hesitations, Churchill told the Chiefs of Staff:

This is an example of the fatuity of Planning Staffs playing upon each other's fears, each Service presenting its difficulties at the maximum, and Americans and Englishmen vying with each other, in the total absence of one directing mind and commanding willpower. I regard the matter as serious in the last degree. We have told the Russians that they cannot have their supplies by the Northern convoy for the sake of 'Husky' and now 'Husky' is to be abandoned if there are two German divisions (strength unspecified) in the neighbourhood.

'What Stalin would think of this,' Churchill added, 'when he has 185 German divisions on his front, I cannot imagine.'[1]

The Chiefs of Staff discussed Churchill's minute that same day, reporting back to him that they entirely shared his views.[2] They also sent a telegram to the Combined Chiefs of Staff in Washington, 'resolutely' opposing the view that if Sicily were garrisoned by two German divisions then operation 'Husky' had little prospect of success. To abandon the invasion of Sicily solely because the number of Germans in the island had reached 'a small predetermined fraction of our own strength' would, the Chiefs of Staff insisted, be 'unthinkable'.[3]

The Americans were also hesitating to send further troops to Britain for 'Sledgehammer', the cross-Channel bridgehead still planned for the autumn of 1943. 'If it is only a question of taking a bridgehead, and we feel capable of doing it,' Churchill minuted to the Chiefs of Staff on April 9, 'it would be better to try it ourselves, and let them come in later in the year when larger numbers are available.' 'Of course,' Churchill wrote, 'if the Americans send us no troops we have

[1] Prime Minister's Personal Minute, D.72/3, 'Most Secret', 8 April 1943: Churchill papers, 4/397A.
[2] Chiefs of Staff minute, 8 April 1943: Churchill papers, 4/298.
[3] Chiefs of Staff Telegram (W) 567, 8 April 1943: Churchill papers, 4/298. On April 25 Lord Halifax informed Churchill that after discussion with the British Joint Staff Mission, which had discussed this telegram at the Combined Staffs on April 24, he had sent a copy of the telegram to Harry Hopkins 'strictly privately and confidentially'. Halifax reported: 'He had not seen it, and it seemed doubtful whether either he or President would in the ordinary course.' Halifax added: 'Harry was anxious to see it and will no doubt do his best to help.' (Telegram No. 1937 from Washington, 'Secret and Personal', 25 April 1943: Churchill papers, 20/110.)

a good reason to give Russia for inaction. However, all planning should go ahead.'

In the Far East, the pace of planning operation 'Anakim' for the reconquest of Burma had also provoked Churchill's anger. On April 9, in his minute to the Chiefs of Staff Committee about 'Sledge-hammer', he also complained that the 'lamentable failure and air of feebleness and incompetence' of the Burmese campaign preparations 'makes one doubt whether with the present High Command in India, and especially with those engaged in command at the front, there is the life and grip to conduct a big operation'.[1] The only news that pleased him came from Montgomery, who telegraphed on April 9 that the Eighth Army had captured a total of 20,000 prisoners since March 20, that he hoped to be in Sfax in the morning, and that in addition 'much booty' had been taken.[2] There was also good news from the Enigma decrypts. ' "Boniface" shows clearly,' Churchill telegraphed to Alexander two days later, 'the dire condition of the enemy, particularly in fuel.'[3]

On April 9 Churchill was enormously relieved to learn, from Field Marshal Dill in Washington, that the United States Joint Chiefs of Staff had informed Eisenhower that they were in 'complete agreement' with the British Chiefs of Staff, about the need to go ahead with the invasion of Sicily, even if there were two German divisions in the island.[4]

On April 10 Churchill learned from Cripps, Sinclair and Portal that it was thought feasible to send Stalin through Africa the 375 Hurricanes and 285 Airacabras and Kittyhawks which were to have gone on the cancelled Arctic convoys JW54 and JW55. 'We are working day and night,' Churchill telegraphed at once to Stalin, 'to make a plan for sending you all these aircraft as rapidly as possible by other routes.' The Airacobras and Kittyhawks would be able to go via Gibraltar and North Africa to Abadan on the Persian Gulf. The Hurricanes, with less range, would go by sea to Takoradi in West Africa, or to Casablanca, be assembled there, 'tropicalised', and fly on to Teheran. If Tunis were conquered 'soon', the Hurricanes would be sent through the Mediterranean, for assembly in Egypt or Basra. Each

[1] Prime Minister's Personal Minute, D.73/3, 'Most Secret', 9 April 1943: Churchill papers, 4/397A.

[2] 'Most Secret', unnumbered, sent 2.08 p.m., received 3.20 p.m., 9 April 1943: Churchill papers, 20/109. Sfax was captured on 10 April 1943.

[3] Prime Minister's Personal Telegram, T.498/3, 11 April 1943: Churchill papers, 4/396.

[4] Joint Staff Mission Telegram, JSM 870, 9 April 1943: Churchill papers, 4/298.

route presented particular problems, especially for the provision of spare parts. 'Nevertheless,' Churchill promised, 'we shall overcome these difficulties.' He also offered Stalin, 'for your operations against German armour on the Russian front', sixty of the Hurricanes which, with their 40 millimetre cannon, had 'met with success' in Tunisia against Rommel's tanks.[1]

In a further telegram to Stalin on April 11, Churchill reported on the victories in North Africa. 'Great pains are being taken,' he wrote, 'for a heavy toll of an escape by sea.' There were 25,000 prisoners 'so far', apart from killed, estimated 'from 5,000 to 10,000'. As to Britain's air offensive over Germany, Churchill reported: 'Last night 502 went to Frankfurt.' He had already sent Stalin a short film of the effect of the bombing, and some photographs. 'I am having these sent regularly to you,' he explained, 'as they might please your soldiers who have seen so many Russian towns in ruins.'

Special 'priority cargoes', Churchill told Stalin, would soon be on their way to the Persian Gulf. These cargoes would include some of the specially selected medicines and medical appliances which had been purchased by Clementine Churchill's Aid to Russia fund, Churchill explained, 'which will shortly reach three million pounds and has been raised by voluntary gifts from both poor and rich', and was proof of the 'warm regard of the British people for the Russian people'.[2]

Stalin responded warmly to Churchill's offers, and messages. 'We are delighted,' he telegraphed, 'that you are not giving respite to Hitler.'[3] Churchill was now pressing for the first trans-Mediterranean convoy to start as soon as possible after the capture of Tunis. Code-named 'Sandwich', this convoy would carry some of the aircraft promised to Stalin. It should be made clear to Admiral Cunningham, Churchill minuted to Pound on April 13, 'the immense political consequences attaching to the swift movement of this traffic'. He should 'make a special operation of it, as if it were a Malta convoy in the difficult days'.[4]

The time had come to decide on whether a cross-Channel landing

---

[1] Prime Minister's Personal Telegram, T.491/3, 'Secret and Personal', 10 April 1943: Churchill papers, 20/109. These Hurricanes were known in Tunisia as 'tankbusters'.

[2] Prime Minister's Personal Telegram, T.500/3, 'Personal and Secret', 11 April 1943: Cabinet papers, 120/858.

[3] 'Personal and Secret', 12 April 1943: Cabinet papers, 120/683.

[4] Prime Minister's Personal Minute, M.264/3, 'Most Secret', 13 April 1943: Churchill papers, 4/397A.

of any sort was possible in the autumn of 1943. At a Staff Conference
in the late afternoon of April 13, Churchill learned for the first time
that most of the landing craft previously earmarked for a cross-
Channel landing in 1943 were, under the recommendations of the
Chiefs of Staff, to be sent to North Africa to meet the needs of the
Sicily landings. 'He had not realized hitherto,' Churchill told the
Chiefs of Staff, 'and it had certainly not been made clear at Casa-
blanca, that the mounting of "Husky" would entail this sacrifice.'

In reply, Brooke explained that the landing craft additional to those
envisaged at Casablanca were needed to 'maintain the momentum of
the "Husky" assault' and in view of the 'probable advantages to be
reaped from a rapid exploitation of a quick success'. For this reason,
the Chiefs of Staff had come to the conclusion 'that it would be wrong
to stint the "Husky" plan for the sake of being able to mount a comparatively small-scale cross-Channel operation'.

Churchill accepted the Chiefs of Staff's arguments, agreeing with
them that the requirements of the Sicily landing and its exploitations
'should have priority'. To this end, he also approved the Chiefs of
Staff's recommendation for the despatch to North Africa of additional
landing craft from the United Kingdom. But it would be necessary,
he warned, to inform the War Cabinet 'that there could now be no
"Sledgehammer" this year'.[1]

The question now to be answered was whether operation 'Bolero',
the build-up of Anglo-American forces in Britain for a major cross-
Channel invasion, should 'mark time', as Churchill minuted for the
Chiefs of Staff Committee, 'or is it to be stopped altogether?' Churchill's own answer was clear. 'Surely,' he asked, 'a steady build-up
should go on for 1944 so as to take advantage of any collapse on the
part of the enemy.'

Churchill added that he did not propose to inform Stalin of these
'developments', hoping that events in Tunisia and Sicily 'and thereafter' would, as Churchill phrased it, 'show substantial results'.[2]

On the day after the Staff Conference at which the abandonment
of 'Sledgehammer 1943' had been mooted, Churchill noted for his
senior advisers that as 'practically all our landing craft' were being
sent for the invasion of Sicily, and as 'hardly any American troops'
would arrive in Britain to be trained before the end of the summer,
'we must recognize that no important cross-Channel enterprise is possible this year'. This, he added, 'is the fact which dominates action'.
It should not however become 'widely known'. Powerful camouflage

---

[1] Chiefs of Staff Committee No. 75 (Operations) of 1943, 6.30 p.m., 13 April 1943: Cabinet
papers, 79/60.
[2] Prime Minister's Personal Minute, D.76/3, 14 April 1943: Churchill papers, 4/397A.

and cover operations should, he wrote, continue, 'in order to pin the enemy to the French coast and not to discourage our Russian Allies'. There should therefore be 'no sudden or violent stop' to the build-up of forces under the 'Bolero' plan. This build-up must inevitably suffer, however, with the ending of a 1943 cross-Channel programme. As Churchill minuted:

... we must not use money and effort unduly for projects which are now impossible in 1943, and about which there is no fixed plan for 1944. The tempo of 'Bolero' should be altered, but it should not be closed down. We should aim at a steady building up of American forces in this country for an overseas campaign in 1944. A precise plan should be made to slow down 'Bolero' in such a way as to ensure steady progress for a target date not in 1943 but in 1944.[1]

There was to be no 'Second Front' in 1943. At the same time, and indeed on the same day as this minute, Churchill learned that the Germans were embarked upon a project which might give them a considerable advantage in 1944. On April 15 General Ismay reported to Churchill details, culled from five separate Intelligence reports, of the development by German scientists of a long-range rocket, known to be at an experimental stage. Someone was needed, Ismay wrote, to establish the facts and, 'if the evidence proves reliable', to devise counter-measures. Ismay proposed that Churchill's son-in-law Duncan Sandys should be entrusted with the task, the Chiefs of Staff having considered that Sandys was 'very suitable' for the task.[2] Churchill accepted this advice.[3]

News of a possible German rocket weapon reached Churchill on the same day as grave news of a different and yet equally disturbing kind. Details had been released by the Germans of a mass grave discovered by German troops in the Katyn forest, not far from the Soviet city of Smolensk. In this grave had been found the corpses of more than 8,000 Polish officers, most of whom had been shot in the back of the neck. It was known that these officers had been interned by the Soviet authorities in the winter of 1939, after Soviet forces had occupied eastern Poland.

---

[1] Prime Minister's Personal Minute, M.271/3 (to Sir James Grigg, General Brooke and the Chiefs of Staff Committee), 15 April 1943: Churchill papers, 4/397A.
[2] Chiefs of Staff Committee No. 91 of 1943, 15 April 1943: Cabinet papers, 79/27.
[3] While it was indeed true that the Germans were developing a rocket (later known as the V2), they were also developing a less powerful aerodynamic missile (the V1 or 'flying bomb'). For many months there was confusion between the two in the Intelligence reports, and in the event, the V1 was used before the V2. The initial 'V' stood for *Vergeltungswaffe*, (retaliation weapon).

The evidence seemed to point to their murder at that time or shortly after, on Soviet orders. The Commander-in-Chief of the Polish forces in the west, General Sikorski, and the Polish Ambassador in London, Count Raczynski, were convinced that the Polish officers had been murdered when in Soviet custody.

On April 15 Sikorski and Raczynski went to 10 Downing Street to see Churchill, who in the presence of Sir Alexander Cadogan told them that Britain was willing to try to mediate between the Poles in London and the Soviet Government, but also warned his visitors against provoking the Soviets. 'Alas,' Churchill told them, 'the German revelations are probably true. The Bolsheviks can be very cruel.' [1]

Against Churchill's advice, Sikorski protested publicly on the following day about the Katyn murders, implying strongly that the blame for the murders lay with Russia. Stalin reacted by accusing the Poles of collusion with Hitler, and breaking relations with them. [2] This led Churchill to telegraph direct to Stalin, about Sikorski: 'His position is one of great difficulty. Far from being pro-German or in league with them, he is in danger of being overthrown by the Poles who consider that he had not stood up sufficiently for his people against the Soviets. If he should go, we should only get somebody worse.' [3]

Henceforth, the Katyn forest massacre was to stand as a barrier between Polish–Soviet relations, forcing the British to seek a precarious balance between the nation for which they had gone to war in September 1939, and the nation which, since June 1941, had borne the brunt of the fighting against Germany.

Churchill's problems of April 15, whether the German rocket preparations, the Katyn quarrel between Sikorski and Stalin, or the postponement of a cross-Channel landing from 1943 to 1944, heightened the contrast between the daily victories reported from Tunisia, and the time that would be needed to secure Hitler's total defeat. On April 16, Churchill wrote to his son Randolph:

Randolph dear, I can see no reason why the war should not be very long, and it would be folly to indulge in comfortable hopes of an early ending. Nevertheless the rascals are getting it pretty hot from the Air as well as from the Russians. They probably have a big disaster facing them in Africa, and I think they are now convinced they cannot win. What a change this is from the days when Hitler danced his jig of joy at Compiègne!

Churchill ended his letter to Randolph with family news, and on a

---

[1] Cadogan diary and notes, 15 April 1943: David Dilks (editor), *op. cit.*, pages 520–1.

[2] 'Personal and Most Secret', 21 April 1943: Churchill papers, 20/110.

[3] Prime Minister's Personal Telegram, T.580/3, 'Personal and Most Secret', 24 April 1943: Churchill papers, 20/110.

personal note. 'Your Mother sends her love,' he wrote. 'Sarah continues her toil in the Photographic Section. Mary has been posted to the heavy battery in Hyde Park, and Diana's event is expected in June. I am going to spend Easter at Chartwell, which I have not seen for many months. The valley must be lovely now.' [1]

---

[1] Letter of 16 April 1943: Churchill papers, 1/375. Sarah Oliver was serving in the Photographic Interpretation section of the Royal Air Force. Diana Sandys' daughter Celia was born on 8 May 1943.

22
Victory in the Gulf of Tunis

A T the Combined Chiefs of Staff meeting in Washington on April
16, General Marshall outlined a plan to invade Sicily while
the Germans still held the Tunisian Tip. 'Personally,' Churchill
telegraphed to Marshall on the following day, 'I think your idea
splendid and real war. A stitch in time saves nine.' [1] To Stalin,
Churchill explained that a 'short pause' was now necessary in Tunisia
while Alexander regrouped his armies in the north, and Montgomery
'brings up the mass of artillery which he habitually uses in his battles'.
But 'very soon', Churchill added, 'the largest battle we have yet fought
in this war will begin', and having once begun it would not stop 'till
Africa is cleared of Axis forces'. Churchill also reported 'three good
blows' on Spezia, Stuttgart and the Skoda works at Pilsen and
Mannheim. The raid on Stuttgart, he noted, 'was a flaming success'. [2]
In these three raids, however, Britain had lost 81 bombers and 'about
500 highly-trained air personnel'. Churchill added, 'I repeat my assurance that the attacks will continue throughout the summer on an ever
increasing scale.' [3]

Churchill made no reference in his telegram to Stalin to the Soviet
leader's earlier requests for a cross-Channel operation in 1943. All
that might be possible, he minuted for the Chiefs of Staff Committee
on April 18, was 'an amphibious feint' designed to bring about an air
battle, and thus give air force units based in Britain a part to play 'in
the general process of attrition'. Meanwhile, he urged that there must
be a 'gradual building up' of forces in Britain, and 'long-term study'
of the cross-Channel attack in 1944. Plans should also go ahead for a

[1] Prime Minister's Personal Telegram, T.531/3, 'Personal', 17 April 1943: Churchill papers,
20/110.
[2] After a Cabinet meeting two days later, Sir Alexander Cadogan noted in his diary later:
'We seem to have been rather promiscuous in our bombing, and to have made some bosh-
shots—particularly at Stuttgart!' (Cadogan diary, 19 April 1943: David Dilks, editor, *op. cit.*,
page 521.)
[3] Prime Minister's Personal Telegram, T.534/3, No. 393 to Moscow, 'Personal and Secret', 17
April 1943: Churchill papers, 20/110.

possible 'Jupiter' operation against northern Norway in January 1944 'or whatever is the best winter month'.[1]

Churchill also sought his advisers' views on the possibility of an attack on the Dodecanese Islands, operation 'Handcuff', in the autumn of 1943 from which, he explained to Roosevelt, 'strong pressure' would have to be put on the Turks for the use of their air bases.[2]

'The battle in Tunisia is begun': with these words, Churchill informed Stalin of Alexander's final offensive. 'It is intended,' Churchill explained, 'to carry matters to a conclusion if possible by continuous pressure.'[3] Thirty hours later, Churchill heard from Alexander that the fighting had been 'very fierce' and that 'the enemy put in four counter-attacks, all of which were beaten off'. Many Germans had been killed, and 'some 800 prisoners taken'.[4]

As the fighting continued, the German resistance intensified. 'All indications are,' Alexander telegraphed to Churchill on April 23, 'that enemy will offer bitter resistance in his present positions, but a good start has been made.'[5] Two days later he reported on the struggle in a hopeful tone. 'Enemy continues to resist desperately,' he telegraphed to Churchill towards midnight on April 25, 'but this evening there are definite signs that he is weakening.' More than 1,200 prisoners had been taken. The German infantry strength had been 'much reduced'. Alexander commented: 'Enemy is unlikely to be able to stand our prolonged pressure, but he will continue to offer bitter and most stubborn resistance until his troops are exhausted.'[6]

What Alexander sensed in the war zone was confirmed by what Churchill learned from the decrypted German messages. 'Boniface', he telegraphed to Alexander on April 26, 'clearly shows the enemy's anxiety, his concern over his ammunition expenditure, and the strain upon his air force'. Churchill added: 'It is a great comfort in these

[1] Prime Minister's Personal Minute, D81/3, 'Most Secret', 18 April 1943: Churchill papers, 4/397A.
[2] Prime Minister's Personal Telegram, T.595/3, Prime Minister to President, No. 286, 26 April 1943: Churchill papers, 20/110.
[3] Prime Minister's Personal Telegram, T.550/3, No. 402 to Moscow, 'Personal and Secret', sent 9.10 a.m., 20 April 1943: Churchill papers, 20/110.
[4] MA/328, 'Personal and Most Secret', received 3.15 p.m., 21 April 1943: Churchill papers, 20/110.
[5] MA/335, 'Personal and Most Secret', received 4.15 p.m., 23 April 1943: Churchill papers, 20/110.
[6] MA/342, 'Personal and Most Secret', 25 April 1943 (received 4 a.m., 26 April 1943): Churchill papers, 20/110.

anxious days to know that you are conducting this great battle your-self.'[1]

A further message from Alexander on April 28 reported that the Eighth Army was 'undoubtedly tired', with the 51st Division and the two New Zealand divisions no longer capable of 'full offensive action' until they had been 'nursed'. Montgomery however, Alexander added, 'understands the great importance of continuing to exercise hard pres-sure', and the offensive would continue. Heavy cloud over German positions and heavy rain in the area of the Allied airfields had pre-vented the bombers making 'any contribution' for the previous five days. 'With settled weather,' Alexander pointed out, the bombers 'should help to reduce or cut off the enemy's present limited intake by air and sea.'[2]

With the battle in Tunisia at its height Churchill found himself forced to act as a mediator between the Soviet Government and the Poles on the matter of the Katyn forest killings near Smolensk in 1940. Sikorski and Stalin having taken up strong public positions against each other, Churchill tried to modify an impending Polish communiqué which was, he minuted to Eden, 'a declaration of mortal war'. In Churchill's opinion, and in this he was given strong support by Smuts, conciliation was 'the only line of safety for the Poles and indeed for us'. There was 'no use', Churchill added, 'prowling morbidly round the three-year-old graves of Smolensk'.

On the night of April 27, Churchill had redrafted the communiqué which the Polish Government was about to issue, writing it as if coming from the Poles. Its aim was to put aside the issue of Katyn, and a looking forward to Polish–Soviet co-operation in the war against Germany. 'If you can get the Poles to adopt this line,' Churchill minuted to Eden on the morning of April 28, 'it is important that it should come from them and not seem to be inspired by us.' In talking to the Poles, Churchill added, 'you can point out that they can always run the Smolensk story if all else fails'.[3]

At 3 o'clock on the afternoon of April 28 Churchill and Eden saw Sikorski. 'You will see,' Churchill telegraphed to Roosevelt, 'that we have persuaded them to shift the argument from the dead to the living and from the past to the future.' He was therefore sending Stalin a message 'feeling sure it will be in accordance with your views'.[4]

---

[1] Prime Minister's Personal Telegram, T.592/3, 'Most Secret and Personal', 26 April 1943: Churchill papers, 20/110.

[2] MA/361, 'Personal and Most Secret', 28 April 1943: Churchill papers, 20/111.

[3] Prime Minister's Personal Minute, M.323/3, 28 April 1943: Churchill papers, 4/397A.

[4] Prime Minister's Personal Telegram, T.608/3, Prime Minister to President, No. 289, 'Personal and Most Secret', 28 April 1943: Churchill papers, 20/111.

Churchill's message to Stalin began with a rebuke to the Soviet leader for having broken off relations with the Poles without giving Churchill time to report on the course of his earlier talks with Sikorski. 'I had hoped,' Churchill wrote, 'that, in the spirit of our Treaty last year, we should always consult each other about such important matters, more especially as they affect the combined strength of the United Nations.' The Poles, Churchill reported to the Soviet leader, had been urged not to make 'charges of an insulting character' against the Soviet Government. 'I am glad to tell you,' he added, 'that they have accepted our view and that they want to work loyally with you.' In return, they wished to have the dependants of the Polish Army in Persia, and the fighting Poles still in the Soviet Union, to join those Poles whom Stalin had already allowed to go to Persia. 'We think the request is reasonable,' Churchill commented, asking Stalin to consider it 'in a spirit of magnanimity'. For its part, Britain would ensure 'proper discipline' in the Polish Press in Great Britain. Matters 'to our joint detriment' must be stopped and 'will be stopped'.

Churchill then referred to a recent statement by Goebbels that the Soviet Union intended to set up a Polish Government on Russian soil 'and deal only with them', and he warned: 'We should not, of course, be able to recognize such a Government and would continue our relations with Sikorski who is far the most helpful man you or we are likely to find for the purposes of the common cause.' Churchill added: 'I expect this will also be the American view.'

Churchill ended his telegram to Stalin:

My own feeling is that the Poles have had a shock and that after whatever interval is thought convenient, the relationship established on July 30, 1941, should be restored. No-one will hate this more than Hitler and what he hates most is wise for us to do.

We owe it to our Armies now engaged, and presently to be more heavily engaged, to maintain good conditions behind the fronts. I and my colleagues look steadily to the ever closer co-operation and understanding of the USSR, the USA and the British Commonwealth and Empire, not only in the deepening war struggle but after the war. What other hope can there be than this for the tortured world? [1]

The Polish communiqué as redrafted by Churchill was issued on the night of April 28. 'The Polish Government and people look to the future,' it declared, and went on to appeal, as Churchill had indicated to Stalin it would, for the release of Poles still in Russia who wished to take part in the Polish war effort, as well as for the release of 'tens of

[1] Prime Minister's Personal Telegram, T.606/3, No. 452 to Moscow, 'Personal and Most Secret', 28 April 1943: Churchill papers, 20/111.

thousands' of Polish orphans and children 'for the education of whom they would take full responsibility and which now—in view of the German mass slaughter—are particularly precious to the Polish people'.[1] Churchill had prevented a full breach between Stalin and the Poles, but the hatreds which Katyn created were to poison the relations between the Soviet Union and Poland for the rest of the war, and beyond. Churchill, his fears of a worsening relationship with Stalin given unexpected substance by the Katyn episode, sought, even at the moment of crisis, to encourage the Soviet leader, expressing, in a telegram on May 2, his 'utmost satisfaction and admiration' for Stalin's 'splendid' May Day speech of the previous day. 'I particularly appreciate,' Churchill wrote, 'your reference to the united blow of the Allies,' and he added: 'You may indeed count on me to do everything "to break the spine of the Fascist beast",' Stalin's words in the speech.[2]

Churchill's telegram went on to tell Stalin of the most recent British bombing raids over Germany. 'We gave Duisburg 1,450 tons,' he wrote, 'the heaviest yet launched in a single raid,' and he then set out details of the fighting in Tunisia. In sending Stalin this telegram, Churchill also telegraphed to the British Ambassador in Moscow on May 2:

I think it would be a pity that our Polish discussions with Stalin should interrupt the more or less weekly flow of friendly messages I have been sending him about operations. I am sure these give him pleasure and maintain our indispensable contact. In giving him this you may, if you like and if the going is good, say I should like him to give me a fighting Pole for every German I catch in Tunisia from now on, and a Polish dependant, woman, or child, for every Italian. Such jokes are in questionable taste, but there are moments and situations when they have their uses.[3]

'I like your joke,' replied Sir Archibald Clark Kerr, 'and shall enjoy putting it to him, for I think he will like it too.'[4]

The Ambassador saw Stalin on May 7. 'I tried this on Stalin last night,' he telegraphed to Churchill on the following morning. 'Although (somewhat helped by Molotov) he began by missing the point a little, when he got it, it gave him a good laugh.' Stalin would not 'clinch' Churchill's deal however, 'for he claimed that you would catch many more Germans than he had of fighting Poles to give you, and that no Italian was worth a Polish woman and that would not be fair

[1] Full text in Prime Minister's Personal Telegram, T.609/3, Prime Minister to President, No. 290, 28 April 1943: Churchill papers, 20/111.

[2] Prime Minister's Personal Telegram, T.632/3, 'Personal and Most Secret', No. 479 to Moscow, despatched at 3.20 a.m., 3 May 1943: Churchill papers, 20/111.

[3] Prime Minister's Personal Telegram, T.633/3, No. 480 to Moscow, 'Personal and Most Secret', despatched 12.30 a.m., 3 May 1943: Churchill papers, 20/111.

[4] No. 333 from Moscow, 'Personal and Secret', 3 May 1943: Churchill papers, 20/111.

on him'. In any case, Stalin told the Ambassador, Churchill would need all the Italians he could catch to build roads: 'That was all that Italians could do.'[1]

On April 22 Churchill and his wife drove down to Chartwell, to spend the Easter weekend. Kathleen Hill and Elizabeth Layton accompanied him to take dictation. 'Last night he came walking into the office,' Elizabeth Layton wrote on April 26, 'and said, by way of being chatty, that he did hope I should be able to have a nice hot bath in the morning.' 'Dear boss knows that we are doing our own cooking,' she added, 'and one day he asked us what we were having. We said "salad" and he was horrified—"But you must have more than that."'[2]

At a Staff Conference in London on April 22, before Churchill had set off for Chartwell, the two Commanders-in-Chief, India, General Wavell and Air Chief Marshal Peirse, as well as the Commander-in-Chief, Eastern Fleet, Admiral Sir James Somerville, were present at a discussion of Far Eastern strategy. It seemed 'unlikely', Churchill told them, that sufficient shipping would be available to carry out operation 'Anakim', against Japanese forces in Burma, in 1943. 'At the same time,' Churchill pointed out, 'Burma appeared a disadvantageous area in which to fight the Japanese.' Britain would be dependent on long lines of poor communication, malaria would take 'a heavy toll of our forces', and Britain's superiority in aircraft, tanks and artillery could not be used 'with effect' in jungle warfare, 'which particularly favoured the Japanese'.

Wavell agreed that 'Anakim' was 'a most difficult and unattractive Operation and likely to be costly'. 'Undoubtedly the best way to defeat the Japanese,' Churchill commented, 'was by bombing Japan from bases in Russia and China.' This could not, however, be undertaken until after the defeat of Germany. Meanwhile, 'he was inclined to think that we should concentrate on the support of China by the largest possible air transport service', and at the same time try to find the 'most favourable' locality for attacking the Japanese 'by-passing Burma and making full use of our sea power'.[3]

[1] No. 353 from Moscow, 'Personal and Secret', 8 May 1943: Churchill papers, 20/111.
[2] Elizabeth Layton, letter of 26 April 1943: Nel papers.
[3] Staff Conference, 22 April 1943, Chiefs of Staff Committee No. 84 (Operations) of 1943: Cabinet papers, 79/60.

At the very moment when the Burmese campaign envisaged for 1943 was being abandoned, Churchill was concerned at the possibility that the Pacific might supersede Europe as the main focus of America's future war effort. The United States Chiefs of Staff had recently invited Wavell, together with Peirse and Somerville, to Washington. 'If they went,' Churchill told the War Cabinet on April 29, 'there would be a grave danger that the main emphasis of the war would be altered and greater emphasis put on the Pacific.'

As the American commanders from the Burma and China theatres were going to Washington, it would be 'awkward', Churchill pointed out, if Britain refused to allow Wavell, Peirse and Somerville to go, 'and later, things went wrong'. He therefore thought that they ought to go, but with 'political support'. That political support would be himself, and he would take General Brooke with him, as well as the Minister of War Transport. They would discuss the planned recapture of Burma, Britain's strategy in the Far East, and the question of the conquest of Sicily 'and what should follow it'.

Churchill's proposal to go once more to Washington came as a shock to his colleagues, some of whom asked, as the minutes of the War Cabinet recorded, 'whether it was really necessary that the Prime Minister should undertake this journey, about which they showed no enthusiasm'. But when, as the minutes noted, Churchill 'made it clear that he was sure he ought to go', the War Cabinet gave its assent. He would travel, Churchill said, by sea, 'since his doctors did not regard it as suitable that he should fly at a great height, which might be necessary at this time of year'.[1] That same day Churchill telegraphed to Roosevelt, putting Sicily before Burma in his order of priorities:

It seems to me most necessary that we should all settle together now first 'Husky' and exploitation thereof, and secondly the future of 'Anakim' in light of Burma campaign experiences and shipping stringency. There are also a number of other burning questions which you and I could with advantage bring up to date. I think I could manage to be with you by Tuesday, 11th May. I would bring Wavell, Peirse and Admiral Somerville as well as Pound, Brooke, Portal, Mountbatten and Leathers. Please say whether you would like this or whether you would prefer to send your people over here, which of course would be easier for us.[2]

'What is essential,' Churchill telegraphed to Hopkins on May 2, 'is that our plans should be made and thrashed out and decisions taken

[1] War Cabinet No. 62 of 1943, 29 April 1943, Confidential Annex: Cabinet papers, 65/34.
[2] Prime Minister's Personal Telegram, T.613/3, Prime Minister to President, No. 291, 'Personal and Secret', 29 April 1943: Churchill papers, 20/111.

as at Casablanca.' His telegram continued: 'I am conscious of serious divergences beneath the surface which, if not adjusted, will lead to grave difficulties and feeble action in the summer and autumn. These difficulties we must forestall.' [1]

On April 30, as he began to plan for this new American visit, Churchill learned from Alexander that the Tunisian offensive had had to be temporarily suspended. Montgomery had told Alexander that day that 'extreme difficulties of the ground', and the strong German artillery concentration against the Eighth Army in the coastal sector, meant that Montgomery's impending operations 'would have been very costly in casualties and were not certain of success'. Alexander had therefore cancelled them. The next offensive would not begin until May 4. 'I have every hope,' Alexander added, 'that this attack will lead to decisive results.'

In his telegram, Alexander gave Churchill a description of the nature of the Tunisian battle. 'As an instance of the desperate nature of the enemy's resistance,' he wrote, 'fifty men of the Hermann Goering Division had just surrendered, when one of them persuaded them to take up arms again, and the whole party started fighting and had to be shot to a man.' [2]

Studying the Enigma decrypts, Churchill learned of the success of British air attacks on the port of Tunis. 'Boniface shows the decisive reactions produced upon the enemy,' he telegraphed to Tedder on May 2, 'and that the little enemy ships are also important.' [3] These 'little' ships were those in which, as the Enigma decrypts showed, supplies of fuel and ammunition were still reaching Tunis. Larger ships were finding it impossible to get through.

In a telegram to Stalin on May 3, Churchill gave an indication of the scale of the casualties on both sides. 'Since we entered Tunisia,' he wrote, 'we have taken about 40,000 prisoners; in addition, the enemy have suffered 35,000 dead and wounded. The casualties in the First Army have been about 23,000, and in the Eighth Army about 10,000. The total Allied casualties are about 50,000 of which two-thirds are British.' Churchill also told Stalin of the difficulties of the terrain. 'The peculiar mountainous character of the country,' he explained, 'with flat plains commanded by rugged, upstanding peaks, each of which is a fortress, aids the enemy's defence and slows up our advance. I hope however to have good news for you be-

---

[1] Prime Minister's Personal Telegram, T.629/3, 'Personal and Most Especially Secret', 2 May 1943: Churchill papers, 20/111.

[2] MA/367, 'Personal and Most Secret', 30 April 1943: Churchill papers, 20/111.

[3] Prime Minister's Personal Telegram, T.630/3, OZ 1251, 'Personal', 'Most Secret', 2 May 1943: Churchill papers, 20/111.

fore the end of this month. Meanwhile the whole campaign is most costly to the enemy on account of his additional losses in transit.' [1]

On May 4, as a result of an Enigma decrypt, British destroyers sank the *Campobasso* off Cape Bon and on the following day the United States Air Force sank the 6,000 ton *San Antonio*: these were the last large merchant ships to try to reach Tunis. As Churchill had foreseen, however, the Germans continued to try to use smaller craft, and even planned, as an Enigma decrypt showed on May 6, to use U-boats to ferry fuel. [2]

In the Battle of the Atlantic, the fortunes of war had turned decisively in favour of the Allies. On May 2, the Government Code and Cypher School at Bletchley had decrypted a telegram from the Japanese Ambassador in Berlin, reporting to his masters in Tokyo that Hitler, while hopeful of a new U-boat offensive, was complaining that because the war had started too soon, 'we have been unable to dominate the seas'. [3] Two days later, in a lengthy battle, two U-boat packs attacked and sank twelve merchant ships in convoy. [4] This success, the last on such a scale, was achieved however with the loss of seven of the U-boats. Not only did the Enigma decrypts confirm this loss, but also gave evidence of the growing U-boat fears both of Allied aircraft and of the surface escorts. [5]

On the night of May 4 Churchill set off for the United States, leaving London by train for the Clyde. On the following morning, as the train steamed northwards, Churchill summoned Elizabeth Layton to take dictation. 'He worked all morning,' she noted in her diary, 'and the time flew. In his tiny cabin the only place to sit was on the bed, trying not to sit on his feet, and it was a horrid moment when I got cramp in one leg.'

Work continued until the mid afternoon, when the train reached the Clyde. There Churchill boarded the *Queen Mary* for the voyage across the Atlantic. Hardly had he settled into his cabin, than the

---

[1] Prime Minister's Personal Telegram, T.632/3, No. 479 to Moscow, 'Personal and Most Secret', despatched 3.20 a.m., 3 May 1943: Churchill papers, 20/111.

[2] Hinsley and others, *British Intelligence in the Second World War*, *op. cit.*, volume 2, page 612.

[3] Decrypt of 2 May 1943: F. H. Hinsley and others, *British Intelligence in the Second World War*, *op. cit.*, volume 2, page 572.

[4] There were forty-one U-boats in two packs, seventy merchant ships in the convoy.

[5] F. H. Hinsley and others, *British Intelligence in the Second World War*, *op. cit.*, volume 2, page 570.

dictation began again—a letter to the Prime Minister of Northern Ireland on his retirement.[1]

Also on board the *Queen Mary* were about 5,000 German prisoners-of-war, captured in North Africa, and on their way to camps in Canada. The ship sailed that afternoon. On the main deck, in the room next to Churchill's cabin, a Map Room had been established by Captain Pim. 'I must tell you that we all of us worked like Trojans all the way over,' Elizabeth Layton wrote to her parents. 'We (Mr Kinna and I) produced the most huge documents which were distributed to the others to scratch their heads over.'[2]

Among those whom Churchill had asked to accompany him to Roosevelt were Beaverbrook and Harriman. At lunch on the first day, according to Harriman's notes, Beaverbrook suggested that Churchill ought to drive through the streets of New York, and be recognized by the populace, when the *Queen Mary* docked. When Harriman countered that the Secret Service would not like it at all, Churchill answered: 'One can always do what one wants to if it takes people by surprise. There is not time for plotters to develop their nefarious plans.'[3]

On May 6, at a Chiefs of Staff meeting on board ship, the urgent purpose of the voyage was confirmed. 'There is no doubt,' General Brooke noted in his diary, 'that, unless the Americans are prepared to withdraw more shipping from the Pacific, our strategy in Europe will be drastically affected.' It was now clear, Brooke added, that larger American land and air forces had gone to the Pacific than to Europe, 'in spite of all we have said about the necessity of defeating Germany first'.[4]

That evening, the night duty officer informed Churchill that a German submarine, heading west from the French port of Brest, seemed likely to cross the *Queen Mary*'s course about fifteen miles ahead. Churchill hastened to reassure Harriman, with whom he was still playing bezique: 'Pound says we are just as likely to ram the submarine as it is to see us first.' Churchill added that he had arranged for a machine gun to be fixed in his own lifeboat, should they be forced to abandon ship. Harriman's account of the ensuing conversation continued:

---

[1] Elizabeth Layton, 'Diary of Events', 5 May 1943: Nel papers.
[2] Elizabeth Layton, letter of 19 May 1943: Nel papers.
[3] Harriman notes: Abel and Harriman, *op. cit.*, page 202.
[4] Brooke diary, 6 May 1943: Bryant, *op. cit.*, volume 1, page 607. His aim in going to Washington, Churchill telegraphed to Stalin two days later from 'mid-Atlantic', was to settle 'further exploitation in Europe' after the invasion of Sicily, 'and also to discourage undue bias towards the Pacific', as well as to discuss the offensive against Japan in the Indian Ocean. (Prime Minister's Personal Telegram, T.674/3, 8 May 1943: Churchill papers, 4/394A.)

Churchill: I won't be captured. The finest way to die is in the excitement of fighting the enemy. (Then, after a moment's thought) It might not be so nice if one were in the water and they tried to pick me up.

Harriman: Prime Minister, this is all very disquieting to me. I thought you told me that the worst a torpedo could do to this ship, because of its compartments, was to knock out one engine room, leaving sufficient power to steam at twenty knots.

Churchill: Ah, but they might put two torpedoes in us. You must come with me in the boat and see the fun.[1]

On May 6, Alexander launched his major attack on either side of the Medjez–Tunis road, telegraphing to Churchill that same day of 'stiff' German opposition, but also of 'indications of enemy withdrawing'. His telegram ended: 'Our troops are enthusiastic about the effective and very strong air support and report prisoners' morale shaken.'[2] 'I am delighted at the successes of the Anglo-American troops,' Stalin telegraphed that same day, 'and I wish them still more successes.'[3]

From London on May 6, on the authority of the Chiefs of Staff, the British Military Mission in Russia was sent a note of British casualty figures from 3 September 1939 to 31 March 1943. These included 30,540 deaths in action at sea, 38,894 Army deaths, and 23,588 Air Force deaths: a total of 93,022 known deaths, apart from those soldiers, sailors and airmen who had been reported missing. More than 20,000 merchant seamen had also been killed.

These figures, the Mission was told, should be communicated to the Russian General Staff.[4]

Just before dinner on May 7, news reached the *Queen Mary*, as Brooke noted in his diary, of further 'good progress' in Tunisia.[5] This was a telegram from Alexander, informing Churchill that advanced units of the First United States Armoured Division had 'entered Bizerta' at four o'clock that afternoon.[6] That same day the British First Army entered Tunis.

That evening, Churchill again played bezique, his favourite card game, with Harriman, who noted in his diary:

He talked a lot during bezique and afterward, when we went alone to the War Room, about the amount of effort that was being put into protecting this ship. He spoke of the tremendous courage and risks of the merchant seamen. He didn't like the idea that he personally was given all the protection

---

[1] Harriman notes: Abel and Harriman, *op. cit.*, page 205.

[2] MA/394, 'Most Secret and Personal', 6 May 1943: Churchill papers, 20/111.

[3] 'Personal and Most Secret', 6 May 1943: Churchill papers, 20/111.

[4] Telegram No. 76940, 6 May 1943: War Office papers, 202/912.

[5] Brooke diary, 7 May 1943: Bryant, *op. cit.*, volume 1, page 308.

[6] MA/402, 'Personal', 'Most Secret', 7 May 1943: Churchill papers, 20/111.

but explained that everything in war was relative and the value of the party to the war as against the individual lives was the basis for it.

He spoke about the losses of the British merchant seamen—21,000 out of perhaps 100,000—relatively much greater than the losses of the armed services. He went over the map of the Atlantic again and the location of the submarines, the convoys and their escorts. He said: 'I think perhaps it is time for us to attempt to get the Portuguese to give us use of the Azores. Will the President support me? It will save perhaps 1,000,000 tons of shipping.'

News had just reached the *Queen Mary* of the sinking of thirteen ships in a convoy of fifty between Newfoundland and Greenland. 'It is sad to think of these convoys,' Churchill told Harriman, 'the ships, and their priceless cargoes.' [1] During the attack, Brooke noted in his diary, five German submarines had been sunk by the escorting warships. [2]

On May 8, Churchill received from Alexander further details of the capture of Bizerta and Tunis. The Axis front 'has completely collapsed and disintegrated', Alexander reported. As many as 20,000 prisoners had been taken, 'besides many guns, lorries and dumps'. The work of the Royal Air Force had been 'quite magnificent, and all troops are in terrific heart'. [3]

'Overjoyed at your splendid news,' Churchill telegraphed to Alexander from on board ship. 'History will admire your handling of these great armies.' [4] On May 8, to prevent the escape of Germans across the water to Sicily, Admiral Cunningham launched operation 'Retribution', signalling to the ships under his command: 'Sink, burn and destroy. Let nothing pass.' As a result of this naval vigilance, only 653 Germans are known to have escaped.

Within two days it became clear that the victory in Tunisia was substantial, including, as Alexander telegraphed to Churchill on May 10, '50,000 prisoners already counted through cages, and still coming in', as well as 'nine German generals so far'. [5] To Attlee and Eden, Churchill telegraphed on May 10, three years to the day since he had become Prime Minister: 'I feel strongly that the bells should be rung for the Victory of the Gulf of Tunis as we did after Alamein.' [6] The bells were rung.

---

[1] Harriman diary and notes: Abel and Harriman, *op. cit.*, pages 203–4.

[2] Brooke diary, 7 May 1943: Bryant, *op. cit.*, volume 1, page 608.

[3] MA/414, IZ 1686, 'Personal and Most Secret', 6.30 p.m., 8 May 1943: Churchill papers, 20/111.

[4] Prime Minister's Personal Telegram, T.669/3, 'Most Secret and Personal', 9 May 1943: Churchill papers, 20/111.

[5] MA/423, 'Personal and Most Secret', 10 May 1943: Churchill papers, 20/111.

[6] 'Pencil' No. 30, 'Personal and Most Secret', 10 May 1943: Churchill papers, 20/128.

23
Washington, May 1943:
The Search for the Way Forward

WHILE on board the *Queen Mary*, Churchill and the British Chiefs of Staff discussed what should be the British strategic plan, and approach to the Americans, now that North Africa was under Allied control. Churchill's first thoughts were towards the Far East, and it was in anticipation of a dispute with the Americans in this distant theatre that he prepared a note for the Chiefs of Staff, based on his and their agreement that a landing in Burma would be 'physically impossible' for 1943. Churchill told the Chiefs of Staff that he approved their search 'for variants or alternatives'. 'Going into swampy jungles to fight the Japanese,' he wrote, 'is like going into the water to fight a shark. It is better to entice him into a trap or catch him on a hook and then demolish with axes after hauling him out on to dry land. How then to deceive and entrap the shark?'

Churchill then proposed the seizure of 'some strategic point or points' which would force the Japanese to counter-attack 'under conditions detrimental to them and favourable to us'. The 'surest way' to make a successful landing, he commented, 'is to go where you are not expected', and he pointed to the crescent from Moulmein to Timor as the area across which one or more points could be chosen to land 30,000 or 40,000 men. This crescent would include, he wrote, the Andaman islands, Mergui 'with Bangkok as its objective', the Kra Isthmus, an assault on Northern Sumatra as set out earlier by the Chiefs of Staff Committee, the 'southern tip' of Sumatra, and Java. Churchill finished his note on May 8. 'I should be very glad,' he ended, 'to have a preliminary talk with the Chiefs of Staff on the issues cursorily discussed in this Paper tomorrow evening at 6 p.m., if possible.' [1]

This 'preliminary talk' took place at 11.30 in the morning of May 10. Opening the discussion, Churchill told the three Chiefs of Staff

[1] 'Notes on "Anakim"', Chiefs of Staff Paper (Trident) No. 8, 'Most Secret', 8 May 1943: Cabinet papers, 99/22.

and the three Far Eastern Commanders-in-Chief, that all were agreed as to the 'inadvisability' of launching operation 'Anakim' that summer. He himself 'felt much attracted to the idea of by-passing Burma and launching out eastwards across the sea'. The right course, ventured Brooke, was to draw up with the Americans 'a combined plan for the defeat of Japan', and then study 'such operations from India as would fit into the long-term plan'.

Wavell told the meeting that he was 'inclined to think' that the most promising direction for an operation in those regions was the northern tip of Sumatra and Penang. In discussing this with the Americans, Churchill commented, 'we should not decry the importance of this theatre of operations'. An operation against Sumatra and Malaya, he thought, 'would have similar merits to the "Torch" operation', and he would like to have it 'thoroughly studied'.

Pound and Brooke both replied that the scale of such an operation would be similar to that of 'Anakim', nor could it be carried out without 'impinging' on both the Mediterranean and cross-Channel plans. 'The Naval forces required,' they said, 'could not be made available until Italy had been eliminated from the war.'

Churchill was 'disinclined to accept this view', he said, if it were to be applied to the 'whole winter of 1943–44'. Surely, he asked, it would be possible to mount the operation in March 1944, 'by which time Italy should be out of the war'. A study of the Sumatra-Penang operation should, he concluded, 'be set on foot', as a British operation, 'with a provisional date of March 1944'.[1]

The Chiefs of Staff Committee met again on May 10, at 5.30 in the afternoon, when Brooke explained the reasons underlying the Chiefs of Staff's proposals to follow the conquest of Sicily with an attack on mainland Italy. If mainland Italy proved impossible, the Chiefs of Staff advised that Sardinia should be the target after Sicily.

In reply, Churchill stated that if mainland Italy proved impossible, he would prefer to undertake an operation against Axis forces in Greece rather than to capture Sardinia, but Brooke stressed both the threat to northern Italy from Sardinia, and the use of Sardinia and Corsica as 'stepping stones towards southern France'. He hoped nevertheless, Churchill remarked, that operations in Greece 'would continue to be studied'. Churchill also told the Committee that he was in 'complete agreement' with the Chiefs of Staff's proposed line to be taken in conversation with the Americans, 'namely, that nothing should prevent us adhering to our main policy for the defeat of Germany first, and that the greatest step which we could take in 1943

[1] Chiefs of Staff Committee (Trident), 9th Meeting, 11.30 a.m., 10 May 1943: Cabinet papers, 99/22.

towards this end would be the elimination of Italy'.[1] This had been the conclusion of the Chiefs of Staff Committee held on the morning of May 4, their last day in London, with Brooke in the chair, when it had been agreed that Britain's 'main offensive effort' after Sicily 'should continue to be made in the Mediterranean theatre'.[2]

At the afternoon meeting on the *Queen Mary* on May 10, the Chiefs of Staff Committee had gone on to discuss 'possible operations for India in 1943–44', when Churchill said that the Americans 'would undoubtedly expect us to do something in the Far East theatre in place of "Anakim"'. They would, he thought, 'welcome the idea of an operation to capture the point of Sumatra and Penang'. The Chiefs of Staff reiterated, however, 'that the essential point was to maintain pressure against Germany', and pointed out that at Casablanca 'we had not committed ourselves to carry out operation "Anakim"', and that Britain should now press, not for Sumatra and Penang, but for 'the development of the air route to China'. Britain would find herself in difficulties with the Americans, he pointed out, if she were, on the one hand, to use the argument that the Mediterranean operations were designed to assist an eventual cross-Channel landing, and, on the other hand, to press for an operation in the Far East which would absorb the landing craft required for the cross-Channel attack.

Churchill made no further comment on the dispute, merely repeating that he was 'anxious to have a complete study made' of operations against northern Sumatra and Penang, the calculations to include 'the minimum possible assault landing craft' required.[3]

After four days sailing westward, the *Queen Mary* reached the waters patrolled by United States' warships. 'Since yesterday,' Churchill telegraphed to Roosevelt on May 10, 'we have been surrounded by US Navy and we all greatly appreciate high value you evidently set upon our continued survival. I look forward to being at White House with you tomorrow afternoon and also to going to Hyde Park with you at weekend. The voyage has been so far most agreeable and staff have done vast amount of work.'[4]

On May 11, Churchill learned from Alexander that the number of

---

[1] Chiefs of Staff Committee (Trident) 10th Meeting, 5.30 p.m., 10 May 1943: Cabinet papers, 99/22.

[2] Chiefs of Staff Committee No. 93 (Operations) of 1943, 10.30 a.m., 4 May 1943: Cabinet papers, 79/60. Those present were Brooke, Pound, Portal, Mountbatten and Ismay, Captain C. E. Lambe (Admiralty), Brigadier W. Porter (War Office), Air Commodore W. Elliot (Air Ministry) and Brigadier M. W. McLeod (Headquarters, Combined Operations).

[3] Chiefs of Staff Committee (Trident), 10th Meeting, 5.30 p.m., 10 May 1943: Cabinet papers, 99/22.

[4] 'Pencil' No. 36, 'Personal and Secret' ('Message from Naval not former naval person to President'), No. 294 from Prime Minister to President, 10 May 1943: Premier papers, 4/72/2, folio 660.

German and Italian prisoners was likely to exceed 100,000. 'No one has got away,' Alexander added, 'except a mere handful by air.'[1] At noon that day, the *Queen Mary* reached the United States. 'It is an added pleasure to me,' Alexander had telegraphed in answer to Churchill's congratulations, 'to be able to produce results which will assist you in your great work.'[2]

Churchill spent the night of May 11 in the White House, and on the following afternoon, in the President's oval study, the 'Trident' conference began. '"Torch" was over,' Churchill commented in his opening remarks, 'Sicily was near; what should come next?' The 'great prize', he believed, was to get Italy out of the war 'by whatever means might be the best'. Once Italy were out of the war, the Turkish Government would allow the Allies to use bases in Turkey to bomb the Roumanian oilfields at Ploesti. Another 'great effect' of the elimination of Italy would be felt in the Balkans, 'where patriots of various nationalities were with difficulty held in check by large Axis forces', including twenty-five or more Italian divisions. If these withdrew, either Germany would have to give up the Balkans, or withdraw large forces from the Russian front to fill the gap. 'In no other way could relief be given to the Russian front on so large a scale this year.'

The defeat of Italy would also eliminate the Italian fleet, releasing British warships from the Mediterranean 'to proceed either to the Bay of Bengal or the Pacific to fight Japan'. A second object in the defeat of Italy was 'the taking of weight off Russia'. Britain and America 'should never forget' that there were 185 German divisions on the Russian front. Churchill added: 'We had destroyed the German army in Africa, but soon we should not be in contact with them anywhere. The Russian effort was prodigious, and placed us in their debt.' The 'best way of taking the weight off the Russian front in 1943' he reiterated, 'would be to get, or knock, Italy out of the war, thus forcing the Germans to send a large number of troops to hold down the Balkans'.

A third object, Churchill told the meeting, was 'to apply our vast armies, air forces and munitions to the enemy'. The British alone had

---

[1] MA/427, IZ 1709, 'Personal and Most Secret', 8.15 p.m., 11 May 1943: Churchill papers, 20/111. Alexander's estimate of the likely number of prisoners was rapidly exceeded; the number of unwounded prisoners held by May 25 was 238,243; the final total was calculated at the time at 244,500. (Sir David Hunt, letter to the author, 23 July 1985.)

[2] CON/1, IZ 1706, 'Personal and Most Secret', 9.15 a.m., 11 May 1943: Churchill papers, 20/111.

thirteen divisions in north-west Africa. If Sicily were 'completed' by
the end of August, 'what should these troops do between that time
and the date, seven or eight months later, when the cross-Channel
operation might first be mounted?'

With the cross-Channel invasion most likely to take place in March
or April 1944, the problem to be resolved in Washington seemed to be
what to do with the large victorious armies between August 1943 and
March 1944. 'They could not possibly stand idle,' he told the President, 'and so long a period of apparent inaction would have a serious
effect on Russia, which was bearing such a disproportionate weight.'

Churchill then spoke in greater detail about 'Round-up', telling the
President, as the minutes of the meeting recorded:

. . . that he could not pretend that the problem of landing on the Channel
coast had been solved. The difficult beaches, with the great rise and fall of
tide, the strength of the enemy's defences, the number of his reserves and the
ease of his communications, all made the task one which must not be
underrated. Much however would be learnt from Sicily. He wished to make
it absolutely clear that His Majesty's Government earnestly desired to
undertake a full-scale invasion of the Continent from the United Kingdom as
soon as a plan offering reasonable prospects of success could be made.

Churchill then spoke of the need to make use of 'the large forces
standing in India'. The difficulties of fighting in Burma had become
'apparent'. The jungle prevented the use of the 'modern weapons'
available. The monsoon strictly limited the campaign season. Nor
were there any means of bringing sea power to bear. He therefore
suggested, as a possible alternative to the reconquest of Burma, an
operation against 'the tip of Sumatra and the waist of Malaya at
Penang'. The time had also come, Churchill believed, to study 'the
long-term plan' for the defeat of Japan. He would like to state 'once
more' the British determination 'to carry the struggle home to Japan'.

Churchill asked that all these proposals for action in the Far East
should be studied by the Staffs, led by the United States Chiefs of
Staff, based upon the assumption 'that Germany would be out of the
war in 1944', enabling the Allies to concentrate upon the 'great
campaign' against Japan in 1945.

In reply, Roosevelt stated that 'everyone was agreed' that there
was 'no possibility' of a cross-Channel enterprise in 1943. He also
shared Churchill's view that the operation must be carried out 'on the
largest scale' in the spring of 1944, but was worried that this date
might be set back by a campaign in Italy. Churchill, in reply, was
emphatic, first that it was 'imperative' to use the armies which would
have been victorious on Sicily to do something after August 1943,

rather than sit idle for six months, and second that it was not necessary to occupy all Italy. 'If Italy collapses,' he added, 'the United Nations would occupy the ports and airfields needed for further operations into the Balkans and Southern Europe.' [1]

Even as Churchill set out his confident assertions about what the Allied armies would do in Sicily and Italy, the news from North Africa gave cause for considerable jubilation in London and Washington. An Enigma decrypt from General von Arnim stated curtly: 'We have fired our last cartridge. We are closing down for ever.' [2] A few hours later, Alexander telegraphed from Tunisia to Churchill at the White House: 'The end is very near. Von Arnim has been captured, and prisoners will most likely be over 150,000. All organized resistance has collapsed, and only pockets of enemy are still holding out.' [3] A second telegram followed on May 13: 'Sir, it is my duty to report that the Tunisian campaign is over. All enemy resistance had ceased. We are masters of the North African shores.' [4] That same day, King George VI wrote to Churchill of 'how profoundly I appreciate the fact' that the initial conception and successful prosecution of the campaign in Africa 'are largely due to your vision and to your unflinching determination in the face of early difficulties'. [5] From 10 Downing Street came a letter from Clementine Churchill:

My Darling Winston,

How I wish that in this hour of Victory I were with you—so that we could rejoice together & so that I could tell you what I feel about *your* North African Campaign. You must be deeply moved by these events although you planned them & knew beforehand that they could be achieved.

I'm worried at the importance given by the Press (notably The Times) to the presence of Wavell & his East Indian Naval & Air Colleagues in your Party. I'm so afraid the Americans will think that a Pacific slant is to be given to the next phase of the War—I have cut out the piece of the Times which disturbs me. *Surely* the liberation of Europe *must* come first. I wonder what impression Wavell has now made upon you. I have never met him but I understand he has a great deal of personal charm. This is pleasant in civilized times but not much use in total War. [6]

[1] 'Trident', 'Minutes of First Meeting, held in the White House, 2.30 p.m., May 12, 1943', 'Most Secret': Cabinet papers, 99/22.

[2] Quoted in Cadogan diary, 12 May 1943: David Dilks (editor), *op. cit.*, page 530.

[3] MA/436, 'Personal', 'Most Secret', 12 May 1943: Churchill papers, 20/111.

[4] MA/439, 'Personal', repeated to Washington as Alcove No. 201, 13 May 1943: Churchill papers, 20/111.

[5] 'Alcove No. 199', 'Personal', 13 May 1943: Churchill papers, 20/111.

[6] A former officer in the Western Desert writes: 'Wavell was a great man but had no personal charm at all, or only on *very* long acquaintance. His cold taciturnity was what most prejudiced Churchill against him.' (Letter to the author, 23 July 1985.) On 6 October 1943, at a farewell dinner for Wavell before he left for India, Churchill said: 'We send out to India in this time of

'Do re-assure me,' Clementine Churchill ended, 'that the European front will take 1st place all the time.'[1]

While Churchill was in Washington he received news which gave considerable confidence to the Allied preparations. Three months before 'Trident', during the early phases of preparation for the invasion of Sicily, 'a somewhat startling cover plan', as Ismay described it to Churchill, had been devised in London.[2] This plan depended upon the landing on the coast of Spain of a body which would appear to be that of a British Staff officer killed in a plane crash while carrying with him a document giving details of Allied landings, not in Sicily, but elsewhere.

The idea for this deception came from Flight Lieutenant Charles Cholmondley of M.I.5, who had been acting as a liaison officer with Colonel Bevan's deception team, the London Controlling Section. As soon as Cholmondley's plan had been approved by the Chiefs of Staff, Ismay had told Bevan, as Bevan later recalled:

. . . that I must see Mr Churchill and get him to pass it. So down I went one morning at half past nine, found him in bed smoking a cigar and dictating to his secretaries. I handed him a piece of paper—one sheet of foolscap as usual—to explain what we intended to do. He read it and I said, well, of course there's a possibility that the Spaniards might find out that this dead man was in fact not drowned at all from a crashed air-craft, but was a gardener in Wales who'd killed himself with weed-killer. However Bernard Spilsbury had explained to me that this was very unlikely because it was a very difficult technical job to find out the cause of death; weed-killer gets into the kidneys and is very difficult to diagnose. Apparently it would take you three weeks to a month just to find out what it was.

The other point I stressed was that of course the wind and the tide might be wrong and consequently the body wouldn't be washed ashore; whereupon he said to me, well, in that case you'll have to take him on another swim, won't you.[3]

---

crisis one of our foremost citizens and one of our greatest soldiers, a man of the highest courage, of very wide culture, a man who, although professionalised in the duties of the officer and of the commander, has nevertheless a wide field of learning, of reading, and is, as I say, capable of wielding the pen with almost equal effect to the way in which he wields the sword.' ('Speeches at the Farewell Dinner in Honour of Field Marshal the Viscount Wavell before leaving to take up his post as Viceroy of India,' 6 October 1943: Churchill papers, 20/99.)

[1] Letter of 13 May 1943: Spencer-Churchill papers.

[2] Ismay minute of 14 April 1943: quoted in Michael Howard, *Grand Strategy*, volume 4, August 1942–September 1943, London 1972, page 370.

[3] 'Interview with Mr. John Bevan', 9 May 1967. This interview was conducted by Randolph Churchill at his home, Stour, in Suffolk. It was one of the first, and last interviews which Randolph Churchill undertook in connection with what would, but for his premature death in October 1968, at the age of 57, have been his own Second World War volume of the Churchill biography.

The deception plan, code name Operation 'Mincemeat', was intended to give the Germans definite proof that following the conquest of Tunisia, Allied forces under General Montgomery would invade, not Sicily, but the Greek Peloponnese, with a view to an advance through the Balkans. A second Allied army, under Alexander, would invade elsewhere. The 'Mincemeat' deception was to take the form of a letter from the Vice-Chief of the Imperial General Staff, General Nye, to Alexander, telling him that the idea of using Sicily as the 'cover plan' for his operation had been rejected in favour of using it for the landings in Greece. Thus any build-up of activity against Sicily was shown to be a mere cover operation for one of two landings elsewhere.

A second letter in the dead man's briefcase, from Mountbatten, was to make it clear that Sardinia was the second of the two amphibious operations being planned. A reference to the Germans in the Nye letter stated bluntly: 'we stand a very good chance of making him think we will go for Sicily—it is an obvious objective and one about which he must feel nervous'.

The two letters were duly written, Mountbatten's dated April 21 and General Nye's dated April 23. The body was then given the documents of an imaginary Major Martin, and, on April 30, was floated ashore from a submarine off the coast of Spain.

The London Controlling Section, the Chiefs of Staff, and Churchill, waited anxiously for any clue that Nye's letter had reached the German High Command. All went according to plan. On May 9, after the Spaniards had found the body, and allowed the Germans to copy the letters, the German High Command in Berlin received its first appreciation of the two letters. This was followed by a second appreciation on May 14. Both appreciations accepted the letters as genuine, and 'anticipated' Greece and the Balkans as the locations of Allied landings 'on a fairly large scale'. Sicily was firmly relegated to the status of 'cover operation'. During May 14, Hitler himself, at a conference with Admiral Doenitz, who had just returned from Italy, told Doenitz: 'The Fuehrer does not agree with the Duce that the most likely invasion point is Sicily. Furthermore, he believes that the dis-covered Anglo-Saxon order confirms the assumption that the planned attack will be directed mainly against Sardinia and the Peloponnese.'

These German exchanges were unknown in London, but, as Colonel Bevan's assistant, Lady Jane Pleydell Bouverie, later recalled, 'Enigma told us that the Germans were falling for it.'[1] It did so on May 14, only two weeks after the body had floated ashore, in a 'most secret' message sent from the German High Command to Naval Group

---

[1] Lady Jane Bethell recollections: in a conversation with the author, 17 June 1985.

Command South. In this message the 'possible starting points' for Allied landing operations were pinpointed in Greece, with Kalamata and Cape Araxos, both of which had been mentioned in Nye's letter, being specifically referred to. The German High Command message went on to order a series of measures 'to reinforce rapidly the defensive strength of the areas which are specifically threatened': these included laying of minefields off Kalamata and other Greek ports, the installation of port defences and the possibility of installing operational U-boat bases.[1]

An Enigma decrypt of this German message reached London that very day.[2] To Churchill, who was in Washington, Brigadier Hollis at once telegraphed: ' "Mincemeat" swallowed rod, line and sinker by right people and from best information they look like acting on it.'[3]

As the Combined Chiefs began their discussions in Washington about future Anglo-American strategy, Roosevelt took Churchill to his mountain retreat at Shangri-La, in the Allegheny mountains. While relaxing there, Churchill learnt that General Marshall's idea of an acceleration of the Sicily landing had been 'turned down' at Eisenhower's headquarters. 'I hope,' he minuted to the Chiefs of Staff, 'we shall not be blamed on the same lines as Hitler is, for having neglected to come on into England immediately after the collapse of France.' It 'may well be', he commented, that a quarter of the force 'launched now' could achieve what the whole force would have difficulty in doing 'two months hence'.[4]

Returning to Washington, Churchill, Roosevelt and their Chiefs of Staff met on the afternoon of May 14 to discuss the India-Burma-China theatre. Churchill again pressed, as he had done in his shipboard memorandum of May 8, for an 'Asiatic "Torch"', and suggested specifically the possibility of seizing 'the northern tip of Sumatra'. Churchill was supported by Wavell, who felt that if it were possible to place strong air forces on northern Sumatra, and protect them, 'a bad situation would be created for the Japanese and cause them considerable air loss'. Air Chief Marshal Peirse also supported the northern Sumatra plan, describing it as having 'considerable merit

---

[1] Ewen Montagu, *The Man Who Never Was*, London 1953, page 104. It was with Lieutenant-Commander Montagu's indispensable support that Cholmondley's original idea for the 'mincemeat' deception had been transformed into reality. The German General sent to the Peleponnese to prepare for the non-existent assault was Rommel; in the first week of June, a group of German motor torpedo boats was ordered from Sicily to the Aegean. This fact was likewise revealed through Enigma.

[2] CX/MSS/257/T4: Hinsley and others, *British Intelligence, op. cit.*, volume 3, part 1, page 78.

[3] 'Alcove' No. 217, 14 May 1943: Cabinet papers, 120/88.

[4] Prime Minister's Personal Minute, D (T) 12/3, 15 May 1943: Churchill papers, 4/397A.

because it extends our own cover eastwards and interferes with the Japanese shipping lanes'.

Opposition came from the American General, 'Vinegar' Joe Stilwell, who said that operations against Sumatra or Malaya 'would have no bearing on the opening of the Burma Road, and would thus greatly prolong the period during which no steps were being taken to open it'. The Chinese, Stilwell declared, 'were suspicious of the British, and it would be necessary for the British to prove that they were in earnest'. The effect of the cancellation of 'Anakim' would be 'very bad' on the Chinese people, nor would the development of an air supply route be an adequate substitute. To this Churchill replied that 'he was not prepared to undertake something foolish purely in order to placate the Chinese. He was not prepared to make war that way. He would do anything that was sensible to help the Chinese in exactly the same way as he would do anything that was sensible to help the Russians; but he did not see any particular value in carrying out costly operations to no purpose.'

Roosevelt then asked about the possibility of using the 'Anakim' forces, intended for Burma, for an advance towards China instead, opening the Burma Road as they advanced, but Wavell replied that a force advancing in that manner could not be sustained. Upper Burma was 'the most malarial country in the world', Wavell declared, 'and if operations were continued there in the rainy season, 25 per cent casualities per month must be expected'.[1]

Churchill was distressed by what he saw as a lack of drive in the Far Eastern theatre. Two weeks later he sent Attlee a file on the air bases in Assam, urging that their development 'with the utmost exertion is a matter of supreme urgency and importance in this theatre'. His message ended: 'I am disquieted about the way in which our affairs in this theatre have been conducted and the opportunity should be taken of gripping the whole situation and injecting new vim into all proceedings.'[2]

Churchill spent most of May 18 preparing his speech for the United States Congress. Beginning that morning at 9.30, he dictated until 4.30 in the afternoon, 'without a break', Elizabeth Layton wrote to her parents. There was then further dictation from mid-

---

[1] 'Trident', 'Revised Minutes of Second Meeting held in the White House, 2 p.m., May 14th, 1943', 'Most Secret': Cabinet papers, 99/22.
[2] 'Most Secret', 26 May 1943, Annex to Chiefs of Staff Committee No. 114 (Operations) of 1943, 28 May 1943: Cabinet papers, 79/61.

night until 2.30 in the morning: a total of nine and a half hours dictation.[1]

Addressing Congress shortly after midday on May 19, Churchill warned the assembled Senators and Representatives that although, after Gettysburg, no one doubted 'which way the dread balance of war would incline', nevertheless far more blood had been shed after Gettysburg 'than in all the fighting which went before'.

Churchill ended his address:

If we wish to abridge the slaughter and ruin which this war is spreading to so many lands and to which we must ourselves contribute so grievous a measure of suffering and sacrifice, we cannot afford to relax a single fibre of our being or to tolerate the slightest abatement of our efforts. The enemy is still proud and powerful. He is hard to get at. He still possesses enormous armies, vast resources, and invaluable strategic territories.

War is full of mysteries and surprises. A false step, a wrong direction, an error in strategy, discord or lassitude among the Allies, might soon give the common enemy power to confront us with new and hideous facts. We have surmounted many serious dangers, but there is one grave danger which will go along with us till the end; that danger is the undue prolongation of the war. No one can tell what new complications and perils might arise in four or five more years of war. And it is in the dragging-out of the war at enormous expense, until the democracies are tired or bored or split, that the main hopes of Germany and Japan must now reside.

'We must destroy this hope,' Churchill declared, 'as we have destroyed so many others, and for that purpose we must beware of every topic however attractive and every tendency however natural which turns our minds and energies from this supreme objective of the general victory of the United Nations.' His oration ended: 'By singleness of purpose, by steadfastness of conduct, by tenacity and endurance such as we have so far displayed—by these, and only by these, can we discharge our duty to the future of the world and to the destiny of man.'[2]

'Your address to Congress was grand,' Clementine Churchill wrote on the following day, '& a master-piece of "walking delicately". It warmed me to hear your voice so strong, resonant & resolute.'[3]

Lord Halifax, who acted as Churchill's host at the British Embassy when Roosevelt was away from Washington, noted that when he sug-

---

[1] Elizabeth Layton, letter of 19 May 1943: Nel papers.
[2] Speech of 19 May 1943: BBC Written Archives Centre (the speech was broadcast live from Congress, unlike any of Churchill's speeches in the House of Commons).
[3] Letter of 20 May 1943: Spencer-Churchill papers.

gested that there might be questions about the re-payment of Britain's Lend Lease debt, Churchill had said to him: 'Oh, I shall like that one. I shall say, yes by all means let us have an account if we can get it reasonably accurate, but I shall have my account to put in too, and my account is for holding the baby alone for eighteen months, and it was a very rough brutal baby I had to hold. I don't quite know what I shall have to charge for it.'

Halifax was intrigued by Churchill's new mood. 'I have never seen him in better heart or form,' he wrote, 'an amazing contrast to the very tired and nerve-strained PM I saw last August in England.' [1]

On the evening of Wednesday May 19, at their third meeting, Churchill and Roosevelt were told by their Chiefs of Staff that some 'tentative conclusions' on future strategy would most probably be ready 'for the week-end'. Agreement had been reached that day, Brooke reported, for the build-up in England 'of a sufficient force to secure a bridgehead on the Continent from which further offensive operations could be carried out'. Churchill 'indicated his pleasure' that a cross-Channel operation 'had finally been agreed upon'. [2]

On May 21 Churchill sent Attlee and Eden an account of the progress of the 'Trident' meetings. 'The Staffs,' he reported, 'have been engaged in perpetual discussions sometimes four meetings a day.' At first the differences had seemed 'insuperable' and it had looked 'like a hopeless breach'. But by 'patience and perseverance' these difficulties had been overcome. 'The fact that the President and I have been living side by side seeing each other at all hours,' Churchill added, 'that we are known to be in close agreement, and that the President intends to decide himself on the ultimate issues—all this together with the priceless work of Hopkins had exercised throughout a mollifying and also a dominating influence on the course of Staff discussions.'

The essence of those discussions, Churchill explained, was that Britain would have 'a free hand' in the Mediterranean until November, and that 'thereafter' the Allies concentrate on a combination of cross-Channel landing and cross-Channel invasion, formerly when separate, 'Sledgehammer' and 'Round-up', now to be called 'Roundhammer', and to take place 'by May first'. [3]

In this way, on 21 May 1943, in Washington, it was decided that the cross-Channel landings were to take place by 1 May 1944: the

[1] Letter of May 1943: Lord Birkenhead, *Halifax: The Life of Lord Halifax*, London 1965, page 537.

[2] 'Trident', 'Minutes of Third Meeting, held in the White House, 6 p.m., May 19, 1943', 'Most Secret': Cabinet papers, 99/22.

[3] 'Pencil' No. 165, 'Most Secret and Personal', 21 May 1943: Churchill papers, 20/128.

next Spring season, and without any delay being incurred in the event of the Italian campaign leading to an opening up of possibilities in the Balkans.

By coincidence, on the day of Churchill's telegram to Attlee and Eden, the British involvement in the Balkans was about to take a new twist, with the imminent despatch of a British Mission to the Yugoslav partisan leader, Josip Broz Tito, with a view to undertaking 'joint actions of sabotage' against the Germans.[1] One of the two British officers who was to be parachuted behind German lines to make contact with Tito, and to coordinate the sabotage, was Churchill's former Research Assistant, Bill Deakin. Not knowing if he would survive his hazardous mission, Deakin wrote to Churchill from Cairo on May 21:

My dear Mr. Churchill,

I am leaving tomorrow morning for the Balkans to try and make contact with the Yugoslav partisans. You may remember our talk when you were here in Cairo. I have done as you said, and asked the Embassy to pass this letter to you direct. I am glad to go, and hope to be able to establish a useful liaison, and in any case send back information of value.

It will be some time before I can extricate myself from the Balkans again, but am looking forward with very great pleasure to seeing you again.

I do not need to tell you now after five years how much I have appreciated all your kindness and generosity. You may not realize how much the many personal touches have been valued. . . .[2]

Churchill was to follow the course of Deakin's mission, and of Tito's fighting, with close attention, watching through the Enigma decrypts to see how far the partisan activities were succeeding in pinning down German forces, and drawing them away from other fronts.

Three days after Deakin's letter, during the fifth meeting of Churchill and Roosevelt with the British and American Chiefs of Staff, Churchill pointed out that the 'prime factor' to be kept in mind in deciding how to follow up a success in Sicily was the position in the Balkans, 'where 34 Axis Divisions were held in play by rebels', who would become 'much more active' if the Allies could gain touch with them through the Adriatic port of Durazzo, 'or any other suitable point'.[3]

On the afternoon of May 21, at the fourth 'Trident' meeting of

[1] F. W. D. Deakin, *The Embattled Mountain*, London 1971, page 219.
[2] Letter of 21 May 1943: Churchill papers, 2/464.
[3] 'Trident', 'Minutes of 5th Meeting, held in the White House, 4.45 p.m., 24th May 1943', 'Most Secret': Cabinet papers, 99/22.

Churchill, Roosevelt and their Chiefs of Staff, there was discussion of the combined Anglo-American bomber offensive from the United Kingdom. Roosevelt wanted 'occasional raids' on the smaller German towns 'where factories were known to exist'. It would 'greatly depress the Germans', he said, 'if they felt even the smaller towns could not escape'. General agreement, noted the minute, was expressed with this view.[1]

On May 24 the Staff Conversations came to an end, their draft conclusions being submitted to Churchill and Roosevelt. One recommendation was for the occupation of the Portuguese islands of the Azores, Operation 'Lifebelt', a move which the British and American Chiefs of Staff described as 'essential to the efficient conduct of the anti-U-boat war'. It was also proposed to strengthen the air forces engaged in the 'Bay of Biscay Offensive' against the U-boats, and to increase the number of aircraft engaged in convoy protection. A combined 'US-British air offensive' against Germany was also approved, aimed at 'the progressive destruction and dislocation of the German military, industrial and economic system, and the undermining of the morale of the German people to a point where their capacity for armed resistance is fatally weakened'.

The Combined Chiefs of Staff produced their Final Report on May 25. With regard to the date and scale of the cross-Channel operation, they now 'resolved' that twenty-nine divisions, with the possibility of one French Division added 'at a later date', should be gathered for the cross-Channel landings, the 'target date' for which was set as 1 May 1944.

For the Mediterranean, the Combined Chiefs of Staff advised the exploitation of 'Husky' in such a way as 'to eliminate Italy from the war and to contain the maximum number of German divisions', using all the forces available up to 1 November 1943, after which four American and three British divisions would be 'held in readiness for withdrawal' to take part in the cross-Channel operation.[2] After this withdrawal of forces to Britain, a total of 19 British and Allied, 4 United States and 4 French Divisions—27 Divisions in all—would be available for garrisons and operations in the Mediterranean area 'subsequent' to the conquest of Sicily.[3]

With their Final Report completed, the British and American Chiefs

[1] 'Trident', 'Minutes of 4th Meeting, held in the White House, 5 p.m., 21st May 1943, 'Most Secret': Cabinet papers, 99/22.
[2] This was later increased to four American and four British divisions, the maximum for which shipping was available.
[3] Combined Chiefs of Staff Paper No. 242/6, 'Final Report to the President and Prime Minister', 'Most Secret', 25 May 1943: Premier papers, 3/443/4, folios 2–23 (circulated to the War Cabinet as Chiefs of Staff Paper Ni. 281 (O) of 1943, 3 June 1943).

of Staff prepared to present them to Roosevelt and Churchill. Brooke noted in his diary: 'At 4.45 p.m. we went to the White House, first to be photographed and then to attend Conference with President and PM.' Brooke was worried that Churchill had not accepted the Combined Chiefs of Staff report in its entirety, and feared that he had 'created a situation of suspicion in the American Chiefs that we had been behind their backs. . . .' 'There are times,' Brooke added, 'when he drives me to desperation. Now we are threatened by a redraft by him, and more difficulties tomorrow. . . .' [1]

In fact, Churchill's wish to make alterations in the Final Report of the Combined Chiefs of Staff concerned his fear that the American desire to invade Sardinia would not be as beneficial as going straight from Sicily to Italy. If Italy were to go 'out of the war', Churchill explained at the meeting with the British and American Chiefs of Staff on May 24, then the Italian divisions in the Balkans would have to withdraw, and Germany would then 'either have to fill the gap, or retire to the Danube'. The 'effect on Turkey' would also be 'very important', Churchill argued, and he added: 'None of these effects could possibly accrue from an operation against Sardinia.' [2]

On May 25 Churchill decided to challenge the American preference for Sardinia but Hopkins, in whom he confided his intentions, warned that it would need another week of argument in Washington to obtain a clear-cut decision, and even then the decision Churchill wished for could not be guaranteed. 'I was deeply distressed at this,' Churchill recalled eight years later. [3] What Churchill could not reveal in his memoirs, nor apparently even to Hopkins at the time, was that only eleven days earlier the Germans had convinced themselves that Sardinia was to be the object of an Allied attack; and had done so as a result of Britain's own initiative in trying to conceal from them that Sicily was to be the real target.

Churchill now planned to fly from Washington to Algiers, to discuss the post-Sicily strategy with Eisenhower himself and the other Commanders-in-Chief in North Africa. He was convinced that, once in Algiers, he would be able to secure a decision to follow up the conquest of Sicily with an immediate invasion of Italy; as General Marshall himself had earlier advocated the invasion of Sicily as soon as possible after victory in North Africa, or even earlier. Churchill therefore asked Roosevelt if Marshall could accompany him to Algiers. He would feel

---

[1] Brooke diary, 24 May 1943: Bryant, *op. cit.*, volume 1, page 626.

[2] 'Trident', 'Minutes of 5th Meeting, held in the White House, 4.45 p.m., 24th May 1943', 'Most Secret': Cabinet papers, 99/22.

[3] Winston S. Churchill, *The Second World War*, volume 4, London 1951, page 724.

'awkward', he said, in discussing these matters with Eisenhower 'without the presence of a United States representative on the highest level'. Roosevelt agreed, a decision which, Churchill told Roosevelt, was a source of 'great satisfaction'.[1]

'In our May talks in Washington,' Churchill informed Smuts eight weeks later, 'we found serious American misgivings lest we should become deeply involved in the Mediterranean, and a hankering for winding up the campaign there with the capture of Sardinia. This we combated, and as our forces in the Mediterranean far outnumber the American we were able to have the matter left open till after the capture of Sicily. Not being satisfied with this,' Churchill added, 'I requested the President to send General Marshall with mc to North Africa, and there upon the spot to convince Eisenhower and others that nothing less than Rome could satisfy the requirements of this year's campaign.'[2]

On the afternoon of May 25 Roosevelt and Churchill gave a joint Press Conference. When Roosevelt told the assembled newspapermen that the combination of the day and night bombing of Germany by United States and British aircraft was achieving 'a more and more satisfactory result', Churchill remarked, amid laughter: 'It's like running a twenty-four-hour service.' The air weapon, he added, 'was the weapon these people chose to subjugate the world. This was the weapon with which they struck at Pearl Harbour. This was the weapon with which they boasted—the Germans boasted they would terrorize all the countries of the world. And it is an example of poetic justice that this should be the weapon in which they should find themselves most out-matched and first out-matched in the ensuing struggle.'

As to the war at sea, Churchill pointed out, the surplus of new building over sinking over the past six months had been 'substantial'. The 'killings of U-boats' had improved and reached 'a very high pitch—never better than in the last month'.

When the Press Conference was over, and the journalists began to leave 'rather slowly', as the White House transcript noted, 'the Prime Minister climbed onto his chair and gave the "V" for Victory sign with his fingers, which was accompanied by much applause'.[3]

*   *   *

[1] 'Trident', 'Minutes of 6th Meeting, held in the White House, 11.30 a.m., 25th May 1943', 'Most Secret': Cabinet papers, 99/22.

[2] Prime Minister's Personal Telegram, T.1043/3, 16 July 1943: Churchill papers, 20/131.

[3] 'Confidential', 'Press Conference No. 899', Executive Office of the President, 4.03 p.m., 25 May 1943: Premier papers, 4/72/2, folios 609–26.

The greatest victory at 'Trident' was one of which the Press knew nothing. It was an agreement that development on the atom bomb should be a joint enterprise. Almost a year earlier, in June 1942, Churchill had discussed just such an agreement with Roosevelt at Hyde Park: 'My whole understanding,' Churchill later wrote, 'was that everything was on the basis of fully sharing the results as equal partners. I have no record, but I shall be very much surprised if the President's recollection does not square with this.' [1]

Following this unwritten and unrecorded agreement, it had been intended to set up a full-scale atom bomb production plant in Britain, with American help and expertise, under the general direction of the Lord President of the Council, Sir John Anderson, the code for the project being 'Tube Alloys'. Within less than two months, however, it had become clear, as Anderson informed Churchill, that the production plant for the bomb 'would have to be on such a huge scale that its erection in this country will be out of the question during the war. Even the erection and operation of a pilot plant would cause a major dislocation in war production.' Meanwhile, Anderson warned, 'the Americans have been applying themselves with enthusiasm and a lavish expenditure, which we cannot rival, to experimental work over the whole field of Tube Alloys. They are working on four alternative methods, and are making increasingly rapid progress. It is still considered probable that our method is the best; but it has little chance so long as work on it is handicapped by the limited resources available in this country.'

In these circumstances Anderson had come to the conclusion, after discussion with his Consultative Council and with Lord Cherwell, 'that we might now make up our minds that the full scale plant for production according to the British method can only be erected in the United States and that, consequently, the pilot plant also will have to be designed and erected there. The immediate effect of this would be that, whilst certain of the more academic research work would continue to be carried on in this country, we would move our design work and the personnel concerned to the United States.' Henceforth, work on the atom bomb 'would be pursued as a combined Anglo-American effort'. Anderson added: 'I make this recommendation with some reluctance, as I should like to have seen the work carried forward in this country. We must, however, face the fact that the pioneer work done in this country is a dwindling asset and that, unless we capitalise it quickly, we shall be rapidly outstripped. We now have a real con-

[1] Prime Minister's Personal Telegram T.233/3, 'Personal, Immediate and Most Secret', 27 February 1943: Premier papers, 3/139/8A, folios 537–9.

tribution to make to a "merger". Soon we shall have little or none.' [1]

Anderson sent Churchill this proposal on July 30. On the following day Churchill accepted it, minuting in the margin, 'As proposed.' [2]

The Americans agreed in principle to such a joint development, but six months later, Anderson warned Churchill that the United States authorities concerned 'have received an order which restricts interchange of information on this subject by the application of the principle that they are to have complete interchange on design and construction of new weapons and equipment only if the recipient of the information is in a position to take advantage of it in this war'. Anderson added: 'It appears that this principle is being interpreted to mean that information must be withheld from us over the greater part of the field of tube alloys. At the same time, the United States authorities apparently expect us to continue to exchange information with them in regard to those parts of the project in which our work is further forward than theirs.' This development, Anderson told Churchill, 'has come as a bombshell and is quite intolerable'. Anderson had discussed the American order with Cherwell. Both were agreed 'that an approach to President Roosevelt is urgently necessary'. [3]

Churchill made no comment, except to write at the top of Anderson's letter the word 'Symbol', in a circle.

While Churchill was at 'Symbol', Anderson telegraphed to him with further alarming news. He had just seen an American memorandum making it clear 'that there is to be no further interchange of information in regard to many of the most important processes'. The 'pretext' for this policy, Anderson explained, was secrecy, 'but one cannot help suspecting', he wrote, 'that the US Military authorities who are now in complete control, wish to gain an advance upon us, and feel that, having now benefited from the fruits of our early endeavours, they will not suffer unduly by casting us aside'.

Both he and Cherwell 'regard the position as most serious', Anderson wrote, and he added: 'We hope you will be able to prevail upon the President to put matters right. If not, we shall have to consider drastic changes in our programme and policy.' [4]

As Anderson and Cherwell wished, Churchill had raised the matter at Casablanca. 'I may be obtaining most satisfactory personal assurances,' he telegraphed to Anderson on January 23, 'but it is thought

[1] 'Most Secret', 'Very urgent', 30 July 1942: Premier papers, 3/139/8A, folios 566–7.
[2] Note initialled 'WSC, 31 vii': Premier papers, 3/139/8A, folio 567.
[3] 'Tube Alloys', 'Most Secret', 11 January 1943: Premier papers, 3/139/8A, folios 562–3.
[4] 'Telescope' No. 151, 'Immediate' sent at 12.59 a.m., 20 January 1943: Premier papers, 3/139/8A, folio 560.

better not to telegraph instructions from here'.[1] Churchill had discussed the conflict with Harry Hopkins, who told him that all would be 'put right' as soon as Roosevelt returned to the United States. This assurance came to nothing, however, for, as Churchill telegraphed to Hopkins on February 15, 'at present the American War Department is asking us to keep them informed of our experiments while refusing altogether any information about theirs'.[2]

The impasse continued, so much so that in March 1943 Churchill proposed warning Hopkins that 'I must shortly commit myself to full scale action, towards which we have made some progress in the last three months'. 'Time is passing,' Churchill warned. 'No information is being exchanged.'[3] Two weeks later, Churchill telegraphed again to Hopkins: 'I am much concerned about not hearing from you about tube alloys. That we should each work separately would be a sombre decision.'[4]

The only information which the Americans wished to exchange, Cherwell informed Churchill on April 7, was on the separating plant for light uranium, 'in which we are well ahead'.[5]

Churchill now asked Anderson for a report on what would be involved in Britain pressing forward with atomic bomb research and production 'at full speed ourselves'. Churchill added: 'I should like a rough estimate of the financial cost and the manpower required, so far as possible year by year, until the projects are completed. The figures for manpower should be split up into skilled and unskilled labour. If it were possible to give me some idea of what other projects would be affected, and to what extent, it would be most helpful.'

Churchill understood, from Lord Cherwell, that it was 'likely to be six or nine months' before Britain could begin the actual construction of an atomic bomb, even if 'the highest priority' were given to the work of designing and planning. 'In my view,' Churchill added, 'we cannot afford to wait, and the necessary staff should be directed to draw out detailed plans for putting these projects into effect, with the necessary time tables and estimates, etc.'[6]

[1] 'Stratagem' No. 196, 'Hush Most Secret', 23 January 1943: Churchill papers, 20/127.
[2] Prime Minister's Personal Telegram, T.178/3, 'Personal and Secret', 15 February 1943: Premier papers, 3/139/8A, folio 556.
[3] 'Personal and Most Secret', 'In a locked box', 18 March 1943: the words 'I must shortly commit myself to full scale action towards which' were omitted. The sentence 'No information is being exchanged' was replaced by 'collaboration appears to be at a standstill'. (op. cit., folio 526).
[4] Prime Minister's Personal Telegram, T.434/3, 'Personal and Secret'. 1 April 1943: Premier papers, 33139/8A, folio 523.
[5] 'Tube Alloys', 'Summary', 7 April 1943: Premier papers, 3/139/8A, folio 511.
[6] Prime Minister's Personal Minutes, M.270/3, 15 April 1943: Premier papers, 3/139/8A, folios 502–3.

For Britain to manufacture the atomic bomb without the United States would require, at the least, independent sources of uranium and heavy water. For these, the Canadian connection was indispensable. On May 13, however, Anderson telegraphed to Churchill: 'I have just received most disturbing information regarding completeness of American control of uranium and heavy water supplies.'[1] Two days later, a second telegram from Anderson confirmed that any British hope of an independent atomic bomb was a chimera. Under a contract which the United States Government had placed in Canada, Anderson explained, and had placed 'with the knowledge' of the Canadian Government, 'the United States Government have secured entire output of Canadian uranium mines for the next two years. A similar position has also arisen in regard to the Canadian production of heavy water.'[2]

Churchill discussed the atomic bomb crisis with Lord Cherwell. 'Can England afford to neglect so potent an arm while Russia develops it?' Cherwell asked. 'In cooperation,' he added, 'undoubtedly America and England can complete these projects faster than if each works alone.' There was also the risk that Britain and America might lose the war 'if Germany completes the work first'. Cherwell went on to ask: 'What is the objection to continued complete collaboration? We have had frank and intimate exchange of information for many months and it has worked well. Our contributions are considerable. (We showed the United States the best method to extract 25; we persuaded them the 49 process was feasible.) What reason has emerged for excluding us now?'[3]

The logic of America's raw material control, and of the danger of a German victory, was irresistible. No independent British production was possible, certainly not within the time remaining.

On May 26 Churchill telegraphed to Anderson from Washington: 'Tube Alloys. Conversation with the President entirely satisfactory.'[4] In a further telegram that day, Churchill explained to Anderson what had been achieved. 'The President agreed,' Churchill wrote, 'that the exchange of information on Tube Alloys should be resumed and that the enterprise should be considered a joint one, to which both countries would contribute their best endeavours.'

Roosevelt's agreement, Churchill added, was based, as he under-

[1] 'Alcove' No. 197, 'Most Secret', sent at 1.55 p.m., 13 May 1943: Premier papers, 3/139/8A, folio 497.

[2] 'Alcove' No. 236, 'Immediate', 'Most Secret', sent at 9.40 a.m., 15 May 1943: Premier papers, 3/139/8A, folio 495.

[3] 'Note on Tube Alloys', undated, marked by Churchill, 'Yes': Premier papers, 3/139/8A, folio 494.

[4] 'Pencil' No. 251, sent at 7.20 a.m., 26 May 1943: Premier papers, 33139/8A, folio 493.

stood it, 'upon the fact that this weapon may well be developed in time for the present war and that it falls within the general agreement covering the interchange of research and invention secrets'.[1]

Unlike the agreement of June 1942, which had failed, that of May 1943 succeeded: Britain and the United States were now partners in a deadly race. 'I am very grateful,' Churchill telegraphed to Hopkins two weeks later, 'for all your help in getting this question settled so satisfactorily. I am sure that the President's decision will be to the best advantage of both our countries.' Churchill added: 'We must now lose no time in implementing it.'[2]

On the morning of May 26, Marshall and Churchill flew by flying boat from Washington to Newfoundland, together with General Brooke. Also with them were his doctor, newly ennobled as Lord Moran, and General Ismay, Churchill's Private Secretary Leslie Rowan, his shorthand writer Patrick Kinna, and two detectives.[3] 'Trident' was at an end; Churchill, who had been out of England for three weeks, now set his course once more for Africa.

---

[1] 'Pencil' No. 405, 'Most Secret', 26 May 1943: Premier papers, 3/139/8A, folio 492.

[2] Prime Minister's Personal Telegram T.760/3, 'Most Secret and Personal', 10 June 1943: Premier papers, 3/139/8A, folio 489.

[3] 'Pencil' No. 245, 'Most Secret and Personal', 25 May 1943: Churchill papers, 20/112. The two detectives were Inspector Thompson and Sergeant Dudgeon.

24
'Trident' in Africa

THE flight from Washington to Newfoundland took eight and a half hours. After refuelling, the flying boat set off towards Gibraltar, a flight of 3,000 miles across the Atlantic Ocean. It was already dark, and Churchill was ready to sleep. As he later recalled:

The large double bed in the bridal suite of the Boeing was most comfortable, and I slept sound for a good many hours. All at once there was a sudden shock and bump. I awoke. Something had happened. There were no consequences, which after all are what is important in air journeys. Nevertheless, being thoroughly awake, I put on my zip suit and went forward down the long central gallery of our spacious machine, and climbed the staircase to the navigating controls. I sat in the co-pilot's seat. It was by now a lovely moonlight night. After a while I asked the pilot what caused the bump. 'We were struck by lightning,' he said, 'but there's nothing wrong.' This was good news. We had not caught fire or broken up in the air; there was no need to make a forced landing a thousand miles from anywhere. I had always wondered why aircraft did not mind being struck by lightning. To a groundsman it would seem quite a dangerous thing. Afterwards I learned that there had been a good deal of anxiety.[1]

At four in the afternoon of May 27, Churchill's flying boat reached Gibraltar. He had been airborne for seventeen hours. On May 28, having shown General Marshall something of 'the Rock', Churchill and his travel companions flew from Gibraltar to Algiers. This time, they flew in Churchill's new aircraft, a Lancaster bomber converted for his use, and known as a York. 'Very comfortable,' Brooke noted in his diary, 'with a special cabin for PM, dining rooms, berths for four besides PM, and lavatory.'[2]

After a three-hour flight, the York reached Algiers, where Eisenhower awaited it at the airfield, together with General Alexander and Admiral Sir Andrew Cunningham. That night, at dinner, Churchill

[1] Winston S. Churchill, *The Second World War*, volume 4, London 1951, page 727.
[2] Brooke diary, 28 May 1943: Bryant, *op. cit.*, volume 1, page 633.

and Brooke 'were busy', Brooke noted in his diary, 'trying to impress on Eisenhower what is to be gained by knocking Italy out of the war'. In Brooke's view, now in harmony with Churchill's, Eisenhower did not 'begin to realize the possibilities that lie ahead of us in this theatre. . . .'[1]

That night, while Churchill slept in Algiers, his former research assistant, Bill Deakin, together with a fellow-officer, Captain Stuart, and their two radio operators, sergeants Walter Wroughton and Peretz Rosenberg, parachuted into Yugoslavia. This was operation 'Typical'. The four men landed near Mount Dormitor at the very moment when the German army was seeking to crush altogether the already surrounded partisan troops.[2]

'I have no more pleasant memories of the war,' Churchill later wrote, 'than the eight days in Algiers or Tunis.'[3] 'I've just received your message,' Clementine Churchill wrote from London on May 30, 'saying that you are resting in the sunshine & cool breezes, & that you will not be returning for another week. Altho' I long to see you I'm sure this is very sensible as Washington must have been a strain & a racket—& then the altitude of the air journey.'[4] Churchill had been 'quite dead when he first arrived from America', Eden told Oliver Harvey a week later, 'and could hardly move, but the sun and the bathing had gradually revived him'.[5]

On the afternoon of May 29 Churchill met his pre-war friend, General Georges, who had just come out of France. In 1939 Georges had been Commander of Operations in north-east France, with the title of Generalissimo. After discussing with Georges the means of reconciliation between Giraud and de Gaulle, Churchill telegraphed to Eden, urging him to fly out to North Africa to join him. Eden was 'much better fitted than I am', Churchill telegraphed to Attlee, 'to be

---

[1] Brooke diary, 28 May 1943: Bryant, *op. cit.*, volume 1, page 633.

[2] During the night of 10 June 1943, Tito, his staff and an escort battalion, together with the British mission, escaped the German encirclement, and joined up with some 8,000 partisans who had broken through the German ring. Captain Stuart, a fluent Serbo-Croat linguist, was killed in a German air attack on 9 June 1943, the day before the breakout. More than a hundred partisans were also killed in this attack, in which both Tito and Deakin were wounded.

[3] Winston S. Churchill, *The Second World War*, volume 4, London 1951, page 729.

[4] Letter of 30 May 1943: Spencer-Churchill papers.

[5] Harvey diary, 5 June 1943: John Harvey (editor), *op. cit.*, pages 263–5.

best man at the Giraud-de Gaulle wedding'.[1] De Gaulle himself arrived on the following day.

At five on the afternoon of May 29 Churchill and Brooke discussed future military operations with Eisenhower and Marshall.[2] According to the official record of the meeting, Eisenhower opened the discussion by giving an account of his plans for the capture of the Italian island of Pantelleria, halfway between Tunisia and Sicily. Code-named 'Hobgoblin', the assault was planned for June 11. Churchill told the meeting: 'the operation would provide a very useful experiment as to the extent to which coast defences could be neutralised by air attack. There was a school of thought in the United Kingdom which thought that air forces could knock out coast defences sufficiently to admit practically unopposed landings.'

Eisenhower then gave an account of his plans for 'Husky' itself, the invasion of Sicily, after which the discussion turned to what would happen after the capture of Sicily. If Sicily 'proved to be an easy proposition', Eisenhower told the meeting, 'we ought to go directly into Italy'. Eisenhower also spoke of the cross-Channel invasion of Europe, which he called, somewhat surprisingly, 'a drop in the bucket' and 'unnecessary'. It was Churchill who, in reply, 'emphasized', as the minutes recorded, 'that both the British people and the British Army were anxious to fight across the Channel'.

As the discussion continued, Eisenhower re-iterated that if Sicily 'were polished off easily', he would be willing 'to go straight to Italy'. If Sicily were to be conquered 'within a week', he would at once cross the Straits of Messina 'and establish a bridgehead'.[3]

'The meeting was of good value,' Brooke noted in his diary, 'and I think went a long way towards securing the action after Sicily that we look for.'[4] 'It looks as if complete agreement will be reached,' Churchill telegraphed to Roosevelt, 'when we resume the conference on Monday.'[5]

A second meeting was arranged for the afternoon of Monday May 31. Before it began Churchill circulated a note in which he stressed the advantages that would accrue to the Allies should Italy be made 'to quit the war'. If the battle went against the Germans in Russia, he said, and 'our action upon or in Italy is also successful', the Germans

[1] 'Pencil' No. 417, 29 May 1943: Cabinet papers, 120/86.

[2] Other British officers present included Cunningham, Alexander, Tedder and Ismay.

[3] 'Minutes of a Meeting held at General Eisenhower's Villa, Algiers, at 1700 hours, 29th May 1943', 'Most Secret', Chiefs of Staff paper No. 290 (O) of 1943, 5 June 1943: Cabinet papers, 99/22, folios 225–7.

[4] Brooke diary, 29 May 1943: Bryant, op. cit., volume 1, page 634.

[5] Prime Minister's Personal Telegram, T.723/3, Prime Minister to President, No. 298, 'Most Secret and Personal', 30 May 1943: Churchill papers, 20/112.

might be forced 'by events' to withdraw to the Alps and the Danube, 'as well as making further withdrawals on the Russian front, and possibly evacuating Norway'. All these results, he said, might be achieved in 1943 'by bold and vigorous use of the forces at our disposal'. No other action 'of the first magnitude', he added, 'is open to us this year in Europe'.[1]

At the meeting of May 31, Churchill later wrote, General Marshall 'was in no way hostile to these ideas', but he did not want a clean-cut decision to be taken until after the attack on Sicily had begun, and when it might be known whether the Germans intended to resist in south Italy, or to withdraw as far north as the River Po. The Allies should exercise 'great discretion' in choosing what to do after the conquest of Sicily.[2]

Churchill was not convinced by this argument. As the minutes of the meeting recorded, he told Marshall and Eisenhower that he 'very passionately wanted to see Italy out of the war and Rome in our possession'. To realize this result, he would be willing to send eight additional divisions. Additional anti-aircraft units, he said, 'could be secured from the United Kingdom', used for post-Sicily operations, 'and still be brought back for their rendezvous in May 1944': the cross-Channel invasion.

A further reason for 'knocking Italy out of the war', commented Eden, was that it would 'go a long way' to winning Turkey to the Allied side. The Turks would become 'much more friendly when our troops had reached the Balkan area'. But to this argument, Churchill reacted 'emphatically', as the minutes noted, telling the meeting that he was not advocating sending an army into the Balkans 'now or in the near future'. An actual army in the Balkans was not needed, Eden replied, to influence the Turks, but only the Turkish realization 'that we were able to constitute an actual and immediate threat to the Balkans'.[3]

After the meeting of May 31, Admiral Cunningham told Brooke that Churchill's 'latest idea' was to go on from Algiers to Moscow. That night, at a dinner given by Eisenhower, Eden drew Brooke aside 'to ask me', as Brooke noted, 'about the Moscow plan'. Brooke told Eden, 'I considered we should stop PM at all costs owing to the strain on his health.'[4] The Moscow visit was not mentioned again.

---

[1] 'Background Notes by the Prime Minister and Minister of Defence', 31 May 1943, Chiefs of Staff Committee paper No. 290 (O) of 1943, 5 June 1943: Cabinet papers, 99/22, folios 231–2.

[2] Winston S. Churchill, *The Second World War*, volume 4, London 1951, page 738.

[3] 'Revised Minutes of a Meeting held at General Eisenhower's Villa, Algiers, at 1700 hours, 31st May 1943', 'Most Secret', Chiefs of Staff Committee paper No. 290 (O) of 1943, 5 June 1943: Cabinet papers, 99/22, folios 228–30.

[4] Brooke diary, 31 May 1943: Bryant, *op. cit.*, volume 1, page 638.

On June 1 Churchill flew in his York to a military aerodrome, where he attended a briefing of an American airforce squadron about to set off to bomb the defences of Pantelleria Island, between Tunisia and Sicily. He then watched the bombers take off on their mission, before flying on in his York to Tunis. From the airfield at Tunis he was driven to Carthage, where a vast number of troops had been assembled in the Roman amphitheatre. 'It was a most wonderful setting,' Brooke noted, 'for the PM's address to the men. . . .' That evening, at dinner, Churchill told the assembled guests: 'Yes, I was speaking from where the cries of Christian virgins rent the air whilst roaring lions devoured them—and yet—I am no lion and certainly not a virgin.'[1]

On June 2 Churchill travelled through much of the Tunis battle area, examining a German tank, and once more addressing the troops. Flying back from Tunis to Algiers, he took the controls of the York for a while, 'and gave us', Brooke noted, 'somewhat of a swaying passage for a bit'.[2]

The third and final meeting of the Algiers conference took place on the afternoon of June 3. The first decision was to proceed with operation 'Soapsuds', the bombing of the Roumanian oilfields at Ploesti.[3] It was also agreed to consider bombing the marshalling yards in Rome. 'He would not only raise no objection to the bombing,' Churchill told the meeting, 'but he would even suggest that it should be done.' Rome, Eden pointed out, like Naples, was on the supply lines to Sicily. The bombing of the yards, added Marshall, 'should be executed by a very large force of aircraft'.

Montgomery, who had arrived in Algiers on the previous evening, then spoke of the plans for the invasion of Sicily. 'His officers,' he said, 'were completely happy about the whole thing.' As to post-Sicily, Churchill now told the meeting that he did not think they should attempt to draw up a 'formal' plan. It was 'understood', he said, that the post-Sicily plan 'would be in General Eisenhower's hands', and that Eisenhower would recommend to the Combined Chiefs of Staff 'whichever operation seemed best'. However, 'he felt everyone agreed that it would be best to put Italy out of the war as soon as possible'. The capture of Rome, 'with or without the disappearance of Italy

---

[1] Brooke diary, 1 June 1943: Bryant, *op. cit.*, page 639.

[2] Brooke diary, 2 June 1943: Bryant, *op. cit.*, page 639.

[3] Three weeks later, Churchill telegraphed to Roosevelt: 'On reflection, I thought "Soapsuds" was inappropriate for an operation in which so many brave Americans would risk or lose their lives. I do not think it is good for morale to affix disparaging labels to daring feats of arms. I am very glad that the United States Chiefs of the Staff have agreed with ours to substitute "Tidal Wave" for "Soapsuds". I wish all our problems were as simply settled.' (Prime Minister's Personal Telegram, T.895/3, Prime Minister to President, No. 330, 'Personal and Most Secret', 26 June 1943: Churchill papers, 20/113.)

from the war', would be a 'very great achievement' for the Allied forces in the Mediterranean. But, he reiterated, one could only tell about the possibilities of the Italian project after the invasion of Sicily, when Eisenhower would report to the Combined Chiefs of Staff. If any differences were to arise as to post-Sicily, 'they would be settled between the two Governments'.

Churchill ended by expressing his 'full confidence' in Eisenhower, and his admiration of the manner in which the General had handled 'his many great problems'.[1] 'We have had long, most agreeable and fruitful discussions,' Churchill telegraphed to Roosevelt a few hours later, 'and I am *not* aware of the slightest difference existing between the British and American outlooks.'[2]

Behind these confident words lay the realization that General Marshall, upon whom the post-Sicily decision depended, had still not fully committed himself to the Italian landing, and that for the moment, nothing was fixed for post-Sicily, except to wait and see, and to rely upon Eisenhower's recommendations. Churchill was certain, however, that Eisenhower would follow the British plan. 'There are many obstacles,' Churchill summed up the conference in a telegram to Smuts, 'but I feel now that all has been made to flow in the right direction.'[3]

One unexpected gain of the Algiers visit was the agreement reached in the city on June 3 between Giraud and de Gaulle. Both men agreed, after three days of discussion, to set up a French Committee of National Liberation, under their joint presidency. 'I have now heard from Macmillan,' Churchill telegraphed to Roosevelt, 'that the Bride and Bridegroom have at last physically embraced. I am entertaining the new Committee at luncheon today, but I will *not* attempt to mar the domestic bliss by any intrusions of my own.'[4] 'Best of luck,' Roosevelt replied, 'in getting rid of our mutual headache.'[5]

The reconciliation luncheon took place on June 4. 'At the end of lunch,' Brooke noted in his diary, 'PM made an excellent speech in French, followed by Giraud and de Gaulle. Anthony Eden then spoke and finally old Georges said a few words. Photos were taken and then they departed.'[6]

In a telegram to Roosevelt, summing up the de Gaulle-Giraud

---

[1] 'Minutes of a meeting held at General Eisenhower's Villa, Algiers, at 1700 hours, 3rd June, 1943', 'Most Secret', Chiefs of Staff paper, 290 (O) of 1943, 5 June 1943: Churchill papers, 4/298.

[2] Prime Minister's Personal Telegram, T.734/3, Prime Minister to President, No. 290, 'Personal and Most Secret', 5 June 1943: Churchill papers, 20/112.

[3] Prime Minister's Personal Telegram, T.744/3, 7 June 1943: Churchill papers, 4/394A.

[4] Prime Minister's Personal Telegram, T.734/3, Prime Minister to President, No. 299, 'Personal and Most Secret', 4 June 1943: Churchill papers, 20/112.

[5] 'Most Secret', 5 June 1943: Churchill papers, 20/112.

[6] Brooke diary, 4 June 1943: Bryant, *op. cit.*, volume 1, page 643.

reconciliation, Churchill pointed out that, within the Committee of National Liberation, if de Gaulle 'should prove violent or unreasonable', he would be in a minority of five to two, 'and possibly completely isolated'. The Committee was therefore 'a body with collective authority', with which, in Churchill's opinion, 'we can safely work'. The setting up of the Committee, Churchill added, 'brings to an end my official connection with de Gaulle as leader of the Fighting French which was set out in the letters exchanged with him in 1940'; Churchill now proposed 'in so far as is necessary, to transfer those relationships, financial or otherwise, to the Committee as a whole'. But throughout North Africa, the 'supreme and ultimate power', Churchill noted, rested with Eisenhower.

Churchill added, in his telegram to Roosevelt, that he would have liked to stay another week in Algiers, 'as the weather was delicious and the bathing was doing me no end of good'.[1] 'The Prime Minister and I,' Eden later recalled, 'enjoyed some bathing expeditions that were so agreeable that we more than once lamented our failure to take two days holiday.'[2] The time had come for Churchill to leave Algiers. He had been out of England for almost a month. That afternoon, June 4, he flew in the York, first to Gibraltar, and then, at 10.30 that same evening, to Britain. Because of the bad weather, the flight from Gibraltar had continued in the Liberator, instead of in the more comfortable Boeing Clipper flying boat to which they had intended to transfer. Another Clipper was flying from Lisbon to Plymouth that same day, along a similar flightpath. This unarmed plane was shot down, and all its passengers killed, among them the British actor, Leslie Howard. A month later in a Liberator taking off from Gibraltar, General Sikorski was killed, together with his daughter, and two British Members of Parliament, Victor Cazalet and Brigadier Whiteley.

The first information that Sikorski had been killed was brought to Churchill by the Head of the Central Department of the Foreign Office, Frank Roberts. 'I remember taking him the news,' Roberts later recalled. 'He wept.'[3]

---

[1] Prime Minister's Personal Telegram, T.740/3, Prime Minister to President, No. 300, 'Personal and Most Secret', 6 June 1943: Churchill papers, 20/112.

[2] Eden memoirs, The Reckoning, op. cit., page 389.

[3] Sir Frank Roberts, recollections: in conversation with the author, 16 February 1985. The canard that Churchill had any part in Sikorski's death is totally without foundation.

25

Stalin's Disappointment

CHURCHILL was back in London on the morning of June 5. 'We have been rather anxious about you,' his daughter Diana wrote on the following day, 'since they got Leslie Howard.' [1] At noon on June 5, Churchill presided over a meeting of the War Cabinet at 10 Downing Street, giving an account of his travels to Washington, Algiers and Tunis. General Marshall, he said, 'who had not previously been specially enthusiastic about operations in the Mediterranean, had been greatly influenced by what he had seen and heard in North Africa and it seemed likely that he would return to the United States a convinced supporter of the projected operations in this theatre'. [2]

That afternoon Churchill went to Chequers, where his wife, and his daughter Sarah, his brother Jack, Brendan Bracken and Lord Cherwell made up the small weekend gathering. [3] Among those on duty at Chequers that weekend was Churchill's secretary, Marian Holmes, who noted in her diary: 'After dinner, we all adjourned upstairs to the Long Gallery. A projectionist comes down every weekend. We were shown a film called "The Moon is Down" and some films, apparently not yet ready for public showing, of the PM's visit to Washington. During this the PM and Brendan Bracken kept up an amusing commentary. After the film, we returned to the office downstairs and the PM did a little dictation, packing me off to bed at 1 a.m.' [4]

During the weekend, Churchill prepared a statement that he was to make in the House of Commons on June 8. On the Sunday morning he dictated to Kathleen Hill, then to Marian Holmes, who noted in her diary:

The PM worked in the office after lunch. He said 'What is your name

[1] Letter of 6 June 1943: Churchill papers, 1/375.
[2] War Cabinet No. 81 of 1943, 5 June 1943: Cabinet papers, 65/34.
[3] 'Chequers List, Weekend 5–7 June 1943': Chequers papers.
[4] Marian Holmes diary, 5 June 1943: Marian Walker Spicer papers.

again?' 'Miss Holmes.' He obviously didn't hear me and turned to John Martin for enlightenment. Mr Martin said 'You know—Sherlock Holmes.' 'Ah,' said the PM, 'Miss Sherlock!' I hope the tag doesn't stick.[1]

After dinner, we all adjourned to the Long Gallery to see some excellent newsreels. This was followed by a sentimental Mickey Rooney film. The PM couldn't stand it and soon walked out and downstairs to the office, hotly pursued by Mr Martin and me.

The PM dictated the statement until 2 a.m. He was most kind. For instance, when I had to read various bits of the statement over to him he murmured 'Very clear' by way of encouragement. After he had gone to bed, I remained in the office to type out the statement and got to bed at 4.15 a.m.[2]

On Tuesday, June 8, Churchill made his statement in the House of Commons, surveying the whole war scene, and pointing out that democratic nations like Britain and the United States 'do not become exhausted by war. On the contrary, they get stronger as it goes on,' and he added:

It may well be that those guilty races who trumpeted the glories of war at the beginning will be extolling the virtues of peace before the end. It would certainly seem right, however, that those who fix, on their own terms, the moment for beginning wars should not be the same men who fix, on their own terms, the moment for ending them.

These observations, Churchill commented, were of a 'general character', but not without 'their particular application'.

During his speech on June 8 Churchill also set out his impressions of the 'intimacy and strength' of the ties 'now uniting the British and United States Governments and the British and American peoples', telling the House of Commons:

All sorts of divergences, all sorts of differences of outlook and all sorts of awkward little jars necessarily occur as we roll ponderously forward together along the rough and broken road of war. But none of these makes the slightest difference to our ever-growing concert and unity, there are none of them that cannot be settled face to face by heart-to-heart talks and patient argument.

My own relations with the illustrious President of the United States have become in these years of war those of personal friendship and regard, and nothing will ever happen to separate us in comradeship and partnership of thought and action while we remain responsible for the conduct of affairs.[3]

Harold Nicolson, listening to Churchill's speech, noted 'understate-

---

[1] The nickname did stick. When Commander Thompson came into Churchill's room on 31 July 1943, Churchill said to him: 'You can say anything in front of Miss Sherlock. Her withdrawal from the room is not required.'

[2] Marian Holmes diary, 6 June 1943: Marian Walker Spicer papers.

[3] *Hansard*, 8 June 1943, columns 560–70.

ment of our victory, rather than jubilation', but 'in a way', he added, 'I think the House liked it better even than his most triumphant oratory. It was so eminently strong, powerful, sincere and confident.'[1]

In the smoking room after his speech, Churchill was 'in splendid form', Nicolson noted. 'He had been much amused by a story of an American chaplain who, when a German major complained of the lack of organization in the prisoners' cages, replied, "It is no good talking to me. I came out here to bury you guys."'[2]

In a telegram to Churchill, Eisenhower wrote of how happy 'all in North Africa' had been, not only to have had 'the benefit of your inspiring and dauntless courage amongst us', but to have been able to provide Churchill with 'some small respite from your many cares'. Eisenhower added: 'I hope that events may so turn that we can provide you with an even better tonic. Neptune was only shaking his trident, preparatory to plunging it into the soft under belly.'[3]

Reading the Enigma decrypts, Churchill learned of an Allied attempt to land on the island of Lampedusa, south of Sicily. He had previously been told nothing about this proposed operation. 'One would like to know about these things as they occur,' he telegraphed to Admiral Cunningham on June 9.[4] It was from his own son that Churchill learned, in a letter from Algiers, that Brigadier Stirling 'is back from Malta where he went to organize a small & abortive attack on Lampedusa'.[5] That day, as confirmation of the scale of the Allied victory in North Africa, it was announced that the total number of German and Italian prisoners exceeded a quarter of a million. Nor was the follow-up slow in coming. On June 11 Churchill telegraphed to Roosevelt with the text of a message just intercepted, sent from the Italian garrison on the island of Pantelleria, to Malta. The message read: 'Beg to surrender owing to lack of water.'[6] The capture of Pantelleria, operation 'Hobgoblin', cleared the way for the invasion of Sicily. 'Many congratulations,' Churchill telegraphed to Eisenhower. 'How does our centime account stand? I hope I have to pay you a lot.

---

[1] Nicolson diary, 8 June 1943: Nigel Nicolson, (editor), op. cit., page 299.

[2] Nicolson diary, 8 June 1943: Nigel Nicolson, (editor), op. cit., pages 299–300.

[3] 'Most Secret', Message 091928 B, 10 June 1943: Premier papers, 4/72/3, folio 893.

[4] Prime Minister's Personal Telegram, T.758/3, OZ 1616, 'Personal and Most Secret', 9 June 1943: Churchill papers, 20/112.

[5] Letter of 8 June 1943: Churchill papers, 1/375. The raid had been carried out from Malta by eight men in a motor torpedo boat. The aim was to try to capture the radar station. The alarm having been given immediately after the men had landed, they were driven off by machine gun and mortar fire. Two men were missing. Churchill learned these details from Cunningham on June 10. (Signal No. 092342 of 10 June 1943, 'Most Secret': Churchill papers, 20/112.)

[6] Prime Minister's Personal Telegram, T.782/3, Prime Minister to President, No. 307, 'Secret', 11 June 1943: Churchill papers, 20/112.

I am a buyer of the article at this price.' In humorous vein, Churchill added: 'Give my love to Joan of Arc.'[1]

The news of the capture of Pantelleria was one of the topics discussed when Eden went to see Churchill at 10 Downing Street on June 11. 'We thought it a good omen,' Eden noted in his diary.[2] There was however a big cloud on the horizon that day, Stalin's expected but fierce reaction to the further delay to the Second Front. In a telegram from Stalin to Roosevelt, Stalin protested that now, in May 1943, Roosevelt and Churchill had abandoned the decision to open a cross-Channel second front by September 1943, and that the Anglo-American invasion of western Europe had been postponed until the spring of 1944. 'In other words,' Stalin wrote, 'the opening of the second front in Western Europe which once was put off from 1942 to 1943, is now again being postponed until spring of 1944.'

Stalin's telegram, of which he sent a copy direct to Churchill, continued:

This decision creates quite exceptional difficulties for the Soviet Union, which has been waging war for already two years under the greatest strain against the main forces of Germany and her satellites. This decision leaves also the Soviet Army, which is fighting not only for its own country, but for its Allies as well, to combat nearly single-handed a still very strong and dangerous enemy.

Should I explain what a painful impression this new postponement of the second front will make on the people and the army of the Soviet Union? Should I explain what a disturbing effect will have the fact that our army, which made so heavy sacrifices, will again be left without serious support on the part of the Anglo-American forces?

The Anglo-American decision, Stalin added, was taken without the Soviet Union's participation, and without 'any attempt' to consider the question 'together'.[3]

This 'castigation we have both received from Uncle Joe', Churchill telegraphed to Roosevelt on June 12, 'was naturally to be expected', and he added: 'In my opinion the best answer will be to knock Italy out of the war and let him feel the relief which will come to him thereby.' As to Stalin's complaint about not participating in the decision, that, Churchill wrote, 'is the limit, in view of the efforts we have

---

[1] Prime Minister's Personal Telegram, T.486/3, No. 3287 to Algiers, 'Personal and Secret', 11 June 1943: Churchill papers, 20/112. Churchill had said, while in Algiers, that there were only 3,000 Italians on Pantelleria, and offered Eisenhower five centimes for every Italian captured above 3,000. The wager cost Churchill 65 francs (i.e. there were 9,500 Italians on the island, and captured).

[2] Eden diary, 11 June 1943: Eden memoirs, *op. cit.*, page 393.

[3] 'Personal and Secret', Kremlin, 11 June 1943: Churchill papers, 20/112.

made to bring about a tripartite conference'. This both Churchill and Roosevelt had indeed done, with first Khartoum in the Sudan, and then Scapa Flow, in the Orkneys, as possible meeting places. Churchill now proposed a further effort to meet Stalin, telling Roosevelt:

I will of course come anywhere you wish to a rendezvous, and I am practising every day with my pistol to make head against the mosquitoes. Nevertheless I once again beg you to consider Scapa Flow, which is safe, secret and quite agreeable in July and August. If you could come there in a battleship I do not think it would be difficult for him to join us.

This, Churchill thought, was the moment to make such a suggestion to Stalin. 'If you have any better idea,' he told Roosevelt, 'pray share it with me. He ought I think at least to have an offer.' [1]

Replying direct to Stalin on June 13, Churchill set out the argument against a cross-Channel invasion in 1943:

It would be no help to Russia if we threw away a hundred thousand men in a disastrous cross-Channel attack such as would, in my opinion, certainly occur if we tried under present conditions and with forces too weak to exploit any success that might be gained at very heavy cost. In my view and that of all my expert military advisers, we should, even if we got ashore, be driven into the sea, as the Germans have forces already in France superior to any we could put there this year, and can reinforce far more quickly across the main lateral railways of Europe than we could do over the beaches or through any of the destroyed Channel ports we might seize. I cannot see how a great British defeat and slaughter would aid the Soviet Armies. It might however cause the utmost ill-feeling here if it were thought it had been incurred against the advice of our military experts and under pressure from you.

'You will remember,' Churchill added, 'that I have always made it clear in my telegrams to you that I would never authorize any cross-Channel attack which I believed would lead only to useless massacre.'

The best way for Britain and America to help Russia, Churchill continued, 'is by winning battles and not by losing them'. If Italy could be knocked out of the war by the end of 1943, 'as is my earnest and sober hope', far more Germans would be drawn off the Russian front 'than by any other means'. Moreover, he explained, reiterating the reasons and arguments of the past weeks:

The great attack which is now not far off will absorb the capacities of every port under our control in the Mediterranean, from Gibraltar to Port Said inclusive. If Italy should be forced out of the war, the Germans will have to occupy the Riviera front, make a new front either on the Alps or the Po, and above all provide for the replacement of the numerous Italian divi-

[1] Prime Minister's Personal Telegram, T.795/3, Prime Minister to President, No. 309, 'Most Secret and Personal', 12 June 1943: Churchill papers, 20/112.

sions now in the Balkans.[1] The moment for inviting Turkish participation in the war, active or passive, will then arrive. The bombing of the Roumanian oil-fields can be carried through on a decisive scale.

'Already,' Churchill reminded Stalin, 'we are holding in the west or south of Europe the larger part of the German Air Force, and our superiority will increase continually. We are also ruining a large part of the cities and munition centres of Germany.'

Churchill went on to express to Stalin his 'firm belief' that Britain and America would confront Russia, before the end of the year, 'with results which will give you substantial relief and satisfaction'. As to Stalin's complaint that he had not been consulted by Churchill and Roosevelt in their recent decisions, Churchill told Stalin:

I fully understand the reasons which prevented you from meeting the President and me at Khartoum, whither we would have gone in January, and I am sure you were right not to relinquish even for a week the direction of your immense and victorious campaign. Nevertheless the need and advantages of a meeting are very great. I can only say that I will go at any risk to any place that you and the President may agree upon. I personally believe that Scapa Flow, our main Naval harbour in the North of Scotland, would be the most convenient, the safest and, if desired, the most secret.

If Stalin could come by air to Scapa Flow 'at any time in the summer', he could be sure that every arrangement would be made to suit his wishes, and he would have 'a most hearty welcome from your British and American comrades'.[2]

This telegram to Stalin, Churchill informed the British Ambassador in Moscow, was 'a soft answer', and he went on to tell the Ambassador that 'no apology is called for from us'. The Anglo-American strategy and offensive in the Mediterranean was probably the cause which was delaying the German offensive against Russia, 'and if so, is of enormous service to them'. Churchill's telegram continued:

You should adopt a robust attitude to any further complaints. They themselves destroyed the second front in 1939 and 1940 and stood by watching with complete indifference what looked like our total obliteration as a nation. We have made no reproaches, and we did our best to help them when they were in turn attacked. Nothing will induce me in any circumstances to allow what at this stage I am advised and convinced would be a useless massacre of British troops on the Channel beaches in order to remove Soviet suspicions. I

[1] At that moment, no one thought that the Germans could be lured into fighting in southern Italy.
[2] Prime Minister's Personal Telegram, T.803/3, draft, Prime Minister to President No. 310, 'Most Secret and Personal', 13 June 1943. The telegram as finally sent seven days later, with Roosevelt's approval, was Prime Minister's Personal Telegram, T.852/3, No. 741 to Moscow, 'Personal and Most Secret', 20 June 1943: Churchill papers, 20/113.

am getting rather tired of these repeated scoldings, considering that they have never been actuated by anything but cold-blooded self-interest and total disdain of our lives and fortunes.

'At the proper time,' Churchill added, 'you might give Stalin a friendly hint of the danger of offending the two Western powers whose war-making strength is growing with every month that passes and who may play a helpful part in the Russian future. Even my own long-suffering patience is not inexhaustible.' [1]

On Monday June 14 Churchill and his wife left Chequers, not for London, but for Chartwell, where they had decided to spend the day. No Private Secretary accompanied them, only Marian Holmes to take dictation. In her diary she recalled the day's events:

. . . it has been an experience coping alone with the PM and Mrs C. and surrounded by boxes of papers. The first thing he asked when the car drew up was 'Is my secretary here?' It was a cold lunch during which the PM discussed the sex of the little white kitten. Sent some despatch boxes up to No. 10 with the Despatch Rider. PM and Mrs C went out to visit his goldfish. After tea, I drove back to town with the PM. He dictated most of the way and it was a balancing act, as we were driven at great speed, trying to keep despatch boxes from falling on the flowers, finding the right papers and taking dictation on them all at the same time. Back at No. 10, sorted the papers, transcribed the shorthand notes, and got to bed at 2 a.m. [2]

On June 11, British bombers had dropped more than 2,000 tons of bombs on Düsseldorf and Munster. On June 12, the tiny Italian island of Lampedusa, halfway between Tunisia and Malta, surrendered to the Allies, and so, on June 13, did its north-eastern neighbour, Linosa island. Churchill studied the reports of these captures, and sought to

[1] Prime Minister's Personal Telegram, T.851/3, 'Most Secret and Personal', 16 June 1943: Churchill papers, 20/113. When, ten months later, Churchill learned that the Moscow newspapers had published a Tass message from London to the effect that Franco Spain had been a German supply base since 1939, Churchill commented, in a telegram to Sir Archibald Clark Kerr: 'All the same it was a very good thing that Franco did not let the Germans through to attack Gibraltar and get across into North Africa. This has to be considered too and you might remind our friends, as opportunity serves, that at that time we were absolutely alone in the world [and the Soviet were feeding Germany with essential war munitions.] So don't let's all be too spiteful about the past.' In sending this telegram, Churchill deleted the words in square brackets (Prime Minister's Personal Telegram, T.921/4, 'Personal and Secret', 23 April 1944: Premier papers, 3/405/8, folio 159).

[2] Marian Holmes diary, 14 June 1943: Marian Walker Spicer papers.

apply such lessons as were possible to the cross-Channel landing, now less than a year away. In connection with the cross-Channel landing, he minuted to the Chiefs of Staff Committee on June 14, it was 'very important that the softening effects produced on the garrison of Pantelleria by the prolonged preparatory bombings should be carefully appreciated and collated': bearing in mind the closure of the German-held Channel ports, 'it is essential that full consideration should be given to this newly emerging and important factor'. Commenting on the critical attitude of 'Bomber' Harris towards the bombardment of forts, Churchill wrote: 'The opinion of C.-in-C. Bomber Command is influenced by the fact that he wishes everything concentrated on the bombing of Germany, and he would consider the opening of large-scale military operations in Europe a disaster. This may be natural from his point of view, but we must not allow such localised opinions to obstruct our thoughts.'[1]

It was in connection with Britain's bomber raids over Germany that, on June 22, a Staff Conference discussed the dropping of tin foil strips to simulate a bombing raid on the German radar screens, and thus create confusion and cover for a real raid elsewhere. This scheme, known as 'Window', had been mooted by Professor Lindemann in 1937, and put forward by Churchill at that time to the Government's Air Defence Research Committee, on which Churchill served. In 1942, with Churchill's backing, Lindemann authorized experiments which made it clear that 'Window' would not only be effective but, as Portal told the Staff Conference on June 23, 'would save one third of our bomber casualties'. This estimate was supported by the Assistant Director of Intelligence at the Air Ministry, Dr R. V. Jones. In answer to Churchill's question as to whether the Germans might themselves use 'Window' in conjunction with renewed heavy air raids on Britain, Portal felt that given the 'small scale' of German offensive now possible, the balance of advantage lay with Britain. It was therefore agreed to begin 'full scale use' of 'Window' within the month.[2] Churchill sought, however, one final delay in the decision. 'Although every preparation should be made to open the window,' he minuted to Portal on the following day, 'I should like to be consulted again in a few days before the step is taken.'[3] A week later, Churchill was still hesitant to commit himself. 'This is one of those cases,' he minuted to Portal, 'which ought

[1] Prime Minister's Personal Minute, D.97/3, 14 June 1943: Churchill papers, 4/397A.

[2] 'Staff Conference held on 22nd June, 1943', Chiefs of Staff paper No. 325 (O) of 1943, 'Most Secret', 22 June 1943: Churchill papers, 4/2, and Secretary's Standard File, 'Most Secret', 23 June 1943: Cabinet papers, 79/88.

[3] Prime Minister's Personal Minute, M.413/3, 'Most Secret', 24 June 1943: Churchill papers, 4/397A.

to be proved three-ply before the plunge is taken. You must excuse my being cautious, but I feel it my duty to be completely convinced.'[1]

Churchill was finally convinced, on July 17, when the Chiefs of Staff reiterated that 'the time had now come to launch the operation', both because of the moral effect of decreased casualities, and because 'we should be able to drop about one-third more bombs on Germany in a given period'.[2] 'Window' was first used a week later, during a bombing raid on Hamburg on July 24, when it was immediately successful. British bomber losses dropped almost to half. It was quite a short-lived success, however, as the German night fighters and radar defences developed effective counter-measures, with the result that British bomber losses were again to grow, and, within eight months, to exceed those of the pre-'Window' era.[3]

Another decision which was reached at the Staff Conference of June 23 was to despatch additional military supplies to the partisans in Yugoslavia. Enigma decrypts had made it clear that as many as thirty-three German, Italian, Croat and Bulgarian Divisions were being held down in Yugoslavia, most of them by Tito's partisans. Churchill there-fore directed that a number of additional aircraft be used in the dropping of supplies: 'this demand', Churchill had explained to Ismay on the previous day, 'has priority even over the bombing of Ger-many'.[4] The air resources needed to send up to five hundred tons a month of arms and equipment to the Yugoslav partisans would be 'a small price to pay', Churchill told the Staff Conference, 'for the diversion of Axis forces caused by resistance in Yugoslavia'. Every effort should be made, he said, 'to increase the rate of delivering supplies. It was essential to keep this movement going.'[5]

Even as the Staff Conference was authorizing this diversion of Brit-ish effort in order to draw off German forces from the eastern front, Stalin was replying to Churchill's 'soft' answer with strong accusations of Allied perfidy. 'It goes without saying,' Stalin wrote, 'that the Soviet Government cannot put up with such disregard of the most vital

[1] Prime Minister's Personal Minute, M.432/3, 2 July 1943: Churchill papers, 20/104.
[2] Chiefs of Staff Committee No. 160 of 1943, 'Secretary's Standard File', 'Most Secret', 15 July 1943: Cabinet papers, 79/88.
[3] On the first series of 'Window' raids, called by the Royal Air Force 'the Battle of Hamburg', 20,000 German civilians were killed. 'Window', however, was only one of the special features of this new style attack.
[4] Minute of 22 July 1943, circulated in Chiefs of Staff Paper No. 336 (O) of 1943, 23 June 1943: Cabinet papers, 80/71.
[5] Staff Conference of 23 July 1943, Chiefs of Staff Committee No. 135 (Operations) of 1943, 23 June 1943: Cabinet papers, 79/62. The Ministers present were Churchill (in the Chair), Lord Selborne and Lord Cherwell. Cadogan was present representing Eden. Also present for the Yugoslav discussion were Major Morton and Lord Glenconner.

Soviet interests in the war against the common enemy.' A cross-Channel invasion would 'save millions of lives in the occupied regions of Western Europe and Russia', and would reduce the 'colossal sacrifices' of the Soviet armies, in comparison with which, Stalin reflected, 'the losses of the Anglo-American troops could be considered as modest'.[1] Stalin's telegram was resented by those who saw it: 'another ugly message', was Oliver Harvey's comment, and he added: 'It has a nasty taste.'[2]

Stalin made no mention in his reply of the proposed meeting with Churchill and Roosevelt. But that same evening, Churchill learned from Averell Harriman that Roosevelt had suggested, rather than a Tripartite meeting, that he and Stalin should meet alone, in Alaska. Churchill replied in anguish on the following morning: 'You must excuse me expressing myself with all the frankness that our friendship and the gravity of the issue warrant. I do not underrate the use that enemy propaganda would make of a meeting between the heads of Soviet Russia and the United States at this juncture with the British Commonwealth and Empire excluded. It would be serious and vexatious, and many would be bewildered and alarmed thereby.'

Churchill still believed that he, Roosevelt and Stalin should meet together. He told the President that such a Tripartite meeting, at Scapa Flow 'or anywhere else on the globe that can be agreed', not only of the three leaders but of their Staffs, coming together for the first time, 'would be one of the milestones of history'. Churchill added: 'If this is lost, much is lost.' Nevertheless, he ended, 'whatever you decide I shall sustain to the best of my ability here.'[3]

Churchill was caught between Stalin's rebukes and Roosevelt's whims, combatting each in turn. On June 26 he answered Stalin's further complaint about the cross-Channel landing. This time he abandoned the 'soft' approach of six days earlier, reminding Stalin that:

Although until 22nd June, 1941, we British were left alone to face the worst that Nazi Germany could do to us, I instantly began to aid Soviet Russia to the best of our limited means from the moment that she was herself attacked by Hitler. I am satisfied that I have done everything in human power to help you. Therefore the reproaches which you now cast upon your Western Allies leave me unmoved. Nor, apart from the damage to our military interests, should I have any difficulty in presenting my case to the British Parliament and nation.

[1] 'Personal and Most Secret', 24 June 1943: Churchill papers, 20/113.
[2] Harvey diary, 26 June 1943: John Harvey (editor), op. cit., page 269.
[3] Prime Minister's Personal Telegram, T.885/3, Prime Minister to President, No. 328, 'Personal and Most Secret', 25 June 1943: Premier papers, 3/366/1, folios 57–8.

Churchill went on to stress that 'powerful Nazi forces' had been drawn into the campaign in North Africa, and that the German uncertainty 'as to where the blow will fall and what its weight will be' had already, 'in the opinion of my expert advisers', led to the delaying of Hitler's third attack on Russia, 'for which it seems great preparations were in existence six weeks ago'. Churchill's telegram ended:

It may even prove that you will not be heavily attacked this summer. If that were so, it would vindicate decisively what you once called the 'military correctness' of our Mediterranean strategy. However, in these matters we must await the unfolding of events.

Thus not only on the one hand have the difficulties of the cross-Channel attack continually seemed greater to us and the resources available have not been forthcoming, but a more hopeful and fruitful strategic policy has opened to us in another theatre, and we have the right and duty to act in accordance with our convictions, informing you at every stage of the changes in our views imposed by the vast movement of the war.[1]

In a telegram to Sir Archibald Clark Kerr, the British Ambassador in Moscow, Churchill wondered what the Ambassador could gather of the reactions 'to my patient reply to Stalin's offensive message'. Churchill added: 'Personally I feel that this is probably the end of the Churchill-Stalin correspondence from which I fondly hoped some kind of personal contact might be created between our countries.' There was 'certainly no use', Churchill believed, in making the correspondence 'a vehicle of recrimination'.[2]

The bombing of Germany continued to mount in intensity. In June, as part of the 'Battle of the Ruhr', the Royal Air Force made seven major attacks on the cities of the Ruhr, dropping 15,000 tons of bombs in twenty nights. On Sunday June 27, at Chequers, Richard Casey was among Churchill's guests. 'Tonight at Chequers,' he noted in his diary, 'in the course of a film showing the bombing of German towns from the air (made up from films taken during actual bombing raids) very well and dramatically done, WSC suddenly sat bolt upright and said to me, "Are we beasts? Are we taking this too far?"' It was, Casey added, a 'momentary reaction from the very graphic presentation. I said that we hadn't started it, and that it was them or us.'[3]

[1] Prime Minister's Personal Telegram, T.894/3, 'Personal and Most Secret', 26 June 1943: Churchill papers, 20/113.

[2] Prime Minister's Personal Telegram, T.903/3, 'Personal and Secret', 29 June 1943: Churchill papers, 20/114.

[3] Casey diary, 27 June 1943: Lord Casey, *Personal Experience 1939–1946*, London 1962, page 166.

26

'We all go the same way home'

ON the evening of 29 June 1943, Duncan Sandys presented Churchill, Eden, Brooke and Lord Cherwell with the photographic evidence that the Germans were well advanced with their new rocket weapon. 'Arrived at conclusion that a definite threat exists,' Brooke noted in his diary, 'and that we should bomb Peenemunde experimental station at earliest possible date.' [1] No hint of this new danger came into Churchill's speech on June 30, when he received the Freedom of the City of London at the Guildhall. But he did point out a danger that had only just passed, the German submarine campaign in the Atlantic, which had reached its climax in May, 'packs of fifteen or twenty U-boats' concentrating their efforts to disrupt the trans-Atlantic convoys. During May, more than thirty U-boats had been destroyed, 'many of them foundering with their crews into the dark depths of the sea'. As a result of the onslaught upon them, 'the U-boats have recoiled to lick their wounds and mourn their dead'. June had been the 'best month' for British merchant ships of any that had been known 'in the whole forty-six months of the war'. [2]

What Churchill could not say was that the collapse of the U-boat successes arose to a considerable extent out of a triumph of cryptography: the overcoming of difficulties which, in March, April and May, had led to sometimes disastrous delays in reading of the modified form of Enigma used by the U-boats in the Atlantic. [3] By a remarkable cryptographic success, this modified Enigma had, as Churchill knew, been broken in December 1943, and by the end of June the sinkings dropped below the danger level. [4] This had important repercussions in releasing warships and merchant ships for service in all theatres of war: including operation 'Priceless', as the post-Sicily move was now known,

[1] Brooke diary, 29 June 1943: Bryant, *op. cit.*, volume 1, page 651.
[2] Speech of 30 June 1943: Churchill papers, 9/194.
[3] Dir/C Archive, 2634 of 19 March 1943: Hinsley and others, *British Intelligence in the Second World War*, *op. cit.*, page 750.
[4] Sixty merchant ships had been sunk in March, thirty-four in April, thirty-one in May and eleven in June.

and operation 'Overlord', the new codename for the cross-Channel invasion of 1944.

Eisenhower and his Staff, in Algiers, were still worried about the dangers of too stiff an opposition on Sicily, fearing a fierce and prolonged struggle for control of the island. Puzzled by Eisenhower's renewed hesitations, set out now in a request for further study of the Sicily plans by the British and American Planning Staffs, Churchill minuted to the Chiefs of Staff Committee:

The Supreme Commander seems to be getting more than ever 'sicklied o'er with the pale cast of thought'. It is quite right for Planning Staffs to explore mentally all possible hypotheses, but happily human affairs are simpler than that.

We must first fight the battle which is in the hands of Alexander and Montgomery. Supposing that all goes well or that there is even a collapse, the next step will show itself quite clearly.

If, on the other hand, the Sicilian operation were to fail, 'no question of the next step arises', Churchill wrote, and he went on to ask: 'why is this poor man torturing himself in this unhappy manner?'

Noting that Eisenhower and his Staff seemed to want to go back to the Sardinia landing, operation 'Brimstone', instead of Sicily, Churchill added:

We cannot allow the Americans to prevent our powerful armies from having full employment. Eisenhower seems now to be wriggling away to 'Brimstone'. We must stiffen them all up and allow no weakness. I trust the Chiefs of Staff will once again prevent through the Combined Chiefs of Staff this weak shuffling away from the issue by the American generals. They are simply wrapped up in their staff work.

The British 'must preserve to ourselves', Churchill insisted, 'the full power to judge and launch once we know what "Husky" tastes like'. He did not like the new American attitude, telling the Chiefs of Staff: 'Strong guidance must be given.'[1] Three days later, Brooke noted in his diary: 'USA looks at present like trying to close the Mediterranean theatre if they can after Sicily.'[2]

On July 3 the Allies began intense bombing raids on military airfields in Sicily, the prelude to invasion, the details being left, as Churchill explained to Macmillan, 'to Ike's discretion'. This was at Roosevelt's request.[3] 'You know my hope,' Churchill telegraphed to

---

[1] Prime Minister's Personal Minute, D.114/3, 'Most Secret', 2 July 1943: Churchill papers, 20/104.
[2] Brooke diary, 5 July 1943: Bryant, *op. cit.*, volume 1, page 670.
[3] Prime Minister's Personal Telegram, T.972/3, No. 1210 to Algiers 'Personal and Most Secret', 7 July 1943: Churchill papers, 20/114.

Alexander that same day, the eve of the invasion of Sicily, 'that you will put your right paw on the mainland as soon as possible. Rome is the bull's-eye.' [1]

Throughout the first week of July, the Enigma decrypts had shown the pressure exerted on German military dispositions by the partisan fighting in both Yugoslavia and Greece. Britain was now very much involved in these activities, sending in by parachute both emissaries and supplies. This too seemed to augur well for the post-Sicily operations. 'I presume you have read the "Boniface" about the recent heavy fighting in Yugoslavia,' Churchill telegraphed to Alexander on July 7, 'and the widespread sabotage and guerrilla beginning in Greece.' Albania also, he added, 'should be a fertile field'. All this had grown up 'with no more aid from Britain than the dropping of a few bundles by parachute'. Churchill's reflection ended: 'If we can get hold of the mouth of the Adriatic so as to be able to run even a few ships into Dalmatian or Greek ports, the whole of the Western Balkans might flare up with far-reaching results. All this is however hunting in the next field.' [2] Four days later, however, seeking further details of the effect of the partisan activities, Churchill minuted to Brigadier Menzies: 'Let a 2,000–3,000 word digest be made of the "Boniface" about Yugoslavia, Albania and Greece during the last two months or thereabouts, showing the heavy fighting and great disorder going on in those regions and assembling also the intelligence about the number of Partisans, & c., and of Axis troops involved or contained.' This latter, Churchill added, 'should be in tabular form as an annex to the digest, with dates, & c. I wish to have an absolutely factual presentation of the whole scene and balances.' [3]

On July 5 the Germans finally launched their third offensive in three years on the Russian front. More than two hundred German divisions were now in action in the east. In the west, the Sicily landings were 'imminent', as Churchill telegraphed to Stalin on July 8, and he added: 'Much depends on the first impact. I will let you know how the battle goes as soon as I can see clearly.' Meanwhile, Churchill reported, 'we have sunk 50 U-boats for certain in 70 days'. [4]

[1] Prime Minister's Personal Telegram, T.971/3, 'Personal and Most Secret', 7 July 1943: Churchill papers, 20/114.

[2] Prime Minister's Personal Telegram, T.971/3, 'Personal and Most Secret', 7 July 1943: Churchill's paper, 20/114.

[3] Prime Minister's Personal Minute, D.122/3, 'Most Secret', 11 July 1943: Churchill papers, 20/104.

[4] Prime Minister's Personal Telegram, T.975/3, No. 843 to Moscow, 'Personal and Most Secret', 8 July 1943: Churchill papers, 20/114. On July 14 Churchill reported to Roosevelt that 7 U-boats had been sunk in 36 hours, 'the record killing of U-boats yet achieved in so short a

The worst phase of the Battle of the Atlantic was over. The new victories, whereby Britain's food and supply lifelines were made secure, came from a variety of causes. One was the reinforcement of the convoy escorts by special destroyer support groups. Another was the closing of the air cover gap, which had existed from south of Greenland to north of the Azores, by use of long-range, shore-based Liberator aircraft. Another was the improved tactics and weaponry, the weaponry including more effective depth charges and the 'Hedgehog' ahead-firing weapon. Centimetric radar, and improved ship-borne wireless direction finding equipment which could pick up direct the bearing of the U-boats, also contributed to the turn of the Atlantic tide of battle. So too did the now effectively and finally broken German naval Enigma, the decrypts of which revealed both the pattern of U-boat patrol lines, and the scale of U-boat losses.[1] Hence Churchill's confident, and accurate, assertion in his telegram to Stalin.

On the evening of Friday, July 9, Churchill drove to Chequers, to await the first news of the Sicily landings, timed for the early hours of the following morning. 'I am thinking a great deal of our partnership and friendship,' Churchill telegraphed to Roosevelt, on July 9, 'now that our second great venture is launched.'[2]

Throughout July 10, reports of the battle reached Churchill at Chequers. 'This is our greatest venture so far,' he telegraphed to the Dominion Prime Ministers as soon as the attack began.[3] 'Both the British and United States armies seem to be getting ashore all right,' he telegraphed to Stalin a few hours later.[4] 'The PM was in bubbling form,' Marian Holmes noted in her diary.[5] That night, Syracuse, the first port to be attacked, was under Allied control. 'It is a tremendous feat,' Churchill telegraphed to Eisenhower two days later, 'to leap on shore with nearly 200,000 men.'[6]

---

time'. (Prime Minister's Personal Telegram, T.1031/3, Prime Minister to President, No. 363, 'Personal and Secret', 14 July 1943: Churchill papers, 20/115.)

[1] F. H. Hinsley and others, *British Intelligence in the Second World War*, volume 2, London 1981, pages 566–7.

[2] Prime Minister's Personal Telegram, T.995/3, Prime Minister to President, No. 355, 'Personal and Most Secret', 9 July 1943: Churchill papers, 20/114.

[3] Prime Minister's Personal Telegram, T.1003/3, 'Most Secret and Personal', 10 July 1943: Churchill papers, 20/115.

[4] Prime Minister's Personal Telegram, T.1004/3, 'Personal and Secret', 10 July 1943: Churchill papers, 20/115.

[5] Marian Holmes diary, 10 July 1943: Marian Walker Spicer papers.

[6] Prime Minister's Personal Telegram, T.1020/3, No. 3859 to Algiers, 'Personal and Secret', 10 July 1943: Churchill papers, 20/115.

The success of the Sicily landing immediately encouraged Churchill to press, as the next step, for the rapid invasion of Italy. As far as the preparations for the cross-Channel landing in the spring of 1944 were concerned, troops did not have to be transferred back to Britain until November or December. This gave Britain and America 'five months in hand', Churchill minuted to the Chiefs of Staff Committee on July 13, 'to use all our strength against Italy'. The Polish troops in Persia should be brought to Egypt for this task. These Poles wished to fight, he added, 'and once engaged will worry less about their own affairs, which are tragic'.[1] That same day, in a further minute to the Chiefs of Staff Committee, Churchill asked why it was necessary to land at the toe of Italy: 'why should we crawl up the leg like a harvest bug, from the ankle upwards?' he asked. 'Let us rather strike at the knee.'

Churchill's idea was to land 'as high up Italy' as the air bases on Sicily would allow. His minute continued:

Let the Planners immediately prepare the best scheme possible for landing on the Italian west coast with the objective the port of Naples and the march on Rome, thus cutting off and leaving behind all Axis forces in Western Sicily and all ditto in the toe, ball, heel and ankle. It would seem that two or three good divisions could take Naples and produce decisive results if not on the political attitude of Italy then upon the capital. Tell the Planners to throw their hat over the fence; they need not be afraid there will not be plenty of dead weight to clog it.

This work, Churchill added, 'is of the utmost urgency'. He wished to put his suggestion to Roosevelt and Eisenhower 'in the next few days'. His minute ended with a Shakespearian quotation, from *Julius Caesar*:

> There is a tide in the affairs of men
> Which taken at the flood leads on to fortune;
> Omitted, all the voyage of their life
> Is bound in shallows and in miseries.
> On such a full sea are we now afloat
> And we must take the current when it serves
> Or lose our ventures.[2]

From South Africa, a telegram from Smuts urged the capture of Rome as the next step: 'its possession', Smuts wrote, 'may mean the transformation of the whole war situation this year, and the chance of finishing it next year'.[3] The British and Americans had agreed in

[1] Prime Minister's Personal Minute, D.126/3, 'Action this Day', 13 July 1943: Churchill papers, 20/104.
[2] Prime Minister's Personal Minute, D.127/3, 'Action this day', 13 July 1943: Churchill papers, 20/104. The quotation is from Act IV, Scene 3.
[3] No. 930 from South Africa, 'Most Secret and Personal', 14 July 1943: Churchill papers, 20/115. Churchill sent copies of this telegram to Roosevelt, Marshall and Eisenhower.

May, Churchill told Smuts, to take the decision about an invasion of
Italy as soon as it was seen how the fighting in Sicily had gone, and
provided the Sicily campaign was not 'severe and prolonged'. The
moment was now approaching 'when this choice must be made'. How
it would be made, Churchill could not tell, but he was hopeful, telling
Smuts:

I believe the President is with me: Eisenhower in his heart is naturally for
it. I will in no circumstances allow the powerful British and British-controlled
armies in the Mediterranean to stand idle. I am bringing the very fine Polish
army from Persia into Syria, where it can also participate.

The situation in the Balkans is also most hopeful, and I am sending you a
report from the Middle East Headquarters showing the Italian forces on the
verge of collapse. Not only must we take Rome and march as far north as
possible in Italy, but our right hand must give succour to the Balkan Patriots.
In all this there is great hope provided action is taken worthy of the opportunity. I am confident of a good result, and I shall go all lengths to
procure the agreement of our Allies. If not, we have ample forces to act by
ourselves.[1]

Churchill's fears about American hesitations led him to persevere
in his suggestion for another meeting with Roosevelt. 'I must say, the
PM doesn't let the grass grow under his feet,' was Oliver Harvey's
comment. The meeting, to be held at Quebec, was, Harvey added, 'to
discuss the next stage of operations in view of the unexpected feebleness
of Axis resistance on Sicily'. Churchill, he added, 'is anxious to pin
the Americans down before their well-known dislike of European operations except cross-Channel gets the better of them again, and they
pull out their landing craft and send off their ships to the Pacific'.[2]

News of a closing of the gap between the British and American
positions reached Churchill on July 17: a message from the United
States Chiefs of Staff in Washington to Eisenhower, suggesting, after
Sicily, a direct amphibious landing operation against Naples. Reading
this message, Churchill at once telegraphed to General Marshall:
'Post—"Husky". I am with you heart and soul.'[3] General Marshall's
view, Churchill informed Smuts, 'is a great relief to me', and he added:
'We all go the same way home.'[4]

At a conference with his senior advisers on July 17, Eisenhower
decided, however, against the amphibious landing against Naples, for
lack of sufficient air cover for the naval force. But it was 'the consensus
of the meeting', he reported direct to Churchill on the following day,

[1] Prime Minister's Personal Telegram, T.1043/3, 16 July 1943: Churchill papers, 20/131.
[2] Harvey diary, 16 July 1943: Oliver Harvey (editor), op. cit., page 276.
[3] Prime Minister's Personal Telegram, T.1054/3, 17 July 1943: Churchill papers, 20/131.
[4] Prime Minister's Personal Telegram, T.1058/3, 18 July 1943: Churchill papers, 20/131.

'that if we once get firmly established in the toe we should use every possible expedient to drive rapidly toward the vital features of the region'.[1] Churchill still hoped however for at least a detailed examination of a scheme involving a more northerly landing. As he explained to the Chiefs of Staff Committee on July 18:

> ... it should be borne in mind the enormous advantage of using both hands in a boxing match. If the enemy are threatened in the south and crowd troops into the toe, ball and heel, all these troops can be cut off and left behind and made to surrender later. We ought to feint with our right and reach out far to the north with our left; but the blow should be with the left and to the north.

It was this combination, Churchill explained, on which a view should be expressed, 'although the final decision must rest with the people on the spot'.[2]

In the east, Hitler's third Russian offensive was being checked and turned back. On July 19 the War Cabinet were told of the 'very reassuring news' of a Russian counter-offensive at Orel, which 'had regained all the ground that had been lost in the recent German offensive north of Kursk'. Two further Russian offensives had also been launched.[3] That day, a second, heavier American bombing raid was launched against railway yards at Rome, with 700 planes dropping 800 tons of bombs. 'It is understood,' John Martin had already informed Churchill, 'that the Pope has a good shelter.'[4] In Sicily, further Allied advances made the post-Sicily decisions, as Churchill telegraphed to Roosevelt, 'all the more urgent'.[5]

Churchill was already aware that if the proposed Italian campaign were to prosper, its continuing success might become impossible if the seven divisions then in the Mediterranean, and needed for the cross-Channel invasion in May 1944, were to be withdrawn. Even with the transfer of these seven divisions, he wrote for the Chiefs of Staff Committee on July 19, it might be felt that the forces available in the United Kingdom 'will not be equal to the task of landing and maintaining themselves on land'. If so, Churchill wanted the northern Norway landing, operation 'Jupiter', to be considered instead of 'Overlord' for the spring of 1944. 'In my view it is a preferable alternative,' he wrote, 'and, in all probability, the only one which will be open in the west.'

[1] No. 142 from Algiers, 'Personal and Most Secret', 18 July 1943: Churchill papers, 20/115.

[2] Prime Minister's Personal Minute, D.132/3, 'Most Secret', 18 July 1943: Churchill papers, 20/104.

[3] War Cabinet No. 101 of 1943, 19 July 1943: Cabinet papers, 65/35.

[4] Minute of 16 July 1943: Premier papers, 3/14/3, folio 369.

[5] Prime Minister's Personal Telegram, T.1066/3, Prime Minister to President, No. 371, 'Personal and Most Secret', 19 July 1943: Churchill papers, 20/115.

Churchill then set out what he believed to be the 'right strategy' for 1944. This was in two parts. The first was the 'maximum' post-Sicily advance through Italy. This advance should be continued 'certainly' as far as the River Po, 'with an option to attack westwards in the south of France or north-eastwards towards Vienna'. At the same time, the Allies should seek 'to procure the expulsion of the enemy from the Balkans and Greece'. The second part of the strategy for 1944 was the northern Norway expedition, with 'Overlord' used as a cover. Churchill then explained why he felt that 'Jupiter' should replace 'Overlord':

I do not believe that 27 Anglo-American divisions are sufficient for 'Overlord' in view of the extraordinary fighting efficiency of the German Army, and the much larger forces they could so readily bring to bear against our troops even if the landings were successfully accomplished. It is right for many reasons to make every preparation with the utmost sincerity and vigour, but if later on it is realised by all concerned that the operation is beyond our strength in May and will have to be postponed till August 1944, then it is essential that we should have this other considerable operation up our sleeves.

'We cannot allow our Metropolitan forces,' Churchill added, 'to remain inert.'[1]

The Germans, commented Churchill at a Staff Conference held on the evening of July 19, 'must be finding the position most baffling, and would find it hard to dispose their limited resources against the threat of an amphibious attack on the long Italian coastline'. The 'temptation' to reinforce Sicily and the toe of Italy would be strong, 'and we must do our utmost to encourage him to move his divisions into this area'. After this, 'we could then contain him there with our right hand, and hit out at Naples with our left', with the object of cutting off the Germans in the south. If Naples were guarded, and the Germans were 'relatively weak' in the South, Britain should 'content' herself with 'a "pedestrian" advance northwards and increased support to the Balkans'. This decision, he saw, could be taken in two or three weeks, in the light of developments, German dispositions, and the recommendations of the Commander-in-Chief.

An advance on to the mainland of Italy, commented Brooke, would be the prelude to 'extensive land operations' there, which would inevitably affect the date of 'Overlord' and of operations in the Indian theatre.[2]

[1] Prime Minister's Personal Minute, D.134/3, 'Most Secret', 19 July 1943: Churchill papers, 20/104.
[2] Staff Conference, Chiefs of Staff Committee No. 165 (Operations) of 1943, 10.30 p.m., 19 July 1943: Cabinet papers, 79/62.

Following this Staff Conference, the Chiefs of Staff informed their American opposite numbers that any scheme for a landing on the Italian mainland 'must entail certain changes and retentions in the Mediterranean at the expense of operations in Burma and across the Channel'. This, Brooke noted in his diary, 'will not be greeted with great joy'.[1] Churchill, meanwhile, had also sought a means to advance his alternative to the possible postponed 'Overlord', the northern Norway expedition.

In his minute of July 19, Churchill urged the Chiefs of Staff to examine a scheme, for use in northern Norway, to turn icebergs into floating air bases, massive and unsinkable. These iceberg bases, including installations built out of frozen wood pulp, had been given the codename 'Habbakuk'. For the northern Norway expedition, Churchill wrote, ' "Habbakuk" would be an invaluable aid'.[2]

Churchill also believed that these floating ice stations could be used in the war against Japan, the future strategy of which he also wished to discuss with Roosevelt at Quebec. In his minute of July 19 Churchill set out his strategic thinking about the Japanese war, based on the assumption that 'Hitler and Mussolini are disposed of in 1944'. As Churchill envisaged:

Obviously we should probably carry the war through Burma, Java and Sumatra into the Malay Peninsula, while the United States undertook the mastery of various islands and the reconquest of the Philippines. We should probably also require to take Formosa in combination, and to establish landings and air power in China. If Russia comes in on our side, as is a 51–49 probability, the great air attack on Metropolitan Japan could be made from Russian and Chinese bases. How very convenient it would be to supplement or anticipate this by refuelling station provided by a number of 'Habbakuks' prepared in Alaska or the Aleutians and towed into position in these very cold waters.

There was also, in Churchill's mind, another reason why the Allies should come to a decision about Far Eastern strategy as soon as possible. As he explained to the Chiefs of Staff, it was 'vital' for the British armed forces 'to know beforehand that this task lies ahead', as well as the methods by which 'some would be chosen to go and others to return home'. Churchill added: 'If soldiers know their fate, they make up their minds to it. But if things are sprung on them suddenly

---

[1] Brooke diary, 20 July 1943: Bryant, *op. cit.*, volume 1, page 672.

[2] The code name 'Habbakuk' had been chosen by Churchill, from the Biblical text: 'Behold ye among the heathen, and regard, and wonder marvellously: for I will work a work in your days which ye will not believe, though it be told you.' The idea of a floating iceberg met with widespread scepticism, so much so that one scientist proposed using the term 'milli-habbakuk' as a new unit for measuring impracticability.

and an indefinite vista of separation from home opens out before them, the greatest difficulties will arise.'[1]

On the following day, in a letter to General MacArthur, Churchill wrote of how he 'looked forward to the days when, having cleared up our troubles here, we can come with all our needful forces and aid you in your great task'. It was his hope, Churchill added, to 'neutralize or destroy' the Italian fleet by the end of 1943, and, with the ships thus freed, 'to constitute a powerful Eastern British Fleet in the Indian Ocean and the Bay of Bengal'. There was also the Soviet perspective. 'I am of opinion on the whole,' Churchill added, 'that once Stalin has been relieved of the pressure of the German Army,—out of which he has cut a good part of the guts—he will most likely come into the War against Japan, whose hyena attitude he has thoroughly understood. This of course would open very large possibilities for the attack by air upon Japan itself.'

'All this,' Churchill noted, 'is rolling forward in the future.' He could assure MacArthur that he was 'under no delusions' about the Japanese: 'They are a terrible foe,' he wrote, 'and their military qualities extort admiration from the most reluctant minds.'[2] The war against Japan, Churchill asserted in a paper for the War Cabinet on July 21, might take 'several years' and would require 'a large proportion' of Britain's best troops. 'The heart-burnings which will arise about this will be fierce,' he added. 'However, if it is all laid down beforehand and made public beforehand, and if it conforms to the soldier's broad sense of justice, the difficulties will be mitigated.'[3]

[1] Prime Minister's Personal Minute, D.134/3, 'Most Secret', 19 July 1943: Churchill papers, 20/104.

[2] 'Private and Secret', 20 July 1943: Churchill papers, 20/94.

[3] 'Morale and the War against Japan' and 'The Two-Stage Ending and Demobilization', War Cabinet Paper No. 327 of 1943, 'Secret', 21 July 1943: Cabinet papers, 66/39.

27

From Sicily to Italy

_____

CHURCHILL was not looking forward to the conference at Quebec. If the Americans persisted in their reluctance to follow through the conquest of Sicily by a substantial campaign in Italy, and if Molotov, or some other senior Soviet figure, were present to support them, 'the PM feels', Oliver Harvey noted, 'he might well be overwhelmed'.[1]

On 21 July 1943 the Quebec meeting was given the codename 'Quadrant'. On the following day, from London, the Chiefs of Staff urged upon their American counterparts the Naples plan, now codenamed 'Avalanche'. But in Washington, where the plan was meeting with opposition, it was decided that, although it could go ahead if Eisenhower so wished it, he could not be sent any further troops to carry it out. The bulk of the forces to be employed would therefore have to be British. 'A very disappointing wire from American Chiefs of Staff,' Brooke noted in his diary in July 24. 'Marshall absolutely fails to realize the strategic treasures that lie at our feet in the Mediterranean and hankers after cross-Channel operations. He admits the one object must be to eliminate Italy and yet is always afraid of facing the consequences of doing so.'[2]

Churchill and Brooke were prepared to face those consequences. They were also increasingly aware of what the treasures might be, both in Italy, and across the Adriatic. 'I am sending you by an officer,' Churchill had telegraphed to Alexander on July 22, 'a full account which I have had prepared from "Boniface" and all other sources of the marvellous resistance put up by the so-called Partisan followers of Tito in Bosnia and the powerful cold-blooded manoeuvres of Mihailovic in Serbia. Besides this there are the resistances of the guerrillas in Albania and recently in Greece.' The Germans had not only been reinforcing the Balkan peninsula with divisions, Churchill noted, 'but

[1] Harvey diary, 20 July 1943; John Harvey (editor), _op. cit._, pages 277-8.
[2] Brooke diary, 24 July 1943: Bryant, _op. cit._, volume 1, page 673.

they have been continually improving the quality and mobility of these divisions and have been stiffening up the local Italians'.

Basing his figures upon Enigma, Churchill informed Alexander that there were in Yugoslavia 9 German, 17 Italian, 5 Bulgarian and 8 Croat divisions. On the Greek mainland, there were a further 6 German, 8 Italian and 2 Bulgarian divisions. 'The enemy,' he commented, 'cannot spare these forces, and if Italy collapses the Germans could not bear the weight themselves.'

'Great prizes,' Churchill told Alexander, 'lie in the Balkan direction.' Nevertheless, he continued, 'all being said and done, no objective can compete with the capture of Rome which in its turn gives, a stage later, all the advantages hoped for from a Balkan liberation'. Alexander should do his 'utmost' to solve the problem of continuing the war in Italy by whatever he felt were 'the best manoeuvres'. The fall of Italy, Churchill declared, the effect upon 'the other German satellites', and the 'subsequent utter loneliness of Germany', these, Churchill believed, 'may conceivably produce decisive results in Europe especially in view of the vast strength evinced by the Russian armies'.[1]

From Alexander came news, on the following morning, of further military successes in Sicily, and of resolute plans to exploit success. 'We are prepared to jump a bridgehead on to mainland at first opportunity,' Alexander wrote. 'You may rest assured that we consider "Husky" only a base for an extension of an advance into Italy.'[2]

The Americans, however, stood firmly behind the cross-Channel landing, and now even tried to accelerate it. On July 24 Henry Stimson, the Secretary for War, was in London, 'passionately advocating an early shock offensive across the Channel', as Oliver Harvey noted in his diary. 'On this, I'm thankful to say, the PM will refuse absolutely to budge,' Harvey added, and he went on: 'On military matters he is instinctively right as he is wrong on foreign affairs. As a war minister he is superb, driving our own Chiefs of Staff, guiding them like a coach and four, applying whip or brake as necessary, with the confidence and touch of genius.'[3]

Since his return from Washington, Churchill, anxious to keep his promise to Roosevelt to obtain facilities for allied aircraft on the Azores,

[1] Prime Minister's Personal Telegram, T.1083/3, 'Secret. For you alone', 22 July 1943: Churchill papers, 20/115.

[2] 'Special unnumbered message', 'Most Secret', sent 8 p.m., 22 July 1943: Churchill papers, 20/115.

[3] Harvey diary, 24 July 1943: John Harvey (editor), *op. cit.*, pages 278–9.

for use in the Battle of the Atlantic, had watched with perturbation the efforts by Portugal to spin out negotiations about the British occupation of the Azores. By the last week of July his patience was exhausted, and on July 24 he minuted to Eden: 'August 20 was fixed as the date when ultimate sanction could be applied. But then came this hope of parley, invoking the Alliance and so forth, and I certainly had the impression that the goods were going to be delivered in July.' Churchill's minute continued:

Now, after all this vast verbiage and haggling, Ambassador Campbell talks of September 1 as being a date rather too early to be insisted upon, and the Portuguese have ample argumentative munitions to spread the matter out into the winter weather.

The time has come to let them know that this nonsense must cease. Every form of ceremony and civility has been exhausted. We must have the facilities in these islands by August 15. They ought to be told this, and the expedition should be prepared in accordance with what was agreed at Washington and what the Staffs have worked out, and should sail so as to strike by August 20 or whatever is the earliest date now possible in consequence of the new forms of 'Post-Husky'.

'I do not think that time has been wasted in the discussions,' Churchill ended, 'but now we cannot go on waiting any longer, and we ought to tell them exactly what they are up against and that unless they agree to offer the facilities freely and without fail by August 15, we will take our own measures in our own time'. [1]

At the Chiefs of Staff Committee on July 26, with Brooke presiding, it was agreed to inform the Portuguese that the British convoy must arrive in the Azores 'not later than 15th September', and that if this date were refused, 'we should withdraw our Delegation, leaving the Portuguese completely in the dark as to what we intended to do next'. The 'Lifebelt' force had, in fact, been 'stood down' as a result of the continuing negotiations. The Chiefs of Staff advised that it should be 'remounted', in order to be able to reach the Azores 'before the weather became too bad'. [2]

In Burma, continual fighting had led to hardly any territorial success. A 'vast expenditure of force', Churchill minuted to the Chiefs of Staff on July 24, was required 'for these trumpery gains', and he

---

[1] Prime Minister's Personal Minute, M.514/3, 24 July 1943, Chiefs of Staff Committee No. 172 (Operations) of 1943, 26 July 1943, Annex II: Cabinet papers, 79/63.

[2] Chiefs of Staff Committee No. 172 (Operations) of 1943, 26 July 1943: Cabinet papers, 79/63.

was scathing in his comments on the commanders on the spot who, he wrote, 'seem to be competing with one another to magnify their demands and the obstacles they have to overcome'. Churchill proposed a new commander for the 'army against Burma', Brigadier Wingate, whose exploits in Palestine against the Arab revolt, and in Abyssinia against the Italians, he both knew and admired. Three months earlier General Nye, the Vice Chief of the Imperial General Staff, had informed Churchill of the 'extremely encouraging' operations being carried out by Wingate's Long Range Penetration Group, operations, Nye added, which demonstrated 'that British and Indian troops, when well-trained and confident, are really masters of the Japanese'.[1]

Of Wingate's qualities, Churchill wrote in his minute to the Chiefs of Staff on July 24:

He is a man of genius and audacity, and has rightly been discerned by all eyes as a figure quite above the ordinary level. The expression 'The Clive of Burma' has already gained currency. There is no doubt that in the welter of inefficiency and lassitude which has characterised our operations on the Indian front, this man, his force and his achievements stand out; and no mere question of seniority must obstruct the advance of real personalities to their proper stations in war.

Wingate, Churchill added, 'should come home for discussion here at an early date'.[2] Orders were given for Wingate to return by air.

At the end of July Churchill was troubled by a series of telegrams from the British Military Mission in Russia about the sentences meted out to British merchant seamen found guilty of drunken and disorderly conduct in northern Russia. These telegrams 'about the ill-treatment of our people in North Russia', Churchill wrote, had troubled him. 'The only way to deal with this kind of thing,' he minuted for the Chiefs of Staff Committee on July 25, 'is for ostentatious preparations to be made to withdraw the whole of our personnel without saying anything to them (the Russian authorities).' Churchill's minute continued: 'Let a plan be made for this. As soon as the local Russians see that we are off they will report to Moscow and will of course realise that the departure of our personnel means the end of the Arctic convoys. If anything brings them to their senses, this will. If not, any way we had better be out of it as it only causes friction.' Churchill added: 'Experience has taught me that it is not worth while arguing with Soviet people. One simply has to confront them with the new fact and await their reactions.'[3]

[1] Minute of 19 March 1943: Cabinet papers, 79/26, folios 191–2.
[2] Prime Minister's Personal Minute, D.140/3, 'Most Secret', 24 July 1943: Churchill papers, 20/104.
[3] Prime Minister's Personal Minute, D.141/3, 25 July 1943, circulated as Chiefs of Staff Paper No. 214 of 1943, 'Secret', 25 July 1943: Cabinet papers, 79/63. The original minute is in Cabinet papers, 120/683.

At a meeting of the Chiefs of Staff Committee on the following day it was pointed out, by Patrick Dean of the Foreign Office, that Britain was not in 'a strong position' as regards the sentenced merchant seamen 'since we could not legally claim that there was any alternative jurisdiction to which they were subject'. The Foreign Office would however make 'strong representation' as regards the severity of the sentences.[1] In a note to Churchill, the three Vice-Chiefs of Staff pointed out that the 24 Allied merchant vessels and 700 seamen then in North Russia could not be brought back to Britain 'until the dark period in November—and then only by means of a major operation'. They were, meanwhile, 'at the request of the Russians', running cargoes between Archangel and the Kola Inlet. At the same time, the success of Britain's own plans to destroy the German naval units in the Arctic region, depended 'upon the existence of adequate facilities in North Russia', and the retention of almost all the existing naval personnel.[2]

On the afternoon of July 25, at Chequers, on a seat in the orchard, Churchill discussed future Mediterranean strategy with Brooke. 'We are both in complete agreement,' Brooke noted, 'but fully realize the trouble we shall have with the Americans.'[3] 'I trust,' Churchill telegraphed to Roosevelt that day, 'we can keep all important options in this theatre open until we meet.'[4]

That evening, at Chequers, Churchill, his wife, his daughters Mary and Sarah, Brooke, and the duty Private Secretary, John Martin, watched a film, Sous les toits de Paris. Marian Holmes, who was also present, noted in her diary how, as they were watching the film:

. . . the telephone beside my chair in the Long Gallery rang. (The arrangement with our two telephonists at Chequers was that if there was an urgent call while we were watching an after-dinner film, they would give an almost imperceptible ring on the telephone as a signal to me to go downstairs to the office and take the message.) On this occasion it was the BBC Monitoring Service who asked me to inform the PM that Mussolini had resigned. I

---

[1] Chiefs of Staff Committee No. 118 of 1943, 26 July 1943: Cabinet papers, 79/27. On this occasion the Chiefs of Staff Committee consisted of the three Vice Chiefs of Staff (Lieutenant General A. E. Nye, Vice-Admiral Sir Neville Syfret and Air Marshal Sir Douglas Evill).

[2] 'Secret', 'Difficulties in North Russia' (signed E. N. Syfret and Air Marshal Sir Douglas Evill): Cabinet papers, 120/683.

[3] Brooke diary, 25 July 1943: Bryant, op. cit., volume 1, page 677.

[4] Prime Minister's Personal Telegram, T.1105/3, Prime Minister to President, No. 378, 'Personal and Most Secret', 25 July 1943: Churchill papers, 20/116.

rushed back upstairs to the Long Gallery and whispered the message to John Martin who informed the PM. The film was stopped, the lights went on, and the PM announced the good news. Everybody clapped. Back in the office, I took down the Proclamations over the scrambler telephone and read them to the PM and then to Mr Eden over the telephone.[1]

After Mussolini's resignation, King Victor Emmanuel assumed supreme command of the Italian armed forces, and Marshal Badoglio became Prime Minister. Churchill and Eden discussed over the telephone what should be done. 'He made it plain,' Eden noted in his diary, 'that he wanted to treat with King and Badoglio. I said I thought it likely this Government would not last.'[2]

Churchill and Roosevelt exchanged views by telegram of the possible peace proposals which might come from Italy. Roosevelt wished to insist on the use 'of all Italian territory and transportation against the Germans in the north and against the whole Balkan peninsula'.[3] Churchill added to this the surrender of the Italian fleet, the withdrawal of all Italian forces from southern France, Corsica, Yugoslavia, Albania and Greece, and the use of air bases in Italy 'on which we can base the whole forward air attack on South and Central Germany'.[4]

There was now a possibility, Churchill minuted to Brooke on July 26, that 'large distances' might have to be covered by British troops in Italy in the near future, 'especially if our front broadens out into the northern part of Italy and the valley of the Po'.[5] That same day, in Rome, Marshal Badoglio formed his Government, from which all the Fascist leaders were excluded. Then, as one of its first actions, the new Government dissolved the Fascist Party, and abolished the Fascist Grand Council. 'These are stirring times,' Cadogan noted in his diary. 'PM is keeping his head, but Washington are going off the rails with excited abuse of Badoglio and the King.'[6] 'Now Mussolini is gone,' Churchill telegraphed to Roosevelt, 'I should deal with any non-Fascist Italian Government which can deliver the goods.'[7]

Speaking in the House of Commons on July 27, Churchill said that the choice was in the hands of the Italians. If they wished, they could

---

[1] Marian Holmes diary, 25 July 1943: Marian Walker Spicer papers.

[2] Eden diary, 25 July 1943: Eden memoirs, *The Reckoning*, *op. cit.*, page 400.

[3] President to Prime Minister, No. 324, 'Personal and Most Secret', 26 July 1943: Churchill papers, 20/116.

[4] Prime Minister's Personal Telegram, T.1119/3, Prime Minister to President, No. 383, 'Personal and Secret', 26 July 1943: Churchill papers, 20/116. Also War Cabinet paper No. 339 of 1943: Churchill papers, 23/11.

[5] Prime Minister's Personal Minute, M.528/3, 26 July 1943: Churchill papers, 20/104.

[6] Cadogan diary, 26 July 1943: David Dilks (editor), *op. cit.*, page 546.

[7] Prime Minister's Personal Telegram, T.1119/3, Prime Minister to President No. 383, 'Personal and Secret', 26 July 1943: Churchill papers, 20/131.

have a negotiated peace and the revival of 'their former democratic and parliamentary institutions'. But if they chose 'that the Germans are to have their way' in Italy, as hitherto, then no choice was open to the Allies but to continue to make war upon Italy 'from every quarter'. North and south, from the sea and from the air, 'and by amphibious descents', the Allies would endeavour 'to bring the utmost rigour of war increasingly upon them'. Britain's 'prime and capital foe', Churchill stressed, 'is not Italy but Germany'.[1]

'I thought the PM's speech the most statesman-like of his utterances,' noted Henry Channon, usually a sharp critic, 'for he avoided cheap jibes or wit at the expense of the fallen Duce, and he deplored too much jubilation. It was restrained and subtle, and prepared the Commons for greater things to come.'[2]

When, or whether, negotiations for unconditional surrender were to begin, Churchill now looked for independent British action in one remote corner of Italy's empire, the island of Rhodes. 'We ought to get there quickly, if it is humanly possible,' he minuted to the Chiefs of Staff on July 27, 'as I need this place as part of the diplomatic approach to Turkey.'[3]

There was also action to be taken to increase the size and standing of Britain's military mission with Tito's partisans in Yugoslavia. On July 28 Churchill proposed sending a Conservative MP, Fitzroy Maclean. 'What we want,' Churchill explained to Eden, 'is a daring Ambassador-Leader with these hardy and hunted guerrillas.'[4] That same day he telegraphed to Alexander, who was about to launch an attack on the Sicilian city of Palermo: 'Important as this battle would have been in ordinary circumstances, its effect will be redoubled now. No one can tell what its consequences far beyond the battlefield may be. This is a decisive moment in the war, and your armies may strike a resounding blow.' Churchill added: 'I thank God you are there and that all is in your hands.'[5]

Armistice negotiations with Italy were discussed at the Defence Committee on July 28. As a result of the discussion, Churchill was authorized to telephone Roosevelt. The Germans, who were able to listen in to the trans-Atlantic telephone, recorded the brief discussion:

[1] *Hansard*, 27 July 1943, column 1397–1402.
[2] Channon diary, 27 July 1943: Robert Rhodes James (editor), *op. cit.*, page 373.
[3] Prime Minister's Personal Minute, D.144/3, 'Action this Day', 'Secret', 27 July 1943: Churchill papers, 20/104.
[4] Prime Minister's Personal Minute, M.530/3, 'Action this Day', 28 July 1943: Churchill papers, 20/104.
[5] Prime Minister's Personal Telegram, T.1141/3, 'Personal and Most Secret', 28 July 1943: Churchill papers, 20/116.

Churchill: We do not want proposals for an armistice to be made before we
           have been definitely approached.
Roosevelt: That is right.
Churchill: We can also wait quietly for one or two days.
Roosevelt: That is right.[1]

'I was so glad to hear your voice again,' Churchill telegraphed to
Roosevelt on the following day, 'and that you were in such good
spirits.'

Churchill's main concern as the discussions on an Italian armistice
went forward was for the future of the British prisoners-of-war in Italy.
He vividly remembered the transfer, to Britain's detriment, of released
German pilots from France to Germany after the fall of France in
1940, and was much afraid that the tens of thousands of British
prisoners-of-war in Italy might somehow likewise be taken by the
Germans. As he told Roosevelt in his telegram of July 29:

Discarding etiquette, I have sent a direct message to the King of Italy
through Switzerland emphasising our vehement and savage interest in this
matter. I am most grateful for your promise to put the screw on through the
Pope or any other convenient channel. If the King and Badoglio allow our
prisoners and key men to be carried off by the Huns without doing their
utmost to stop it, by which I mean using physical force, the feeling here
would be such that no negotiations with that Government would stand a
chance in public opinion.[2]

The War Cabinet was 'quite clear', Churchill explained, that 'we
ought not to broadcast armistice terms to the enemy'. It was for their
'responsible Government', he explained. 'to ask formally for an
armistice on the basis of our principle of unconditional surrender'.

The armistice terms were unequivocal, including immediate cessation of 'all hostile activity' by the Italian armed forces, and a pledge
by Italy to 'use her best endeavours to deny to the Germans facilities
that might be used against the United Nations', as well as the transfer
of the Italian Fleet and Italian aircraft 'to such points as may be
designated by the Allied Commander-in-Chief, with details of disarmament to be prescribed by him'.[3]

'We have not bombed Northern Italy for the last two days,'
Churchill telegraphed to Eisenhower on July 29, 'because we wanted
to give them a taste of relief, but unless they formally ask for an

[1] Percy Ernest Schramm (editor), *Kriegstagebuch des Oberkommandos der Wehrmacht*, Frankfurt-
on-Main 1965, volume 3, 1943, page 854.
[2] Prime Minister's Personal Telegram, T.1143/3, Prime Minister to President, No. 387,
'Personal and Most Secret', 29 July 1943: Churchill papers, 20/116.
[3] Prime Minister's Personal Telegram, T.1156/3, Prime Minister to President, No. 332,
'Personal and Secret', 30 July 1943: Churchill papers, 20/116.

Armistice in the immediate future, we intend to give them all manner of Hell.' Churchill also told Eisenhower of the 'great battle' which was about to begin in Eastern Sicily: 'The destruction of the three German divisions now facing the Fifteenth Army Group, happening at this time of all others, may well produce decisive effects in every quarter.' [1] From Spain, the British Naval Attaché, Captain Hillgarth, had written privately to Churchill on July 28, of the impact of the Italian situation on Spain: 'Sicily has impressed everyone and delighted most. Mussolini's resignation and what it presages has stunned opponents. The bombing of Rome went down almost as well as the bombs.' [2]

It was not clear who in Italy would offer, or be able, to make peace. 'I told the Press today,' Roosevelt telegraphed to Churchill on July 30, 'we have to treat with any person or persons who can best give us first disarmament and second assurances against chaos,' and that after an armistice Churchill and Roosevelt 'could say something about self-determination in Italy at the proper time'.[3] Churchill also gave instructions, to both the cinema newsreels and the BBC, that their reports on Italy, 'should not contain sneers at the King of Italy—Badoglio Government on the grounds of their Fascist antecedents'. They have 'completely abolished Fascism', he explained, 'and they want to make peace'.[4]

Throughout July 30 and 31, the question of the Italian armistice terms filled the telegrams between Churchill, Roosevelt and Eisenhower. 'Eisenhower keeps on making broadcast appeals to surrender,' noted Oliver Harvey, 'only more or less approximate to the official terms.' [5] But Churchill was less troubled than was the Foreign Office by Eisenhower's approach, and on July 31 he minuted to Eden:

Many things in life are settled by the two-stage method. For instance, a man is not prevented from saying, 'Will you marry me, darling?' because he has not got the marriage contract, drawn up by the family solicitors, in his pocket. Personally I think the terms which Eisenhower may now offer are much more likely to be understood by an envoy, and thus be capable of immediate acceptance, than the legal verbiage of the Instrument of Surrender, and they will look much better if published. If we get emergency

[1] Prime Minister's Personal Telegram, T. 1142/3, No. 4157 to Algiers, 'Personal and Secret', 29 July 1943: Churchill papers, 20/116.
[2] 'Secret and Personal', 28 July 1943: Premier papers, 4/21/2, folios, 231–2.
[3] President to Prime Minister, No. 334, 'Personal and Secret', 30 July 1943: Churchill papers, 20/116.
[4] Prime Minister's Personal Minute (to the Minister of Information), M.549/3, 1 August 1943: Churchill papers, 20/104.
[5] Harvey diary, 30 July 1943: John Harvey (editor), *op. cit.*, pages 281–2.

terms it means that the Italians will have given themselves up to us, lock, stock, and barrel. There would be nothing improper in our requiring them to hand over the pull-through and other cleaning materials afterwards.[1]

As to the nature of the Italian authority with which the Allies would be prepared to negotiate, here too Churchill held a moderate attitude, informing Roosevelt on July 31:

My position is that once Mussolini and the Fascists are gone I will deal with any Italian authority which can deliver the goods. I am not in the least afraid for this purpose of seeming to recognise the House of Savoy or Badoglio, provided they are the ones who can make the Italians do what we need for our war purposes. Those purposes would certainly be hindered by chaos, Bolshevisation, or civil war. We have no right to lay undue burdens on our troops. It may well be that after the armistice terms have been accepted both the King and Badoglio will sink under the odium of surrender and that the Crown Prince and a new Prime Minister may be chosen.

I should deprecate any pronouncement about self-determination at the present time, beyond what is implicit in the Atlantic Charter. I agree with you that we must be very careful not to throw everything into the melting-pot.[2]

Throughout the discussions on an Italian armistice, the Battle of the Atlantic had continued to go against the Germans. 'The July canaries to date number 35,' Churchill told Roosevelt with reference to the number of U-boats sunk that month, 'making a total of 85 in the 91 days since May 1', and he commented: 'Good hunting.'[3]

The Italian Government remained uncertain of how to react to any possible Allied offer of an armistice. 'Whether they will dare to provoke the Germans or not,' Churchill minuted on August 1, 'remains to be seen.'[4] Through the British Embassy in Switzerland came a request, originating from the Vatican, that in the continuing Allied bombardments over Italy, Rome should not be bombed again until the new Italian Government 'has had time to establish its authority'.[5] Churchill commented, in a minute to Eden:

I do not understand why, if we are to bomb the cities of Northern Italy, the populations of which are the most favourable to the Allies and the most violently anti-German, we should not continue to bomb military objectives

[1] Prime Minister's Personal Minute, M.544/3, 31 July 1943: Churchill papers, 20/104.

[2] Prime Minister's Personal Telegram, T.1163/3, Prime Minister to President, No. 394, 'Personal and Most Secret', 31 July 1943: Churchill papers, 20/116.

[3] Prime Minister's Personal Telegram, T.1161/3, Prime Minister to President, No. 392, 'Personal and Secret', 31 July 1943: Churchill papers, 20/116.

[4] Prime Minister's Personal Minute, M.549/3 (to the Minister of Information), 1 August 1943: Churchill papers, 20/104.

[5] Telegram No. 232 from the Holy See, No. 3675 from Berne to the Foreign Office: Churchill papers, 20/104.

on the outskirts of Rome. Many people think that bombing Rome was the final blow to Mussolini. I do not put it so high, but I cannot see any reason why, if Milan, Turin and Genoa are to be bombed, Rome should be specially exempted.

The bombing of Rome was to be authorized, Churchill pointed out, from Eisenhower's headquarters, and was to be carried out almost entirely by United States forces. 'Do you suggest we should interfere with this?' he asked Eden. 'They have no need to ask our renewed position.'[1] 'I have no objection to the bombing of Rome,' Eden replied, 'as previously agreed between us & Eisenhower.'[2]

On the afternoon of August 1, the offensive in Sicily was renewed. 'The Canadians have made a successful debut,' Alexander telegraphed to Churchill on August 2, 'and are fighting well.'[3] On August 3, as the advance in Sicily continued on all fronts, the Red Army began its second major offensive in the East, striking at the German salient around Kharkov. Three weeks later, Kharkov was in Russian hands. For the German army, the dream of conquering Russia turned into a nightmare, as the Red Army began to drive relentlessly westward.

As the Allies advanced across Sicily, discussions continued between Churchill and Roosevelt on the terms to be eventually offered to Italy. To suggestions that Rome might be declared an Open City, Churchill had intended to telegraph to Roosevelt on August 3: 'Surely there would be the utmost danger that any such bargain would encourage the Italians to make a try for a neutralization of Italy itself.' The 'best opinion' in Britain, he had added, was 'much disturbed by suspicion we are giving them a lull'.[4] This telegram was never sent. Without consulting Churchill, Roosevelt had already committed himself in principle to the Open City proposal. On learning this, Churchill telegraphed again, urging delay. He had considerable hopes, he ex-plained, that 'in a few months Rome will be in our hands, and we shall need to use its facilities for the northward advance'. If Rome had been declared an Open City, Churchill pointed out, 'it will be practically impossible for us to take away its status when we want to use it and its communications and airfields ourselves'. It was the view of the British Chiefs of Staff, Churchill added, that the creation of

[1] Prime Minister's Personal Minute, M.557/3, 1 August 1943: Premier papers, 3/14/3, folio 248.
[2] Foreign Secretary's Minute, PM 43/260, 2 August 1943: Premier papers, 3/14/3, folio 247.
[3] MA/346, 'Most Secret and Personal', 2 August 1943: Churchill papers, 20/116.
[4] Prime Minister's Personal Telegram, T.1181/3, Prime Minister to President No. 398, 'Personal and Most Secret', 3 August 1943: Premier papers, 3/14/3, folio 243.

Rome as an Open City 'would paralyse the whole further campaign'. A decision, Churchill hoped, could be held over, 'if you so desire it', until he and Roosevelt had met.[1]

That same day, Churchill prepared to leave London on the first stage of his journey to Quebec. 'I am off on another journey to confer with the President,' he telegraphed to Smuts before he left, 'but hope to be back early in September.' Churchill added: 'We are in heavy battle today in Sicily and I hope confidently for a good result.'[2] On the following day, Catania fell to the British forces, and two weeks later, all Sicily was under Allied control.

In making his plans to travel across the Atlantic to the Canadian port of Halifax, Churchill was concerned that there should be no interruption in the receipt of the Enigma decrypts and other Intelligence which he normally received from Brigadier Menzies. To ensure that this would continue to reach him, he had minuted to his Private Office three days before his departure:

It will be very necessary for me to be kept fully informed during these critical days. Particularly I must have good 'C' stuff. At any moment a larger crisis may arise, and risks may have to be run. Subject to this all possible economies should be practised and enforced.

Make sure that full pouches by air including 'C' stuff await me at H. There will be time for a long read up in the train.[3]

Nine hours before he was to leave London, Churchill presided over a meeting of the Pacific War Council, its first meeting in 1943. The Dutch and Chinese were the two other Pacific powers represented, the latter by the Chinese Foreign Minister, Dr T. V. Soong. Speaking of the war in Europe, Churchill said 'that we were in the process of striking at the under-belly of the Axis'. This process had so far produced 'the disappearance of Mussolini and he was hopeful that, in due course, the elimination of Italy would follow'. Mussolini and all his paraphernalia had disappeared overnight—like snow at Easter. It was not impossible that a similar spasm might convulse the present German regime'. This, however, could not be relied upon. 'We must press on,' Churchill declared, 'and continue to engage the enemy with unrelenting vigour wherever possible.'

[1] Prime Minister's Personal Telegram, T.1201/3, Prime Minister to President, No. 403, 'Personal and Most Secret', 4 August 1943: Churchill papers, 20/117.

[2] Prime Minister's Personal Telegram, T.1193/3, 'Most Secret and Personal', 'For your eye alone', 4 August 1943: Premier papers, 4/84/2A, folio 348.

[3] Minute initialled 'WSC', 1 August 1943: Cabinet papers, 120/93.

Turning to the Far East, Churchill stated that it was still British policy to open the Burma Road 'as soon as possible'. The lines of communication from India were, he said, 'the baffling difficulty'. Given the 'considerable land slides which had taken place', it would not be possible, in his view, to open the Burma Road for the next fifteen months, 'even if there were no enemy in Burma'. At the same time, with reference to the possibility of operations in Lower Burma, he preferred, he said, 'a stroke more adventurous and further flung'. But whatever strategy was decided upon, he had 'pledged his word that the entire forces of the British Commonwealth would, at the earliest possible moment, be hurled into the battle against Japan'.[1]

On the evening of August 4 Churchill had planned to dine alone with his wife and daughter Mary, both of whom were to accompany him to Quebec. Half an hour before dinner was to begin, he learned that Brigadier Wingate, whom he had first met in November 1938, had just arrived in London from Burma. Ten days earlier Churchill had asked for Wingate to come back by air; he was at the moment at Downing Street, still in what Ismay recalled as 'the somewhat disreputable thin khaki' in which he had just flown home.[2]

Churchill asked to see Wingate at once, to learn about the possibilities of a renewed offensive in Burma, of which the Commanders-in-Chief in India had repeatedly stressed the difficulties. 'We had not talked for half an hour,' Churchill later recalled, 'before I felt myself in the presence of a man of the highest quality. He plunged at once into his theme of how the Japanese could be mastered in jungle warfare by long-range penetration groups landed by air behind the enemy lines. This interested me greatly. I wish to hear much more about it, and also to let him tell his tale to the Chiefs of Staff.'[3]

Churchill asked Wingate to stay to dinner, when he entranced the three Churchills with his tales of jungle fighting. Eventually Churchill said to him: 'You must come with me tonight and tell all this to the President,' to which Wingate replied: 'I have no clothes. I have nothing but my tropical kit.' 'Oh, don't bother about that,' Churchill answered, 'I'll lend you some. I've plenty.'

Wingate replied: 'But, sir, I've not seen my wife for a long time,' to which Churchill answered: 'Of course, you must bring her too.'[4]

[1] Pacific War Council, 1st Meeting of 1943, 3 p.m., 4 August 1943: Cabinet papers, 99/26.
[2] The Memoirs of General the Lord Ismay, London 1960, page 305.
[3] Winston S. Churchill, The Second World War, volume 5, London 1951, page 62.
[4] Lord Moran, diary and notes, 4 August 1943: Moran, op. cit., pages 106–7.

Before reaching Downing Street, Wingate had known nothing of Churchill's imminent departure for Quebec. Unperturbed, he agreed to accompany him. Lorna Wingate, who had intended to travel to London on the following day to see her husband, was telegraphed by one of Churchill's Private Secretaries, and told to be on the platform at Waverley Station, Edinburgh, early the following morning: why, she could not be told.

Shortly before midnight, the Churchills left Downing Street for Addison Road station, in west London, to board their night train to Scotland. As they waited for the moment of departure, Churchill strode up and down the platform singing:

> 'I go away
> This very day
> To sail across the sea—
> Matilda!' [1]

---

[1] Gerald Pawle, *The War and Colonel Warden* (Based on the recollections of Commander C. R. Thompson), London 1963, page 243.

28
August 1943:
The Quebec Conference

FIFTEEN minutes after midnight, as 5 August 1943 opened, 'Colonel Warden', 'Mrs Warden', and 'Lieutenant M. Warden' were among the passengers leaving London by train for Scotland. Churchill and his wife and their daughter Mary were three of more than two hundred Britons setting off for the Quebec conference, codename 'Quadrant'. At 5.30 on the afternoon of August 5, this formidable team, including the three Chiefs of Staff, sailed in the *Queen Mary* from the Clyde.

Churchill and the Chiefs of Staff used the five-day voyage to discuss every aspect of the war plans for the year ahead: the twice-postponed and much-awaited cross-Channel invasion, 'Overlord', the Mediterranean, and the Far East. Among those who participated in these discussions were the Chief of Combined Operations, Lord Louis Mountbatten, and the Minister of War Shipping, Lord Leathers. It was Churchill's first opportunity, Ismay later recalled, to learn from his advisers the full details of the 'Overlord' plan, including the progress made towards creating an artificial harbour which was to be assembled in England, taken across the Channel, and then used to enable the Allied forces to get ashore, and to be supplied, across what had hitherto been open beaches. The plan was presented to Churchill by Brigadier K. G. McLean, who, with two other officers from General Morgan's Staff, had been working since the Casablanca Conference to devise a workable plan to land on the Normandy beaches: a location favoured by Mountbatten, and supported by Morgan.

McLean and the two other officers 'came to me', Churchill later recalled, 'as I lay in my bed in the spacious cabin, and, after they had set up a large-scale map, explained in a tense and cogent tale the plan which had been prepared for the cross-Channel descent upon France'.[1]

[1] Winston S. Churchill, *The Second World War*, volume 5, London 1952, page 67.

The cross-Channel landing plan which Brigadier McLean explained depended, as he told Churchill, upon the establishment on the Normandy coast of one, or two, artificial harbours, created by blockships which would cross the Channel under their own power, and then be sunk in pre-arranged positions, forming thereby a continuous breakwater within which supply ships could dock and unload. The plan of these artificial harbours had come two months earlier from Morgan's Naval Chief of Staff, Commodore J. Hughes-Hallett, Churchill himself having put the idea forward in May 1942.

All this Churchill examined and absorbed. Ismay later recalled:

If a stranger had visited his bathroom, he might have seen a stocky figure in a dressing-gown of many colours, sitting on a stool and surrounded by a number of what our American friends call 'Top Brass', while an Admiral flapped his hand in the water at one end of the bath in order to simulate a choppy sea, and a Brigadier stretched a lilo across the middle to show how it broke up the waves. The stranger would have found it hard to believe that this was the British High Command studying the most stupendous and spectacular amphibious operation in the history of war.[1]

Churchill had once more arranged for a Map Room to accompany him on his travels, and once again Captain Pim had been in charge of setting it up, adjoining Churchill's quarters on the main deck.[2] On the second day out, August 6, Pim later recalled:

I got up early to collect the news from various sources available for the Prime Minister and arrived in his cabin about twenty minutes past six, only to find that he had forestalled me by almost an hour. Putting back the clocks three hours as we did during the first day out resulted in his early awakening and in the absence of any newspapers there was a general search for news of any sort. Just after breakfast he again came into the Map Room in his multi-coloured dressing gown saying, 'Put your finger on Aderno and on Paterno'— both towns in Sicily which we had just heard had been captured from the enemy.

It was always a source of pleasure to the Prime Minister to mark in china-graph pencil in very considerable detail advances made by the various Divisions and Brigades, and if just a little bit of wishful thinking was included and the advance portrayed somewhat optimistically, at least no harm resulted.[3]

---

[1] Ismay memoirs, *op. cit.*, page 308.

[2] Pim was accompanied by three other members of the Map Room staff, Lieutenant-Commander D. W. Jones RNVR, Lieutenant F. de Vine Hunt, RNVR and Mrs E. Meyer. Pim and his staff, who saw Churchill every day when he was in London, were to travel with him to all subsequent conferences. Lieutenant-Commander Baird-Murray, one of the Map Room staff at the Annexe, later recalled: 'It was sometimes disconcerting when reporting to him at 8 a.m. as he lay in bed, as Nelson, his big black cat was usually jumping about on the bed playing with his toes moving about under the blanket, but nevertheless no detail however small escaped him.' (Letter to the author, 11 April 1978.)

[3] Pim recollections: Pim papers.

During August 6 the Chiefs of Staff discussed, as Brooke noted in his diary, 'how best to tackle the Mediterranean situation with the American Chiefs of Staff'.[1] 'If things go well with us in the Balkans,' Churchill minuted that same day, 'and the Russian advance continues on the main front, could we not, by the air, assist Russian landings in Roumania or a Russian attempt to regain the Crimea?' This would involve air bases in Turkey, and possibly 'partial control' of the Dardanelles, 'so as to enable us to prevent any traffic helpful to the enemy going through, and possibly get some British submarine flotillas with a few parent ships to work in the Black Sea?' This, Churchill added, would be 'an effective way of giving our right hand to Russia . . .'[2]

On August 6, in Tangier, an Italian diplomat, Signor Berio, approached the British Diplomatic Representative in the port, with authorisation from Marshal Badoglio to open negotiations with the British. 'We are entitled to regard it as an offer by the Badoglio Government to negotiate on terms,' Eden telegraphed to Churchill, and he went on to ask: 'should we not then reply that, as is well known, we insist on unconditional surrender, and the Badoglio Government must as a first step notify us that Italy surrenders unconditionally? Subsequently, at a later stage, if the Badoglio Government was to do this, we should then inform them of the terms on which we should be prepared to cease hostilities against Italy.'[3]

Churchill minuted on Eden's telegram: 'Don't miss the bus,' and he added: 'If they surrender immediately we should be prepared to accord conditions as acts of grace and not as a bargain.' Churchill then telegraphed to Eden from the *Queen Mary*: 'We agree with course you have taken. Badoglio admits he is going to double-cross someone, but his interests and the mood of the Italian people make it more likely Hitler will be the one to be tricked.' Allowance should be made, Churchill added, for the difficulties of his position. 'Meanwhile the war should be carried forward against Italy in every way that the Americans will allow. We do not have to ask their permission about bombing the towns of Northern Italy, and Harris should be limited only by weather.'[4]

To Eden, Churchill minuted that same day about his belief that Russian anxieties concerning the rearming of Italy were unfounded: 'Obviously however the Russians will not remain contented with the

[1] Brooke diary, 6 August 1943: Bryant, *op. cit.*, volume 1, page 693.
[2] Prime Minister's Personal Minute, D(Q) 1/3, 6 August 1943: Churchill papers, 20/104.
[3] 'Concrete' No. 20, 7 August 1943: Cabinet papers, 120/98.
[4] 'Welfare' No. 10, 8 August 1943: Cabinet papers, 120/94.

present state of the Straits, and I do not suppose they have forgotten that we offered them Constantinople in the earlier parts of the late war.' Turkey's 'greatest safety', Churchill re-iterated, 'lies in the active association with the United Nations. As you know, the time may come very soon when we shall ask her to admit our air squadrons and certain other forces to protect them in order to bomb Ploesti and gradually secure the control of the Straits and the Black Sea.'[1]

During August 7, Churchill urged the Chiefs of Staff Committee, before 'we meet the Americans', to agree upon a 'general plan' for offensive operations in South-East Asia. His hope was that a specially constituted South-East Asia Command, under a British Supreme Commander, should be set up. It would then, he argued, be given a chance of 'proving our zeal in this theatre of war, which by its failures and sluggishness is in a measure under reasonable reproach'.

Churchill also suggested that Wingate should tell his story to the United States Chiefs of Staff, 'and thus convince them that we mean business in this sector. . . .'[2] At 6.30 on the evening of August 7, at the first meeting of the Chiefs of Staff Committee at which Churchill presided during the voyage, Brooke warned that the operation of Wingate's specially devised Long-Range Penetration Force 'would have to be backed up by the main advance, so as to make good what he had gained'. Wingate's ideas, Brooke added, 'gave shape to our plans for Upper Burma, but it must be remembered that if they were carried out, and we occupied Northern Burma, it would be essential to carry on in that theatre the following year and complete its conquest'.[3]

Among those on board the *Queen Mary* was Captain Maurice Vernon, a member of Combined Operations, and an expert on amphibious operations in the Indian Ocean area. On the night of August 8 he was summoned to Churchill's cabin, shortly after midnight, to discuss a possible landing on the Andaman Islands. Vernon's nephew later wrote: 'Directly he was ushered in, Churchill began to question him about this operation. Vernon replied that it was not feasible with the equipment, etc. giving the technical reasons, also that he could see little point in it. Churchill countered with all kinds of reasons in favour of it, cross-examining him very sharply, but Vernon refused to alter his opinion (he had been warned that this proposal might come up and had done his homework thoroughly).

[1] Prime Minister's Personal Minute, M.580/3, 6 August 1943: Cabinet papers, 120/714.
[2] Prime Minister's Personal Minute, D(Q) 2/3, 'Most Secret', 7 August 1943: Churchill papers, 20/104. Circulated as Chiefs of Staff Paper (Q) No. 6, 7 August 1943: Premier papers, 3/366/3, folios 111–12.
[3] Chiefs of Staff Committee (Quadrant), 4th Meeting, 8 August 1943: Premier papers, 3/366/3.

After about fifteen minutes Churchill said, "Are you still of the same opinion?" Vernon replied, "Yes Sir, but of course if you are determined to mount it, we will do our best." Churchill, "Well you are the expert and now I have heard what you have to say I accept your decision." ' [1]

On Sunday August 8 Churchill spent more than an hour with Wingate, and then a further hour with the Director of Plans, who was also on board.[2] After lunch he spent an hour with Brooke, again discussing a possible landing on the northern tip of Sumatra.[3] That night he dined with Averell Harriman and Ismay.[4] Among his minutes on August 8 was one which dealt with a problem which had long concerned him, the choice of operational codenames. Having studied a 'specimen list' of codenames under consideration, he minuted to Ismay:

I have crossed out on the attached paper many unsuitable names. Operations in which large numbers of men may lose their lives ought not to be described by code-words which imply a boastful and over-confident sentiment, such as 'Triumphant', or, conversely, which are calculated to invest the plan with an air of despondency, such as 'Woebetide', 'Massacre', 'Jumble', 'Trouble', 'Fidget', 'Flimsy', 'Pathetic', and 'Jaundice'. They ought not to be names of a frivolous character, such as 'Bunnyhug', 'Billingsgate', 'Aperitif', and 'Ballyhoo'. They should not be ordinary words often used in other connections, such as 'Flood', 'Smooth', 'Sudden', 'Supreme', 'Fullforce', and 'Fullspeed'. Names of living people—Ministers or commanders—should be avoided; e.g. 'Bracken'.

After all, the world is wide, and intelligent thought will readily supply an unlimited number of well-sounding names which do not suggest the character of the operation or disparage it in any way and do not enable some widow or mother to say that her son was killed in an operation called 'Bunnyhug' or 'Ballyhoo'.

Proper names are good in this field. The heroes of antiquity, figures from Greek and Roman mythology, the constellations and stars, famous racehorses, names of British and American war heroes, could be used, provided they fall within the rules above. There are no doubt many other themes that could be suggested.

Care should be taken in all this process. An efficient and a successful administration manifests itself equally in small as in great matters.[5]

On the afternoon of August 9 the *Queen Mary* reached the Canadian

---

[1] 'Incident as told to Mr Eversley Belfield by his uncle Capt. Maurice Vernon, OBE, DSC': Letter to the author, 31 December 1981.
[2] Prime Minister's Engagement Cards, 8 August 1943.
[3] Brooke diary, 8 August 1943: Bryant, *op. cit.*, volume 1, page 694.
[4] Prime Minister's Engagement Cards: 8 August 1943.
[5] Prime Minister's Personal Minute, D(Q) 4/3, 8 August 1943: Churchill papers, 20/104.

port of Halifax. From there, studying the most recent reports from Italy, Churchill telegraphed to Eden: 'Badoglio must state that he is prepared to place himself unreservedly in the hands of the Allied Governments, who have already made it plain that they desire Italy to have a respectable place in the new Europe.' The object of this, Churchill added, was to convey to the Italian Government 'the feeling that, while they have to make the formal act of submission, our desire is to treat them with consideration, so far as military exigencies allow. Merely harping on "unconditional surrender" with no prospect of mercy held out even as an act of grace may well lead to no surrender at all.' The expression 'honourable capitulation' had, Churchill added, 'also been officially used by the President, and I do not think it should be omitted from the language we are now to use'. Eisenhower had already agreed, Churchill pointed out, that Italian prisoners-of-war in Tunis would be returned to Italy 'provided Allied prisoners are speedily set free'.[1]

Churchill also telegraphed to Attlee on August 9, about a suggestion made to him earlier by Leo Amery, that Lord Louis Mountbatten should be appointed to the South-East Asia Command. 'All would depend,' Churchill added, 'upon whether the Americans liked the idea. Personally I think he might well be acceptable to the President. He knows the whole story from the top; he is young, enthusiastic and triphibious.'[2] Churchill telegraphed to Attlee and Eden two days later that Mountbatten's appointment 'would I think command public interest and approval and show that youth is no barrier to merit'.[3]

From Halifax, Churchill travelled by train to Quebec. 'Crowds collect wherever we stop,' John Martin wrote home, 'and wave and cheer the PM and return his V sign.'[4] Rumours, preceding the train, were of an important personage on his way, though as Martin noted, 'some said it was the Pope, others Stalin'.[5] The train journey took all night and all day. Quebec was reached at six in the evening of August 10. Awaiting Churchill there was a telegram from Stalin, congratulating him on the victory in Sicily, and agreeing that a Three-Power meeting was 'absolutely desirable'.[6] 'I was very glad to hear again from Bruin in the first person,' Churchill telegraphed to Eden and Attlee on August 11.[7] 'You will see,' he telegraphed to Roosevelt

[1] 'Welfare' No. 22, 'Most Secret and Personal', 10 August 1943: Churchill papers, 20/129.
[2] 'Welfare' No. 9, 'Secret and Private', 9 August 1943: Churchill papers, 20/129.
[3] 'Welfare' No. 64, 'Most Secret and Personal', 11 August 1943: Churchill papers, 20/129.
[4] Letter of 10 August 1943, 'in the train': Martin papers.
[5] Letter of 16 August 1943: Martin papers.
[6] 'Concrete' No. 81, 'Most Secret', 10 August 1941: Churchill papers, 20/117.
[7] 'Welfare' No. 55, 'Most Secret', 11 August 1943: Cabinet papers, 120/89.

on the following day, 'I am restored, if not to favour, at any rate to the court.' [1]

While in Quebec, Churchill lived at the Citadel, the summer residence of the Governor-General, the upstairs floor of which was being prepared for Roosevelt, with ramps fitted wherever necessary for his wheelchair. 'The holding of the conference at Quebec,' Churchill telegraphed to the King on the morning of August 11, 'is most timely, as there is a lot of fretfulness here, which I believe will soon be removed.' He was to meet the Canadian Cabinet that morning, and the Quebec Cabinet in the afternoon.

As a result of the discussion with Wingate on board the *Queen Mary*, 'I look,' Churchill informed the King, 'for a new turn being given to the campaign in Upper Burma.' As to the prospects of a meeting with Stalin, 'Your Majesty will have noticed that I have heard from the Great Bear, and that we are on speaking, or at least growling, terms again.' [2]

Churchill was pleased with the appointment of Wingate as commander of the special Long Range Penetration Group. 'Brigadier Wingate is a remarkable man,' he telegraphed to Attlee and Eden on August 11, 'and he also in his Jungle sphere would fit in with my ideas of vigour and inventiveness in this decayed Indian scene.' [3]

While in Quebec on August 11, Churchill sent Stalin congratulations on the most recent Soviet victories in the Kharkov region. 'The defeats of the German Army on this front,' he wrote, 'are milestones to our final victory.' The Anglo-American success in Sicily, Churchill added, would be exploited to the full, 'without prejudice' to the cross-Channel invasion. As to the bombing of Germany, 'eighty percent of the houses are down'; he was sending Stalin 'a small stereoscopic machine' together with 'a large number' of photographic slides of the damage done by British bombing to German cities. 'They give one a much more vivid impression than anything that can be gained from photographs,' Churchill noted. 'I hope you will find half an hour in which to look at them.' Meanwhile, the bombing of Berlin was continuing; a raid about to be launched would be 'the heaviest ever known'. [4]

---

[1] Prime Minister's Personal Telegram, T.1219/3, Prime Minister to President, No. 409, 'Personal and Most Secret', 12 August 1943: Churchill papers, 20/117.

[2] 'Welfare' No. 54, 'Most Secret and Personal, With humble duty', 11 August 1943: Churchill papers, 20/129.

[3] 'Welfare' No. 64, 'Most Secret and Personal', 11 August 1943: Churchill papers, 20/129.

[4] According to Air Chief Marshal Harris, in a note to Churchill on 3 November 1943, the figures for devastation (in acres) were Hamburg, 6,200 out of 8,382; Essen, 1,030 out of 2,630; Cologne, 1,785 out of 3,320. Coventry had 100 acres devastated, out of 1,922. Harris added: 'Berlin has 480 acres devastated, inner London 600.' (Secret, 3 November 1943: Air Ministry papers, 14/3507.) Lord Cherwell's statistical tables showed the largest percentages of destruction

On the Atlantic front, Churchill informed Stalin, U-boat sinkings for May, June and July had been 'at a rate of almost one a day'. This had substantially reduced the Allied shipping losses and would facilitate 'the establishment of the large scale Anglo-American front which I agree with you is indispensable to the shortening of the war'.[1]

At six on the evening of August 11 Churchill and his daughter Mary left Quebec by train, for Hyde Park, Roosevelt's home on the Hudson river. Reaching Niagara Falls on the morning of August 12, they were driven across the Falls bridge to the United States. Asked by a journalist what he thought of the Falls, Churchill replied: 'I saw them before you were born. I came here first in 1900.' 'Do they look the same?' he was asked. 'Well,' he replied, 'the principle seems the same. The water still keeps falling over.'[2]

From Niagara, Churchill and his daughter continued by train to Hyde Park, arriving at the siding there at 6.30 in the evening, twenty-four hours after leaving Quebec.[3] Clementine Churchill had remained in Quebec, having been, as Churchill explained to Roosevelt from Quebec, 'so much exhausted by the journey and sleeplessness that Moran feels she ought to rest here for the next few days'. She had much wanted to make the journey. 'I am sure however,' Churchill added, 'that she must regather her strength.'[4]

At Hyde Park, on August 12 Churchill and his daughter dined with Roosevelt and his wife. Harry Hopkins was among the guests. 'Oppressively hot,' John Martin noted in his diary on the following day, Friday August 13. 'Swim. Picnic lunch at Mrs R's cottage (hot dogs).'[5]

While he was at Hyde Park, Churchill wrote to Roosevelt about Yugoslavia. A series of Enigma decrypts revealed the murder by German forces, not only of Tito's partisans, but of several thousand Yugoslav civilians. 'I am not sure that your people have quite realized,' Churchill wrote, 'all that is going on in the Balkans and the hopes and horrors centred there. You might find it convenient to keep it by you. Much of it is taken from the Boniface sources, and it cer-

---

of large cities as 74% (Hamburg), 54% (Cologne), 51% (Hanover), 41% (Düsseldorf) and 39% (Essen). Note and Tables of 6 November 1943: Premier papers, 3/14/1.

[1] 'Welfare' No. 44, 'Most Secret and Personal', Prime Minister's Personal Telegram, T.1218/3, 11 August 1943: Churchill papers, 20/117. Sent as Foreign Office No. 1084 to Moscow, 'Decypher Yourself', 12 August 1943: Cabinet papers, 120/858.

[2] Winston S. Churchill, *The Second World War*, volume 5, London 1952, page 73.

[3] 'August 11–16, 1943: Quebec–Niagara Falls and Hyde Park', White House Itineraries: Thompson papers.

[4] 'Welfare' No. 61, Prime Minister's Personal Telegram, T.1222/3, 'Most Secret and Personal', 11 August 1943: Churchill papers, 20/129.

[5] John Martin diary, 13 August 1943: Martin papers.

tainly makes one's blood boil. I must add,' Churchill wrote, 'that I am not in any way making a case for the employment of an Allied Army in the Balkans but only for aiding them with supplies, agents and Commandos. Once the Adriatic is open we should be able to get into close contact with these people and give them aid sufficient to make it worth their while to follow our guidance.'[1]

Churchill stayed two nights at Hyde Park. 'Each day', John Martin wrote, 'we had a picnic lunch in a cottage in the woods—hot dogs and hamburgers cooked on the spot, corn on the cob, fish chowder, huge slices of water melon etc', as well as 'a refreshing swim in the open air pool', an essential bonus in the damp, sticky heat.[2] 'It was so hot,' Churchill later recalled, 'that I got up one night because I was unable to sleep and hardly able to breathe, and went outside to sit on a bluff overlooking the Hudson. Here I watched the dawn.'[3]

While Churchill was at Hyde Park, the first meeting of the British and American Chiefs of Staff took place in Quebec, the city given the codename 'Abraham' for the duration of the conference. 'Please make sure,' Churchill telegraphed to Ismay that Friday, 'that an account of the opening meeting reaches me in my train somewhere on the journey back to "Abraham".'[4]

While at Hyde Park, Churchill and Roosevelt discussed the future Commands in Europe and South-East Asia. Churchill had earlier offered General Brooke the Supreme Command of the cross-Channel forces, but Roosevelt wanted Marshall, on the principle, which Churchill later set out for Attlee, 'that the Commands should go to whichever country has substantially the largest number of troops employed'. Churchill accepted this.[5] For his part, and on the same principle, Roosevelt accepted Churchill's nominee, Mountbatten, as Supreme Commander in South-East Asia. 'I am sure the plan you have in mind is the best,' Churchill wrote to Roosevelt on the following day.[6] 'There is no doubt,' Churchill telegraphed to Attlee a week later, repeating his sentiments about Wingate, 'of the need of a young and vigorous mind in this lethargic and stagnant Indian scene.'[7]

Several other decisions were also reached at Hyde Park that Saturday. One was to ensure the full sharing of all work on the atomic bomb, an issue which, until June, had been a source of divided counsel and friction. Churchill and Roosevelt agreed to a 'Tube Alloy'

[1] 'Mr President', 13 August 1943: Premier papers, 3/353, folios 92–3.
[2] Letter of 16 August 1943: Martin papers.
[3] Winston S. Churchill, *The Second World War*, volume 5, London 1952, page 73.
[4] Prime Minister's Personal Minute, D(Q) 11/3A, 13 August 1943: Churchill papers, 20/104.
[5] 'Welfare' No. 558, 'Most Secret and Personal', 2 September 1943: Churchill papers, 20/129.
[6] 'For you alone', 15 August 1943: Churchill papers, 20/94.
[7] 'Welfare' No. 326, 'Most Secret and Personal', 22 August 1943: Churchill papers, 20/129.

memorandum which placed the research and manufacture of the bomb in the United States, but as a joint project with no secrets withheld from either side. In the Articles of Agreement, the first one laid down that Britain and the United States 'will never use this agency against each other'. The second article stated: 'we will not use it against third parties without each other's consent'; the third, 'that we will not either of us communicate any information about Tube Alloys to third parties except by mutual consent'. In the fourth article of agreement, covering the post-war industrial and commercial advantages of atomic research and development, Churchill, as the article noted, 'expressly disclaims any interest in these industrial and commercial aspects beyond what may be considered by the President of the United States to be fair and just in harmony with the economic welfare of the world'.[1]

A second decision reached at Hyde Park was to 'make a renewed final offer' to Stalin for a Tripartite meeting, with Alaska as the meeting place. 'If he accepts,' Churchill wrote to Roosevelt on the following day, 'it will be a very great advantage: if not, we shall be on very strong ground,' and he added: 'we must mind the Japanese do not get us(!)'[2]

Churchill stayed at Hyde Park for the whole of August 14. A further session, a second picnic, and dinner. During the dinner, at which Averell Harriman was present, Churchill spoke of his hopes that the 'fraternal relationship' of Britain and the United States would be perpetuated in peacetime. Harriman noted that Churchill 'liked the idea of a loose association better than a formal treaty': it would be an association 'flexible enough to adjust itself to historical developments'. One of the dinner guests was apprehensive. As Harriman noted: 'Mrs Roosevelt seemed fearful this might be misunderstood by other nations and weaken the UN concept.' The PM did not agree, arguing that 'any hope of the UN would be in the leadership given by the intimacy of the US and Britain in working out misunderstandings with the Russians—and the Chinese too', he conceded, 'if they become a nation'.[3]

'We travelled in a most comfortable special train,' noted John Martin, 'with observation cars and long baths, air conditioned.'[4] The same train that had brought them to Hyde Park took them back to Quebec, where they arrived on the morning of August 14. Within 'three minutes' of reaching the Citadel, so an official communique reported, 'Mr Churchill started work in his famous map room. . . .'[5]

---

[1] 'Articles of Agreement', 19 August 1943: Premier papers, 3/139/8A, folios 356–9.
[2] 'For you alone', 15 August 1943: Churchill papers, 20/94.
[3] Harriman notes: Abel and Harriman, *op. cit.*, page 222.
[4] Letters of 13 and 14 August 1943: Martin papers.
[5] *Montreal Gazette*, 16 August 1943.

Churchill had also to break the news to Brooke he was not to be the Supreme Commander of 'Overlord'. 'He had just returned from being with the President and Harry Hopkins at Hyde Park,' Brooke noted in his diary on April 15. 'Apparently,' Brooke added, Marshall had 'pressed hard' for the appointment of Eisenhower, 'and, as far as I can gather, Winston gave in, in spite of having previously promised me the job. He asked me how I felt about it, and I told him that I could not feel otherwise than disappointed.'[1] Brooke later recalled August 15 as 'a black day', adding bitterly: 'He offered no sympathy, no regrets at having to change his mind, and dealt with the matter as if it were one of minor importance ...'[2] Churchill, however, in his memoirs, recalled: 'He bore the great disappointment with soldierly dignity.'[3]

Among the official papers which Churchill saw while in Quebec was one concerning operation 'Firebrand'. The word meaning nothing to him, he at once asked Brigadier Jacob to explain. The answer was, a proposed operation to take Corsica. This was the first Churchill had heard of such a plan. 'What troops is it proposed to use and when is it timed?' he asked Brooke, adding: 'We cannot allow ourselves to be kept in ignorance of such important strategic and political movements in the Mediterranean.'[4]

On the morning of August 16 Churchill received a telegram, through London, with details of an Italian request to change allegiance from the German to the Allied side. The request had been made in Madrid on the previous day by General Castellano, Chief of Staff to the Chief of the Italian General Staff, in a conversation with the British Ambassador, Sir Samuel Hoare. Castellano told Hoare that he came with the 'full authority' of Marshal Badoglio, to say that Italy would 'accept unconditional surrender' provided she could join the Allies 'in fighting the Germans'. If the answer was yes, Castellano himself would give 'at once' the fullest possible information about the deployment of German forces in Italy.[5]

Churchill received this report while he was still in bed. He at once prepared a draft reply to the Italians, and then summoned the Chiefs

---

[1] Brooke diary, 15 August 1943: Bryant, *op. cit.*, volume 1, page 706.
[2] Brooke recollections, Bryant, *op. cit.*, volume 1, page 707.
[3] Winston S. Churchill, *The Second World War*, volume 5, London 1952, page 76.
[4] Prime Minister's Personal Minute, M(Q) 12/3, 16 August 1943: Churchill papers, 20/104.
[5] Telegram No. 1404 from Madrid to Foreign Office, 15 August 1943.

of Staff to read it to them.[1] He then sent a copy of his draft to Roosevelt, for the President's approval.

Churchill's proposed message was a strong encouragement to the Italians to come to terms, while rejecting any prior bargain. 'The Italians know quite well,' Churchill wrote, 'that British and United States Governments do not seek to deny Italy her respected place in Europe.' By taking its own independent action against the 'common enemy', Churchill added, 'the Italian Government, Army and people could, without any bargains, facilitate a more friendly relationship with the United Nations'. Churchill's proposed message ended with the sentence: 'In particular we state that if Allied troops arrive at any point where they find Italians fighting Germans, we shall aid Italians to our utmost.'

In sending Roosevelt this draft message, Churchill added: 'Eden should be here tomorrow and we can discuss whole position together. I send you this budget in order that you may see the way my mind is working.' The Combined Chiefs of Staff, Churchill reported, were at this very moment considering 'the practical steps and timings to make an Italian turnover effective'.[2] Roosevelt replied that same day to say that he 'heartily approved' of Churchill's proposed answer.[3]

The Combined Chiefs of Staff, in their deliberations, favoured the despatch of instructions to Eisenhower, instructing him to send two officers, one American and one British, to Lisbon, in order to negotiate with Castellano. When Roosevelt reached Quebec on August 17, he and Churchill agreed to this course, which was, they explained to Stalin, 'a measure of military diplomacy'.[4] The same day, August 17, Castellano met Eisenhower's emissaries, General Bedell Smith and General Strong, at the British Embassy in Lisbon. No difficulty was made over the idea of unconditional surrender; it was clear that Badoglio's intention was to change sides while guarding against the dangers which might arise from German reaction.[5] Castellano was given a document setting out the Allied military terms, and arrangements were made, on Churchill and Roosevelt's instructions, for secret wireless contact to be maintained between them. These were such terms: 'passive resistance' throughout Italy, 'minor sabotage' par-

[1] Brooke diary, 16 August 1943: Bryant, *op. cit.*, volume 1, page 707.

[2] Prime Minister's Personal Telegram, T.1232/3, 16 August 1943: Churchill papers, 20/133. Churchill sent a copy of this telegram to Attlee as 'Welfare' No. 156, 16 August 1943: Cabinet papers, 120/94.

[3] Personal Message from British Chargé d'Affaires, Washington, 16 August 1943: Churchill papers, 20/133. Churchill sent a copy of Roosevelt's reply to Attlee as 'Welfare' No. 171, 17 August 1943: Cabinet papers, 120/94.

[4] Prime Minister's Personal Telegram, T.1239/3, 19 August 1943: Churchill papers, 20/132.

[5] Sir David Hunt, then a British officer involved in these negotiations, has given an account of them in his book, *A Don at War*, London 1966, pages 214–25.

ticularly of communications and airfields used by the Germans, safeguard of Allied prisoners-of-war, no Italian warships or merchant shipping to fall into German hands, the Germans not to be allowed to take over the Italian coast defences, and Italian formations in the Balkans to 'march to the coast' with a view to being 'taken off to Italy by the United Nations'.[1]

Meanwhile, the battle in Sicily continued unabated; among the documents which Churchill studied on August 16 was a telegram from Eden about the possibility of declaring Rome an Open City, which, Eden wrote, I should 'still prefer not to'. Even if such a declaration were made, Eden advised, 'we should have to reserve the right to cancel the agreement if the enemy ever use the city of Rome in the course of military operations in Italy'.[2] 'I agree,' Churchill replied, and he added: 'Present line I am taking with President and United States authorities is that we pay no attention to unilateral declaration about Rome being an open city but continue to bomb remorselessly. The Combined Chiefs of Staff take this view strongly and I understand that orders have now been given to resume Rome bombing.'[3]

On August 17 Churchill received a telegram from Alexander, announcing the Anglo-American victory in Sicily. 'By 10 a.m. this morning,' Alexander telegraphed, 'the last German soldier was flung out of Sicily and the whole island is now in our hands.'[4] The capture of the island had taken thirty-eight days.

That same night, 571 British heavy bombers struck at Peenemünde, centre of German rocket and flying bomb research and development, the unravelling of which had been supervised by Churchill's son-in-law, Duncan Sandys. Considerable damage was done, setting back the German rocket programme by many months.

On August 17, Roosevelt and Hopkins arrived at Quebec, followed soon afterwards by Eden and Brendan Bracken. During August 17, while the British and American Chiefs of Staff were examining the detailed aspects of war strategy on all its fronts, Churchill prepared his own statement on war policy. In it he stressed the need both to make comprehensive plans for the defeat of Japan, and to decide upon the future scale of operations in Italy. In the Far East, to Brooke's annoyance, Churchill again pressed for the seizure of the tip of Sumatra, having 'found with a pair of dividers', Brooke later recalled,

[1] Instructions to General Eisenhower, 17 August 1943, sent to Stalin in Prime Minister's Personal Telegram, T.1240/3, 19 August 1943: Churchill papers, 20/133.

[2] 'Concrete' No. 221, 'Most Secret', 15 August 1943: Premier papers, 3/14/3.

[3] 'Most Secret and Personal', 'Action this Day', 16 August 1943: Premier papers, 3/14/3.

[4] MA/423, 'Personal', 'Most Secret', 17 August 1943: Churchill papers, 20/117.

'that we could bomb Singapore from this point and he had set his heart on going there'.[1] 'He is insisting on capturing the tip of Sumatra island,' Brooke noted in his diary, 'irrespective of what our general plan of war against Japan may be.'[2]

In his statement of August 17, Churchill suggested that a Task Force of 30,000 men should be prepared for the Sumatra plan, operation 'Culverin'. Admiral King, to whom Churchill had explained his ideas on the previous night, had seemed 'greatly interested'. From what King told Churchill, it was clear that American operations in mid-1944 would put a considerable strain on the power of Japan 'to move large reinforcements over great distances'. At present there were only 6,000 Japanese troops in the Sumatra tip, able to exercise, Churchill wrote, none but 'the most loose, partial and spasmodic surveillance of the enormous, undeveloped and roadless areas involved'.

Turning to Europe, Churchill's emphasis was on the need to give the fullest priority to 'Overlord'. By capturing Naples in the near future, Churchill wrote, 'we shall have a first-rate port in Italy', and other harbours, like Brindisi and Taranto, 'will fall into our possession thereafter'. The ability of the Allied armies to use such harbours 'supersedes the need of landing-craft', which could therefore be released, both for 'Overlord' and for the Indian theatre. At the same time, the 'disappearance of the Italian Fleet as a factor' would enable 'a great diminution' to be made in the Allied naval strength in the Mediterranean, with no more than a 'detachment' of the landing Fleet required for 'minor descents across the Adriatic', and operation 'Accolade', the capture of Rhodes and other islands in the Aegean.

In Italy, Churchill continued, even by limiting the Allied military advance to a line from Leghorn to Ancona, Britain and America would still be able to supply arms and equipment by air to the French underground forces in Savoy and the French Alps, and to the partisans in the Balkans, aiming thereby to 'stimulate' their activities. If the Allies were to go north of the Leghorn–Ancona line, however, then, as General Maitland Wilson had pointed out, many more divisions would be needed to hold the wider geographic area, the line of the Po, or of the Alps. 'If we cannot have the best,' Churchill commented, 'these are very good second bests,' and he went on to state, as his basic principle for the Italian strategy: 'It may be necessary for us to accept these limitations in order that the integrity of Operation "Overlord" should not be marred.'[3]

*   *   *

[1] Brooke recollections: Bryant, *op. cit.*, volume 1, page 712.

[2] Brooke diary, 19 August 1943: Bryant, *op. cit.*, volume 1, page 712.

[3] Prime Minister's Personal Minute, D(Q) 13/3, 'Most Secret', 17 August 1943: Churchill papers, 20/104.

'Our greatest danger,' Churchill telegraphed to Alexander on August 19, in congratulating him on the 'brilliantly executed' victory in Sicily, 'is that the Germans should enter Rome and set up a Quisling–Fascist Government.' 'Scarcely less unpleasant,' Churchill added, 'would be the whole of Italy sliding into anarchy.' He doubted if the Badoglio Government could hold 'their double-faced position' until the date fixed for 'Avalanche', so that 'anything' that could be done to bring 'Avalanche' forward 'without endangering military success' would, Churchill noted, be 'most helpful'.[1]

'Everything possible is being done to put on "Avalanche" at the earliest possible date,' Alexander replied. 'We realise here very clearly that every hour gives enemy more time to prepare and organise against us.'[2] That same day, Churchill and Roosevelt informed Stalin: 'We shall begin our invasion of Italy probably before the end of this month', and 'about a week later' would make 'our full scale thrust' at Naples, operation 'Avalanche'.[3]

A second initiative, taken by Churchill and Roosevelt on August 18, was to invite Stalin to a conference in Alaska. Stalin had suggested Archangel or Astrakhan as the meeting place.[4] Neither, he was told, was 'suitable'. If Alaska were possible, they added, Churchill would 'remain on this side of Atlantic for as long as may be necessary'.[5]

On the afternoon of August 19, Churchill and Roosevelt met the British and American Chiefs of Staff, who presented the conclusions of five days of continuous discussion. 'We gave them results of our work,' Brooke noted in his diary, 'and got our agreements accepted by them fairly easily.'[6] These 'agreements' covered every aspect of strategy. The 'overall strategic concept' remained the defeat of Germany before Japan. The Combined Chiefs of Staff also concluded that 'Overlord' should be the 'primary United States–British ground and air effort against the Axis in Europe', with its target date set for 1 May 1944. The aim of 'Overlord' was not only to land in northern France, but to undertake further operations from northern France 'designed to strike at the heart of Germany and to destroy her military forces. . . .'

[1] 'Welfare' No. 214, Prime Minister's Personal Telegram, T.1238/2, 'Most Secret and Private', War Office Telegram No. 60571, 19 August 1943: Churchill papers, 20/117.

[2] MA/443, IZ 2929, 20 August 1943: Churchill papers, 20/117.

[3] 'Welfare' No. 217, Prime Minister's Personal Telegram, T.1239/3, 'Most Secret and Personal', 19 August 1943: Churchill papers, 20/117.

[4] Telegram of 8 August 1943: Cabinet papers, 120/113.

[5] 'Welfare' No. 209, Prime Minister's Personal Telegram, T.1241/3, 'Personal and Most Secret', 18 August 1943: Cabinet papers, 120/113.

[6] Brooke diary, 19 August 1943: Bryant, op. cit., volume 1, page 712.

The Combined Chiefs of Staff were also agreed, as between 'Overlord' and operations in the Mediterranean, that wherever there was a shortage of resources, 'available resources will be distributed and employed with the main object of ensuring the success of "Overlord"'. Only if circumstances were to render 'Overlord' impossible would the Allies consider the northern Norway landing, operation 'Jupiter', as an alternative, expanded to include 'an entry into southern Norway'.

In Italy, 'unremitting pressure' was to be maintained against the German forces, and the creation of what the Combined Chiefs of Staff described as 'conditions required for "Overlord"'. The Combined Chiefs of Staff also proposed, in order to create 'a diversion in connection with "Overlord", an Allied lodgment' in southern France, in the Toulon–Marseilles area, with exploitation northward. Operations in the Balkans, however, would be 'limited' to sending supplies by air and sea to the guerrillas, to 'minor Commando forces', and to the bombing of strategic objectives.[1]

In discussing with Roosevelt the Combined Chiefs of Staff report on August 19, Churchill expressed his worry lest 'Overlord' were to be carried out against too formidable a German military defence. To guard against this, he wanted a rule laid down, as prepared by General Morgan, whereby if there were more than twelve mobile German divisions in France at the intended moment of the Allied landing, that landing would not take place. Nor, Morgan had advised, should the Germans be capable of a build-up of more than fifteen divisions 'in the succeeding two months'.[2]

Churchill's primary fear was casualties. 'We had the most solemn warnings of what might happen,' Harry Hopkins told Lord Moran on the following day. 'The old, old story of enormous casualties and the terrific strength of the German fortifications.' But having given his warnings, Churchill accepted that 'Overlord' should go ahead. He 'wished to emphasize', as the minutes of the meeting recorded, 'that he strongly favoured "Overlord" for 1944', and he asked that every effort should be made 'to add at least 25 per cent to the initial assault'. There were nine months, he pointed out, in which to ensure an increase in the number of landing craft available. The beaches selected

---

[1] 'Progress Report to the President and Prime Minister', 19 August 1943, Combined Chiefs of Staff Paper 319: Churchill papers, 23/12. A revised version (CCS 319/2) was issued on 21 August 1943 and a final version (CCS 319/5) on 27 August 1943.

[2] On 6 June 1944 (D Day) the fighting power of the German divisions in France did not exceed General Morgan's limits; nor, in fighting power, did the build-up in the succeeding two months significantly exceed his limits: it was the tenacity of the German defenders that was to prove the obstacle until the August breakthrough, and again at Arnhem, and on the Siegfried Line.

were 'good', he told the meeting, 'but it would be better if at the same time a landing were to be made on the inside beaches of the Cotentin peninsula'. Churchill added: 'The initial lodgment must be strong, as it so largely affects later operations.'

As to Italy, Churchill told this first plenary meeting that he wanted it to be 'definitely understood' that he was not committed to an advance into northern Italy, beyond the Ancona–Pisa line. He also spoke of the proposed diversion in southern France, saying that he would be 'hesitant' in putting British or American divisions into an area where considerable resistance might be expected, and that he doubted if French divisions 'would be capable of an operation of the kind suggested'. Churchill thought, as an alternative to an Anglo-American landing in the south of France, supplies might be flown in for French underground fighters who might be operating in the mountains. 'This mountain area,' Churchill noted, 'would constitute an excellent rendezvous point for Frenchmen who objected to being sent into Germany and who might take refuge there.' Churchill's phrase to the Conference was,—'air-nourished guerilla warfare'.

Roosevelt then asked if plans had been made for Allied action in the event of a German withdrawal from the Balkans 'to the line of the Danube', but Brooke did not think there would be 'any surplus from our main operation'. Commando forces, Churchill pointed out, could operate 'in support of the guerrilla on the Dalmatian coast'.

Turning to the Far East, Churchill called the attack on Sumatra 'the great strategic blow which should be struck in 1944'. 'Culverin', he said, would be the 'Torch' of the Indian Ocean. Roosevelt replied, however, as Brooke had earlier complained, that the Sumatra operation 'would be heading away from the main direction of our advance to Japan'. Churchill was not convinced, telling Roosevelt 'that nevertheless it would greatly facilitate the direct advance'. The alternative would be to 'waste the entire year', with nothing to show for it but the Burmese port of Akyab, for the capture of which a plan existed, 'and the future right to toil through the swamps of Southern Burma'. The Sumatra project, Churchill added, was strategically of the highest importance. He would compare it, 'in its promise of decisive consequences, with the Dardanelles operation of 1915'.[1]

On Friday, August 20 Churchill and Roosevelt, Hopkins and Harriman, left Quebec for the Governor-General's country retreat, a log cabin on the Grand Lac de l'Épaule. There, in the morning, they

---

[1] 'Minutes of First Meeting of the President and Prime Minister with the Combined Chiefs of Staff, held at 1730, 19th August, at the Citadel, Abraham: Churchill papers, 23/12. 'Abraham' was the codename for Quebec. These minutes were subsequently printed as Chiefs of Staff Paper No. 513 (O) (Part A) of 1943, 'Most Secret', 11 September 1943.

fished. Before leaving Quebec, Churchill had urged the British Chiefs of Staff to make a more detailed study of his Sumatra plan. 'I am still studying it myself,' he wrote, and he went on to tell the Chiefs of Staff that it was 'not possible to come to any decision with the Americans' about the campaign in Burma. The Chiefs of Staff, Churchill warned, should 'beware of creating a situation where I shall certainly have to refuse to bear any responsibility for a decision which is taken on their level. This would entail the whole matter being referred to the War Cabinet at home after our return. I remain absolutely where I was at the last Conference, and where we all were, that a campaign through Rangoon up the Irrawaddy to Mandalay and beyond would be most detrimental and disadvantageous to us.' The capture of Akyab without such a campaign, he added, 'is only an act of waste and folly'.

Churchill's aim, he told the Chiefs of Staff, was to see Britain, 'at this time next year', masters of the tip of Sumatra, with Wingate 'in touch with the Chinese in Yunnan', communications in Upper Burma improved 'as far as possible', and a 'free option' as to where to 'strike next amphibiously, having regard to the reactions from the enemy, which by then will have been apparent'. [1]

After lunch in the log cabin, Churchill and Roosevelt discussed the relative merits of Sumatra and Burma as the main area of the next main British thrust in the Far East. Harriman, who was present, noted that Sumatra 'did not particularly appeal to the President'. Harriman added that Roosevelt 'used most of the glasses and salt cellars on the table, making a V-shaped diagram to describe the Japanese position in the quadrant from Western China to the South Pacific, indicating the advantages of striking from either side, thereby capturing the sustaining glasses, and the disadvantages of trying to remove the outer ones one by one'. [2]

In a telegram to Attlee on August 20, Churchill reported that Roosevelt and Marshall were 'very keen' on Mountbatten's appointment to South East Asia Command. 'There is no doubt,' he wrote, 'of the need of a young and vigorous mind in this lethargic and stagnant Indian scene.' The 'difficulties' about the South East Asia Command had been 'cleared up to our satisfaction', Churchill added, and he went on to explain: 'Broad strategic plans and major assignments of forces and supplies will be decided by the Combined Chiefs of Staff, subject to the approval of their respective Governments. But all operational control will be vested in the British Chiefs of Staff, acting under His Majesty's Government, and all orders will go through them.' [3]

[1] Prime Minister's Personal Minute, D(Q) 15/3, 20 August 1943: Churchill papers, 20/104.
[2] Harriman notes for 20 August 1943: Abel and Harriman, op. cit., page 224.
[3] 'Welfare' No. 326, 'Most Secret and Personal', 22 August 1943: Churchill papers, 20/129.

Returning to Quebec, Churchill and Roosevelt dined with Eden and Cordell Hull. During the dinner Roosevelt outlined his plan for an international security organization, to be set up by Britain, China, Russia and the United States as soon as the war was over, 'to cover', as Eden recalled, 'the interim period before the final peace treaties could be signed'.[1] Eden noted in his diary that Cordell Hull 'appeared anxious to go to bed'. When he eventually rose to go, about midnight, 'W. was scandalized and explained in reply to Hull's protest that it was late, "Why, man, we are at war!"' [2]

On August 23, at the second Plenary, the Combined Chiefs of Staff proposed, and Churchill and Roosevelt accepted, that plans should be made to defeat Japan within twelve months after the collapse of Germany.

During the course of this second Plenary, Roosevelt asked if a study was being made with regard to 'an emergency entrance of the Continent', in the event of a premature German collapse, and indicated, as the minutes recorded, 'that he desired United Nations' troops to be ready to get to Berlin as soon as did the Russians'.

Once more, Churchill stressed that British acceptance of the cross-Channel invasion 'included the proviso' that it could only be carried out 'in the event that certain conditions regarding German strength were met'. These included the number of German divisions to be in France and a 'definite superiority' over the German fighter force at the time of the initial assault. The Allies, he said, should have 'a second string to their bow' in the event of these conditions not being met: he again suggested operation 'Jupiter' in northern Norway, and this was accepted by Roosevelt. Churchill added that he did not 'in any way' wish to imply that he was not 'wholeheartedly' in favour of 'Overlord', but at the same time, he wished to emphasize that its launching was dependent upon certain conditions 'which would give it a reasonable chance of success'. General Marshall pointed out, to allay Churchill's worries, that there would be four and a half divisions in the initial assault rather than a force of three divisions 'which had been suggested at the last conference with the President and the Prime Minister'.[3]

On the last night of the Quebec conference, August 23, Churchill

[1] Eden recollections: Eden memoirs, *The Reckoning*, *op. cit.*, page 402.
[2] Eden diary, 20 August 1943: Eden memoirs, *The Reckoning*, *op. cit.*, page 402.
[3] 'Minutes of Second Meeting ... held at 1730, 23rd August, at the Citadel, Quebec': Churchill papers, 23/12. These minutes were subsequently printed as Chiefs of Staff Paper (No. 513) (O) (Part A) of 1943, 'Most Secret', 11 September 1943: Cabinet papers, 99/23.

was, as Sir Alexander Cadogan noted, 'in very good form, but that resulted in our being kept up till 1.30'. At one moment, he wrote, Churchill was 'pacing about haranguing us' when Harry Hopkins said suddenly: 'Now I'll tell *you*, Mr PM, what's going to happen.' Churchill halted 'and looked enquiring'. 'Your pants is coming down,' said Hopkins.[1]

The Quebec conference ended on August 24. 'There seems to be general satisfaction,' Brigadier Jacob telegraphed that day to General Hollis, 'though I can't see what has been decided which takes us much beyond "Trident". However,' Jacob added, 'I think much suspicion has been dissipated. They realize we are not bluffing on "Overlord" and there has been a much more realistic approach to Burma operations.' An operation against the 'Sumatra tip', Jacob added, 'looks a certainty' though 'for some reason' the Americans wanted British operations 'confined to Burma'.[2]

That evening, just before dinner, Churchill read an appreciation by one of Alexander's staff officers, that six divisions could not be installed across the Straits of Messina or in Naples until the beginning of December. 'The lateness of this forecast sent him quite mad,' Brooke noted in his diary, 'and during a twenty minutes' talk I failed to calm him. I must now go to see him at 10 a.m. to discuss this situation further.'[3]

Throughout the Quebec conference, Churchill and Roosevelt had received detailed reports from Eisenhower of the continuing negotiations for the unconditional surrender of Italy. Details of these negotiations were passed on regularly to Stalin. He, however, took offence at this procedure. Hitherto, he telegraphed to Churchill and Roosevelt on August 22, 'Great Britain and the United States make agreements' but the Soviet Union was 'just a passive observer', receiving information about these agreements. 'I have to tell you,' he warned, 'that it is impossible any longer to tolerate such situation.' A military–political commission should therefore be set up, with representatives of Britain, the Soviet Union and the United States, to consider the question of all States who wished to dissociate themselves from Germany. 'I propose to establish this commission,' Stalin added, 'and to assign Sicily at the beginning as its place of residence.'[4]

Stalin's sense of urgency could be understood by rumours reaching the Foreign Office in London at that very moment. 'Finland wants to

---

[1] Cadogan diary, 23 August 1943: David Dilks (editor), *op. cit.*, pages 554–5.
[2] 'Welfare' No. 356, 'Most Secret', 24 August 1943: Cabinet papers, 120/89.
[3] Brooke diary, 24 August 1943: Bryant, *op. cit.*, volume 1, page 719.
[4] Telegram of 22 August 1943: Churchill papers, 20/133.

get out of the war,' noted Oliver Harvey on August 23, 'and Hungary is ready to surrender unconditionally.' [1]

Stalin's telegram reached Quebec on August 24. That night Churchill and Roosevelt dined together, with Harriman and Eden. 'The Prime Minister and President were particularly annoyed,' Harriman noted, 'because they had attempted to keep him fully informed.' Harriman, Eden and Ismay took the view that 'one can't be annoyed with Stalin for being aloof and then be dismayed with him because he rudely joins the party'. When Eden suggested that Stalin's telegram was 'not so bad', Churchill commented: 'There is no need for you to attempt to smooth it over in the Foreign Office manner.' [2] Later in the evening, Churchill said that he foresaw 'bloody consequences in the future', using 'bloody' in the literal sense. 'Stalin is an unnatural man,' he warned. 'There will be grave troubles.' [3]

'The black spot at the present time,' Churchill telegraphed to Attlee on August 25, 'is the increasing bearishness of Soviet Russia,' and he added that Roosevelt had been 'much offended' by the force of Stalin's message. Stalin had 'of course', Churchill noted, 'studiously ignored our offer to make a further long and hazardous journey in order to bring about a tripartite meeting. In spite of all this I do not think his manifestations of ill temper and bad manners are preparatory to a separate peace with Germany as the hatreds between the two races have now become a sanitary cordon in themselves.'

It was 'disheartening', Churchill commented, to make 'so little progress' with the Russians, but he was sure that the War Cabinet would not feel 'that I myself or our Government as a whole have been wanting in any way in patience and in loyalty'.

Russia apart, Churchill was not dissatisfied with the results of the Quebec conference. As he told Attlee and the War Cabinet in his telegram of August 25: 'Everything here has gone off well. We have secured a settlement of a number of hitherto intractable questions— e.g., the South-East Asia Command, "Tube Alloys", and French Committee recognition.' On this last Churchill added, 'we all had an awful time with Hull, who has at last gone off in a pretty sulky mood, especially with the Foreign Secretary, who bore the brunt'.

He was feeling 'rather tired', Churchill told Attlee 'as the work of the Conference has been very heavy and many large and difficult questions have weighed upon us'. He hoped that the War Cabinet

[1] Harvey diary, 23 August 1943: John Harvey (editor), *op. cit.*, pages 285–6.

[2] A week later, after Eden had returned to London, Oliver Harvey noted in his diary: 'The PM, he thinks, is now getting dangerously anti-Russian.' (Harvey diary, 30 August 1943: *supra*, page 288.)

[3] Harriman notes for 24 August 1943: Abel and Harriman, *op cit.*, page 226.

'will think it proper for me to take two or three days' rest'.[1] Churchill proposed going with his wife and daughter for four days to a retreat and fishing camp in the Laurentian mountains, the home of a Canadian officer, Colonel F. W. Clarke, situated more than seventy miles from Quebec.

On the morning of August 25, Brooke found Churchill 'still in a very peevish and difficult mood' about the rate of build-up of British divisions for the crossing of the Straits of Messina and the Naples landing.[2] These were operations 'Baytown' and 'Avalanche'. The December date, Churchill telegraphed to Alexander on the morning of August 26, 'has filled me with the greatest concern, and I hope you will be able to reassure me'. Assuming that the landings were successful, he wrote, 'and that we are not defeated in the subsequent battles, I cannot understand why two and a half months or more will be required to get ashore, or why it should be necessary, once we have obtained an effective port and bridge-head at "Avalanche", to march all the "Baytown" divisions through Calabria instead of sending some at least of them round by sea'.

If the liberation of Rome were to be delayed for more than three months, Churchill wrote, 'no one can measure the consequences'. As Churchill saw it, these consequences were, first, 'no effective help can come to enable the Italians in Rome to turn against the Germans, and the dangers of a German Quisling Government being installed, or alternatively sheer anarchy supervening, will be aggravated and prolonged'. Secondly, 'if your rate of build-up is no more than twelve divisions by December 1, and these only in the Naples area, what is to prevent the Germans in the same time from bringing far larger forces against them?'

Roosevelt was also 'much distressed' by the December date, Churchill told Alexander. 'I hope however,' he ended, 'you will chase these clouds away.'[3]

Churchill's tiredness was a cause of concern to his doctor, who reported to Eden on August 26. 'He is worried,' Eden noted in his diary, 'says that he appears to be unduly depressed by troubles that are not immediate and unable to shake them off.' Later, when Eden saw Churchill, he noted: 'He did not look well and was a bad colour. He said to me that he felt the need for a longer change. I urged him to take it.'

Churchill also spoke to Eden about Eden's imminent return flight

---

[1] 'Welfare' No. 421, 'Most Secret and Personal', 25 August 1943: Cabinet papers, 120/113.
[2] Brooke diary, 25 August 1943: Bryant, *op. cit.*, volume 1, page 719.
[3] Prime Minister's Personal Telegram, T.1253/3, War Office telegram 62930, 'Secret, Private and Confidential', 26 August 1943: Churchill papers, 20/117.

to England by flying boat, together with Brooke, Portal and Mountbatten. 'I don't know what I should do if I lost you all,' Churchill commented. 'I'd have to cut my throat. It isn't just love, though there is much of that in it, but that you are my war machine. Brookie, Portal, you and Dickie. I simply couldn't replace you.' [1]

On August 26, Churchill left Quebec for the Laurentian mountains, to a mountain retreat on the Montmorency river, La Cabane de Montmorency, and a fishing camp on the Lac des Neiges, four thousand feet above sea level. 'This mountain air should bring new life to him,' Lord Moran noted, after Churchill had initiated him into the art of line fishing. 'When night fell,' Moran added, 'Winston came out on the wooden pier, gazing up at the Aurora Borealis. This quiet life is doing him good, but he feels he is playing truant.' [2]

On the following afternoon Anthony Eden and Cadogan drove over from their retreat to Churchill's. As they approached, they met John Martin and a detective. 'They said,' Cadogan noted in his diary, 'PM was "shooting the rapids" in a canoe, and they had come to pick him up!' [3] That night, Brooke and Portal also motored over from their mountain retreat an hour and a half's drive away, for dinner. Among Churchill's other guests were Eden, Cadogan and Moran. [4]

Churchill realized how much he needed his lakeside holiday. 'Should like to arrive Washington Wednesday 1st in time for dinner instead of Monday 30th,' he had telegraphed to Roosevelt on August 26. 'Hope this will not be inconvenient to you. I feel I require a little more rest.' [5] Roosevelt approved, warning Churchill only about the results of his fishing: 'Be sure to have the big ones weighed and verified by Mackenzie King.' [6] Churchill went one better, sending the biggest fish he caught to Roosevelt at Hyde Park.

With his daughter Mary, Churchill continued his fishing amid the quiet lakelands. 'Subaltern and I have caught a few,' Churchill telegraphed to Roosevelt on the afternoon of August 27, 'and the change and air are doing us all good.' Portal and Brooke 'have won great victories on the same front'. The British Cabinet, Churchill added, 'have cabled expressing pleasure at the satisfactory result of our Conference and urging me to take a holiday as all is quiet in England'. [7]

[1] Eden diary, 26 August 1943: Eden memoirs, *The Reckoning*, *op. cit.*, page 404.
[2] Moran notes for 26 August 1943: Moran, *op. cit.*, pages 114–15.
[3] Cadogan diary, 27 August 1943: David Dilks (editor), *op. cit.*, page 556.
[4] Brooke diary, 27 August 1943: Bryant, *op. cit.*, page 721.
[5] 'Welfare No. 435', Prime Minister's Personal Telegram, T.1255/3, 26 August 1943: Churchill papers, 20/117.
[6] 'Welfare No. 435', Prime Minister's Personal Telegram, T.1257/3, 27 August 1943: Churchill papers, 20/117.
[7] 'Personal and Most Secret', 27 August 1943: Cabinet papers, 120/89.

In the solitude at La Cabane, Churchill worked on the broadcast he had agreed to give to the Canadian people. He also dealt more briefly than usual with various queries which had been sent on to him. To a telegram from Attlee about the terms of surrender for Italy, he minuted briefly: 'I think Attlee's telegram settles this satisfactorily.'[1] To a note from Eden about the question of appointing a 'political adviser' for 'Overlord' he minuted equally briefly: 'I really don't want to be brought into this. Will you settle?'[2]

The mountain expedition was comfortable as well as relaxing. 'We lived in comfortable log houses,' John Martin wrote home, 'complete with electric light, sanitation, hot baths and a blazing log fire to sit round at night.'[3] Churchill remained at this retreat throughout August 28. 'Fishing' is the main note in his engagement card for that day.[4] There was fishing again on August 29, a Sunday.[5] At lunch, Cadogan was among the guests. 'WSC in terrific form,' he noted in his diary, 'singing Dan Leno's songs and other favourites of the Halls of forty years ago, together with the latest Noël Coward.'

Cadogan spent some time going through Churchill's broadcast, 'and got one or two things altered. He luckily then went to sleep.' That evening, Cadogan added, there was 'more singing at dinner'.[6]

On August 30 Churchill telegraphed to the King: 'I am benefitting from the outdoor life and change.'[7] That afternoon he went over his broadcast with Cadogan and, as Cadogan noted, 'concocted some more'. That evening, Churchill sat up talking with Ismay and Leslie Rowan until 3.45 in the morning.[8]

For Churchill's Private Office in London, their master's journeys were causing some concern. 'Please telegraph urgently details and times of future movements,' they telegraphed to Rowan on August 30, 'in order transmission of news may be arranged, particularly information from "C".'[9]

On the morning of August 31 Churchill returned to Quebec, where, from the Citadel, he made his broadcast to the Canadian people. 'Here at the gateway of Canada,' he proclaimed, 'in mighty lands which have never known the totalitarian tyrannies of Hitler and Mussolini, the spirit of freedom has found a safe and abiding home.'

---

[1] Prime Minister's Personal Minute, M (Q) 28/3, 27 August 1943: Churchill papers, 20/104.
[2] Prime Minister's Personal Minute, M (Q) 30/3, 27 August 1943: Churchill papers, 20/104.
[3] Letter of 29 August 1943: Martin papers.
[4] Saturday 28 August 1943: Prime Minister's Engagement Cards.
[5] Sunday 29 August 1943: Prime Minister's Engagement Cards.
[6] Cadogan diary, 29 August 1943: David Dilks (editor), op. cit., page 556.
[7] 'Welfare No. 472', 'With humble duty', 30 August 1943: Churchill papers, 20/129.
[8] Cadogan diary, 30 August 1943: David Dilks (editor), op. cit., pages 556–7.
[9] 'Concrete' No. 636, 'Most Secret', 30 August 1943: Cabinet papers, 120/93.

Churchill had been concerned, while at La Cabane, to make some favourable references to the Soviet Union's part in the Allied cause and deliberations. It would not have been suitable, he explained in his broadcast, for her to have been represented at a conference which had dealt so much with 'heating and inflaming the war against Japan'. As the Soviet Union had a five-year treaty of non-aggression with Japan, he explained, 'it would have been an embarrassing invitation for us to send'. But 'nothing is nearer to the wishes of President Roosevelt and myself', Churchill added, 'than to have a threefold meeting with Marshal Stalin'. If that meeting had not yet taken place, it was certainly not 'because we have not tried our best, or have not been willing to lay aside every impediment and undertake further journeys for that purpose'. There was no step which Britain and America might take in Europe, or might be forced to take by the 'unforeseeable course' of the war, 'about which we should not wish to consult with our Russian friends and allies in the fullest confidence and candour'.

To judge by the latest news from the Russian battle fronts, Churchill remarked, 'Marshal Stalin is certainly not wasting his time. The entire British Empire sends him our salutes on this brilliant summer campaign, and on the victories of Orel, Kharkov, and Taganrog, by which so much Russian soil had been relieved and so many hundreds of thousands of its invaders wiped out.'

Churchill also spoke to his Canadian listeners about the cross-Channel invasion. 'You would certainly not wish me to tell you when that is likely to happen,' he said, 'or whether it be soon or late; but whenever the great blow is struck, you may be sure that it will be because we are satisfied that there is a good chance of continuing success, and that our soldiers' lives will be expended in accordance with sound military plans' and not squandered for political considerations of any kind.'

Africa was 'cleared'. Mussolini was overthrown. The whole of the Balkans was 'aflame'. In occupied Europe the Germans were hated 'as no race has ever been hated in human history', and with good reason. 'We see them sprawled over a dozen once free and happy countries, with their talons making festering wounds, the scars of which will never be effaced.' But Nazi tyranny and Prussian militarism, 'those two loathsome dominations', might well foresee and dread 'their approaching doom'.[1]

Before Churchill made his speech, Ismay later recalled, he had been complaining 'that original composition was a terrible strain', but, Ismay added, 'his speech certainly gave no indication that his powers

[1] Broadcast of 31 August 1943: Churchill papers, 9/195.

were on the decline. It was magnificent in form, substance and delivery'.[1] That night, Churchill left Quebec by train for Washington.
His visit to the mountain, he wrote to the Countess of Athlone before
leaving, was 'the first real holiday I have had since the war began, and
I can imagine no more pleasant place in which I could have spent it'.
Even at La Cabane, there had been one immediate link with the war.
'I sympathize with you both,' Churchill wrote to Colonel Clarke and
his wife, 'in your anxieties about your gallant son who is a prisoner of
war.'[2] Churchill had also learned while at La Cabane of the death of
his aunt, Lady Leslie, and of the imminent death of his friend and pre-
war supporter, Sir Henry Strakosch.[3]

The ending of the Quebec conference marked the last stage in the
fixing of a joint Anglo-American strategy for the wars against
Germany and Japan. Churchill, Roosevelt and their advisers had established the early summer of 1944 as the date for the cross-Channel
invasion, with General Marshall as Supreme Commander. They had
ensured that some form of Italian campaign would be pursued, with
the Ancona–Pisa line as the northern limit of its action. They had agreed
on that most secret of secrets, the manufacture of the atom bomb, with a
pledge of 'full and effective interchange of information and ideas', and
with agreement 'never to use this agency against each other' and not to
use it against third parties 'without each other's consent'.[4]

At Quebec, Churchill and Roosevelt had also established the South-
East Asia Command, with Lord Louis Mountbatten as Supreme
Commander, and with Wingate as head of the Long Range Pene-
tration Group to act behind Japanese lines. They had given formal
Anglo-American recognition to the French Committee of National
Liberation, with de Gaulle and Giraud as its leaders.[5] They had
accepted Soviet participation in any armistice negotiations in western

---

[1] *The Memoirs of Lord Ismay, op. cit.*, page 318.

[2] Letter of 31 August 1943: Churchill papers, 20/94.

[3] In his will, published on 5 February 1944, Strakosch left Churchill £20,000.

[4] 'Articles of Agreement', 19 August 1943: Churchill papers, 4/299. Implementation of this
agreement was the responsibility of a specially established Combined Policy Committee, on
which the British representatives were Field Marshal Dill and Colonel J. J. Llewellin, British
Minister Resident in Washington. The Committee held its first meeting on 8 September 1943.
As a result of the Quebec agreement, as Sir Michael Perrin (a member of the 'Tube Alloys'
Directorate from 1941 to 1945) has commented, 'the presence of individual scientists from the
UK was allowed in some of the different laboratories, particularly Los Alamos where the actual
bomb was made, and they were able to make significant contributions'. (Sir Michael Perrin,
letter to Sir John Martin, 14 July 1977.)

[5] To the end of the Quebec Conference, however, Cordell Hull had refused to use the actual word
'recognition', so that the American and British formulations remained at variance with each other.

Europe, and invited Stalin to a tripartite meeting. Churchill suggested Algiers or Casablanca, but noted that Sicily, being 'conquered enemy territory', therefore 'commends itself to the Russians'.[1]

---

[1] 'Welfare' No. 571, (Churchill to Attlee and Eden), 2 September 1943: Churchill papers, 20/129.

29

The War in the Mediterranean, 'Improvise and dare'

REACHING Washington from Quebec on the afternoon of 1 September 1943, Churchill was told that Marshal Badoglio had agreed to the Allied surrender terms. He also learned, from Stalin, that the Soviet Union agreed to an Anglo-American request that the French National Liberation Committee should be represented on the Allied commission for negotiations with Italy.[1] That night, summoned to the White House, Sir Alexander Cadogan found Churchill 'very excited about Italian armistice negotiations'. Joined at midnight by General Marshall, Churchill, Ismay and Cadogan discussed the next military move and agreed, as Cadogan noted in his diary, to authorize Eisenhower to send an air-borne Division at the 'appropriate moment' to near Rome.[2] 'We highly approve your decision. . . .', Churchill and Roosevelt telegraphed to Eisenhower an hour after midnight.[3]

The Italian landing, operation 'Avalanche', was imminent. 'I hope you realize,' Churchill telegraphed to Attlee and Eden on September 2, 'the extreme hazard and gravity of the great battle impending at "Avalanche". Owing to the delays the Germans may be nearly as strong as us and able to build up quicker.' The Italian landing, he added, 'is the biggest risk we have yet run, though I am fully in favour of running it'. The Italian armistice, Churchill noted, 'would be blown sky high if we lost the battle and were driven back to the sea'. An 'equally unpleasant' situation would arise if the Germans 'seized Rome and set up a Quisling government', having made prisoners of the American Airborne Division. The 'overwhelming need' was

---

[1] 'Concrete' No. 683, 31 August 1943: Cabinet papers, 120/101.

[2] Cadogan diary, 1 September 1943: David Dilks (editor), op. cit., page 558.

[3] 'Welfare' No. 567, 'Personal, Secret', sent at 1 a.m. on 2 September 1943: Churchill papers, 20/129.

to win the battle in Italy 'and get Italians fighting Germans, and the Italian people and armies throughout Italy tearing up and obstructing the communications of the enemy'.[1]

The invasion of the mainland would begin 'almost immediately', Churchill and Roosevelt telegraphed to Stalin on September 2, and the 'heavy blow called "Avalanche" would be struck in next week or so'. Meanwhile, Eisenhower would be authorized to accept the Italian unconditional surrender on behalf of the Soviet Union, as well as of Britain and the United States, as 'matters are moving so fast'.[2]

September 3 marked the fourth anniversary of the day on which Britain had declared war on Germany. On the morning of that anniversary, Churchill learned from Alexander that operation 'Baytown' had begun, with British and Canadian forces landing on the Italian mainland opposite Sicily. The Canadians had captured Reggio and its airfield. The battle, Alexander noted, 'appears to be going well'.[3]

That same day, in the afternoon, Churchill learned from Alexander that the armistice had been signed between the Italians and the Allies, the Italian signatories having agreed to talk that same evening to arrange, as Alexander explained, the 'best resistance which Italian forces can contribute to our operations'.[4] The 'minor' enemy of more than three years had become an ally.

In searching for an acceptable location for the tripartite meeting between Stalin, Roosevelt and himself, on September 3 Churchill proposed Edinburgh or London, or both. The agenda, he telegraphed to Attlee and Eden, should include the question 'if we win what are we to do with Germany? Is it to be divided, and if so how.' There was also the question, which Maisky had raised earlier, of 'whether there should be spheres of influence or whether both the Anglo-Americans and the Russians should play over the whole field'. There would be 'no question', Churchill warned, 'of our disinteresting ourselves in any part of the world for out of this might immediately come the cause of a new war'.[5]

The question of location immediately proved a difficult one. Roosevelt 'now feels Edinburgh and London equally awkward from point of view of local American politics', Churchill informed Attlee and Eden later on September 3. 'I protested strongly against this ban

---

[1] 'Welfare' No 577, 2 September 1943: Churchill papers, 20/129.
[2] Prime Minister's Personal Telegram, T.1271/3, 2 September 1943: Churchill paper, 20/131.
[3] MA/493, 'Concrete' No. 720, 'Most Secret', 3 September 1943: Churchill papers, 20/117.
[4] MA/494, 'Concrete' No. 722, 'Most Secret', 3 September 1943: Churchill papers, 20/117. The actual surrender of Italy was signed by Marshal Badoglio on 28 September 1943, at Malta, on board the battleship *Nelson*. On 13 October 1943 the Royal Italian Government declared war on Germany.
[5] 'Welfare' No. 582, 3 September 1943: Cabinet papers, 120/96.

but I do not think that it is likely to be overcome on account of it being election year.' In these circumstances, Churchill now proposed Casablanca 'or somewhere thereabouts'.[1]

Churchill remained in Washington for five days. 'I deliberately prolonged my stay in the United States,' he later recalled, 'in order to be in close contact with our American friends at this critical moment in Italian affairs.'[2] 'Winston will, I think, settle down in US!' Cadogan noted in his diary.[3] 'The PM has a beautifully cool air-conditioned room,' John Martin wrote home on September 4, 'but we work next to him (and sleep) in the atmosphere of a hot-house and the constant transition from one to the other is a Bad Thing.'[4]

On September 4 Churchill was the guest at a Washington Press lunch, and, as Cadogan noted, 'did awfully well in reply to questions'.[5] That evening he and Roosevelt worked on their respective messages to Stalin, with Cadogan acting as adviser. 'I was there till 8,' Cadogan wrote home to his wife, 'running between the PM in bed and the President in his study.' Cadogan added: 'The PM's sleeping arrangements have now become quite promiscuous. He talks with the President till 2 a.m., and consequently spends a large part of the day hurling himself violently in and out of bed, bathing at unsuitable moments and rushing up and down corridors in his dressing gown.'[6] 'The President and I,' Churchill informed Attlee and Eden, 'talked together up till two a.m. this morning and on the very best of terms.'[7]

On September 5 Churchill sent the messages to the Soviet leader which Roosevelt had read and approved. In the first message, Churchill reported on the successful landing opposite Sicily, and the 'imminent' landing further north, telling Stalin that although he believed 'we shall get ashore' further north, 'I cannot foresee what will happen in Rome or throughout Italy.' The 'dominant aim', Churchill added, 'should be to kill Germans and to make Italians kill Germans on the largest scale possible in this theatre'.[8]

In a second telegram to Stalin on September 5, Churchill expressed his concern to know 'what your wishes are about the future', and to give Stalin 'our views so far as they are formed'. To this end, Churchill said, he was willing 'if necessary' to go to Moscow. If however Stalin

[1] 'Welfare' No. 593, 3 September 1943: Cabinet papers, 120/96.
[2] Winston S. Churchill, *The Second World War*, volume 5, London 1952, page 110.
[3] Cadogan diary, 3 September 1943: David Dilks (editor), *op. cit.*, page 558.
[4] Letter of 4 September 1943: Martin papers.
[5] Cadogan diary, 4 September 1943: David Dilks (editor), *op. cit.*, pages 558–9.
[6] Letter of 4 September 1943: David Dilks (editor), *op. cit.*, page 559.
[7] 'Welfare' No. 604, 'Most Secret and Personal', 5 September 1943: Churchill papers, 20/129.
[8] Prime Minister's Personal Telegram, T.1290/3, 'Welfare' No. 606, 'Most Secret', 5 September 1943: Churchill papers, 20/117.

wished to go into the technical details 'of why we have not yet invaded France across the Channel and why we cannot do it sooner in greater strength than is now proposed', he would welcome a separate technical mission of Soviet generals and admirals, and this could be held in London, or in Edinburgh. At such a meeting of military experts, which could take place in October, 'the fullest possible exposition of our thought, resources, and intentions could be laid before them and thrashed out'.[1] To Smuts, Churchill telegraphed that same day:

I think it inevitable that Russia will be the greatest land power in the world after this war which will have rid her of the two military powers, Japan and Germany, who in our lifetime have inflicted upon her such heavy defeats. I hope, however, that the 'fraternal association' of the British Commonwealth and the United States together with sea and air power, may put us on good terms and in a friendly balance with Russia at least for the period of re-building. Further than that I cannot see with mortal eye, and I am not as yet fully informed about the celestial telescopes.[2]

On September 5 Churchill left Washington by train for Boston. The train left Washington at ten o'clock in the evening. 'He then started to compose his speech,' Elizabeth Layton wrote to her mother, 'and P. Kinna and I laboured away alternately. We packed the Old Man off at about 2.30, then I did the speech form, and we both went to bed at 4.30.'[3] John Martin and Sir Alexander Cadogan had both been in attendance as the speech was fashioned. 'I had various brushes with him while he was in bed on the train,' Cadogan noted in his diary on the following day; 'he had wanted to leave China out of the Great Four in a most pointed and wounding way. He changed it,' Cadogan added, 'with much blasphemy.'[4]

Reaching Boston on the morning of September 6, Churchill was driven to Harvard, where he received an honorary degree. 'The PM in Oxford doctor's cap and gown,' John Martin wrote home, 'looked like a genial Henry VIII.'[5]

In his acceptance speech Churchill spoke of how 'the long arm of destiny' had twice in his lifetime reached out to the United States and twice the United States had responded. The price of greatness was responsibility. One could not rise to be 'in many ways the leading community in the civilized world', without being involved in its problems,

[1] Prime Minister's Personal Telegram, T.1291/3, 'Welfare' No. 613, 'Most Secret', 5 September 1943: Churchill papers, 20/117.
[2] Prime Minister's Personal Telegram, T.1287/3, No. 1149 to South Africa, 'Most Secret and Personal', 'For you alone', 5 September 1943: Churchill papers, 20/117.
[3] Elizabeth Layton, letter of 6 September 1943: Nel papers.
[4] Cadogan diary, 6 September 1943: David Dilks (editor), op. cit., page 559.
[5] Letter of 7 September 1943: Martin papers.

'convulsed by its agonies and inspired by its causes'. Churchill added:

We do not war primarily with races as such. Tyranny is our foe, whatever trappings or disguise it wears, whatever language it speaks, be it external or internal, we must for ever be on our guard, ever mobilized, ever vigilant, always ready to spring at its throat. In all this, we march together. Not only do we march and strive shoulder to shoulder at this moment under the fire of the enemy on the fields of war or in the air, but also in those realms of thought which are consecrated to the rights and the dignity of man.

During his speech, Churchill had a message for the youth of America. 'Even elderly Parliamentarians like myself,' he said, 'are forced to acquire a high degree of mobility. But to the youth of America, as to all the Britons I say: "You cannot stop. There is no halting place at the point we have now reached in our journey. It must be world anarchy or world order."'

Churchill went on to stress the need for the closest possible Anglo-American intimacy, both during the war and after it. Both countries shared common conceptions of what was 'right and decent'. Both had 'a marked regard for fair play', especially to the weak and poor. Both share 'a stern sentiment of impartial justice, and above all the love of personal freedom'. The 'gift of a common tongue' was, he urged, 'a priceless inheritance' which might some day become the foundation of a common citizenship. 'I like to think,' Churchill said, 'of British and Americans moving about freely over each other's wide estates with hardly a sense of being foreigners to one another.' He did not see why they should not try 'to spread our common language even more widely throughout the globe'.

The war, Churchill warned, was entering perhaps, for the British and Americans, 'upon its most severe and costly phase'. But, he continued:

I am here to tell you that, whatever form our system of world security may take, however the nations are grouped and ranged, whatever derogations are made from national sovereignty for the sake of the large synthesis, nothing will work soundly or for long without the united effort of the British and American peoples.

If we are together nothing is impossible. If we are divided all will fail. I therefore preach continually the doctrine of the fraternal association of our two peoples, not for any purpose of gaining invidious material advantages for either of them, not for territorial aggrandisement or the vain pomp of earthly domination, but for the sake of service to mankind and for the honour that comes to those who faithfully serve great causes.[1]

Churchill's speech was 'very good', Cadogan noted in his diary.[2]

[1] Speech of 6 September 1943: Harvard University, Cambridge, Massachusetts, printed as War Cabinet paper No. 398 of 1943, 20 September 1943: Churchill papers, 23/11.
[2] Cadogan diary, 6 September 1943: David Dilks (editor), *op. cit.*, page 559.

'Dear old man,' noted Elizabeth Layton, 'he made a simply wonderful speech—he just had them all in the palm of his hand. It was one of his very best deliveries—one felt he was completely master of everything he said and that even a bomb wouldn't have shaken him. He was as calm and firm as a rock, and he made the most of every little point. He made one good crack—a typical Winston touch. He said, speaking of modern times, "the infernal combustion engine—I mean the *internal* combustion engine"—which pleased the audience highly. It sounded like a slip, but I ha'e me doots.'[1] It emerged that Patrick Kinna had heard the 'slip' being rehearsed on the train from Washington.[2]

During the journey back to Washington, Elizabeth Layton wrote to her mother, 'I was sitting beside him when suddenly he said how long had it been since I saw you.' Learning that Miss Layton's mother had specially flown from Vancouver to Montreal in order to be with her daughter for a while, 'he said he'd like to pay half your fare, but that I was to say it came from me'.[3] He understood, he said, why Miss Layton herself had gone to Britain after the outbreak of war, telling her: 'I know—you just wanted to be *in it.*'

'I should like a tabular report of the reactions of all important American newspapers to my Harvard statement,' Churchill minuted to Brendan Bracken, 'showing which are for and which against.'[4] That day, at John Martin's request a digest of the press comment had already been completed by a member of the British Embassy staff in Washington, the Oxford philosopher Isaiah Berlin. 'The speech,' wrote Berlin, 'the importance of which is being grasped, is likely to provide a cardinal text for concrete discussion of the Anglo-American future.' It had come at a moment when there was 'a strong sense of Anglo-American solidarity (tacitly acknowledged even by those who most condemned it) in the face of a disturbingly aloof Russian attitude'. Berlin noted however that the speech had encountered 'several accidental handicaps' and he went on to explain: 'The White House announcement that the speech would contain little of political significance deflected the attention of editors and political commentators.' At the same time, 'a number of train wrecks occurred within this same twenty-four hours, one of them

---

[1] Elizabeth Layton, letter of 6 September 1943: Nel papers.
[2] Elizabeth Layton, letter of 18 October 1943: Nel papers.
[3] Elizabeth Layton, letter of 6 September 1943: Nel papers. The cost of the fare was $200, towards which Churchill paid $100.
[4] Prime Minister's Personal Minute, M(Q)37/3, 10 September 1943: Churchill papers, 9/196.

the most sensational in many years, and monopolized headlines'.[1]

Churchill's speech, declared the *New York Times*, 'has opened up a vast and hopeful field of discussion. Down the grim corridors of war light begins to show.'[2]

On the afternoon of September 6, Churchill returned by train to Washington. 'Winston enjoyed himself hugely,' Cadogan wrote of the 17 hour journey, 'making V-signs from the train window at all the engine drivers on the line and at all the passers-by. He quite unnecessarily rushes out on to the rear platform of the car, in a flowered silk dressing-gown, to attract and chat with anyone he can find on the platform at stopping-places.'[3]

On reaching Washington at eight in the morning of September 7, Churchill was shown a telegram from Alexander reporting continued advances up the toe of Italy. The Eighth Army, Alexander reported, 'are in good heart and very satisfied with progress, operations and maintenance'.[4] In reply, Churchill expressed his concern for the build-up after the 'Avalanche' landing, now planned for Salerno on September 9. 'Surely,' Churchill telegraphed, 'if you can get port of Naples in working order you should be able to push in two divisions a week.' On a front which would be about 170 miles long, 'one never can tell if given time Germans may not bring real punch to bear. . . .'[5]

Churchill now waited in Washington for the Salerno landing. 'On this landing,' Lord Moran noted, 'he has been building all his hopes. There are no doubts of any kind in his mind; anyway he admits none. It *must* succeed, and then Naples will fall into our hands.' On the evening of September 6, Churchill had talked 'of meeting Alex in Rome before long'. The capture of Rome, Moran added, 'has fired his imagination; more than once he has spoken about Napoleon's Italian campaign'.[6]

While awaiting news of the Salerno landing, Churchill put to Roosevelt a proposal for maintaining the Combined Anglo-American

[1] On 30 August 1943 the Lackawanna Limited, travelling between New York and Chicago, was in collision with a freight train; twenty-seven passengers were killed. On 6 September 1943 the Congressional Limited, a luxury train running from Washington to New York, was derailed in north east Philadelphia: initially, 150 passengers were reported killed. Two days later, the death toll was confirmed at seventy-nine; one of the worst disasters in United States railway history.

[2] Isaiah Berlin, 'American Press Comment on Mr Churchill's Harvard Speech of September 6th, 1943', 10 September 1943: Churchill papers, 9/196.

[3] Letter of 7 September 1943: David Dilks (editor), *op. cit.*, pages 559–60.

[4] MA/525, 'Most Secret and Personal', 6 September 1943: Churchill papers, 20/117.

[5] 'Welfare' No. 640, Prime Minister's Personal Telegram, T.1297/3, 'Personal and Private', 7 September 1943: Churchill papers, 20/117.

[6] Moran diary and notes, 7 September 1943: Moran, *op. cit.*, page 118.

Chiefs of Staff after the war, 'on, say, a ten-year footing', as he explained to Attlee, Eden, the Chiefs of Staff Committee and the King on September 7. Roosevelt had 'liked the idea at first sight', Churchill reported. 'It involves no treaty and can be represented simply as a war-time measure.' Once set up and maintained for some years in peace, it would have 'such great advantages to both sides that it might well become permanent'. There would be a 'complete interchange' of officers in the colleges, similarly of training and weapons, 'continued sharing of research and inventions', mutual accommodation at bases, all this 'springing up under the guise of military needs but in fact weaving the two countries together as the one ultimate bulwark against another war'.

Churchill's telegram ended:

There is no doubt that Americans have a high respect for us now and have become deeply conscious of our military efficiency and strength. This is a great change from pre-Pearl Harbour and even from pre-Alamein days. I hope our countries wll be pleased at the brilliant fruition of our plans and efforts. However, our chickens are not yet hatched though one can hear them pecking at their shells.[1]

The long-awaited Italian surrender took place on the afternoon of September 8. That night, German forces began to occupy Rome. Marshal Badoglio, and the Italian Royal family, made their escape in the early hours of September 9, driving to the Adriatic port of Pescara, and then being taken in two corvettes to Brindisi. There, protected by the Allied occupation forces, they set up an anti-Fascist Italian Government.

As Badoglio and the King were on their way to Brindisi, units of the Italian Fleet, including the flagship *Roma*, and four other battleships, pursued their course for Malta, seeking safety under the British guns which had so recently been their target. Attacked by German aircraft, *Roma* was sunk. In the early hours of September 9, operation 'Avalanche', the Salerno landings, began and, on the heel of Italy, part of the British 1st Airborne Division, carried in naval warships, was admitted to Taranto by the Italians.

The first setback in the Allied plans came with the cancellation of Eisenhower's planned airborne assault near Rome, originally timed to co-incide with the Salerno landing. The operation had been postponed, Alexander informed Churchill, 'as no, repeat no, arrangement for its reception has been made by Italians and we have reason to believe the Germans are in occupation of airfields'.[2]

---

[1] 'Welfare' No. 650, 'Most Secret and Personal', 7 September 1943: Churchill papers, 20/129.
[2] MA/104, 'Most Secret', 8 September 1943: Churchill papers, 20/118.

In Washington, Cadogan had noted on September 8: 'The PM, oddly enough, is fairly calm, or was when I saw him last this afternoon.'[1] On learning from General Maitland Wilson of his imminent attack on Rhodes, Churchill telegraphed: 'Good. This is a time to play high. Improvise and dare.'[2] But that same morning, in a memorandum for Roosevelt and the Combined Chiefs of Staff, Churchill warned that, even if it proved possible for the Allies to advance north of Naples, and beyond Rome, the possibility of a strong German counter-attack by the end of the year 'cannot be excluded'. What was needed, when the Allied troops reached the main German positions, was to build 'a strong fortified line of our own', in order to remain on the defensive until the spring of 1944, when a decision could be made to make an offensive 'if the enemy were weak', or to threaten an offensive, or to stand on the defensive.

Churchill also saw opportunities in an advance up Italy for the Balkan theatre, to give greater help to the 'Patriot' partisans:

If we can get an agreement between the Patriots and the Italian troops it should be possible to open quite soon one or more good ports on the Dalmatian coast, enabling munitions and supplies to be sent in by ship and all forces that will obey our orders to be raised to good fighting condition. The German situation in all this theatre will become most precarious, especially from the point of view of supplies. When the defensive line across Northern Italy has been completed it may be possible to spare some of our own forces assigned to the Mediterranean theatre to emphasize a movement north and north eastward from the Dalmatian ports.

For the moment, Churchill urged, the 'utmost efforts' should be made to organize the attack upon the Germans throughout the Balkan peninsula 'and to supply agents, arms, and good direction'. There should also be 'improvised expeditionary forces and garrisons' for 'various minor ventures', including Rhodes and several other of the Dodecanese Islands off the Turkish coast, a French National Committee expedition against Corsica, and some Allied help to the Italians in Sardinia, to procure 'the disarmament of any German units there'.[3]

Churchill, Pound, Dill and Ismay were among those who discussed Churchill's memorandum with Roosevelt, Marshall, King, Arnold and others at the White House on the afternoon of September 9. The meeting began by a discussion of the 'considerable odds in favour of

[1] Letter of 8 September 1943: David Dilks (editor), *op. cit.*, page 560.
[2] Prime Minister's Personal Telegram, T.1304/3, 'Welfare' No. 669, OZ 2722, 9 September 1943: Churchill papers, 20/118.
[3] 'Welfare' No. 674 (to Attlee, Eden and Brooke), 'Personal', 9 September 1943. Churchill papers, 20/129.

the acquisition of the Italian Fleet', and Churchill hoped that, when-ever it might arrive, this Fleet 'would be treated with respect by the Allies'. This, he said, 'was very important for the future'. Churchill then read out his memorandum, in which, writing of the 1944 cam-paign in Italy, he stressed the need to be 'very chary of advancing northward beyond the narrow part of the Italian peninsula'. 'Of course,' Churchill added, 'if the Germans retreat to the Alps another situation is presented, but, failing that, it would seem beyond our strength, having regard to the requirements of "Overlord", to broaden out into the plains of Lombardy.'

Churchill went on to suggest the construction of a 'strong fortified line of our own', making use of Italian military labour, and with Italian troops 'naturally' taking part in defending it. Thus, by the spring of 1944, 'we should be able in this theatre either to make an offensive if the enemy were weak, and anyhow to threaten one, or, on the other hand, stand on the defensive, using our air-power, which will in the meanwhile have been built up, from behind our fortified line, and divert a portion of our troops for action elsewhere, either to the west or to the east'.

In reading out this memorandum, Churchill paused at the Balkan section to 'consider briefly' the forces that might be available to, and on, the Dalmatian coast. The 75,000 to 80,000 men of the Polish Army, 'now well equipped', were, he said 'burning to engage the enemy'. Then there was the New Zealand Division. The time would come when all that was required in the Balkans were garrison forces 'with a few of our mobile columns. We would be settling down to action in a friendly area.' Roosevelt agreed: in the Balkans, he said, 'we should be prepared to take advantage of any opportunity that presented itself'.[1]

That evening, Alexander telegraphed to Churchill that 'Commando now holds half Salerno. . . .', and, at the heel of Italy, 'first contingent of British 1st Airborne entered Taranto this evening. . . .'[2]

For some months, Dudley Pound's work had suffered as a result of a stroke. While in Washington, the effects of the stroke became

---

[1] On September 12 the Minister of State, Cairo, Richard Casey, telegraphed to Churchill: 'SOE have dropped into Balkans to date, for the maintenance and stimulation of guerrillas, the equivalent of one and a half million pounds sterling in gold and local currencies.' Of this one million had gone into Greece, 440,000 pounds to Mihailovic and his Chetniks, and 'only small amounts' to Tito, and to Albania. In August, SOE had dropped 245 tons of ammunition, 79 individuals and 26 wireless sets into Yugoslavia and Greece (MOS 84, 'Personal and Secret', 12 September 1943: Churchill papers, 20/118).

[2] MA/111, 'Most Secret', 'Personal', sent 9.40 p.m., 9 September 1943: Churchill papers, 20/118.

more pronounced. Nine years later, Churchill recalled the evening of September 9:

In the White House the President and I sat talking after dinner in his study, and Admiral Pound came to see us upon a naval point. The President asked him several questions about the general aspects of the war, and I was pained to see that my trusted naval friend had lost the outstanding matter-of-fact precision which characterised him. Both the President and I were sure he was very ill. Next morning Pound came to see me in my big bed-sitting-room and said abruptly, 'Prime Minister, I have come to resign. I have had a stroke and my right side is largely paralysed. I thought it would pass off, but it gets worse every day and I am no longer fit for duty.' I at once accepted the First Sea Lord's resignation, and expressed my profound sympathy for his breakdown in health. I told him he was relieved at that moment from all responsibility, and urged him to rest for a few days and then come home with me in the *Renown*. He was completely master of himself, and his whole manner was instinct with dignity. As soon as he left the room I cabled to the Admiralty placing Vice-Admiral Syfret in responsible charge from that moment pending the appointment of a new First Sea Lord.[1]

'Can nothing be done, Charles?' Churchill asked Lord Moran that night. 'Will he get better?'[2]

---

[1] Winston S. Churchill, *The Second World War*, volume 6, London 1952, page 118.
[2] Moran notes for 9 September 1943: Moran, *op. cit.*, pages 118–19.

30
September 1943, Returning Home

WHILE Churchill was in Washington on 9 September 1943, he received a telegram from Stalin, proposing Moscow as the meeting place for the Allied Foreign Ministers, and Teheran for the three leaders.[1] 'I should have preferred Cyprus or Khartoum,' Churchill replied, 'but I defer to your wishes.' On this meeting, Churchill added, 'may depend not only the best and shortest method of finishing the war, but also those good arrangements for the future of the world which will enable the British, American, and Russian nations to render a lasting service to humanity'.

Of the battle in Italy, Churchill informed Stalin: 'We have got a substantial force ashore and are engaging the Germans.'[2] That night German troops completed their occupation of Rome. In the eastern Mediterranean, British forces occupied the Italian island of Kastelorizo.[3] But two British officers who were parachuted on Rhodes failed to obtain the Italian authorities' agreement to surrender the island.

Twice on September 10, Churchill telephoned Eden to discuss the day's developments. Eden was angered at what he called Roosevelt's 'alacrity' in accepting Moscow for the Foreign Ministers' conference. He was also worried that Churchill, 'by prolonging his stay in Washington', was strengthening the American impression 'that militarily all the achievements are theirs'.[4]

During September 10 Churchill was introduced to the senior members of the British Embassy staff in Washington, members of the

---

[1] Telegram of 8 September 1943: Churchill papers, 20/132.

[2] 'Welfare No. 681', Prime Minister's Personal Telegram, T.1313/3, 'Most Secret and Personal', 10 September 1943: Churchill papers, 20/118.

[3] Also known as Castelrosso.

[4] Eden diary, 10 September 1943: Eden memoirs, *The Reckoning*, op. cit., page 405.

many British delegations and missions then in the American capital.[1]
There was now a 'chance', he told them, not only of 'freeing Italy
from the Nazi yoke', but of bringing Italy into the war against
Germany, and of 'definitely turning the Italians against the Germans
for many years to come'. The capture of the Italian port of Taranto
was 'very important', opening up as it did 'the way to the Adriatic
and the Balkans, where it was to be hoped the Italian troops would
now be able to establish friendly contact with the patriot forces in
Greece and Yugoslavia'. The German position in the Balkans, he
forecast, 'would certainly greatly deteriorate'.

Speaking of the Soviet Union, Churchill said that 'he was prepared
to be patient with the Russians and would not be deterred by harsh
words from his efforts to reach agreement with them'. He was 'always
prepared', he said, 'to be snubbed for his country'. He hoped 'before
long' to bring about a Three-Power meeting between himself, Roosevelt and Stalin 'at which progress could be made with laying the
foundation for the future'. He was 'convinced', however, 'that we
should do much better with the Russians if we first got on to intimate
terms with the US. It was important not to allow the Russians to try
to play the US and the UK off against each other.'[2]

On September 10, Roosevelt left Washington for Hyde Park. Before
he left he said to Churchill, as Ismay later recalled: 'Winston, please
treat the White House as your home. Invite anyone you like to any
meals, and do not hesitate to summon any of my advisers with whom
you wish to confer at any time you wish. Please break your journey to
Halifax at Hyde Park and tell me all about it.'[3]

Churchill did as Roosevelt had suggested, and at a meeting at the
White House on September 11, pressed the American Chiefs of Staff
for a swifter reinforcement of the Allied troops already in Italy. The
existing pace of reinforcement was, he said, 'unacceptable'. General
Marshall agreed to accelerate the current plans. 'Even the acceleration

---

[1] Among them Colonel J. J. Llewellin (Minister Resident for Supply), Field Marshal Sir John
Dill and Commander R. Coleridge (Joint Staff Mission), Admiral Sir Percy Noble (British
Admiralty Delegation), Lieutenant-General Sir G. N. Macready (British Army Staff), Air
Marshal Sir William Welsh (Royal Air Force Delegation), Sir Girja Bajpai (Indian Agent
General), G. Archer (British Raw Materials Mission), Hon. D. Bowes Lyon (Political Warfare
Executive), Hon. R. H. Brand (British Food Mission), Sir Richard Fairey (British Air Commis-
sion), J. F. Leckie (Board of Trade Delegation), J. Maclay (British Merchant Shipping Mission),
E. Melville (British Colonies Supply Mission), Professor D. Robertson (UK Treasury Delegation),
and General Sir Walter Venning (British Ministry of Supply Mission).

[2] 'Record of a meeting held at the British Embassy Washington on September 10th, 1943',
Washington, 11 September 1943: Cabinet papers, 120/89. The transcript of this meeting was
subsequently printed for the War Cabinet as War Cabinet Paper No. 430 of 1943, 'Secret', 5
October 1943: Premier papers, 3/366/8, folios 176–80.

[3] Ismay recollections: Ismay memoirs, *op. cit.*, page 319.

of one division by a fortnight,' Churchill urged, 'might make a big difference.' [1]

Half an hour before midnight on September 11, Churchill, his wife and daughter, left Washington for the overnight journey to Hyde Park. At 9.30 on the morning of September 11 they were greeted by Roosevelt, with whom they spent the day. The news from Salerno was of a hold-up in the landing. 'It looked,' Ismay later recalled, 'as though no headway was being made, and the Prime Minister was most upset. It reminded him of the Suvla landing in the Gallipoli campaign, when the troops got ashore successfully but failed to move inland for two or three days, thus giving the enemy time to concentrate against them.' [2]

September 12 was the Churchills' thirty-fifth wedding anniversary. The day 'passed very happily', Mary Churchill later recalled, 'my mother confiding to me that my father had told her that "he loved her more and more every year"'. At dinner that night, Roosevelt proposed their health, 'and afterwards drove us all down to the little railway station near Hyde Park, where we took our leave of him'. [3]

At 10.30 that night Churchill's train left for Halifax, which it reached at noon on September 14, a journey of more than thirty-seven hours. [4]

While Churchill was travelling through Maine and Quebec, German parachutists in central Italy seized Mussolini, whom Marshal Badoglio had interned, and took him to see Hitler. Henceforth, a Fascist Government on the shores of Lake Garda maintained the fiction of Mussolini's rule. Badoglio hurried south, where he was eventually installed under the Allied aegis in Brindisi. The Salerno landings began to gain ground. Italy had become a battlefield.

Throughout September 13 Churchill was travelling by train towards Halifax. He was unhappy with the news that had reached him from the Mediterranean. During the journey he dictated a telegram to General Maitland Wilson:

> The capture of Rhodes by you at this time with Italian aid would be a fine contribution to the general war. Let me know what are your plans for this. Can you not improvise the necessary garrison out of the forces in the Middle East? What is your total ration strength?

---

[1] 'Minutes of a Meeting held at the White House, on 11th September, 1943': Churchill papers, 23/12.
[2] Ismay recollections: Ismay memoirs, *op. cit.*, page 319.
[3] Mary Churchill diary and recollections: Mary Soames, page 340.
[4] 'September 11–14, 1943', White House Itinerary: Thompson papers.

This is a time to think of Clive and Peterborough and of Rooke's men taking Gibraltar.[1]

Churchill also telegraphed to the Chiefs of Staff Committee, insisting that 'our prime duty is to accelerate the build-up in Italy', and he added: 'We must on no account be guilty of failing to nourish the battle.' In his telegram, Churchill cast about for reserves of un-utilized troops, seeking to move the maximum numbers to the Italian battle zone. 'We must at all costs,' he said, 'avoid letting our forces stand idle or be frittered away.' Troops should be sent from Sicily and North Africa. As for the operation against Rhodes, 'to my certain knowledge there is the best part of an Army Corps in Cyprus and at least two divisions, apart from the Poles, in Syria'. Churchill's telegram ended with a final reference to Rhodes and the Dodecanese: 'This is the moment,' he wrote, 'for intensification of effort and for running small-scale risks audaciously. If we fail to profit by our good fortune now, we shall lose in History the credit we have so painfully gained.'[2]

Searching for a means of influencing the battle at Salerno, Churchill telegraphed that day to General Alexander:

I hope you are watching above all the Battle of 'Avalanche', which domin-ates everything. None of the commanders engaged has fought a large-scale battle before. The Battle of Suvla Bay was lost because Ian Hamilton was advised by his C.G.S. to remain at a remote central point where he would know everything. Had he been on the spot he could have saved the show. At this distance and with time-lags I cannot pretend to judge, but I feel it my duty to set before you this experience of mine from the past.

Nothing should be denied which will nourish the decisive battle for Naples.

Ask for anything you want, and I will make allocation of necessary supplies with highest priority irrespective of every other consideration.[3]

By the time Churchill's telegram reached Italy, Alexander was already on his way to Salerno. 'I feel sure you will be glad to know,' he replied, 'that I have already anticipated your wise advice and am now here with Fifth Army. Many thanks for your offer of help. Everything possible is being done to make "Avalanche" a success. Its fate will be decided in the next few days.'[4]

[1] 'Welfare' No. 716, Prime Minister's Personal Telegram, T.1331/3, Passed to Middle East as OZ 2770, 'Personal and Most Secret', 13 September 1943: Churchill papers, 20/118.

[2] 'Welfare' No. 720, 'Most Secret and Personal', 13 September 1943: Churchill papers, 20/129.

[3] 'Welfare' No. 721, 'Prime Minister's Personal Telegram, T.1334/3, War Office Telegram No. 69100, sent at 7 a.m., 14 September 1943: Churchill papers, 20/118.

[4] 'Concrete' No. 896, MA/142, 'Personal', 4.43 a.m., 15 September 1943: Cabinet papers, 120/102.

During September 14, while Churchill was still on his way to Halifax, the Italian garrison on Rhodes surrendered to the Germans. Kastelorizo and Samos received small British garrisons. Churchill's hopes of a swift seizure of Rhodes, the prize, were dashed. 'Situation Rhodes deteriorated too rapidly for us to take action,' Maitland Wilson telegraphed to Churchill in reply to his earliest message. 'Italians surrendered town and harbour after light bombing.' The Eighth Indian Division, which had been 'trained and rehearsed' to seize Rhodes, was 'now diverted' to the Central Mediterranean, its ships and landing craft having been dispersed, Wilson explained, 'by order of Admiralty'.[1]

During his thirty-seven hour journey to Halifax, Churchill informed Eden that any 'differences' which might emerge during the Foreign Ministers' conference in Moscow should be left 'for the ultimate crush' at the personal meeting of the Heads of Government. Churchill still hoped to persuade Stalin to come for this meeting of leaders to Cairo, Khartoum, Cyprus or, 'if we can get it', Rhodes. If it was felt better to use ships as the base for the leaders themselves, then Churchill suggested Beirut harbour, Haifa or Alexandria 'for the personal meeting'. Only 'if all else fails', he told Eden, would Roosevelt feel able to go as far as Teheran, 'but this is really hard measure and should be resisted so far as possible'.[2] 'I still hope,' Churchill telegraphed to Stalin that same day, 'you will consider Egypt, or perhaps a Syrian port like Beirut, or a shipboard conference in one of the harbours of Egypt or the Levant, or possibly at Cyprus,' where each leader would 'have a ship'. Wherever they chose, the Press would be 'entirely banished' and the whole place 'sealed off' by a cordon, 'so that we are not disturbed in any way in these conversations upon which, I repeat, the hopeful future of the world depends'.[3]

To the Chiefs of Staff, Churchill sent on September 14 a rebuke concerning their hesitations to initiate action in the Balkans. Considering the 'many immense holes' made in the German system in the Balkans, Churchill wrote, 'a negative attitude on our part would be wrong' and he went on to explain:

I have never contemplated heavy-footed operations of 'being drawn into a fresh campaign with inadequate forces', but it would be folly not to exploit the

---

[1] CIC/119, 'Private and Personal', 14 September 1943: Churchill papers, 20/118.
[2] 'Welfare No. 722', 'Most Secret and Personal', 14 September 1943: Churchill papers, 20/129.
[3] 'Welfare No. 731', 'Most Secret and Personal', 14 September 1943: Churchill papers, 20/129.

highly favourable possibilities now offered to us without in any way prejudicing the build up in Italy. We should certainly try to obtain some seaports on the eastern side of the Adriatic and excite and sustain the patriot activities to the utmost. There seems at this distance to be a lack of energy and enterprise in the Middle East Command. Although we cannot fight a Balkan campaign ourselves we ought to use enough force to stimulate others to do it.

Any further 'serious defeats' inflicted on the Germans by the Russians would, Churchill added, have 'great effects' in the Balkans, where it was 'far from certain' that the Germans might not have to withdraw to the River Sava and the Danube before the end of the year. Nor should 'psychological factors' be overlooked. In Italy these had proved 'overwhelming' and produced results 'far beyond reach of our physical resources'. The Balkans were an 'even more explosive' area. Changes might 'easily' take place in Hungary, Roumania and Bulgaria 'which would open the passage of the Dardanelles and the Bosphorus to Russian supplies across the Black Sea'.[1]

In a second telegram to the Chiefs of Staff, dictated during his train journey to Halifax, Churchill expressed his dissatisfaction at the proposed rate of transfer of troops to the Italian mainland. 'It is now four months since I suggested that the Polish Corps should be brought from the Levant,' he wrote. 'Why can it not be employed before January?' Nor, Churchill had been told, could the First Armoured Division be ready for action until mid-January, as it had become 'disorganized' in the previous months. 'It is a scandal,' he wrote, 'that our best division should be mauled and melted down in this way.'[2]

Churchill also dictated a telegram to his son during the long train journey, Randolph being with Alexander's army in southern Italy. Signed 'Air Commodore Spencer', Churchill's message contained the tantalizing sentence: 'I hope to drop in upon you one of these fine days.'[3]

Churchill had one more message to send before reaching Halifax. It was headed 'On the train' and it began: 'Dear Franklin'. In his letter, Churchill told the President how much he had 'enjoyed this trip', and what a pleasure it had been to him, his wife and their daughter 'to receive your charming hospitality at the White House and at Hyde Park'. Churchill's letter ended: 'You know how I treasure the friendship with which you have honoured me and how profoundly I

---

[1] 'Welfare No. 730', 14 September 1943: Churchill papers, 20/129.
[2] 'Welfare No. 730', 14 September 1943: Churchill papers, 20/129. The answer to Churchill's question about the Polish Corps was, (a) that it had not finished equipping, owing to its low priority and (b) a shortage of shipping.
[3] 'Welfare No. 733', War Office Telegram No. 69188, 'Most Secret', 14 September 1943: Churchill papers, 1/375.

feel that we might together do something really fine and lasting for our two countries and, through them, for the future of all.'[1]

Churchill reached Halifax shortly before midday on Tuesday September 14. Three hours later he sailed on the battleship *Renown* for England. 'My father was in relaxed and genial form,' Mary Churchill later recalled.[2]

That evening, after dinner in the Admiral's cabin, Churchill called for a box of matches, and demonstrated to those present the disposition of Kitchener's forces at the Battle of Omdurman in 1898. He also commented that he had been under fire for the first time in his life on his twenty-first birthday. Commander Thompson, who was present, noted that Mary Churchill 'whose own twenty-first birthday it was next day, pointed out excitedly that she had beaten her father by just over a year'.[3]

On September 15 British paratroopers and a South African Spitfire squadron had occupied the island of Kos, in the Dodecanese. On the following day, Leros was captured. But German control over Rhodes was complete.

On September 16 Churchill received a long telegram from Alexander, who had just returned from a visit to the Salerno beach-head. He had been able 'to cheer them up', he reported, and to give certain directions, to 'hold what we have gained', to consolidate key positions 'at all costs' by digging, wiring and mining, to reorganize all scattered and mixed units and formations, to form local reserves and as strong a mobile reserve as possible, and to inform the troops of the 'rapid approach' of the Eighth Army.[4] Alexander's telegram ended: 'We shall regain the initiative and start to gain key points as soon as we are strong enough to do so. God's blessing on our enterprise and a little luck will secure success to our arms.' This reassuring telegram crossed with one from Churchill to Alexander, sent from *Renown* on September 16, after Churchill had learned from Alexander of the reinforcements on their way to the Salerno beach-head: 'My feeling about "Avalanche",' Churchill wrote, 'is expressed in Foch's maxim, "Cramponnez partout". The Navy are quite right to throw their heavy ships in, for this is a battle of far-reaching significance. My feeling is you are going to win.'[5]

On September 16, as Churchill and Alexander exchanged tele-

[1] Letter of 13 September 1943: Churchill papers, 20/94.

[2] Mary Churchill recollections: Mary Soames, page 340.

[3] Gerald Pawle, *The War and Colonel Warden* (based on the recollections of Commander C. R. Thompson), London 1963, page 251.

[4] MA/163, 'Concrete' No. 909, 16 September 1943: Churchill papers, 20/118.

[5] 'Welfare' No. 758, Prime Minister's Personal Telegram, T.1350/3, 'Hush, Most Secret', 16 September 1943: Churchill papers, 20/118.

grams, Eighth Army patrols made their first fleeting contact with units of the Salerno beach-head, whereupon the German army commander at Salerno accepted defeat and began to withdraw. 'Every good wish,' Churchill telegraphed to Alexander late that night. 'Please continue to keep me informed. I am in mid-ocean, but can receive fully at all hours.' Churchill added: 'I am glad to feel you have taken a personal grip of "Avalanche" build-up.'[1] 'I do not wish to mislead you by being over-optimistic,' Alexander telegraphed on September 17, 'but I am satisfied that we now have situation in hand and will be able to carry out our future operations according to plan.'[2]

Studying Alexander's daily telegraphic reports, Churchill now felt 'easier', as he informed Roosevelt on September 18, about the Salerno landings. But he went on to warn Roosevelt that 'the quality of German resistance shows how hard we shall have to fight in "Overlord"'.[3]

Churchill worked on board ship, dictating telegrams, and preparing the speech that he would make on his return to London. Elizabeth Layton later wrote home recalling those sea-borne days:

He was doing his speech to Parliament, and what a huge one it was! I shall never forget working by that bedside. It was a very nice cabin with lots of room. But, as usual, the cigar kept going out, and he got a fit of wanting to light it with a candle (this does happen sometimes) So it was one continuous 'Light the candle'—and then of course it must be blown out away from the bed so that none of the smell reaches him. As soon as one had got settled down again and two more words written, the blasted old cigar would be out and the performance have to be gone through again.

One day I was walking on the quarter-deck when suddenly there was a Marine saying, 'The PM would like to see you at once.' Of course there had been a good sea-breeze and I was looking more impossibly untidy than you could possibly conjure up—even the good old combs had been blown out. But I went rushing straight up 'as is' and seized book and pencil, knowing it was some more speech. It was, and as I settled down breathless, pink and tousled he looked up gravely and said, 'I do hope I haven't disturbed you in the middle of your tea.'[4]

On the morning of Sunday September 19 *Renown* reached the Clyde. It was more than six weeks since Churchill had left England for 'Quadrant'. The voyage had taken exactly 109 hours. He had received, as he told Roosevelt, 'five or six thousand words a day by

[1] 'Welfare No. 764', Prime Minister's Personal Telegram, T.1349/3, 'Most Secret', 17 September 1943: Churchill papers, 20/118.

[2] MA/178, 'Most Secret', 'Personal', 17 September 1943: Churchill papers, 20/118.

[3] 'Welfare No. 767', Prime Minister's Personal Telegram, T.1354/3, Prime Minister to President No. 416, 'Most Secret and Personal', 18 September 1943: Churchill papers, 20/118.

[4] Elizabeth Layton, letter of 18 October 1943: Nel papers.

wireless' and had been able to send replies 'every night by one or other of the escort vessels. Therefore I was in full touch the whole time.'[1]

Before leaving ship, Churchill addressed the ship's company, and then attended Divine Service. 'I must say I've seldom felt so moved by anything,' Elizabeth Layton wrote home, 'those dear sailors lined up, the Old Man singing away, the Padre (he was a marvellous man) in his robes, the few (brass) instruments forming a small band which somehow sounded very quiet and touching.'[2]

Awaiting Churchill at the quayside was a telegram from Alexander, which began: 'I can say with full confidence that the whole situation has changed in our favour and that the initiative has passed to us. . . .'[3]

A despatch from Britain's former Ambassador to Japan, Sir Robert Craigie, was also awaiting Churchill. In his Final Report, Craigie wrote of the coming of war with Japan as having been a disaster for Britain. Reading this, Churchill minuted to Eden that Japan's attack on the United States had been 'a blessing' for Britain, having brought America 'wholeheartedly and unitedly into this war'. Churchill added: 'Greater good fortune has rarely happened to the British Empire than this event which has revealed our friends and foes in their true light, and may lead, through the merciless crushing of Japan, to a new relationship of immense benefit to the English-speaking countries and to the whole world.'[4]

[1] Prime Minister's Personal Telegram, T.1409/3, Prime Minister to President No. 422, 'Personal and Most Secret', 25 September 1943: Churchill papers, 20/119.

[2] Elizabeth Layton, letter of 21 September 1943: Nel papers. The padre, Henry Lloyd (later Dean of Truro), had won the DSO while serving in the aircraft carrier *Illustrious* in the Mediterranean.

[3] MA/183, 'Most Secret', sent 18 September 1943, received in London, 1 a.m., 19 September 1943: Churchill papers, 20/118.

[4] Prime Minister's Personal Minute, M.588/3, 'Secret', 19 September 1943: Churchill papers, 20/104.

31
Rhodes, 'An immense but fleeting opportunity'

CHURCHILL returned to London on the evening of 20 September 1943. During the train journey, Dudley Pound, whose health had further deteriorated during the sea voyage, submitted his letter of resignation. At Euston Station, Churchill was greeted, as Captain Pim recalled, 'by all his colleagues in the Cabinet and cheering crowds and was obviously in the best of form'.[1] Also at Euston was an ambulance, which took the sick Pound to the Royal Masonic Hospital.

On the following day, September 21, Churchill gave the House of Commons an account of his journeyings, and of the recent developments in each of the war zones. He was particularly concerned to answer the criticisms that had been made, that time had been lost in making the Salerno landing because of 'futile' negotiations with the Italian Government. 'I have seen it said,' Churchill told the House, 'that forty days of precious time were lost in these negotiations, and that in consequence British and American blood was needlessly shed around Salerno. This criticism is as ill-founded in fact as it is wounding to those who are bereaved.' The timing of the attack on Italy, Churchill added, was fixed 'without the slightest reference to the attitude of the Italian Government'. The provisional date of the operation 'was settled long before any negotiations with them had taken place, and even before the fall of Mussolini'. That date had depended, he explained, upon the availability of the landing craft which had earlier been used for the landings in Sicily, and he went on to tell the House:

The condition and preparation of the landing-craft were the sole but

[1] Pim recollections: Pim papers.

decisive limiting factors. It had nothing to do with 'wasting time over the negotiations', nothing to do with the Foreign Office holding back the generals while they worried about this clause or that clause and so forth. There was never one moment's pause in the process of carrying out the military operations, and everything else had to fit in with that main-line traffic.

When I hear people talking in an airy way of throwing modern armies ashore here and there as if they were bales of goods to be dumped on a beach and forgotten, I really marvel at the lack of knowledge which still prevails of the conditions of modern war.

Churchill then made what he called 'a momentary digression', commenting 'that this class of criticism which I read in the newspapers when I arrived on Sunday morning reminds me of the simple tale about the sailor who jumped into a dock, I think it was at Plymouth, to rescue a small boy from drowning. About a week later this sailor was accosted by a woman, who asked, "Are you the man who picked my son out of the dock the other night?" The sailor replied modestly, "That is true, ma'am." "Ah," said the woman, "you are the man I am looking for. Where is his cap?"'

Churchill's speech, which he had been preparing during the voyage home, lasted for more than two and a half hours, with an hour's break for lunch in the middle. He had found in America, he said, the feeling 'that the war was being well managed, that the central direction made good plans and that highly competent and resolute officers were entrusted with their execution in every part of the globe. It is my hope that this conviction is generally shared at home. . . .' [1]

Harold Nicolson, who was present for both halves of Churchill's speech, wrote that evening to his sons:

He began, as always, in a dull, stuffy manner, reciting dates and chronology, reading slowly from the typescript on the box. But as he progressed, he began to enliven his disclosure with the familiar quips and gestures. His most characteristic gesture is strange indeed. You know the movement that a man makes when he taps his trouser pockets to see whether he has got his latchkey? Well, Winston pats both trouser pockets and then passes his hands up and down from groin to tummy.

Later in his letter, Nicolson described how:

At the end of the first act, and before we adjourned for luncheon, he did an amusing thing. He referred to Italy and expressed pleasure that the Italian

[1] Speech of 21 September 1943: *Hansard*, 21 September 1943, columns 69–105.

people, 'rescued from their state of servitude', could now take 'their rightful place among the democracies of the world'. 'The satellite States,' he continued, 'suborned and overawed . . .' and then he raised his arm as if about to deliver the most terrific thunderbolt from his rich armoury of rhetoric, but he dropped his arm suddenly and took off his spectacles, '. . . may perhaps be allowed to work their passage home', he concluded, grinning. It is in this that one finds his mastery of the House. It is the combination of great flights of oratory with sudden swoops into the intimate and conversational. Of all his devices it is the one that never fails.[1]

As he left the Chamber, Churchill saw Sir Patrick Donner, a Conservative MP who had been one of his younger and more active supporters in the previous struggle against the India Bill. Donner's wife had recently died, and Churchill hastened to speak to him, and to offer his sympathy. 'When ill eight years ago,' Donner wrote later that same day, 'it was you sent flowers to me and today it was again you who comforted me with words of consolation. It is in truth your greatness of heart that makes so many of us devoted to you.'[2]

On September 24, following the death of Sir Kingsley Wood, Churchill appointed Sir John Anderson as the new Chancellor of the Exchequer. Attlee replaced Anderson as Lord President of the Council. Beaverbrook returned to the Government, but not to the War Cabinet, as Lord Privy Seal. 'Except for you and me,' Churchill commented to Eden, 'this is the worst Government England ever had!'[3]

On September 25, as Allied forces approached the port of Naples on the western coast of Italy, and were poised to occupy the air base of Foggia on the eastern side, Churchill again sent Eisenhower a plea for action to seize Rhodes, the island which was, in Churchill's words, 'the key both to the Eastern Mediterranean and the Aegean'. It would be 'a great disaster', Churchill added, 'if the Germans are able to consolidate there'.[4]

A short while later, Churchill telegraphed to Eisenhower with a note of what he called 'the priorities which I assign in my own mind'

[1] Harold Nicolson, letter to Ben and Nigel Nicolson, 21 September 1943: Nigel Nicolson (editor), op. cit., page 320.

[2] Letter of 21 September 1943, House of Commons: Churchill papers, 2/464.

[3] As reported by Sir Alexander Cadogan, Cadogan diary for 25 September 1943: David Dilks (editor), op. cit., pages 562–3.

[4] Prime Minister's Personal Telegram, T.1411/3, No. 5224 to Algiers, 'Most Secret, Personal and Private', 25 September 1943: Churchill papers, 20/119.

to the various 'desirable objectives', including Rhodes, for which he had previously pressed. 'Four-fifths of our effort,' he wrote, 'should be the build-up of Italy. One-tenth should be our making sure of Corsica (which will soon finish) and in the Adriatic. The remaining tenth should be concentrated on Rhodes. This of course applies to the limiting factors only. These, I presume, are mainly landing-craft and assault shipping, with light naval craft.'

'I send this,' Churchill added, 'as a rough guide to my thought only because I do not want you to feel I am pressing for everything in all directions without understanding how grim are your limitations.' [1]

Churchill's concern was whether these limitations were exaggerated. He considered himself 'perfectly free to give up the Rhodes stroke if the conditions are too bad', he minuted for the Chiefs of Staff four days after his telegram to Eisenhower, but he wished to add 'that I doubt the figure of 350 first-line aircraft for the Greece-Aegean area'. What did the Air Staff say, he asked, and he added: 'Rhodes is a big prize.' [2]

At the Chiefs of Staff Committee on September 30, Sir Charles Portal 'expressed similar views', as the minutes noted, to Churchill's enquiry, telling Brooke, Syfret and Ismay 'that he felt it was quite wrong to consider withdrawing from Kos [3] and Leros because the enemy air threat to these islands had increased'. Britain had in the Mediterranean alone, Portal added, 'more aircraft than were in the whole German air force and our policy should be to fight the enemy wherever the opportunity offered'. [4]

Churchill's travels, and events in the Mediterranean, were taking their toll of his strength. 'PM seems terribly tired,' Marian Holmes wrote in her diary on September 27. [5] 'He raised the roof with John Peck over some matter,' she noted two days later, adding: 'He was alternately nice and ill-tempered.' [6]

On September 28 Churchill had to decide whether, as suggested by

---

[1] Prime Minister's Personal Telegram, T.1415/3, No. 5225 to Algiers, 'Personal and Private', 25 September 1943: Churchill papers, 20/119.

[2] Prime Minister's Personal Minute, D.159/3, 'Action this Day', 29 September 1943: (Chiefs of Staff Committee No. 231 (Operations) of 1943, 30 September 1943, Annex: Cabinet papers, 79/65).

[3] Various spellings for this island include Kos, Cos and Coo. On 4 October 1943 the Chiefs of Staff Committee noted 'that the Prime Minister had directed that in future the Island was to be known as Kos and not Cos. . . .' (Chiefs of Staff Committee No. 236 (Operations) of 1943, 4 October 1943: Cabinet papers, 79/65.)

[4] Chiefs of Staff Committee No. 231 (Operations) of 1943, 30 September 1943: Cabinet papers, 79/65.

[5] Marian Holmes diary, 27 September 1943: Marian Walker Spicer papers.

[6] Marian Holmes diary, 29 September 1943: Marian Walker Spicer papers.

Roosevelt, the Allies should declare Rome an 'Open City'. Churchill based his decision in part on an Enigma decrypt of a German message. This message stated that the previous Italian open city terms 'were never to hamper' German rail and road communications. This secret German decision, Churchill informed Eden, was no doubt 'understood' by Roosevelt 'to give us equal freedom'.[1]

Eden agreed with Churchill's decision, and approved Churchill's telegram to Roosevelt, sent that same day, informing the President, without any reference to Enigma, that 'We think it would be a mistake to talk about making Rome an open city as it may hamper our forward movement and will anyway not bind the enemy.'[2]

In the last week of September, Churchill had also been thinking of the possibility of some British military initiative in Greece should the Germans be unable to maintain their presence there, and should the Greeks appeal to Britain 'to send in forces to keep order throughout the country'. The Prime Minister, Ismay informed the Foreign Office on October 4, 'contemplates a relatively small and strictly limited military commitment of about 5,000 men for the purpose of keeping order *in Athens only*'. Ismay himself had underlined the words in italics, and he added: 'This token force of course would be well within our power.'[3]

Churchill had invited down to Chequers on the weekend Colonel Myers, whom he had questioned closely on the situation in Greece, Myers having just arrived in London after many months as British liaison officer with the Greek Communist forces. Myers had shown Churchill, as he later recalled: 'A pair of stereoscopic aerial photographs of the Asopos railway viaduct lying at the bottom of the gorge it had spanned, after we had blown it up shortly before our other widespread demolitions in conjunction with the invasion of Sicily. He chuckled delightedly.'

Myers' account continued:

I told him I thought that his recent speech at Quebec, in which he had said he looked forward to the Greek King's return to Greece, had made my job more difficult. 'Surely,' I said, 'what happened to their King is a Greek affair and it is not for us to interfere.' He asked me what he had said at Quebec and I produced an extract of his speech out of my attaché case, which he looked through. He politely said that he agreed with what he had said; so I left it at that.

[1] Prime Minister's Personal Minute, M.609/3, 'Action this Day', 28 September 1943: Premier papers, 3/14/3, folio 299.
[2] Prime Minister's Personal Telegram, T.1439/3, Prime Minister to President No. 424. 'Personal and Secret', 28 September 1943: Premier papers, 3/14/3, folio 300.
[3] Letter of 4 October 1943, Chiefs of Staff Committee No. 236 (Operations) of 1943, 4 October 1943, Annex 1: Cabinet papers, 79/65.

I then produced a draft of the broadcast over the BBC which I was proposing to make to the andartes before I left London in a few days time. It contained a message of good cheer from Mr Churchill. It was entirely non-political and had already been approved by SOE and the Foreign Office. Churchill read it through in silence and at the end said, 'Well, that's alright, perfectly harmless. Would you like me to add a bit of pep to it?' I said I would be very pleased if he would. Whereupon he got out his fountain pen filled with red ink and slowly started scratching away. Afterwards I was given what he had written to read and comment. I found that he had added a paragraph almost exactly on the lines I had suggested at lunch, affirming and justifying our policy towards Greece.[1]

'The Greek people must be masters of their destinies,' Churchill's handwritten amendment read. 'They alone can decide their future form of Government. England, always their friend, will never interfere in their home politics and will always champion their sovereign rights.' Britain had 'obligations of honour' to King George because he fought for the Allied cause. 'These we must discharge. They do not in any way affect the full freedom of the Greek people to settle their own affairs once conditions of tranquillity and orderly politics are re-established.'[2]

In preparation for the Heads of Government conference at Teheran, Churchill informed Stalin that the cover plan was to indicate Cairo as the location of the talks. 'Accordingly,' he telegraphed to Stalin on September 25:

I suggest for your consideration that I make preparations at Cairo in regard to accommodation, security, etc., which are bound to be noticed in spite of all praise-worthy efforts to keep them secret. Then perhaps only two or three days before our meeting we should throw a British and a Russian Brigade around a suitable area in Teheran including the airfield, and keep an absolute cordon till we have finished our talks.

We would not tell the Persian Government nor make any arrangements for our accommodation until this moment comes. We should of course have to control absolutely all outgoing messages. Thus we shall have an effective blind for the world Press and also for any unpleasant people who might not be as fond of us as they ought.

Churchill continued, with regard to the Teheran deception plan:

[1] Brigadier E. C. W. Myers, in Phyllis Auty and Richard Clogg (editors), *British Policy Towards Wartime Resistance in Yugoslavia and Greece*, London 1975, pages 160–1. Twenty years earlier, Myers had described this meeting with Churchill in his book *Greek Entanglement*, London 1955, pages 228 ff. In August 1943, at the suggestion of Brigadier Myers, the Greek guerilla groups, known as the andartes, had sent six representatives, three of them communist, three of them non-communist republicans, to Cairo, for an Anglo-Greek discussion on the political future of Greece.

[2] Manuscript note: Premier papers, 3/211/5.

I suggest also that in all future correspondence on this subject we use the expression 'Cairo Three' instead of 'Teheran' which should be buried, and also that the code name for the Operation should be 'Eureka' which I believe is Ancient Greek. If you have other ideas let me know, and we can then put them to the President. I have not said anything to him about this aspect yet.[1]

On September 25, Soviet forces entered Smolensk, one of the cities which the Germans had captured in their first offensive, in the autumn of 1941. Churchill telegraphed immediately to Stalin: 'Eden and I wish to send you our personal congratulations on the grand news about Smolensk.'[2]

The Russians had for some while been demanding the renewal of the Arctic convoys, as Churchill informed Roosevelt on September 28.[3] With 'Overlord' set for May 1944, Churchill had already urged upon his own advisers the despatch of 'at least five full convoys' to Russia before the 'Overlord' operations began.[4]

On the night of September 29, Churchill learned that the *Tirpitz* had been disabled by an attack made on her by six British midget submarines, two of which had penetrated the German defences.[5] The damage to the *Tirpitz* made the sailing of the Arctic convoys much less hazardous. On September 30 Churchill minuted to Eden, 'let me see your list of grievances about the treatment of our people in North Russia, so that I can combine the two to best advantage'.[6]

For four days the Admiralty examined the whole question of the renewal of the Arctic convoys. Despite the immobilization of the *Tirpitz*, there were several other problems, which Churchill set out in a telegram to Stalin on October 1, problems which entailed 'very great difficulties' in renewing the convoys to Russia:

First the Battle of the Atlantic has begun again. The U-boats have set about us with a new kind of acoustic torpedo, which has proved effective against the escorting vessels when hunting U-boats. Secondly, we are at very full stretch in the Mediterranean, building up an army in Italy of about

---

[1] Prime Minister's Personal Telegram, T.1408/3, 'Personal and Most Secret', 'For your eye alone', 25 September 1943: Cabinet papers, 120/113.

[2] Prime Minister's Personal Telegram, T.1413/3, 25 September 1943: Churchill papers, 20/132 Stalin replied: 'I very much appreciate the congratulations you and Mr Eden sent on the occasion of the recapture of Smolensk' (Kremlin, 26 September 1943: Churchill papers, 20/119).

[3] Prime Minister's Personal Telegram, T.1440/3, Prime Minister to President, No. 425, 'Personal and Most Secret', 28 September 1943: Churchill papers, 20/119.

[4] Prime Minister's Personal Minute, M.605/3, 'Most Secret', 27 September 1943: Churchill papers, 20/104.

[5] Both their Commanding Officers, Lieutenant Cameron and Lieutenant Place, were captured by the Germans. Both received the Victoria Cross.

[6] Prime Minister's Personal Minute, M.620/3, 'Action this Day', 30 September 1943: Churchill papers, 20/104.

600,000 men by the end of November, and also trying to take full advantage of the Italian collapse in the Aegean islands and the Balkan peninsula. Thirdly, we have to provide for our share of the war against Japan, in which the United States are greatly interested, and whose people would be offended if we were lukewarm.

Notwithstanding these problems, the first convoy, Churchill told Stalin, would leave for Archangel on November 12, with three subsequent convoys, each of thirty-five ships, being sent at twenty-eight-day intervals. This was, however, 'no contract or bargain', Churchill explained, 'but rather a declaration of our solemn and earnest resolve'.

Churchill then asked Stalin to read a note prepared by the Foreign Office and the Admiralty, of 'the difficulties we have experienced' in North Russia, and the need to allow 150 visas to British personnel needed to replace those whose 'state of health' made it 'very necessary to relieve them without further delay'. Nor had visas been granted for the small medical unit which Britain wished to send. 'Please remember,' Churchill pointed out, 'that we may have heavy casualties.'

Churchill also urged Stalin to end the restrictions imposed on British personnel and seamen in North Russia, restrictions 'which seem to me inappropriate for men sent by an ally to carry out operations of the greatest interest to the Soviet Union'. These restrictions included censorship of the private Service mail, and special passes to move between British shore stations, or from British ships to British shore stations. Churchill added:

The imposition of these restrictions makes an impression upon officers and men alike which is bad for Anglo-Soviet relations, and would be deeply injurious if Parliament got to hear of it. The cumulative effect of these formalities has been most hampering to the efficient performance of the men's duties, and on more than one occasion to urgent and important operations. No such restrictions are placed upon Soviet personnel here.

'I trust indeed,' Churchill ended, 'that you will find it possible to have these difficulties smoothed out in a friendly spirit, so that we may help each other, and the common cause, to the utmost of our strength.'[1]

Stalin, replying two weeks later, challenged Churchill's statement that the convoys were not a part of any 'contract or bargain'. The supplies sent to Russia were, he insisted, 'an obligation, which, by special agreement between our countries, the British Government undertook in respect of the USSR, which bears on its shoulders, already for the third year, the enormous burden of struggle with the common enemy of the Allies—Hitlerite Germany'.

[1] Prime Minister's Personal Telegram, T.1464/3, 1 October 1943: Churchill papers, 20/132.

Stalin rejected the argument for an increase in British personnel, as those in north Russia were not, he wrote, adequately employed, 'and for many months have been doomed to idleness'. But he did agree to the private Service mail being censored by the British authorities themselves.[1]

The first part of Stalin's reply, about Britain's 'obligation', the Foreign Office found 'outrageous', so much so that Cadogan held it up for a night before passing it to Churchill.[2] As Eden was even then on his way to Moscow, it fell to Churchill to deal with Stalin's message, which it was decided to return 'unread' to the Soviet Ambassador, Maisky's successor Feodor Gousev, without 'receiving' it, and thus without the need to comment on it. The 'Soviet machine', Churchill telegraphed to Roosevelt on October 16, 'is quite convinced it can get everything by bullying, and I am sure it is a matter of some importance to show that this is not necessarily always true'.[3] Two days later, Stalin's telegram was returned to the Soviet Ambassador, unread. To Eden, who had just reached Moscow, Churchill telegraphed that evening about his talk with Gousev:

... we had a short discussion about the Moscow Conference and the Second Front. I explained to him that this kind of operation could not be undertaken on impulse and that I was always ready to arrange for a meeting between British and Russian military experts who would go into the facts and figures, upon which everything depended and without which discussion was futile.

I spoke to him earnestly about the great desire we had to work with Russia and to be friends with her, how we saw that they should have a great place in the world after the war, that we should welcome this and that we would do our best also to make good relations between them and the United States. I further said how much I was looking forward to a meeting with Marshal Stalin if it could be arranged and how important this meeting of the Heads of the British, American and Soviet Governments was to the future of the world.

I then turned to the message which Monsieur Gousev had delivered to Sir Alexander Cadogan for me from Marshal Stalin about the proposed resumption of British convoys to North Russia with British and American supplies. I said very briefly that I did not think this message would help the situation, that it had caused me a good deal of pain, that I feared any reply which I could send would only make things worse, that the Foreign Secretary was in Moscow and I had left it to him to settle the matter on the spot and that therefore I did not wish to receive the message, which I then handed back to him in an envelope. Monsieur Gousev opened the

---

[1] Telegram of 13 October 1943, 'Personal and Secret': Churchill papers, 20/121.

[2] Cadogan diary, 14 October 1943: David Dilks (editor), *op. cit.*, pages 566–7.

[3] Prime Minister's Personal Telegram, T.1640/3, Prime Minister to President, No. 459, 'Personal and Most Secret', 16 October 1943: Churchill papers, 20/121.

envelope to see what was inside it and, recognising the message said he had been instructed to deliver it to me. I then said 'I am not prepared to receive it' and got up to indicate in a friendly manner that our conversation was at an end.

We had a little talk in the doorway about his coming to luncheon in the near future and discussing with Mrs Churchill some questions connected with her Russian Fund, which I told him had now reached four million pounds. I did not give Monsieur Gousev a chance of recurring to the question of the convoys or of trying to hand me back the envelope so he went off with it, and it can be treated as nul et non avenu.[1]

Cadogan later recalled that Churchill 'had an amiable conversation with M. Gousev, said that the Foreign Secretary would deal with the question of convoys in Moscow, handed back the offending message in an envelope and ushered the Ambassador to the door'. Cadogan noted that Churchill even used 'the correct phrase "nul et non avenu", found in handbooks on diplomacy', for a refusal to accept the telegram.[2]

Before Eden had left for Moscow, he had attended a War Cabinet at which General Smuts, just arrived from South Africa, had been present at Churchill's invitation. During the meeting, Eden was angered when Churchill, as Oliver Harvey noted in his diary, 'kept saying such things as "we don't know in what condition Germany will be after the war". "We musn't weaken Germany too much—we may need her against Russia" (Hear, hear, from Smuts). "We must destroy Prussianism".' The Cabinet, Harvey added, 'were horrified at all this'.[3]

That same day, Churchill had to deal with a Soviet request for the recognition of the post-war western frontiers of Russia. Nearly two years had passed since Stalin had first pressed for such recognition. 'It should be remembered,' Churchill minuted to Eden on October 6, 'that the reason why we sheered off making this agreement and substituted the Twenty Years' Treaty was the perfectly clear menace of very considerable division of opinion in the House of Commons. I know of no reason for supposing that this same opposition might not manifest itself again, perhaps in an even stronger form. The opponents would have the advantage of invoking very large principles against us.'

[1] Prime Minister's Personal Telegram, T.1659/3, 'Personal and Most Secret', 'For you eye alone', Telegram No. 1634 to Moscow, SU/43/108, 18 October 1943: Foreign Office papers 954/26, folio 26.

[2] Cadogan notes concerning 18 October 1943: David Dilks (editor), op. cit., page 567.

[3] Harvey diary, 6 October 1943: John Harvey (editor), op. cit., pages 304–5. The War Cabinet minutes of this meeting, War Cabinet No. 135 of 1943, held at 5.30 p.m. on 5 October 1943, make no reference, even in the Confidential Annex (Cabinet papers, 65/40) to Churchill's remarks as reported by Harvey, who was not present, but presumably had been told them by Eden.

Churchill remained convinced that territorial issues should be decided upon, not during the war itself, but at the post-war Peace Conference. As he explained to Eden:

At a Peace Conference, the position can be viewed as a whole, and adjustments in one direction balanced by those in another. There is therefore the greatest need to reserve territorial questions for the general settlement. This is even more true of the United States position, especially in an election year. It would be well therefore to have the American attitude clearly deployed before we adopt a new position in advance of the Twenty Years' Treaty.

As far as Poland was concerned, of her pre-war eastern frontier Churchill had long been a critic. 'I think,' he told Eden, 'we should do everything in our power to persuade the Poles to agree with the Russians about their Eastern frontier, in return for gains in East Prussia and Silesia. We could certainly promise to use our influence in this respect.'[1]

On October 1, the day before his departure for India, Mountbatten attended his last Staff Conference, and was 'wished every success' by Churchill on his appointment as Supreme Allied Commander, South East Asia Command. This Command, Churchill declared, 'was essentially a British Command'. Although the Staff was composed of both British and American personnel, 'the interests in this theatre were overwhelmingly British'. As agreed at 'Quadrant', jurisdiction over the Command would be exercised 'solely' by the British Chiefs of Staff, who would be 'the sole channel for communication with the Supreme Allied Commander'.[2] Mountbatten's instructions, sent at the end of the month, set out as his 'prime duty' to engage the Japanese 'as closely and continuously as possible in order by attrition to consume and wear down the enemy's forces, especially his Air Forces, thus making our superiority tell and forcing the enemy to divert his forces from the Pacific theatre; and secondly, but of equal consequence, to maintain and broaden our contacts with China, both by the Air route and by establishing direct contact through Northern Burma inter alia by suitably organized, Air-supplied ground forces of the greatest possible strength'.[3]

*   *   *

[1] Prime Minister's Personal Minute, M.647/3, 'Most Secret', 6 October 1943: Premier papers, 3/399/6, folio 92.

[2] Staff Conference, 12 noon, 1 October 1943, Chiefs of Staff Committee No. 233 (Operations) of 1943: Cabinet papers, 79/65.

[3] 'Directive by the Prime Minister and minister of defence', 'Most Secret', sent as COSSEA No. 1, OZ 3331, 29 October 1943: Cabinet papers, 120/707.

On October 1 British units entered Naples. In the same week, Sardinia and Corsica came under Allied control. 'I rejoice with you at the brilliant turn our affairs in the Mediterranean have taken,' Churchill telegraphed to Eisenhower on October 2, 'and that Sardinia and Corsica have fallen as mere incidents in the campaign.'[1] That same day, in a telegram to Alexander praising 'your master-stroke in seizing Taranto', Churchill added: 'have studied the plan you have sent home by your officer, and note that you have already accomplished the first and second phases of it. I hope the third phase will be accomplished by the end of the month or thereabouts, and that we shall meet in Rome.'

'Everything in "Boniface",' Churchill told Alexander, 'goes to show that the enemy's object is to gain time and retire northward without serious losses.' For this reason, he hoped that Montgomery, despite the need for a two week halt to bring up supplies, would keep his patrols and light forces 'in touch with the enemy's rearguards'.[2]

Replying on October 3 from his new headquarters at Bari, Alexander assured Churchill that 'the Germans will be harassed and continuous pressure applied to his rearguards all the time by light mobile forces and air forces when we cannot reach him with our main bodies'.[3] That same day, the Germans launched an attack on the island of Kos. 'We rely on you to defend this island to the utmost limit,' Churchill telegraphed to the senior British officer on the island. 'Tell your men the eyes of the world are upon them.'[4] 'I am sure I can rely upon you,' he telegraphed to Air Chief Marshal Tedder, 'to turn on all your heat from every quarter, especially during this lull in Italy.'[5] But by the following day, Cos was in German hands. 'It may well be,' Churchill minuted to the Chiefs of Staff Committee on October 6, about the plans to capture Rhodes, 'that the moment of panic after Italy's collapse has been lost.'[6]

At a Staff Conference on the afternoon of October 6, Churchill suggested that Eisenhower meet his own Commanders-in-Chief, Mediterranean, as well as the Commanders-in-Chief, Middle East, in order

---

[1] Prime Minister's Personal Telegram, T.1483/3, No. 5341 to Algiers, 'Most Secret', 2 October 1943: Churchill papers, 20/119.

[2] Prime Minister's Personal Telegram, T.1481/3, 'Personal and Most Secret, also Private', 'To be transmitted through "C"', 2 October 1943: Churchill papers, 20/119.

[3] 'Special unnumbered message', 'Most Secret', 3 October 1943: Churchill papers, 20/120.

[4] Prime Minister's Personal Telegram, T.1495/3, 3 October 1943: Churchill papers, 4/396.

[5] Prime Minister's Personal Telegram, T.1497/3, 3 October 1943: Churchill papers, 4/396.

[6] Prime Minister's Personal Minute, D.164/3, 6 October 1943: Churchill papers, 20/104.

to discuss what action could be taken 'to restore the situation in the Dodecanese'. Churchill told the conference:

We were in danger of suffering a vexatious setback in this theatre. Although it was admittedly a theatre of secondary importance we could not afford, particularly in view of the repercussions it would have throughout the Balkans and in Turkey, to see our forces mauled in the way they had been at Kos and to allow the Germans to retain this trophy undisturbed. It was of particular importance that we should retain our hold on the fortress of Leros which we had picked up at no cost.

Brooke warned that there was a 'a grave danger' that Britain would find herself 'drawn into an amphibious campaign in the Eastern Mediterranean' which would absorb resources 'which might be badly needed in Italy'. Against an estimated twenty-two German divisions in Italy, Britain was assembling in Italy a force of nineteen or twenty divisions, comprising British, American, Canadian, New Zealand, Indian and Polish formations. By 'diverting resources to the Eastern Mediterranean', Brooke declared, 'we should be running an increased risk of a setback in Northern Italy'.

In support of action, Air Chief Marshal Sir Sholto Douglas, Air Officer Commanding-in-Chief, Middle East, stated that Britain's commitment in the Middle East could be limited 'to the capture of Rhodes and Kos and the recapture of Leros, should the garrison be overwhelmed'. With Rhodes, Kos and Leros 'in our possession', Douglas stated, 'we could control the Aegean Sea'.[1]

In a telegram to the Combined Chiefs of Staff, and to the British Chiefs of Staff, sent on October 5, Eisenhower had warned that if an attempt were made to capture Rhodes, the operation, 'however desirable in itself', would be 'bound to place calls on us for a very considerable and continuing diversion of air effort from the main operations in Italy'. Eisenhower added: 'I consider any material diversion highly prejudicial to the success of Italian operations. It is repeated that these operations will probably assume the aspect of a major bitter battle.'[2]

With Rhodes and Kos now securely in German hands, Eisenhower's warning could not be brushed aside lightly. After reading it, Churchill telegraphed to Roosevelt in considerable anguish on October 7, sending one copy of his telegram to Eisenhower, another to Maitland Wilson, and a third to Alexander:

[1] Staff Conference, Chiefs of Staff Committee No. 239 (Operations) of 1943, 3 p.m., 6 October 1943: Cabinet papers, 79/65. Those present at this Staff Conference were Churchill (in the Chair), Eden, Brooke, Portal, Admiral of the Fleet Sir Andrew Cunningham (First Sea Lord designate) Vice-Admiral Sir Nevill Syfret, Air Chief Marshal Sir W. Sholto Douglas and Ismay.

[2] NAF 438, Telegram No. W.1750/3464, 'Secret', 5 October 1943: Cabinet papers, 105/141.

What I ask for is the capture of Rhodes and the other islands of the Dodecanese, and the movement northward of our Middle Eastern air forces and their establishment in these islands and possibly on the Turkish shore, which last might well be obtained, thus forcing a diversion on the enemy far greater than that required of us. It would also offer the opportunity of engaging the enemy's waning air-power and wearing it down in a new region. This air-power is all one, and the more continually it can be fought the better.

Rhodes, Churchill added, was 'the key to all this'. The present plan of taking it was 'not good enough' however. A policy was needed which would be carried out 'with vigour and celerity, requiring the best troops and adequate means'. The diversion from the main theatre would only be temporary, but the results 'may well be of profound and lasting importance'. Churchill's telegram ended:

I beg you to consider this and not let it be brushed aside and all these possibilities lost to us in the critical months that lie ahead. Even if landing-craft and assault ships on the scale of a division were withheld from the build-up of 'Overlord' for a few weeks without altering the zero date it would be worth while. I feel we may easily throw away an immense but fleeting opportunity. If you think well, would you very kindly let General Marshall see this telegram before any decision is taken by the Combined Chiefs of Staff.[1]

Churchill's conviction that an attack on Rhodes was likely to succeed derived from his reading of the Enigma decrypts. As he explained to Alexander on October 7: 'Everything in "Boniface" shows the enemy are retiring to Northern Italy and that the forces immediately in front of you are only trying to gain time by inflicting as much damage as possible while retreating.' There should therefore be 'plenty of time' Churchill added, 'to take Rhodes with good troops which can be relieved by garrison troops and sent on to join you before you come up against the main German forces in the North'.[2]

The Joint Planning Staff did not support Churchill's view of the feasibility of the capture of Rhodes and Kos. The plan put forward by the Commanders-in-Chief Middle East to recapture Rhodes, they wrote on October 6, 'is unlikely to succeed'. The recapture of Cos was, in their view, 'not tactically feasible with the forces at present being assembled for Rhodes'.[3]

At a further Staff Conference on October 7, Churchill reiterated his

---

[1] Prime Minister's Personal Telegram, T.1523/3, Prime Minister to President, No. 438, 'Personal and Most Secret', 7 October 1943: Churchill papers, 20/120.

[2] Prime Minister's Personal Telegram, T.1531/3, 'Personal and Most Secret', 'Through "C"', 7 October 1943: Churchill papers, 20/120.

[3] Joint Planning Staff Paper No. 358 (Final) of 1943, 'Situation in the Aegean', 'Most Secret', 6 October 1943: Cabinet papers, 79/65.

desire for the capture of Rhodes, 'done properly and by first-class troops'. Such troops, he said, could be one of the divisions 'now destined for Italy'. The diversion of a 'first class division' from Italy, warned Brooke, 'would leave us open to a serious danger of being successfully counter-attacked when we reached the Pisa line, and of being thrown back, possibly even as far as Rome'.

In place of an attack on Rhodes, Brooke suggested British military support 'for the guerilla forces now in Albania and Yugoslavia', with a view to forcing the Germans to withdraw from Greece. 'If this were achieved,' he said, 'the Aegean Islands would fall into our hands.' Moreover, Brooke argued, should the troops used in this Balkan operation 'be urgently required in Italy', they could be withdrawn 'more easily' from the western Balkans than from Rhodes.

According to Portal, 'considerable pressure could be brought to bear on the Balkans' by the bombing of such cities as Sofia, Budapest and Bucharest. The bombing of Sofia, he said, 'might result in our being able to compel the Bulgarians to withdraw the eight divisions they now had in Greece', a withdrawal which 'could have considerable effect on the whole German position in the area'. This bombing proposal was supported by Eden.

As the Staff Conference came to an end, Churchill told the meeting that 'a cardinal strategic decision was now at issue. It was intolerable that the enemy, pressed on all fronts, could be allowed to continue to pick up cheap prizes in the Aegean.' Rhodes, Churchill added, 'was the key and every effort should be made to capture it provided our position in Italy was not imperilled. The matter required further and urgent study.'[1]

Churchill now proposed flying to Tunis, to Eisenhower's headquarters. 'PM has ordered his plane to be ready to take him to Tunis tonight!' Cadogan noted in his diary on October 7. 'He is excited about Kos, and wants to lead an expedition into Rhodes!'[2] Brooke was annoyed, noting in his diary on October 8:

I can now control him no more. He has worked himself into a frenzy of excitement about the Rhodes attack, has magnified its importance so that he can no longer see anything else and has set his heart on capturing this one island even at the expense of endangering his relations with the President and the Americans and the future of the Italian campaign. He refused to listen to any arguments or to see any dangers.[3]

Churchill's dictation that night was to Marian Holmes, who noted

[1] Staff Conference, Chiefs of Staff Committee No. 241 (Operations) of 1943, 7 October 1943: Cabinet papers, 79/65.
[2] Cadogan diary, 7 October 1943: David Dilks (editor), op. cit., page 565.
[3] Brooke diary, 8 October 1943: Bryant, op. cit., volume 2, page 51.

in her diary: 'The PM said he had had a bad day, a very bad day. In a rather confiding way he said "The difficulty is not winning the war; it is in persuading people to let you win it—persuading fools." He seemed distressed and said he felt "almost like chucking it in". He had been trying to persuade the Americans to invade Rhodes.' [1]

On October 8, Churchill received Roosevelt's reply to his telegram of October 7. 'I do not want,' it began, 'to force on Eisenhower diversions which limit the prospect for the early successful development of the Italian operations to a secure line north of Rome.' Nor should there be any 'diversion of forces or equipment', Roosevelt urged, that might 'prejudice "Overlord" as planned'. The American Chiefs of Staff 'agree', he added. [2] Churchill replied at once:

I earnestly pray that my views may receive some consideration from you at this critical juncture, remembering how fruitful our concerted action has been in the past and how important it is for the future.

I am sure that the omission to take Rhodes at this stage and the ignoring of the whole position in the Eastern Mediterranean would constitute a cardinal error in strategy. I am convinced also that if we were round the table together this operation could be fitted into our plan without detriment either to the advance in Italy, of which, as you know, I have always been an advocate or to the build-up of 'Overlord', which I am prepared faithfully to support.

Churchill added that he was 'willing to proceed' immediately to Eisenhower's headquarters in Tunis, with General Brooke, 'if you will send General Marshall, or your personal representative, to meet me there, and we can then submit the results of a searching discussion to you and your Chiefs of Staff'. He and Brooke could be in Tunis, Churchill added, in two days' time, on the afternoon of October 10, a Sunday. [3]

In a second telegram on October 8, Churchill pointed out that the delay involved in the Rhodes plan in landing craft reaching Britain was of about six weeks, and this 'nearly six months before they would actually be needed' for 'Overlord'. It also involved only

[1] Marian Holmes diary, 7 October 1943: Marian Walker Spicer papers. On the following day, while on his way to Chequers, Churchill had gone to the Royal Masonic Hospital to see Sir Dudley Pound. At the hospital, and at the request of King George VI, he placed in Pound's hands the insignia of the Order of Merit. Pound, the victim of two severe strokes, was unable to speak, but, as Commander Thompson recalled, 'he recognized the Prime Minister, and grasped his hand'. (Gerald Pawle, *The War and Colonel Warden* based on the recollections of Commander C. R. Thompson, London 1963, page 253.) Thirteen days later, on Trafalgar Day, Pound died.

[2] President to Prime Minister, No. 379, 'Personal and Most Secret', 8 October 1943: Churchill papers, 20/120.

[3] Prime Minister's Personal Telegram, T.1535/3, Prime Minister to President, No. 441, 'Personal and Most Secret', 8 October 1943: Churchill papers, 20/120.

nine landing craft. 'There ought, I think, to be some elasticity,' he added, 'and a reasonable latitude in the handling of our joint affairs.' [1]

Replying on October 9, Roosevelt reiterated his and the American Chief of Staffs' opposition to a campaign against Rhodes. The 'problem is', he wrote, 'are we to enter into a Balkan campaign, starting with the southern tip, or is there more to be gained, and with security, by pushing rapidly to the agreed-upon position north of Rome?' As to the meeting which Churchill proposed on October 10 in Africa, 'this', Roosevelt wrote, 'would be in effect another meeting of the Combined Chiefs of Staff, necessarily involving only a partial representation and in which I cannot participate. Frankly, I am not in sympathy with this procedure under the circumstances.' [2]

Churchill gave up his plan to fly to Tunis. 'At your wish,' he telegraphed to Roosevelt, 'and as you cannot send General Marshall, I have cancelled my journey, which I told Harry on the telephone I would never undertake without your blessing.'

General Wilson's plan to attack Rhodes on October 23, operation 'Accolade', was still to go ahead, but without any forces diverted from Italy, unless Eisenhower were to give his approval, which now seemed unlikely. Wilson considered his forces were sufficient, Churchill told Roosevelt, 'but I am doubtful whether they are not cut too fine'. Cancellation of 'Accolade', however, would involve the loss of Leros, 'and the complete abandonment by us of any foothold in the Aegean, which will become a frozen area, with most unfortunate political and psychological reactions in that part of the world instead of great advantages'. [3]

Churchill had begun his telegram to Roosevelt by thanking the President 'very much for your kindness in giving so much of your time and thought to the views which I ventured to set before you', and he ended:

I fully agree with all you say about the paramount importance of the build-up in Italy, and I have given every proof of my zeal in this matter by stripping the British Middle Eastern Command of everything which can facilitate General Eisenhower's operations, in which we also have so great a stake. [4]

To General Wilson, who had gone to Tunis for a conference of

---

[1] Prime Minister's Personal Telegram, T.1540/3, Prime Minister to President, No. 443, 'Personal and Most Secret', 8 October 1943: Churchill papers, 20/120.

[2] President to Prime Minister, No. 381, 'Personal and Most Secret', 9 October 1943: Churchill papers, 20/120.

[3] Prime Minister's Personal Telegram, T.1552/3, Prime Minister to President, No. 445, 'Personal and Most Secret', 9 October 1943: Churchill papers, 20/120.

[4] Prime Minister's Personal Telegram, T.1552/3, Prime Minister to President, No. 445, 'Personal and Most Secret', 9 October 1943: Churchill papers, 20/120.

Middle East Commanders-in-Chief, Churchill telegraphed that same day:

You should press most strongly at the conference for further support for 'Accolade'. I do not believe the forces at present assigned to it are sufficient, and if you are left to take a setback it would be bad. It is clear that the key to the strategic situation in the next month in the Mediterranean is expressed in the two words 'Storm Rhodes'. Do not therefore undertake this on the cheap. Demand what is necessary, and consult with Alexander.

Chuchill's telegram ended: 'I am doing all I can.'[1]

At the meeting of the Commanders-in-Chief held in Tunis on October 9, it was decided that further reinforcements could not be spared for the Rhodes attack. The Germans, Eisenhower pointed out in a telegram to the Combined Chiefs of Staff and to the British Chiefs of Staff, had reacted to the Italian armistice 'even more strongly than expected', and had brought air force reinforcements from both Russia and France, 'which at once resulted' in almost complete German control 'of the air, and consequently, of the sea in the Aegean'. Eisenhower added, in explanation of the Tunis Conference discussions: 'All of us are agreed that if Rhodes is not captured and held there is no chance of restoring the local air situation sufficiently to allow surface forces and maintenance shipping to defend and maintain the islands we still hold.' But the Conference, having examined the available Allied forces, was agreed, Eisenhower reported, 'that our resources in the Mediterranean are not large enough to allow us to undertake the capture of Rhodes and at the same time secure our immediate objectives in Italy. We must therefore choose between Rhodes and Rome. To us it is clear that we must concentrate on the Italian campaign.'[2]

The decisive factor in the Tunis decision was one which had not been foreseen forty-eight hours earlier, the German decision to give up the withdrawal northward, which 'Boniface' had so faithfully monitored, and to hold a line well south of Rome.[3]

---

[1] Prime Minister's Personal Telegram, T.1549/3, OZ 3120, 'Personal and Most Secret', 9 October 1943: Churchill papers, 20/120.

[2] NAF 384, Telegram Nos. 686 and 687, 'Secret', 9 October 1943: Cabinet papers, 105/140.

[3] This German decision, one former Staff Officer writes, 'spelled success for the Allied Mediterranean strategy'. Hitherto, he adds, 'we had been failing, since the enemy were successfully withdrawing. Now Hitler, as if written into the part, sprang to our rescue and guaranteed that we should achieve our object of "containing the maximum number of German divisions". We needed his collaboration, and we not only got it but retained it until May 1945.' (Sir David Hunt, letter to the author, 23 July 1985.)

In a telegram to Churchill on October 9, when the Tunis discussions had ended, Eisenhower referred to the effect of these 'drastic changes' in the German plan on the operation against Rhodes. 'It is personally distressing to me,' Eisenhower wrote, 'to advise against a project in which you believe so earnestly but I feel I would not be performing my duty if I should recommend otherwise.' All the Commanders-in-Chief, Eisenhower ended, 'share this attitude'.[1]

Churchill still hoped that 'Accolade' might somehow be possible, and Maitland Wilson also felt that something might be done at 'a later date'. Wilson also believed, as he telegraphed to Churchill on October 10, that the holding of Leros and Samos was 'not impossible'.[2] Churchill replied at once: 'Cling on if you possibly can. It will be a splendid achievement.' If, after everything had been done, 'you are forced to quit, I will support you, but victory is the prize'.[3]

Churchill accepted that the evacuation of Leros might have to take place. He would not interfere with Maitland Wilson's judgement. 'I will not waste words,' he telegraphed to Roosevelt, 'in explaining how painful this decision is to me.' 'You should now try,' he telegraphed to Alexander, 'to save what we can from the wreck. . . .'[4]

'Can nothing be done even to regain Kos?' Churchill asked Admiral Cunningham on October 10.[5] But the answer was a gloomy one. 'Without the Turkish airfields,' Cunningham replied, 'the recapture of Kos would have to be undertaken almost without air cover.' The air effort required to have a 'reasonable prospect of success', Cunningham added, 'can only be provided at cost of compromising main battle in Italy'.[6] 'We left no stone unturned to meet your wishes,' Alexander telegraphed to Churchill that same day, 'and I am only so sorry and disappointed we could not find the way.'[7]

The focus of attention now turned again to Italy. To Eden, who was in Algiers on his way to Moscow, Churchill telegraphed on October 10: 'We must bow before the new fact of the German intention to reinforce the south and fight the battle south of Rome.' But still he hankered after the possibility of the recapture of Kos, using, as

[1] Telegram No. 681, 9 October 1943: Churchill papers, 20/120.

[2] CIC/134, IZ 3724, 'Personal and Most Secret', 10 October 1943: Churchill papers, 20/120.

[3] Prime Minister's Personal Telegram, T.1576/3, OZ 3138, 'Personal and Most Secret', 10 October 1943: Churchill papers, 20/120.

[4] Prime Minister's Personal Telegram, T.1571/3, Prime Minister to President, No. 449, 'Personal and Most Secret', 10 October 1943: Churchill papers, 20/120.

[5] Prime Minister's Personal Telegram, T.1566/3, Naval Signal No. 100215/A, 'Most Secret and Personal', 10 October 1943: Churchill papers, 20/120. Admiral Sir John Cunningham had just been appointed Commander-in-Chief, Mediterranean in succession to his cousin, Admiral Sir Andrew Cunningham, Dudley Pound's successor as First Sea Lord.

[6] Naval Signal No. 100504/A, 10 October 1943: Churchill papers, 20/120.

[7] MA/636, 'Most Secret', 10 October 1943: Churchill papers, 20/120.

Cunningham, had made clear they would have to use, the Turkish airfields. The Turks, he wrote, had already shown themselves 'unexpectedly co-operative' in the matter of both the islands, straining Turkish neutrality and provoking German protest. 'If we are extricated from those islands,' Churchill told Eden, 'making no effort, all this will be chilled and frozen again.' [1] But on the following day, in a telegram to Alexander, Churchill accepted the inevitable. 'I quite understand,' he wrote. 'Situation had been changed by new enemy movements and intentions.' [2] Three days later, British forces were to be forced to withdraw from Simi, which the Germans occupied on the following day. To General Wilson, Churchill telegraphed on October 11 that it would be a 'great triumph' if he could keep Leros 'safely', and he added: 'I am very pleased with the way in which you used such poor bits and pieces as were left you. "Nil desperandum."' [3]

---

[1] Prime Minister's Personal Telegram, T.1573/3, Foreign Office No. 2229 to Algiers, 'Personal and Secret', 10 October 1943: Churchill papers, 4/396.

[2] Prime Minister's Personal Telegram, T.1581/3, 11 October 1943: Churchill papers, 4/396.

[3] Prime Minister's Personal Telegram, T.1616/3, 'Personal and Most Secret', 11 October 1943: Churchill papers, 20/121.

32

The Channel *versus* the Mediterranean

C HURCHILL'S Private Office and secretaries witnessed a world of work which had many lighter moments. Four entries in Marian Holmes' diary for mid October give a flavour of these evening, and sometimes morning, sessions:

Wed. 13th Oct. '43
PM was entertaining. When I went in he said 'I aint seen you for a long time'. He accidentally lit his cigar at the wrong end. 'Oh Lor'! Look what I've done.' He read a newspaper account of his own statement in the House today and acted it out gesticulating wildly towards the fire as if he were delivering the speech all over again.

Friday 15th Oct. 1943, Chequers
PM arrived with Mr Rowan about 8 p.m. After work had finished late in the office he seemed reluctant to go to bed and wanted to talk. He was so amusing—Mr Rowan and I were spellbound. He talked about the Transfiguration and St Peter being expected to make some comment. He reminisced about his bout with paratyphoid and Randolph being prepared 'to make the supreme sacrifice'.

Saturday, 16th Oct. '43
PM working from bed. Went in at 10 a.m. and emerged at 1.15 with packets of work. Inadvertently blew his cigar candle out in his face. Faux pas no. 1 today.

Sunday 17th Oct. '43
We had a film on the Battle of Britain produced by the Americans. PM had a stag party dinner which didn't break up until midnight. Afterwards he worked a little and then had some records of martial music played in the Great Hall. Bed at 2.30 a.m.[1]

On October 12 Churchill announced in the House of Commons that Portugal had granted Britain 'certain facilities' in the Azores, for

[1] Marian Holmes, diary entries for 13, 15, 16 and 17 October 1943: Marian Walker Spicer papers.

the protection of British merchant shipping in the Atlantic; these included naval and air facilities. This, Churchill said, was the 'latest application' of the Anglo-Portuguese Treaty of 1373.[1] He could make no reference to his many weeks of intense telegraphic discussion with Roosevelt about the Azores, and about a possible British military landing, should the Portuguese refuse to grant the British the facilities they sought. Even then, there were to be many further weeks of haggling with the Portuguese Government, until it agreed to let American as well as British aircraft operate from the Azores.

Churchill had accepted that the cross-Channel landing must go ahead, whatever opportunities might or might not exist for further military action in Italy and the Balkans. Since his arrival in Britain, however, General Smuts had continued to take a critical view of 'Overlord'. On October 13 Smuts put his worries to the King, who wrote to Churchill on the following day of how Smuts wanted Britain 'to go on fighting' in the Mediterranean theatre of war, '& not to switch over to a new front like "Overlord"'. The King's letter continued:

I have thought about this matter a lot since then & am wondering whether we three could not discuss it together, I have always thought that your original idea of last year of attacking the 'underbelly of the Axis' was the right one, & you convinced President Roosevelt & Gen. Marshall to carry out 'Torch'. The present situation as we know has turned out even better than we could have ever hoped for last year & would it not be possible to carry on there. Look at the present position in the Mediterranean. The whole of North Africa is ours, we command the Mediterranean Sea itself, Sicily, Sardinia & Corsica, half the mainland of Italy is ours. Italy is now at war with our enemy Germany; Roumania & Hungary are trying to get into touch with us.

What we want to see is Greece & Yugoslavia liberated; then Turkey may come in with us & may be we shall see the 3 Great Powers, Great Britain, USA & USSR fighting together on the same front!!

Let this country be the base from which all bombing operations will take place in an ever increasing intensity on Germany.

The King's letter ended:

I was so impressed by what Smuts said that I felt I must pass it on to you. I know there are many difficulties for a change of plan at this late hour, but you, F.D.R. & Stalin are to meet in the near future.

I am alone here for dinner tonight, & if there is any possibility of Smuts & you joining me, it would give us all a very good opportunity of talking these things over undisturbed.

Would 8.30 p.m. or 8.45 p.m. suit you best?[2]

---

[1] 'Azores (British Facilities in), Agreement with Portugal': *Hansard*, 12 October 1943: columns 716–18.

[2] Letter of 14 October 1943, from Buckingham Palace: Churchill papers, 20/92.

Churchill accepted the King's invitation to dine that night. But in his letter of acceptance he set out his position, and that of the Government, with terse clarity, and in four short sentences, telling the King:

There is no possibility of our going back on what is agreed. Both the US Staff and Stalin would violently disagree with us.

It must be remembered that this country is the only base from which our Metropolitan Fighter Air Force can make its weight tell. I think there are resources for both theatres.[1]

That night, Smuts and Churchill dined with the King at Buckingham Palace. 'We discussed the whole strategy of the war at length,' the King wrote in his diary, '& W thinks it possible to arrange for Overlord & the Balkans too. The USSR know that we & the USA are definitely going to do the former but if the situation in the Medn warrants it we shall go on there, & the divisions will not be withdrawn until later.'[2]

Soviet demands for a meeting of the three leaders were now linked to accusations that neither Britain nor the United States were serious about the cross-Channel operation, or willing to take risks to maintain the convoy system. The Russians, Churchill telegraphed to Roosevelt a week later, after a Soviet complaint about the 'Quadrant' meeting in Quebec, 'ought not to be vexed if the Americans and British closely concert the very great operations they have in hand for 1944 on fronts where no Russian troops will be present'. Nor, he added, 'do I think we ought to meet Stalin, if ever the meeting can be arranged, without being agreed about Anglo-American operations as such'.[3]

Churchill now pressed Roosevelt for a final decision about the 'High Commands'. Although at Quebec these Commands had been allocated according to the numbers of troops involved, with the cross-Channel invasion to be commanded by an American, no actual appointments had yet been made. 'Unless there is a German collapse,' Churchill telegraphed to Roosevelt on October 17, 'the campaign of 1944 will be far the most dangerous we have undertaken, and per-

---

[1] Letter of 14 October 1943, 'Copy of letter sent in the Prime Minister's own hand': Churchill papers, 20/92.

[2] King George VI, diary, 14 October 1943: John W. Wheeler-Bennett, *King George VI, op. cit.*, page 596.

[3] Prime Minister's Personal Telegram, T.1707/3, Prime Minister to President, No. 471, 'Personal and Most Secret', 23 October 1943, sent to Eden in Moscow as Foreign Office, Telegram No. 118 Extra, 23 October 1943: Cabinet papers, 120/113.

sonally I am more anxious about its success than I was about 1941, 1942 or 1943.'[1]

To maintain the security of the artificial harbours being prepared for the cross-Channel landing, and so essential to its success, the Joint Intelligence Sub-Committee decided, on October 11, that the code-word 'Mulberry' should be adopted 'to cover all reference to artificial harbours in connection with Operation "Overlord"'.[2] To Eden, who was in Moscow, Churchill pointed out on October 18, the efforts Britain was making in preparation for the cross-Channel invasion, the 'delays' in which the Russians continued to complain of, even though, at Quebec, its date had been set for May 1944.

Churchill went on to point out to Eden, for his Soviet hosts, that Britain was about to bring the 50th and 51st Divisions, as well as the 1st Airborne Division, back to Britain from Sicily, 'where', Churchill pointed out, 'they are needed for the Italian battle', in order to prepare them for the cross-Channel operation. Also earmarked for return was the 7th Armoured Division, known, from its formation sign, as the Desert Rats. Yet the cross-Channel operation, Churchill added, 'cannot take place for seven months at the earliest' and only then upon the 'hypothetical conditions which will probably not be fulfilled' of not more than twelve mobile German divisions being in France and the Low Countries at the time of the landing, and no more than fifteen 'first quality' divisions being able to be transferred from Russia during the first two months. Everything showed, Churchill wrote, 'that the German troops are fighting with their customary skill and tenacity' and he added: 'I do not view the prospects for the 1944 campaign with a complacent eye.'[3]

It was not only with fears that the cross-Channel invasion might fail, but with worries lest opportunities might also be missed elsewhere, that Churchill returned, on October 19, to thoughts of a renewed initiative in the Mediterranean. Having studied reports of partisan activity in Yugoslavia and Greece, and having met one of the organizers of the resistance in Greece, Brigadier Myers, Churchill asked the Chiefs of Staff to carry out a study of the situation in the Mediterranean 'with particular reference to the growing resistance to Germany, both active and potential, which is developing in varying degrees in all the Balkan countries'.

---

[1] Prime Minister's Personal Telegram, T.1655/3, Prime Minister to President, No. 464, 'Personal and Most Secret', 17 October 1943: Churchill papers, 20/121.

[2] Joint Intelligence Committee Paper No. 416 (Operations) (Final) of 1943, 'Most Secret', 11 October 1943: Cabinet papers, 79/66. The codeword 'Flowerpot' was chosen at the same time for all artificial harbours in connection with South-East Asia command.

[3] Prime Minister's Personal Telegram, T.1659/3, 'Personal and Most Secret', 'For your eye alone', 18 October 1943: Churchill papers, 20/121.

In his minute to the Chiefs of Staff Committee, Churchill noted, in relation to the 'engagements' into which Britain had entered at Quebec with regard to 'Overlord' and South East Asia: 'Nevertheless, we must not shrink from taking a stern view of the policy we ought to adopt as opportunities open themselves to us for exploiting successes in any theatre of war.' Churchill's minute continued:

We cannot lightly disregard the difficulties facing the Germans and their satellites in the Balkan countries and the chance that may lie within our grasp to bring Turkey more actively on our side.

Pray let this enquiry be conducted in a most secret manner and on the assumption that commitments into which we have already entered with the Americans, particularly as regards 'Overlord', could be modified by agreement to meet the exigencies of a changing situation.

If the Chiefs of Staff advocate a forward policy in the Balkans, I should like to know, in broad terms, what this will involve. It may well be that we need not recant on 'Overlord' except as regards emphasis and the balance of our effort.[1]

Reading this minute, Brooke noted in his diary, 'I am in many ways entirely with him, but God knows where this may lead us regards clashes with the Americans.'[2]

At 10.30 that night Churchill's minute was one of the items on the agenda at a Staff Conference. Those present included the three Chiefs of Staff, Attlee, Cadogan, Lyttelton, and Field Marshal Smuts. During the discussion, Churchill expressed his concern at 'the effect the arrangements being made for "Overlord" were having on operations in the Mediterranean', telling the Staff Conference:

It was unsound to miss present opportunities for the sake of an operation which could not take place for another seven months, and which might, in fact, have to be postponed to an even later date. He felt that by tying ourselves to undertake Operation 'Overlord' there was a serious risk that we should undertake two operations, each employing approximately equal forces and neither being strong enough for the purpose for which it was required. We would thus give the enemy an opportunity of concentrating and defeating our forces in detail.

As far as operation 'Overlord' was concerned, Churchill continued, 'he was not afraid of the Channel crossing or of the landing on the enemy coast'. He felt that we should 'probably' be able to effect a landing, and 'in the first instance we might make progress'. His worries were for later on, as he went on to explain:

[1] Prime Minister's Personal Minute, D.178/3, 'Most Secret', 19 October 1943: Churchill papers, 20/104.

[2] Brooke diary, 19 October 1943: Bryant, *op. cit.*, volume 2, page 55.

He felt that by landing in Northwest Europe we might be giving the enemy the opportunity to concentrate, by reason of his excellent roads and rail communications, an overwhelming force against us and to inflict on us a military disaster greater than that of Dunkirk. Such a disaster would result in the resuscitation of Hitler and the Nazi regime.

Smuts supported Churchill, feeling that the 'events of the last year' in North Africa, Sicily and Italy 'now offered a clear run in to victory provided we did not blunder'. The cross-Channel operation could be a 'very dangerous one' unless large German forces could be diverted to oppose operations elsewhere, and he cited 'both Italy and the South of France'. Brooke was likewise cautious. It was 'quite wrong', he said, 'to try to wage war on the principle of a series of "lawyers' contracts"', and he went on to recall that at the 'Quadrant' meeting 'he had refused to agree to a definite contract and had for example insisted that the question of the withdrawal of divisions from the Middle East for operation "Overlord" should be reviewed in the light of the situation prevailing when the time for their withdrawal came'.

Brooke also noted that, in a recent telegram from Italy, 'General Alexander had pointed out that large numbers of landing craft were required for maintenance purposes, and that as our forces advanced into mountainous areas and communications became canalised, landing craft were essential to enable us to get round the enemy flanks'.

Churchill then reminded the Staff Conference 'that he had only agreed to Operation "Overlord" being launched provided certain conditions regarding size of the enemy land and air forces and probable rate of build-up were fulfilled'. In addition to the possibility of the German forces exceeding these limits, he pointed out, 'there was always the possibility of a slackening in the efforts of the Russians on the Eastern front'. A 'guarantee from the Russians that they would continue to push on', Churchill argued, 'would be an essential condition to "Overlord"'.

Both Portal and Cunningham remarked that the Russians 'might regard our operations in the Mediterranean with great favour' if they thought they were undertaken 'with the object of opening the Dardanelles'—shades of 1915! Summing up, Churchill felt that the meeting was agreed:

(i) To reinforce the Italian theatre to the full.
(ii) To enter the Balkans.
(iii) To hold our position in the Aegean Islands.
(iv) To build-up our air forces and intensify our air attacks on Germany.
(v) To encourage the steady assembly in this country of United States troops, which could not be employed in the Pacific owing to the shortage of shipping, with a view to taking advantage of the softening in the

enemy's resistance due to our operations in other theatres, though this might not occur until after the spring of 1944.

'Unfortunately,' Churchill commented, 'we could not take a unilateral decision regarding the future strategy of the Allied nations. A further meeting with the Americans would therefore be necessary.' Churchill added:

He, however, felt so strongly that our strategy, as at present agreed, was wrong in that it exposed our forces in the various theatres to defeat in detail, and at the same time led to our missing great opportunities now in order to build-up forces for an operation which could not take place for some months, and would in all probability be postponed, that he was prepared to reopen the matter with the Americans. If, as a result, the latter wished to transfer the bulk of their forces to the Pacific, he would be prepared to accept this providing they would leave the forces already in this country and would build-up their Air Force for operations against Germany as already promised. He did not, however, think the shipping position would permit them to employ the greater part of their Army in areas other than Europe.[1]

The outcome of this Staff Conference was to call for a meeting of the Combined Chiefs of Staff as soon as possible, and, as Cadogan noted, 'before the "Big Boys" meet'.[2] On the following day, in a telegram to Roosevelt, Churchill sounded a warning note, pointing out the 'changes' that had taken place since Quebec and the need for a 'full conference' of the Combined Chiefs of Staff in North Africa, possibly while Churchill and Roosevelt were themselves on their way to their meeting with Stalin. 'We will go wherever you wish,' Churchill wrote, 'but is there any reason why we should not meet again at Anfa?'[3]

In a telegram to Eden on October 20, Churchill set out what he considered had become the 'grave defects' of the Anglo-American plans for 1944. 'Neither the force built up in Italy,' he wrote, 'nor that which will be ready in May to cross the Channel, is adequate for what is required. . . .' Churchill was 'determined', he wrote, to have this situation 'reviewed'. His telegram continued:

If it lay with me to decide, I would not withdraw any troops from the Mediterranean and would not debouch from the narrow leg of Italy into the valley of the Po, and would engage the enemy strongly on the narrower front while at the same time fomenting Balkan and Southern France disturbances. In the absence of a German collapse, I do not think we should

[1] Staff Conference, Chiefs of Staff Committee No. 254 (Operations) of 1943, 19 October 1943: Cabinet papers, 79/66.
[2] Cadogan diary, 19 October 1943: David Dilks (editor), *op. cit.*, page 569.
[3] Prime Minister's Personal Telegram, T.1670/3, Prime Minister to President, No. 467, 'Personal and Most Secret', 20 October 1943: Churchill papers, 20/121.

cross the Channel with less than forty divisions available by the sixtieth day, and then only if the Italian front were in strong action with the enemy. I do not accept the American argument that our metropolitan Air Forces can flatten everything out in the battle zone or on its approaches. This has not been our present experience.

'All this,' Churchill added, 'is for your internal consumption, and not for deployment at this stage.' It was to show Eden 'the dangers of our being committed to a lawyer's bargain for "Overlord" in May for the sake of which we may have to ruin the Italian and Balkan possibilities' and yet, in northern France, have 'insufficient forces to maintain ourselves after the thirtieth or fortieth day'.

Churchill wanted Eden to find out 'what the Russians really feel' about the Balkans, and he went on to ask:

Would they be attracted by the idea of our acting through the Aegean involving Turkey in the war, and opening the Dardanelles and Bosphorus so that British Naval forces and shipping could aid the Russian advance and so that we could ultimately give them our right hand along the Danube? How great an interest would they feel in our opening the Black Sea to Allied warships, supplies, and Allied military forces, including Turkish? Have they any interest in this right-handed evolution, or are they still set only on our attacking France?—observing that of course in any circumstances the steady building up of forces in England will hold large German forces in the West.

'It may be,' Churchill reflected, that for political reasons the Russians would not want Britain to develop a 'large-scale' Balkan strategy. Their desire that Turkey should enter the war showed, however, their interest in the 'South-Eastern' theatre. Churchill's telegram continued:

I remain convinced of the great importance of our getting a foothold in the Aegean by taking Rhodes, re-taking Kos, and holding Leros, and building up an effective air and naval superiority in these waters. Do the Russians view with sympathy our effort to hold Leros and desire to take Rhodes? Do they understand the effect this has upon Turkey, and how it opens the possibility of a naval advance into the Black Sea?

Churchill's telegram ended: 'Again, all the above is simply for your inner thoughts.' [1]

Churchill's 'inner thoughts' had turned decisively towards a continuation and if possible an intensification of the Italian, Balkan and Eastern Mediterranean war, and he was now hesitating about 'Overlord'. But in a telegram from Moscow, Eden made it clear that the Soviet Union would brook no change of emphasis or plan:

[1] Prime Minister's Personal Telegram, T.1677/3, Foreign Office No. 1663 to Moscow, 'Personal and Most Secret', 20 October 1943: Churchill papers, 20/121.

'Overlord' must go ahead. On this both Molotov and Marshal Voroshilov were insistent when they met Eden, Cordell Hull and Harriman on October 21, 'after a hearty lunch given by Mr Molotov'.[1]

That evening, Stalin himself, in conversation with Eden, admitted, as Eden's diary recorded, 'that the Anglo-American campaign in Italy had helped the Soviet Union; the Germans no longer moved fresh reserves to the Soviet front'.[2] 'I am quite clear,' Eden telegraphed to Churchill on the following day, 'that they are completely and blindly set on our invading Northern France and that there is absolutely *nothing* that we could suggest in any other part of the world which would reconcile them to a cancellation of, or even a postponement of "Overlord".' The Russians had asked him 'again and again', Eden reported, 'When would the operation start?'[3]

Churchill's hesitations about 'Overlord' had not led him to neglect any of the preparations essential for its success. One of these was the need to decide finally on the personnel who were to command the various aspects of the invasions. 'I am hoping this can be settled soon,' Churchill telegraphed to Roosevelt on October 22, and he added: 'To give "Overlord" the best chance, the Commanders should be at it now. The eye of the master maketh the horse fat.'[4]

'Whatever happens,' Churchill ended, 'we have got to meet soon.'[5] On the following day he telegraphed again, stressing that the reason for wanting an early conference was his worries about the follow-up prospect of 'Overlord'. Churchill began by setting out the developments which would have taken place in the three months between his 'Quadrant' meeting with Roosevelt at Quebec and the proposed Big Three 'Eureka' conference at Teheran, pointing out to Roosevelt:

In these ninety days events of first magnitude have occurred. Mussolini has fallen; Italy has surrendered; its Fleet has come over; we have successfully invaded Italy, and are marching on Rome with good prospects of success. The Germans are gathering up to 25 or more divisions in Italy and the Po Valley. All these are new facts.

[1] 'Space' No. 48, 'Most Secret', Moscow, 21 October 1943: Churchill papers, 20/121.
[2] Eden diary and notes, 21 October 1943: Eden memoirs, *The Reckoning, op. cit.*, page 412.
[3] Telegram No. 1149 from Moscow, 'Most Secret', 22 October 1943: Churchill papers, 20/121.
[4] Xenophon, *Oeconomicus*, chapter 12, section 20: 'The King, you know, had happened on a good horse, and wanted to fatten him as speedily as posssible. So he asked one who was reputed clever with horses what is the quickest way of fattening a horse. "The master's eye" replied the man. I think we may apply the answer generally, Socrates, and say that the master's eye in the main does the good and worthy work.' ('If you want to make men fit to take charge you must supervise their work and examine it, and be ready to reward work well carried through, and not shrink from punishing carelessness as it deserves.')
[5] Prime Minister's Personal Telegram, T.1693/3, Prime Minister to President, No. 469, 'Personal and Most Secret', 22 October 1943: Churchill papers, 20/121.

Churchill then set out the worries which he had first expressed at the Staff Conference four days earlier, and which were now even more deeply troubling him:

Our present plans for 1944 seem open to very grave defects. We are to put 15 American and 12 British divisions into Overlord and will have about 6 American and 16 British or British-controlled divisions on the Italian front. Unless there is a German collapse Hitler, lying in the centre of the best communications in the world, can concentrate at least 40 to 50 divisions against either of these forces while holding the other. He could obtain all the necessary forces by cutting his losses in the Balkans and withdrawing to the Sava and the Danube without necessarily weakening his Russian front.

In examining the question of how Britain and America had come to their strategic decisions for 1944, Churchill reminded the President:

The disposition of our forces between the Italian and the Channel theatres has not been settled by strategic needs but by the march of events, by shipping possibilities, and by arbitrary compromises between the British and Americans. The date of Overlord itself was fixed by splitting the difference between the American and British view. It is arguable that neither the forces building up in Italy nor those available for a May Overlord are strong enough for the tasks set them.

Churchill's telegram continued:

The British Staffs and my colleagues and I all think this position requires to be reviewed, and that the Commanders for both fronts should be named and should be present. In pursuance of Quadrant decisions we have already prepared two of our best divisions, the 50th and the 51st now in Sicily, for transfer to Overlord. Thus they can play no part in the Italian battle to which they stood so near, but will not come into action again for seven months and then only if certain hypothetical conditions are fulfilled which may very likely not be fulfilled.

Early in November a decision must be taken about moving landing craft from the Mediterranean to Overlord. This will cripple Mediterranean operations without the said craft influencing events elsewhere for many months. We stand by what was agreed at Quadrant but we do not feel that such agreements should be interpreted rigidly and without review in the swiftly changing situations of war.

'Personally,' Churchill informed Roosevelt, 'I feel that if we make serious mistakes in the campaign of 1944, we might give Hitler the chance of a startling come-back.' A German prisoner-of-war then being held in custody in London, General von Thoma, had been 'overheard', Churchill told Roosevelt, 'saying "Our only hope is that they come where we can use the Army upon them"'. 'All this,'

Churchill commented, 'shows the need for the greatest care and foresight in our arrangements, the most accurate timing between the two theatres, and the need to gather the greatest possible forces for both operations, particularly Overlord.'

Churchill went on to tell Roosevelt:

I do not doubt our ability in the conditions laid down to get ashore and deploy. I am however deeply concerned with the build-up and with the situation which may arise between the thirtieth and sixtieth days. I feel sure that the vast movement of American personnel into the United Kingdom and the fighting composition of the units requires to be searchingly examined by the commander who will execute 'Overlord'.

I wish to have both the High Commands settled in a manner agreeable to our two countries, and then the secondary commands, which are of very high importance, can be decided, I repeat I have the greatest confidence in General Marshall, and that if he is in charge of 'Overlord' we British will aid him with every scrap of life and strength we have.

'My dear friend,' Churchill continued, 'this is much the greatest thing we have ever attempted, and I am not satisfied that we have yet taken the measures necessary to give it the best chance of success. I feel very much in the dark at present, and unable to think or act in the forward manner which is needed.' It was for these reasons, Churchill ended, 'I desire an early conference.'[1] To Alexander, Churchill telegraphed on October 24: 'Naturally I am made anxious by the departure while your battle is on of our two fine divisions, 50th and 51st, in pursuance of "Quadrant" decisions. I should like to have your feelings about the strength of your Army for the tasks which lie immediately ahead.'[2]

Each day's secret news and dispositions made clear the impact which preparations for 'Overlord' were having on the Italian campaign. 'Naturally,' Churchill telegraphed to General Marshall on October 24, 'I feel in my marrow the withdrawal of our 50th and 51st Divisions, our best, from the edge of the Battle of Rome in the interests of distant "Overlord",' and he added: 'We are carrying out our contract, but I pray God it does not cost us dear.'

Churchill had still not heard from Roosevelt of Marshall's formal and public appointment, to command the cross-Channel forces. 'I do hope to hear of your appointment soon,' he wrote. 'You know I will back you through thick and thin and make your path smooth here.'

In spite of his grave doubts, Churchill's work for 'Overlord' was

[1] Prime Minister's Personal Telegram, T.1707/3, Prime Minister to President, No. 471, 'Personal and Most Secret', 23 October 1943: Churchill papers, 20/122. Sent to Eden in Moscow as Foreign Office telegram No. 118 Extra, 23 October 1943: Cabinet papers, 120/113.

[2] Prime Minister's Personal Telegram, T.1716/3, 'Personal and Secret. For Your Eye Alone', 'Through "C"', 24 October 1943: Churchill papers, 20/122.

continuous and wholehearted. It was essential, he told Marshall, 'to mystify and baffle' the Germans as to the meaning of the Allied movements. 'More tell-tale even than the movement of divisions,' Churchill wrote, 'is that of landing craft. We know from "Boniface" that this has already been noticed.' He was therefore giving directions 'for an elaborate cover plan' to be made.[1]

From Italy, Churchill learned on October 25 of Alexander's 'anxiety' about the number of German Divisions being brought into Italy, and of the German ability 'to maintain strong forces in the area south of Rome'. For this reason, Alexander was 'keen' to build up the Allied air forces in Italy.[2] The reduction in landing craft, Alexander warned a Commander's conference on October 25, was 'so serious as to preclude us from taking advantage, other than with minor forces, of the enemy's inherent weakness, which is the exposure of his two flanks to turning movements from the sea'. As for a 'stabilised front south of Rome', Alexander added, this 'cannot be accepted, for the capital has a significance far greater than its strategic location, and sufficient depth must be gained before the Foggia airfields and the port of Naples can be regarded as secure'. This being so, the seizure of 'a firm defensive base north of Rome' became imperative. Moreover, Alexander argued, 'we cannot afford to adopt a purely defensive role, for this would entail the surrender of the initiative to the Germans'.[3] 'We shall have to have an almighty row with the Americans,' Brooke noted in his diary, 'who have put us in this position with their insistence to abandon the Mediterranean operations for the very problematical cross-Channel operations.' Now, Brooke commented, 'we are beginning to see the full beauty of the Marshall strategy! It is quite heart-breaking when we see what we might have done this year if our strategy had not been distorted by the Americans.'[4]

At ten in the morning of October 26, Churchill discussed Alexander's report with Brooke, and the 'best methods', as Brooke noted in his diary, 'of getting Americans to realize that we must for the present concentrate on the Mediterranean'.[5] At a meeting of the Chiefs of Staff later that morning, a telegram was prepared for despatch to Washington, which the Chiefs of Staff discussed with Churchill at midday. In their telegram, which Churchill approved,

---

[1] Prime Minister's Personal Telegram, T.1719/3, War Office telegram, OZ 3351, 'Personal and Most Secret' (through Field Marshall Dill), 24 October 1943: Churchill papers, 20/122.

[2] MA/682, IZ 3966, 'Most Secret and Private', 25 October 1943: Churchill papers, 20/122.

[3] Churchill sent a copy of Alexander's paper to Anthony Eden, who was then in Moscow. Prime Minister's Personal Telegram, T.1737/3, No. 142 Extra to Moscow, 'Personal and Most Secret', sent 6.44 p.m., 26 October 1943: Churchill papers, 20/122.

[4] Brooke diary, 25 October 1943: Bryant, *op. cit.*, volume 2, page 56.

[5] Brooke diary, 26 October 1943: Bryant, *op. cit.*, volume 2, pages 56–7.

the Chiefs of Staff gave as their considered opinion that Eisenhower and Alexander 'must be backed to the full' in Italy, so that the 'momentum' of their offensive could be restored 'until Rome and the airfields to the north have been captured. For this they must have the resources they require, even if the 'Overlord' programme is delayed: the 'crux' of the problem was landing craft. Yet 56 British and 48 American landing craft were due to leave the Mediterranean 'within the next few weeks' and many had already been withdrawn from the battle in preparation for the voyage to Britain, as part of the 'Overlord' preparations; this, the Chiefs of Staff insisted, would be a 'grave military error'.[1]

'This is what happens,' Churchill telegraphed to Eden, 'when battles are governed by lawyers' agreements made in all good faith months before and persisted in without regard to the ever-changing fortunes of war.' The battle in Italy, Churchill added, 'must be nourished and fought until it is won. We will do our very best for "Overlord" but it is no use planning for defeat in the field in order to give temporary political satisfaction.' It should be made clear to Stalin, Churchill insisted, that the assurances Eden had given 'about May "Overlord"', subject to the already specified conditions, must also be 'modified by the exigencies of battle in Italy'. Nothing, Churchill ended, 'will alter my determination not to throw away the battle in Italy at this juncture, so far as the King's Armies are concerned. Eisenhower and Alexander must have what they need to win the battle, no matter what effect is produced on subsequent operations. This may certainly affect the date of "Overlord".'[2]

On the following day Churchill telegraphed to Roosevelt, with reference to Alexander's warning:

We must not let this great Italian battle degenerate into a deadlock. At all costs we must win Rome and the airfields to the north of it. The fact that the enemy have diverted such powerful forces to this theatre vindicates our strategy. No one can doubt that by knocking out Italy we have enormously helped the Russian advance in the only way in which it could have been helped at this time. I feel that Eisenhower and Alexander must have what they need to win the battle in Italy, no matter what effect is produced on subsequent operations.[3]

Feeling against 'Overlord' had become widespread among those who knew of it. Alexander's survey of the war in Italy made it clear,

[1] Chiefs of Staff No. 907 of 1943, War Office telegram No. OZ 3384, 26 October 1943: Cabinet papers, 65/40.

[2] Prime Minister's Personal Telegram, T.1737/3, 'Extra No. 142', 'Most Secret and Personal', 26 October 1943: Churchill papers, 20/122.

[3] Prime Minister's Personal Telegram, T.1739/3, Prime Minister to President, No. 475, 'Personal and Most Secret', 26 October 1943: Churchill papers, 20/122.

Cadogan noted in his diary on October 26, 'Germans *may* mass to defeat us there in detail,' in which case, Cadogan added, 'all this "Overlord" folly must be thrown "Overboard".'[1] It was 'folly', Brooke told the War Cabinet on October 27, 'to withdraw forces from Italy until it was clear that we were in a position to carry out "Overlord" successfully'. But 'our power to carry out "Overlord" successfully' depended, Brooke declared, 'upon the success of our operations in Italy'. For this reason, 'sufficient forces' must be sent to Italy 'to ensure success' there.

Smuts, who was present as a full member of the War Cabinet, while agreeing that 'Overlord' was 'bound to be carried out' as the 'last big show in the war', also argued that the war in Italy should be the priority 'until we reached a line which we could hold with perfect safety'. He could not see 'Overlord' being possible until August 1944. Meanwhile, 'our air attacks on Germany', Smuts believed, 'might bring Germany to her knees in twelve months'.[2]

Cadogan, who was present at this meeting of the War Cabinet, noted that the 'whole Cabinet', and Smuts 'particularly', had been 'very definite' that Britain '*can't* be tied, in changing circumstances, to the Quebec decisions'. Churchill, he noted, 'will fight for "nourishing the battle" in Italy and, if necessary, resign on it'.[3]

Suddenly, but not unexpectedly, the date of the cross-Channel invasion was in jeopardy, and the principal decision of the Quebec conference was in disarray. Even Lord Beaverbrook, so long an advocate of as early as possible a Second Front, bowed to what now seemed the inevitable. After listening, in Brooke's presence, to a 'long discourse' by Churchill and Smuts on October 27, he stated, as Brooke noted in his diary, 'that he had always been an ardent supporter of the cross-Channel operation but now that we were committed to the Mediterranean, we should make a job of it'.[4]

Churchill telegraphed to Roosevelt that same day, October 27:

Hitherto we have prospered wonderfully, but I now feel that the year 1944 is loaded with danger. Great differences may develop between us and we may take the wrong turning. Or again we may make compromises and fall

---

[1] Cadogan diary, 26 October 1943: David Dilks (editor), *op. cit.*, page 570. Curiously, there was a codename 'Overboard', which perhaps Cadogan knew. It had been invented to express 'the general principle that the number of divisions required to capture the number of ports required to maintain those divisions is always greater than the number of divisions that those ports can maintain'.

[2] War Cabinet No. 147 of 1943, 10 Downing Street, 6 p.m., 27 October 1943, Confidential Annex: Cabinet papers, 64/40.

[3] Cadogan diary, 27 October 1943: David Dilks (editor), *op. cit.*, pages 570–1.

[4] Brooke diary, 27 October 1943: Bryant, *op. cit.*, volume 2, page 57.

between two stools. The only hope is the intimacy and friendship which has been established between us and between our High Staffs. If that were broken I should despair of the immediate future.

The specific reason for Churchill sending this word of warning was a Soviet request for a Soviet military representative to sit in at the meetings of the Anglo-American Joint Staffs. But his deeper worries were of a fatal rift in Anglo-American strategic thought. 'I must add,' he told Roosevelt, 'that I am more anxious about the campaign of 1944 than about any other with which I have been involved.' [1]

Churchill's anxieties were not lessened by a reply from General Marshall, reporting the view 'here' in Washington, that Eisenhower already had 'adequate troops to fight in Italy without taking undue risks'. Marshall added that Eisenhower had said himself that the more Germans he could 'contain' in Italy 'the better the chances of "Overlord" will be'. [2] From Russia, however, Eden, having reported to Stalin that Churchill would do his 'best' to launch 'Overlord' but was 'not prepared to risk a defeat in Italy', noted that Stalin 'took it all very well'. [3] Churchill sent copies of Eden's telegram to the King and to Smuts.

In a further telegram on October 29, Eden reported Stalin's approval of the proposed diversionary attack, as proposed at Quebec, against southern France at the time of the cross-Channel invasion. This, Stalin thought, was 'a good idea since the more we made Hitler disperse the better'. These, Stalin added, 'were just the tactics he had employed on the Russian front', but he wanted to know whether there would be enough landing craft for both operations. Stalin also told Eden that the Soviet Armies 'would not have had the success they had won, had the Germans been able to move from the West the 40 divisions which were pinned by the mere threat of our invasion'. The Soviet Union, Stalin said, 'fully understood this contribution to our cause'. Eden added:

I said that as the Marshal well knew my Prime Minister was just as keen on hurting Hitler as he was. M. Stalin fully acknowledged this but added with a gust of laughter that Mr Churchill had a tendency to take the easy road for himself and leave the difficult jobs to the Russians. I refused to acknowledge this and referred to the difficulties of naval operations and our recent heavy losses in destroyers. M. Stalin becoming serious again said that his people talked little about naval operations but they had a full realisation of their difficulties.

[1] Prime Minister's Personal Telegram, T.1747/3, Prime Minister to President, No. 476, 'Personal and Most Secret', 27 October 1943: Churchill papers, 20/122.

[2] War Office telegram, IZ 4009, 'Most Secret', 'Personal', 27 October 1943: Churchill papers, 20/122.

[3] 'Space No. 105', Moscow, 'Most Secret', 28 October 1943: Churchill papers, 20/122.

Throughout the discussion, Eden noted, Stalin had seemed 'in excellent humour'.

Stalin had asked Eden how long a delay in 'Overlord' the campaign in Italy might now involve.[1] Eden could give no precise answer, but Churchill did, telegraphing to Eden that same day, for use 'in discussion' with Stalin:

There is of course no question of abandoning 'Overlord', which will remain our principal operation for 1944. The retention of landing-craft in the Mediterranean in order not to lose the Battle of Rome may cause a slight delay, perhaps till July, as the smaller class of landing-craft cannot cross the Bay of Biscay in the winter months and would have to make the passage in the spring. The delay would however mean that the blow when struck would be with somewhat heavier forces, and also that the full bombing effort on Germany would not be damped down so soon. We are also ready at any time to push across and profit by a German collapse.[2]

In an earlier telegram to Eden on October 29, Churchill had accepted Stalin's request for 'a share in the Italian fleet', while pointing out that the Italian warships were 'quite unsuited' for Arctic waters. As for the battleships for which Stalin had asked, Churchill pointed out that it was Britain's intention to use the 'newest vessels' of the Italian fleet in the war against Japan, 'and the Russians will surely understand that we ought not to prejudice that'.[3]

In a third telegram to Eden on October 29, Churchill set out his wider plan for the Soviet Union and its fleet:

Most especially secret and for your own thought and perhaps fly-throwing: if it were decided that on the defeat of Hitler Russia would play her part against Japan a great design might come into being, as a part of which the fitting out under the Soviet flag and manning with Russian sailors of a substantial naval force at some Pacific base in our possession and the participation of this force of surface ships in the final phase of the war might come into view.[4]

At a Staff Conference on October 29, the Soviet request for 'a portion of the Italian fleet' was approved. It was also agreed, at Churchill's suggestion, that Britain would offer a flotilla of submarines in support of the Russians in the Black Sea.[5]

[1] 'Space' No. 108, Moscow, 'Most Secret and Personal', 29 October 1943: Churchill papers, 20/122.
[2] Prime Minister's Personal Telegram, T.1764/3, 'Most Secret and Personal', No. 174 to Moscow, 29 October 1943: Churchill papers, 20/122.
[3] Prime Minister's Personal Telegram, T.1758/3, 'Most Secret', No. 171 to Moscow, 29 October 1943: Churchill papers, 20/122.
[4] Prime Minister's Personal Telegram, T.1769/3, 'Extra No. 181', 'Most Secret and Personal', 29 October 1943: Churchill papers, 20/122.
[5] Staff Conference, Chiefs of Staff Committee No. 264 (Operations) of 1943, 29 October 1943: Cabinet papers, 79/68.

On Friday October 29 Churchill went to Chequers for the weekend. That evening the film was 'Gentleman Jim', 'interrupted', as Marian Holmes noted in her diary, 'when I had to descend to the office to take down an urgent telegram'.[1]

The urgent telegram was to Roosevelt. It was sent because no reply had yet reached Churchill from Stalin about the Three Power Conference. 'It is very awkward waiting about for an answer from U.J.,' Churchill explained to the President. 'It is urgent to get dates settled and preparations made.' Whatever Stalin decided, Churchill suggested, he and the President could meet at Casablanca between November 15 and November 20. 'I have a great wish and need to see you,' Churchill added. 'All our troubles and toils are so much easier to face when we are side by side.'[2]

If Stalin could not come, the question arose of some less senior Russian, possibly a General. 'A triple conference is excellent,' Churchill telegraphed to Eden, who was still in Moscow, 'but an irresponsible Russian observer at a conference on the conduct of purely Anglo-American operations would be most injurious.'[3]

Churchill had now to try to coordinate with Eden the various changing plans for meeting, as well as the military problems outstanding. 'If I speak to you on the telephone,' he telegraphed to Eden on November 2, 'Leros will be called Byron; Wilson, Jumbo; and Eisenhower, Idaho.' Russia or Stalin, he added, 'will be called Sealskin', and Turkey would be called Christmas.[4]

Churchill's two requests to Roosevelt for the name of the Commander-in-Chief for 'Overlord' had as yet gone unanswered. On October 30 Roosevelt informed Churchill that he could not make Marshall available 'immediately', but that he was 'none the less anxious that preparations proceed on schedule', as agreed at Quebec, 'with target date May 1'. Roosevelt added that Churchill might care to consider 'the early appointment' of a British Deputy Supreme Commander, who would receive 'the same measure of support' as would 'eventually' be accorded to Marshall, and that whoever was approached 'could well carry the work forward'. Roosevelt's own suggestion for the Deputy was 'Dill, Portal, or Brooke'.[5] That same day, it

[1] Marian Holmes diary, 29 October 1943: Marian Walker Spicer papers.

[2] Prime Minister's Personal Telegram, T.1767/3, 'Personal and Most Secret', Prime Minister to President No. 477, 29 October 1943: Premier papers, 3/136/1, folio 127.

[3] Prime Minister's Personal Telegram, T.1808/3, 'Personal and Most Secret', 1 November 1943: Premier papers, 3/136/1, folio 111.

[4] Prime Minister's Personal Telegram, T.1815/3, 2 November 1943: Premier papers, 3/136/1, folio 104.

[5] President to Prime Minister, No. 403, 'Personal and Most Secret', 30 October 1943: Churchill papers, 20/122.

was agreed that, before the meeting with Stalin, Churchill and Roosevelt should meet, on October 20, in Cairo. 'Every facility exists in Cairo,' Churchill pointed out, 'for the full Staffs to be accommodated and to meet for business, and they can easily come out to your villa whenever desired.'[1]

On October 30 Field Marshal Smuts arrived at Chequers with his son. The after-dinner film was 'Sky's the Limit' with Fred Astaire. 'When the PM went out of the office,' Marian Holmes noted, 'FM Smuts told us we "let the PM work much too hard and much too late at night". We must remember Mr Churchill was not young any more.'[2] On the following day, however, as Marian Holmes noted, 'The PM worked hard all morning. He was in high spirits and seemed to have an insatiable thirst for work. He began, but did not finish, the jingle "There was a young lady of Crewe".'[3]

At the beginning of November, Churchill was angered to learn that the Turkish Government was unwilling to contemplate providing air bases for Britain to use for the protection of Leros and the recapture of Kos. He had wanted to reply that, in that case, 'our interest in Turkey lapses'. On the afternoon of November 3 he sent for Cadogan, to whom he showed the telegram in which this phrase appeared. Cadogan persuaded Churchill to change this to: 'We cannot plead Turkey's case with the Soviets.'[4] The telegram, sent to Eden on November 3, also warned Turkey that the provision of British military equipment would be 'stopped at once', and pointed out that both Britain and Russia wished Turkey to declare war on Germany before the end of the year. 'This may be the last chance,' Churchill added, 'for Turkey to come in on the side of the victorious nations.' If she were to come into the war now, 'she gains the greatest possible guarantee of the integrity of her interests and possessions'.[5] On November 4 Roosevelt agreed to join Churchill and Stalin 'in making immediate demand on Turkey for use of air bases and later pressing Turkey to enter the war', provided, Roosevelt added, that no British or American resources would be committed to the Eastern Mediterranean 'which in the opinion of the Commanders responsible are necessary for "Overlord" or for operations in Italy'.[6]

[1] Prime Minister to President, No. 403, 'Personal and Most Secret', 30 October 1943: Churchill papers, 20/122.
[2] Marian Holmes diary, 30 October 1943: Marian Walker Spicer papers.
[3] Marian Holmes diary, 31 October 1943: Marian Walker Spicer papers.
[4] Cadogan diary, 3 November 1943: David Dilks (editor), *op. cit.*, page 573.
[5] Prime Minister's Personal Telegram, T.1838/3 No. 1752 to Cairo, 'Most Secret and Personal', 3 November 1943: Churchill papers, 20/123.
[6] President to Prime Minister, No. 407, 'Personal and Most Secret', 4 November 1943: Churchill papers, 20/123.

The spectre of 'Overlord' was omnipresent. On November 4, first Churchill and Brooke, and then the War Cabinet, discussed Eisenhower's forecast that he would not be able to occupy the line necessary to protect the Rome airfields until January or even February 1944 if the existing programme of withdrawing landing craft for 'Overlord' were adhered to.[1] With the War Cabinet's approval, Churchill telegraphed to Roosevelt that same day, expressing 'the increasing anxiety' of the British Government about the withdrawal of landing craft from the Mediterranean 'at this critical juncture'. 'We feel entitled,' Churchill wrote, 'to ask our American Allies to attach weight to our earnest representations in view of the very great preponderance of British troops deployed against the enemy in Italy, with proportionate losses, and also in view of the clear opinions of the United States Commander-in-Chief under whom we serve.'

Churchill went on to try to mitigate American suspicions by telling Roosevelt that 'by various intense efforts' the British had every hope that an additional seventy-five landing craft could be produced in the United Kingdom 'by the date fixed for 'Overlord'' '[2]

In deference to British wishes, on November 6 the American Chiefs of Staff authorized Eisenhower to retain in Italy sixty-eight of the landing craft scheduled for 'an early departure' to Britain. Roosevelt sent Churchill this news by telegram that same day.[3] Churchill replied at once, to say how 'greatly relieved' he was, as were his colleagues and the British Chief of Staff.[4] Churchill immediately told Alexander of the American decision. 'I hope therefore,' he wrote, 'that this will enable you to achieve your full plan and at any rate spend Christmas in Rome.'[5]

If December 15 was to be the last date for the retention of the landing craft, Alexander warned, it would not allow him 'to carry out the whole of my plan'.[6] Churchill replied at once, telling Alexander to make his plans on the basis that the landing craft would 'stay on till January 15'. Churchill added: 'I am pretty certain this will be agreed at our conference.'[7]

---

[1] War Cabinet No. 150 of 1943, 4 November 1943, Confidential Annex: Cabinet papers, 65/40.
[2] Prime Minister's Personal Telegram, T.1848/3, Prime Minister to President, No. 490, 'Most Secret and Personal', 4 November 1943: Churchill papers, 20/123.
[3] President to Prime Minister, No. 409, 'Personal and Most Secret', 6 November 1943: Churchill papers, 20/123.
[4] Prime Minister's Personal Telegram, T.1872/3, Prime Minister to President, No. 493, 'Personal and Most Secret', 6 November 1943: Cabinet papers, 120/113.
[5] Prime Minister's Personal Telegram, T.1874/3, 'Purely Personal', 'Through "C"', 6 November 1943: Churchill papers, 20/123.
[6] 'Most Secret', 9 November 1943: Churchill papers, 20/124.
[7] Prime Minister's Personal Telegram, T.1916/3, 'Personal and Most Secret', 'despatched through "C"', 9 November 1943: Churchill papers, 20/124.

Alexander, making immediate dispositions based upon the landing craft that were to be retained, began to study and to plan details of a seaborne divisional operation in the Rome area, to be launched, he told Churchill, when the Allied armies were 'within supporting distance of such a landing'.[1]

Britain was in the middle of Churchill's feared cleft stick, unable because of 'Overlord' to intensify the Italian campaign, but still at least six months away from 'Overlord'. In 'Overlord', as Churchill saw, the military balance would tilt in America's favour, weakening British control on all future military decision making. On November 6, he minuted for Sir James Grigg and Brooke that on the cross-Channel D day it was 'fixed' for the Americans to have fifteen divisions and Britain twelve. His minute continued:

> Now it seems to me a great pity that we cannot make our quota equal or, if possible, one better. So much depends upon the interpretation given to the word 'division'. I should like to be able to tell them: 'We will match you man for man and gun for gun on the battlefront,' and also that we have made extra exertions for this. In this way we shall maintain our right to be effectively consulted in operations which are of such capital consequence.
>
> For the above purpose I would run considerable risks with what is left in the island. If necessary the Home Guard could be largely mobilized during the period when all the regular troops have left the country, and the resulting decline in the factory munition output accepted.

Churchill noted that Britain had won its argument about retaining the landing craft in Italy 'entirely by mentioning that we had preponderance on the battlefront'. She ought to have 'at least equality' in the other 'most critical task'. The announcement that Britain had raised its contribution, he added, 'would sweeten all the discussions which are now proceeding and might well enable us to secure any necessary retardation of D day'.[2]

Churchill was angered on November 9 when he learned of Roosevelt's apparent wish to give Marshall the joint command of the Mediterranean and cross-Channel operations. That day, Churchill telegraphed to Dill, for the attention of Admiral Leahy, the Chairman of the American Chiefs of Staff Committee:

> You should leave Admiral Leahy in no doubt that we should never be able to agree to the proposals of putting the 'Overlord' and Mediterranean Commands under an American Commander-in-Chief.
>
> As we shall have approximately 14–15 British or British-controlled divis-

---

[1] 'Private', 'Most Secret', 10 November 1943: Churchill papers, 20/124.

[2] Prime Minister's Personal Minute, M.786/3, 'Most Secret', 6 November 1943: Churchill papers, 20/104.

ions in Italy and at least 16 ready for 'Overlord', total 30, in the Spring of 1944, and the United States will not have more than 7–8 American or American-controlled divisions in Italy and 15 in 'Overlord', total 22–23, apart from the large British naval and air forces which we shall possess in the Western theatres, such an arrangement would not be conformable to the principle of equal status which must be maintained among the great Allies.

I cannot accept a combination of the two Commands under one Commander-in-Chief. This would place him above the Combined Chiefs of Staff and would also affect the constitutional control of the movements of forces by the President as United States Commander-in-Chief and by the Prime Minister acting on behalf of the War Cabinet. I should certainly never be able to accept responsibility for such an arrangement. Hitherto we have successfully prevented any carping here at the fact that we have been fighting and sustaining casualties in Tunis, Sicily and Italy on something like a $2\frac{1}{2}$ to 1 basis, although we are serving loyally under a United States general. If I were to attempt to propose anything such as is suggested above, there would be an explosion. However, this will not occur while I hold my present office.[1]

Dill saw Leahy on November 10, and informed him of Churchill's opposition to a 'unified' command. 'If that is the opinion of the Prime Minister,' Leahy replied, 'there is nothing more to be said about it.' Dill also saw Hopkins, who said that he was 'disappointed'. But both men now knew 'how useless it would be to return to the charge', Dill reported to Churchill, 'and I hope they won't.'[2] Nor did they. The proposal, Dill reported, 'came from the White House and had never received any proper consideration by the US Chiefs of Staff'. Dill added: 'I do not think you need take it too seriously.'[3] But Churchill was convinced that he had to take seriously anything that might later lead to trouble or difficulties. His, in the last resort, was the responsibility for anything that was overlooked. That same day, apologizing to a friend for a harsh altercation, he wrote: 'I have a great many things to vex and worry me, and I suppose at the end of fifty months of war one tends to get easily nettled.'[4]

[1] Prime Minister's Personal Telegram, T. 1899/3, War Office telegram OZ 3614, 'Personal and Secret', 8 November 1943: Churchill papers, 20/123.

[2] FMD/56, War Office incoming telegram, IZ 4258, 'Personal', 9 November 1943: Churchill papers, 20/124.

[3] FMD/55, War Office incoming telegram, IZ/4242, 'Most Secret', 'Personal', 8 November 1943: Churchill papers, 20/124.

[4] 'Private', 8 November 1943 (to Richard Law): Churchill papers, 20/94.

33

Prelude to Teheran

A T the Mansion House on 9 November 1943, Churchill warned
that 'this is no time for relaxation or soft thoughts on the joys
of peace and victory'. Hitler, he pointed out, still had 400 divisions
'under his command or control'. Churchill also spoke of the achievements of the Red Army, telling his listeners that, although 'in Sicily
and Italy, Great Britain has had the honour to bear the greatest part
and to pay the heaviest price', while the Americans, Australians and
New Zealanders had carried out many 'brilliant actions' in the Far
East, nevertheless, 'I gladly admit, and indeed proclaim, that the outstanding event of this famous year has been the victorious advance
of the Russian armies from the Volga westward across the Dnieper,
thus liberating, as Marshal Stalin has told us, two-thirds of the occupied Russian soil from the foul invader.' In this process, Churchill
declared, 'the Russian Soviet armies have inflicted deep and dire injury
upon the whole life and structure of the German military power.
That monstrous juggernaut engine of German might and tyranny has
been beaten and broken, outfought and outmanoeuvred, by Russian
valour, generalship, and science, and it has been beaten to an extent
which may well prove mortal.' [1]

Three days before his Mansion House speech, the British Ambassador in Moscow, Sir Archibald Clark Kerr, had informed Churchill
of Soviet dissatisfaction at the progress of the war in Italy, and its
effect on the eastern front. At a meeting on November 6, Clark Kerr
reported, Molotov had told Harriman that 'Stalin and Soviet military
authorities were disturbed and much dissatisfied because the Germans
were moving divisions from Italy and the Balkans to the Russian front. At
the Kremlin dinner on October 30 Mr Eden had expressed the hope
that Kiev and Rome would soon be taken. Kiev had now fallen and
the Soviet Government could not understand why the Italian front
was inactive enough to permit of the withdrawal of German troops

[1] Speech of 9 November 1943, recorded: BBC Written Archive Centre.

which would be turned against the Red Army.' Molotov had gone on to say 'that he shared the dissatisfaction his people felt and that the question was not a purely military one, it had political significance also'.[1]

In his reply, Churchill assured Clark Kerr that his wish had always been 'to sustain and press to the utmost the campaign in Italy and to attract to that front and hold upon it as many Divisions as possible'. He was 'glad to say' that agreement had been reached by the Combined Staffs 'that no more landing craft shall be withdrawn until December 15'. This would enable 'greater power to be put into the whole of our operations'. Churchill continued:

You may tell Molotov in strict confidence for Stalin only that I am going myself very shortly to this front and I will do everything in human power to animate the forward movement on which my heart is set at this moment. Moreover, by making new intense exertions at home I hope to make up by additional building of landing craft for the delay in sending home the others. You should convey all the above verbally from me.

As to the Russian concern about the transfer of troops from Italy to the eastern front, Churchill pointed out to Clark Kerr, also for transmission to Molotov, that half of the German strength in Italy 'is in Northern Italy and Istria separated from our front by some 300 miles'. It was from that half 'that the withdrawals back to South Russia have been made'. These withdrawals have been rendered possible, 'not by any inactivity on our fighting front, but by a diminution of the risks to internal security due to the passive attitude of the Italians in Northern Italy'.[2]

To resolve the growing conflicts over strategy, Churchill had been pressing for three separate meetings. One was a meeting of senior British, American and Soviet military figures, the second was a meeting between himself and Roosevelt, and the third was a meeting of himself, Roosevelt and Stalin. The first two were to be held in Cairo, the third, if Stalin would agree to make the journey, in Teheran. 'It is very difficult,' Churchill telegraphed to Stalin on November 11, in urging him to go to Teheran, 'to settle things by triangular correspondence, especially when people are moving by sea and air.'[3] The military meetings in Cairo were to come first. 'I attach great importance,' Churchill telegraphed to Clark Kerr in Moscow, 'to the Russian delegation being a powerful, authoritative expert body.'[4]

---

[1] No. 1259 from Moscow, 'Personal and Most Secret', 'Decypher Yourself', 6 November 1943: Cabinet papers, 120/683.

[2] 'Most Secret and Personal', undated draft: Cabinet papers, 120/683.

[3] Prime Minister's Personal Telegram, T.1932/3, No. 1840 to Moscow, 'Most Secret and Personal', 11 November 1943: Cabinet papers, 120/113.

[4] Prime Minister's Personal Telegram, T.1945/3, No. 1853 to Moscow, 'Most Secret and Personal', 12 November 1943: Churchill papers, 20/124.

On November 11 Churchill was 'not well enough', as he wrote to Sir Edward Bridges, to preside over the Cabinet.[1] On the following morning, following several days of inconclusive telegraphic exchanges, it was Roosevelt who finally learned that Stalin was willing to go to Teheran. 'Thus endeth a very difficult situation,' he telegraphed at once to Churchill that morning, 'and I think we can be happy.' Churchill added: 'Am just off. Happy landing to us both.'[2]

At noon on November 12, Churchill left London by train for Plymouth, and for the battleship *Renown*. 'I was feeling far from well,' he later recalled, 'as a heavy cold and sore throat were reinforced by the consequences of inoculations against typhoid and cholera.'[3] Accompanied by his daughter Sarah, Churchill sailed from Plymouth shortly after six o'clock that evening.[4] Also on board were the new First Sea Lord, Admiral Sir Andrew Cunningham, the American Ambassador, Gilbert Winant, two members of Churchill's Defence Staff, General Ismay and General Hollis, his doctor Lord Moran, his Intelligence adviser Desmond Morton, his Principal Private Secretary John Martin, and his son Randolph.[5]

During their first day at sea, *Renown* was lashed by heavy seas, the quarterdeck being under water 'most of the time', as Captain Pim recalled.[6] Pim, who was again in charge of Churchill's travelling map room, was asked by Churchill to work out the total mileage of his travels since September 1939. Up to their departure from Plymouth, Churchill's total distance by sea and air was, Pim calculated, 111,000 miles. He had spent 792 hours at sea, and 339 hours in the air.[7] In a brief note written on November 13 from Downing Street, Clementine Churchill wrote: 'I hope this may catch you at Gibraltar, refreshed & not knocked about by the Atlantic. You have been away only 24 hours and the place seems dead.' Clementine added: 'I see bad news from Leros. I hope it will not worry you too much.'[8] This news was of a German landing at one end of the island. But on

---

[1] Prime Minister's Personal Minute, C(S) 1/3, 'Most Secret and Personal', 15 November 1943: Churchill papers, 20/104.

[2] President to Prime Minister No. 418, 'Personal and Secret', 12 November 1943: Cabinet papers, 120/113.

[3] Winston S. Churchill, *The Second World War*, volume 5, London 1952, page 287.

[4] Prime Minister's Engagement Cards, Friday 12 November 1943: Thompson papers.

[5] Prime Minister's Engagement Cards, Saturday 13 November 1943: Thompson papers. During the journey, Winant learned to his relief that his son, missing some time previously while pilot of an American aircraft in an attack on Germany, was a prisoner-of-war. (Pim recollections: Pim papers.)

[6] Pim recollections: Pim papers.

[7] Pim recollections: Pim papers.

[8] Letter of 13 November 1943: Spencer-Churchill papers.

November 14 Maitland Wilson assured Churchill that the British troops 'are somewhat tired but full of fight and well fed'. The ammunition situation, however, had become 'acute'.[1]

On November 14, Soviet forces entered Zhitomir. 'I am at sea,' Churchill telegraphed to Stalin as soon as he learned the news. 'All congratulations on your continued triumphant advance.'[2] The news from Leros remained hopeful, despite further German landings. 'No doubt enemy also very tired . . .,' Wilson telegraphed on November 15, as Churchill reached Gibraltar.[3] There, Harold Macmillan came on board. 'The PM was in excellent form,' he noted in his diary, 'and asked a great deal about the French situation. He is still violently anti de Gaulle but as always, if you maintain a point with energy, he is prepared to listen.' Churchill told Macmillan that he feared de Gaulle's xenophobia, 'and there is no denying', Macmillan noted, 'this is very strong'. But new arrivals from France were joining de Gaulle in Algiers, 'by no means slavish or adulatory supporters of de Gaulle', bound together 'in a fierce spiritual unity—not to be neglected'. Macmillan added: 'we managed to get to bed at a reasonably early hour—1.30 a.m. Last night, they told me, he sat up till 5 a.m.'[4]

On the morning of November 16, Macmillan joined Churchill in his cabin. The two men talked together for three and a half hours, Churchill explaining to Macmillan his feeling that the Mediterranean position 'has not been exploited with vigour and flexibility'. This, Macmillan felt, was due in part to the 'extreme rigidity' of the Americans. 'It is of course,' he added, 'infuriating for Winston, who felt that all through the war he is fighting like a man with his hands tied behind his back, and yet no one but he, and that with extraordinary patience and skill, could have enticed the Americans into the European war at all.'

Talking about de Gaulle's ascendancy over the French National Committee, from the co-Presidency of which Giraud had withdrawn a week earlier, Churchill told Macmillan that what he feared 'is a sort of de Gaulle dictatorship, hostile to Britain, and mischievous if not dangerous'.[5]

Shortly after midday on November 16, *Renown* reached Algiers.

---

[1] 'Grand' No. 25, CIC/176, War Office incoming telegram, IZ/4361, 'Most Secret', 'Personal', 14 November 1943: Churchill papers, 20/124.

[2] 'Frozen' No. 2, Prime Minister's Personal Telegram, T.1962/3, 'Personal and Most Secret', 14 November 1943: Churchill papers, 20/124.

[3] 'Grand' No. 38, CIC/182, War Office incoming telegram, IZ/4372, 'Personal', 15 November 1943: Churchill papers, 20/124.

[4] Macmillan diary, 15 November 1943: *War Diaries, Politics and War in the Mediterranean, January 1943–May 1945*, London 1984, pages 293–4.

[5] Macmillan diary, 16 November 1943: *War Diaries, op. cit.*, page 294.

Churchill did not go ashore, but received on board 'various callers during the day', as John Martin noted in his diary, among them Admiral Sir John Cunningham and General Bedell Smith.[1] During the afternoon, Macmillan noted in his diary:

Somebody rashly remarked that the Services were better co-ordinated in this war than in the last. The Chiefs of Staff system was a good one. 'Not at all,' said Winston. 'Not at all. It leads to weak and faltering decisions—or rather indecisions. Why, you may take the most gallant sailor, the most intrepid airman, or the most audacious soldier, put them at a table together—what do you get? The sum total of their fears!'[2]

The news from Leros was now very bad. The situation had 'deteriorated' and the 'enemy was reinforced', Wilson reported to Churchill on November 16. 'Situation is undoubtedly very precarious,' he added, 'and troops are very tired, and continuous dive bombing inevitably affects morale.'[3]

Renown left Algiers after dark on November 16. At dawn, as the battleship passed Pantelleria, a German reconnaissance aircraft was sighted, and action stations were sounded, but no attack took place. Reaching Malta, Churchill went ashore, as Lord Gort's guest at the Governor's Palace. He was still feeling unwell, and for his two days in Malta had to spend most of his time in bed; while there, he studied a report of the Allied Bomber Force which, now based at Foggia in southern Italy, was striking at industrial targets in eastern Germany, part of operation 'Pointblank'. Churchill minuted for the Chiefs of Staff Committee:

It is surely altogether wrong to build up the Strategic Air Force in Italy at the expense of the battle for Rome. The strategic bombing of Germany, however important, cannot take precedence over the battle, which must ever rank first in our thoughts. Major tactical needs must always have priority over strategic policy. I was not aware until recently that the build-up of the Army had been obstructed by the forward move of a mass of strategic air not connected with the battle. This is in fact a departure from all orthodox military doctrine, as well as seeming wrong from the point of view of common sense.[4]

'The monstrous block of air,' Churchill minuted a week later, 'in its eagerness to get ahead, has definitely hampered the operations of the Army.'[5]

---

[1] John Martin diary, 16 November 1943: Martin papers.
[2] Macmillan diary, 16 November 1943: *War Diaries, op. cit.*, page 295.
[3] 'Grand' No. 46, CIC/185, 'Personal', 16 November 1943: Churchill papers, 20/124.
[4] Prime Minister's Personal Minute, D(S) 5/3, 17 November 1943; Churchill papers, 20/104.
[5] Prime Minister's Personal Minute, D(S) 9/3, 'Most Secret', 24 November 1943: Churchill papers, 20/104.

On the morning of November 18 General Ismay, who had remained on board *Renown*, reported to Churchill at the Governor's Palace. Later he recalled:

When I reported to him early next morning, he was in bed with a feverish cold and evidently finding Gort's spartan regime a trifle unsatisfying. His first words were pathetic. 'Do you think you could bring me a little bit of butter from that nice ship?' Apparently he had also experienced a shortage of hot water for his bath. 'I only want a cupful of hot water,' he complained, 'but I can't get it.' Knowing how much he enjoyed wallowing in a bath full to overflowing, I suggested that he had made a mistake in leaving the *Renown*. He ignored my observation, and went on to say that Alexander, Tedder and John Cunningham were all in the island and that he would like to have a meeting with them and the three Chiefs of Staff as soon as they could be collected. Even if he had been at death's door, he would not have forgone the chance of a talk with the commanders in the Mediterranean. We all managed to squeeze into his none too large bedroom, and the topics discussed included the progress and prospects of the campaign in Italy, plans for the capture of Rhodes, and guerrilla operations in Yugoslavia.[1]

Churchill's new journey co-incided with the last phase of the battle of Leros. 'Leros has fallen,' General Wilson telegraphed to Churchill on November 17, 'after a very gallant struggle against overwhelming air attack.' It was, he added, 'a near thing between success and failure. Very little was needed to turn the scale in our favour and to bring off a triumph.'[2] On receiving this bad news Churchill replied: 'I approve of your conduct of the operations there. Like you, I feel this is a serious loss and reverse, and, like you, I feel I have been fighting with my hands tied behind my back.' It was his hope, Churchill added, to have 'better arrangements made' as a result of the coming conference.[3]

'I know you will be deeply unhappy about Leros,' Clementine Churchill wrote from Downing Street. 'I fear Samos must go too? & all to be begun again I suppose.'[4] It was, Churchill commented two days later, Germany's 'first success since Alamein'.[5]

As Clementine Churchill realized, the fall of Leros caused her husband 'deep unhappiness', so much so that she wrote to him again, a few days later: 'but never forget that when History looks back your vision & your piercing energy, coupled with your patience & magnanimity, will all be part of your greatness. So don't allow yourself to

---

[1] Ismay memoirs, *op. cit.*, page 333.

[2] 'Grand' No. 58, 'Personal' IZ/4415, 17 November 1943: Churchill papers, 20/124.

[3] 'Frozen' No. 32, Prime Minister's Personal Telegram, T.1990/3, OZ/3792, 'Secret', 18 November 1943: Churchill papers, 20/124.

[4] Letter of 18 November 1943: Spencer-Churchill papers.

[5] Memorandum of 20 November 1943: Churchill papers, 23/11.

be made angry—I often think of your saying, that the only worse thing than Allies is *not* having Allies!' [1]

'Leros was a poignant blow,' Churchill commented to the King, 'and the weather paralyses our offensive in Italy.' For the moment, he added, 'we are in the trough of the wave but I think it will soon come better'. [2]

On November 18 Churchill was still in Malta. 'I am laid up with a sore throat for the moment,' he telegraphed to Eden, 'and am remaining here today and probably tomorrow.' [3] There was a sudden emergency that day, when Roosevelt, from on board the USS *Iowa*, sent Churchill a telegram, with the information that the Cairo meeting place was 'known to enemy through press and radio'. Roosevelt added: 'Propose meeting place be changed to Khartoum.' [4]

On receipt of this telegram, Churchill at once conferred with Eisenhower, Sir Andrew Cunningham, and Sir John Cunningham. 'We all agreed it would be better to go through with the Cairo rendezvous,' Churchill replied, and he added:

We had of course always thought that the news was bound to leak directly we got there, and the fact that it has leaked a few days earlier should not therefore very much affect our plans. We would be well dispersed at Cairo. Enemy aircraft have to fly 100 miles over land before reaching us and arrangements have been made already to strengthen fighter and gun defences of enclave in which we propose to live. In addition we could if necessary have alternative residences.

If however you remain of opinion that we should not go through with Cairo, your suggestion of Khartoum would not I fear be feasible. Apart from fact that accommodation there is inadequate, it is 1,000 miles from Cairo and off our route and it would be very difficult to move necessary staffs.

One possibility, Churchill suggested, was to hold the meeting in Malta. 'We are of course nearer the enemy here,' Churchill explained, 'but defences are good.' [5]

At a meeting of the Chiefs of Staff Committee, held at San Antonio Palace, Malta, on November 18, Churchill spoke of the 'unsatisfactory situation' in the Balkans, where, 'after the initial shock of Italy's surrender, the Germans seemed to have recovered themselves and to be pressing back the Partisans at almost all points'. Fresh efforts should

---

[1] Letter of 23 November 1943: Spencer-Churchill papers.
[2] 'Frozen' No. 106, 'Most Secret and Personal', 24 November 1943: Churchill papers, 20/130.
[3] 'Frozen' No. 33, 'Personal and Most Secret', 18 November 1943: Churchill papers, 20/130.
[4] Telegram of 17 November 1943: Warren Kimball (editor), *Churchill and Roosevelt, The Complete Correspondence*, Princeton 1984, volume 2, page 601. (Text first published in *Foreign Relations of the United States, Teheran Conference*, Washington, 1961, page 96.)
[5] 'Special Unnumbered Signal', 'Most Secret', 18 November 1943: Cabinet papers, 120/113.

be made, he said, 'to gain control of the Adriatic. Our large air superiority should enable this to be done.'[1]

That night, the largest British bombing force yet to be sent over Germany bombed Mannheim, Ludwigshafen and Berlin.[2] On November 19 Churchill was well enough to visit the Malta dockyard, and to see the substantial bomb damage to the town. During the drive, as John Martin wrote in a letter home, Churchill received 'a tumultuous welcome from hundreds—or thousands—of Maltese'. Then, at the Governor's palace, 'Winston appeared like Mussolini on the balcony and beamed upon a large cheering crowd in the square below.'[3]

The problem of whether to continue with the Cairo talks, or to switch the location to Malta, was resolved on November 19. 'All authorities here,' Churchill telegraphed to Roosevelt that day, 'strongly recommend adhering to Pyramid area and that air raid danger is slight.' Churchill added: 'Everything is prepared and all precautions are taken in present position and I hope that you will decide to come there.'[4]

That night Churchill sailed on *Renown* for Alexandria. On the morning of November 20, the battleship steamed off the Libyan coast, within sight of Benghazi, Derna, Tobruk and Sidi Barrani.[5] Churchill, with the loss of Leros much on his mind, set down his thoughts on the war in the Mediterranean. Since the landing in Italy, he wrote, the campaign had taken 'an unsatisfactory course'. The build-up and advance of the army in Italy had been 'extremely slow', even allowing for bad weather. Nor was there 'sufficient preponderance' over the Germans in the front line. Two of the best British divisions, and some of the 'vitally-needed' landing craft, had already been sent back to the United Kingdom. The land campaign had 'flagged', and there was now no prospect of taking Rome in 1943.

The Germans had even been able, Churchill wrote, to transfer several divisions from Italy to the Russian front. 'We have therefore failed to take the weight of the attack off the Soviets.' Side by side with this, the Allies had also 'failed' to give any 'real measure of support' to the partisans in Yugoslavia and Albania. 'These forces,'

---

[1] Chiefs of Staff (Sextant), Preliminary Meeting, 18 November 1943: Premier papers, 3/136/5.

[2] Two weeks before this raid, Sir Arthur Harris had written to Churchill about the comparative destruction of British and German cities. Inner London had lost 600 acres to aerial bombardment, he wrote, compared with 480 acres in Berlin. At Coventry, 100 out of the city's 1,922 acres had been destroyed, in contrast to Hamburg, where 6,200 out of 8,382 acres had been destroyed. 'There remains,' Harris wrote, ' "The Central Complex", Leipzig, Chemnitz, Dresden. . . .' (Minute of 3 November 1943: Premier papers, 3/14/1.)

[3] Letter of 2 December 1943: Martin papers.

[4] 'Special Unnumbered Signal', 'Most Secret', 19 November 1943: Cabinet papers, 120/113.

[5] Pim recollections: Pim papers.

Churchill noted, 'are containing as many divisions as the British and American Armies put together.' But despite Allied air and naval superiority in the mouth of the Adriatic, 'yet no ships with supplies have entered the ports taken by the Partisans'. A 'complete neglect to do anything effective', Churchill concluded, 'has taken place in this extremely` important Balkan theatre'. With 'great cruelty' the Germans were mopping up many of the partisan forces. 'We shall certainly be rightly accused of short-sightedness or even worse in all this affair,' Churchill commented.

The débâcle had occurred, Churchill argued, because of the 'imaginary line' drawn down the Mediterranean 'which relieves General Eisenhower's armies of all responsibility for or interest in the Dalmatian coast and the Balkans'. These were assigned to the Middle East Command under General Wilson, 'but he does not possess the necessary force'. That one Command had the forces but not the responsibilities, and the other the responsibilities but not the forces, 'is certainly a very bad arrangement and reflects severely on our conduct of the war'. The fall of Kos and Leros had been taken 'with great composure by the High North African Command because it is out of their parish'.

If the 'artificial line of division' between Eisenhower and Wilson was one cause of the failure, the other, Churchill argued, was 'the shadow of Overlord'. The decisions at the 'Quadrant' conference to transfer troops from the Mediterranean to Britain in preparation for Overlord had been maintained 'with inflexible rigidity and without regard to the loss and injury to the allied cause created thereby'. The Italian landings, 'the successful invasion of the mainland of Europe', had not been allowed to alter the Quadrant decision. 'We have protested ceaselessly,' Churchill noted, 'but as we could not obtain agreement we have so far carried out the Quadrant decisions.' There was now a situation, Churchill warned, where 'a fixed target date' for the cross-Channel landing 'will continue to wreck and ruin the Mediterranean campaign: that our affairs will deteriorate in the Balkans and that the Aegean will remain firmly in German hands'. All this was to be accepted, 'for the sake of an operation fixed for May upon hypotheses that in all probability will not be realized at that date and certainly not if the Mediterranean pressure is relaxed'.

Churchill went on to warn of the 'discouraging and enfeebling effect' on the Mediterranean and Italian operations of the fact 'that it is now common knowledge in the Armies that the theatre is to be bled as much as necessary for the sake of an operation elsewhere in the Spring'; and he proposed 'for action' that all further movement of British troops and British and United States landing craft from the

Mediterranean should be stopped, that 'all possible energy' should be used to take Rome, that Turkey should be brought into the war using the 'necessary Air detachments', that an expedition should be prepared to take Rhodes in January 1944 'using the Turkish airfields', and that a port or ports should be seized on the Dalmatian coast of Yugoslavia, to carry 'a regular flow of airborne supplies' to the partisans, with British forces used 'to aid and animate the resistance in Yugoslavia and Albania and also to capture islands like Corfu and Argostoli'.[1]

Churchill put his plan to remedy the situation to the Chiefs of Staff Committee in a minute on the following day. 'The centre point of my thought,' he wrote, 'is the capture of Rome at the beginning of January and the capture of Rhodes at the end.'[2] Commenting on Churchill's minute, the Chiefs of Staff stated that 'Broadly speaking, we entirely agree with your general thesis', including 'the importance of capturing Rome and subsequently Rhodes'. It would 'probably not be possible to do Rhodes' however, they wrote, before February. As to Churchill's advocacy of a bridgehead on the Dalmatian coast, 'We think we can do just as much, and, at the same time avoid an unlimited commitment, by smuggling in material at many points on the coast and by air.'[3]

Renown reached Alexandria on the morning of November 21. Churchill flew at once to Cairo, where he was to stay in the villa of Lord Moyne, the Minister Resident. Arrangements had already been put into force to protect him and Roosevelt in the event of a German air or parachute attack. 'Risk small in view of precautions taken,' was the view of the Commanders-in-Chief Middle East. There was however a 'remote possibility' that low flying German aircraft might reach the 'target'. To meet this danger, three Spitfire squadrons, three Hurricane squadrons and one night fighter squadron were in readiness, at airfields around Cairo. A total of eighty-two anti-aircraft guns were 'deployed in target area', as Ismay reported to Churchill. A radar warning system covered the 'whole coast', and special arrangements had been made for Observer Posts inland. Five infantry battalions and one troop of armoured cars were guarding the conference area.[4]

[1] 'Future Operations in the European and Mediterranean Theatre', 'Minute by the Prime Minister', 20 November 1943, circulated in Cairo on 22 November 1943 as Chiefs of Staff (Sextant), Paper No. 1 (Revise): Cabinet papers, 80/77, folios 216–17. Argostoli is a harbour on the island of Cephalonia.

[2] Prime Minister's Personal Minute M(S) 6/3, 21 November 1943, circulated as Chiefs of Staff (Sextant), Paper No. 6, 'Future Operation in the Aegean'; Premier papers, 3/136/5, folio 62.

[3] 'Most Secret', 23 November 1943 (signed A. F. Brooke, C. Portal, A. B. Cunningham): Premier papers, 3/136/6, folios 30–4.

[4] 'Most Secret', 20 November 1943: Premier papers, 3/136/2, folios 16–18.

On the morning of November 22, Churchill was at the airport to greet Roosevelt, with whom he both lunched and dined.[1] He also saw the Chinese nationalist leader, Chiang Kai-shek, who pressed upon Churchill the need, while in Cairo, to agree to a major amphibious operation across the Bay of Bengal.

The Cairo Conference, code name Sextant, opened on the morning of November 23, the first plenary session being held in Roosevelt's villa. It was devoted to the Far East, and to a discussion, in which both Mountbatten and Churchill participated for Britain, of a military assault in northern Burma, as well as of the use, in the Bay of Bengal, of the substantial naval forces surrendered by the Italians, including five modernized battleships and four heavy armoured cruisers. Mountbatten also spoke of the 'natural difficulties' of the terrain, with the Allied lines of communication running through 'one of the most difficult countries in the world'. There were plans, however, for Wingate to make 'three thrusts' with his Long Range Penetration Groups in February, in order, by the use of gliders, to 'disrupt and muddle the Japanese'.

Churchill spoke hopefully of this Far Eastern offensive, telling the conference that these were 'important military operations of a much greater magnitude than ever previously contemplated for this theatre'. The plans had not yet been examined by the Chiefs of Staff, he said, but this would be done 'at the earliest opportunity, possibly the same day'. In all, Churchill told the conference, 'there was an Allied force of approximately 320,000 men who would apply pressure on the enemy' in Burma. They would have 'a qualitative as well as a quantitative supremacy over the enemy'. He had 'high hopes of these operations', Churchill added, 'the success of which largely depended on surprise and secrecy and ignorance on the part of the enemy as to the lines of approach and the points of attack'.[2]

'All contacts with the President are favourable,' Churchill telegraphed to Eden on November 23, 'and I feel much easier in my mind about the larger issues of the war.'[3] Plans were also going ahead to meet Stalin in Teheran. 'I hope we can be with you as long as possible,' Churchill telegraphed from Cairo, 'so that there may be a real chance to get together and also to have a full interchange of views on all aspects of the war between the Principals and High Staffs.'[4]

[1] Prime Minister's Monthly Engagement Cards, 22 November 1943: Ward Thompson papers.
[2] '"Sextant" Conference', 'Minutes of First Plenary Meeting, held at the Villa Kirk, on Tuesday, 23rd November, 1943, at 11.00': Cabinet papers, 80/77, folios 263–4.
[3] 'Frozen' No. 88, 23 November 1943: Churchill papers, 20/130.
[4] Prime Minister's Personal Telegram, T.2000/3, 23 November 1943: Churchill papers, 20/131.

To Churchill's surprise, he discovered that Roosevelt had never seen the Sphinx or the Pyramids. He at once went on a reconnaissance visit with his daughter Sarah to see if it would be possible for Roosevelt to drive up to them in a car. 'Finding we could drive right round them,' Sarah Churchill wrote to her mother that evening, 'we went back and got the President and all three of us bumbled along for a second tour. It was a lovely drive, and the President was charming— simple and enthusiastic. I think he enjoyed himself—I think he appreciated the trouble Papa took. Papa loved showing them to him. It really is wonderful how they both get on—they really like and understand each other. . . .' [1]

At the Sphinx, Churchill later recalled, the two men 'examined this wonder of the world from every angle', gazing at her in silence for several minutes as the evening shadows fell. 'She told us nothing,' Churchill added, 'and maintained her inscrutable smile. There was no use waiting longer.' [2]

The second plenary meeting in Cairo, held at eleven o'clock on the morning of November 24, was devoted to Europe, and to the conflicting claims of the Mediterranean and cross-Channel theatres.

It was opened by Roosevelt, who said that the 'logistic problem' to be decided was, 'whether we would retain "Overlord" in all its integrity and, at the same time, keep the Mediterranean ablaze'. In his view, he added, 'Premier Stalin would be almost certain to demand both the continuation of action in the Mediterranean and "Overlord".'

Churchill then spoke of the 'series of disappointments' of the past two months. In Italy 'the campaign had flagged', nor was there 'a sufficient margin of superiority to give us the power to force the enemy back'. The winter had been bad, and the departure from the Mediterranean 'of certain units and landing craft had, it seemed, a rather depressing effect on the soldiers remaining to fight the battle'. He had agreed 'but with a heavy heart' to the return of seven divisions from the Mediterranean theatre. In preparation for embarkation, the 50th and 51st British Divisions, 'which were first class troops', had had their equipment removed. It was also 'a lamentable fact' that, across the Adriatic, 'virtually no supplies had been conveyed by sea to the 222,000 followers of Tito'. These 'stalwarts', Churchill added, 'were holding as many Germans in Yugoslavia as the combined Anglo-

---

[1] Letter of 23 November 1943: Sarah Churchill, *Keep on Dancing, An Autobiography*, London 1981, page 69.

[2] Winston S. Churchill, *The Second World War*, volume 5, London 1952, page 371 (Churchill has misdated the visit to the Sphinx to his return to Cairo after the Teheran conference: Sarah Churchill's letter makes it clear that the visit took place on 23 November 1943).

American forces were holding in Italy south of Rome'. Considering
that 'the Partisans and Patriots had given us such a generous measure
of assistance at almost no cost to ourselves', Churchill said, 'it was of
high importance to ensure that their resistance was maintained and
not allowed to flag'.

Churchill then spoke of the 'black picture' in the eastern Mediterranean. 'When Italy fell,' he said, 'cheap prizes were open to us,
and General Wilson had been ordered to "improvise and dare". Although we had not been able to seize Rhodes, we had occupied Kos,
Leros, Samos and others of the smaller islands.' But Leros had been
recaptured, 'and we had lost 5,000 first-class troops, with four cruisers
and seven destroyers either sunk or damaged'. Taking into account
'the German soldiers drowned and those killed by air attack and in
the battle', Churchill said, 'neither side could claim any large superiority in battle casualties. The Germans, however, were now re-established in the Aegean.'

If Turkey put her air fields at the Allies' disposal and Rhodes were
'once more in our possession', Churchill said, the other Aegean islands
'would become untenable to the enemy'. This was one reason why it
was important to bring Turkey into the war, but beyond that, 'the
effect on Hungary, Roumania and Bulgaria would be profound. All
this might be done at quite a small cost—say, two divisions and a few
landing craft.' Churchill hoped that a meeting between himself and
the Turkish Prime Minister 'could be arranged on the way back from
meeting Premier Stalin'.

Churchill then spoke of the inability of the British to provide the
ships and landing craft for operation 'Culverin' in the Far East. 'If,'
he said, 'it was thought by the United States Chiefs of Staff that
"Culverin" was the best contribution to the Pacific war, then our
resources would have to be made up by help from America. If, on the
other hand, "Culverin" was thought to be too costly, it might be
better to bring back from the South-East Asia Theatre to the Mediterranean sufficient landing craft for an attack on Rhodes.' Thus,
Churchill said, the 'sequence' which he now envisaged would be 'first
Rome then Rhodes'.

There was no British plan to advance into the Valley of the Po,
Churchill told Roosevelt. Instead, the British idea was 'that the
campaign in Italy should have the strictly limited objective of the
Pisa-Rimini line'. Nor would any 'regular formations' be sent to
Yugoslavia. 'All that was needed there,' Churchill explained, 'was a
generous packet of supplies, air support and, possibly, a few Commandos. This stepping-up of our help to the Patriots would not involve
us in a large additional commitment.' Only when 'we had reached

our objective in Italy' would the time come 'to take the decision whether we should move to the left or to the right'.

Turning to the cross-Channel landing, Churchill told the conference: '"Overlord" remained top of the bill, but this operation should not be such a tyrant as to rule out every other activity in the Mediterranean; for example, a little flexibility in the employment of landing craft ought to be conceded.' Seventy additional Tank landing craft had been ordered to be built in British shipyards. 'We must see if we can do even better than this.'

Churchill went on to explain that Alexander 'had asked that the date of the return of the landing craft for "Overlord" should be deferred from mid-December to mid-January'. The resources which were 'at issue' between the American and British Staffs would, Churchill suggested, probably be found to amount 'to no more than 10 per cent of the whole, excluding those in the Pacific', and he went on to ask: 'Surely some degree of elasticity could be arranged.' Nevertheless, he wished 'to remove any idea that we had weakened, cooled or were trying to get out of "Overlord". We were in it up to the hilt.'

Churchill then set out 'the programme he advocated': Rome in January, Rhodes in February, supplies to the Yugoslavs, the 'opening of the Aegean' subject to the outcome of an approach to Turkey, and 'all preparations for "Overlord" to go ahead full steam within the framework of the foregoing policy for the Mediterranean'.

Roosevelt, commenting on the difficulty of telling what the state of German military capability would be 'from month to month', spoke of a possible Russian advance to the boundaries of Roumania 'in a few weeks'. The Russians, he added, 'might suggest that we stage an operation at the top of the Adriatic with a view to assisting Tito'.[1]

'I am making good progress with the President and his high officers,' Churchill telegraphed that day to the King, 'and I am pretty sure all will end up harmoniously.'[2]

While the Cairo conference was in progress, Anthony Eden arrived from London. With him he brought a letter for Churchill from his wife. 'Anthony brings you this letter with my dear love,' she wrote. 'I'm more lonely this time than ever before, because I have tasted of the excitement & interest of travel in War Time in your company.'[3]

There was a lighter moment at Cairo on Thanksgiving Day,

[1] '"Secret" Conference', 'Minutes of Second Plenary Meeting, held at the Villa Kirk, on Wednesday, 24th November, 1943, at 11.00': Cabinet papers, 80/77.
[2] 'Frozen' No. 106, 'Most Secret and Personal', 24 November 1943: Churchill papers, 20/130.
[3] Letter of 23 November 1943: Spencer-Churchill papers.

November 25, when Roosevelt not only entertained Churchill to the traditional turkey feast, but carved the turkey himself. 'An immense turkey,' John Martin wrote home to his wife, 'and an Army band.' [1] After the meal, Sarah Churchill, who was the only woman present, danced with Roosevelt's son Elliott and with Harry Hopkins' son Robert.

Eden, who had reached Cairo in time for the Thanksgiving dinner, discussed with Churchill the problems of reaching agreement with the Americans. In his diary, Eden recorded Churchill's impressions of the American President and his methods:

FDR was 'a charming country gentleman', but business methods were almost non-existent, so W had to play the role of courtier and seize opportunities as and when they arose. I am amazed at patience with which he does this. W admits that our war progress in the last two months has been below level of events. He showed me memoranda he had prepared for our Chiefs of Staff and repeated many times that during the last two months he had felt to be fighting with hands tied behind his back. [2]

On November 25 the British Chiefs of Staff set out their thoughts on the need for an active Mediterranean strategy, which was, they wrote, 'not only fully justified but positively essential'. While not in any way wishing to 'recoil from' or sidetrack 'our agreed intention to attack the Germans across the Channel in the late spring or early summer of 1944', or 'even earlier' if a German collapse seemed imminent, they argued that it would be wrong to regard 'Overlord' on a fixed date 'as the pivot of our whole strategy on which all else turns'. With the Germans in their 'present plight', the Chiefs of Staff wrote, 'the surest way to win the war in the shortest time is to attack them remorselessly and continuously in any and every area where we can do so with superiority'. The number of places at which such an attack could be carried out depended 'mainly on the extent to which they are stretched. Our policy is therefore clear; we should stretch the German forces to the utmost by threatening as many of their vital interests and areas as possible and, holding them thus, we should attack wherever we can do so in superior force.'

The Chiefs of Staff then proposed 'action in the Mediterranean' whereby the offensive in Italy would be 'nourished and maintained until we have secured the Pisa-Rimini Line'. They also proposed the placing of Allied policy on Yugoslavia, Greece and Albania 'on a regular military basis' with an intensification of measures 'to nourish the Partisan and irregular forces in these countries', as well as an attempt to bring Turkey into the war before the end of 1943, the

[1] Letter of 26 November 1943: Martin papers.
[2] Eden diary, 25 November 1943: Eden memoirs, *The Reckoning*, op. cit., page 424.

opening of the Dardanelles 'as soon as possible' and doing 'everything possible to promote a state of chaos and disruption in the satellite Balkan countries'.[1] If these measures involved putting back the date at which the 'Overlord' forces had to be in Britain, 'this should be accepted since it does not by any means follow that the date of the invasion of France will be put back to the same extent'.[2]

At a meeting of the Combined Chiefs of Staff on the following day, November 26, Eisenhower, who opened the discussion, supported the British Chiefs of Staff, telling them and the American Chiefs of Staff that, from the perspective of the Russian advance and the 'Pointblank' bombing offensive, 'Italy was, in his view, the correct place in which to deploy our main forces and the objective should be the Valley of the Po. In no other area could we so well threaten the whole German structure including France, the Balkans and the Reich itself. Here also our air would be closer to vital objectives in Germany.'

Eisenhower then told the Combined Chiefs of Staff that, after the Italian offensive, 'the next best method of harrying the enemy was to undertake operations in the Aegean'. There were sufficient forces in the Mediterranean, he said, 'to take action in this area provided it is not done until after the Po line has been reached. It could then be undertaken while the forces in Italy were reorganising for thrusts either to the east or west.' When these Aegean operations were undertaken, Eisenhower added, 'it would be necessary to bring Turkey into the war'.

On the assumption, Eisenhower continued, that 'only limited means were available' for action in Italy and the Mediterranean, he considered 'that only the line north of Rome could be achieved and that after that he would have to maintain a strategic defensive with strong local offensive action. Lack of landing craft would prevent him from amphibious turning movements designed to cut off enemy forces. The time to turn to the Aegean would be when the line north of Rome had been achieved.' Eisenhower added: 'German reactions to our occupation of the islands had clearly proved how strongly they resented action on our part in this area. From here the Balkans could be kept aflame; Ploesti would be threatened and the Dardanelles might be opened. Sufficient forces should be used for operations in the Aegean and no unnecessary risks run.'

On the assumption that he could advance to the Po line, Eisenhower told the Combined Chiefs of Staff that he would propose action to

[1] Following his advocacy of supplies for the Yugoslav partisans, on November 25 Churchill informed Ismay that one of 'the first practical duties' of the Staff Conference was 'to make sure that the Yugoslav guerrillas are properly supplied'. (Prime Minister's Personal Minute, D.(S) 11/3 25 November 1943: Churchill papers, 20/104.)

[2] 'Note by the British Chiefs of Staff', Combined Chiefs of Staff Paper no. 409, 'Most Secret', 25 November 1943: Cabinet papers, 122/1245.

establish small garrisons in the islands on the eastern coast of the Adriatic 'from which thrusts as far north as possible could be made into Yugoslavia and the Patriots furnished with arms and equipment'. If only Rome was reached, however, 'it would not be possible to thrust as far up as the Adriatic as he would have liked'.

Eisenhower's support for the continuation of the Italian campaign was emphatic: as the minutes recorded, he 'stressed the vital importance of continuing the maximum possible operations in an established theatre since much time was invariably lost when the scene of action was changed, necessitating, as it did, the arduous task of building up a fresh base'.[1]

The meetings of the Combined Chiefs of Staff at Cairo had come to no firm conclusions. The United States Chiefs of Staff, Ismay reported to Churchill, 'would probably agree to the policy of keeping the Mediterranean theatre aflame throughout its length and breadth, provided the bill is not too big, realizing that to enable this to be done, "Overlord" must be postponed'.

Ismay also told Churchill that the United States Chiefs of Staff had not been allowed even to discuss the question of the Far Eastern offensive, operation 'Buccaneer', but that it was 'tolerably certain' that Roosevelt had given 'a definite undertaking' to Chiang Kai-shek 'that this operation will, in fact, take place'.

Ismay noted, in conclusion, that 'it looks as though we can do all you want in the Mediterranean theatre (including the Balkans and Aegean) and also "Buccaneer", provided that "Overlord" is postponed until the 15th July'.[2]

Ismay had already explained to Churchill, however, two days earlier, 'that no firm decisions would be taken on these matters' until after the Teheran conference, when the Combined Chiefs of Staff meetings would resume again in Cairo.[3]

While he was in Cairo, Churchill had to deal with a domestic issue, the release of some of those who had been interned in May and June 1940 under Regulation 18B. As he telegraphed to Attlee and Morrison from Cairo on November 25:

[1] '"Sextant" Conference', 'Minutes of Meeting held in Conference Room 1, Mena House, of Friday, 26th November, 1943, at 14.30', Combined Chiefs of Staff, 131st Meeting: Premier papers, 3/136/5.
[2] Note of 28 November 1943, Chiefs of Staff (Sextant), Paper No. 14, Annex I: Premier papers, 3/136/5, folio 74.
[3] Note of 26 November 1943, Chiefs of Staff (Sextant), Paper No. 14, Annex II: Premier papers, 3/136/5, folios 74–5.

On no account should we lend any countenance to the totalitarian idea of the right of the Executive to lock up its political opponents or unpopular people. The door should be kept open for the full restoration of the fundamental British rights of habeas corpus and trial by jury on charges known to the law. I must warn you that departure from these broad principles because the Home Office have a few people they like to keep under control by exceptional means may become a source of very grave difference between us and the totalitarian-minded folk. In such a quarrel I am sure I could carry the majority in the House of Commons and the mass of the nation. Anyhow, I would try. It seems to me you have a perfectly good line in deploring the fact that such powers are thrust on you and in proclaiming your resolve to use them with the utmost circumspection and humanity. Do not quit the heights.[1]

'I am sure,' Churchill commented acerbicly in a separate telegram to Morrison, 'we shall not need to go to Stalin for help in defending the principles of British liberty and humanity. Any unpopularity you have incurred through correct and humane exercise of your functions will be repaid in a few months by public respect.'[2]

On November 26 Churchill prepared to leave Cairo. To Madame Chiang Kai-shek he sent through his daughter Sarah some 'tiny trinkets' including a 'sprightly and sagacious' cat, noting that 'Like the ancient Egyptians I am very fond of cats', and wishing Madame Chiang a 'safe and prosperous return to Chungking, and better still to Peking, where I hope to visit you if the war ends before I get too old'.[3] That night, Eden gave Churchill a small dinner party, noting in his diary that Churchill 'was in tremendous form'. 'Much discussion about the past,' Eden added, 'and my poor old resignation came up again together with 1940 and War Office experiences.'[4] Sarah Churchill was also present that evening, as were the British Ambassador to Cairo, Sir Miles Lampson, and Sir Alexander Cadogan, who wrote in his diary: 'PM talked to the whole table from 8.30 till 11.30. Then to me and A and Miles from 11.30 till 1.35. Then expressed surprise at having a sore throat!'[5]

On the morning of November 27 Churchill prepared to leave Cairo by air for Teheran. 'W had lost his voice,' Eden noted in his diary, 'I think from too much talk last night, and was sorry for himself until he

[1] 'Frozen' No. 145, 'Most Secret and Personal', 25 November 1943: Churchill papers, 20/130.
[2] 'Frozen' No. 136, 'Most Secret and Personal', 25 November 1943: Churchill papers, 20/130.
[3] Letter of 26 November 1943: Churchill papers, 2/464.
[4] Eden diary, 26 November 1943: Eden memoirs, *The Reckoning*, op. cit., page 425.
[5] Cadogan diary, 26 November 1943: David Dilks (editor), op. cit., page 578.

had a stiff whisky and soda, at 8.45 a.m.'[1] Flying in his York across the Dead Sea, the Tigris and the Euphrates, Churchill and Eden reached Teheran that afternoon, after a five and a half hour journey. 'The plane is very noisy,' Sarah Churchill wrote to her mother, 'so more throat strain.'[2]

At Mehrabad airport, outside Teheran, 'The crew were lined up as he alighted,' J. H. Colegrave later recalled. 'He caught the pilot a smack across his ankles with his stick and said "a bloody bad landing".'[3] Nine years later, Churchill published his own recollections of the journey from the airport:

As we approached the city the road was lined with Persian cavalrymen every fifty yards, for at least three miles. It was clearly shown to any evil people that somebody of consequence was coming, and which way. The men on horseback advertised the route, but could provide no protection at all. A police car driving a hundred yards in advance gave warning of our approach. The pace was slow. Presently large crowds stood in the spaces between the Persian cavalry, and as far as I could see there were few, if any, foot police.

Towards the centre of Teheran these crowds were four or five deep. The people were friendly but non-committal. They pressed to within a few feet of the car. There was no kind of defence at all against two or three determined men with pistols or a bomb. As we reached the turning which led to the Legation there was a traffic block, and we remained for three or four minutes stationary amid the crowded throng of gaping Persians.

If it had been planned out beforehand to run the greatest risk and have neither the security of quiet surprise arrival nor an effective escort the problem could not have been solved more perfectly. However, nothing happened. I grinned at the crowd, and on the whole they grinned at me. In due course we arrived at the British Legation, which lay within a strong cordon of British-Indian troops.[4]

The British delegation was to stay at the British Legation, whose grounds adjoined those of the Soviet Embassy. At Stalin's insistence, the American delegation were housed in a building in the grounds of the Soviet Embassy, to avert an assassination plot which the Soviets claimed to have uncovered. In a telegram to Stalin on November 23, from Cairo, Churchill had proposed that Roosevelt stay at the British Legation, but his suggestion had been ignored.[5] 'The Soviets had once

---

[1] Eden diary, 27 November 1943: Eden memoirs, *The Reckoning, op. cit.*, page 426.

[2] Sarah Churchill, letter of 4 December 1943: Sarah Churchill, *Keep on Dancing, An Autobiography*, London 1981, page 70.

[3] J. H. Colegrave recollections: letter to the author, 15 January 1982. Colegrave was a Staff Officer at 'Paiforce' (Persia and Iran Force) headquarters in Teheran.

[4] Winston S. Churchill, *The Second World War*, volume 5, London 1952, pages 302–3.

[5] 'Frozen' No. 85, 'Most Secret', 'Following for Marshal Stalin from Premier Churchill', 23 November 1943: Cabinet papers, 120/113.

more got what they wanted,' Ismay later recalled. 'I wonder if micro-phones had already been installed in anticipation!'[1]

Having lost his voice, Churchill was unable to dine as planned with Stalin and Roosevelt, so 'the dinner of the three great ones was off', Cadogan noted in his diary, 'and they are all dining separately (PM in bed)'.[2] As Sarah Churchill explained to her mother:

Papa was really very tired and his voice almost completely gone. Uncle Joe was already there and he—Papa—wanted to start right there and then. However, Moran and I went into action, got our heads bitten off; but finally, luckily, no meeting and he had dinner in bed like a sulky little boy and was really very good. He was nervous and apprehensive, I think. After all, this was the high jump and it was frightening not to be feeling well and to have practically no voice. Still, they say a bad dress rehearsal—a good performance and after a good night's sleep, he never looked back.[3]

On the morning of November 28 Churchill hoped to have a talk with Roosevelt, to prepare for their first meeting with Stalin that afternoon. 'PM and President *ought* to have got together, with their Staffs, *before* meeting the Russians,' Cadogan noted in his diary, 'but that,' he added, 'through a series of mischances has not happened.'[4] Instead, an hour before the first meeting of the Big Three, Roosevelt and Stalin had their first meeting, without Churchill being invited. Hopkins, who was present, later told Lord Moran that Roosevelt had 'made it clear that he was anxious to relieve the pressure on the Russian front by invading France', as if to distance himself from Churchill's hopes of a more vigorous Mediterranean strategy. Listening to Hopkins, Moran 'felt that the President's attitude will encourage Stalin to take a stiff line in the conference'.[5]

[1] Ismay memoirs, *op. cit.*, page 337.

[2] Cadogan diary, 27 November 1943: David Dilks (editor), *op. cit.*, pages 578–9.

[3] Sarah Churchill, letter of 4 December 1943: Sarah Churchill, *Keep On Dancing, An Auto-biography*, London 1981, page 70.

[4] Cadogan diary, 28 November 1943: David Dilks (editor), *op. cit.*, page 579.

[5] Moran notes, 28 November 1943: Moran *op. cit.*, pages 134–5.

34

The Teheran Conference: 'Impending doom for Germany'

———

THE first meeting of the Teheran Conference opened in the Soviet Embassy at half past four on the afternoon of 28 November 1943, two days before Churchill's sixty-ninth birthday. Once more, Churchill used Major Birse as his interpreter.[1] 'It was a thrilling experience,' recalled General Ismay, 'to see the Big Three sitting round the same table at long last.'[2] They represented, Churchill told the meeting, probably 'the greatest concentration of worldly power that had ever been seen in the history of mankind'.

Roosevelt, who as the only Head of State, presided, spoke of the 'many plans which had been mooted', the cross-Channel expedition, a 'very big expedition in the Mediterranean', 'increasing the strength of our attack on Italy, the Balkans, the Aegean, Turkey, and so forth'. The most important task of the Conference would be to decide 'which of these to adopt', the 'governing object' would be for the Anglo-American armies 'to draw the greatest weight off the Soviet forces'.

Stalin, who spoke next, told the two western leaders, in answer to the question of how the Anglo-American forces could best help Russia:

The Soviet Government had always felt that the Italian campaign had been of great value to the Allied cause in that it opened the Mediterranean. But Italy was not a suitable jumping-off ground for the invasion of Germany. The Alps stood between. Therefore nothing was to be gained by concentrating large numbers of troops in Italy for the invasion of Germany. Turkey would be a better point of entry than Italy; but it was a long way from the

---

[1] 'The notes I took at the time,' Birse later wrote, 'had, for security reasons, to be destroyed.' ('Teheran, November 1943', letter to Churchill, 12 June 1947, Churchill papers, 4/391A.)

[2] Ismay memoirs, *op. cit.*, page 337.

heart of Germany. He believed that North or North-West France was the place for Anglo-American forces to attack, though it was of course true that the Germans there would resist desperately.

Churchill then told Stalin that the cross-Channel invasion was absorbing most of the 'preparation and resources' of Britain and the United States. Both 'were resolved to do it in 1944'. The operations in the Mediterranean had been 'of a secondary character', although they constituted 'the best contribution we could make in 1943'. Stalin disagreed. He had never regarded the operations in the Mediterranean 'as being of a secondary character', he said. 'They were of the first importance, but not from the point of view of invading Germany.'

The discussion turned to the details of Overlord, which would be carried out, Churchill explained, by thirty-five divisions, nineteen United States and sixteen British. But these forces could not be ready until the early spring or summer of 1944, which was 'still six months away'. Both he and Roosevelt had been asking themselves 'what could be done during these six months with the resources available in the Mediterranean that would best take the weight off Russia', without postponing the cross-Channel invasion 'for more than perhaps a month or two'.

The plan, Churchill explained, was to capture Rome in January, and at the same time to destroy or capture ten or eleven German divisions. Churchill added:

... we had not contemplated going into the broad part of the leg of Italy, still less invading Germany across the Alps. The general plan was first to capture Rome and seize the airfields north of it, which would enable us to bomb Southern Germany, and then to establish ourselves on a line towards Pisa-Rimini. After that the possibility of establishing a Third Front in conformity with, but not in substitution for, the cross-Channel operation would have to be planned.

There were two 'possibilities', Churchill told Stalin. One was to move into southern France. The second, 'suggested by the President', was to move 'from the head of the Adriatic north-east towards the Danube'. Both these could take place at the same time as the cross-Channel landing. The question remained, 'what should be done in the next six months?' Churchill then explained why he felt that there was 'much to be said' for giving aid to Tito, who was 'holding a number of German divisions', and doing 'much more' for the Allied cause than his fellow Yugoslav Mihailovic, commander of the Chetniks. There could be 'great advantage', Churchill believed, in supporting Tito 'with supplies and guerilla activities', as the Balkan theatre was one of the areas 'where we could stretch the enemy to the utmost'. Then, Churchill said, there was the question of Turkey. If Turkey was to enter the war on the side of the allies, it would open up the Dardanelles to the passage of Allied escort vessels already in the Mediterranean, and thus enable 'a ceaseless flow of supplies' to reach the Soviet Black Sea ports. Churchill then asked Stalin a series of questions:

How could we persuade Turkey to come into the war? If she came in, what should she be asked to do? Should she merely give us her bases, or should she attack Bulgaria and declare war on Germany? Should she move forward or should she stay on the Thracian frontier? What would be the effect on Bulgaria, who owed a profound debt to Russia for rescuing her in former days from the Turkish yoke? How would Roumania react? They were already putting out genuine peace-feelers for unconditional surrender. Then there was Hungary. Which way would she go? There might well be a political landslide among the satellite States which would enable the Greeks to revolt and hustle the Germans out of Greece. All these were questions on which the Soviets had a special point of view and special knowledge. It would be invaluable to know what they thought about it all. Would these plans in the Eastern Mediterranean be of sufficient interest to the Soviet Government to make them wish us to go ahead, even if it meant a delay of one to two months from May 1 in launching 'Overlord'?

The British and American Governments, Churchill added, had deliberately kept their minds open on the Turkish question 'until they knew what the Soviet Government felt about these problems'.

Roosevelt now briefly intervened, to remind Churchill and Stalin of the 'further projects' of moving up to the Northern Adriatic and then north-east to the Danube. Churchill agreed that such an advance would be possible 'once we had taken Rome and destroyed the German armies south of the Apennines . . .'. Whether the plan chosen at this stage should be against the South of France or, 'in accordance with the President's idea, north-east from the head of the Adriatic' were operations, Churchill told the conference, which, if Stalin considered them 'with favour', should be further examined. But neither move was to be at the expense of the cross-Channel invasion, as Churchill made clear; on this the minutes of the meeting are conclusive:

Marshal Stalin addressed the following questions to the Prime Minister:
Question: 'Am I right in thinking that the invasion of France is to be undertaken by thirty-five divisions?'
Answer: 'Yes. Particularly strong divisions.'
Question: 'Is it intended that this operation should be carried out by the forces now in Italy?'
Answer: 'No. Seven divisions have already been, or are in process of being, withdrawn from Italy and North Africa, to take part in "Overlord". These

seven divisions are required to make up the thirty-five divisions mentioned in your first question. After they have been withdrawn about twenty-two divisions will be left in the Mediterranean for Italy or other objectives. Some of these could be used either for an operation against Southern France or for moving from the head of the Adriatic towards the Danube. Both these operations will be timed in conformity with "Overlord". Meanwhile it should not be difficult to spare two or three divisions to take the islands in the Aegean.'

Stalin immediately picked up the idea of a landing in the south of France, expressing his preference for it, as opposed to Roosevelt's northern Adriatic proposal. He also said that it would be 'worthwhile' to take the Aegean islands if this could be done with three or four divisions. He did not expect Turkey to agree to enter the war.[1] He would prefer to 'forgo' the capture of Rome if, by doing so, a south of France landing could be launched 'by, say, three divisions', some two months before the cross-Channel landings. The two invasions 'could then join hands'. Churchill replied, however, that it would be 'impossible for us to forgo the capture of Rome. To do so would be regarded on all sides as a crushing defeat, and the British Parliament would not tolerate the idea for a moment.'

Roosevelt spoke next, suggesting that military experts should examine the possibility of operations against Southern France 'on the timing put forward by Stalin', the 'governing factor' being that Overlord should be launched 'at the prescribed time'.

This 'governing factor' of Roosevelt's was in contrast to his agreement in Cairo that 'Overlord' might have to be delayed until mid-July because of the conflicting military needs of operation 'Buccaneer' in the Far East, as well as Mediterranean and Aegean needs. In reply to this, Churchill told Roosevelt and Stalin:

He did not disagree in principle with these views. The suggestions that he had made for minor help to Yugoslavia and Turkey did not, he said, conflict in any way with that general conception. At the same time, he wished it to be placed on record that he could not in any circumstances agree to sacrifice the activities of the armies in the Mediterranean, which included twenty British and British-controlled divisions, merely in order to keep the exact date of May 1 for 'Overlord'. If Turkey refused to come into the war it could not be helped. He earnestly hoped that he should not be asked to agree to any such rigid timing of operations as the President had suggested.

Angered by the course the discussion was taking, Churchill suggested a break. 'Would it not be right,' he asked, 'for the Conference to meditate over all that had been said and to continue their discussions on the following day?' Roosevelt agreed to a pause, and to

[1] Turkey did not declare war on Germany until January 1945.

military discussions among the experts. But Stalin commented that he had not expected that military questions would be discussed at the Conference, and he had not brought his military experts with him'. Nevertheless, he added, Marshal Voroshilov, who was present, 'would do his best'.

At the end of this first meeting of the Big Three, Churchill told Roosevelt and Stalin 'that, although we were all great friends, it would be idle for us to delude ourselves that we saw eye to eye on all matters. Time and patience were necessary.'[1]

That night Roosevelt was the host at a dinner party to which both Churchill and Stalin, as well as Eden and Molotov, were invited. Roosevelt, as Eden noted in his diary, 'was not feeling well' and seemed to be 'below par' in the conversation 'at our end of the table': indeed, Hopkins told Eden that he was afraid Roosevelt 'was going to faint'. As a result of Roosevelt's indisposition, 'dinner broke up early'. Before it did so, Churchill and Eden, Roosevelt and Hopkins, Stalin and Molotov, sat in a circle with their coffee and cigars. After a while, as Eden noted in his diary, Churchill remarked: 'I believe that God is on our side. At least I have done my best to make Him a faithful ally.' The translation finished, Stalin looked up, grinned, and commented: 'And the devil is on my side. Because, of course, everyone knows that the devil is a Communist—and God, no doubt, is a good Conservative.'[2]

After coffee and cigars, Roosevelt went to bed. Remaining in the American villa, Churchill led Stalin to a sofa and suggested that the two men 'talk for a little on what was to happen after the war was won'.[3] Eden was also present. This was 'a historical meeting', Churchill pointed out; 'so much' depended upon the friendship of the three heads of Government and the decisions reached at the Conference. First, replied Stalin, they should consider 'the worst that might happen'. He thought that Germany 'had every possibility of recovering from this war and might start on a new war within a comparatively short time. He was afraid of German nationalism. This was a possibility and allowances must be made for it.' After Versailles, Stalin added, 'peace seemed assured, but Germany recovered very quickly. We must therefore establish a strong body to prevent Germany starting a new war. He was convinced that she would recover.'

Churchill then asked 'how soon' Germany would recover, to which Stalin replied that he thought 'it might be within fifteen to twenty years'.

[1] 'Eureka', '1st Meeting', 'Minutes of First Plenary Meeting held at the Soviet Embassy, Teheran, at 4.30 p.m. on Sunday, 28th November 1943': Cabinet papers, 80/77.

[2] The Eden memoirs, *The Reckoning*, *op. cit.*, page 427.

[3] Winston S. Churchill, *The Second World War*, volume 5, London 1952, page 317.

The world must be made safe 'for at least fifty years', Churchill commented. 'If it was only for fifteen to twenty years, then we would have betrayed our soldiers.'

Stalin then suggested that he and Churchill should consider 'the economic side of the question'. The Germans, he said, 'were an able people, very industrious and cultured, and they would recover quickly'.

Certain measures would have to be 'enforced', Churchill replied. 'He would forbid all aviation, civil and military, and he would forbid the General Staff system.'

Stalin then asked Churchill whether he would also forbid 'the existence of watchmakers' and furniture factories which could easily be turned into factories for 'making parts of shells and into aircraft factories'. The Germans, Stalin added, 'had produced toy rifles which had been used for teaching hundreds of thousands of men how to shoot'.

In reply, Churchill told Stalin: 'nothing was final. The world rolled on. We had now learnt something. Our duty was to make the world safe at least fifty years (a) by disarmament, (b) by preventing rearmament, (c) by supervision of German factories, (d) by forbidding all aviation, and (e) by territorial change of a far-reaching character.' This, Stalin thought, 'was correct, but Germany would work through common countries'.

It all came back, Churchill commented, 'to a question of whether Great Britain, the United States and the USSR kept a close friendship and supervised Germany in their mutual interest'. They should 'not be afraid', he said, 'to give orders as soon as they saw any danger'.

There had been control after the last war, Stalin noted, 'but it had failed', to which Churchill replied: 'people were inexperienced. The last war was not to the same extent a national war and Russia was not a party at the peace conference. It was different this time. He had a feeling that Prussia should be isolated and reduced, that Bavaria, Austria and Hungary might form a broad, peaceful cow-like confederation. He thought Prussia should be dealt with more severely than the other parts of the Reich, so that the latter would not want to go in with Prussia.'

All this, Stalin thought, 'was very good but insufficient', to which Churchill commented 'that Russia would have her army. Great Britain and the United States navies and air forces.' In addition, all three Powers 'would have their other forces, all strongly armed, and they must not assume any obligation to disarm. They were the trustees for the peace of the world. If they failed, there would be, perhaps, a hundred years of chaos. If they were strong they would carry out their trusteeship.'

He would 'think it over', Stalin remarked.

There was 'more than merely keeping the peace', Churchill continued. 'The three Powers should guide the future of the world. He was not a Communist and he did not want to enforce any principles on other nations. But he asked for freedom and for the right of all nations to develop as they liked. He said that they must keep friends in order to ensure happy homes in all countries.'

Stalin then asked 'what was to happen with Germany'; to which Churchill replied 'that he was not against toilers in Germany, but only against the leaders and against dangerous combinations'. There were 'many toilers in the German divisions, who fought under orders', Stalin remarked, and he went on to tell Churchill that when he asked German prisoners who came from the working classes 'why they fought for Hitler, they replied that they were executing orders'. Stalin added: 'He shot such prisoners.'

Churchill then suggested that he and Stalin should discuss the Polish question. Stalin agreed, and invited Churchill to begin. 'We had declared war on account of Poland,' Churchill said. 'Poland was therefore important to us. Nothing was more important than the security of the Russian western frontier. But he had given no pledges about frontiers. He wanted heart-to-heart talks with the Russians about this.' When Stalin 'felt like telling us what he thought about it', Churchill added, 'the matter could be discussed and they could reach some agreement, and the Marshal should tell him what was necessary for the defence of the western frontiers of Russia'.

To this, Stalin replied that 'he did not feel the need to ask himself how to act. So far his heart did not feel stimulated.' He meant, the notes of the meeting commented, 'that the Prime Minister should become more precise'.

Churchill then set out what he had in mind. After the war in Europe, 'which might end in 1944, the Soviet Union would be overwhelmingly strong and Russia would have a great responsibility for hundreds of years in any decision she took with regard to Poland. Personally, he thought Poland might move westwards like soldiers taking two steps left close. If Poland trod on some German toes, that could not be helped, but there must be a strong Poland. This instrument was needed in the orchestra of Europe.'

Stalin answered Churchill by saying that 'the Polish people had their culture and their language, which must exist. They could not be extirpated.'

Agreeing with this, Churchill then asked Stalin 'if we were to draw frontier lines', to which Stalin replied: 'Yes.' The minutes of the meeting continued:

THE PRIME MINISTER said he had no power from Parliament, nor he believed had the President, to define any frontier lines. He suggested that they might now, in Teheran, see if the three Heads of Government, working in agreement, could form some sort of policy which might be pressed upon the Poles and which we could recommend to the Poles, and advise them to accept.
MARSHAL STALIN said we could have a look.
THE PRIME MINISTER said we should be lucky if we could.
MARSHAL STALIN asked whether it would be without Polish participation.
THE PRIME MINISTER replied in the affirmative and said that this was all informally between themselves, and they could go to the Poles later.
MARSHAL STALIN agreed.
Mr EDEN said he had been much struck by what the Marshal had said that afternoon to the effect that Poles could go as far west as the Oder. He saw hope in that and was much encouraged.
MARSHAL STALIN asked whether we thought he was going to swallow Poland up.
Mr EDEN said he did not know how much the Russians were going to eat. How much would they leave undigested?
MARSHAL STALIN said the Russians did not want anything belonging to other people, although they might have a bite at Germany.
Mr EDEN said what Poland lost in the east she might gain in the west.
MARSHAL STALIN said possibly they might, but he did not know.
THE PRIME MINISTER demonstrated with the help of three matches his idea of Poland moving westwards, which pleased Marshal Stalin.[1]

On November 29 Churchill invited Roosevelt to lunch with him before the second plenary session of the conference that afternoon. Roosevelt declined, sending Averell Harriman to explain to Churchill 'that he did not want Stalin to know that he and I were meeting privately'. That afternoon, however, before the plenary session, it was Roosevelt and Stalin who met privately, with Churchill excluded from their discussion of the method of post-war government. Then, at 3.30, Churchill and the British delegation crossed into the Russian compound for a short ceremony, the handing over by Churchill to Stalin of the specially made Sword of Stalingrad. Inscribed on the blade of the sword, in English and in Russian, were the words: 'To the steel-hearted citizens of Stalingrad, the gift of King George VI, in token of the homage of the British people.'[2] 'PM made a short speech,'

[1] 'Record of Conversation between the Prime Minister and Marshal Stalin at Teheran on 28th November, 1943', 'Teheran Conference', Section 1, 'Most Secret': Cabinet papers, 120/113.
[2] The sword is on permanent display in Stalingrad (now Volgograd) at the Museum of the Defence of Stalingrad.

Cadogan noted, 'and handed it to Stalin. Latter replied shortly, kissed the scabbard and handed it to Voroshilov—obliquely, so that the sword slipped out of the scabbard and the pommel hit V on the toe.' [1] A Russian guard of honour then escorted the sword from the room, and the Big Three returned to the conference table for their second plenary session.

The military advisers having met all morning, General Brooke was the one who reported the results of their deliberations. Unless 'something was done' in the Mediterranean between now and the launching of 'Overlord', he warned, the Germans would be able to transfer troops from Italy to Russia or northern France. Three possibilities had been discussed, he said: advancing 'up the leg' of the Italian peninsula, strengthening the partisans in Yugoslavia so that they could hold down German divisions in the Balkans, and getting Turkey into the war. Marshall added that the 'variable and question-able factor in almost every one of the problems facing the Allies was landing craft'. But Stalin was not impressed. 'Who will command "Overlord"?' were his first words, and when Roosevelt replied that this had not been decided, Stalin retorted that the operation 'would come to nought' unless one man was placed in charge both of the preparation for it, and its execution.

Churchill then reiterated the British view, that 'at least' sufficient landing craft should be retained in the Mediterranean to transport two divisions. 'With a landing force of this size,' he said, 'we could help forward the advance up the leg of Italy by outflanking move-ments, and thus avoid the slow laborious methods of frontal attack.' Secondly, Churchill told Stalin, 'these landing-craft would enable us to take Rhodes and open the Aegean simultaneously with the entry of Turkey into the war'. It would also 'enable us five or six months hence to conduct the operation into Southern France in co-operation with "Overlord" '. Churchill added:

Clearly, all these operations would require the most careful timing and study, but there seemed to be a good hope that all the operations that he had mentioned could be carried through. On the other hand, it was obvious that landing-craft sufficient to transport two divisions could not be kept in the Mediterranean without setting back the date of 'Overlord' for perhaps six to eight weeks, or alternatively, without recalling from the East the assault craft and ships which had been sent there for operations against the Japanese. This placed us on the horns of a dilemma. It was a case of balancing one problem against the other.

The object of all the Mediterranean operations envisaged, Churchill

[1] Cadogan diary, 29 November 1943: David Dilks (editor), *op. cit.*, page 580.

reiterated, was 'to take the weight off Russia and to give the best possible chance to "Overlord" '. There was 'no question' of using large forces in the Mediterranean. The Yugoslav, Albanian and Greek partisans were already tying down twenty-one German divisions. Roumania 'was already trying desperately hard to surrender unconditionally'.

Stalin spoke next. The entry of Turkey into the war, the support of Yugoslavia, and the capture of Rome were, he said, 'relatively unimportant'. If the Conference had been convened to discuss military matters, ' "Overlord" must come first', and should take place 'some time in May, and no later'. As a 'supporting operation', the assault on the South of France, whether before, during or even after 'Overlord', would be 'definitely helpful'. But the capture of Rome, and other operations in the Mediterranean, 'could only be regarded as diversions'. Roosevelt did not dissent; instead, he again supported Stalin in warning that any eastern Mediterranean expeditions, 'even though initially they might entail only two or three divisions, there was always the possibility that they might develop into a bigger commitment involving the despatch of larger forces. In this event, even the later date of "Overlord" would be prejudiced.'

For his part, Stalin was emphatic, telling Churchill and Roosevelt that he was 'not prepared to agree to any delay in "Overlord" beyond the month of May'. Churchill reminded him, however, of the three conditions, set out many months earlier, upon which the launching of 'Overlord' depended: first, that there must be a 'satisfactory reduction' in the strength of the German fighter forces in north-west Europe before the assault; second, that German reserves in France and the Low Countries must not on the day of the assault be more than 'about twelve full-strength first-quality mobile divisions'; and third, that it must not be possible for the Germans to transfer from other fronts more than fifteen first-quality divisions during the first sixty days of the operation.

In response to this, Stalin asked Churchill if 'the Prime Minister and the British Staffs really believe in "Overlord" ', to which Churchill replied that, provided these conditions were met, 'it will be our stern duty to hurl across the Channel against the Germans every sinew of our strength'.[1]

Churchill then set out for Stalin his reasons for wanting Turkey to be brought into the war. 'If our efforts to bring Turkey in were unsuccessful,' he said, 'that would be the end of the matter, and we should have to let it drop.' It 'must not be overlooked', however, 'that

---

[1] 'Eureka', '2nd Meeting', 'Minutes of Second Plenary Meeting held at the Soviet Embassy, Teheran, on Monday, 29th November, 1943, at 4 p.m.': Cabinet papers, 80/77.

our failure to bring Turkey in would be a relief to the Germans'. There was 'a further point about Turkey', Churchill told Stalin. If Turkey came in to the war on the Allied side, he stressed, 'and we captured Rhodes and subsequently turned the Germans out of the other Aegean Islands, our troops and air forces in Egypt could all move forward into action instead of remaining in their present defensive role'. Churchill added, as the minutes recorded: 'He begged that the issue of Turkey should not be lightly turned aside.'

The second plenary was at an end. 'They don't seem to have made *any* progress on their operational talks,' Cadogan noted in his diary after talking to Eden, 'rather the reverse, as the President promises everything that Stalin wants in the way of attack in the West, with the result that Winston, who has to be more honest, is becoming an object of suspicion to Stalin. . . .' [1]

That night Stalin was the host to Churchill and Roosevelt at a dinner in the Soviet Embassy. They were joined by Roosevelt's son Elliott. During the dinner, as Churchill later wrote, after much chaff by Stalin and even teasing of Churchill:

... the Marshal entered in a genial manner upon a serious and even deadly aspect of the punishment to be inflicted upon the Germans. The German General Staff, he said, must be liquidated. The whole force of Hitler's mighty armies depended upon about fifty thousand officers and technicians. If these were rounded up and shot at the end of the war German military strength would be extirpated. On this I thought it right to say, 'The British Parliament and public will never tolerate mass executions. Even if in war passion they allowed them to begin they would turn violently against those responsible after the first butchery had taken place. The soviets must be under no delusion on this point.'

Stalin, however, perhaps only in mischief, pursued the subject. 'Fifty thousand,' he said, 'must be shot.' I was deeply angered. 'I would rather,' I said, 'be taken out into the garden here and now and be shot myself than sully my own and my country's honour by such infamy.'

At this point the President intervened. He had a compromise to propose. Not fifty thousand should be shot, but only forty-nine thousand. By this he hoped, no doubt, to reduce the whole matter to ridicule. Eden also made signs and gestures intended to reassure me that it was all a joke. But now Elliott Roosevelt rose in his place at the end of the table and made a speech, saying how cordially he agreed with Marshal Stalin's plan and how sure he was that the United States Army would support it. At this intrusion I got up and left the table, walking off into the next room which was in semi-darkness. I had not been there a minute before hands were clapped upon my shoulders from behind, and there was Stalin, with Molotov at his side, both grinning broadly, and eagerly declaring that they were only playing, and that nothing

[1] Cadogan diary, 29 November 1943: David Dilks (editor), *op. cit.*, page 580.

of a serious character had entered their heads. Stalin has a very captivating manner when he chooses to use it, and I never saw him do so to such an extent as at this moment. Although I was not then, and am not now, fully convinced that all was chaff and there was no serious intent lurking behind, I consented to return, and the rest of the evening passed pleasantly.[1]

Speaking about unconditional surrender, Stalin said, as Eden reported to London on the following day, that 'he thought this bad tactics vis-à-vis Germany', and suggested that the Allies work out 'terms' together, and make these terms known to the German people. Eden added that Churchill 'agrees that this is a better suggestion'.[2]

The dinner over, Churchill returned to the British Embassy, where he was joined by Eden and Clark Kerr, the British Ambassador to Russia. Lord Moran, who went to see if Churchill 'needed anything', found the Prime Minister talking 'in a tired, slow voice, with his eyes closed'. There might, he said, in the future, 'be a more bloody war. I shall not be there. I want to sleep for billions of years.' Britain would need to be 'supreme' in the air. 'If we are strong in the air,' he said, 'other countries, remembering this war, will hesitate to attack us. Moscow will be as near to us as Berlin is now.'

Eden and Clark Kerr retired to bed. The doctor remained a few moments longer with Churchill. The doctor's account continued:

He could not rid himself of that glimpse of impending catastrophe. Blurred and ill-defined as it was, it stuck in his mind. He pulled up abruptly, so that he stood looking down at me, his eyes popping.

'I believe man might destroy man and wipe out civilization. Europe would be desolate and I may be held responsible.'

He turned away with a gesture of impatience:

'Why do I plague my mind with these things? I never used to worry about anything.'

His face became very grave.

'Stupendous issues are unfolding before our eyes, and we are only specks of dust, that have settled in the night on the map of the world. Do you think,' he demanded abruptly, 'my strength will last out the war? I fancy sometimes that I am nearly spent.'

He said no more as he got into bed. I hung about for a few minutes and then asked him whether he wanted his light put out. He did not answer. He was already asleep.[3]

During their discussions on November 29 Stalin had made what Churchill described in a minute to the British Chiefs of Staff, as the 'momentous declaration' that the Soviet Union 'would enter the war

---

[1] Winston S. Churchill, *The Second World War*, volume 5, London 1952, page 330.

[2] 'Frozen' No. 538, 'Most Secret', sent at 10.30 a.m., 30 November 1943: Premier papers, 3/197/2, folio 25.

[3] Lord Moran, notes for 29 November 1943: Moran, *op. cit.*, pages 136–41.

against Japan the moment Germany was defeated'. This made it necessary, Churchill minuted to the Chiefs of Staff that evening, for the
'Bucaneer' operation in the Far East to be entirely American, to enable
Britain to 'strengthen amphibious operations' during the Italian campaign 'and for any operation against the South of France', the project
favoured by Stalin. Churchill also asked his Chiefs of Staff: 'Cannot
also more landing-craft etc., be sent across the Atlantic to increase the
"lift" for Overlord and keep the May date?' [1]

At 8.45 on the morning of November 30, the three British Chiefs of
Staff, together with Ismay and Dill, met at the British Legation in
Teheran, to discuss the points which they intended to put to the United
States Chiefs of Staff at a joint meeting, set for three quarters of an hour
later. At this early morning discussion, the British Chiefs of Staff decided
to propose to the United States Chiefs of Staff seven strategic points for
discussion, representing the British point of view. The first of these was
that an operation 'shall be mounted' in the South of France, timing and
scope to be decided later, 'maybe after "Overlord" '.
    There followed, as the other strategic points, an advance in Italy to
the Pisa-Rimini line; assistance to the partisans in Yugoslavia 'but
no forces other than Commandos to be used'; operations in the Aegean
to be 'entirely dependent' upon Turkey entering the war, and no
more landing craft to be kept away from 'Overlord' for the specific
purposes of operations in the Aegean; for the Italian advance, landing
craft to be kept in the Mediterranean until the 15 January 1944;
because of the Italian campaign, the earliest date of 'Overlord' not
now to be possible before June 1; and, finally, a question to the Americans about 'Buccaneer', would it be affected by Stalin's statement
about Russia coming in against Japan 'once Germany is out'? [2]
    Putting these points to the United States Chiefs of Staff, Brooke
stressed that in Italy 'we should not stay in the position now reached
and must advance further'. Hence the British Chiefs of Staff's wish to
advance north of Rome, to the Pisa-Rimini line, even if this had a
'repercussion' on the 'Overlord' date. If, Brooke pointed out, the
landing craft due to return to 'Overlord' were to stay in the Mediterranean until 15 January 1944, for the Italian campaign, then 1
June 1944 would be 'the earliest date possible' for 'Overlord', because
of the need for repairing the landing craft and using them for training
purposes. Admiral Leahy disputed this, arguing that even if the

---

[1] Minute of 29 November 1943: Churchill papers, 4/318.
[2] Chiefs of Staff meeting, British Legation, Teheran, 8.45 a.m., 30 November 1943: Premier
papers, 3/136/5.

landing craft were retained in the Mediterranean until 15 February 1944, ' "Overlord" would still be possible by the 15th May'.

Turning to 'Buccaneer', Brooke noted that thirty-two landing craft were involved.[1] These had not been mentioned in the 'Overlord' equation. Portal, speaking of the recent increase in German fighter production, warned that 'Overlord' could face 'a very strong fighter force acting against it'. From the 'air point of view', Portal added, 'a June or July date for "Overlord" would seem to be better, as regards weather, than one in May'.

Ismay, commenting on the earlier decision, at 'Trident' to carry out 'Overlord' on 1 May 1944, pointed out that the Russians had not been given this precise date, but only told that 'Overlord' was scheduled for 'some time in May'.[2]

A May date for 'Overlord' was receding. The next suitable moon period after May 8, pointed out the Chief of Combined Operations, General Laycock, a week later, 'occurs between 5th June and the 10th'.[3]

That morning, disturbed by the divergences which were opening up between the British, Soviet and American viewpoints, Churchill asked to see Stalin alone. Stalin agreed, and, at a meeting attended only by the two leaders and their interpreters, Churchill explained his reasons for wanting to see further military action in the Mediterranean during the six months before 'Overlord'. There were nine or ten British divisions in Italy, Churchill explained. 'I want to use them all the time.' Churchill then pointed out to Stalin that American determination to undertake an amphibious operation against the Japanese in the Bay of Bengal in March, operation 'Buccaneer', was affecting the timing of 'Overlord' just as much as the Mediterranean strategy. 'I was not keen about it,' Churchill told Stalin. 'If we had the landing-craft needed for the Bay of Bengal in the Mediterranean, we should have enough to do all we wanted there and still be able to keep an early date for "Overlord".' The choice was not between the Mediterranean and the date of 'Overlord', but between the Bay of Bengal and the date of 'Overlord'. In Italy, the British army had been 'somewhat disheartened' by the removal of three British and four American divisions, 'all in preparation for "Overlord" '. It was for that reason 'we had not been able to take full advantage of Italy's collapse'. But, Churchill pointed out, 'it also proved the earnestness of our preparations for "Overlord" '.[4]

---

[1] Twenty landing craft Tanks and twelve landing craft Infantry.

[2] Combined Chiefs of Staff, 182nd Meeting, British Legation, Teheran, 9.30 a.m., 30 November 1943: Premier papers, 3/136/5.

[3] R. E. Laycock, note dated 5 December 1943: Premier papers, 3/136/5.

[4] Four British divisions were to leave Italy for 'Overlord': the 7th Armoured, the 1st Airborne, and the 50th and 51st Infantry.

'A great battle was impending in Italy,' Churchill told Stalin. There were about half a million men under Alexander; thirteen or fourteen Allied divisions against nine or ten German divisions. The weather had been bad and bridges had been swept away, 'but in December we intended to push on, with General Montgomery leading the Eighth Army'. An amphibious landing would be made near the Tiber. At the same time 'the Fifth Army would be fiercely engaged holding the enemy. It might turn into a miniature Stalingrad.'

It was not the Italy campaign however, but 'Overlord' on which Stalin's attention was fixed, and on which his worries were focused. Churchill assured Stalin that he had urged Roosevelt to decide on the name of the 'Overlord' Commander-in-Chief 'before we all left Teheran'. As the discussion continued, however, Stalin raised the spectre of a breach between the Allies, even of Russia pulling out of the war. The notes of the interpreter, Major Birse, recorded Stalin's warning:

. . . the Red Army was depending on the success of our invasion of Northern France. If there were no operations in May 1944 then the Red Army would think that there would be no operations at all that year. The weather would be bad and there would be transport difficulties. If the operation did not take place he did not want the Red Army to be disappointed. Disappointment could only create bad feeling. If there was no big change in the European war in 1944 it would be very difficult for the Russians to carry on. They were war-weary. He feared that a feeling of isolation might develop in the Red Army. That was why he had tried to find out whether 'Overlord' would be undertaken on time as promised. If not, he would have to take steps to prevent bad feeling in the Red Army. It was most important.

Churchill assured Stalin that the cross-Channel invasion 'would certainly take place', but he reiterated the British proviso that the landings depended upon the Germans not bringing into France 'larger forces than the Americans and British could gather there'. If the Germans had forty to fifty divisions in France, 'I did not think the force we were going to put across the Channel could hold on.' But if the Red Army 'engaged the enemy', and the British 'held them in Italy', and if, possibly, Turkey entered the war, 'then I thought we could win'.

Stalin told Churchill that the 'first steps' of the cross-Channel invasion 'would have a good effect' on the Red Army, which could itself attack the Germans in May and June. The Germans, he said, 'were afraid of the Red Army advance. The Red Army would advance if it saw that help was coming from the Allies.' [1]

[1] 'Record of Conversation between the Prime Minister and Marshal Stalin at the Soviet Embassy, 12.45 p.m., 30th November, 1943', 'Most Secret', War Cabinet Paper No. 9 of 1944, 7 January 1944: Cabinet papers, 120/113.

Churchill and Stalin then proceeded to Roosevelt's villa for luncheon, where Stalin raised the question of Russia's desire for a warm-weather port. 'I had always thought it a wrong thing,' Churchill later wrote, 'capable of breeding disastrous quarrels, that a mighty land-mass like the Russian Empire, with its population of nearly two hundred millions, should be denied during the winter months all effective access to the broad waters.' [1]

Holding this view, Churchill was able to tell Stalin that there were 'no obstacles' to Russia having a warm-water port. He expected, he said, 'that Russia would sail the ocean with her Navy and merchant fleet and we would welcome her ships'. The Russian 'grievance' would be met, because, Churchill declared, 'the government of the world must be entrusted to satisfied nations, who wished nothing more for themselves than what they had. If the government were in the hands of hungry nations,' Churchill warned, 'there would always be danger.' Peace would be kept 'by people who live in their own way and were not ambitious. Our power placed us above the rest. We were like rich men in their habitations.' [2]

Shortly after this luncheon had ended, the third plenary session of the Teheran conference began: 'agreement had been reached', Roosevelt told the assembled gathering, 'on the main military problems'. The Joint Chiefs of Staff recommended, as Brooke explained, that the cross-Channel invasion would be launched in May, with a 'supporting operation' against the South of France. The 'danger period' for 'Overlord', Stalin commented, would be 'at the time of deployment from the landings'; he would therefore undertake to organize 'a large scale Russian offensive in May', in order to prevent any movement from the east 'of any considerable German forces'. Roosevelt then told the conference that the Commander for 'Overlord' would be named 'within three or four days'.

Churchill then suggested that the Staffs should draft a conference communiqué. 'The note to be sounded,' he said, 'was brevity, mystery, and a foretaste of impending doom for Germany.' [3] Churchill's wish was met. 'Our Military Staffs,' the communiqué read, 'have joined in our round table discussions, and have concerted our plans for the destruction of the German forces. We have reached complete agreement as to the scope and timing of the operations which will be undertaken from the east, west and south.'

[1] Winston S. Churchill, *The Second World War*, volume 5, London 1952, page 336.
[2] 'Record of a Conversation between the Prime Minister, President Roosevelt and Marshal Stalin at Luncheon on 30th November, 1943', 'Teheran Conference', Section 3, 'Most Secret': Cabinet papers, 120/113.
[3] 'Eureka', '3rd Meeting', 'Minutes of Third Plenary Meeting held at the Soviet Embassy, Teheran, on Tuesday, 30th November, 1943, at 4 p.m.': Cabinet papers, 80/77.

At the end of this session, the discussion turned to the question of deception, Stalin explaining to Churchill and Roosevelt 'that the Russians had made considerable use of deception by means of dummy tanks, aircraft and airfields. Radio deception had also proved effective.' He was 'entirely agreeable', Stalin added, 'to the Staffs collaborating with the object of devising joint cover and deception schemes'.

Churchill and Stalin were in agreement, Churchill commenting 'that truth deserved a bodyguard of lies'. This phrase was to become the key of a new and most secret operation, 'Bodyguard', the deception plans for 'Overlord', to which Stalin was, within a few months, to make his contribution.[1]

That night, Churchill was host at the third dinner of the conference. It was his own birthday dinner: he was sixty-nine. 'The speeches,' Ismay later recalled, 'started directly we sat down and continued almost without interruption until we got up.'[2] In his toasts, Churchill praised Roosevelt for having by his courage and foresight prevented 'a revolutionary upheaval in the United States in 1933'. As for Stalin, 'he would be ranked with the great heroes of Russian history and had earned the title "Stalin the Great" '.[3]

The toasts and joviality continued all evening. Sarah Churchill, who was present, wrote to her mother of how, 'when Papa during one of the many toasts remarked, "England is getting pinker", Joe interjected: "It is a sign of good health." '[4] Lord Moran recorded two further toasts:

> PM: 'I drink to the Proletarian masses.'
> Stalin: 'I drink to the Conservative Party.'[5]

After dinner, when Roosevelt and most of the other guests had left, Stalin stood talking for a while. Randolph Churchill, who with his sister Sarah had been invited to join them, went over to Stalin who, Lord Moran noted, 'was almost boisterous'.[6] 'There could not have been greater cordiality,' John Martin wrote, 'and Uncle Joe enjoyed himself as much as anybody.'[7] At one point in the conversation, as Birse later recalled, Stalin 'noticed a portrait of King George V, but

---

[1] The origin of the phrase 'Bodyguard of Lies', Churchill later told one of his Private Secretaries, was Stalin himself, who had called it 'a Russian proverb'. Churchill's use of it in the discussion must have been meant, the Private Secretary later reflected, to please Stalin 'by quoting his own phrase back at him'. (Sir David Hunt, letter to the author, 24 July 1985.)

[2] Ismay memoirs, op. cit., page 340.

[3] Harriman recollections: Abel and Harriman, op. cit., page 276.

[4] Sarah Churchill, letter of 4 December 1943: Keep On Dancing, op. cit., page 71.

[5] Lord Moran, notes for 30 November 1943: Moran, op. cit., page 143.

[6] Lord Moran, notes for 30 November 1943: Moran, op. cit., page 143.

[7] John Martin, letter of 2 December 1943: Martin papers.

mistaking it for King Edward VII, he said: "That King was exactly like our Czar. He was a good King; he allowed me to come to England." ' [1]

On the following day there was a small birthday parade for Churchill, made up of British troops, Indian troops and employees of the Anglo-Persian Oil Company. J. H. Colegrave, who was present, later recalled how Churchill, 'wearing one of his inimitable uniforms, walked down the single rank of this very small parade, and accepted his presents with tears streaming down his face'. [2]

The military strategy for 1944 having been agreed, the discussions at Teheran turned to the detailed problems arising from it. At luncheon on the following day, December 1, it was agreed to try to persuade Turkey to enter the war on the side of the Allies. 'If Turkey refused,' Churchill remarked, 'she would forfeit her chance to sit at the Peace Conference and would be treated as other neutrals. We would say that Great Britain had no further interest in her affairs and would stop the supply of arms.'

The luncheon discussion then turned to the Soviet request for a share of the Italian Fleet, which had surrendered to the British. Such a request, commented Churchill, 'was a very small thing after all the efforts that Russia was making or had made'. He would like to see the Italian ships go to the Black Sea, and 'perhaps he might at the same time send some of His Majesty's Ships with them'. Stalin's comment: 'Good.' Churchill then continued, as the minutes recorded:

The Prime Minister said that Russia must have complete control of the Black Sea. He and the President needed time to arrange the matter with the Italians, for they (the Italians) were helping with some of their smaller ships in patrol work, and some of their submarines were carrying important supplies. The matter would have to be so arranged that there would be no mutiny in the Italian fleet and no scuttling of ships. He suggested that a couple of months would be enough for him and the President to handle the Italians like a cat handling a mouse. 'In two months a battleship and a cruiser: would that do?'

Stalin agreed, asking only that the transfer date be at the end of January, to which both Roosevelt and Churchill assented. Churchill also offered British help, 'if we got into the Black Sea', with the work 'of cleaning the Russian ships of their foul bottoms'. The fall of

[1] 'Teheran: November 1943', letter of 12 June 1947: Churchill papers, 4/391A.
[2] J. H. Colegrave recollections: letter to the author, 15 January 1982.

Sebastopol and the loss of the dry docks there 'must have made this difficult for the Russians', he said. 'We should be glad to help.'

This, Stalin said, 'would be a good thing'. The discussion continued, still on a naval note:

The Prime Minister went on to say that he would like to put four or five submarines into the Black Sea, especially if there were a chance of drowning some of the Germans and Roumanians who were now in the Crimea. But we would abide by Marshal Stalin's wishes. We had no ambitions in the Black Sea.

Marshal Stalin replied that that was good, and that he would be grateful for any help.

The Prime Minister said that this was one of the things which might be asked of Turkey if she only accepted strained neutrality. We had between thirty and forty submarines in the Mediterranean. Turkey should let us slip them through the Dardanelles by night. Our submarine officers would think it an honour to fight side by side the Soviet Black Sea fleet. It would only be a small contribution, but we would like to make it.

American submarines, Churchill added, 'were sinking a lot of Japanese ships in the Pacific, and we in the Mediterranean had been sinking a very large number of Italian and German ships. We thought submarine warfare wicked, but we would like to do a lot more of it.' [1]

After luncheon, the Big Three returned to the conference table, where Poland was the principal subject of their discussion. Stalin spoke strongly against the Polish Government in exile, in London: 'he was by no means sure', he said, that it was ever likely to become 'the kind of Government it ought to be'. The talk then turned to frontiers with Stalin referring to 'the matter of the three matches', when Churchill had demonstrated the movement westward of Russia's frontier to the Curzon line of 1920, and Poland's frontier, by way of compensation, to the River Oder, thus transferring the eastern regions of Germany to Polish sovereignty. The minutes of the meeting continued:

THE PRIME MINISTER said that it would be a great help if round that very table we could learn what were the Russian ideas about the frontiers. He would then be glad to put the matter before the Poles and to say frankly that he thought the conditions fair. His Majesty's Government (he was only speaking for His Majesty's Government) would be prepared to tell the Poles that the plan was a good one and the best that they were likely to get, and that His Majesty's Government would not argue against the Soviet Government at the peace table. Then we could get on with the President's

---

[1] 'Record of a Conversation at Luncheon in the Soviet Embassy, Teheran, on 1st December 1943', 'Teheran Conference', Section 4, 'Most Secret': Cabinet papers, 120/113.

idea of resuming relations. What we wanted was a strong and independent Poland, friendly to Russia.

MARSHAL STALIN said that that was true, but that the Poles could not be allowed to seize the Ukraine and White Russian territory. That was not fair. According to the 1939 frontier the soil of the Ukraine and White Russia was returned to the Ukraine and to White Russia. Soviet Russia adhered to the frontiers of 1939, for they appeared to be ethnologically the right ones.

Mr EDEN asked if this meant the Ribbentrop-Molotov line.

MARSHAL STALIN said: 'Call it whatever you like.'

M. MOLOTOV remarked that it was generally called the Curzon Line.

Churchill then produced a map, on which were marked both the Curzon Line and the 1939 Polish-Soviet border, and he indicated on it 'the line of the Oder'. The discussion then focused on the city of Lvov, with Eden suggesting that, under Lord Curzon's line, Lvov was intended to be inside the Polish frontier.[1] Stalin disagreed. Churchill's map, he said, 'had not been drawn right'. Lvov 'should be left on the Russian side'. The line should go 'westward' of Lvov, towards the town of Przemysl. The discussion continued, as the minutes recorded:

MARSHAL STALIN here remarked that he did not want any Polish population, and that if he found any district inhabited by Poles he would gladly give it up.

PRESIDENT ROOSEVELT asked if he might put a question. Did the frontier of East Prussia and the territory east of the Oder approximate to the size of the eastern provinces of Poland itself?

MARSHAL STALIN said that he did not know and that it had not been measured.

THE PRIME MINISTER suggested that the value of this land was much greater than the Pripet Marshes. It was industrial and it would make a much better Poland. We should like to be able to say to the Poles that the Russians were right, and to tell the Poles that they must agree that they had had a fair deal. If the Poles did not accept, we could not help it. And here he made it clear that he was speaking for the British alone, adding that the President had many Poles in the United States who were his fellow-citizens.

[1] Between 1918 and 1939 Lvov (Lwów, Lemberg) had been apart of independent Poland. Between 1779 and 1917 it had been part of the Austrian Empire, later Austria-Hungary. The Curzon Line was the name given to the line recommended by the Supreme Council of the Allied Powers on 8 December 1919, as Poland's eastern frontier. The course which the line took derived from the decision of the Allied Powers to include only ethnographically Polish regions within the frontiers of the new Polish State. On 12 July 1920 the British Foreign Secretary, Lord Curzon, sent a Note to the Soviet Government proposing that this line should be the eastern frontier of Poland. According to the Note: 'This line runs approximately as follows: Grodno, Jalovka, Nemirov, Brest-Litovsk, Dorohusk, Ustilug, east of Hrubieszow, Krilow and thence west of Rava-Ruska, east of Przemysl to the Carpathians.' On 16 August 1945, a treaty signed in Moscow defined the Soviet-Polish frontier essentially as that of the Curzon Line, with certain small adjustments (see map 8, pages 1362-3).

MARSHAL STALIN said again that if it were proved to him that any district were Polish, he would not claim it, and here he made some shadowing on the map west of the Curzon Line and south of Vilna, which he admitted to be mainly Polish.

At this point the meeting again broke up, and there was a prolonged study of the Oder Line on a map. When this came to an end—

THE PRIME MINISTER said that he liked the picture, and that he would say to the Poles that if they did not accept it they would be fools, and he would remind them that but for the Red Army they would have been utterly destroyed. He would point out to them that they had been given a fine place to live in, more than 300 miles each way.

MARSHAL STALIN said that it would indeed be a large, industrial State.

THE PRIME MINISTER said that it would be a State friendly to Russia.

MARSHAL STALIN replied that Russia wanted a friendly Poland.

THE PRIME MINISTER said to Mr Eden, with some emphasis, that he was not going to break his heart about this cession of parts of Germany to Poland or about Lvov.

Mr EDEN said that if Marshal Stalin would take the Curzon and Oder Lines as a basis on which to argue that might provide a basis.

At this point M. MOLOTOV produced the Russian version of the Curzon Line, and a text of a wireless telegram from Lord Curzon giving all the place names.

THE PRIME MINISTER asked whether M. Molotov would object to the Poles getting the Oppeln district.

M. MOLOTOV replied that he did not foresee any objection.

The Poles, Churchill remarked, 'would be wise to take our advice, they were getting a country 300 miles square, and he was not prepared to make a great squawk about Lvov'. Then, turning to Stalin, Churchill added 'that he did not think that we were very far off in principle'.

Would the transfer of the population be possible on a voluntary basis, asked Roosevelt. 'Probably it would be,' was Stalin's reply. The discussion on Poland was at an end.[1]

The discussion then turned to Finland, which was still allied to Germany. The British, said Churchill, wanted two things, 'first, that Russia should be satisfied with her frontiers; second, that the Finns should be free and independent and live as well as they could in those very uncomfortable regions'. He had been 'sympathetic' to Finland, he said, in the days of the Russo-Finnish war, but 'he had turned against her when she came into the war against the USSR'. That, he said, had been 'disgraceful'.

Russia must have 'certain things', Churchill declared: 'Security for

---

[1] 'Record of a Conversation at Luncheon at the Soviet Embassy, Teheran, on 1st December, 1943', 'Teheran Conference', Section 5, 'Most Secret': Cabinet papers, 120/113.

Leningrad and its approaches', while her position 'as a permanent naval and air power' in the Baltic 'must be assured'. As Molotov spoke of the twenty-seven months' bombing and bombardment of Leningrad by the Finns and the Germans, Churchill declared: 'Great Britain's policy was to make the western frontier of Russia secure.'

As to Stalin's demand for compensation from Finland, Churchill replied that 'it was easy enough to do damage, but very hard to repair it, and it was bad for any one country to fall into tribute to another. It did not work and could not be done.' So far as Germany was concerned, the Soviet Government should take 'all her machines' to repair the ruin done to the Soviet industries, not as indemnities, but as reconstruction, 'whereas the Finns were only poor little musk rats and ermine and they had nothing to give'. The conversation continued:

MARSHAL STALIN said that the Finns might perhaps be given an opportunity to repay the damage they had done in, say 5 to 8 years.
THE PRIME MINISTER said: No more than that, adding that experience showed large indemnities did not work.
MARSHAL STALIN proposed to occupy a region of Finland if the Finns did not pay, but if they did pay the Russians would withdraw within the year.
THE PRIME MINISTER said that he had not yet been elected a Soviet commissar, but that if he were he would advise against this. There were much bigger things to think about.
MARSHAL STALIN asked whether Finns would accept all the other points.
THE PRIME MINISTER replied that we were behind the Russians and ready to help them at every turn, but we must think of the May battle.[1]

With Churchill's reference to the Anglo-American cross-Channel plans for May 1944, the conversation turned to the question of post-war Germany. This section of the discussion began with a description by Roosevelt of an American plan for splitting Germany into five separate self-governing regions, with two more regions, Kiel-Hamburg and the Ruhr-the Saar, to be governed by the United Nations. He was only 'throwing this out', Roosevelt said, 'as an idea which might be talked over'. Churchill's response was emphatic:

THE PRIME MINISTER suggested that he might use the American idiom and say that the President had 'said a mouthful', and that Mr Roosevelt's plan was a new one to him. In his opinion there were two things: one constructive and the other destructive.

[1] 'Record of a Conversation at the Soviet Embassy, Teheran, on 1st December, 1943', 'Teheran Conference', Section 7, 'Most Secret': Cabinet papers, 120/113.

He had two clear ideas in his mind. First was the isolation of Prussia. What was to be done to Prussia after that was only secondary. Then he would like to detach Bavaria, Wurtemburg, Palatinate, Saxony and Baden.

Whereas he would treat Prussia harshly, he would make things easier for the second group, which he would like to see work in with what he called a Danubian Confederation. The people of these parts of Germany were not the most ferocious, and he would like to see them live, and in a generation they would feel different. South Germans were not going to start another war, and we would have to make it worth their while to forget Prussia. He did not much mind whether there were one or two groups, and he asked Marshal Stalin whether he would be prepared to go into action on this front.

Stalin replied that while he would be 'prepared to go with action' on these lines, he preferred 'a plan for the partition of Germany' on Roosevelt's lines, as being 'more likely to weaken Germany'. Fundamentally, Stalin argued, there was 'no difference' between North Germans and South Germans, 'for all Germans fought like beasts'. Nor should Austria be included in any such combination. Austria had existed independently before, 'and could do so again'. It was 'far better', he believed, 'to break up and scatter the German tribes'. They would always want to reunite, however, and would have to be 'neutralised' by various economic measures, 'and in the long run by force if necessary. That was the only way to keep the peace.' But if the Allies were to make 'a large combination with Germans in it, trouble was bound to come'. Germans, Stalin added, 'would always want to reunite and to take their revenge. It would be necessary to keep ourselves strong enough to beat them if ever they let loose another war.'

As the meeting was drawing to a close, Churchill brought the discussion back to Poland. He did not ask for any agreement, he said, nor was he 'convinced on the matter himself', but he would 'rather like to get something down on paper'. Churchill then produced the following formula:

It was thought in principle that the home of the Polish State and nation should be between the so-called Curzon Line and the line of the Oder, including for Poland East Prussia (as defined) and Oppeln; but the actual tracing of the frontier line required careful study, and possibly disentanglement of population at some points.

With such a formula, Churchill told Stalin and Roosevelt, he could say to the Poles: 'I do not know if the Russians would approve, but I think that I might get it for you. You see you are being well looked after.' Churchill added, however, that 'we should never get the Poles to say that they were satisfied. Nothing would satisfy the Poles.'

Stalin's only comment—'with a grin' as the minutes recorded—was that 'the Poles in London seem to be most reasonable people'. He then said that Russia would like to have the warm-water port of Königsberg, in East Prussia, and he sketched on the map a possible border line between Russia and Poland in East Prussia. 'This,' he said, 'would put Russia on the neck of Germany.' 'If he got this,' Stalin added, he would be 'ready enough' to agree to Churchill's formula about Poland.[1] 'What about Lvov?' Churchill asked, to which Stalin replied that, 'he would accept the Curzon Line.'[2] These were the final sentences of the Teheran conference.[3]

During the luncheon, Churchill, Roosevelt and Stalin also agreed to the contents and texts of five 'military conclusions'. These were, one, that the partisans in Yugoslavia should be supported by supplies and equipment 'to the greatest possible extent, and also by commando operations'; two, that it was 'most desirable' for Turkey to come into the war on the side of the Allies 'before the end of the year'; three, that if Turkey, while at war with Germany, was attacked by Bulgaria, 'the Soviet Union would immediately be at war with Bulgaria'; four, that operation 'Overlord' would be launched 'during May 1944', in conjunction with an operation against Southern France, while at 'about the same time', Soviet forces would launch an offensive 'with the object of preventing German forces from transferring from the Eastern to the Western Front'; and five, that the military staffs of Britain, Russia and the United States would 'keep close touch with each other' in regard to future operations in Europe, and, in particular, in order to concert 'a cover plan to mystify and mislead the enemy as regards these operations. . . .'[4]

'We have had a grand day here,' Churchill telegraphed to Attlee, 'and relations between Britain, United States and USSR have never been so cordial and intimate. All war plans are agreed and concerted.'[5]

---

[1] In 1945 Königsberg and northern East Prussia were incorporated into the Soviet Union (and Königsberg renamed Kaliningrad). Southern East Prussia was incorporated into Poland.

[2] The Russians had earlier made it clear that they considered, under the Curzon Line, that Lvov was not a part of Poland, but took the south-eastern border down only to Przemysl (where it was to end, also, in the final border lines of 1945).

[3] 'Record of a Conversation at the Soviet Embassy, Teheran, on 1st December, 1943', 'Teheran Conference', Section 8, 'Most Secret': Cabinet papers, 120/113.

[4] 'Military Conclusions of the Teheran Conference', 'Most Secret', initialled 'WSC, JVS, FDR', 1 December 1943: Premier papers, 3/136/10, folios 5–6.

[5] 'Frozen' No. 546, 'Most Secret and Personal', 1 December 1943: Churchill papers, 20/130.

35

'Stranded amid the ruins of Carthage'

ON the morning of 2 December 1943, Churchill left Teheran by air for Cairo where he stayed at the Casey Villa. 'The house had been beautifully fitted out for us,' Elizabeth Layton wrote home, 'with everything the Old Man likes in the way of telephones, bells, buzzers, flyswats, mosquito nets, and the like.' The 'Old Man', Elizabeth Layton added, 'was in a wonderful frame of mind. We were never growled at—at least, seldom.'[1]

At eleven in the morning of December 4, the third plenary meeting of 'Sextant' opened in Cairo. Roosevelt was accompanied by Hopkins and the American Chiefs of Staff; Churchill and Eden by the British Chiefs of Staff and Ismay. Commenting on Stalin's promise to make war on Japan 'the moment Germany was defeated', Churchill suggested that this 'would give us better bases than we could ever find in China, and make it all the more important that we should concentrate on making "Overlord" a success'. He would have preferred July 1944 for 'Overlord', he said, 'but he was determined nevertheless to do all in his power to make the May date a complete success'. 'Overlord' was a task 'transcending all others', he declared. A million American troops were to be 'thrown in', and half a million or more British. 'Terrific battles' were to be expected, on a scale 'far greater than we had experienced before'.

In order to give 'Overlord' the 'greatest chance of success', Churchill continued, it was necessary for the landing in the South of France 'to be as strong as possible'. The 'critical time' would come at about the thirtieth day, 'and it was essential that every possible step should be taken by action elsewhere to prevent the Germans from concentrating a superior force against our bridgeheads'.

Sir Andrew Cunningham now stated that if 'Overlord' and 'Anvil',

[1] Elizabeth Layton, letter of 12 December 1943: Nel papers.

the code name given to the proposed South of France landing, were both to go ahead, Britain's naval resources would not be adequate to undertake a third amphibious operation at the same time.

The south of France landing, Churchill commented, should be planned on the basis of an assault force 'of at least two divisions'. As for the operations in South East Asia, these 'must be judged in their relation to the predominating importance of "Overlord"'. He was 'astounded' at the demands for 'Buccaneer' which had reached him from Mountbatten. 'Although there were only 5,000 Japanese in the Island,' Churchill remarked, '58,000 men were apparently required to capture it. As he understood it, the Americans had been fighting the Japanese successfully at odds of two and a half to one. In the face of Marshal Stalin's promise that Russia would come into the war, operations in the South-East Asia Command had lost a good deal of their value; while, on the other hand, their cost had been put up to a prohibitive extent.'

In suggesting that Britain's offensive plan for the Far East should be suspended, and the priority of resources given to 'Overlord' and 'Anvil', Churchill was supported by Brooke, who told the conference: 'The Mediterranean was of the greatest importance. It would be fatal to let up in that area. We should go on hitting the Germans as hard as we possibly could, and in every place that we could.'

Roosevelt, in an attempt to preserve Britain's Far Eastern offensive, now spoke of the ease with which 'Buccaneer' could be carried out; far from 58,000 troops being needed, he thought that 14,000 'would be ample'. Brooke 'demurred', however, to Roosevelt's reasoning, feeling that 'it might be found that the proper strategy was to divert landing craft from "Buccaneer" to the Mediterranean', and to increase the South of France landing 'to, say a three-division assault'.

Admiral King spoke of the availability of at least two divisions for the 'Anvil' landing. As to the new construction of landing craft in the United States, he said, 'nothing would be sent to the Pacific'. This, Churchill observed, was 'a fruitful decision'. It might be 'proper strategy', Portal observed, to get from South East Asia command the forces for at least a three division landing in the South of France. 'Surely,' Brooke added in support of Portal, 'it would be better to employ all the "Buccaneer" resources to strengthen up the European front.'

Churchill, Brooke and Portal were in agreement; Mountbatten's offensive would have to wait until after the monsoon, whatever pledges had been made to Chiang-Kai-shek that the offensive would be launched in the spring.

With 'Anvil' now set, at Britain's insistence, to replace 'Buccaneer', the talk turned to the Aegean Sea, and to what Churchill called the 'great political reactions' if Turkey were to enter the war. Bulgaria, Roumania and Hungary 'might all fall into our hands', he said, adding: 'we ought to make these German satellites work for us'. Churchill continued: 'If we could get a grip on the Balkans there would be a tremendous abridgement of our difficulties. The next Conference might perhaps be held at Budapest!' All this, Churchill said, 'would help "Overlord"'. He himself 'was not apprehensive about the landing; but the critical period would be at about the 30th day. It was therefore essential that the Germans should be held at every point, and that the whole ring should close in together.'

It was Roosevelt who then summed up the discussion, setting out the priorities on which there was, as he called it, 'general agreement': First, that 'Nothing should be done to hinder "Overlord"'; second, that 'Nothing should be done to hinder "Anvil"'; third, 'By hook or by crook we should scrape up sufficient landing craft to operate in the Eastern Mediterranean if Turkey came into the war'; and, fourth, that Mountbatten should be told 'to go ahead and do his best with what had already been allocated to him'.

Churchill's only comment was that it might be necessary 'to withdraw resources' from Mountbatten's offensive, in order to 'strengthen up' both 'Overlord' and 'Anvil'. 'He could not agree with this,' Roosevelt said, adding: 'We had a moral obligation to do something for China and he would not be prepared to forgo the amphibious operation except for some very great and readily apparent reason.' This 'very good reason', commented Churchill, 'might be provided by "Overlord"', where the present assault was planned on only a three and a half Division basis, 'whereas we had put nine Divisions ashore in Sicily on the first day'. The 'Overlord' plan, Churchill added, 'was at present on a very narrow margin'.[1]

On his first day in Cairo, Churchill had welcomed the Turkish President, Ismet Inönü, to the Egyptian capital. After three days of talks, however, Inönü refused to agree to bringing Turkey into the war. His country was not ready militarily, he insisted. The most he would agree to was that British aircraft might be allowed to operate from Turkish bases. Such operations, he said, could begin in two months' time. The first British 'experts' could leave for Turkey at once. 'But the experts must be sent in thousands,' Churchill commented during his first meeting with Inönü on December 4. 'They

[1] 'Minutes of Third Plenary Meeting, held at Villa Kirk, on Saturday, 4th December, 1943, at 1100': Cabinet papers, 80/77.

could come in mufti. It was important to diminish the risk which
would arise when the Germans attacked.' [1]

At the second meeting with Inönü on December 4, a meeting at
which Roosevelt was also present, Churchill told the Turkish President: 'In a few months, perhaps six, German resistance might be
broken, and Turkey, if she did not accept the invitation now, might
find herself alone, not on the Bench, but wandering about in Court.'
It would be 'dangerous', Churchill added, 'if Turkey now missed the
chance of joining the English-speaking peoples, numbering, excluding
coloured races, some two hundred million souls'. By associating herself
with the United Nations now, Churchill added, Turkey 'would also
be associated with Russia, one of the strongest military powers in the
world, if not the strongest, at any rate in Europe and Asia'. His 'own
opinion', Churchill said, and he reminded Inönü that 'he had been
associated with European politics for about 35 years', was that the
entry of Turkey into the war, 'arranged in the right way and at the
right time', would bring about a series of 'landslides' in Roumania,
Hungary and Bulgaria. That 'would be most fruitful and welcome'. A
Bulgarian declaration of war on Turkey, he assured Inönü, 'would
automatically mean a Russian declaration of war on Bulgaria'. [2]

The discussion continued on December 5, when Churchill pressed
Inönü to consider entering the war 'about the end of February'. The
issue then discussed was whether the Turkish preparations, including
the arrival of British personnel, might provoke Germany to declare
war before Turkey was ready. It was, Churchill said, 'a vicious circle.
We were satisfied that no preparations could be effective without the
introduction of personnel, while the Turks refused the introduction of
personnel because of the danger of provoking Germany. Thus no
preparation could be made against Germany being provoked.' [3]

Churchill and Inönü met again, without Roosevelt, on December
6. A decision was needed, Churchill reiterated, by February 1944. 'If
Turkey lost four or five months,' he warned, 'matters would proceed
without the Turks.' Turkey, replied Inönü, 'was now on a peace
footing. To get on a war footing they would require the necessary
equipment.' [4] This question of equipping the Turks was then discussed
at Roosevelt's villa, by Churchill, Inönü, and the President. If the

---

[1] 'Anglo-American–Turkish Conversations in Cairo', 'Record of Informal Meeting held at
President Inönü's Villa, 4th December 1943', 'Most Secret': Cabinet papers, 120/113.

[2] 'Anglo-American–Turkish Conversations in Cairo', 'Record of Meeting held at President
Roosevelt's Villa on 4th December at 5 p.m.', 'Most Secret', Cabinet papers, 120/113.

[3] 'Anglo-American–Turkish Conversations in Cairo', 'Record of Meeting held at President
Roosevelt's Villa on the 5th December at 3 p.m.', 'Most Secret': Cabinet papers, 120/113.

[4] 'Anglo-American–Turkish Conversations in Cairo', 'Record of a Meeting held at 4 p.m. on
6th December at President Inönü's Villa', 'Most Secret': Cabinet papers, 120/113.

Allies sent twenty air squadrons, Inönü declared, 'it would not be possible to say that Turkey was ready'. 'The Allies seemed to think that the Turkish Government should act in spite of risks,' he added, to which Churchill reiterated: 'The war was going on, and the moment for Turkey would pass.' [1]

Churchill's final meeting with Inönü took place on the morning of December 7. The Turkish Government, Inönü remarked, 'saw Germany as stretching from the Crimea to Rhodes, with Turkey encircled, and they felt that Germany had fresh forces with which she could attack'. Turkey feared she would be at war with Germany 'without a minimum of essential supplies'. 'It would be easy,' Churchill replied in some exasperation, 'for Turkey to make prohibitive conditions, and in that case the Allied forces must be sent elsewhere.' The war would 'move westwards', and Turkey would then 'lose the chance of coming in and reaping the advantages which entry into the war would promise her'.

Churchill's arguments were in vain. The most to which Inönü would agree was for British 'experts' to go to Ankara, followed by more British Officers 'to continue the conversations'. [2]

Inönü's agreement to allow Turkish air bases to be used by British aircraft, an operation codenamed 'Saturn', gave at least the prospect of a British attack on Rhodes, using the Turkish air bases for the necessary air cover. But the decisive factor in any attack on Rhodes would be landing craft, as Churchill noted for the Chiefs of Staff Committee. These landing craft would have to be used against Rhodes—operation 'Hercules'—before the end of February, as after that all landing craft would be needed for the south of France landing. [3]

While in Cairo, Churchill was again a victim of ill health. 'PM not too well, and cried off dinner,' Cadogan noted in his diary on December 4, of the first dinner in honour of President Inönü. 'However,' Cadogan added, 'he appeared in his rompers just as I hoped we might be going home. Turks and others left soon after, and we got away about 12.15.' [4] The illness was stomach ache. 'Your telegram just came,' Clementine Churchill wrote to her husband two days later, 'saying you have gippie tummy & absolute whirl of business. I do hope the tummy

[1] 'Anglo-American-Turkish Conversations in Cairo', 'Record of Meeting held at President Roosevelt's Villa at 5 p.m. on 6th December 1943', 'Most Secret': Cabinet papers, 120/113.

[2] 'Anglo-American-Turkish Conversations in Cairo', 'Record of a Meeting at Casey Villa on 7th December 1943, Morning', 'Most Secret': Cabinet papers, 120/113.

[3] 'Operation "Saturn" ', 'Most Secret', Prime Minister's Personal Minute, D (S) 12/3A, 6 December 1943: Churchill papers, 20/104. Telegraphed to London as Frozen No. 435, 9 December 1943: Cabinet papers, 120/113.

[4] Cadogan diary, 4 December 1943: David Dilks (editor), op. cit., pages 582–3.

will yield to treatment; I fear it can be rather obstinate. . . .'[1]

At the fourth plenary, held at eleven o'clock on December 5, 'Buccaneer' remained the point in dispute. When Churchill suggested that the difficulty might be overcome by bringing Mountbatten's offensive forward to January, General Marshall replied 'that this would not be possible'. Mountbatten had given a date in the middle of March. If that date was adopted, Admiral Leahy remarked, 'the landing craft could not be returned to the European theatre till the beginning of May'.

Churchill then spoke disparagingly about Mountbatten's plans. 'If a superiority of 10 to 1 was required,' he said, 'this, in fact, made the conduct of war impossible.' Both 'Overlord' and 'Anvil' were 'known to be of great importance', he added, 'and will be seemingly affected by a diversion such as "Buccaneer"'. 'Buccaneer' should therefore be postponed. The 'right thing', suggested Brooke, 'seemed to be to take what was required for the European Theatre, and then see what could be done with what was left in South-East Asia'.

Churchill supported Brooke, adding that 'we should be doing wrong strategically if we used vital resources such as landing craft on operations of comparatively insignificant importance, instead of using these resources to strengthen up "Overlord" and "Anvil", where it looks like we are working to a dangerously narrow margin'. It was then agreed that the Combined Chiefs of Staff would 'initiate further studies' concerning the scope of 'Overlord' and 'Anvil', 'with a view to increasing the assaults in each case'. At the same time, the combined Chiefs of Staff would ask Mountbatten 'what amphibious operations he could do on a smaller scale than "Buccaneer" if the bulk of landing craft and assault shipping were withdrawn from South-East Asia during the next few weeks'.[2]

' "Buccaneer" is off,' Roosevelt informed Churchill after the fourth plenary session, and Churchill at once gave the news to Ismay, with the comment: 'He is a better man that ruleth his spirit than he that taketh a city.'[3] The reduction of the proposed scale of operations in the Bay of Bengal, Churchill informed Stalin on the following day, was to permit the reinforcement of amphibious craft for the operation against southern France. Orders had also been given, as a result of these further discussions in Cairo, 'to divert certain landing craft from the Pacific' for the southern France operation.[4]

A second agreement reached by Churchill and Roosevelt, and also

---

[1] Letter of 6 December 1943: Mary Soames, *Clementine Churchill, op. cit.*, page 342.

[2] 'Minutes of Fourth Plenary Meeting held at the Villa Kirk, on Sunday, 5th December, 1943, at 11.00': Cabinet papers, 80/77.

[3] Winston S. Churchill, *The Second World War*, volume 5, page 364.

[4] Prime Minister's Personal Telegram, T.2013/3, 'Frozen' No. 371, 6 December 1943: Churchill papers, 20/125.

telegraphed to Stalin, was the decision to give 'the highest strategical priority' to a bomber offensive against Germany 'with the objective of destroying German air combat strength, the German military, industrial and economic system, and preparing the way for a cross-Channel operation'; the two leaders had also ordered the 'utmost endeavours', as Churchill told Stalin, 'to increase production of landing craft in UK and the USA for reinforcement of "Overlord" ', and further orders had been issued to divert certain landing craft from the Pacific 'for the same purpose'.[1]

Among those who saw Churchill on December 5 was Harold Macmillan, who had flown to Carthage from Algiers. 'I have made it clear,' Churchill told Macmillan, 'that, as regards the present Government, all resignation will be gratefully received!' 'Does that mean,' asked Randolph Churchill, 'that anyone can join who wants to?' 'No,' replied Churchill with a grin, 'but you can join the queue.'

There were so many issues to be resolved, Macmillan noted: the Turks 'being very sticky', the Chinese, the Russians, the Greeks, the Yugoslavs, the Italians, the French, 'all these questions are bobbing about for settlement, like those little celluloid balls on shooting galleries at the seaside. It is a fantasy and a miracle—and more and more, in spite of everything, Winston begins to dominate the scene.'[2]

On December 6, Churchill drove with Roosevelt to the Pyramids. During the drive Roosevelt said, 'almost casually' as Churchill later recalled, that he had decided upon the 'Overlord' commander. He could not spare General Marshall from Washington, he explained, and so proposed to nominate Eisenhower for the command. This Churchill accepted without demur.[3]

That evening, at the fifth and final plenary meeting, Roosevelt read out the conclusions of the Combined Chiefs of Staff. 'Overlord' and 'Anvil' were to have the priority. An attempt was to be made to bring Turkey into the war. 'Buccaneer' was to be postponed.[4] When military historians came to 'adjudge' the decision of the 'Sextant' conference, Churchill commented, 'they would find them fully in accordance with the classic articles of war'. He wished also to express his 'deep sense of gratitude' to his United States colleagues. The 'Anvil' operations had been 'a great contribution made by them' to the Conference. He was 'convinced', Churchill added, that the 'Anvil' operation 'would contribute largely to the success of "Overlord" '.[5]

[1] 'Frozen' No. 371, 'Most Secret', 6 December 1943: Cabinet papers, 120/858.
[2] Macmillan diary, 5 December 1943: War Diaries, op. cit., page 318.
[3] Winston S. Churchill, The Second World War, volume 5, London 1952, pages 369–70.
[4] Combined Chiefs of Staff Paper, No. 426/1, 6 December 1943.
[5] 'Minutes of Fifth Plenary Meeting held at the Villa Kirk, on Monday, 6th December, 1943, at 19.30': Cabinet papers, 80/77.

The second Cairo conference was at an end. First to leave the city was Roosevelt, at eight in the morning of December 7, followed at noon by President Inönü. As Eden later recalled:

On the airfield President Inönü embraced Mr Churchill in farewell. This attention delighted the Prime Minister, who said as we drove back into Cairo: 'Did you see, Ismet kissed me.' My reply, perhaps rather ungracious, was that as this seemed to be the only gain from fifteen hours of hard argument, it was not much to be pleased with. Mr Churchill said no more to me, but that night, when he went to bed he remarked to his daughter Sarah: 'Do you know what happened to me today, the Turkish President kissed me. The truth is I'm irresistible. But don't tell Anthony, he's jealous.' [1]

Before dinner, Churchill saw Harold Macmillan again. '7 pm,' he noted in his diary. 'Saw PM. He was in bed. He is tired, but triumphant since at the last moment his policy—his strategical policy, has triumphed. The Far East adventure is postponed, and all will be concentrated (as far as may be) on the Mediterranean and north European campaigns.' [2]

That night, at dinner, Brooke found Churchill 'in tremendous form', asking each of those present to say when they thought Germany would be defeated. Both Brooke himself, and Dill, opted for March 1944, thus making the cross-Channel landings unnecessary. General Marshall also predicted March, 'and, if not then, November'. [3]

While still in Cairo, Churchill submitted to a punishing schedule of talks and appointments. On December 8 his first meeting, at ten in the morning, was about aid to Tito's partisans. Those present included two members of Britain's mission to Tito, Brigadier Fitzroy Maclean and Bill Deakin, now a Major. Shortly after midday Churchill called on King Farouk, then lunched with Eden and the King of Greece. Following his afternoon sleep, he had talks first with General Wilson, then, once more, with Harold Macmillan. At dinner at the British Embassy the guests included Field Marshal Smuts, General Brooke, Maclean, Deakin, Lord Jellicoe—who had been in the Leros battle— and Julian Amery, who was serving with the partisans in Albania. After dinner, there was a further discussion with Macmillan. [4] 'Winston was in great form and holding forth to a circle of these young men,' Macmillan noted. [5] But Smuts had formed a different impression of Churchill's condition, pulling Brooke aside while Churchill was presiding over the conversation 'to tell me', as Brooke noted in his diary, 'that he was not at all happy about the condition

[1] Eden recollections of 7 December 1943: Eden memoirs, *The Reckoning*, op. cit., page 429.
[2] Macmillan diary, 7 December 1943: *War Diaries*, op. cit., page 321.
[3] Brooke diary, 7 December 1943: Bryant, op. cit., volume 2, page 110.
[4] Prime Minister's Engagement Cards, entry for 8 December 1943: Thompson papers.
[5] Macmillan diary, 8 December 1943: *War Diaries*, op. cit., page 322.

of the PM'. Smuts told Brooke that he considered Churchill 'worked far too hard and exhausted himself', and added that 'he was beginning to doubt whether he would stay the course; that he was noticing changes in him'.[1]

On December 9 Churchill lunched with Brooke, to discuss the Mediterranean command in the wake of Eisenhower's appointment to command 'Overlord'. Brooke noted in his diary: 'he was looking very tired and said he felt very flat, tired and pains across his loins'. As the discussion continued, Brooke wrote, Churchill 'kept on harping back and repeating details which were of no consequence, and I saw that it was useless in his tired state to discuss large issues'.[2]

Churchill was indeed tired, so much so that he noticed, in Cairo, 'that I no longer dried myself after my bath, but lay on the bed wrapped in my towel till I dried naturally'.[3] At no time since the war began had he been so exhausted. He had, however, to telegraph on December 9 to Mountbatten, to explain that planning for the post-monsoon operations could not possibly be on the scale which Mountbatten had proposed for the now abandoned operation 'Buccaneer':

Everyone here has been unpleasantly affected by your request to use 50,000 British and Imperial troops of which 33,700 combatant against 5,000 Japanese. I was astounded to hear of such a requirement and I cannot feel sure you are getting competent military advice. The Americans have been taking their islands on the basis of two and a half to one and that your Generals should ask for six and a half to one had produced a very bad impression. Even the detailed figures with which I have been furnished do not remove it.

While 'such standards' prevail, Churchill added, 'there is not much hope of making any form of amphibious war'.[4]

On December 10 Churchill had another busy schedule. In the morning there were meetings with both King Peter of Yugoslavia and the Regent of Iraq, followed by a Press conference. At lunch Yugoslavia was the issue, with the head of SOE, General Gubbins, Brigadier Maclean and Major Deakin being invited to the discussion of future support for Tito. Greece was the theme in the afternoon, with several Greek statesmen to see. There followed dinner at the British Embassy, at which Smuts, Eden, Cadogan, Casey and Randolph Churchill were among those present. Another of the guests, Julian Amery, wrote to his father a few days later:

[1] Brooke diary, 9 December 1943 (recalling 8 December 1943): Bryant, op. cit., volume 2, page 111.
[2] Brooke diary, 9 December 1943: Bryant, op. cit., volume 2, page 112.
[3] Winston S. Churchill, The Second World War, volume 5, London 1952, page 372.
[4] Prime Minister's Personal Telegram, T.2020/3, 'Frozen' No. 433, 'Most Secret and Personal', 9 December 1943: Churchill papers, 20/125.

Among his (the PM's) better remarks was a reply to a question about his future plans 'I am the victim of caprice and travel on the wings of fancy'. And on France 'the destinies of a great people cannot be determined for all time by the temporary deficiencies of its technical apparatus'. He told us that he had been on the point of using this at Teheran and had only just remembered in time that it had originally been coined by Trotsky.[1]

That night, at 1 a.m., Churchill left Cairo for the westward flight to Tunisia, the prelude, as he hoped, to a visit to the British troops in Italy. 'PM very tired and flat,' noted Brooke after the eight and a half hour flight. 'He seemed to be in a bad way; the Conference has tired him out and he will not rest properly and insists on working.'[2]

Matters had been made worse by the flight from Cairo ending at the wrong airport. Brooke later recalled how 'they took him out of the plane and he sat on his suit-case in a very cold morning wind, looking like nothing on earth. We were there about an hour before we moved on and he was chilled through by then.'[3]

Churchill had been sitting on his official boxes, as he later recalled, 'worn out'. A message came that Eisenhower was waiting at an airfield forty miles away. Churchill returned to the York, and after a ten minutes flight was at the correct destination. 'I am afraid,' he said to Eisenhower as they drove towards The White House, Eisenhower's Villa near Carthage, 'I shall have to stay with you longer than I had planned. I am completely at the end of my tether, and I cannot go on to the front until I have recovered some strength.'[4]

Throughout December 11, Churchill slept. As he did so, General Brooke decided to intervene in the proposed visit to the Italian front. As he later recalled:

I felt that a trip to Italy in December with snow and seas of mud, living in cold caravans, would finish him off. I discussed the matter with Moran who entirely agreed. I therefore tackled Winston in the evening and told him that he was wrong in wanting to go to Italy. I granted that the troops would be delighted to see him and that he would enjoy the trip, but said that I did not think he had any right to risk his health in this way when he had such far more important matters in front of him connected with the war. I was beginning to make a little progress, and then I foolishly said: 'And what is more, Moran entirely agrees with me.' He rose up on the elbow in his bed, shook his fist in my face and said: 'Don't you get in league with that bloody old man!'[5]

[1] Julian Amery, *Approach March, a venture in autobiography*, London 1973, page 270.
[2] Brooke diary, 11 December 1943: Bryant, *op. cit.*, volume 2, page 114.
[3] Brooke recollections (of 11 December 1943): Bryant, *op. cit.*, volume 2, page 115.
[4] Winston S. Churchill, *The Second World War*, volume 5, London 1952, page 373. Eisenhower's villa was also known as La Maison Blanche.
[5] Brooke recollections (of 11 December 1943): Bryant, *op. cit.*, volume 2, page 115.

That night, Churchill dined with Eisenhower, Brooke, Lord Moran, Air Chief Marshal Tedder, two members of his staff, 'Tommy' Thompson and John Martin, and two of his children, Randolph and Sarah.[1] On going to bed, Churchill felt a pain in his throat, and went at once to Moran's bedroom for advice. 'It's pretty bad,' he told the doctor. 'Do you think it's anything? What can it be due to?' But Moran reassured the Prime Minister, and sent him back to bed. 'For a man with his strong constitution,' Moran noted, 'he never seems to be long without some minor ailment. Probably in the morning I shall hear no more of this pain.'[2]

Churchill awoke in the early hours of the morning, in considerable discomfort. Brooke noted in his diary:

I was dog-tired last night and sleeping like a log at 4 am when I was woken by a raucous voice re-echoing through the room with a series of mournful, 'Hulloo, Hulloo, Hulloo!' When I had woken sufficiently I said, 'Who the hell is that?' and switched on my torch. To my dismay I found the PM in his dragon dressing-gown, with a brown bandage wrapped round his head, wandering about in my room. He said he was looking for Lord Moran and that he had a bad headache.

I led him to Moran's room and retired back to bed. But for the next hour the whole house resounded with the noise of people waking up and running round.[3]

In the morning, the pain had gone, but Churchill's temperature was 101°. Lord Moran at once telegraphed to Cairo for two nurses and a pathologist. On the afternoon of December 13, Colonel Pulvertaft, the pathologist, arrived, and did a blood count: it was normal. 'He seemed timid about blood sampling,' Pulvertaft later recalled, 'but gratified that they were painless.'[4] Later in the day a portable X-ray machine was brought from Tunis. It showed a shadow on the lung. Churchill had pneumonia. He was at once put on the new antibiotic sulphonamide, made by May and Baker, and already known as M & B.

Churchill remained in bed. 'My master is unwell,' John Martin wrote home, 'and future movements remain uncertain.'[5] Work had begun again, however, and soon proceeded, as Patrick Kinna later recalled, 'at an alarming pace'. The doctors present 'protested about the volume of work being done by the PM—but to no avail'.[6] 'Am stranded amid these ancient ruins with a temperature,' Churchill

---

[1] Prime Minister's Engagement Cards, 11 December 1943: Thompson papers.
[2] Moran notes for 11 December 1943: Moran, *op. cit.*, page 148.
[3] Brooke diary, 12 December 1943: Bryant, *op. cit.*, volume 1, page 116.
[4] Professor Pulvertaft, recollections: letter to the author, 26 February 1985.
[5] John Martin, letter of 13 December 1943: Martin papers.
[6] Patrick Kinna recollections: letter to the author, 18 January 1985.

telegraphed to Eden on December 13, 'and must wait till I am normal.' He also telegraphed to Macmillan, asking him to come to see him 'to report on latest from Algiers front'.

During December 13 Churchill saw a telegram sent from the British Ambassador in Angora, Sir Hughe Knatchbull-Hugesson, to the Foreign Office, reporting Turkish hesitations about the proposed British presence at Turkish airfields from February 15, as agreed in Cairo. The Turks, it appeared, were afraid of German retaliation. Referring to this in his telegram to Eden, Churchill wrote:

Am sure you should tell Knatchbull to put the screw on hard at Angora. They must be left under no illusions that failure to comply when request is made on February 15 is the virtual end of the alliance and that making impossible demands is only another way of saying no. Meanwhile, insist on the instalment of expert personnel going through punctually.

You should ask the staffs to report upon the possibilities of the Germans being able to gather enough forces for a further separate invasion of Turkey. I believe this to be absolute rubbish. Ambassador will no doubt use his judgment as to times and circumstances of imparting this information.

Churchill ended on a personal note, 'Good luck to speech', as Eden prepared to give the House of Commons an account of the Cairo and Teheran conferences.[1]

On the evening of December 13, Harold Macmillan and Desmond Morton arrived in Tunis from Algiers, summoned by the ailing Prime Minister. On reaching the Maison Blanche they found Sarah Churchill, Lord Moran, John Martin, Francis Brown and Tommy Thompson. 'They seemed very fussed about the PM's condition,' Macmillan noted in his diary, and he added: 'He insisted on seeing me, but seemed weak and drowsy. I escaped as soon as I could, as I felt sure he was seeing too many people.'[2]

On December 14 Macmillan noted in his diary: 'PM is definitely worse, and has got pneumonia, and they fear pleurisy.' General Maitland Wilson had arrived from Cairo; Churchill asked him and Macmillan to discuss the organization of the Mediterranean command, which Wilson was to head, and to write him a report. 'In spite of his temperature (101°),' Macmillan noted, 'he dealt with this in the evening and wrote a long telegram to the Cabinet about it.'[3] In the telegram, sent to Attlee that evening, Churchill set out the argument of Brooke and Eisenhower that if Alexander succeeded Eisenhower as Supreme Commander in the Mediterranean, it would be impossible for him, at the same time, 'to fight the battles which will take place in

---

[1] 'Frozen' No. 468, 13 December 1943: Churchill papers, 20/130.
[2] Macmillan diary, 13 December 1943: *War Diaries, op. cit.*, page 326–7.
[3] Macmillan diary, 14 December 1943: *War Diaries, op. cit.*, page 327.

Italy after the conquest of Rome'. Alexander himself 'saw this', Churchill added. He therefore proposed that General Maitland Wilson succeed Eisenhower. Wilson was sixty-four. Despite his age, 'I am satisfied,' Churchill told Attlee, 'that for the great co-ordinating task which will be entrusted to him, he has all the qualifications and the necessary vigour.' This was also Brooke's view. As to the cross-Channel invasion, Churchill proposed Tedder as Eisenhower's Deputy Supreme Commander, 'on account of the great part the air will play in this operation', with either Alexander or Montgomery to command the Expeditionary Army. Eisenhower, he noted, 'would prefer to have Alexander', but he, Churchill, had not yet made up his mind.[1]

Meeting on the following afternoon, the War Cabinet were divided between Montgomery and Alexander, but a majority favoured Montgomery 'both on merits and from the point of view of its reception by public opinion'. Those who supported Alexander stressed not only his achievements, 'but also the capacity he has shown to work smoothly with the Americans'.[2] General Eisenhower would also have preferred Alexander, Churchill told Roosevelt a week later, 'but the War Cabinet', he explained, 'consider that the public confidence will be better sustained by the inclusion of the well known and famous name of Montgomery, and I agree with them as the operations will be to many people heart-shaking'.[3]

During December 14, Churchill's illness had continued to cause alarm. 'Moran seems very worried,' Macmillan noted. 'He is telegraphing all over the place for specialists.'[4] 'My fever still continues,' Churchill telegraphed to Eden, 'and the weather is foul.'[5] That night, Churchill's heart began to show signs of strain. Lord Moran took alarm, telling Macmillan on the following day 'that he thought the PM was going to die last night'.[6] 'If I die,' Churchill told his daughter Sarah, 'don't worry—the war is won.'[7]

Wednesday December 15 saw Churchill's condition deteriorate. 'PM is worse,' Macmillan noted in his diary. 'His pulse is very irregu-

[1] 'Frozen' No. 479, 'Personal and Secret', 14 December 1943: Churchill papers, 20/130.
[2] War Cabinet No. 170 of 1943, 15 December 1943, Confidential Annex: Cabinet papers, 65/40.
[3] Prime Minister's Personal Telegram, T.2045/3, Prime Minister to President, No. 514, Frozen No. 770, 21 December 1943: Churchill papers, 20/125.
[4] Macmillan diary, 14 December 1943: War Diaries, op. cit., page 327.
[5] 'Frozen' No. 480, 14 December 1943: Churchill papers, 20/130.
[6] Macmillan diary, 15 December 1943: War Diaries, op. cit., page 327.
[7] Lady Audley (Sarah Churchill), recollections: in conversation with the author, 25 May 1981.

lar.' Brigadier Bedford, a heart specialist, arrived that morning from Cairo. 'He seems sensible,' Macmillan noted, 'and gives us comfort. He is giving digitalis to try to calm the heart.' [1] Daily bulletins on Churchill's condition were now being sent to his wife in London.

On the afternoon of December 15 Randolph Churchill arrived. 'His presence will do no good,' noted Macmillan, 'as he will talk to his father about French politics!' Randolph was followed by another visitor, Lieutenant-Colonel Buttle, 'the great M & B specialist', commented Macmillan. Colonel Buttle had been flown from Italy. 'He is an expert on how to give the stuff,' Macmillan added. 'He seems clever, determined, rather gauche and rude—just the chap we need. I had a long talk with him and begged him to be firm and *forbid* telegrams or visitors.' [2]

There were several telegrams Colonel Buttle could not forbid. One to Roosevelt began: 'Am stranded amid the ruins of Carthage, where you stayed, with fever which has ripened into pneumonia. All your people are doing everything possible but I do not pretend I am enjoying myself.' [3] Churchill also minuted to Air Chief Marshal Tedder and General Wilson about 15 extra fighter squadrons to be sent to Turkey, 'on the assumption Rome is taken in the middle of January'. 'Let me have a list,' he added, 'of the fighter squadrons in the Mediterranean.' [4] In a telegram to Eden, Churchill commented on the Foreign Office's distress at Turkey's continuing reluctance to see British aircraft operate from Turkish bases after February 15, the date agreed in Cairo. 'On no account break with Turkey at this stage,' Churchill counselled. 'Continue to nag and press for importations of material and specialists up to February 15th. I doubt if they can refuse to allow this. I am trying to get some more air squadrons out of this opulent Mediterranean Command.' Churchill added: 'Pray act in the Turkish business without further reference to me.'

The second part of Churchill's telegram to Eden concerned Eden's speech. Illness had not curbed Churchill's sense of history:

I am glad the speech went well, but surely when you say that *only* a geographical accident preserved us from the fate of France you are forgetting the RAF, the Royal Navy and the spirit of the British people. The sea spaces between Denmark and Oslo are greater than those between Calais and Dover

---

[1] Before the war, Bedford had been Consultant for Heart Diseases at the Middlesex Hospital in London.

[2] Macmillan diary, 15 December 1943: *War Diaries, op. cit.*, page 327.

[3] Prime Minister's Personal Telegram, T2032/3, Prime Minister to President, No. 511, 'Personal and Most Secret', 15 December 1943: Churchill papers, 20/125.

[4] Prime Minister's Personal Minute, M (S) 12/3, 'Most Secret', 'Most Immediate', 15 December 1943: Churchill papers, 20/104.

but they were quite easily traversed by the Germans on account of the Norwegians having no sea power and air power. Neither do I agree that even if we had remained attached to the Continent we should have shown ourselves so rotten as the French.[1]

At six o'clock that evening a nurse summoned Lord Moran to Churchill's bedside. 'I don't feel well,' Churchill told him. 'My heart is doing something funny—it feels to be bumping all over the place.' The Prime Minister, Moran noted, was 'very breathless and anxious looking. I felt his pulse: it was racing and very irregular. The bases of his lungs were congested and the edge of his liver could be felt below the ribs.'

Moran gave Churchill more digitalis. 'As I sat by his bedside listening to his quick breathing,' he wrote, 'I knew that we were at last right up against things.'[2] Churchill had suffered a heart attack, 'what is called "fibrillation"', Macmillan noted. 'It was not very severe,' he added, 'but has alarmed them all.'[3]

For four hours Moran sat by Churchill's bedside, waiting for the Prime Minister's heart to resume its normal rhythm. 'A man feels pretty rotten, I imagine,' Moran noted, 'when he fibrillates during pneumonia, but the PM was very good about it.' At half past ten the palpitations ceased, with Churchill at last 'comfortable and drowsy'.[4] On the morning of December 16 Macmillan noted: 'PM much better today. His pulse is steadier, and the lung is clearing a little. The experts seem to think he is through the crisis.' That afternoon, Macmillan and Morton returned to Algiers. 'I saw PM before going,' Macmillan noted. 'He was cheerful, though rather weak.'[5] 'PM distinctly better,' noted John Martin, as yet another specialist, Professor John Scadding, arrived from Cairo.[6] Scadding was Physician for chest diseases at the Brompton Hospital, London. 'We have quite an assembly of medical talent,' Martin wrote to his wife, 'and everything possible is being done for him.'[7]

Colonel Pulvertaft, who had been with Churchill now for three days, found him 'co-operative, and interested in haematology. Wanted one to remain with him to do daily blood counts.'[8]

---

[1] 'Frozen' No. 485, 'Most Secret', 15 December 1943: Churchill papers, 20/130.
[2] Moran, notes for 15 December 1943 (mis-dated 14 December 1943): Moran, op. cit., pages 150–1.
[3] Macmillan diary, 15 December 1943: War Diaries, op. cit., page 327.
[4] Moran notes, 15 December 1943 (mis-dated 14 December 1943): Moran, op. cit., pages 150–1.
[5] Macmillan diary, 16 December 1943: War Diaries, op. cit., pages 327–8.
[6] John Martin diary, 16 December 1943: Martin papers.
[7] John Martin, letter of 16 December 1943: Martin papers.
[8] Professor Pulvertaft, recollections: letter to the author, 26 February 1985.

Churchill was much concerned, also, about Brendan Bracken, who had been taken ill in London on December 13 with an acute abcess. 'What is the latest news of Brendan?' he telegraphed to Clementine Churchill on December 16. 'Give him my best wishes.'[1] That same afternoon, Bracken telegraphed to Churchill from his own sick bed:

I am greatly grieved by the news of your illness. But I am comforted by long experience of your power to overcome any impediment to your capacity to strengthen England. Obey the doctors, paint lots of pictures and take the rest you so greatly deserve. Everything is going well here. The House is placid and the Treasury is rolling up money through forfeited election deposits. Woolton has made a splendid start and Anthony has had two field days in the House.[2]

The theme 'obey the doctors' was repeated by others, including Roosevelt, who telegraphed from the Potomac: 'The Bible says you must do just what Moran orders, but at this moment I cannot put my finger on the verse and the chapter.'[3] 'I hope for the future,' General Marshall telegraphed from Honolulu, 'Lord Moran's word will be law....'[4]

Churchill decided to read a novel, or rather to have a novel read to him. His choice of author was Jane Austen, the novel, *Pride and Prejudice*, and the reader, his daughter Sarah.

'It is cruel that the PM's triumphant journey should end in this way,' Sir Alan Lascelles wrote to Clementine Churchill from Buckingham Palace, but he added that the King and Queen 'hope that good may come out of evil, and that, in the long run, this spell of comparative rest may be a blessing in disguise to him'. It was a 'great comfort', Lascelles ended, 'to know that there are such competent doctors, and nurses, on the spot to look after him'.[5]

Clementine Churchill asked Leslie Rowan to reply to this letter for her, as she was in the midst of preparations for her departure to Lyncham airport, 'a slow disagreeable drive through swirling fog', as Mary Churchill, who accompanied her mother to Lyneham, later recalled.[6] From the control tower, Mary watched her mother's take-off. Clementine Churchill was accompanied by her secretary, Grace Hamblin, and Churchill's former Junior Private Secretary, Jock Colville, who, after more than two years in the Royal Air Force, had returned to Churchill's Private Secretariat.

[1] 'Frozen' No. 496, 16 December 1943: Churchill papers, 20/139.
[2] 'Grand' No. 622, 'Personal and Most Secret', 16 December 1943: Churchill papers, 20/139.
[3] President to Prime Minister, No. 420, 'Personal and Secret', 17 December 1943: Churchill papers, 20/125.
[4] 'Grand' No. 710, R-7123, 20 December 1943: Churchill papers, 20/125.
[5] Letter of 16 December 1943: Spencer-Churchill papers.
[6] Mary Soames, *Clementine Churchill, op. cit.*, page 342.

Clementine Churchill, Jock Colville and Grace Hamblin arrived at Carthage on the afternoon of December 17. 'He sent for me,' Colville noted in his diary, 'and I found, instead of a recumbent invalid, a cheerful figure with a large cigar and a whisky and soda in his hand.' [1] 'The joy of seeing him,' Clementine Churchill wrote to Mary, 'was overcast by the change I saw in him. But when later in the evening I mentioned this to Sarah and Lord Moran, they both said that if I had seen him 48 hours earlier I would indeed have been shocked, and that they thought he was now looking remarkably better.'

Churchill and his wife dined alone. It was nearly six weeks since they had last seen each other. After dinner they were joined by Sarah and Randolph. 'At eleven o'clock,' Clementine Churchill reported to Mary, 'Lord Moran came in to say "Goodnight" and then I saw that he wanted us all to go so we did. Of course we had really stayed rather too long without knowing it, and I rather wish that Lord Moran or the Nurse had come in before and told us as it appears that they were secretly fussing. But Papa showed no signs of fatigue, and once or twice when I got up to go to bed, he would not let me go.'

Clementine Churchill did finally get to bed, but at one o'clock in the morning, as she told Mary, 'I saw a light under his door, and went into the passage and saw the night nurse who said: "He is awake and feeling very cheerful and having beef tea—come in and see him." So I did, and sat with him for a quarter of an hour, after which he went to sleep and I returned to my bed.'

At 3.15 in the morning, while Clementine Churchill slept, Churchill had another attack of auricular fibrillation, 'a slight one', Clementine Churchill explained to her daughter later that day. 'The doctors are disappointed but not surprised,' she wrote, and added: 'Papa is very upset about it as he is beginning to see that he cannot get well in a few days and that he will have to lead what to him is a dreary monotonous life with no emotions or excitements. Yesterday morning, before my arrival, because he felt well again, he was as happy as a lark, and began to smoke again, which of course is wrong; but Lord Moran agrees that it is not as bad for him as it would be for most patients. The smoking has of course been quite cut out to-day.'

Churchill quickly recovered from his early morning setback. Only one person at a time was allowed to see him, but, as Clementine Churchill wrote, 'there has been a constant stream of people all day', so much so that 'I have not done more than poke my nose round the corner of the door'.[2] During the day Churchill dictated a telegram to Roosevelt about the new commands. The telegram began with thanks

---

[1] Colville diary, 17 December 1943: Colville papers.
[2] Clementine Churchill, letter of 18 December 1943: Spencer-Churchill papers.

for Roosevelt's own message. 'I have hearkened unto the voice of Moran,' he wrote, 'and made good progress, but I am fixed here for another week.'

During December 18 Churchill received news from Sir Archibald Sinclair of the most recent air attack on Berlin, carried out by 482 Lancasters, escorted by 15 Mosquitoes. Twenty-five of the Lancasters were lost. Drifting low cloud at their base on return had resulted in 34 crashes, but from these, '16 entire crews are safe'.[1] 'I hope the fog clearing apparatus saved some lives,' Churchill telegraphed to Sinclair that afternoon, and he added: 'Compliment officers and crews from me on all this series of great attacks.'[2]

During December 18 Churchill had a long conversation with Brooke, who had flown to Tunis from Italy: both men were agreed, Churchill told Roosevelt, that Eisenhower should command the cross-Channel invasion, with Maitland Wilson as his successor in the Mediterranean. 'I beg most earnestly,' Churchill added, 'that I may soon have your reply upon these proposals, or at least upon the key ones, as the Commander of "Overlord" is urgently required. . . .'[3]

During his discussion with Brooke, Churchill went in some detail into the question of landing craft. It appeared that many of the landing craft available in the Mediterranean were being used 'in purely supply work', as Churchill minuted to the Chiefs of Staff on the following day, 'to the prevention of their amphibious duties'. The 'stagnation' of the Italian campaign, he wrote, 'is becoming scandalous'. Brooke's visit to Italy 'has confirmed my worst forebodings'. Churchill added:

The total neglect to provide amphibious action on the Adriatic side and the failure to strike any similar blow on the west have been disastrous.

None of the landing-craft in the Mediterranean have been put to the slightest use for three months, neither coming home in preparation for 'Overlord', nor for 'Accolade', nor in the Italian battle. There are few instances, even in this war, of such valuable forces being so completely wasted.

'The impending change of command,' Churchill ended, 'should correspond with a vigorous amendment in these respects.'[4]

[1] 'Grand' No. 641, 'Most secret', 17 December 1943: Premier papers, 3/14/2, folio 44.
[2] 'Frozen' No. 722, 'Most Secret', 18 December 1943: Premier papers, 9/14/2, folio 49. There had been previous attacks that month on Berlin (December 2), Leipzig (December 3), Emden (December 11) and Kiel (December 13).
[3] Prime Minister's Personal Telegram, T.2038/3, 'Frozen' No. 726, 18 December 1943: Churchill papers, 20/125. Roosevelt gave his approval two days later. Eisenhower would be Supreme Commander of 'Overlord', with Tedder as his Deputy Supreme Commander. Maitland Wilson would be Supreme Commander, Mediterranean, and General Eaker would command the Allied Air Force, Mediterranean.
[4] 'Frozen' No. 736, 19 December 1943: Churchill papers, 20/130. 'Accolade' was the projected assault on the Aegean Islands, principally Rhodes.

That evening Brooke went to say goodbye to Churchill. 'Clementine was sitting on the bed with him,' he noted in his diary, 'and Randolph was also there.' Churchill, added Brooke, 'was in very good form, but objecting to having to spend a week in bed before going on to Marrakesh for his fortnight's recuperation'.[1]

[1] Brooke diary, 18 December 1943: Bryant, *op. cit.*, volume 2, page 125.

36

Plans for Anzio

'PAPA much better today,' Clementine Churchill reported to her daughter Mary on 19 December 1943. 'Has consented not to smoke, and to drink only weak whisky and soda.'[1] While he was still in bed in Carthage, Churchill scrutinized the reports of several projects, among them operation 'Penitent', a series of naval and commando raids against the Dalmatian coast of Yugoslavia. 'The results are certainly satisfactory,' he minuted to Tedder on December 19. 'I am very glad to know from you and the Admiral that everything possible will be done to keep this coast open.'[2] Reading in his intercepts that the Turkish Foreign Minister 'is under the impression that we alone are putting on the pressure' about the use of Turkish air bases, Churchill telegraphed to Eden: 'It seems the United States should make a parallel démarche. . . .'[3]

'I am delighted that you are really so much better,' Roosevelt telegraphed to Churchill on December 20, 'and I wish I could be with you at the Flower Villa at Marrakesh. I hope you have sent for your brushes.' Roosevelt also signalled his approval of Clementine Churchill's presence. 'I feel relieved,' he wrote, 'that she is with you as your superior officer.'[4] 'Papa very refractory and naughty this morning,' Clementine Churchill wrote to Mary that same day, 'and wants to leave this place at once. All doing our best to persuade him that complete recovery depends on rest and compliance with regulations. Progress continued.'[5] That day Major-General Evelegh,

---

[1] Clementine Churchill, letter of 19 December 1943: Mary Soames, *Clementine Churchill*, *op. cit.*, page 344.

[2] Prime Minister's Personal Minute, M (S), 13/3, 'Most Secret', 'Immediate', 19 December 1943: Churchill papers, 20/104.

[3] 'Frozen' No. 740, 19 December 1943: Churchill papers, 20/130.

[4] President to Prime Minister, No. 421, 'Personal and Most Secret', 20 December 1943: Churchill papers, 20/125.

[5] 'Health Bulletin for Monday December the 20th', 20 December 1943: Mary Soames, *Clementine Churchill*, *op. cit.*, page 345.

commanding the 6th Armoured Division, arrived to take over command of the defence of the Maison Blanche. 'There is apparently a flap in high circles,' noted an officer in the Coldstream Guards, 'because the Germans are thought to know that Churchill is here.'[1]

During December 20, Churchill read a report from one of the British officers with the Yugoslav partisans. This report reinforced his view that the time had come for Britain to press King Peter 'towards procuring the dismissal' of General Mihailovic. 'I still think this a most necessary step,' he informed Eden, 'and I see one of our officers with Mihailovic considers that it would be accepted by his commanders or some of them.' Among those who had become involved in Yugoslav policy was Churchill's son Randolph, who was preparing to be parachuted into Yugoslavia to join the partisans under Tito's command. In a note for his father, written shortly before he set off, Randolph urged the 'immediate repudiation' of Mihailovic by the British Government, 'and if possible' by King Peter. He also urged the 'immediate return' of Fitzroy Maclean from Italy to Tito's headquarters, to try to obtain 'the maximum military advantage' from the situation, as well as to explore what advantage might be gained for King Peter by the 'new situation' that would be 'created upon the dismissal of Mihailovic'.

Churchill approved his son's approach, which 'seems to me sound', he told Eden, 'and to represent to a large extent your point of view and mine'. A friendly message from Tito to Churchill, wishing him a speedy recovery, seemed, Churchill told Eden, an opportunity to send Tito a welcoming reply.[2]

In his telegram to Eden of December 20 Churchill also set out his thoughts on the post-war frontiers of Poland, and on what he saw as the need to put to the London Poles, without delay, the frontier line discussed at Teheran. Churchill was certain that it was in Poland's best interests to accept these frontiers, and to accept them at once. As he told Eden:

I think you should now open the Polish frontier question with the Poles, stating it is as my personal wish and that I would have done it myself but for my temporary incapacitation. You should show them the formula and the rough line on the map on the eastern side, and the line of the Oder including the Oppeln district on the west. This gives them a magnificent piece of country three or four hundred miles across each way and with over 150 miles of seaboard, even on the basis that they do not begin till west of Königsberg.

[1] Elston Grey-Turner, diary entry for 20 December 1943: 'Pages from a diary', *British Medical Journal*, volume 281, 20 November–7 December 1980, page 1693.

[2] 'Frozen' No. 976, 29 December 1943: Churchill papers, 20/130. Randolph Churchill's note was dated 25 December 1943.

The Poles should understand of course that these are only very broad, tentative suggestions, but that they would be most unwise to let them fall to the ground. Even if they do not get Lemberg I should still advise their acceptance and that they put themselves in the hands of their British and American friends to try to turn this plan into reality. You should put it to them that by taking over and holding firmly the present German territories up to the Oder they will be rendering a service to Europe as a whole as well as making for themselves a secure, solid and integral homeland which, on the basis of a friendly policy towards Russia and close association with Czechoslovakia, would give a chance for the rebirth of the Polish nation brighter than any yet seen.

Churchill's telegram to Eden continued with a warning to the Poles, and recognition of the effect which the continuing westward advance of the Red Army would have on all frontier discussions:

Once we know that they will accept and endorse these proposals we will address ourselves to the Russians and endeavour to make matters firm and precise. On the other hand if they cast it all aside I do not see how His Majesty's Government can press for anything more for them. The Russian armies may in a few months be crossing the frontiers of pre-war Poland, and it seems of the utmost consequence to have friendly recognition by Russia of the Polish Government and a broad understanding of the post war frontiers settlement agreed before then.

'I shall be most interested to hear,' Churchill ended, 'what their reaction is.'[1]

The Polish reaction was hostile, Eden reported to Churchill. The view of the Polish Prime Minister, Stanislaw Mikolajczyk, was that as a 'reward for Polish suffering', Poland should emerge from the war 'her eastern provinces intact and her western provinces increased'. Nonetheless, Eden commented, 'We are pegging away and I do not despair.'[2]

As Churchill worked and recuperated in Eisenhower's seaside villa, a 'little gun boat', as Clementine Churchill wrote to Mary, 'patrols up and down in front of the house in case a German submarine should pop up its nose and shoot up the Villa'. Of course, she added, 'if the enemy knew we were here they could wipe out the place with dive bombers from the airfields near Rome. It is less than two hours' flight from here to the toe of Italy . . .'[3] That evening Clementine Churchill returned to the villa after a sightseeing tour of the Tunis battlefields

[1] 'Frozen' No. 762, 20 December 1943: Churchill papers, 20/130.
[2] Telegram of 22 December 1943: Eden memoirs, *op. cit.*, page 434.
[3] Clementine Churchill, letter of 20 December 1943: Mary Soames, *Clementine Churchill, op. cit.*, page 345.

and 'found Papa sitting up in bed looking very pink and mischievous and announcing he had had a hot bath with Dr Bedford's consent'. Clementine added: 'Your father has taken a great deal of trouble to seduce Dr Bedford, and Lord Moran is quite jealous.' After the bath Churchill played 'innumerable games of bezique with Randolph. In spite of all this he was not really exhausted though when bed-time came he was looking a little pale and wan.' [1]

On the morning of December 21 Churchill was feeling well enough to send for Patrick Kinna and continue with dictation. Details of the arrest of three Vichy French leaders by General de Gaulle's French National Committee in Algiers had been given to him by Randolph: 'exaggerated accounts', Jock Colville called them, and he added: 'Winston almost had apoplexy and Lord Moran was seriously perturbed.' [2]

In a telegram to Eden, Churchill pointed out that it was to one of the three Frenchmen, Boisson, 'we owe the delivery of Dakar', and that the second, Peyrouton, had been invited to Algiers by Giraud, his journey being approved by the State Department. 'I certainly did say to both of them,' Churchill noted, ' "March against the Hun and count on me".' Were de Gaulle to proceed 'to extremities against them, it will be necessary for me to make this public', Churchill added. As for the third Frenchman under arrest, Flandin, no 'specific obligation' existed, Churchill wrote, but:

... having acquainted myself in detail with his actions over the last ten years, I am of the opinion that for the French Committee to proceed against him would be proof that they are unfit to be considered in any way the trustees of France, but rather that they are small, ambitious intriguers endeavouring to improve their position by maltreating unpopular figures. It does not lie with the present House of Commons to reproach Flandin with his telegram to Hitler after Munich because, as you know, the vast majority of our Party highly approved that act and Mr Chamberlain's action far exceeded that of Flandin. Please also acquaint yourself with the details of Flandin's ministerial record under Vichy and his successful burking of Laval's attempts to bring about a French alliance with Germany and an expedition from Dakar to the Chad area. [3]

In a telegram to Roosevelt, Churchill raised the possibility of making the three Frenchmen an offer of asylum. 'Pray let me know if there is any way in which we could help,' he asked Roosevelt, pointing out that in February 1943, at Algiers, he had, 'in supporting your policy

---

[1] Clementine Churchill, letter of 21 December 1943: Mary Soames, *Clementine Churchill, op. cit.*, page 345.
[2] Colville diary, 21 December 1943: Colville papers.
[3] 'Frozen' No. 779, 21 December 1943: Churchill papers, 20/130.

and that of General Eisenhower', encouraged these three men 'to hold firm in their posts and aid us in our struggle for Tunis, saying also in that case "Count on me"'. The American obligation, Churchill pointed out, was 'even stronger'.[1]

Roosevelt shared Churchill's anger. 'It seems to me,' he telegraphed in reply to Churchill's message, 'that this is the proper time in which to abandon the Jeanne D'Arc complex and return to realism. I too am shocked by high handed arrests at this time.' Roosevelt had therefore instructed Eisenhower to inform the French Committee 'to take no action against Boisson, Peyrouton, or Flandin.[2] Churchill approved of Roosevelt's decision, noting that de Gaulle's action raised 'the whole question of our relations with France', and he went on to tell the President:

France can only be liberated by British and American force and bloodshed. To admit that a handful of émigrés are to have the power behind this all-powerful shield to carry civil war into France is to lose the future of that unfortunate country and prevent the earliest expression of the will of the people as a whole. In fact, we would be lending ourselves to a process of adding to the burdens and sacrifices of our troops and of infringing our fundamental principle 'All Governments derive their just powers from the consent of the governed'.[3]

In accepting the two main changes in command which Churchill had sent him, the Supreme Command to Eisenhower for 'Overlord', and to Wilson for the Mediterranean, Roosevelt made no reference to the proposal that Montgomery should command the cross-Channel expeditionary force under Eisenhower, or Alexander the armies in Italy, under Wilson. 'Both these appointments,' Churchill telegraphed to Roosevelt on December 21, 'are an essential part of any announcement that could be made on January one.'[4] Realising, however, that Roosevelt would not make up his mind until General Marshall had returned from Honolulu to Washington, Churchill telegraphed that same day to Marshall: 'Do hasten back to the Capitol as much necessary structure hangs in mid-air pending your arrival. Our Chiefs

[1] Prime Minister's Personal Telegram, T.2043/3, 'Frozen' No. 780, 21 December 1943: Churchill papers, 20/125.

[2] President to Prime Minister, No. 423, 'Frozen' No. 816, 23 December 1943: Churchill papers, 20/125.

[3] Prime Minister's Personal Telegram, T.2052/3, 'Frozen' No. 814, 23 December 1943: Churchill papers, 20/125.

[4] Prime Minister's Personal Telegram, T.2045/3, Prime Minister to President No. 514, 'Frozen' No. 770, 21 December 1943: Churchill papers, 20/125..

of Staff are fretting for clear cut decision. The war in Italy languishes and the Turk is stalling.'[1]

On the evening of December 21 Churchill had three unusual visitors: Air Vice Marshal Boyd, General Neame and General O'Connor, each of whom had been taken prisoner of war by the Germans, and had escaped. After three and a half months in hiding, the three officers had managed to cross through the German lines in Italy. Their arrival in Tunis caused 'great excitement', Clementine Churchill reported to Mary. 'First of all,' she explained, 'Papa wanted to get up and go into the dining room in his dressing gown to have dinner with them. Thank Goodness he gave way about that and consented to have his dinner in bed. Then he said he would get up after dinner and go and join the men in the dining room, and he was putting a toe to the floor when he sank back on to his pillow and said "Let them come in here".'[2]

Churchill's continuing tiredness did not alarm him. 'I am getting stronger every day,' he telegraphed to Harry Hopkins on December 22, 'and hope to leave for Flower Villa after Christmas.'[3] Colville noted in his diary that day that Randolph was causing 'considerable strife in the family and entourage. But the PM likes playing bezique with him.'[4] 'Very good progress,' Clementine Churchill reported on December 23, 'I think the only anxiety is impatience to be well too soon.'[5]

A sequence of priorities had emerged, in which 'Overlord' could not take place until the early summer. Rome, if the Americans were to agree, could be much sooner; on this both Churchill and his Chiefs of Staff were united. On December 22 the Chiefs of Staff informed Churchill by telegram that they were 'in full agreement' with him that the 'present stagnation' in Italy 'cannot be allowed to continue'. The solution, they added, 'as you say, clearly lies in making use of our amphibious power to strike round on the enemy's flank and open up the way for a rapid advance on Rome'.

The Chiefs of Staff pointed out that at present, although Eisenhower planned a landing 'behind the enemy just south of Rome', he would have 'little more than one division for this task'. This would mean waiting until the Fifth Army was 'within supporting distance' of the intended landing place. If more landing craft could be made available, however, a stronger force could then be landed 'without waiting for

---

[1] Prime Minister's Personal Telegram, T.2047/3, 'Frozen' No. 785, 21 December 1943: Churchill papers, 20/125.

[2] Clementine Churchill, letter of 23 December 1943: Spencer-Churchill papers.

[3] Prime Minister's Personal Telegram, T.2046/3, 'Frozen' No. 789, 22 December 1943: Churchill papers, 20/125.

[4] Colville diary, 22 December 1943: Colville papers.

[5] 'Health Bulletin', 23 December 1943: Mary Soames, *Clementine Churchill*, op. cit., page 346.

the main army to arrive within supporting distance'. Such a landing, the Chiefs of Staff believed, 'would have a more far-reaching effect on the whole progress of the campaign, and would be much more likely to open the way for a rapid advance'.[1]

The landing favoured by both Churchill and the British Chiefs of Staff was of two divisions. This would require, in all, eighty-eight landing craft. There were in the Mediterranean that December a total of a hundred and four such craft, but by the middle of January, sixty-eight were due to be sent away, in preparation for 'Overlord', leaving only thirty-six, with a possible fifteen more arriving from the Indian Ocean. The Chiefs of Staff now proposed keeping all the existing landing craft in the Mediterranean for an extra three weeks, to be used 'for the launching of a two-divisional amphibious assault', designed to capture Rome and then to advance to the Pisa-Rimini line.[2]

'In no case,' Churchill telegraphed to the Chiefs of Staff on December 23, after he had seen both Eisenhower and Alexander, 'can we sacrifice Rome for the Riviera. We must have both.'[3] But it was also clear to Churchill that Eisenhower, with his new 'Overlord' perspective, regarded the Riviera landings in the South of France as of greater importance than Anzio. As to the operation against Rhodes, 'I am resigning myself,' Churchill telegraphed to Maitland Wilson on December 23, 'to "Hercules" being pinched out by greater events.'[4] Giving up the operation against Rhodes, however, Churchill telegraphed to Eden, should 'in no way' slacken the effort 'to bring Turkey in, as once we have the Turkish airfields many things will be possible even without "Hercules"'.[5]

On the evening of December 24 Churchill left his sick bed for the first time, to hold a conference in the dining room with Maitland Wilson, Alexander, Tedder and others on the problem of the Anzio landings, 'and, in particular', Colville noted, 'the question of providing landing craft'. Among those at the Conference was Captain Power, the Deputy Chief of Staff, Plans, to Admiral Sir John Cunningham. Power had already argued, in a paper of which Cunningham approved, that the landing craft could be retained in the Mediterranean for an extra three weeks or a month, without impeding their 'Overlord' dates or training. Their crews, 'being good seamen', Power wrote, 'should

[1] 'Grand' No. 736, 22 December 1943: Cabinet papers, 120/127.
[2] Chiefs of Staff, draft telegram to the Joint Staff Mission, 24 December 1943, 'Grand' No. 806, 24 December 1943: Cabinet papers, 120/127.
[3] 'Frozen' No. 806, 23 December 1943: Churchill papers, 20/130.
[4] Prime Minister's Personal Telegram, T.2053/3, 'Frozen' No. 827, 23 December 1943: Churchill papers, 20/125.
[5] 'Frozen' No. 829, 23 December 1943: Churchill papers, 20/130.

require very brief instruction and training before they master the new problem'.[1]

The conference ended at midnight. Half an hour later Churchill telegraphed to the Chiefs of Staff and to the First Sea Lord that all were agreed that the Anzio landing 'must be carried out on a sufficient scale to ensure success, namely, at least a two-divisional assault'. The target date would be 'about January 20'. The assumption was 'that Rhodes is not on'. To achieve success at Anzio, all fifty-six British landing craft due to leave the Mediterranean in January and on February 1 for 'Overlord' should be delayed 'for not more than one month'.[2]

Churchill was now feeling well enough to contemplate flying to Marrakech on December 26. But Clementine Churchill urged him to reconsider the date. Her thoughts were with those who would have to travel with him, as she explained in a letter written on Christmas Eve:

My Darling One,

May I plead with you to make the 27th our *first* flying day?—*Not* on the grounds of your health for I believe that is being well taken care of, but on the grounds of kindness of heart.

It is of course quite different with General Alexander. *Everything* must give way to war exigencies.

But this is a question only of personal wishes & Christmas means so much to the great mass of humanity & those who are not fortunate in being together like ourselves value their little celebrations with their comrades while they think of their wives & children at home.[3]

Churchill deferred to his wife's advice. He also prepared for a conference of considerable strategic importance, called for Christmas Day. That morning, five Commanders-in-Chief converged upon Carthage: Eisenhower, Maitland Wilson, Alexander, Tedder and Admiral Sir John Cunningham. The conference was to discuss operation 'Shingle', the Anzio landing now planned for January 20. Churchill was determined that the Anzio landing should go ahead. 'It would be folly,' he told the Conference, 'to allow the campaign in Italy to drag on' and for the Allies to face 'the supreme operations "Overlord" and "Anvil" with our task in Italy half-finished.' Success at Anzio 'should decide the battle of Rome, and possibly achieve the destruction of a substantial part of the enemy's army'.

Eisenhower, speaking next, said that although he had not yet had an opportunity to study the 'Overlord' operation, he 'felt strongly, however, that the right course was to press on in Italy, where the Germans were

---

[1] 'Frozen' No. 887: Cabinet papers, 120/122.
[2] Colville diary, 24 December 1943: Colville papers. Among the others present were Air Vice Marshal Park and General Gale (the Quartermaster General).
[3] Letter dated 'Christmas Eve', 24 December 1943: Spencer-Churchill papers.

still full of fight'. Anything short of a 'bold venture' such as Anzio would 'quicken up' their successful prosecution of the campaign.

The discussion then turned to the availability of landing craft. The 'only course', Churchill said, was to delay 'for about three weeks' the despatch of the fifty-six landing craft about to be sent to the United Kingdom for 'Overlord'. General Alexander said he was 'prepared to take on Operation "Shingle" with confidence' if given two divisions for the assault. General Wilson, who said he was in agreement with the 'general conception' of the operation, 'emphasized the importance of putting in a force of sufficient strength at the outset'.

It was agreed to go ahead with 'Shingle', it being clearly under-stood, as the notes of the Conference stated, 'that nothing should be allowed to interfere with the May date of "Overlord" or "Anvil"'. [1] Thus the Teheran decisions began to take shape.

Churchill's concept of a renewed initiative had prevailed. 'We can-not go to other tasks,' he explained to Attlee when the conference was ended, 'and leave this unfinished job behind us.' The case for 'finishing up Rome job', he added, 'is not the capture of the City, important though that be, but the violation of portion of enemy's army in Italy and securing of a line protecting Naples–Foggia airfields from counter attack'. At the morning's conference, Churchill told Attlee, Eisenhower had expressed himself 'strongly in this sense' while General Bedell Smith was 'confident' that the matter of landing craft 'can be adjusted by drastic arrangement'. Tedder and Wilson 'concur', Churchill ended, 'and General Alexander is fully prepared to carry out operation'. [2]

All that remained was to secure Roosevelt's approval. The landing at Anzio, Churchill explained to the President, would need eighty-eight landing craft: 'Nothing less than this will suffice.' This would delay the departure of some of the landing craft needed for 'Overlord' from mid-January to February 5, as agreed at Teheran. Churchill explained, however, that by 'various expedients' it was believed 'that the lost three weeks can be recovered and the existing prescribed build-up for "Overlord" maintained'. The Anzio landing, he believed, 'should decide the battle of Rome and possibly achieve destruction of a substantial part of enemy's army'.

Churchill then set out his reasons for being so strong an advocate of the Anzio landing. Having kept these fifty-six landing craft in the Mediterranean so long, 'it would seem irrational to remove them for the very week when they can render decisive service', and he added:

---

[1] Record of the Conference of 25 December 1943 (General Hollis to War Cabinet Offices). 'Frozen' No. 897, 25 December 1943: Churchill papers, 4/340.

[2] 'Frozen' No. 892, 25 December 1943: Churchill papers, 20/130. Churchill sent this same telegram to Eden, and also to Ismay for the Chiefs of Staff Committee.

What also could be more dangerous than to let the Italian battle stagnate and fester on for another three months thus certainly gnawing into all preparation for and thus again affecting Overlord. We cannot afford to go forward leaving a vast half finished job behind us. It therefore seemed to those present that every effort should be made to bring off 'Shingle' on a two division basis around January 20th, and orders have been issued to General Alexander to prepare accordingly. If this opportunity is not grasped we must expect the ruin of Mediterranean campaign of 1944. I earnestly hope therefore that you may agree to the three weeks delay in return of the 56 landing craft and that all the authorities should be instructed to make sure that the May 'Overlord' is not prejudiced thereby.[1]

On Christmas Day, the five Commanders-in-Chief and their staffs were Churchill's guests at a festive luncheon; 'a soporific lunch of turkey and plum pudding', John Martin wrote to his wife. 'The PM was up for it and in good form, proposing a whole series of toasts.' It was Churchill's first meal outside his bedroom since he had been taken ill. 'The PM,' Martin added, 'is remarkably well and has begun doing a good deal of work in the last two or three days. The doctors are quite unable to control him and cigars etc have now returned. I was amazed to find him dictating their bulletin.'[2]

Just as the Christmas lunch had begun, two further visitors had reached Carthage, Harold Macmillan and Desmond Morton, both summoned from Algiers to discuss the most recent actions of the French National Committee. 'The old boy presided at a festive gathering,' Macmillan wrote in his diary, '(having just had a two-hour military conference in his bedroom) clothed in a padded silk Chinese dressing-gown decorated with blue and gold dragons—a most extraordinary sight.' Macmillan's account continued:

It was indeed an odd way of spending Christmas. In the best Russian style (and looking in his strange costume rather like a figure in a Russian ballet) the PM proposed a series of toasts with a short speech in each case. (In spite of looking rather grumpily at me, he proposed mine in most eulogistic terms).

After luncheon (which ended nearer to 4 p.m. than 3 p.m.) I managed to escape with Alex for a short walk (and delightful talk).

At about 5.30, just before the PM went to sleep, he sent for me. He was obviously very tired, as he had worked all the time since luncheon, dictating a résumé of the military decisions taken in the morning and on a telegram embodying them to his colleagues and the President.

He only kept me for a few minutes. He was very sleepy, and I left him, thereby earning a good word from poor Mrs Churchill, who does her best to make him spare himself.[3]

[1] Prime Minister's Personal Telegram T.2060/3, Prime Minister to President, No. 521, 'Frozen' No. 893, 25 December 1943: Churchill papers, 20/125.
[2] Letter dated 'Christmas Day', 25 December 1943: Martin papers.
[3] Macmillan diary, 25 December 1943: *War Diaries, op. cit.*, page 338.

That evening there was a cocktail party, 'through the midst of which', Jock Colville noted in his diary, 'the PM walked as if in perfect health . . .'.[1]

That same evening, when the cocktail party was over, Churchill discussed with Macmillan how to handle the French National Committee 'in its present mood'. On the previous day Churchill had set out his view in a telegram to Eden. His theme was to use pressure against the Committee:

My constant purpose is the restoration of the greatness of France, which will not be achieved by the persecution mania of the Committee, nor by their violent self-assertion of French dignity, nor will France be helped by De Gaulle's hatred of Britain and the United States. In order to bring home to the Committee the unwisdom of their present attitude and the harm which it will do their country and themselves, a stern pressure should now be maintained. This is more likely to bring them to reason than smooth diplomatic conversations. As I shall be forced to remain in these parts for the best part of a month, I propose myself to see various members of the Committee and of the resistance groups and possibly De Gaulle himself, but I want a harder atmosphere established.

The French National Committee, Churchill warned, must not be allowed to 'start up civil war in France behind our lines'.[2]

In his discussion on the evening of December 25, Churchill 'was obviously rather embarrassed', Macmillan noted, 'and really almost pathetically so. He actually asked for my views and gave me ten minutes free run to explain the present French situation as I saw it.' When Macmillan had finished, Churchill said to him: 'Well—perhaps you are right. But I do not agree with you. Perhaps I will see de Gaulle. Anyway you have done very well.' Macmillan's account continued:

Then he took my hand in his in a most fatherly way and said, 'Come and see me again before I leave Africa, and we'll talk it over.'

He is really a remarkable man. Although he can be so tiresome and pigheaded, there is no one like him. His devotion to work and duty is quite extraordinary.[3]

It was the Anzio landing which dominated Churchill's work that night, and in a telegram to the Chiefs of Staff Committee, sent on the following morning, he stressed that there was 'not the slightest chance' of landing two divisions at Anzio unless all fifty-six landing craft due

[1] Colville diary, 25 December 1943: Colville papers.
[2] 'Frozen' No. 875, 25 December 1943: Churchill papers 20/130.
[3] Macmillan diary, 25 December 1943: War Diaries, op. cit., pages 338–9.

to leave the Mediterranean in mid-January were held back another
three weeks. 'The success of Anzio,' he wrote, 'depends on the strength
of the initial landing. If this is two full divisions plus paratroops it
could be decisive, as it cuts the communications of the whole of the
enemy forces facing the Fifth Army. The enemy must therefore an-
nihilate the landing force by withdrawals from the Fifth Army front
or immediately retreat.'

On the three week delay in the departure of the landing craft for
'Overlord', Churchill told the Chiefs of Staff, 'depends the success or
ruin of our Italian campaign'.[1]

[1] 'Frozen' No. 901, 26 December 1943: Cabinet papers, 120/122.

37

Convalescence at Marrakesh: 'Full steam ahead'

A S Churchill prepared to fly from Carthage to Marrakesh, he learned that both Eisenhower and Montgomery had expressed themselves 'entirely dissatisfied' with the plans for 'Overlord', so much so, Churchill informed the Chiefs of Staff 'in strictest secrecy' on 26 December 1943, that it was 'very likely', once they had examined the plan in detail, that they 'will propose a delay'.

The Teheran 'contract' stipulated 'during May' for the cross-Channel assault. But if the 'responsible commanders' were to require 'the June moon around 6th June', Churchill wrote, the 'extra week' might have to be conceded. 'I am fighting the case on the Teheran line', Churchill added, but Eisenhower had spoken 'of telegraphing himself to Stalin', to demand 'a reasonable measure of delay'.[1]

Eisenhower's wish to delay 'Overlord' until the first week of June 1944 had a direct bearing on the Anzio landing, giving a week or two extra time for the landing craft needed for Anzio to be ready for their despatch to Britain. The Chiefs of Staff noted that May 5 was the date for the 'present plan' of 'Overlord', owing to moon and tide conditions. These conditions, they wrote, 'do not recur till early June'.[2]

Churchill was against the May 5 date. 'I am fighting this issue entirely on Teheran basis,' he stressed. 'This assumed May 20 rather than May 5, which is an altogether new date. Our contract with Stalin would be fulfilled by any date up to May 31.' It seemed to Churchill, however, 'from what I have heard from Eisenhower', that June 3, 'which is the corresponding moon phase, would be perfectly permissible, especially if it were asked for by the commanders now nominated for the operation'.[3]

*   *   *

[1] 'Frozen' No. 902, 26 December 1943: Churchill papers, 20/130.
[2] 'Grand' No. 581, 27 December 1943: Churchill papers, 4/340.
[3] 'Frozen' No. 945, 28 December 1943: Churchill papers, 20/130.

At midday on December 26 the Principal Medical Officer of the Royal Air Force in North Africa, Air Commodore Kelly, went to see Churchill to discuss the need for oxygen during the flight to Marrakesh, and to show him the oxygen apparatus. 'He was lying propped up in bed, surrounded by documents,' Kelly later recalled. 'He looked at the oxygen apparatus and asked me to explain how it worked. This I did. He then said: "Will you do a trial run on me now." I turned the oxygen on to 3,000 ft. and after a minute or so I asked him could he taste it? He removed the mask from his face and said: "I'll have you know, my boy, that I took oxygen before you were born. Do you think oxygen will be necessary?" I replied: "Prime Minister, no weather report can be entirely relied on for a flight of 5 hours over mountainous country. As a measure of prudence it ought to be available. If it is not available there may be an unpleasant incident." '

Churchill asked Kelly to accompany him on the flight. 'We leave in the morning,' he said, 'if the weather is fine.' [1]

On the morning of December 27 Churchill dressed, for the first time since his illness, and prepared to leave for the airfield, and for Marrakesh. As he was leaving the door of the villa, a telegram was put into his hand, reporting the sinking of the *Scharnhorst*. He immediately stopped and dictated a telegram to Stalin. 'The Arctic convoys to Russia have brought us luck,' the telegram began. 'Yesterday enemy attempted to intercept with battle cruiser *Scharnhorst*. Commander-in-Chief Admiral Fraser with the *Duke of York* (35,000 ton battleship) cut off *Scharnhorst*'s retreat and after an action sank her.' [2] It was an interception, though Churchill could not say so, made possible by the Enigma decrypts. [3]

Stalin replied with congratulations, and the words, 'I shake your hand firmly.' 'I am glad,' he added, 'you are recovering.' [4]

Going from the villa to the car, Churchill found walking difficult. One of those who watched was Captain Elston Grey-Turner, medical officer of the 2nd Battalion, Coldstream Guards, who noted in his diary: 'He was dressed in RAF uniform, of which Mrs Churchill very sweetly fastened the belt for him. He carefully inspected the Guard,

---

[1] Air Vice Marshal Thomas J. Kelly, CBE, MC, MD, 'The Prime Minister's Journey to Marrakesh, December 27th, 1943', typescript, 10 October 1962.

[2] Prime Minister's Personal Telegram, T.2061/3, 'Frozen' No. 926, 27 December 1943: Churchill paper, 20/125.

[3] The Staff Officer (Intelligence) on board the *Duke of York* was Lieutenant Commander Edward Thomas, RNVR, subsequently one of the authors of the multi-volume official history, *British Intelligence in the Second World War: Its Influence on Strategy and Operations* (by F. H. Hinsley, with E. E. Thomas, C. F. G. Ransom and R. C. Knight).

[4] 'Grand' No. 882, 29 December 1943: Churchill papers, 20/125.

and then they drove off to our cheers. Mrs Churchill gave us a beaming smile as she passed.'[1]

On the flight, it had been intended to fly at 4,000 feet, to avoid undue strain on Churchill's heart. After breakfasting on the plane, Churchill read papers for a while, and then lay down on the bed in his cabin. For three hours there were no problems, but then, at about eleven o'clock, as Air Commodore Kelly recalled, 'the weather became bad and the visibility nil'. Kelly's account continued:

We were flying at about 4,000 ft. The Prime Minister got anxious and began sending up frequent messages to the captain of the aircraft as to our height, position, and what weather reports we were getting from the pilot of the Liberator flying ahead. The messages were going up so frequently that at one time there were three or four of us waiting to talk to the captain of the aircraft to get information for the Prime Minister. A message came back that the weather was very bad and bumpy. The Prime Minister said: 'If I were not on this aircraft it would be flying at 19,000 ft. It is ridiculous keeping it low, it will crash into the mountains.' He told Mrs Oliver to go and tell the captain to go higher, but as she was leaving the cabin he said to her: 'It is my wish but do not give an order.'

The aircraft prepared to climb to 10,500 feet. 'I went into the Prime Minister's cabin,' Kelly recalled, 'got the apparatus ready, and began to give him oxygen. He first of all held the mask to his face himself, but later asked me to strap it round his neck. From time to time he pulled it on one side to send some message to the captain of the aircraft. I set the oxygen at about 10,000 ft. We climbed gradually. The Prime Minister's colour became perfectly normal, and he went on taking oxygen. When we were at 10,500 ft. I pushed the regulator up higher.'

'Sit at the end of my bed, Kelly,' Churchill asked, as the aircraft continued to climb, reaching 12,000 feet. By 12.45, after crossing the mountains, it entered a cloudless region. The aircraft then went down to 5,000 feet, whereupon Churchill wanted to discontinue the oxygen, 'but I advised him to continue it', Kelly recalled, 'and remain lying down until 13.00 hours, as I was afraid that if he discontinued the oxygen suddenly it might have a bad effect on his heart'.

At one o'clock the oxygen was turned off. Ten minutes later, Kelly recalled, 'we had a very good lunch, and the PM was in great form'.[2]

---

[1] Elston Grey-Turner, diary entry for 27 December 1944: *British Medical Journal*, 20–7 December 1980, page 1694.

[2] Air Vice Marshall Thomas J. Kelly, CBE, MC, MD, 'The Prime Minister's Journey to Marrakesh, December 27th, 1943', typescript, 10 October 1962. At dinner that night, as he was leaving the dining room, Churchill put his hand on Kelly's shoulder and said: 'Kelly, you have rendered me a great personal service today, I am very grateful to you.'

At about four o'clock that afternoon Churchill landed at Marrakesh, and was driven to the Villa Taylor, 'Flower Villa' as he and Roosevelt had called it. There, with the United States Army as both his guards and his hosts, Churchill lived, as he informed Roosevelt, 'in the lap of luxury, thanks to overflowing American hospitality'. Lord Beaverbrook had just flown in from London. 'I propose to stay here in the sunshine,' Churchill added, 'till I am quite strong again.'

On Churchill's second day at Marrakesh, Roosevelt approved the principle of the Anzio landings, while pointing out that he could not agree 'without Stalin's approval' to any use of forces or equipment elsewhere 'that might delay or hazard the success of "Overlord" or "Anvil" '.[1] Churchill was delighted and a little surprised that the Americans had accepted that the Anzio landing was to take place. 'I thank God for this fine decision,' he told Roosevelt, 'which engages us once again in whole-hearted unity upon a great enterprise.' The Chiefs of Staff would be telegraphing that day 'in full' to their American opposite numbers. 'Meanwhile,' Churchill added, 'here the word is "Full Steam Ahead".'[2]

That night, relaxing with Beaverbrook, who had flown out to join him, Churchill played poker, 'unruly but amusing', Jock Colville noted, and he added: 'The PM was wildly rash but successful.'[3]

Three issues clouded the sun on December 29. The first was when Churchill learned of a plan to move British Commando forces from the Mediterranean to the United Kingdom, as additional forces for 'Overlord'. At the Cairo conference Churchill had obtained American agreement that these forces, numbering about 5,000, should remain in the Mediterranean 'for action' as he reminded Brooke on December 29, 'to help the Yugoslavs, or possibly later on help in Greece'. Churchill added: 'It is not right to pillage the Mediterranean by pulling out all the plums. We must not become more Yankee than the Americans.' It had already been decided that some Special Air Service personnel were to be parachuted behind German lines as part of

[1] President to Prime Minister, No. 427 'Grand' No. 864, 'Personal and Secret', 28 December 1943: Churchill papers, 20/125.
[2] Prime Minister's Personal Telegram, T.2071/3, 'Frozen' No. 949, 28 December 1943: Churchill papers, 20/125.
[3] Colville diary, 28 December 1943: Colville papers.

'Overlord'. There was plenty of time, Churchill noted, 'to organise this from the resources in Great Britain'.[1]

Churchill's second concern was the danger that the needs of operation 'Buccaneer' in Burma would set back the May 1944 date for 'Overlord'. The Russians had 'a right to know' the approximate date for 'Overlord' before the Cairo conference ended. It was for the Americans to provide 'the sole means of carrying out the amphibious operation in the South of France which the Americans and the Russians so strongly desire. We have no objection to this, but the provision of the necessary landing-craft goes beyond anything we had previously asked for Mediterranean affairs.' It was for the Americans to say 'how these are to be provided, i.e., whether they should come from "Buccaneer" or across the Atlantic at the expense of the Pacific, or by a greater effort of new construction'. These facts, Churchill added, 'appear to dominate the date of "Overlord"'.[2]

Churchill's third cause for concern on December 29 came when he read a statement by a United States Senator, Edward Johnson, that 'It will come as a shock to Americans that three-quarters of the troops in "Overlord" will be American'. Churchill telegraphed at once to Harry Hopkins: 'This statement does not present the facts fairly.' The initial attack, Churchill calculated, 'will be delivered by sixteen British and nineteen American divisions, and it is only after several months that the American build-up will make a large change. In fact we start very nearly fifty-fifty. In the Mediterranean which should also be considered, we have a large plurality, and I am sure that, considering our much smaller population, you will find we shall do our full share.'

If Hopkins had the means of correcting Senator Johnson's statement, Churchill added, 'I should be obliged, as it is so much better we each keep our own crowds in order rather than issue contradictions across the ocean. The comradeship is magnificent at the front and in the staff organisation.'[3]

'Everyone here thinks Johnson's statement very bad,' Hopkins replied, enclosing a statement by the American Chiefs of Staff stressing that, while the exact proportion of British and American troops was 'a military secret which the Germans would like to know', both countries 'were going to hit the common enemy with everything available'.[4]

[1] 'Frozen' No. 962, 29 December 1943: Churchill papers, 20/130.

[2] 'WSC, 29.11.43': Churchill papers, 4/318.

[3] Prime Minister's Personal Telegram, T.2083/3, 'Frozen' No. 975, 29 December 1943: Churchill papers, 20/131.

[4] 'Grand' No. 930, 'Personal and Secret', 31 December 1943: Churchill papers, 20/125. Two days later Churchill criticized a Signal Corps report of an action in the Bay of Biscay which

That night, at dinner, Churchill was in a reminiscing mood, making, Colville noted, 'the first apologia I have ever heard him make for the Baldwin Government'. The effect of the climate of public opinion on people, Churchill remarked, was 'overpowering'. The war, however, would be known in history as 'The Unnecessary War'.[1]

Roosevelt's acceptance of the Anzio landing, which Churchill had already acknowledged on December 28, was mentioned again on December 30, when Churchill informed the President: 'The sun is shining today, but nothing did me the same good as your telegram showing how easily our minds work together on the grimly simple issues of this vast war.' Churchill added: 'Alexander reports he has arranged satisfactory plans with Clark for "Shingle". He is using the British 1st and the American 3rd Divisions, with paratroops and armour. I am glad of this. It is fitting that we should share equally in suffering, risk and honour.'[2]

On the eastern front, the Red Army had renewed its advance in the Kiev salient, covering sixty miles in five days. 'I am so glad you have retaken Korosten, whose loss you told us about at Teheran,' Churchill telegraphed to Stalin on December 30. His telegram continued, in amicable vein: 'I only wish we could meet once a week. Please give my regards to Molotov. If you will send me the music of the New Soviet Russian Anthem, I could arrange to have it played by the BBC on all occasions important Russian victories were announced.'[3] That same day Churchill asked Eden to try 'to run an additional Russian

---

stated 'that the eleven German destroyers were sighted by United States Navy Liberators', but which did not state, as Churchill informed Brendan Bracken, that the cruisers which sank three of them were British. Churchill added: 'I am sure it is important for the good will of the two countries that fairly balanced statement should be made and that British receive their due share of notice from our own papers.' ('Frozen' No. 1007, 31 December 1943: Churchill papers, 20/130.) There had been five German destroyers and six torpedo boats; one destroyer and two of the torpedo boats had been sunk. The Liberators had been guided in their successful attack by Enigma decrypts (F. H. Hinsley and others, *British Intelligence in the Second World War*, volume 3, part 1, page 250).

[1] Colville diary, 29 December 1943: Colville papers.

[2] Prime Minister's Personal Telegram, T.2086/3, 'Frozen' No. 980, Prime Minister to President No. 528, 29 December 1943: Churchill papers, 20/125.

[3] Prime Minister's Personal Telegram, T.2089/3, 'Frozen' No. 990, 30 December 1943: Churchill papers, 20/125. The Staff Officer (Intelligence) on board the *Duke of York* writes: 'We had the music of the new Russian National Anthem at the beginning of December 1943. The marine band practised every day just above my cabin!' (Edward Thomas, notes for the author, 23 May 1985.)

convoy' beyond those already arranged for before 'Overlord'. 'Pray let me know what is involved in this,' he added, 'observing that anyhow the Commanders may choose up to as late as May 31' for 'Overlord'.[1]

'Overlord' itself now began to engage Churchill's attention for the first time. 'I have not hitherto given detailed attention to operation "Overlord",' he explained to the Chiefs of Staff in a telegram from Marrakesh on December 30, 'but I trust every kind of improvisation will be used in addition to regular landing ships and craft.' He then set out the first of what were to be many such ideas. 'For instance,' he asked, 'have you any plans for a reverse Dunkirk in which, during fine weather, after the shore defences have been knocked out and while we have complete command of air, 1,000 small vessels of all kinds came from the Thames and every tiny creek and carry infantry and stores to many beaches.'

As to the Teheran 'contract' with the Russians, Churchill informed the Chiefs of Staff that this 'would be fulfilled' by the May 31 date. Churchill added: 'In my opinion it would be a *bona fide* execution of it if we fixed June 3, which is the corresponding moon phase to May 5, for the actual assault. It is however better to work to May 5, and thus have a month to spare.'

Churchill also asked the Chiefs of Staff to 'fly out' to him a short summary 'of COSSAC plan', as Montgomery was going to be with him on the following day.[2] This plan, drawn up by the Anglo-American Joint Staffs in London, under General Sir Frederick Morgan, constituted the initial plan for 'Overlord'. Churchill was sent a summary of it on December 31. That same day, he was joined by both Montgomery and Eisenhower. Eisenhower had brought bad news: of the eighty landing craft 'now likely to be available' for the Anzio landing, 'a proportion' would not be operationally fit.[3]

It was New Year's Eve. 'We saw the New Year in early,' Jock Colville noted, 'so that General M could go to bed early. Punch was brewed, the PM made a little speech, the clerks, typists and some of the servants appeared, and we formed a circle to sing Auld Lang Syne.'[4]

* * *

---

[1] 'Frozen' No. 997, 30 December 1943: Churchill papers, 20/130.

[2] 'Frozen' No. 994, 30 December 1943: Churchill papers, 20/130. COSSAC was Major General Frederick Morgan, Chief of Staff, under Supreme Allied Commander.

[3] Prime Minister's Personal Telegram, T.2096/3 (to General Maitland Wilson), 'Frozen' No. 1019, 31 December 1943: Churchill papers, 20/125.

[4] Colville diary, 31 December 1943: Colville papers.

For New Year's Day a picnic had been planned in the Atlas mountains two hours' drive from Marrakesh. Montgomery was among the picnic guests. After the picnic, as the cars climbed up into the mountains to a viewpoint which Churchill knew from his pre-war visit, Montgomery got out of the car and, 'to keep himself in training' as he put it, began to walk straight up the hill. 'I warned him,' Churchill later recalled, 'not to waste his vigour, considering what was coming. I emphasised the truths that energy of mind does not depend on energy of body; that energy should be exercised and not exhausted; that athletics are one thing and strategy another. These admonitions were in vain. The General was in the highest spirits; he leaped about the rocks like an antelope, and I felt a strong reassurance that all would be well.'[1]

That afternoon, on waking from his sleep, Churchill gave Montgomery the summary of the cross-Channel invasion plans which had reached Marrakesh earlier that day.[2] 'He said, "Here's the plan, I want your views on it,"' Montgomery later recalled. 'I said, "I'm not your military adviser: the Chiefs of Staff are. They're the people you've got to ask for advice on this plan,"' to which Churchill replied: 'I know. But I want your views on it.'[3]

On returning from the picnic site, Churchill asked Montgomery what he had thought of the 'Overlord' plan. The general replied, as Churchill recalled: 'This will not do. I must have more in the initial punch.'[4] Churchill's reaction, according to General Hollis, was: 'Very well then. If you don't like Morgan's plan, do one of your own!'[5]

Montgomery at once prepared a written note for Churchill, making 'the very serious criticism', as Churchill telegraphed to the Chiefs of Staff Committee on the following day, 'that the proposal to move so many divisions in over the same narrow strip of beaches would be quite impracticable and would lead to inextricable confusion'. Montgomery also considered that the Channel Islands should be re-taken 'in order inter alia to provoke the air battle'. Churchill added:

I was interested to hear from General Montgomery that it is only the initial assault that requires the special craft and that he landed large numbers of troops from liners as much as five miles out without using special landing craft at all. Moreover the weather was none too good at 'Husky'. I do not consider that the principle of 'reverse Dunkirk' should be lightly discarded. I was encouraged to hear General Montgomery's arguments that many landing

[1] Winston S. Churchill, *The Second World War*, volume 5, London 1952, page 393.
[2] This was Chiefs of Staff Paper No. 416 (O) of 1943.
[3] Field Marshal Viscount Montgomery of Alamein, in conversation with the author, 1968.
[4] Winston S. Churchill, *The Second World War*, volume 5, London 1952, page 393.
[5] Hollis recollections: James Leasor, *War at the Top*, London 1959, page 269.

points should be chosen instead of concentration as at present proposed through one narrow funnel.

In his telegram to the Chiefs of Staff Committee, Churchill also had a point to make about the nomenclature being used in advance of the cross-Channel landing:

I hope that all expressions such as 'Invasion of Europe' or 'Assault upon the Fortress of Europe' may be eliminated henceforward. I shall address the President again on this subject shortly pointing out that our object is the liberation of Europe from German tyranny, that we 'enter' the oppressed countries rather than 'invade' them and that the word 'invasion' must be reserved for the time when we cross the German frontier. There is no need for us to make a present to Hitler of the idea that he is the defender of a Europe we are seeking to invade.[1]

On the last day of 1943 Churchill had learned that Roosevelt was suffering from 'a mild case' of influenza.[2] He replied to the President, on New Year's day:

I am so sorry about your influenza. I earnestly hope you will defer to McIntyre's advice and show that attitude of submission to the medical faculty which you have so sedulously enjoined on me.

Flower Villa is perfect. The doctors want me to stay here for the next three weeks. The weather is bright, though cool. The cook is a marvel. We go for picnics to the mountains. Last night Eisenhower was with us on his way to you, and I had long talks with him. Montgomery is here now on his way to England. I think we have a fine team, and they certainly mean to pull together.

'Accept all my best wishes,' Churchill ended, 'for a New Year which will not only be marked by triumph but will open wider doors to our future work together. Clemmie and Sarah also send their salutations.'[3]

During January 1, Clementine Churchill sent her daughter Mary an account of the invalid of Marrakesh:

He is gaining strength every day, but very slowly indeed. He is disappointed that his recovery is slow; but when in the end he is quite well, the slowness of his convalescence may be a blessing in disguise, as it may make him a little more careful when he has to travel. For instance, when we came

---

[1] 'Frozen' No. 1052, 2 January 1944: Churchill papers, 20/179.

[2] President to Prime Minister, No. 430, 'Grand' No. 929, 31 December 1943: Churchill papers, 20/146.

[3] Prime Minister's Personal Telegram, T.3 of 1944, 'Frozen' No. 1026, 1 January 1944: Churchill papers, 20/154.

from Tunis here, the doctors did not wish him to fly above five thousand feet, but he insisted on going up to twelve thousand, to get above the clouds which of course made it safer as we were over mountainous country. He had oxygen and I think really it has turned out all right, but yesterday he said sadly, 'I am not strong enough to paint.'

But this morning, New Year's Day, he came early into my room, and said 'I am so happy. I feel so much better.' So don't be anxious, but we must all realise that he really needs great care. He is not staying in bed now more than he does in his ordinary life. This is his day: He works in bed all the morning and gets up just in time to go for an expedition or for lunch in the garden, after which he goes for a drive. Then he goes back again to bed till dinner. We try to prevent him sitting up late, but I am afraid he does. . . .[1]

That night, Churchill listened for a while to two gramophone records, *Pirates of Penzance* and *Patience*. Both were part of a complete set of Gilbert and Sullivan operas which his daughter Mary had given him as a Christmas present. 'I read, and brooded on the flowing music,' he wrote to her on the following morning. 'On the whole one of the happiest hours I have had in these hard days! How sweet of you to have the impulse! How clever to have turned it into action and fact!'[2]

Montgomery returned to England after dinner on January 1, to work on the revision of the 'Overlord' plan. That same day, Churchill invited de Gaulle to visit him 'during my convalescence', and to stay overnight. 'This,' Churchill wrote, 'would give us an opportunity of long-needed talks.'[3]

At dinner that night, Churchill and Beaverbrook 'went over the whole course of the last war and this', Colville noted in his diary. At one moment Churchill turned to Commander Thompson with the words: 'But, Tommy, you will bear witness that I do not repeat my stories so often as our dear President of the United States.' Speaking of his own Chiefs of Staff, Churchill commented: 'They may say I lead them up the garden path, but at every stage of the garden they have met delectable fruit and wholesome vegetables.'[4]

On January 3, Captain Pim, summoned by the message 'pray join me forthwith at Marrakesh', arrived at the Villa Taylor with his map room and staff. That night, at dinner, where the guest of honour was the local French commander, Pim found Churchill 'in great heart and considerably better that I had anticipated he would be'. The air

---

[1] Letter of 1 January 1944: Mary Soames, *Clementine Churchill*, *op. cit.*, page 347.
[2] Letter of 2 January 1944, to 'Darling Mary' from 'Your ever loving Father, W': Soames papers.
[3] Prime Minister's Personal Telegram, T.6/4, 'Frozen' No. 1029, 1 January 1944: Churchill papers, 20/154.
[4] Colville diary, 2 January 1944: Colville papers.

of Marrakesh, with its warm sunshine by day and crisp cold nights, 'must be the most beneficial possible for an invalid'.[1]

On January 4 Soviet forces crossed into pre-war eastern Poland, driving the Germans westward. That same day, the Czechoslovak President in exile, Eduard Beneš, visited Churchill in Marrakesh. As his main purpose was to convey the Soviet thinking on the post-war Polish frontiers, Churchill referred to the visit in his telegram to Stalin that morning, in which he combined praise and news:

> The splendid advances you are making beyond Vitebsk and west and south-west of Kiev fill our hearts with joy. I hope before the end of the month to make a small contribution at which I have been labouring here. Meanwhile everything is going full blast for 'Overlord'. General Montgomery passed through here on his way to take up his Command of the Expeditionary Group of Armies. He naturally has his own ideas about the details of the plan, but he is full of zeal to engage the enemy and of confidence in the result.
>
> President Beneš is coming to see me to-day. He is a wise man and should be a help in bringing the Poles to reason.
>
> I am getting stronger every day. Beaverbrook is with me and sends his warmest greetings. My son Randolph is flying in by parachute to Tito with Brigadier Maclean, the head of our mission, so I shall be kept well informed. All officers have been instructed to work in the closest harmony with any mission you may send. Many thanks for your help about the Greeks.[2]

Churchill's discussion with Beneš lasted for four and a half hours. He was instructed by Stalin, he said, to give Churchill 'the most friendly greetings on his behalf'. The talks then focused on Poland, Churchill reported that night to Eden:

> We went over the map of the Polish eastern frontier in great detail. In the north the Russians are ready to follow the Curzon line conceding Lomza and Bialystok but they must have Lemberg in the south. On the other hand they give to the Poles East Prussia from Königsberg exclusive and also the line of the Oder including the bulk of Oppeln.[3]

The approximate frontiers discussed at Teheran had become the Soviet's firm demands. 'Stalin is determined to have Lvov,' noted Colville.[4] It was in the west, from Germany, that Poland must seek its compensation. 'I think you should take the Poles in hand on this line,' Churchill told Eden, 'and as matters are urgent you might if necessary fly them out to me here towards the end of next week.'

[1] Pim recollections: Pim papers.

[2] Prime Minister's Personal Telegram, T.15/4, 'Frozen' No. 1092, 4 January 1944: Churchill papers, 20/154. Stalin had urged the Greek Communist guerillas to work with the Greek Government in exile.

[3] 'Frozen' No. 1104, 4 January 1944: Churchill papers, 20/179.

[4] Colville diary, 4 January 1944: Colville papers.

'I am getting stronger every day,' Churchill ended, 'but Max is down now with Gippy tummy and temperature. All my thoughts are on "Shingle" which as you may well imagine I am watching intensely.'[1]

Reporting to Roosevelt about his talk with Beneš, Churchill commented that the Czech leader 'may be most useful in trying to make the Poles see reason and in reconciling them to the Russians, whose confidence he has long possessed'. On the map which Beneš had brought, Churchill explained, the Soviet proposals for the post-war Polish frontiers had been marked 'with pencil marks by UJ'. The new borders, as marked by Stalin, gave Poland 'a fine place to live in' in Germany's eastern regions, 'more than 300 miles square with 250 miles of seaboard on the Baltic'. Churchill added:

As soon as I get home I shall go all out with the Polish Government to close with this or something like it, and having closed they must proclaim themselves as ready to accept the duty of guarding the bulwark of the Oder against further German aggression upon Russia, and also they must back the settlement to the limit. This will be their duty to the Powers of Europe who will twice have rescued them. If I can get this tidied up early in February a visit from them to you would clinch matters.

Churchill also reported that, as far as Czechoslovakia was concerned, the Russians were 'agreeable to Beneš having his old pre-Munich frontier back', other than 'a little territory to the eastward' to link Czechoslovakia with Russia. That 'little territory', though Churchill did not say so, was Sub-Carpathian Ruthenia, with a largely non-Czech population, which had been incorporated in Czechoslovakia at the creation of the new State after the First World War.[2]

In his telegram to Roosevelt, Churchill also sent some personal news of Marrakesh. 'The weather is lovely,' he wrote, 'both bracing and bright. We set out every day to the foot of the Atlas and have a picnic in olive groves by some mountain stream. You would enjoy it very much.'[3]

On January 4, in conference with Mark Clark, Alexander learned that the removal of all but six of the Tank Landing Craft after the initial Anzio landing 'will not allow us to put the two divisions ashore complete with their essential fighting vehicles'. With only six tank landing craft 'left to us', it would take twenty-one days to land the fighting vehicles required if the two divisions were to meet the

[1] 'Frozen' No. 1104, 4 January 1944: Churchill papers, 20/179.
[2] Today Sub-Carpathian Ruthenia is part of the Soviet Union.
[3] Prime Minister's Personal Telegram, T.26/4, 'Frozen' No. 1120, 6 January 1944: Churchill papers, 20/154.

Germans 'on equal terms'. 'We are willing,' Alexander telegraphed to Churchill that day, 'to accept any risks to achieve our object but if the two divisions get sealed off by the Germans we obviously cannot leave them there without any support . . .' These facts were causing him 'grave concern', Alexander told Churchill, 'and I must therefore ask for your help and assistance'. Alexander added: 'My experience of combined operations is that the initial assault to get ashore can be effected but the success of the operation depends on whether the full fighting strength of the expedition can be concentrated in time to withstand the inevitable counter-attack. For "Shingle" two divisions are the minimum force to put ashore in face of likely German resistance.' [1]

On January 4 Churchill proposed flying to Malta to discuss the Anzio landing with Alexander, 'but strong pressure', Colville noted, 'was brought against his doing so'.[2] Instead, General Bedell Smith and General Gale flew to Marrakesh to discuss the question of the availability of landing craft, despite the demands of 'Overlord'. 'Bedell Smith is quite sure it will be all right,' Churchill telegraphed to Alexander on January 5, 'and is going to telephone to me and telegraph to you tonight.' [3]

Returning to Algiers, Bedell Smith sent Churchill his calculations later that day. A total of 94 landing craft would be available for the Anzio landing, 'of which the maximum that can be serviceable will be 90'. Of the 94 available, 33 would have to return to the United Kingdom to refit in time for 'Overlord', the first 20 on February 6, the remaining 13 on February 16.[4] On this basis, the Anzio landing could go ahead.

'I am getting much stronger every day,' Churchill telegraphed to Hopkins, 'and am thinking now only of "Shingle".' [5] To the Chiefs of Staff, who wished to press the Americans for three landing craft from the Far East to be held back temporarily from the 'Overlord' preparations on behalf of 'Shingle', Churchill wrote: 'Believe me they will not give way and will make a point of insisting on their view against all our arguments. . . .' 'I see all the danger signals in their message,' Churchill warned, and he advised caution, telling the Chiefs of Staff: 'I do not recommend resistance which may cost us much in other directions.' As it was now almost certain, Churchill added,

[1] MA/956 (sent as M/250 to Commander-in-Chief, Mediterranean), 4 January 1944: Churchill papers, 4/340.

[2] Colville diary, 4 January 1944 (written on 22 January 1944 for security reasons, Colville 'having decided to write no word of future operations in this diary, however securely I may keep it at No. 10'): Colville papers.

[3] M.254, 5 January 1944: Churchill papers, 4/340.

[4] Telegram No. 24380 (from Algiers), 5 January 1944: Churchill papers, 4/340.

[5] Prime Minister's Personal Telegram, T.16/4, 5 January 1944: Churchill papers, 20/183.

that the June date would be chosen for 'Overlord', you certainly have enough in hand'.[1]

At dinner on the night of January 5, President Beneš expressed himself 'confident', as Colville noted, that the war could end 'any day after May 1st'. Churchill then put it to the vote round the table 'whether Hitler would still be in power on September 3rd 1944'. Churchill, Beaverbrook and Colville were among those who answered 'yes'. The 'noes' included Beneš, Lord Moran, John Martin, General Hollis, Tommy Thompson and Sarah Churchill.[2] Lord Beaverbrook, noted John Martin, 'has become an established part of the household'.[3]

During his visit on January 5, General Bedell Smith had told Churchill that he and Montgomery were both convinced 'that it is better to put in a much heavier and broader "Overlord" than to expand "Anvil". . . .' In reporting this to Roosevelt on January 6, Churchill added: 'As you know, I have always hoped that the initial assault at "Overlord" could be with heavier forces than we have hitherto mentioned.' It also seemed 'very probable', Churchill noted, 'from what I have heard', that the June moon, June 3, 'will be the earliest practicable date'. He did not see 'why we should resist this' if the Commanders 'feel they have a better chance then'.

The problem was Stalin, and the Teheran pledge; but Churchill reminded Roosevelt that 'in conversation with UJ we never mentioned such a date as 5th May, or even 8th May, but always spoke to him around 20th. Neither did we at any time dwell upon the exact phase of the operation which should fall on any particular day.' If the early June date were now 'accepted as final, I do not feel that we shall in any way have broken faith with him'. The operation would 'anyhow' begin in May 'with feints and softening bombardments, and I do not think UJ is the kind of man to be unreasonable over 48 hours'. By June, also, the ground in the east would be 'drier for UJ's great operations', and in the west the British and Americans would be able to make 'a much heavier attack and with much better chances of success'. When Eisenhower had presented his own 'final conclusions', Churchill suggested, then was the time to tell Stalin 'all the story in all its strength, including any modification of "Anvil", with the authority of the responsible Commanders behind our statement'.[4]

Churchill telegraphed to Attlee the same day, urging the need for having 'in hand' an extra Arctic convoy, 'as a sweetener to UJ if

[1] 'Frozen' No. 1146, 6 January 1944: Churchill papers, 20/179.

[2] Colville diary, 5 January 1944: Colville papers.

[3] John Martin, letter dated 6 May 1944: Martin papers.

[4] Prime Minister's Personal Telegram, T.29/4, 'Frozen' No. 1121, 6 January 1944: Churchill papers, 20/154.

"Overlord" goes back 28 days as seems more than probable'.[1] A further gesture was to be made to Stalin in expediting the transfer to the Soviet navy of several of the Italian warships which had earlier surrendered to the British. The ships requested by Russia were one battleship, one cruiser, eight destroyers and four submarines for North Russia, as well as 40,000 tons of merchant shipping for the Black Sea.[2] 'You started this up at Moscow,' Churchill telegraphed to Eden on January 7, 'and we clinched the matter at Teheran. It is far more important to convince Stalin that when we say a thing we mean business than to study the frills and flounces of the Italians.' Churchill added: 'I am particularly anxious to make good on this Italian ship business with the Russians because I may require some easement you know of in respect of "Overlord" dates, and also we want friendly consideration from the Russians in the Polish business.'[3] If it proved 'too risky' to send the warships before 'Overlord' and 'Anvil', Churchill suggested five days later, 'why do we not meanwhile lend UJ at least one of our battleships we have laid up for want of manpower, say *Malaya*, and suggest to the Americans they lend a cruiser, or possibly we could do both'. Such an offer, he argued, 'would certainly show the greatest goodwill on our part which is indeed deserved by their splendid victories'.[4]

To Churchill's surprise, an acrimonious dispute ensued, with Stalin insisting upon the Italian ships. After nearly a month of intensive telegraphic correspondence, Stalin accepted in place of the Italian ships, a British battleship and an American cruiser, but he did so 'somewhat grudgingly', Churchill told the War Cabinet when all was finally settled on February 7, and had also 'complained' that there was 'no mention of the 8 destroyers and 4 submarines for which he had asked'. These would therefore be provided by the Admiralty. The submarines, Churchill pointed out, 'would be modern vessels, and we should require them later on for use against Japan'.[5] This decision, Churchill telegraphed to Roosevelt, would, he hoped, 'quiet the growl on this subject for some time'.[6]

*   *   *

[1] 'Frozen' No. 1138, 6 January 1944: Churchill papers, 20/129.

[2] President to Prime Minister, No. 437, 'Grand' No. 1252, 9 January 1944: Churchill papers, 20/154.

[3] 'Frozen' No. 1155, 7 January 1944: Churchill papers, 20/129.

[4] 'Frozen' No. 1209 (to Eden, A. V. Alexander and Admiral of the Fleet Sir Andrew Cunningham), 10 January 1944: Churchill papers, 20/129.

[5] War Cabinet No. 16 of 1944, 7 February 1944, Confidential Annex: Cabinet papers, 65/45.

[6] Prime Minister's Personal Telegram, T.271/4, Prime Minister to President No. 462, 'Personal and Most Secret', 9 February 1944: Churchill papers, 20/156. One of Churchill's concerns had been the effect of the transfer on the morale of the Italian navy (Premier papers, 3/472).

On January 7 and 8 Churchill presided in Marrakesh over a final conference of all those concerned with the Anzio landings, including Maitland Wilson, Alexander and Bedell Smith. 'Everyone is in good heart,' he reported to Roosevelt when the conference was over, 'and the resources seem sufficient. Every aspect was thrashed out in full detail by sub-committees in the interval between the two conferences.'[1] 'I am deeply conscious,' Churchill wrote to General Mark Clark when the conferences were ended, 'of the importance of this battle, without which the campaign in Italy will be regarded as having petered out ingloriously.' In order to gain maximum advantage of the much-disputed landing craft, Churchill added, 'One thing I beg you, namely, to do everything in your power to start off on the 22nd if the weather is good. Every day gained increases the use you will have of these invaluable landing craft.' The earlier they could start, the more they could do, before being transferred to their 'Overlord' duties. 'I know you will do everything in human power,' Churchill ended.[2]

On the evening of January 7, Fitzroy Maclean and Randolph Churchill reached Marrakesh, their parachute drop into Yugoslavia having been briefly postponed because of bad weather. 'My unchanging object,' Churchill had informed Eden on the eve of their visit, 'is to get Tito to let the King come out and share the luck with him and bring in the old Serbian core.' The dismissal of Mihailovic, Churchill believed, was 'an essential preliminary'.[3] Next to the Anzio landing, Colville noted in his diary that night, 'the Yugoslav problem, with its intricacies about abandoning Mihailovic and reconciling King Peter to Tito, has been our chief interest out here'.[4]

To Tito, Churchill wrote from 'Africa' on January 8, that he had learned 'all about your valiant efforts' from Major Deakin, 'who is a friend of mine'. Fitzroy Maclean, he added, 'is also a friend of mine, and a colleague in the House of Commons'. Joining Maclean at Tito's headquarters would soon be Churchill's son Randolph 'who is also a member of Parliament'. Churchill's telegram continued:

One supreme object stands before us; namely, to cleanse the soil of Europe from the filthy Nazi Fascist taint. You may be sure that we British

[1] Prime Minister's Personal Telegram, T.40/4, 'Frozen' No. 1173, 8 January 1944: Churchill papers, 20/154.

[2] 'Africa', 'Secret and Personal', 8 January 1944: Churchill papers, 20/137.

[3] 'Frozen' No. 1132, 6 January 1944: Churchill papers, 20/179.

[4] Colville diary, 7 January 1944: Colville papers. Churchill's view was supported by the Chiefs of Staff Committee at their meeting in London on January 11. By encouraging 'both Mihailovic and Tito', they felt, 'we ran the risk of falling between two stools'. Britain's object was to 'contain German forces in Yugoslavia', a matter which was of 'great importance to our whole European strategy'. It 'would seem', the Chiefs of Staff concluded, 'that the best way of achieving this object would be to break with Mihailovic and give our full support to Tito'. Chiefs of Staff Committee No. 8 (Operations) of 1944: Cabinet papers, 79/69.

have no desire to dictate the future government of Yugoslavia. At the same time we hope that all will pull together as much as possible for the defeat of the common foe, and afterwards settle the form of government in accordance with the will of the people.

The British Government, Churchill told Tito, would give no further military support to Mihailovic 'and will only give help to you'. Britain would however remain 'in official relations' with King Peter II, who, as a boy, had escaped 'the treacherous clutches' of the Regent, Prince Paul, 'and came to us as a representative of Yugoslavia and as a young prince in distress'. There would, Churchill hoped, be 'an end to polemics on either side, for these can only help the Germans'.[1]

'Your message to Tito,' Stalin telegraphed to Churchill a few days later, 'whom you thus encourage with your support, will have great significance.'[2]

For Churchill the question of Poland's future frontiers also loomed large during his sojourn in Marrakesh, for the Polish Government in exile was reluctant to accept the loss of its pre-war eastern regions, on which Stalin now insisted. On January 7 Churchill informed Eden of his current thoughts:

I rather contemplate telling the world that we declared war for Poland and that the Polish nation shall have a proper land to live in but we have never undertaken to defend existing Polish frontiers, and that Russia, after two wars which have cost her between 20 and 30 millions of Russian lives, has a right to the inexpungeable security of her Western frontiers.

Moreover, without the Russian armies Poland would have been destroyed or liquidated to a servile condition and the very existence of the Polish nation blotted out. But the valour and prowess of the Russian armies are liberating Poland and no other forces in the world could have done it. Poland is now assigned a position as a great independent nation in the heart of Europe with a fine seaboard and better territory than she had before. If she does not accept this, Britain has discharged to the full her obligations and the Poles can make their own arrangements with the Soviets.

Churchill was in a stern mood towards the Poles. 'I do not think we should give them the slightest hope of further help or recognition,' he told Eden, 'unless they cordially support the decisions which we and our Soviet ally have reached.' The Poles must be 'very silly', he wrote, 'if they imagine we are going to begin a new war with Russia for the sake of the Polish Eastern frontier'.

Churchill ended his telegram to Eden with an emphatic conclusion.

[1] Prime Minister's Personal Telegram, T.50/4, 'Personal and Most Secret' 8 January 1944 (sent to Stalin and Roosevelt on 10 January 1944, to Roosevelt as Prime Minister to President No. 544): Cabinet papers, 118/86.
[2] 'Personal and Secret', 14 January 1944: Premier papers, 3/14/2, folio 19.

'Nations who are found incapable of defending their country,' he wrote, 'must accept a reasonable measure of guidance from those who have rescued them and who offer them the prospect of a sure freedom and independence.' It was not explained, however, what form that 'freedom and independence' would take, or how it would be maintained.[1] Stalin's attitude to the Poles was clear. If one was to judge by the most recent declaration of the Polish 'emigrant' Government, he telegraphed to Churchill on January 8, 'there is no foundation for reckoning on the possibility of bringing these circles to reason. These people are incorrigible.'[2] 'We are watching almost from hour to hour the marvellous advances of the Soviet Armies,' Churchill telegraphed to Stalin on January 9, and he added: 'I am well enough to go home quite soon, and propose to do utmost to bring Poles to reason, on lines of your talk with Beneš.'[3]

On January 10 the Soviet Government publicly proposed the 'Curzon Line' as its frontier with Poland.

At Marrakesh, the conferences over, Churchill continued to regain his strength for the return to Britain. 'We have been for several more picnics,' Clementine Churchill wrote home on January 10. 'In fact we go out every day when it is fine, but we can rarely go any distance because your Father works all the morning.'[4]

Churchill's work on January 10 included a note for the War Cabinet on the expression 'Unconditional Surrender', as first used by Roosevelt at the Casablanca conference, and endorsed by Churchill in the conference communiqué. By 'Unconditional Surrender', Churchill explained, 'I mean that the Germans have therefore no *rights* to any particular form of treatment. For instance, the Atlantic Charter would not apply to them as a *matter of right*. On the other hand, the victorious nations owe it to themselves to observe the obligations of humanity and civilization.'

It would be 'perhaps well', Churchill commented, to look at what was 'actually going to happen' to Germany before deciding whether 'more precise' statements should be made to 'induce them to surrender'. First, he pointed out, 'they are to be completely disarmed and deprived of all power to re-arm'. Second, 'they are to be prohibited from all use of aviation, whether civil or military, and from practising the art of flying'. Third, 'large numbers of persons alleged

[1] 'Frozen' No. 1163, 'Most Secret and Personal', 7 January 1944: Churchill papers, 20/179.
[2] 'Grand' No. 1243, 'Personal and Most Secret', 8 January 1944: Churchill papers, 20/154.
[3] Prime Minister's Personal Telegram, T.48/4, 'Frozen' No. 1204, 9 January 1944: Premier papers, 3/14/2, folio 21.
[4] Letter of 10 January 1944: Mary Churchill, *Clementine Churchill*, *op. cit.*, page 349.

to be guilty of atrocities are to be handed over for judgement to the countries where their crimes were committed'. Stalin had mentioned at Teheran 'that he would certainly require at least four million Germans to work for many years in building up the ruin they had caused in Russia'. Churchill commented: 'I have no doubt the Russians will insist upon the handing over to them of vast quantities of German machinery to make up in a generous fashion for what has been destroyed. It may well be that similar claims will be made by others of the victorious powers. In view of the great severity practised upon immense numbers of French, Italian and Russian prisoners-of-war and internees, such retribution would not appear to be devoid of justice.'

Fourth, Churchill pointed out, the British, American and Russian Governments 'are I understand agreed that Germany is to be decisively broken up into a number of separate States. East Prussia and Germany east of the River Oder are to be alienated forever and the population shifted. Prussia itself is to be divided and curtailed. The Ruhr and other great centres of coal and steel must be put outside the power of Prussia.' Fifth, 'the entire core of the German Army comprised in the General Staff must be entirely broken up, and it may well be that the Russians will claim that very large numbers of the General staff of the Germany Army shall be either put to death or interned for many years'.[1] These five points might show, Churchill concluded, 'that a frank statement of what is going to happen to Germany would not necessarily have a reassuring effect upon the German people and that they might prefer the vaguer terrors of "unconditional surrender" . . .'[2]

Reading Churchill's note, Clement Attlee expressed his agreement with its conclusions, but, commenting on Churchill's statement that 'the British, United States and Russian Governments are agreed that Germany is to be decisively broken up into a number of separate states', Attlee wrote: 'I do not recall that we have ever taken so definite a decision. For myself, while desiring the decentralization of Germany and the severance of certain areas, I am sceptical as to the efficacy of a partition enforced by the victors.'[3] This 'certainly was the President's view', Churchill noted, '& that of M. Stalin. I did not commit HMG beyond "the isolation of Prussia".'[4]

---

[1] Churchill noted at this point: 'I have myself wished to publish a list of some 50 to 100 outlaws of first notoriety with a view to dissociating the mass of the people from those who will suffer capital punishment at the hands of the Allies and of avoiding anything in the nature of mass executions. This would tend to reassure the ordinary people. But these proposals were scouted at Teheran as being far too lenient. . . .'

[2] 'Note by the Prime Minister', 10 January 1944: Premier papers, 3/197/2, folios 30–3.

[3] 'Secret', 25 January 1944: Premier papers, 3/197/2, folio 34.

[4] Note of 26 January 1944: Premier papers 3/197/2, folio 34.

Churchill now prepared to welcome de Gaulle to the Villa Taylor. On January 10 Duff Cooper, the British Representative with the French National Committee, arrived in Marrakesh from Algiers, with Lady Diana Cooper. 'From various quarters,' Churchill telegraphed that day to Harry Hopkins, 'I have derived the impression that de Gaulle is much more involved in the collective strength of the Committee and the Assembly and that he may well become more reasonable. I certainly desire to make the best of him for the common cause. . . .' [1]

General de Gaulle's visit caused a certain trepidation. 'I am rather nervous,' Clementine Churchill wrote to her daughter Mary, 'as de G has again perpetrated one of his chronic incivilities by sending Papa (who really has worked for the French at all these Conferences and also to keep the President sweet, who simply loathes de G) a boorish message.' [2] The message was that it would be 'most inopportune' for General de Lattre de Tassigny to accept an invitation to dine with Churchill and stay the night. 'The PM was furious,' Colville noted in his diary on January 11, 'and said that in that case he would not see de Gaulle. Duff Cooper with difficulty pacified him, and the conversation merely became a heated discussion between Mrs C (very anti-French), the PM (temporarily anti-French) and the Duff Coopers arguing the other way.' [3]

On the morning of January 12, as Duff Cooper was preparing to leave Marrakesh, he was summoned by telephone to the Villa Taylor. He described the sequel in his diary:

I got over to him in half an hour. He was in bed, and had apparently worked himself up again about de Gaulle. He suggested sending him a note to the airfield to say he was sorry he had been troubled to come so far but that he would not be able to see him after all. I strongly dissuaded him from this course, pointing out that we knew nothing of the reason which had caused de Gaulle to prevent de Lattre from coming here. He might have perfectly good reasons for having done so. De Lattre had not yet received an official appointment and de Gaulle might wish to consult the PM as to what was to be done with him. Alternatively, he might have thought that Giraud would be annoyed at a junior officer receiving such an invitation when he was not invited.

This worked, but Winston then said he would receive de Gaulle on a purely social basis, would talk about the weather and the beauty of the place and then say 'good-bye'. This was better, but I suggested that Palewski would probably ask me whether there were going to be serious conversations after

[1] Prime Minister's Personal Telegram, T.52/4, 'Frozen' No. 1219, 'Private and Confidential', 10 January 1944: Churchill papers, 20/154.

[2] Letter of 12 January 1944: Lady Soames papers.

[3] Colville diary, 11 January 1944: Colville papers.

lunch—what was I to say? He said he didn't mind having a talk if de Gaulle asked for it, but that he would not take the initiative. Nor would he see him alone. If he did, de Gaulle would misrepresent what he had said. I must be present and Max too, and de Gaulle could bring whom he liked. I should have to alter my plans and stay over till tomorrow.

Duff Cooper stayed, and de Gaulle arrived, together with his Chef de Cabinet, Gaston Palewski. Duff Cooper recorded the meeting in his diary: 'All passed off well. Winston was in a bad mood when de Gaulle arrived and was not very welcoming. He had just read of the shooting of Ciano, de Bono, etc. which had rather shocked him. As lunch proceeded, however, Winston thawed.'[1]

The British Consul in Marrakesh, Bryce Nairn, had been invited to the meeting as Churchill's interpreter. At first, however, Churchill spoke French to de Gaulle, while Nairn waited for the moment of serious discussion, when his interpreter's services would be called for. But when Churchill turned away from de Gaulle for a moment it was not to ask Nairn to translate for him, but to say to Duff Cooper, 'in a very audible whisper' as Nairn later recalled: 'I'm doing rather well. Aren't I?'

'Everyone, General de Gaulle setting the example, burst out laughing,' Nairn wrote. Churchill then continued, still in French. Later he paused once more to turn to Duff Cooper with the words: 'Now that the General speaks English so well, he understands my French perfectly.'

'The General laughed heartily,' Nairn wrote, 'and the Prime Minister went on talking in French. . . .'[2] As Churchill and de Gaulle spoke, Duff Cooper was able to explain to Palewski 'the delicacy of the situation and of the PM's irritation over the de Lattre episode'. Then, as Duff Cooper noted in his diary:

When the ladies left, Winston invited de Gaulle to sit next to him, but things were still tricky. We then moved out into the garden—Winston, Max, the British Consul and me on the one side—de Gaulle and Palewski on the other. The conversation lasted about two hours. Winston was admirable, I thought, and de Gaulle very difficult and unhelpful. He talked as though he were Stalin and Roosevelt combined. Winston dealt first with the prisoners

[1] Duff Cooper diary, 12 January 1944: Churchill papers, 4/52 (sent by Duff Cooper to Churchill when Churchill was writing his war memoirs) Count Ciano, who in 1930 had married Mussolini's daughter Edda, and was Italian Foreign Minister from 1936 to 1943, and Marshal de Bono, one of Mussolini's associates in the March on Rome, had both voted against Mussolini at a meeting of the Fascist Grand Council on 25 July 1943. On 8 January 1944 they were among six 'traitors' tried by a Tribunal of Italian Fascists at Verona, northern Italy. All six were found guilty of treason, although both Ciano and de Bono had refused to seek an accommodation with Badoglio or the King after the July 1943 vote; all six were shot on 11 January 1944. Many Italians were shocked at Mussolini's rejection of his daughter Edda's pleas for clemency on behalf of her husband.
[2] 'Notes on Mr Churchill's visit to Marrakesh in 1944': Churchill papers, 4/326.

question—talked about Georges—about Syria—always on the line 'Why should we quarrel? Why can't we be friends?' De Gaulle did very little towards meeting him half way, but they parted friends and the Prime Minister agreed to attend the review on the following day.[1]

When de Gaulle had gone, Bryce Nairn found himself alone with Churchill in the drawing room: 'he was striding up and down when suddenly he stopped', Nairn later recalled, 'and with what I thought was rather a challenging look, said: "There is no doubt about it! C'est un grand animal!" I knew what the Prime Minister meant and I bowed in agreement.'[2]

Two weeks later, Churchill gave an account of his talk with de Gaulle to some of his friends at the Other Club.[3] Among those present was Colin Coote, who noted:

His meeting with De Gaulle had obviously been stormy, but finished more satisfactorily than it had begun. It must not be forgotten that Beaverbrook, who was present throughout, is always grit in the oil of Franco-British relations.

Anyway, Winston said he found De Gaulle difficult and touchy and that he finally said to him, 'Look here! I am the leader of a strong, unbeaten nation. Yet every morning when I wake my first thought is how I can please President Roosevelt, and my second is how I can conciliate Marshal Stalin. Your situation is very different. Why then should your first waking thought be how you can snap your fingers at the British and Americans?' Apparently this went well.[4]

The fullest account of Churchill's conversation with de Gaulle is Churchill's own report of it to Roosevelt. Their talk, Churchill wrote, 'consisted mainly of a prolonged complaint and lecture by me, in good manners and bad French, upon his many follies'. Churchill's account continued:

I explained how foolish he was to create needless antagonism with you and me and that he hindered the interests of France thereby.

I spoke of Boisson, Peyrouton and Flandin, saying that we had entered into obligations towards the first two and that these must be respected by the French Committee. About Flandin I said that if they were going to draw the line of impurity at Flandin, they would be making so wide a schism in France that the resultant friction in any territory that might be liberated would hamper our military operations and was therefore a matter of concern to us.

---

[1] Duff Cooper diary, 12 January 1944: Churchill papers, 4/52. (Sent by Duff Cooper to Churchill when Churchill was writing his war memoirs.)

[2] 'Notes on Mr Churchill's visit to Marrakesh in 1944': Churchill papers, 4/326.

[3] A dining club, founded by Churchill and F. E. Smith in 1911, and meeting once a fortnight while Parliament was in session. Its history was later written by Colin Coote.

[4] Colin Coote notes, 27 January 1944: Coote papers.

De Gaulle, in reply showed me the report of the bitter debate in his Assemblée the day before printed in the local newspaper, and certainly there is no doubt that the pressure comes from there and also by messages from France. I remarked that it was an odd way to restore the greatness of France by proving how many Frenchmen had behaved badly.

I then complained to him about the Lebanon &c.—how unwise it was for a nation having great colonies to act in this high-handed manner at a time when two of her principal Allies had no colonial possessions worth speaking of, and could therefore afford to take a very detached view.[1] I spoke also of my regret that General Georges, who was an old friend of mine, had been dismissed, and made it clear to him that we had confidence that General Giraud would not allow French troops to be used for our detriment, but that we had not yet the same confidence in the French Committee nor, by implication, in its Head. He seemed upset by this.

The impression I tried to create was that they would have to work their passage in order to regain from us that confidence which might be of marked advantage to them. I made no commitments of any kind.[2]

French efforts to assert control of the Lebanon in such a way as to retain that control after the war continued to anger Churchill. 'After all,' he minuted to Eden on May 7: 'We are pledged to the cause of Lebanese independence.'[3] Two months later Churchill minuted again: 'We must not forget that both we and the French have promised independence to the people of Syria and the Lebanon, and the same sort of relations, as we have in Iraq—so much and no more. We cannot go back on this.'[4]

Among the other matters with which Churchill had to deal on January 12 was the news of continued Portuguese reluctance to allow American troops to be based in the Azores. The Americans should be supported 'vigorously', Churchill telegraphed to Eden, and he added: 'There is no need for us to be apologetic in dealing with any of these neutrals who hope to get out of Armageddon with no trouble and a good profit.'[5]

---

[1] On 11 November 1943 French Marines had arrested the President of the Lebanese Republic and dissolved the Chamber of Deputies. From Cairo, the Minister of State, Richard Casey, had telegraphed to Churchill: 'the criminally foolish thing that the French have now done has shocked opinion in the Middle East. People are asking if this is the Middle Ages or the World Powers Atlantic Charter. It will need all the pressure we can bring to bear on the French Committee of Liberation at Algiers to make them untangle the knot they have tied.' During subsequent fighting, at least sixteen Lebanese were killed, and on November 21, in clashes between French and British forces, a Royal Army Ordnance Corps Major had been killed. (Major-General Sir Edward Spears, *Fulfilment of a Mission: The Spears Mission to Syria and Lebanon 1941–1944*, London 1977, chapters 16–21.)

[2] Prime Minister's Personal Telegram, T.176/4, Prime Minister to President, No. 559, 'Personal and Most Secret', 30 January 1944: Churchill papers, 20/155.

[3] Prime Minister's Personal Minute, M.517/4, 7 May 1944: Premier papers, 3/423/1, folio 20.

[4] Prime Minister's Personal Minute, M.855/4, 13 July 1944: Premier papers, 3/423/1, folio 18.

[5] 'Frozen' No. 1254, 12 January 1944: Churchill papers, 20/179.

Churchill also had harsh words for those Cabinet Ministers who were pressing him to implement the 1939 Palestine White Paper, whereby it had been proposed, as of May 1944, to create an Arab majority Government in Palestine, thus making even a partitioned Jewish State impossible. 'Surely we are not going to make trouble for ourselves in America,' Churchill telegraphed to Attlee and Eden, 'and hamper the President's chances of re-election for the sake of this low-grade gasp of a defeatist hour. The Arabs have done nothing for us during this war, except for the rebellion in Iraq.'[1] 'Obviously,' Churchill minuted to the Chiefs of Staff Committee two weeks later, 'we shall not proceed with any plan of partition which the Jews do not support.'[2]

As well as Portugal and Palestine, there was also more Polish business to attend to on January 12. The Poles should be told, Churchill instructed Eden, that it was his counsel that they should 'adopt in principle' the frontier proposals 'which it seems are not unacceptable to the Soviets'. Having been ceded so much German territory, up to the River Oder, 'it would be a sacred duty for Poland', Churchill declared, 'to guard the line of the Oder in the interests of the Russian State and thus receive from them the friendship and support without which their Polish future is most precarious'. Churchill added:

As we are the only unbroken power that went to war with Germany and as we did so for the sake of Poland I wish to make it absolutely clear that I personally should regard this settlement as a full discharge of all our promises and obligations to Poland and that if it were not accepted in a loyal spirit and recommended by the Polish Government in London I should certainly not take any further responsibility for what will happen in the future. In this I also speak for His Majesty's Government.

Churchill went on to warn Eden that the 'consequences of a failure' to reach the basis of an agreement with Russia 'as to the Eastern frontier now may well be the establishment by the Russians in Warsaw of a rival Polish Government and results may occur in Poland of a most lamentable kind. Whereas a settlement now might speedily bring about a cessation of the agony which Poland is suffering.' Churchill added:

There could be no question in any case of our quarrelling with the Russians if the kind of proposals now put forward were rejected. Considering that Russia has lost perhaps thirty millions of citizens in the two devastating wars of the last twenty-five years they have the right as well as the power to have their Western frontiers properly secured.[3]

[1] 'Frozen' No. 1256, 12 January 1944: Churchill papers, 20/179.
[2] Prime Minister's Personal Minute, 25 January 1944: Churchill papers, 20/152.
[3] 'Frozen' No. 1246, 12 January 1944: Churchill papers, 20/179.

That evening, at the Villa Taylor, Diana Cooper spoke to Clementine Churchill about what would happen after the war. 'I never think of after the war,' Clementine replied. 'You see, I think Winston will die when it's over.' Diana Cooper remonstrated gently, 'that people lived to ninety or might easily, in our lives, die that day; but Clementine seemed,' she recalled, 'quite certain and quite resigned to his not surviving long into peace'. 'You see,' she said, 'he's seventy and I'm sixty and we're putting all we have into this war, and it will take all we have.' [1]

On January 13 de Gaulle invited Churchill to review the French troops in Marrakesh, the two men standing side by side on the saluting base. 'First there were Senegalese troops on foot,' Elizabeth Layton later recalled, 'black as pitch, in reddish uniforms with red fezes, and bayonets on their rifles, hopelessly out of step but obviously tough soldiers. Fighters roared low overhead. Next came the Foreign Legion, also on foot. . . .' [2] Duff Cooper, who was also present, noted in his diary:

Winston was in the uniform of an Air-Commodore. I could see that he was very much moved by the loud cries of 'Vive Churchill', which predominated even over the cries of 'Vive de Gaulle'. I couldn't help thinking, as I watched them standing together taking the salute, of the incident 24 hours earlier when Winston had said that he would not receive de Gaulle at all. After Winston had left, de Gaulle made a short speech in appreciation of the privilege they had enjoyed in having the Premier Ministre Britannique at their review and extolling the alliance. [3]

The 'alliance' was shaky, nevertheless, and when Churchill learned, eight days later, that the words 'République Française' were to be included on new banknotes to be issued by the French National Committee, he minuted to Eden: 'I have no doubt that the President's position is that he will not allow a de Gaulle-headed committee to be considered synonymous with "République Française". I see no great harm in the French realizing how far they have been led into estranging important personalities.' Churchill's minute continued:

There is a real danger that should we liberate considerable areas of France, the French National Committee will hurry along behind trying to peg out monopolistic claims for themselves with de Gaulle trying to hoist the Croix de Lorraine on every town hall. They really have got to convince us of their loyalty and efficiency. It is too easy for this handful of émigrés to call themselves the Government of France and write off everyone else as 'impure'. As you know, I still hope to bring them all together. [4]

[1] Diana Cooper, *Trumpets from the Steep*, London 1960, page 182.
[2] Elizabeth Nel, *Mr Churchill's Secretary*, London 1958, page 133.
[3] Duff Cooper diary, 13 January 1944: Churchill papers, 4/52.
[4] Prime Minister's Personal Minute, M.11/4, 21 January 1944: Churchill papers, 20/152.

As soon as the march past had ended, Churchill was on his way to another picnic in the Atlas mountains, two hours' drive from Marrakesh. 'It took place at a very beautiful spot,' noted Duff Cooper, 'and everyone enjoyed it. Winston was in a heavenly mood—very funny and very happy.' [1]

The picnic spot was at a place known as the Pont Naturel, overlooking a deep gorge through which, as Jock Colville noted, 'a stream ran, falling from rock to rock into limpid blue pools'. 'The PM,' Colville added, 'insisted on being carried down, scrambling over the rocks.' [2] That evening Churchill was again joined by Harold Macmillan. 'PM was in a most mellow mood,' he noted in his diary, largely because the de Gaulle visit 'had gone off satisfactorily'. At the morning's review, Macmillan added, 'Winston had been much moved by the enthusiasm of his reception.' Churchill also spoke of the continuing authority, in Allied controlled Italy, of King Victor Emmanuel and Marshal Badoglio. 'He is all for keeping them at present,' Macmillan recorded. In Churchill's own words: 'When I want to lift a pot of hot coffee I prefer to keep the handle.' [3]

During January 13 Churchill found time to send a telegram to Stalin: the music of the new Soviet national anthem had been received, 'and will be played before 9 pm News on Sunday night by the full Symphony Orchestra of the BBC'. [4] The BBC should make it clear, Churchill telegraphed to Brendan Bracken on the following day, that this music 'has been sent to me personally at my request by Marshal Stalin', and should play it 'on all occasions when news of Russian victories is received. [5] Stalin was delighted to learn of Churchill's efforts, sending back a message, through the British Ambassador in Moscow, that he hoped 'that you would set about learning the new tune and whistling it to members of the Conservative Party'. [6]

Churchill had decided that he should be in London when the Anzio landing took place, and, much as he would have liked an-

---

[1] Duff Cooper diary, 13 January 1944: Churchill papers, 4/52.

[2] Colville diary, 13 January 1944: Colville papers.

[3] Macmillan diary, 13 January 1944: *War Diaries, op. cit.*, page 361.

[4] Prime Minister's Personal Telegram, T.59/4, 'Frozen' No. 1266, 13 January 1944: Churchill papers, 20/154.

[5] 'Frozen' No. 1086, 14 January 1944: Churchill papers, 20/179.

[6] No. 267A from Moscow to the Foreign Office, 'Secret and Personal', 3 February 1944:

other two weeks' convalescence, left Marrakesh at midday on January 14, flying to Gibraltar. There, after hearing from General Maitland Wilson and Admiral Sir John Cunningham of the final details of the Anzio plan, he went on board the battleship *King George V*, for the return voyage to England. One ominous piece of news which reached him that day was a message from Roosevelt, reporting an American Intelligence message that Marshal Graziani had, early in December, 'urged Hitler to hold Cassino at any cost and that the time had come to try to throw us back to the Sangro by a very large counter-attack along the Adriatic'. This information, Roosevelt noted, 'comes from a good but not sure source. I am merely passing it on to you for what it is worth.' [1]

Reading each day the Enigma decrypts, Churchill noticed in one, as he telegraphed to Alexander on January 12, a movement of German troops 'which will surely be agreeable to you'. His telegram mentioned: 'I am, indeed, disappointed that my health does not allow me to come to your Headquarters. I hope, however, you will not fail to keep me fully informed. I shall be moving homeward very soon.' [2]

Each day that Churchill was on board *King George V* steaming back to Britain, Soviet troops were pressing westward. On January 15 the Red Army opened a new offensive, west of Leningrad, driving towards the Baltic. This raised in Churchill's mind the question of the Baltic States, and, as he reminded Eden on January 16, 'the very strong line I took against our committing ourselves to their

---

Churchill papers, 20/156. It was not a Soviet tune, however, but a scheme for a British National Health Service, that Churchill was preparing for the Conservative Party (of which he had been leader for just under four years). In a speech to the Royal College of Physicians in London on 2 March 1944, he set out his reasons for such a substantial change in Party policy. 'The discoveries of healing science must be the inheritance of all,' he said. 'That is clear. Disease must be attacked, whether it occurs in the poorest or the richest man or woman, simply on the ground that it is the enemy; and it must be attacked just in the same way as the fire brigade will give its full assistance to the humblest cottage as readily as to the most important mansion.' The British Government, Churchill added, 'have adopted the policy outlined in the remarks of Lord Beaconsfield on health and the laws of health, and that is the course upon which we have embarked. Our policy is to create a national health service in order to ensure that everybody in the country, irrespective of means, age, sex, or occupation, shall have equal opportunities to benefit from the best and most up-to-date medical and allied services available.' (Speech of 2 March 1944: Churchill papers 9/204.) The Cabinet had given its approval to a national health scheme on 9 February 1944, when Churchill told his Ministers that in their speeches they should stress that it 'was put forward for public discussion and that constructive criticism would be welcomed'. (War Cabinet No. 17 of 1944, 9 February 1944: Cabinet papers, 65/41, 'reaffirmed' at War Cabinet No. 21 of 1944, 15 February 1944: Cabinet papers, 65/41.)

[1] President to Prime Minister, No. 442, 'Grand' No. 1368, 'Personal and Secret', 14 January 1944: Churchill papers, 20/154.

[2] Special unnumbered Telegram of 12 January 1944: Churchill papers, 4/340.

absorption in Russia' during discussions on the subject at the beginning of 1942. 'I ask myself,' Churchill's minute to Eden continued, 'how do all these matters stand now?' and he went on to answer his question:

Undoubtedly my own feelings have changed in the two years that have passed since the topic was first raised during your first visit to Moscow. The tremendous victories of the Russian armies, the deep-seated changes which have taken place in the character of the Russian State and Government, the new confidence which has grown in our hearts towards Stalin—these have all had their effect. Most of all is the fact that the Russians may very soon be in physical possession of these territories, and it is absolutely certain that we should never attempt to turn them out. Moreover, at Teheran when Stalin talked about keeping East Prussia up to Königsberg, we did not say anything about the Baltic States, which clearly would be comprised in the Russian dominions in any such solution.

We are now about to attempt the settlement of the eastern frontiers of Poland, and we cannot be unconscious of the fact that the Baltic States, and the questions of Bukovina and Bessarabia, have very largely settled themselves through the victories of the Russian armies. At the same time any pronouncement on the topic might have disastrous effects in the United States in the election year, and there is no doubt that we should ourselves be subject to embarrassing attacks in the House of Commons if we decided the fate of the countries.

As far as he could 'make out', Churchill noted, 'the Russian claim in no way exceeds the former Tsarist boundaries; in fact, in some parts it falls notably short of them'.[1] It would be 'far' better, Churchill told Eden, 'to shelve it all until we reach the discussions which we shall have to have after the defeat of Hitler'. But this might not be possible, as the negotiation which would soon take place about Poland might 'directly or indirectly' affect these other regions as well.[2]

On the day of this minute to Eden, in which he conceded in effect the Soviet Union's claim to the Baltic States, Churchill also telegraphed to Stalin to inform him that there would be an additional Arctic convoy of twenty ships, leaving Britain in mid-March, 'without prejudice' to 'Overlord'. 'I am at present at sea,' Churchill added,

---

[1] Nine days later Eden minuted to Churchill: 'The boundaries now asked for by the Russians fall short of the boundaries of Tsarist Russia in that the whole of Finland and most of Poland formed, of course, part of Imperial Russia.' (Foreign Secretary's Minute, PM/44/21, 25 January 1944: Premier papers, 3/399/6, folios 72–6.)

[2] Prime Minister's Personal Minute, M (S) 31/1, 16 January 1944: Churchill papers, 20/152.

'but you may be sure that on reaching home I shall make success of "Overlord" my first care.'[1]

Meanwhile, 'Shingle' continued to cause Churchill some concern, not its planning aspects, but the possibility that it might, when successful, be represented, as he telegraphed to General Wilson, as a 'purely American victory'. 'No one is keener than I am,' Churchill wrote, 'in working with the Americans in the closest comradeship.' But in General Mark Clark's Fifth Army, he noted, 'which is at least one-half British', it was General Clark who conducted the operations. Two other Americans were in charge of the Tactical Air and Strategical Air. An American Admiral was to command the Naval Squadron, and, as a recent telegram informed him, an American General had been designated Military Commander of Rome.

'It is a short-sighted policy,' Churchill wrote, 'by all these means to conceal the fact that more than half the troops engaged, even on the Fifth Army and "Shingle" fronts, will be British, that the Eighth British Army is also in action, and that Alexander and his Staff are responsible for the whole planning and control of the operations, because,' Churchill warned, 'this will only lead to a feeling of bitterness in Great Britain when the claim is stridently put forward, as it surely will be, that "the Americans have taken Rome".' It was 'most desirable', Churchill told Wilson, 'that an even balance should be maintained and the credit, of which there will be enough for all, fairly shared'.[2] On the following day, British troops of the Fifth Army launched three separate attacks across the Garigliano and Rapido rivers, hoping to draw the Germans' attention away from preparations being made for the Anzio landing.

On board ship on January 17, 'the PM went all Harrovian after lunch', Jock Colville noted in his diary, 'and said that the lines "God give us bases to guard and beleaguer, etc" had always inspired him greatly, despite the fact that he detested football'. During the day he spent 'an hour or more in the Gunroom, answering questions from the delighted Subs and Midshipmen'.[3]

One of those Midshipmen was Tony Barter, who wrote to his parents of Churchill's visit to the Gunroom:

[1] 'Frozen' No. 1278, 16 January 1944: Churchill papers, 20/179. This telegram was sent from London two days later as Prime Minister's Personal Telegram, T.71/4, 'Personal and Most Secret', No. 137 from Foreign Office to Moscow: Churchill papers, 20/154.

[2] Prime Minister's Personal Telegram, T.66A/4, 'Most Secret', 16 January 1944: Churchill papers, 20/154.

[3] Colville diary, 17 January 1944: Colville papers.

He stayed an hour, during which time we continuously fired questions at him on every imaginable subject to do with the war. He's got a mind just like an encyclopaedia: you ask a question & the answer comes out pat! He was most interesting & tried to answer every question, talking of Russia, Italy, France, the Beveridge Report, U-boats, & hosts of other subjects.

On Russia he was most illuminating & is definitely certain that she has abandoned the Comintern Pact, which pleases him very much. He made many jokes, the best remark being that 'Now we have at last persuaded the Conservative Party to sing the "Red Flag", the Russians produce a new National Anthem!'

He seemed amazingly well & has terrific personality which seems to radiate from him. He has enormous shoulders & a few wisps of white hair, but not the baby face that seems to come out in some of his photos.

Afterwards he took us in his Map Room where he has maps of all the war theatres, complete with flags. He described everything for about half an hour, taking each front in turn, including the Atlantic. On talking of the U-boats his eyes lit up & he waxed most enthusiastic.[1]

Shortly before midnight the *King George V* dropped anchor at Plymouth, where, John Martin noted, John Peck was waiting 'with PM's train'.[2] Actually, it was King George VI's personal train, code-name 'Rugged', which had brought John Peck, Charles Barker and Marian Holmes to Plymouth.[3] 'Unlike previous home-comings, there were no political, strategic or diplomatic dramas—the atmosphere was one of immense relief the PM was back alive and well and truly in control of events.'[4]

---

[1] Letter from Midshipman A. P. Barter, RNVR, to his parents, 21 January 1944: Barter papers.

[2] Martin diary, 17 January 1944: Martin papers.

[3] Marian Holmes diary, 17 January 1944: Marian Walker Spicer papers. Charles Barker, the Chief Clerk at 10 Downing Street, had been with Churchill since 1940. Jock Colville writes: 'Efficient and entertaining, he was popular with the Private Secretaries. An expert on old silver. He had two intelligent men, Pat Kinna and Donald MacKay, working under him and jointly they kept the office in apple-pie order.' (John Colville, *The Fringes of Power, Downing Street Diaries 1934–1955*, London 1985, page 247, note 1.)

[4] Sir John Peck, letter to the author, 13 January 1985.

38

Anzio: 'The Hun is still very tough'

TRAVELLING overnight from Plymouth, Churchill reached London on the morning of 18 January 1944, where the Cabinet awaited him at Paddington Station, and 'the PM', noted Marian Holmes, 'emerged to a battery of camera-men and press'.[1] Two hours later he was in the House of Commons for Prime Minister's Question Time. At noon, in his room in the House of Commons, he gave the War Cabinet an account of his travels, 'leaving at 1.28', Colville noted, 'to lunch with the King at 1.30'. Colville added: 'Plus ça change, plus c'est la même chose, I observe.'[2] 'I have now got home again safely,' Churchill telegraphed to Roosevelt later that day, 'and am all right except for being rather shaky on my pins.'[3]

Some of Churchill's efforts that day were observed by Harold Nicolson, others by the King's Private Secretary, Sir Alan Lascelles. As Nicolson wrote that night to his sons:

I happened to have been told that Winston had arrived home that morning, but the rest of the House were wholly unaware of that fact. We were dawdling through Questions and I was idly glancing at my Order Paper when I saw (saw is the word) a gasp of astonishment pass over the faces of the Labour Party opposite. Suddenly they jumped to their feet and started shouting, waving their papers in the air. We also jumped up and the whole House broke into cheer after cheer while Winston, very pink, rather shy, beaming with mischief, crept along the front bench and flung himself into his accustomed seat. He was flushed with pleasure and emotion, and hardly had he sat down when two large tears began to trickle down his cheeks. He mopped at them clumsily with a huge white handkerchief.

A few minutes later he got up to answer questions. Most men would have been unable, on such an occasion, not to throw a flash of drama into their

[1] Marian Holmes diary, 18 January 1944: Marian Walker Spicer papers.

[2] Colville diary, 18 January 1944: Colville papers.

[3] Prime Minister's Personal Telegram, T.76/4, Prime Minister to President, No. 547, 'Personal and Most Secret', 18 January 1944: Churchill papers, 20/154.

replies. But Winston answered them as if he were the youngest Under-Secretary, putting on his glasses, turning over his papers, responding tactfully to supplementaries, and taking the whole thing as conscientiously as could be. I should like to say that he seemed completely restored to health. But he looked pale when the first flush of pleasure had subsided, and his voice was not quite so vigorous as it had been.

Later in his letter, Nicolson wrote:

Tommy Lascelles told me that when that morning Winston had been to see the King, he (Tommy) had met him at the Palace door. Tommy asked after his health. 'I'm quite all right,' said Winston, 'quite all right. Only I'm a little groggy still on my pins.' 'Would you like the lift?' asked Tommy. 'Lift?' said Winston—and ran up the stairs two at a time. When he reached the top, he turned round to Tommy and cocked a snook.[1]

Both Yugoslavia and Japan were the subjects of Churchill's enquiries on January 19. 'We ought to assert domination of the Dalmatian coast,' he minuted to the Chiefs of Staff Committee that day. 'It is within easy reach of our commanding Air Force in Italy.' After the Anzio landings, it 'ought to be easy to organize a circus of, say 2,000 commando men and a dozen or so light tanks, and go round and clean up every single island the Germans have occupied, killing or capturing their garrisons. A plan should be made for this which we could consider and then present to the Supreme Commander for his consideration. Pray let work be begun upon this at once.' Churchill added: 'We are letting the whole of this Dalmatian coast be sealed off from us by an enemy who has neither the command of the air nor the sea. How can he garrison the islands in any strength to resist a concentrated attack?'[2]

When the Chiefs of Staff Committee met on the afternoon of January 19, Churchill, who presided, favoured the opening of 'the maximum possible threat' on the Mediterranean coastline 'between Genoa and the Spanish Frontier', using for this purpose such amphibious resources as were available after strengthening 'Overlord'. At the same time, he said, a successful Anzio landing 'would give us an opportunity of deploying large forces in Northern Italy and, perhaps, forcing the Germans to withdraw behind the Alps'. It would then be 'open to us', he declared, 'to turn left into France, or to pursue the Germans towards Vienna, or to turn right towards the Balkans'.[3]

[1] Letter of 18 January 1944: Nigel Nicolson (editor), *op. cit.*, pages 344–6.
[2] Prime Minister's Personal Minute, D.4 of 1944, 'Most Secret', 19 January 1944: Churchill papers, 20/152.
[3] Staff Conference, Chiefs of Staff Committee No. 16 (Operations) of 1944, 19 January 1944: Cabinet papers, 79/69.

On January 19 a British Corps under Lieutenant-General Philip Christison began its advance down the Arakan coast of Burma. Also planning to be in action later on, Mountbatten had reported to Churchill two days earlier, were Wingate's troops, 'in fine fettle and eager for the fray'.[1]

At a meeting of the Defence Committee on the night of January 19, to discuss future strategy in the war against Japan, Churchill stated his strong preference for a substantial British operation in northern Sumatra, Operation 'Culverin', as opposed to a British contribution to the naval war in the Pacific. If the United States Chiefs of Staff required the presence of British naval forces in the Pacific, he said, 'they would, of course, be provided' as had been agreed at the Cairo Conference. But it appeared that this would then preclude offensive action 'of any consequence' by the British in the Indian Ocean. 'He was dismayed at the thought that a large British army and airforce would stand inactive in India during the whole of 1944.'[2]

Returning from this meeting of the Defence Committee, Churchill told Colville that 'his heart was giving him trouble'. Colville added: 'He ascribed it to indigestion, but evidently he must now go warily.'[3]

On January 20 Alexander reported to Churchill from Italy that the Fifth Army offensive was 'in full swing', that a bridgehead had been established across the Garigliano river, and that offensive operations were developing from it. At the same time, all preparations for the Anzio landing were 'complete'.[4]

On the morning of January 20 Churchill had his first meeting with the London Poles since his return from Teheran and Marrakesh, and his discussions with Stalin about Poland. The three Poles present were the Prime Minister, Stanislaw Mikolajczyk, the Foreign Minister, Tadeusz Romer, and the Ambassador in London, Edward Raczynski. Eden and Cadogan were also present. 'PM gave it them hot and strong, poor dears,' Cadogan noted in his diary, 'but that's right.'[5]

The meeting began with Churchill asking the Polish Government 'to accept in principle' the Russian proposal regarding the Curzon Line, it being 'clearly understood' that that would leave Lvov in Russia, and 'to take the compensation offered them' in East Prussia,

[1] SC/45, 'Personal and Private', Delhi, 17 January 1944: Churchill papers, 20/154.
[2] War Cabinet Defence Committee (Operations) No. 3 of 1944, 19 January 1944: Cabinet papers, 69/6.
[3] Colville diary, 19 January 1944: Colville papers.
[4] MA/1019, IZ 469, 'Personal', 20 January 1944: Churchill papers, 20/154.
[5] Cadogan diary, 20 January 1944: David Dilks (editor), op. cit., page 598.

Danzig, Pomerania, up to the Oder Line and in Upper Silesia. He asked the Polish Government 'not only to accept this in principle but with enthusiasm'. He quite understood that 'that would be particularly hard for them, but, as a friend of their country, he was convinced that this was the best that they could hope to obtain. Personally, he thought it offered a fair solution. Poland would obtain valuable territory in exchange for a region including the Pripet Marshes, which could be of little value to them. It would cast on Poland the responsibility of rendering great service to the future of Europe: they would be the guardians of Europe against Germany on the east and that would ensure a friendly Russia.' Moreover, Churchill told the Poles, 'the territory which they would then possess would enable Poland to live as a strong and independent State.'

'If it were said that the Polish move to the west would bring them in conflict with Germany,' Churchill continued, 'his answer would be that the United Nations would see to it that all unwanted Germans would be removed from the territory transferred to Poland, and that Germany herself would be disarmed and mutilated to an extent that would render it impossible for her to commit any further aggression against Poland.' It was 'unthinkable' that Britain should go to war with the Soviet Union over the Polish eastern frontier, 'and the United States would certainly never do so'. After all, Churchill argued, Britain 'never entered the war for the eastern frontiers of Poland, and it was useless to imagine that we could embark on a conflict with Russia on that issue'. He was making these remarks to the Polish Prime Minister in private conversation, but 'he would not hesitate if necessary to repeat them in public'.

Mikolajczyk, in reply, said that the Polish Government by their last declaration had meant to make it plain 'that they regarded the question of frontiers as open for discussion'. Churchill 'admitted this', and went on to observe 'that the subsequent Soviet rejoinder was of a harsh nature'. If a 'settlement could be reached', Churchill added, then in his view it should be 'agreed' by Britain, the United States and the Soviet Union, the Three Great Powers, 'and defended by them'.

Churchill agreed with Mikolajczyk that the frontier changes envisaged would certainly involve large transfers of population, 'but he was bound to say that he thought they afforded the best hope to Poland'. After 'generations of servitude' Poland had been given her freedom at the end of the last war. 'Now she had again been brutally overrun, but he felt that there was a chance now of setting up an independent Poland in a compact territory with an ample seaboard. It would not be necessary for the Polish frontier to be pushed farther west towards the Oder than the Poles desired, but on their western frontier the Poles would have the high duty of standing guard against future German aggression with the guarantee of the three Great Powers.' It 'must be remembered', Churchill added, 'that the Russians had certain rights in the matter, having lost in this war and the last perhaps as many as 20 million men. Britain alone could never have restored Poland to independence. It was the Russian army that had made possible the rebuilding of a strong and independent Poland.'

Churchill then told the Poles that Britain 'felt we had the right to ask of Poland this great service of defending Europe against German eastward expansion; that was the way in which the Polish Government should put it to their people, rather than representing it as a surrender'. He felt that there was 'not much room' for negotiation; if Poland received the Curzon Line on the one hand and compensation in the north and west on the other, 'it would be a good escape from the present dilemma'.

Churchill then asked the Poles to consider 'what, after all, was the alternative?' Under the present proposals it might well be that a Pole in Lvov would have to be transferred to Oppeln, 'and that no doubt might involve inconvenience and disturbances'. But that would 'surely be better for them than to wait while the Russian army rolled on and leave their ultimate fate to the decision of the Soviet Government'. It would be much better to transfer Poland westward, 'as it were', even though that meant encroachment on what was now German territory. The Great Powers would 'see to it' that Germany after the war 'would be in no position to take revenge on her neighbour'.

Mikolajczyk replied that he 'quite realized' the strength of Churchill's arguments, but he must emphasize another point, which was that 'the proposals under consideration would expose Poland to very serious real losses in the shape of mines, oilfields, forests, agricultural land, etc. His position would be impossible unless he could tell the Polish nation that Poland would emerge from the war undiminished'.

Churchill replied that he proposed to send a telegram to Stalin 'informing the latter of what he had just said to the Polish Prime Minister, and telling him that that would be the attitude of His Majesty's Government at any Peace Conference'. He hoped that Mikolajczyk might enable him to say that the Poles were willing to discuss in principle on the basis of the Curzon Line 'on the understanding that Poland would receive compensation in the west'. He would in that event 'protest strongly against the Soviet tendency to call in question the authority of the Polish Government recognized by His Majesty's Government. The attempt to undermine another Government was inadmissible. One or more members of the Polish

Government might not be to the Soviet liking, but no Government had the right to dictate to another concerning its composition.'

If negotiations on these lines could be opened, Churchill told Mikolajczyk, he hoped diplomatic relations might be resumed. Mikolajczyk 'would have to take the risk and incur the odium of saying to his people that he thought this was the right course'. These questions, Churchill added, were better reserved for settlement at the Peace Conference. 'But it must be remembered that the Russian armies were pressing forward, and if nothing was done it was difficult to know what situation might face us. If, on the other hand, an agreement could be reached now the situation could be held.'

Mikolajczyk replied that he 'fully realized' all this, but he had to state his own difficulties. He was ready to accept the fact that a change of frontier was inevitable, but there were two great difficulties in the cession of Vilna and Lvov. As regards Vilna, Churchill pointed out that Britain had opposed its award to Poland at the last peace settlement, and that as regards Lvov, 'though that might be a Polish city, it must be admitted that the surrounding country was not predominantly Polish'. It must also be remembered that under these proposals Poland would receive as compensation in East Prussia Danzig, Silesia and Oppeln.

Mikolajczyk then referred to the Soviet Government's apparent desire to interfere in Polish internal affairs. From this he deduced that the Soviets 'really wished to incorporate Poland in the Soviet Union'. That, Churchill observed, 'would be an argument for reaching a settlement now: if the matter were delayed that might be indeed the ultimate result', and he reminded Mikolajczyk that he had already said that he would press Stalin in this point of dealing with the Polish Government in London.

At the end of their discussion, Churchill told Mikolajczyk that 'all these matters must be dealt with very urgently; if not, we might be overtaken by events which would be difficult to remedy'. He hoped Mikolajczyk would give him 'as full a contribution as possible which he could use in his telegram to Marshal Stalin. He fully understood that this would be difficult, but he hoped that in this critical moment M. Mikolajczyk would be equal to the occasion.' [1]

As Churchill had warned Mikolajczyk, that 'occasion' was being created by military facts. For more than three weeks, the Red Army had been advancing westward, liberating from the German yoke the towns and villages of pre-war Poland which, under the Teheran and

---

[1] 'Agreed record of a conversation between M. Mikolajczyk, Mr Romer, Count Raczynski, Mr Churchill, Mr Eden and Sir Alexander Cadogan. . . .', London, 20 January 1944: *Documents on Polish-Soviet Relations*, volume 2, London 1967, document No. 83, pages 144–9.

Marrakesh maps, were to become a part of post-war Russia. The western Allies had no equivalent military presence: their only foothold in Europe was in southern Italy. Even in Italy they did not have the momentum which the Red Army had created by such supreme effort and weight of numbers in the east. The Anglo-American plans for Italy had, moreover, no political implications, beyond the establishment of a non-Fascist Government in Italy. The battle in Italy, in as much as it could affect the wider issues, would do so only by drawing men and aircraft away from the eastern front, and making the advance of the Red Army that much quicker. It was to this end, as much as any other, that the Anzio landing had been planned: to liberate Rome, and to help Russia.

The Anzio landing was made on the morning of January 21. 'We have launched the big attack,' Churchill telegraphed to Stalin that afternoon, 'against the German armies defending Rome which I told you about at Teheran. The weather conditions seem favourable. I hope to have good news for you before long.'[1]

The landing itself began in the early hours of January 22. 'We have made a good start,' Alexander telegraphed to Churchill at nine o'clock that morning. 'We have obtained practically the whole of our bridgehead and most of the divisional supporting weapons will be ashore tonight I hope.'[2] By midnight, 36,000 Allied troops and 3,000 vehicles were ashore. 'All your good news augurs well for impending climax,' Churchill telegraphed to Alexander on January 23. 'I presume Eighth Army is holding everything pinned on its own front, even at some cost.'[3]

During January 23, while awaiting the outcome of the Anzio landings, Churchill's thoughts were also with the future cross-Channel landing, now scarcely four months distant. That day he gave instructions for a committee to be set up, to meet weekly, with himself in the Chair, to keep the preparations for 'Overlord' 'under constant survey'.[4] On January 24, he held a Staff Conference on one of the main features of 'Overlord' preparations, the artificial breakwaters, code name 'Gooseberry', which were to be towed across the Channel to the landing grounds. He had been 'disturbed', Churchill told the meeting, by recent reports, and 'feared some of the projects were lagging behind schedule'. He also directed that a 'census' should be taken of all tugs of 600 horse-power or over. Everyone concerned,

---

[1] Prime Minister's Personal Telegram, T.92/4, 'Secret, Operational', No. 160 from Foreign Office to Moscow, 21 January 1944: Churchill papers, 20/154.

[2] MA/1026, 'Most Secret and Personal', 22 January 1944: Churchill papers, 20/155.

[3] Prime Minister's Personal Telegram, T.116/4, 'Personal and Most Secret', 23 January 1944: Churchill papers, 20/155.

[4] Prime Minister's Personal Minute (to Ismay and Bridges), D 6/4, 23 January 1944: Cabinet papers, 21/1512.

Churchill said, 'should press on with the study and implementation of plans for all the projects under review', and be prepared to report again in 'greater detail' in a week's time'.[1]

Henceforth, a Committee was to meet each week with Churchill in the Chair, the task of which, as Churchill informed the War Cabinet, was 'to speed up and stimulate "Overlord" preparations in all aspects other than tactical and strategic', and to 'review and adjust their impact on war programmes and on the civil life of the community'.[2] Whatever the problems, Ismay later recalled, 'the Chairman's fiery energy and undisputed authority dominated the proceedings'. Everything, he added, 'had to be done at once, if not sooner; the seemingly slothful or obstructive were tongue-lashed; competing differences were reconciled; priorities were settled; difficulties which at first appeared insuperable were overcome; and decisions were translated into immediate action'.[3]

Churchill's sense of priorities was seen again at the Staff Conference of January 31, the last Staff Conference before the coming into effect of the 'Overlord' Committee, when he said that while it would be 'wrong' to jeopardize the operation by using too few ships, 'it would be equally wrong to use more than the minimum necessary in view of the very severe strain on all our resources'.[4]

As Churchill awaited the news from Anzio, he had news of a more personal nature, telegraphing to Stalin: 'Brigadier Maclean and my son Randolph have safely parachuted into Tito's headquarters.'[5]

On January 23, Alexander telegraphed to Churchill that the build-up at Anzio was 'proceeding satisfactorily', with further reinforcements expected to land on the following evening. 'I have stressed the importance,' Alexander added, 'of strong-hitting, mobile patrols being boldly pushed out to gain contact with the enemy, but so far have not received reports of their activities.'[6] 'Thank you for all your messages,' Churchill replied. 'Am very glad you are pegging out claims rather than digging in beach-head.'[7]

[1] War Cabinet Chiefs of Staff Committee, Staff Conference, 'Most Secret', 24 January 1944: Churchill papers, 4/333.
[2] War Cabinet Paper No. 68 of 1944, 'Secret', 31 January 1944: Churchill papers, 23/13.
[3] Ismay memoirs, op. cit., page 345.
[4] War Cabinet, Chiefs of Staff Committee, No. 29(0) of 1944, Staff Conference, 31 January 1944: Churchill papers, 4/333.
[5] Prime Minister's Personal Telegram, T.130A/4, 'Most Secret and Personal', Foreign Office No. 192 to Moscow, 24 January 1944: Churchill papers, 20/155. This telegram was 'endorsed' by the War Cabinet at six o'clock that evening: War Cabinet No. 10 of 1944, 24 January 1944: Cabinet papers, 65/41.
[6] MA 1028, IZ 548, 7.40 p.m. 23 January 1944: Churchill papers, 20/155.
[7] Prime Minister's Personal Telegram, T.128/3, OZ 409, 5.25 a.m., 24 January 1944: Churchill papers, 20/155.

'On late duty,' Colville noted in his diary on the night of January 24. 'The operations in Italy monopolized attention.'[1] 'My impressions are,' Alexander telegraphed to Churchill on January 25, 'that the enemy are still in process of concentrating units to hold us but are not yet in a position to launch any serious counter attack.'[2] 'I am thinking of your great battle night and day,' Churchill replied on January 26.[3]

From Anzio itself, the news was not hopeful. 'French and 2nd US Corps,' General Wilson reported on January 26, 'after meeting heavy resistance are renewing advance first light tomorrow directed on Mount Castellone.'[4] 'I have no fresh divisions in reserve out of the line,' Alexander warned half an hour later, 'except New Zealand division which I am keeping in GHQ reserve for final throw.'[5]

On January 27 General Wilson reported to Churchill that British and United States troops were only 'one mile short' of Cisterna and Campoleone.[6] There was another warning note from Alexander, however, who telegraphed that same day that he was 'not satisfied with speed of our advance'.[7] That evening, at the Other Club, Churchill spoke about the Anzio battle to his journalist friend Colin Coote, who noted:

About the new landing he said, 'It hasn't succeeded yet, the battle hasn't happened yet. But we are ahead of schedule in landing stuff and we ought to win when the battle comes. We have more men, more guns, more armour and complete air mastery.'

He was greatly impressed with the fighting on the Garigliano and the Rapido. Again and again he said, 'The Germans are fighting magnificently. Never imagine they are crashing. Their staff work is brilliantly flexible. They improvise units out of unrested remnants and those units fight just as well as the fresh ones. I don't know how the Russians have beaten the main German armies if they are all like the German army in Italy. Of course, we like to think the Germans in Italy are their crack troops but I am not so sure.'

Churchill also spoke to Coote about the Allied troops in Italy. Coote noted:

About the Allied troops in Italy he said, 'There is no shirking. Everyone was mad keen on this new operation. The Americans are fighting very

[1] Colville diary, 24 January 1944: Colville papers.
[2] MA/1032, 'Most Secret and Personal', IZ 595, 25 January 1944: Churchill papers, 20/155.
[3] Prime Minister's Personal Telegram, T.139/4, 26 January 1944: Churchill papers, 20/183.
[4] Unnumbered, sent 6.30 p.m., 26 January 1944, 'Strictly Personal': Churchill papers, 20/155.
[5] 'Special Unnumbered signal', 'Most Secret', 'Strictly Personal', sent 6.55 p.m., 26 January 1944: Churchill papers, 20/155.
[6] 'Received through "C's" Channel', 27 January 1944: Churchill papers, 20/155.
[7] MA/1037, 'Most Secret and Personal', IZ 655, 27 January 1944: Churchill papers, 20/155.

bravely and their 3rd division in particular are first-class troops. General Clark is first-class.' He was insistent on the fact that casualties were beginning to be heavy. 'British and American blood is flowing in great volume.' The Americans lost a third of a division when they were driven back over the Rapido last week.

He said the French, about a quarter of whom were white troops, were fighting extremely well. They had endured 4,000 casualties without flinching. This was a lot for two divisions. General Juin was showing all the traditional French military skill, and his (Winston's) heart was warmed by the proof of French military recovery.[1]

One of Churchill's main concerns that evening was Poland. For several days he had been working with Eden and the Foreign Office on the message he had promised to Stalin about the Polish frontier, and his own negotiations with the Polish leaders in London. 'There seems to be very little doubt,' he had minuted to Eden and Cadogan on January 26, 'that the Polish Government is willing to consider the cession of territory mentioned to me by them on the basis of equivalent compensations and suitable guarantees.'[2] At a meeting of the War Cabinet on the previous day, Churchill had warned that if no settlement was reached between Russia and Poland, 'we had to face the fact that when the Russians reached Warsaw they would probably set up a Polish Government, based on a plebiscite, having every aspect of democratic and popular foundation, and in full accord with the Russian view'. 'Nor,' Churchill added, 'ought we to ignore the fact that only Russian sacrifice and victories held out any prospect of the reconstruction of a Free Poland.'[3]

Colin Coote's account of Churchill's remarks on the evening of January 27 included his concerns about Poland:

About the Russo-Polish business, he exclaimed, 'If only I could dine with Stalin once a week, there would be no trouble at all. We get on like a house on fire.' The Americans have been silly to expose themselves to a rebuff by proferring their 'good offices'. We had not made that mistake. We were quietly doing our best to patch things up with the full realisation that what the Russians wanted would have to happen, but that what they wanted was, on the whole, moderate. The Poles had been very foolish about the Katyn graves. The Russian investigations into this matter might or might not be convincing, but that was of no practical importance.

[1] 'Memo by Mr Colin Coote. Other Club, 27th January 1944': Camrose papers. Four days later Churchill telegraphed to de Gaulle and Giraud: 'Accept my compliments on the magnificent way in which your troops are fighting in the present battle. It is a comfort to have strong French Army formations alongside British & Americans in the line. It reminds us of old times, and is the herald of new times'. (Prime Minister's Personal Telegram, T.184/4, No. 117 to Algiers, 31 January 1944: Churchill papers, 20/155.)

[2] Prime Minister's Personal Minute, M.32/4, 26 January 1944: Churchill papers, 20/152.

[3] War Cabinet No. 11 of 1944, 25 January 1944, Confidential annex: Cabinet papers, 65/45.

'I gathered,' Coote added, 'that this matter was not going very well.' [1]

Churchill finally telegraphed to Stalin on January 28 that he had advised the Polish Government 'to accept the Curzon Line as a basis for discussion'. But he also had words of caution for the Soviet Union. While 'everyone would agree', he wrote, 'that Soviet Russia has the right to recognize or refuse recognition to any foreign Government, do you not agree that to advocate changes within a foreign Government comes near to that interference with internal sovereignty to which you and I have expressed ourselves as opposed?' Churchill added: 'I may mention that this view is strongly held by His Majesty's Government,' and he went on with a clear warning of the dangers that lay ahead, as the 'successful advance' of the Soviet Army continued. The creation in Warsaw, he wrote, 'of another Polish Government different from the one we have recognised up to the present, together with disturbances in Poland, would raise issues in Great Britain and the United States detrimental to that close accord between the three Great Powers upon which the future of the world depends.'

'I should like myself to know from you,' Churchill added, 'what steps you would be prepared to take to help us all to resolve this serious problem. You could certainly count on our good offices, for what they are worth.' [2] Two days later, there was evidence of these 'good offices' when, in asking Eden about the Katyn Forest massacre, Churchill explained: 'All this is merely to ascertain the facts, because we should none of us ever speak a word of it.' [3]

Anglo-Soviet relations had reached a turning point: Britain was prepared to urge the Poles to accept Stalin's concept of what the Polish-Soviet frontiers should be, but was not prepared to endorse a Soviet sponsored or Soviet controlled Government in Poland. Churchill was thus presented with the need to act simultaneously against the deepest wishes of both Stalin and Mikolajczyk, while seeking to reconcile their differences. From January 1944 until January 1945 he faithfully pursued this exhausting task, seeking to reconcile what in the end proved to be the irreconcilable, as, from day to day, Soviet troops liberated more and more Polish soil, and the Polish Government in London struggled to assert demands from a basis of dwindling power.

With so many concerns, Churchill had few moments for relaxation.

---

[1] 'Memo. by Mr Colin Coote. Other Club, 27th January 1944': Camrose papers.

[2] Prime Minister's Personal Telegram, T.163/4, No. 227 to Moscow, 'Most Secret and Personal', 28 January 1944: Churchill papers, 20/183.

[3] Prime Minister's Personal Minute, M.51/4, 30 January 1944: Premier papers, 3/353, folio 82. On receiving a detailed report of the Katyn massacre from Sir Owen O'Malley, Churchill informed his Private Office: 'This should be circulated to the War Cabinet Ministers only, in a box, from hand to hand.' (Minute of 3 March 1944: Premier papers, 3/353, folio 81.)

One such moment occurred during the weekend beginning on Friday January 28, at Chequers. 'After-dinner film "The Nelson Touch",' Marian Holmes noted in her diary on the Friday night, and she added: 'PM did little work. He was in a reminiscent mood. With John Peck, Tommy Thompson and me as audience, he talked about his early life. As a young subaltern in India, he found himself often at a loss to understand references in conversation. He decided to be better informed. He began to spend after-lunch siesta time lying on his charpoy reading, beginning with Gibbon's "Decline and Fall" and Macaulay's Essays and on through the classics. He talked about polo being the other great occupation of his life then.'[1]

On the Saturday Churchill drove to Blenheim Palace for lunch, returning to Chequers at 5.30 that afternoon. After a little dictation, and then dinner, there was another film, the 'new Deanna Durbin'.[2] On the Sunday, Churchill worked in bed all morning. 'Tried unsuccessfully', noted Marian Holmes, 'to induce the PM to take his medicine'.[3]

Churchill remained at Chequers on Monday January 31. Once more, Marian Holmes recorded the activities of the day: 'PM worked from bed all morning. Finally got my lunch at 2.40. PM was in marvellous spirits. John Peck, Elizabeth Layton, Tommy T. and I sat and dozed in the afternoon. Suddenly, the PM said we would go back to town & we got ready in a rush. PM joined us in the Gt. Hall, drank some whisky & soda and said it was "good as a stirrup cup".'[4]

It had become clear during January 27 that the Anzio landing had not achieved its purpose of surprise, with the main body of the army unable to link up with the bridgehead, and the bridgehead itself not expanding as initially planned. 'It will be unpleasant if you get sealed off there,' Churchill telegraphed to Alexander on January 28, 'and cannot advance from the south', and if the four divisions ashore at Anzio were unable to take Cisterna or Campoleone, or to break out of the bridgehead.[5] Cisterna, Alexander telegraphed to Churchill on January 31, was in his view 'a key point and essential for development of further operations'.[6] But it remained in German hands. 'The situ-

[1] Marian Holmes diary, 28 January 1944: Marian Walker Spicer papers.
[2] Marian Holmes diary, 29 January 1944: Marian Walker Spicer papers.
[3] Marian Holmes diary, 30 January 1944: Marian Walker Spicer papers.
[4] Marian Holmes diary, 31 January 1944: Marian Walker Spicer papers.
[5] Prime Minister's Personal Telegram, T.161/4, OZ 551, 'Personal and Most Secret', 28 January 1944: Churchill papers, 20/155.
[6] MA/1068, IZ 749, 'Personal and Most Secret', 31 January 1944: Churchill papers, 20/155.

ation as it now stands,' signalled Admiral Sir John Cunningham, 'bears little relation to the lightening thrust envisaged at Marrakesh. . . .'[1]

After the War Cabinet on January 31, Cadogan noted in his diary that Churchill was 'v despondent' about the landing. 'Said this had now become an American operation, with no punch in it.' The clinging to the beachhead at Anzio, Churchill added, was 'a bad prospect for this operation and a bad omen for greater operations later'.[2] 'In fact,' Churchill told Smuts a month later, 'instead of hurling a wild cat on to the shore all we got was a stranded whale and Suvla Bay over again.'[3]

A telegram from Alexander to Churchill on February 2 gave a gloomy picture. German resistance had increased, and was especially strong opposite the 3rd United States Division at Cisterna and the 1st British Division at Campoleone. No further offensive was possible until these points were captured. The 3rd Division had fought hard for Cisterna during the last two or three days. The men were tired and were still about a mile from the town. A brigade of the 1st Division was holding Campoleone railway station, but they were in a very long and narrow salient and were being shot at 'by everything from three sides'. Alexander ended, however, in hopeful vein. 'We shall presently be in a position,' he wrote, 'to carry out a properly co-ordinated thrust in full strength to achieve our object of cutting the enemy's main line of supply to 14 Corps, for which I have ordered plans to be prepared.'[4]

On February 3 the Germans launched an offensive against the Anzio beachhead, at the very moment when Churchill had to consider the long-term problem of an American proposal to transfer fighter aircraft from the Mediterranean to China, on the assumption of reverting to what Maitland Wilson had called a 'purely defensive' front in Italy.[5] Such an assumption, Churchill told the Chiefs of Staff Committee, 'is I think disastrous' and he went on to explain: 'I never

[1] At Marrakesh, on the morning of 25 December 1943, Sir John Cunningham had been present, with Eisenhower, Maitland Wilson, Alexander and Tedder, at a conference presided over by Churchill, at which the Anzio landing had been discussed in detail, as a prelude to the capture of Rome and the destruction of 'a substantial part' of the German forces in Italy (see pages 620–2).

[2] Cadogan diary, 31 January 1944: David Dilks (editor), op. cit., pages 601–2.

[3] Prime Minister's Personal Telegram, T.413/4, 'Strictly Secret and Personal, For Your Eyes Alone', 27 February 1944: Churchill papers, 20/158. Two days later Churchill told the Chiefs of Staff: 'We hoped to land a wild cat that would tear out the bowels of the Boche. Instead we have stranded a vast whale with its tail flopping about in the water!' (Brooke diary, 29 February 1944: Bryant, op. cit., volume 2, pages 159–60.) Churchill was referring to the summer of 1915, when British troops had landed unopposed on the plain north of the Gallipoli bridgehead, but where the Generals had failed to take advantage of their initial success, and instead of advancing, had dug in, giving the Turks two days in which to bring up adequate reinforcements.

[4] MA 1069, 'Most Secret and Personal', IZ 796, 2 February 1944: Churchill papers, 20/155.

[5] Telegram IZ 794, 46308, 2 February 1944: Churchill papers, 20/152.

imagined that Alexander would not be free to push on to the north and break into the Po Valley.'

The Americans should be pressed 'most strongly' not to withdraw 'any air forces' from the Mediterranean to China. If they did so, Churchill told the Chiefs of Staff, 'we should replace those forces from home', where the 4,000 British and American fighters constituted an 'overwhelming' force for 'Overlord'. To bring the armies in Italy 'to a standstill', Churchill argued, 'would be most short-sighted and would simply enable the enemy to transfer divisions rapidly from North Italy to oppose the "Overlord" landing'.[1]

In order to help 'Overlord', Churchill had considered, both at Marrakesh and in London, the arming of French resistance forces. He had discussed this in detail with one of its strongest advocates, General d'Astier de la Vigerie, de Gaulle's Minister of the Interior. Their first talk was at a meeting at 10 Downing Street on January 27, to which d'Astier de la Vigerie was invited, together with Sir Archibald Sinclair, Sir Charles Portal, Lord Selborne, Ismay, Desmond Morton, and two experts on clandestine activities.[2] If the 'bands of patriots' now in the Maquis were not armed, de la Vigerie warned those present, 'there was danger of their disappearnce'. At present they were killing two Germans to every one of their own number who was killed, 'but they could not go on much longer without help'. They were subject to attack, he added, 'not only by the German occupying forces in France, but by those French elements who had been seduced by the Germans to do their handiwork'.

In urging Portal to make as many aircraft as possible available to supply the French resistance, Churchill told the meeting that he 'wished and believed it possible to bring about a situation in the whole area between the Rhone and the Italian Frontier and between the Lake of Geneva and the Mediterranean comparable to the situation in Yugoslavia'. Churchill added: 'Brave and desperate men could cause the most acute embarrassment to the enemy and it was right that we should do all in our power to foster and stimulate so valuable an aid to Allied strategy.'[3]

After his second talk with de la Vigerie, Churchill explained to Roosevelt:

This is a remarkable man of the Scarlet Pimpernel type and fairly fresh from France, which he has revisited three or four times. He has made very

---

[1] Prime Minister's Personal Minute, D.31/4, 'Most Secret', 3 February 1944: Churchill papers, 20/152.

[2] These were both members of SOE, H. Sporborg and Brigadier E. E. Mockler-Ferryman.

[3] 'Minutes of a Meeting held at No. 10 Downing Street, SW1, at 3. p.m., on Thursday, 27th January 1944', 'Most Secret': Premier papers, 3/185/1.

strong appeals to me to drop more arms by air for their resistance movements. I hope to be able to do more in February. He says that in Haute Savoie, south of Geneva between Grenoble and the Italian frontier, he has over 20,000 men all desperate, but only one in five has any weapon. If more weapons were available, very large numbers more would take to the mountains. As you know, I am most anxious to see a guerrilla à la Tito started up in Savoy and the Alpes Maritimes.[1]

'I want extra efforts made,' Churchill minuted to the Minister of Economic Warfare, Lord Selborne, on February 2, 'to improvise additional sorties to the Maquis on nights when conditions are favourable.' The supplies dropped in March should be 'double' those planned for February. 'I am told,' Churchill wrote, 'that the stocks of ammunition in the Maquis are far below what is reasonable, even for the few weapons they possess.' De La Vigerie 'has also asked me to send in some concentrated food and vitamins'. Churchill's minute ended: 'You should consult with the French about all this and arrange to pack accordingly your containers to be dropped in March.'[2]

One area in which Britain could help the French resistance was in the proposed operation 'Caliph', an idea put forward by Churchill to land 5,000 commandos at Bordeaux twenty or thirty days after D Day, 'when everyone is all out'.

The Joint Planning Staff had discussed operation 'Caliph' on the evening of February 1. Bordeaux, they noted on February 2, 'lies about 40 miles up a river which has quite heavy defences at its mouth'. A detailed examination of the whole coastline had been made eighteen months earlier, 'and it is a very unpromising area in which to attempt to capture a reasonable size port'. Nor could shipping and army administrative units be found for 'Caliph' except 'at the expense of Italy and "Anvil" '. The Joint Planning Staff concluded, in their note of February 2, that 'Caliph' could only be carried out 'if "Anvil" is cancelled'.[3] Churchill was disappointed by this conclusion. 'Some rapid dictation from the PM,' Marian Holmes noted in her diary. 'Somehow today he looks 10 years older.'[4]

Churchill returned to his advocacy of 'Caliph' on February 3, when he minuted to the Chiefs of Staff Committee that such a landing should be possible as the German air forces 'would all have been drawn in to the northward'. Such a force, he believed, 'let loose in the south and centre of France would instantly arouse widespread revolt and would

[1] Prime Minister's Personal Telegram, T.176/4, Prime Minister to President, No. 559, 'Personal and Most Secret', 30 January 1944: Churchill papers, 20/155.

[2] Prime Minister's Personal Minute, D.62/4, 'Most Secret', 2 February 1944: Premier papers, 3/185/1.

[3] Brief No. 382, 'Most Secret', 2 February 1944: Defence papers, 2/120.

[4] Marian Holmes diary, 2 February 1944: Marian Walker Spicer papers.

be of measureless assistance to the main battle'.[1] Instead of the American plan to put an extra division into the south of France landing, it would be 'far better', Churchill told Ismay, to devote any such extra forces to the Bordeaux landing, as this 'affords an opportunity for the French to come in behind our armour'.[2]

At Chequers, Churchill saw General Donovan, head of the United States Office of Strategic Services, who had just arrived from the Anzio beachhead. 'Operationally they have great courage,' Churchill remarked that weekend, 'administratively none.'[3] From General Wilson, Churchill learned that although, in the first phase of the battle, the American commander of the beachhead, General Lucas, had achieved complete surprise, he had failed to 'take advantage of it'.[4] 'The battle in Italy has not gone as I had hoped or planned,' Churchill telegraphed to Stalin on February 8. 'Although the landing was a brilliant piece of work and achieved complete surprise,' he explained, 'the advantage was lost and now it is a question of hard slogging.' The Germans had, however, Churchill pointed out, 'brought five additional divisions to the south of Rome', so that a total of seventeen German divisions were being 'actively engaged' on the Italian front. 'We have good hopes of a satisfactory outcome,' Churchill added, 'and anyhow the front will be kept aflame from now on.'[5]

'All this has been a disappointment to me,' Churchill telegraphed to Field Marshal Dill on February 8. 'Nevertheless,' he added:

... it is a great advantage that the enemy should come in strength and fight in South Italy, thus being drawn far from other battlefields. Moreover, we have a great need to keep continually engaging them, and even a battle of attrition is better than standing by and watching the Russians fight. We should also learn a good many lessons about how not to do it which will be valuable in 'Overlord'.[6]

---

[1] Prime Minister's Personal Minute, D.28/4, 'Most Secret', 2 February 1944: Cabinet papers, 119/3.

[2] Prime Minister's Personal Minute, D.34/4, 5 February 1944: Churchill papers, 20/152.

[3] Colville diary, 5 February 1944: Colville papers.

[4] 'Special Un-numbered signal from Algiers', 'Most Secret and Private', 5 February 1944: Churchill papers, 20/156.

[5] Prime Minister's Personal Telegram, T.255/4, 'Personal and Most Secret', 8 February 1944: Churchill papers, 20/156.

[6] Prime Minister's Personal Telegram, T.256/4, OZ 709, 'Personal and Most Secret', 8 February 1944: Churchill papers, 20/156.

39

The Polish and Italian Stalemates

O N 3 February 1944 news reached London that two towns in
eastern Poland, Rovno and Lutsk, had both been liberated by
Soviet troops.[1] At a meeting of the Defence Committee that day,
Churchill stated that it was 'a matter of high public importance' for
the Air Staff to give greater assistance to resistance movements in
occupied Europe, 'even at some small expense to the other responsibilities of the Royal Air Force'. Treble the existing allocation of
aircraft for Poland, he said, should be accorded. 'An extra 12 aircraft
for Poland at this stage might make a considerable difference,' he
said, and he went on to explain: 'Now that the Russians were
advancing into Poland it was in our interest that Poland should be
strong and well-supported. Were she weak and overrun by the
advancing Soviet armies, the result might hold great dangers in the
future for the English speaking peoples.'[2]

On February 5 it was again the Polish question which thrust itself
forward, when Stalin replied to Churchill demanding the exclusion of
'pro-fascist imperialist elements' from the Polish Government, and the
inclusion of 'people of a democratic turn of mind'. Stalin added: 'I
remember, by the way, that in May last year you wrote to me that
the composition of the Polish Government could be improved and
that you would busy yourself in this direction. At that time you did
not think that this would be interference in the internal sovereignty of
Poland.'[3] Stalin's telegram crossed with one from Churchill to Sir
Archibald Clark Kerr in Moscow, stating that on receipt of Stalin's

[1] Both towns are in the Volhynia, one of the easternmost regions of inter-war Poland. The
Polish spellings are Równe and Łuck.

[2] War Cabinet, Defence Committee (Operational), No. 4 of 1944, 3 February 1944: Cabinet
papers, 96/6.

[3] 'Personal and Most Secret', Prime Minister to President No. 566, 5 February 1944: Foreign
Office papers, 954/20, folios 42–4.

telegram 'I will see Mikolajczyk and try my best to get him to remodel his Government and drop all talk of Riga'—the Polish-Soviet Treaty of Riga of 1921 which had established Poland's inter-war eastern frontier. If the Poles did not agree, Churchill added, he would propose a direct Anglo-Soviet 'understanding' on the Polish settlement. 'In other words,' Churchill explained, 'we would make the best bargain we could for our unreasonable clients and let the clients know that if at the proper time they do not accept it we would withdraw from the case.' Churchill also wanted Stalin to know that the Polish Division in England which was preparing for 'Overlord' had shown 'a most sensible attitude' and was 'very steady behind Mikolajczyk', and that another Polish division 'had already entered the line against the Germans in Italy'.[1]

Also on February 5, Churchill reported to Roosevelt on the interview between Clark Kerr and Stalin, which made Churchill feel 'more hopeful than I have yet been' about the Polish question. In answer to Churchill's questions about the future Polish Government:

U.J. replied that of course Poland would be free and independent and he would not attempt to influence the kind of Government they cared to set up after the war. If Poland wished to ask for a guarantee she would get it. She could count upon all the help she needed in expelling the Germans. All Poles would be free to move out of the regions to be assigned to Russia and he would ask for the same freedom on behalf of the Ukrainians now west of the Curzon Line. The Poles need have no anxiety about their position when Poland west of the Curzon Line was occupied by the Red Armies. Of course the Polish Government would be allowed to go back and to establish the broadbased kind of Government they had in mind. Poland was their country and they were free to return to it.

The 'greatest inducement' to Mikolajczyk, Churchill added, would be 'the possiblity of his going back to Warsaw after the advance of the Russian armies to the westward had passed it, and being able to constitute there a Polish Government and State'.[2]

On Sunday, February 6, the Polish Prime Minister, Stanislaw Mikolajczyk, went to Chequers with his Foreign Minister, Tadeusz Romer and the Polish Ambassador to London, Count Edward Raczynski, for their second discussion of the Polish frontier question in three weeks. On the British side, with Churchill, were Eden, Lord Cherwell and Sir Owen O'Malley, the British Ambassador to the Polish Government. Their task was to reach agreement on the text of

---

[1] Prime Minister's Personal Telegram, T.220/4, 'Personal and Most Secret', 5 February 1944: Churchill papers, 20/156.
[2] Prime Minister's Personal Telegram. T.216/4, 5 February 1944: Churchill papers, 20/183.

another message from Churchill to Stalin, in which Britain would try at the same time both to satisfy Stalin's demands and safeguard the needs of the Polish Government.

At the start of the meeting, Churchill asked the Poles 'to work on the basis that the US, Britain and the USSR would co-operate for many years to come in the task of maintaining world order and unity'. Eden then read out two telegrams from Clark Kerr, sent three days earlier, in which he pointed out that Stalin, in answer to Churchill's message of January 28, had stated 'without hesitation' that, after the war, 'Poland would certainly be free and independent, as much so as Czechoslovakia, and he would not try to influence either country's choice of government'. Stalin had also told the British Ambassador that the Polish Government in London 'would be allowed to return to Poland and establish a broad-based Government, which could function administratively in the liberated areas'.

Mikolajczyk then noted that in reply to an appeal which he had made to the Polish underground movement on January 6, he had received a message, dated January 19, 'saying that the partisans realized the difficulties of the position and desired to establish good neighbourly relations with Russia, but that they stood firm by the Polish eastern frontier as fixed by the Treaty of Riga and demanded that the Soviet troops occupying eastern Poland should respect the sovereign rights of the Polish state'. This, Mikolajczyk thought, would be the 'predominant note' in any message sent from Poland in reply to Churchill's present proposals.

Information from 'Communist circles in Warsaw', said Mikolajczyk, was of preparations to establish a Committee of National Liberation. If 'matters were allowed to drift', Churchill warned, 'such a Committee would undoubtedly be established and the Polish Government would have no say in the matter'. It was 'no use', Churchill told Mikolajczyk, talking of 'negotiating about frontiers'. The Curzon Line was 'the best that the Poles could expect and all that he would ask the British people to demand on their behalf'.

Mikolajczyk then asked about those parts of Poland that had been a part of Austria-Hungary before 1914, and not specifically referred to by the Curzon Line: this was the region of which Lvov was the capital. The Russians, Churchill replied, 'must have Lvov'. The Poles would retain Przemysl. Mikolajczyk was 'sceptical' however, of Stalin's assurances to Clark Kerr, remarking that he suspected that the Russians 'were purposely trying to make the Polish Government refuse their terms in advance'.

Churchill persevered in his line of argument, commenting that 'had not the Russians won great victories, Poland would have no future at all'. He would 'do his utmost for Poland, but if he could not reach agreement with the Polish Government, he would have to make his own position clear to the Russians and to come to an understanding with them'. For this 'he would take full responsibility before Parliament and the world'.

There were three courses open, Churchill said: an agreement 'in which all parties joined', an Anglo-Russian agreement 'in which he would endeavour to settle the frontier problem and to procure humane treatment for the Poles', and 'To do nothing, while the Russian steamroller moved over Poland, a communist Government was set up in Warsaw and the present Polish Government was left powerless to do anything but make its protests to the world at large'.

Mikolajczyk reverted yet again to the territorial aspect, telling Churchill and Eden: 'He could not publicly announce that he would accept the Curzon Line.' In that case, Churchill replied, 'he must look at the matter from the British point of view and make his own agreement with Stalin'. He must 'say frankly', Churchill added, 'that, while the Polish troops over here had made themselves both loved and respected, the people of Poland had been unable to maintain their independence throughout the centuries, and even during their short period of freedom, had not had a record of which they could be proud. Now they had a fine opportunity if they were prepared to take it. If they were not, he would certainly make the agreement without them.'

When Eden then pressed Mikolajczyk to agree at least to say that he would be prepared to negotiate 'on the basis' of the Curzon Line, Mikolajczyk replied that 'while it might look as if only the frontier line were in question, he was convinced that his Government were in reality defending the independence of Poland itself'. The Polish Government, Churchill retorted, had 'no power' to defend the areas east of the Curzon Line, and he went on: 'It was arguable whether they had a moral right, since, after the last war, Poland had occupied Vilna by an act of war against the wishes of the Allied Governments. On the other hand, the Russians, in view of the blood they had shed, had a moral right to the security of their western frontiers.'

Churchill then told the Poles that Stalin had 'demanded' Königsberg 'and the part of East Prussia lying to the east of it'. This, commented Mikolajczyk, 'showed that the Russian scale of demands was increasing and would increase'. They had started asking for the Curzon Line, 'then for a change in the Polish Government, and now for half of East Prussia'. But Churchill was not impressed by this line of argument, telling the Poles that 'Poland had taken many wrong turns in her history and that a refusal now might be the most

fatal and disastrous of all'. If the Poles rejected Stalin's offer of negotiations on the basis of the Curzon Line as Poland's eastern frontier,
'he would certainly explain their views' to the Soviet Government,
but he would also 'state the British view', and make a separate
agreement with the Russians. If, in making this agreement, the
Soviet Government 'should refuse to guarantee Poland her rights,
her independence and adequate territory, he would certainly resist'.
But he would not 'exert the strength of Britain for Poland's exact
frontiers; he was struggling for the life of the Polish nation and for
a home for the Polish people'. These, Churchill added, 'were the
great objectives'.

The meeting was coming to an end. He was 'very grateful' to
Churchill 'for all he had done', Mikolajczyk declared, but he could
not go so far as Churchill proposed 'without abandoning Poland's
moral right and losing the support of his people'.[1] The final topic was
a Polish request for arms to the Polish Underground Army 'in view of
the general rising against the Germans, the time of which was approaching'. When Churchill replied that the British Government had
already decided 'to treble for the next three months the load to be
carried to Poland by air', Mikolajczyk 'expressed his thanks for this
decision'.[2]

At the War Cabinet the following afternoon of February 7,
Churchill told his colleagues 'that it might well prove beyond the
powers' of the Polish Government to agree 'at the present time' to the
frontier settlement proposed. What Britain might do, he suggested,
was to say to the Russians 'that we regarded a settlement on the basis
of the Curzon Line as reasonable, and would support their claims to
such a frontier at the Peace Conference'.[3]

'Eden and I had a long day with the Poles on Sunday,' Churchill
telegraphed to Stalin on February 8, 'and are working hard. In two
or three days I will report to you further.'[4] It was 'clear', Churchill
minuted to Eden on the following day, 'that unless we can speedily
get a settlement with Russia in which they are included, the disintegrating forces inside Poland will bring everything to confusion,
out of which only the Russian-fostered Communist element will

[1] 'Record of a meeting held at Chequers on Sunday, February 6th, 1944, at 3 p.m.': Foreign
Office papers, 954/20, folios 54–9.
[2] 'Notes on the conversation between Mikolajczyk and Mr Churchill at Chequers. . . .', 6
February 1944, record 'agreed by both parties': *Documents on Polish-Soviet Relations*, volume 2,
London 1967, document No. 96, pages 165–71. Also Premier papers 3/472.
[3] War Cabinet No. 16 of 1944, 7 February 1944, Confidential Annex: Cabinet papers,
65/45.
[4] Prime Minister's Personal Telegram, T.255/4, 'Personal and Most Secret', 8 February 1944:
Churchill papers, 20/156.

emerge as a Russian Puppet Government. *Now*, in these days, may be their last chance of remaining a factor in Polish affairs.' 'Failing this,' Churchill added, 'it seems to me we should make an agreement with Russia about the Poles, assuring them of our support if reasonable terms are offered & observed.'[1]

Within the Foreign Office, Owen O'Malley protested that the British insistence that Poland accept the Curzon Line in return for British support for her independence was 'morally indefensible'. 'I do not agree with Ambassador O'Malley's suggestion,' Churchill minuted to Eden, 'that the proposals I have made are "morally indefensible", and I have given good reasons why. They are in my opinion no more than what is right and just for Russia, without whose prodigious exertions no vestige of Poland would remain free from German annihilation or subjugation.' The Curzon Line, Churchill pointed out, 'was considered a fair frontier for Poland on the East in 1920, apart altogether from the extra-ordinary compensations now offered to Poland at the expense of Germany'. Churchill's telegram to Stalin was, he said, 'aimed at securing a *modus vivendi* and the possibility of a reconstitution of the Polish State even during the war', and he added: 'I am certainly prepared to defend on their merits the proposals now made to Poland for a Polish National Home.'

In his protest, O'Malley had stressed the tyrannical nature of the Soviet regime. 'If of course,' Churchill commented, 'the view is adopted that Russia is going to present herself as a new Nazi Germany ideologically inverted, we shall have to make what head we can against another tyranny, and this would have to be borne in mind when considering the position which a chastened Germany would occupy. In any case I should not bring such matters to an issue on the question of the Curzon Line.' Churchill ended his minute: 'I notice that Sir Owen O'Malley quotes the Poles as declaring that this is "another Munich". Whatever may be said about this taunt, and there is much, it certainly does not lie in the mouths of the Poles, who jumped on the back of Czechoslovakia in that moment of agony and helped to rend her in pieces, to use such language to the representatives of this country which has so valiantly toiled, sword in hand, against wrongdoing, and will still fight against aggression with whatever strength is left it.'[2]

*   *   *

[1] Prime Minister's Personal Minute, M.89/4, 9 February 1944: Foreign Office papers, 371/39422, folio 134.

[2] Prime Minister's Personal Minute, M.117/4, 15 February 1944: Foreign Office papers, 954/20, folios 69/71.

In a brief moment of relaxation, on February 7 Churchill was among the guests at a private room in the Savoy at the twenty-first birthday party of Clementine Churchill's cousin Judy Montagu. 'There was an extremely good conjuror who appeared at the end of dinner,' Jock Colville noted, 'and whom the PM declared to be the best he had ever seen.'[1]

At the Chiefs of Staff meeting on February 7, Brooke spoke of the 'considerable merit' of a landing on the Atlantic coast of France, but did not feel that Bordeaux was 'a suitable port'; his preference was for a port further north than Bordeaux, one, for example, in the Brest peninsula, 'from which a thrust could be developed from an unexpected direction' against the German forces opposing 'Overlord'.[2]

On the afternoon and evening of February 8, Churchill was almost continuously in conference with General Brooke and his senior military advisers. Their first discussion was operation 'Caliph', the proposed landing at Bordeaux twenty or thirty days after the 'Overlord' D-Day.

At a Staff Conference that evening, Churchill presented what he called the 'attractions' of 'Caliph'. First, it made use of 'available forces which might not otherwise be employed'. Secondly, by mounting the operation from North West Africa, it avoided the passage through the Straits of Gibraltar, so that the force 'would reach its objective by an uninterrupted sea route where enemy observation would be difficult'. Thirdly, Churchill told the Chiefs of Staff, 'he envisaged the subsequent support of the operation by carriers and commandos from the United Kingdom'.

The French, Churchill told the Staff Conference, were 'pressing to be allowed to co-operate to as large an extent as possible in the liberation of France, and here was an opportunity'. He also felt, in regard to the British troops that would be available over and above the 'Overlord' and 'Anvil' landings, 'that no forces should be allowed to remain idle'. He was 'not necessarily wedded to the choice of Bordeaux as the place for the force to land', Churchill explained, but he did look to the 'low-lying territory' in that part of France.[3]

That night there was a second Staff Conference, with Attlee, Eden, Sinclair and Cripps present, at which the discussion was about the airborne forces available for 'Overlord'. The plan to land gliders in daylight, he thought, was 'an unnecessarily hazardous operation'. Brooke suggested that casualties to gliders and glider tugs might be

[1] Colville diary, 7 February 1944: Colville papers.
[2] Chiefs of Staff Committee No. 37 (Operations) of 1944, 7 February 1944: Cabinet papers, 79/70.
[3] Staff Conference, Chiefs of Staff Committee No. 39 (Operations) of 1944, 6 p.m., 8 February 1944: Cabinet papers, 79/70. Those present were Churchill (in the Chair), Brooke, Portal and Andrew Cunningham. The meeting was held at 10 Downing Street.

reduced if bombers were employed to escort them, and to bomb the German anti-aircraft defences during the time they were passing over them. 'No effort should be spared,' Churchill urged, 'to ensure that casualties were reduced to a minimum and, in particular, that the possibility of landing gliders in the dark should be examined.' [1]

On February 9, Churchill's late night dictation began at 12.45 a.m. and continued until 2.45 when Marian Holmes, the secretary to whom he did this particular night's dictation, told him that she was meant to be on duty on the following morning. He asked, 'working for me?' to which she replied, 'No. In the office.' He then told her: 'In that case you must be sure to sleep till noon,' and ringing the bell for Jock Colville, instructed him: 'She mustn't come on duty until lunchtime.' [2]

At a meeting of the Chiefs of Staff on the evening of February 9, concern was expressed at the 'divergence of thought between ourselves and the Americans' over the South of France landing, which Churchill and the British Chiefs of Staff now wished either to postpone, or to cancel altogether. At the meeting, Churchill spoke of the 'negative character' of Roosevelt's reply to a suggestion that the American Chiefs of Staff should come to London for a conference on 'Overlord' and 'Anvil'. Churchill also asked his Chiefs of Staff that, in the planning for 'Overlord', the lessons of the Anzio landing would be 'taken to heart', when, as he said, 'over 18,000 vehicles had already been crammed into the congested beachhead'. There was, he said, 'a strong tendency in all our plans to allow a large margin against accidents'. [3]

From Anzio itself the news continued to be distressing. On February 10 the 1st British Division was under such severe German attack that it was 'forced', as Alexander telegraphed to Churchill, 'to give some ground'. Alexander added that the Germans 'are fighting as hard and as bitterly as I have ever known them to'. [4] Churchill expressed his own concern in a telegram to Alexander that same day, mentioning 'how great a disappointment' had been caused in both Britain and the United States by the 'standstill' at Anzio. His telegram continued:

I do not of course know what orders were given to General Lucas, but it is a root principle to push out and form contact with the enemy. The spectacle

[1] Staff Conference, Chiefs of Staff Committee, 40th Meeting (Operations) of 1944, 10 p.m., 8 February 1944: Cabinet papers, 79/70. This meeting was held in the Cabinet War Room.

[2] Marian Holmes diary, 9 February 1944: Marian Walker Spicer papers. After Churchill had gone to bed that night, Marian Holmes continued typing out his dictation until five in the morning. She then slept, as instructed, until noon.

[3] Chiefs of Staff Committee No. 42 (Operations) of 1944, 10.15 p.m., 9 February 1944: Cabinet papers, 79/70.

[4] MA/1089, IZ 988, 'Most Secret and Personal', 10 February 1944: Churchill papers, 20/156.

of 18,000 vehicles accumulated ashore by the 14th day for only 70,000 men or less than 4 men to a vehicle including drivers and attendants, though they did not move more than 12 or 14 miles, is most astonishing. Moreover I gather we are still stronger than the enemy, and naturally one wonders why over 70,000 British and Americans should be hemmed in on the defensive by what are thought to be at most 60,000 Germans.

The ease with which the enemy moved their pieces about on the board and the rapidity with which they adjusted the perilous gaps they had to make on their southern front is most impressive. It all seems to give us very awkward data in regard to 'Overlord'.

The problem of Alexander's relationships with his subordinate American commanders was one which had troubled Churchill considerably. As he told Alexander in his telegram of February 10:

I have a feeling that you may have hesitated to assert your authority because you were dealing so largely with Americans and therefore urged an advance instead of ordering it. You are however quite entitled to give them orders, and I have it from the highest American authorities that it is their wish that their troops should receive direct orders. They say their Army has been framed more on Prussian lines than on the more smooth British lines, and that American Commanders expect to receive positive orders which they will immediately obey. Do not hesitate, therefore, to give orders just as you would to our own men. The Americans are very good to work with and quite prepared to take the rough with the smooth.

Churchill went on to tell Alexander that if he was not 'satisfied' with leaving General Lucas in command at the bridgehead, 'you should put someone there whom you can trust'.[1] Amongst American Corps Commanders, Alexander replied, Lucas 'is probably their best', but he added that 'all American higher Commanders lack the years of practical battle experience we have had and this is an undoubted weakness when it comes to fighting difficult battles against veterans'.[2] It had been decided in Washington to ask one of the American Generals in Italy to enquire into who should be sacked for the hesitations of the Americans on the bridgehead. 'When I suggested that Clark might be the man to ask,' Dill informed Churchill on February 9, 'Marshall said Clark might be the man to go.'[3]

⁕   ⁕   ⁕

[1] Prime Minister's Personal Telegram, T.284/4, 'Personal and Most Secret', 'To be sent through "C",,' 10 February 1944: Churchill papers, 20/156.

[2] 'Special Unnumbered', 'Most Secret', 'Strictly Personal', received 12 February 1944: Churchill papers, 20/157.

[3] FMD/119, 'Private', 9 February 1944: Churchill papers, 20/156. In the event it was General Lucas who was replaced, by General Truscott, 'a young American Divisional Commander, whom everyone speaks of most highly' (Churchill to Smuts, Prime Minister's Personal Telegram, T.413/4, 27 February 1944: Churchill papers, 20/158).

In mid-February Roosevelt informed Churchill of possible peace overtures from Bulgaria, and asked if, while 'conversations' opened in Istanbul, the Anglo-American bombing of Bulgaria could be suspended 'for a limited period'.[1] After discussing this suggestion with Eden, Churchill replied that they were both agreed that the bombing of Bulgarian targets 'should not be stopped'. Churchill added: 'If the medicine has done good, let them have more of it.'[2] On the following day, February 12, Churchill warned Roosevelt against any 'conversations' with the Bulgarians in Istanbul. 'If the Bulgarian Government really mean business,' he wrote, 'they should be told to send a fully qualified mission to meet representatives of the three Powers,' possibly in Cairo or Cyprus. At the same time, Soviet agreement 'to our proposed line of action' should be secured.[3]

Churchill did not allow such peace talk to deflect his concerns for the impending cross-Channel landings, about which he had no illusions. 'The war in Europe might last longer than some people in this country thought,' Churchill told a Staff Conference on February 14. 'We might be involved in heavy operations on the continent in the coming autumn.'[4]

In the Far East, American forces were invading the Japanese-held atoll of Kwajalein in the Marshall Islands. Among the Marines killed during the assault was an 18-year-old private, Stephen P. Hopkins, one of the three sons of Harry Hopkins. 'Dear Harry,' Churchill and his wife telegraphed on February 13, 'please accept our most profound sympathy with you in your hour of grief.'[5] Of Hopkins himself, Churchill wrote to Roosevelt: 'He is an indomitable spirit. I cannot help feeling very anxious about his frail body and another operation. I shall always be grateful for any news about him, for I rate him high among the Paladins.'[6]

Beginning on February 15, the Allied forces in Italy, desperate to link up with the Anzio bridgehead, sought to break through the

---

[1] President to Prime Minister No. 463, 'Personal and Most Secret', 9 February 1944: Churchill papers, 20/156.

[2] Prime Minister's Personal Telegram T.280/4, Prime Minister to President, No. 575, 'Personal and Most Secret', 11 February 1944: Churchill papers, 20/156.

[3] Prime Minister's Personal Telegram, T.290/4, Prime Minister to President, No. 576, 'Personal and Most Secret', 12 February 1944: Churchill papers, 20/156.

[4] Staff Conference, Chiefs of Staff Committee No. 48 (Operations) of 1944, Cabinet War Room, 10 p.m., 14 February 1944: Cabinet papers, 79/70.

[5] Prime Minister's Personal Telegram, T.300/4, Prime Minister to President, No. 578, 'Personal', 13 February 1944: Churchill papers, 20/156.

[6] Prime Minister's Personal Telegram, T.299/4, Prime Minister to President, No. 577, 'Personal and Most Secret', 13 February 1944: Churchill papers, 20/156.

German positions at Monte Cassino. But after three days of intense fighting, many casualties, and fierce air bombardment, the monastery heights were still in German hands. On February 16 the Germans launched their make-or-break counter attack on the Anzio bridgehead. As a result of the Enigma decrypts, the scale and direction of the counter-attack was known accurately, and well enough in advance, to be effectively checked, and then repulsed.[1]

That same morning, in the House of Commons, Churchill answered an 'inspired question', as Colville described it, about British casualties in Italy, 'so as to give some ammunition for countering the American view that American troops are doing all the fighting'. Colville added: 'Actually it is the unenterprising behaviour of the American Command at Anzio that has lost us our great opportunity there.'[2] A week later, on learning that the bridgehead army, in which there were over 50,000 British troops, was called the '6th United States Corps', Churchill minuted to Brooke: 'This really is a shame, and greatly increases the need for calling it either "The Sixth Allied Army" or "The Bridgehead Army".' Churchill added: 'I cannot agree that this term "The 6th United States Corps" should continue, as it is most unfair to our troops who have lost three men to four American in the fighting.'[3]

On the afternoon of February 16, as bitter fighting continued at Anzio and Monte Cassino, Churchill held his third meeting with the Polish Government, to discuss Poland's future frontiers. Two days earlier he had told the War Cabinet that the Poles were apparently 'hankering' after a line intermediate between the Curzon Line and the Riga Line, 'which there was no chance that Stalin would accept'.[4] At the War Cabinet on February 15, when the subject arose yet again, Ernest Bevin had asked whether Churchill could 'press' Stalin to agree to a boundary line which would leave Lvov inside Poland. But Churchill had replied that there was 'no chance' of Stalin accepting it, 'and that, on balance, it was inadvisable to make the suggestion'.[5]

On February 16, Churchill, Eden, Cadogan and O'Malley met

---

[1] F. H. Hinsley and others, *British Intelligence in the Second World War*, op. cit., volume 3, Part 1, pages 190–3. Also known from Enigma were the German efforts to reinforce the Dalmatian Coast. '"Boniface" reports have been received that the islands off the Dalmatian Coast are being equipped with naval guns', Churchill telegraphed to Maitland Wilson. 'All this points to the urgency of your organising the Commando Operations about which I have telegraphed to you.' (Prime Minister's Personal Telegram, T.304/4, 13 February 1944: Churchill papers, 20/183.)

[2] Colville diary, 16 February 1944: Colville papers. The question was asked by Patrick Buchan-Hepburn, Churchill's former Political Secretary (in 1929). The figure given by Churchill, for British, Dominion and Indian casualties in Italy since the landings of 3 September 1943 and 12 February 1944, were 7,635 killed, 23,283 wounded, and 5,708 missing. He made no reference to American or other casualties. (*Hansard*, 16 February 1944, columns 175–6.)

[3] Prime Minister's Personal Minute, M.163/4, 23 February 1944: Churchill papers, 20/152.

[4] War Cabinet No. 20 of 1944, 14 February 1944, Confidential Annex: Cabinet papers, 65/45.

[5] War Cabinet No. 21 of 1944, 15 February 1944, Confidential Annex: Cabinet papers, 65/45.

Mikolajczyk, Romer and Raczynski at 10 Downing Street. It was not only Lvov in the south, but also Vilna in the north, which the Poles insisted upon keeping as a part of Poland. Commenting on this, Churchill pointed out that it would be 'quite impossible' for the Poles to retain Vilna 'in view of the incorporation of Lithuania in the Soviet Union'.[1] When Mikolajczyk complained that with the Soviet Union at Königsberg, Poland 'would not only be encircled, but fully controlled by Russia', Churchill was not convinced. On the same analogy, he said, 'the British south coast ports could be controlled from France'. What hope was there 'in any case', he asked, 'that Poland could resist Russia unless she had the aid of other countries. Poland would in any case have to live within gunshot of the Russians.'

Once more Churchill reiterated the British position, that if no agreement was reached between Poland and Russia soon, the Russians, advancing rapidly, would set up a 'puppet government' in Poland. They would hold a plebiscite, he warned, 'under which the opponents of Soviet plans would be unable to vote'. The Polish Government, still in London, would have no influence on events. 'Poland would then be little more than a grievance and a vast echoing cry of pain.'

If the Curzon Line frontier proposals were rejected, Churchill declared, and no arrangement made between the Polish Government and Stalin, the Poles 'would have no place of their own to live in, no compensation from the broken power to the West and no agreement'. He added, of the prospect now of a 'homogeneous home' for Poland, by agreement with Russia:

The Poles might say they did not trust the Russians. If the Russians did in fact prove untrustworthy it would indeed be a bad prospect for all the world but worst of all for the Poles. Britain would always do her best against tyranny in whatever form it showed itself. But Britain, though better situated, was not much bigger than Poland. We would do our best, but this would not save Poland. The Prime Minister had heard talk of a second Munich. No Pole should say this because the Poles had participated in the pillage of Czechoslovakia. The Prime Minister also felt quite differently towards our foe Germany and towards Russia, without whose armies there would have been no means of re-creating a Polish state. After 1940 Britain would have held on, keeping the seas and bombarding Germany, if necessary for years, but Poland would have been gradually liquidated.

If the Polish Government were to accept the Curzon Line, sign an agreement with Stalin, and return to Warsaw, 'they would be

[1] Vilna (Wilno, Vilnius) had been the Lithuanian capital from 1918 to 1920, when it had been seized by Polish forces and incorporated into Poland. In 1939 it reverted to Lithuania, which was itself annexed by the Soviet Union in 1940. From 1941 to 1944, when under German occupation, Vilna was the scene of the murder of tens of thousands of Jews. Since 1945 the city has been the capital of the Lithuanian Soviet Socialist Republic of the Soviet Union.

protected', Churchill said, 'by the goodwill of the Allies and if they were seriously ill-treated by the Russians this would be most offensive to all the Allies'. Their 'best hope' lay in going back, in 're-assembling the elements of the Polish nation and ensuring their support'.

It was Eden who reminded the Poles that the Russians were 'already across or near' to the demarcation line which the Polish Government were now asking for 'so far to the east'.

Churchill now urged that the Polish Government put its case into Britain's hands, and that the Poles agree to allow the eastern regions which Stalin wished to annex to be seen as 'a military zone for war purposes', to be occupied by Russia 'to safeguard the lives of their people and to ensure co-operation with the Russians against Germany'. The Poles would 'still be free' to put forward arguments in regard to Vilna and Lvov 'later on'. The Polish Government should also agree to a 'broad-based' government being set up in Warsaw. On these terms, Churchill would seek a settlement with Stalin which would enable the Polish Government to return to Warsaw. 'The Russian word might be hard,' Churchill explained, 'but he had not, in his experience, known them to go back on the letter of their word.' He had, however, to reach 'some arrangement' with Stalin 'before the Russians occupied Poland'. Churchill added:

Poland had no chance of getting out of the German grip without the Russians. British and American strength was mainly in the sea and in the air, and in financial and other resources. He doubted whether the United States would be ready to go on fighting in Europe for several years to liberate Warsaw. It was no use expecting us to do more than we could.

Churchill then warned Mikolajczyk that Europe could not be plunged into 'endless wars' arising out of the intermingling of ten million people of different races: the races of Russia, Poland and Germany would have to be 'disentangled' as had been done in the Graeco-Turkish exchange of population in 1922.[1] Churchill 'pressed' the Polish Government to accept his proposals, and let him send them to Stalin 'with their goodwill'. His remarks continued, as he addressed himself with passion to the three Polish representatives:

[1] Following the Treaty of Lausanne (1 April 1924) between Greece and Turkey, a population exchange was carried out. 'By an extraordinary series of provisions,' Churchill wrote in his First World War memoirs, 'all the Greek inhabitants of Turkey, and a still large but smaller number of Turkish inhabitants of Greece, were reciprocally combed out and transported to their natural sovereignties. Turkey lost a great mass of citizens who had for centuries played a vital part in the economic life of every Turkish village and township. Greece, impoverished and downcast, received an accession of nearly one and a quarter million refugees who, under the pressure of misfortune and privation, have already become a new element of national strength.' (Winston S. Churchill, *The World Crisis: The Aftermath*, London 1929, page 438.)

His heart bled for them, but the brutal facts could not be overlooked. He could no more stop the Russian advance than stop the tide coming in. It was no use saying something which would only make the Russians more angry and drive them to the solution of a puppet Government in Warsaw. He did not wish to rush the Poles and if they wished for forty-eight hours to consider his new draft, well and good. But he hoped they could reply by tomorrow night and that any suggestions they might have to make would be on practical lines. If the Russians then refused, the Poles would lose nothing, if they accepted, the Poles would gain a lot.

In reply, Mikolajczyk said that the Poles 'saw no practical guarantee in return for their concessions'. They had not been encouraged by a recent 'bad' article in *Pravda*. The 'broad based' Government which Churchill wanted them to accept was also a stumbling point.

The meeting of February 16 was coming to an end without an agreement. In the last moments, Churchill again appealed to the Poles to 'accept his advice and give him the most they could with which to reply to Marshal Stalin'. The minutes of the meeting recorded his final plea:

By his reference to establishing a broad based Government in Poland (which M. Mikolajczyk had questioned) the Prime Minister had not of course meant that the Polish Government would at once reform their Government according to Russian wishes. He had merely thought that they would naturally wish to strengthen themselves by selecting elements from the whole population.

The Poles must rejoice at the advance of the Russian Armies, dangerous though this might be to them, since it was their only hope of liberation from the Germans. There was no reason to suppose that Russia would repeat the German desire to dominate all Europe. After the war Great Britain and the United States of America would maintain strong forces and there were good hopes of the world settling down into a peace of thirty or forty years which might then prove much more lasting.[1]

Throughout February 17 and February 18 the Foreign Office drafted and redrafted the British proposals to Stalin about Poland, seeking to evolve a formula acceptable to the Polish Government. By the afternoon of February 18, O'Malley, on whom the principal task devolved, had produced what Cadogan called 'an ingenious draft, which he thinks he can put across the Poles'.[2] 'We have been wrestling continuously with the Poles,' Churchill telegraphed to Stalin on February 18, 'and I am glad to say we have at last produced some

---

[1] 'Record of a Meeting held at 10 Downing Street on Wednesday, 16th February, 1944, at 5.30 p.m.', 'Most Secret': Foreign Office papers, 954/20, folios 74–7.

[2] Cadogan diary, 18 February 1944: David Dilks (editor), *op. cit.*, page 607.

15. With his daughter Mary at Quebec, August 1943; far left, Detective Inspector Thompson

16. With Clementine Churchill at Quebec, August 1943

17. Presenting the Sword of Stalingrad to Joseph Stalin, Teheran, 29 November 1943. Between them is Marshal Voroshilov. Far left, Eden. To the right, Stalin's interpreter, Pavlov, and Molotov. The sword was the gift of King George VI 'to the steel-hearted citizens of Stalingrad' (page 577)

18. Roosevelt, Churchill and Stalin, at Churchill's sixty-ninth birthday party, British Embassy, Teheran, 30 November 1943. Far right, Churchill's interpreter, Birse; bottom right, Anthony Eden. During the dinner Stalin told Churchill: 'England is getting pinker. It is a sign of good health' (pages 586–7)

19. Churchill, recuperating at Carthage, after giving a Christmas Day lunch to his visitors, 25 December 1943 (page 622). Front row: Eisenhower, Churchill and General Sir Henry Maitland Wilson. Back row (in uniform): Air Chief Marshal Sir Arthur Tedder, Admiral Sir John Cunningham, General Sir Harold Alexander, General Sir Humfrey Gale, Brigadier-General Leslie Hollis and General Bedell Smith

20. Returning home, January 1944, on board the battleship *King George V*. With Churchill is his daughter Sarah. The journey from Gibraltar to Plymouth took four days (pages 651–4)

21. Examining the damage to Kitchener's statue, 21 February 1944, after bombs had fallen on Horse Guards Parade. 'We have just had a stick of bombs around 10 Downing Street,' Churchill told Roosevelt, 'and there are no more windows . . .' (page 689)

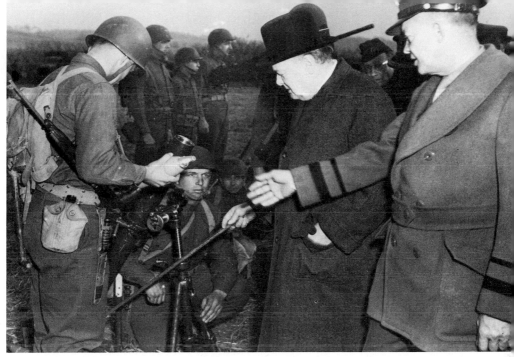

22. With Eisenhower, 23 March 1944, on a tour of inspection of United States troops in southern England, preparing for the Normandy landings. Churchill told the men of one unit: 'I thank God you are here, and from the bottom of my heart I wish you good fortune and success' (page 717)

23. Inspecting United States troops preparing for the Normandy landings. On his return to London, Churchill learned that General Wingate had been killed in Burma: 'This man of genius,' Churchill called him, 'who might well have been a man of destiny' (page 717)

24. Making the final preparations for the Normandy landings: General·
Brooke, General Eisenhower, Churchill and Air Chief Marshal Sir Arthur
Tedder

25. Churchill with General Montgomery, 12 June 1944, at the start of
Churchill's first visit to the Normandy beaches (pages 806–7)

26. Churchill returns to Normandy, 22 July 1944. With him are Lieutenant-General O'Connor, Field Marshal Smuts, General Montgomery and General Brooke. This photograph was taken just as a German aircraft flew overhead (page 860)

27. Churchill and Montgomery, with British troops near Caen, 22 July 1944

28. Churchill with General Ismay, awaiting the flying bombs at an anti-aircraft site south of London. 'Is there anything on the cards?' Churchill asked. There was not (pages 836–7)

results.' But he went on to warn Stalin 'that these proposals will very likely split the Polish Government'.[1]

Amid these Polish entanglements, Churchill was also troubled by domestic politics. After lunch on February 18 he learned that the Government candidate at West Derbyshire, Lord Hartington, a Major in the Coldstream Guards, had been defeated by the Independent Labour candidate, Charlie White, by 4,500 votes.[2] 'This caused a pall of blackest gloom to fall on the PM,' noted Colville, who went on to explain that Churchill was 'personally affected by this very emphatic blow to the government' in view of the letter which he had written to Hartington, 'in which he lauded the political record of the Cavendish family'.[3] Colville added that there had also been 'trouble' at Brighton two weeks earlier, when Churchill had written 'another long letter' to the Government candidate, who had 'only scraped home in the safest of Tory seats'.[4] That afternoon, Colville wrote:

Sitting in a chair in his study at the Annexe, the PM looked old, tired and very depressed and was even muttering about a General Election. Now, he said, with great events pending, was the time when national unity was essential: the question of annihilating great states had to be faced; it began to look as if democracy had not the persistence necessary to go through with it, however well it might have shewn its capacity of defence.[5]

In this pessimistic mood, Churchill went to Chequers for the weekend. There, he wrote to the Chiefs of Staff Committee to revive plans for operation 'Jupiter', the plan for a British landing in northern Norway. Here again his mood was sombre. 'In the event of "Overlord" not being successful,' he wrote, 'or Hitler accumulating forces there quite beyond our power to tackle, it would perhaps be necessary to adopt the flanking movements both in "Jupiter" and from Turkey and the Aegean in the winter of 1944/45.'[6]

Among the luncheon guests at Chequers on February 19 was Admiral Cooke of the United States Navy, who showed Churchill photographs of the American attack on the Kwajalein atoll. In describing the landing, and the naval contribution, Cooke stressed

[1] Prime Minister's Personal Telegram, T.334/4, 'Most Secret and Personal', 18 February 1944: Churchill papers, 20/157.

[2] In 1918 and again in 1922 White's father had been elected as a Liberal MP, but had been defeated by Lord Hartington's father in 1923. In 1938 White had stood unsuccessfully, as the Labour candidate. In 1945 he was re-elected as a Labour MP (with a majority of 156).

[3] Lord Hartington, defeated by 11,775 votes to 16,336, was killed in action in Belgium on 9 September 1944, four months after his marriage to Kathleen Kennedy, daughter of Joseph and brother of John, Robert and Edward Kennedy.

[4] So safe, indeed, that Teeling was re-elected in 1945 with a larger majority.

[5] Colville diary, 18 February 1944: Colville papers.

[6] Prime Minister's Personal Minute, D.49/4, 19 February 1944: Churchill papers, 20/152.

'the great value of short-range bombardment, at, say, 2,000 yards'. In telling Sir Andrew Cunningham of this on the following day, Churchill commented:

The beaches in our case will not be convenient for that, I presume. Nevertheless the greater the power that can be brought to bear the better. Here is the time to use the *Ramillies* class; and, as I have said, men can be taken off other ships in order to work up a bombardment for the actual event of the landing, after which they can return to their duties.

A meeting of the Defence Committee was set up for February 28, to discuss this naval aspect. In the event, a force of six battleships, two monitors and twenty-two cruisers, as well as many destroyers, two-thirds of them British, took part in the naval bombardment.

On February 20, while Churchill was still at Chequers, the Polish Government accepted the text of Churchill's 'message' to Stalin. In a covering note, Churchill explained to Stalin that the message had been seen by both Mikolajczyk and Romer, 'has been written in close consultation with them, and is despatched with their agreement'. Churchill added: 'I earnestly hope that it may be the means of reaching a working arrangement between Poland and Soviet Russia during the war, and that it may become the foundation of a lasting peace and friendship between the two countries as part of the general settlement of Europe.' [1]

The Polish Government was ready, Churchill explained in the message itself, to declare that the Riga Line, the Polish–Soviet border of 1921, 'no longer corresponds to realities' and was ready to discuss with the Soviet Government, 'as part of a general settlement, a new frontier between Poland and the Soviet Union, together with the future frontiers of Poland in the north and west'. As any public statement of this willingness would, however, 'immediately be repudiated' by 'a large part' of their people abroad, as well as by the Underground Movement in Poland 'with which they are in constant contact', any such settlement could only formally be agreed 'when the victorious Powers are gathered around the table at the time of an armistice or peace'. Meanwhile, the 'vigorous prosecution of the war' would be greatly assisted if the Soviet Government could 'facilitate the return of the Polish Government to the territory of liberated Poland at the earliest possible moment', followed by the establishment 'from time to time' of the 'civil administration' of the Polish Government 'in given districts'. The Polish Government, Churchill added, were 'naturally very

---

[1] Prime Minister's Personal Telegram, T.351 A/4, No. 458 to Moscow, 'Most Secret and Personal', 20 February 1944: Churchill papers, 20/157.

anxious' that these districts should include 'such places' as Vilna and
Lvov.

Churchill went on to tell Stalin that he had informed the Poles,
'and they clearly understand that you will not assent' to leaving Vilna
and Lvov 'under Polish administration'. He wished however to 'assure'
the Poles that the area to be placed under Polish civil administration
'will include at least all Poland west of the Curzon Line'. He had
already told them that Königsberg and part of East Prussia were to
become a part of Russia, and he told Stalin:

> The information came as a shock to the Polish Government, who see in
> such a decision a substantial reduction in the size and in economic importance
> of the German territory to be incorporated in Poland by way of compensation.
> But I stated that in the opinion of His Majesty's Government this was a
> rightful claim on the part of Russia.
> Regarding as I do this war against German aggression as all one and as a
> thirty years' war from 1914 onwards, I reminded M. Mikolajczyk of the fact
> that the soil of this part of East Prussia was dyed with Russian blood
> expended freely in the common cause. Here the Russian armies advancing in
> August 1914 and winning the battle of Gumbinnen and other actions had,
> with their forward thrusts and with much injury to their mobilization, forced
> the Germans to recall two Army Corps from the advance on Paris, which
> withdrawal was an essential part in the victory of the Marne. The disaster at
> Tannenberg did not in any way undo this great result. Therefore it seemed
> to me that the Russians had an historic and well-founded claim to this
> German territory.[1]

The Polish Government, Churchill continued, while unable to
admit 'any right of a foreign intervention' as far as its composition
was concerned, was willing to include 'none but persons fully determined to co-operate with the Soviet Union'. Such a Government,
Churchill commented, might be allowed to 'come about naturally',
and to await its 'formal' resumption of relations with the Soviet Union
'at the time of the liberation of Warsaw, when it would arise naturally
from the circumstances attending that glorious event'.

In accordance with the assurances 'I have received from you',
Churchill added, an agreement between Britain and the Soviet Union
could now contain an undertaking:

> . . . first to recognise and respect the sovereign independence and territorial
> integrity of the reconstituted Poland and the right of each to conduct its
> domestic affairs without interference;
> secondly, to do their best to secure in due course the incorporation in

---

[1] Churchill had written an account of the Russo-German struggle of 1914 in his book *The
Eastern Front*, first published in 1931, and re-issued in 1937 as *The Unknown War: the Eastern
Front*.

Poland of the Free City of Danzig, Oppeln Silesia, East Prussia west and south of a line running from Königsberg and of as much territory up to the Oder as the Polish Government see fit to accept;

thirdly, to effect the removal from Poland, including the German territories to be incorporated in Poland, of the German population; and fourthly, to negotiate the procedure for an exchange of population between Poland and the Soviet Union, and for the return to their mother-country of nationals of the Powers in question.

All these Anglo-Soviet undertakings 'on the part of Poland' should, Churchill told Stalin, be drawn up in such a form 'that they could be embodied in a single instrument or exchange of letters'. Churchill also informed Stalin that should such a settlement 'become a fact and be observed in the spirit by all parties to it', he had told the Polish Ministers that Britain would support that settlement 'at the conference after the defeat of Hitler', and would also 'guarantee that settlement in after years to the best of our ability'.[1]

This telegram, Churchill hastened to inform Roosevelt, had been 'textually agreed' with the Poles. 'You will see,' he added, 'that it achieves in essentials, without actually saying so, the settlement outlined at Teheran.'[2] For Stalin, however, the Churchill message was unsatisfactory and unacceptable. 'I saw Stalin tonight,' Sir Archibald Clark Kerr telegraphed to Churchill on February 28. 'It was not a pleasant talk. He attempted to dismiss with a snigger the position of the Polish Government as described in the Prime Minister's message.' When Clark Kerr pointed out to Stalin that the Polish Government had said that 'they would not disavow our action', Stalin remarked: 'Is that serious? How handsome of them!' The Polish Government, Stalin insisted, 'did not want a settlement'. He asked for two things 'only', the Curzon Line and the reconstruction of the Polish Government. He would 'not agree' that the Polish Government should not accept the Curzon Line 'now', or that the reconstruction of their Government 'should await their return to Warsaw'.

It was, the Ambassador commented, a 'dreary and exasperating conversation. No argument was of any avail.'[3] Churchill's initiative had failed. His pressures on the Poles had been in vain.

*   *   *

[1] Prime Minister's Personal Telegram, T.352/4, No. 459 to Moscow, 'Most Secret and Personal', 20 February 1944: Churchill papers, 20/157.

[2] Prime Minister's Personal Telegram, T.353/4, Prime Minister to President, No. 584, 'Personal and Most Secret', 20 February 1944: Churchill papers, 20/157.

[3] Telegram No. 557 from Moscow, 'Most Secret', sent at 11.32 p.m., 28 February 1944: Foreign Office papers, 954/20, folios 119–20; enclosed in Prime Minister's Personal Telegram, T.419/4, Prime Minister to President, No. 595, 'Personal and Secret', 29 February 1944: Churchill papers, 20/158.

On the night of February 20, twenty-five German bombers, flying over London, dropped one of their bombs in Whitehall and two on the Horse Guards Parade. 'We have just had a stick of bombs around 10 Downing Street,' Churchill telegraphed to Roosevelt on the following day, 'and there are no more windows. Clemmie and I were at Chequers and luckily all the servants were in the shelter.' But four people had been killed outside.[1]

On the morning of February 21, Churchill inspected the bomb damage: the crater in Horse Guards Parade, the shrapnel marks on Kitchener's statue, and the broken windows of Downing Street. A photographer, Captain Horton, recorded the scenes and the damage.[2]

While at Chequers, Churchill had prepared a survey of the war for the House of Commons, his first major speech on the war in five months: 'The PM told me it was a great effort to him to make these speeches now,' Jock Colville noted in his diary.[3] 'He is looking well again,' wrote Harold Nicolson after Churchill had spoken, 'but has a slight cough. He is not of course as vigorous or as pugnacious as in 1940. But he has no need to be. He is right to take the more sober tone of the elder statesman.'[4]

Churchill spoke for nearly an hour and twenty minutes, stressing the Anglo-American bombing of Germany as 'our chief offensive effort at the present time', and telling the House that 38,300 British pilots and aircrew had been killed and over 10,000 aircraft lost since the beginning of the war.[5] The most recent four raids, 'during the 48 hours beginning at 3 a.m. on 20th February', in which 9,000 tons of bombs had been dropped on Germany by British and American bombers, 'constitute the most violent attacks which have yet been made on Germany, and they also prove the value of saturation in every aspect of the air war'. Leipzig and Stuttgart had been the targets. The air offensive, he added, 'constitutes the foundation upon which our plans for overseas invasion stand', and he went on to tell the House:

[1] Prime Minister's Personal Telegram, T.355/4, Prime Minister to President, No. 586, 'Personal and Most Secret', 21 February 1944: Churchill papers, 20/157. Three days later Churchill wrote to Eisenhower (in inviting him to lunch): 'The windows have been repaired and the house is weather proofed after the bombing' (Letter of 24 February 1944: Churchill papers, 20/137).

[2] Photographs, and note by John Martin, 'PM. Attached are the photographs taken by Capt. Horton at No. 10 this morning,' 21 February 1944: John Martin papers.

[3] Colville diary, 22 February 1944: Colville papers.

[4] Nicolson diary, 22 February 1944: Nigel Nicolson (editor), op. cit., page 352.

[5] Churchill also gave the figure of 41,000 for the Royal Navy personnel killed since the outbreak of war.

This air power was the weapon which both the marauding States selected as their main tool of conquest. This was the sphere in which they were to triumph. This was the method by which the nations were to be subjugated to their rule. I shall not moralise further than to say that there is a strange, stern justice in the long swing of events.

During the course of his speech, Churchill referred to the British Government's decision to support Tito and not Mihailovic in Yugoslavia. Tito's partisans, he said, 'are the only people who are doing any effective fighting against the Germans now', and he told the House:

For a long time past, I have taken a particular interest in Marshal Tito's movement, and have tried, and am trying, by every available means, to bring him help. A young friend of mine, an Oxford don, Captain Deakin, now Lieut.-Colonel Deakin, D.S.O., entered Yugoslavia by parachute nearly a year ago and was for eight months at Marshal Tito's headquarters. On one occasion, both were wounded by the same bomb. They became friends. [Laughter.] Certainly, it is a bond between people, but a bond which, I trust, we shall not have to institute in our own personal relationships. From Colonel Deakin's reports we derived a lively picture of the whole struggle and its personalities. Last Autumn, we sent a larger Mission under the hon. and gallant Member for Lancaster (Brigadier Fitzroy Maclean). Having joined the Foreign Secretary and myself at Cairo to report, he has now re-entered Yugoslavia by parachute. I can assure the House that every effort in our power will be made to aid and sustain Marshal Tito and his gallant band.

Churchill made no reference to the fact that his son Randolph had been parachuted into Yugoslavia with Fitzroy Maclean. Nor of course could he mention that he had recently given instructions to prevent his exchange of messages with Maclean from being read by American Intelligence.[1]

In his speech, Churchill also described the battle in Italy, of which he said: 'On broad grounds of strategy, Hitler's decision to send into the south of Italy as many as eighteen divisions, involving, with their maintenance troops, probably something like half a million Germans, and to make a large secondary front in Italy, is not unwelcome to the Allies.' After all, Churchill added: 'We must fight the Germans somewhere, unless we are to stand still and watch the Russians.' The 'wearing' battle in Italy, he added, occupied German troops who, as a result,

[1] This was a recurring theme of Churchill's minutes at this time. Nor would he allow Maclean's Mission to be put under the Combined Chiefs of Staff. 'I do not wish the Combined Chiefs of Staff,' he minuted to Ismay on February 26, 'or the United States Chiefs of Staff, to sit in judgement on my telegrams or the Foreign Secretary's, to Brigadier Maclean.' (Prime Minister's Personal Minute, D.60/4, 26 February 1944: Churchill papers, 20/152.)

'could not be employed in other greater operations, and it is a prelude to them'.

During his speech, Churchill warned of future air attacks over Britain 'either by pilotless aircraft or possibly rockets, or both'. But he made it clear that Britain had 'long been watching this with the utmost vigilance' and was 'striking at all evidences of these preparations when the weather is suitable for such action and to the maximum extent possible without detracting from the strategic offensive against Germany'. This, though he did not say so, was Operation 'Crossbow'.

Speaking of Poland, Churchill told the House that it was 'reasonable and just' for Russia to have the Curzon Line, and for Poland to obtain 'compensation' from Germany in the north and west. At Teheran, he said, Stalin had assured him that he wanted 'a strong, integral, independent Poland as one of the leading powers of Europe'. Churchill also explained to the House the meaning of the phrase 'unconditional surrender', which had been much criticised for its harsh overtones. As Churchill explained:

Unconditional surrender means that the victors have a free hand. It does not mean that they are entitled to behave in a barbarous manner, nor that they wish to blot out Germany from among the nations of Europe. If we are bound, we are bound by our own consciences to civilisation. We are not to be bound to the Germans as a result of a bargain struck. That is the meaning of 'unconditional surrender'.

During the course of his speech, Churchill was critical of the internal political discussions in the House of Commons and elsewhere, referring to the 'little folk who frolic alongside the juggernaut of war to see what fun or notoriety they can extract from the proceedings'. The theme of his speech, and of his mood, had been clearly expressed in his opening words: 'This is no time for sorrow or rejoicing. It is a time for preparation, effort and resolve.' As to the future course of the war, he said, it had been agreed at Teheran 'to fall upon and smite the Hun by land, sea and air with all the strength that is in us during the coming Spring and Summer', and he ended his speech:

It is to this task that we must vow ourselves every day anew. It is to this ordeal that we must address our minds with all the moral fortitude we possess. The task is heavy, the toll is long and the trials will be severe. Let us all try our best to do our duty. Victory may not be so far away, and will certainly not be denied us in the end.[1]

On February 22 the British Chiefs of Staff met Eisenhower, to work out an agreed position on the relationship between Italy and

[1] Speech of 22 February 1944: *Hansard*, 22 February 1944, columns 679–700.

'Overlord', Eisenhower, as Ismay informed Churchill, 'representing the US Chiefs of Staff'. As a result of the agreement reached at this meeting, a telegram was sent to Washington 'in line', Ismay told Churchill, 'with the views which you yourself have expressed', ensuring 'that the Italian campaign has over-riding priority' while 'Overlord' would get 'all the extra landing craft that can be employed profitably'. At the same time, Ismay added, 'in deference to the US Chiefs of Staff', the telegram 'does not entirely close the door on "Anvil"'.[1]

Even as the planning for 'Overlord' went ahead, the future strategy of the war against Japan continued to be a source of contention. On February 25, at a midday meeting with the Chiefs of Staff, Churchill 'was still insisting', as General Brooke noted in his diary, 'on doing the North Sumatra operation and would not discuss any other'. According to the detailed minutes of the meeting, however, it is clear that Churchill's sense of urgency arose from his just having learned of the reported movement of major units of the Japanese Fleet to Singapore. To counter this, he said, Britain should concentrate 'as large a fleet as possible in the Indian Ocean', a move which would 'rule out for the time being' the despatch of major British naval units to the Pacific, where the Americans, he commented, 'appeared to be using steam hammer methods to crack nuts'.

Of the reported move of the Japanese Fleet to Singapore, Churchill commented: 'we could not ignore the menace which this Japanese fleet stationed at Singapore would constitute to the main supply routes from Great Britain to Australia, from the Cape to Australia and to our oil supplies in the Persian Gulf'. Britain 'could not take risks', Churchill warned, 'about the security of Ceylon, India and the trade routes in the Indian Ocean'. Nor could she 'ignore the possibility of a Japanese expedition to capture Ceylon'.[2]

That afternoon at three o'clock, when Eden, Oliver Lyttelton and Attlee were also present, together with several of Mountbatten's staff, 'The whole party were against the Chiefs of Staff,' Brooke noted, and he added: 'Thank God I have now got Andrew Cunningham to support me. It makes all the difference from the days of poor old Dudley Pound.'

Churchill told this meeting, as the minutes recorded, 'that we could not reach our final decision in this country at once. There was now a new factor of great significance. It appeared that the Japanese had

[1] Chiefs of Staff Committee No. 55 (Operations) of 1944, 22 February 1944, Annex 111, 23 February 1944: Cabinet papers, 79/70.
[2] 'Minute of a Meeting held in the Prime Minister's Map Room on Friday, 25th February, 1944 at 12 noon', 'Most Secret', Chiefs of Staff Committee No. 61 (Operations) of 1944, 'Secretary's Standard File': Cabinet papers, 79/89.

moved or were in process of moving the major part of their main fleet to Singapore. It was necessary to form an opinion as to the reasons which had led the Japanese to take this step.'

There were, Churchill pointed out, several possibilities. 'It might be that the move was a temporary one. It might be that rumours had reached the Japanese which led them to believe that we intended to attack Sumatra. The move may have been caused by consideration for Japanese public opinion. The spirit of the Japanese people was not likely to be improved by the sight of their main fleet lying idle in home waters while the American fleet was inflicting successive painful blows on Japan further south. The Japanese might even contemplate offensive action in the Bay of Bengal.'

One thing was 'certain', Churchill told the Chiefs of Staff, 'that was that so long as the Japanese Navy remained at Singapore, the "Culverin" operation could not be undertaken unless we could ourselves collect in the Bay of Bengal a sufficiently large fleet to enable us to do battle with the Japanese Fleet and defeat them. On the other hand, so long as the Japanese Fleet remained at Singapore, the position of the Americans in the Pacific was enormously improved, and he could not believe that in these circumstances the United States Navy would require assistance in the Pacific from the Royal Navy.'

All preparations for 'Culverin' should proceed, Churchill argued, 'on the basis of the Japanese Fleet leaving Singapore, and not being able to return there by the date of "Culverin"'. He was still 'convinced', Churchill added, 'that "Culverin" was the only operation which offered a prospect of employing, during the next 12 months, the large British forces available, in useful activity against the enemy'. Churchill ended his arguments in favour of 'Culverin' by telling the Chiefs of Staff Committee that:

In the first place, he believed that the Commanders and Staffs were overestimating the naval requirements for the operation. Secondly, the move of the Japanese Fleet had altered the strategic picture. Thirdly, there was a preference among the Staffs in this country for fighting the Japanese in the Pacific. It was, however, easy to find reasons against any operation, and he was not prepared, at this stage, to reach a final conclusion. It was essential that as strong a force as possible should be collected in the Bay of Bengal.[1]

That afternoon the discussion lasted for two and a half hours. 'I got very heated at times,' Brooke noted. 'Winston pretended that this was all a frame-up against his pet Sumatra operation and took it almost as a personal matter. . . .'

[1] Chiefs of Staff Committee No. 62 of 1944, 'Minutes of Meeting held in Prime Minister's Map Room on Friday, 25th February 1944 at 3 p.m.', 'Most Secret', 'Secretary's Standard File'; Cabinet papers, 79/89.

That evening Churchill telephoned Brooke and invited him to dinner. As Brooke noted in his diary:

I thought it was to tell me that he couldn't stick my disagreements any longer and proposed to sack me. On the contrary, we had a tête-à-tête dinner at which he was quite charming, as if he meant to make up for some of the rough passages of the day. He has astonishing sides to his character. We discussed Randolph, my son Tom, his daughters, my daughters, the President's unpleasant attitude lately, the fact that we may have to go to America soon, the Italian front, the air-raids etc.

After dinner there was a further Chiefs of Staff meeting, with Churchill in the Chair. 'PM in much more reasonable mood,' Brooke noted, 'and I think that a great deal of what we have been doing has soaked in. I hope so at least.'[1]

At this evening meeting on February 25, Churchill spoke of the Anglo-American proposal to put Britain's major effort, not in the Bay of Bengal, but in the Pacific. 'He saw inherent dangers in this policy,' Churchill told the Chiefs of Staff. 'It was not a nice prospect for us to tail along at the heels of the American fleet and when great victories had been won, to be told that all the credit was due to United States forces.' Churchill added: 'The idea of sending British forces to Australia was not attractive, particularly as the Australians had expressed the intention of only maintaining three divisions in the field—a very poor contribution.'

Churchill then set out what he saw as the scale of 'Culverin', explaining to the Chiefs of Staff:

His own idea was a kind of Anzio bridgehead in the tip of Sumatra to establish airfields from which we could control vital communications. If the arguments as between the Indian Ocean strategy and the Australia East to West strategy were evenly balanced, he felt that the Indian Ocean should not be lightly abandoned. He considered our policy should be to build up the Eastern Fleet as fast as possible and then to take a view as to the next step.[2]

Churchill's mention of Anzio arose not merely as a comparison, but because Anzio was also much on his mind. During this evening meeting he asked Brooke whether it might not be possible for Alexander to 'take charge of the bridgehead operations during the critical phase ahead'. Churchill also suggested 'that consideration should be given to the mounting of another amphibious operation with a view to relieving pressure on the bridgehead'. Brooke, somewhat angered

---

[1] Brooke diary, 25 February 1944: Bryant, *op. cit.*, volume 2, pages 155–6.
[2] President to Prime Minister, No. 480, 'Personal and Most Secret', 25 February 1944: Churchill papers, 20/157.

by both suggestions, 'undertook to examine' the proposal to put Alexander in charge of the bridgehead operations, and said, of the proposal for another amphibious operation, 'that all possibilities of this nature were being studied'. Nothing came of either suggestion.

Brooke's opposition to the Sumatra operation was shared by Roosevelt. 'I fail to see,' he telegraphed to Churchill on February 25, 'how an operation against Sumatra and Malaya, requiring tremendous resources and forces, can possibly be mounted until after the conclusion of the war in Europe.' For Roosevelt, the Anglo-American priority was on mainland Asia, 'a vigorous and immediate campaign' in Upper Burma.[1] Churchill deferred to Roosevelt's insistence. 'I have given the President a personal assurance,' he telegraphed to Mountbatten that same day, 'that you will not withdraw or withhold any forces from the campaign in Upper Burma for the sake of "Culverin" or any other amphibious operation.'[2] These assurances, Churchill assured Roosevelt, were 'most positive'. His telegram ended: 'How I wish we could have a talk.'[3]

In Italy, the troops at Anzio were still trapped on their bridgehead, while those at Monte Cassino could make no advance. Rome, which Churchill had hoped to see in Allied hands in January, remained a distant goal. On February 27 Churchill telegraphed to Smuts:

Naturally I am very disappointed at what has appeared to be the frittering away of a brilliant opening in which both fortune and design had played their part. I do not in any way however repent of what has been done. As a result the Germans have now transferred into the south of Italy at least eight more divisions, so that in all there are eighteen south of Rome. It is vital to the success of 'Overlord' that we keep away from that theatre and hold elsewhere as many German divisions as possible, and hard fighting in Italy throughout the spring will provide for the main operation a perfect prelude and accompaniment.

'My confidence in Alexander is undiminished,' Churchill added, 'though if I had been well enough to be at his side as I had hoped at the critical moment I believe I could have given the necessary stimulus. Alas for time, distance, illness and advancing years.'[4]

At a meeting of the Chiefs of Staff Committee on the afternoon of February 29, Churchill 'emphasized the importance', as the minutes

[1] 'Minutes of a Meeting held in the Prime Minister's Map Room on Friday, 25th February, 1944, at 10 p.m.', 'Most Secret': Cabinet papers, 79/89.
[2] Prime Minister's Personal Telegram, T.397/4, 'Most Secret and Personal', OZ 1041, 25 February 1944: Churchill papers, 20/157.
[3] Prime Minister's Personal Telegram, T.395/4, Prime Minister to President No. 592, 'Personal and Most Secret', 25 February 1944: Churchill papers, 20/157.
[4] Prime Minister's Personal Telegram, T.413/4, 'Strictly Secret and Personal, For Your Eyes Alone', 'No Distribution—PM's instructions', 27 February 1944: Churchill papers, 20/158.

noted, of providing Maitland Wilson 'with sufficient resources to enable the present battle to be carried to a successful conclusion'. The collapse of the Anzio beachhead, Churchill warned, 'would not only expose our remaining forces in Italy to defeat, but would jeopardize "Overlord" by enabling the Germans to send reinforcements from Italy to France, and by filling the Anglo-American Expeditionary Force with grave forebodings'.

The discussion turned to the tank landing craft which Maitland Wilson still needed for his supplies and reinforcements. Of 84 which had been available when 'Shingle' had been launched, 8 had been sunk or damaged, 20 had returned to the United Kingdom for 'Overlord', and a further 13 were due 'now' to return to the United Kingdom.[1]

Six hours later the Chiefs of Staff Committee met again, with Eisenhower present. When the problem was explained to him, Eisenhower agreed that the first 26 tank landing craft due to be returned from 'Shingle' to 'Overlord' should remain in the Mediterranean, and that he would accept for 'Overlord' 26 from the United States 'knowing that their crews were not as well trained as the Mediterranean crews'. This proposal Churchill 'warmly endorsed'.[2]

The failures in Italy made Churchill even more vigilant for 'Overlord', now a mere three months away. The 'Overlord' battle, he minuted to the Chiefs of Staff Committee on the last day of February 1944, 'must be the chief care of all concerned, and great risks must be run in every other sphere and theatre in order that nothing should be withheld which could contribute to its success'. When the 'air plan' for 'Overlord' has been made by Eisenhower and Tedder, 'the utmost endeavour will naturally be made', he wrote, 'by the British and United States Chiefs of Staff, jointly and severally, to comply with all requests and meet all needs so far as the general conduct of the war renders this possible'.[3]

Writing in his telegram to Smuts about his critics at home, the 'little folk' as he described them, who had become 'more active', Churchill added: 'Their chirpings will presently be stilled by the thunder of the cannonade.'[4]

---

[1] Chiefs of Staff Committee No. 69 (Operation), 4 p.m., 29 February 1944: Cabinet papers, 79/71.
[2] Staff Conference, Chiefs of Staff Committee, No. 70 (Operations) of 1944, Prime Minister's Upper Map Room, 10 p.m., 29 February 1944: Cabinet papers, 79/71.
[3] Prime Minister's Personal Minute, M.194/4, 29 February 1944: Churchill papers, 20/152.
[4] Prime Minister's Personal Telegram, T.413/4, 27 February 1944: Churchill papers, 20/158.

40

'The war weighs very heavy on us all'

A S part of a new German air offensive, there were four German air raids on London in March 1944, the first on the night of March 1–2.[1] As during earlier bombardments, Churchill instructed Captain Pim to inform him whenever there was news of German aircraft making for London from the French coast. Pim later recalled how, on learning that a raid was imminent:

The Prime Minister's only reaction was to have his coat and tin hat got ready so that as soon as the guns opened fire he might proceed to the roof of the building to get a better view of the proceedings. On more than one occasion he replied to my reports 'Let 'em come. We can deal with 'em.' The question of taking shelter never seemed to enter his head and it was only as a result of much pressure by his personal staff that he could be made to realise that there was some modicum of personal danger. When the All Clear had sounded he often went out to see what damage had been done and to encourage those who had suffered.[2]

On the evening of March 1, Churchill held his first weekly Wednesday meeting of the 'Overlord' Preparation Committee.[3] That same day, learning of the success of the Fourteenth Army against the Japanese in

[1] The other London raids in March 1944 were on the nights of March 14–15, 21–2 and 24–5. There was also one raid on Hull and one on south-west and south Wales. In all, 279 civilians were killed.

[2] Pim recollections for March 1944: Pim papers.

[3] The Ministers present were Attlee (Lord President of the Council), Bevin (Labour and National Service), Lyttelton (Production), Morrison (Home Secretary), Beaverbrook (Lord Privy Seal), A. V. Alexander (Admiralty), Grigg (War Office), Sinclair (Air Ministry), Cripps (Aircraft Production), Leathers (War Transport), Llewellin (Food), Portal (Works), Gwilym Lloyd George (Fuel and Power) and Cherwell (Paymaster General). One of their tasks, Churchill told them, would be 'the arrangements for clearing civilian hospitals to provide for military casualties', as well as the effect on labour supply in Britain 'of the proposed suspension of civil travel between Great Britain and Ireland'. (War Cabinet, Committee on 'Overlord' Preparations, 1st Meeting, 10 Downing Street, 6 p.m., 2 February 1944: Cabinet papers, 98/40.)

Burma, he telegraphed to Mountbatten: 'It is a sign of the new spirit in your Forces and will, I trust, urge everyone to keep closer to the enemy.' Churchill also commented on the use of the word 'Jap' in official communiqués. He would, he said, prefer the word 'Japanese', as 'Jap' was 'too familiar for the rascals'.[1] 'Let me know when and where you are going to attack with untiring energy,' Churchill asked Mountbatten three days later, and he added: 'Do not weary of well doing. Keep close to the enemy. Get on with the job. All good wishes.'[2]

On March 1, with his thoughts on the preparations for 'Overlord', Churchill sent his congratulations to Sir Stafford Cripps, the Minister of Aircraft Production, upon the output of aircraft for the previous month, 'and upon beating the programme'. Churchill's message ended: 'Pray convey to all those who have achieved or exceeded their programme my best thanks.'[3]

Also on March 1, Churchill was asked by Ismay to approve a request which had come from General Alexander and General Eaker for the bombing of marshalling yards at Florence, situated only a mile from the Duomo. The destruction of the yards, they argued, 'would have a considerable effect on North–South railway traffic, as well as destroying the principal locomotive repair shops in Italy'. After Air Chief Marshal Sir John Slessor proposed that 'only the most experienced and accurate bomber squadrons should be employed' in the attack, the Chiefs of Staff were of the opinion that the attack should go ahead. Ismay put all this to Churchill, who noted on Ismay's minute: 'Certainly Bomb'.[4]

From Russia had come details of severe sentences imposed upon two British naval ratings, Prior and Loades, from the Royal Navy shore establishment at Archangel. The two men, after a drunken brawl, had been sentenced by a Soviet court to four and three years' penal servitude in Siberia. Eden asked Churchill to telegraph direct to Stalin in protest. 'Alas,' Churchill replied on March 3, 'I cannot send such a telegram which would embroil me with Bruin on a small point when so many large ones are looming up.' Stalin's only response, Churchill added, would be 'an insulting, argumentative answer'. Churchill's advice was to have some questions asked in Parliament about the sentences, 'and trouble created'. 'A little anti-Russian feeling in the House of Commons,' he told Eden, 'would be salutary at the

[1] Prime Minister's Personal Telegram, T.428/4, 'Personal and Most Secret', 1 March 1944: Churchill papers, 20/158.

[2] Prime Minister's Personal Telegram, T.446/4, 4 March 1944: Churchill papers, 20/158.

[3] Prime Minister's Personal Minute, M.199/4, 1 March 1944: Churchill papers, 20/152.

[4] 'Most Secret', Minute of 1 March 1944, note of 2 March 1944: Premier papers, 3/14/3, folio 259.

present time.' [1] On the following day, Churchill received a telegram from Stalin about Poland. 'I have studied the detailed account of your conversations with members of the émigré Polish Government,' Stalin wrote, 'and have come more and more to the conclusion that such people are not capable of establishing normal relations with the USSR'. Merely to raise the question of 'certain Soviet territories', including Lvov and Vilna, was 'insulting for the Soviet Union'. [2]

The impasse with Russia was complete. 'We certainly do have plenty to worry us,' Churchill telegraphed to Roosevelt on March 4, 'now that our respective democracies feel so sure the whole war is as good as won.' [3] The time had come, he believed, for the Polish Prime Minister to visit the United States. 'It may at any rate make the Russians more careful,' Churchill told Roosevelt, 'if they see that Poland is not entirely without friends.' [4] Jock Colville noted in his diary that Churchill was 'disturbed by the attitude of Russia' and that he felt like telling the Russians: 'Personally I fight tyranny whatever uniform it wears or slogans it utters.' [5]

In the last week of February, Churchill had received two long telegrams from Roosevelt about post-war international economic relations, or, as one of the two telegrams phrased it, about 'a manifest need for United Nations machinery for joint planning of the procedures by which consideration should be given to the various fields of international economic co-operation, the subjects which should be discussed, the order of discussion, and the means of co-ordinating existing and prospective arrangements and activities'. [6] Churchill had not answered this telegram. Nor had he replied to a second telegram from Roosevelt that same day, calling for 'immediate consideration' of the relationship between the United Nations economic planning system and the existing Anglo-American Combined Boards. [7] Lord Halifax pressed for an answer, through Eden. But on March 4, from Chequers, Churchill minuted to Eden:

[1] Prime Minister's Personal Minute, M.207/4, 3 March 1944: Churchill papers, 20/152. Churchill later telegraphed to Sir Archibald Clark Kerr: 'I am indeed indignant at the way our men are treated, and you should make this clear to Molotov. I do not wish however to complicate my personal correspondence with Stalin' (Prime Minister's Personal Telegram, T.543/4, No. 703 to Moscow, 'Personal and Secret', 13 March 1944: Churchill papers, 20/159).

[2] 'Secret and Personal', 3 March 1944: Churchill papers, 20/158.

[3] Prime Minister's Personal Telegram, T.453/4, Prime Minister to President, No. 601, 'Personal and Most Secret', 4 March 1944: Churchill papers, 20/158.

[4] Prime Minister's Personal Telegram, T.457/4, Prime Minister to President, No. 604, 'Personal and Most Secret', 4 March 1944: Churchill papers, 20/158.

[5] Colville diary, 4 March 1944: Colville papers. Churchill embodied this phrase in a speech which he made a year later, on 15 March 1945.

[6] President to Prime Minister, No. 476, 'Personal and Most Secret', 24 February 1944: Churchill papers, 20/157.

[7] President to Prime Minister, No. 477, 'Personal and Most Secret', 24 February 1944: Churchill papers, 20/157.

I cannot believe any of these telegrams come from the President. They are merely put before him when he is fatigued and pushed upon us by those who are pulling him about.

The main thing is to tell Ambassador Halifax to be calm and phlegmatic, and if anything is running rather loose, let it flap and break if necessary, and let us see what happens. All this frantic dancing to the Amerian tune is silly. They are only busy about their own affairs and the more immobile we remain the better. My recommendation is to let it all rip for a bit.[1]

That weekend at Chequers, Churchill and his wife were joined by two other members of their family, Churchill's brother Jack and Randolph's wife Pamela. The other guests included Air Marshal Sir Arthur Conyngham, Harold Macmillan, and General Ismay. Sarah Churchill and Lord Cherwell arrived on the Sunday.[2] Jock Colville, the duty Private Secretary, noted in his diary on the Saturday night:

Late at night, after the inevitable film, the PM took his station in the Great Hall and began to smoke Turkish cigarettes—the first time I have ever seen him smoke one—saying that they were the only thing he got out of the Turks. He keeps on referring to the point that he has not long to live and tonight, while the gramophone played the Marseillaise and Sambre et Meuse, he told Coningham, Harold Macmillan, Pug, Tommy and me that this was his political testament for after the war: 'Far more important than India or the Colonies or solvency is *the Air*. We live in a world of wolves—and *bears*.' Then we had to listen to most of Gilbert and Sullivan on the gramophone, before retiring at 3.0 a.m.[3]

On the morning of March 6 the Chiefs of Staff Committee learned that the Soviet Union had agreed to participate in full in the Anglo-American deception plan for 'Overlord'.[4] This plan, known as 'Bodyguard', had been taken to Moscow on January 30 by the British and American officers responsible for it, Colonel Bevan and Lieutenant Colonel Baumer.[5] The Soviet part in 'Bodyguard' was threefold: to time its summer 1944 offensive after the cross-Channel D-Day, in order to confuse the Germans as to where the first offensive would fall; to appear to be about to mount a major Anglo-Soviet landing in northern Norway with a view to opening up a supply route to Sweden in order to establish air bases in southern Sweden, to cover an am-

---

[1] Prime Minister's Personal Minute, M.220/4, 4 March 1944: Churchill papers, 4 March 1944. The two Roosevelt telegrams were President to Prime Minister Nos. 476 and 477.

[2] 'Chequers List of Guests for Weekend March 3–6': Chequers papers.

[3] Colville diary, 4 March 1944: Colville papers.

[4] Chiefs of Staff Committee No. 76 (Operations) of 1944, 11 a.m. 6 March 1944: Cabinet papers, 79/71. Present at this meeting were Brooke (in the Chair), Portal, Andrew Cunningham, Ismay, and Major-General R. E. Laycock, Chief of Combined Operations.

[5] 'Report by Colonel Bevan and Lt. Col. Baumer regarding their visit to Moscow', London Controlling Section Paper No. 10 of 1944, 'Top Secret', 2 April 1944: Cabinet papers, 79/73.

phibious assault on Denmark from Britain; and to appear to be about to mount a Russian amphibious operation against the Black Sea coast of Rumania and Bulgaria.[1]

The Soviet Union accepted its part in the overall deception plan, making the crucial 'Bodyguard' a tripartite plan: a 'three nation document' as the Soviet representatives had asked.[2]

On March 6 Churchill lunched with Eisenhower and Bedell Smith to discuss the progress of the preparations for 'Overlord'. Meanwhile, in Burma, the 15th Corps offensive had been halted by the Japanese. 'Regrouping is now in active progress,' Mountbatten telegraphed from Delhi, 'for resumption of offensive at earliest possible moment.'[3] That same day, the first of 7,500 men of Wingate's Long Range Penetration Group were dropped by glider deep inside upper Burma, to harass the Japanese lines of communication. The landing places were a hundred miles behind the Japanese lines, and nearly three hundred miles from the nearest supply base, all supplies being sent in by an American 'Air Commando' of 250 machines.[4] In Russia, a new offensive was launched that day by the Red Army, on the 3rd Ukrainian Front. It could only be a matter of months before Soviet forces reached, and crossed, the Curzon Line, resolving the Polish frontier question by force of events. The 'latest evidence' of Stalin's attitude, Churchill told the War Cabinet that day, was 'that he was unlikely to be influenced by argument'.[5]

A reply had nevertheless to be sent to Stalin's rejection of Churchill's message on Poland. 'The proposals I submitted to you', Churchill pointed out in a telegram to Stalin on March 7, 'make the occupation by Russia of the Curzon Line a *de facto* reality in agreement with the Poles the moment your armies reach it', and this reality would be supported by the British Government 'at the armistice or peace conferences'. He had no doubt, Churchill added, that it would be 'equally supported' by the United States. 'Force can achieve much,' Churchill continued, 'but force supported by the goodwill of the world can achieve more.' All that Britain asked was for Stalin to agree to a 'working relationship' with the Polish Government, 'which we shall

[1] 'Plan "Bodyguard", Overall Deception Policy for the War against Germany', Chiefs of Staff Paper No. 779 (Operations) (Final), 'Most Secret', 'Restricted', 23 January 1944: Cabinet papers, 80/77.

[2] At a meeting with Bevan and Baumer on 14 February 1944. The three Soviet representatives during these negotiations were Lieutenant General F. Kuznetsov (Chairman), Major-General Slavin, and Vladimir Dekanosov (Russian Foreign Office).

[3] SC/58, Delhi, 6 March 1944: Churchill papers, 20/158.

[4] Churchill sent these details to Roosevelt when the drop was completed (Prime Minister's Personal Telegram, T.555/4, Prime Minister to President, No. 620, 'Personal and Most Secret', 14 March 1944: Churchill papers, 20/159).

[5] War Cabinet No. 29 of 1944, 6 March 1944, Confidential Annex: Cabinet papers, 65/41.

continue to recognise as the Government of the Ally for whom we declared war upon Hitler'. He would be 'very sorry indeed' if Stalin rejected this, and the War Cabinet had asked him to say 'that they would share this regret'. 'Our only comfort,' Churchill added, 'will be that we have tried our very best.' [1]

Stalin had told Clark Kerr of the 'danger' that the Polish question would make 'a rift' between the two leaders. 'I shall try earnestly to prevent this,' Churchill told Stalin. 'All my hopes for the future of the world are based upon the friendship and co-operation of the Western Democracies and Soviet Russia.' [2]

In sending this telegram to the British Ambassador in Moscow, Churchill also sent instructions for its delivery to Stalin. Clark Kerr should point out to Stalin, Churchill said, that if Stalin continued to refuse to come to an arrangement with the Polish Government, there would be 'a considerable movement of opinion' in Britain 'and all pro-Polish sympathizers will become active'. There would also be 'a strong recrudescence of Polish sentiment' in the United States. Clashes between the Polish underground movement 'and the Soviet troops as they advance' would be 'a source of continued embarrassment to us all'. At the same time, Britain's relationship with 'the Polish Government now in London' would continue to be 'that we formally recognize them as the Government of Poland. We could not therefore recognize any other Polish Government which might be set up.'

Controversy over Poland, Churchill warned, would reveal to the world 'a marked divergence on policy' between the Soviet Union 'and the two Western Allies'. All this, he added, 'casts its shadow over the great operations which all three of us are to launch from different points in accordance with the Teheran agreements'. Churchill went on to tell Clark Kerr, in preparation for his interview with Stalin:

You should not fail to emphasize the gravity of divergence in its bearing upon the future but you should avoid anything that could be construed as a change of policy or change of heart, let alone anything like a threat. It may well be however that the Russian treatment of Poland will prove to be a touchstone and make all sorts of far more important things more difficult.

In a final sentence, drafted by Sir Alexander Cadogan, and accepted by Churchill without amendment, the Ambassador was in-

[1] Churchill had originally written: 'Our only comfort will be that we have tried our very best, but that is not much comfort when hope is chilled.' The Foreign Office persuaded him to delete the last ten words. (Prime Minister's Personal Minute, M/226/4, enclosure, 'Prime Minister to Marshal Stalin': Foreign Office papers, 371/39393.)

[2] Prime Minister's Personal Telegram, T.473/4, 'Most Secret and Personal', 7 March 1944: Churchill papers, 20/158.

structed to tell Stalin that the present situation of 'doubt and uncertainty, while the Red Army is approaching the Curzon Line, may present grave dangers and embarrassments to the conduct of the war by the United Nations'.[1]

The Soviet imbroglio had deepened Churchill's sombre mood. 'The PM says this world ("this dusty and lamentable ball") is now too beastly to live in,' Jock Colville noted in his diary on March 7. 'People act so revoltingly that they don't deserve to survive.'[2]

From Moscow, Clark Kerr urged several modifications in Churchill's instructions for his talk with Stalin. 'Any remark by myself,' he wrote, 'about the casting of a shadow over the coming operations would, I fear, suggest to Stalin's suspicious mind that we were not going to live up to our promises made at Teheran.' It was also important, Clark Kerr believed, for Churchill to add, when he made his statement to Parliament that no favourable results had been achieved, 'that the door is still open'.[3] 'You have my authority,' Churchill replied, 'to tell Marshal Stalin that I should like to be able to say in Parliament that the door is still open, but whether I can do so will depend on his reply.' As for the other modifications of the message, Churchill told Clark Kerr, neither he nor Eden wished to change it. 'This is our position,' Churchill informed the Ambassador, 'and we should stand firm by it.' The War Cabinet, he added, 'is solid and stiff'. Churchill's last words were: 'Appeasement has had a good run.'[4]

At a meeting with Molotov ten days later, Clark Kerr was surprised to learn, as he reported to Churchill, that the Soviet Government's 'acceptance of the Curzon Line' had been 'designed as a concession' in order to secure agreement with Poland. The Curzon Line, Molotov said, 'had found little favour with the Ukrainians and White Russians'. The Ukrainians were claiming that certain regions west of the line—west of the River Bug—'were purely Ukrainian'. Clark Kerr would 'remember', Molotov added, the speech by Nikita Khrushchev at the Ukrainian Supreme Council 'demanding for instance Kholm and Hrubieszow'—two cities on the western side of the Bug. In their turn, White Russians were claiming Bialystok. Recent developments had 'sharpened these claims which were becoming more and more articulate'.[5]

[1] Prime Minister's Personal Telegram, T.472A/4, 'Most Secret and Personal', 7 March 1944: Churchill papers, 20/158.

[2] Colville diary, 7 March 1944: Colville papers.

[3] No. 645 from Moscow, 'Most Secret and Personal', 8 March 1944: Churchill papers, 20/158.

[4] Prime Minister's Personal Telegram, T.517/4, No. 660 from Foreign Office to Moscow, 'Most Secret', 'Most Immediate', 'Decypher Yourself', 10 March 1944: Foreign Office papers, 954/20, folio 136.

[5] No. 757 from Moscow, 'Most Secret and Personal', 20 March 1944: Foreign Office papers, 1954/20, folios 145–6.

In a final attempt to persuade Stalin to come to an agreement with the Polish Government, which Stalin was now describing as an 'exile' Government, Churchill telegraphed on March 21 that he would have 'very soon' to make a statement in Parliament about the Polish position, and that this would involve him saying both 'that we continue to recognize the Polish Government, with whom we have been in continuous relations since the invasion of Poland in 1939' and that 'we now consider all questions of territorial change must await the Armistice or Peace Conference of the victorious powers', and that meanwhile 'we can recognize no forcible transferences of territory'. Churchill's telegram ended with 'the earnest hope that the breakdown which has occurred between us about Poland will not have any adverse effect upon our co-operation in other spheres where the maintenance of our common action is of the greatest consequence'.[1] In sending this telegram to Roosevelt, Churchill noted: 'I have today sent the following reply to UJ,' and he added, in exasperation: 'So what!'[2]

On March 8 Attlee sent Churchill a series of notes, pointing out that, on existing plans, the 'Overlord' landing might turn into a static, besieged bridgehead, as Anzio had done. It would then serve as a fortified area against which the Germans would throw 'an increasing concentration' of forces, drawing them away from Russia, Italy and the Balkans, but not as a springboard for offensive action. Such a springboard, Attlee argued, would require the capture of 'considerable territory in order to give space to bring over land and air forces'. This second scheme, which Attlee preferred, 'involves', he told Churchill, 'taking very vigorous action and accepting great risks'.[3]

Churchill agreed with Attlee's notes, and used them in his discussion with his advisers. 'As you know,' he minuted to the Chiefs of Staff on March 11, 'I am in sympathy with their general tenor.'[4]

As the 'Overlord' preparations continued, Churchill was alert to any possible breach of security. Reading an article in the *Evening Standard* in which the Canadian Minister of Munitions was reported to have hinted at major allied military operations 'within the next

---

[1] Prime Minister's Personal Telegram, T.624/4, No. 787 to Moscow, 'Personal and Most Secret', 21 March 1944: Foreign Office papers, 954/20, folios 148–9.

[2] Prime Minister's Personal Telegram, T.630/4, 'Personal and Most Secret', 21 March 1944: Churchill papers, 20/160.

[3] Minute by the Lord President, 8 March 1944: Chiefs of Staff Committee Paper No. 246 (Operations) of 1944, 12 March 1944.

[4] Prime Minister's Personal Minute, D.80/4, 11 March 1944: Chiefs of Staff Committee Paper No 246 (Operations) of 1944, 12 March 1944.

three or four months', Churchill telegraphed to the Canadian Prime Minister: 'As the time for the return to the Continent approaches, it is of vital importance that Ministers and senior officials in Service and Civil Government Departments should avoid making reference in any public statements which might give an indication of, or clue to the timing, scope or direction of forthcoming operations.' Silence was equally important for another reason. 'As you are aware', Churchill added, 'elaborate "cover plans" have been devised and are now being put into operation in order to persuade the enemy that the date, selected area and scale of the forthcoming return to the Continent are other than those decided upon.'[1]

The preparations for 'Overlord' also enabled Churchill to continue to seek better relations with de Gaulle. On March 10 he telegraphed to Duff Cooper, in Algiers: 'You may let de Gaulle know privately that I am much in favour of the Leclerc division fighting in the main battle here and from my talks with Eisenhower I gather he has the same view. I am therefore working in this sense to overcome the difficulties of transportation etc, and I am pretty confident I can succeed.'[2]

That same day, in a telegram to General Spears in Beirut, Churchill warned him against 'too much a pro-native and anti-French line'. 'I told you in Cairo,' Churchill wrote, 'that I had no wish to destroy French influence in Syria and the Lebanon,' and he added:

Our relations with the French National Committee are improving. The personal leadership of General de Gaulle is being merged in the Committee in which he has several times sustained serious defeats. He also has to struggle with his Assembly. He is becoming increasingly encadré which is healthy in itself. In the process he has become more reasonable and my relations with him are much better than they were before we met at Marrakesh.[3]

Throughout the 'Overlord' preparations, Churchill kept in regular personal contact with both Eisenhower and Bedell Smith. Since his return from Marrakesh, Churchill explained to General Marshall on March 11, he had 'looked carefully' into four principal aspects of the cross-Channel plan: the 'Mulberry' floating harbour 'and all connected with it', the airborne assault 'including method of glider attack', the inshore bombarding naval squadrons, and the Air Command arrangements. Churchill added:

I have presided at a series of meetings at which either Ike or Bedell has been present, and I am satisfied that everything is going on well. Ike and

[1] Prime Minister's Personal Telegram, T.480/4, 7 March 1944: Churchill papers, 20/183.
[2] Prime Minister's Personal Telegram, T.524/4, 'Most Secret', 10 March 1944: Churchill papers, 20/159.
[3] Prime Minister's Personal Telegram, T.527/4, 'Most Secret', Personal and Private', 10 March 1944: Churchill papers, 20/159.

Bedell will probably tell you they are well pleased. I am hardening very much on this operation as the time approaches in the sense of wishing to strike if humanly possible, even if the limiting conditions we laid down at Moscow are not exactly fulfilled.

'I hope a chance may come for us to have a talk before long,' Churchill added, and he ended: 'Every good wish.'[1] 'I am greatly re-assured,' Marshall replied, 'to have this indication of your personal interest and strong leadership in all that pertains to "Overlord".'[2]

Marshall's earlier fears of Churchill being lukewarm to 'Overlord' could also have been dispelled by a study of Churchill's daily probing of all aspects of the preparations. 'How do we stand about the inshore bombardment plans?' he minuted to the First Sea Lord and Ismay on the day of his telegram to Marshall. 'Could you let me have a note showing the position at this moment? I can then settle whether another evening meeting is necessary.'[3]

From the Far East, General Lumsden, Churchill's liaison officer with General MacArthur, had been visiting Britain to discuss the war in Burma, China and the Pacific. Churchill had spoken to Lumsden several times, had brought him into the Staff conferences, and had sent him to formations and units being trained for 'Overlord' in order to see the methods that were to be employed in the attack. On March 12 Lumsden returned to the Pacific. Before he left, Churchill gave him a letter for General MacArthur. The first part dealt with 'Overlord':

This is of course a momentous operation. I am sure that it would not have succeeded in 1942 or 1943; but in 1944 with all the experience we have gained, the extra training the troops have received and the enormous amount of new tackle we have contrived and gathered, I have good confidence in the results. It is our duty to engage the enemy on the broadest fronts possible and make him burn and bleed.

The incalculable factor is the Air. We shall be using Air power to an extent never before imagined. Indeed before 'Overlord' starts the enemy's fighter defence will be strained to the utmost or husbanded only at disastrous cost to himself. You will have read my references to Air power in my last speech in Parliament. Since then both British and American Air Forces have been making long journeys into Germany in great numbers, often with hardly any loss at all. It is not true to say that Air can prevent movement but it should certainly hold the hostile rail-heads at arm's length. However all this will be plain enough before the summer is past.

As to the situation at Anzio and Monte Cassino, where the Anglo-

[1] Prime Minister's Personal Telegram, T.533/4, 'Personal, Private and Most Secret', 11 March 1944: Churchill papers, 20/159.
[2] SH/56, Ref No. 298, 'Top Secret', 15 March 1944: Churchill papers, 20/159.
[3] Prime Minister's Personal Minute, M.263/4, 11 March 1944: Churchill papers, 20/152.

American forces were still being held by the Germans, Churchill told MacArthur:

> If Hitler likes to play on a front of 20 Divisions in Italy, we are quite agreeable and we could not have a better preliminary to 'Overlord' than this heavy fighting continuing without rest or pause which keeps his troops away from the decisive theatre and enables us to use troops who could never have got there anyway.[1]

In a discussion on Far East strategy on March 13, Churchill again raised with the Chiefs of Staff his preference that the 'centre of gravity' of Britain's future operations should be the Indian Ocean and not the South-West Pacific. 'He very much favoured a direct attack across the comparatively short width of the Indian Ocean,' he said, 'but his case would fall to the ground if he could not prove that the punch that could be delivered across the Indian Ocean was not greater than that which would be delivered by going right round Australia.' Nothing should be 'said to Australia', however, 'which would give them any justification for saying that we were committed, until we had come to an agreement on the future with the Americans'. These were all 'weighty matters affecting our future', Churchill added, and he was therefore 'very averse to taking a decision which closed the door while such great operations were impending in the European theatre'.[2]

On March 13 Churchill lunched again with Eisenhower and Bedell Smith.[3] That same day he circulated to all members of the Cabinet a note on the dangers of 'unauthorized disclosures of information'. The 'only safe rule', Churchill declared, was 'never to mention' Cabinet discussion or decisions 'even in the form of guarded allusions, except to those who must be informed of them for reasons of State....'[4] Churchill's scrutiny was felt in small matters as well as large. On the day after his lunch with the two American Generals he minuted to Attlee and others:

> General Bedell Smith mentioned to me yesterday the very high and extortionate prices now being charged to American officers over here for flats and small houses. A medium-sized flat, he said, was twenty-eight pounds a week and the small house that he occupied was thirty-five pounds a week. There is no reason why the Americans should not pay a fair and equitable price for accommodation, which they are quite willing to do, but I do not

---

[1] 'Personal, Private and Confidential', 12 March 1944: Churchill papers, 20/137. General Lumsden was killed in January 1945 when a Japanese suicide plane struck the battleship *New Mexico* in the Gulf of Lingayen.

[2] Chiefs of Staff Committee No. 79 (Operations) of 1944, 'Secretary's Standard File', 'Most Secret', 13 March 1944: Cabinet papers, 79/89.

[3] Desk diary, 13 March 1944: Churchill papers, 20/191.

[4] 'Confidential', 13 March 1944: Churchill papers, 23/23.

think extortion or profiteering should be allowed.

I am not certain who deals with this, but would you very kindly give it your attention and let me know, first, about the facts, and, secondly, whether there is any remedy.[1]

Churchill now contemplated another meeting with Roosevelt, and suggested Bermuda, on March 25. This journey had the code name 'Quintette'. 'Pray let me have the possibilities of the return route by air from Quintette,' he minuted to Portal on March 13.[2] 'It is more than 90 days since we and our Staffs parted,' he telegraphed to Roosevelt, 'and many things, military and political, have happened meanwhile, not all unsatisfactory by any means.' Churchill added: 'We are now approaching the decisive venture.'

One of the decisions to be reached, Churchill noted, was: 'what is the latest date on which a decision can be taken as to whether "Overlord" is or is not to be launched on the prescribed date?' Following that, if the conditions 'definitely stipulated' for the launching of 'Overlord' were not present, that is 'if 20 to 25 mobile German divisions are already in France on the date in question, what are we going to do?'[3]

In the political sphere there was, Churchill wrote, 'a big field for you and me to browse over', including '(1) Our policy in Italy and the Balkans, (2) Our attitude towards de Gaulle and the French National Committee, (3) What can we do for Poland?, (4) What can we do to de Valera?' Churchill ended: 'There are various other topics which will readily occur to us both.'[4]

This telegram was never sent. In its place, Churchill sent a shorter proposal for a Bermuda meeting. 'I wonder,' he telegraphed, 'whether you would care to spend Easter with me at Bermuda. I can arrive there on the 5th and we could separate on the 11th or earlier if you are pressed.' Churchill added: 'I would not suggest bringing the great Staffs but only the principals on the scale with which we went to Teheran. It is not so much that there are new departures in policy to be taken but there is a need after more than ninety days of separation for checking up and shaking together.'[5]

[1] Prime Minister's Personal Minute, M.279/4, to the Lord President (Attlee), the Chancellor of the Exchequer (Sir John Anderson), the Minister of Works and Buildings (Lord Portal) and the Minister of Health (H. Willink).

[2] Prime Minister's Personal Minute, M.274/4, 13 March 1944: Premier papers, 3/367.

[3] These conditions had been laid down on 30 July 1943 by Lieutenant-General Frederick Morgan, Chief of Staff, Supreme Allied Commander (Chief of Staff Paper No. 416, Operations, of 1943). The Russians had been informed of them by General Ismay on 20 October 1943, in Moscow. (Joint Intelligence Committee Report No. 210, Operations, Final, of 1944, 20 May 1944: Cabinet papers, 79/74).

[4] 'Personal and Most Secret', undated draft: Premier papers, 3/367, folios 24–6.

[5] Prime Minister's Personal Telegram, T.597/4, Prime Minister to President, No. 624, 'Personal and Most Secret', 'No distribution', 18 March 1944: Premier papers, 4/75/2, folio 762.

On March 13, having talked to Lord Moran, Brooke wrote in his diary: 'Medically it is all wrong that he should go.'[1] On the following day Brooke noted that Churchill was 'apparently' prepared to put off the date of his departure to the end of March 'but still hopes to go to Bermuda'. Brooke added:

I had another interview with Moran yesterday to try and stop the PM on medical grounds. He tells me he is writing to the PM to tell him that there are three good reasons why he should not go:
(a) He may become a permanent invalid if he does.
(b) Owing to his very recent go of pneumonia he is quite likely to get another if he exposes himself to the hardships and fatigues of a journey, and
(c) he is liable to bring on a heart-attack. . . .[2]

During March 14 Churchill received a telegram from Field Marshal Dill, in Washington, on America's emerging Pacific strategy. 'Unquestionably these weighty matters cannot be fully resolved,' Dill wrote, 'without a full dress Conference for the purpose.' But he added: 'For this the time is hardly ripe.'[3]

That night Churchill gave a now customary monthly Tuesday dinner to the King, in the small downstairs dining room at 10 Downing Street. During the dinner the air-raid siren sounded, and, as John Martin wrote to his wife, who was in Oxford with their newborn son, 'all had to go down to the air-raid shelter' together with members of the domestic staff 'in their night attire'. Martin himself was 'posted at the telephone getting the latest news every few minutes'. At one point he was told that there had been a German aircraft over Oxford, 'whereupon the PM informed the King of my special reason for concern'.[4] It was 'a very heavy night' of bombing, Elizabeth Layton wrote home, and Churchill 'Kept dodging out and coming back to say no one must move'. The King, she added, 'was in terrific form—obviously enjoying himself to the limit—and very animated. There were continuous roars of laughter and poor Mr Martin, struggling with the telephone to find out what was going on, looked quite distracted.'[5]

In a letter to his son Randolph, in Yugoslavia, Churchill was to describe the new blitz in its 'local' aspects, the bombing itself, Mary Churchill at her anti-aircraft battery, and the imminent pilotless aircraft:

The bombing has been on a very modest scale. But they have put a good

[1] Brooke diary, 13 March 1944: Bryant, *op. cit.*, volume 2, page 164.
[2] Brooke diary, 14 March 1944: Bryant, *op. cit.*, volume 2, page 165.
[3] FMD/160, 'Private', 14 March 1944: Churchill papers, 20/159.
[4] Letter of 14 March 1944: Martin papers.
[5] Elizabeth Layton, letter of 25 March 1944: Nel papers.

deal more pepper in the bombs, and the fragmentation is remarkable. They straddled No. 10 a month ago, with one bomb in Parliament Street and another just in front of the Kitchener Statue. This made quite a small crater, but I should think 5 or 6 hundred scars, some quite big holes, were made on our garden front and the Treasury. All the windows came in, and a large part of the roof, and several ceilings were down. However we did not have to suspend holding our Cabinets here, and only missed lunching downstairs on one day. Another good straddle was at the bottom of St. James's Street, which really made a frightful mess with about three bombs.

The raids are very fine to look at now because of the brilliant red flares which hang seemingly motionless in the air, and the bright showers of incendiaries. Every now and again the rocket batteries hurl their flaming prongs upwards. I have had my watch-tower put in order over the Annexe, so that there is enough overhead cover to stop the splinters while not impeding the view. Sometimes I go to Maria's battery and hear the child ordering the guns to fire.

All these impressions make me feel Winston Junior is better in the country. I am sure you will approve. We think they will very likely start up their secret weapon in the near future, but we have got it pretty well marked down and do not think it will amount to more than a severe nuisance.[1]

On March 15 General Alexander launched his third offensive in the Cassino mountains, preceded by a heavy air bombardment, 'the greatest concentration of fire power', Alexander informed Churchill, 'which has ever been put down and lasting for six hours'. But the German troops had retained their ability to continue to fight once the assaulting forces came on. 'I doubt if there are any other troops in the world who could have stood up to it and then gone on fighting with the ferocity they have,' Alexander reported to Churchill five days later. Men of the Gurkha regiment had managed to fight their way well up towards the monastery, but on slopes so steep that supplies could not reach them even by air, and they had to be withdrawn. A bridgehead was established over the river Rapido, and a large part of the town of Cassino was taken, but the monastery itself remained in German hands.

There was now no chance of linking up with the Anzio bridgehead, Alexander reported, until the middle of May. The objective, Rome, had thus receded still further, making more difficult the Allied involvement with internal Italian politics. The problem, as Colville noted in his diary on March 15, was 'whether to go on supporting the King of Italy and Badoglio', or to accept the claims 'of the so-called

[1] Letter of 4 April 1944: Churchill papers, 1/381.

"Six Parties" at Naples'. Churchill, he added, was 'adamant' in support of the King and Badoglio, 'largely because he thinks any new regime would try to court favour from the Italian populace by standing up to the Allies'. Roosevelt, however, 'now seems to be veering in the opposite direction'.[1] In a telegram to Roosevelt, which the War Cabinet discussed and approved that day, Churchill stated that while the War Cabinet agreed with the United States on the need for 'a more broadly based' Government in Italy, it believed 'that we should wait until we had captured Rome before parting company with the King'. Should the capture of Rome be delayed, however, 'for, say, 2 or 3 months', the question of timing might have to be reviewed.[2]

Scrutinizing the operational telegrams from the Mediterranean, Churchill took up with the Chiefs of Staff each decision which might weaken the Italian campaign. Learning on March 16 that four squadrons of British fighter aircraft were to be moved from Italy to Britain, he at once minuted that the 'great plethora' of fighter aircraft in Britain, 'upward of 6,000', did not justify 'depriving' the Mediterranean of these four squadrons. Churchill added: 'I am entirely against robbing the Mediterranean. Indeed, I thought they might well have had half a dozen squadrons from here.'[3]

In reply, it was General Hollis of his Defence Staff who pointed out that there were in fact not nearly 6,000, but a total of 4,156 fighters in Britain at Eisenhower's disposal, and that of these 'only about 2,700' would be available for the actual assault, the rest being employed in the escort of heavy bombers, or in defensive duties.[4] The American Chiefs of Staff eventually agreed, as Portal informed Churchill, that while seven British fighter squadrons would have to return from the Mediterranean to Britain, a total of forty-two American squadrons would remain in the Mediterranean.[5]

In Burma, mid-March saw a Japanese offensive aimed at capturing the Imphal plain. Mountbatten at once sent the Chiefs of Staff an appeal for extra air transport. 'Chiefs of Staff and I are backing you up to the full,' Churchill telegraphed in reply on March 17. 'I have telegraphed to the President. In my view nothing matters but the battle. Be sure you win.'[6] That same day Churchill sent Roosevelt Mountbatten's request for thirty United States transport aircraft, to

---

[1] Colville diary, 15 March 1944: Colville papers.

[2] War Cabinet No. 35 of 1944, 15 March 1944, Confidential Annex: Cabinet papers, 64/41.

[3] Prime Minister's Personal Minute, D.86/4, 16 March 1944: Premier papers, 3/281/7.

[4] 'Top Secret', 18 March 1944: Premier papers, 3/281/7.

[5] 'Top Secret', 6 April 1944: Premier papers, 3/281/7.

[6] Prime Minister's Personal Telegram, T.584/4, OZ 1426, 'Personal and Secret', 17 March 1944: Churchill papers, 20/159.

be diverted from the China run, 'the Hump'. 'We trust the United States Chiefs of Staff will agree,' he wrote. 'The stakes are pretty high in this battle and victory would have far-reaching consequences.' [1]

Roosevelt agreed to Mountbatten's request, 'so I hope', Churchill telegraphed, 'you will win this battle in the north. It is of very great importance.' With the Far East much in mind, Churchill told Mountbatten that he still remained 'entirely opposed to shifting the centre of gravity against Japan from the Indian Ocean to the Pacific, at any rate for the next eighteen months'. He had agreed to send a Mission to reconnoitre the Australian bases, in order that possibilities for a Pacific operation could be 'explored', but this 'in no way implies any decision to change the existing policy'. Meanwhile, 'Do not let anything take your eye off the battle.' [2]

With his Indian Ocean priority much in mind, and conscious of the Chiefs of Staff opposition to the Sumatra operation, on March 17 Churchill asked the Chiefs of Staff to consider an operation elsewhere in the Dutch East Indies. He was still searching for a Far Eastern strategy that would enable British forces, operating from India, to make use of the Bay of Bengal, and to conduct operations which could be effective against the Japanese in the regions nearest to India. Such a strategy would also enable Britain to act in a region where she would not, as in the Australian and Western Pacific theatre, be subordinate to the United States. That day, after a discussion with Churchill about American strategy in the Pacific, Brooke, annoyed, noted in his diary how:

He then informed us that he had discovered a new island just north-west of Sumatra called Simalur. He had worked out that the capture of this island would answer as well as the tip of Sumatra and would require far less strength. However, by the time he had asked Portal for his view, he found out that from the point of view of the air he had little hope of building up his aerodromes and strength before being bumped off. From Cunningham he found out that from a naval point of view, with the Jap fleet at Singapore, he was courting disaster.

'I began to wonder,' Brooke added, 'whether I was in Alice in Wonderland or qualifying for a lunatic asylum. . . .' [3]

Meanwhile, Churchill's main thoughts were steadily on the cross-Channel plans. 'I am hardening for "Overlord" as the time gets nearer,'

[1] Prime Minister's Personal Telegram, T.582/4, Prime Minister to President, No. 622, 17 March 1944: Churchill papers, 20/183.

[2] Prime Minister's Personal Telegram, T.594/4, 'Personal, Secret, Private and Confidential', 18 March 1944: Churchill papers, 20/159.

[3] Brooke diary, 17 March 1944: Bryant, op. cit., volume 2, page 166.

he telegraphed to Roosevelt on March 18. 'Perhaps Marshall will show you a telegram I sent him.'[1] As part of his 'Overlord' concerns, Churchill still hoped to see plans made for a possible seizure of Bordeaux twenty or more days after a successful D-Day. In defence of this operation, code name 'Caliph', Churchill minuted to the Chiefs of Staff Committee on March 17:

... in circumstances when the enemy's air force is either completely absorbed or grounded, as it may well be, we should be most unwise not to throw in a secondary attack in order to seize important harbours and penetrate into a country thoroughly friendly and eager to revolt. Four or five divisions should certainly be assigned to this, and any resources in North Africa should be considered as available. The 1st and 6th Armoured Divisions and certain French divisions are naturally in one's mind.

'I ask,' Churchill added, 'that this should be energetically pursued.' There could be 'no doubt', however, 'that the possession of overwhelming air power is the priceless foundation of our offensive leap across the water, and to go outside its range in the first instance would be most improvident and silly'.[2]

On March 19, amid his daily budget of Enigma messages, Churchill read one which made it clear that the Germans intended to make, as he informed General Wilson, 'an important effort' to recover the island of Vis, off the Adriatic coast of Yugoslavia. The decrypt showed that the attack would be made by 'air-borne troops and landing craft'. This island, off the Yugoslav coast, was held by the Yugoslav partisans, with British help. 'Having started up there,' Churchill telegraphed to Wilson, 'we ought surely to carry it through. I hope it will not become another Kos. Such an event would bring great discouragement among the Partisans.'[3]

Wilson replied that everything was arranged for 'immediate naval and air support' for Vis, where the garrison of 3,500 partisans had been reinforced by twenty-four British-manned anti-aircraft guns. There were also two British Commandos based on the island 'carrying out frustration attacks against shipping'. The situation in Italy, however, Wilson warned, 'renders it impossible to detach any British formation to hold this island'.[4]

[1] Prime Minister's Personal Telegram, T.597/4, Prime Minister to President, No. 624, 'Personal and Most Secret', 18 March 1944: Premier papers, 4/75/2, Part 2, folio 762.
[2] Prime Minister's Personal Minute, D.89/4, 17 March 1944: Churchill papers, 20/152.
[3] Prime Minister's Personal Telegram, T.609/4, 19 March 1944: Churchill papers, 20/183. The decrypt was CX/MSS/T127/69, VL 8803.
[4] 'Most Secret and Personal', 21 March 1944: Churchill papers, 20/160.

Churchill was determined not to let Vis fall. 'You have on your ration strength in Italy, North Africa and Levant,' he replied, 'upwards of 1¾ million men.' According to an earlier telegram, 'you contemplate a considerable pause before renewing the offensive in Italy'. In these circumstances 'I think you ought to be able to make sure that Vis is properly defended', and that 'the small body of troops required to ensure this is forthcoming'.[1] Wilson replied that same day, that he was 'taking steps' to reinforce Vis at the 'earliest possible' moment.[2] He also intended to attack the German-held island of Hvar 'next week'. To this news Churchill replied with a single word: 'Good.'[3]

On March 20 the War Cabinet learned of further Russian successes on the eastern front, with two new offensives in the Kowel and Luck Regions, both deep inside inter-war Poland. Further south, Russian forces had reached the river Dneister on a sixty-mile front.[4] 'I must congratulate you again,' Churchill telegraphed to Stalin on the following day, 'on all the wonderful victories your Armies are winning. . . .'[5] At Monte Cassino, however, the Germans held firm despite repeated attacks by the 2nd New Zealand and 4th Indian Division.

The disappointments of Monte Cassino added to the daily pressures of war. 'PM this morning confessed he was tired,' Cadogan noted in his diary on March 21, and he added: 'he's almost done in'.[6] 'The war weighs very heavy on us all just now,' Churchill telegraphed to Alexander.[7]

Roosevelt was also still ill. 'The old attack of grippe having hung on and on,' he telegraphed to Churchill on March 21, 'leaving me with an intermittent temperature', and his doctor had ordered 'a complete rest of about two or three weeks'. He could not therefore get to Churchill's suggested conference at Bermuda in early April, al-

[1] Prime Minister's Personal Telegram, T.624/4, 'Personal and Most Secret', 22 March 1944: Churchill papers, 20/160.
[2] 'Special unnumbered Signal', Cairo, 22 March 1944: Churchill papers, 20/160.
[3] Prime Minister's Personal Telegram, T/641/4, 'Most Secret and Personal', 23 March 1944: Churchill papers, 20/160.
[4] War Cabinet No. 36 of 1944, 20 March 1944: Cabinet papers, 65/41.
[5] Prime Minister's Personal Telegram, T.625/4, 'Personal and Most Secret', 21 March 1944: Churchill papers, 20/160.
[6] Cadogan diary, 21 March 1944: David Dilks (editor), op. cit., pages 611–13.
[7] Prime Minister's Personal Telegram, T.623/4, 'Personal and Secret', 21 March 1944: Churchill papers, 20/160.

though a meeting of their staffs would, he felt, 'be most useful'. Roosevelt added: 'I am glad you feel hardened about "Overlord". Its accomplishment may synchronize with a real Russian breakthrough.'[1] 'I am indeed grieved and trust rest will do you good,' Churchill replied, and he added: 'I do not think the Staff Meeting worth while without your being there. I hope you are still planning your visit here for the great event after you are fully recovered.'[2]

During March 21 Sir John Anderson suggested to Churchill that the time had come to give 'full information' about 'Tube Alloys'—the atom bomb research programme—to the three Service Ministers and to the War Cabinet. Churchill minuted, however, 'I do not agree,' asking in a note in the margin of Anderson's request: 'What can they do about it?'[3] Anderson, as Lord Cherwell later wrote to Churchill, 'was perturbed by your decision', but as a result of it the atomic bomb 'was never discussed at Cabinet or in the Defence Committee' at any time before the dropping of the bombs on Hiroshima and Nagasaki a year and a half later.[4]

In his note of March 21, Anderson had also suggested that there was 'much to be said for communicating to the Russians in the near future the bare fact that we expect, by a given date, to have this devastating weapon: and for inviting them to collaborate with us in preparing a scheme for international control'. Churchill minuted in the margin: 'On no account.'[5]

On March 21, Maitland Wilson had strongly advised the Chiefs of Staff Committee by telegram against the withdrawal of any forces from Italy, 'particularly Air forces', until after the capture of Rome.[6] Wilson's advice was supported by the Joint Planning Staff who, that same day, recommended that 'Anvil' should now be cancelled.[7] This recommendation was discussed on the morning of March 22 by the Chiefs of Staff, Eisenhower, Tedder and Bedell Smith. It was 'recog-

---

[1] President to Prime Minister, No. 506, 'Personal and Secret', 21 March 1944: Premier papers, 4/75/2, folio 761.
[2] Prime Minister's Personal Telegram, T.621/4, Prime Minister to President, No. 629, 'Most Secret and Personal', 21 March 1944. Premier papers, 3/367. Roosevelt had contemplated a visit to London to coincide with D-Day. It was a project that did not come to pass.
[3] 'Tube Alloys', 'Most Secret', 21 March 1944: Premier papers, 139/2, folio 140.
[4] Lord Cherwell, 'Events Leading up to the Use of the Atomic Bomb, 1945', 'Secret', 28 January 1953: Churchill papers, 4/379.
[5] 'Tube Alloys', 'Most Secret', 21 March 1944: Premier papers, 139/2, folio 142.
[6] MEDCOS No. 73, 'Top Secret', 21 March 1944: Cabinet papers, 105/153.
[7] Joint Planning Staff Paper No. 68 (Final) of 1944, 'Top Secret', 21 March 1944: Cabinet papers 79/71.

nized in Washington', Eisenhower told the meeting, that a continuance of the battle in Italy 'on the present scale' would absorb a large part of the resources required for 'Anvil', but would, from the point of view of 'Overlord', provide 'as good if not a better diversion than "Anvil" itself'.

In his opinion, Eisenhower told the British Chiefs of Staff, 'the time had come to cancel "Anvil" in its present conception of a two divisional assault'. At the same time, it was 'most important' that the abandonment of the existing date for 'Anvil' should not lead to a 'diminution of our offensive effort in Italy'. Any instructions to Maitland Wilson, Eisenhower stressed, should place emphasis 'on the importance of maintaining the highest possible tempo of offensive action, with the object of giving the greatest possible assistance to "Overlord" by containing the maximum enemy forces away from the "Overlord" lodgment area'.[1]

The instruction was sent that same day, first to the Joint Staff Mission in Washington, using the exact words, which Eisenhower had used.[2] In Washington, Wilson's appeal, and the support given to it by both Eisenhower and the British Chiefs of Staff, led to a reversal of American policy. The American Chiefs of Staff telegraphed to London on March 24 that, in view of Wilson's appreciation 'that he will be unable to amalgamate the bridgehead and main line in Italy before 15 May, we agree that a date for "Anvil" concurrent with "Overlord" cannot be met and that "Anvil" must therefore be delayed'.[3]

Anglo-American strategy was, momentarily at least, in harmony. Italy, not the south of France, was to be the war zone in which German troops were to be pinned down during the initial stages of 'Overlord'.

Churchill was told of this decision by the Chiefs of Staff on the early evening of March 22, and gave it his approval.[4] Brooke, who was present, noted in his diary:

He was in a good mood, and all went well beyond wasting an hour with interruptions of every description. Had we seen the last wire to Stalin? What was happening in Hungary? Why would we use the word 'intensive' when the correct word was 'intense'? He had had a lovely view of last night's raid

[1] Chiefs of Staff Meeting No. 95 (Operations) of 1944, 10.30, 22 March 1944: Cabinet papers, 79/71.
[2] Chiefs of Staff (W) 1229, Z 1582, 'Top Secret' 'Immediate' 22 March 1944: Cabinet papers, 122/1245.
[3] Combined Chiefs of Staff, 465/13, 'Top Secret', 24 March 1944: Cabinet papers, 122/1245.
[4] Staff Conference, Chiefs of Staff Committee No. 96 (Operations) of 1944, 6 p.m., 22 March 1944: Cabinet papers, 79/71.

from the roof. He was going to broadcast on Sunday night. What a strain we had been having for the last three years. Why could not Wilson be more intelligent? etc.? All these were sandwiched in between each paragraph of the Minutes he was looking through.

'Thank Heaven,' Brooke added, 'Roosevelt cannot meet him in Bermuda so our trip next week is off.' [1]

At midday on March 23 Churchill set off by train with Eisenhower on a two-day inspection of American troops in Britain. 'I thank God you are here,' he told the men of one airborne unit, 'and from the bottom of my heart I wish you good fortune and success.' [2] Before leaving London, Churchill had received a telegram from Mountbatten, to say that Wingate had sent a 'hysterical' message complaining 'that Press accounts of operations had been distorted' and that the name of his Force had been suppressed. [3] Churchill replied at once, to say that he did not think Wingate's message 'hysterical' and he told Mountbatten: 'I propose to mention his name in my broadcast on Sunday. . . .' If Mountbatten agreed, Churchill added, he would make 'direct representations' to Roosevelt for the additional air forces which Wingate had asked for. [4] 'I propose to mention General Wingate's name in my broadcast on Sunday,' Churchill reiterated to the Chiefs of Staff Committee, before setting off on his tour of inspection. [5]

Churchill's telegram to Mountbatten was sent just after midday on March 23. On the following day, Wingate was killed in an air crash, on the way to his troops. But Churchill could make no reference to this in his broadcast, because, when Mountbatten telegraphed the first news that Wingate was missing, he asked him 'to make no mention of this in your broadcast, as there is a definite chance he may be alive'. [6] 'I am deeply grieved and stricken by your news,' Churchill replied. 'You should keep it secret till after the battle is decided.' [7] 'This is a very heavy blow to me,' Churchill telegraphed to Field Marshal Dill, 'for you know how much I had counted upon this man of genius, who might well have been a man of destiny.' [8]

*   *   *

[1] Brooke diary, 22 March 1944: Bryant, volume 2, *op. cit.*, page 173.

[2] Speech of 23 March 1944: Churchill papers, 9/166.

[3] SC/65, 'Personal and Private', 23 March 1944: Churchill papers, 20/160.

[4] Prime Minister's Personal Telegram, T.644/4, 'Most Secret and Private', 23 March 1944: Churchill papers, 20/160.

[5] Prime Minister's Personal Minute, D.94/4, 23 March 1944: Churchill papers, 20/152.

[6] SAC/1276, IZ 2847, 'Personal', 25 March 1944: Churchill papers, 20/160.

[7] Prime Minister's Personal Telegram, T.670/4, OZ 1695, 'Personal and Most Secret', 28 March 1944: Churchill papers, 20/160.

[8] Prime Minister's Personal Telegram, T.672/4, OZ 1694, 'Personal and Most Secret', 28 March 1944: Churchill papers, 20.160.

While Churchill was inspecting the American and British troops, now within six weeks of their greatest test, a further telegram from Moscow revealed that Foreign Office intervention on behalf of the two imprisoned British naval ratings, Loades and Prior, had been in vain. Churchill's reaction, John Peck later recalled, 'closely resembled minor volcanic activity. There would be continuous and barely perceptible seismic rumblings while he dealt with other matters, punctuated by a series of molten and sulphurous explosions'. During these 'explosions', Peck added, 'Leslie Rowan and I thought it wiser not to carry out, exactly, some of his instructions such as "Gimme Stalin", "Clear the Line". . . .'[1]

On March 25 Stalin's reply about Poland reached London, a 'violent reply', Cadogan noted in his diary.[2] That evening Churchill telephoned to Eden. 'He seems to have enjoyed his trip with the American troops,' Eden noted, 'but much perturbed by very bad message from Uncle Joe. . . .'[3] In his telegram, which had been sent from Moscow on March 23, Stalin described Churchill's own previous telegrams on Poland as 'full of threats against the Soviet Union'. Such a 'method of threats', he added, was 'not only incorrect in the mutual relations of allies', but also 'harmful'. If Churchill were to state in the House of Commons his opposition to the transference of territories 'carried out by force', this would be taken, Stalin warned, 'as an undeserved insult directed at the Soviet Union'. Stalin added: 'Of course you are free to make whatever statement you please in the House of Commons—that is your affair. But if you do make such a statement, I shall consider that you have committed an unjust and unfriendly act towards the Soviet Union.' As to Churchill's wish that failure over the Polish question would not influence 'our collaboration' in other spheres, 'I fear,' Stalin wrote, 'that the method of threats and discrediting, if it continues in the future, will not conduce to our collaboration.'[4]

In an earlier telegram from Sir Archibald Clark Kerr, Churchill had learned that, through Andrei Vyshinski, the Soviet Government had insisted that the British substitutes for the Italian ships be brought to Russian ports by British and American crews. Russian crews could only be trained for the task with difficulty if they came to British ports

---

[1] Sir John Peck recollections, letter to the author, 22 October 1984. A month later Churchill minuted to Sir James Grigg and Brooke, about the Russian treatment of General Martel: 'They treat all our people like dogs'. (Prime Minister's Personal Minute, M.442/4, 19 April 1944: Churchill papers, 20/144.) Martel had been head of the British Military Mission at Moscow in 1943.

[2] Cadogan diary, 25 March 1944: David Dilks (editor), *op. cit.*, page 613.

[3] Eden diary, 25 March 1944: Eden memoirs, *The Reckoning, op. cit.*, page 439.

[4] 'Personal and Most Secret', sent 23 March 1944, received 25 March 1944: Churchill papers, 20/160.

for the purpose; such had been Vyshinski's argument. Angered by the Soviet attitude to each British request and action, Churchill now wished to instruct Clark Kerr to tell Vyshinski that it was 'not agreed' that the training of Russian crews would be more difficult in Britain than in Russia. The experts on British-built ships and equipment were in Britain, 'not in Russia'. Churchill wanted to add, with his first direct reference in a telegram to Russia to the two imprisoned British seamen:

Moreover in Britain there would be no danger of sailors guilty of some drunken brawl being sent off for several years of penal servitude. In order to preserve the best relations between the proletariats of both countries, it is most important that another 3,000 British sailors should not be exposed to the misfortunes which have overtaken Seamen Loades and Prior (Repeat Loades and Prior) who are now we are told travelling eastwards to Siberia to serve long terms of imprisonment for petty offences.

If the Soviet Union was not prepared to send Russian crews to Britain, Churchill had intended to end his telegram, 'we would wish to know as soon as possible', so that the active ships 'could return to operational service, and the older ones placed in care and maintenance'.[1]

Churchill showed this telegram to Eden and Bridges: it was never sent to Moscow since, at the War Cabinet at which it was considered, it was felt that it should be redrafted 'in the shortest and least argumentative form'. Later in the discussion, Churchill told the War Cabinet that he felt that the sentences on the two seamen 'were unjustifiably severe, and that everything must be done to secure a modification of them'.[2]

On Saturday March 25, at Chequers, Churchill prepared his first broadcast speech for more than a year.[3] 'PM arrived at 10 p.m.,' wrote Marian Holmes, who, with Elizabeth Layton, was waiting to take the dictation. 'Immediately', she noted, 'we went into the Hawtrey Room and he started dictating his broadcast for tomorrow night. Elizabeth and I took it in turns. The PM seemed very tired but sweet-tempered and solicitous. No film tonight—too busy. Got to bed at 3.30 a.m.'[4]

Work on the broadcast continued at Chequers throughout Sunday March 26. 'By 5 o'clock in the afternoon,' Marian Holmes noted in her diary, 'we got the final draft of the PM's broadcast. Eliz. and I pitched in to putting it into speech form. We completed it by 8 o'clock.

---

[1] Prime Minister's Personal Telegram, T.654/4, 'Top Secret and Personal', 25 March 1944: Churchill papers, 20/160. Following further protests., Loades and Prior were released from labour camp (having served three months of their sentence).

[2] War Cabinet No. 40 of 1944, 27 March 1944, Confidential Annex: Cabinet papers, 65/45.

[3] Marian Holmes diary, 25 March 1944: Marian Walker Spicer papers.

[4] Marian Holmes diary, 25 March 1944: Marian Walker Spicer papers.

The PM broadcast to the nation from the study at 9 p.m. for 50 minutes.'[1]

During Churchill's broadcast, there was no hint of his bitterness towards Stalin, nor of his vexation over the sentences on the two seamen, as he told his listeners that the Red Army's advance of 900 miles in a single year, from Stalingrad to the Dniester river, 'constitutes the greatest cause of Hitler's undoing'. The people of Russia had been fortunate 'in finding in their supreme ordeal of agony a warrior leader, Marshal Stalin, whose authority enabled him to combine and control the movements of armies numbered by many millions upon a front of nearly 2,000 miles, and to impart a unity and a concert to the war direction in the East which has been very good for Russia and for all her Allies'.

Speaking of the fighting in Burma, Churchill made no reference to Wingate by name. 'Our men are at the helm,' he said. 'Our airborne operations enable us to attack the Japanese in the rear.' In nearly every combat 'we are able to count three or four times more Japanese dead, and that is what matters, than we have ourselves suffered in killed, wounded or missing'.

Much of Churchill's speech was devoted to post-war reforms: to education, agriculture, 'the vigorous revival of healthy village life', employment and housing. But he concluded with a reference to military events: 'The hour of our greatest effort and action is approaching.' It would require, he warned, 'from our own people here, from Parliament, from the Press, from all classes, the same cool, strong nerves, the same toughness of fibre, which stood us in good stead in those days when we were all alone under the blitz'. Churchill ended:

And here I must warn you that in order to deceive and baffle the enemy as well as to exercise the forces, there will be many false alarms, many feints, and many dress rehearsals. We may also ourselves be the object of new forms of attack from the enemy. Britain can take it. She had never flinched or failed. And when the signal is given, the whole circle of avenging nations will hurl themselves upon the foe and batter out the life of the cruellest tyranny which has ever sought to bar the progress of mankind.[2]

Churchill's broadcast was not universally well received. 'The PM broadcast, indifferently I thought,' was Colville's comment in his diary that night.[3] 'People seem to think that Winston's broadcast last night was that of a worn and petulant old man,' Harold Nicolson noted in his diary on March 27, and he added: 'I am sickened by the absence

[1] Marian Holmes diary, 26 March 1944: Marian Walker Spicer papers.
[2] Broadcast of 26 March 1944: Churchill papers, 9/166.
[3] Colville diary, 26 March 1944: Colville papers.

of gratitude towards him. The fact is that the country is terribly war-weary, and the ill-success of Anzio and Cassino is for them a sad augury of what will happen when the Second Front begins.'[1]

Churchill's health gave cause for concern to those who worked with him most closely. On the morning of March 28, at a meeting of the Chiefs of Staff Committee, Brooke noted in his diary:

We found him in a desperately tired mood. I am afraid that he is losing ground rapidly. He seems quite incapable of concentrating for a few minutes on end, and keeps wandering continuously. He kept yawning and said he was feeling desperately tired.[2]

Churchill lunched that day with the King, and, in the evening, discussed with Beaverbrook and Bracken the Government's surprising defeat in the House of Commons, earlier that day, by a single vote. The defeat had come on an amendment by the Tory Reform Committee, a group of back bench MPs, seeking equal pay for men and women under the Education Code.[3] The Government's view had been that the issue of equal pay was a far larger one than could be dealt within a Bill of limited application. In the Map Room that night, Churchill told Captain Pim that he feared the Germans would not explain that the defeat of the Government had been on a single clause of a Bill on Education but would 'hail' the vote 'as a sign that Britain was war weary and that the Government no longer had their support in the war effort'.[4]

That night Churchill was up until two in the morning discussing the defeat with R. A. Butler, the President of the Board of Education, who had been in charge of the Bill. Butler offered Churchill his resignation, but this Churchill refused to accept.

On the following morning, March 29, Churchill continued with his duties as before, seeing Lord Cherwell at 9.30, answering Prime Minister's questions in the House of Commons at 11.30, making a Commons statement at noon on the Education Bill, lunching with Sir Stafford and Lady Cripps, Lord and Lady Cranborne, General Gott's widow and others at 1.30, seeing the United States Air Force General, Ira Eaker, at 3, and after his late afternoon sleep, dining with General Montgomery at 8.30.[5] The most difficult moment of the day had been in the House of Commons, immediately after Question Time, when

[1] Nicolson diary, 27 March 1944: Nigel Nicolson (editor), *op. cit.*, page 356.
[2] Brooke diary, 28 March 1944: Bryant, *op. cit.*, volume 2, page 175.
[3] The amendment (to Clause 82 of the Education Bill) had been put by a Conservative woman MP, Thelma Cazalet Keir (whose brother Victor Cazalet had been killed in the same air crash in which Sikorski died).
[4] Pim recollections: Pim papers.
[5] Prime Minister's Engagement Cards, 29 March 1944.

he announced that the Education Bill defeat could be debated on the following day, and would be regarded by the Government as a Vote of Confidence. 'If the Government do not secure an adequate majority,' he warned, 'it will entail the usual constitutional consequences.' [1] 'The House gasped at the hard (but just) terms,' Henry Channon noted in his diary, 'and the rebels looked foolish. . . .' As for Churchill, Channon wrote, 'He looked tired, wounded, and was barely audible.' [2] 'Everybody was ruffled and annoyed,' Harold Nicolson wrote to his sons and he added:

The only person who really enjoyed it was Winston himself. He grinned all over. A man came up to him in the smoking-room and said that he thought it exaggerated to make them all swallow their vote, and could some other means not be devised whereby confidence could be reaffirmed? 'No,' said Winston. 'Not at all. I am not going to tumble round my cage like a wounded canary. You knocked me off my perch. You have now got to put me back on my perch. Otherwise I won't sing.' [3]

On the following day, March 31, the vote was taken. 'The Government got its majority of over 400 and the PM was radiant,' Colville noted in his diary. 'I thought it was cracking a nut with a sledgehammer,' he added. [4]

'I have had some little trouble here which has been coming to a head for some time,' Churchill informed Roosevelt, 'which at length forced me to fall back upon the House of Commons which as usual showed itself steadfast in the cause and put all malignants in their proper places.' It was an 'immense comfort' for him, Churchill added, 'to feel this mighty body behind me when troubles like Singapore, Tobruk and untimely yearnings for reconstruction come along'. [5]

To his son Randolph, Churchill wrote of the Education Bill debate:

I was sure you would be interested in the House of Commons racket. I am the child of the H. of C., and when I was molested by a number of cheeky boys I ran for succour to the old Mother of Parliaments and she certainly chased them out of the backyard with her mop. A mere Vote of Confidence would have been an empty bouquet. What the malcontents did not like was being made to eat their words. [6]

*   *   *

[1] House of Commons, 29 March 1944: *Hansard*, column 1452.
[2] Channon diary, 29 March 1944: Robert Rhodes James (editor), *Chips, op. cit.*, page 390.
[3] Nicolson letter, 2 April 1944: Nigel Nicolson (editor), *op. cit.*, page 358.
[4] Colville diary, 30 March 1944: Colville papers. The vote was 425 to 23.
[5] Prime Minister's Personal Telegram, T.698/4, Prime Minister to President, No. 635, 'Most Secret and Personal', 1 April 1944: Churchill papers, 20/160.
[6] Letter of 4 April 1944: Churchill papers, 1/381.

On March 30 Soviet forces advanced to within sixteen miles of the Hungarian frontier. That night Churchill left London by train for Yorkshire, for a visit to the 21st Army Group which was preparing for 'Overlord', working on the train until three in the morning. During the night, 950 British bombers struck deep into Germany, most of them against Nuremberg. But nearly one in ten were shot down.

Churchill's principal concern during March 31 was the criticism, some of it in the House of Commons, of the 'modifications' in the Atlantic Charter implied in any Soviet territorial expansion westward. Britain was being 'blamed', Churchill minuted to Eden, 'for departing from idealistic principles', and he added:

Actually all this is done for the sake of Russia, which is resolved to seize the Baltic States and take what she wishes from Poland and Roumania. Nor do we know that a second series of demands may not follow her further military victories. Any division between Britain and the United States will make us powerless in this matter. Together we can probably control the situation.[1]

Among the telegrams in Churchill's box on March 31 was one, from the Foreign Office to Washington, which contained a Soviet proposal for the future administration of liberated France.[2] Reading this, Churchill suggested to Eden that this proposal provided Britain with an opportunity to propose a tripartite commission in respect of the occupied countries in the east of Europe, including 'particularly' the Baltic States, the liberated districts of Poland, and the conquered territories of Rumania and Bulgaria 'as they fall later'. Churchill added:

It must be borne in mind that in Italy the Russians have had no losses at all, and we have had four times the military losses and at least twenty times the naval losses of the United States. Yet the Russians claim equality with Britain and the United States. We have agreed to this but now with regard to France, where we have already had very heavy losses, I do not think we ought to concede tripartite control of the territories immediately behind our armies unless an equal measure is given in the east. The matter should be handled with the Americans first. It would be of immense advantage if we had a say in the treatment to be meted out to liberated Poland.[3]

It should also be made clear, Churchill told Eden in a further minute that day, that Russia's own view, as far as Poland was concerned, was 'that there should be no territorial aggrandisement

[1] Prime Minister's Personal Minute, M.322/4, 31 March 1944: Churchill papers, 20/152.
[2] 'Citizen' No. 101 of 30 March 1944.
[3] Prime Minister's Personal Minute, M.329/4, 'Action this day', 31 March 1944: Churchill papers, 20/152.

beyond the frontiers of the Ribbentrop–Molotov Line', and he commented crossly: 'I am getting a little tired of being told by the Left Wing that we have fallen below their altruistic standards, when Britain seeks nothing for herself and the only cause of trouble is the Soviet desire for territory.'

In this same minute of March 31, Churchill suggested a conciliatory gesture to Stalin. In preparing the text of his statement to Parliament on Poland, Churchill wrote, it 'might be well' to send it to Clark Kerr first, for him to show to Molotov, 'saying that the substance of this must be imparted to Parliament but that if there is any phrase or passage which the Soviet Government find injurious to them, we should be glad at least to have it pointed out to us so that we can see if the same thing could be said in a different way'.[1]

Churchill's anger at the tone of Stalin's message did not deflect him from his hope of a compromise. 'I have a feeling that the Soviet bark may be worse than its bite,' he telegraphed to Roosevelt on April 1, 'and that they have a great desire not to separate themselves from their British and American Allies.' Although 'unwilling to say anything to us of a reassuring nature' about Poland, it might be, Churchill wrote, that 'they will in fact watch their step very carefully'. An invitation from Roosevelt to Mikolajczyk to visit the United States would, Churchill added, 'show the Russians the interest which the United States takes in the fate and future of Poland'.[2]

In Yorkshire on the morning of March 31, Churchill inspected men of the Royal Army Service Corps, then, men of the Guards Armoured Division, saw a tank display, and went for a ride in a 'Cromwell'. Before lunch he saw an exhibition of a lorry driving through water, and, as Colville noted in his diary, 'met an old and very decrepit man, Colonel Wormald', with whom Churchill had charged, in 1898, at the battle of Omdurman.[3]

After lunch on the train, Churchill continued to Harrogate, where the local population gave him, as Colville noted, 'a rousing reception'. He then inspected the 15th Scottish Division 'and saw some battle practice'.[4] That evening he returned south by train, reaching

[1] Prime Minister's Personal Minute, M.330/4, 31 March 1944: Churchill papers, 20/152.
[2] Prime Minister's Personal Telegram, T.693/4, Prime Minister to President, No. 632, 'Personal and Most Secret', 1 April 1944: Churchill papers, 20/160.
[3] Frederick William Wormald, born in 1869, had been commissioned in the 7th Hussars in 1891. He died in 1948.
[4] Colville diary, 31 March 1944: Colville papers.

Chequers at 11.15 p.m. where his wife, his brother, and Brendan Bracken awaited him.[1] At dinner in the train, noted Colville, 'he spent most of the time repeating the Lays of Ancient Rome and Marmion, which was a remarkable feat of memory but rather boring.'[2]

'I often think of our trek together up the Nile, which was quite a picnic compared with what our soldiers have to encounter in these days,' Colonel Wormald wrote on the following day. 'Do you remember pulling me off my valise just as I was about to roll over onto a scorpion?' and he added: 'I was very glad to see you looking so well. I hope you did not find it too cold upon the Wolds, and that you will take care of yourself. We can't do without you, you know!'[3]

Churchill's concern as Spring came to London focused more and more upon 'Overlord'. 'As you know,' he telegraphed to Roosevelt on 1 April 1944, 'I harden for it the nearer I get to it,' and he added: 'Eisenhower is a very large man.'[4] But Soviet policy constituted a continual worry which was even accentuated as D-Day drew nearer. As Churchill explained to Eden on April 1, 'once we get on to the Continent with a large commitment, they will have the means of blackmail, which they have not at present, by refusing to advance beyond a certain point, or even tipping the wink to the Germans that they can move more troops into the West.' Although he had tried 'in every way to put myself in sympathy with these Communist leaders', Churchill wrote, 'I cannot feel the slightest trust or confidence in them. Force and facts are their only realities.'

As to the Polish issue, Churchill told Eden:

The great thing at this stage is not to argue with them. Let us give them two or three months of perfectly simple answers to questions they may ask. Whenever possible let the answers be given by the two Ambassadors, or by Churchill and Roosevelt signed together. I am anxious to save as many Poles as possible from being murdered. It is perfectly clear that to argue with the Russians only infuriates them.

The British attitude to Russia, Churchill believed, should be 'to relapse into a moody silence'. Britain's communications to Russia should be delivered 'in the most urbane and detached manner and no argument entered upon at all', and he ended:

[1] 'List of Guests for Weekend, March 31–April 3, 1944': Chequers archive.
[2] Colville diary, 31 March 1944: Colville papers.
[3] Letter of 1 April 1944: Churchill papers, 2/498.
[4] Prime Minister's Personal Telegram, T.698/4, Prime Minister to President, No. 635, 'Most Secret and Personal', 1 April 1944: Churchill papers, 20/160.

I do not know how long we shall be able to keep this up, but it is clear to me that at present their feeling is we must flatter and kowtow to them, and they may be disagreeably surprised if we simply do not come to the party. Meanwhile every effort must be made to reach complete understanding with the United States and Poland is an extremely good hook.

I write the above without the slightest wish to go back on our desire to establish friendly relationships with Russia, but our and especially my very courteous and even effusive personal approaches have had a bad effect. This is why I take this line.[1]

April 1 was Clementine Churchill's fifty-ninth birthday. That night, at Chequers, she and her husband were joined for the family party by Duncan and Diana Sandys, Sarah and Mary Churchill, Jack Churchill and Jock Colville. 'The clocks were advanced to double summer time,' Colville noted in his diary, 'and we sat up till 4.30.' While Churchill worked, 'I played Gilbert and Sullivan and old music-hall songs (which are the PM's choice of music) on the gramophone.'[2] That night Churchill telegraphed to Yugoslavia to his son Randolph, his only child not at Chequers:

I was delighted to receive your letter, and I have sent all enclosures to their destinations. The more you can write me the better, especially descriptive letters, so that I can picture your daily life.

Members of Parliament henceforward have the right to speak in any constituency. The House of Commons this week has showed itself a rock on which war can be waged. Their kindness to their servant is beyond description.

I am keeping Winston with me in the country where he is safe from the London bombings and has room to play about. He comes to see me every day, and his mother sees him every week. He expressed great pleasure at your letter. Mary is in action two or three nights a week.

Much love from us all.[3]

On April 2 it was announced from Moscow that Russian troops had entered Rumania, and that Russia had no desire to acquire new territory, or to change Rumania's social structure. But the inter-war border between Rumania and the Soviet Union had been crossed some months earlier. By this announcement, the Soviets signalled that the large provinces of Bessarabia and Northern Bukovina, Rumanian from 1918 to 1940, were to be considered an integral part of the Soviet Union. Before 1914, Bessarabia had belonged to Tsarist Russia, Northern Bukovina to Austria–Hungary.

*   *   *

[1] Prime Minister's Personal Minute, M.338/4, 1 April 1944: Churchill papers, 20/152.
[2] Colville diary, 1 April 1944: Colville papers.
[3] Prime Minister's Personal Telegram, T.699/4, 'Private Personal and Secret', No. 203 to Cairo, sent at 4.20 a.m., 2 April 1944: Churchill papers, 20/160.

On April 2 Churchill agreed that, where necessary, anti-aircraft defences could be moved to the 'Overlord' ports from less vulnerable areas. 'It is quite understood,' he minuted, 'that the British public will take their share of anything that is going.' [1] On the following day Churchill gave his now regular lunch to Eisenhower and Bedell Smith. There were no other guests. Among the problems to be resolved was the destruction of the French railway network in the areas leading to the 'Overlord' beaches, in order to create a 'railway desert'. This problem was discussed at the War Cabinet on the following day, when Portal said that between 20,000 and 40,000 French civilians might be killed if the plan were to go ahead. Churchill told his colleagues: 'He felt some doubts as to the wisdom of this policy.' [2] That evening Churchill wrote to Eisenhower:

My dear General,
The Cabinet to-day took rather a grave and on the whole an adverse view of the proposal to bomb so many French railway centres, in view of the fact that scores of thousands of French civilians, men, women, and children, would lose their lives or be injured. Considering that they are all our friends, this might be held to be an act of very great severity, bringing much hatred on the Allied Air Forces. It was decided that the Defence Committee would consider the matter during this week, and that thereafter the Foreign Office should address the State Department and I should myself send a personal telegram to the President.
The argument for concentration on these particular targets is very nicely balanced on military grounds.

'The advantage to enemy propaganda,' Churchill added, 'seems to me very great, especially as this would not be in the heat of battle but a long time before.' [3]

On April 4 Churchill told the House of Commons the number of war dead since September 1939: 120,958 British soldiers, sailors and airmen, 49,730 civilian casualties in the United Kingdom, and 26,317 merchant seamen: a total of 197,005 United Kingdom deaths. [4] For Churchill, these were not mere statistics. 'The prospect of the 2nd Front worries him,' Jock Colville noted in his diary that night, 'though he says he is "hardening to it".' [5]

---

[1] Prime Minister's Personal Minute, D.106/4 (to the Chiefs of Staff, and Vice Chiefs of Staff), 2 April 1944: Churchill papers, 20/152.
[2] War Cabinet No. 42 of 1944, Confidential Annex: Cabinet papers, 65/46.
[3] 'Personal and Private', 3 April 1944: Churchill papers, 20/137.
[4] House of Commons, 4 April 1944: Hansard, columns 1817–18. The other military, naval and air dead included 12,298 Australians, 9,209 Canadians, 5,912 Indians, 5,622 New Zealanders and 3,107 South Africans.
[5] Colville diary, 4 April 1944: Colville papers.

41

April 1944: A Multitude of Problems

AS the planning of 'Overlord' proceeded, with only two months left before D-Day, Churchill and his Chiefs of Staff were confronted by new American pressures.

Still determined to launch an attack on the south of France, and to do so after 'Overlord', the United States Chiefs of Staff had made it clear that while they were prepared to release landing craft from the Pacific for 'Anvil', they were not willing to do so in order to help the Italian campaign.

Instead of cancelling 'Anvil', as the British Chiefs of Staff had asked, the Americans had delayed it until 10 July 1944. As a result of the delayed but still considerable switch of resources which this involved, it was clear, Brooke explained to the Chiefs of Staff on April 1, that operations in Italy 'would virtually be at a standstill during the most critical phase of "Overlord"', and that the eight weeks preparatory period for the postponed 'Anvil' 'would come just at the wrong time strategically'.[1]

'Difficulties again with our American friends,' Brooke noted in his diary four days later, 'who still persist in wanting to close down operations in Italy and open new ones in South of France, just at the most critical moment. . . .'[2] In a minute to the Chiefs of Staff Committee, Churchill commented bitterly: 'The campaign in the Aegean was ruined by stories of decisive battles in Italy. The decisive battles in Italy were ruined by pulling out seven of the best divisions at the critical time,' for 'Overlord'. He now feared that the future campaign in Italy would also be ruined, first, by what he called Alexander's 'desolating delay' in renewing the offensive, and second by the

---

[1] Chiefs of Staff Committee No. 107 (Operations) of 1944, 1 April 1944: Cabinet papers, 79/73.

[2] Brooke diary, 5 April 1944: Bryant, *op. cit.*, volume 2, page 177.

'shadow' of the South of France landing, 'which will spoil all operations after 14th May'. Churchill added: 'We shall therefore be reduced
to stalemate paralysis in Italy and building up a tardy "Anvil".' 'We
must be very careful,' Churchill warned, that, for the sake of accepting
landing craft from the 'sacred Pacific, we do not commit ourselves to
the complete frittering away both of "Anvil" and the march on
Rome'.[1]

Problems great and small continued to beset Churchill during the
first week of April. On April 6, he learned that the Americans were
about to send an Intelligence Mission to Mihailovic, at the very
moment when Britain was withdrawing its officers from Mihailovic's
headquarters, and putting all its political support behind Marshal
Tito. Churchill at once instructed SOE in Cairo to delay 'by every
reasonable means' any arrangements to fly the American Mission
into Yugoslavia, 'the greatest courtesy being used to our friends and
Allies in every case, but no transportation'.[2] The despatch of an American mission at such a time, he telegraphed to Roosevelt that same
day, 'will show throughout the Balkans a complete contrariety of action
between Britain and the United States'. The Russians, he added, 'will
certainly throw all their weight on Tito's side which we are backing
to the full. Thus we shall get altogether out of step.'[3]

A third issue pressing upon Churchill as D-Day drew nearer was
the problem of British Communists passing military secrets to the
Soviet Union. He had already given instructions for all known Communists to be investigated, and wherever it was felt that national security was at risk, to be removed from Government departments. The
issue arose again on April 6, in connection with those members of the
French National Committee who might be Communists, and who, as
part of the South of France landing preparations, would be sent to
England to work with their British and American opposite numbers.
On April 6 Churchill telegraphed to Duff Cooper, in Algiers:

I suppose you realize that we are weeding out remorselessly every single
known Communist from all our secret organizations. We did this after having
to sentence two quite high-grade people to long terms of penal servitude for
their betrayal, in accordance with Communist faith, of important military
secrets. If therefore the French Committee or any representatives sent here

[1] Prime Minister's Personal Minute, D.109/4, 5 April 1944: Churchill papers, 20/152.
[2] Prime Minister's Personal Telegram, T.728/4 (to Mr Broad, Cairo), 6 April 1944: Churchill
papers, 20/183.
[3] Prime Minister's Personal Telegram, T.729/4, Prime Minister to President, No. 638, 'Personal and Most Secret', 6 April 1944: Churchill papers, 20/161. Roosevelt replied to Churchill
that it was an entirely intelligence gathering mission with 'no political function whatever', and
agreed that it should not be sent (President to Prime Minister, No. 515, 'Personal and Top
Secret', 8 April 1944: Churchill papers, 20/161).

are infected with Communism, they will certainly not be made party to any British or, I expect, American secrets.[1]

'You will remember,' Churchill minuted to the Minister of State at the Foreign Office and Sir Alexander Cadogan a week later, 'that we are purging all our secret establishments of Communists because we know they owe no allegiance to us or to our cause and will always betray secrets to the Soviet, even while we are working together. The fact of the two Communists being on the French Committee requires extremely careful treatment of the question of imparting secret information to them.'[2]

To Duff Cooper, Churchill telegraphed ten days later that he should 'encourage' de Gaulle 'not to worry too much about Communists'. A Russian or a Yugoslav Communist, Churchill wrote, 'may be a hero; but many French Communists were traitors to France before Russia came into the war'. Churchill added: 'I thought it was a mistake when he put Communists into the Committee and certainly their presence there makes a bar against confidential information being imparted.'[3]

On Good Friday, April 7, General Brooke was among the senior British and American officers who went to St Paul's School, which had been taken over by Montgomery's invasion staff, to hear for the first time full details of the D-Day landings. This Good Friday meeting, which had been given the code name Exercise 'Thunderclap', heard first Admiral Ramsay and then Air Marshal Leigh-Mallory explain the naval and air plans. After lunch, the military commanders, among them Bradley and Dempsey, gave their accounts. After Montgomery had summed up, Brooke noted in his diary, 'the PM turned up and addressed a few remarks to the meeting. He was looking old and lacking a great deal of his usual vitality.'[4]

'On Good Friday I gave a good talk,' Churchill telegraphed to Roosevelt five days later, 'to all the Generals, British and American, who were gathered at General Montgomery's Headquarters, expressing my strong confidence in the result of this extraordinary but

[1] Prime Minister's Personal Telegram, T.730/4, 'Personal and Most Secret', No. 324 to Algiers, 6 April 1944: Churchill papers, 20/161.

[2] Prime Minister's Personal Minute, M.401/4, 13 April 1944: Churchill papers, 20/152.

[3] Prime Minister's Personal Telegram, T.935/4, 'Personal and Secret', 23 April 1944: Churchill papers, 20/163.

[4] Brooke diary, 7 April 1944: Bryant, op. cit., volume 2, pages 179–80. General Kennedy noted in his diary a few days later: 'Winston spoke without vigour. He did not look up much while he spoke. There was the usual wonderful flow of fine phrases, but no fire in the delivery. I thought he was going to burst into tears as he stepped down to sit beside Eisenhower and Monty and the Chiefs of Staff while the officers filed out of the room. But I heard afterwards that members of the audience who saw him on that day for the first time were tremendously impressed and inspired.' (Bernard Fergusson, editor, The Business of War, The War Narrative of Major-General Sir John Kennedy, London 1957, page 328.)

magnificent operation.' 'I do not agree,' Churchill added, 'with the loose talk which has been going on on both sides of the Atlantic about the unduly heavy casualties which we shall sustain. In my view it is the Germans who will suffer very heavy casualties when our band of brothers gets among them.'[1]

From Exercise 'Thunderclap', Churchill was driven to Chequers for the Easter weekend. There, for the first time, a Map Room had been set up by Captain Pim, to show the Pacific theatre.[2] On Saturday, April 8 the three Joint planners assembled at Chequers for a Staff Conference to discuss British policy in the war against Japan. Also present was Mountbatten's Army Chief of Staff, the American General A. C. Wedemeyer, with four other members of the South East Asia Command.[3] The meeting began at 11.30 in the morning, with Brigadier Sugden explaining the military, naval and air arrangements that were needed for an attack on the northern tip of Sumatra. Churchill then asked 'what had happened' to his own proposal to capture the island of Simeulue, also known as Simalur, 'and to base air forces there with which to attack Singapore'. In reply, Air Commodore Dawson said that it was indeed intended, during the 'first phase' of the capture of Sumatra, to capture Simalur 'for use as an advanced naval base'. But he also warned that 'weather conditions' on Sumatra, with low cloud after midday 'on one day out of two', would be 'most unfavourable to our air operations'.

Churchill told the Staff Conference that he had been considering 'what other islands in the Western Pacific' could be captured, to provide air bases 'from which to attack the enemy and to support operations forward'. He had in mind, he said, 'the capture of a series of islands, thus providing a series of tangent circles of air cover'. From a 'glance at the map', Christmas Island 'possessed attractions from this point of view'. But although, according to Captain Grantham, there were only two thousand Japanese soldiers on the islands and no aircraft, the whole coast 'was composed of high cliffs', making any assault difficult.

Churchill then spoke of his continuing preference for the 'Culverin' strategy, using British troops based in India to strike across the Bay of Bengal, as opposed to the use of British forces based on Australia to support the left flank of the American advance in the western Pacific, as agreed upon at the Cairo Conference. General Wedemeyer sup-

---

[1] Prime Minister's Personal Telegram, T.795/4, Prime Minister to President, No. 643, 'Private, Personal and Most Secret', 12 April 1944: Churchill papers, 20/161.

[2] Pim recollections: Pim papers.

[3] Private Office Diary (typescript), 8 April 1944. The Joint Planners present were Captain Grantham RN, Air Commodore Dawson and Brigadier Sugden; the officers from South East Asia Command were Major-General Macleod, Captain Goodenough RN, Lieutenant-Colonel Cary USAAF, and Lieutenant-Colonel de Chassiron.

ported Churchill, suggesting that after the northern tip of Sumatra had been seized, it might be 'desirable to go for the Sunda Straits and Borneo'. Our operations should be timed, he added, 'to assist the effort being made by the Americans in the Pacific'. But Churchill warned that 'it would be wrong' in these operations for Mountbatten 'to count on receiving land forces from Europe'. Most of the Indian forces which he hoped to see returned to India 'had suffered losses in the battle in Italy and it was unlikely that they could be used for the purpose'. The planning of 'Culverin' should not be carried out, Churchill warned, 'on any assumption of the availability of additional land forces being sent from Europe', but by 'establishing ourselves in the islands', he concluded, in urging that the planning enquiries should go ahead, 'we obtained great advantage at small cost'.

The meeting ended with the Joint Planning Staff being instructed to 'examine and report on' the potentialities as air bases of Simalur, Nias, Batu, Christmas Island, Timor and the islands of the Malay Barrier, on the assumption that operations would begin in November 1944, provided the operations in northern Burma were successful, and the deep water harbours in northern France in Allied hands by September 1944.[1] 'Winston was in very good form,' Guy Grantham later recalled, 'gave us an excellent late lunch and with many anecdotes.' [2]

There were problems in the first week of April much nearer home. In Cairo, at the end of March, a mutiny of Greek troops had led to the resignation of the Greek Prime Minister, Emmanuel Tsouderos. These troops had then declared their loyalty to the Greek Communists, who in rivalry to the Greek Government in exile in Cairo, had set up a Committee of National Liberation in the Greek mountains. Eden having just taken three weeks' leave of absence on doctor's orders, Churchill was in charge of the Foreign Office when the news of this mutiny reached London. 'This is an occasion,' he telegraphed on April 6 to Philip Broad, a Foreign Office representative with the Greek Government in exile, 'for you to show those qualities of imperturbability and command which are associated with the British diplomatic service.' [3]

Two days later, on April 8, Churchill learned that a Greek destroyer at Alexandria had refused to obey orders to go to sea unless a Greek Government were formed which contained Communist representatives. In Cairo, the 4,500 men of the 1st Greek Brigade who had

---

[1] 'Minutes of a Staff Conference held at Chequers. . . .', 'Top Secret', 8 April 1944: Cabinet papers, 78/21.

[2] Sir Guy Grantham recollections: letter to the author, 8 January 1985.

[3] Prime Minister's Personal Telegram, T.728/4 (to Mr Broad, Cairo), 6 April 1944: Churchill papers, 20/183.

mutinied against their officers, took up defensive positions around its camp. Churchill at once telegraphed from Chequers to the commander of the British troops in Egypt, General Paget:

A mutinous brigade threatening its officers should certainly be surrounded and forced to surrender by stoppage of all supplies. Why do you leave out water? Will this not bring the desired result quicker? Obviously these troops should be disarmed. I agree that the hope of getting them to Italy may have to be abandoned. Keep me fully informed of plans for disarming. We cannot tolerate political revolutions carried out by foreign military formations for which we are ultimately responsible. In all cases large numbers of British troops should be used so as to overawe, and thus minimise bloodshed.[1]

'You will have achieved success,' Churchill telegraphed to Paget on the following day, 'if you bring the Brigade under control without bloodshed. But brought under control it must be. Count on my support.'[2] It was a 'lamentable fact', Churchill telegraphed to Reginald Leeper, the British Ambassador to the Greek Government, that the Greek soldiers, who were about to raise the name of Greece 'high in the world' on the battlefields of Italy, 'should have signalized this opportunity by an undignified, even squalid exhibition of indiscipline which many will attribute to an unworthy fear of being sent to the front'.[3] Not only the military and diplomatic, but also the naval aspect of the Greek revolt came under Churchill's scrutiny that weekend. On April 9 he minuted to the First Lord and First Sea Lord:

Make sure you have ample forces available in Alexandria to enforce discipline upon the mutinous Greek ships. It is always wise on these occasions to have ample plurality. This minimises the risk of having to use force and makes it the more effective should evil conduct prevail. Make sure the mutinous Greek destroyers do not loose off their torpedoes in all directions. This can probably be done by training the harbour guns upon them and letting them know beforehand the weight of metal they might have to face. It would be better to use the fortress guns than to get our destroyers close enough to be mauled. Take your time about it; but even a heavy shot or two might show them what they are up against.[4]

In the next two weeks Churchill repeated these instructions several times. On April 14 he learned that the Greek mutineers might be prepared to negotiate. 'Do not show yourself over-eager to parley,' he

[1] Prime Minister's Personal Telegram, T.753/4, 'Personal and Secret', 8 April 1944: Churchill papers, 20/161.
[2] Prime Minister's Personal Telegram, T.766/4, OZ 1868, 'Personal and Top Secret', 9 April 1944: Churchill papers, 20/161.
[3] Prime Minister's Personal Telegram, T.764/4, 'Personal and Secret', 9 April 1944: Churchill papers, 20/161.
[4] Prime Minister's Personal Minute, M.389/4, 9 April 1944: Churchill papers, 20/152.

telegraphed to Leeper. 'Simply keep them rounded up by artillery and superior force and let hunger do its part.' [1] 'No treaty with mutineers,' he telegraphed to Paget. 'They must surrender and be disarmed.' [2]

On the evening of April 23, the mutinous Greek ships were boarded by Greek sailors loyal to the King. On the following day, British troops, under Paget's command, surrounded the Greek camp, and in the ensuing 'battle' one British officer was killed. The Greek brigade then surrendered. There had been no Greek casualties. [3]

Among the guests at Chequers on April 9 was the Polish Prime Minister, Mikolajczyk, the American Ambassador, Gilbert Winant, and the American Under Secretary of State, Edward Stettinius. Both England and America, Churchill assured Mikolajczyk in the presence of the two Americans, 'would never allow the loss of independence by Poland', nor would they rest 'until Poland had recovered it'. Although he had not changed his mind, Churchill said, about the Curzon Line, or the 'restitution of Poland with compensations in the west, the American support for Poland was stronger'. Churchill went on, at dinner, to urge that the Polish Government 'should immediately dismiss' its Commander-in-Chief, General Sosnkowski, whose anti-Soviet statements had caused such offence in Moscow. But this Mikolajczyk refused to do. He also pointed out that the Russians had raised the status of their Polish division, renaming it the Polish Army, and that they intended, after crossing the Curzon Line, to set up a Government in Lublin. 'Mr Churchill reacted strongly to this,' the minutes recorded, 'saying: "We shall not recognize any Government set up by the Soviets in this way."'

At the end of their discussion, Churchill assured Mikolajczyk 'that neither England nor America would ever allow Poland to lose her independence and to become a satellite State'. They would 'never', he added, 'suffer any kind of tyranny in Europe'. [4]

The Polish Government, Churchill wrote in a minute to Sir Owen

[1] Prime Minister's Personal Telegram, T.808/4, 'Personal and Secret', 14 April 1944: Churchill papers, 20/162.

[2] Prime Minister's Personal Telegram, T.823/4, OZ 1966, 'Personal', 14 April 1944: Churchill papers, 20/162.

[3] CIC/35, 'Personal from General Paget to Prime Minister', IZ 3490, 24 April 1944: Churchill papers, 20/163. Churchill sent the text of Paget's telegram to Roosevelt that same day, as Prime Minister's Personal Telegram, T.946/4, Prime Minister to President, No. 660, 24 April 1944: Churchill papers, 20/163.

[4] 'Notes on a conversation between M. Mikolajczyk and Mr Churchill. . . .', 9 April 1944: *Documents on Polish–Soviet Relations, 1939–1945*, volume 2, document No. 124, pages 220–4.

O'Malley, had 'lost a great opportunity' by not accepting the Soviet proposals for the Curzon Line. But, he added, 'it seems to me this opportunity had now returned', if the Poles were to dismiss General Sosnkowski, 'the Soviet bugbear'.[1]

Churchill remained at Chequers throughout Easter Monday, April 10, lunching with Winant and Stettinius, who had stayed overnight. At 6.30 that afternoon, following his usual sleep, Churchill held a meeting on the naval construction programme and naval shipbuilding, with the First Lord, the Controller and Lord Cherwell, all of whom remained for dinner.[2]

On April 9, while Churchill had been at Chequers, the Vice-Chiefs of Staff had met to consider four telegrams from the Joint Staff Mission in Washington, reporting on the withdrawal of the American offer of landing craft from the Pacific. These landing craft had been intended for an early 'Anvil' landing in the south of France, which Britain had opposed. In accepting this British opposition, and agreeing that 'Anvil' was not to take place before or simultaneously with 'Overlord', the American offer of landing craft was withdrawn.[3]

In a minute that Easter Sunday to Churchill, the Vice-Chiefs of Staff pointed out that the withdrawal of the American offer of landing craft from the Pacific, together with the present programme of transferring landing craft from the Mediterranean to Britain, for 'Overlord', would leave Maitland Wilson with 'something a little less than one divisional assault lift in the Mediterranean'. Their minute continued: 'The amphibious operations open to him, therefore, will be restricted in scope to an amphibious cat's claw in Italy, or the maintenance of a threat against the South of France, with the possibility of a descent in that area with a smaller force than that contemplated for the original "Anvil" if, when the time came, this would best help "Overlord".'[4]

A telegram for Maitland Wilson from Brooke, approved at the Chiefs of Staff Committee on Easter Sunday, informed him that '"Anvil" in its original conception is cancelled', that the United States Chiefs of Staff 'have withdrawn their offer to divert US landing craft

---

[1] Prime Minister's Personal Minute, M.394/4, 10 April 1944: Churchill papers, 20/152.
[2] Private Office diary, 10 April 1944.
[3] Chiefs of Staff Commitee No. 115 (O) of 1944, 11.30 a.m. Easter Sunday, 9 April 1944: Cabinet papers, 79/73.
[4] Minute of 9 April 1944: Chiefs of Staff Committee No. 115 (O) of 1944, Annex: Cabinet papers, 79/73.

from the Pacific to the Mediterranean', and that Wilson's 'object' was now '(i) To give the greatest possible assistance to "Overlord" by containing the maximum enemy forces away from the "Overlord" lodgment area; (ii) to launch, as early as practicable, a co-ordinated, sustained all-out offensive to join the bridgehead with the main line in Italy.' [1]

On April 11 Churchill left Chequers for London. That evening there was a meeting of the Chiefs of Staff Committee, attended by Alexander, to discuss the timing of the next Allied offensive at Anzio. May 14, Alexander told them, was 'the earliest practicable date for the attack' for joining up the bridgehead with the main front. [2]

'General Alexander has arrived home,' Churchill telegraphed to General Marshall on the following day, 'and has convinced us that an all-out sustained major offensive cannot be launched earlier. Moreover the timing of this great battle will accord harmoniously with the date of "Overlord".' As a result of Alexander's new date, Churchill pointed out, all available British, American and Allied forces 'will be in heavy action on both fronts simultaneously'. [3]

Churchill was disappointed by the further month's delay, but deferred to Alexander's arguments. 'He defended his actions or inactions with much force,' Churchill told Roosevelt, 'pointing out the small plurality of his army, its mixed character, there being no fewer than seven separate nationalities against the homogeneous Germans, the vileness of the weather and the extremely awkward nature of the ground. At latest by the date in my immediately following he will attack and push everything in as hard as possible. If this battle were successful or even raging at full blast it would fit in very well with other plans.' [4]

The Italian campaign was to resume on May 14. 'Although the fighting at the bridgehead and on the Cassino front has brought many disappointments,' Churchill told Marshall in his telegram of April 12, 'you will I trust recognize that at least eight extra German divisions have been brought into Italy down to the south of Rome and heavily mauled there.' The Enigma decrypts, Churchill pointed out, showed that Hitler had been saying 'that his defeats in South Russia are due to the treacherous Badoglio collapse of Italy which has involved thirty-

[1] 'Most Secret and Private', draft telegram, 9 April 1944, Chiefs of Staff Committee No. 115 (O) of 1944, Appendix 1: Cabinet papers, 79/73.
[2] Chiefs of Staff Committee No. 118 (Operations) of 1944, 'Secretary's Standard File', 12 April 1944: Cabinet papers, 79/89.
[3] Prime Minister's Personal Telegram, T.783/4, OZ 1895, 'Personal and Most Secret', 12 April 1944: Churchill papers, 20/161.
[4] Prime Minister's Personal Telegram, T.936/4, Prime Minister to President, No. 657, 'Personal, Private and Top Secret', 24 April 1944: Churchill papers, 20/163.

five divisions'. 'At any rate,' Churchill added, 'I believe that our action in Italy has played a large part in rendering possible the immensely important advances made in South Russia, which as a further benefit are convulsing the Satellites.'

Churchill now addressed the question of what the Allied object in Italy should be, telling Marshall, in support of his renewed plea for landing craft to be transferred at once from the Pacific to the Mediterranean:

At the moment my own position is as follows. We should above all defeat the German army south of Rome and join our own armies. Nothing should be grudged for this. We cannot tell how either the Allied or enemy armies will emerge from the battle until the battle has been fought. It may be that the enemy will be thrown into disorder, and that great opportunities of exploitation may be open. Or we may be checked, and the enemy may continue to hold his positions south of Rome against us with his existing forces. On the other hand, he may seek to withdraw some of his Divisions to the main battle in France. It seems to me we must have plans and preparations to take advantage of the above possibilities.

Regarding 'Anvil', Churchill explained:

I believe that whatever happens on the mainland of Italy, the enemy forces now detached to the Riviera can in the meanwhile be fastened there by feints and threats. One thing that alarms me, however, is lest our Directive to General Wilson should make him fall between two stools. This would mean that we should be denied the exploitation of any victory gained south of Rome (and victories are wonderful things) or the power to pin down German divisions in Italy, and yet on the other hand not be able to make a major operation out of 'Anvil'.

If the march on Rome were successful, Churchill added, 'I would not now rule out either a vigorous pursuit northward of the beaten enemy nor an amphibious cat's-claw higher up to detain him or cut him off.' Plans and preparations ought to be contrived 'to render possible either this or "Anvil" in one form or another'. If thirty-four German divisions could be kept in the western Mediterranean theatre, Churchill commented, 'the forces there will have made an immense contribution to "Overlord"'. He had 'hardened very much upon "Overlord"', Churchill told Marshall, 'and am further fortified by the evident confidence of Eisenhower, Brooke and Montgomery'.

When the Italian campaign had been renewed, Churchill told Marshall, and the 'first results' of 'Overlord' were known, it would be necessary to decide 'whether to go all out for "Anvil" or exploit the results of the victory in Italy'. But it had to be recognized that this option 'will not exist' unless the landing craft from the Pacific 'are now assigned to the Mediterranean'.

Churchill ended his telegram on a personal note, sending 'Every good wish' to Marshall, King and Arnold, the American Joint Chiefs of Staff.[1] 'How I wish we were all together,' Churchill wrote, 'but I trust we shall be reassembled before the supreme struggle begins.'[2] Marshall was not impressed, nor helpful, replying that preparations for 'Anvil' 'must be made now, even though they may be at the partial expense of future operations in Italy after the bridgehead had been joined to the main line'. Nor, he told Churchill, could any more landing craft be spared from the Pacific, as this would result 'in the loss of the renewed momentum which means so much towards shortening the period of the war in the Pacific'.[3]

That night, after late duty at Downing Street, Jock Colville echoed the earlier comments of General Brooke when he noted in his diary: 'Struck by how very tired and worn out the PM looks now.'[4]

After nearly four years as Prime Minister, three serious illnesses, and many setbacks, there seemed to be no end to the intractable problems and difficult decisions: 'Anvil' versus a vigorous follow-up campaign in Italy, the American refusal to transfer landing craft then lying unused in the Pacific in order to make sure of success in Italy, the Bay of Bengal versus the Pacific as the regions for Britain's Far Eastern offensive, the future of Poland, Yugoslavia and Greece demanding time and decisions, Anglo-American relations requiring a constant watch, Anglo-Soviet relations at a low ebb, de Gaulle clamant, 'Overlord' looming, the German secret weapon imminent. No day passed without one or other, or several, of these issues demanding urgent discussion.

The present was beset with problems, and the future looked bleak. On April 13 Churchill again questioned the bombing of French railways in the 'Overlord' zone as an essential prelude to the landings themselves. 'PM scared of casualties to the French entailed by this policy,' Brooke noted in his diary.[5] 'This slaughter was likely to put the French against us,' Churchill warned the Defence Committee that

---

[1] On 17 April 1944 Churchill telegraphed to General Arnold: 'The Chief of the Air Staff has just informed me that you have very kindly allocated a C.54 to be fitted out for my use on long-distance flights. This will solve many of our transport difficulties for important passengers as well as myself and add greatly to our comfort and convenience. I am most grateful. Please accept my best thanks.' (Prime Minister's Personal Telegram, T.848/4, OZ 1987, 'Personal', 17 April 1944: Churchill papers, 20/162.)

[2] Prime Minister's Personal Telegram, T.783/4, OZ 1895, 'Personal and Most Secret', 12 April 1944: Churchill papers, 20/161.

[3] W/22810, 'Top Secret', 'Urgent', 14 April 1944: Churchill papers, 20/162.

[4] Colville diary, 12 April 1944: Colville papers.

[5] Brooke diary, 13 April 1944: Bryant, op. cit., volume 2, page 182.

evening, 'and he was doubtful if the results achieved by the plan would justify it. There was a limit to the slaughter and the resulting anger and resentment which it would arouse among Frenchmen beyond which we could not go.' [1] Two weeks later, the War Cabinet supported Churchill's doubts that the 'strategic advantages' of the plan would justify its continuance, and concluded that 'it was certainly wrong on humanitarian grounds', and it might, on balance, 'well do more evil than good'. [2] He 'had not fully realized,' Churchill told the War Cabinet when the matter was raised again, 'that our use of air power before "Overlord" would assume so cruel and remorseless a form.' It was 'clear', he added, 'that great slaughter would inevitably result. . . .' [3] All depended upon Roosevelt, to whom Churchill telegraphed directly:

I am satisfied that all possible care will be taken to minimise this slaughter of friendly civilian life. Nevertheless the War Cabinet share my apprehensions of the bad effect which will be produced upon the French civilian population by these slaughters, all taking place so long before 'Overlord' D-Day. They may easily bring about a great revulsion in French feeling towards their approaching United States and British liberators. They may leave a legacy of hate behind them.

He had 'just now' received a telegram from Duff Cooper, the British Ambassador to the French National Committee at Algiers, Churchill noted, 'which I am pretty sure represents a serious wave of opinion in France', and he continued:

It may well be that the French losses will grow heavier on and after D-Day, but in the heat of battle, when British and United States troops will probably be losing at a much higher rate, a new proportion establishes itself in men's minds. It is the intervening period that causes me most anxiety. [4]

Roosevelt did not defer to Churchill's view. 'I am not prepared,' he replied, 'to impose from this distance any restriction on military action by the responsible commanders that in their opinion might militate against the success of "Overlord" or cause additional loss of life to our Allied forces of invasion.' [5]

Churchill had also seen King Peter of Yugoslavia on the previous day, and as he telegraphed to Molotov on April 14, had advised him

[1] War Cabinet Defence Committee No. 6 of 1944, 13 April 1944, Confidential Annex: Cabinet papers, 69/6.

[2] War Cabinet No. 58 of 1944, 27 April 1944, Confidential Annex: Cabinet papers, 65/46.

[3] War Cabinet No. 61 of 1944, 2 May 1944, Confidential Annex, Cabinet papers, 65/46.

[4] Prime Minister's Personal Telegram, T.1044/4, Prime Minister to President, No. 669, 'Personal and Top Secret', 7 May 1944: Churchill papers, 20/164.

[5] President to Prime Minister, No. 537, 'Personal and Top Secret', 11 May 1944: Churchill papers, 20/164.

to dismiss the Puric Government, in which Mihailovic was Minister of War, and to form a small administration composed of people 'not particularly obnoxious to Tito but still preserving a certain relation with the Serbian nation'. Such a step, Churchill pointed out, would 'automatically' deprive Mihailovic of his position of Minister of War. 'My only object in Yugoslavia,' Churchill told Molotov, 'is the united action of the three elements, Serbians, Croats and Slovenes of all classes and politics, into an intense effort to kill the Germans or drive them out and to get into friendly touch with any guerrillas who may take to the mountains from Hungary as well as with any Roumanians who choose to side with them on the eastern frontiers of Yugoslavia.'[1]

Churchill sent this telegram in his capacity as acting Foreign Secretary in Eden's absence. 'PM dictated telegram to Molotov telling him what we are doing,' Cadogan noted in his diary, and he added: 'PM rather fractious—or depressed. Hadn't had his afternoon sleep, I think—planned to take it in car on the way to Chequers this evening.'[2]

At a Staff Conference before he left London, Churchill suggested that Britain should make 'one last attempt' to induce the American Chiefs of Staff 'to keep open' their offer of additional landing craft for the Mediterranean. Brooke pointed out, however, that the American attitude was that once the Anzio bridgehead and the main front line in Italy had been joined, 'we should assume a defensive strategy in Italy and concentrate our attention on preparations for "Anvil"'. Brooke added:

In his opinion, this strategy would be absolutely wrong. Our aim was to destroy or contain the maximum number of German formations in the Mediterranean and thus prevent their participation in the operations opposing 'Overlord'. It might well be that, after the bridgehead had been joined, the enemy would have decided seriously to oppose our advance on a line south of Rome at a time when better weather, easier geographical conditions, and the organisation we had already built up to support our forces in that theatre would permit us to engage him on favourable terms. In such circumstances it would be folly to divide our forces with the consequent risk of being forced on to the defensive in Italy and in any bridgehead we might establish in the South of France.

Cunningham went even further, urging a 'clear-cut decision now'

---

[1] Prime Minister's Personal Telegram, T.819/4, 'Most Secret', No. 1130 to Moscow, 14 April 1944: Churchill papers, 20/162. Four days later, Churchill wrote to his son, who was still behind German lines in Yugoslavia: 'The Serbians are a valiant and powerful race, accustomed to centuries of torment. They have a large peasant proprietary and there can be no united Yugoslavia without their willing accord. A Balkan State without a Crown is an unimpressive political unit. They will need all their united forces and powerful connections to keep their independence.' (Letter of 18 April 1944: Churchill papers, 1/381.)

[2] Cadogan diary, 14 April 1944: David Dilks (editor), op. cit., pages 618–19.

to abandon 'Anvil', even if this resulted in the loss of landing craft which might otherwise be obtained from the Pacific. The cancellation of 'Anvil' would, he said, 'at the least, ease the minds of Commanders and remove the shadow of the dead hand of "Anvil", which was at present exerting a serious influence on operations in Italy'.[1]

Churchill was not ready to leave London that evening until nearly eight o'clock. Among the telegrams which he sent that day was one to Roosevelt, which revealed yet further problems with the Americans. In this telegram, Churchill urged that the American Chiefs of Staff revoke their recent decision not to increase the programme for the manufacture of landing craft. Such an increase, Roosevelt had explained, would involve 'interference' with other programmes.[2] This American decision, Churchill replied, if persisted in, would limit Britain's power to help in the war against Japan. 'I hope you will bear this in mind,' Churchill added, 'if there are any complaints hereafter.'[3] Roosevelt, on receiving this telegram, instructed his Staff neither to acknowledge it, nor to reply to it.[4]

Churchill knew nothing of this decision, and on April 16, as pressed to do by the British Chiefs of Staff, he telegraphed direct to Marshall about the 'absurd shortage' of the LST tank landing craft:

How it is that the plans of two great empires like Britain and the United States should be so much hamstrung and limited by a hundred or two of these particular vessels will never be understood by history.[5] I am deeply concerned at the strong disinclination of the American Government even to keep the manufacture of LSTs at its full height so as to have a sufficient number to give to us to help you in the war against Japan. The absence of these special vessels may limit our whole war effort on your left flank, and I fear we shall be accused unjustly of not doing our best, as we are resolved to do.

Churchill also sought to influence Marshall not to let strategic planning of 'Anvil' affect the battle in Italy, telling Marshall: 'What I cannot bear is to agree beforehand to starve a battle or have to break it off just at the moment when success, after long efforts and heavy

---

[1] Staff Conference, Chiefs of Staff Committee No. 123 (Operations) of 1944, 4.45 p.m., 14 April 1944: Cabinet papers, 79/73.

[2] President to Prime Minister, No. 520, 'Personal and Secret', 14 April 1944: Churchill papers, 20/162.

[3] Prime Minister's Personal telegram, T.822/4, Prime Minister to President, No. 645, 'Top Secret and Personal', 14 April 1944: Churchill papers, 20/183.

[4] Warren F. Kimball, *Churchill & Roosevelt, The Complete Correspondence*, Princeton, New Jersey, 1984, volume 3, page 91.

[5] In his diary on 19 April 1944, Brooke also referred to history in connection with the United States landing craft. 'History,' he wrote, 'will never forgive them for bargaining equipment against strategy and for trying to blackmail us into agreeing with them by holding a pistol of withdrawing craft at our heads. . . .' (Brooke diary, 19 April 1944: Bryant, *op. cit.*, volume 2, page 184.)

losses, may be in view. Our forces in Italy are not much larger than those of the enemy. They comprise seven or eight different races, while the enemy is all German. The wet weather has hitherto restricted the full use of our superiority in artillery, in armour, and in the air.' Churchill's telegram continued: 'Alexander tells me that he strikes out north-east, not south-east, from the Anzio beach-head shortly after his main thrust across the Rapido. Thus,' as he explained to Marshall:

. . . there will not necessarily be a moment when we shall pause and say, 'Halt here. Go over to the defensive. All aboard for "Anvil".' Nor will there necessarily be an exact moment when the cutting of supplies for the Italian battle for the sake of 'Anvil' can be fixed beforehand in imagination. A half-hearted undercurrent sets in with an army which has a divided objective, part to the front and part to the rear. This infects all the rearward services, who cannot help knowing. Remember the terrible bleeding the armies in Italy got when their seven best divisions were taken for 'Overlord'.

Of course, if the battle goes wrong early and we are hung up before other enemy lines of defence and forced to go over to a general defensive no doubt strong forces could then be spared, but the drain of feeding the bridgehead would continue to press on our landing-craft, and without your Pacific landing-craft there will be no two-division lift for any amphibious operations, 'Anvil' or other.

Therefore it seems to me we must throw our hearts into this battle, for the sake of which so many American and British lives have already been sacrificed, and make it, like 'Overlord', an all-out conquer or die. It may well be that by May 31 we shall see many things which are now veiled from us. I regret having to forgo such an hour of choice.

Churchill's telegram to Marshall continued:

Dill tells me that you had expected me to support 'Anvil' more vigorously in view of my enthusiasm for it when it was first proposed by you at Teheran. Please do me the justice to remember that the situation is vastly changed. In November we hoped to take Rome in January, and there were many signs that the enemy was ready to [retire] northwards up the Italian peninsula. Instead of this, in spite of our great amphibious expedition, we are stuck where we are, and the enemy has brought down to the battle south of Rome the eight mobile divisions we should have hoped a full-scale 'Anvil' would have contained. Thus there has been cause for rejoicing as well as bitter disappointment.[1]

On April 15, at Chequers, Churchill pondered the question of who should succeed Sir Harold MacMichael as High Commissioner in

[1] Prime Minister's Personal Telegram, T.843/4, OZ 1985, 'Most Secret and Personal', 16 April 1944: Churchill papers, 20/162.

Palestine. The half million Jews of Palestine feared a High Commissioner who might be unsympathetic towards their hopes of eventual statehood. Churchill had long favoured the setting up of a Jewish State in Palestine. After a Royal Commission in 1936 had proposed the partition of Palestine into two separate states, one Jewish and one Arab, the Zionist leadership inside and beyond Palestine, including Dr Weizmann, had been prepared to accept Statehood on those terms. The Foreign Office had not supported the Royal Commission's advocacy of partition, being in favour of self-determination for the majority Arabs, and an end to Jewish immigration on a scale capable of securing in due course a Jewish majority. Such was the policy of the 1939 Palestine White Paper, to which Churchill had been, and remained, opposed. He therefore suggested that Weizmann himself should succeed MacMichael, and, failing Weizmann, another British Jew, Lord Melchett. As Churchill minuted to the Colonial Secretary:

We have plenty of time in which to settle this appointment. I do not think it should be of a departmental character. It should certainly be one to give satisfaction to the Jews and, at the same time, do justice to the Arabs. I wonder if Dr Weizmann would take it? He had rendered great service by his science to the Allied cause. He would certainly take a world-wide view. It might ruin him with the Jews, but it would, in the first instance, quell a good deal of the trouble in the United States. You can depend on Weizmann. He would not take on a job if he did not mean to stick to the conditions which would have to be imposed.

The present Lord Samuel, when Governor of Palestine, held the scales there evenly, and got much abused by fellow Jews.[1]

Another possibility would be Lord Melchett, if his health were good enough to stand it, but Weizmann would be better. I believe both of them would be ready to work towards your partition scheme. I do not believe at all in Colonial Office officials or military men in this particular task so full of world politics.[2]

Four days after writing this minute, Churchill presided at a meeting of the Defence Committee, at which Brooke spoke of the Palestine repercussions which might follow the political crisis which had just arisen in Egypt, with King Farouk wishing to dismiss his Prime Minister and choose another more amenable to the royal wishes. The Jews, warned Brooke, 'who we knew were forming a secret army in Palestine, might well seize on such a moment to create trouble'. Churchill's reply was emphatic: 'He did not believe there would be

---

[1] Lord Samuel, then Sir Herbert Samuel, had been High Commissioner of Palestine from 1921 to 1925.

[2] Prime Minister's Personal Minute, M.429/4, 'Most Secret', 15 April 1944: Churchill papers, 20/152.

any general trouble with the Jews,' and he went on to tell the Committee that there were 'a small number of extremists who were likely to cause trouble and there might be some murders': a general rising was, however, 'most unlikely'. It might be advisable, Churchill said, 'to tell Dr Weizmann that if such murders continued and the campaign of abuse of the British in the American papers did not stop, we might well lose interest in Jewish welfare'.[1]

On April 17 the Secretary of State for War, Sir James Grigg, sent Churchill a letter from Montgomery, suggesting a special Church Service for the 'hallowing' of the Armed Forces of the Crown. Such a Service, Montgomery believed, would be particularly impressive if the King were to allow the Coronation regalia to be used. Churchill opposed Montgomery's suggestion. A day of prayer, he felt, ought not to be ordained until after the battle had started. He had earlier expressed his fears, to the War Cabinet, that such a day of prayer in advance of the battle might have rather a depressing effect on the soldiers. He would certainly 'never advise' the King to allow the Coronation regalia to be used in such circumstances, he minuted to Grigg, and he went on, in censorious vein:

I am of opinion that the Army Council should instruct General Montgomery to bring to an end his public tours and civic receptions. We are getting very near the great battle, and a bad effect will be produced if it is thought that the General immediately responsible is spending his time at demonstrations which are more appropriate after the victory than before. Let not him that girdeth on his harness boast himself as he that putteth it off. There is a mass of intricate Staff work to be done, and the Army Council, yourself and the C.I.G.S. are directly responsible for seeing that this is not relegated to second place. If anything were to go seriously wrong and it were found that something had been neglected, the General would come in for heavy criticism.[2]

One problem as 'Overlord' drew near was the question of some public pronouncement as to the future of a defeated Germany. On April 15 Cadogan had asked Churchill if there could be some public clarification about the term 'unconditional surrender'. Certain British generals, he said, felt that some clear message of intent was needed. 'I may say I think it all wrong,' Churchill replied on April 19, 'for the generals to start

---

[1] War Cabinet Defence Committee (Operations), 7th meeting of 1944, 'Top Secret', 19 April 1944: Cabinet papers, 69/9.
[2] Prime Minister's Personal Minute, M.433/4, 18 April 1944: Churchill papers, 20/152.

shivering before the battle,' and he added: 'This battle has been forced upon us by the Russians and by the United States military authorities. We have gone in wholeheartedly, and I would not raise a timorous cry before a decision in the field has been taken.'

As to the actual terms of surrender contemplated by the Allies, these, 'if stated in detail', Churchill noted, were 'not of a character' to reassure the Germans, and he went on to explain:

Both President Roosevelt and Marshal Stalin at Teheran wish to cut Germany into smaller pieces than I had in mind. Stalin spoke of very large mass executions of over 50,000 of the Staffs and military experts. Whether he was joking or not could not be ascertained. The atmosphere was jovial but also grim. He certainly said that he would require 4,000,000 German males to work for an indefinite period to rebuild Russia. We have promised the Poles that they shall have compensation both in East Prussia and, if they like, up to the line of the Oder. There are a lot of other terms implying the German ruin and indefinite prevention of their rising again as an armed Power.[1]

On April 19 the United States Chiefs of Staff at last agreed that 'we must throw everything we have in the Mediterranean into the battle in Italy in order to reduce the German capability to move forces to oppose "Overlord"'. As Churchill and the British Chiefs of Staff had urged for so long, Italy, not the south of France, was henceforth to be the priority. Since Eisenhower's cross-Channel assault 'is not now be supported by a landing in southern France', Marshall telegraphed to Churchill, 'every possible deceptive effort—air, sea and ground—in the Mediterranean will have to be utilized to hold the Germans in southern France during the critical days of "Overlord"'.[2] 'I can see nothing to dislike in Marshall's telegram,' Field Marshal Dill informed Churchill, 'except the fact that he still finds it impossible to provide the landing craft which are so sorely needed in the Mediterranean.' As to putting these issues direct to Roosevelt, Dill was doubtful. 'The President, as you know, is not military minded,' he wrote, 'and you will, in my view, gain little by referring purely military questions to him.'[3]

Of the decision to give priority to the Italian campaign, Churchill telegraphed to Roosevelt on April 24: 'I am very glad at what has happened in Italy. It seems to me that we have both succeeded in gaining what we sought. The only thing now lacking is a victory.'[4]

---

[1] Prime Minister's Personal Minute, M.446/4 (in reply to Cadogan's minute, PM44/252 of 15 April 1944): Churchill papers, 20/152.
[2] W/24751, 'Top Secret', 'Urgent', 19 April 1944: Churchill papers, 20/162.
[3] FMD/194, IZ 3495, 'Private and Personal', 24 April 1944: Churchill papers, 20/163.
[4] Prime Minister to President No. 657, 'Personal, Private and Top Secret', Prime Minister's Personal Telegram, T.936/4, 24 April 1944: Churchill papers, 20/163.

Cadogan, dealing with Churchill daily in Eden's absence, was worried, as Brooke and Colville had been, by the Prime Minister's state of health. 'PM, I fear, is breaking down,' he noted in his diary after a War Cabinet on April 19. 'He rambles without a pause, and we really got nowhere. . . .' Cadogan added: 'I really am fussed about the PM. He is *not* the man he was twelve months ago, and I really don't know whether he can carry on.'[1] But carry on he did. On April 20, Cadogan had gone to see him at ten in the morning—to find 'He and Clemmie playing Bezique'.[2] After this brief relaxation, Churchill was in the House of Commons to answer questions, and then lunched with two Americans, John J. McCloy, the Assistant Secretary for War, and Lieutenant General Joseph T. McNarney, the Deputy Chief of Staff. 'Our conversation,' McNarney wrote a week later, 'materially added to our understanding of conditions', giving him and McCloy 'a better understanding of the situation. We were greatly reassured by all we saw in England and by your courage and confidence.'[3] Early that evening, Churchill presided over the War Cabinet, after which he saw Gilbert Winant about Ireland, saw Cadogan after dinner to discuss Foreign Office matters, and then spent the rest of the evening preparing his speech for the Empire Affairs debate on the following day.[4] At one moment, reverting to the possibility that Lord Cranborne might succeed Eden as Foreign Secretary, and Eden become First Lord of the Treasury, Churchill told Colville that the 'trouble' about Cranborne was 'that when he wasn't ill he would be obstinate. It would be a question of a fortnight's illness alternating with a fortnight's obstinacy.'[5]

On April 21 Churchill went to the House of Commons where he was to wind up the debate on Empire Affairs. 'We spent the day at the H of C,' Jock Colville noted in his diary, 'while the PM listened to the debate on Empire affairs and prepared his own speech. He re-wrote it in a last-minute feverish rush and wasn't even able to have his afternoon sleep in the bed which he had had specially installed in his room at the House. Nevertheless he made a good speech, shewing more vigour than he has of late and presenting a fine apologia for the British Commonwealth and Empire. The House approved.'[6]

[1] Cadogan diary, 19 April 1944: David Dilks (editor), *op. cit.*, pages 621–2.
[2] Cadogan diary, 20 April 1944: David Dilks (editor), *op. cit.*, page 622.
[3] Letter of 27 April 1944 (Washington): Premier papers, 4/69/2.
[4] Private Office diary, 20 April 1944.
[5] Colville diary, 20 April 1944: Colville papers.
[6] Colville diary, 21 April 1944: Colville papers.

In his speech, Churchill referred to the Dominions and the outbreak of the war in 1939, declaring: 'The darkest moment came. Did anyone flinch? Was there one cry of pain or doubt or terror? No, Sir, darkness was turned into light and into a light which will never fade away.' 'When peace returns,' Churchill added, 'and we should pray to God it soon may, the Conferences of the Prime Ministers of the Dominions, among whom we trust India will be reckoned and with whom the Colonies will be associated, will, we hope, become frequent and regular facts and festivities of our annual life.' [1]

Following his speech, Churchill spent an hour in the Smoking Room, talking to Members of Parliament. [2] Among those who was also in the Smoking Room and Lobbies was Churchill's Parliamentary Private Secretary, Harvie Watt, who wrote to Churchill that many Members had expressed the view 'that you seemed to be in better form than you have been for some time'. Harvie Watt added that Edgar Granville, 'who is usually critical', had described Churchill's speech, 'as a masterpiece and a gem of its kind'. [3]

On the following morning Sir Alexander Cadogan, summoned to see Churchill at 10.30, found him having breakfast in bed. 'Said he was tired after his speech yesterday,' Cadogan noted in his diary. [4] During the day, Churchill again raised the possibility of following the cross-Channel landing with a landing on the French Atlantic coast, operation 'Caliph'. As he minuted to the Chiefs of Staff Committee on April 22, reiterating the plan which he had first put forward on February 2:

Even a small force would be better than none. Cannot a dozen auxiliary carriers, no longer required in the narrow waters, and bombarding vessels which have done their part, be made available? There never was such a chance for a surprise descent into a population eager to revolt. It is a fine country for armoured cars and tanks. Look how the Germans overran it in 1940. The French ought to have a show in France and not merely be made to send more divisions to Italy. This would of course all have to fit in with General Wilson's plans for amphibious feints, &c., in the Mediterranean.

I am sure that even if as few as 50,000 troops were landed around Bordeaux by a surprise operation, they would liberate the city and enable reinforce-

[1] *Hansard*, 21 April 1944, columns 577–88. The first and second British Commonwealth Conferences were held in London in 1948 and 1949. At the third Conference also held in London, in 1951, the word 'British' was dropped. Subsequent Commonwealth conferences were held in London (1961 and 1965), Lagos (1966), London (1966), Singapore (1971), Ottawa (1973), Kingston, Jamaica (1975), London (1977), Lusaka, Zambia (1978), Melbourne (1981), New Delhi (1983) and the Bahamas (1985).

[2] Private Office diary, 21 April 1944.

[3] 'Report by the Parliamentary Private Secretary', 21 April 1944: Harvie Watt papers.

[4] Cadogan diary, 22 April 1944: David Dilks (editor), *op. cit.*, pages 622–3.

ments to sail up the Gironde. The effect upon the enemy would be profound. If this is neglected I am sure that we shall lay ourselves open to justifiable criticism. To hold the enemy tightly gripped at one point, and having nothing planned in either diversion or picking up easy gains is certainly difficult to defend.[1]

Churchill's desire to see an Atlantic coast landing examined by the Joint Planning Staff had not been followed up when first he had put it forward, at the beginning of February, largely because 'Anvil' had seemed at that time to call for the main effort of resources. It was now examined, as Churchill again asked, and was found, as Colonel Capel Dunn wrote to Ismay on April 22, 'far the most attractive' of the various operations proposed to help 'Overlord'.[2] 'I feel,' Capel Dunn added, 'that we have not been as quick on this as we would have wished,' and he went on to tell Ismay: 'I do not know how much of the above you will think it wise at this stage to pass on to the Prime Minister. It would, perhaps, be a pity for him to become too enamoured of one particular operation only to be disappointed later by it being found to be impracticable.'[3]

The Joint Planning Staff went ahead, however, to inform the American Chiefs of Staff that 'an opportunity may arise' at some point after '"Overlord" D + 20' to enable a port on the west coast of France 'to be seized at little cost, thereby opening up a further point of entry into France'. The Joint Planners added: 'We cannot tell whether or when conditions required for its success will arise, but we are sure plans should be prepared now to enable us to seize the opportunity if it comes.'[4]

The ideas of Churchill and his Joint Planning Staff about 'Caliph' were in harmony.

Throughout these trying, troubled days, with 'Overlord' looming, Churchill had continued his talks with the Polish Government, but on April 23 he warned Mikolajczyk that 'British–Russian relations remained cold and questions of primary importance could not be settled'.[5] Churchill was also puzzled, and disturbed, by the recent agreement between the Soviet Union and Japan about the northern half of the island of Sakhalin. Eden, shortly before his short leave of absence from the Foreign Office, had written to Churchill that he

[1] Prime Minister's Personal Minute, D.128/4, 'Most Secret', 22 April 1944, Chiefs of Staff Committee No. 360 (Operations) of 1944, Annex: Cabinet papers, 122/1257.

[2] The other operations examined by the Joint Planning Staff were, the Istrian Peninsula, the Gulf of Genoa, and the South of France ('Anvil').

[3] Minute 44/292, 'Top Secret', 22 April 1944: Cabinet papers, 119/3, folio 27.

[4] Draft Telegram to Joint Staff Mission, Washington, 'Top Secret', 24 April 1944, Joint Planning Staff Paper No. 119 of 1944: Cabinet papers, 79/73.

[5] 'Notes on a conversation between M. Mikolajczyk and Mr Churchill. . . .', 23 April 1944: *Documents on Polish–Soviet Relations 1939–1945*, volume 2, 1943–1945, London 1967, pages 227–8, document No. 128.

believed the agreement to be 'good' for Britain.[1] In reply, on Eden's return, Churchill pointed out that at Teheran, however, Stalin had said that Russia would declare war on Japan 'as soon as possible'. Japan's territorial sacrifice under the new agreement showed, Churchill commented, that the Japanese Government 'hope to delay a Russian breach'. As to Russian motives, 'personally', Churchill wrote, 'I thought the business looked rather suspicious,' and he added: 'They are cashing in on the fact that Britain and the United States are at war with Japan, which causes Japan embarrassment. They are getting their own quarrels with Japan settled. This will put them in a better position to drive a hard bargain with us when Hitler is defeated before they embark upon hostilities with Japan. It may, of course, be part of a deception scheme to lull the Japanese into a false sense of security. Personally I do not like it.'[2]

That same day, April 23, Churchill read a telegram from Clark Kerr to the Foreign Office, reporting the publication in Moscow newspapers on April 20 of a Tass message from London, to the effect that Franco Spain had been a German supply base since 1939, and describing the presence of German technical experts in Spain. The Tass source was a Spanish anti-Franco newsletter in London.[3] Churchill at once telegraphed direct to Clark Kerr: 'All the same it was a very good thing that Franco did not let the Germans through to attack Gibraltar and get across into North Africa. This has to be considered too and you might remind our friends, as opportunity served, that at that time we were absolutely alone in the world [and the Soviets were feeding Germany with essential war munitions]. So don't let's all be too spiteful about the past.'[4]

On the evening of April 25, as preparations for 'Overlord' continued, Churchill held a Staff Conference at 10 Downing Street to discuss the 'Mulberry' harbours. 'He would be among the first on the bridgehead if he possibly could', Churchill told Colville that day, and 'what fun', he added, 'it would be to get there before Monty'.[5]

On April 25 Churchill had a further meeting with the Polish Prime Minister, Mikolajczyk. The purpose of the meeting was to hear a

[1] Foreign Secretary's Minute, PM/44/204 of 1944, 5 April 1944.

[2] Prime Minister's Personal Minute, M.458/4, 23 April 1944: Churchill papers, 20/152.

[3] Telegram No. 1019 from Moscow, 21 April 1944: Premier papers, 3/405/8, folio 160.

[4] Prime Minister's Personal Telegram, T.921/4, 'Personal and Secret', 23 April 1944: Premier papers, 3/405/8, folio 159.

[5] Colville diary, 25 April 1944: Colville papers.

report from Zygmunt Berezowski, the Representative of the Polish Underground, who had just been smuggled out of German-occupied Poland. The Polish people, Berezowski said, put its trust in Britain, and in Churchill, and relied on his 'firm backing' for ensuring Poland's 'independence, and her territorial integrity'. To this Churchill replied: 'Assistance for assuring independence—yes: for the integrity of her frontiers—no.' British policy would not change. 'I stand for the Curzon Line', he said, and reiterated that this would leave Vilna and Lvov 'outside Polish territory'. It would however, and this he had made clear several times before, also provide Poland 'with a broad access to the sea and valuable territories at Germany's expense as a compensation'. Should the Poles 'wish it', Churchill said, they could have 'as far as the Oder Line'. Such a solution, he added, 'would give you a considerable and compact territory and an adequate seat for your nation'. Berezowski replied by recounting 'the role played in the nation's life' by Lvov and Vilna, declaring that 'the Polish nation would never accept a decision so injurious to her country', and stating that the Poles would if necessary 'meet it with active resistance'. To this Churchill replied gravely, even 'gloomily' as the minutes noted: 'Of course; a decision to resist, whatever might be the consequences, is the privilege of every nation, and it cannot be refused even to the weakest.'[1]

On the evening of April 28, Churchill was driven to Chequers for the weekend. 'The PM arrived alone in his car,' Jock Colville noted in his diary, 'fast asleep with his black bandage over his eyes and remained asleep in the stationary car before the front door.'

At dinner that night Field Marshal Smuts was the main guest. After dinner, Colville noted, 'there was a film, Smuts went to bed, and the PM worked till 1.30. . . .' The papers in Churchill's box that night included a minute by the Minister of War Transport, Lord Leathers, about the use of the ocean liner, the *Mauritania*, then a troopship, for 'repatriating' British women and children evacuees who had been sent to Canada and the United States in the summer of 1940. Churchill noted: 'There must not be more people on this ship, with the women and children, than can be carried in the boats.'[2]

---

[1] 'Note on a conversation. . . .', 25 April 1944: *Documents on Polish Soviet Relations, 1939–1945*, volume 2, 1943–1945, London 1967, document No. 129, pages 228–9.

[2] Prime Minister's Personal Minute, M.466/4, 28 April 1944: Churchill papers, 20/152. The *Mauritania*, sailing from New York, reached Liverpool safely. The author, then aged $7\frac{3}{4}$, was among its passengers.

Having gone to bed on April 28 at the unusually early hour, for him, of 1.30, Churchill slept on the morning of April 29 until a quarter to twelve.[1] But the tiredness which now dogged him did not weaken his grasp of events, or his capacity to deal with them. On April 29 he proposed to Eisenhower a compromise on the 'Overlord' bombing dispute: the American Air Force would produce a plan, in conjunction with the Directorate of Bomber Operations in the Air Ministry, 'for the employment of the Strategical Air Force in such a way that not more than, say, 100 French lives should be sacrificed on any target'. If this plan proved 'vastly inferior' to the Marshalling Yards Plan, the British Government 'could be more easily convinced that the political disadvantages must be overriden in favour of the military advantages'.[2]

That same day, in a telegram to Roosevelt, Churchill explained the final decision about the Italian campaign. The object of the Italian battle, code name 'Diadem', was not the taking of Rome, 'good though that would be', or even the joining of the bridgehead with the main force, 'which is indispensable'. The 'prime purpose' was the destruction of the German armed forces, and if by mid-May 'we find the enemy before us in present strength, I have every hope we shall be so closely engaged and entangled with them, we being the superior force, that much of the life may be struck out of this German Army'. Meanwhile, everything not needed for the Italian battle was being prepared 'for the biggest amphibious operation we can mount'. Like the United States Chiefs of Staff, Churchill continued:

... I too fear a sudden and swift withdrawal through the tunnels of the Alps, but I do not consider on the whole that it is very likely. Hitler is obstinate by habit vide Stalingrad, The Crimea, Tunis etc. and also he would be very much afraid of his position in the Balkans. If he let us get swiftly up to the north of Italy he would not be able to tell which way we would go. Moreover he must now be very expectant of an 'Overlord' move in the favourable moon and tide period at the beginning of May, as indeed was originally aimed at by us. Notwithstanding this, he has made no move to withdraw the eight extra divisions sucked down to the south of Rome by the 'Shingle' Operation and our joint fighting there.[3]

In France, resistance movements were to receive special supplies of arms during the 'April moon': Churchill received details of these from

[1] Private Office Diary, 28 April 1944: and Colville diary, 29 April 1944: Colville papers.
[2] 'Secret', 29 April 1944: Churchill papers, 20/137.
[3] Prime Minister's Personal Telegram, T.1000/4, Prime Minister to President, No. 668, 'Top Secret and Personal', 29 April 1944: Churchill papers, 20/163.

Desmond Morton.[1] Throughout France, more than 35,000 active members of the Maquis had been identified, district by district, including Brittany and the Loire, but not in the regions near the landings themselves.[2]

On April 14 Montgomery had completed the tactical instructions to the two armies which were to land in Normandy, warning that the main bodies of men must not be 'so stretched that they would be unable to hold on against determined counter-attack'. On the other hand, he wrote, 'having seized the initiative by our initial landing, we must ensure that we keep it'. Armoured units and brigades must be 'concentrated quickly as soon as ever the situation allows after the initial landing on D-Day'.

Speed and boldness were required, Montgomery wrote, 'and the armoured thrusts must force their way inland', in order to establish 'firm bases well in advance of our main bodies', bases which, 'if their location is carefully thought out', the Germans would be unable to bypass. As the main bodies moved forward, 'their task will be simplified by the fact that armoured forces are holding firm on important areas in front'.[3] Reading Montgomery's instructions on April 30, Churchill commented: 'For what my opinion is worth, it seems to be exactly the spirit in which the execution should proceed, and I only wish that a similar course had been attempted when the forces landed at Anzio.'[4]

In preparation for 'Overlord', the Royal Air Force flew 11,000 sorties over Germany and German-occupied Europe in May 1944, dropping 37,000 tons of bombs. A further 63,000 tons were dropped by the United States Strategic Air Forces.

Churchill lunched on May 1 with Eden, Smuts and Eisenhower. During the meal, Eisenhower told Churchill that the Royal Navy had 'landed' him with some last minute problems concerning the provision of the material and craft required for the artificial harbours. 'I think he was sorry he had,' Eden noted in his diary, 'because afterwards he received so much advice.' Eden added:

Smuts tried to break party up from 2.30 p.m. and got up from table. He and I talked at window, Smuts making occasional sorties to the table to replace the stopper on the brandy bottle. W. ignoring all and continuing to address Ike on the way to handle British Admiralty, pretty good stuff based on years of experience.

[1] Prime Minister's Personal Minute, DM/8 of 1944, 'Top Secret', 30 April 1944: Churchill papers, 20/152.
[2] 'Most Secret', 'Low Countries & France' (map), 'Mâquis': Cabinet papers, 80/79, folio 164.
[3] Tactical instructions, 14 April 1944: *The Memoirs of Field Marshal the Viscount Montgomery of Alamein, KG*, London 1958, pages 234–6.
[4] 'Personal and Most Secret', 30 April 1944: Churchill papers, 20/137.

Smuts lectured me on W., said: 'He may be mentally the man he was, he may be, but he certainly is not physically. I fear he over-estimates his strength, yes, he over-estimates his strength and he will wear himself out if he is not careful.' Some of which W. may have heard and was probably meant to hear.[1]

That evening, at Chequers, Smuts, the principal guest of the week-end, was joined by the New Zealand Prime Minister, Peter Fraser. Jock Colville noted in his diary:

There was the usual film: excellent American fighter combat films and a weird ghost story called 'Halfway House'. The evening was finally marred by the arrival of an offensive telegram from Molotov, who quite unjustifiably claimed we were intriguing behind the back of the Russians in Roumania. This set the PM off on his gloomy forebodings about the future tendencies of Russia and, as he looked at his watch just before 2.00 a.m. and dated the last minute awaiting his signature, he said: 'I have always not liked the month of May; this time I hope it may be all right.'[2]

On May 2 Churchill set out his thoughts on this Soviet protest, challenging Molotov's charge that Britain was trying to work against Russia in Roumania, by means of a secret Mission to Marshal Antonescu's government. It was a charge, he believed, that required his personal intervention. 'You have got hold of a mare's nest' were Churchill's opening words, and he went on to the tell Molotov:

What I am astounded at is that you should have imagined for one moment that we are in any intrigue with the Roumanian Government or anybody in Roumania, or that we have any evil interest in Roumania to the detriment of your operations and of the common cause, or that we have any secrets with Roumania to which we will not make you partners at any moment. The fact that you should harbour these thoughts shows how difficult it is working together, even when the greatest combined military operations in the world are impending.

The British Government, Churchill reiterated, considered the Soviet Union 'our leaders' in Rumanian policy. But, he added, 'Of course if you do not believe a single word we say it would be better to leave things run out as they will.' It was because of 'the tremendous business

[1] Eden diary, 1 May 1944: Eden memoirs, *The Reckoning, op. cit.*, page 442.

[2] Colville diary, 30 April 1944: Colville papers. The political crisis of 1915, in which Churchill had been forced to leave the Admiralty, had taken place in May. Of that occasion Churchill later wrote: 'The change from the intense executive activities of each day's work at the Admiralty to the narrowly measured duties of a counsellor left me gasping. Like a sea-beast fished up from the depths, or a diver too suddenly hoisted, my veins threatened to burst from the fall in pressure. I had great anxiety and no means of relieving it; I had vehement convictions and small power to give effect to them. I had to watch the unhappy casting-away of great opportunities, and the feeble execution of plans which I had launched and in which I heartily believed. I had long hours of utterly unwonted leisure in which to contemplate the frightful unfolding of the War. At a moment when every fibre of my being was inflamed to action, I was forced to remain a spectator of the tragedy, placed cruelly in a front seat.' (*Strand*, December 1921–January 1922 reprinted in Winston S. Churchill, *Thoughts and Adventures*, London 1932.)

we have in hand together' that Churchill hoped Molotov would give up his suspicions and work with Britain to secure surrender terms in Roumania satisfactory to all the Allies.[1]

It emerged, as Eden explained to the War Cabinet a week later, that an SOE mission to the Roumanian opposition leader, Dr Maniu, had been captured by the Roumanian Government. Eden told the War Cabinet that in October 1943, in Moscow, Molotov had 'encouraged' Eden to send this mission, but that the Soviet Government 'had not actually been informed' of its despatch. On first being given these details Churchill minuted to Eden: 'Molotov's reaction was wrongful; but it is by no means certain that he will not find a briar patch of reproachful words and accusations into which to retreat.'[2]

After a further complaint from Molotov on May 10, Churchill told the War Cabinet that he 'felt that he could not continue to correspond with M. Molotov whose attitude led him to despair of the possibility of maintaining good relations with Russia'.[3]

'Never forget,' Churchill minuted to Eden on May 2, 'that Bolsheviks are crocodiles.'[4] But they were crocodiles, however, who had to be fed: in the previous eight months Britain had convoyed 191 ships to Russia's northern ports, with more than a million tons of war stores, including aviation fuel.[5] 'The moment we have got over the crisis of "Overlord",' Churchill assured Stalin on May 3, 'I shall be making plans to send you more.' He had already given directions for the matter to be studied, so that another convoy could be sent 'if the course of the battle allows'.[6]

'Evidently,' Churchill noted on May 4, 'we are approaching a showdown with the Russians about their Communist intrigues in Italy, Yugoslavia and Greece,' and he suggested the possibility of recalling the British Ambassador from Moscow 'for consultation'. America had already recalled its Ambassador, Averell Harriman. 'I

[1] Prime Minister's Personal Telegram, T.1026/4, 'Personal and Top Secret', 2 May 1944: Churchill papers, 20/164.

[2] Prime Minister's Personal Minute, M.513/4, 'Private and Confidential', 7 May 1944: Churchill papers, 20/152. As leader of the Roumanian National Peasant Party, Dr Maniu was allowed to participate in the national elections in 1946. He was later arrested, however, and despite protests from the British and United States Governments, was sentenced on 11 November 1947 to solitary confinement for life.

[3] War Cabinet No. 63 of 1944, 11 May 1944, Confidential Annex: Cabinet papers, 65/46. Churchill's final comment on the Roumanian episode: 'It is erroneous to suppose that one must always be doing something. The greatest service SOE can render to us is to select with great discrimination their areas and occasions of intervention' (Prime Minister's Personal Minute, M.580/4, to Eden, 21 May 1944: Churchill papers, 20/152).

[4] Prime Minister's Personal Minute, M.483/4, 2 May 1944: Churchill papers, 20/152.

[5] Fifty were British ships, the rest United States ships.

[6] Prime Minister's Personal Telegram, T.1028/4, 'Personal and Most Secret', 3 May 1944: Churchill papers, 20/164.

do not think,' Churchill wrote, 'they would very much like a period in which they had neither a British nor an American Ambassador there,' and he added: 'I must say their attitude becomes more difficult every day.' [1]

Clark Kerr had already reported twice on Soviet proposals for a Yugoslav–Bulgarian 'Link-up' after the war. [2] 'I have read both these telegrams,' Churchill minuted to Cadogan on May 5. 'How do they strike you? How should we feel towards a Bulgar Yugoslav *bloc*? It certainly does not seem very pleasant at first sniff.' [3] On the following day, at Chequers, it was Britain's links with Tito's Communists that was under scrutiny, when Churchill was in conference with three men just arrived from German-occupied Yugoslavia, two of the British representatives with Mihailovic, Colonel W. S. Bailey and Colonel Hudson, together with Fitzroy Maclean, Churchill's principal emissary with Tito. [4] The 'order is', Churchill telegraphed to Macmillan in Algiers that evening, 'that all forms of aid go to Marshal Tito's war against the Germans, and no help at any time is given to Mihailovic'. All that remained to send to the Mihailovic area was 'an air load or two of stuff' to make sure that the British officers with Mihailovic 'get safely out of the country'. [5]

On May 4, Churchill had expressed to Eden his worries about Soviet involvement in Greece. 'We ought to watch this movement carefully,' he minuted. 'After all, we lost 40,000 men in Greece and you were very keen on that effort at the time. I do not think we should yield to the Russians any more in Greece.' [6] That morning, at a meeting of Dominion Ministers, John Curtin, the Prime Minister of Australia, had asked 'how seriously we took the risk that after the defeat of the Nazis, Communist or Leftist organizations might move into control in Germany?' and had gone on to tell the meeting: 'We had been informed that in the Balkans the Russians were developing Communist cells. In France the Communists were, it appeared, the one really organized party. In Italy, Mussolini, who had been anti-Communist in policy, was no longer in power, and the pendulum of ordinary public opinion was apt to swing from one side to the other. Personalities counted. If the Communist Party, whatever might be said against it, could throw up personalities who would attract public attention and support as the Nazis had done, they might well appeal to oppressed and discontented elements.' Curtin had in his mind, he said, 'a strong resurgence of Russian nationalism of

[1] Prime Minister's Personal Minute, M.498/4, 4 May 1944: Churchill papers, 20/152.
[2] Telegram No. 1117 and 1118 from Moscow.
[3] Prime Minister's Personal Minute, M.502/4, 5 May 1944: Churchill papers, 20/152.
[4] Private Office diary, 6 May 1944. Colonel Bailey and Ambassador Stevenson were also present.
[5] Prime Minister's Personal Telegram, T.1041/4, 'Personal and Secret', No. 958 to Algiers, 6 May 1944: Churchill papers, 20/164.
[6] Prime Minister's Personal Minute, M.493/4, 4 May 1944: Churchill papers, 20/152.

which there appeared to be so many signs, with the Communist Party in other countries acting as it were as Russian diplomatic agents'.

Curtin went on to tell Churchill and the Dominion Prime Ministers: 'We should aim at establishing as early as possible some kind of stable Government in the countries which had been overrun. He did not overlook the difficulties, and he fully accepted that in countries such as Yugoslavia or Greece, those who fought the enemy must, whatever their party allegiance, receive our support during the war, and might thereby consolidate their local political position for the post-war period.' It was clear, Curtin ended, that 'all post-war adjustments would primarily depend on how far we could succeed in our arrangements with Russia and how far Russia in fact sincerely intended to collaborate'.[1]

With Curtin's remarks much in mind, Churchill minuted to Eden later that day:

A paper should be drafted for the Cabinet and possibly for the Imperial Conference setting forth shortly, for that is essential, the brute issues between us and the Soviet Government which are developing in Italy, in Roumania, in Bulgaria, in Yugoslavia and above all in Greece. It ought to be possible to get this on one page.

I cannot say there is much in Italy, but broadly speaking the issue is: Are we going to acquiesce in the communization of the Balkans and perhaps of Italy? Mr Curtin touched upon this this morning and I am of opinion on the whole that we ought to come to a definite conclusion about it and that, if our conclusion is that we resist the communist infusion and invasion, we should put it to them pretty plainly at the best moment that military events permit.

'We should of course,' Churchill added, 'have to consult the United States first.'[2]

In the Far East, the Japanese, driving north-westward into India from the Chindwin river, were halted at Kohima, on the mountain pass into Assam, after ferocious fighting in which four thousand Japanese were killed. South of Kohima, at Imphal, 60,000 British and Indian soldiers faced, also on Indian soil, a relentless pressure. 'Let nothing go from the battle that you need for victory,' Churchill telegraphed to Mountbatten on May 4, and he added: 'I will not accept denial of this from any quarter, and will back you to the full.'[3]

At this very moment of battle inside the north-eastern frontier of

[1] PMM(44) 6th meeting, 'Meeting of Prime Ministers', 'Secret', 11.30 a.m., 4 May 1944, Cabinet papers, 99/28.
[2] Prime Minister's Personal Minute, M.497/4, 4 May 1944: Churchill papers, 20/152.
[3] Prime Minister's Personal Telegram, T.1034/4, 'Personal and Top Secret', OZ 2382, 4 May 1944: Churchill papers, 20/164.

India, Churchill received a telegram from Mountbatten about American demands that he should devote the resources of South East Asia Command to the capture of northern Burma.[1] 'This is a very serious telegram,' Churchill minuted to Ismay for the Chiefs of Staff Committee, 'casting its shadow upon the whole of our affairs in SEAC.' Churchill's minute continued with a bitter comment. 'The American method of trying to force particular policies,' he wrote, 'of the withholding or giving of certain weapons, such as carrying airplanes or LSTs, in theatres where the command belongs by right of overwhelming numbers to us, must be objected to at the right time and strongly protested against.'

Churchill added: 'what with our own differences and the uncertainty of American action, we are not unfolding a creditable picture to history'.[2]

It was General Hollis who pointed out to Churchill that the United States Chiefs of Staff proposed sending Mountbatten a directive, instructing him 'to undertake the most vigorous action to capture Upper Burma during the remainder of this dry season, throughout the monsoon and next fall, in order to increase the capacity of the air transport line to China and expedite the laying of a pipe line to that country'. To this, Mountbatten had replied, in two telegrams to the Chiefs of Staff in London, that he doubted his ability either to capture and secure Myitkyina, or to recapture Upper Burma, 'without substantial reinforcements, which cannot be found for him before the defeat of Germany'.[3] The Chiefs of Staff supported Mountbatten, and, as Hollis told Churchill, proposed that the Americans should agree to a strategy whereby long range aircraft would 'fly direct from Calcutta to China without staging at Myitkyina'. Long range transport aircraft, Hollis pointed out, 'can only, however, be provided from American resources'. In the view of the Chiefs of Staff, if the United States view of Mountbatten's strategic goal were to prevail, it was unlikely, whatever his current success, that any resources would become available for other projects in the Bay of Bengal, 'at any rate in 1944'.[4]

Replying to Hollis on the following day, for the Chiefs of Staff Committee, Churchill reiterated his distaste for the strategy laid down by the United States Chiefs of Staff:

It is to be observed that we have now come back to the old policies which we unitedly condemned as foolish when we went to the United States in May and in August of last year. We are to plunge about in the jungles of

[1] SEACOS No. 152, 3 May 1944.
[2] Prime Minister's Personal Minute, D.139/4, 5 May 1944: Cabinet papers, 120/707.
[3] SEACOS No. 134 and SEACOS No. 152.
[4] Chiefs of Staff Minute, COS 748/4, 'Top Secret, 6 May 1944: Cabinet papers, 120/707.

Burma, engaging the Japanese under conditions which though improved are still unfavourable to us, with the objective of building a pipe-line or increasing the discharge over the 'hump'.

Churchill then set out his hopes for a more active policy in southern Burma, where ten British divisions were confronted by nine Japanese divisions:

The fact that India, with 2 million men on her ration strength, can only support the equivalent of ten divisions on the Burma frontier, i.e. 2 hundred thousand men, is not one that can pass without searching scrutiny. It is indeed a disgrace that so feeble an army is the most that can be produced from the enormous expense entailed. The North-West Frontier seems to be quiet and conditions there are favourable. The internal peace of India can be left in the main to the police. Yet we are informed that out of this immense force only a tenth can be found for the major battle required from India. This is a lamentable fact discreditable to all concerned, including ourselves if we leave it without remedy.

Churchill was particularly reluctant to accept the American strategic directive to Mountbatten if it involved, as clearly it would, an end to the operations which he had hoped to see mounted across the Bay of Bengal. 'I am not prepared at this moment,' he wrote, 'to exclude an enterprise like the capture of Simalur and the establishment of an Air base there, nor any of these naval operations such as Admiral James Somerville executed upon Sabang, another of which I believe is already in contemplation.' Churchill's minute ended:

For Simalur, which is a virtually undefended island at the present time, I require:
(a) a fleet ready to give battle to the main Japanese Navy should it still be stationed at Singapore. This should certainly be available by then and is probably on the spot now.
(b) the temporary use of air-borne carrier forces sufficient for the capture of the island and the mounting of a defensive Air Force.
(c) 7 fighter squadrons defensive and 2 or 3 long-range bomber squadrons.

'The above,' Churchill ended, 'will have effects upon Japanese movement and fighting strength out of all proportion to the small forces we require to engage them.' [1]

That weekend at Chequers, Churchill dictated a minute to General Hollis, in which he deprecated the growing number of military missions which, he had been told, were being sent to Algiers. He also, with D-Day now less than a month away, had a proposal for the employment of these officers:

I certainly expressed myself strongly against these military missions to Algiers,

[1] Prime Minister's Personal Minute, D.142/4, 7 May 1944: Cabinet papers, 120/707.

from what I heard about them at the Gibraltar conference, and I greatly regret that they should have piled themselves up and ensconced themselves at Algiers, where they are not needed in any way, but only add to the horribly bloated staffs which are lurking there, most of them away from all participation in the war. I certainly wish this matter to be taken up with a view to recalling and putting to some useful work these highly paid and no doubt highly skilled and experienced officers. The best thing would be to form a Sacred Legion of about 1,000 Staff officers and let them set an example to the troops in leading some particularly desperate attack. Anyhow, the missions should be liquidated.[1]

After dinner on May 7, and after 'the usual film', as Brooke noted in his diary, 'Winston took me down to the little study where the secretaries work.' There, he sat by the fire and drank soup. 'He looked very old and very tired,' Brooke added. The conversation then turned to health, and ill-health, as Brooke recorded:

He said Roosevelt was not well and that he was no longer the man he had been; this, he said, also applied to himself. He said he could still always sleep well, eat well and especially drink well, but that he no longer jumped out of bed the way he used to, and felt as if he would be quite content to spend the whole day in bed. I have never yet heard him admit that he was beginning to fail.[2]

The dispute with the United States Chiefs of Staff over Mountbatten's proposed advance in northern Burma was discussed at a Staff Conference on May 8. The conclusion was emphatically against the American demands. 'What we wanted,' Churchill told the meeting, was a decision 'to bring to an end, if possible, the continued pressure to increase our commitment in Burma.' What the Americans wanted in northern Burma, Churchill told the Conference, 'appeared to close the door on the operation, which he favoured, for the capture of the island of Simalur this autumn'. Churchill then stated, as a personal comment: 'at present we had no plans to carry out any operations whatever in South-East Asia during the coming autumn and winter. This was deplorable, and he would continue to press for operations to be undertaken which, while involving small commitments for us, should exhaust the Japanese resources.'[3]

Strategic disagreement with the United States in the Far East persisted, so much so that on May 9 Churchill minuted to the Chiefs of Staff Committee, in support of Mountbatten's fighting on the Indian frontier: 'We cannot on any account throw away this battle. I am quite willing to telegraph to the President pointing out to him the

[1] Prime Minister's Personal Minute, D.147/4, 7 May 1944: Churchill papers, 20/152.
[2] Brooke diary, 7 May 1944: Bryant, op. cit., volume 2, pages 187–8.
[3] Staff Conference, Chiefs of Staff Committee No. 149 (Operations) of 1944, 'Top Secret', 8 May 1944: Cabinet papers, 79/74.

disastrous consequences to his own plans for helping China which would follow the casting away of this battle.' [1]

'Winston terribly tired,' Brooke noted after this Staff Conference; 'required great patience to handle him, but got what we wanted through.' [2]

Churchill was indeed tired, but it was a tiredness arising as much from his fears for the outcome of the Normandy landings, as from physical exhaustion. With less than a month to D-Day these worries were considerable, reflecting words which he had written to his wife nearly thirty years earlier, on the eve of the First World War. Peering into the future then, he told her, 'Everything is ready as it has never been before. And we are awake to the tips of our fingers. But war is the Unknown & the Unexpected!' [3] Going to the House of Commons one evening with John J. McCloy, Roosevelt's Assistant Secretary for War, Churchill showed him the destroyed Chamber and spoke about his early Parliamentary career. 'Suddenly,' McCloy later recalled, 'he referred to the number of his early contemporaries who had been killed during what he called the hecatombs of World War I.' Churchill then described himself 'as a sort of "sport" in nature's sense as he said most of his generation lay dead at Passchendaele and the Somme. An entire British generation of potential leaders had been cut off and Britain could not afford the loss of another generation.' He then said, McCloy recalled, 'that if I felt, or if my Chief, Mr Stimson, felt that he was using all his efforts to avoid such another slaughter as had taken place in World War I due to inadequately equipped men it was not a false accusation. The Americans should understand this as it was extremely important that in the coming post-war period both Britain and the United States should have vigorous and competent leaders at hand to ensure the peace and democratic government.' [4]

Churchill had spoken, McCloy added, 'with great conviction and vigour'. It was a conviction that led him to scrutinize not only the dangers that might lie ahead for the Allies on D-Day, but the threat to civilian life of Allied bombing policy both in France and Italy. Reading on May 7 of a Royal Air Force plan to reduce Rome to starvation by bombing food convoys on their way to Rome at the hours when these convoys were known to be travelling, he minuted to Eden and the Chiefs of Staff Committee: 'In my opinion the military authorities should be instructed to be very careful not to bomb any

---

[1] Prime Minister's Personal Minute D.150/4, 9 May 1944: Churchill papers, 20/152.
[2] Brooke diary, 8 May 1944: Bryant, *op. cit.*, volume 2, page 188.
[3] Letter of 28 July 1914: Spencer-Churchill papers.
[4] John J. McCloy recollections: letter to the author, 26 April 1982.

convoys on this route between the hours mentioned, unless there is some important military object which they will be called upon to explain thereafter,' and he added: 'It looks as if some stupid and spiteful person of the fourth grade has got hold of this matter.'[1] The bombing of entirely military targets in Italy was likewise the subject of Churchill's critical scrutiny. Reading the report of an air attack on the Italian village of Sonnino, where 45 people had been killed, among them 30 children, he minuted to Eden: 'They ought not to treat co-belligerent populations in the same way as enemy populations—that is to say, making sure they bring no bombs home if they cannot find the right target.'[2]

Churchill's worries about D-Day were parallelled by his concern about future Soviet influence in Europe. In the second week of May, he received a telegram from Stalin in praise of 'Overlord', 'which of course', Stalin wrote, 'will demand a enormous effort, but which also promises enormous positive results for the whole course of the war'.[3] The same day, Eden sent Churchill details of a Moscow radio broadcast of April 29, stating that the 'increasing blows' now being struck against the German invaders by Polish patriots 'were being obstructed by traitors in Poland' who took their orders from General Sosnkowski.[4] Angered by this Soviet accusation against the underground army of the London Poles, Churchill minuted to Eden: 'I fear that very great evil may come upon the world. This time at any rate we and the Americans will be heavily armed. The Russians are drunk with victory and there is no length they may not go.'[5]

Churchill's anger was even clearer on the draft telegram to Molotov, which he dictated and sent to Eden, but which, on Eden's advice, he

---

[1] Prime Minister's Personal Minute, M.511/4, 7 May 1944: Churchill papers, 20/152. News of the bombing proposal had reached London in two telegrams (Numbers 309 and 310 of 3 May 1944) sent to the Foreign Office from the British Ambassador to the Holy See.

[2] Prime Minister's Personal Minute, M.521/4, 7 May 1944: Premier papers, 3/14/3, folio 281. Sonnino, which lay halfway between the Anzio bridgehead and the main Italian front, had been given as an 'alternative target' for a force of American Bostons which had been sent to attack a target thirty miles to the north-west. This attack had been prevented by bad weather. 'We do not know why Sonnino was selected as an alternative target,' the Vice Chief of the Air Staff, Sir Douglas Evill, minuted to Churchill on May 6. 'It does not itself appear to be a centre of communications although it is surrounded by a number of communication targets underlined in red on the map which had been frequently attacked. It is reasonable to assume however that the responsible commander had evidence that there was some installation there, such as a military dump, radar station or headquarters which made him select it as an alternative bombing target.' (Minute of 6 May 1944: Premier papers, 3/14/3, folio 282.)

[3] 'Personal and Most Secret', 8 May 1944: Churchill papers, 20/164.

[4] Foreign Secretary's Minute, PM/44/305, 4 May 1944: Foreign Office papers, 954/20, folios 167–8.

[5] Prime Minister's Personal Minute, M.537/4, 8 May 1944: Foreign Office papers, 954/20, folio 168.

did not send. During the course of the telegram Churchill had intended to tell Molotov:

One of the greatest obstacles to Anglo-Soviet friendship and collaboration is the Soviet opinion that we will put up with anything. I have the honour to assure you this is not the case. If you want a wordy warfare to begin between our two countries on the subject of Poland, you have only to continue the present declarations of the Moscow radio broadcast on this subject. We shall start talking to our people and to the world, which will listen, not only on the broadcast but in Parliament. A series of very reasonable talks will be given by the B.B.C. both from British and Polish sources. This will be a sad preliminary to the great operations which are pending; but the responsibility will not lie on us.

Churchill had intended to continue his telegram to Molotov:

On June 22, 1941 I spoke up at once for you in your heroic resistance to the German onslaught. I will not hesitate to speak for Poland too. We have always shown ourselves the greatest respect for Soviet Russia since she was attacked by Germany, and have always admired the manner with which she defended herself. I earnestly trust you may think of the common cause in these days when we all need each other's assistance to finish this cruel war.

There were people 'here and in many countries' Churchill added, 'who warn us that if we and the Americans get on to the Continent, a cessation of effort by Russia will lead to our sustaining a great defeat. We spurn these men. But should you not also on your part make some contribution to the unity of the three great Powers, on which the future peace of the world depends?' [1]

---

[1] 'Prime Minister to Monsieur Molotov', 'Personal and Secret', unsent draft, 8 May 1944: Foreign Office papers, 954/20, folios 169–71.

42

'Events which no one could foretell'

AT midday on 1 May 1944 Churchill welcomed the Dominion
Prime Ministers to London, on the first day of a two-week
conference. They were gathered together, he told them at their
opening meeting at 10 Downing Street, 'in the most deadly climax of
the conflict of nations, at a time when, though we need no longer fear
defeat, we are making the most intense efforts to compel an early
victory'.[1]

That afternoon, during a superb survey of the war, Churchill explained, in the utmost secrecy, the difficulties confronting Britain's
strategy, not only because of a shortage of landing craft and in particular tank landing craft, but because, as he phrased it, 'the Americans had not been very forthcoming in providing craft for the European theatre'.

Although the Washington Conference of December 1941 had,
Churchill explained, led to agreement between Britain and America
on 'the wisdom of the overall strategic concept of concentrating first
against Germany while maintaining our position in the Pacific', even
so 'the United States had put their major strength in the Pacific'.

Speaking of the 'great Operation about to be launched' across the
Channel, Churchill told the Dominion Prime Ministers that it would
use between 3,000 and 4,000 vessels, and nearly 11,000 aircraft, 'a
great bombardment fleet and an air shield of unsurpassed power'.
'We should not again experience the distressing conditions of a
Namsos,' he said, referring to the Norwegian campaign of April 1940
when the landings had been caught by superior German forces. 'The

---

[1] 'Meeting of Prime Ministers', PMM (44) 1st Meeting, 'Confidential', 12 noon, 1 May
1944: Cabinet papers, 99/28. The Prime Ministers present represented Britain, Canada, Australia, New Zealand, India, Rhodesia and South Africa. The Government of India was represented by the Maharaja of Jammu and Kashmir.

boot was on the other leg now.' Nevertheless, he warned, 'it was a difficult operation to cross the Channel. Had it not been so, we might not now be holding a conference in London.'

Turning to the Mediterranean, Churchill told the Dominion Premiers that 'we had had much difficulty in getting the Americans to agree to invade Sicily, and then to continue the campaign in Italy. Many Americans had regarded the Mediterranean campaign as an unorthodox departure, and some of their Officers were still to be found who said that if we had established a bridgehead in Northern France in 1943, or even in 1942, we should by now be in Berlin. They had wanted to be content in the Mediterranean with the capture of Sardinia.'

Churchill then gave the Dominion Premiers an account of the Anglo-American strategic dispute, where so much had depended on the American willingness to provide the necessary LST, Landing Ship Tank, landing craft. As Churchill explained:

He himself had been against a campaign in Northern France in 1942 and 1943. We had not then had experience of large-scale land operations, and the time was not ripe. He had therefore persuaded the Americans to agree to an Italian campaign. He had at the same time ardently wished to secure control of the Aegean, for which purpose the capture of Rhodes was indispensable.

At the time of the Italian collapse we had secured a number of islands at little or no cost, and the provision of a certain number of LST and two or three Brigades would have been sufficient for the capture of Rhodes, and for the opening of a route to the Dardanelles and the Black Sea. However, the resources had not been forthcoming. It was said that they were all required for the battle in Italy. In the event, many of the LST had been used for the build-up of the Strategic Air Force, which, though it was now doing excellent work, might well have been delayed three months in order to allow us to secure the rich prizes that were offered in the Aegean.

After the Cairo Conference the landing at Anzio had been planned. It had not been exploited in the manner conceived, but it had led to one unexpected result: Hitler decided to cling on to Rome as he had clung on to Stalingrad, to Tunisia, and to the Crimea, and he had sent down eight fresh Divisions to the Italian battle. This had led to the equalising of the forces in that theatre, but had reduced the forces available to oppose 'Overlord'.

Recently the Americans had expressed the fear that the Germans might rapidly disengage themselves from the Italian front, and withdraw their forces through the tunnels under the Alps into France. They had therefore exerted presure on us to prepare for an amphibious assault by two Divisions in Southern France, and had offered us 26 LST for the purpose. The operations that would be conducted after the landing in the South of France remained somewhat nebulous.

We had taken the view that nothing should be allowed to detract from the full exploitation of our coming offensive in Italy. Subject to this, we were prepared to undertake the largest possible amphibious operation, either in the Gulf of Genoa or the Gulf of Lions, or wherever might prove most advantageous, but we were not prepared to mar the integrity of the battle, in which we hoped to engage heavily all the German forces in Italy. The Americans had withdrawn their offer of landing craft, but there was some reason to suppose that they might now relent.

Speaking of the Allied bombing offensive over Germany, Churchill told the Dominion Premiers: 'We knew what it meant to be bombed and we didn't much like it. We stuck it out, but there was no doubt that at the time it was the principal topic of conversation. What we received was child's play compared to what we were now giving Germany.'[1] The German retaliation, Churchill added, 'was petty'.

Churchill ended his survey as he had begun it, with the impending cross-Channel assault. 'Great forces were about to be set in motion,' he said, 'and all we could do now was to await results.'

Speaking after Churchill, the Canadian Prime Minister, William Mackenzie King, said that in listening to Churchill 'it had again been borne in upon him how wise Mr Churchill had been in putting off the time of the invasion of Northern Europe. He knew how great the pressure had been for the launching of an attack. It was perhaps the greatest of the many great things that Mr Churchill had done that he had withstood this pressure until the time was ripe.'

Field Marshal Smuts agreed with Mackenzie King. 'He had always been anxious about operations in North-West Europe,' he said, 'remembering how for four years we had been locked in the struggle on the Western Front in the last war.' Smuts was still concerned with the dangers which the cross-Channel landing would pose, telling the meeting: 'The stage was now set and we could but hope that the enemy had been sufficiently weakened to allow us to venture on this last great move. Nevertheless, we should be undertaking great risks. Our forces were dwindling and we must face the fact that the issue would depend upon the Americans. Last time we had had at our side the veteran French Army, extremely well led. Now we should be fighting alongside troops who had no experience of battle and who would be pitted against a veteran army. We could not regard the situation lightly.'

Smuts also spoke in defence of Churchill's Mediterranean strategy. 'There was a time,' he said, 'when the Mediterranean was looked upon as a side-show, and it was only the efforts and persuasive power of Mr Churchill which had made possible the amazing results which

[1] Between 1940 and 1945, a total of 60,595 British civilians lost their lives in bombing and rocket raids. The German civilian casualties during those same years were in excess of 500,000.

had been achieved. Italy had been knocked out, together with some 80 divisions and a great fleet. A route had been cleared to the East.'

He was 'much concerned', Smuts told the Dominion Premiers, 'lest we should be led to minimise the results which might flow from activity in the Mediterranean. He was all for prosecuting the Italian campaign with the utmost vigour. There should be no breaking off in what was not a side-show but part of a major operation. He felt, however, that more should have been made of the situation in the Balkans where there was a mass of brave men who could most advantageously be brought into the battle front against Germany.'

The last comment of the meeting came from the Australian Prime Minister, John Curtin, who asked whether, if there was a 'stalemate' in north-western Europe, the Americans might not, in their disappointment, 'turn more decisively to the Pacific, where the going would appear to be better'. This situation, Churchill replied, 'would have to be faced if it arose', but, he added, 'he doubted whether the Americans, who were a stubborn people when roused, would draw back from the struggle. It must be remembered that we were out for the complete destruction of Germany, and great nations could not be completely destroyed without paying an exacting price. We were the servants of events which no one could foretell. He could give no guarantee that "Overlord" would bring about a speedy end to the struggle.' [1]

Speaking to the Dominion Prime Ministers again, on the morning of May 2, during their discussion of military strategy with the Chiefs of Staff, Churchill 'pointed to the absolute necessity that all troops should be thrown into the closest action with the enemy wherever contact could be made'. Speaking of the Italian front, and the American pressure that Britain should 'break off the campaign as soon as the Anzio bridgehead joined up with the main battle front', Churchill noted that the Americans 'had been somewhat inclined to treat the question in a bargaining spirit, but there were signs that they would relent. He believed that they had come to realize that they had placed themselves by their attitude in a position which would be historically indefensible.'

The Prime Minister of New Zealand, Peter Fraser, wondered whether the threat of resuming the offensive in Italy might be 'enough', and not the offensive itself, to which Churchill replied: 'The enemy must be made to bleed and burn at every point throughout the summer at whatever cost.' This applied, he said, 'both to the land and to the air'. [2]

---

[1] 'Meeting of Prime Ministers', PMM (44) 2nd Meeting, 'Secret', 5.30 p.m., 1 May 1944: Cabinet papers, 99/28.
[2] 'Meeting of Prime Ministers', PMM (44) 3rd Meeting, 'Top Secret', 11.30 a.m., 2 May 1944: Cabinet papers, 99/28.

At the next day's meeting of the Dominion Prime Ministers, Peter Fraser warned about Allied involvement in the Balkans, a region, he said, 'of seething factions who would turn to whoever would give them the most support or hold out to them most hope for the future'. There had 'never been any question', Churchill replied, 'of major action in the Balkans', and he went on to tell the Prime Ministers:

It was merely a question of assistance by Commandos and air action. Due priorities must prevail in the application of resources. We were, however, operating in the islands on the Dalmatian coast. We held Vis, and had recently captured Korcula, where we killed or captured 1,000 Germans. We had then evacuated it, and hoped to recapture it again shortly, thus causing more loss to the enemy. When the position was eased in Italy, we certainly might do more in this direction, and run increased quantities of equipment in to Tito, but nothing we would do there would be comparable to the main operations elsewhere.

The Germans had 23 divisions in Italy and 21 in Yugoslavia, Smuts pointed out, a sign of the 'enormous importance' they still attached to the southern front. Smuts added, bitterly: 'In his opinion, we had not done justice to our successes in the Mediterranean. Owing to the switch-over of forces to the North-West, which in itself was a daring action in the middle of a war, we had deprived ourselves of the means of exploiting our victories. We had lost the Greek islands; we had given too little help to the Partisans; and we were in danger of leaving the whole field clear in the South-East of Europe to the Russians.' The military strategy 'should not be such', Smuts declared, 'as to hinder our political strategy'. He recognised that the 'switch-over' had been pressed by the Americans and by the Russians, but the result might well mean that 'our post-war policy in South-East Europe would be prejudiced'.

Churchill, in thanking Smuts for his survey, went on to 'admit' that if he had had 'his own way' the lay-out of the war would have been different. His 'inclination', Churchill told the Dominion Premiers, 'would have been in favour of rolling up Europe from the South-East, and joining hands with the Russians. However, it had proved impossible to persuade the United States to this view. They had been determined at every stage upon the invasion in North-West Europe, and had constantly wanted us to break off the Mediterranean operations.'

The decisions of the Teheran Conference, Churchill pointed out, 'now bound us to the great operations which were impending'. If these were not successful, he warned, 'we must either set our teeth and prepare for a longer war, or else reduce the severity of the terms which we were prepared to offer to the enemy. He was in no doubt which course we should adopt.' [1]

At the fifth meeting of the Dominion Prime Ministers, held at 10 Downing Street on the morning of May 5, there was some discussion about the problems of Communism, and its probable hostile role in the post-war world. Communism, Churchill commented, 'was a quasi-religious movement with a quality of its own. It was the whole life and soul of many of its votaries. The main movement was a profound movement of equalitarianism enforced without regard to any form of morals we had known; and like all totalitarian Governments it made the mistake that the individual under it was not free.' He himself was 'confident', Churchill added, 'that the spirit of freedom in the world would face up to the brutish regimentation of Communism. The best counter in experience to all violent movement from the left was the improvement of basic conditions for all.' [2]

At the ninth meeting of the Dominion Prime Ministers, held on May 9, Churchill spoke of his worries about the future of Europe, a continent, he said, which was 'the storm centre, the place where the weather came from'. He could not 'ignore the probability', he said, 'that the United States Government would be under strong and continuous pressure from America to withdraw troops from Europe, and that after one Presidential election we might find there were no United States troops left in that continent. It was in those circumstances that he felt that one of our endeavours must be to build some entity in Europe and to give a sense of self-preservation to the countries of that continent.' It must be remembered, he pointed out, that at Teheran 'both Russia and the United States had been strongly in favour of the dismemberment of Germany'. For this reason he attached the 'greatest importance' to what he called 'the three Great Armed Powers', the United States, the Soviet Union and Great Britain, 'acting as a Peace Executive or Steering Committee' on a World Council, whereby 'facts would be established, action taken and warnings issued'. Churchill added: 'If that warning was disregarded orders would be given to the States of the world to call up the forces which they were under obligation to provide against the offender.' Once the 'great machine' of a World Council had been 'set in motion', Churchill declared, 'with the power at its disposal he felt that there was little danger that a larger

[1] 'Meeting of Prime Ministers', PMM (44) 4th Meeting, 'Top Secret', 11.30 a.m., 3 May 1944: Cabinet papers, 99/28.
[2] 'Meeting of Prime Ministers', PMM (44), 7th Meeting, 'Secret', 11 a.m., 5 May 1944: Cabinet papers, 99/28.

State would persist in action likely to lead to the breaking of the peace'.[1]

Wednesday, 10 May 1944 marked the fourth anniversary of Churchill's premiership. 'May God grant you *many* years to lead us,' wrote Eric Long, 'not only to Peace & Victory but then to lead us to contentment. . . .'[2]

Throughout the following morning Churchill awaited news of the imminent offensive in Italy. Shortly before noon he received a telegram from General Alexander:

Everything is now ready, all plans and preparations are complete. Our object is the destruction of the enemy south of Rome and we have every hope and every intention of doing that. We expect and are ready for extremely heavy and bitter fighting. I shall send you our private code word when the attack is launched.[3]

The private code word was 'Zip'. That night, a few minutes after eleven o'clock Alexander's message came: ' "Zip", repeat "Zip".'[4] Operation 'Diadem' had begun.

On May 12, as the Allied troops in Italy met fierce German opposition, Churchill left London, with Smuts, Mackenzie King and Sir Godfrey Huggins, the Prime Minister of Southern Rhodesia, for a tour of inspection of troops preparing for 'Overlord'. At Lydd, on the south coast, they witnessed a series of demonstrations, rejoining the train for Ascot, where they were joined by the New Zealand Prime Minister, Peter Fraser. That night, still on his train, Churchill was joined for dinner by Eisenhower.[5] Ten days earlier, at Eden's request, Churchill had made a personal appeal to Eisenhower to provide extra vehicles for the Leclerc Division. 'Let me remind you of the figures of Anzio,' Churchill wrote, 'viz., 125,000 men with 23,000 vehicles, all so painfully landed to carry them, and they only got twelve miles.' Churchill added: 'Forgive me for making this appeal, which I know you will weigh carefully and probe deeply before rejecting.'[6] Eisenhower had agreed

---

[1] 'Meeting of Prime Ministers', PMM (44) 9th Meeting, 'Secret', 11.30 a.m., 9 May 1944: Cabinet papers, 99/28.

[2] Letter of 10 May 1944: Churchill papers, 2/495. Eric Long, the son of the 1st Viscount Long, had fought at the Dardanelles in 1915. A Conservative MP from 1927 to 1931, from 1939 to 1943 he was Officer Commanding the 75th Searchlight Regiment, Royal Artillery. His only brother was killed in action on 27 January 1917. His elder son, Lieutenant Walter Reginald Basil Long, was drowned while on active service in Greece, 28 April 1941, aged 22. His nephew (whom he succeeded as third Viscount) was killed in action in north-west Europe on 23 September 1944.

[3] MA/1251, IZ 3866, 'Personal for Prime Minister', time of arrival, 11.35 a.m., 11 May 1944: Churchill papers, 20/164.

[4] MA/12567, IZ 3873, 'Personal for Prime Minister', time of arrival, 11.05 p.m., 11 May 1944: Churchill papers, 20/164.

[5] Private Office Diary, 12 May 1944.

[6] 'Top Secret', 'Personal', 2 May 1944: Churchill papers, 20/137.

that any deficiencies in the Leclerc Division's vehicle situation, including provision for maintenance, 'will be met from American sources'.[1]

One of the questions which Eisenhower and Churchill discussed on May 12 was the use of French resistance troops in the follow-up of the landings. Yet no arrangement existed between the French National Committee and the British and French Governments for the employment of French forces outside or inside France. That night Churchill telegraphed to Roosevelt:

> . . . General Eisenhower says that he attaches great importance to the action to be taken by the French Resistance Groups on and after D-Day, and undoubtedly we must take care that our joint troops do not suffer heavier losses owing to the fact that no agreement has been made for the employment of the French Resistance Groups. The French Committee state that the Resistance Army numbers 175,000 men and they intend to incorporate them officially in the French Army under the name of French Forces of the Interior.
>
> I therefore propose to you that General de Gaulle, together with one or two of his Committee, should be invited to come here on say 18th May in the utmost secrecy; that you should either entrust your case to General Eisenhower or send over someone specially to meet them; that we should discuss outstanding matters affecting military and political collaborations together face to face, showing all our substantial reasons against any extreme demands but endeavouring to reach a working arrangement. The Foreign Secretary or I would conduct the discussion with de Gaulle and any of your representatives you may choose. We will make the best proposals we can to you without agreeing to anything until we have heard from you. It may be that no agreement will be reached because they are unreasonable, in which case we have done our best, and he will have put himself hopelessly in the wrong. In any case we shall have done our duty by the soldiers and you will have the fullest opportunity of seeing the best lay-out we can get for you to consider.[2]

Roosevelt approved Churchill's negotiations with de Gaulle, on condition that, 'in the interest of security', de Gaulle were kept in the United Kingdom, 'until the "Overlord" landing has been made'.[3] But Churchill, aware that this would be offensive to de Gaulle, proposed, after a talk with Bedell Smith, 'to wait for D-Day' before inviting de Gaulle to Britain.[4] After D-Day, Churchill added two days later, 'we might even get him into a friendly mood'.[5]

---

[1] 'Top Secret', 10 May 1944: Premier papers, 3/180/9, folio 448.

[2] Prime Minister's Personal Telegram, T.1071/4, Prime Minister to President, No. 674, 'Personal and Top Secret', 12 May 1944: Churchill papers, 20/183.

[3] President to Prime Minister, No. 538, 'Personal and Most Secret', 13 May 1944: Churchill papers, 20/164.

[4] Prime Minister's Personal Minute, M.548/4 (to Eden), 4 May 1944: Churchill papers, 20/152.

[5] Prime Minister's Personal Minute, M.555/4 (to Eden, Eisenhower and the Chiefs of Staff Committee), 16 May 1944: Churchill papers, 20/152.

On May 13 Churchill, still in his train, returned to the south coast, to Cosham, where he and his guests were taken on a tour of inspection of Spithead and in Southampton Water of naval preparation for 'Overlord'. Returning through London, where Smuts, Mackenzie King, Fraser and Huggins left the train, Churchill continued by train to Chequers. That weekend, reading of the Dominion Prime Ministers' Conference, Jock Colville noted 'the great tribute paid by the Dominions PMs to our own Prime Minister's leadership', adding:

Whatever the PM's shortcomings may be, there is no doubt that he does provide guidance and purpose for the Chiefs of Staff and the FO on matters which, without him, would often be lost in the maze of inter-departmentalism or frittered away by caution and compromise. Moreover he has two qualities, imagination and resolution, which are conspicuously lacking among other Ministers and among the Chiefs of Staff. I hear him very much criticized, often by people in close contact with him, but I think much of the criticism is due to the inability to see people and their actions in the right perspective when one examines them at quarters too close.[1]

From Italy, on May 14, news came of the first success of operation 'Diadem', when French troops of the 5th Army broke through the German defence line south of the Liri valley, and captured Ausonia. On the following day, American troops captured Spigno.

In London on May 15, Churchill attended the final conference on D-Day preparations at Montgomery's headquarters in St Paul's School. The King and Smuts, both of whom had earlier doubted the wisdom of the cross-Channel assault, were also present, together with the Chiefs of Staff and the senior officers of SHAEF, the Supreme Headquarters, Allied Expeditionary Force. The first speaker was the King, then Churchill, who used the phrase 'I am hardening on this enterprise'. This, Ismay later wrote to Churchill, he had taken to mean 'that the more you thought about it, the more certain you were of success'.[2]

After Churchill had spoken, Eisenhower told the gathering of the general plan, followed first by Montgomery, then by General Sir Humfrey Gale, the Chief Administrative Officer. Ismay later recalled, of General Gale's presentation:

---

[1] Colville diary, 13 May 1944: Colville papers.

[2] General Ismay, 'Notes on Pre-D Day Events', 23 November 1950', Churchill papers, 4/335. Churchill spoke, General Kennedy wrote in his diary, 'for about half an hour in a robust and even humorous style, and concluded with a moving expression of his hopes and good wishes. He looked much better than at the last conference, and spoke with great vigour, urging offensive leadership and stressing the ardour for battle which he believed the men felt.' (Bernard Fergusson, editor, *The Business of War, The War Narrative of Major-General Sir John Kennedy*, London 1957, page 328.)

In his desire to give an idea of the magnitude of the undertaking, he revealed that the number of vehicles to be landed within the first twenty days was not far off two hundred thousand. The Prime Minister winced. He had been amused, but shocked, by the tale—probably apocryphal—that in the 'Torch' operation, twenty dental chairs had been landed with the first flight at Algiers. I had never had the courage to tell him of another tale—probably equally apocryphal—that the first crates to be unpacked on the beaches at Anzio were found to contain harmoniums and hymn books. He was of course aware that there could not be any substantial changes in the loading tables at this late hour, but the first instruction which he gave me as we drove away from St Paul's was to write to Montgomery and tell him that the Prime Minister was concerned about the large number of non-combatants and non-fighting vehicles which were to be shipped across the Channel in the early stages. . . . [1]

On May 17 Ismay wrote to Montgomery to explain Churchill's concern at what he had heard at the St Paul's briefing, that, for example, '2,000 officers and clerks were to be taken over to keep records', and that on D-Day plus 20 'there will be one vehicle to every 4.84 men'. [2] Two days later, Churchill discussed the loading scales with Montgomery, who explained, as Churchill reported to Brooke, 'that he was only taking 50 per cent of his establishment and in these the fighting vehicles predominate over the trucks'. This, Churchill added, 'is quite all right'. Churchill made no mention of the clerks. [3]

At the end of the St Paul's briefing, Churchill had spoken privately to Admiral Ramsay, Allied Naval Commander-in-Chief of the Expeditionary Force, and asked Ramsay to make a plan for him to witness the first day's bombardment, and to land briefly on one of the landing beaches. On the following day Ramsay wrote to Churchill:

Briefly the plan is that you should embark in H.M.S. 'Belfast', Flagship of Rear-Admiral F. Dalrymple Hamilton, in Weymouth Bay in the late afternoon of D-1, the ship being called in on her passage from the Clyde for the purpose, and rejoining her squadron at full speed.

I consider that nothing smaller than a cruiser is suitable for you during the night and the approach. She is one of the bombarding ships attached to the centre British Force. Next day, it should be possible to transfer you to a destroyer which has completed her bombardment and which is due to return to England to re-ammunition. You could make a short tour of the beaches, with due regard to the unswept mine areas, before returning in her.

I shall not make any detailed arrangements until I know that the above arrangements are satisfactory to you. You told me not to mention this plan to the First Sea Lord and I have not done so, but you will appreciate that, as Supreme Commander, it was essential that General Eisenhower should know

[1] Ismay recollections: Ismay memoirs, *op. cit.*, page 352.
[2] 'Top Secret and Personal', 17 May 1944: Churchill papers, 4/335.
[3] Prime Minister's Personal Minute, M.586/4, 21 May 1944: Churchill papers, 20/152.

of what was in the air, and I must tell you that he is very averse to your going. You mean so much to the Nation at this stage in the war that I venture to suggest that any risk to your life, even though it may be small, should not be taken unnecessarily. While heartily sympathizing with your wish I feel that a visit to the other side as soon as the channels are swept and the situation stabilized would be more appropriate.[1]

Churchill persevered in his efforts to be with the bombarding force. Ismay, who had learned of Churchill's intentions by chance when he saw him in deep consultation with Ramsay, was opposed to them 'not so much', Ismay later recalled, 'by the risk involved, but at the prospect of the Prime Minister being cut off from communication with the outside world at a time when critical and immediate decisions might have to be taken'. Ismay's objections were 'abruptly silenced' however, he later recalled, 'by the whispered promise that, if I kept my mouth shut, he would take me with him'.[2]

The D-Day preparations now entered their final three weeks. On May 16, Churchill said farewell to the Dominion Prime Ministers: 'we do not know how long victory will be denied', he told them, 'or what tribulations we shall have to ask our people to endure, but we are absolutely sure that they will not be found unequal to the tests and the trials, however long and heavy. . . .'[3] Three days later, after his talk with Montgomery about the loading scales, Churchill wrote in Montgomery's private message book: 'On the verge of the greatest adventure with which these pages have dealt, I record my confidence that all will be well, and that the organization and equipment of the Army will be worthy of the valour of the soldiers and the genius of their chief.'[4]

For four days, Alexander had carried out his advance on the main Italian front without a parallel attack from the Anzio bridgehead. 'There is some opinion here,' Churchill telegraphed, 'that it would have been better for the Anzio punch to be let off first.' Churchill added, however, that he and Brooke agreed with Alexander that 'it is better to keep the threat of the compressed spring working on the enemy in the present phase'.[5] Alexander replied on the following evening: 'I weighed very carefully the pros and cons of an Anzio break-out, and among many factors two influenced me most. Firstly,

[1] 'Top Secret and Personal', 16 May 1944: Churchill papers, 20/136.

[2] Ismay recollections: Ismay memoirs, *op. cit.*, page 352.

[3] 'Meeting of Prime Ministers', PMM (44) 16th Meeting, 'Confidential', 16 May 1944: Cabinet papers, 99/28.

[4] Field Marshal Bernard L. Montgomery, *Ten Chapters, 1942–1945*, London 1946, facsimile message of 19 May 1944.

[5] Prime Minister's Personal Telegram T.1086/4, sent at 6.25 p.m., 17 May 1944: Churchill papers, 20/164.

the enemy's reserves in that area were too strong, with 90th Division and 26th Division, and I wanted to draw them away first. As you know, 90th Division has been drawn down to main battle area, and part of 26th Division has also been moved. Secondly, the German expected Anzio to be the major thrust, and to gain surprise I did what he did not expect.' When the 'right moment' came, Alexander added, 'the Americans will punch out to get astride the enemy's communications to Rome'.[1]

On May 18, after severe fighting which had lasted for six days, the town and monastery of Monte Cassino fell at last to Alexander's army, with Polish troops taking the monastery itself. The Poles were 'elated', Wilson telegraphed to Churchill, at their hard won success, as the fighting has been 'very severe'.[2] 'I am very glad the battle is going so well,' Churchill replied, 'and hope it will be pressed with unflagging energy against an enemy whose foundations may not be solid.'[3] The capture of Cassino was 'a trophy', Churchill telegraphed to Stalin, noting that the Poles had 'fought bravely' losing several thousand men, and that the French had 'distinguished themselves'. He hoped, Churchill commented, that between thirty to thirty-five German divisions would be kept in the Italian theatre and 'away from "Overlord" '. As for 'Overlord' itself, 'all our thoughts are wrapt up in this. All the commanders are confident and the troops most eager.'[4]

From Washington, Roosevelt wrote to Churchill on May 20, having been ill and out of action for several weeks: 'Remember what I told old Moran to make you do—obey his orders.' Thus, Roosevelt added, 'the Commander-in-Chief in one country orders around a mere Minister of Defence in another country'.[5]

On May 20 Churchill's Junior Private Secretary, Jock Colville, left Downing Street for three months' active duty in the Royal Air Force. He was replaced during his absence by the twenty-seven year old

[1] 'Top Secret and Private', sent at 5.20 p.m., 18 May 1944: Churchill papers, 20/164.
[2] 'Top Secret and Personal', 18 May 1944: Churchill papers, 20/164.
[3] Prime Minister's Personal Telegram, T.10088/4, 'Personal and Secret', 18 May 1944: Churchill papers, 20/164.
[4] Prime Minister's Personal Telegram, T.1096/4, 'Personal and Top Secret', 19 May 1944: Churchill papers, 20/164.
[5] Letter of 20 May 1944, signed 'With my affectionate regards, As ever yours, FDR': Churchill papers, 20/146. This letter was delivered to Churchill on May 24. In his memoirs he wished to quote it, but wrote: 'Alas, I cannot find it.' (Winston S. Churchill, *The Second World War*, volume 5, London 1952, page 553.)

Christopher Dodds, who had been at the Admiralty since 1939. Dodds later recalled Churchill's 'incredible energy—the enormous energy of the man', as well as 'his capacity to argue the military case'.

At their first meeting, Churchill said to Dodds, 'I hear you were at Dakar.' 'Yes,' replied Dodds, 'I'm afraid I was,' to which Churchill commented: 'Well it wasn't *your* fault.' [1]

May 20 was the day on which Churchill learned from the Joint Intelligence Committee that the two prior conditions for launching 'Overlord' had been met. These conditions, laid down a year earlier by General Morgan, were, first, that 'there should be an over-all reduction in the German fighter force between now and the time of the surface assault', and, second, that 'the number of German offensive divisions in reserve must not exceed a certain figure on the target date, if the operation is to have a reasonable chance of success'. These German reserves, Morgan explained, in France and the Low Countries 'as a whole, excluding divisions holding the coast, German Air Force divisions and training divisions, should not exceed, on the day of the assault, twelve full-strength, first-quality divisions'. In addition, Morgan had stated, the Germans 'should not be able to transfer more than fifteen first-quality divisions from Russia, during the first two months'. [2]

'Overlord' could therefore go ahead.

As D-Day approached, Churchill expressed several anxieties, among them, as he minuted to Brooke on May 21, 'the comparatively small number of troops that will be landed' and 'the smallness of the infantry component of the fighting troops'. [3] He had also discussed with Montgomery the question of whether the Germans might use poison gas to repel the landing forces. Not only poison gas, but bacteriological warfare, was a cause for concern. Churchill had already sent Ismay, 'In a locked box', for the Chiefs of Staff Committee, a note by Lord Cherwell of a bacteriological warfare development, 'N' spores, to which there was 'no known cure and no effective prophylaxis'. Animals breathing in 'minute quantities' of these spores were likely to die 'suddenly but peacefully' within a week. They could be used behind enemy lines 'to render towns uninhabitable', and could be stored and scattered in 4lb bombs 'which go into the ordinary incendiary con-

[1] Christopher Dodds recollections: in conversation with the author, 7 February 1985.
[2] Joint Intelligence Committee No. 210 (Operations), (Final) of 1944, 'Most Secret', 20 May 1944: Cabinet papers, 79/74.
[3] Prime Minister's Personal Minute, M.586/4, 21 May 1944: Churchill papers, 20/152.

tainers'. Half a dozen Lancasters could carry enough, 'if spread evenly, to kill anyone found within a square mile and to render it uninhabitable thereafter'.

Referring to the current atom bomb research, Cherwell saw no reason to doubt that the bacteriological weapon 'appears to be a weapon of appalling potentiality; almost more formidable, because infinitely easier to make, than tube alloy'. It was also urgent to prepare countermeasures, 'if any there be', but, Cherwell ended, 'in the meantime it seems to me we cannot afford not to have N-bombs in our armoury'.[1]

That Churchill saw the bacteriological weapon as a deterrent was made clear on March 8, when he minuted: 'I have had most secret consultations with my Military Advisers. They consider, and I entirely agree, that if our enemies should indulge in this form of warfare, the only deterrent would be our power to retaliate.'[2]

On May 18 Churchill had arranged for Cherwell to explain about these 'N' spores to the Chiefs of Staff.[3] Two days later, in a minute to Ismay about poison gas, Churchill wrote: 'As you know, great progress has been made in bacteriological warfare and we have ordered a half million bombs from America for use should this mode of warfare be employed against us.'[4] On the following day Churchill wrote again to Ismay:

I do not myself believe that the Germans will use gas on the beaches, although this is the most potent way in which gas could be used. The reason is that we could retaliate tenfold or more through the greater power of our air forces to deliver upon all their cities. The only reason they are not using gas is that it would not pay them to do so. However, the temptation to use it on the beaches might conceivably be strong enough to override prudence. General Montgomery tells me that he is leaving all his anti-gas equipment on this side and his men are not even to carry gas masks. I agree with this.

It is however worth while considering whether a warning should not be uttered by me and the President such as those we have previously given about the Russians repeating our assurance that we have no intention of using gas but also giving warning that if any form of gas or toxic substances is used upon us or any of our Allies, we shall immediately use the full delivery

[1] 'Most Secret', 25 February 1944: Premier papers, 3/65, folios 25–7.
[2] Prime Minister's Personal Minute, M.246/4: Premier papers, 3/65. Cited in Julian Lewis, 'Churchill & the "Anthrax Bomb" ': Encounter, London, February 1982, pages 18–28.
[3] Prime Minister's Personal Minute, D.160/4, 18 May 1944: Premier papers, 3/65, folio 44.
[4] Prime Minister's Personal Minute, D.162/4, 21 May 1944: Cabinet papers, 120/782. Cited in Julian Lewis, 'Churchill & the "Anthrax Bomb" ': Encounter, London, February 1982, pages 18–28.

power of our Strategic Air Forces to drench the German cities and towns where any war industry exists.[1]

In Italy, on May 23 British and American forces launched their offensive from the Anzio bridgehead. 'Delighted to watch your constant progress,' Churchill telegraphed to Alexander. 'The only thing that matters is the reduction of the enemy's armed forces everywhere. Myself, I think you have got them. All good luck.'[2] That day, in a telegram to Stalin, Churchill pointed out that, 'far from withdrawing under heavy rearguards, as the American staffs thought probable, Hitler has committed himself obstinately to fighting it out south of Rome'. The battle must be considered 'critical'. The Allied forces involved 'do not greatly exceed those of the enemy'.[3] If a part of Hitler's special troops were thrown into the battle, however, 'it all helps "Overlord"'.[4]

During the Foreign Affairs debate in the House of Commons on May 24, Churchill surveyed the world, allied, enemy and neutral. 'I must, therefore,' he said, 'pick my way among heated ploughshares. . . .' Among the countries whose policies Churchill surveyed was Turkey, which had displayed 'an exaggerated attitude of caution', and yet rendered 'good service' by the personal initiative of President Inönü to halt all chrome exports to Germany. In Italy there was the 'hideous prospect of the red-hot rake of the battle-line being drawn from sea to sea right up the whole length of the peninsula'. Italian forces, he pointed out, now equipped by the Allies, 'have played their part in the line on more than one occasion', while Italian ships and aircraft were doing 'important and useful service'. He had praise for Spain, especially at the time of the North African landings in November 1942, when 'the Spaniards remained absolutely friendly and tranquil. They asked no questions, they raised no inconveniences.' He had praise too for the new Greek Government in exile, headed by George Papandreou, who, in conference in the Lebanon, had just persuaded all parties, including the communist EAM and its military wing, the ELAS, to join a single Government and a single under-

[1] Prime Minister's Personal Minute, D.163/4, 'Top Secret', 21 May 1944: Churchill papers, 20/152.

[2] Prime Minister's Personal Telegram, T.1111/4, 'Personal and Most Secret', 23 May 1944: Churchill papers, 20/165.

[3] The ratio of Allied to German Forces was 1.4 to 1.

[4] Prime Minister's Personal Telegram, T.1114/4, 'Personal and Top Secret', 23 May 1944: Churchill papers, 20/165.

ground national army. Thus, Churchill said, Greece had a hope of shaking off 'what I call the diseases of defeat'.[1]

Churchill then spoke of Yugoslavia, of Poland, and of the French Committee of National Liberation in Algiers. All questions of monarchy or republic, or Leftism or Rightism, were, he told the House, 'strictly subordinate to the main purpose we have in mind. In one place we suggest a King, in another a Communist—there is no attempt by us to enforce particular ideologies. We only want to beat the enemy. . . .' Of Russia, Churchill spoke in terms of optimism:

Profound changes have taken place in Soviet Russia; the Trotskyite form of Communism has been completely wiped out. The victories of the Russian Armies have been attended by a great rise in the strength of the Russian State, and a remarkable broadening of its views. The religious side of Russian life has had a wonderful rebirth. The discipline and military etiquette of the Russian Armies are unsurpassed.

Thirty years earlier, Churchill recalled, Britain had begun 'to march forward with the Russians in the battle against the German tyranny of the Kaiser and we are now marching with them, and I trust we shall until all forms of German tyranny have been extirpated'. As to Nazism, the 'other' ideology, 'we intend to wipe that out utterly, however drastic may be the methods required'.[2]

Churchill spoke for an hour and twenty minutes. 'He was as lucid as ever,' Harold Nicolson wrote that night to his sons. 'There were here and there some of the old striking phrases. His humour and charm was unabated. But the voice was not thunderous and three times Members called out to him to "Speak up!".'[3] 'You seemed tired,' Harvie Watt reported to Churchill of the opinion of many

[1] Two days later Churchill telegraphed to Papandreou: 'Thank you for your message announcing the successful conclusion of the Lebanon Conference. I am indeed thankful to learn of the determination of your great and ancient people to bury their differences in the liberation of their country and I congratulate you most warmly on your part in achieving this happy result. May the unity of the Greek people continue long after the Nazi hordes have been driven out.' (Prime Minister's Personal Telegram, T.1126, 26 May 1944: Churchill papers, 20/183.)

[2] *Hansard*, 24 May 1944, columns 762–86. On the following day Churchill telegraphed to Roosevelt, who wished to issue a pronouncement on D-Day itself about the differences between the Allied and Nazi ideologies: 'In truth there is much more between them and us than a philosophy. Nearly all Europe cries for vengeance against brutal tyranny. At Teheran my suggestion for the isolation of Prussia was considered far too modest by you and UJ. Everybody expects complete forcible disarmament of Germany, possibly extending to civil aviation, to be made and maintained. There are other very grave questions open. For instance, how are the Poles going to be compensated if they do not get East Prussia and certain territories up to the line of the Oder in return for the Curzon Line which the Russians will certainly demand?' (Prime Minister's Personal Telegram, T.1123/4, Prime Minister to President No. 680, 'Top Secret and Personal', 25 May 1944: Churchill papers, 20/165.)

[3] Letter of 24 May 1944: Nigel Nicolson (editor), *op. cit.*, pages 372–3.

MPs, 'particularly in the second half of the speech.'[1]

'The PM did very little work,' Marian Holmes noted in her diary that night. 'He said, "I'm fed up to the back teeth with work, so I'll let you off lightly."'[2] On May 25, however, work began again in earnest, with the night secretary, who that night was Marian Holmes, starting work at 11 p.m. and taking Churchill's dictation for two and a half hours. 'At 1.15,' she noted, 'he looked at the clock and said "Tut, tut".'[3]

Churchill was certainly tired after his speech, but could not break off too easily from his work. At ten o'clock that evening, at a meeting of the Chiefs of Staff Committee, he was confronted with a setback in plans for the 'Mulberry' harbour which required an urgent decision: the 'entire Naval pumping resources', he was told, were insufficient for the task of raising 'Phoenixes', the concrete caissons, for the despatch across the Channel. Had the pumping resources 'of the London Fire Brigades for instance' been called upon, he asked.[4]

In a telegram to Marshal Tito on May 25 Churchill had ended: 'Give my love to Randolph should he come into your sphere. Maclean will be coming back soon. I wish I could come myself but I am too old and heavy to jump out in a parachute.'[5] That very day, in Bosnia, German paratroops attacked Tito's headquarters in what they had hoped would be a surprise raid. Enigma decrypts had indicated the German intention, but, for security reasons, no alert had been sent to the British Mission. The British Mission had already concluded, however, on the basis of persistent German photographic air reconnaissance, that an attack was imminent, and had changed their location shortly before the attack.[6] As a result of this foresight, Tito and Randolph escaped into the mountains. 'We are told that British

[1] 'Report by Parliamentary Private Secretary', 26 May 1944: Harvie Watt papers. Five days later, in reply to a request from Thomas Loveday, Vice Chancellor of Bristol University, to have his portrait painted in his capacity as Chancellor of Bristol University, Churchill wrote: 'I should be very ready, if and when an occasion offered, to submit myself for a sitting. But I am afraid I can make no promise in war time, and will hardly be worth painting unless the War stops soon.' (Letter of 31 May 1944: Loveday papers.)

[2] Marian Holmes diary, 24 May 1944: Marian Walker Spicer papers.

[3] Marian Holmes diary, 25 May 1944: Marian Walker Spicer papers.

[4] Chiefs of Staff Committee No. 170 (Operations) of 1944, 10 p.m., 24 May 1944: Cabinet papers, 79/74. When transported across the Channel and then sunk off the Normandy shoreline, the 'Phoenixes' would serve as an artificial harbour.

[5] Prime Minister's Personal Telegram, T.1120/4, No. 52 to Bari, 'Most Secret and Personal', 24 May 1944: Churchill papers, 20/165.

[6] F. H. Hinsley and others, British Intelligence in the Second World War, volume 3, Part 1, London 1984, page 165.

liaison officers are safe,' Harold Macmillan telegraphed to Churchill from Bari on May 26. 'This includes Randolph.' [1]

Even as the D-Day preparations entered their last two weeks, the Foreign Office was seeking to define Britain's attitude towards the central Council or Executive of the main international organization of the post-war world. Eden intended to speak on this theme in the House of Commons. Reading the draft of Eden's speech, Churchill told Eden that, in his view, the Big Three, or the Big Four, would be 'the trustee or steering committee of the whole body in respect of the use of force to prevent war', but they would not, as Eden had suggested, deal with the economic side. Churchill added:

You should make it clear that we have no idea of three or four Great Powers ruling the world. On the contrary, their victory will entitle them to serve the world in the supreme respect of preventing the outbreak of more wars. We should certainly not be prepared ourselves to submit to an economic, financial, and monetary system laid down by, say, Russia, or the United States with her faggot-vote China.

The Supreme World Council or Executive is not to rule the nations. It is only to prevent them tearing each other in pieces. I feel I could argue this very strongly from the point of view of derogation of national sovereignties. [2]

Amid these issues of world significance, Churchill still watched over the humbler elements of war policy, especially those which might affect morale. On May 26, impressed by improvements in the rationing system, he wrote to the Minister of Food, Colonel Llewellin, to praise what had been done, and to maintain vigilance. [3] 'Try to cut out petty annoyances,' he wrote, 'whether in the hotels, the little shops or the private lives of ordinary people. Nothing should be done for spite's sake. The great work of rationing in this country, which has given so much confidence and absence of class feeling, should not be prejudiced by little trumpery regulations which when enforced make hard cases.' [4]

Reading in the *Yorkshire Post* that a householder had been fined one pound, with two guineas costs, for having borrowed coal from a neighbour, Churchill urged the Minister of Fuel and Power, Major Gwilym Lloyd George, to 'put a stop to nonsense like this if it lies in your sphere'. Such acts of 'bureaucratic folly', he added, 'are, I fear, only typical of a vast amount of silly wrong-doing by small officials or committees'. [5]

*   *   *

[1] No. 67 from Bari to Foreign Office, 'Personal and Top Secret', sent 26 May 1944, received 27 May 1944: Churchill papers, 20/165.

[2] Prime Minister's Personal Minute, M.614/4, 25 May 1944: Churchill papers, 20/152.

[3] Llewellin had succeeded Lord Woolton as Minister of Food on 11 November 1943.

[4] Prime Minister's Personal Minute, M.621/4, 26 May 1944: Churchill papers, 20/152.

[5] Prime Minister's Personal Minute, M.638/4, 27 May 1944: Churchill papers, 20/152.

In following the preparations for 'Overlord', Churchill had to consider political as well as strategic needs. In urging Brooke not 'on any account' to let the Polish Division be kept out of the battle front, he wrote: 'Not only is it a magnificent fighting force, but its exploits will help to keep alive the soul of Poland, on which much turns in the future.' He had spoken about this to Bedell Smith, who said he could help in getting more men for this division 'by flying them from Africa and the United States'.[1]

Many captive nations looked to D-Day, whenever it might come, and to Churchill personally, for their salvation, and redress of grievances. On May 26, Eden asked Churchill to see the Belgian Prime Minister, Hubert Pierlot, and his Foreign Secretary, Paul Henri Spaak, who were concerned about their country 'getting much knocked about by our bombardment', the casualties from which had already been 'heavy'. Pierlot, added Eden, 'is not a strong man and is evidently much upset'.[2] Churchill's reaction revealed the bitterness he still felt at Belgium's policy in 1939 and 1940. His reply began:

Considering that there are millions of French and British graves in Belgium, and that she was saved from all the horrors of German incorporation by our exertions, I thought her attitude in the years preceding the war singularly ungrateful and detached. Had she acted vigorously with France, French action might have been stimulated. Anyhow at the outbreak of war, her armies could have been placed in a far better strategical position than was subsequently possible, and the hideous gap at Sedan might have presented a very different aspect to the enemy. Without going so far as to say that Belgian action might have changed the sombre course of events, I have no doubt whatever that, up till the time they were fallen upon and invaded, our account with them was expressed by 'thank you for nothing'. Indeed I think they were the most contemptible of all the neutrals at that time.

Churchill's minute continued:

This however did not prevent me from speaking in more considerate tones about the surrender of the Belgian Army by the King of the Belgians without the slightest regard to what happened to all the forces that had come as fast as they could, in view of Belgian policy, to the rescue of that country. In fact I have very little sympathy with them beyond what I feel for all countries invaded and trampled down by the Huns. I should not be able to see them on this occasion without pointing out some of these historical events. This might not cheer them up at all.

Do you not think, on the whole, it would be better for me to leave them alone?

[1] Prime Minister's Personal Minute, M.632/4, 27 May 1944: Churchill papers, 20/152.
[2] Foreign Secretary's Minute, PM/44/373, 26 May 1944: Premier papers, 3/69A, folios 60–1.

They will get over it very soon. We should only hear complaints about the ill-feeding of the children and the cruel bombing of their cities. I have not got much that is of any use to say on either of these points. However, if you wish me to do anything, I might find an occasion on Thursday, but I advise against it.[1]

Eden persisted, and on the following Thursday, Churchill saw Pierlot and Spaak, for half an hour.[2] 'I will do the best I can with them,' he assured Eden that morning.[3] During the meeting, Churchill gave the Belgian Ministers such assurances as he could that everything possible would be done to avoid civilian casualties, telling the Belgians 'that it was of vital importance to interrupt as much as possible the enemy's lines of communication and bombing was therefore inevitable. He was, however, personally giving continuous attention to the subject and had reason to hope that the losses which had recently been so heavy would in future be considerably less.' In reply, Pierlot said 'that he himself fully realised that bombing was unavoidable and was in consequence very glad to learn that the losses might not be so severe henceforth'. After thanking Churchill 'for his kindness in receiving them', the Foreign Office note of the meeting concluded, 'Monsieur Pierlot and his colleague then left, obviously far happier than on their arrival'.[4]

On May 28 General Eaker was among Churchill's guests at Chequers. He was on his way back to Cairo, giving Churchill a chance to write to Randolph, whose escape with Tito had just been confirmed. 'We are naturally following with some anxiety the news of the attack on Tito's headquarters,' Churchill wrote. 'But today the report is that the airborne Huns have been liquidated.' His letter continued:

I cannot do more than wish you good luck, but you are ever in my thoughts, and in those of all (repeat all) here. We have a lovely day at where we live from time to time, and all is fair with the first glory of summer. The War is very fierce and terrible, but in these sunlit lawns and buttercup meadows, it is hard to conjure up its horrors.

Baby Winston, as you will no doubt have been told by Pamela, has developed German measles. I am ashamed to say I told him it was the fault of the Germans, but I shall labour to remove this impression quite soon.[5]

Among the other guests at Chequers that weekend was a second

---

[1] Prime Minister's Personal Minute, M.639/4, 27 May 1944: Premier papers, 3/69A, folios 58–9.

[2] Private Office Diary, 1 June 1944.

[3] Prime Minister's Personal Minute, M.648/4, 28 May 1944: Premier papers, 3/69A, folio 57.

[4] 'Memorandum', 2 June 1944: Premier papers, 3/69A, folios 37–8. This memorandum was sent to Churchill by Sir Lancelot Oliphant, Ambassador to the Belgian Government in London, who had accompanied the Belgian Prime Minister and Foreign Secretary to Downing Street.

[5] Letter of 28 May 1944: Randolph Churchill papers.

American, Averell Harriman, who was on his way back from Moscow to Washington. Churchill told Harriman of recent efforts to try to smooth matters over with Russia. The British had agreed to 'keep hands off Roumania' while the fighting continued there, while the Russians, in their turn, were willing 'to leave the British a free hand in Greece'. Already the Greek Communists were being 'most co-operative'.[1] 'Due largely to Stalin's recent civil messages,' Harriman reported to Roosevelt, 'the sun is shining again on the Soviet horizon.'[2]

Harriman's report was not entirely accurate. In a minute to Eden on May 28, Churchill had noted, of Clark Kerr's reaction to the Soviet charge of British intrigue in Roumania: 'The Ambassador knows quite well this is a false accusation, yet he cringes before Molotov and thinks we cannot pursue the matter further. Believe me, this is not the way to get on with the Russians.' Against this sentence, Eden noted: 'Yet no one is more effusive to Russians than PM.' Churchill's minute ended: 'It is a terrible mistake to quit this kind of battlefield unsatisfied.'[3]

Towards Greece, Churchill was determined not to allow the Lebanon agreement to lapse, nor Papandreou's authority to weaken. That Sunday he instructed Reginald Leeper, the Ambassador to the Greek Government in exile to let the Greeks know that 'we are going to be pretty rough with them if they continue in their state of fractious and turbulent intrigue'. Papandreou's opponents, Churchill minuted to Eden, should be sent 'to some remote island and their supporters made to feel they are out of it for several months, or even years'. 'If you are not very careful,' Churchill warned Eden, 'these Greek affairs will slop back into the trough.' Papandreou should be prevented at all costs 'from yielding to the weak babble of chatter that is proceeding around him. You cannot be too stiff in handling this situation and making them feel that the "fairy godmother" is capable of giving any of them a good smack over the head.'[4]

That Sunday, which Churchill spent at Chequers, the cross-Channel landing was only nine days away. That day, subordinate Commanders were told of the date of D-Day, and, from that moment, all personnel involved in the landings were 'sealed' in their ships, camps and assembly ports, and all mail impounded. 'Everything here is centred on "Overlord",' Churchill telegraphed to Stalin, 'and

[1] Abel and Harriman, op. cit., pages 328–9.
[2] Report of 29 May 1944: Abel and Harriman, op. cit., page 328.
[3] Prime Minister's Personal Minute, M.647/4, 'Top Secret', 28 May 1944: Foreign Office papers, 371/44001, R 9078/6.
[4] Prime Minister's Personal Minute, M.644/4, 28 May 1944: Churchill papers, 20/152.

everything in human power will be done or risked.'[1] To Roosevelt, who had had to cancel their Bermuda meeting because of ill health, but whom he was urging to make a visit to England after D-Day, Churchill wrote: 'Doctor Churchill informs you that a sea voyage in one of your great new battleships will do you no end of good.'[2]

As the air bombardment of French railway marshalling yards continued, at Roosevelt's insistence, Churchill read each day with consternation the reports of a committee set up to monitor the French reactions to the raids. 'Terrible things are being done,' he minuted to Eden on May 28.[3] On the following day, reading the reports for May 28, he minuted to General Hollis: 'The thing is getting much worse.'[4] To the Deputy Supreme Commander of the Allied Expeditionary Force, Air Chief Marshal Tedder, Churchill disagreed 'that the best targets were chosen', and he warned: 'you are piling up an awful load of hatred'.[5]

On May 23, within a week of the capture of Monte Cassino, Alexander had renewed the offensive in Italy. 'Your battle seems to be approaching its climax,' Churchill telegraphed that day, 'and all thoughts here are with you.'[6] This time, the advance of the Eighth Army was followed within twenty-four hours by a renewed attack by the forces at Anzio. On May 25, contact was made between the beachhead and the main force. Three days later, as the United States forces moved, not against the main German line of retreat, but against the German fortified positions on the road to Rome, Churchill telegraphed to Alexander: 'At this distance it seems much more important to cut their line of retreat than anything else.' A 'cop', Churchill added, 'is much more important than Rome, which would anyhow come as its consequence'.[7] A few hours later Churchill telegraphed again. He would back Alexander up 'whatever happens' but, he added, 'I should feel myself wanting in comradeship if I did not let you know that the glory of this battle, already great, will be measured,

[1] Prime Minister's Personal Telegram, T.1146/4, 'Top Secret and Personal', 28 May 1944: Churchill papers, 20/165.
[2] Prime Minister's Personal Telegram, T.1147/4, Prime Minister to President, No. 685, 'Top Secret and Personal', 28 May 1944: Churchill papers, 20/165.
[3] Prime Minister's Personal Minute, M.649/4, 28 May 1944: Churchill papers, 20/152.
[4] Prime Minister's Personal Minute, D.178/4, 29 May 1944: Churchill papers, 20/152.
[5] Prime Minister's Personal Minute, M.655/4, 29 May 1944: Churchill papers, 20/152.
[6] Prime Minister's Personal Telegram, T.1113/4, 'Top Secret and Personal', sent at 6.01 p.m., 23 May 1944: Churchill Papers, 20/165.
[7] Prime Minister's Personal Telegram, T.1144/4, 'Personal and Secret', sent half an hour after midnight, 28 May 1944: Churchill papers, 20/165.

not by the capture of Rome or the juncture with the bridgehead, but by the number of German divisions cut off. I am sure you will have revolved all this in your mind, and perhaps you have already acted in this way. Nevertheless I feel I ought to tell you that, "It is the cop that counts".' [1]

Churchill's hopes were not fulfilled; General Mark Clark sent out one division towards the main retreating road, but the division was forced to a halt before reaching its objective. The battle towards Rome went well, however, for the Allies, whose forces drew closer and closer to the city: the first capital city under German occupation to be threatened. On May 31 Churchill telegraphed to Alexander:

> The capture of Rome is a vast, world-wide event, and should not be minimised. I hope that British as well as Americans will enter the city simultaneously. I would not lump it in with other towns taken on the same day. Nevertheless, as you rightly state, the destruction of the German Army in the field gives us Rome and the rest thrown in.
>
> How lucky it was that we stood up to our United States Chiefs of Staff friends and refused to deny you the full exploitation of this battle! I will support you in obtaining the first priority in everything you need to achieve this glorious victory. I am sure the American Chiefs of Staff would now feel this was a bad moment to pull out of the battle or in any way weaken its force for the sake of other operations of an amphibious character, which may very soon take their place in the van of our ideas.
>
> All good luck. [2]

On May 31, Churchill held yet another meeting with Mikolajczyk, the Polish Prime Minister, in which he stated that he had never given Stalin 'the slightest grounds for thinking that he was weakening in his support' for the London Poles. He had 'no intention of altering his attitude', Churchill told Mikolajczyk, but he stressed the need for the Poles to 'help themselves to help him help them' by showing 'in every way' as much friendliness to Russia as possible 'in spite of every kind of provocation to act otherwise'. [3] That same day, Churchill proposed formally to Roosevelt a possible agreement with the Soviet Government 'as a practical matter' that the Russians 'would take the lead in Roumanian affairs', while Britain would 'take the lead in Greek affairs', each Government giving the other help in the respective

[1] Prime Minister's Personal Telegram, T.1148/4, 'Personal and Private', sent at 7.05 p.m., 28 May 1944: Churchill papers, 20/165.

[2] Prime Minister's Personal Telegram, T.1159/4, 'Personal and Top Secret', 'Through Special Channel', 8.55 a.m., 31 May 1944: Churchill papers, 20/165.

[3] 'British Minutes of the Conversation between M. Mikolajczyk and Mr Churchill. . . .', 31 May 1944: *Documents on Polish–Soviet Relations*, volume 2, document No. 136, pages 243–6.

countries. Such an arrangement, Churchill explained, 'would be a natural development of the existing military situation since Roumania falls within the sphere of the Russian armies and Greece within the Allied Command under General Wilson in the Mediterranean'. Churchill added:

I hope you may feel able to give this proposal your blessing. We do not of course wish to carve up the Balkans into spheres of influence, and in agreeing to the arrangement we should make it clear that it applied only to war conditions and did not affect the rights and responsibilities which each of the three Great Powers will have to exercise at the peace settlement and afterwards in regard to the whole of Europe. The arrangement would of course involve no change in the present collaboration between you and us in the formulation and execution of Allied Policy towards these countries. We feel however that the arrangement now proposed would be a useful device for preventing any divergence of policy between ourselves and them in the Balkans.[1]

At Churchill's suggestion to the War Cabinet, de Gaulle was to be told about D-Day by Churchill personally, on June 4.[2] 'Otherwise,' Churchill explained to Roosevelt, 'it may become a very great insult to France.' Eisenhower, who agreed with this plan, would tell de Gaulle 'what is necessary' about the landings.[3] Churchill had already obtained the Chiefs of Staff's agreement not to invite de Gaulle to Britain before D-Day, and not to allow, for the sake of maintaining 'Overlord' security, any 'free exchange' of telegrams between the Free French in London and those in Algiers. Churchill had explained to the War Cabinet two weeks earlier: 'If General de Gaulle were invited to this country now he would almost certainly be accompanied by some staff officers and would demand to be allowed to exchange telegrams freely with Algiers. He would almost certainly regard a refusal of this request as an insult and an aspersion on his honour.'[4]

On the morning of June 3 Churchill worked on his train, where he was joined during the morning by Anthony Eden, and Eden's Prin-

---

[1] Prime Minister's Personal Telegram, T.1161/4, Prime Minister to President, No. 687, 'Personal and Top Secret', 31 May 1944: Churchill papers, 20/165.

[2] War Cabinet No. 70 of 1944, 31 May 1944, Confidential Annex: Cabinet papers, 65/46.

[3] Prime Minister's Personal Telegram, T.1174/4, Prime Minister to President, No. 688, 'Personal and Top Secret', 1 June 1944: Churchill papers, 20/165.

[4] Staff Conference, Chiefs of Staff Committee No. 163 (Operations) of 1944, 18 May 1944: Cabinet papers, 79/84.

cipal Private Secretary, Pierson Dixon.[1] At lunchtime Ernest Bevin arrived. After luncheon Churchill, Smuts and Bevin visited Southampton, where they saw the embarkation of troops of the Tyneside Division. They then embarked on a motor launch and saw an assembly of landing craft. 'These are wonderful sights to see,' Churchill telegraphed to Roosevelt on the following day, 'with all these thousands of vessels.'[2] Churchill, Smuts and Bevin then continued in the launch to Portsmouth, visiting Eisenhower's headquarters on the way back to Churchill's train.[3] Waiting for the train at its siding was Eden, together with Pierson Dixon, who noted in his diary how, at eight that evening:

PM arrived accompanied by Smuts, Bevin, Geoffrey Lloyd, Duncan Sandys, Pug Ismay and Tommy Thompson. After he had changed from his Trinity House uniform to the cooler drill of a Colonel of the Hussars, we had a very convivial dinner in the dining saloon. It was a very pictorial scene—the two old warlords [Churchill and Smuts], fat, gross Ernie Bevin and Anthony, very elegant, next to him, and the lesser fry at the ends of the narrow table. The food was admirable, with 1926 champagne and a grand old brandy out of balloon glasses. The talk was mostly about British and S. African politics at the beginning of the century; the PM very genial. E. Bevin, who likes Anthony, became very affectionate towards him at the end of the evening, and their friendliness provoked the PM to say that he was ready to give up the leadership to either, or both of them at any time.[4]

Late that night Churchill received news that de Gaulle would be arriving from Algiers on the following morning.[5]

On the night of June 3, because of the worsening weather, Eisenhower postponed the launching of the operation for at least twenty-four hours, setting the new D-Day on the morning of June 6 when there was a forecast of a brief spell of better weather. Bedell Smith telephoned the news to Ismay in the early hours of the morning. Summoned soon afterwards by Churchill, Ismay told him of the postponement, and of the new date.

In the early hours of June 4, de Gaulle reached England from Algiers. He was greeted by a letter from Churchill which read:

[1] In his diary, Dixon described Churchill's train, to which he and Eden had been escorted by a CID man some two hundred yards from the station, around a curve. 'It consisted of two saloons,' he wrote, 'one with a bedroom at one end and a tiny office and telephone at the other; the other saloon doing service as dining-room and conference-room.' Churchill, added Dixon, 'was, audibly, having his bath when we arrived'. (Pierson Dixon diary, 3 June 1944: Piers Dixon, *Double Diploma, The Life of Sir Pierson Dixon, Don and Diplomat*, London 1968, pages 89–90).

[2] Prime Minister's Personal Telegram, T.1192/4, Prime Minister to President, No. 692, 'Personal and Top Secret', 4 June 1944: Churchill papers, 20/165.

[3] Private Office diary, 3 June 1944.

[4] Pierson Dixon diary, 3 June 1944: *op. cit.* Pierson Dixon's son Piers later married Churchill's grand-daughter Edwina Sandys.

[5] Private Office diary, 3 June 1944.

My dear General de Gaulle,

Welcome to these shores! Very great military events are about to take place. I should be glad if you could come to see me down here in my train, which is close to General Eisenhower's Headquarters, bringing with you one or two of your party. General Eisenhower is looking forward to seeing you again and will explain to you the military position which is momentous and imminent. If you could be here by 1.30 p.m., I should be glad to give you dejeuner and we will then repair to General Eisenhower's Headquarters. Let me have a telephone message early to know whether this is agreeable to you or not.[1]

Short before one o'clock on Sunday June 4, General de Gaulle reached Churchill's train. Eden, who was present, later recalled:

I arrived in time to walk down the railway line with de Gaulle. The Prime Minister, moved by his sense of history, was on the track to greet the General with arms outstretched. Unfortunately de Gaulle did not respond easily to such a mood. He was offended at the failure to make any agreement with the French Committee for the civil administration of France, and may also have been genuinely uncertain about the purpose of this somewhat strange railway meeting. Mr Bevin and Field-Marshal Smuts were other guests on the train. Smuts, usually so invaluable as a soothing influence, was handicapped by a previous statement of his which the French remembered with bitterness, to the effect that France would never be a great power again.[2]

At the start of their discussion, Churchill told de Gaulle that he had felt that it would have been 'a very bad thing' in the history of the two countries if an operation 'designed to liberate France' had been undertaken by British and American forces 'without the French being informed'. He also explained that the reason for the bombing of the French railways, 'which to our regret had caused such loss of life', was that it had enabled the Allies to limit 'the number of enemy divisions that could be used against us at any given moment while our front was building up'.

Churchill then explained to de Gaulle how the landings would be carried out, and their scale. It was 'clearly an affair of momentous importance', de Gaulle replied. 'He had himself thought that now was the moment to carry it out.' The discussion turned to the future civil administration of France. The minute recording Churchill's words read:

[1] 'Top Secret', 4 June 1944: Churchill papers, 20/137.
[2] Eden memoirs, *The Reckoning, op. cit.*, page 452.

He must warn the General that the part of France at first liberated might not be big, and might contain only a few French people, under heavy fire. The President had said that General Marshall would be able to speak with General de Gaulle on all military affairs, but he had twice refused to give his consent to conversations between representatives of the three countries on political matters. The Prime Minister was free to talk *à deux*. But he felt sure that, if General de Gaulle were to express the wish to visit the President, he would be made most welcome. We should be glad to forward such a message, and he would suggest that when the battle was launched the General should send his representative in Washington to inform the President that he desired to come. But the President had been unwilling to send a representative to the present conversations.

This procedure, de Gaulle felt, was 'humiliating'. Churchill replied that he himself had told the President on three or four occasions in the past that he would like to visit him 'but the President had declined'. He, Churchill, 'had taken it *en camarade*'.

De Gaulle's grievance was that no agreement on the civil administration of liberated France had been reached many months earlier. Churchill urged him, despite his grievance, to go to Roosevelt now. As he told de Gaulle:

> ... whether or not General de Gaulle visited the President was a matter for the General himself to decide. But he himself strongly advised him to do so. After all, the United States and Great Britain were two great nations who were willing to risk the loss of scores of thousands of their men in an operation designed to liberate France. He felt that it was General de Gaulle's duty to do everything to bind these nations to France, and he would be very sorry for France if General de Gaulle were to do otherwise. He must tell him bluntly that, if after every effort had been exhausted the President was on one side and the French National Committee of Liberation on the other, he, Mr Churchill, would almost certainly side with the President, and that anyhow no quarrel would ever arise between Britain and the United States on account of France. As regards the Civil Affairs agreement, he would sum up the view of His Majesty's Government as follows: If General de Gaulle wanted us to ask the President to agree to give him the title deeds of France, the answer was 'No'. If he wanted us to ask the President to agree that the Committee of National Liberation was the principal factor with whom we should deal in France, the answer was 'Yes'.

De Gaulle replied that he 'quite understood' that in case of disagreement between the United States and France, 'Britain would side with the United States', to which Churchill commented that 'he had expressed his own personal opinion which he had little doubt would be endorsed by the House of Commons in view of the relations subsisting through the Anglo-American society and brotherhood-in-arms which nothing could break'.[1]

'I did not like this pronouncement,' Eden later recalled, 'nor did Mr Bevin, who said so in a booming aside. The meeting was a failure.'[2] But Churchill did not veer from his view of the primacy not only of Anglo-American relations, but of his own personal relations with Roosevelt. 'Our personal friendship,' he had telegraphed to the President shortly before the meeting with de Gaulle, 'is my greatest stand-by amid the ever increasing complications of this exacting war.'[3] And in an account of his conversation with de Gaulle, sent to Roosevelt four days later, Churchill reported: 'I repeatedly told de Gaulle and he acknowledged it without irritation that failing an agreement, I stand with you.'[4] Churchill added: 'I think it would be a great pity if you and he did not meet. I do not see why I should have all the luck.'[5]

Marian Holmes, who accompanied Churchill on the train, noted how, when Churchill had returned to the train from a visit of inspection to the troops, he 'looked anxious, but he was amiable', and she added: 'He had been striving for this moment for four years.'[6]

On the evening of June 4, Churchill returned by train to London, and to No. 10 Annexe. 'Went in to the PM at 10.30 p.m.' noted Marian Holmes that Sunday night, 'and didn't emerge until 3.45 a.m. He drives himself far too hard and he nearly fell asleep over the papers.'[7]

At one point during the evening's work, Churchill went to his Map

[1] 'Record of Conversation between the Prime Minister and General de Gaulle on the 4th June, 1944', War Cabinet Paper No. 297 of 1944, 'Top Secret', 9 June 1944: Churchill papers, 4/335.

[2] Eden memoirs, *The Reckoning*, op. cit., page 452.

[3] Prime Minister's Personal Telegram, T.1192/4, Prime Minister to President, No. 462, 'Personal and Top Secret', 4 June 1944: Churchill papers, 20/165.

[4] Sir Patrick Reilly, British Minister in Paris during the last two years of Churchill's second Premiership, and subsequently Ambassador to France, writes: 'De Gaulle's account of his meeting with Churchill on June 4 (*Mémoires de Guerre*, volume 2, pages 223–4) has had a continuing impact in France. He makes Churchill end the tirade referred to above with the words: "We are going to liberate Europe, but it is because the Americans are with us to do it. For, let me tell you! Anytime we have to choose between Europe and the open seas (le grand large) we shall always be for the open seas. Anytime I have to choose between you and Roosevelt, I will always choose Roosevelt." The phrase "le grand large" is still often quoted as proof that the British can never be good Europeans. There is no evidence in any other known account of this conversation that Churchill used it, or used language which could be plausibly represented by it. If indeed he did use such language, Churchill unwittingly gave de Gaulle a valuable argument in justifying his double veto of British membership of the EEC' (Sir Patrick Reilly, letter to the author, 17 June 1985).

[5] Prime Minister's Personal Telegram, T.1215/4, Prime Minister to President, No. 694, 'Personal and Top Secret', 8 June 1944: Churchill papers, 20/166.

[6] Marian Holmes diary, 6 June 1944: Marian Walker Spicer papers.

[7] Marian Holmes diary, 4 June 1944: Marian Walker Spicer papers.

room, where, for nearly four years, he had watched the progress, and regress, of so many battles. 'While I sat in my chair in the Map Room of the Annexe,' he later wrote, 'the thrilling news of the capture of Rome arrived.' [1]

At 7.15 that evening, Allied forces had entered the Piazza Venezia, in the centre of the Italian capital. 'How magnificently your troops have fought!' Churchill telegraphed that day to Roosevelt, and he added: 'I hear that relations are admirable between our armies in every rank there, and here certainly it is an absolute brotherhood.' [2]

While Churchill slept, Eisenhower called a further conference to re-examine the weather prospects. The conference met at four in the morning, and gave its final approval to Eisenhower's decision to go ahead on the morning of June 6.

On the morning of June 5, having no visitors, Churchill worked in bed.[3] As he worked, he was handed a letter from his wife. 'I feel so much for you,' she wrote, 'at this agonizing moment—so full of suspense, which prevents one from rejoicing over Rome!' [4]

That day, Churchill lunched with the three Chiefs of Staff and Ismay. 'He really is an incorrigible optimist,' Admiral Cunningham noted in his diary.[5] 'I found him over-optimistic as regards prospects of the cross-Channel operation,' was Brooke's diary comment, 'and tried to damp him down a bit.' In Italy, Brooke added, 'he now believes that Alex will wipe out the whole of the German forces'.[6] As soon as the remaining German divisions south of Rome had been trapped, 'we shall decide', Churchill informed Stalin, 'how best to use our armies in Italy to support the main adventure'. Poles, British, Free French and Americans had all 'broken or beaten in frontal attack the German troops opposite them', and there were 'various important options' which would soon have to be considered.[7]

Churchill was clear in his own mind what those options were. As soon as the Allied forces had entered Rome on the night of June 4, his thoughts had focused on the possible movement of Allied troops from Italy to the Atlantic coast of France. In the early hours of June 5 he had dictated a draft telegram to Roosevelt, for the approval of the

[1] Winston S. Churchill, *The Second World War*, volume 5, London 1952, page 558. In the fighting in Italy since February 16, 6,695 British Dominion and Indian troops had been killed. (*Hansard*, 27 June 1944, statement by Churchill.)

[2] Prime Minister's Personal Telegram, T.1192/4, Prime Minister to President, No. 462, 'Personal and Top Secret', 4 June 1944: Churchill papers, 20/165.

[3] Private Office diary, 5 June 1944.

[4] Letter of 5 June 1944: Spencer–Churchill papers.

[5] Cunningham diary, 5 June 1944: Cunningham papers.

[6] Brooke diary, 5 June 1944: Bryant, *op. cit.*, volume 2, page 205.

[7] Prime Minister's Personal Telegram, T.1194/4, 'Personal, Private and Top Secret', 5 June 1944: Churchill papers, 20/165.

Chiefs of Staff. 'Tonight our joint forces have entered Rome,' Churchill's draft began. 'If it should prove that the bulk of the German Army south of Rome is mauled, cut-off, stripped of its heavy weapons,' he added, 'it may well be that we can afford in a few weeks to begin to move troops from Italy either to prepare to deliver some form of "Anvil" or far better to come round and strike at the Biscay ports.' Churchill's draft telegram continued:

The reason why it is better to strike between Bordeaux and St Nazaire rather than on the Riviera is that the first course will be in intimate relation with the main battle and that it is possible not only to gain new ports for direct transatlantic debarkation, but to join hands with Eisenhower when he has landed and deployed. The distances are so much less. In fact it may be said that an action 500 miles distant will not influence the main battle till that main battle is decided.

The size of the 'Caliph' force which Churchill had in mind was between twelve and fourteen divisions, including four or five French divisions, two or three American divisions 'for which no berthing accommodation can be found in the British Isles' and five or six divisions from Italy.[1]

The Chiefs of Staff were opposed to Churchill sending this telegram to Roosevelt. Their reasons, set out in a draft minute which Hollis sent to Churchill two days later, foreshadowed an imminent conflict with the United States over Mediterranean strategy: 'Anvil' *versus* 'Diadem'. While stressing that 'we must not cut into the planned "Overlord" build-up', the Chiefs of Staff went on, with equal emphasis: 'We must not do anything which will rob General Alexander of the full fruits of his victory.' This desire to see 'Diadem' succeed would in Italy 'probably mean', the Chiefs of Staff commented, 'resisting the desire on the part of the American Chiefs of Staff to withdraw troops from the Italian battle in readiness for "Anvil" on which they are still set'.

The Chiefs of Staff were concerned not to let the Germans 'do to us in the Adriatic what they did in the Aegean'. The boot, they wrote, 'must be on the other leg'. As for 'Anvil', the Chiefs of Staff shared Churchill's preference for a landing on the Atlantic coast of France, though they believed, in regard to 'the actual point of attack', that somewhere like Quiberon Bay 'would pay a better dividend than further to the South', as suggested by Churchill.[2]

Churchill deferred to the Chiefs of Staff, and the telegram to Roosevelt remained unsent.

On the afternoon of June 5, Churchill learned from Maitland

---

[1] Draft telegram, Prime Minister's Personal Minute, D.183/4, 'Top Secret', 5 June 1944: Defence papers, 2/120.

[2] Chiefs of Staff Minute, COS 977/4, 'Top Secret', 6 June 1944: Defence Ministry papers, 2/120.

Wilson that 2,500 Yugoslav partisans and 2,000 British troops based on the island of Vis had just launched a 'powerful raid' on the island of Brac. 'Further raids of all scales,' Wilson reported, 'will follow against other islands.'[1] It was on Vis that Tito was about to find refuge, following the surprise German attack on his headquarters. In a minute to Eden on June 5, pointing out that the island was 'under the protection of British naval and air forces and cannot be defended otherwise', he suggested that first Dr Ivan Subasic, and then King Peter should go to Vis 'and settle there'. They had 'as much right to do this as Tito', who might be 'strengthened' by the King's presence 'at a time when he particularly needs support'. Churchill added: 'At any rate, it seems to me that we have some good cards if we play them well.'[2]

Tito decided to remain on Vis only for two or three weeks until the situation allowed him to return to the mainland. But he told Fitzroy Maclean he would be glad, while on Vis, to 'talk things over' with the Ban of Croatia, 'if he would come to Vis'.[3]

At the War Cabinet at 6.30 that evening, Churchill spoke of de Gaulle's apparent refusal either to broadcast, or to allow French liaison officers to accompany the Allied forces across the Channel, as no agreement on civil affairs had been reached with the British and Americans. Churchill told the War Cabinet that he was 'extremely dissatisfied' with de Gaulle's attitude: 'It might even be necessary to indicate that an aeroplane would be ready to take him back to Algiers forthwith.'[4]

The problems of Italy, of Yugoslavia, and even of de Gaulle, could not overshadow the dangers of D-Day. In his telegram to Stalin on June 5, Churchill described the impending cross-Channel assault. 'The difficulties of getting proper weather conditions are very great,' he explained, 'especially as we have to consider the fullest employment of the air, naval, and ground forces in relation to tides, waves, fog and cloud.' With 'great regret' Eisenhower had been 'forced to postpone for one night, but the weather forecast has undergone a most favourable change and tonight we go. We are using 5,000 ships, and have available 11,000 fully mounted aircraft.'[5]

That evening, Churchill dined alone with his wife. Then he went to the Map Room to examine the final dispositions and plan of attack.

[1] 'Top Secret and Personal', time of arrival 2.15 p.m., 5 June 1944: Churchill papers, 20/165.
[2] Prime Minister's Personal Minute, M.685/4, 5 June 1944: Churchill papers, 20/152.
[3] Bari to Algiers, No. 117, repeated to Foreign Office, 'Top Secret', 6 June 1944: Churchill papers, 20/166.
[4] War Cabinet No. 72 of 1944, 5 June 1944, Confidential Annex: Cabinet papers, 65/46.
[5] Prime Minister's Personal Telegram, T.1194/4, 'Personal, Private and Top Secret', 5 June 1944: Churchill papers, 20/165.

Shortly before she went to bed, Clementine Churchill joined him in the Map Room. 'Do you realize,' Churchill said to her, 'that by the time you wake up in the morning twenty thousand men may have been killed?'[1]

[1] Recollections of Commander C. R. Thompson: Gerald Pawle, *The War and Colonel Warden*, London, page 302. Between 6 and 28 June 1944, a total of 7,704 soldiers were killed in action in Normandy. Of these, 4,868 were United States Army, 2,443 British Army and 393 Canadian Army (Air Ministry papers, 14/3507, minute of 3 July 1944). The numbers of Allied dead on D-Day itself were approximately 3,000. On D-Day itself, the US First Army reported 1,465 dead. (Chester Wilmot, *The Struggle for Europe*, London, 1952, page 293.) No equivalent British figures exist.

43

'Overlord' and beyond

A T two o'clock on the morning of 6 June 1944 six gliders of 6
Airborne Division landed in Normandy, near two bridges
spanning the Canal de Caen and the River Orne. Both bridges were
captured intact. Half an hour later, 3 and 5 Parachute Brigades began
to drop east of the River Orne. 'Overlord' had begun. At dawn, troops
of the Second British Army, and the First United States Army, were
put ashore on the Normandy beaches. The 'Bodyguard' deception
had worked, and the Germans were unprepared.

The first reports reached Churchill when he woke up. The glider
landings, he learnt, had been unopposed, and the assault forces 'were
proceeding according to plan, although weather in the Channel was
not wholly favourable'. Churchill also learned that morning that 1,374
aircraft of Bomber Command had flown over Normandy throughout
the night, dropping nearly 6,000 tons of bombs on coastal batteries
and other military targets in the Caen and Cherbourg areas.[1] At
dawn, the United States Air Force struck at the shore defences.

During the morning, Churchill watched the progress of the landings
in his Map Room, the assault on the beaches being plotted for him
minute by minute by Captain Pim and the Map Room staff. Each
landing had reached its immediate objective, with only one exception:
V American Corps, landing at 'Omaha' beach north-west of
Bayeux, had met severe resistance. 'This vast operation,' Churchill
told the House of Commons at noon, 'is undoubtedly the most complicated and difficult that has ever taken place.'[2]

'Everything has started well,' Churchill telegraphed to Stalin that
afternoon. 'The mines, obstacles, and land batteries have been largely
overcome. The air landings were very successful, and on a large scale.

[1] Cabinet War Room Record No. 1738 for the 24 hours ending 7 a.m., 6 June 1944: Cabinet
papers, 100/11.
[2] *Hansard*, 6 June 1944, columns 1207–10.

Infantry landings, are proceeding rapidly, and many tanks and self-propelled guns are already ashore.'[1]

After his House of Commons statement, Churchill lunched with the King, and with him drove first to Allied Air Headquarters in St. James's Square, and then to Eisenhower's headquarters, 'where', John Martin noted, 'the latest position was shown on large maps'.[2]

During June 6 Roosevelt sent Churchill a gift: two electric typewriters.[3]

At 6.15 that evening Churchill made a further statement in the House of Commons about the continuing progress of the landings. The operation was proceeding, he said, 'in a thoroughly satisfactory manner'. The airborne landings had been 'on a scale far larger than anything that has been seen so far in the world'. General Eisenhower's 'courage', he added, 'is equal to all the necessary decisions that have to be taken in these extremely difficult and uncontrollable matters'.[4]

That evening Churchill dined in bed, and worked in bed afterwards.[5] Soon after midnight, he telephoned Eden 'in a rage', as Eden noted in his diary, because Bevin and Attlee had both supported Eden's view that Britain should now discuss the civil administration of France with the French National Committee. Admiral Raymond Fernard, the French National Representative in the United States, had arrived in London with a message from Roosevelt to de Gaulle. Negotiations were clearly possible. Eden noted in his diary:

Argument continued for forty-five minutes, perhaps longer. I was accused

---

[1] Prime Minister's Personal Telegram, T.1203/44, 'Personal and Top Secret': Churchill papers, 20/166.

[2] Letter of 8 June 1944: Martin papers.

[3] Churchill had earlier made enquiries about this typewriter, having admired the typescript on a letter from General McNarney. The two typewriters, wrote Roosevelt, were being shipped 'without delay which I hope you will accept as a gift from me and as a symbol of The strong bond between the people of America and Great Britain'. (Letter dated 6 June 1944, The White House, Washington: Premier papers, 4/69/2.) A member of Churchill's staff noted on June 12: 'The machine is of course of the "Noisy" variety, and would therefore be useless for dictation straight on to the machine.' Jock Colville had already minuted to Churchill that although the typewriter produced good results, 'frequent mechanical breakdowns and prohibitive cost made it unpopular with firms in this country'. Churchill commented: 'Pretty good all the same. Can't we get a couple for high class work in our office?' (Notes of 17 and 22 May 1944: Premier papers, 4/69/2.)

[4] *Hansard*, 6 June 1944, columns 1323–4. Eisenhower's particular courage, though Churchill could not say so, was his decision to launch the invasion on the basis of the forecast of a brief spell of better weather on June 6. Another Commander might have felt the need for a longer favourable forecast than that given to Eisenhower on June 3.

[5] Private Office Diary, 6 June 1944.

of trying to break up the Government, of stirring up the press on the issue. He said that nothing would induce him to give way, that de Gaulle must go. Said I had no right to 'bully' him at a time like this and much more. There would be a Cabinet tomorrow. House of Commons would back him against de Gaulle and me and any of Cabinet who sided with me, etc. etc. FDR and he would fight the world. I told him that I heard that Fernard had arrived with a personal message from FDR to de Gaulle. He did not like that. I didn't lose my temper and I think that I gave as good as I got. Anyway I didn't budge an inch.

Two hours later, at two in the morning, Brendan Bracken telephoned Eden to say that Churchill had called Bracken a 'lackey' of the Foreign Office for supporting Eden, but that 'in the middle, a message from FDR came inviting de Gaulle to United States'.[1]

On June 7 German troops were cleared from 'Omaha' beach, and most of the remaining German coastal batteries were silenced by naval bombardment. That morning Churchill learned from the Cabinet War Room record that British assault troops had established 'a substantial bridgehead', and that a convoy of ten Allied troop ships, on its way to the beachhead, had passed through the Straits of Dover 'without interference'. A total of 2,656 heavy bomber sorties had been flown over the German positions. Naval and air opposition had been slight. The American assault troops at 'Omaha' beach, however, had faced 'considerable opposition'.[2]

During June 7 Churchill sent an account of the development of the battle to Stalin. 'We had expected to lose about 10,000 men,' he confided. Of the events of the previous night, Churchill told the Soviet leader: 'There was a tank engagement of our newly landed armour with fifty enemy tanks of the 21st Panzer-Grenadier Division late last night towards Caen, as the result of which the enemy quitted the field. The British 7th Armoured Division is now going in, and should give us superiority for a few days.' Churchill added: 'The question is, how many can they bring against us in the next week? The weather outlook in the Channel does not seem to impose any prohibition on our continued landings. Indeed, it seems more promising than before.' All the commanders, Churchill wrote, were 'satisfied that in the actual landing things have gone better than we expected'.

He too was 'well satisfied' by the situation. 'By tonight we hope to have the best part of a quarter of a million men ashore, including a considerable quantity of armour (tanks) all landed from special ships or swimming ashore by themselves,' Churchill also told Stalin:

---

[1] Eden diary, 6 June 1944: Eden memoirs, *The Reckoning, op. cit.*, page 455.
[2] Cabinet War Room Record No. 1739 for the 24 hours ending 7 a.m., 7 June 1944: Cabinet papers, 100/11.

Most especially secret. We are planning to construct very quickly two large synthetic harbours on the beaches of this wide, sandy bay of the Seine estuary. Nothing like these has ever been seen before. Great ocean liners will be able to discharge and run by numerous piers supplies to the fighting troops. This must be quite unexpected by the enemy, and will enable the build-up to proceed with very great independence of weather conditions.[1]

The fall of Rome was also much in Churchill's mind; he hoped that news of it, and of the Normandy landings, 'will cheer your valiant soldiers after all the weight they have had to bear, which no one outside your country has felt more definitely than I'.[2]

Churchill's concern for Russian needs was not merely emotional. As soon as he learned, on June 7, that the British naval bombardment off the Normandy coast had led to far fewer naval losses than had been anticipated, he at once instructed the Ministers involved to organize a convoy to Russia that month, 'and to run them regularly thereafter as long as the Americans will send anything or there is anything due from us. . . .'[3]

That evening, as the battle of Normandy continued for its second day, the War Cabinet met to discuss what Churchill described as 'the difficulties which had arisen with de Gaulle' over the appointment of French liaison officers with the Allied troops already landed in France. Churchill also pointed out that it had been 'noticeable' that, in his D-Day broadcast de Gaulle had omitted any reference to the share of the Americans in the Allied landings. For their part, the Americans were 'quite unable', in his view for 'good reason', to recognise the French National Committee as the 'authoritative government of France'.

After a long discussion, it was agreed to ask de Gaulle to enter into discussions, in search of 'a reasonable basis of agreement', and then to 'commend it' to the United States.[4]

On the morning of June 8, the Cabinet War Room record reported that, in spite of earlier problems in that sector, British troops had captured Bayeux and were 'within about three miles of Caen'. Allied airborne troops had been 'successfully reinforced'. Landing craft were

[1] Successful though the two Mulberry habours were, when a Channel gale blew up in the third week of June, almost no unloading was possible. As a result of the gale, the American Mulberry was destroyed, and the British one sufficiently damaged to hold up reinforcements for several more weeks.

[2] Prime Minister's Personal Telegram, T.1216/4, 'Personal and Top Secret', 7 June 1944: Churchill papers, 20/166.

[3] Prime Minister's Personal Minute M.693/4 (to the Minister of Production, Minister of War Transport, First Lord and First Sea Lord), 7 June 1944: Churchill papers, 20/152.

[4] War Cabinet No. 73 of 1944, 7 June 1944, Confidential Annex: Cabinet papers, 65/42.

already returning from the beaches to reload, and minesweepers had swept three channels, each two miles wide, into the assault area. One tank landing ship had been torpedoed, but all its occupants saved.[1]

On the morning of June 8, as the Normandy battle entered its third day, Churchill urged Members of Parliament not only to 'maintain morale' when they went to their constituencies that weekend, but to give 'strong warnings against over-optimism', and against the idea 'that these things are going to be settled with a run'. Although 'great dangers lie behind us', he added, 'enormous exertions lie before us'.[2] The 'concentration of German reinforcements to oppose us', Churchill told Alexander on June 8, 'has been lower than we expected. But of course there is a deadly battle ahead and afterwards a prolonged struggle.'[3]

With the capture of Rome still much on their minds, the Chiefs of Staff had set out for Churchill their determination not to do 'anything which will rob General Alexander of the full fruits of his victory'. This, they warned him on June 7, 'will probably mean resisting the desire on the part of the American Chiefs of Staff prematurely to withdraw troops from the Italian battle in readiness for "Anvil" on which they are still set'.[4] At a meeting of the Chiefs of Staff on the following morning, with Brooke presiding, it was felt that an examination should be made of 'the possibilities of exploiting the Italian situation by an advance eastward, based eventually on Trieste'. As for the 'most favourable area' for amphibious assaults in support of 'Overlord', this, the Chiefs of Staff agreed with Churchill, 'appeared to be the Brittany coast north of the Loire', although the strength of the German defences would make an assault 'extremely hazardous' unless developments elsewhere forced the Germans 'to thin out their defences'.[5]

Operations in Italy had been considered in detail by the Joint Planning Staff, which, in its report on June 7, suggested that, after a 'full scale offensive by land', the best course in Italy would be a 'bold landing in the Istrian area', in order then to 'direct our effort' towards south-east Austria. Such an advance, the Joint Planners believed, would serve three purposes: it would be 'a threat to the whole enemy position in South-East Europe and to Austria which could not be

---

[1] Cabinet War Room Record No. 1740, 7 a.m., 8 June 1944: Cabinet papers, 100/11.

[2] *Hansard*, 8 June 1944, column 1522.

[3] Prime Minister's Personal Telegram, T.1220/4, 'Personal and Top Secret', 8 June 1944: Churchill papers, 20/166.

[4] Chiefs of Staff Minute, 979/4, Chiefs of Staff Committee No. 184 (Operations) of 1944, 7 June 1944, Annex: Cabinet papers, 79/75.

[5] Chiefs of Staff Committee No. 185 (Operations) of 1944, 10.30 a.m., 8 June 1944: Cabinet papers, 79/75.

ignored', it would make 'the most use' of the Yugoslav partisans, and it would both 'benefit from and assist' a Soviet advance south of the Carpathian mountains.[1]

At a second meeting of the Chiefs of Staff Committee on June 8, with Churchill in the Chair, Portal suggested 'exploiting a further success' in Italy by 'an advance into Istria'. If, Portal argued, 'we called a halt' on the Pisa-Rimini line and began to transfer forces by sea to northern France, 'we should suffer the disadvantages that these forces would be out of action for many weeks at a critical stage of the war'. The 'possibilities open to us of exploiting the situation eastwards from northern Italy', Churchill agreed, 'ought certainly to be examined'.[2]

That afternoon Churchill and his wife accompanied the King and Queen to Churchill's Map Room, where, in addition to the maps, Captain Pim had arranged for models to be on display of all the landing craft and methods employed in putting troops and lorries ashore.[3] During the day, Churchill received a note from one of his most persistent Labour Party critics, Emanuel Shinwell. 'I should like you to know,' Shinwell wrote, 'that at this time, when the thoughts of all of us are turned on grave events, I and others, whose views do not always accord with Government policy, are with you and your colleagues to a man.'[4]

In sending this letter to Churchill, Harvie Watt noted that 'no reply is required'.[5] But Churchill did reply, as soon as the pressure of events was relaxed a little:

My dear Shinwell,
Thank you very much for your kind letter. I know well that your patriotic sentiments have been profoundly stirred by the glorious events of the last fortnight. Very heavy fighting lies ahead in France but I expect our power to reinforce is greater than the enemy's—at any rate for some time to come.
Meanwhile Stalin is sure to get on the move.[6]

Churchill's letter was marked 'Secret', for he knew that the next Soviet offensive, as agreed upon at Teheran, was imminent.

*   *   *

[1] Joint Planning Staff Paper No. 144 (Final), 'Top Secret', 7 June 1944: Cabinet papers, 79/76.
[2] Chiefs of Staff Committee No. 186 (Operations), 12 noon, 8 June 1944: Cabinet papers, 79/75.
[3] Pim recollections: Pim papers.
[4] Letter of 8 June 1944: Churchill papers, 20/146.
[5] Note of 9 June 1944: Churchill papers, 20/146.
[6] 'Secret', 15 June 1944: Churchill papers, 20/146.

By the morning of June 9, British and American forces on the Normandy beaches had made their first contact, although the Americans were, as reported by the Cabinet War Room record, 'about 24 hours behind schedule'. Heavy German opposition had been encountered 'along the whole British front', particularly to the north and north west of Caen, so much so that the British forward line 'has remained substantially unchanged during the past 24 hours'. An attack by German Panzers, the record noted, 'has had some success at one point'.[1]

A particular Allied failure was the inability to secure sufficient terrain to set up on French soil air-strips for the war in the air. All but a fragment of those forces had therefore to continue to operate from bases in southern England. 'You were at that time,' Ismay wrote to Churchill six months later, 'expressing the view (though I cannot find it recorded in writing) that we might have to be content for some time to come with securing the "smaller and the large lunette", i.e. the Cherbourg and Brest Peninsulas.'[2]

That afternoon, accompanied by Eden, Churchill again visited Eisenhower's headquarters in southern England. Then, with Eden, he saw Ivan Subasic, the former Ban, or Governor, of Croatia, and urged him to go out to Vis and to discuss with Tito the formation of a Yugoslav Government of all groups and parties. 'I am still strongly supporting Tito,' Churchill telegraphed to Maitland Wilson, 'but as he has come into our sphere of protection on an island on which he has no more right to live than King Peter or the Ban of Croatia, it seems that here is a place to try and knock together these jangling Yugoslav heads and try to get the unity of the country against the Huns, which is our overall objective.' King Peter could 'watch events from Malta', Churchill added, 'but I personally think that it is a case of taking the Kingdom of Heaven by storm'. 'In fact,' Churchill told Wilson, 'it seems to me a God-sent opportunity and the last chance.'

In the event, King Peter went to Malta and Dr Subasic went to Vis, where, on June 17, he and Tito signed an agreement that King Peter's Royal Government and Tito's National Liberation Committee would collaborate closely. Tito told Subasic that he did not intend to impose Communism on Yugoslavia after the war. But he made no reference to the possibility of King Peter's return to Yugoslavia once the war was over, nor did he show any wish to meet the King.

In his telegram to Wilson on June 9, Churchill had also asked about his son:

---

[1] Cabinet War Room Record No. 1741, for the 24 hours ending 7 a.m., 9 June 1944: Cabinet papers, 100/11.

[2] 'Secret' 13 December 1944: Cabinet papers, 120/170.

Is it not rather a pity to bring Randolph out of Yugoslavia at a moment when he has evidently a chance of making lasting contact with the Partisan Forces whose hazards and hardships he is sharing? If it is thought he is doing no good where he is and an opportunity comes of bringing him out, do so. But do not bring him back out of any consideration for me or because a price has been put on his head. Let Service considerations alone prevail. This is what I know he would wish.[1]

Churchill's telegram to Wilson crossed with one from Randolph, to say that he had arrived in Bari that morning by a daylight pick-up operation which was evacuating surplus personnel of the Anglo-American and Russian military missions. His plan was to return to the 8th Yugoslav Corps in three or four days. His telegram continued:

The last fortnight has been extremely interesting and at times exciting and I have learned more in these few days about the Partisan movement than I had in the previous four months.

As a result of a fortnight with nothing to drink, very little to eat or smoke and 20 or 30 miles a day over mountain country I am fitter than ever before.

It looks as if the Hun offensive is now petering out. He is retreating to his towns and main lines of communication and the Partisans are rapidly re-occupying their former areas. I believe that conditions will soon return to normal.

Randolph also reported to his father on the effect of the news of D-Day among the Yugoslavs:

The opening of the Second Front has thrilled the Partisans and has raised our prestige to an extraordinary extent. I can now do most useful work in consolidating our relations with them. You can imagine how much my thoughts have been with you in these last few days and how thankful I am that all seems to have gone so well.[2]

On June 9, Churchill decided to make plans to cross over to France in three days' time. 'We do not wish in any way to be a burden to you or on your headquarters,' he wrote in a draft telegram for Brooke to send to Montgomery, 'or in any way to divert your attention from the battle. All we should require is an ADC or a Staff Officer to show us round. We shall bring some sandwiches with us.'[3] 'Will meet you and give you full picture,' Montgomery replied, and he added: 'Road not (repeat not) 100 per cent safe owing to enemy snipers including women. Much enemy bombing between dusk and dawn.' Believing the message came from Brooke, Montgomery ended: 'Essential PM

---

[1] Prime Minister's Personal Telegram, T.1230/4, 'Personal and Top secret', 9 June 1944: Churchill papers, 20/166.

[2] No. 130 from Bari to the Foreign Office, 'Personal', 9 June 1944: Churchill papers, 20/166.

[3] Prime Minister's Personal Minute, M.702/4, 'Top Secret', 9 June 1944: Premier papers, 3/339/1, folio 123.

should go only where I take him and you must get away from here in early evening. Am very satisfied with progress of operations.'[1]

On the morning of June 10 the Cabinet War Room record reported that, almost everywhere in the Normandy beachhead, 'progress has been slow in face of stiff enemy opposition, including that of considerable armoured forces'.[2] But still the Germans hesitated to commit all their forces in France to the slowly widening beachhead, the effect of the 'Bodyguard' deception plans having kept Calais as a possible landing point even after the Normandy landings. In Norway too, Anglo-Soviet cooperation in the 'Bodyguard' deception had led to German nervousness as to an imminent landing. At the same time, another essential feature of the 'Bodyguard' plan, the Soviet agreement to postpone the next eastern offensive until after D-Day, was now about to reap its own reward, with the first of the Soviet summer offensives launched that day on the Finnish front.

'I have just heard from Marshal Stalin,' Churchill telegraphed to Tito, 'that he has opened his offensive today. One united heave and we may be freed from the agonies of War, and the menace of tyranny.'[3] 'The whole world,' Churchill telegraphed to Stalin that day, 'can see the Teheran design appearing in our concerted attacks upon the common foe.'[4]

By the late afternoon of June 10 Churchill was able to send Stalin a confident progress report of the Normandy landings. Nearly 400,000 men were ashore, together with 'a large superiority in tanks and a rapidly growing mass of artillery and lorries'. In Italy, he reported, Alexander was 'chasing the beaten remnants of Kesselring's army northward swiftly'. Six or seven German divisions were retreating northward. 'He is on their track while mopping up the others.'[5]

In newly liberated Rome, however, the news was less good, at least politically, when Marshal Badoglio was replaced as Prime Minister by 'this wretched old Bonomi', as Churchill called him in a minute to Eden. Churchill added: 'We have lost the only competent Italian with whom we could deal.'[6] The Turks, maintaining their neutrality, had also vexed him. 'Turkey should become a belligerent,' he wrote to

[1] 'Personal for CIGS from General Montgomery', 9.30 a.m., 10 June 1944: Premier papers, 3/339/11, folio 122.

[2] Cabinet War Room Record No. 1742, for the 24 hours ending 7 a.m., 10 June 1944: Cabinet papers, 100/11.

[3] Letter of 10 June 1944: Churchill papers, 20/166.

[4] Prime Minister's Personal Telegram, T.1246/4, 'Personal and Top Secret', 10 June 1944: Churchill papers, 20/166.

[5] Prime Minister's Personal Telegram, T.1246/4, 'Personal and Top Secret', 10 June 1944: Churchill papers, 20/166.

[6] Prime Minister's Personal Minute, M.705/4, 10 June 1944: Churchill papers, 20/152.

Eden, 'or she will definitely be in default with the Alliance. By continuing their present pusillanimous policy, they are preparing a dark day for themselves.' [1]

By the morning of June 11 the Cabinet War Room record reported that all the Allied bridgeheads in Normandy had been joined 'into one continuous front' and the German pressure north and east of Caen had been resisted.[2] Caen, however, remained stubbornly in German hands. For Churchill, the main problem of the day was not military but political, a telegram from Roosevelt, with the news that the American Government was 'unwilling' to allow Britain to come to any agreement with the Soviet Union about Roumania and Greece, as proposed by Churchill on May 31. 'In our opinion', Roosevelt told Churchill, this would result both in the 'persistence of division' between Britain and Russia, and in 'the division of the Balkan region into spheres of influence despite the declared intention to limit the arrangement to military matters'. The Americans preferred to set up a 'consultative machinery' to dispel misunderstandings and 'restrain the tendency towards the development of exclusive spheres'.[3] Churchill disagreed vehemently, replying that same day:

I am much concerned to receive your message. Action is paralysed if everybody is to consult everybody else about everything before it is taken. Events will always outstrip the changing situations in these Balkan regions. Somebody must have the power to plan and act. A Consultative Committee would be a mere obstruction, always overridden in any case of emergency by direct interchanges between you and me, or either of us and Stalin.

The Russians, Churchill pointed out, had been 'ready to let us take the lead' in the recent Greek crisis. It had been dealt with effectively, and without bloodshed. 'I always reported to you, and I always will report to you. You shall see every telegram I send. I think you might trust me in this.' The agreement with Russia had meant that the Communist forces of EAM 'and all its malice' could be controlled 'by the national forces of Greece'. Otherwise, Churchill warned, 'civil war and ruin to the land you care about so much'. Churchill added:

---

[1] Prime Minister's Personal Minute, M.704/4, 'Top Secret', 10 June 1944: Churchill papers, 20/152.

[2] Cabinet War Room Record No. 1743, for the 24 hours ending 7 a.m., 11 June 1944: Cabinet papers, 100/11.

[3] President to Prime Minister, No. 557 'Personal and Top Secret', 11 June 1944: Churchill papers, 20/166.

Your telegrams to me in the recent crisis worked wonders. We were entirely agreed, and the result is entirely satisfactory. Why is all this effective direction to be broken up into a committee of mediocre officials such as we are littering about the world? Why can you and I not keep this in our own hands, considering how we see eye to eye about so much of it?

If it became necessary to consult other Powers 'in these difficulties', Churchill warned, and a 'set of triangular or quadrangular telegrams got started the only result would have been chaos or impotence'.[1] Roosevelt deferred to Churchill's argument. But he noted: 'We must be careful to make it clear that we are not establishing any post-war spheres of influence.'[2]

The American Chiefs of Staff had reached Britain, to be near the Normandy operations. That day, the Joint Staff Mission in Washington warned the British Chiefs of Staff and Churchill that 'Overlord' was 'the last chance we shall have to put across to the American public the magnitude of the British military effort'. The Mission warned: 'we must make the most of this since Anglo-American relations in the future will so largely depend on American appreciation of the blood, sweat and tears which Great Britain and the Dominions have shed'. Churchill and the Chiefs of Staff were told that the American newspapers, 'with their human interest stories' about American units and individuals in 'Overlord', were already leaving an impression 'in the mind of the average American' that the 'major part' in these operations was 'being played by the United States forces'.[3]

On June 11 the American Chiefs of Staff dined with Churchill on his train, which was 'stabled at Ascot' for the night.[4] Brooke joined the train after dinner, and the following morning they proceeded in the train to Dover. Unable to cross to France on June 6 because of the King's opposition, Churchill now, on D + 6, set out for the Normandy beaches. 'It is a wonderful sight,' he telegraphed to Stalin two days later, 'to see this city of ships stretching along the coast for nearly fifty miles and apparently secure from the air and the U-boats which are so near.'[5]

Brooke, who accompanied Churchill, recorded in his diary how, off the French coast:

[1] Prime Minister's Personal Telegram, T.1259/4, Prime Minister to President, No. 700, 'Secret, Personal and Private', 11 June 1944: Churchill papers, 20/166.
[2] President to Prime Minister, No. 560, 'Personal and Top Secret', 13 June 1944: Churchill papers, 20/166.
[3] JSM No. 96, 'Secret', 11 June 1944: Cabinet papers, 105/46.
[4] Private Office Diary, 11 June 1944.
[5] Prime Minister's Personal Telegram, T.1281/4, No. 1799 to Moscow, 'Personal and Top Secret', 18 June 1944: Churchill papers, 20/166.

Everywhere the sea was covered with ships of all sizes and shapes, and a scene of continuous activity. We passed through rows and rows of anchored tank landing-ships and finally came to a 'Gooseberry', namely a row of ships sunk in a half crescent to form a sort of harbour and provide protection from the sea. Here we were met by Admiral Vian, who took us in his Admiral's barge from which we changed into a 'Dukw'. This ran us straight on to the beach and up another road.[1]

Montgomery, 'smiling and confident', Churchill later recalled, 'met me at the beach as we scrambled out of our landing craft'. The weather, Churchill added, 'was brilliant'.[2]

Field Marshal Smuts had also come to see the beachhead. Travelling by jeep, Churchill, Smuts and Brooke were driven to Montgomery's headquarters, about five miles inland. There, Montgomery gave them an explanation on the map of his dispositions and plans. Churchill later recalled:

We lunched in a tent looking towards the enemy. The General was in the highest spirits. I asked him how far away was the actual front. He said about three miles. I asked him if he had a continuous line. He said 'No.' 'What is there then to prevent an incursion of German armour breaking up our luncheon?' He said he did not think they would come. The staff told me the chateau had been heavily bombed the night before, and certainly there were a good many craters around it. I told him he was taking too much of a risk if he made a habit of such proceedings. Anything can be done once or for a short time, but custom, repetition, prolongation, is always to be avoided when possible in war. He did in fact move two days later, though not till he and his staff had had another dose.

It continued fine, and apart from occasional air alarms and anti-aircraft fire there seemed to be no fighting. We made a considerable inspection of our limited bridgehead.[3]

The countryside seemed little affected, Churchill noted, either by the privations of four years of occupation or by the ravages of six days of battle. 'We are surrounded,' Churchill commented as they drove to General O'Connor's headquarters, 'by fat cattle lying in luscious

---

[1] Brooke diary, 12 June 1944: Bryant, *op. cit.*, volume 2, page 213. The 'Dukw', or DUKW, was an amphibious vehicle, based on the standard 2½ ton United States army truck, which took personnel from the landing craft to the shore. The prototype had been produced by General Motors in 1942, and it was first used during the landings in Sicily in July 1943. The name derives from the General Motors code, in which D = 1942, U = Utility, K = Front-wheel drive, and W = Six-wheel.

[2] Winston S. Churchill, *The Second World War*, volume 6, London 1954, pages 10–11.

[3] Winston S. Churchill, *The Second World War*, volume 6, London 1954, page 11. One of those 'air alarms' was real, and caught by the cameraman. Montgomery, looking at the photographs twenty-five years later, recalled: 'A German came over. There was an air battle. Everyone was rather alarmed. Winston was rather pleased. There was shelling. Everything was happening.' (Field Marshal Viscount Montgomery of Alamein, in conversation with the author, 1969.)

pastures with their paws crossed.'[1] Brooke's account of the journey continued:

We then returned to Courseulles, having watched a raid by Hun bombers on the harbour, which did no harm. We re-embarked in Admiral Vian's barge and did a trip right along the sea-front, watching the various activities. We saw tank landing-craft unloading lorries, tanks, guns, etc., on to the beaches in a remarkably short time. We then went to the new harbour being prepared west of Hamel. There we saw some of the large 'Phoenixes' being sunk into place and working admirably. Also 'Bombardons' to damp down waves, 'Whales' representing wonderful floating piers, all growing up fast.

Close by was a monitor with 14″ gun firing away into France. Winston said he had never been on one of His Majesty's ships engaging the enemy and insisted on going aboard. Luckily we could not climb up owing to seaweed on the bilges, as it would have been a very noisy entertainment had we succeeded. Then we returned to our destroyer and went right back to the east end of the beach where several ships were bombarding the Germans.[2]

Churchill later recalled the sequel:

The bombardment was leisurely and continuous, but there was no reply from the enemy. As we were about to turn I said to Vian, 'Since we are so near, why shouldn't we have a plug at them ourselves before we go home?' He said, 'Certainly,' and in a minute or two all our guns fired on the silent coast. We were of course well within the range of their artillery, and the moment we had fired Vian made the destroyer turn about and depart at the highest speed. We were soon out of danger and passed through the cruiser and battleship lines. This is the only time I have ever been on board a naval vessel when she fired 'in anger'—if it can be so called. I admired the Admiral's sporting spirit.[3]

'After doing laborious duty,' Churchill informed Roosevelt two days later, 'we went and had a plug at the Hun from our destroyer, but although the range was 6,000 yards he did not honour us with a reply.'[4]

On the three-hour sea voyage back to Portsmouth, Churchill slept. Then, on the train back to London, he dined with Brooke, Smuts, Marshall, and King, the two Americans having also spent the day on the beachhead, visiting the American positions. 'We dined together in a happy mood,' Churchill recalled. 'They were highly pleased with

[1] Brooke diary, 12 June 1944: Bryant, *op. cit.*, volume 2, page 214.
[2] Brooke diary, 12 June 1944: Bryant, *op. cit.*, volume 2, pages 214–15.
[3] Winston S. Churchill, *The Second World War*, volume 6, London 1954, page 12.
[4] Prime Minister's Personal Telegram, T.1282/4, Prime Minister to President, No. 703, 'Personal and Top Secret', 14 June 1944: Churchill papers, 20/166.

all they had seen on the American beaches, and full of confidence in the execution of our long-cherished design.' [1]

Churchill returned from the Normandy beachhead sunburnt and contented.[2] That evening he was dining with his wife and daughter Mary, Lord Beaverbrook and Oliver Lyttelton, when Captain Pim informed them that the first German flying bomb was on its way.[3] In the Map Room that night, Churchill received the latest news of the arrival of this secret weapon: three waves of pilotless aircraft crossed the Channel coast during the night. The first had consisted of ten, the second of thirteen and the third of four flying bombs. Only four of the twenty-seven reached as far as Greater London. One, falling in Bethnal Green, killed two people. At a meeting of the Chiefs of Staff on the following morning, Air Marshal Bottomley, who gave these details, added that the flying bombs 'appeared to be about the size of a Spitfire', and flew at between 230 and 250 miles an hour. The Germans 'had made a great effort to produce some reply to "Overlord"', Portal commented, and he went on to point out that to neutralize the forty-two launching sites would need 'a large air effort' of some 3,000 Flying Fortresses. Such attacks, he argued, should not however be allowed 'to interfere with the prosecution of "Overlord"'.[4]

On the morning of June 14, the Chiefs of Staff Committee were informed that a total of sixty-seven launching sites, or 'Ski' sites as they were called, had now been discovered, with a further ten suspected sites 'under examination'.[5] One piece of good news that morning was a Joint Intelligence Committee report that the Germans, still fearing 'subsidiary operations' in both the Pas de Calais and south and south-western France, had not yet moved their two armoured Divisions from the South of France. The Germans also still thought 'that diversionary operations threaten against southern Norway'.[6]

On the night of June 15, more than 150 flying bombs reached

---

[1] Winston S. Churchill, *The Second World War*, volume 6, London 1954, page 12. On June 16 Churchill received a telegram from his son. 'It is kind of your Generals to be so worried about my welfare,' Randolph wrote, and he added: 'I am grieved that they allow you to be exposed to much greater dangers in Normandy while we have been poodle-faking in the Balkans.' (No. 165 from Bari, sent 15 June 1944, received 16 June 1944: Churchill papers, 20/189.)

[2] 'The boss has a frightful fit on, of not wanting to work,' Elizabeth Layton noted four days later (Elizabeth Layton, letter of 16 June 1944: Nel papers).

[3] Pim recollections: Pim papers.

[4] Chiefs of Staff Committee No. 191 (Operations) of 1944: 10.30 a.m., 13 June 1944: Cabinet papers, 79/76.

[5] Chiefs of Staff Committee No. 193 (Operations) of 1944, 11 a.m., 14 June 1944: Cabinet papers, 79/76.

[6] Joint Intelligence Sub-Committee Report No. 250 (Operations) (Final) (Limited Circulation) of 1944, 12 June 1944: Cabinet papers, 79/76.

[7] 'Note on the "spread" of the V-1s during June and July 1944': Premier papers, 4/84/1, folio 168.

Britain, fifty of which exploded in the London area.[7] Only twenty had been destroyed while on their journey, twelve by anti-aircraft fire and eight by fighters.[1] That night, hearing sounds 'of unusual and very adjacent aerial activity', John Peck telephoned to Christopher Dodds, who was the Duty Private Secretary and asked: 'Is this what I think it is?' to which Dodds replied: 'Yes.'[2]

Churchill had already gone to bed, and Dodds was talking with Brendan Bracken. 'We heard a V1 go overhead,' Dodds later recalled, 'and Brendan suggested that we go outside to find out if there was anything to be seen, so that we could put the PM in the picture later. As we reached the door leading to St James's Park, we met the PM, who had already been out to see for himself,' an episode, Dodds reflected, 'exemplifying the PM's energy and (hair-raising!) disregard for personal danger'.[3]

A new era of the war had begun. 'Hitler has started his secret weapon upon London,' Churchill informed Stalin on the following day. 'We had a noisy night.'[4] What Churchill did not tell Stalin was that some of the 'particularly heavy' anti-aircraft guns, as Air Marshall Bottomley told the Chiefs of Staff Committee, on the morning of June 16, which it had been intended to use against the flying bombs, 'were now employed in "Overlord" and would not therefore be available'.[5] At five o'clock that evening, at a Staff Conference called by Churchill to discuss measures to be taken to counter the flying bomb, it was agreed to ask Eisenhower to take 'all possible measures' to neutralize the supply and launching sites, 'subject to no interference with the essential requirements of the battle in France'. It was also agreed that there should be no air-raid warning for a single bomb, and that at night the sounding of the sirens should be 'reduced to a minimum'.[6]

On June 18 more than sixty people, many of them serving officers, were killed when a flying bomb fell on the Guards Chapel during a service. That evening, Churchill presided over another Staff Conference in his Map Room, at which Sir Roderick Hill, Air Marshal Commanding the Air Defence of Great Britain, explained that as the

---

[1] Chiefs of Staff Committee Meeting No. 196 (Operations) of 1944, 11 a.m., 16 June 1944: Cabinet papers, 79/76.

[2] Sir John Peck recollections: letter to the author, 13 January 1985.

[3] Christopher Dodds recollections: letter to the author, 25 May 1985.

[4] Prime Minister's Personal Telegram, T.1302/4, 'Personal and Top Secret', 16 June 1944: Cabinet papers, 120/858.

[5] Chiefs of Staff Committee No. 196 (Operations) of 1944, 11 a.m., 16 June 1944: Cabinet papers, 79/76.

[6] Staff Conference, Chiefs of Staff Committee Meeting No. 197 (Operations) of 1944, 5 p.m., 16 June 1944: Cabinet papers, 79/76.

flying bombs flew at between 300 and 330 miles an hour, 'our fighters had only a comparatively small margin of speed', nor could there be simultaneous fighter and gun defensive action 'without each seriously impeding the effectiveness of each other'.

Churchill suggested that the fighters might be given 'a free run by day and the AA guns at night'. He also supported Herbert Morrison's suggestion that Admiralty kites should be used 'to thicken up the balloons'.

There were other problems: bad weather over Calais, said Tedder, meant that only 'blind attacks' could be carried out over the rocket launching sites. In summing up the discussion, Churchill stated 'that it should be our policy to hit the supply and launching sites as hard as we could without detriment to the battle of Normandy; but there was no need to anounce this policy publicly'. The public, Churchill added, 'should be encouraged to sleep in the safest available places at night, but by day to carry on with their normal tasks'.[1]

On June 19 Churchill presided at a meeting of the Crossbow Committee to discuss the flying bombs. 'He was at his best,' Admiral Cunningham noted in his diary, 'and said the matter had to be put robustly to the populace, that their tribulations were part of the battle in France, and that they should be very glad to share in the soldiers' dangers.'[2]

The routing of aircraft over London to deal with the flying bomb was, the Committee was told, 'causing the general public unnecessary anxiety'. But of the 700 flying bombs fired at Britain so far, 200 had been shot down, 112 by anti-aircraft guns and 88 by fighters.[3]

In his diary, Admiral Cunningham noted that the Crossbow Committee agreed that, when the flying bombs did come over, the air raid sirens should be sounded as little as possible, 'as the PM said one must have sleep, and you either woke well rested or in a better land!!'[4]

On June 17, Churchill telegraphed to Stalin with the news that 550,000 Allied troops were now ashore on Normandy, and that General Marshall had just told him 'that the power of the enemy to launch a great-scale counter-attack in the next few days has been largely

[1] Staff Conference, Chiefs of Staff Committee No. 200 (Operations), 6 p.m., 18 June 1944: Cabinet papers, 79/76.

[2] Cunningham diary, 19 June 1944: Cunningham papers.

[3] War Cabinet Crossbow Committee, CBC(44) 1st Meeting, 'Top Secret', Defence Map Room, No. 10 Annex, 5 p.m. 19 June 1944: Cabinet papers, 98/36.

[4] Cunningham diary, 19 June 1944: Cunningham papers.

removed through Rommel throwing in strategic reserves prematurely to feed the battle-line'. The Allies had sustained about 30,000 casualties 'and have certainly inflicted more upon the enemy'. Three days earlier, 'we held 13,000 prisoners', Churchill added, 'and many more have been taken since'. Churchill's telegram ended: 'All good wishes in these stirring times.'[1]

On the day of Churchill's telegram to Stalin, Hitler travelled to France for a conference with his two senior Generals of the Normandy front, Rundstedt and Rommel, both of whom urged a withdrawal from Normandy towards the Seine. As in Russia, however, and as in Italy, Hitler rejected this military advice; his troops were to fight for every mile.

Two days later, on June 19, at a meeting of the Crossbow Committee, Brooke found Churchill 'in very good form, quite ten years younger', he wrote, 'all due to the fact that the flying-bombs have again put us into the front line'.[2]

Churchill's much improved mood arose largely as a result of his relief that the D-Day landings had not led to a far greater slaughter.

At the War Cabinet on June 19, Ministers were told that 526 civilians had been killed in the first week, just ended, of these attacks. A 'series of conferences', Churchill reported to the War Cabinet, was being held, to determine the 'best means' of countering this new form of attack.[3] These conferences, a smaller version of the Crossbow Committee, were held in Churchill's own Map Room, 'so that it will be convenient for me', as he minuted to Brigadier Jacob, 'to go into them at any time'.[4] Duncan Sandys, the Joint Parliamentary Secretary at the Ministry of Supply, was Chairman. It was under Sandys' supervision two years earlier that the British had 'discovered' the flying bomb and then located its manufacturing and launching sites. 'The Committee will report daily,' Churchill instructed, 'or as often as may be necessary, to me, the Home Secretary, the Secretary of State for Air and the Chiefs of Staff.'[5]

On June 20 news reached London of a general uprising by French resistance forces in southern France. Their urgent need was for arms.

---

[1] Prime Minister's Personal Telegram, T.1302/4, 'Personal and Top Secret', 17 June 1944: Cabinet papers, 120/858.

[2] Brooke diary, 19 June 1944: Bryant, *op. cit.*, volume 2, page 220.

[3] War Cabinet No. 80 of 1944, 19 June: Cabinet papers, 65/42.

[4] Prime Minister's Personal Minute, D.198/4, 21 June 1944: Churchill papers, 20/152.

[5] Prime Minister's Personal Minute, M.736/4, 'Top Secret', 22 June 1944: Churchill papers, 20/152. The Sandys Committee's three other members included Air Marshal Bottomley, Deputy Chief of the Air Staff, Air Marshal Hill, Air Officer Commanding Air Defence of Great Britain, and General Pile, General Officer Commanding Anti-Aircraft Command. The Committee's Secretary was Brigadier Jacob.

'You should visit General Bedell Smith tomorrow morning,' Churchill instructed Desmond Morton, 'saying that you have come from me, and see what he thinks can be done. We will do our part.'[1] To Lord Selborne, the Minister responsible for SOE, Churchill minuted that same day, at Morton's suggestion:

The Maquis has started upon guerrilla warfare and is in temporary control of certain areas of southern France. The Germans are reacting strongly with fully armed troops. Every effort must be made to supply the Maquis at once with rifles, Bren guns, Piat guns, mortars and bazookas, with ammunition and whatever else is needful to prevent the collapse of the movement and to extend it. What is being done about this? Have you any difficulty in getting men to repack containers with the right sort of weapons? Could General Wilson help from North Africa? Pray tell me if I can help you to accelerate action.[2]

The 'Bodyguard' deception continued to be effective. The Allied advance in Italy, reported the Joint Intelligence Committee on June 19, had 'increased the enemy's fears' of a landing on the South French coast, to such an extent that German ground forces in southern France had been maintained 'at the same strength as on 6th June'. The German fears of landings in Norway had also been maintained, so much so that German naval and ground strength in Norway had remained 'unaltered' since the cross-Channel landings.[3]

On the morning of June 20, Portal reported to the Chiefs of Staff Committee that, by six o'clock that morning, twenty-six flying bombs had reached London, and a further twenty-seven had been shot down, in the previous twenty-four hours.[4] On June 21, while dictating a telegram to Roosevelt about the need for a 'cordial agreement' on post-war Anglo-American oil policy, Churchill broke off his line of argument to inform the President:

At this moment a flying bomb is approaching this dwelling. We think we are getting the best of them. We have received the greatest consideration from Eisenhower and Spaatz, and I have given it out that nothing is to

[1] Prime Minister's Personal Minute, D.M. 11/4, 20 June 1944: Churchill papers, 20/152.
[2] Prime Minister's Personal Minute, M.733, 20 June 1944: Premier papers, 3/185/1, folio 33. A note by Patrick Kinna on this minute states: 'Major Morton advises that his draft minute has been despatched unaltered.' Nine days later, following a further request from Lord Selborne for air support for SOE operations in France in support of the Maquis, Churchill minuted to Morton: 'Take every step to secure the fulfilment of Lord Selborne's wishes, and draft minutes for me to sign whenever these may be necessary' (Prime Minister's Personal Minute, D.M.13/4, 29 June 1944: Premier papers, 3/185/1, folio 4).
[3] Joint Intelligence Sub-Committee Report No. 260 (Operations), (Final), (Limited Circulation), 'German appreciation of Allied intentions in the West', 19 June 1944: Cabinet papers, 79/71.
[4] Chiefs of Staff Committee No 201 (Operations), 10.30 a.m., 20 June 1944: Cabinet papers, 79/71.

impede the battle. This perpetual bombardment is a new feature, but I do not think it will seriously affect production in London. Up to date there are 7,000 casualties of which half are light. The Guards Chapel, where 300 occurred, was a sad episode. General Bedell Smith was invited by Colonel Ivan Cobbold, who was killed, to attend the Service but did not go.

I consider the battle on land is progressing favourably, but the weather has not been kind for June. Bomb has fallen some way off, but others are reported.

'We have exploded more than half our visitors today,' Churchill told Roosevelt, 'by fighter aircraft harmlessly.'[1]

From Stalin came news on June 21 that 'in not more than a week' would begin the 'second round' of the Soviet summer offensive. 'I hope,' Stalin telegraphed to Churchill, 'our offensive will render essential support to the operations of the Allied armies in France and Italy.'[2] Stalin's own troops had just crossed the River Bug, and entered the town of Chelm, on the Polish side of the Curzon Line. From there, on June 22, a Polish Committee for National Liberation was set up, under Soviet auspices. Its mission, announced that night over Radio Moscow, was to 'direct the fight' of the Polish people for liberation, to 'achieve independence', and to 'rebuild the Polish State'. A few days later, this Committee moved to Lublin. Henceforth, the London Poles and the Lublin Poles were in direct confrontation. The London Polish leaders, who had just returned from Washington, went to see Churchill on June 22. 'Roosevelt considers his own influence with Stalin and his possibilities of obtaining concessions as greater than Churchill,' Mikolajczyk had reported to his Government's Delegate in Poland on the previous day.[3]

On the evening of June 22 Churchill worked at No. 10 Annexe. 'Sat in the study for ages', noted Marian Holmes, 'listening to the PM talking with Anthony Eden and Harold Macmillan. When they finally left, the PM gave me some dictation. After the heavy raids of the past few nights, doodlebugs started coming over again about 2 a.m. It was very noisy. The PM asked me if I were frightened. I said "No". How can one feel frightened in his company?'[4]

[1] Prime Minister's Personal Telegram, T.1329/4, Prime Minister to President, No. 708, 21 June 1944: Churchill papers, 20/167.

[2] 'Personal and Top Secret', 21 June 1944: Churchill papers, 20/167.

[3] Dispatch of 21 June 1944: *Documents on Polish-Soviet Relations, 1939–1945*, volume 2, document No. 147, pages 269–70.

[4] Marian Holmes diary, 22 June 1944: Marian Walker Spicer papers. Sir John Colville writes: 'The slow throb of the flying bombs, a sound quite distinct from that of ordinary aircraft, became a familiar sound to Londoners. Waiting for the throb to stop, which meant that the engine had cut and the flying bomb was about to dive eastwards, was inappropriately reminiscent of the children's game, musical chairs. The tension was for many greater than in the "blitz" of 1940-41.' (Note for the author, March 1986.)

44

'The first major strategic and political error'

IN the aftermath of 'Overlord' there was a serious Anglo-American disagreement on future Allied strategy in the Mediterranean. The British Chiefs of Staff, and Churchill, were determined to follow up Alexander's successes in Italy with further advances there, and beyond. The United States Chiefs of Staff, however, were equally determined to proceed with the 'Anvil' landing in the South of France, and to launch it by August 15.

In an attempt to retain Italy as the principal theatre of Allied exertions after 'Overlord', the Joint Planning Staff had already given their opinion that if the forces at Alexander's disposal were to 'remain intact' during the late summer and autumn of 1944, a force of four to five divisions should undertake an amphibious assault on Trieste, and an overland advance to Trieste, followed by 'the capture of the Ljubljana area'. Ten divisions could then be deployed to ensure 'further exploitation towards the Hungarian-Austrian border', an advance which could be carried out 'with progressively dwindling forces'. The choice of direction in which to exploit the advance would have to be made 'nearer the time', but it would probably be desirable, the Joint Planners advised, 'at an early stage to seize Zagreb'.

The Joint Planners then set out the 'best possible timing' for the Istria-Ljubljana operation: crossing the Piave line in early October 1944, securing the Udine-Gorizia-Trieste area in early November, and securing Ljubljana in January 1945, for a further advance in March or April. 'It is of vital importance', the Joint Planners concluded, 'to the Germans to prevent the Allies advancing from Italy towards Austria or Hungary'; they would therefore try to hold the line in great strength, 'compelling' them 'to withdraw forces from other fronts'. To this end, 'we should require to retain in Italy some twenty divisions'.[1]

[1] Joint Planning Staff Paper 161 (Final) of 1944, 'Exploitation from Northern Italy' 15 June 1944: Cabinet papers, 79/76.

Maitland Wilson, who was also seeking to preserve the Italian campaign as a principal theatre of war, telegraphed to Eisenhower on June 19 to point out 'certain disadvantages' in the South of France landing, one of which was that it would involve halting the Allied Army in Italy 'in front of the Pisa-Rimini line and breaking up a force which has proved itself to be a first class fighting machine and in which co-operation between ground and air has reached an exceptional and increasing degree of efficiency after months of hard work'. In addition, Maitland Wilson argued, the 'switch' from Italy to 'Anvil' would involve a six-week break in offensive operations 'in which the Germans would be given a breathing space and an opportunity to rest and regroup their forces'.

Maitland Wilson favoured the capture of Florence before the end of June, an attack 'with 14 divisions' towards Bologna in mid-July, a bridgehead across the Po in early August, crossing the Adige and reaching 'the line Venice-Verona' at the end of August, and, during September, 'an advance on Trieste and the Ljubljana Gap', preferably in conjunction with 'amphibious and airborne resources'.[1]

Eisenhower rejected Wilson's arguments, pointing out in a telegram to Marshall on June 20 that Wilson's telegram 'seems to discount the fact that the Combined Chiefs of Staff have long ago decided to make Western Europe the base from which to conduct decisive operations against Germany. To authorize any departure from this sound decision seems to me ill advised and potentially dangerous'. Eisenhower added: 'In my opinion to contemplate wandering off overland via Trieste to Ljubljana repeat Ljubljana is to indulge in conjecture to an unwarrantable degree at the present time. Certainly it involves dispersion of our effort and resources. Even granted successful achievement of this objective by autumn, I am unable to repeat unable to see how the over-riding necessity for exploiting the early success of "Overlord" is thereby assisted.'

This was 'the moment', Eisenhower told Marshall, 'for definite coordinating action to be taken by the Combined Chiefs of Staff in relation to the whole campaign in Western Europe'. Wilson, he added, 'should be directed to undertake Operation "Anvil" at the earliest possible date'.[2]

While awaiting Eisenhower's reply to Wilson's telegram of June 19, the Joint Planning Staff examined the telegram in detail. Though not disagreeing with Wilson's desire to retain the initiative in Italy, and

[1] Telegram B.12995, 'Top Secret', 'Urgent', 19 June 1944: Cabinet papers, 122/1246.
[2] Telegram S. 54239, 'Top Secret', 'Personal for General Marshall's eyes only', 20 June 1944: Alfred D. Chandler (editor), *The Papers of Dwight David Eisenhower, The War Years*, volume 3, Baltimore and London 1970, document 1765, pages 1938-9.

to seek to push beyond Trieste, the Joint Planners did feel that 'the combination of weather, terrain and lack of roads' would 'combine to limit drastically our rate of advance', as well as limiting the forces that could be built up east of the Julian Alps for exploitation. An amphibious operation at the head of the Adriatic, they added, 'presents very considerable difficulties'.[1]

On the afternoon of June 21 Churchill called a Staff Conference to learn the views of Field Marshal Smuts, who was about to leave London for South Africa. Smuts spoke with enthusiasm of Wilson's plan, being in favour, he said, 'of extending our right hand across the Balkans towards the Russians, and the development of a threat to Austria from bases in the Trieste-Venice area'. This plan, Smuts added, 'might well result in the loss to Germany of the whole of the Balkans'. Churchill told the meeting:

He was not prepared to see General Alexander's armies attempting to storm the Alps or to work their way westwards along the narrow Mediterranean shore. He saw no great advantage in landing operations in the region of Toulon and Marseilles in view of the time it would apparently take to mount and launch them, and of the overland distance to Bordeaux, although Allied inactivity in this area would forfeit to us the value of the guerilla activities of the southern Maquis. A landing at Sète looked attractive on the map but had been crabbed on account of the beaches. He would like more information on this point. A coup de main at Bordeaux still had certain attractions but might not prove practicable.

He liked the idea of ripping open the coast and small ports north-west from Havre in direct support to 'Overlord'; this suggestion must be further studied. On the other hand, the attractions of an advance into southern Austria though the Ljubljana gap were strong, particularly as this might well clear Greece and the Balkans and result in the collapse of Hungary, and act as a stimulant to the Turks. An Allied offensive in this area could not fail to draw German reserves which would otherwise be directed towards the Eastern or North-Western Front.

From Brooke came a word of warning. As regards Alexander's plans, he said, 'the country in Istria was well adapted for defence and we must beware lest the Germans should succeed in containing us there with smaller forces than were deployed against them'.[2]

At a meeting of the Chiefs of Staff Committee on June 22, Lieutenant-General J. A. H. Gammell, Maitland Wilson's Chief of Staff, explained that the 'speed of advance' of Wilson's plan 'depended to a

[1] Joint Planning Staff Paper No. 170 (Final) of 1944, 'Mediterranean Operations' 21 June 1944: Cabinet papers, 79/76.
[2] Chiefs of Staff Committee No. 203 (Operations) of 1944, 2.45 p.m., 21 June 1944: Cabinet papers, 79/76.

great extent on the availability of landing-craft for maintenance purposes'. In fact, Gammell pointed out, Alexander would depend 'to a great extent' on the continued use of these landing craft even 'for the maintenance of his offensive across the Pisa-Rimini line'. This offensive would need 14 divisions with 6 in immediate reserve. If it were decided to mount 'Anvil' early in August, Gammell warned, 'this decision would quickly begin to affect operations in Italy', three United States and four French divisions then in Italy being 'earmarked' for 'Anvil'.[1]

At a Staff Conference that same evening, Churchill and his advisers accepted that the needs of the battle in Normandy, 'extending to the battle in Brittany', must continue to have 'absolute priority'. Any surplus, Churchill believed, should be used for an amphibious thrust in the Trieste area, in order to influence the 'speeding up of Alexander's advance' in Italy. The 'only worthwhile alternative' to Trieste, Churchill told the Staff Conference, 'seemed to him to be to transfer forces to operate in closed tactical relation to the battle in Normandy by introducing them on the Biscay coast north or south of the Loire'.

Churchill was 'not at all attracted', he stated, 'by the prospects of an "Anvil" type operation on the south coast of France'. This area was 'too far removed' from Eisenhower's battle front for a landing there 'to have any tactical effect on "Overlord" '. The continued 'threat' of an amphibious operation somewhere in the south of Europe, 'culminating at the appropriate moment in a landing at the head of the Adriatic in the Trieste area' should, Churchill said, be 'more effective strategically' than 'Anvil' would be 'in drawing and keeping divisions away from the western front'.

It was Churchill's view, as he told the Staff Conference of June 22, that the Germans 'would probably be more sensitive to a thrust developing from the head of the Adriatic than to an advance up the Rhone Valley'. Another argument 'against "Anvil" ' was, he said, that an enormous 'tail' would be needed to develop a new base in the South of France. Wilson had already estimated that an 'Anvil' landing could not take place before August 15 and it would then be forty to sixty days, Churchill pointed out, before the force would be strong enough to 'brush aside more than the lightest resistance'. His 'preference', Churchill concluded, was to see Alexander 'continue his advance into northern Italy', across both the Po and the Piave rivers.

Brooke then told the Staff Conference that he had 'always been strongly in favour' of allowing Alexander to develop 'the full weight of his advance into northern Italy', particularly as the Germans

[1] Chiefs of Staff Committee No. 204 (Operations) of 1944, 10.30 a.m., 22 June 1944: Cabinet papers, 79/76.

showed every intention 'of attempting to fight it out'. The danger was that having crossed the Po, he might not be able to 'deploy or maintain' all the forces at his disposal, as, with the 'difficult country on Italy's north-eastern frontier', and with the onset of winter, the Germans might 'succeed in containing the Allied army with relatively weaker forces, thus neutralizing our strategy'.[1]

'We had a long evening of it listening to Winston's strategic arguments,' Brooke noted in his diary. 'In the main he was for supporting Alexander's advance on Vienna. I pointed out that, even on Alex's optimistic reckoning, the advance beyond the Pisa-Rimini line would not start till after September; namely, we should embark on a campaign through the Alps in winter.' Brooke added, in spite of his support for the basic strategic concept, 'It was hard to make him realise that, if we took the season of the year and the topography of the country in league against us, we should have three enemies instead of one. We were kept up till close on 2 a.m. and accomplished nothing.'[2]

Brooke's criticisms were being answered by Wilson and Alexander that same day, when they discussed the Italian strategy with Field Marshal Smuts, who had gone to Italy on his way back to South Africa. On June 23 Smuts telegraphed to Churchill:

As regards plan for Alexander's advance, he and Wilson agree that there will be no difficulty in his break through to the Po and thereafter swinging east towards Istria, Ljubljana, and so on to Austria. Alexander favours an advance both by land and sea, while Wilson favours the latter and thinks three seaborne divisions with one or two airborne divisions would suffice and make possible capture of Trieste by beginning of September. Thereafter the advance will reopen eastward, gathering large Partisan support and perhaps forcing the enemy out of the Balkans. The co-operation between our and the Russian advance towards Austria and Germany would constitute as serious a threat to the enemy as Eisenhower's advance from the west, and the three combined are most likely to produce early enemy collapse.[3]

All now awaited Eisenhower's answer to Maitland Wilson's telegram of June 19. Four days after receiving this telegram, Eisenhower was ready to reply to it, and to reject it, informing the American Chiefs of Staff on June 23: 'Our forces in Italy do not directly threaten any area vital to the enemy, who, therefore, has the initiative in deciding whether or not to withdraw out of Italy.' An advance on Ljubljana and Trieste, Eisenhower added, while it would 'probably

---

[1] Staff Conference, Chiefs of Staff Committee No. 206 (Operations) of 1944, 10.30 p.m., 22 June 1944: Cabinet papers, 79/76.

[2] Brooke diary, 22 June 1944: Bryant, op. cit., volume 2, pages 222–3.

[3] Telegram of 23 June 1944: Churchill papers, 4/347.

contain a considerable amount of German strength', would not necessarily divert 'any appreciable number of German divisions from France'. Nor would it provide 'an additional port' which could be used 'to assist in the deployment of divisions in the area'. The advance on Ljubljana, Eisenhower warned, 'would have little positive effect until 1945'.

Wilson was 'fully prepared' to carry out 'Anvil', Eisenhower added, 'if the decision is made to do so'. A week earlier, Eisenhower had told Wilson that he agreed with the Combined Chiefs of Staff, 'that a quick and successful operation at Bordeaux, if such were possible, is preferable to a similar operation in southern France'.[1] Now he put his support behind 'Anvil' telling Wilson, and the American Chiefs of Staff: 'This opens up another gateway into France, which, if not the best in geographical location, is the best we can hope to obtain at an early date. The possession of such a gateway I consider vital.' Eisenhower added, in further opposition to Wilson's view: 'France is the decisive theater. This decision was taken long ago by the Combined Chiefs of Staff. In my view, the resources of Great Britain and the US will not permit us to maintain two major theaters in the European war, each with decisive missions.'[2]

On June 24 the strategic dispute was brought to a climax by a message from the United States Chiefs of Staff. 'General Wilson's proposal,' they wrote, 'for commitment of Mediterranean resources to large scale operations in northern Italy and into the Balkans is unacceptable to the United States Chiefs of Staff.' The 'essential requirement' was to support 'Overlord' and to exploit the successes it had already obtained at the 'earliest possible' moment. This could only be achieved 'by seizing another major port in France'.[3]

If 'Anvil' were to be launched on August 15, Wilson telegraphed to the British Chiefs of Staff on June 24, it would be necessary to begin to withdraw resources from Alexander in four days' time. 'This,' Wilson warned, 'will affect his capacity to continue the battle in Italy.'[4]

It was too late for effective argument. In a second message from Washington on June 24, the United States Chiefs of Staff sent the British Chiefs of Staff their draft instructions for Wilson, stating that 'Anvil' would be launched 'at the earliest possible date', and gave August 1 as the 'target date' towards which Wilson should aim. Those

---

[1] S.53967, 'Top Secret', 16 June 1944: Alfred D. Chandler (editor), *The Papers of Dwight D. Eisenhower, The War Years*, volume 3, Baltimore and London 1970, document No. 1755.

[2] SCAF 53, S,54425, 'Top Secret', 23 June 1944: Cabinet papers, 122/1246.

[3] United States Chiefs of Staff Memorandum, CCS 603, sent to London as JSM 111, IZ 4741, 'Top Secret', 8.21 p.m., 24 June 1944: Cabinet papers, 122/1246.

[4] MEDCOS, 131, 'Top Secret', 24 June 1944: Cabinet papers, 122/1246.

resources not required for 'Anvil' could be used in Italy. But 'Anvil' was to absorb a three division assault, an airborne lift for the equivalent of one division, 'and a build-up to at least ten divisions as quickly as the resources made available to you will permit', bearing in mind 'the vital support of the "Overlord" operation'.[1]

'I have just read Memorandum CCS 603 from the United States Chiefs of Staff,' Churchill telegraphed to Roosevelt on June 25, 'and also the immediately following containing the proposed draft orders. These very grave questions will immediately be examined by the British Chiefs of Staff and by the War Cabinet. I earnestly hope you will consent to hear both sides. Our answer will be given within 48 hours.'[2]

The 'Anvil'–Adriatic dispute was not one which revolved entirely upon an Anglo-American axis. The Joint Planning Staff, in a report to Churchill and the Chiefs of Staff Committee on June 25, put their support firmly behind 'Anvil', 'especially', they wrote, 'as General Eisenhower has stated that the possession of a further major port is vital'.[3]

From the Supreme Headquarters of the Allied Expeditionary Force in London, Eisenhower informed the United States Chiefs of Staff, and Maitland Wilson on June 26 that his two British colleagues, Admiral Ramsay and Montgomery, 'share my conviction with regard to the importance of "Anvil" '.[4] That same day, June 26, the British Chiefs of Staff obtained Churchill's approval for their reply to the United States Chiefs of Staff, and for its 'immediate despatch'.[5] In their telegram, Brooke, Portal and Cunningham informed their opposite numbers in Washington, Marshall, King and Arnold, that the withdrawal of forces from Italy to 'Anvil' was 'unacceptable to us'.

Even if 'Anvil' were postponed until the end of August, the British Chiefs of Staff asserted, 'the withdrawal of additional resources from General Alexander' would 'almost certainly prejudice operations for the destruction of the German forces in Italy', and they went on to urge that 'Anvil' be abandoned altogether. If the Italian campaign were successful, the British Chiefs of Staff pointed out, Alexander would be able to 'extend a hand' from northern Italy to the French

---

[1] JSM 112, IZ 4742, 'Top Secret', 8.23 p.m., 24 June 1944: Cabinet papers, 122/1246.
[2] Prime Minister's Personal Telegram, T.155/4, Prime Minister to President, No. 714, 25 June 1944: Churchill papers, 4/347.
[3] Joint Planning Staff Memorandum, 173 (Final) of 1944: 'Top Secret', 25 June 1944: Cabinet papers, 79/76.
[4] SCAF 54, Telegram No. S,54597, 'Top Secret', 26 June 1944: Cabinet papers, 122/1246.
[5] Staff Conference, Chiefs of Staff Committee No. 210 (Operations) of 1944, 6 p.m., 26 June 1944: Cabinet papers, 79/76.

resistance forces in southern France. 'It seems to us,' they concluded, 'that the Germans must divert more divisions to defend Northern Italy than to stem an advance up the Rhone Valley, which will be too late to threaten anything this summer.' [1]

On the following day the United States Chiefs of Staff replied. The British proposal, they wrote, was 'unacceptable'. Their telegram ended: 'The US Chiefs of Staff do not consider there exists any reason for engaging in further discussion which can only be for the purpose of further delaying a decision which must be made. The wording of the directive we have proposed in CCS 603 gives sufficient latitude to the Commanders concerned, both as to resources and target date. We ask that it be sent to General Wilson immediately.' [2]

This telegram from the United States Chiefs of Staff reached London on June 28. Brooke noted in his diary:

This morning the American reply to our wire arrived, a rude one at that! They still adhere to 'Anvil' being carried out and want it at once. They argue that we have derived benefit out of the Italian campaign in spite of the fact that they were always opposed to it, but state that the reason for its success is attributable to Hitler's error in deciding to fight for Southern Italy. They forget that this is exactly what we kept on telling them would happen. [3]

The British Chiefs of Staff met, at eleven o'clock on the morning of June 28, to discuss the American reply. It was agreed, the minutes of the meeting recorded, 'that there was nothing in the memorandum from the US Chiefs of Staff to affect the conclusion reached at the Staff Conference earlier in the week that the right strategy in the Mediterranean was to continue to develop the full power of the Allied offensive in Italy and to maintain the threat of an assault on the South Coast of France'. In view of the 'latest reports', the minutes noted, there could be 'no doubt that an advance into Northern Italy would present a very serious threat to the Germans, and would probably draw in further German divisions'.

It was their intention, the Chiefs of Staff noted, that Alexander should destroy the German forces opposed to him, 'and by his advance northward, present a threat which would compel the Germans to divert additional resources to this theatre'. Strong and continued pressure on the Italian front, the Chiefs of Staff believed, could exert, in this way, 'a direct effect on the German campaigns in the East and

[1] Chiefs of Staff Telegram, COS(W) 130, 'Top Secret', 26 June 1944: Cabinet papers, 122/1246.
[2] United States Chiefs of Staff Memorandum, 27 June 1944, sent as JSM, 114, IZ.4790, 'Top Secret', 27 June 1944: Cabinet papers, 105/46.
[3] Brooke diary, 28 June 1944: Bryant, *op. cit.*, volume 2, pages 224–5.

West, whereas "Anvil", if launched, could have no direct effect for a considerable time and would entail an almost immediate reduction in the power of the offensive in Italy'.[1]

Hardly had this meeting ended, than the Chiefs of Staff, and Churchill, were given information of an exceptionally secret sort, which 'provided decisive confirmation' that their Italian strategy was the correct one. This information came in the form of a German naval message, decrypted at Bletchley, and prepared for circulation to those with knowledge of the most secret source of British Intelligence at nine o'clock that same morning, June 28. The message was a directive from the German Supreme Command, sent on June 17 to the German Naval authorities on the island of Elba. The message, which revealed that the Germans intended to do everything possible to hold the line in Italy, began:

The Fuehrer has ordered the Apennine position as the final blocking line, since the enemy's entry into the Po plain would have incalculable military and political consequences. In large parts of the Apennine position, nothing has, so far, been done in the way of defence works. It is therefore desired that the misconception—existing in the minds of both commanders and men—that there is a fortified Apennine position should be scotched once for all. The conduct of C. in C. South West (Kesselring) is therefore to be directed towards gaining time until adequate development of the Apennine position is achieved, a task which will require mighty labour for some months to come.

In a summary of the rest of this decrypt, the Director of Naval Intelligence, E. G. N. Rushbrooke, noted: 'Hitler's directive continued by stating that it was vital that Elba should not be evacuated, as otherwise there would be danger in the coastal flank. The capture of Leghorn and Ancona would enable the supply and preparation of leapfrog landings which would outflank the Apennine position.'

In a comment on the decrypt, likewise circulated on June 28 to those who had access to this most secret source, Rushbrooke noted that on June 8, before Hitler's directive, the Germans had been planning the evacuation of Elba.[2]

As circulated on June 28, this decrypt was headed: 'Hitler orders Apennine positions as "final blocking line".'[3] Pondering its clear instruction to Kesselring to defend the northern Apennines with the utmost exertion because an Allied breakthrough into northern Italy

---

[1] Chiefs of Staff Committee No. 213 (Operations) of 1944, 11 a.m., 28 June 1944: Cabinet papers, 79/76.

[2] The Allied landing on Elba took place on 17 June 1944, the German forces on the island being overcome two days later.

[3] Special Intelligence Summary No. 2419/12, 9 a.m., 28 June 1944. The decrypt was CX/MSS/T.228/49, the comment on it, SI 2387. This was not an Enigma, but a Fish decrypt.

would have 'incalculable military and political consequences', Churchill and his advisers realized that if Alexander's army were to remain at its present strength, not lose five Divisions to the South of France, and remain on the offensive, the Germans would be forced to send more and more reinforcements down into Italy to check the Allied advance. Not the South of France, but Italy, was shown by this decrypt to be the area in which the Germans felt vulnerable, and which Hitler was determined to defend to the last. Brooke noted in his diary:

And now we have the most marvellous information indicating clearly the importance that Hitler attaches to Northern Italy, his determination to fight for it and his orders to hold a line south of the Pisa-Rimini line whilst this line is being developed. Kesselring's Army is now a hostage to political interference with military direction of operations. It would be madness to fail to take advantage of it and would delay the conclusion of the war.[1]

Hitler's directive confirmed the Italian strategy favoured by Churchill and his Chiefs of Staff. 'We spent most of the day drafting a reply,' Brooke wrote in his diary, 'refusing to withdraw forces at present for a landing in Southern France with the opportunities that lie in front of us. Winston is also sending a wire to the President backing up our message.'[2]

'It would be a grave strategic error,' Brooke, Portal and Cunningham telegraphed to the United States Chiefs of Staff on June 28, 'not to take advantage of destroying the German forces at present in Italy and thus drawing further reserves on to this front.' Their argument was not based upon general strategic consideration alone, but, as they explained, on a 'Boniface' decrypt which 'completely vindicates our estimate of the enemy reaction to a full scale campaign in Italy and establishes the correctness of our plan'. This was the Hitler directive circulated that same morning.[3]

In their telegram to the United States Chiefs of Staff, Brooke, Portal and Cunningham pointed out that Alexander's offensive had already drawn four German reserve divisions 'on to his front'. The destruction of Kesselring's army 'cannot fail', the British Chiefs of Staff added, 'to draw further divisions away from "Overlord", and moreover will draw them away earlier than they would be by an "Anvil" launched about the end of August'.

To 'divide our air forces' between Italy and the South of France, the British Chiefs of Staff warned, 'would be a violation of the principle of concentration of force'. However much Eisenhower was responsible

---

[1] Brooke diary, 28 June 1944: Bryant, *op. cit.*, volume 2, pages 224-5.
[2] Brooke diary, 28 June 1944: Bryant, *op. cit.*, volume 2, pages 224-5.
[3] Boniface of 28 June 1944, from G2, TAY 175, paragraph 1.

for the success of 'Overlord' itself, they added, 'we cannot admit that he has any responsibility for European strategy as a whole'.[1]

To reinforce the arguments of the Chiefs of Staff, Churchill prepared the note which, with their approval, he was to send to Roosevelt. In it, he warned of the possible difficulties that might confront an 'Anvil' landing. 'It is as easy to talk of an advance up the Rhône valley as it is of a march from Italy to Vienna,' Churchill wrote, 'but very great hazards, difficulties and delays may menace all such projects. Once we are committed to the landing at Marseilles, all the enemy troops along the Riviera, at present 7 or 8 divisions, can be brought to oppose us.' It would always be possible for the German High Command 'to move any forces they have in Italy through the tunnels under the Alps or till winter comes along the great motoring roads which have been made over them, and intercept our northward advance at any point they chose. The country is most formidable. Without the enemy withdrawing a single division from the "Overlord" battle, we could be confronted with superior forces at every step we advance up the Rhône valley.'

Churchill then referred to Wilson's telegram of June 19, and Smuts's telegram of June 23, both holding out the possibility that 'Alexander could have possession of Trieste by the end of September'. Churchill's note continued:

Whether we should ruin all hopes of a major victory in Italy and all its fronts and condemn ourselves to a passive role in that theatre, after having broken up the fine Allied army which is advancing so rapidly through that peninsula, for the sake of 'Anvil' with all its limitations, is indeed a grave question for His Majesty's Government and the President, with the Combined Chiefs of Staff, to decide. For my own part, while eager to do everything in human power which will give effective and timely help to 'Overlord', I should greatly regret to see General Alexander's army deprived of much of its offensive power in northern Italy for the sake of a march up the Rhone valley, which the Combined Chiefs of Staff have themselves described as unprofitable, in addition to our prime operation of 'Overlord'.[2]

In his note of June 28, Churchill proposed two areas of maximum Allied activity; first, an immediate reinforcement of 'Overlord', including landings as far west as St. Nazaire in Brittany and the seizure of Bordeaux, and 'next' a plan in Italy that would 'do justice to the great opportunities' of the Mediterranean commanders. 'Anvil', he wrote, should be replaced by 'minor diversions and threats to hold

---

[1] Chiefs of Staff Memorandum, COS(W) 135, 'Memorandum by the British Chiefs of Staff', 'Top Secret', 28 June 1944: Cabinet papers, 122/1246.

[2] Chiefs of Staff Paper, COS (44) 571 (O) (Revise), 'Top Secret', 28 June 1944: Cabinet papers, 122/1246.

the enemy around the Gulf of Lions'. Italy and Normandy should be the priority. No landing craft or troops should be withdrawn from Italy to support a landing in the south of France. 'Let us resolve not to wreck one great campaign for the sake of another,' he pleaded. 'Both can be won.'[1]

That night, Churchill sent Roosevelt a copy of this note. 'Please remember,' he wrote in a covering telegram, 'how you spoke to me at Teheran about Istria, and how I introduced it at the full Conference. This has sunk very deeply into my mind, although it is not by any means the immediate issue we have to decide.' Churchill wondered whether Roosevelt would really involve himself in the intricacies of the decision. 'I most earnestly beg you,' he wrote, 'to examine this matter in detail for yourself.' Churchill added: 'I am shocked to think of the length of the message I shall be sending you tonight. It is a purely personal communication between you and me in our capacity as Heads of the two Western Democracies.'[2]

In sending Roosevelt the strategic arguments of the British Chiefs of Staff, and his own, Churchill added: 'Please also take into consideration the very important information which General Menzies is sending you separately on my instructions.'[3] This information was the decrypt of June 28. A 'careful and patient discussion', Churchill telegraphed to Roosevelt on June 29, 'is indispensable, and not an overriding decision by either side.'[4]

On the afternoon of June 29 a special meeting of the Combined Chiefs of Staff was convened in Washington to try to resolve the dispute. Speaking of the decrypt which showed that the Germans had decided to send south as many troops as were needed to hold the line in Italy, General Marshall commented 'that "Boniface" was, of course, of immense value. However, it must be borne in mind that if we had always given full value to "Boniface" reports it was doubtful if "Overlord" would ever have been launched.'[5]

---

[1] Prime Minister's Personal Telegram, T.1376/4, Prime Minister to President, No. 718, 'Strictly Private, Personal and Top Secret', 28 June 1944: Churchill papers, 20/167. This telegram had previously been circulated to and approved by both the War Cabinet and the Chiefs of Staff Committee, entitled 'Operations in the European Theatres, Note by the Prime Minister and Minister of Defence', Chiefs of Staff Paper No. 571 (O) (Revise), 'Top Secret', of 28 June 1944: Churchill papers, 23/13.

[2] Prime Minister's Personal Telegram, T.1375/4, Prime Minister to President, No. 717, 'Strictly Personal and Top Secret', 28 June 1944: Churchill papers, 20/167.

[3] Prime Minister's Personal Telegram, T.1376/4, Prime Minister to President, No. 718, 'Strictly Private, Personal and Top Secret', 28 June 1944: Churchill papers, 20/167.

[4] Prime Minister's Personal Telegram, T.1378/4, Prime Minister to President, No. 719, 'Personal and Top Secret', 29 June 1944: Churchill papers, 20/167.

[5] 'Record of a Meeting of the Combined Chiefs of Staff, held on Thursday, the 29th June 1944, at 2.30 p.m.': MM(S) (44) 53, 'Top Secret', 29 June 1944: Cabinet papers, 122/1246.

Shocked by this dismissal of Britain's most secret source, the three British representatives present 'made it clear', as they reported at once to the Chiefs of Staff in London, 'that this was not a fair argument'.[1]

In his reference to 'Overlord' and 'Boniface', General Marshall was referring to the fact that on the eve of D-Day the British had learnt through 'Boniface' of a German build-up of sixty divisions against 'Overlord'. It was actually not only the decrypts, but also agents, who had revealed this; the particular role of 'Boniface' had been to tell of certain last-minute reinforcements of Normandy. On paper, these sixty German divisions were more than the planners of 'Overlord', General Morgan, the British Chiefs of Staff, and Churchill, had agreed to be the maximum for 'Overlord' to take place at all, and there had indeed been some last-minute anxiety on that score. Military Intelligence in the War Office had brought re-assurance however, by pointing out that while the German build-up looked formidable and therefore a reason to cancel 'Overlord' in terms of the actual number of German divisions, the true sum of their strength was about the same as in the original British stipulations.

Marshall's comment about 'Boniface' and 'Overlord' was thus unfair and shortsighted, in that the two cases were not at all similar: in the 'Overlord' case it was a matter of a straightforward numerical adjustment to an accurate but misleading figure; in the current Italian case, it was a precise and unambiguous Hitler directive for future action.

The United States Chiefs of Staff remained insistent upon 'Anvil', the British Chiefs of Staff remained equally insistent in their opposition to 'Anvil', minuting to Churchill on June 30: 'We consider that "Anvil" at the expense of the Italian campaign is the wrong strategy,' and, 'far from helping "Overlord" may well delay progress in Normandy.' But they feared a break with the Americans if, by pressing for the Italian campaign, Britain were to lay herself open 'to suspicion that we are seeking by delay to make "Anvil" impossible'. Having agreed to 'Anvil', they added, 'we must reluctantly agree that the Operation should be carried out, and, having agreed, we are determined to back it to the full and to leave nothing undone to ensure its success'.[2]

Roosevelt himself now rejected Churchill's appeal. 'My interests and hopes,' he replied on June 29, 'centre on defeating the Germans

[1] JSM 118, 'Top Secret', IZ 4837, 11.35 p.m., 29 June 1944: Cabinet papers, 122/1246. The British representatives on the Combined Chiefs of Staff were Admiral Sir Percy Noble, General G. N. Macready and Air Marshal Sir William Welsh.

[2] Minute dated 30 June 1944, Chiefs of Staff Committee No. 217 (Operations) of 1944, 30 June 1944, Annex: Cabinet papers, 79/77.

in front of Eisenhower and driving on into Germany, rather than on limiting this action for the purpose of staging a full major effort in Italy.' Even with five divisions withdrawn from Italy for the South of France operation, Roosevelt asserted, there would be sufficient Allied forces in Italy 'to chase Kesselring north of Pisa-Rimini and maintain heavy pressure against his Army. . . .'

In rejecting the British proposal, Roosevelt made no reference to the Hitler directive decrypt which seemed to Churchill and his Chiefs of Staff to be the decisive factor.

Roosevelt also told Churchill that, for 'purely political considerations' in the United States, 'I should never survive even a slight setback in "Overlord" if it were known that fairly large forces had been diverted to the Balkans.' [1]

This was a misconception. Neither Churchill nor the Chiefs of Staff had suggested advancing into the Balkans, but rather, by landing at Istria and Trieste, moving north-east through the Ljubljana gap towards Vienna, Roosevelt's own suggestion at Teheran.

Roosevelt's telegram reached London in the early hours of June 30. The Americans, noted Brooke, 'now begin to own the major strength on land, in the air and on the sea. They, therefore, consider that they are entitled to dictate how their forces are to be employed. We shall be forced into carrying out an invasion of southern France, but I am not certain that this need cripple Alexander's power to finish crushing Kesselring.'

At the Chiefs of Staff Committee that morning, however, with Brooke in the chair, it was felt, as the minutes recorded, that 'by dividing our air forces between two theatres', the pressure which could be maintained on the Germans 'would be on a reduced scale in both, and the advance of our land forces would be proportionately slower'. [2]

At the Staff Conference that evening, Churchill reminded the Chiefs of Staff Committee that when future operations in the Mediterranean had been discussed at Cairo and Teheran, 'it had been the President who had suggested the possibility of our striking North-East from the head of the Adriatic'. At the same time, Eisenhower had 'stressed the importance of continuing the maximum possible operations in an established theatre', since much time was 'invariably lost when the scene of action is changed, necessitating as it does, the arduous task of building up at a fresh place'.

Churchill pointed out that Alexander had recently reported 'that

[1] President to Prime Minister, No. 579, 'Personal and Top Secret', 29 June 1944: Churchill papers, 20/167.
[2] Chiefs of Staff Committee No. 216 (Operations) of 1944, 11 a.m., 30 June 1944: Cabinet papers, 79/76.

American troops, some of them who were actually in contact with the enemy, were already being withdrawn in preparation for "Anvil", and that the present uncertainty regarding future operations in the Mediterranean was causing his army to "look over their shoulder" '.

There was a 'danger', Churchill warned, 'that by undertaking two operations in the Mediterranean theatre, both would be doomed to failure. General Alexander would be forced on to the defensive, whilst the "Anvil" force struggled slowly forward up the Rhone Valley, an area which abounded in defensive positions.' [1]

At ten that evening the Chiefs of Staff met Churchill for a final discussion on how to proceed. Churchill told them that he had ordered the Clipper and the York to stand by, 'so we may be flying off to Washington before we are very much older'. Brooke noted in his diary, 'but I doubt it. Winston will realize there is nothing more to be gained by argument.'

'We left Winston with "Pug",' Brooke noted, 'drafting a telegram which we are to see tomorrow morning and discuss with him at 11 a.m.' [2]

Churchill's telegram to Roosevelt was discussed by the Chiefs of Staff on the following day. 'We are deeply grieved by your telegram,' it began, and continued with a solemn protest against the South of France landings and abandonment of a major Italian offensive. The splitting up of the Italian campaign into two operations, 'neither of which can do anything decisive', was, Churchill added, 'in my humble and respectful opinion, the first major strategic and political error for which we two have to be responsible'. At Teheran, Churchill pointed out, 'you emphasized to me the possibilities of a move eastward when Italy was conquered, and mentioned particularly Istria. No one involved in these discussions has ever thought of moving armies into the Balkans; but Istria and Trieste in Italy are strategic and political positions, which as you saw yourself very clearly might exercise profound and widespread reactions, especially now after the Russian advances.'

After Teheran, Churchill added, 'I was made doubtful about "Anvil" by General Eisenhower's dislike of it.' Eisenhower had then argued, and Churchill quoted from one of the records of the meeting, that it was of 'vital importance' to continue 'the maximum possible operations in an established theatre, since much time was invariably lost when the scene of action was changed, necessitating, as it did, the

---

[1] Staff Conference, Chiefs of Staff Committee No. 217 (Operations) of 1944, 10 p.m., 30 June 1944: Cabinet papers, 79/77.

[2] Brooke diary, 30 June 1944: Bryant, *op. cit.*, volume 2, pages 225–6.

arduous task of building up a fresh base'. Those had been Eisenhower's words. Montgomery too, Churchill reminded Roosevelt, had explained at Marrakesh 'that it would take ninety days for a force landed at "Anvil" to influence the "Overlord" operation'. Both these opinions, Churchill added, 'expressed so decidedly' as they had been, 'make me less confident about an "Anvil" operation', and he went on to tell Roosevelt:

I doubt whether you will find that three American divisions, supported by seven French 80 percent native divisions from Morocco, Algeria and Tunis, will have any important strategic effect on the tremendous battle Eisenhower and Montgomery are fighting 500 miles away to the North. It seems more likely to prove a cul-de-sac into which increasing numbers of United States troops will be drawn, and I fear that further demands will be made even upon what is left to us in Italy. It would no doubt make sure of de Gaulle having his talons pretty deeply dug into France.

I should not be frank if I did not assure you that I fear a costly stalemate for you unless far more American divisions, at the expense of Eisenhower, are thrust into 'Anvil' to make it good at all costs by the great power of the United States.

The American decision to proceed with the landings in the South of France meant that 'little account' was to be taken of Alexander's operations in Italy. Churchill pointed out that Alexander had already warned him, in a telegram on June 28, of the effect on troop morale of the news and dispositions for 'Anvil'. The Americans had already ordered back two units 'which are actually in contact with the enemy', and, as Alexander warned, 'the ghost of "Anvil" hangs heavily over the battle-front'. The 'air effort' was also about to be curtailed, and the French troops no longer appeared to be 'putting their hearts' into the fighting, but 'have their eyes turned in another direction'.

Churchill then deprecated Roosevelt's suggestion 'that we should lay our respective cases before Stalin', pointing out that Stalin, on a 'long-term political view', might prefer that the British and Americans 'should do their share in France in this very hard fighting that is to come, and that East, Middle and Southern Europe should fall naturally into his control'.

Churchill's telegram of July 1 ended:

What can I do Mr President, when your Chiefs of Staff insist on casting aside our Italian offensive campaign, with all its dazzling possibilities, relieving Hitler of all his anxieties in the Po basin (vide Boniface), and when we are to see the integral life of this campaign drained off into the Rhone Valley in the belief that it will in several months carry effective help to Eisenhower so far away in the North?

If you still press upon us the directive of your Chiefs of Staff to withdraw so many of your forces from the Italian campaign and leave all our hopes there dashed to the ground, His Majesty's Government, on the advice of their Chiefs of Staff, must enter a solemn protest. I need scarcely say that we shall do our best to make a success of anything that is undertaken. We shall therefore forward your directive to General·Wilson as soon as you let us know that there is no hope of reconsideration by your Chiefs of Staff or by yourself. Our Chiefs of Staff are letting yours know the corrections on points of detail which they think necessary in the previous draft.

It is with the greatest sorrow that I write to you in this sense. But I am sure that if we could have met, as I so frequently proposed, we should have reached a happy agreement. I send you every personal good wish. However we may differ on the conduct of the war, my personal gratitude to you for your kindness to me and for all you have done for the cause of freedom will never be diminished.[1]

'I have done my very best in your affairs,' Churchill telegraphed that same day to Alexander.[2] But neither Churchill's arguments nor the Chiefs of Staff's unanimity were of avail. Roosevelt and the American Combined Chiefs of Staff insisted upon the landing in the South of France.

'We are still convinced,' Roosevelt replied to Churchill on July 2, 'that the right course of action is to launch "Anvil" at the earliest possible date.' As to Italy, 'even if we clear the Po valley we gain very little in the destruction of Germans as they can retreat even further north'. As to Istria, the country there, Roosevelt wrote, 'has bad combat terrain in the winter time—worse than southern France', and he added: 'Therefore I am compelled by the logic of not dispersing our main efforts to a new theatre to agree with my Chiefs of Staff. . . .' Roosevelt ended his telegram: 'I honestly believe that God will be with us as he has in "Overlord" and in Italy and in North Africa. I always think of my early geometry "A straight line is the shortest distance between two points".'[3]

Roosevelt again made no reference to the decrypt of June 28, which had so influenced British strategic thinking. The argument was at an end. On July 2, Maitland Wilson was ordered to prepare to attack the South of France on August 15. 'Anvil', given the codename 'Dragoon' to maintain security, was now the prime task of the Allied forces in the Mediterranean.

[1] Prime Minister's Personal Telegram, T.1392/4, Prime Minister to President, No. 721, 'Personal and Top Secret', 1 July 1944: Churchill papers, 20/167.

[2] Prime Minister's Personal Telegram, T.1397/4, 'Personal and Top Secret', 'To be sent through "C",' 1 July 1944: Churchill papers, 20/167.

[3] President to Prime Minister, No. 577, 'Personal and Top Secret', 2 July 1944: Churchill papers, 20/167.

Churchill, his Chiefs of Staff, and his military commanders in the Mediterranean, had lost their favoured strategy, and were now to watch in growing frustration, and mounting anger, as the Army in Italy, deprived of its full fighting strength, was cheated of its opportunity both to destroy the substantial German forces that were to have been sent against it, and to break through to the Po valley, and beyond, even to Austria. 'It seems to me', Churchill minuted to Ismay for the Chiefs of Staff Committee on July 2, on re-reading the United States Chiefs of Staff directive to Maitland Wilson, that the insertion of the words 'at least' in the ten division build-up of troops which Wilson was asked to prepare for in the South of France, as well as the 'super-priority given to "Anvil", will completely ruin any plans Alexander can make', and Churchill went on to ask: 'Can we not now fight to get him at any rate a fixed force?'[1]

---

[1] Prime Minister's Personal Minute, D.211/4, 2 July 1944: Churchill papers, 20/153.

45
'Heavy burdens'

O N 23 June 1944, while the discussion of strategy in the West was at its most intense, the main Soviet summer offensive was launched in the central sector of the Eastern Front, between Vitebsk and Gomel, thus fulfilling in its entirety the Anglo-American-Soviet agreement reached by the 'Bodyguard' negotiators in Moscow in February. Within a week, Soviet forces had liberated Minsk, the principal city of White Russia. 'On July 17 alone,' Churchill later recalled, '57,000 German prisoners were marched through Moscow—who knows whither?' [1]

Russia's central front offensive, so essential a part of the Anglo-American strategic plan in France, served nevertheless to emphasize yet again the imminent political problems which would come with liberation and control.

On June 22 Roosevelt telegraphed to Churchill, his telegram both inspired and drafted by Cordell Hull, to protest against Churchill's earlier message, on May 31, that 'the Soviet Government would take the lead in Roumanian and the British in Greek affairs'. [2] 'I am a bit worried,' Roosevelt's telegram read, 'and so is the State Department,' and he added:

I think I should tell you frankly that we were disturbed that your people took this matter up with us only after it had been put up to the Russians and they had inquired whether we were agreeable. Your Foreign Office apparently sensed this and has now explained that the proposal 'arose out of a chance remark' which was converted by the Soviet Government into a formal proposal. However, I hope matters of this importance can be prevented from developing in such a manner in the future. [3]

---

[1] Winston S. Churchill, *The Second World War*, volume 6, London 1954, page 72.
[2] Prime Minister's Personal Telegram, T.1161/4, Prime Minister to President, No. 687, 'Personal and Top Secret', 31 May 1944: Churchill papers, 20/165.
[3] President to Prime Minister, No. 565, 'Personal and Top Secret', 22 June 1944: Churchill papers, 20/167.

Replying on June 23, Churchill defended his support for the Soviet initiative in Roumania and the British initiative in Greece, telegraphing to Roosevelt, on the day on which the Red Army's main offensive had begun:

The Russians are the only Power that can do anything in Roumania, and I thought it was agreed between you and me that on the basis of their reasonable armistice terms, excepting indemnities, they should try to give coherent direction to what happened there. In point of fact we have all three co-operated closely in handling in Cairo the recent Roumanian peace-feelers.

On the other hand, the Greek burden rests almost entirely upon us, and has done so since we lost 40,000 men in a vain endeavour to help them in 1941. Similarly, you have let us play the hand in Turkey, but we have always consulted you on policy, and I think we have been agreed on the line to be followed.

It would be quite easy for me, on the general principle of slithering to the Left, which is so popular in foreign policy, to let things rip, when the King of Greece would probably be forced to abdicate and EAM would work a reign of terror in Greece, forcing the villagers and many other classes to form Security Battalions under German auspices to prevent utter anarchy.[1] The only way I can prevent this is by persuading the Russians to quit boosting EAM and ramming it forward with all their force. Therefore I proposed to the Russians a temporary working arrangement for the better conduct of the war. This was only a proposal, and had to be referred to you for your agreement.

Roosevelt's opposition to this proposal seemed to Churchill to be unjust. His telegram continued:

I cannot admit that I have done anything wrong in this matter. It would not be possible for three people in different parts of the world to work together effectively if no one of them may make any suggestion to either of the others without simultaneously keeping the third informed. A recent example of this is the message you have sent quite properly to Uncle Joe about your conversations with the Poles, of which as yet I have heard nothing from you.[2]

'I am not complaining at all of this,' Churchill added, 'because I know we are working for the general theme and purposes, and I hope you will feel that has been so in my conduct of the Greek affair.'

[1] EAM was the political and ELAS the military arm of the Greek Communist and Left Wing resistance. 'There seems to be no limit to the baseness and treachery of ELAS,' Churchill had minuted to Eden on 6 February 1944, 'and we ought not to touch them with a barge pole ' (Prime Minister's Personal Minute, M.75/4, 6 February 1944: Churchill papers, 20/152). 'Obviously giving them weapons will not increase their efforts against the Germans,' Churchill minuted to the Chiefs of Staff eight days later, 'but only secure the domination of these base and treacherous people after the war.' (Prime Minister's Personal Minute, D.45/4, 'Most Secret', 14 February 1944: Churchill papers, 20/152.) The strongly anti-Communist resistance group, EDES, was led by General Zervas.

[2] Six days earlier, on June 17, Roosevelt had informed Stalin in detail of his own and his officials' discussions with Mikolajczyk, which had taken place in Washington between June 5 and June 14. As a result of this reference in Churchill's telegram, Roosevelt sent Churchill, on

It was not only in Greece, but also in Yugoslavia, that Britain had taken an independent initiative. As Churchill explained to Roosevelt:

I have also taken action to try to bring together a union of the Tito forces with those in Serbia, and with all adhering to the Royal Yugoslav Government, which we have both recognised. You have been informed at every stage of how we are bearing this heavy burden, which at present rests mainly on us. Here again nothing would be easier than to throw the King and the Royal Yugoslav Government to the wolves and let a civil war break out in Yugoslavia, to the joy of the Germans. I am struggling to bring order out of chaos in both cases and concentrate all efforts against the common foe. I am keeping you constantly informed, and I hope to have your confidence and help within the sphere of action in which initiative is assigned to us.

These were strong words, indicating Churchill's anger at Roosevelt's translation of what Churchill saw as essential 'spheres of action' into what Roosevelt regarded as malignant 'spheres of influence'. After some words of congratulation for the 'brilliant fighting' of the American troops in the Cherbourg Peninsula as well as in Italy, Churchill ended: 'We have immense tasks before us. Indeed I cannot think of any moment when the burden of the war has laid more heavily upon me or when I have felt so unequal to its ever-more entangled problems.' [1]

The Far East was also proving fertile ground for a breach with the Americans. On June 24 the Chiefs of Staff discussed future operations in that theatre. Churchill, who still sought a major British offensive against Malaya and the liberation of British territory conquered by Japan, was distressed, as he minuted to Ismay, that in the American strategic plan Mountbatten and the South-East Asia Command 'are either cut out altogether or subordinated to General MacArthur'. Churchill added:

The political importance of our making some effort to recover British territory must not be underrated. Rangoon and Singapore are great names in the British eastern world, and it will be an ill day for Britain if the war ends without our having made a stroke to regain these places and having let the whole Malay Peninsula alone until it is eventually evacuated as the result of an American-dictated peace at Tokyo, even though there is a very small British force in the American Armies. [2]

June 26, a copy of his message to Stalin. Mikolajczyk's 'first immediate concern', Roosevelt had told Stalin, 'is the vital necessity for setting up the fullest kind of collaboration between the forces of the Polish underground and the Red Army in the common struggle against our enemy'.

[1] Prime Minister's Personal Telegram, T.1342/4, Prime Minister to President, No. 712, 'Personal and Top Secret', 23 June 1944: Churchill papers, 20/167.

[2] Prime Minister's Personal Minute, D.203/4, 'Top Secret', 24 June 1944: Churchill papers, 20/152.

Churchill dictated this minute while he was at Chequers on June 24. That night a flying bomb—they were being nick-named 'bumble-bombs' and 'doodle bugs'—fell in a field four miles away. It made, John Martin noted, 'a surprisingly loud noise', and on the following day he and Clementine Churchill went to see the crater. 'We trespassed into a farm,' he wrote, 'and were turned back by a fierce woman. . . .'[1] During the weekend Churchill telegraphed to Stalin, congratulating the Soviet leader on 'the opening results of your immense operations'. The western Allies would not cease, he added, 'by every human means', to broaden those of their fronts that were in action, 'and to have the fighting kept at the utmost intensity'.

Churchill then gave Stalin an account of the battle in Normandy. 'We have had three or four days of gale,' he wrote, 'most unusual in June, which has delayed the build-up and done much injury to our synthetic harbours in their incomplete condition.' Churchill added: 'We have provided the means to repair and strengthen them. The roads leading inland from the two synthetic harbours are being made with great speed by bulldozers and steel networks unrolled.' Thus, with Cherbourg, a 'large base' would be established 'from which very considerable armies can be operated irrespective of weather'. Churchill's account continued: 'We have had bitter fighting on the British front, where four out of the five Panzer divisions are engaged. The new British onslaught there has been delayed a few days by the bad weather, which delayed the completion of several divisions. The attack will begin tomorrow.'

Turning to German claims about the effects of the flying bombs, Churchill told Stalin:

You may safely disregard all the German rubbish about the results of their flying bomb. It has had no appreciable effect upon the production or life of London. Casualties during the seven days it has been used are between ten and eleven thousand. The street and parks remain full of people enjoying the sunshine when off work or duty. Parliament debates continually throughout the alarms. The rocket development may be more formidable when it comes. The people are proud to share in a small way the perils of our own soldiers and of your soldiers, who are so highly admired in Britain.[2]

'I shall send you a telegram presently,' Churchill told Stalin, 'about the various strategic possibilities which are open in this quarter,' and he added: 'The over-riding principle which, in my opinion, we should follow, is the continuous engagement of the largest possible number of

---

[1] Letter of 25 June 1944: Martin papers. The missiles were also called 'buzz-bombs'.
[2] Prime Minister's Personal Telegram, T.1357/4, 'Personal and Top Secret', 25 June 1944: Churchill papers, 20/167.

Hitlerites on the broadest and most effective fronts. It is only by hard fighting we can take some of the weight off you.'[1]

On June 24 Churchill returned to London from Chequers. The flying bombs were now a daily and a nightly hazard. That night, Elizabeth Layton was the secretary on duty at the Annexe. 'I sat by Pappa for several hours while he worked and occasionally dictated,' she wrote home. 'There was dead silence in the room except for an occasional rustle. I sat absolutely still and just thought. Then far in the distance I would hear the familiar rattling roar, then slowly it would get louder till it seemed right overhead. Then sometimes it would cut out. Pappa would never move a muscle, just go calmly on reading, and I would merely sit (with one eye on him). Then CRASH.' Elizabeth Layton watched Churchill's reaction. '*Complete* boredom prevailed. Once he looked up and said, "Does this make you nervous?" after a particularly loud one, and I could assure him with absolute truth that it didn't.'[2]

The flying bombs continued to bring civilian death on a scale unknown since the Blitz, with 1,935 civilians killed, and nearly 6,000 injured, in the first sixteen days of bombardment. 'This new form of attack imposed upon the people of London,' Churchill later recalled, 'a burden perhaps even heavier than the air raids of 1940 and 1941. Suspense and strain were more prolonged. Dawn brought no relief, and cloud no comfort. The man going home in the evening never knew what he would find; his wife, alone all day or with the children, could not be certain of his safe return. The blind, impersonal nature of the missile made the individual on the ground feel helpless. There was little that he could do, no human enemy that he could see shot down.'[3]

On June 30 Churchill and his wife spent the day visiting defences against the flying bombs. 'It really was rather fun,' noted Elizabeth Layton, 'Master and Mistress sitting amid the corn, cameras snapping on every side, rather anxious Generals rushing about, "Is there anything on the cards?" and there wasn't!'[4] Later that afternoon,

[1] Prime Minister's Personal Telegram, T.1357/4, 'Personal and Top Secret', 25 June 1944: Churchill papers, 20/167.

[2] Elizabeth Layton, letter of 25 June 1944: Nel papers. Churchill's concern for his personal secretaries was expressed in many ways. 'He would never let us carry things,' Kathleen Hill later recalled, 'or run up and down stairs quickly. He was afraid we would get a heart attack.' (Kathleen Hill recollections: conversation with the author, 15 October 1982.)

[3] Winston S. Churchill, *The Second World War*, volume 6, London 1954, page 35.

[4] Elizabeth Layton, letter of 1 July 1944: Nel papers.

Churchill and his wife visited a second anti-aircraft site, at Marlpit, just below Chartwell, where Mary Churchill was stationed. Here the guns engaged one bomb but did not shoot it down. Two other bombs flew over but the guns did not fire because fighters were in action. Neither of the bombs were shot down. Churchill then went to Chartwell, his first visit there that year. It was, Elizabeth Layton noted, 'shut up and rather desolate'.[1] Churchill stayed there for an hour before returning to London.[2]

That night, less than a mile from Chartwell, twenty-four babies and eight staff at a children's home were killed by shell fragments fired from an anti-aircraft battery at a flying bomb.[3]

On June 26 Churchill learned, from the Joint Intelligence Committee, of the continuing success of the main 'Bodyguard' deception plan. Almost three weeks after the Normandy landings it was clear, the Committee reported, 'from our Intelligence and from the German dispositions as a whole', that the Germans still expected 'a large scale landing between the Pas de Calais and the Seine'. For this reason, the Report continued, 'he is reluctant materially to reduce his army strength protecting this part of the Channel coast in order to reinforce Normandy, realising that any rapid movement of formations back across the Seine is no longer likely to be possible'.

German fears of 'large scale' landings on the Mediterranean coast remained 'very much alive'. German fears of Allied amphibious operations against south and south-west Norway 'remain but are decreasing'.[4]

In the east, the new Soviet offensive was continuing its swift advances: 'we shall not give the Germans a breathing space', Stalin telegraphed to Churchill on June 27.[5] On June 28 the Red Army entered Bobruisk, killing 16,000 German soldiers and taking 18,000 prisoner. 'This is the moment,' Churchill telegraphed to Stalin three days later, 'for me to tell you how immensely we are all here impressed

---

[1] Elizabeth Layton, letter of 1 July 1944: Nel papers.

[2] Private Office diary, 20 June 1944.

[3] Prime Minister's Personal Minute, M.777/4, 1 July 1944: Churchill papers, 20/153. Five of the babies were only one month old. The oldest was eleven months. All were at the London County Council Residential School at Weald House. There is a communal grave at Edenbridge. The inscription on the memorial stone reads: 'In Memory of the Nurses, Staff and Children of the LCC Residential School at Weald House, Crockham Hill, killed by enemy action on June 30, 1944.'

[4] Joint Intelligence Committee Paper No. 276 (O) (Final) of 1944, 'Top Secret', 'German Appreciation of Allied Intentions in the West', 26 June 1944: Cabinet papers, 79/76.

[5] 'Personal and Secret', 27 June 1944: Churchill papers, 20/167.

with the magnificent advances of the Russian Armies which seem, as they grow in momentum, to be pulverizing the German Armies which stand between you and Warsaw, and afterwards Berlin. Every victory that you gain is watched with eager attention here.' Churchill added: 'I realize vividly that all this is the second round you have fought since Teheran, the first which regained Sebastopol, Odessa and the Crimea and carried your vanguards to the Carpathians, Sereth and Pruth.'

That morning the news from the eastern front was of further Russian advances. In Italy, Alexander continued to push Kesselring's forces northward. In Normandy, more than three-quarters of a million British and American troops were now ashore, and 50,000 Germans had been taken prisoner. 'The enemy is burning and bleeding on every front at once,' Churchill telegraphed to Stalin, 'and I agree with you that this must go on to the end.' [1]

At a meeting of the War Cabinet on July 3, with Churchill in the chair, Herbert Morrison set out details of the extent of the previous two weeks' flying bomb attacks. The weight of high explosives dropped on London in the last two weeks of June, he reported, was almost as heavy as that dropped in October 1940, 'the worst fortnight of the 1940–41 raids'. The total number of those killed in the last two weeks of June 1944 was 2,000. The total number seriously injured in that same two-week period was 7,403, 'compared', Morrison noted, 'with 16,456 for the whole month of September 1940'.

Morrison also pointed out to the War Cabinet that many flying bombs fell in daylight, 'when people were going about their business', that the bombs had a high blast effect, and that 'many casualties were due to broken glass'. The Minister of Aircraft Production, Sir Stafford Cripps, added that the attacks 'were having a serious effect on output'. [2]

After listening to these two alarming reports, Churchill told the War Cabinet that, 'subject to the overriding needs of the Battle of France', all Britain's available resources 'must be used' to try to counter the flying bombs. It was also 'necessary to consider', he said, whether counter measures should not be used against Germany 'in view of the deliberate use of this weapon of an indiscriminate character'. Churchill added:

[1] Prime Minister's Personal Telegram, T.1396/4, No. 1967 to Moscow, 'Personal and Top Secret', 1 July 1944: Cabinet papers, 120/858.
[2] War Cabinet No. 85 of 1944, 3 July 1944: Cabinet papers, 65/43.

It was for consideration whether we should not publish a list of, say, 100 of the smaller towns in Germany, where the defences were likely to be weak, and announce our intention of destroying them one by one by bombing attack. It would, of course, be necessary to take account of the extent to which a policy of this kind would divert our air power from the support of our Allies in France and from targets, such as oil installations, factories, depots, flying bomb sites, attacks on which directly crippled the enemy's general war effort or his power to launch flying bomb attacks. There would also have to be some consultation with the United States and Soviet Governments before such a policy was adopted.

Sir Archibald Sinclair opposed such an attack as Churchill proposed, fearing that there would be a 'grave risk' of reprisals in the form of the shooting of any British air crews who fell into German hands.[1]

At the Chiefs of Staff Committee on July 5, it was 'generally agreed', both that gas would not be an effective weapon against flying bomb installations, and that the use of gas as a reprisal, such as Churchill had suggested would, as Brooke expressed it, 'play into the enemy's hand, by diverting still more of our bomber effort away from attacks on military targets'.[2]

Portal had already given his view two days earlier, pointing out that if Britain were to obliterate a hundred of Germany's smaller towns, as Churchill had suggested, and assuming that these attacks were 'completely successful', less than two per cent of the German population would be affected. Portal added: 'We could not hope to keep pace with the Germans on a campaign of reprisals.'[3]

Meanwhile, as the flying bomb attacks went on unabated, the measures to combat them were accelerated. It was found that heavy guns could shoot them down even though the bombs flew below the height at which heavy guns were thought to be effective. To avoid shooting the bombs down over London, their target area, a gun line was established on the North Downs. To the south and east of London a balloon barrage was created which succeeded in catching in its nets more than two hundred flying bombs. British bombers also struck at the launching sites across the Channel, difficult though these were to locate and to hit, and even harder to find because of the unfavourable weather. This bad weather, Churchill told the House of Commons on July 6, had, in Normandy, 'robbed us in great part of the use of our immense superiority'.

During his speech of July 6, Churchill reported that in all, up to six

---

[1] War Cabinet No. 85 of 1944, 3 July 1944, Confidential Annex: Cabinet papers, 65/47.
[2] Chiefs of Staff Committee, No. 222 (O) of 1944, 5 July 1944: Cabinet papers, 79/77.
[3] Chiefs of Staff Committee, No. 220 (O) of 1944, 4 July 1944: Cabinet papers, 79/77.

o'clock that morning, 2,754 flying bombs had been launched, and 2,752 civilians killed. He was 'sure of one thing', he said, 'that London will never be conquered, and will never fail, and that her renown, triumphing over every ordeal, will long shine among men'.[1]

Whilst the flying bomb brought death back to London on a scale approaching the Blitz, those with access to the most secret sources of information were trying to piece together whatever they could about a potentially far more dangerous rocket weapon. On June 22 the British Air Attaché in Stockholm had reported that a German missile which had crashed in Sweden but failed to explode was not a flying bomb but a missile equipped with a turbo-compressor.[2] On June 26 a fortnightly report of the Assistant Chief of Air Staff (Intelligence) revealed that, according to the recent interrogation of German prisoners-of-war, the weight of this new weapon was between fifteen and twenty tons.[3]

Mystery surrounded this new weapon. It was not until July 7 that expert examination of the one which had fallen by accident in Sweden was to reveal that it was rocket-propelled, without wings, weighing at least five tons and possibly 'considerably more'.[4] In speaking about the flying bomb in the House of Commons on July 6, Churchill described it as 'a weapon literally and essentially indiscriminate in its nature, purpose and effect', and he continued: 'The introduction by the Germans of such a weapon obviously raises some grave questions, upon which I do not propose to trench today.'[5] That same day, in studying the note by the Air Staff opposing retaliatory raids as reprisals for the flying bombs, Churchill sent Ismay a minute for the Chiefs of Staff Committee, asking, in the first of seven numbered paragraphs, '1. I want you to think very seriously over this question of poison gas.' Churchill added, in explaining the limitations on the use of poison gas as he envisaged them: 'I would not use it unless it could be shown either that (a) it was life or death for us, or (b) that it would shorten the war by a year.' Churchill's minute continued:

2. It is absurd to consider morality on this topic when everybody used it in the last war without a word of complaint from the moralists or the Church. On the other hand, in the last war the bombing of open cities was regarded

[1] *Hansard*, 6 July 1944, columns 1322–32.
[2] Air Attaché, Stockholm, telegram A.370 of 22 June 1944: F. H. Hinsley and others, *British Intelligence in the Second World War*, volume 3, part 1, London 1984, page 445.
[3] Chiefs of Staff Paper No. 573 (Operations) of 1944, 26 June 1944: Cabinet papers, 121/213.
[4] Air Attaché, Stockholm, telegram Z.391 of 7 July 1944: F. H. Hinsley and others, *British Intelligence in the Second World War*, volume 3, part 1, London 1984, page 445.
[5] *Hansard*, 6 July 1944, columns 1322–39.

as forbidden. Now everybody does it as a matter of course. It is simply a question of fashion changing as she does between long and short skirts for women.

3. I want a cold-blooded calculation made as to how it would pay us to use poison gas by which I mean principally mustard. We will want to gain more ground in Normandy so as not to be cooped up in a small area. We could probably deliver 20 tons to their 1, and for the sake of the 1 they would bring their bomber aircraft into the area against our superiority, thus paying a heavy toll.

4. Why have the Germans not used it? Not certainly out of moral scruples or affection for us. They have not used it because it does not pay them. The greatest temptation ever offered to them was the beaches of Normandy. This they could have drenched with gas greatly to the hindrance of our troops. That they thought about it is certain and that they prepared against our use of gas is also certain. But the only reason they have not used it against us is that they fear the retaliation. What is to their detriment is to our advantage.

5. Although one sees how unpleasant it is to receive poison gas attacks, from which nearly everyone recovers, it is useless to protest that an equal amount of High Explosives will not inflict greater cruelties and suffering on troops or civilians. One really must not be bound within silly conventions of the mind whether they be those that ruled in the last war or those in reverse which rule in this.

Churchill then turned to the rocket danger which now seemed imminent, informing the Chiefs of Staff Committee:

6. If the bombardment of London really became a serious nuisance and great rockets with far-reaching and devastating effect fell on many centres of Government and labour, I should be prepared to do anything that would hit the enemy in a murderous place. I may certainly have to ask you to support me in using poison gas. We could drench the cities of the Ruhr and many other cities in Germany in such a way that most of the population would be requiring constant medical attention. We could stop all work at the flying bomb starting points. I do not see why we should always have all the disadvantages of being the gentlemen while they have all the advantages of being the cad. There are times when this may be so but not now.

7. I quite agree it may be several weeks or even months before I shall ask you to drench Germany with poison gas, and if we do it, let us do it 100 per cent. In the meanwhile, I want the matter studied in cold blood by sensible people and not by that particular set of psalm-singing uniformed defeatists which one runs across now here now there. Pray address yourself to this. It is a big thing and can only be discarded for a big reason. I shall of course have to square Uncle Joe and the President; but you need not bring this into your calculations at the present time. Just try to find out what it is like on its merits.[1]

[1] Prime Minister's Personal Minute, D.217/4, 6 July 1944: Cabinet papers, 120/775.

On July 8 the Chiefs of Staff Committee, at its morning meeting with Brooke presiding, discussed what the minutes described as Churchill's request 'that a comprehensive examination be made of the question of employing gas against Germany'. Portal, the only member of the Chiefs of Staff to speak on this issue, said that he was 'not convinced' that the use of gas would produce the results suggested in Churchill's minute. 'It was very difficult', Portal told the meeting, 'to achieve a heavy concentration of gas over a large area', nor did he believe that the use of gas against launching sites 'would stop flying bomb attacks'.

The Air Staff had always been of the opinion, Portal added, that 'to achieve the best effect', gas should be used in continuation with 'high explosive'. Existing preparations allowed for approximately one-fifth of Britain's bomber effort 'to be employed on dropping gas if it was decided to use this form of warfare'.

In their conclusion, the Chiefs of Staff asked the Vice Chiefs to carry out not only Churchill's request for an enquiry into the possible use of poison gas, but also to include in their examination 'considera-tion of the possibilities of biological warfare'.[1] In a minute to Churchill after the meeting however, General Hollis made no reference to the biological aspect of the Chiefs of Staff Committee instruction, but only to Churchill's original request about poison gas. Hollis's minute read: 'Prime Minister, Reference your minute at flag "A" (D.217/4) about the use of gas, the Chiefs of Staff this morning directed the Vice-Chiefs of Staff to go into this matter with the greatest care and thoroughness, bringing into consultation all interested authorities. A report will be submitted to you as soon as possible.'[2]

Churchill's suggestion that he might one day ask the Chiefs of Staff to 'drench' the cities of the Ruhr, and other cities, with poison gas had been written on a day when the flying bomb peril, and the danger of rockets of unknown speed and power, was much on his mind, but when the Chiefs of Staff Committee had dismissed retaliatory attacks as ineffective. It was nearly four years since Churchill had seen the intensity of Germany's air bombardment of Britain's cities, of which Morrison had reminded the War Cabinet on July 3. The flying bomb, and the rocket weapon that was known to be in preparation, repre-sented a new, and possibly more intense and prolonged threat to British lives.

At the time of his 'poison gas' minute of July 6, Churchill was also distressed at the previous week's decision, insisted upon by Roosevelt, and the United States Chiefs of Staff, to withdraw troops from Italy

---

[1] Chiefs of Staff, 227th Meeting (Operations), 8 July 1944: Cabinet papers, 79/77.
[2] Chiefs of Staff Secretariat, Minute 1140/4, 8 July 1944: Cabinet papers, 120/775.

for the South of France. On the morning of Thursday July 6, in the minute immediately preceding his request for an enquiry into the possible use of poison gas, Churchill had also minuted to Ismay, for the Chiefs of Staff Committee, about the new situation in Italy as a result of the American decision:

The one thing to fight for now is a clean cut so that Alexander knows what he has and we know what we have a right to give him. Let them take their seven divisions—three American and four French. Let them monopolise all the landing craft they can reach. But let us at least have a chance to launch a decisive strategic stroke with what is entirely British and under British command.

I am not going to give way about this for anybody. Alexander is to have his campaign. If the Americans try to withdraw the two divisions still left with him, I shall ask you to send the 52nd division from the United Kingdom to bridge the gap. I hope you realise that an intense impression must be made upon the Americans that we have been ill-treated and are furious. Do not let any smoothings or smirchings cover up this fact. After a little, we shall get together again; but if we take everything lying down, there will be no end to what will be put upon us.

'The Arnold–King–Marshall combination,' Churchill added, 'is one of the stupidest strategic teams ever seen. They are good fellows and there is no need to tell them this.' [1]

At a Staff Conference on the evening of July 6, Churchill asked, as the minutes recorded, that steps should be taken 'to protect General Alexander from having his forces progressively drained away to supply the needs of "Anvil"'. Neither Brooke, Eden nor Cunningham referred to this in their diaries. Churchill's suggestion at the meeting was that he should tell Roosevelt that, 'while we wished good fortune to "Anvil", which was his operation, and we would loyally support the decisions which had been reached, we must ask to be allowed to retain intact the remaining resources available for the war in Italy'.

Churchill told the Staff Conference of July 6 that he believed Alexander might reach Bologna by the middle of August, and capture Trieste by the middle of September. 'Everything possible,' he said, 'should be done to support General Alexander at this juncture,' and he proposed the transfer to Italy of the 'good Indian division' stationed in Persia. Brooke opposed this, telling the Staff Conference, as the minutes recorded:

. . . that he thought the Prime Minister had underestimated the military task that confronted us in Persia. The maintenance of law and order in that country presented a more difficult problem that had been suggested. It was not the Persian Government, or the Persian Army, that involved us in this

[1] Prime Minister's Personal Minute, D.218/4, 6 July 1944: Churchill papers, 20/153.

commitment, but the Kurdish and other tribes, who were themselves frequently in revolt against the Persian Government. He could not advise the removal of a division now stationed in Persia to assist General Alexander. We could not replace such a division from India, since there was urgent need to relieve the forces that had been engaged in fighting so long and so hard in Burma.

The minutes of the Staff Conference also recorded Brooke's remark, that while he 'recognized the importance of preventing "Anvil" from draining away General Alexander's resources in Italy, he questioned the wisdom of demanding an undertaking from the Americans that the forces in Italy should be maintained at a particular level before it became clear that they intended to drain away Alexander's resources. We did not want to put predatory ideas into their heads.' [1]

The Staff Conference of July 6 had been held in the underground Cabinet War Room because of the dangers of flying bombs. As well as the three Chiefs of Staff, three Ministers, Attlee, Eden and Lyttelton were also present: 'a deplorable evening', Eden noted in his diary. [2] 'There is no doubt the PM was in no state to discuss anything,' was Admiral Cunningham's diary comment, and he added: 'Very tired and too much alcohol.' [3] The meeting had begun, according to Brooke's diary, with Churchill, tired as a result of his flying bomb speech, abusing Montgomery, 'because operations were not going faster', and because 'apparently Eisenhower had said that he was over-cautious'.

'I flared up,' Brooke's account continued, 'and asked him if he could not trust his generals for five minutes instead of belittling them. He said that he never did such a thing. I then reminded him that in front of a large gathering of Ministers, he had torn Alexander to pieces for lack of imagination and leadership in continually attacking at Cassino. He was furious with me, but I hope it may do some good in the future.'

As well as the discussion about Alexander, Churchill had brought up various proposals, including the raising of a 'Home Guard' in Egypt as a force to deal with disturbances in the Middle East. It was not until after midnight, Brooke noted, 'that we got on to the subject we had come to discuss—the war in the Far East'. Brooke's account continued:

---

[1] Staff Conference, Chiefs of Staffs Committee No. 225 (Operations) of 1944, 10 p.m., 6 July 1944: Cabinet papers, 79/77.
[2] Eden diary, 6 July 1944: Eden memoirs, *The Reckoning, op. cit.*, page 461.
[3] Cunningham diary, 6 July 1944: Cunningham papers.

Here we came up against all the old arguments that we have had put up by him over and over again. Attlee, Eden and Lyttelton were there. Fortunately they were at last siding with us against him. This infuriated him more than ever and he became ruder and ruder. He finished by falling out with Attlee and having a real good row with him concerning the future of India. We withdrew under cover of this smoke-screen just on 2 a.m., having accomplished nothing beyond losing our tempers and valuable sleep.[1]

Although not mentioned by Brooke, another issue discussed at the Staff Conference of July 6 was a proposal by the Chiefs of Staff to form a British naval force in Australia to operate on the left flank of MacArthur's advance in the south-west Pacific. Churchill, and also Eden, still preferred operation 'Culverin', the landing in northern Sumatra, with a view to being able to move from there to the re-conquest of Malaya.

As Churchill told the meeting:

The British contribution to the recapture of our Empire in the Far East was minute. The shame of our disaster at Singapore could, in his opinion, only be wiped out by our recapture of that fortress. He still favoured an operation in November of this year for the capture of the island of Simalur, to the followed by the capture of the tip of Sumatra. We would then obtain air domination of Singapore and Malaya.

When that stage had been reached, Churchill added, 'he did not believe that the Japanese, with the Americans on their flank in the Philippines, would be able to prevent our assaulting and capturing Singapore'. He was not convinced by the argument that the necessary land forces 'could not be made available'. There were 'enormous forces in the Indian Army on our payroll', he said, 'and it would be a scandal not to make use of these forces. We should find ourselves in a most humiliating position in the Far East, if the Americans could turn round and claim that they alone had defeated Japan.'

Brooke, Cunningham and Portal were emphatic however that Britain did not have the land forces available for such an operation until some time after the end of the war against Germany.[2] That evening Eden noted in his diary that Churchill had 'kept muttering that resources were available and ended up by accusing us all of trying to corner the Prime Minister or take it out on him. . . .'[3]

With the Staff Conference over, and his hopes for both Italy and

[1] Brooke diary, 6 July 1944: Bryant, *op. cit.*, volume 2, pages 229–30.
[2] Staff Conference, Chiefs of Staff Committee No. 225 (Operations) of 1944, 10 p.m., 6 July 1944: Cabinet papers, 79/77.
[3] Eden diary, 6 July 1944: Eden memoirs, *The Reckoning, op. cit.*, page 461.

the Far East frustrated, Churchill returned to the Annexe for his nightly dictation session. 'PM in mellow mood,' Marian Holmes noted, 'and quite chatty for him. Loads of work and got to bed finally at 3.40 a.m.' [1]

At the War Cabinet on the following day, July 7, held once more in the underground Cabinet War Room because of the danger of flying bombs, Alexander, who had just arrived in London, gave an account of the winter campaign in Italy. When he had done so, Churchill expressed the War Cabinet's 'highest admiration' for Alexander's achievements, and the 'fullest confidence that he would achieve still further success'. [2] As Alexander left, the discussion turned to the nature of the World Organization to be set up after the war. Churchill, as Cadogan noted, 'announced he had to lunch with a "Royal Person" and would have to leave at 12.30, so he took various other items and then left us to "the Peace of the World about which, in present circumstances, I am rather lukewarm" '. This, Cadogan added, was 'hopeless and very naughty'. If Churchill was going to 'evade the issue and snipe', Cadogan noted, the British Delegation to Washington to discuss the World Organization would be 'very uncomfortable'. [3]

Churchill's luncheon was with the Duchess of Kent, at her home in Buckinghamshire. From there, he went on to Chequers for the weekend. While he was at Chequers, Soviet forces entered Vilna, and Allied forces entered Caen.

It was also on July 7 that Churchill learned of the full extent of the mass murder of the Jews at Auschwitz, where Jews were being gassed at a rate of about 12,000 a day. The Jewish Agency for Palestine of which Dr Weizmann was the head, had therefore appealed to the Allies for the bombing of the railway line leading from Budapest to Auschwitz, along which, at that very moment, they had information that hundreds of thousands of Hungarian Jews were being deported to their deaths. 'Get anything out of the Air Force you can,' Churchill minuted at once to Eden, 'and invoke me if necessary.' [4] Eden immediately passed the bombing request to Sinclair, who replied after making

[1] Marian Holmes diary, 6 July 1944: Marian Walker Spicer papers.

[2] War Cabinet No. 88 of 1944, 7 July 1944: Cabinet papers, 65/43.

[3] Cadogan diary, 7 July 1944: David Dilks (editor), op. cit., pages 645–6.

[4] Prime Minister's Personal Minute, M.800/4, 7 July 1944: Premier papers, 4/51/10, folio 1364.

enquiries, that 'interrupting the railways' was 'out of our power',
while
bombing the gas chambers themselves could only be done by day,
which meant that it would have to be a United States Air Force
operation.[1] Churchill was not shown this reply, but he was told, as
indeed was true, that the deportation of Jews from Hungary to
Auschwitz had been halted in the second week of July, as a result of
world-wide public protest, including that of the Pope, the King of
Sweden, and the International Red Cross.[2] On July 11, having read
further details of the fate of the Jews deported to Auschwitz in the
past two years, and said by two recent escapees from the camp to
number 1,700,000 murdered men, women and children, most of them
gassed, some of them even burned alive, Churchill minuted to
Eden:

> There is no doubt that this is probably the greatest and most horrible
> crime ever committed in the whole history of the world, and it has been done
> by scientific machinery by nominally civilized men in the name of a great
> State and one of the leading races in Europe. It is quite clear that all con-
> cerned in this crime who may fall into our hands, including the people who
> only obeyed orders by carrying out the butcheries, should be put to death
> after their association with the murders has been proved.[3]

On his return from Chequers to London on July 10 Churchill
presided at a meeting of the War Cabinet, where, Brooke noted, he
was 'in good and affable mood'.[4] After dinner there was a meeting
with the Chiefs of Staff, who felt that Alexander could make his future,
if more limited, plans, 'in confidence that there will be no further
withdrawals from his forces'. The Chiefs of Staff also felt that, 'on the
whole, it would be better not to reopen this particular issue with the
US Chiefs of Staff'. The British Chiefs of Staff remained opposed,
however, to 'Anvil', and during the meeting Churchill expressed his
'full agreement' with their proposal 'that it should be made clear to
the United States Chiefs of Staff that we profoundly disagreed with
operation "Anvil", and that the only reason why we had given way
to their views in this matter was because we did not wish them to

---

[1] Letter of 15 July 1944: Foreign Office papers, 371/42809, WR 277, folios 147–8. The United
States War Department had already turned down the same request on June 26, and was to do
so again on several subsequent occasions.
[2] There is a detailed account of the origin of the request to bomb Auschwitz and its repercussions in Martin Gilbert, *Auschwitz and the Allies*, London 1981.
[3] Prime Minister's Personal Minute, M.844/4, 11 July 1944: Foreign Office papers, 371/42809,
WR 274.
[4] Brooke diary, 10 July 1944: Bryant, *op. cit.*, volume 2, pages 231.

think that by delaying tactics, we were trying to gain our point by the effluxion of time, as indeed we could easily have done'.

Churchill accepted the advice of the Chiefs of Staff that the Americans should not be asked to give a specific guarantee about withdrawing more forces from Italy. Were Alexander's campaign to go wrong, Brooke told the meeting, 'we could resist any attempt to withdraw forces from him on strategic grounds when the time comes'. Churchill urged the Chiefs of Staff, however, to make 'every effort' to find all possible additional forces to replace those being withdrawn from Italy, and he suggested that troops might be found from Egypt and Palestine.[1]

Following this meeting, Admiral Cunningham wrote in his diary: 'PM in very sweet and chastened mood, probably remembering last Thursday.'[2]

In Normandy, the German retention of Caen had impeded the whole thrust of the Allied advance. On July 8 the Allies launched their attack on the city, dropping more than two thousand tons of bombs on the German defences. The British infantry then advanced, but did so only with difficulty across the rubble and bomb craters which the air assault had created. By July 10 the Germans had been driven out of all but a small section of the city. 'Many congratulations on your capture of Caen,' Churchill telegraphed that night to Montgomery.[3] 'Thank you for your message,' Montgomery replied on the following evening. 'We wanted Caen badly. We used a great weight of air-power to ensure quick success, and the whole battle area leading up to Caen is a scene of great destruction. The town itself also suffered heavily. All today the 9th and 10th Panzer Divisions have been attacking furiously . . .'[4]

On July 11, Churchill sent Stalin an account of the Normandy battle:

We have about a million and fifty thousand men in Normandy, with a vast mass of equipment, and rising by 25,000 a day. The fighting is very hard, and before the recent battles, for which casualties have not yet come in, we and the Americans had lost 64,000 men. However, there is every evidence that the enemy has lost at least as many, and we have besides

[1] Staff Conference, Chiefs of Staff Committee No. 229 (Operations) of 1944, 10 July 1944: Cabinet papers, 79/77.

[2] Cunningham diary, 10 July 1944: Cunningham papers.

[3] Prime Minister's Personal Telegram, T.1424/4, 'Personal and Secret', 9.30 p.m., 10 July 1944: Churchill papers, 20/168.

[4] M47, 'Most Immediate', received 9.15 p.m., 11 July 1944: Churchill papers, 20/168.

51,000 prisoners in the bag. Considering that we have been on the offensive, and had the landing from the sea to manage, I consider that the enemy has been severely mauled. The front will continue to broaden and the fighting will be unceasing.

Churchill also told Stalin that Alexander was 'pushing very hard' in Italy, where he hoped to break into the Po Valley, and that 'the Londoners are standing up well to the bombing', which looked like becoming 'chronic'. His telegram ended: 'Once more, congratulations on Vilna.' [1]

At a meeting of the 'Crossbow' Committee on the evening of July 11, to discuss the continuing depredations of the flying bomb, it was learned that 10,000 houses had already been destroyed, 'as compared with 63,000 during the whole of the 1940/41 blitz'. If, Churchill told the Committee, 'he became convinced of the necessity for it, he was quite prepared to threaten the heaviest possible scale of gas attack on Germany if the indiscriminate attack on London was not stopped'. He was not convinced, however, 'that the present scale of attack on London justified such a serious step'.

Turning to home defence measures, the Committee was told, by Sir Frederick Pile, General Officer Commanding-in-Chief, Anti-Aircraft Command, that more than 1,500 anti-aircraft guns were now deployed against the flying bombs. He had 'the greatest confidence' in the Anti-Aircraft Command, Churchill told the Committee, and he realized 'that a very fine job had been done in such a short time in re-deploying such a large number of guns'. [2]

That night, Eden found Churchill 'in a mellow mood'. As their discussion ended at two in the morning, Churchill said to Eden: 'You and I have some heavy burdens to bear together.' [3]

---

[1] Prime Minister's Personal Telegram, T.1429/4, No. 2079 to Moscow, 'Personal and Top Secret', 11 July 1944: Churchill papers, 20/168.

[2] 'Crossbow' Committee, 5th Meeting of 1944, 10.30 p.m., 11 July 1944: Cabinet papers, 98/36.

[3] Eden diary, 11 July 1944: Eden memoirs, *The Reckoning, op. cit.*, page 467. On the following evening Marian Holmes noted: 'PM was very weary but in a sweet & mellow mood. A strange black and white cat was asleep in the other armchair. PM told me that the cat had "pounded on the window and demanded entry and the poor pussy has been sleeping ever since". The PM loves cats and he kept making sucking noises at the sleeping mog.' (Marian Holmes diary, 12 July 1944: Marian Walker Spicer papers.)

46
July 1944, Dangerous Times

ONE of the issues confronting Churchill and Eden in July was Britain's war debts to the United States. At the War Cabinet on 18 July 1944, Churchill argued 'that we could not reasonably regard our sterling indebtedness as on the same footing as ordinary commercial debts to a bank. We had no assets to set against our debt and we started at a heavy disadvantage when it was remembered that over and above the problems presented by our overseas indebtedness. Great Britain had to import and to pay for half her food supplies and most of her raw materials.' 'Unquestionably,' Churchill argued, 'by developing our export trade we should ease our obligations to the sterling area, and help in solving the post-war problem of unemployment. But a lot would have to come back in imports to feed the workers who had produced our exports.'

In the context of Britain's indebtedness to the United States, Churchill was also worried about 'the risk that (e.g. in regard to India) if we accepted the financial help of the United States we might also be parting with political authority and control'. Finance, he warned, was 'interwoven with the power and the sovereignty of the State'. He also felt 'strongly', he told his colleagues, that in any ultimate settlement of the problem of her indebtedness, Britain 'must press that the fullest weight should be given to the contribution we had made to the victory of the Allies and to the preservation of those who were fighting with us. Their survival would be very largely due to the fact that we had held the enemy at bay for a year and a half single-handed and to the assistance we had given in men, money and materials. Those considerations could not be ignored, and we should be entitled to present the other side of the account in terms of these imponderables when the question of settlement was under consideration.' [1]

Another of Churchill's concerns was the Far East, and in particular

[1] War Cabinet No. 93 of 1944, 18 July 1944: Cabinet papers, 65/43.

the danger, as he saw it, that the war there might last 'well into 1945'. The Chiefs of Staff had recommended a Pacific strategy involving the use of bases in Australia to launch an attack on the island of Amboina, between Australia and the Philippines. Such a strategy, Churchill told a Staff Conference on July 14, 'meant condemning the vast forces that were at our disposal in India to inaction, save for those that would be engaged in the swamps of Burma'. It was 'clear', Churchill added, 'that the forces that would be engaged in the Pacific would be very small. Until after the defeat of Germany the only British land contribution would be one Special Service Brigade. It was true that the proposal envisaged the use of Australian divisions, but these would be in the theatre and available in any case, and he did not believe that the offer of these Dominion forces would appear to the Americans to be a very substantial contribution.'

Churchill went on to tell the Staff Conference that the strategy recommended by the Chiefs of Staff 'assumed the defeat of Germany this year. Of course it was true that the Germans were now faced with grave difficulties and they might give up the struggle. On the other hand, such evidence as there was seemed to show that they intended to continue that struggle, and he believed that if they tried to do so, they should be able to carry on well into next year.' The Far Eastern strategy recommended by the Chiefs of Staff, Churchill continued, 'aroused no enthusiasm in him. The only advantages which it appeared to offer were that it was designed to give the Dominion forces now serving under General MacArthur a better chance of continuing to take an active part in the war, and that General MacArthur's Command would be brought under the direction of the Combined Chiefs of Staff. He was still convinced the right course was to mount an operation from Ceylon at the earliest possible date to capture the North of Sumatra, and thereafter to advance against Malaya and recapture Singapore.'

Eden supported Churchill's preference for 'Culverin', but pointed out that 'neither the necessary troops nor the necessary landing craft could be found in time'. Despite 'Culverin's' 'obvious attractions', added Attlee, 'there was no chance of it taking place within a measurable time'.[1]

On July 15 Churchill learned that 3,600 civilians had now been killed by flying bombs, and a further 10,000 seriously injured. The number of destroyed homes had risen to 13,000.[2] But at the War

---

[1] Staff Conference, Chiefs of Staff Committee No. 236 (Operations) of 1944, 14 July 1944: Cabinet papers, 79/77.

[2] 'Crossbow' Committee Paper No. 22 of 1944, 'Crossbow', 'Top Secret', 15 July 1944: Cabinet papers, 79/77.

Cabinet on the following day it was agreed, in view of the needs of the battle of France, 'that it was important that there should be the least possible interruptions of work owing to these attacks'. For this reason, at the Staff Conference later that day, it was agreed 'that the air raid warning should not be sounded on the approach of a single aircraft'.[1] Had each flying bomb's approach been heralded by a warning siren, 'the whole of London', as Ismay minuted to Churchill a year later, 'would have been in a perpetual state of warning practically throughout the 15th/16th July'.[2] Twelve days later, at 9.41 in the morning, a single flying bomb fell on Lewisham, in South London, arriving without any siren being sounded, according to the Staff Conference decision. So heavy was the death toll that, on Herbert Morrison's insistence, Churchill agreed that the sirens could be sounded even for a single bomb.[3]

On July 16 Soviet forces entered Grodno, a town which lay only a few miles east of the Curzon Line. That same day, the Red Army began its offensive in the direction of Lvov, crossing the River Bug, and reaching the Curzon Line at its southern end. During the day Churchill telegraphed twice to Roosevelt, to urge another meeting of the Big Three, whose previous meeting had been at Teheran more than six months earlier. The first telegram read:

When are we going to meet and where? That we must meet soon is certain. It would be better that U.J. came too. I am entirely in your hands. I would brave the reporters at Washington or the mosquitos of Alaska! Surely we ought now to fix a date and then begin negotiating with U.J. His Majesty's Government would wish to propose 'Eureka II' for the last ten days of August. For details see my immediately following telegram. Failing this, Casablanca, Rome or even Teheran present themselves and many other places too. But we two must meet, and if possible three. Please let me have your ideas on all this.[4]

Churchill's second telegram read:

We suggest that the first attempt should be to arrange a meeting between us three at Invergordon, where each could have his battleship as headquarters besides a suitable house on land, the King would entertain us before, after or during the meeting either at Langwell, which he could borrow from the Duke of Portland, or at Balmoral if a night journey is acceptable. The weather might well be agreeable in Scotland at that time. Secrecy, if desired, and security in

[1] Note by John Peck: Premier papers, 4/84/1, folios 158–9.
[2] Minute of 4 July 1945: Premier papers, 4/84/1, folio 166.
[3] Note by John Peck: Premier papers, 4/81/1, folios 158–9.
[4] Prime Minister's Personal Telegram, T.1449/4, Prime Minister to President, No. 732, 'Personal and Top Secret', 16 July 1944: Premier papers, 4/75/2, Part 2, folio 736.

any case can be provided. U.J. might be able to fly or could certainly come by sea in the *Royal Sovereign*, which has now become a part of his fleet. Anyhow please let me know what you think. Remember you have my standing offer and Mackenzie King's for Quebec if that is easiest for you.[1]

In reply, Roosevelt suggested September 10 or September 15 for the meeting. 'I am rather keen about the idea of Invergordon or a spot on the west coast of Scotland,' he wrote, and he added: 'I like the idea of the battleship.' The dates would also suit him as they would 'get me back in plenty of time for the Election. Although that is in the lap of the Gods.'[2]

Churchill was at Chequers throughout the weekend beginning Friday July 14. Working after dinner on the Friday, noted Marian Holmes, 'PM was amusing on the subject of a certain general. "A useless pupstick, puffing and blowing. He should be swatting flies in his wife's boudoir. I've turned the other cheek so often I ain't got no more cheeks to turn." He was in a marvellously entertaining mood. Bed early at 1.30 a.m.'[3]

For some weeks, Churchill had been under pressure from the Greek Government in Cairo to withdraw the British missions attached to the Communist EAM partisans in Greece. That Saturday, at Chequers, he had a long talk with Colonel Woodhouse, who had just returned from Greece, where he was with one of the EAM groups.[4] After Woodhouse had argued that the British missions were, as Churchill recalled, 'a valuable restraint' on the Communist forces, and also that it might be 'difficult and dangerous to get them out', Churchill agreed to let them stay; 'but I feared', he later wrote, 'that one day they would be taken as hostages and I asked for them to be reduced'.[5]

On July 15, while saying goodbye to two of his guests who were returning to London, and 'still in merry mood', Marian Holmes noted, 'he said rather mischievously, "would you like to go round the corner before you leave? Only common prudence you know." '[6] On Sunday July 16, after dinner and a film, Churchill had fallen deep into conversation with Lord Cherwell. 'It was getting very late (at least early in the morning),' Marian Holmes noted, and she added:

John Peck and Tommy T went out to get themselves a drink. Instead of

---

[1] Prime Minister's Personal Telegram, T.1450/4, Prime Minister to President, No. 779, 'Personal and Top Secret', 16 July 1944: Premier papers, 4/75/2, Part 2, folio 735.

[2] President to Prime Minister, No. 585, 'Personal and Top Secret', 17 July 1944: Churchill papers, 20/168.

[3] Marian Holmes diary, 14 July 1944: Marian Walker Spicer papers.

[4] Prime Minister's Engagement Cards, entry for Saturday, 15 July 1944. Woodhouse was accompanied by Brigadier Armstrong, former commander of the British Military Mission to Mihailovic.

[5] Winston S. Churchill, *The Second World War*, volume 6, page 97.

[6] Marian Holmes diary, 15 July 1944: Marian Walker Spicer papers.

coming back into the office they made efforts to dislodge the Prof. and get both him and the PM off to bed. They stood in the entrance Hall where the PM and Prof. couldn't see them but as the office door was wide open, I could both see and hear them. They looked so funny—Tommy so small and wearing the Prof's huge bowler hat and John so tall wearing a brass bowl, putting on an act and trying to make me laugh out loud. PM and Prof finally took the hint and went to bed. During the evening, the PM asked me to get him a whisky and soda from the drinks tray in the Great Hall. John Peck told me afterwards that while I was out of the room the PM said 'That's a damned pretty girl—lovely. Sort of girl who'd rather die than have secrets torn out of her.'[1]

Churchill left Chequers for London on the morning of Monday, having said goodbye to his two grandchildren, 'young' Winston and Celia Sandys. 'Accompanied the PM in the car,' noted Marian Holmes. 'The children were waving goodbye and yelling "Don't go, Grandpa!". The PM said "What a world to bring children into". The chauffeur touched 70 mph and the PM was dictating. Quite a balancing act with the despatch boxes and papers. The PM dictated a letter to Baby Winston and asked if I would type it on the new electric typewriter. For posterity?'[2] The new electric typewriter was the D-Day gift from Roosevelt.

In Normandy, on July 17, Field Marshal Rommel was severely wounded when his car was attacked by low-flying fighters. Lunching alone with Churchill that day, Eden found him 'in pretty good spirits', but 'my face fell when W said that when coalition broke up we should have two or three years of opposition and then come back together to clear up the mess!'[3] 'Mr Churchill used to enjoy this tease,' Eden later recalled, 'and practise it in diverse forms, whether I fell for it or not.'[4]

Randolph Churchill, having returned briefly to London to give his father an account of the partisan war, had returned to Yugoslavia in the third week of July. On approaching the airstrip in Croatia, the plane had stalled and crashed and then burst into flames. Randolph's batman, Douglas Sowman, had been among those killed. The crew of four, three passengers, and three Royal Air Force sergeants also perished.[5] Among the passengers who were killed was Air Commodore

[1] Marian Holmes diary, 16 July 1944: Marian Walker Spicer papers.

[2] Marian Holmes diary, 17 July 1944: Marian Walker Spicer papers.

[3] Eden diary, 17 July 1944: Eden memoirs, *The Reckoning, op. cit.*, page 463.

[4] Eden recollections: Eden memoirs, *The Reckoning, op. cit.*, page 463.

[5] AOC/1, Balkan Air Force to Air Ministry Whitehall, 'Top Secret', 'Most Immediate', 17 July 1944: Churchill papers, 20/168.

Carter, deputy to the commander of the Balkan Air Force. The nine survivors of the crash included the journalist Philip Jordan and the novelist Evelyn Waugh; both, 'although shaken and burned', Randolph reported to his father, 'are with me and safe. I am shaken but OK, repeat OK.'[1]

'We all thank God you are alive,' Churchill replied, and he added: 'I grieve for the death of the faithful Sowman and will convey the tidings to Mrs Sowman. . . .'[2] Randolph was, in fact, 'rather more bruised and shaken than I first thought', he informed his father on the following day.[3] But no bones were broken, and he left hospital a day later. 'Very happy to learn that Randolph has come through all right,' Roosevelt telegraphed to Churchill ten days later, and there were also messages of relief at Randolph's good fortune from King Peter of Yugoslavia, from the Ban of Croatia, and from Dr Weizmann.[4]

'It seems remarkable,' Bill Deakin wrote to Churchill from Bari, 'that anyone survived.'[5] Air Commodore Carter had 'commanded all the fighters at Alamein', Randolph wrote to his father in his own account of the crash, 'and entertained you to lunch when you visited all the pilots a month before the battle'. As for Sowman, 'he had been my daily companion for 18 months and had become a real friend'.[6]

On July 17 the War Cabinet had heard Eden argue in favour of sending back to Russia the 1,500 Russians then held as prisoners-of-war in Britain. Eden's proposal had been accepted. During the discussion, however, Churchill had said that the ambivalent position of these Russians, as former allies of the Germans, should be shown in the most 'extenuating' light, and if possible 'their return should be

---

[1] The two pilots who were killed were Flight Lieutenant D. E. Jones Gardiner, 267 Squadron, Australia, and Captain H. W. Volms, 28 Squadron, South African Air Force, South Africa No. 1360 from Algiers (Randolph Churchill to Christopher Dodds, 30 July 1944: Churchill papers, 20/150). In 1947, Philip Jordan became Press officer at 10 Downing Street.

[2] Prime Minister's Personal Telegram, T.1460/4, 'Personal and Most Secret', 17 July 1944: Churchill papers, 20/168.

[3] No. 348 from Bari, 18 July 1944: Churchill papers, 20/168. Churchill did not limit his condolences to the Sowman family to letters. He was 'anxious', as Christopher Dodds wrote to the War Office, that the 'limit of financial assistance' should be given to Sowman's widow, Joan. 'Her husband', Dodds wrote, 'was a very loyal and courageous man who, belonging to an ordinary Army Unit, voluntarily learned parachute jumping' in order to accompany Randolph into Yugoslavia. (Letter of 19 July 1944, to A. C. W. Dew: Churchill papers, 20/150.)

[4] 'Letters and Telegrams Received by the Prime Minister on Major Randolph Churchill's air crash in Yugoslavia', 'Confidential', undated: Churchill papers, 20/150. Roosevelt's telegram was President to Prime Minister No. 589, 'Personal and Secret', 27 July 1944.

[5] Letter of 19 July 1944: Churchill papers, 2/464.

[6] Letter of 21 July 1944: Churchill papers, 20/150.

delayed'.[1] Four days after this meeting, Lord Selborne had protested to Eden against sending the Russians back, arguing that most of them had only joined the German ranks under incredible duress and even enforced starvation. On reading Selborne's protest, Churchill minuted to Eden: 'I think we dealt rather summarily with this at Cabinet and the point put by the Minister of Economic Warfare should certainly be reconsidered. Even if we are somewhat compromised, all the apparatus of delay must be used. I think these men were tried beyond their strength.'[2]

On an issue of domestic concern, Churchill sent a minute to his War Cabinet colleagues that day about a 'singular fact'. Up to six o'clock on July 15 the total estimated launches of flying bombs had been 3,582. Up to that same moment, 3,583 British civilians had been killed by the flying bombs. Although Radar did not necessarily 'plot every flying bomb launched' and the total number of those killed 'is swollen by deaths in hospital', the figures, Churchill wrote, 'are so extraordinary that they deserve the attention of my colleagues'.[3]

On July 18, at a meeting of the 'Crossbow' Committee held in the undergound Cabinet War Room, Dr R. V. Jones warned that there might already be in existence as many as a thousand of the far more powerful missile than the flying bomb, the V2 rocket, weighing more than eleven tons, and capable of a speed of about 4,000 miles an hour: involving a flight of only three to four minutes from its launching site in Europe to London.

Pondering the information about this new German rocket, Churchill suggested to the 'Crossbow' Committee, as its minutes recorded, 'that we had to some extent been caught napping', but Portal replied that 'all action that could be thought of had been taken as far as could be done without harming the essential interests of "Overlord" '.

Portal also told the Committee, in a paragraph deleted before the minutes were circulated, that 'the position for us would be much more serious if all the enemy's efforts had been concentrated on increasing the severity of the attack by flying bombs'.

At the end of the discussion, Churchill said that if rocket attacks should develop, 'he was prepared, after consultation with the United States and the USSR, to threaten the enemy with large scale gas attacks in retaliation, should such a course appear profitable'. He had already instructed the Chiefs of Staff, Churchill added, 'to carry out a purely military examination of the probable effects of such an attack on the enemy'.[4]

[1] War Cabinet No. 91 of 1944, 17 July 1944: Cabinet papers, 65/43.
[2] Prime Minister's Personal Minute, M.896/4, 26 July 1944; Premier papers, 3/364/8, folios 293–5.
[3] War Cabinet Paper No. 392 of 1944, 'Secret', 17 July 1944: Churchill papers, 23/13.
[4] 'Crossbow' Committee No. 7 of 1944, 18 July 1944: Cabinet papers, 98/36.

On the day after this meeting of the 'Crossbow' Committee, Churchill asked Stalin if British rocket experts could go at once to Poland, as soon as Soviet forces had moved west of Lvov, to see the evacuated and abandoned German experimental rocket station at Debice, between Lvov and Cracow. 'Parliament will require me to convince them that everything possible is being done', Churchill told Stalin, and he went on to explain that a bomb which had fallen in Sweden and failed to detonate had given 'a good deal' of information about the bomb, but 'traces of the Polish experiment' would give 'an invaluable supplement'.[1]

On the evening of July 18 Churchill had seen Mikolajczyk, at the latter's urgent request, who handed Churchill translations of coded messages, received from Poland, which showed that a bitter struggle was in progress in Poland between the advancing Soviet forces, and the Polish Underground forces loyal to the London Government.

Mikolajczyk wanted Churchill to telegraph to Stalin, to point out that Polish Underground forces had co-operated with the Red Army in the final assault and liberation of Vilna. Churchill told the Polish Prime Minister: 'it would be of no use to telegraph to Marshal Stalin on a matter of this kind. A rebuff would be the only result. The Russians would never admit that a number of men from the Underground Movement had played an important part in the liberation of Vilna.' Mikolajczyk then explained 'that his desire was that these Polish troops should be allowed to go on fighting' and that they should 'advance with the forward Russian troops towards the West'. He 'fully understood' what he called the 'delicacy' of the position in Vilna in view of the Soviet Government's declaration that Lithuania was a Soviet Socialist Republic.

Churchill then asked Mikolajczyk, as Sir Owen O'Malley's note of the conversation recorded, 'why he went on pressing so hard in this matter of Vilna. He must know that there was no hope of Poland obtaining what she wished in that quarter. The Poles had seized Vilna after the last war against the wishes of the Allies at that time. He feared that Poland had already missed many opportunities of coming to terms with Russia and this continued persistence on Vilna could do Poland no good. It would be much better if M. Mikolajczyk would go to see Marshal Stalin.'

Mikolajczyk saw no point in such a visit, telling Churchill that 'the

[1] Prime Minister's Personal Telegram, T.1468/4, No. 2165 to Moscow, 'Personal and Top Secret', 19 July 1944: Churchill papers, 20/168.

truth was that the Soviet Government wished Poland to be the Number 17th Soviet Socialist Republic'. Churchill replied 'that he did not believe this'. If Mikolajczyk were first to agree to discuss these matters in Moscow, both Churchill and O'Malley explained, Churchill would then be willing to send a message to Stalin 'expressing his hope' that Stalin would agree to see him. But for Britain to take the initiative on her own account 'would be quite useless'.[1]

To try to help the London Poles, on July 19 Churchill drafted a message to be sent, for publication, to Alexander. The message read: 'Pray convey to General Anders and his gallant Polish Divisions my sincere compliments on the capture of Ancona. Here in this distant theatre Polish Divisions are striking at the German foe and furthering the inflexible resolve of the President of the United States, Marshal Stalin and His Majesty's Government, that Poland shall be strong, independent and free.'[2]

On reading this, Eden asked Churchill to replace the words 'the President of the United States, Marshal Stalin and His Majesty's Government' by the phrase 'the United Nations', lest the Russians felt 'that HM Government are using this occasion as a pretext for interferring once more in the Polish-Russian dispute and that they may resent this', in which case the effect of the telegram 'may be to worsen rather than to improve Russo-Polish relations'.[3] Churchill was not convinced, minuting to Eden on the following day:

Nobody cares a damn about the United Nations. I leave it to you either to send the telegram as drafted or to suppress it altogether. If my judgment is any use, I think Stalin will be quite content. The words quoted are his own.[4]

On July 20, Churchill also telegraphed to Stalin, reporting that a 'new cycle' of Arctic convoys would begin in August, asking Stalin to make 'comradeship' with the Polish Government 'if it really strikes hard and true against the Germans', and ending: 'I hope that you and the President and I may have a meeting somewhere or other before the winter closes in. It will be worth it to the poor people everywhere.'[5]

To Harry Hopkins, who was back at the White House after his

[1] Sir Owen O'Malley to Anthony Eden, 'Secret', 18 July 1944: Foreign Office papers, 954/20, folios 203–5.
[2] Draft telegram, 'Prime Minister to General Alexander': Foreign Office papers, 954/20, folio 207.
[3] Valentine Lawford to Leslie Rowan, 'Secret and Immediate', 19 July 1944: Foreign Office papers, 954/20, folio 208.
[4] Prime Minister's Personal Minute, M.887/4, 20 July 1944: Foreign Office papers, 954/20, folio 212.
[5] Prime Minister's Personal Telegram, T.1476/4, No. 2175 to Moscow, 'Personal and Secret', 'Decypher Yourself', 20 July 1944: Churchill papers, 20/168.

operation, and hoping to join Roosevelt at the new conference, Churchill telegraphed with foreboding that 'although we look like winning the War, a most formidable set of problems is approaching us from every side, and personally I do not feel that anything but duty would make me encounter them'. Churchill warned Hopkins:

Our affairs are getting into a most tangled condition. We have to deal with the affairs of a dozen States, some of which have several civil wars brewing and anyhow are split from top to bottom, by means of the concerted action of three great Powers or four if you still include China, every one of which approaches the topic from a different angle and in a different mood.

As we can only meet at intervals of six months it is very hard for anyone to have a policy. There are economic, financial and political issues of the utmost stress and consequence advancing in a steady parade.

'However,' Churchill added, 'the war news makes amends for much. We look like getting a fine Anglo-American victory in the next few days.' [1]

The second phase of 'Overlord' was imminent. Codenamed 'Cobra', this operation involved a British assault against German positions between Caen and Falaise, in order to pin down as many German forces as possible while the Americans broke out from the Cherbourg peninsula. Churchill was eager to see the Anglo-American forces on the eve of this imminent offensive, and prepared to make his second visit to Normandy, including the newly liberated Caen. At 3.15 on the afternoon of July 20 he flew in a United States Army Dakota from Heston airport to Cherbourg.[2] That same day, in East Prussia, a German officer exploded a bomb at Hitler's headquarters, wounding the Führer, but failing to kill him. In the aftermath of the plot, hundreds of German officers and civilians were executed on Hitler's orders, and the wounded Rommel, implicated in the plotters' designs, was forced to commit suicide.

Churchill spent the afternoon of July 20 under American auspices, visiting Cherbourg, where he inspected the damage to the port and the measures being taken to reopen it. At Cherbourg he saw Harry Hopkins' son Robert. 'He was in great form,' Churchill telegraphed to Hopkins senior, 'and sent you his love.' [3]

From Cherbourg, Churchill visited an unfinished flying bomb

[1] Prime Minister's Personal Telegram, T.1466/4, 'Personal and Top Secret', 19 July 1944: Churchill papers, 20/142.
[2] 'PM's Movements': Churchill papers, 4/344.
[3] Prime Minister's Personal Telegram, T.1477/4, 21 July 1944: Churchill papers, 20/168.

launching site, 'an elaborate creation of concrete', John Martin wrote home, 'only 60% complete and apparently intended for launching bombs in the direction of Bristol'.[1] From there, Churchill drove to 'Utah' beach, one of the American landing sites, where he embarked in a motor torpedo boat and was taken the two and half hour journey to the main British landing beach at Arromanches. The sea was 'very rough', John Martin wrote, so much so that Churchill had to go below decks and take seasickness pills.[2] At Arromanches, Churchill went on board HMS *Enterprise*, to dine and sleep, his host being Captain Peachey.

On July 21 Churchill visited Montgomery's headquarters near Blay, and afterwards lunched with General Naylor at the Headquarters, Lines of Communication. There he also met General Gale and General Graham. In the afternoon he visited a general hospital, a field bakery and a medium artillery battery 'engaged in bombarding enemy positions'.[3] The battery was part of the 121 Field/Medium Regiment, Royal Artillery, whose regimental history recorded Churchill's visit as 'a famous occasion in the Regiment's history', describing it:

Mr Churchill watched one of the guns in action (A Troop number 4 gun); he stood by the layer and had rounds fired until he was satisfied that he understood the gun drill. Then he went up to the OP on point 103 in a Jeep, and watched an AGRA concentration fall on the enemy along the Tilly-Villers Bocage road.[4] He gave great joy to the batmen and cooks and fatigue men of 276 Battery by stopping his car on his way back and having his photograph taken with them.[5]

After Churchill had left, the Commander of the Regiment, William Stirling, wrote to him: 'I know how much you enjoy getting near the battle, but also I would like to tell you how tremendously pleased, heartened and honoured every soldier was by your visit. It means very much to them that you should wish to come and see them at work in their gun pits.' After Churchill had left them, Stirling added, 'we moved over to help in the American attack'.[6]

That evening, Churchill returned to HMS *Enterprise*, once more to dine and sleep.[7] During the night there was, as John Martin noted,

[1] John Martin, letter of 24 July 1944: Martin papers.
[2] Private Office Diary, 20 July 1944.
[3] Private Office Diary, 21 July 1944.
[4] OP = Observation Point. AGRA = Army Group Royal Artillery.
[5] Sergeant R. W. Morris and others, *121 Field/Medium Regiment, Royal Artillery, 1939–1946*, Guildford 1946, page 78.
[6] Letter of 23 July 1944: Churchill papers, 20/146.
[7] Private Office Diary, 21 July 1941.

an 'alarm of human torpedoes'.[1] But no such German suicide attack took place.

On the morning of July 22 Churchill returned from HMS *Enterprise* to the shore, lunching with Montgomery at his headquarters. After lunch, accompanied by Montgomery he visited Caen, and then the battle area. In the course of the afternoon he also called at 2nd Army Headquarters and met the four Corps Commanders, as well as General Omar Bradley of the United States Army.[2] That night Churchill again dined and slept in HMS *Enterprise*.[3] 'I enjoyed my day with you enormously,' he wrote to Montgomery that night, '& I hope that fruitful results will come from my more intimate impressions of the war scene, & from another opportunity of having a good talk with you.'[4]

On July 23 Churchill again lunched with Montgomery at Headquarters, after which he made a tour of Royal Air Force landing strips in the battle area, being flown in a captured German aircraft piloted by Air Vice Marshal Broadhurst.[5] In an address to British airmen at one of his stops, he made a brief reference to the Hitler bomb plot. 'They are shooting each other,' he said. 'I cannot help that. It might be that the fighting might come to an end earlier than we have the right to say.'[6]

From France, Churchill flew that evening to Northolt, then drove to Chequers, where Gilbert Winant was his dinner guest.[7] Winant had welcome news, an assurance from Roosevelt about Britain's meat contract with the Argentine, which Churchill had feared would be in conflict with the meat imports of the United States. 'I would not do anything in the world,' Roosevelt had telegraphed direct to Churchill, 'to cut down the supply of meat to England. Heaven knows that it is already quite short enough.'[8]

There was a second telegram awaiting Churchill on his return. It was from Stalin, announcing that Lublin had been 'occupied today' by Soviet troops, 'who are continuing to advance'. Stalin added that he had decided to 'establish contact' with the Polish Committee of National Liberation. This Committee, which now made Lublin its Headquarters, intended, Stalin wrote, 'to undertake the setting up of administration on Polish territory, and this, I hope, will be accom-

---

[1] John Martin diary, 21 July 1944: Martin papers.

[2] The four Corps Commanders were Generals Bucknall, 30th Corps, Ritchie, 12th Corps, Simmonds and O'Connor (the General who had earlier escaped from German captivity).

[3] Private Office Diary, 22 July 1944.

[4] Letter of 22 July 1944, HMS *Enterprise*: Montgomery papers.

[5] Private Office Diary, 23 July 1944.

[6] Address of 23 July 1944: Montgomery papers.

[7] Private Office Diary, 23 July 1944.

[8] President to Prime Minister, No. 588, 'Personal and Top Secret', 23 July 1944: Churchill papers, 20/168.

plished'. He would certainly not 'refuse' to see Mikolajczyk, Stalin added, but it would be 'better' if he were to address himself to the Polish National Committee, whose attitude towards him would be 'friendly'.[1]

From Chequers, Churchill hastened to encourage Stalin to agree to a meeting of the Big Three in the north of Scotland in the second week of September, asking him to consider 'the great advantages and simplifications of all our joint affairs which would flow as at Teheran from a threefold meeting'. Of the situation in Normandy, Churchill told Stalin that since the landing the Allies had lost 110,000 men, the Germans, 'at least 160,000 including 60,000 prisoners'. More than 1,400,000 Allied troops were ashore. One of the two 'synthetic' harbours had been destroyed 'by the fury of the storm in June', but the other 'has delivered up to 11,000 tons in a day and is an astonishing sight to see'.

The South of France landing, Churchill told Stalin, was to begin on August 15. In Italy, Alexander hoped to cross the Po Valley and to reach Trieste 'before the winter sets in'. He would then 'give his right hand to Marshal Tito whom we are helping in every way possible'.

Churchill ended his telegram with 'heartfelt congratulations on the irresistible onward marches of the Soviet Armies and on the enormously important conquests you have made'.[2]

In his telegram to Stalin, Churchill had made no reference to Poland. But at the War Cabinet that night he said that he was 'strongly' of the opinion that Mikolajczyk should see Stalin 'without delay' and without 'any barrier' to his making contacts thereafter with the Polish Committee of National Liberation. Churchill also told his colleagues that the Poles 'who were now co-operating with the Russians were neither Quislings nor Communists'. The Russians might soon be in Warsaw, 'and every day's delay', he stressed, 'thus strengthened the position of the local Poles, and placed the Polish Government in London at a greater disadvantage if no contacts were established'. If contact was not made now, he warned, 'the alternative Government, with Russian backing, would be well in the saddle when the peace settlement was reached and would claim with some plausibility to be representative of Poland'.[3]

Churchill also saw Mikolajczyk on July 25, when he 'strongly insisted' on Mikolajczyk's 'speedy flight to Moscow', in order to discuss 'the whole complex of Polish-Soviet relations and to find a way out

[1] 'Personal and Top Secret', 23 July 1944: Churchill papers, 20/168.

[2] Prime Minister's Personal Telegram, T.1487/4, No. 2217 to Moscow, 'Personal and Top Secret', 24 July 1944: Premier papers, 4/75/2, Part 2.

[3] War Cabinet No. 95 of 1944, 24 July 1944, Confidential Annex: Cabinet papers, 65/47.

from the present blind-ally'. Mikolajczyk agreed to fly to Moscow on the following evening. He also asked Churchill for an 'assurance' that in the event of the failure of the negotiations 'he and the Polish Government could count on the full support of the British Government'. Churchill replied 'positively', as the minutes recorded, 'saying that M. Mikolajczyk could depend on it'.[1]

It was of the 'utmost importance', Churchill telegraphed to Roosevelt on the following day, 'that we do not desert the orthodox Polish Government'. The 'great hope', Churchill wrote, 'is fusion of some kind between Poles relying on Russia and Poles relying on USA and GB'. 'We are sure,' Churchill added, 'that UJ will be much influenced by your view of these things.'[2] On the eastern front, the conditions for a settlement were rapidly being created by the advance of the Red Army, which, crossing the Curzon Line in the north, entered Bialystok on July 27. That same day, in the south, the Red Army entered Lvov, which the London Poles had insisted upon being an integral part of post-war Poland. Churchill telegraphed that day to Stalin to tell him that 'Mikolajczyk and his colleagues have started', and that he was sure that Mikolajczyk 'is most anxious to help a general fusion of all Poles on the lines on which you and I and the President are, I believe, agreed'. His telegram continued:

I believe that Poles who are friendly to Russia should join with Poles who are friendly to Great Britain and the United States in order to establish the strong, free, independent Poland, the good neighbour of Russia and an important barrier between you and another German outrage. We will all three take good care there are other barriers also.

Churchill's telegram ended:

It would be a great pity and even a disaster if the Western Democracies found themselves recognising one body of Poles and you recognising another. It would lead to constant friction and might even hamper the great business which we have to do the wide world over. Please therefore receive these few sentences in the spirit in which they are sent, which is one of sincere friendship and our Twenty Years Alliance.[3]

On July 24 the Joint Intelligence Committee had reported that,

[1] 'Two conversations held by M. Mikolajczyk, the first with Mr Eden, the second with Mr Eden and Mr Churchill . . .', *Documents on Polish Soviet Relations 1939–1945*, volume 2, document 167, pages 298–9.

[2] Prime Minister's Personal Telegram, T.1493/4, Prime Minister to President, No. 735, 'Personal and Top Secret', 26 July 1944: Churchill papers, 20/168.

[3] Prime Minister's Personal Telegram, T.1505/4, 'Personal and Top Secret', 27 July 1944: Churchill papers, 20/169.

more than five weeks after the Normandy landings, the Germans were 'still apprehensive' of a second major landing somewhere between the River Seine and the Franco-Belgian frontier. There had been 'no considerable transfer' of German forces from the Pas de Calais, which remained 'strongly garrisoned'. This was, however, partly to protect the 'Crossbow' flying bomb sites.[1] On the following day, July 25, operation 'Cobra' was launched in Normandy. Within a few days, the Americans succeeded in breaking out of the Cherbourg peninsula, enabled to do so by a major British assault on the far more heavily defended German positions between Caen and Falaise. That week, behind the German lines in Poland, an experimental V2 rocket failed to explode, was hidden in a river by the Polish underground, salvaged, dismantled, and then flown out of Poland, together with a Polish engineer. The flight was in a Royal Air Force Dakota which made the dangerous journey for that sole purpose. In Britain, the parts of the bomb proved invaluable in anticipating the imminent heavier German rocket attack. The Polish engineer was flown back to Poland. Later he was caught by the Gestapo, and shot.

Over Britain, the number of flying bombs had decreased as a result of Allied bombing of their main launching sites, and the destruction of the missile while in flight.[2] But the V2s remained a constant danger, nor had Churchill forgotten his long minute of July 6 about the possible use of poison gas as a deterrent. On July 25 he minuted to Ismay: 'On July 6 I asked for a dispassionate report on the military aspects of threatening to use lethal and corrosive gases on the enemy if they did not stop the use of indiscriminate weapons. I now request this report within three days.'[3] In fact, unknown to Churchill, the Vice-Chiefs of Staff, meeting on July 13, had considered Churchill's minute, and instructed the enquiry into 'the question of employing gas against Germany' to be made by the Joint Planning Staff. At the suggestion of the Chiefs of Staff, this enquiry was to include, not only gas warfare, as Churchill had asked, but also 'consideration of German readiness to undertake bacteriological warfare'.[4]

Equally unknown to Churchill, the enquiry had been put in train on July 16, so that when the Chiefs of Staff met on July 26 to consider Churchill's second minute, they were able to provide their report, not 'within three days' as he had asked, but within a few hours.[5] In its

---

[1] Joint Intelligence Committee Report No. 321 (Operations) of 1944, 'Final', 'Limited Circulation', 'Top Secret', 24 July 1944; Cabinet papers, 79/78.

[2] Only 712 flying bombs were launched in the week ending 29 July 1944. Of these, 372 had been destroyed, and 234 had reached London.

[3] Prime Minister's Personal Minute, D.234/4, 25 July 1944: Cabinet papers, 120/775.

[4] Chiefs of Staff Committee No. 234 (Operations) of 1944, Confidential Annex, 13 July 1944: Cabinet papers, 79/89.

[5] Chiefs of Staff Committee No. 248 (Operations) of 1944, 26 July 1944: Cabinet papers, 79/78.

first eight and a half pages, the report argued against the use of gas. In a one and a half page section, it also dealt, as the Chiefs of Staff had proposed, with bacteriological warfare. 'If the claims of "N" are substantiated,' the report stated, 'its use could probably make a material change in the war situation, but there is no likelihood of a sustained attack being possible before the middle of 1945.' The report continued: 'There is no known prophylactic against "N". If it can be used in practice, the effect on morale will be profound.' On the other hand, the report concluded, 'It is improbable that the Germans will initiate biological warfare. There is no evidence to show whether they are in a position to retaliate in kind, were we to initiate it.' [1]

Ismay sent Churchill a copy of this report. In relation to the Joint Planning Staffs eight and a half page opposition to the use of gas, Churchill minuted in reply: 'I am not at all convinced by this negative report. But clearly I cannot make head against the parsons and the warriors at the same time. The matter should be kept under review and brought up again when things get worse.' [2]

The question of using poison gas as a deterrent was not in fact raised again, even when the rocket attacks began. The Joint Planning Staff's comprehensive critique had been effective.

Churchill now made plans to leave Britain again, for the Italian front. 'The only thing that will delay me in London,' he telegraphed to Alexander on July 25, 'is a serious worsening of the bombing. This is quite possible.' [3] 'I may be around the Mediterranean one of these days after the Parliament has risen,' Churchill telegraphed to Randolph two days later. 'But there is a lot going on.' [4] One of Churchill's problems that week, as he explained to Montgomery, was an announcement from Eisenhower's headquarters that the British had sustained 'quite a serious set-back' in Normandy. 'I am not aware,' Churchill telegraphed to Montgomery, 'of any facts that justify such a statement.' Nor did it have any justification: the Commandos had been forced back 1,000 yards at one point. But the word 'set-back' had created, Churchill wrote, 'a good deal of talk here. I should like to know exactly what the position is, in order to maintain confidence among wobblers or critics in high places.' [5]

[1] Chiefs of Staff Paper No. 661 (Operations) of 1944, 26 July 1944: Cabinet papers, 80/85.

[2] Prime Minister's Personal Minute, D.238/4, 29 July 1944: Cabinet papers, 120/775.

[3] Prime Minister's Personal Telegram, T.1489/4, 'Personal and Top Secret', 25 July 1944: Churchill papers, 20/168.

[4] Prime Minister's Personal Telegram, T.1506/4, 'Personal and Top Secret' (through Duff Cooper), 27 July 1944: Churchill papers, 20/150.

[5] Prime Minister's Personal Telegram, T.1509/4, 'Personal and Private, also Top Secret', 27 July 1944: Churchill papers, 20/169.

Montgomery sent Churchill details of how his policy 'since the beginning' had been to draw the main German armoured strength into his eastern flank, 'and to fight it there', so that the fighting on the western flank could proceed the easier. 'In this I have succeeded.' As a result, 'the Americans are going great guns'.[1] Churchill at once telegraphed to Montgomery, whose troops were preparing to attack the German defences at Falaise:

I wish you all success in your impending venture. I am very glad that the Americans had a good success to-day. It would be fine if this were matched by a similar British victory. I realise that you have the main weight of the enemy against you and I am sure you will overcome them. This is the moment to strike hard.

'Thank you so much,' Churchill ended, 'for your kindness and hospitality.'[2]

In the last week of July there was much concern in the War Cabinet about the impending German V2 rocket attacks, now codenamed 'Big Ben'. Churchill had followed closely the various counter-measures being studied by Duncan Sandys, Lord Cherwell, and the 'Crossbow' Committee. 'We must be sure,' he minuted to Sinclair, Sandys and Portal on July 28, 'that heavy and immediate counter-attacks fall on every point of the enemy's rocket organization as soon as it takes shape.' The defeat of the rocket attack, he wrote, 'will be a victory calculated to remove one of the enemy's last hopes'.[3] That day, Brooke noted in his diary:

At 3 p.m. another Cabinet meeting which lasted two hours, and at which we spent all our time discussing rockets and flying bombs. All this should have been finished yesterday. Winston relating all his old reminiscences connected with the various Cabinet appointments he has held, none of which have any bearing on the points under discussion. I remain very fond of him, but, by Heaven, he does try one's patience![4]

The rocket danger could not be shaken off however, and on August 1 the Chiefs of Staff Committee, with Brooke in the Chair, sought assurances from 'C' 'that the best possible measures were being taken to infiltrate agents into the area through which material would have

---

[1] 'Top Secret', 27 July 1944: Churchill papers, 20/169.
[2] Prime Minister's Personal Telegram, T.1504/4, 27 July 1944: Churchill papers, 20/194.
[3] Prime Minister's Personal Minute, M.903/4, 'Top Secret', 28 July 1944: Churchill papers, 20/153.
[4] Brooke diary, 28 July 1944: Bryant, *op. cit.*, volume 2, page 245.

to be moved before an attack could be launched'.[1] So nervous were those who knew of the rockets' possible power that on August 2 the British Chiefs of Staff informed the American Chiefs that German attacks by flying bombs 'and possibly in the future by rockets' would 'at best impede and at worst may seriously interrupt British war effort'. In developing their plans for the campaign in France, the British Chiefs added, 'please ensure that due weight is given to the elimination of this threat'.[2]

Public concern about the flying bombs was one of the subjects with which Churchill intended to deal in a speech which he was to give in the House of Commons on August 2. On July 29 he dictated 3,500 words of the speech to Marian Holmes, telling her, as she noted in her diary, 'You need not type it tonight as I won't open my eyes until Big Ben strikes ten tomorrow.'[3] On August 1, Churchill worked on the speech again. Marian Holmes noted the further progress in her diary:

He dictated 1,000 words before dinner. He was in the most sweet and amiable mood. After dinner, Liz Layton and Jo Sturdee were mobilised to help. The speech came out in dollops to be typed into speech form. While I was with him, the PM read part of his speech to Brendan Bracken, Duncan Sandys and Leslie Rowan. 'I've only half the life in me these days' he said. Brendan Bracken assured him he had never looked better. Sat typing up the speech until 7 a.m.[4]

On August 2, in giving the House of Commons a survey of the war, Churchill dwelt at some length upon the flying bomb, pointing out that 4,500 tons of these bombs had been launched against Britain between June 5 and July 31. During the same period, he reported, the Allied Air Force had dropped 48,000 tons of high explosives on Germany. Of course, he said, it might be that there was less loss of life when 'important military objectives' were the target than when a weapon was used 'which has no other object than the indiscriminate slaughter of the civilian population'.[5] A total of 5,735 flying bombs had been sent over Britain, killing 4,735 people. About 17,000 houses had been totally destroyed. Nearly a million people, including 225,000 mothers with children, had been evacuated from London. But 'hundreds of the best expert brains we have' were 'constantly rivetted' on the problem of how to prevent and mitigate the effects of the new bombardment.

[1] Chiefs of Staff Committee No. 254 (Operations) of 1944, 1 August 1944: Cabinet papers, 79/78.
[2] 'Future Operations in France', Combined Chiefs of Staff Paper No. CCS 640, 'Top Secret', 2 August 1944: Cabinet papers, 122/340.
[3] Marian Holmes diary, 29 July 1944: Marian Walker Spicer papers.
[4] Marian Holmes diary, 1 August 1944: Marian Walker Spicer papers.
[5] On 28 July 1944, fifty-six Londoners had been killed, and more than a hundred seriously

At one point in his speech, Churchill spoke of idealism and ideology. 'While I cherish idealism,' he said, 'as a cheerful light playing over the thoughts and hopes of men and inspiring noble deeds, ideology too often presents itself as undue regimentation of ideas and may very likely be incompatible with freedom.' For that reason, he had 'rejoiced' to see the Fascist ideology overthrown in Italy. For this reason, he praised the 'friendly contact' between Tito and the Government of Dr Subasic in Yugoslavia, and the 'broadly representative' Government of George Papandreou in Greece. Britain would work for the unity of any forces gathering together for 'the cleaning of their soil from the foul German invader'. As for the July 20 bomb plot against Hitler by German officers, Churchill told the Commons:

Not only are those once proud German armies being beaten back on every front and by every one of the many nations who are in fighting contact with them, every single one, but, in their homeland in Germany, tremendous events have occurred which must shake to their foundations the confidence of the people and the loyalty of the troops. The highest personalities in the German Reich are murdering one another, or trying to, while the avenging Armies of the Allies close upon the doomed and ever-narrowing circle of their power. We have never based ourselves on the weakness of our enemy but only on the righteousness of our cause. Therefore, potent as may be these manifestations of internal disease, decisive as they may be one of these days, it is not in them that we should put our trust, but in our own strong arms and the justice of our cause.[1]

Churchill ended his speech with a peroration reminiscent of the clarion calls of 1940:

Let us go on then to battle on every front. Thrust forward every man who

---

injured, when a V1 fell on the street market at Lewisham (Home Office papers, 186/2405). There was a rumour at the time that the casualties were higher than officially admitted. These figures were confirmed however by a report compiled by the Home Office (Inspector General's Branch, Civil Defence Department), dated 7 August 1946.

[1] Eden had sent Churchill a memorandum on the bomb plot (Foreign Office papers, 371/30912, C 5202/48/18), but this is closed to public inspection until the year 2018. Among those who advised the Foreign Office on the implications of the plot was Eden's friend John Wheeler-Bennett, who wrote on July 25: 'It may now be said with some definiteness that we are better off with things as they are today than if the plot of July 20th had succeeded and Hitler had been assassinated. In this event the "Old Army" Generals would have taken over and, as may be deduced from the recent statement from the Vatican as to the Pope's readiness to mediate, would have put into operation through Baron von Weizsäcker a peace move, already prepared, in which Germany would admit herself defeated and would sue for terms other than those of Unconditional Surrender. By the failure of the plot we have been spared the embarrassments, both at home and in the United States, which might have resulted from such a move and, moreover, the present purge is presumably removing from the scene numerous individuals who might have caused us difficulty, not only had the plot succeeded, but also after the defeat of a Nazi Germany.' (Foreign Office papers, 371/39062, C.9896, 'Top Secret', written 25 July 1944, received in the Foreign Office, 28 July 1944.)

can be found. Arm and equip the Forces in bountiful supply. Listen to no parley from the enemy. Vie with our valiant Allies to intensify the conflict. Bear with unflinching fortitude whatever evils and blows we may receive. Drive on through the storm, now that it reaches its fury, with the same singleness of purpose and inflexibility of resolve as we showed to all the world when we were all alone.[1]

'Everyone agrees that your speech was a tremendous success,' Duncan Sandys wrote, and he added: 'It was worth the time and labour you devoted to it.'[2]

His speech over, Churchill returned to the Annexe, and his Map Room, where he found Captain Pim listening to a wireless report of the speech itself. Eager to know what information had come in from the war front during the previous two hours, Churchill, as Pim later recalled, 'sat down in his chair, and starting a fresh cigar said, "Now, Pim, tell me all about the war."'[3]

[1] *Hansard*, 2 August 1944, columns 1459–1485.
[2] Letter of 3 August 1944: Churchill papers, 20/146.
[3] Pim recollections of 2 August 1944: Pim papers.

47

August 1944: 'These thorny matters'

STALIN had not accepted Churchill's invitation to a Three Power Conference in Scotland; his presence in Russia was essential, he said, at a time of such rapid military advances. But he did telegraph to Churchill on 28 July 1944 with apparent approval for what he described as 'the unification of Poles friendly disposed towards Great Britain, the USSR and the United States'.[1] This seems to be the best ever received from UJ,' Churchill telegraphed to Roosevelt.[2] That same evening Churchill also telephoned Eden. 'He took a more cheerful view of UJ's reply on Poles than I did,' Eden noted in his diary. 'He may be right. Truth is that, like many communist messages, it is capable of several interpretations.'[3]

The Stalin message of July 28, while welcoming the 'unification' of Poles 'friendly' to Britain, Russia and America, had also said that 'a good start' had been made towards this by the creation of the National Committee: the Communist-based 'Lublin' Poles. It had also castigated those 'Polish elements who are not capable of unification with democratic forces'.[4] Eden showed a more immediate grasp of the ambiguities and dangers than Churchill. For Stalin's previous messages had made it clear that in the Soviet leader's view these 'elements' were present not only in the ranks of the London Poles, in Britain, but also among the underground forces in Poland who were loyal to the London Poles.

The crisis was to arise more quickly than either Churchill or Eden could expect. On July 29, Moscow radio station broadcast an appeal to the population of Warsaw, telling them that the 'guns of liberation'

[1] 'Personal and Top Secret', 28 July 1944: Churchill papers, 20/169.
[2] Prime Minister's Personal Telegram, T.1530/4, 30 July 1944: Churchill papers, 20/184.
[3] Eden diary, 30 July 1944: Eden memoirs, *The Reckoning, op. cit.*, page 466.
[4] 'Personal and Top Secret', 28 July 1944: Churchill papers, 20/169.

were now within hearing and calling upon them to join battle with the Germans 'as in 1939', this time for 'decisive action'. Moscow radio declared: 'For Warsaw, which did not yield but fought on, the hour of action has already arrived.' Referring to 'the German plan' systematically to destroy the city, Radio Moscow ended: 'all is lost that is not saved by active effort'.[1] On July 31, two days after this broadcast, Soviet tanks broke into the German defences on the eastern side of the River Vistula, opposite Warsaw, and came to within fifteen miles of the river. The same day, the Polish underground command ordered a general uprising against the German forces in the capital.

More than a year earlier, in April 1943, the surviving Jews in the Warsaw ghetto had challenged with vastly inferior weapons the Germans who sought to deport them to the death camps: an heroic act of hopeless defiance. Now 40,000 of Warsaw's one million Poles were joined in their desperate endeavour by several thousand surviving Polish Jews in hiding, and rose up against the German occupation forces, seeking to establish a Polish authority in the city before the arrival of the Russians: to liberate themselves, and then to be their own masters, at the very moment when their Prime Minister, Mikolajczyk, was on his way to Moscow to negotiate with Stalin. But once again, as against the Jews, the German forces were overwhelming.

Speaking in the House of Commons on August 2, before news of the Warsaw uprising had reached the West, Churchill made a public plea for Polish understanding of the Soviet point of view, calling the present time 'a hopeful moment' for Poland, 'for whose rights and independence we entered the war against Germany'. He and Eden and others had done their best, he said, 'late into the night', to promote Mikolajczyk's visit to Moscow, and he added:

The Russian Armies now stand before the gates of Warsaw. They bring the liberation of Poland in their hands. They offer freedom, sovereignty and independence to the Poles friendly to Russia. This seems to me very reasonable, considering the injuries which Russia has suffered through the Germans marching across Poland to attack her. The Allies would welcome any general rally or fusion of Polish Forces, both those who are working with the Western Powers and those who are working with the Soviet. We have several gallant Polish divisions fighting the Germans in our Armies now and there are others who have been fighting in Russia. Let them come together. We desire this union and it would be a marvellous thing if it could be proclaimed, or at least its foundations laid, at the moment when the famous capital of Poland,

---

[1] Radio Moscow, broadcast of 29 July 1944, text telegraphed from Churchill to Roosevelt in Prime Minister's Personal Telegram, T.1637/4, Prime Minister to President, No. 761, 'Personal and Top Secret', 19 August 1944: Churchill papers, 20/170.

which so valiantly defended itself against the Germans, has been liberated by the bravery of the Russian Armies.[1]

Warsaw had not yet been liberated. Nor had it yet finished the task of trying to defend itself against the Germans. On August 3 Russian forces crossed the River Vistula near Sandomierz, 120 miles south of Warsaw. East of the Vistula, they were only twelve miles from the city. But Warsaw itself remained in the German grip and on August 4 German forces, amounting to one and a half divisions, began to attack the insurgents from strongpoints within and around the city. A division of elite troops, the Hermann Goering division, was being hurried from Italy, and two SS divisions were also on their way. At that same moment, Russian air activity over Warsaw ceased, although Soviet forces were less than twelve miles away to the east, across the Vistula. On August 4 the insurgents appealed for Allied help. Churchill at once telegraphed to Stalin:

At urgent request of Polish Underground Army we are dropping, subject to weather, about sixty tons of equipment and ammunition into the southwest quarter of Warsaw, where it is said a Polish revolt against the Germans is in fierce struggle. They also say that they appeal for Russian aid, which seems to be very near. They are being attacked by one and a half German divisions. This may be of help to your operation.[2]

Stalin replied at once; an answer, as Churchill later described it, both 'prompt and grim'.[3] Even as Polish underground forces battled with the Germans throughout Warsaw, Stalin told Churchill:

I think that the information which has been communicated to you by the Poles is greatly exaggerated and does not inspire confidence. One could reach that conclusion even from the fact that the Polish emigrants have already claimed for themselves that they all but captured Vilna with a few stray units of the Home Army, and even announced that on the radio. But that of course does not in any way correspond with the facts. The Home Army of the Poles consists of a few detachments, which they incorrectly call divisions. They have neither artillery nor aircraft nor tanks. I cannot imagine how such detachments can capture Warsaw, for the defence of which the Germans have produced four tank divisions, among them the Hermann Goering Division.[4]

On the same day that he sent his telegram, Stalin also replied to Churchill's suggestion to send six British submarines to the Baltic Sea to help the Soviet naval offensive. The sending of these submarines, Stalin wrote, 'would be an excellent measure which would constitute yet another blow against the Germans'.[5] Six days later, however,

---

[1] *Hansard*, 2 August 1944, column 1482.
[2] Prime Minister's Personal Telegram, T.1547/4, Foreign Office Telegram No. 2374 to Moscow, 'Personal and Top Secret', 4 August 1944: Foreign Office papers, 954/20, folio 236.
[3] Winston S. Churchill, *The Second World War*, London 1954, volume 6, pages 115–16.
[4] 'Personal and Top Secret', 5 August 1944: Churchill papers, 20/169.
[5] 'Personal and Top Secret', 5 August 1944: Churchill papers, 20/169.

Churchill had to report to Stalin that 'owing to external mining both our own and the enemy's' in the Skaggerak and Kattegat, sending the submarines was 'not a practicable proposition'. He was sorry, Churchill added, that the White Sea–Baltic Sea canal had been too badly damaged by the Germans, as 'We should like to be with you'.[1]

On the night of August 4, thirteen British aircraft had been despatched from southern Italy to central Poland, which lay at the extreme limit of their range. Five out of the thirteen had failed to return. According to Air Marshal Slessor, had these planes been sent to Warsaw, 'the losses would almost certainly have been greater'. At a meeting of the Chiefs of Staff Committee three days later, with Brooke presiding, it was decided to tell the Polish Government in London, in answer to their appeal for help, 'that it is not a practicable operation for aircraft to drop the supplies required'.[2] The light anti-aircraft guns with which the Germans were 'liberally equipped', Ismay explained in a note to the Foreign Office on August 7, would be 'lethal' at the low height from which drops would have to be made over Warsaw itself, if the aircraft were to have any hope 'of being able to drop the arms in the right streets and squares of a large city at night'. In Portal's view, Ismay explained, these tactical difficulties and the losses of 'a third of the aircraft despatched', amounted 'to a virtual impossibility' of meeting the request from the Polish President to Churchill for further help.[3]

On July 25 the American forces under General Omar Bradley had launched their offensive southwards, and by the first week of August broke into Brittany. The Canadians under General Crerar, and the British Second Army under General Dempsey, were likewise moving forward. In Italy, the 8th Army had reached the outskirts of Florence; but the preparations now being made for 'Dragoon', the imminent landing in the South of France, had begun to be felt on the Italian front. On August 2, Maitland Wilson warned Eisenhower that 'heavy troop withdrawals from Fifth Army in favour of "Dragoon" are causing deep concern to me in my efforts to keep the battle in Italy going'.[1] On August 4, Alexander's forces entered Florence. But then,

[1] Prime Minister's Personal Telegram, T.1606/4, Chain No. 3, 'Personal and Top Secret', 11 August 1944: Churchill papers, 20/170.
[2] Chiefs of Staff Committee No. 262 (Operation) of 1944, 7 August 1944: Cabinet papers, 79/79.
[3] Letter of 7 August 1944, Chiefs of Staff Committee No. 262 (Operations) of 7 August 1944, Annex: Cabinet papers, 79/79.
[4] NAF 756, Telegram No. FX 78053, 'Top Secret', 'Priority', 2 August 1944: Cabinet papers, 122/1308.

because of the transfer of American and French Divisions to the forces gathering for 'Dragoon', there was a three-week pause in his offensive. Future air force cover and support would also be 'substantially reduced', Maitland Wilson reported on the following day, in order to provide 'the necessary air cover and support for "Dragoon"'.[1]

Eisenhower, with the Cherbourg peninsula now under his control, seemed momentarily to turn against 'Dragoon' himself, although from another perspective. On August 4 Brooke wrote in his diary: 'Today Eisenhower has asked for the famous South of France landing to be cancelled and that same force to be transferred to Britanny instead.' Brooke added: 'This is actually what we suggested to the Americans and they had turned it down. It is by far the best solution.'

Later that same day, after a Staff Conference, Brooke noted: 'Winston did not keep us long. Told us that Ike had lunched with him and read a paper with the suggestion that the South of France landing should be transferred to Brittany, which Winston thoroughly agreed with.'[2]

In the ensuing discussion, Brooke told Churchill that he too 'entirely agreed with the proposal', though he was against telegraphing to this effect to Roosevelt, as it could 'only have the effect of swinging the Americans against us'. Churchill disagreed, and after further discussion, the Chiefs of Staff, as the minutes of the meeting recorded, agreed that Eisenhower's suggestion should be put 'earnestly' to Roosevelt.

Brooke, Portal and Cunningham then approved a draft telegram from Churchill to Roosevelt.[3] The telegram began:

The course of events in Normandy and Brittany, and especially the brilliant operations of the United States Army, give good prospects that the whole Brittany peninsula will be in our hands within a reasonable time. I beg you will consider the possibility of switching 'Dragoon' into the main and vital theatre, where it can immediately play its part at close quarters in the great and victorious battle in which we are now engaged.

I cannot pretend to have worked out the details, but the opinion here is that they are capable of solution. Instead of having to force a landing against strong enemy defences we might easily find welcoming American troops at some point or other from St Nazaire north-westward along the Brittany peninsula. I feel that we are fully entitled to use the extraordinary flexibility of sea and air-power to move with the moving scene.

The arrival of the ten divisions assigned to the South of France,

[1] MEDCOS 167, Telegram No. FX, 79396, 'Top Secret', 5 August 1944: Cabinet papers, 122/1308.

[2] Brooke diary, 4 August 1944: Bryant, *op. cit.*, volume 2, pages 247–8.

[3] Staff Conference, Chiefs of Staff Committee No. 260 (Operations) of 1944, 4 August 1944: Cabinet papers, 79/78.

with their landing craft, on the Atlantic coast, could, Churchill believed, 'be achieved rapidly', and if the landing 'came off' would be 'decisive for Eisenhower's victorious advance by the shortest route right across France'.[1]

'I have some very important matters to put before you,' Churchill telegraphed to Montgomery in Normandy on August 4, 'and therefore will arrive at your Headquarters around 12.30 tomorrow Saturday, always weather permitting.' Admiral Cunningham would be coming with him. 'After luncheon we wish to go on to Eisenhower.'[2] In a telegram to Eisenhower in southern England announcing his impending visit, Churchill reported that he had telegraphed to Roosevelt 'backing up your suggestion about switching "Dragoon" directly into the Brest Peninsula to reinforce your Armies', and he went on to ask: 'Why should we bash in the back door when we have the latchkey of the front door?'[3]

Churchill now pressed Cunningham to embark upon a series of naval initiatives around the Brest peninsula and the Atlantic coast. On August 4, as he made his plans to visit Montgomery and Eisenhower in France, he minuted to Cunningham: 'What are the Navy doing on the western flank of the Armies? I should have thought that they would be very lively all along the Atlantic shores of the Brest Peninsula, driving off all enemy vessels, isolating the Channel Islands from all food or escape of the German garrison, being ready at Quiberon Bay or elsewhere to join hands with the advancing American columns.' Churchill's minute continued:

We shall soon be possessed of harbours or inlets at which bases for E-boats and destroyers could be established dominating the waters round the Brest Peninsula and greatly helping the movements of the land forces. As it is, they seem to be doing very little except to fight on the north-eastern flank. There are plums to be picked in the Brest Peninsula. Admiral Ramsay must not weary of well-doing.

Cunningham had already commented to Churchill that Eisenhower had not asked for any such naval activity. To this Churchill replied:

[1] Prime Minister's Personal Telegram, T.1556/4, Prime Minister to President, No. 742, 'Personal and Top Secret': Churchill papers, 20/169.
[2] Prime Minister's Personal Telegram, T.1554/4, 'Personal and Top Secret', 'Through "C"', 4 August 1944: Churchill papers, 20/169.
[3] Prime Minister's Personal Telegram, T.1555/4, 'Personal and Top Secret', 4 August 1944: Premier papers, 3/339/11, folio 105.

'It is not the least use telling me that General Eisenhower has not asked for anything. He is very busy with the land battle and knows very little about the sea.' Churchill's minute ended: 'I am convinced that opportunities are passing.' [1]

'Am off to Normandy tomorrow morning,' Churchill telegraphed to Roosevelt late on August 4. 'I shall be in full touch all the time,' he added, 'and will communicate as usual, which is saying a lot.' As to the military situation, 'things are everywhere approaching a climax', Churchill wrote, 'and almost always a climax in our favour'. [2] 'It looks as though we may soon have the whole of Brittany in our hands,' the Chiefs of Staff telegraphed to Maitland Wilson, 'and that it may be possible to land considerable forces at various ports on that coast without opposition.' If events were to 'take this course', he added, 'we feel strongly that far the best strategy is to switch "Dragoon" or at least as much as possible of "Dragoon" to ports in Brittany at the earliest possible moment'. [3]

The Chiefs of Staff saw an urgent strategic need in the switch of the new offensive from the South of France to Brittany. The 'rapid progress on our western flank in France', they explained to the Joint Staff Mission in Washington, 'and particularly the practical certainty that the ports on the Brittany coast will soon be in our hands, gives us priceless opportunities to concentrate in that decisive theatre the greatest possible force in the shortest possible time'. As for 'Dragoon', the Chiefs of Staff added, it was 'fairly certain to involve an opposed landing and in any event cannot exercise any direct effect on the main battle for a considerable time. The Brittany coast on the other hand is almost certain to afford us unopposed landings at points within a few days' march of the main battle.'

The Chiefs of Staff asked the Joint Staff Mission to 'put the above' immediately to the United States Chiefs of Staff, 'and ask for their agreement'. [4] 'We shall do our best,' Brigadier Cornwall-Jones, British Secretary of the Combined Chiefs of Staff replied, 'but I am afraid we shall have a sticky time.' [5]

On the morning of August 5 Churchill flew by Dakota from Northolt for France, to see Montgomery. After an hour and fifteen minutes

---

[1] Prime Minister's Personal Minute, M.921/4, 'Top Secret', 4 August 1944: Churchill papers, 20/153.

[2] Prime Minister's Personal Telegram, T.1561/4, Prime Minister to President, No. 744, 'Personal and Top Secret', 5 August 1944: Cabinet papers, 120/144.

[3] COSMED 165, Telegram No. 4191, 'Top Secret', 4 August 1944: Cabinet papers, 122/1308.

[4] COS(W) 229, OZ 4205 to JSM Washington, 'Top Secret', 'Most Immediate', 5 August 1944: Cabinet papers, 105/61.

[5] LETOD 247, 'Top Secret', 'Most Immediate', 6 August 1944: Cabinet papers, 122/1308.

the plane arrived over the Cherbourg peninsula, but was then recalled, as fog on the landing strip at which Churchill was expected had caused a preceding plane to crash, and all of its occupants had been killed.

Churchill's plane flew back to Britain, landing at Thorney Island, from where he was driven to Eisenhower's forward headquarters at Sharpener Camp. Churchill and Eisenhower then lunched together, 'the PM taking delight', as Eisenhower's Naval Aide-de-Camp, Captain Butcher, noted in his diary, 'in feeding milk to the General's black kitten, Shaef, from a saucer on the dinner table at his place'.[1] After luncheon, Churchill and Eisenhower were joined in conference by General Bedell Smith, Admiral Ramsay and Admiral Tennant.[2] The meeting began with Churchill proposing the switch to Brittany. 'To my surprise,' Cunningham noted in his diary, 'found Eisenhower dead against it and had never sent a message putting it forward.' It was 'very apparent', Cunningham added, 'that the PM knowingly or not had misled the Chiefs of Staff and bounced them into sending their telegram to the United States Chiefs of Staff'.[3]

Eisenhower had certainly changed his mind, but, at the Sharpener Camp meeting, as Captain Butcher noted in his diary, had been 'surprised to find' that his own Chief of Staff, General Bedell Smith, 'agreed with the PM'. Butcher also noted that 'Ike lost the usual support of his former ally, his great friend Admiral Cunningham who sided with the PM', but, to counter Bedell Smith and Cunningham, had the 'ardent backing' of Admiral Ramsay and Admiral Tennant.

The discussion about the switch from the South of France to Brittany continued all afternoon. 'Ike argued so long and patiently,' Butcher noted, 'that he was practically limp when the PM departed and observed that although he had said "no" in every language, the Prime Minister, undoubtedly, would return to the subject in two or three days' time and simply regard the issue as unsettled.'[4] It was 'apparent', Cunningham reported to the Chiefs of Staff two days later, that at the meeting on August 5 Eisenhower had been 'opposed' to the switch from the South of France to Brittany. His view 'appeared to be' that rather than 'gamble on the availability of sufficient port capacity' in the Brittany peninsula, 'he would prefer the certainty of a battle in the South of France'.

Eisenhower had 'agreed' however, Cunningham told the Chiefs of Staff, 'to keep the matter open for four days in order to see what

[1] Diary entry for 7 August 1944 (referring to 5 August 1944): Captain Harry C. Butcher, *Three Years with Eisenhower*, London 1946, page 545.

[2] Private Office Diary, 5 August 1944.

[3] Cunningham diary, 5 August 1944: Cunningham papers.

[4] Diary entry for 7 August 1944 (referring to 5 August 1944): Captain Harry C. Butcher, *Three Years with Eisenhower*, London 1946, pages 545–6.

progress was made in Brittany, particularly as regards the capture of ports and the state of these ports when captured'.[1] 'He is now keeping an open mind on the question,' the Chiefs of Staff reported in a telegram to the Joint Staff Mission in Washington, 'and proposes to see how things develop in Brittany in the next four days before deciding whether to recommend a switch.'[2]

To reinforce the request of the British Chiefs of Staff to their United States opposite numbers, and while waiting to see what Eisenhower would decide as a result of his four days' wait 'to see how things develop in Brittany', Churchill telegraphed on August 6 to Harry Hopkins, in the hope that Hopkins would explain the Brittany proposal to General Marshall.

'I am grieved to find,' Churchill wrote, 'that even splendid victories and widening opportunities do not bring us together on strategy,' and he went on to tell Hopkins:

The brilliant operations of the American Army have not only cut off the Brest peninsula, but in my opinion have to a large extent demoralised the scattered Germans who remain there. St Nazaire and Nantes, one of your major disembarkation ports in the last war, may be in our hands at any time. Quiberon Bay, Lorient, and Brest will also soon fall into our hands. It is my belief that the German troops on the Atlantic shore south of the Cherbourg peninsula are in a state of weakness and disorder and that Bordeaux could be obtained easily, cheaply, and swiftly.

The possession of these Atlantic ports, together with those we have now, will open the way for the fullest importation of the great armies of the United States still awaiting their opportunity. In addition the ten divisions now mounted for 'Dragoon' could be switched into St Nazaire as soon as it is in Allied possession, in this case American possession. Thus Eisenhower might speedily be presented with a new great port, as well as with a new army to operate on his right flank in the march.

In the Toulon–Marseilles area, Churchill added, 'the enemy will at the outset be much stronger than we are', and the line of advance ran 'cross-grained' to the lie of the country, 'which abounds in most formidable rocky positions, ridges and gullies'. It would not be until 'probably ninety days' after the landings that these forces could influence Eisenhower's battle. 'Of course we are going to win anyhow,' Churchill commented, 'but these are very hard facts.' Churchill added:

There are still three or four days in which the decision to send to S. Nazaire the forces now destined and largely loaded for 'Dragoon' could be reconsidered. I admit the arguments against late changes in plans, but they ought

[1] Chiefs of Staff Committee No. 262 (Operations) of 1944, 7 August 1944: Cabinet papers, 79/79.
[2] OZ 4238, 'Top Secret', 'Most Immediate', 7 August 1944: Cabinet papers, 122/1308.

to be fairly weighed against what seems to us to be the overwhelming case for strengthening the main battle, and thus possibly finishing up Hitler this year.

Churchill asked Hopkins to put his views before General Marshall, 'if you feel able to embroil yourself'.[1]

On August 7 Churchill again flew to France. This time, despite his departure having been delayed for more than three hours because of bad weather in Normandy, he was able to land shortly after lunch. He then drove to see Montgomery at 21 Army Group Headquarters, from where he proceeded to the headquarters of the United States 12th Army Group, where General Bradley awaited him. The battle was then at its height however, and, sensing the tension, Churchill cut short his visit after an hour and returned by air to his original airstrip. At that moment, Eisenhower arrived from Britain, and the two men were able to talk together for twenty minutes, before Churchill flew back to Northolt, 'and so', as his Private Office diary recorded, 'to the Annexe for dinner'.[2]

Awaiting Churchill in London was the answer to his appeal to Hopkins. 'While there has been no reply as yet from the President,' Hopkins reported, 'to your message relative to the same matter, I am sure his answer will be in the negative.' The supply problem of Brittany would be found 'insurmountable'. No one knew the condition of the Brittany ports. 'To change the strategy now would be a great mistake and I believe would delay rather than aid our sure conquest of France.' The movement north from 'Anvil' would be 'much more rapid' than Churchill anticipated. The Germans 'have nothing to stop us'. The French would 'rise and assassinate large numbers of Germans, including, I trust, Monsieur Laval'. 'A tremendous victory is in store for us.'[3]

On the afternoon of August 7, the Joint Staff Mission put Britain's case against 'Dragoon' to the United States Chiefs of Staff, and 'did our best', as they reported back to London, 'to drive home the arguments' of the British Chiefs of Staff. Were the 'Dragoon' resources to be switched to the north from the south, they argued, it 'would lead to earlier victory and so to the end of the war'. But the arguments, although prolonged, were unsuccessful, with Marshall telling the Joint Staff Mission that he had 'never known a case' in which the United States Chiefs of Staff 'were all so unanimous'. To make a change now, Marshall argued, 'would be to cause the utmost confusion everywhere

[1] Prime Minister's Personal Telegram, T.1568/4, 'Personal, Private and Secret', 6 August 1944: Churchill papers, 20/169.
[2] Private Office Diary, 7 August 1944.
[3] Hopkins to Churchill, No. 36, 'Personal and Secret', 7 August 1944: Churchill papers, 20/169.

and in the event we might fall between two stools'. The Joint Staff Mission added: 'We could not budge them.' Unless Eisenhower himself 'comes up very strongly in support of the proposal', the Joint Staff Mission doubted whether it would be possible 'to shake the United States Chiefs of Staff in their views'.[1]

In a memorandum prepared that day for their British opposite numbers, the United States Chiefs of Staff were emphatic that 'the situation had not changed sufficiently' to warrant 'such a radical change in our plans'. They were also 'convinced', as they informed the British Chiefs of Staff, 'that "Dragoon" will be successful in its landing phase'. They also expected 'a rapid advance up the Rhône Valley, aided to the fullest extent by the French resistance groups', an operation which 'may well contribute the knock-out punch to the German army in France'. For this reason it would be 'extremely unwise', they warned, 'to change our plans at this late date when all indications point to the complete success of the "Dragoon" operation'.[2] This emphatic rejection of the Brittany operation reached the British Chiefs of Staff on August 8, and was read out at their morning meeting.[3] That same day, Roosevelt telegraphed direct to Churchill. He had consulted by telegraph with his Chiefs of Staff, he said, and was 'unable to agree' that the resources allocated to 'Dragoon' should be 'considered available' for a move into France through the Brittany ports. It was his own considered opinion that 'Dragoon' should begin as planned.[4] 'I pray God that you may be right,' Churchill replied. 'We shall of course do everything in our power to help you achieve success.'[5]

When the British Chiefs of Staff met on the morning of August 9, they had in front of them not only the memorandum from the United States Chiefs of Staff, opposing the switch to Brittany, but a telegram from Eisenhower expressing himself 'strongly opposed to a cancellation or major modification of "Dragoon" ' which should itself be 'pushed energetically and speedily'.[6] Eisenhower's four days of 'open mind' had been to no avail. In these circumstances, the British Chiefs of Staff concluded, 'there would be no further point in continuing to

---

[1] JSM 180, IZ 5728, 'Most Immediate', 10.45 p.m., 7 August 1944: Cabinet papers, 105/46.
[2] CCS 603/16, sent to London as JSM 176, IZ 5682, 'Top Secret', 5 August 1944: Cabinet papers, 105/46.
[3] Chiefs of Staff Committee No. 263 (Operations) of 1944, 10.30 a.m., 8 August 1944: Cabinet papers, 79/79. The United States Chiefs of Staff Memorandum had been telegraphed to London as JSM 180.
[4] President to Prime Minister, No. 596, 'Personal and Top Secret', 8 August 1944: Churchill papers, 20/169.
[5] Prime Minister's Personal Telegram, T.1585/4, Prime Minister to President, No. 745, 'Personal and Top Secret', 8 August 1944: Churchill papers, 20/169.
[6] SCAF 61, FWD 12704, 'Top Secret', 8 August 1944: Cabinet papers, 122/1308.

press the United States Chiefs of Staff to agree to the proposed modifications in the plan'.[1]

The Brittany diversion was dead; 'Anvil', earlier given the codename 'Dragoon' for security reasons, was less than a week away. It should proceed, Eisenhower was instructed on August 10, 'as originally planned'.[2]

On August 6 Churchill learned that the Greek Communists were only prepared to accept the Lebanon Charter subject to the resignation of the man who had negotiated it, George Papandreou.[3] Churchill at once minuted to Eden:

Surely we should tell M. Papandreou he should continue as Prime Minister and defy them all. The behaviour of EAM is absolutely intolerable. Obviously they are seeking nothing but the communisation of Greece during the confusion of the war, without allowing the people to decide in any manner understood by democracy.

We cannot take a man up as we have done Papandreou and let him be thrown to the wolves at the first snarlings of the miserable Greek Banditti. Difficult as the world is now, we shall not make our course easier by abandoning people whom we have encouraged to take on serious jobs by promises of support.

The British Parliament, Churchill pointed out, had accepted the Papandreou Government and the Lebanon Charter. 'How would we look at the next stage,' Churchill asked Eden, 'if we threw Papandreou over for the sake of some other poor wretch connected with the fortunes of Greece?' Should matters go 'downhill', Churchill added, and the EAM Communist movement 'became master', Britain would have to reconsider keeping any of its Missions there 'and put the Greek people bluntly up against Bolshevism'. Either Britain supports Papandreou, 'if necessary with force as we have agreed, or we disinterest ourselves entirely in Greece'.[4]

Churchill now proceeded to make plans to send a British military force to Greece. An Enigma decrypt, of August 1, had shown the

---

[1] Chiefs of Staff Committee No. 267 (Operations) of 1944, 10.30 a.m., 9 August 1944: Cabinet papers, 79/79.

[2] Combined Chiefs of Staff Telegram, 77500, WAR 78677, 10 August 1944: Cabinet papers, 122/1309.

[3] Telegrams No. 569, 571, 572 and 573 from the British Chargé D'Affaires to the Greek Government (Cairo) to the Foreign Office.

[4] Prime Minister's Personal Minute, M.932/4, 'Top Secret', 6 August 1944: Churchill papers, 20/153.

accelerating pace of the German withdrawal from southern Greece. On August 6 Churchill minuted to Brooke:

It may be that within a month or so we shall have to put 10,000 or 12,000 men into Athens with a few tanks, guns and armoured cars. You have a division in England which has above 13,000 troops. Such a force could be embarked now and would probably be in time for the political crisis, which is of major consequence to the policy of His Majesty's Government. Such a force could be supported by ground troops from the airfields of the Delta, and by scrapings and combings from the 200,000 tail we have in Egypt.

I repeat there is no question of trying to dominate Greece or going outside the immediate curtilage of Athens, but this is the centre of government and, with the approaches to it, must be made secure. Bren gun carriers would be very useful. If you have a better plan, let me know it.

It is to be presumed that the Germans have gone or are streaking away to the north, and that the force landed at the Piraeus would be welcomed by the great majority of the population of Athens, including all notables.

'The utmost secrecy,' Churchill stressed, 'must enwrap this project.' [1]

Three days after Churchill wrote this minute, Eden told the War Cabinet of the 'political importance of maintaining our position in Greece', and of avoiding a Communist coup d'état immediately the Germans withdraw. Were the Greek Communist forces, 'who were strongly armed', to seize power, Eden warned, 'a massacre might follow'. This would be 'very injurious to our prestige', and might even 'add Greece to the post-war Balkan Slav bloc which now showed signs of forming under Russian influence, and from which we were anxious to keep Greece detached'.

Eden told the War Cabinet that 'the case for despatching a force' to Greece, the main force to Athens but perhaps a 'simultaneous' force to Salonica, was 'very strong'.

Giving details of a 'special force' to be prepared in the Mediterranean, Brooke feared that ten thousand men 'might prove insufficient'. Attlee felt that the troops that were sent could go 'ostensibly, at any rate, in connection with the arrangements for relief'. The discussion ended with 'general agreement' that a special force should be organized to be despatched to Greece 'in the event of a German withdrawal'. It was also agreed that Eden would tell the United States of this decision, but that 'at the present stage should *not* inform the Russian Government of our intentions in this matter'. [2]

Half an hour later, at a further meeting of the War Cabinet with

---

[1] Prime Minister's Personal Minute, M.932/4, 'Top Secret', 6 August 1944: Churchill papers, 20/153.
[2] War Cabinet No. 103 of 1944, 5.30 p.m., 9 August 1944, Confidential Annex: Cabinet papers, 65/47.

many Cabinet Ministers present, it was learned that three Polish aircraft, flying from bases in southern Italy, had succeeded in dropping weapons to the Polish Underground Army in Warsaw. 'It would clearly be much easier,' the minutes recorded, 'for help to be sent by the Russians instead of from Western Europe; but a previous approach had been coldly received.' [1] On August 10 it appeared that Stalin was willing to help. 'I am so glad to learn that you are sending supplies yourself,' Churchill telegraphed. 'Anything you feel able to do will be warmly appreciated by your British friends and Allies.' As to Stalin's talks in Moscow with Mikolajczyk, 'I am very glad,' Churchill told Stalin, 'that you brought both sides together. Undoubtedly an advance has been made towards our common goal. I share your hope that the business will go better in the future.' [2]

The actual result of Stalin's talks with Mikolajczyk was not as auspicious as Churchill's hopeful comments suggested, for, as Stalin had told him when it was proposed that Mikolajczyk should be Prime Minister of post-war Poland, the Polish Government of which he was already the Prime Minister would have only four portfolios in a Cabinet of eighteen. Now, Stalin wrote, it was up to Mikolajczyk to reach agreement on this basis with the Polish Committee of National Liberation, and its leader, Boleslaw Bierut. [3]

For three days in mid-August, Churchill and his senior advisers devoted their mental energies to an attempt to evolve a strategy for the war in the Far East. At issue were two conflicting claims, those of the Pacific and the Bay of Bengal theatres. Mountbatten, who had come to London to advise on how he would employ amphibious resources 'if these were made available for operations in South East Asia Command', told the Chiefs of Staff Committee on August 7 that in view of the Japanese strength in Burma, forces 'could not be withdrawn from Burma to undertake operations in other areas'. [4]

On the morning of August 8, at the first of five Staff Conferences in the course of two days, Churchill argued that 'an operation for the capture of Rangoon' would result in diverting Japanese forces from northern Burma. He was 'horrified', Churchill said, to learn that operation 'Vanguard' could not be launched before the spring of 1945 'and

---

[1] War Cabinet No. 104 of 1944, 6 p.m., 9 August 1944: Cabinet papers, 65/43.

[2] Prime Minister's Personal Telegram, T.1603/4, 'Personal and Top Secret', 10 August 1944: Churchill papers, 20/170.

[3] 'Personal and Top Secret', 8 August 1944: Churchill papers, 20/169.

[4] Chiefs of Staff Committee No. 262 (Operations) of 1944, 11 a.m., 7 August 1944: Cabinet papers, 79/79.

felt that the possibility of speeding up the operation should be examined. Rangoon was in itself an important objective', he said, 'and its capture would open up possibilities of further operations such, for example, as an advance on Moulmein or Bangkok or to the Kra Isthmus or Malay Peninsula'. Britain's 'general strategy' in the Far East, Churchill felt, 'might be to recapture the many valuable possessions we had lost in that area'.

Mountbatten spoke of the need to pursue operation 'Champion', aimed at opening up the air and supply routes from northern Burma to Chiang Kai-shek's forces in China. Commenting on this, Churchill told the Chiefs of Staff Committee that 'while he agreed that we were under an obligation to protect the air route to China, he deprecated a policy which would result in the whole effort of the British/Indian forces being bogged down in Burma. He thought the effort required to guard the air route was disproportionately costly, though he agreed that this must be maintained as, if supplies were cut off, the Generalissimo's forces would wither'.

Brooke supported 'Vanguard' and the capture of Rangoon, as against 'Champion' and its campaign in northern Burma, fearing that the latter held out 'the gloomy prospect of "eating the porcupine quill by quill" '. Once Rangoon was captured, Churchill commented, he would leave the remaining Japanese forces in Burma 'to rot away' and release Mountbatten's forces for other operations.[1]

The discussion continued that afternoon. Mountbatten told the Chiefs of Staff Committee that the 'actual capture' of Rangoon 'could perhaps be done with resources now available', but that a follow-up would be necessary, and these forces could only come 'from outside South East Asia'. Brooke suggested that 'Vanguard' itself should be postponed until November 1945, and 'Champion' carried out in its place. But Churchill preferred, instead of 'Champion', his earlier favourite project, 'to seize the tip of Sumatra' while maintaining 'only the minimum forces in Burma to secure the air route to China'.[2]

At a third meeting of the Chiefs of Staff that day, Oliver Lyttelton spoke in favour of the capture of Rangoon, as being the only operation which would eventually result in the release of forces from Burma 'for operations in other theatres', giving Britain an option to undertake either a Bay of Bengal or a South-West Pacific strategy. Churchill supported this veiw, urging that preparations 'should be begun at once', and asking that in the meanwhile 'we should make the greatest offer

---

[1] Staff conference, Chiefs of Staff Committee No. 264 (Operations) of 1944, 11 a.m., 8 August 1944: Cabinet papers, 79/79.

[2] Staff Conference, Chiefs of Staff Committee No. 265 (Operations) of 1944, 6 p.m., 8 August 1944: Cabinet papers, 79/79.

of naval assistance within our power to the United States, ascertaining from them the way in which the forces could be most effectively employed'. If the Americans adhered to their present speed of advance, he said, 'they would be launching an immense amphibious stroke aimed at the heart of Japan early next year. It was possible that they could employ such a mass of seaborne air forces as would enable them to dominate the Japanese land based air forces. Such a bold stroke commanded the imagination.'[1]

The next Staff Conference to discuss the Pacific took place just after midday on August 9, when it was agreed 'to plan and prepare for the capture of Rangoon at the earliest moment, extreme efforts being made to attack before the end of 1944, whether Germany had surrendered or not'. At the same time, four British Indian divisions from the Mediterranean and two British divisions from France or Britain were to be moved to South-East Asia Command. If the attack on Rangoon was not launched before these reinforcements arrived, they and all other forces available should be used instead for 'the best variants' of operation 'Culverin', 'as a step', Churchill explained, 'towards the recapture of Singapore'.[2]

The final Staff Conference on the Pacific met that night, when the attack on Rangoon, operation 'Vanguard', was given priority. At the same time, it was agreed that plans should also be made 'for the recapture of Malaya in readiness for the time when the necessary forces became available'. If Germany's 'organized resistance' were to 'collapse early', then it would be necessary to review the situation, and to decide between the operations against Rangoon, and other operations, principally 'Culverin', 'which may then seem more profitable'. The 'greatest offer of naval assistance' would at the same time be made to the United States Chiefs of Staff, 'it being impressed upon them', as the conclusions of the meeting noted, 'that it is our desire to share with them in the main operations against the mainland of Japan or Formosa'.[3]

These were the decisions for which Churchill had fought.

At the beginning of the second week of August, Churchill learned that Roosevelt was unwilling to come to a conference in Britain, giving as his reason the fact that Stalin, who did not wish to leave Russia, would be unable to join them. Roosevelt was also concerned about the forthcoming Presidential election in November. 'As you know,' he

---

[1] Staff Conference, Chiefs of Staff Committee No. 266 (Operations) of 1944, 10.30 p.m., 8 August 1944: Cabinet papers, 79/79.

[2] Staff Conference, Chiefs of Staff Committee No. 268 (Operations) of 1944, 12.30 p.m., 9 August 1944: Cabinet papers, 79/79.

[3] Staff Conference, Chiefs of Staff Committee No. 269 (Operations) of 1944, 10.30 p.m., 9 August 1944: Cabinet papers, 79/79.

reminded Churchill, 'domestic problems are unfortunately difficult for three months to come.'[1] 'I most deeply regret your inability to visit Scotland,' Churchill replied on August 10, and he added: 'The King seemed very disappointed when I told him.'

Determined to hold a meeting as soon as possible, Churchill suggested a return to Quebec. 'MacKenzie King assured me he would be enchanted,' Churchill wrote. 'I have no doubt all could be arranged to your comfort and convenience.' Churchill went on to explain to Roosevelt, who was then visiting the Aleutian Islands, why he felt that a meeting was now urgent:

There are several serious matters in the military sphere which must be adjusted between our Staffs. I too would greatly welcome a few frank talks with you on matters it is difficult to put on paper. We have to settle the part the British Empire should take in the war against Japan after Germany's unconditional surrender. The situation in Burma causes me much anxiety. We have suffered very heavy losses through disease and the prospect of the whole forces of the British-Indian Army being tied down indefinitely in the worst part of the country is unattractive. Other tangled questions arise about the position of Alexander's Army in Italy including whether it is to be bled white for 'Dragoon' and thus stripped of all initiative.

'It is impossible,' Churchill told Roosevelt, 'to resolve these thorny matters by correspondence and I am sure that if we and the Staff were together, good working agreements could be reached.'

Churchill ended his telegram: 'It will be a very great pleasure for me to see you again. I do hope your tour has done you good. Let me know your wishes as soon as possible.'[2]

---

[1] President to Prime Minister No. 595, 'Personal and Top Secret', 8 August 1944: Premier papers, 4/75/2, Part 2, folio 711.

[2] Prime Minister's Personal Telegram, T.1600/4, Prime Minister to President, No. 750, 'Personal and Top Secret', 10 August 1944: Premier papers, 4/75/2, Part 2, folios 702–3.

48

Italian Journey

I N Italy Alexander's forces had been much depleted since early July as a result of 'Anvil'. By the beginning of August seven divisions in all had left his command, reducing the Fifth Army alone from nearly a quarter of a million men to only 153,000 men. Alexander still sought, however, to conduct offensive operations, and succeeded on the night of 10 August 1944 in forcing the Germans to withdraw from Florence. That night, Churchill left Northolt airport in his specially converted York, for Italy, accompanied by Lord Moran, Brigadier Jacob, Commander Thompson, Leslie Rowan, John Peck, Sawyers the valet and a detective.[1] In much of the telegraphic correspondence about the visit, Churchill was described as 'Colonel Kent'.[2] 'I do hope,' Oliver Lyttelton wrote that day, 'you will get a little rest with the brush as well as the binoculars,' and he added: 'I am much relieved about the Pacific strategy.'[3]

Churchill's first landing was in Algiers, where he stayed in Duff Cooper's villa. De Gaulle, whom Churchill had invited to see him, refused to come. Churchill, noted Pierson Dixon, 'was justly incensed'.[4] One welcome visitor was Randolph Churchill, still not fully recovered from the damage to his knees and spine during the air crash in Croatia. 'No reference was made by either of us to family matters,' Churchill wrote to his wife. 'He is a lonely figure by no means recovered as far as walking is concerned. Our talk was about politics, French and English, about wh there was plenty of friendly badinage & argument.'[5]

Randolph Churchill had at this time become estranged from his wife Pamela, who remained in Churchill's family circle, to Randolph's

[1] Prime Minister's Personal Telegram, T.1590/4 (to Alfred Duff Cooper), 'Personal and Top Secret', 9 August 1944: Churchill papers, 20/169.

[2] Prime Minister's Personal Telegram, T.1591/4 (to Generals Wilson and Alexander), 'Personal and Top Secret', 9 August 1944: Churchill papers, 20/169.

[3] Letter of 10 August 1944: Premier papers, 4/75/1, folio 15.

[4] Pierson Dixon diary, 11 August 1944: Piers Dixon, *op. cit.*, page 97.

[5] Letter of 12 August 1944: Mary Soames, *Clementine Churchill, op. cit.*, page 353.

considerable distress. 'Randolph's marriage is going wonky,' Harold
Nicolson wrote to his sons three weeks later, 'and Winston is terribly
distressed. The old boy is tremendously domestic and adores his
family.'[1]

During his talk with Randolph in Algiers, Churchill had spoken
critically about de Gaulle, having been 'considerably affronted', as
Churchill's Private Office noted, by de Gaulle's refusal to meet him.[2]
Shortly before Churchill flew on that night to Italy, Randolph sent
him a letter, urging a conciliatory attitude towards de Gaulle. Although
de Gaulle's conduct was 'deplorable', Randolph wrote, 'after all he is a
frustrated man representing a defeated country. You as the un-
challenged leader of England and the main architect of victory can
well afford to be magnanimous without fear of being misunderstood'.[3]
'Naturally at times like this,' Churchill wrote to his wife six days later,
about de Gaulle's 'insolent' attitudes, 'I do not let them influence my
political judgement, but I feel that de Gaullist France will be a France
more hostile to England than any since Fashoda.'[4]

After lunch in Algiers, Churchill flew on to Naples where he was
the guest of General Wilson at the Villa Rivalta, overlooking the Bay
of Naples.[5] At dinner, with Wilson, Macmillan and Pierson Dixon,
the talk was of Italy. Eden had instructed Pierson Dixon, as Dixon
noted, 'to encourage Churchill to agree to a peace treaty being signed
with Italy'. But Dixon's efforts were to no avail. 'Talk after dinner,'
Dixon noted in his dairy, 'with the PM, who showed himself very
tough about Italy and quite against, and determined to reform the
various Allied and British organisations. Italy had done us great
damage and must be punished and be ground down. I asked him
what "working her passage" meant. Answer, 3 or 4 years. I tried to
counter these extreme views but without much success.' Dixon added:

> The PM very critical of the FO. But not entirely consistent in his criticisms.
> One was that the FO were always wanting to do something, thus contravening
> the maxim of Talleyrand: 'Surtout pas trop de zèle.' But we were also accused of
> being inconclusive. 'If you ask the FO to write you a paper, you add up the
> paragraphs with odd numbers, and you get one opinion; add up the paragraphs
> with even numbers and you get another: and no conclusion.[6]

[1] Harold Nicolson letter of 31 August 1944: Nigel Nicolson, editor, *op. cit.*, page 397. Randolph
Churchill's marriage to Pamela Digby was dissolved in 1946.

[2] 'Diary of Visit to Italy', 11 August 1944: notes written up each night by John Peck and Leslie
Rowan.

[3] Letter of 11 August 1944: Churchill papers, 1/381.

[4] 'Private', 17 August 1944: Spencer-Churchill papers.

[5] The Villa's name can also be spelt Riv'Alta. Churchill described it to his wife as 'A very
comfortable guest-house, formerly the villa of a wealthy Fascist, now in a concentration camp'
(Letter of 17 August 1944: Spencer-Churchill papers).

[6] Pierson Dixon diary, 11 August 1944: Piers Dixon, *op. cit.*, page 98.

That night General Wilson left at 11.30, and Macmillan an hour later, after which Churchill went to bed. 'We have asked all concerned,' noted the Private Office, 'to co-operate in sparing the Prime Minister after-dinner meetings or work late at night.'[1] On the following morning Churchill received the copy of an appeal from the Poles in Warsaw to the Allies. It was their tenth day of fighting against the Germans. 'We are conducting a bloody fight,' the message read. 'The town is cut by three routes.' Each route was 'strongly held' by German tanks, and the buildings along them 'burnt out'. Two German armoured trains on the city's periphery, and artillery from the Praga suburb on the east bank of the Vistula, 'fire continuously on the town, and are supported by air forces'.

The Polish message noted that only one 'small drop' had come from the Allies. 'On the German-Russian front silence since the 3rd. We are therefore without any material or moral support. . . .' The message continued:

The soldiers and the population of the capital look hopelessly at the skies, expecting help from the Allies. On the background of smoke they see only German aircraft. They are surprised, feel deeply depressed, and begin to revile.

We have practically no news from you, no information with regard to the political situation, no advice and no instructions. Have you discussed in Moscow help for Warsaw? I repeat emphatically that without immediate support, consisting of drops of arms and ammunition, bombing of objectives held by the enemy, and air landing, our fight will collapse in a few days.

With the above-mentioned help the fight will continue.

I expect from you the greatest effort in this respect.

Churchill at once sent on this message to Stalin, whose troops were, at one point, only twelve miles from Warsaw across the Vistula, and several of whose operational airfields were within only ten or twelve minutes' flight from the city. 'They implore machine guns and ammunition,' Churchill telegraphed. 'Can you not give them some further help, as the distance from Italy is so very great?'[2]

At noon on August 12, Marshal Tito came to see Churchill at the Villa Rivalta. Pierson Dixon, who was present throughout their discussion, noted in his diary:

[1] 'Diary of Visit to Italy', 11 August 1944.
[2] Prime Minister's Personal Telegram, T.1609/4, 'Personal and Top Secret', 12 August 1944: Churchill papers, 20/170.

Tito was cautious, nervous and sweating a good deal in his absurd Marshal's uniform of thick cloth and gold lace. Fitzroy and I sat opposite. The PM pitched into Tito a good deal towards the end, and told him that we could not tolerate our war material being used against rival Yugoslavs. But Tito must have known that there was no real threat against him, since we have consistently done nothing but court him. But he evidently thought it politic not to turn a deaf ear to the appeal.[1]

During their conversation, Churchill 'suggested' to Tito, as the minutes of the meeting recorded, 'that the right solution for Yugoslavia was a democratic system based on the peasants, conditions in the peasant holdings being gradually improved'. To this, Tito replied that 'as he had several times stated publicly, he had no desire to introduce the Communist system into Yugoslavia, if only for the reason that it was to be expected that most European countries after the war would be living under a democratic system from which Yugoslavia could not afford to differ'.

Developments in the 'small countries', Tito told Churchill, 'depended on relations between the great Powers and relations between Great Britain, Russia and United States had greatly improved. Yugoslavia should be able to profit from this improvement and develop along democratic lines. It was true that the Soviet Government had a Mission with the Partisans, but this Mission, far from expressing any idea of introducing the Soviet system into Yugoslavia, had expressed views in the contrary sense.'

When Churchill said he would like to see Tito 'reaffirm publicly his statement about Communism', Tito replied that he was 'reluctant to do so at this moment since such a statement might give the impression that it had been forced on him and weaken his position'.

When Tito mentioned that he favoured a federation for Yugoslavia, but not a Balkan federation, Churchill, as the minutes noted, 'sounded a note of warning about Panslavism'.[2]

Pierson Dixon's account continued:

We went straight from the conference into a lunch in Tito's honour, to which the Commanders-in-Chief and Harold Macmillan came. The PM, looking pasty and ill, lurched to his feet at the end and made a highly laudatory speech about Tito's exploits, welcoming him as an ally. This was a tactical mistake, which undid the good of the sermon at the conference. It was left that Tito should meet the Ban,[3] and that the two of them would have a discussion with the PM the following day.

---

[1] Pierson Dixon diary, 12 August 1944: Piers Dixon, *op. cit.*, pages 99–100.
[2] 'Minutes of Conference at Naples, 12th August 1944, 12 noon–1.15 p.m.', 'Top Secret': Premier papers, 3/512/3.
[3] Dr Ivan Subasic, the former 'Ban', or Governor, of Croatia.

Throughout the talks, Tito's interpreter Olga Humo had sat between the two men. As he left the conference room, Churchill told Pierson Dixon that he had an 'important instruction' to give him. Churchill then explained:

I wish to give Olga a memento of the occasion. These gestures do good. I gave a present to Stalin's daughter. I have certain funds at my disposal for such purposes. Procure by tomorrow morning an ornament (making a vague gesture across his neck which I interpreted to indicate a necklace), and let it be inscribed to commemorate the occasion. Spend about twenty pounds.

A locket was bought, which Dixon had inscribed with the words: 'Olga Humo from Winston S. Churchill, Naples 12th August 1944.'[1]

Two photographers with the United States Army Pictorial Service, Donald Wiedenmayer and Jack Wagers, were now summoned to record the meeting of Prime Minister and partisan leader. When the two leaders had been photographed alone, Churchill himself suggested a second photograph with secretaries, aides and interpreters.[2]

During August 12, Churchill received a formal invitation from Roosevelt for a meeting at Quebec in September. 'We accept with greatest pleasure,' he replied, and added: 'Urgently looking to our meeting.' Churchill also sent Roosevelt a report on the Americans in Normandy. 'How magnificently your troops are fighting,' he wrote, 'and how their logistics have carried them forward.'[3]

That afternoon, Churchill went by admiral's barge to the island of Ischia, where, on a small beach, he bathed for about half an hour in the warm waters of a hot spring. On the return journey he passed, and was recognized by, troops in two convoys of landing craft sailing for 'Dragoon', whereupon the admiral's barge altered course and came down the line of each of the convoys. As he passed the cheering troops, Churchill sent a message to them, 'wishing them every success in their venture'.[4] 'They did not know,' Churchill later wrote, 'that if I had had my way they would be sailing in a different direction.'[5]

That evening, before dinner, Churchill had a short talk with the Ban of Croatia, Dr Subasic. At dinner itself, much of the talk was also about Yugoslavia. Pierson Dixon noted in his diary:

The PM at dinner was very realistic about Tito, who he thought was getting away with too much. At the conference he had said that he intended to send Tito a memo and I had drafted one in the afternoon, which I later

[1] Pierson Dixon diary, 12 August 1944: Piers Dixon, *op. cit.*, pages 98–9.

[2] Donald Wiedenmayer recollection: letter to Randolph Churchill, 10 April 1963. The first of the two photographs is reproduced in this volume.

[3] 'Chain' No. 5, 'Personal and Top Secret', 12 August 1944: Cabinet papers, 120/144.

[4] 'Diary of a Visit to Italy', 12 August 1944.

[5] Winston S. Churchill, *The Second World War*, London 1954, volume 6, page 84.

discussed with Ralph Stevenson.[1] The PM after dinner approved this but stiffened it with statements about the importance of the Serbs and the need for unity if our supplies were to continue.[2]

Churchill's memorandum on August 12 was emphatic that Tito must make 'not only a statement regarding his intention not to impose Communism on the country, but also a statement to the effect that he will not use the armed strength of the Movement to influence the free expression of the will of the people on the future régime of the country'. If any large quantity of the ammunition which had been sent from Britain was used for 'fratricidal strife other than in self-defence', it would affect 'the whole question' of Allied supplies. Nor was Britain satisfied that 'sufficient recognition' had been given by Tito to 'the powers and rights of the Serbian people'.[3]

At 12.45 a.m. Churchill went to bed. An hour later the memorandum was ready to send to Tito. 'It was a great pleasure to meet you today,' Churchill had written in his covering note. 'I promised to write personally. Here it is.'[4]

On the morning of August 13 Churchill worked on the papers in his box, dictating to Patrick Kinna a minute on why he opposed too rapid a peace treaty with Italy. The present Government, Churchill argued, 'hold office only as a result of their own intrigues'. The industrial North, still under German rule, 'has no representation and may easily repudiate what is signed behind their backs'.[5] Soon after eleven o'clock, Churchill left for a visit to Capri. Pierson Dixon, who accompanied him, noted in his diary:

We steamed up to 'Tiberius' rock', a sheer fall of 700 feet down which Tiberius is supposed to have thrown his victims, then on to the Blue Grotto, where all the party, including the PM, disembarked with great zest into little boats and lying flat made the perilous entry into the Grotto. The PM was entranced by the effect of the azure water and referred to it frequently during the tour.

I expressed surprise to our boatman that there were so many boats hanging about the entrance to the Grotto waiting for tourists in war time. He replied that the Germans had come over to the island in great numbers and that there had been no lack of tourists throughout the war.

[1] Ralph Stevenson was the British Ambassador to the Yugoslav Government in Exile. From 1939 to 1941 he had been Eden's Principal Private Secretary. He was knighted in 1946.

[2] Pierson Dixon diary, 12 August 1944: Piers Dixon, op. cit., page 100.

[3] Memorandum of 12 August 1944: Piers Dixon, op. cit., page 100.

[4] Letter of 12 August 1944: Churchill papers, 20/138.

[5] Prime Minister's Personal Minute, M (K) 5/4, 13 August 1944: Churchill papers, 20/153.

We steamed on to a cove at the western end of the island, where a rustic restaurant had been taken over for lunch.

We undressed on the rocks, the PM under a large umbrella on a small platform—a fine sight with his valet attending him and half a dozen American military police dotted about the rocks on guard. After the swim we had a huge lunch in the rustic restaurant. The PM was in holiday mood and talked about chewing-gum defacing the features, demonstrated how to light a cigar without interrupting his conversation and enquired about the arrangements for the Capri water supply.

On the return journey to Naples, another outgoing convoy was passed: American landing craft escorted by six British destroyers. 'We steamed from ship to ship,' Dixon noted, 'and as we passed each destroyer the PM stood up in the prow of the motor launch. Each time he got a tremendous reception from the men lining the decks.' Dixon's account continued:

Half way across Fitzroy Maclean met us by arrangement, bearing a letter from Tito and a report on a conference in the morning between Tito and our military representatives. Fitzroy was a brave sight, in his kilt, boarding the launch. The rest of the voyage was complicated, as the PM was trying to read Tito's letter and Fitzroy's report in the intervals of saluting the destroyers. I read the documents and scribbled out on a sheet of notepaper the main points and the agenda for the conference we were to have with Tito and the Ban as soon as we returned. The PM meanwhile went to sleep for 20 minutes.

Both Tito and the Ban were waiting when Churchill got back to the villa at 5, 'but the PM kept them for half an hour', Pierson Dixon noted, 'perhaps deliberately'. There was then a conference from 5.45 to 7.15, 'in the course of which', Pierson Dixon wrote, 'it became apparent that Tito had swallowed the Ban, who, whenever he was asked for his opinion, merely reiterated or embroidered Tito's views. Tito did, however, make certain concessions of form such as agreeing that the amalgamated navy should be called the Royal Yugoslav Navy and promised to meet the King. A fusion and cessation of civil war was achieved: poor Mihailovic passed over in silence.' [1]

Speaking of the region of Istria, which, as he pointed out, 'still remained Italian', Churchill told Tito and Subasic: 'It might be a good thing to remove the territory from Italian sovereignty.' This would be decided, however, he said, 'at the peace', either at a peace conference or, if there were no peace conference, 'by a meeting of the principal Powers, at which Yugoslavia would have an opportunity to state her claim'.

[1] Pierson Dixon diary, 13 August 1944: Piers Dixon, *op. cit.*, pages 101–2.

As to Communism, Tito reiterated that he was 'entirely averse to imposing any régime on the people'.[1]

After the Conference, there were drinks on the terrace of the villa, and Churchill presented Olga Humo with her inscribed locket. There was then a session with the photographers. 'When the moment came for Tito and the Ban to be photographed on either side of the PM,' Dixon noted, 'there was an embarrassing pause before the two leaders sat down, broken by Tito waving the Ban to the place of honour on the PM's right, with the remark, "the Ban must sit there, as we mustn't get Mr Churchill into trouble with the Conservative Party".'[2]

Pierson Dixon later recalled how Churchill was in reminiscent mood, telling Tito of the journey he had made before the First World War with the then Prime Minister, Asquith, along the Dalmatian Coast.[3] 'Asquith,' Churchill told Tito, 'never mentioned politics except once during the forty days on tour.'[4]

On the night of August 13, 'after doing a certain amount of work', as his secretariat noted, Churchill went to bed at 12.45.[5] On the following morning he telegraphed to both Roosevelt and Stalin to report on the talks with Tito and Subasic. He had told both the Yugoslav leaders, he said, 'that we had no thought but that they should combine their resources so as to weld the Yugoslav people into one instrument in the struggle against the Germans'.[6] 'Marshal Tito promised to issue a statement,' Churchill informed King George VI, 'repudiating any desire to communize the country.'[7] 'You will have read about the interviews with Tito,' Churchill wrote to his wife three days later. 'I think the old Ban and he got on almost too well together. It may well be a case of Tito first, the Ban second and the King nowhere. However, the great thing is to unite all forces against the Germans. Unhappily Tito is now using the bulk of the ammunition we gave him to fight the Serbs.' However, Churchill added, 'the meeting did a lot of good, and made Tito, I think, more desirous of respecting our wishes'.[8]

*   *   *

[1] 'Minutes of Meeting, Naples, 13th August 1944, 5.30–6.45 p.m., 'Top Secret': Premier papers, 3/512/3.

[2] Pierson Dixon diary, 13 August 1944: Piers Dixon, *op. cit.*, pages 103–4.

[3] On 29 June 1944 Sir Edward Bridges had asked Churchill how the two world wars should be described. Bridges' suggestions were 'War of 1914–18' and 'War of 1939–4?'; 'First World War' and 'Second World War'; or 'Four Years' War' and 'Five (or six, or seven) Years' War'. Churchill had chosen 'First World War' and 'Second World War'. Minutes of 24 and 29 June 1944: Premier papers, 4/69/2, folio 684.

[4] Pierson Dixon recollections: Piers Dixon, *op. cit.*, page 104.

[5] 'Diary of a Visit to Italy', 13 August 1944.

[6] Prime Minister's Personal Telegrams T.1617/4, and T.1618/4, 'Chain' Nos 32 and 33, 'Personal and Top Secret', 14 August 1944: Churchill papers, 20/170.

[7] 'Chain' No. 30, 'Personal and Top Secret', 14 August 1944: Churchill papers, 20/180.

[8] 'Personal', 17 August 1944: Spencer-Churchill papers.

At a meeting of the Chiefs of Staff on August 11, during a discussion of 'assistance to the Poles', Portal pointed out 'that though the Russians had promised to help, operations from the Mediterranean were Poland's only hope until such time as the Russian promises were implemented'. Portal had already asked Air Marshal Slessor 'to ensure that the British contribution to such operations was considerable'.[1] Effective air support, however, Sir Douglas Evill told the Chiefs of Staff Committee on August 12, 'could only be provided by Russian tactical aircraft operating at short range'.[2] No such support had yet been forthcoming.

From Italy, Churchill followed the continuing Polish resistance. After reading a note in *The Times* of August 12 headed 'Second Martyrdom of Warsaw', he telegraphed to Eden, who was in London:

It certainly is very curious that the Russian Armies should have ceased their attack on Warsaw and withdrawn some distance at the moment when the underground army had revolted. It would only be a flight of 100 miles for them to send in all the necessary quantities of ammunition and machine guns the Poles need for their heroic fight.

I have been talking to Slessor, trying to send all possible from here. But what have the Russians done? In my opinion it would be better if you sent a message to Stalin through Molotov drawing attention to the implications that are afoot in many quarters and asking the Russians to send all help. Last night 28 aircraft did the flight from Italy which is 700 miles. Three were lost. It was the fourth flight made from here under these quite exceptional conditions.

The suggestion that the Polish patriots in Warsaw were deserted will if it gets afoot be a matter of great annoyance to the Russians but can easily be prevented by operations well within their power. I think it is better that you should do it through Molotov rather than I should do it through Stalin as it is more impersonal.[3]

There was 'some risk', Eden told the War Cabinet that day, that 'bitterness as a result of the difficulties of the Polish Underground Army in Warsaw might lead to something being said which would exacerbate Polish-Russian relations'. But there was no way, the War Cabinet decided, in which Britain could accede to a Polish Government request to recognize the Polish Underground Army as

[1] Chiefs of Staff Committee No. 272 (Operations) of 1944, 11 August 1944: Cabinet papers, 79/79.
[2] Chiefs of Staff Committee No. 273 (Operations) of 1944, 12 August 1944: Cabinet papers, 79/79. Air Marshal Sir Douglas Evill, Vice-Chief of the Air Staff, was in the chair at this meeting, at which the other two Vice-Chiefs, Lieutenant-General Sir Archibald Nye and Vice Admiral Sir Neville Syfret, were the other members of the Committee present.
[3] 'Chain' No. 34, 14 August 1944: Churchill papers, 20/180.

having 'belligerent status', particularly as Poland 'was in the area of Russian operational responsibility'.[1]

On the night of August 14, a further twenty-six aircraft were sent from Italy to drop supplies on Warsaw. Eight had not returned. As a result of this rate of loss, Slessor decided to drop further supplies, not over Warsaw itself, but over the nearby Kampinos forest, and, as the Chiefs of Staff Committee were told on the following day, 'to carry on such operations as far as losses would allow'. The Americans, Portal told the committee, had hoped to carry out a supply dropping operation with American heavy bombers the previous day, 'but had been unable to clear the matter with the Russians'. The Chiefs of Staff were also told that Clark Kerr 'had discussed this question with the Russians, whose attitude towards affording assistance to the Poles fighting in Warsaw had been unhelpful'.[2]

There was also an American dimension to the limitations on aid to the Poles. 'In view of the unfeasibility of day operations to Warsaw,' the Joint Staff Mission reported to London, 'and the commitment of all available XVth Air Force resources to "Dragoon",' the United States Chiefs of Staff were of the opinion that the 'best solution' with regard to 'acceptance of responsibility for helping the Poles in Warsaw' was that it would be undertaken by Stalin, plus 'the minimum night effort' of the special operations unit of the Anglo-American air force. 'Dragoon', which the British had seen endanger their Italian plans, now also took its toll of Warsaw.[3]

At about 11.30 on the morning of August 14 Churchill left the Villa Rivalta once more for a swim, this time driving to a point on the coast beyond Cumae and then embarking on the Prince of Piedmont's launch for the sea voyage back towards Naples. Pierson Dixon, who was present, noted in his dairy how:

. . . the Admiral had selected a nice safe point off-shore. This was rejected as too dirty and too public by the PM, who directed the launch to steam out to the open sea, where we had a fine clean bathe. The PM showing traces of having been a fine swimmer, floated majestically around. For several minutes on end he remained practically immobile on his back, aided in this by his own corpulence and the unusual buoyancy of this part of the Mediterranean. On the way back the PM, wrapped in a large towel, smoking a cigar and

[1] War Cabinet No. 106 of 1944, 14 August 1944: Cabinet papers, 65/43.
[2] Chiefs of Staff Committee No. 277 (Operations), 16 August 1944: Cabinet papers, 79/79.
[3] JSM 199, IZ 5929, 15 August 1944: Cabinet papers, 105/46.

drinking cocktails, spoke generally about Italy, recalling his own early visits and deploring the folly of the people in letting themselves be dragged to destruction by Musso.[1]

Pierson Dixon also noted how, 'with every new day', Churchill's attitude to the Italian people 'softened'. Later he recalled the following conversation:

PM. 'D'you think they like that?' (Making a V sign to an enthusiastic group of Italians at the pier.)
PD. 'Yes, though I believe the sign also has an improper connotation in Mediterranean lands.'
PM. 'I know that, but I have superseded that one—V for victory.'[2]

After lunch at the Villa Rivalta, Churchill left Naples by air with Brigadier Jacob and Commander Thompson, flying in General Wilson's aeroplane to Corsica, and landing at Ajaccio, three hours after leaving Naples. In a letter to his wife three days later, Churchill wrote, of Ajaccio: 'Do you remember when we went to see Napoleon's house there in 1910?'[3]

Proceeding to Ajaccio harbour, Churchill went aboard HMS *Royal Scotsman*. His arrival on board this converted merchant ship, carrying six assault landing craft on her davits, was witnessed by a young naval officer, Christopher Harland, who later recalled how, as officer of the watch at the time of Churchill's arrival, 'we already had on board Admiral Sir John Cunningham—Naval Commander-in-Chief, Mediterranean, General Sir Henry Maitland Wilson & other senior staff waiting to welcome him'. Harland added:

At about 1745, the PM duly arrived on the jetty, dressed in a white-coloured tropical-type rig with khaki topee on his head. I had quickly alerted my Captain & all the top brass, who came down to the quarter-deck, and Admiral Cunningham dashed down the gangway to greet the PM. (The first & last time I ever saw a full admiral running!) When the PM stepped on board, he saluted the quarter-deck by raising his khaki topee, & then shook hands with my Captain, & all others present, apart from me. I, of course, was standing rigidly to attention, telescope under arm, looking straight ahead etc.

As my Captain and all the top brass made as if to usher the PM away

---

[1] Pierson Dixon diary, 14 August 1944: Piers Dixon, *op. cit.*, page 105.

[2] Pierson Dixon recollections: Piers Dixon, *op. cit.*, page 105.

[3] 'Private', 17 August 1944: Spencer-Churchill papers. In fact 1913. Churchill, then First Lord of the Admiralty, had sailed on the Admiralty yacht *Enchantress* for Venice, along the Dalmatian coast, then to Malta, Sicily, Ajaccio and Marseilles. Among his guests was the Prime Minister, H. H. Asquith, and Asquith's daughter Violet. A cartoon in *Punch* on 21 May 1913 showed Churchill in a deckchair on the *Enchantress*, lying back smoking a cigar, asking Asquith, who was reading a newspaper: 'Any home news?', to which Asquith replies: 'How can there be with you here?'

up the ladder to get on with the war, he turned round to me, shook me warmly by the hand & said 'How do you do?' I replied 'How do you do, Sir' in, I hope, not too astonished a way, because I was, of course, thrilled at this gesture—one of those many small things, typical of the man, which, as in this case, sent morale rocketing.[1]

That night, Churchill dined with Cunningham and Wilson on board HMS *Largs*. Several senior United States officers were present, among them General Eaker, joined after dinner by General Somervell, and the United States Under Secretary for War, Robert P. Patterson. That night, Churchill slept on board the *Royal Scotsman*.[2]

While Churchill slept, Allied forces landed on the south coast of France at many points between Toulon and Nice. 'Anvil', now 'Dragoon', had begun.

Three United States divisions, seven French divisions, and a mixed British and American airborne division, constituting the specially formed Seventh Army, took part in the attack, under the command of General Patch. The three American divisions involved had earlier been withdrawn from Alexander's forces in Italy, together with considerable air forces. For the actual landing, three divisions took part. Opposing them were three German divisions, but with a substantial inferiority of air power. At the same time, more than twenty-five thousand armed French resistance fighters, nurtured by British support in weapons, supplies and training, prepared to attack the German lines of communications.

'Reports received up to noon today', Maitland Wilson telegraphed to the British Chiefs of Staff on August 15, indicated that both the commandos and the airborne force had 'all landed successfully'. In addition, all the assault landings were 'on schedule and successfully accomplished against light opposition'. Air opposition was also 'light'. At sea, no opposition at all had been reported.[3]

That morning, Churchill embarked in the destroyer HMS *Kimberley* to look at the progress of the landing to which he had been so opposed. Two days later he wrote to his wife:

The journey takes five hours, and a little after one o'clock we found ourselves in an immense concourse of ships all sprawled along 20 miles of coast with poor St Tropez in the centre.

It had been expected that the bombardment would continue all day, but the air and the ships had practically silenced the enemy guns by 8 o'clock. This rendered the proceedings rather dull. We traversed the whole front and saw the panorama of the beautiful shores with smoke rising from many fires

---

[1] Christopher Harland (formerly Lieutenant, RNVR), letter to the author, 7 December 1981.
[2] 'Diary of a Visit to Italy', 14 August 1944: Thompson papers.
[3] MEDCOS No. 172, 'Top Secret', 'Emergency', 15 August 1944: Cabinet papers, 122/1309.

started by the shelling and artificial smoke being loosed by the landing troops and the landing craft drawn up upon the shore. But we saw it all from a long way off. If I had known beforehand what the conditions would be I would have requested a picket-boat from the *Ramillies*, when I could have gone with perfect safety very much nearer to the actual beaches.

I got frightfully sunburnt, but on the way back I read that novel Berlin Hotel which I thought absolutely thrilling—one of the best I have read 'in years'.[1] We got back to the Headquarters' ship at Ajaccio at about 10, and then heard that all the landings except one had been successful. The three American Divisions were safely ashore without any serious losses. The beaches are now free from fire and further disembarkation of vehicles and cannon, etc., is proceeding smoothly. The whole thing had run like a piece of clock-work. Everybody arrived punctually at exactly the right place'.[2]

'Have just returned from watching the assault from a considerable distance,' Churchill telegraphed to Roosevelt. 'Everything seems to be working like clockwork here, and there have been few casualties so far and none that I know of amongst the mass of shipping deployed.'[3] 'Your Majesty knows my opinion about the strategy,' Churchill telegraphed to King George VI, 'but the perfect execution of the plan was deeply interesting.' There was 'no doubt', he added somewhat mischievously, 'that Eisenhower's operations made a great diversion. The fact that this is the precise opposite of what was intended need not be stressed at the present time.'[4]

To his wife, Churchill wrote in his letter of August 17:

If you reflect upon what I have said at different times on strategic questions you will see that Eisenhower's operations have been a diversion for this landing instead of the other way round as the American Chiefs of Staff imagined. Several German Divisions have gone to the North, but there are still heavy forces in front of the Army. I think it probable that Eisenhower will take Paris before General Patch takes Marseilles. If I had had my way the armies now cast on shore 400 miles from Paris would have come in at St Nazaire in about a week and greatly widened the front of our advance with corresponding security against German movement east of Paris. This will all become blatantly apparent to the instructed. One of my reasons for making public my visit was to associate myself with this well-conducted but irrelevant and unrelated operation.[5]

[1] *Berlin Hotel*, by Vicki Baum, published in 1944, in which a young member of the anti-Nazi underground is the hero. Other characters are a German general in the anti-Hitler plot who commits suicide, a scientist taken to drink because of the evil use his work has been put to, a receptionist at the hotel who falls in love with the hero, and a glamorous actress staying at the hotel who at first appears to sympathize with the hero, then intends to betray him, and finally is shot by him. The book was later filmed by Warner Brothers.

[2] 'Personal', 17 August 1944', Spencer-Churchill papers.

[3] Prime Minister's Personal Telegram, T.1624/4, 'Chain No. 48', 16 August 1944: Churchill papers, 20/170.

[4] 'Chain No. 49', 16 August 1944: Churchill papers, 20/180.

[5] 'Personal', 17 August 1944: Spencer-Churchill papers.

On the morning of August 16 Churchill returned from Ajaccio by air to Naples, the flight taking just under three hours.

Further Enigma decrypts having made it clear that the German withdrawal from Greece was continuing, Churchill and his advisers were faced with the imminent descent upon the capital of Greek communist forces eager to impose their own authority once the Germans had gone. Maitland Wilson had already been informed, Brooke told the Chiefs of Staff Committee in London, 'of the recent Cabinet decision to plan for the early despatch of British forces into Greece, as soon as the Germans had withdrawn'.[1] This operation was to be given the codename 'Manna'.

At lunch on arrival, Churchill discussed operation 'Manna' with Sir John Slessor, Royal Air Force Commander-in-Chief, Mediterranean, General Sir James Gammell, Maitland Wilson's Chief of Staff, and Pierson Dixon. 'Complete agreement reached,' Dixon noted in his diary, 'and the PM sent a telegram to the FO.'[2]

In his telegram, Churchill explained to Eden that arrangements should be made for a British military expedition to Greece. This operation 'must', he wrote, 'be regarded as an operation of reinforced diplomacy and policy, confined to Athens with possibly a detachment at Salonica, rather than an actual campaign'. The arrival of 1,500 British parachutists in the neighbourhood of Athens could be effected, he wrote, 'with complete surprise', probably before the Communist EAM 'had taken any steps to seize the capital'.

Once the landing ground had been secured by the parachutists, the Greek Government would follow 'almost immediately' and within a few hours 'would be functioning in Athens; the people would probably receive the British parachutists with rapture'. The parachutists would be followed by a 'small expedition' not exceeding ten thousand men, entering the Piraeus 'when the mines were out of the way', and relieving the parachutists. The King of Greece, Churchill told Eden, should not start for Athens 'at once', but remain for the time being in Cairo, 'awaiting developments'.[3]

If there were to be 'a long hiatus' after the German authorities had left Athens, Churchill explained to Roosevelt, in defence of 'Manna', it was 'very likely' that the Communist EAM 'and other communist extremists' would attempt 'to seize the city and crush all other forms of Greek expression but their own'. Churchill then set out for Roosevelt the British plan, the preparation of a British force 'not exceeding

---

[1] Chiefs of Staff Committee No. 274 (Operations) of 1944, 14 August 1944: Cabinet papers, 79/79; the War Cabinet decision had been made at War Cabinet No. 103 of 1944.

[2] Pierson Dixon diary, 16 August 1944: Piers Dixon, *op. cit.*, page 106.

[3] 'Chain' No. 56, 16 August 1944: Churchill papers, 20/180.

ten thousand men' which would be sent to Athens to forestall the establishment of 'a tyrannical Communist government'. 'I do not myself expect that anything will happen for a month,' he added, 'and it may be longer, but it is always well to be prepared.' [1]

Roosevelt accepted Churchill's proposal. 'I have no objection,' he replied, 'to your making preparations to have in readiness a sufficient British force to preserve order in Greece when German forces evacuate that country.' There was 'also no objection', Roosevelt wrote, 'to the use by General Wilson of American transport airplanes that are available to him at the time and that can be spared from other operations'. [2]

After lunch on August 16, Churchill again left the Villa Rivalta by admiral's barge, for another swim in the Bay of Naples, this time near the island of Procida. 'We have had altogether four bathes,' Churchill wrote to his wife, 'which have done me all the good in the world. I feel greatly refreshed and am much less tired than when I left England.' [3] 'I am extremely well,' Churchill telegraphed to Attlee that day, 'and the constant movement and clatter is very restful.' [4]

During the boat journey to and from Procida, Churchill discussed with Pierson Dixon the future of Italy. Churchill was still unwilling to proceed with a preliminary peace treaty with the Italian Government. [5] That night, at dinner with Dixon and Macmillan, Churchill spoke of the most recent telegram from Stalin, denouncing the Warsaw uprising as a 'reckless and terrible adventure which is costing the population large sacrifices'. The 'Soviet Command', Stalin added, had come to the conclusion 'that it must dissociate itself from the Warsaw adventure as it cannot take either direct or indirect responsibility for the Warsaw action'. [6]

Churchill made no reply. But in a letter to Eisenhower, congratulating him on the continued advances in Normandy and Anjou, he wrote: 'It seems to me that the results might well eclipse all the Russian victories up to the present.' [7] Churchill added, somewhat mischievously: 'You have certainly among other things effected a very important diversion from our attack at "Dragoon".'

Of the scale and prospects of the operations in France, however,

[1] Prime Minister's Personal Telegram, T.1625/4, Prime Minister to President, No. 755, 'Personal and Top Secret', 17 August 1944: Churchill papers, 20/170.

[2] President to Prime Minister, No. 608, 'Clasp No. 235' from Private Office, 26 August 1944: Churchill papers, 20/170.

[3] Letter of 17 August 1944: Spencer-Churchill papers.

[4] 'Chain' No. 52, 16 August 1944: Churchill papers, 20/180.

[5] Pierson Dixon diary, 16 August 1944, Piers Dixon, op. cit., page 107.

[6] 'Clasp' No. 59, 17 August 1944: Churchill papers, 20/170.

[7] Prime Minister's Personal Telegram, T.1632/4, 'Chain' No. 75, 17 August 1944: Spencer-Churchill papers, 20/170.

Churchill was in no doubt. The 'Ike–Monty operations', he wrote to his wife, 'appear to be the greatest battle of the war and may result in the destruction of the German power in France'. Such a victory, he added, 'will have effects in many directions, one of which undoubtedly will be more mutual respect between the Russians and the Anglo-American democracies'.[1]

On the morning of August 17 Churchill prepared to leave Naples by car for the Cassino battlefield. 'It is very important,' he telegraphed to the King before setting off, 'that we ensure that Alexander's army is not so mauled and milked that it cannot have a theme or campaign.'[2] This would certainly require another conference with Roosevelt, for which, in fact, arrangements were already being made. Roosevelt, as General Hollis telegraphed to Cornwall Jones on August 17, had suggested 'small staffs and short conference, and Prime Minister, before leaving for Italy, did not disagree'. Among the 'certain starters' for the agenda, Hollis added, were the war against Japan, the campaign in Italy, the fusion of 'Overlord' and 'Dragoon' and the zones of occupation in Germany.[3]

How far Roosevelt would be able to absorb himself in these issues was unclear. 'I saw the President this morning,' Lord Halifax reported to Churchill three days later. 'I thought he was a bit pre-occupied with the Election, which he said would be tough and close.' But he was also, Halifax added, 'much looking forward to meeting you', and had suggested that after four or five days at Quebec 'you should go with him to Hyde Park and that the Staffs should bring back from there for final approval whatever they might have worked out on the basis of your first talks'.[4]

'My vigour has been greatly restored,' Churchill told the King in his telegram of August 17, 'by the change and movement and warm weather.'[5] That morning, driving southward through Capua, he was met by Alexander a few miles from Cassino. Alexander then took Churchill up to a point on high ground from which the Monastery, the surrounding hills and the entry to the Liri valley could all be seen. With the aid of a map, Alexander then reconstructed the main features of the battle.

[1] 'Private', 17 August 1944: Spencer-Churchill papers.
[2] 'Chain' No. 68, 17 August 1944: Churchill papers, 20/180.
[3] DOTEL 253, 'Top Secret', 'Immediate', 'Guard', 17 August 1944: Cabinet papers, 120/148.
[4] 'Clasp' No. 139, Washington Telegram No. 4473, 'Guard', 'Personal', 20 August 1944: Cabinet papers, 120/144.
[5] 'Chain' No. 68, 17 August 1944: Churchill papers, 20/180.

Driving down to Cassino itself, Churchill saw the ruins of the town. 'The party did not leave the cars,' the Private Office noted, 'as the whole of the ruins are full of mines and booby-traps and are nowhere safe or even passable.' Churchill then drove back to a roadside olive grove, where a picnic lunch had been laid out, and Generals Wilson and Gammell joined him and Alexander.

After the picnic, Churchill drove to Venafro airfield, flying from there in Alexander's Dakota above the ruins of the Monastery and on to Siena. Churchill then drove to a villa on a hill between Siena and Alexander's headquarters.[1] 'We have now reached Siena and are very comfortable,' Churchill wrote to his wife. 'Alex is gay & charming in spite of the vexation of watching his splendid Army pulled to pieces by American strategy.' He added: 'I hope to remedy this.'[2]

That night, Alexander and General Harding came to dine, and at midnight Churchill went to bed.[3]

Over London and south-east England, the work of the anti-aircraft guns in shooting down flying bombs had continued to improve, forty flying bombs a day being shot down in the week ending August 18, as compared with twenty a day in the previous week. The number of those killed had also fallen, from a weekly average of 800 to a total of 200 deaths that week, bringing the total number of those killed by flying bombs since June 24 to 5,400. Ninety percent of the deaths were in the London area.[4]

On August 18, Churchill had hoped to visit the front line near Florence, 'where fighting is still going on', he explained to his wife. But, 'a thunderstorm and heavy rain is now on', he wrote to her at midday, 'and I do not know how it will affect our plans. (Later—it has spoiled them.)'[5]

On August 19, still unable to visit the front line because of the bad weather, Churchill went to the Headquarters of the United States Fifth Army, at Cecina, where he was met by General Mark Clark. Churchill then drove through the lines of the Royal Air Force personnel to the Headquarters of the 5th Army, where he was received with a guard and band, which he inspected. Mark Clark then ex-

[1] 'Diary of a Visit to Italy', 17 Auguust 1944.
[2] 'Private', 17 August 1944: Spencer-Churchill papers.
[3] 'Diary of a Visit to Italy', 17 August 1944.
[4] 'Crossbow' Committee, 'Thirteenth Report by the Chairman', 'Crossbow' Committee Paper No. 60 of 1944, 'Top Secret', 21 August 1944: Cabinet papers, 79/79.
[5] Letter of 18 August 1944: Spencer-Churchill papers.

plained the situation on the Italian front, and future plans. 'The General seemed embittered,' Churchill later wrote, 'that his army had been robbed of what he thought—and I could not disagree—was a great opportunity. Still, he would drive forward to his utmost on the British left and keep the whole front blazing.'[1]

During Churchill's visit, Mark Clark gave him the Union Jack which had been raised in Rome on the night of its capture by the Fifth Army. 'As this is the first Allied flag to fly in a captured enemy capital in the present war,' Mark Clark wrote, 'it has peculiar historical significance.' It had been raised 'simultaneously' with the Stars and Stripes, on the two flagstaffs to the monument to King Victor Emanuel II in the Piazza Venezia.[2]

From Fifth Army headquarters, Churchill left in a jeep for 34 Division Headquarters. During the drive he stopped to inspect units of the 34th Division and other representatives of the 5th Army, including a Brazilian detachment, and addressed the parade. After lunch, Churchill drove to Leghorn, parts of the route being lined by British and American troops. At Leghorn he embarked in a motor torpedo boat and made a tour of the harbour, seeing the progress of repairing the demolitions made by the Germans and the results of bombing. He then proceeded to the site of a howitzer battery, which was about to fire at enemy gun-sites to the north of Pisa. 'The first round,' noted Churchill's secretariat, 'was fired by the Prime Minister.'[3] The firing of the gun was reported in the *Daily Telegraph* four days later, with a note that 'It was a ranging shot and fell short. The gunnery officer corrected the elevation. . . .' 'It is well known,' Churchill telegraphed to the owner of the *Daily Telegraph*, Lord Camrose, 'that the man who pulls the lanyard which I did has no more to do with aiming the gun than the Archbishop of Canterbury.'[4]

Churchill had hoped to visit a forward observation post on August 19, to witness the result of further bombarding and to get a view of the front line. The visit had to be abandoned, however, because of poor visibility. Returning to Cecina airfield, Churchill flew back to Naples, reaching the Villa Rivalta at seven in the evening.

'Today,' Churchill telegraphed to the President of Brazil, 'I had the honour of inspecting your magnificent troops on the liberated soil of Italy. May I be permitted to express my admiration of the charac-

---

[1] Winston S. Churchill, *The Second World War*, volume 6, London 1954, page 95.
[2] Letter of 19 August 1944: Premier papers, 4/75/1, folio 16.
[3] 'Diary of a Visit to Italy', 18 August 1944.
[4] 'Chain' No. 212, 24 August 1944: Churchill papers, 20/180 (also, Jock Colville to Lord Camrose, 25 August 1944: Camrose papers).

ter, quality and bearing of these soldiers. We are most grateful for your help.' [1] In error, this telegram was sent, not to the President of Brazil but to Roosevelt. 'The cypher people,' Churchill telegraphed to Roosevelt four days later, 'had apparently not realized there was any other President in the World.' [2]

In a telegram to Roosevelt on August 19, Churchill praised 'your grand Fifth Army', but he added, again revealing unhappiness: 'there is a sense of bewilderment at the repeated and ceaseless withdrawals of important and key elements'. [3]

That evening Churchill dined with Alexander and General Harding, Admiral Cunningham and Oliver Lyttelton's son, Captain Anthony Lyttelton. 'The party left the table at 2.30 a.m.,' Commander Thompson noted, 'and went to bed at 3.30 a.m.' [4]

On August 20 Churchill was able to go to the front line. On the way there he inspected and addressed a contingent of the 1st Canadian Division, Armoured Brigade, before going on to lunch at 13 Corps headquarters near San Casciano. After lunch Churchill went to a medium field battery, which he inspected, and then went on to a forward observation post about two miles from the front line on the Arno river. 'He had a good view of Florence,' the Private Office noted, 'which was being occasionally bombarded by the Germans.' He then returned by air to the Villa Rivalta.

That night, Generals Alexander and Harding, and Air Vice Marshal D'Albiac, dined at the Villa. Lord Moyne and Reginald Leeper were also present. [5] 'A discussion on morale and courage followed,' noted Peck and Rowan. 'Point was added to this by the arrival of a large Hornet whose repeated attacks from a low level created considerable confusion before it was brought down and destroyed by the Navy.' [6]

The bitterness of the 'Anvil' depletions could not be assuaged. 'Here was this splendid army,' Churchill later wrote, 'equivalent to twenty-five divisions, of which a quarter were American, reduced till it was just not strong enough to produce decisive results against the immense power of the defensive. A very little more, half what had been taken from us, and we could have broken into the valley of the Po, with all

[1] Prime Minister's Personal Telegram, T.1646/4, 'Chain No. 131', sent on 20 August 1944: Churchill papers, 20/170.
[2] Prime Minister's Personal Telegram, T.1663/4, Prime Minister to President, No. 768, 'Chain No. 194', 'Personal and Top Secret', 24 August 1944: Churchill papers, 20/170.
[3] Prime Minister's Personal Telegram, T.1647/4, 'Chain No. 132', sent on 20 August 1944: Cabinet papers, 120/144.
[4] 'Diary of a Visit to Italy', 19 August 1944.
[5] Lord Moyne was British Minister Resident in the Middle East, and Reginald Leeper British Ambassador to the Greek Government-in-Exile. Both had their offices in Cairo.
[6] 'Diary of a Visit to Italy', 20 August 1944.

the gleaming possibilities and prizes which lay open towards Vienna.' 'That evening,' Churchill recalled, 'Alexander maintained his soldierly cheerfulness, but it was in a sombre mood that I went to bed. In these great matters failing to gain one's way is no escape from the responsibility for an inferior solution.' [1]

For three days British and Canadian forces in Normandy had fought to break the German resistance at Falaise; by nightfall on August 20, eight German divisions had been destroyed. With the closing of the Falaise gap, Normandy, which for six weeks had threatened to become a trap, became at last a springboard.

On the morning of August 21 Churchill flew from Naples, in Alexander's Dakota, to Rome, where he was met by Sir Noel Charles, the High Commissioner for Italy, and driven to the British Embassy, where he was to stay. Both Maitland Wilson and Randolph Churchill arrived before lunch, as did General Brooke and Sir Charles Portal from London, all of whom lunched together at the Embassy. That afternoon, Churchill held a conference with Brooke, Portal and Wilson to discuss what form the British occupation of Greece would take. 'We might have to move in as much as two divisions,' said Brooke, as the German forces on Greece 'might wish to surrender to us on the spot'.

It was 'essential', Churchill told the meeting, that Alexander's operations in Italy 'should not be interfered with to provide troops for Greece'. He was hoping to obtain Roosevelt's approval for the provision of American air transport for a British parachute brigade. [2]

The task of the commander of the forces going into Greece was then defined by Maitland Wilson, and confirmed by Churchill, as threefold: 'To install a Greek Government', 'To accept the German surrender', and 'To open the way for the introduction of relief'.

Churchill then asked 'what action would be taken in Crete'. If the Germans there wished to surrender, Brooke replied, 'it would be easy to arrange to take their surrender', but if they decided to hold out, 'then it would probably be simplest to leave them to rot on the island'. [3]

Immediately after this meeting, Churchill went into conference

---

[1] Winston S. Churchill, *The Second World War*, volume 6 London 1954, page 96.

[2] Roosevelt gave his approval six days later, when he telegraphed to Churchill: 'I have no objection to your making preparations to have in readiness a sufficient British force to preserve order in Greece when the German forces evacuate that country. There is also no objection to the use by General Wilson of American transport aeroplanes that are available to him at that time and that can be spared from his other operation.' (President to Prime Minister No. 608, 26 August 1944, sent as 'Clasp' No. 235 from Churchill's Private Office to Alexander's headquarters in Italy, 'Guard', 26 August 1944: Churchill papers, 20/170.)

[3] 'Minutes of a Meeting held in the British Embassy, Rome, at 3 p.m. on Monday, 21st August, 1944': Premier papers, 3/258/3.

with Rex Leeper and Pierson Dixon to discuss the situation in Greece, after which he spent nearly an hour with the Greek Prime Minister, George Papandreou. According to Churchill's record of the meeting:

He said the EAM had joined his Government because the British had been firm towards them, but the Greek State itself still had no arms and no police. He asked for our help to unite Greek resistance against the Germans. At present only the wrong people had arms, and they were a minority. I told him we could make no promise and enter into no obligations about sending British forces into Greece, and that even the possibility should not be talked about in public; but I advised him to transfer his Government at once from Cairo, with its atmosphere of intrigue, to somewhere in Italy near the headquarters of the Supreme Allied Commander. This he agreed to do.

Churchill noted that, with the five EAM Ministers no longer demanding Papandreou's withdrawal, he was the head 'of a truly national government'. But he went on to warn him against 'subversive influences'. The Greek mutineers, he advised, should not yet be released from custody, and to this Papandreou agreed. He was worried however about the Bulgarian troops who were still on Greek soil. These troops would be ordered back to Bulgaria, Churchill replied, 'as soon as we were able to make sure they would obey us'. The 'best' thing Papandreou could do, Churchill ended, 'was to establish a Greek Government in Greece. Frontier questions must wait for the peace settlement'.

At this point during the conversations between Churchill and Papandreou, Lord Moyne arrived. The discussion then turned to the position of the Greek King. 'We had no intention,' Churchill declared, 'of interfering with the solemn right of the Greek people to choose between monarchy and a republic. But it must be for the Greek people as a whole, and not a handful of doctrinaires, to decide so grave an issue.' Although he personally gave his loyalty to the constitutional monarchy which had taken shape in England, Churchill commented, 'His Majesty's Government were quite indifferent as to which way the matter was settled for Greece provided there was a fair plebiscite.'[1]

Macmillan agreed with Churchill, as he noted in his diary, that the Greek Government should move from the 'poisonous atmosphere of intrigue' in Cairo, to Salerno. It was also agreed that the three British brigades, one of them an airborne brigade, would be kept ready to move from Bari to Athens. 'I fear Anthony may not like the decision,'

---

[1] Meeting of 21 August 1944: Winston S. Churchill, *The Second World War*, volume 6, London 1954, pages 100–1.

Macmillan commented. 'Poor Bob Dixon seems rather alarmed. And of course the President may raise objections. But the PM is determined to have his way and rather bounced everybody by informing Papandreou of the move (though *not* of the plans for sending a military police force).' [1]

In a telegram to Eden, Churchill noted that air forces to support the British force sent to Greece 'can also be found', as Portal had a plan to move 150 British Dakotas from Eisenhower's command to Italy, for the purpose. The task of the British force would be 'to install the Greek Government who should fly in as soon as an airfield is in our hands to accept or effect the surrender of any German troops who capitulate on the spot and to open the way for relief'. [2]

That night Churchill dined at the British Embassy with Papandreou. The other guests included Macmillan and Randolph Churchill. 'Left about 1 a.m.,' Macmillan noted in his diary. 'Winston in very good heart.' [3]

On August 22, the United States Third Army reached Sens, only sixty miles south-east of Paris. Churchill's luncheon guests at the British Embassy in Rome that day included the Italian Prime Minister, Bonomi, and his predecessor, Marshal Badoglio. That afternoon Churchill spent four hours with Macmillan, Sir Noel Charles and Pierson Dixon 'trying', as Churchill telegraphed to Eden, 'to unravel the tangle of our affairs here'. [4] Macmillan was impressed by Churchill's energy. 'The heat was intense,' he wrote in his diary, 'but the PM never flagged. The "whisky" interval (at about 5 p.m.) helped.' [5]

Speaking of the nature of the British and Italian relationship, Pierson Dixon explained the Foreign Office view that a *modus vivendi* was needed 'which would enable us to cease treating Italy as an enemy in the same category as Germany, while not restoring her to the position of an Ally or to full sovereignty'. It would be 'a mistake', Churchill commented, 'to deprive ourselves of any of the rights which we had acquired under the Italian surrender, and premature to relax in any degree the machinery of control set up under the surrender'. Churchill added: 'We should be guided by the precept of Machiavelli that, if one had benefits to confer, they should not be conferred all at

---

[1] Macmillan diary, 21 August 1944: *War Diaries, op. cit.*, page 506.
[2] 'Chain' No. 147, 22 August 1944: Churchill papers, 20/180.
[3] Macmillan diary, 21 August 1944: *War Diaries, op. cit.*, page 506.
[4] 'Chain' No. 162, 22 August 1944: Churchill papers, 20/180.
[5] Macmillan diary, 22 August 1944: *War Diaries, op. cit.*, page 508.

the same time. Any political action should therefore be in the nature of a gesture, such as would in no way limit the powers of the Supreme Commander.'[1]

Macmillan noted in his diary: 'Winston really gave a remarkable demonstration of his powers,' and he explained how:

Winston was like a dog worrying at a bone. But his peculiar method does succeed in eliciting the truth—and throwing over all those sort of bureaucratic Foreign Office proposals which sound all right but are quite obviously unworkable.

Bob Dixon struggled manfully with his brief. His task is to elevate Charles and liquidate your humble. But Winston would have none of it. When Charles cried out piteously, 'But what am I to do?' he replied, 'What do Ambassadors ever do?' He was very scornful of the title 'High Commissioner' when he realised that Charles had no executive functions and that his diplomatic functions were confined to being Ambassador to a shadow government.

He wants me to be head of the Control Commission and run the new policy. He will not have a treaty, but he wants a steady process of relaxation of control. This, he says, is the task of the politician not the diplomat.

We finally broke up at 7 p.m.—all but Winston completely exhausted.[2]

An hour and a half later Churchill dined at the British Embassy with Sir Noel Charles and Macmillan. Lady Diana Cooper was also present.[3] At one o'clock that night, Churchill sent for Brigadier Lush, of the Allied Control Commission, to discuss the nature of Britain's control in the months to come, and the extent to which administrative tasks could be taken over by Italians. 'I told him,' Lush later recalled, 'that we, in the Commission, were most anxious to effect this, not only from our desire to effect freedom of thought and action in Italy, but because we needed the Allied personnel, now engaged in mid and southern Italy, for operational administration as soon as the North fell. We needed every available Allied *and* Italian administrative officer to be ready to move north as soon as the advance began. There was, however, a grave shortage of capable and experienced Italian administrators available who had not been trained in Fascist ways.'

Lush also asked Churchill 'to believe me that, whenever we moved an Allied administrative Officer to give way to an Italian, there was

---

[1] 'Note of Discussion on Italy at the British Embassy, Rome, 22nd August, 1944, 3.30 p.m. to 7.30 p.m.', 'Top Secret': War Office papers, 220/465.

[2] Macmillan diary, 22 August 1944: *War Diaries, op. cit.*, page 508.

[3] 'I was in Rome last week for three weeks to see Winston,' Lord Moyne wrote to his son on September 5. 'He was in very good form and said to be very pleased with his new French word "obvieusement". I was not however fortunate enough actually to hear him use it.' (Letter of 5 September 1944: Moyne papers.)

a howl from the local councils and populations—and in some cases politicians, at the consequent lack of efficiency'. But, Lush assured Churchill, he would do his utmost to 'reduce the "control" in Allied Control Commission', and make Macmillan's job easier, 'always remembering that General Alexander's Army had priority, and that their well being and success must not be jeopardised by deficiencies in law and order, feeding and health of the civilian population caused by political reasons'.

Churchill and Lush then discussed the role of the Allied Control Commission 'when, as we hoped, we broke through that autumn, 'into the Po Valley and the North'. Lush recalled:

I told him of our plans and assured him of their efficiency. He nodded and became cheerful for he was, next day, continuing his participation in the battle, with Alex and his men. He hoped so much to take part in the first stages of an autumnal break through in Italy which would have enabled Alexander to swing to the right—overcome Austria and so alter history. He gave me a cheerful 'good night' at 2 a.m.[1]

That night he sent Eden a full account of what had been decided. Italy, he explained, should now be regarded 'as a friendly co-belligerent and no longer as an enemy state'. To prevent food riots, the Italians should be allowed to resume as far as possible their foreign trade, and no longer be subjected to the Trading with the Enemy Act. They should also receive if possible the benefits of the United Nations Relief and Rehabilitation Agency.[2]

To King George VI, Churchill telegraphed that evening from Rome to offer 'his congratulations on the manner in which Your Majesty's affairs are prospering on the great battlefields of Europe'.[3]

Also on August 22, telegraphing to the First Sea Lord about the need for 'naval reinforcements' in the Mediterranean because of British plans for Greece, Churchill wrote, with a look forward to future strategy: 'I certainly contemplate a move into the Adriatic if General Alexander's impending battle is successful.'[4]

This was Churchill's first reference in a telegram to one of the Chiefs of Staff to the project on which he and Alexander were both keen, to land at the top of the Adriatic, on the Istrian peninsula, and from there to move through the Ljubljana gap into Austria, and to Vienna. On the previous day, Brooke and Portal had discussed with Maitland Wilson the importance, once the forces in Italy crossed the Po and reached the Piave and Isonzo, that 'pres-

---

[1] Brigadier Maurice Lush, recollections: letter to the author, 8 February 1985.
[2] 'Chain' No. 175, 22 August 1944: Churchill papers, 20/180.
[3] 'Chain' No. 160, 'Personal and Private', 22 August 1944: Cabinet papers, 120/144.
[4] 'Chain' No. 167, 22 August 1944: Churchill papers, 20/180.

sure on the Germans should not be relaxed', and were agreed that, in view of the difficulties of the overland route, 'it might be necessary to launch an amphibious operation into Istria'. Such an amphibious operation, they added, 'would be the best way of securing the direct co-operation' of the Yugoslav partisans.[1]

On August 23 French Resistance forces inside Paris rose up in revolt. In the South of France, French troops liberated Marseilles and United States troops entered Grenoble. In the east, Roumania, following King Michael's overthrow of Marshal Antonescu, accepted the Soviet armistice terms, ended hostilities against the Allies, and declared war on Germany. That day, in Rome, Churchill was received in audience by Pope Pius XII. 'We had no lack of topics for conversation,' he later recalled. 'The one that bulked the largest at this audience, as it had done with his predecessor eighteen years before, was the danger of Communism. I have always had the greatest dislike of it; and should I ever have the honour of another audience with the Supreme Pontiff I should not hesitate to recur to the subject.'[2]

'I had an audience with the Pope this morning,' Churchill telegraphed to King George VI, 'and at the outset of a friendly conversation His Holiness asked me to convey to Your Majesty and to the Queen his respectful greetings and his assurance of the revered esteem in which he holds Your Majesties.'[3]

On leaving the Vatican with Lord Moran, Churchill's 'eyes dilated', Moran noted, 'as he declaimed a fine passage from Macaulay's essay on Ranke's *History of the Papacy*, setting forth how the Roman Church in the course of two thousand years had outlived all other institutions. He felt that there must be something in a faith that could survive so many centuries and had held captive so many men.'[4] Churchill lunched that day in the British Embassy. The Prince of Piedmont was the principal guest. 'The PM was in a puckish mood,' noted Pierson Dixon. 'No serious conversation. PM talked mostly about Madam Chiang and the Prince of Piedmont hardly opened his mouth.'[5]

After luncheon, the Italian Cabinet arrived to meet Churchill, and he talked, as his Private Office diary noted, 'to many of them especially

[1] 'Minutes of a Meeting held in the British Embassy, Rome, at 3 p.m. on Monday 21st August, 1944', Annex: Premier papers, 3/258/3.

[2] Winston S. Churchill, *The Second World War*, volume 6, London 1954, page 103.

[3] 'Chain' No. 183, 'Top Secret', 'Guard', 23 August 1944: Premier papers, 4/75/1, folio 226.

[4] Moran notes, 23 August 1944: Moran, *op. cit.*, page 173.

[5] Pierson Dixon diary, 23 August 1944: Piers Dixon, *op. cit.*, page 112.

M. Togliatti, the Communist, and to the new Liberal leader. He also made them an informal speech encouraging them to unite and saying that they would receive all the help we could give them.'

That afternoon Churchill left Rome, flying by air to Alexander's Headquarters near Siena. That evening Churchill dined 'alone' with Brooke, Alexander, Harding and Jacob. 'The rest of the party', as Peck and Rowan noted, 'dined at Alexander's Headquarters.' [1] That evening, reading a report by the Secretary of State for Air and the Minister of Aircraft Production about relative British and German progress on the jet engine, Churchill telegraphed to the Minister of Labour, Ernest Bevin: 'I know how hard pressed you are, but this jet-propelled aeroplane is a feature in which we are definitely behind the Germans,' and he added: 'Catch up as soon as possible.' [2]

To Harry Hopkins, Churchill telegraphed on August 23 for Roosevelt's 'most secret personal information', that Alexander was going to make 'a considerable push in the near future with what he has got left'. Churchill's telegram continued:

You know Harry that I have here the Army of British Empire—British, Canadian, Australian, South African and Indian. The Airborne Army is also representative of whole Empire. They are in grand fettle in spite of unsettlements caused to all ranks by pulling out of key elements which has gone on for 3 months but I hope their action will remind you that they can not possibly be left on side line during later phase of war. I could never consent to this. [3]

Among the papers in Churchill's box that night was the War Office's agreement, after more than four years of hesitation, to the establishment of a Jewish Brigade Group. This force, Churchill explained that day to Roosevelt, would constitute 'what you would call a regimental combat team' and he added: 'this will give great satisfaction to the Jews when it is published and surely they of all other races have the right to strike at the Germans as a recognisable body. They wish to have their own flag which is the Star of David on a white background with two light blue bars. I cannot see why this should not be done. Indeed I think that the flying of this flag at the head of a combat unit would be a message to go all over the world.' If the 'usual objections' were raised, Churchill added, 'I can overcome them.' [4]

*   *   *

[1] 'Diary of a Visit to Italy', 23 August 1944: The 'rest of the party' was Lord Moran, Randolph Churchill, Pierson Dixon, Leslie Rowan, Patrick Kinna, Commander 'Tommy' Thompson, Senior Quartermaster Sergeant Parmenter, Inspector Hughes and Sawyers.

[2] 'Chain' No. 182, 23 August 1944: Churchill papers, 20/180.

[3] Prime Minister's Personal Telegram, T.1653/4, 'Chain' No. 156, 'Personal, Private and Top Secret', 23 August 1944: Cabinet papers, 120/144.

[4] Prime Minister's Personal Telegram, T.1652/4, Prime Minister to President, No. 765, 'Personal and Top Secret', 23 August 1944: Cabinet papers, 118/86.

Alexander's new Italian offensive was to begin on August 26. Having returned to Siena, Churchill spent August 24 visiting the New Zealand Division, driving up and down the lines of about 15,000 men, and lunching with his old friend General Freyberg. From Montgomery, that day, Churchill received news of 200,000 German prisoners and 40,000 German dead since D-Day, as well as 1,500 German tanks destroyed. The left flank of the 21st Army Corp, he added, 'has today reached Honfleur at the mouth of the Seine'.[1] Returning to Siena that evening, Churchill dined with Alexander and Smuts' son Japy. Churchill was, his Private Office noted, 'very tired, and went to bed at 11.30 p.m.'[2]

On August 25 General de Gaulle entered Paris, and the French capital was cleared of the last remaining German troops and snipers. In the South of France, American troops liberated Cannes, Antibes and Grasse, places so well known to Churchill from his pre-war travels. Churchill worked throughout the morning of August 25 at Alexander's headquarters.

That afternoon two American Generals, one of them General Devers, arrived unexpectedly. As Maitland Wilson's deputy, Devers had for 'many weeks', as Churchill later recalled, 'been drawing units and key men ruthlessly from the Fifteenth Army Group, and particularly from the Fifth Army under Mark Clark'. It was known, Churchill added, that the troops to be used in the South of France landing were likely to be raised to an Army Group Command, 'and that Devers would be designated as its chief. Naturally he sought to gather all the forces he could for the great enterprise to be entrusted to him, and to magnify it in every way.' Churchill's account continued:

I saw very soon, although no serious topic was broached, that there was a coolness between him and Alexander. Gay, smiling, debonair, Alexander excused himself after the first few minutes, and left me in the mess tent with our two American visitors. As General Devers did not seem to have anything particular to say to me, and I did not wish to enter upon thorny ground, I also confined myself to civilities and generalities. I expected Alexander to return, but he did not, and after about twenty minutes Devers took his leave. There was of course no public business to be done. I wished him all good luck in his operation, and his courtesy call came to an end. I was conscious however of the tension between these high officers beneath an impeccable surface of politeness.[3]

That night, among the telegrams which Churchill dictated to

[1] M/112, 'Personal and Private', 24 August 1944: Churchill papers, 20/170.
[2] 'Diary of a Visit to Italy', 24 August 1944.
[3] Winston S. Churchill, *The Second World War*, volume six, London 1954, page 105.

Patrick Kinna was one to Smuts, reporting that the Field Marshal's son 'is looking very well', and setting out his continued unhappiness at the weakening of the Italian campaign by the South of France landings:

So far the 'Anvil' abortion has had the opposite effects for which its designers intended it. First it has brought no troops away from General Eisenhower at all. On the contrary, two and a half to three German Divisions of the rearguard will certainly reach the main battle front before the Allied landed troops. Secondly the breaking in full career of these two great armies, the 5th and the 8th, and milking out of the key personnel in them has enforced stagnation here which has led to the withdrawal of three German Divisions from the Italian front including one very strong Panzer of 12,500 active strength. These have gone straight to the Châlons area. Thus about five divisions have been brought against Eisenhower which would not have happened if we had continued our advance here in the direction of the Po and ultimately on the great city.

The 'great city' was Vienna. 'I still hope that we may achieve this,' Churchill told Smuts, and he added: 'Even if the war comes to a sudden end there is no reason why our armour should not slip through and reach it as we can.' [1]

August 26 marked the start of Alexander's new offensive. Churchill, who wished to be as close a witness to it as possible, recalled in his memoirs, written ten years later:

Alexander and I started together at about nine o'clock. His aide-de-camp and Tommy came in a second car. We were thus a conveniently small party. The advance had now been in progress for six hours, and was said to be making headway. But no definite impressions could yet be formed. We first climbed by motor up a high outstanding rock pinnacle, upon the top of which a church and village were perched. The inhabitants, men and women, came out to greet us from the cellars in which they had been sheltering. It was at once plain that the place had just been bombarded. Masonry and wreckage littered the single street. 'When did this stop?' Alexander asked the small crowd who gathered round us, grinning rather wryly. 'About a quarter of an hour ago,' they said.

There was certainly a magnificent view from the ramparts of bygone centuries. The whole front of the Eighth Army offensive was visible. But apart from the smoke puffs of shells bursting seven or eight thousand yards away in a scattered fashion there was nothing to see. Presently Alexander said that we had better not stay any longer, as the enemy would naturally be firing at observation posts like this and might begin again. So we motored two or three miles to the westward, and had a picnic lunch on the broad

[1] Prime Minister's Personal Telegram, T.1676/4, No. 827 from Dominions Office to South Africa, 25 August 1944: Churchill papers, 20/170.

slope of a hillside, which gave almost as good a view as the peak and was not likely to attract attention.

News was now received that our troops had pushed on a mile or two beyond the river Metauro. Here Hasdrubal's defeat had sealed the fate of Carthage, so I suggested that we should go across too. We got into our cars accordingly, and in half an hour were across the river, where the road ran into undulating groves of olives, brightly patched with sunshine. Having got an officer guide from one of the battalions engaged, we pushed on through these glades till the sounds of rifle and machine-gun fire showed we were getting near to the front line. Presently warning hands brought us to a standstill. It appeared there was a minefield, and it was only safe to go where other vehicles had already gone without mishap.

Alexander and his aide-de-camp now went off to reconnoitre towards a grey stone building which our troops were holding, which was said to give a good close-up view. It was evident to me that only very loose fighting was in progress. In a few minutes the aide-de-camp came back and brought me to his chief, who had found a very good place in the stone building, which was in fact an old chateau overlooking a rather sharp declivity. Here one certainly could see all that was possible. The Germans were firing with rifles and machine-guns from thick scrub on the farther side of the valley, about five hundred yards away. Our front line was beneath us. The firing was desultory and intermittent. But this was the nearest I got to the enemy and the time I heard most bullets in the Second World War.

After about half an hour we went back to our motor-cars and made our way to the river, keeping very carefully to our own wheel tracks or those of other vehicles. At the river we met the supporting columns of infantry, marching up to lend weight to our thin skirmish line, and by five o'clock we were home again at General Leese's headquarters . . .[1]

'I took him right up to the front line,' Alexander later recalled. 'You could see the tanks moving up and firing and the machine guns in action a few hundred yards ahead of us. There were quite a lot of shells flying about, and land mines all over the place. He absolutely loved it. It fascinated him—the real warrior at heart.'[2]

Even as Churchill witnessed Alexander's offensive, the United States Chiefs of Staff were pressing for more support for 'Dragoon', informing the Joint Staff Mission that the South of France landing was 'a major operation rendering direct support to "Overlord" and as such to have priority over the Italian campaign'. In support of this view, Marshall, King and Arnold invited 'attention' of the British Chiefs of Staff to the agreement of Cairo in December 1943 that the cross-Channel and South of France operations would be 'the supreme operations for 1944,

[1] Winston S. Churchill, *The Second World War*, volume 6, London 1954, pages 106–7.
[2] Field Marshal Earl Alexander of Tunis, recollections: notes for the author, January 1969.

and that nothing would be undertaken in any other parts of the world to hazard the success of these operations'.[1]

In a telegram to Roosevelt, Churchill pointed out that Alexander had received an urgent message from Eisenhower's headquarters, 'asking for efforts to be made' to prevent the withdrawal of more German divisions from the Italian to the western front. The withdrawal of the German divisions from Italy, Churchill commented, 'was the consequence of the great weakening of our armies in Italy, and has taken place entirely since the attack on the Riviera'.

Four German divisions had already been withdrawn from Italy to France. 'However,' Churchill explained, 'in spite of the weakening process, Alexander began about three weeks ago to plan with Clark to turn or pierce the Apennines. For this purpose the British XIIIth Corps of four divisions has been placed under General Clark's orders, and we have been able to supply him with the necessary artillery, of which his army had been deprived. This army of eight divisions—four American and four British—is now grouped around Florence on a northerly axis.' Churchill's telegram continued:

By skinning the whole front and holding long stretches with nothing but anti-aircraft gunners converted to a kind of artillery-infantry and supported by a few armoured brigades, Alexander has also been able to concentrate ten British or British-controlled divisions representative of the whole British Empire on the Adriatic flank. The leading elements of these attacked before midnight on the 25th, and a general barrage opened and an advance began at dawn on the 26th. An advance of about nine miles was made over a large area, but the main position, the Gothic Line, has still to be encountered. I had the good fortune to go forward with this advance, and was consequently able to form a much clearer impression of the modern battlefield than is possible from the kinds of pinnacles and perches to which I have hitherto been confined.

Churchill ended his telegram to Roosevelt with a reference to the possibilities at the head of the Adriatic, his hopes for which he had already explained to Smuts. 'I have never forgotten your talks to me at Teheran about Istria,' Churchill told Roosevelt, 'and I am sure that the arrival of a powerful army in Trieste and Istria in four or five weeks would have an effect far outside purely military values. Tito's people will be awaiting us in Istria. What the condition of Hungary will be then I cannot imagine, but we shall at any rate be in a position to take full advantage of any great new situation.'[2]

*   *   *

---

[1] Joint Staff Mission Telegram, JSM 222, IZ 6288, 26 August 1944: Cabinet papers, 105/47.
[2] Prime Minister's Personal Telegram, T.1689/4, 'Chain' No. 241, 'Personal and Top Secret', 28 August 1944: Churchill papers, 20/170.

On the morning of August 27 Churchill flew back to Naples. Awaiting him at the airport was Attlee, who had arrived in Italy on the previous day. That afternoon Churchill went in the Prince of Piedmont's launch for a bathe off the island of Procida. That evening he held a conference with Admiral Sir John Cunningham, Maitland Wilson, Slessor, Dixon, and Jacob, on the problem of the employment of Greek air squadrons in Greece, a subject on which he then worked with Dixon from 11 p.m. until 12.45 a.m. The result of these long discussions was an agreement between the Foreign Office and Royal Air Force representatives that the two Greek fighter squadrons stationed in Cyrenaica should be sent to Athens 'some days after the arrival of the first British squadrons'. These were 'experienced units', Churchill explained to Eden, 'who, almost alone among the Greek forces, have a record of steadfast loyalty and good discipline'. Meanwhile, these Greek squadrons should be transferred to Italy, and allowed 'to fight the Germans from Italian soil . . .'.[1]

His work finished shortly before one o'clock, Churchill spent the next two hours of the night talking to Randolph, before going to bed at 3 a.m.

On August 28 Churchill started work at 7.30 in the morning. For three hours he worked, doing 'a considerable amount', as his Private Office Diary noted, before he left for a final bathe off Cumae, in the Bay of Naples. After bathing, Churchill returned to Admiral Morse's barge, passing through the lines of ships in the harbour, and 'being saluted by various crews of British ships of war'. Disembarking in the main harbour, Churchill saw a number of ships, among them a cruiser which had capsized during the bombing. He then drove straight to the airport, for the flight back to Britain, taking off shortly after midday.[2]

As Churchill left Italy, his message to the Italian people was made public. Its aim, he wrote, was to be one of 'encouragement and hope for the Italian people, for whom I have always had, except when we were actually fighting, a great regard'.[3] The message reflected, Pierson Dixon felt, the change from 'animosity and resentment against a former enemy' with which Churchill had arrived in Italy three weeks earlier, to the 'favour' with which he now looked 'on the happy people who had cheered him as he patrolled up and down the Italian peninsula'.[4] It also reflected his abiding personal concern for the restoration and preservation of democratic principles, wherever people and

[1] 'Chain' No. 236, 27 August 1944: Churchill papers, 20/180.
[2] 'Diary of a Visit to Italy', 28 August 1944.
[3] Winston S. Churchill, *The Second World War*, volume 6, London 1954, pages 111–12.
[4] Pierson Dixon recollections: Piers Dixon, *op. cit.*, page 1145.

Governments were prepared to uphold them. One section of Churchill's message to the Italian people read:

... It has been said that the price of freedom is eternal vigilance. The question arises, What is freedom? There are one or two quite simple, practical tests by which it can be known in the modern world in peace conditions, namely:

Is there the right to free expression of opinion and of opposition and criticism of the Government of the day?

Have the people the right to turn out a Government of which they disapprove, and are constitutional means provided by which they can make their will apparent?

Are their courts of justice free from violence by the Executive and from threats of mob violence, and free of all association with particular political parties?

Will these courts administer open and well-established laws which are associated in the human mind with the broad principles of decency and justice?

Will there be fair play for poor as well as for rich, for private persons as well as Government officials?

Will the rights of the individual, subject to his duties to the State, be maintained and asserted and exalted?

Is the ordinary peasant or workman who is earning a living by daily toil and striving to bring up a family free from the fear that some grim police organization under the control of a single party, like the Gestapo, started by the Nazi and Fascist parties, will tap him on the shoulder and pack him off without fair or open trial to bondage or ill-treatment? These simple, practical tests are some of the title-deeds on which a new Italy could be founded.[1]

This message, commented *The Times* in its main editorial on August 30, constituted 'words both of encouragement and warning'. *The Times* added that Churchill had 'all along' shown a 'profound' appreciation of the strategic importance of the Mediterranean. 'The great decision of 1940,' it declared, 'to send armour to Egypt from a Britain expecting invasion was primarily his, and revealed his grasp of the vital truth that, if the Mediterranean were lost to Britain, the way of recovery would be precarious, if not impossible. At the same time events have thoroughly justified his insistence that here the "soft under-belly of the Axis" was to be found.' The 'decisive' defeat imposed upon the Axis in North Africa, Sicily, and Italy was, wrote *The Times*, 'the indispensable preliminary to other allied offensives. Without it the launching of the invasion of Normandy would hardly have been imaginable.'[2]

*   *   *

[1] Message to the Italian people, 28 August 1944: Churchill papers, 2/222.
[2] Leading article 'Italy and the Future', *The Times*, 30 August 1944.

During August 28 Churchill held a further conference, to discuss Greece, with Maitland Wilson, Cunningham and Tedder, who assured him that operation 'Manna', the preparation for a British landing in Athens, 'could be completed within a fortnight', that is, on September 11. 'I am assured,' Churchill minuted to Eden and the Chiefs of Staff Committee on the following day, 'all possible steps are being taken and are being vigorously pushed by the Commanders-in-Chief.' It was 'most desirable', Churchill believed, 'to strike out of the blue without any apparent crisis'. Such would be the 'best way' to forestall the Communists. The Greek Government 'know nothing of this plan and should on no account be told anything. They should be encouraged to wait in hopeful expectancy.'

Churchill then set out the programme 'as I see it' for operation 'Manna', from D minus 1 to D plus 15:

D minus 1.—Inform the members of the Greek Government who are in Italy, of course preventing any leakage.

D Day—Fly in the parachute brigade to the neighbourhood of Athens where they seize the airfield and march into Athens to take possession of the city. They will naturally use as much but no more force than is necessary. Once the airfield is secured, the four squadrons, some British and some Greek, will begin moving in as fast as possible. The Greek Ministers should land as soon as the airfield is ready and follow the advance of the parachutists into Athens. At the same time, the British Fleet preceded by a strong force of minesweepers will operate off the Piraeus.

D plus 3 or 4—Transports carrying armoured tank brigade and the made-up divisions will sail so as to arrive continuously and disembark as fast as possible. On completion of the disembarkation it is hoped that the parachutists may be released as they are required by the army in Italy.

D plus 15—Beginning of the movement in of UNRRA.

'I only hope,' Churchill added, 'the local situation will not break up before we are ready.' [1]

For UNRRA, the United Nations Relief and Rehabilitation Agency, this was to be the first challenge. Churchill was not entirely happy with the financial problems which this new commitment would involve. 'I do not wish to crucify Britain on UNRRA,' he had minuted to Eden three weeks earlier, and he added, 'we will subject ourselves to the same level of self-denial as does the United States.' [2]

During August 28, while still in Naples, Churchill telegraphed to Roosevelt about his impending trans-Atlantic journey. Roosevelt had been anxious to restrict the numbers involved, but, as Churchill ex-

---

[1] Prime Minister's Personal Minute, M.942/4, 29 August 1944: Churchill papers, 20/153.
[2] Prime Minister's Personal Minute, M.920/4, 4 August 1944: Churchill papers, 20/153.

plained, whereas the British members of the conference would be indeed limited to fourteen or fifteen, as Roosevelt wished, it was necessary for the British to bring a clerical staff of forty-two, a cypher staff of thirty and a Royal Marine guard of thirty-six, as well as 'a small contingent' from the British Embassy in Washington. 'These however,' Churchill explained, 'are only the machinery with which I carry on my work and without which I could not leave the country. You have all your great departments immediately under your hand a few hours away by air.'

Reflecting on the most recent military developments, Churchill gave Roosevelt his opinion that the 'glorious events' in France and the Balkans 'have completely altered the whole outlook of the war and with people like the Germans anything might happen. Last time Bulgaria proved the lynch pin which when pulled brought everything crashing down.' As to the American forces, Churchill added, 'I must express my admiration to you not only for the valour but for the astonishing mobility and manoeuvring power of the great armies trained in the United States.' He was looking forward 'immensely' to seeing Roosevelt again, 'and trying to clear up with you in the light of our friendship some of the difficulties which beset even the path of dazzling victory'.[1]

That afternoon, August 28, Churchill left Naples in his York, flying across the sea to the western tip of Sicily, then on to Bizerta and along the north African coast. 'The journey was smooth and uneventful,' Commander Thompson noted, 'until about 5.30 p.m. when we ran into a thunderstorm and for half an hour the flight was very bumpy'. After seven hours in the air, the York landed at Rabat, where it was met by the British Consul-General, Stonehewer Bird.

Churchill had intended to fly on through the night to London. But when further thunderstorms were reported on the route, it was decided to stay in Rabat for the night, Churchill, Lord Moran and Commander Thompson sleeping at the villa of the Consul-General. As three pouches of papers were awaiting Churchill at Rabat, he had, as Thompson noted, 'heaps of reading matter'.[2] Pierson Dixon, who had travelled with Churchill from Naples, noted in his diary: 'Drinks on the terrace overlooking the salt-pan—brilliant flowers. The PM was headachy after the flight, but he mellowed.'[3] Dixon later recalled:

At dinner, despite his headache, Churchill was as communicative as ever. Of Germany, he said that an appeal should be made to the people

---

[1] 'Chain' No. 244, Prime Minister's Personal Telegram, T.1687/4, 'Personal and Top Secret', 28 August 1944: Cabinet papers, 120/144.

[2] 'Diary of a Visit to Italy', 28 August 1944.

[3] Pierson Dixon diary, 28 August 1944: Piers Dixon, *op. cit.*, page 115.

'to overthrow their leaders—only fifty of them, to be treated as war criminals'.

As Churchill surveyed the Balkans, he recalled the many monarchies of his youth—Bulgaria and Roumania, Greece and Yugoslavia. There was now no king in Bulgaria—'She has had no luck in three wars'. In Roumania 'King Carol nearly tried to resist the Germans'.

Churchill continued, as Dixon recorded: 'I have had many kings on my hands. I have fought hard for George and Peter. The King of Italy slipped through my fingers. President Roosevelt supports me: he likes to keep Kings on their thrones.' [1]

Churchill's views on an appeal to the German people had not been confined to after-dinner musing. Five days earlier he had minuted to Ismay:

The best way to bring about the fall of the present High Command in Germany is to draw up a list of war criminals who will be executed if they fall into the hands of the Allies. This list need not be more than fifty to a hundred long (apart from the punishment of local offenders). This would open a gulf between the persons named in it and the rest of the population. At the present moment none of the German leaders had any interest but fighting to the last man, hoping he will be that last man. It is very important to show the German people that they are not on the same footing as Hitler, Goering, Himmler and other monsters, who will infallibly be destroyed. [2]

On 29 August 1944, Churchill flew from Rabat to Britain. After about six hours in the air, and two hours from Britain, 'I had a sudden attack of my former malady,' Churchill informed Roosevelt three days later, 'with a temperature of between 103 and 104 degrees. . . .' [3]

Churchill's plane landed at Northolt shortly before six o'clock in the evening. Clementine Churchill and the Chiefs of Staff were at the airfield to greet him. 'Lord Moran emerged from the aircraft looking agitated,' noted Jock Colville, who was also there, 'and we found that the PM had a temperature of 103°, developed since luncheon.' [4] Admiral Cunningham, who was among those who had gone to the airport to meet Churchill, noted in his diary: 'The York arrived punctually but the PM was hurried to his car by Moran. He certainly looked ill.' [5]

[1] Pierson Dixon recollections: Piers Dixon, *op. cit.*, page 115.
[2] Prime Minister's Personal Minute, D(K)4/4, 23 August 1944: Churchill papers, 20/153.
[3] Prime Minister's Personal Telegram, T.1698/4, Prime Minister to President, No. 773, 'Personal and Top Secret', 31 August 1944: Cabinet papers, 120/144.
[4] Colville diary, 29 August 1944: Colville papers.
[5] Cunningham diary, 29 August 1944: Cunningham papers.

The War Cabinet had been fixed for 6.30 that evening, in order, as Eden noted in his diary, 'that W should have time to get there'. Eden's diary continued:

Looked in at Annexe on chance that he might be arriving and walked into him in passage as I was leaving for Cabinet. He seized my hand. 'Ah, there you are, dear Anthony, come into my room, I want to talk to you.' This was followed by a hurried whisper from Clemmie: 'He has a temperature of 103°.' In his bedroom while undressing and tumbling into bed he told me what had happened: a sudden chill a few hours from home. Fortunately, as he said, for a few hours earlier he would have been stuck at Rabat.

Extracted myself as soon as I could for he showed every desire to discuss all our problems and I felt the whirl of approaching doctors, etc. Slipped out and sent Moran in and went down to Cabinet.[1]

The first medical examination was unambiguous. 'Small patch on lung,' Colville noted.[2] That night Admiral Cunningham wrote in his diary:

The First Lord who went over to Downing Street after dinner said he saw Moran still there & two nurses; a specialist had been sent for. I hope it is only wise precaution it would be a tragedy if anything should happen to him now. With all his faults (& he is the most infuriating man) he has done a great job for the country, & besides there is no one else.[3]

'. . . all is well I hope', Clementine Churchill wrote to their daughter Mary. 'The two beautiful Nurses from St. Mary's Hospital appeared as though by magic—Doctor Geoffrey Marshall the lung specialist took blood tests & X-rays and gave M & B. It *is* a slight attack— there *is* a small shadow on one lung, but in himself he is well. . . .'[4]

---

[1] Eden diary, 29 August 1944: Eden memoirs, *The Reckoning, op. cit.*, page 470.
[2] Colville diary, 29 August 1944: Colville papers.
[3] Cunningham diary, 29 August 1944: Cunningham papers.
[4] Letter of 31 August 1944: Mary Soames, *Clementine Churchill, op. cit.*, page 356.

49

The Warsaw Uprising,
'a black cloud'

O N 18 August 1944, the Communist-controlled National Council in Poland declared Lublin to be the temporary capital of Poland. In Warsaw, the insurgents fought on with growing desperation, against considerable German reinforcements, and without Soviet aid. That same day Churchill telegraphed to Roosevelt:

The refusal of the Soviet to allow the U.S. aircraft to bring succour to the heroic insurgents in Warsaw added to their own complete neglect to fly in supplies when only a few score of miles away constitutes an episode of profound and far reaching gravity. If as is almost certain the German triumph in Warsaw is followed by a wholesale massacre no measure can be put upon the full consequences that will arise. I am willing to send a personal message to Stalin if you think this wise and if you will yourself send a separate similar message.

The 'glorious and gigantic victories' being achieved in France by the British and United States forces could, Churchill told Roosevelt, 'far exceed in scale anything that the Russians have done on any particular occasion', and he added: 'I am inclined to think therefore, that they will have some respect for what we say so long as it is plain and simple. It is quite possible Stalin would not resent it but even if he did we are Nations serving high causes and must give true counsels towards world peace.'[1]

From air bases around Bari, in southern Italy, Royal Air Force bombers had continued to fly nightly sorties to Warsaw, which lay at the very limit of their range, and 145 miles beyond the range of their escorting fighters.[2] On August 17, however, Air Marshal Slessor

[1] Prime Minister's Personal Telegram, T.1634/4, 'Chain' No. 110, Prime Minister to President No. 760, 18 August 1944: Churchill papers, 20/170.

[2] 'Distances', Air Ministry note of 22 August 1944: Air Ministry papers, 20/2710. The distance from Bari to Warsaw was 785 miles, from Cambridge to Warsaw 878 miles.

decided that the losses were too high to impose on regular crews, and from the following day the flights were carried out by volunteer Polish units. Of a total of 182 aircraft sent from southern Italy to Warsaw over a period of three weeks, 35 of them failed to return.[1] On August 18 Churchill telegraphed to Eden, about a further request for non-volunteer air support from the Poles:

I have sent Mikolajczyk's appeal to Air Marshal Slessor, but I do not feel able to press him any further. The losses have amounted to 30% and of course everyone who flies a 700 miles flight knows perfectly well that the Russians could put the supplies in from perhaps only 100 miles away. Should the suppression of the rising be followed by a bloody massacre you cannot expect that this will not make a profound impression upon the world.

Churchill also told Eden that he thought he should speak 'very gravely' to the Soviet Ambassador, 'as well as telegraph to Molotov through Clark Kerr'.[2]

During August 18 Churchill read what he described to Eden as an 'extremely lukewarm telegram' from the American Joint Chiefs of Staff to Eisenhower, deprecating the practicability of flying aid to Warsaw from airfields in Britain, and then landing on Russian airstrips.[3] 'Send me a short report,' Churchill telegraphed to Sinclair that same day, 'on the feasibility and scale of US operations to help Warsaw on the assumption that the Russians are persuaded to give facilities their end. I must know where we are on this. . . .'[4]

The use of Soviet airstrips east of Warsaw was technically feasible, but Stalin refused to make them available for Allied aircraft. To his wife, Churchill wrote on August 18:

You should ask the Private Office to let you see the various telegrams now passing about the Russian refusal either to help or allow the Americans to help the struggling people of Warsaw, who will be massacred and liquidated very quickly if nothing can be done. These messages speak for themselves. If there is a massacre in Warsaw the whole world will criticize the Soviets and will do so with more freedom if the battle in France proves, as I hope, to be a far larger and more intense military event than anything which Russia has produced.

'I am most painfully affected by this Polish incident,' Churchill added.[5] To Lord Selborne, Churchill minuted that same day: 'I have been

---

[1] Air Marshall Sir Douglas Evill, Vice Chief of the Air Staff, to the War Cabinet, War Cabinet No. 117 to 1944, 5 September 1944: Cabinet papers, 65/43.
[2] 'Chain' No. 103, 18 August 1944, Churchill papers, 20/180.
[3] Telegram No. W.80785 of 15 August 1944, referred to in 'Chain' No. 115, 18 August 1944: Churchill papers, 20/180.
[4] 'Chain' No. 117, 18 August 1944: Churchill papers, 20/180.
[5] Letter of 18 August 1944: Spencer-Churchill papers.

very much taken up with Polish affairs, working day and night to bring help to the Poles in Warsaw, though the difficulties are great.'[1]

On August 20, while still on his Italian visit, Churchill had sent Stalin an appeal, drafted by Roosevelt, for Soviet help to the Warsaw insurgents. 'We are thinking of world opinion,' they wrote, 'if the anti-Nazis in Warsaw are in effect abandoned.' They hoped that Stalin would drop 'immediate supplies and munitions to the patriot Poles in Warsaw, or', they added, 'will you agree to help our planes in doing it very quickly? We hope you will approve. The time element is of extreme importance.'[2] This message, Churchill telegraphed to Roosevelt on August 20, 'has been sent to UJ over our two signatures. Our thoughts are one.'

Churchill also sent Roosevelt on August 20 the text of a telegram sent from Moscow by Clark Kerr on August 17, containing a statement by Andrei Vyshinski. 'The Soviet Government,' the statement declared, 'cannot of course object to English or American aircraft dropping arms in the region of Warsaw since this is an American and British affair. But they decidedly object to American or British aircraft, after dropping arms in the region of Warsaw, landing on Soviet territory, since the Soviet Government do not wish to associate themselves either directly or indirectly with the adventure in Warsaw.'[3]

Stalin's reply was uncompromising. 'Sooner or later,' he wrote, 'the truth about the group of criminals who have embarked on the Warsaw adventure in order to seize power will become known to everybody.' His telegram continued:

These people have exploited the good faith of the inhabitants of Warsaw, throwing many almost unarmed people against the German guns, tanks, and aircraft. A situation has arisen in which each new day serves, not the Poles for the liberation of Warsaw, but the Hitlerites who are inhumanly shooting down the inhabitants of Warsaw.[4]

The break between Stalin and the Warsaw insurgents was complete. As each day passed, the Germans regained control over more and more of the city. The slaughter of Poles was on a savage scale, as German artillery and aircraft pounded the areas still under Polish control, forcing the insurgents to take refuge in the sewers. On August 23 Churchill telegraphed from Rome to Brendan Bracken:

[1] Prime Minister's Personal Minute, M(K) 13/4, 18 August 1944: Churchill papers, 20/153. Selborne had asked about the possibility of 'recognizing the Polish Secret Army as an Allied fighting force'. Churchill asked to know 'what is proposed'.

[2] Prime Minister's Personal Telegram, T.1643/4, No. 2602 from Foreign Office to Warsaw, 'Top Secret', 20 August 1944: Churchill papers, 20/170.

[3] Prime Minister's Personal Telegram, T.1641/4, Prime Minister to President, No. 762, 'Personal and Top Secret', 20 August 1944: Churchill paper, 20/110.

[4] Telegram of 22 August 1944, sent by Churchill to Roosevelt as Prime Minister's Personal Telegram, T.1662/4, 'Clasp' No. 185, 23 August 1944: Churchill papers, 20/170.

I see from the papers that the agony of Warsaw has been practically suppressed. There is no need to mention the Soviet behaviour but surely the facts should be given publicity. Is there any stop on this matter? Is there any reason why the consequences of the strange and sinister behaviour of the Russians should not be made public? It is not for us to cast reproaches on the Soviet Government but surely the facts should be allowed to speak for themselves.[1]

At the War Cabinet on August 24, Eden pointed out that Mikolajczyk was doing his utmost to restrain the Polish Government, although he was under 'strong pressure' to make a public protest against Britain's failure to give more effective help to the Underground Army.[2] In Italy, Churchill learned that there was even pressure among the London Poles to replace Mikolajczyk by a Prime Minister who would adopt a more openly anti-Soviet tone. On August 23 Churchill had telegraphed to Eden:

You should warn the Poles most earnestly that the removal of Mikolajczyk would to a very large extent sever the ties which we have with them. Mikolajczyk went under our full encouragement and we are not in the habit of casting away men who have followed our advice. I should regard an attack on Mikolajczyk as an attack on H.M.G. removing the last chance of a solution.[3]

On August 24 Churchill received an 'eye-witness account' of the Warsaw rising, covering the five days from August 11 to August 16. He at once sent a copy by telegram to Roosevelt. Another copy, he explained, had been given to the Soviet Ambassador in London. The account gave many examples of what it called the 'ruthless terror methods' which were being used by the Germans in Warsaw. On August 13, for example, 'the German forces have brutally murdered wounded sick people, both men and women', who were lying in three of the city's hospitals. The inhabitants 'continue to report', the account declared, ' "When we get weapons we will pay them back." '[4]

Churchill still sought some means whereby Stalin would allow British and American aircraft, flying from England, to drop supplies into Warsaw and then fly on to Soviet air bases to refuel. Only in this way could they make the long flight. It was clear that little time was left for such help to be effective. Churchill therefore drafted, for Roosevelt's consideration, a joint telegram to be sent from Prime Minister and President to the Soviet leader. The telegram read:

---

[1] 'Chain' No. 171, 23 August 1944: Churchill papers, 20/180.
[2] War Cabinet No. 110 of 1944, 24 August 1944, Confidential Annex: Cabinet papers, 65/47.
[3] 'Chain' No. 186, 23 August 1944: Churchill papers, 20/180.
[4] Prime Minister's Personal Telegram, T.1656/4, Prime Minister to President, No. 767, 'Personal and Top Secret', 24 August 1944: Cabinet papers, 118/86.

We are most anxious to send American planes from England. Why should they not land on the refuelling ground which has been assigned to us behind the Russian lines without enquiry as to what they have done on the way? This should preserve the principle of your Government's dissociation from this particular episode. We feel sure that if wounded British or American planes arrived behind the lines of your Armies, they will be succoured with your usual consideration. We do not try to form an opinion about the persons who instigated this rising which was certainly called for repeatedly by radio Moscow. Our sympathies are however for the 'almost unarmed people' whose special faith has led them to attack German guns, tanks and aircraft. We cannot think that Hitler's cruelties will end with their resistance. On the contrary it seems probable that that is the time when they will begin with full ferocity. The massacre in Warsaw will undoubtedly be a very great annoyance to us when we all meet at the end of the war. Unless you directly forbid it therefore we propose to send the planes.

If Stalin failed to reply to this, Churchill told Roosevelt in his covering note, 'I feel we ought to go, and see what happens.' The British and American aircraft would make the journey without Stalin's approval. 'I cannot conceive,' Churchill added, 'that he would maltreat or detain them.'[1]

Roosevelt rejected Churchill's suggestion. One reason, he replied on August 26, was Stalin's 'definite refusal' to allow Soviet airfields to be used by Allied planes seeking to drop supplies in Warsaw. The other reason was the 'current American conversations' with the Soviet Union about the future use of Soviet air bases, in Siberia, for use by American bombers on their way to bomb Japan. 'I do not consider it advantageous to the long range general war prospect,' Roosevelt explained, 'for me to join with you in the proposed message to Uncle J.'[2]

Thus, over aid to Warsaw, the Anglo-American unity was broken, leaving Britain alone to take, if it so wished, a step that would only anger the Soviet Union. On August 28, while Churchill was on his way back from Italy, Eden reported to the War Cabinet that messages had reached London from Poland to say 'that the leaders of the Underground Army, as the Russians advanced, were being seized and deported'.[3] On August 29, the British and American Governments declared the Polish Home Army to be a 'responsible belligerent force'. The impasse was complete.

*   *   *

[1] Prime Minister's Personal Telegram, T.1668/4, Prime Minister to President, No. 769, 'Personal and Top Secret', 25 August 1944: Churchill papers, 20/170.

[2] President to Prime Minister, No. 606 of 26 August 1944, 'Clasp', No. 239 of 27 August 1944: Churchill papers, 20/170.

[3] President to Prime Minister, No. 606 of 26 August 1944, 'Clasp' No. 239 of 27 August 1944: Churchill papers, 20/170.

When the War Cabinet met on September 3, in Churchill's absence, they endorsed the idea that Churchill should try to toughen Roosevelt by asking him again to consider an air operation to drop supplies on Warsaw. It was also agreed that Churchill should send another message to Stalin, in the name of the War Cabinet, warning him of the effect of his action on future Anglo-Soviet relations.[1]

Churchill was 'greatly upset' on September 3, Jock Colville noted in his diary, by a telegram from the British Legation to the Vatican, containing the text of a message from the women of Warsaw to the Pope. 'It was truly pathetic,' Colville noted, 'and the PM drafted a telegram to the President suggesting that we might inform Stalin that in default of assistance to Warsaw we should take certain drastic action in respect of our own supplies to Russia.'[2]

On the evening of September 3, Sir Charles Portal went to see Churchill to discuss the possibility of a large-scale operation to Warsaw being carried out by aircraft of Bomber Command from airfields in Britain. As Portal told the Chiefs of Staff Committee on the following morning, Churchill 'had accepted the Air Staff view that such an operation was not practicable'.[3]

The War Cabinet met on the evening of September 4 to discuss the despatch of supplies to Poland. Churchill, who was still unwell, and had spent the day in his bed at No. 10 Annexe, was not expected to attend. Ten years later he recalled how:

When the Cabinet met on the night of September 4 I thought the issue so important that though I had a touch of fever I went from my bed to our underground room. We had met together on many unpleasant affairs. I do not remember any occasion when such deep anger was shown by all our members, Tory, Labour, Liberal alike. I should have liked to say, 'We are sending our aeroplanes to land in your territory, after delivering supplies to Warsaw. If you do not treat them properly all convoys will be stopped from this moment by us.' But the reader of these pages in after years must realise that everyone always has to keep in mind the fortunes of millions of men fighting in a world-wide struggle, and that terrible and even humbling submissions must at times be made to the general aim. I did not therefore propose this drastic step.[4]

At the War Cabinet of September 4, Eden read out the draft of a strongly worded telegram to Stalin, and also an appeal to Roosevelt. 'W was I think tired,' he noted in his diary, 'and did not look at all

[1] War Cabinet No. 492 of 1944, 3 September 1944: Cabinet papers, 65/54.

[2] Colville diary, 3 September 1944: Colville papers.

[3] Chiefs of Staff Committee No. 297 (Operations) of 1944, 11 a.m., 4 September 1944: Cabinet papers, 79/80.

[4] Winston S. Churchill, *The Second World War*, volume 6, London 1954, page 124.

well. He liked the draft messages to UJ and FDR about Polish affairs, though they had been pretty hurriedly scratched up.'[1]

The telegram to Roosevelt again appealed to the American President to take action to aid Warsaw from Russian airfields. The 'only way' to bring material help to the Poles, it declared, was for United States aircraft to drop supplies, 'using Russian airfields for the purpose', and it went on to urge the President to 'authorize your air forces to carry out this operation, landing if necessary on Russian airfields without their consent'.[2] The second telegram, sent to Stalin 'in the name of the War Cabinet', stated that the Soviet Government's action in preventing help from being sent to the Poles 'seems to us at variance with the spirit of Allied co-operation to which you and we attach so much importance both for the present and for the future'.[3] Churchill also sent Roosevelt, on September 4, the text of the appeal of the women of Warsaw to the Pope, in which they declared: 'Warsaw is in ruins. The Germans are killing the wounded in hospitals. They are making women and children march in front of them in order to protect their tanks. There is no exaggeration in reports of children who are fighting and destroying tanks with bottles of petrol.' The women of Warsaw added: 'The Russian armies which have been for three weeks at the gates of Warsaw have not advanced a step.'[4] The problem of Warsaw, Colville noted in his diary that evening, 'is a black cloud in an otherwise azure sky'.[5]

The reply to the appeal to Roosevelt was negative. 'I am informed,' Roosevelt wrote, 'by my Office of Military Intelligence that the fighting Poles have departed from Warsaw and that the Germans are now in full control.' Roosevelt added: 'The problem of relief for the Poles in Warsaw has therefore unfortunately been solved by delay and by German action, and there now appears to be nothing we can do to assist them.'[6]

The German authorities acted in Warsaw with particular savagery. Many thousands of Poles were deported, and several thousand shot.

---

[1] Eden diary, 4 September 1944: Eden memoirs, *The Reckoning*, op. cit., page 473.

[2] Prime Minister's Personal Telegram, T.1740/4, Prime Minister to President, No. 779, 'Personal and Top Secret', 4 September 1944: Churchill papers, 20/171.

[3] Prime Minister's Personal Telegram, T.1741/4, 4 September 1944: Churchill papers, 20/171.

[4] Prime Minister's Personal Telegram, T.1742/4, 4 September 1944: Churchill papers, 20/171.

[5] Colville diary, 4 September 1944: Colville papers.

[6] President to Prime Minister, No. 619, 'Personal and Top Secret', 5 September 1944: Churchill papers, 20/171.

50

Preparing for Quebec

O N 30 August 1944, the United States First Army crossed the Marne and reached Rheims. Châlons too was liberated. Although Churchill had to spend the day in bed, he was well enough in the evening to have an hour and a half discussion with Eisenhower on the future strategy in northern France, and the new Command arrangements which were to come into effect in two days' time.[1] The reason for the American 'mobility', Eisenhower told Churchill, was that the Americans had, as Churchill reported on the following day to Alexander, 'shaken themselves free' from the 'tyranny' of Q stores and supplies, 'and are taking real risks sometimes pushing thirty miles ahead with less than one day's ammunition'. Churchill added: 'This of course fits the situation there, but I was sure that their high mobility could never be achieved by our Gradgrind methods.'[2]

On August 31 Churchill remained in bed, making plans for his next overseas journey, to meet Roosevelt in conference at Quebec, codename 'Octagon', and telegraphing to Roosevelt:

... continuous employment against the enemy will have to be found for the Eighth and Fifth Armies once the German armies in Italy have been destroyed or unluckily have made their escape. This employment can only take the form of a movement first to Istria and Trieste and ultimately upon Vienna. Should the war come to an end in a few months, as may well be possible, none of these questions will arise. Anyhow, we can talk this over fully at 'Octagon'.[1]

[1] Private Office diary, 30 August 1944. Under the new command arrangements, Eisenhower was to move his headquarters from Britain to France, Montgomery to command 21st Army Group and Bradley to command 12th Army Group. These changes were announced on 1 September 1944. On the previous evening, Montgomery had been created Field Marshal (a higher corresponding rank than that of Eisenhower, or of Alexander).

[2] Prime Minister's Personal Telegram, T.1702/4, OZ 4882, 'Personal and Top Secret', 31 August 1944: Churchill papers, 20/171. In Charles Dickens' novel *Hard Times*, Thomas Gradgrind is 'an eminently practical man', who believes in facts and figures and brings up his children Louise and Tom accordingly, 'ruthlessly suppressing the imaginative sides of their nature'. Margaret Drabble (editor), *The Oxford Companion to English Literature*, 5th edition, 1985.

In reply, Roosevelt stated that, after 'breaking' the German forces on the Gothic Line 'we must go on to use our divisions in the way which best aids General Eisenhower's drive into the enemy homeland'. The future deployment of the Allied forces in Italy, Roosevelt insisted, 'depends on the progress of the present battle in Italy, and also in France, where I strongly feel that we must not stint in any way the forces needed to break quickly through the western defences of Germany'.[2]

Before Roosevelt's reply reached him, Churchill had re-iterated his hopes for an active campaign in Italy, when telegraphing to Smuts: 'My object now is to keep what we have got in Italy, which should be sufficient since the enemy has withdrawn four of his best divisions.' With the troops available, Churchill explained, 'I hope to turn and break the Gothic Line, break into the Po Valley, and ultimately advance by Trieste and the Ljubljana Gap to Vienna.' Churchill added: 'Even if the war comes to an end at an early date, I have told Alexander to be ready for a dash with armoured cars.'[3] Vienna was to be the goal.

During August 31 Churchill had four visitors to the Annexe: King George VI, who stayed for an hour, General Brooke, Eden and Lord Camrose.[4] In a note of their conversation, Camrose recorded: 'The Russians were behaving very badly about Warsaw and he savagely attacked the leading article in *The Times* (published yesterday) on the subject.'[5]

As Churchill prepared to leave for Quebec, his family and friends were still welcoming him back from Italy. 'So very glad you are home,' Mary Churchill telegraphed from her anti-aircraft battery near Hastings. 'All well on this doodle-bug point. Hope to see you soon.'[6] From Italy that day came a telegram of thanks from Maitland Wilson. 'All of us here,' he wrote, 'derived from your visit the

---

[1] Prime Minister's Personal Telegram, T.1705/4, Prime Minister to President, No. 774, 'Personal and Top Secret', 31 August 1944: Churchill papers, 20/171.

[2] President to Prime Minister No. 616, 'Personal and Top Secret', 4 September 1944: Churchill papers, 20/171.

[3] Prime Minister's Personal Telegram, T.1706/4, No. 842 from Dominions Office to South Africa, 'Top Secret and Personal. Decypher yourself', 31 August 1944: Churchill papers, 20/171.

[4] Private Office Diary, 31 August 1944.

[5] Lord Camrose, 'Memorandum', 31 August 1944: Camrose papers. In a leading article on 31 August 1944, *The Times* declared that 'the malicious and unfounded rumour was spread that the Russians were deliberately holding back in order to allow a war of extermination to be waged between Poles and Germans'. It was also 'difficult', *The Times* added, 'not to understand Russian reluctance to facilitate the supply of arms to men who are at the same moment proclaiming purposes plainly inconsistent with a friendly attitude towards Russia'. The leader also referred to 'the legitimate sensitiveness of Russia towards independent action by the Powers anywhere in the territories lying between her frontiers and Germany.'

[6] Telegram of 31 August 1944: Churchill papers, 20/149.

same inspiration and encouragement that we experienced during the dark days of this war when your leadership made possible the now imminent victory.'[1]

The few people who knew that Churchill was ill watched his recovery with relief. 'Tonight his temperature is back to normal,' Ambassador Winant reported to Harry Hopkins on September 1, 'and he seems on the way to a quick recovery. But each journey has taken its toll and the interval between illnesses has been constantly shortened.' There was no one he had known in Britain, Winant added, 'who cares so much about friendly relations between Great Britain and the United States, and few people anywhere who have been more loyal in their friendship with the President'.[2] 'My temperature is normal,' Churchill telegraphed to Roosevelt on September 1, 'and I am much better though still eating masses of M and B.'[3] That evening Churchill worked on his papers, and was, Jock Colville noted, 'in tearing form. He had entirely emptied his box.' Churchill gave Colville a survey of the road to D-Day, and beyond, telling his Private Secretary:

> ... it has been like a bull-fight: Torch, Husky etc. were like the preliminaries—the Picadors, the banderillas etc. Then came Overlord, the Matador coming at the crucial moment to make the kill waiting till the bull's head was down and his strength weakened. But 'Dragoon', the landing in the South of France, has been a pure waste: it has not helped Eisenhower at all and, by weakening Alexander's armies, had enabled the Germans to withdraw troops from Italy to Northern France.[4]

Each day, receiving his Enigma decrypts, Churchill studied in his Map Room the places mentioned in them, using maps of the war situation provided by the War Office. 'Dragoon' was making so much progress that on September 1 the War Office map proved useless, to Churchill's chagrin. 'This map shows nothing one wants to see,' he minuted that day to the Director of Military Intelligence. 'We know that the Germans are in Lyons and have a flank guard at Vienne. The 338th Infantry is at Roussillon and I do not even see that on your map. The remnants of the other four have all got past the corner.' In fact, Churchill added, the War Office map 'has absolutely no relations to the situation as disclosed by Boniface. Would you kindly let me have one that is more up to date.'[5]

[1] F/900G, 31 August 1944: Churchill papers, 20/171.

[2] Letter of 1 September 1944: Robert E. Sherwood, *The White House Papers of Harry L. Hopkins*, London, 1949, volume 2, page 806.

[3] Prime Minister's Personal Telegram, T.1713/4, Prime Minister to President, No. 775, 'Personal and Top Secret', 1 September 1944: Premier papers, 4/75/2, Part 2, folio 652.

[4] Colville diary, 1 September 1944: Colville papers.

[5] Prime Minister's Personal Minute, M.955/4, 'Top Secret', 1 September 1944: Churchill papers, 20/153. Access to Churchill's Map Room at the Annexe was restricted to the Map

On September 1 the Royal Air Force and Tito's partisans launched operation 'Ratweek', a seven-day joint attack on German road and rail routes through Yugoslavia, aimed at preventing the evacuation of German troops from Greece and the Balkans. Several railway bridges on the evacuation route were totally destroyed, as were many kilometres of track.[1] At the same time, an unexpectedly rapid advance by the Red Army to the Danube at Turnu Severin made it certain, as Maitland Wilson reported, that, in conjunction with the successes of 'Ratweek', the Germans would be unable to withdraw 'any substantial forces' from the Balkans to assist them either in Italy or in Central Europe.[2]

On September 2 British forces crossed the Belgian frontier. 'How wonderful it is,' Churchill telegraphed to Montgomery, 'to see our people leaping out at last after all their hard struggles.'

Churchill began this letter to Montgomery: 'My dear Field Marshal—to use your new rank for the first time,' and went on to say, of Montgomery's promotion to Field Marshal, 'I am sure no such step has been better earned.' Churchill added: 'There is of course a little reaction in American circles, but here everyone is delighted.' As for Alexander, he would certainly be made a Field Marshal in due course, and, Churchill explained to Montgomery, 'I propose to date it from the capture of Rome which I am sure will be quite agreeable to you. Thus the old order of seniority will be restored.'[3]

Churchill now made the final preparations for his trans-Atlantic journey. 'I propose to give the model of Arromanches to the President for his museum,' he minuted to Captain Pim. 'Pray bring it up-to-date and take it with your Map Room equipment on "Octagon".' A duplicate of the landing beach, Churchill added, 'should be made to stay behind for me'.[4] 'Looking forward much to seeing you,' Churchill telegraphed to Mackenzie King on September 2. 'Am bringing Clemmie with me,' and he added: 'Most Secret. I am at present laid up with a touch of my old complaint but the doctors are confident that, barring accidents, I can keep my engagements.'[5]

Room staff under Captain Pim; to the three Chiefs of Staff; to Ismay and the senior members of Churchill's Defence Staff; to Major Morton, Lord Cherwell and Brendan Bracken; and to Churchill's Private Secretaries, 'apart from such visitors as the Prime Minister may himself invite to inspect the maps'. ('Defence Map Room', 'Secret', 1 November 1943: Premier papers, 4/69/2, folios 489–90.)

[1] A. K. Allen, 'Ratweek', 'Top Secret', 6 September 1944, and Fitzroy Maclean to Air Vice Marshall Elliot, 8 September 1944: Air Ministry papers, 23/852.

[2] NAF 774, 'Top Secret', 8 September 1944: Cabinet papers, 120/148.

[3] Letter of 2 September 1944: Premier papers, 4/84/1, folios 126–7.

[4] 'Personal and Secret', 21 August 1944: Premier papers, 4/75/2, Part 2, folio 855.

[5] Prime Minister's Personal Telegram, T.1728/4, 2 September 1944: Premier papers, 4/75/2, Part 1, folio 286.

In Italy, on September 2, the Fifth Army entered Pisa while, on the eastern side of the peninsula, the Eighth Army broke through the Gothic Line. But two fresh German divisions had been moved to the Adriatic sector to halt the Allied advance. 'These German forces,' Alexander telegraphed to Churchill that day, 'will have to be smashed on the field of battle before Eighth Army can gain its full momentum.' [1] 'I am delighted that you have broken through,' Churchill replied, and he added: 'It is a good thing that the German divisions should be smashed on the field of battle', as this would 'save trouble afterwards'. Churchill also informed Alexander he was arranging 'that when the time comes, as it will very soon', to promote him Field Marshal, in such a way as to preserve his existing seniority over Montgomery. [2]

In western Europe, the advance continued on both the 'Overlord' and 'Dragoon' fronts, with both Brussels in the north and Lyons in the south being liberated on September 3, the fifth anniversary of Britain's declaration of war on Germany. Reporting on 'Dragoon', Maitland Wilson informed the Chiefs of Staff that 50,000 German prisoners had been captured, 'and very heavy losses inflicted on the enemy'. Although one and a half German divisions had escaped to the north, it was only after 'having suffered heavy losses in men and material'. [3]

On September 4, British troops liberated Antwerp. In the previous week, only thirty-seven flying bombs had reached London, nor had a single one been launched since midday on September 1. On August 28, of ninety-four flying bombs which approached the south coast, all but four were destroyed: sixty-five by the anti-aircraft batteries, twenty-three by fighter aircraft, and two by barrage balloons.

It was the future of Greece which now emerged as one of Churchill's principal concerns, and on September 3 he drafted a telegram which he wished to send to Maitland Wilson, about the despatch of a British force under General Scobie to Athens on September 11. Churchill had intended to put several questions to the General:

Can I count on the 11th being kept to? Have you got Scobie with you and have you explained it all to him? Is he good enough for the job? If not, make any changes you think fit. Have you got the extra troops to go in if the parachutists are not strong enough? Is the Admiral all teed up? This operation has got to be a little gem. What is your estimate of the German troops in

[1] MA/1625, IZ/6479, 2 September 1944: Churchill papers, 20/171.
[2] Prime Minister's Personal Telegram, T.1731/4, 'Personal and Top Secret', 3 September 1944: Premier papers, 4/84/1, folio 117.
[3] MEDCOS No. 181, FX 91375, 'Top Secret', 2 September 1944: Cabinet papers, 122/1309.

Athens? How near are the airfields you propose to seize? Are they big enough for troop-carrying planes to land after the parachute phase? Have you got everything you want? Is there any political point on which you are in doubt?

Churchill ended his draft telegram: 'Let me know about all this.' [1] But when the draft was discussed by the Chiefs of Staff, they objected to Churchill's question about September 11, pointing out that it had already been agreed that no date could be fixed for 'Manna' until 'the Germans withdraw or wish to surrender'. [2]

Ismay then wrote to Churchill to explain why Wilson should not be asked to work to the date of September 11. The present German strength in Greece, he pointed out on behalf of the Chiefs of Staff, was 116,000 men on the mainland, 17,000 in the Peloponnese, and 31,000 in Crete. The morale of the Germans on the mainland was 'fair'. In view of this, Ismay added, 'the Chiefs of Staff submit that we should adhere to the original conception of "Manna", namely that it should not be launched until the Germans have either started to crack or to evacuate'. [3]

The Chiefs of Staff decided to ask Churchill to omit his question to Maitland Wilson about September 11, and send the telegram without any fixed date.

Wilson had already set Churchill's mind at rest as to the capacity of General Scobie, and the general planning of the operation. A 'special party' was being sent in, he telegraphed to Churchill on September 4, to provide information on the practicability of an airfield six miles from Athens which was large enough for landing troops in transport aircraft, and 'to confirm that no resistance, especially anti-aircraft, will be encountered'. [4] 'I am much obliged to you and the Admiral,' Churchill replied, 'for making these plans so promptly and effectively.' [5]

The seizure of Athens, Churchill minuted to Ismay on September 4, was to be done 'as a bolt from the blue and not in relation to any particular German movement'. It was of 'great importance,' he added,

[1] Prime Minister's Personal Telegram, T.1729/4, 'Personal and Top Secret', 3 September 1944: Churchill papers, 20/171.

[2] Chiefs of Staff Committee No. 297 (Operations) of 1944, 4 September 1949: Cabinet papers, 79/80.

[3] Minute of 4 September 1944, Chiefs of Staff Committee No. 297 (Operations) of 1944, Annex 1: Cabinet papers, 79/80.

[4] No. 041715 from Caserta, 'Top Secret and Personal', 4 September 1944: Churchill papers, 20/171. This was Hassani airfield, now Athens international airport.

[5] Prime Minister's Personal Telegram, T.1743/4, 5 September 1944: Churchill papers, 20/184.

'not to delay but to forestall events.' If the German forces were 'too strong', however, Maitland Wilson 'must say so'.[1] Churchill also opposed any diversionary landing in the Peloponnese, as had been suggested by the Foreign Office. 'The Greek Government,' Churchill wrote, 'are to go to Athens and nowhere else.'[2]

'This visit of mine to the President,' Churchill had written to his wife on 17 August 1944, 'is the most necessary one that I have ever made since the very beginning, as it is there that various differences that exist between the Staffs, and also between me and the American Chiefs of Staff, must be brought to a decision.'

Churchill wrote these words while he was in Italy. There, in the war-zone, he had reflected on the military and strategic disagreements between Britain and the United States, and on what he saw as an imbalance of effort and reward. Britain, he explained to his wife, had three armies in the field. The first, in France, was fighting 'under American command'. The second, in Italy under General Alexander, was relegated to 'a secondary and frustrated condition' by the United States' 'insistence upon the Riviera landings'. The third, on the Burmese frontier, was fighting 'in the most unhealthy country in the world under the worst possible conditions', in order to guard the American Air line over the Himalayas 'into their very over-rated China'.[3] Thus, Churchill pointed out, 'two-thirds of Britain's forces', those in Italy and Burma, were being 'mis-employed' on behalf of the American Command, and the remaining third, in France, was under American Command.

Churchill ended his letter of August 17: 'These are delicate and serious matters to be handled between friends in careful and patient personal discussion. I have no doubt we shall reach a good conclusion, but you will see that life is not very easy.'[4]

[1] Prime Minister's Personal Minute, D.242/4, 'Urgent', 4 September 1944: Churchill papers, 20/153.

[2] Prime Minister's Personal Minute, D.241/4, 4 September 1944: Churchill papers, 20/153.

[3] Churchill did not exaggerate about the 'unhealthy conditions'. On August 5 he had learned from Lord Moran that, of a total of 98,050 troops serving in northern Burma between September 1943 and February 1944, there had been 3,140 battle casualties, and 47,534 'evacuated sick', of whom 28,909 were due to malaria, 'more than nine times the battle casualties', Moran pointed out, 'from one disease, malaria, alone'. The safeguard since then had been the use of Atebrin, which, among the Australian troops of New Guinea, had reduced the malarial death rate to a tenth the normal mortality in that region. (Letter of 5 August 1944: Premier papers, 4/75/1, folios 87–9.)

[4] Letter of 17 August 1944: Spencer-Churchill papers.

On the morning of September 5 Churchill left London by train for Greenock, on the first stage of his meeting with Roosevelt in Quebec. It was to be their sixth meeting since the summer of 1941. Twenty minutes after the train had left Addison Road station in west London, it slowed down. 'It appeared,' noted Lord Moran, 'that the PM's spectacles had been left behind, and a message was sent to retrieve them.'[1]

The first conference on board the train was about Greece, Churchill being, as Brooke noted in his diary, 'still very much of the opinion that we might be justified in dropping a parachute brigade (about 2,000 to 3,000 strong) near Athens with some 150,000 Germans still in Greece. I had to convince him that such a plan was out of the question and that the dropping of this party was dependent on the Germans evacuating Greece or being prepared to surrender.' Brooke added: 'He was looking much better and in very good form.'[2] As a result of this discussion on the train, Churchill agreed not to refer to September 11 as the date on which 'Manna' should begin, when he telegraphed to Maitland Wilson.[3]

During the afternoon Churchill's train stopped at Carlisle. Churchill's scrambler and telephone were then plugged through to the stationmaster's office, and Churchill telephoned to Eden at the Foreign Office. A report had just reached London, given out over Brussels radio, that Germany had capitulated. 'I shouldn't be at all surprised,' someone said to Moran, 'if we all turned round and went home again.'[4] Admiral Cunningham wrote in his diary, as the train moved north again: 'He sent for me at 17.00 to tell me there was a rumour that Germany had capitulated; also to say that if true he must remain in England & what was to happen if we were two days out & it proved to be true.' The 'only thing to do', Cunningham replied, 'was to turn the ship round & come back'.[5]

Shortly after seven o'clock that evening Churchill's train reached Greenock. 'We are just off . . .' he telegraphed to Roosevelt.[6] With Churchill were his wife, the three Chiefs of Staff, Lord Moran, Lord Leathers, Lord Cherwell, General Ismay, General Hollis, John Martin, Jock Colville and Commander 'Tommy' Thompson. One of the nurses who had been looking after Churchill since his return from

---

[1] Moran notes, 5 September 1944: Moran, *op. cit.*, page 175.

[2] Brooke diary, 5 September 1944: Bryant, *op. cit.*, volume 2, page 267.

[3] Chiefs of Staff Committee (Octagon), 1st Meeting, 6 September 1944 (reporting the discussion of 5 September 1944: Cabinet papers, 120/44).

[4] Moran notes, 5 September 1944: Moran, *op. cit.*, page 175.

[5] Cunningham diary, 5 September 1944: Cunningham papers.

[6] 'Gunfire' No. 1, 5 September 1944: Churchill papers, 20/171.

Italy was also on board, as was Brigadier Whitby, 'the penicillin and M & B man' as Clementine Churchill described him.[1]

'For your information only,' the British Secretariat in Quebec were informed from Downing Street, 'Whitby is specialist and colleague of Moran but it is most important this should not be known nor any deductions drawn.' The telegram added: 'Mrs Pugh is a nurse. This also is not to be made known.'[2]

At 8.30 on the evening of September 5, with four thousand other passengers on board, including many wounded American soldiers, the *Queen Mary* weighed anchor and steamed southward through the Irish Channel.[3]

The journey to Quebec was a time of relaxation as well as preparation for the difficult days ahead. The conversation on the first evening was recorded by Jock Colville, who was present that night at what he described as a 'spacious dinner (oysters, champagne etc.) in the PM's dining room' with Churchill and his wife, Lord Moran, Lord Leathers and Lord Cherwell. The purpose of Cherwell's presence was to reach agreement, if possible, either in Quebec or at Hyde Park, on the joint Anglo-American development of the atom bomb.[4]

The first night's conversation was recorded by Colville in his diary:

Talking about a coming election the PM said that probably the Labour Party would try to stay in the Government (though the rank and file might not let them) until a year or so after the armistice so that they might profit from inevitable disillusionment or at the non appearance of an immediate millennium and might give time for the glamour to fade from a Government which had won the war. But if after that there was a great left-wing majority, let it be so: 'What is good enough for the English people, is good enough for me.'

That night, after dinner, Colville 'played three games of bezique with the PM'.[5]

---

[1] Diary of 6 September 1944: Spencer-Churchill papers. Lionel Whitby was Bacteriologist to the Middlesex Hospital and Consulting Physician in Blood Transfusion to the Army. He was knighted in 1945. Churchill, who liked Whitby very much, called him the 'Vampire' because he was a blood transfusion expert.

[2] 'Strictly Private and Personal', OZ 5073, 7 September 1944: Cabinet papers, 120/145. Churchill's other staff at Quebec consisted of Captain Pim and two of his Map Room assistants (Douglas Murray and Colonel Hughes-Reckitt), four secretaries, Kathleen Hill, Jo Sturdee, Marian Holmes and Elizabeth Layton, two detectives, Bill Hughes and Cyril Davies, and Churchill's Clerical Officer, Charles Barker.

[3] Private Office Diary, 5 September 1944.

[4] 'To contact your people on T.A.' (Tube Alloys), Churchill to Hopkins, 'Chain' No. 156, 'Top Secret', 22 August 1944: Cabinet papers, 120/144. 'The President is delighted that the Prof is coming,' Hopkins replied. Hopkins to Churchill No. 52, 28 August 1944: Cabinet papers, 120/144.

[5] Colville diary, 5 September 1944: Colville papers. That night, Operation 'Bodyguard' was finally cancelled, having served its purpose long after the Normandy landings. (Chiefs of Staff Committee No. 298, Operations, 5 September 1944: Cabinet papers, 79/80.)

On Wednesday September 6 Churchill spent the day in his cabin reading *Phineas Finn*.[1] 'Papa is in low spirits and not very well,' Clementine Churchill wrote to her daughter Mary. 'I hope it is just the M & B working off and perhaps some anti-Malaria tablets which have to be taken for four weeks after leaving Italy and are very depressing.' The *Queen Mary* was north-east of the Azores, and the temperature between 75 and 80 degrees Fahrenheit. 'Papa is, I think, better in himself,' Clementine Churchill wrote, 'but he feels this sticky heat terribly and is very tired.'[2] 'No meeting with PM today,' Admiral Cunningham noted. 'He is very flat, probably as a result of M & B.'[3]

As Clementine Churchill had suggested, Churchill's troubles arose, most probably, from the anti-malaria tablets which he had still to take, following his Italian visit. A month earlier, Churchill had tried to avoid taking these tablets altogether, having been encouraged not to use them by Alexander. 'They upset some people considerably,' Alexander warned. Neither he nor his Staff took them, 'and we have virtually no malaria at my Headquarters. I suggest you tell the doctors to keep their pills.'[4] Lord Moran had not accepted this advice, however. 'General Alexander suggests that the doctors keep their pills,' he had written to Churchill a month earlier, and he added: 'I venture to doubt if General Alexander's views on medical matters have any greater value than mine on military affairs.'[5] 'In view of your salvo,' Churchill replied, 'all unconditionally surrender and have hoisted yellow flag.'[6]

Churchill had taken the pills regularly throughout his Italian visit, and now, as prescribed, continued to take them for four more weeks.[7]

On board the *Queen Mary*, Jock Colville spent much of September 6 trying to master 'the rudiments of the papers on finance in the post-war period'. This, he noted 'is one of the main subjects for discussion with the President'. He also had a further talk with Churchill, writing in his diary:

[1] Private Office Diary, 6 September 1944. Having finished *Phineas Finn*, Churchill read *The Duke's Children*, the first (1869) and last (1880) books respectively in Anthony Trollope's series of four novels charting the erratic progress of a penniless Irishman who, in the course of a tumultuous political and social career in England, arrives at last at peace, fortune and domestic happiness.

[2] Clementine Churchill, letter of 6 September 1944: Spencer-Churchill papers.

[3] Cunningham diary, 6 September 1944: Cunningham papers.

[4] Special Unnumbered Signal, 'Top Secret and Personal', 4 August 1944: Premier papers, 4/75/1, folio 92.

[5] Letter of 5 August 1944: Premier papers, 4/75/1, folios 87–9.

[6] Christopher Dodds to John Martin, Minute of 6 August 1944: Premier papers, 4/71/1, folio 86.

[7] The pills were Atebrin.

The PM says that after all he will not 'beat up' the Americans about 'Dragoon'. He will suggest that the controversy be left to History and add that he intends to be one of the historians!

More talk about a coming election. If the opposition tried to sling mud about the past, they would be warned that the other side, though preferring a truce to recrimination, had a full armoury of mud to sling back. The PM would not regret the loss of any of his Labour colleagues except Bevin, the only one for whose character and capacity he had any real esteem. The others were mediocrities.

On another subject, he said that of all the paper and the theories one read it was wise to pick out certain firm principles (e.g. milk for babies!) and pursue them actively. One of his major tenets was this: we did not enter this war for any gain, but neither did we propose to lose anything through it.[1]

On the morning of September 7 Clementine Churchill sent her husband a short note to greet the new day:

Darling—
How are you this morning?
What a rousing news bulletin this morning! Calais Boulogne Dunkirk Le Havre more & more closely invested—19,000 Prisoners to the poor un-noticed British! Is the Moselle the Frontier between France & Germany? because if so we are in the Reich. . . .[2]

During September 7 Churchill discovered that there were a number of American servicemen on board returning home, whose period of leave was counted from the beginning of their date of embarkation. As some had been waiting on board ship as long as a week, because the *Queen Mary* had been kept waiting for 'Octagon', they were going to lose those days at home. 'May I indicate through your good offices,' Churchill telegraphed to Roosevelt that day, 'this will be made up to them? It would be a pleasure to me if this could be announced before end of voyage and their anxiety relieved.'[3] Roosevelt replied that same day, agreeing to Churchill's request, and thanking him for his 'thoughtfulness'.[4]

At lunch that day, Admiral Cunningham noted in his diary, 'The PM still very flat, not much sparkle about him.'[5] That night, Cherwell and Moran were Churchill's dinner guests. Colville, who was also present, noted in his diary:

---

[1] Colville diary, 6 September 1944: Colville papers.

[2] Letter of 7 September 1944: Spencer-Churchill papers. At this point the Moselle (which flowed into Germany) was still in France.

[3] 'Gunfire' No. 4, Prime Minister's Personal Telegram, T.1752/4, Prime Minister to President, No. 783, 'Personal and Top Secret', 7 September 1944: Churchill papers, 20/171.

[4] 'Cordite' No. 30, President to Prime Minister, No. 621, 'Personal and Top Secret', 7 September 1944: Churchill papers, 20/171.

[5] Cunningham diary, 7 September 1944: Cunningham papers.

The PM produced many sombre verdicts about the future, saying that old England was in for dark days ahead, that he no longer felt he had a 'message' to deliver, and that all that he could now do was to finish the war, to get the soldiers home and to see that they had houses to which to return. But materially and financially the prospects were black and 'the idea that you can vote yourself into prosperity is one of the most ludicrous that ever was entertained'.

Colville added:

The menu for dinner was: oysters, consommé, turbot, roast turkey, ice with canteloupe melon, Stilton cheese and a great variety of fruit, petit fours etc; the whole washed down by champagne (Mumm 1929) and a very remarkable Liebfraumilch, followed by some 1870 brandy: all of which made the conversation about a shortage of consumers' goods a shade unreal.[1]

The *Queen Mary* having entered the Gulf Stream, the weather was hot and sticky, and Churchill was in what Cunningham described as 'his worst mood'.[2] So hot and sticky had the journey become, that Churchill told him the ship had been 'abominably routed'.[3] Churchill then sent for the Commodore and tried to persuade him to change course out of the Gulf Stream. 'As this would have taken him over the Newfoundland Bank,' Cunningham noted, 'he rightly didn't like it. Together we went and convinced the PM.'[4]

Churchill's transatlantic journey co-incided with a turning point in the battle for northern France and for Belgium. Since August 30, when the 1st British Corps had crossed the Seine near Rouen, the Allied advance had been a swift one, despite the tenacious resistance of the German garrison at Le Havre. On September 1 the Canadian Corps had captured Dieppe, and, after overrunning many flying-bomb sites, crossed into Belgium. On September 5, American forces already in Belgium entered Namur and Charleroi. Ploegsteert, where Churchill had served in the trenches in the First World War, was liberated on September 7, as was Ypres. On September 8, Canadian troops entered Ostend, British troops entered Brussels, and the United States 1st Army, having entered Liège, was within twenty miles of the German border.

In preparation for a Staff Conference on September 8, Churchill

[1] Colville diary, 7 September 1944: Colville papers.
[2] Cunningham diary, 8 September 1944: Cunningham papers.
[3] Colville diary, 8 September 1944: Colville papers.
[4] Cunningham diary, 8 September 1944: Cunningham papers.

studied a Joint Intelligence Committee report on Germany's capacity to resist, a report which envisaged an imminent Russian advance from the East, and a renewed Anglo-American thrust in the West, piercing the Siegfried Line before the end of the year.[1] 'Generally speaking,' Churchill minuted to Ismay for the Chiefs of Staff Committee, 'I consider it errs on the side of optimism.' One could already foresee, Churchill warned, 'the probability of a lull in the magnificent advances we have made': indeed, at the 'present time', he pointed out, 'we are at a virtual standstill', and progress 'will be very slow'. Apart from Cherbourg and Arromanches, the Allies had not yet obtained 'any large harbours'. Brest had not yet been taken 'in spite of heavy fighting'. Lorient still held out. No attempt had been made to 'get hold of' Bordeaux. The Germans intended to defend the mouth of the river Scheldt and were still resisting in the northern suburbs of Antwerp. On the line Metz–Nancy, General Patton's army was 'heavily engaged'.

Montgomery, Churchill noted, 'has explained his misgivings as to General Eisenhower's future plan'.[2] He had done so, in a telegram to Brooke, sent to the *Queen Mary* on September 7. The telegram read: 'I am not (repeat not) happy about general strategic plan for further conduct of operations but I do not (repeat not) see how I can do anything more in the matter and must now do the best I can to carry out the orders of the Supreme Commander.' Having prepared this telegram for despatch, Montgomery received Eisenhower's 'directive for future operations', in which, Montgomery pointed out, 'two thrusts are to be made, one via the Ruhr and the other via the Saar'. This means 'that neither thrust will have sufficient resources to be full-blooded'.[3] Nor had the Russians made any progress into East Prussia. Yet the Joint Intelligence Committee forecast assumed 'a decisive Russian offensive' on the eastern front. At present, Churchill noted, that was only 'an assumption'.

Churchill's minute also dealt with the effect of the Roumanian Government's decision to join the Allies. This, Churchill wrote, 'has given the Russians a great advantage and it may well be that they will enter Belgrade and Budapest, and possibly Vienna, before the Western Allies succeed in piercing the Siegfried Line. However desirable militarily such a Russian incursion may be, its political effect upon Central and Southern Europe may be formidable in the last degree.'

Churchill ended his minute with a warning against the Joint

---

[1] Joint Intelligence Sub-Committee Paper (Octagon) 4 (Final) of 1944.

[2] Prime Minister's Personal Minute, D(Octagon) 1 of 1944, 'Top Secret', 8 September 1944: Churchill papers, 20/153.

[3] 'Cordite' No. 20, 'Top Secret', 'Guard', 7 September 1944: Cabinet papers, 120/149.

Intelligence Committee's view that the war could end before the end of the year, telling the Chiefs of Staff:

No one can tell what the future may bring forth. Will the Allies be able to advance in strength through the Siegfried Line into Germany during September, or will their Forces be so limited by supply conditions and the lack of ports as to enable the Germans to consolidate on the Siegfried Line? Will they withdraw from Italy, in which case they will greatly strengthen their internal position? Will they be able to draw on their forces, at one time estimated at between 25 and 35 divisions, in the Baltic States? The fortifying and consolidating effect of a stand on the frontier of the native soil should not be underrated. It is at least as likely that Hitler will be fighting on the 1st January as that he will collapse before then. If he does collapse before then, the reasons will be political rather than purely military.[1]

At the Staff Conference held on board the *Queen Mary* at midday on September 8, Brooke noted that Churchill 'looked old, unwell and depressed. Evidently found it hard to concentrate and kept holding his head between his hands.'[2]

Churchill opened the meeting by telling the Chiefs of Staff how 'very disturbed' he was at their proposal to divert forces from Italy to the Far East, in preparation for operation 'Dracula'. He had hoped, Churchill told the Chiefs of Staff, 'to have their support in resisting all diversion of forces from General Alexander's army until the war in Europe was won'.

Churchill went on to comment that the Chiefs of Staff 'appeared to be working on the assumption that a German collapse was imminent', and that Alexander's 'only problem' would be to 'advance into central Europe' in conditions of a total German collapse.[3] In these circumstances, he agreed, 'the problems which were worrying us would not arise. But it seemed wrong to base our plans on the assumption that Germany was about to collapse. Their resistance in the West had stiffened during the last few days, and the Americans had been sharply checked at Nancy. German garrisons were offering stout resistance at most of the ports; the Americans had failed to take St Nazaire at a time when it might have been had quite cheaply; and the Germans showed every intention of putting up stout resistance in the forts covering the approaches to Antwerp, a port which we badly needed.' Surely, Churchill added, 'with our overwhelming air and sea power we could capture these ports before the Germans could reinforce the garrisons'.

[1] Prime Minister's Personal Minute, D(Octagon) 1 of 1944, 'Top Secret', 8 September 1944: Churchill papers, 20/153.

[2] Brooke diary, 8 September 1944: Bryant, *op. cit.*, volume 2, page 269.

[3] These conditions were codenamed 'Rankin'.

Replying to Churchill, Brooke denied that the Chiefs of Staff had 'ignored' the possibility that German resistance would be prolonged into the winter. They had, however, been 'influenced by the optimistic report' of the Joint Intelligence Committee. 'There should be no question,' Brooke assured Churchill, 'of withdrawing forces from General Alexander (with the exception of the first of the Indian divisions required for "Dracula") until Kesselring's forces had been beaten and driven back across the Piave.'

The fifteen British and Dominion divisions, Brooke believed, 'should be more than enough' to enable Alexander to 'maintain pressure' east of the Piave. The first of the Indian divisions were, however, due to leave Italy for the Far East 'early in October'.

Churchill was angered to hear of the impending further depletion of Alexander's already depleted forces. He had 'understood', he said, 'that the forces for "Dracula" would be found from South-East Asia Command, some three divisions being withdrawn just beforehand from northern Burma. Why then was it proposed to start robbing General Alexander of Indian divisions in a few weeks time? In any case, if "Dracula" could not take place before March next year, why was it necessary to start the moves from Italy nearly six months in advance?'

The answer, said Brooke, was that the shipping programme for sending these additional resources to Mountbatten 'had been very carefully worked out and left no margin'. One of the factors which made it necessary 'to start the move so early', Brooke added, 'was the granting of leave to British and Indian personnel who had been overseas for several years'.

Again, Churchill challenged Brooke's line of argument, declaring that 'the policy of granting leave to men who had been overseas more than a certain time would only be put into effect when the war against Germany was over'. If it were decided to move forces back to India for 'Dracula' before a German collapse, Churchill told Brooke, 'he was quite prepared to cut out the leave period and to promise the units concerned priority for leave as soon as "Dracula" was over'.

The discussion then turned to the possibility of an amphibious operation against the Istrian peninsula. The numbers of landing craft available in the Mediterranean, Brooke warned, 'were likely to prove entirely inadequate'. The additional resources required could only be obtained by withdrawing landing craft from 'Overlord' maintenance, or by retaining in the Mediterranean American tank landing craft which were due to return to the United States for refit, and subsequent employment in the Pacific. 'Such craft as could be spared from "Overlord",' Brooke warned, 'were earmarked for "Dracula"; their employment in an Istrian operation would preclude the launching of "Dracula" until after the monsoon.' It was difficult 'on purely military grounds', Brooke added, to make a case for the retention of American craft for an Istrian operation.

Churchill disagreed, explaining to the Chiefs of Staff 'that he was very anxious that British forces should forestall the Russians in certain areas of central Europe. For instance, the Hungarians had expressed the intention of resisting the Russian advance, but would surrender to a British force if it could arrive in time.' It was 'most desirable for political reasons', Churchill declared, 'that British forces should enter Yugoslavia and advance north and north-east into central Europe', even if 'Rankin' conditions, the collapse of Germany that winter, did not occur.

With the advance of British forces into central Europe in view, Churchill continued, 'he was most disturbed at the suggestion that General Alexander's army should be reduced by the loss of both American and Indian divisions. He would like to see the time-table of the proposed withdrawal of successive Indian divisions, and would resume the discussion of this problem with the Chiefs of Staff the following day.'[1]

Brooke was considerably angered by Churchill's refusal to accept the Joint Intelligence Committee's forecast of a German collapse that winter, a collapse which would enable a rapid transfer of troops from Italy to the Far East. That night Brooke noted in his diary, of the midday meeting:

He began by accusing us of framing up against him and of opposing him in his wishes.

According to him we were coming to Quebec solely to obtain landing-ships out of the Americans to carry out an operation against Istria to seize Trieste, and there we were suggesting that, with the rate at which events were moving, Istria might be of no value!

We also suggested moving troops from Europe for Burma and had never told him that the removal of these forces was dependent on the defeat of Hitler—a completely false accusation! He further said that we had told him only one division was required for Burma, and now we spoke of five—here again a complete misstatement of facts. It was hard to keep one's temper with him, but I could not help feeling frightfully sorry for him. . . .'

Neither Churchill's convictions, nor his capacity for work, had been seriously weakened by the continuing oppressive heat or by the

[1] Chiefs of Staff Committee (Octagon), 4th Meeting, 12.15 p.m., 8 September 1944: Cabinet papers, 120/144. Those present were Churchill (in the Chair), Brooke, Portal, Cunningham, Ismay and Laycock.

[2] Brooke diary, 8 September 1944: Bryant, *op. cit.*, volume 2, pages 269–70.

malaria pills. 'PM gave me a lot of work before dinner,' Marian
Holmes noted in her diary on September 8. 'Couldn't, at one point,
hear at all what he had said. Asked him to repeat it and he exploded.
He then said, "I'm sorry. I didn't mean it."' [1]

That evening, as Churchill was crossing the Atlantic, the first two
V2 rockets landed in England. One fell north of Epping, demolishing
a few wooden huts. The other fell at Chiswick, killing three people
and seriously injuring ten. [2] For security reasons, Churchill was told
that same day, 'no announcement has been made public'. [3]

For the first ten days of this new bombardment, the rockets,
launched from sites near the Hague and in the Scheldt estuary, were
aimed exclusively at Greater London, two hundred miles distant from
the launching sites. The 'secrecy ban', imposed in order to hide the
accuracy of the rocket and the scale of the casualties from the Germans, remained in force for almost ten days, until the secret was
revealed by the *New York Times*. [4] Within two months, 456 people had
been killed by a total of 210 rockets, but a quarter of the deaths were
caused by five rockets which fell in densely populated areas. Fortunately for London, on September 20 the German rocket batteries
went eastward, to avoid being cut off by the Allied armies. The new
launching sites, in Friesland, gave London a respite. [5]

The news reaching Churchill on board the *Queen Mary* gave a
gloomy picture: on September 8, Alexander had reported: 'Heavy
fighting continued today on the Adriatic', with one town, Croce,
having 'changed hands several times' and 'now apparently held partly
by us and partly by the enemy'. [6] A special information telegram from
the Cabinet Office on September 9 reported that, in Italy, 'heavy
rains hamper operations', while in France the Germans had re-
occupied Metz and Nancy, while the 3rd US Army advance had been

[1] Marian Holmes diary, 8 September 1944: Marian Walker Spicer papers.

[2] Chiefs of Staff Committee No. 303 (Operations), 11 a.m., 9 September 1944: Cabinet papers,
79/80.

[3] 'Cordite' No. 53, 'Daily Information Telegram', 'For the Prime Minister', 'Top Secret',
'Most Immediate', 9 September 1944: Cabinet papers, 120/149.

[4] On 6 October 1944 the *New York Times* gave details of the nature and scale of the rocket
attacks, making the 'secrecy ban' impossible to enforce any further. The main argument for
secrecy, the Chiefs of Staff noted on 26 September 1944, 'is that any reference to the attack
would be seized upon by the Germans, and magnified so as to provide sorely needed encouragement for their people', Chiefs of Staff Telegram, COS(W) 348, to Joint Staff Mission,
Washington, OZ 5567, 26 September 1944: Cabinet papers, 105/61.

[5] Crossbow Committee Report No. 76 of 1944, 3 November 1944: Cabinet papers, 98/37.

[6] 'Cordite' No. 32, 'Top Secret', 'Most Immediate', 8 September 1944: Cabinet papers,
120/149.

'hindered by lack of fuel'. Only the Red Army could report success: it had entered Bulgaria, and occupied the Black Sea port of Varna.[1] Two days later, Churchill learned that Soviet military operations against Bulgaria had ceased: 21,000 Bulgarians and 4,000 Germans having been captured in two days' fighting.[2]

There was no way, however, that Britain could either exploit or assist the Soviet success. On the previous day Maitland Wilson had warned that as long as the battle in Italy continued, he had 'no forces to employ in the Balkans' except the small force consisting of a para-chute brigade and an improvised Brigade Group from Alexandria. These, he explained, were being held 'ready to occupy the Athens area and so pave the way for the commencement of relief, and the establishment of law and order and the Greek Government, in the first of the countries which is likely to be liberated'. The only other spare force at Wilson's disposal was the small Land Forces Adriatic 'which are being actively used primarily for commando type opera-tions'.[3]

Throughout the morning of September 9 the weather remained 'oppressively hot', as Churchill's Private Office diary recorded, but by noon the *Queen Mary*, forced to alter course 'to avoid a submarine', had left the Gulf Stream 'and the skies and atmosphere cleared'. That morn-ing, Churchill 'said he felt much better', as Clementine Churchill wrote in her diary.[4] But he was also, as Jock Colville noted, 'irascible'.

'Perhaps foolishly', Colville added, he had taken Churchill a telegram from Attlee about proposals for increasing soldiers' pay in the Japanese war. 'The PM thinks these proposals inadequate and ill-conceived and has said so,' Colville wrote. Attlee's telegram stated, however, that the War Cabinet intended, notwithstanding Churchill's objections, to publish these proposals before his return. 'He was livid,' Colville noted, 'said Attlee was a rat and maintained there was an intrigue afoot. He dictated a violent reply (which was never sent) full of dire threats. Having no pencil or paper with me, I borrowed the PM's red ink pen and scrawled it on the back of the another telegram. To my horror he insisted on reading the production as it was and proceeded to correct what I thought was an illegible semi-shorthand with equal illegibility.'[5]

[1] 'Cordite' No. 53, 'Daily Information Telegram', 'For the Prime Minister', 'Top Secret', 'Most Immediate', 9 September 1944: Cabinet papers, 120/149.
[2] 'Cordite' No. 84, 'Daily Information Telegram', 'For the Prime Minister', 'Top Secret', 'Most Immediate', 10 September 1944: Cabinet papers, 120/149.
[3] NAF 774, 'Top Secret', 'Urgent', FX 93838, 8 September 1944: Cabinet papers, 120/148.
[4] Letter of 10 September 1944: Spencer-Churchill papers.
[5] Colville diary, 9 September 1944: Colville papers.

During September 9 Churchill sent two minutes to the Chief of Staff Committee. In the first, he disagreed with their proposal that British troops should be added to the Australian and New Zealand forces operating in the Far East under General MacArthur. 'As is known,' he minuted, 'I consider that all United Kingdom forces should operate across the Indian Ocean and not in the South-West Pacific.' MacArthur could be assigned only 'a naval component with seaborne air'.[1]

In his second minute to the Chiefs of Staff on September 9, Churchill argued that Britain should have 'powerful forces in Austria and from Trieste northwards at the close of the German war, and should not yield central and southern Europe entirely to Soviet ascendancy or domination'. This was a matter 'of high political consequence, but also has serious military potentialities'. The American General Devers was 'prowling about to pull out linchpins' from Alexander's army in Italy, 'for the sake of his farcical group of armies, of which he seeks to become commander'. Churchill's hopes were to use Alexander's army with not one more division taken from it.

But, as Churchill saw it, the forces under Alexander were threatened in three ways: by the transfer to Southern France of the Army Group under General Devers, by the transfer of three Indian divisions to the Far East beginning on October 15, and by the right of the Americans, if they wished to do so, to withdraw a further four American divisions for use in France. 'Are these withdrawals to take place irrespective of the military situation?' he asked. At least, he urged, let the first withdrawal of the three Indian divisions, needed for 'Dracula' in March, be postponed two months, until mid-December.

Churchill then set out for the Chiefs of Staff the task and opportunity which he envisaged for Alexander's army:

The possibility of making an amphibious descent from Ancona or Venice—if we get it—upon Istria holds a very high place in my thoughts. It is by this means we would widen our front of advance into Austria and Hungary, having the ports of Trieste and Fiume at our disposal. We know from former Bonifaces the great anxiety the German Admiral of the Adriatic has always expressed about Istria. We know that at present it has barely a division. We know that the partisans have actually fought for the outskirts of Fiume, and are increasingly powerful over the whole region. I have asked Tito to make every effort to move his forces northwards instead of using our weapons against his own countrymen.

Churchill then took up the question of landing craft for an assault on Istria, telling the Chiefs of Staff:

[1] Prime Minister's Personal Minute, D(Octagon) 4/4, 'Top Secret', 9 September 1944: Churchill papers, 20/153.

I do not accept the statement that there are no landing craft available as they will all be taken to the Pacific. That is what I understood we were coming to 'Octagon' to discuss with the Americans.

A sufficiency of landing craft in the Adriatic will admit of a right-handed movement of the British forces there, and should have priority so far as concerns the small number of landing craft concerned over the general movement to the Pacific. We ought not to be deprived of amphibious facilities in the northern Adriatic.

The Americans, Churchill pointed out, had constructed the LST tank landing craft 'for the common pool' and had no right to use the fact that they hold them as a means 'of governing British operations'. Churchill added:

Had we known they intended to do this, we would have built our proportion of LSTs rather than concentrate upon other things for the common interest, such as anti-U-boat craft of all kinds and later the materials for synthetic harbours. Of these they have had the benefit, and they ought not to use their monopoly resulting from a proper parcelling out of production against us in an extraneous manner.

However I quite recognise that the Istria enterprise may be affected by the withdrawals of German divisions from the Balkans, and that these troops may stand between Alexander and his goal. About this however we shall be much better informed in a month or six weeks than we are now. I trust therefore that the fullest study with helpful intentions may be given to the Istrian proposition, and that intense efforts should be made not to force withdrawals from Alexander's army during October and November.

'Once again,' Churchill's minute ended, 'I draw attention to the extreme importance on grounds of high policy of our having a stake in central and southern Europe and not allowing everything to pass into Soviet hands with the incalculable consequences that may result therefrom.'[1]

In 1939 Churchill had signed a contract to write a book entitled *Europe Since the Russian Revolution*. His idea had been to describe the 1917 revolution and to tell of its subsequent threat to the stability of Europe. In 1944 his publisher pressed him to deliver the manuscript, but he decided not to do so. 'If we win the war,' he explained, 'it will be followed by a peace conference. If I live and I am still Prime Minister, I shall be a member of that peace conference. I could not write about any of these countries and give a critical and unbiased description of how they behaved in the intervening years, because it would hamper any possibility of amicable agreements.' Churchill added: 'Good arrangements will have to be made. I could not fling out a lot of

[1] Prime Minister's Personal Minute, D(O) 4/4A, 'Top Secret', 9 September 1944: Churchill papers, 20/153.

interesting but essential matter from the old quarrels that have passed, and build upon situations which no longer exist. I certainly should not be on speaking terms with Stalin if I wrote the things I would have written in time of peace. To ask me to do this, is a thing that no reasonable person would do.'

Churchill's note ended: 'Am I to bring up the horrors of the Russian Revolution? My whole outlook is changed. The synopsis which was a living thing then, is now dead. Twenty Years' Alliance with Russia.' [1]

Captain Pim having installed a Map Room on board ship, Churchill frequently visited it during the voyage to see, not only the progress of the war, but also of the *Queen Mary*. On one occasion, finding Sister Pugh looking at the map of the Atlantic, he asked her: 'Well, what do you think of all those?'—the small black markers showing the location of the U-boats.

'I was 24 at the time,' Dorothy Pugh later recalled, 'and he thought that was too young to be married. He was interested in the fact that my husband was serving in the RAF, and whether I was getting regular mail.' [2] For four days, Sister Pugh was not called upon to nurse Churchill, but as the voyage drew to an end, it seemed likely that she would be. When Clementine Churchill lunched with her husband alone on September 9, 'he looked pink and well', she wrote, 'and he said he had weathered the storm. Then suddenly, at 3 o'clock in the afternoon, his temperature was up—not very much, but still, there it was; and he was put to bed with an aspirin. . . .' In the evening, she added, Brigadier Whitby, 'who thank God, came out with us', gave Churchill a blood test. It was negative. But as Churchill was clearly still not fully recovered from his earlier illness, Clementine Churchill cancelled the little dinner party Churchill was to have given that evening, and dined with him alone, 'and after dinner he went straight to bed'. [3]

That night, Jock Colville discussed Churchill's rise in temperature with Lord Moran, who 'does not think seriously of it, probably it is the heat'. But Moran did tell Colville 'that he does not give him a long life and he thinks that when he goes it will be either a stroke or the heart trouble which first shewed itself at Carthage last winter'. Colville commented: 'May he at least live to see victory, complete and absolute, in both hemispheres and to receive his great share of the acclamations. Perhaps it would be as well that he should escape the aftermath.' [4]

[1] 'Note by Mr Churchill on "Europe since the Russian Revolution" ': Churchill papers, 8/710.
[2] Dorothy Pugh recollections: letter to the author, 6 April 1982.
[3] Clementine Churchill, letter of 10 September 1944: Spencer-Churchill papers.
[4] Colville diary, 9 September 1944: Colville papers.

Shortly after midday on September 10, Churchill was well enough to attend a Staff Conference, at which he commented on the ship-board deliberations of the Chiefs of Staff, and tried to co-ordinate his approach and theirs to the imminent discussions with the Americans.

Some of the statements contained in their minute, Churchill said, and in a minute about Mountbatten's needs, 'filled him with consternation'. He had understood from Mountbatten 'that the bulk of the "Dracula" forces would be found from South-East Asia Command—Admiral Mountbatten had said that he would provide three divisions from operations in North Burma—but now it was stated that nearly 400,000 men together with 24,000 vehicles would have to be shipped across the ocean from Europe before we could think of taking Rangoon. This sort of thing would kill "Dracula" stone dead.'

It would also affect the future operations of Alexander's army. The figure of 370,000 men to be shipped from Europe for 'Dracula', Churchill declared, 'must be reduced, and a way must be found of retaining an option on this operation for another month or six weeks'. In discussion with the Americans, Churchill told the Chiefs of Staff, 'our line should be' that, in order to undertake 'Dracula', 'we should require to use forces now engaged in Europe. It was still too soon to say whether these forces could be released, but we should press the Americans to agree to "Dracula" in principle on the assumption that when the time came the necessary resources could be provided.'

Britain's 'object in the Far East', Churchill added, 'should be to engage Japanese forces with the maximum intensity, and at the same time to regain British territory'.[1]

While on board ship, Churchill received a telegram from the Chancellor of the Exchequer, asking for an immediate decision on proposals for a demobilization scheme involving the expenditure of a hundred million pounds.[2] 'This is of course the first time I have seen these proposals,' Churchill replied on September 9, 'and I cannot say my first impressions are favourable.' He had two points to make. First, 'It would be disastrous to make proposals which were rejected by the feeling of Army and of Parliament as inadequate,' and, second, 'At this moment when all forces are being gathered for what may well be the decisive assault on Germany, it would not be a good thing to dwell upon demobilization plans. They should be deferred until undoubted victory has been won. This does not mean till all fighting in Germany is over, but rather till we have broken the German home

---

[1] Staff Conference, Chiefs of Staff Committee (Octagon), 8th Meeting, 12.15 p.m., 10 September 1944: Cabinet papers, 120/144. Those present were Churchill (in the Chair), Lord Leathers (Minister of War Shipping), Brooke, Portal, Cunningham, Ismay and Laycock.
[2] 'Cordite' No. 3, 7 September 1944: Cabinet papers, 120/149.

army and pierced the Siegfried Line and begun invasion. At that time it would be proper to make announcement but not now when battle is rising to its climax.'[1]

Receiving further details of the War Cabinet's plan on September 9, Churchill at once telegraphed to Eden: 'I must pray you to use some consideration to me when I am absent on public duty of highest consequence. Naturally I will take full responsibility to House of Commons for any delay which arises on grounds of policy.' Churchill added: 'I shall be back in a fortnight and we can then go into the whole matter together.'[2] A short while after, Churchill telegraphed again: 'I am sure I may rely on you not to try to hustle me without discussion into approving pay inducements for Japanese war.' His telegram ended: 'My colleagues have really no right to make me responsible for so deadly a matter as inducements for war against Japan without giving me an opportunity of full discussion. The whole future of the war against Japan may be affected. I rely on your aid and friendship in this matter.'[3]

'What I cannot agree without consideration and discussion,' Churchill telegraphed that day to Ernest Bevin, 'is the financial inducements to be offered to men who go into the further gunshots of war against Japan. Failure in this respect to meet military and public demands would be disastrous to whole future of Japanese war. How can we arrive at any decision? How can we know numbers involved until plan is settled here at "Octagon"?' Care must also be taken, Churchill wrote, to make sure that the announcement of such a scheme did not 'clash incongruously with climax of great land battle'; these 'great schemes', he warned Bevin, 'will not win their proper esteem from public if they are dwarfed by military episodes'.[4]

One aspect of the proposed scheme was a substantially increased pay scale for soldiers who fought in the Far East after the end of the war in Europe. A decision on this, Attlee explained to Churchill, was urgent: a week's delay was the maximum.[5] 'If the question of the revised pay was so urgent and vital', Churchill replied, 'I might have hoped I could have seen it before I left so as to have some chance of talking it over with my colleagues. I am most anxious that the increased pay scheme should not be a flop. If so it would result in a great loss of prestige and of the initiative in these matters, and our hand

[1] 'Gunfire' No. 26, 'Personal', 8 September 1944: Cabinet papers, 120/152.
[2] 'Gunfire' No. 34, 'Personal', 'Top Secret', 9 September 1944: Cabinet papers, 120/152.
[3] 'Gunfire' No. 37, 'Private and Personal'. 'Top Secret', 9 September 1944: Cabinet papers, 120/152.
[4] 'Gunfire' No. 39, 'Personal and Top Secret', 9 September 1944: Cabinet papers, 120/152.
[5] 'Cordite' No. 122, 11 September 1944: Cabinet papers, 120/149.

might well be forced into much higher expenditures.' Churchill added: 'To have this most important point pressed upon me suddenly in the middle of my voyage with a demand for immediate assent, subsequently increased to one week, was very disturbing as these matters seem different when one is away and alone from when they are brought to a circle of colleagues'.

The moment he was 'satisfied' that the scheme 'will achieve its purpose', Churchill added, 'namely the contentment of the troops ordered to begin what will seem to them a new war, an announcement can be made.' A delay of a week or ten days in making an announcement was not serious. 'It is really worthwhile avoiding precipitancy', Churchill ended, 'in so delicate and far-reaching a matter and I cannot believe that the British Public are likely to attribute hesitancy or lack of foresight to His Majesty's Government in view of our admittedly successful conduct of the most complicated operations of war.' [1]

From Montgomery, on September 10, came news that the Germans were 'holding strongly' to Boulogne, Calais and Dunkirk. On the right flank, Montgomery added, United States troops, although finding 'very little opposition, cannot get on as they are short of petrol'. [2]

The *Queen Mary* reached Halifax at midday on 10 September 1944. That afternoon, Churchill disembarked. 'Great cheers, and cameras clicking,' noted Marian Holmes in her diary. 'We boarded a Canadian National Railways train. PM stood on the observation platform and joined the crowd in singing "God Save the King" and "Oh Canada". As so often on such occasions, he was deeply moved.' [3]

---

[1] 'Gunfire' No. 86, 'Personal and Top Secret', 12 September 1944: Cabinet papers, 120/152.
[2] M/184, 9 September 1944, sent to 'Octagon' as 'Cordite No. 80', 'Top Secret', 10 September 1944: Cabinet papers, 120/149.
[3] Marian Holmes diary, 10 September 1944: Marian Walker Spicer papers.

51

Quebec, September 1944

AFTER a journey of just over twenty hours, Churchill's train reached Quebec at 9.55 on the morning of 11 September 1944. At Wolfe's Cove station, President Roosevelt's train had arrived on an adjoining track ten minutes earlier, and the President was already sitting in a car waiting to receive the Prime Minister. The two men and their wives drove together to the Citadel. 'Have arrived Quebec,' Churchill telegraphed to his son. 'How are you getting on? Have been laid up since my return with former complaint, but have now recovered.'[1] That same day Churchill learned that Randolph had 'arrived safely' at his destination in Croatia, 'and that Evelyn Waugh accompanied him'.[2]

During this first day in Quebec, Churchill continued with the 'Dracula' debate, minuting to the Chiefs of Staff that Mountbatten had 'repeatedly assured us', that he would withdraw three of his own divisions from Northern Burma for 'Dracula'. Churchill was also convinced, he told the Chiefs of Staff, that adequate forces could reach 'Dracula' from Europe, even if no fighting forces were to leave Italy for the East before December 15. 'By that time we shall know the situation in Europe as we cannot know it in the next few weeks,' he wrote, and he went on to warn that unless these problems could be solved ' "Dracula" must be abandoned', and Britain continue what he described as the 'ruinous and costly campaign' in Central Burma.

It was unnecessary, Churchill added, to go into these details with the United States Chiefs of Staff and other Americans; they must be 'fought out among ourselves with tenacity and diligence both here and at home'.[3] Britain's policy, he minuted to the Chiefs of Staff on the following day, was to give naval assistance 'on the largest scale' to

[1] 'Personal, Private and Top Secret', No. 801 Foreign Office to Caserta, 11 September 1944: Churchill papers, 20/150.

[2] 'Cordite No. 106', 'Private and Top Secret', 11 September 1944: Churchill papers, 20/150.

[3] Prime Minister's Personal Minute, D(O) 5/4, 'Top Secret', 11 September 1944: Churchill papers, 20/153.

the main American operations in the Pacific, but to 'keep our own thrust' for operation 'Dracula' as a preliminary operation, or 'one of the preliminary operations', to a 'major attack' upon Singapore. 'Here,' he added, 'is the Supreme British objective in the whole of the Indian and Far Eastern theatres. It is the only prize that will restore British prestige in this region, and in pursuing it we render the maximum aid to the United States operations by engaging the largest number of the enemy in the most intense degree possible and at the earliest moment.'[1]

The conflict between Burma and Istria was made crystal clear during September 11, when Ismay sent Churchill a telegram, just received from Maitland Wilson, stating that the employment of an airborne division 'to seize the neck of the Istrian peninsula should, if it could be launched, ensure rapid success'.[2] A two division assault, Ismay explained, the scale necessary, would require sixty tank landing craft. If Wilson were to be given 'what he asks for', Ismay added, it would be necessary 'to press the United States Chiefs of Staff' to allow nearly sixty of the tank landing craft then being used for 'Dragoon' in the Mediterranean to remain in the Mediterranean 'after the operation'.[3]

On the morning of September 12, troops of the United States First Army crossed the German frontier west of Aachen.[4] At Quebec all eyes were on this triumphant northern European theatre, but for Churchill, who had warned that the northern impetus might soon falter, the future strategy for the Italian front was also very much in his thoughts. On the morning of September 12, reading his Enigma and other decrypts, Churchill minuted to the Chiefs of Staff, who had sent him progress reports from Eisenhower, Wilson and Mountbatten: 'But see also "Boniface", which declares that a complete withdrawal from Italy and the Balkans has been ordered.'[5]

---

[1] Prime Minister's Personal Minute, D(O) 7/4, 'Top Secret', 12 September 1944: Churchill papers, 20/153.

[2] 'Cordite' No. 67, 9 September 1944: Cabinet papers, 120/149.

[3] Minute of 11 September 1944, Chiefs of Staff Committee (Octagon), 9th Meeting, Annex III: Cabinet papers, 120/144.

[4] Four days later when Allied troops entered Aachen, Churchill telegraphed to Brendan Bracken: 'Please try to introduce Aix-la-Chapelle instead of Aachen, which is pure Hun, into your BBC statement.' ('Gunfire No. 195', 'Personal and Secret', 16 September 1944: Cabinet papers, 120/153.)

[5] Prime Minister's Personal Minute, D(O) 6/4, 'Top Secret', 12 September 1944: Churchill papers, 20/153. This 'Boniface' was misleading; no such 'complete withdrawal' from the Balkans and Italy had been ordered. Substantial withdrawals, however, were called for.

Churchill sent these particular decrypts to Roosevelt. 'Some of the "Boniface" I sent you this morning,' he wrote in a letter to the President later that day, 'appeared to me to be of profound significance. Alexander's battle is a hard one, but now that Clark has crashed into the centre I am hopeful of speedy results.' [1]

On the afternoon of September 12, at the first Conference meeting of the Combined Chiefs of Staff, Brooke told the American Chiefs of Staff that the 'indications' were that the Germans were attempting to withdraw their forces from Greece and Yugoslavia. As a result of Yugoslav Partisan attacks, the Germans might be 'reduced' to 'covering the Ljubljana Gap and endeavouring to hold a line through Yugoslavia and Istria'. In these circumstances, Brooke added, 'any withdrawal' of forces from Alexander's army 'would be most regrettable'.

In reply, Marshall assured Brooke 'that it was not the intention to weaken the 5th Army at the present time'. The seizure of the Istrian peninsula, Brooke continued, 'would be a valuable base for the spring campaign or as a base from which our forces could be introduced into Austria in the event of Germany crumbling. It had not only a military value but also political value in view of the Russian advances in the Balkans.'

Admiral King now told the meeting that 'he too had in mind the possibility of amphibious operations in Istria'. Naval forces, on the other hand, 'were in course of withdrawal for rehabilitation'. Unless a decision to mount an amphibious operation were taken soon, 'the landing craft would lie idle, though required for operations in other parts of the world, for instance, against Rangoon'. The minutes of the meeting continued: 'In reply to a question by General Marshall, Sir Alan Brooke said that General Wilson was planning now for an amphibious operation and the picture should be much clearer in a short time, particularly if the German forces withdrew from North Italy.' There was then 'general agreement that a decision with regard to the launching of an amphibious operation should be made by the 14th October'. [2]

With satisfaction, Brooke noted in his diary that the American Chiefs of Staff 'are prepared to leave tank landing-ships for Istrian venture if required'. He was also pleased that Churchill, in a minute on Pacific strategy, 'now accepts the naval contingent for the Pacific'

[1] Letter of 12 September 1944 (beginning 'My dear Friend' and ending 'Yours always, W'): Churchill papers, 20/138.
[2] Combined Chiefs of Staff, 172 and Meeting, 12 noon, 12 September 1944: Cabinet papers, 120/144.

and 'Dominion Task Force' to serve with MacArthur.[1] Churchill's principal point in this minute, not however mentioned by Brooke in his diary, was that Britain's 'own thrust' was to be against Rangoon, as a preliminary to a 'major attack' on Singapore.[2]

At 6.30 that afternoon, the British Chiefs of Staff went to a Staff Conference with Churchill at the Citadel. During the meeting, Churchill told them that he was 'determined', once operations against Germany had been brought to a successful conclusion, that the British forces in Europe 'should revert to an independent command'. The unity of command under Eisenhower, he explained, had only been agreed upon for military operations: 'he was opposed to unity of command during the occupational period'.[3] Brooke then read to Churchill, for his approval, a draft telegram to Maitland Wilson, with reference to an amphibious operation against the Istrian Peninsula, drafted at the meeting with the United States Chiefs of Staff. The British and American Chiefs of Staff had agreed at this meeting to ask Maitland Wilson that, 'if he wishes to retain for use in the Istrian Peninsula the amphibious lift at present in the Mediterranean, he should submit his plan. . . .' Churchill approved of this telegram.

During this Staff Conference, Churchill also proposed mounting 'Dracula' before the next monsoon, 'if this could possibly be arranged without prejudice to operations in the European theatre'. Britain's 'ultimate object', Churchill reiterated, 'must be the recapture of Singapore'. He wished, however, that he could 'see some way of deferring the decision regarding the eastward move of "Dracula" forces until the middle of October at the earliest'.

Towards the end of the Staff Conference, Portal said that he was anxious for the Royal Air Force 'to play their part in the softening up process against Japan'. Churchill agreed. He was 'determined', he said, 'that we should have our share in operations for the final defeat of Japan'.[4]

One result of this Chiefs of Staff meeting was that Churchill offered Roosevelt the 'British main fleet', including 'our best and most modern battleships, adequately supported by fleet aircraft carriers, escort

---

[1] Brooke diary, 12 September 1944: Bryant, *op. cit.*, volume 2, page 272.

[2] Prime Minister's Personal Minute D(O) 7/4, 'Top Secret', 12 September 1944: Churchill papers, 20/153.

[3] Three days later, Churchill told the Chiefs of Staff Committee that 'the President shared his view that the appointment of Supreme Commander, Allied Expeditionary Force, should terminate with the defeat of Germany': Staff Conference Chiefs of Staff Committee (Octagon) 17th Meeting, 15 September 1944: Cabinet papers, 120/144.

[4] Staff Conference, Chiefs of Staff (Octagon), 11th Meeting, 6.30 p.m., 12 September 1944: Cabinet papers, 120/144.

carriers, cruisers etc', to take part in the major operations against Japan under United States Supreme Command.[1]

Following the Chiefs of Staff meeting on September 12, Churchill mentioned to Portal that he might discuss with Roosevelt that night the vexed question of post-war zones of occupation in Germany and Austria. This remark was overheard by Jock Colville, who noted in his diary: 'Knowing he had not read the briefs on the subject and that there was no time for him to do so before dinner, I volunteered to read them aloud to him in his bath.' Churchill accepted this 'bizarre procedure', Colville added, 'but the difficulties were accentuated by his inclination to submerge himself entirely from time to time and thus become deaf to certain passages'.

As they worked together, Churchill told Colville that he feared the President was now 'very frail'.[2] From Europe, the news that evening was bad: in northern France, the Defence Office telegraphed, 'Enemy resistance increases as Allies approach German frontier.' In Italy, the Germans were 'still resisting strongly' and the 46th Division had been 'in stiff fighting'. Another German rocket, falling on Richmond, had resulted in '30/40 killed or injured'.[3]

The first plenary session of 'Octagon' was held on the morning of September 13. In opening the discussion, Churchill noted that since their meeting in Cairo the affairs of the United Nations had taken 'a revolutionary turn for the good'. Everything which they had touched 'had turned to gold'. On the day before the launching of 'Overlord' they had captured Rome. The results of 'Dragoon', with 80,000 or 90,000 Germans already taken prisoner, were 'most gratifying'. 'He was firmly convinced,' Churchill added, 'that future historians would say that the period since Teheran had shown the successful working of an extraordinarily efficient inter-Allied war machine.'

Roosevelt interrupted at this point, to say 'that some of the credit for the conception of "Dragoon" should be attributed to Marshal

[1] Staff Conference, Chiefs of Staff Committee, COS (Octagon), 11th Meeting, 6.30 p.m., 12 September 1944: Cabinet papers, 120/144.

[2] Colville diary, 12 September 1944: Colville papers.

[3] 'Cordite' No. 137, 'Daily Information Telegram', 'For the Prime Minister', 'Top Secret', 'Most Immediate', 12 September 1944: Cabinet papers, 120/149. The Richmond rocket fell on the Chrysler Motor works at Barnes, killing eight and seriously injuring fourteen. (Home Office papers, 191/198). The fall of the rocket and its effect were unreported in the Press, although an oblique reference to it did appear some days later in an account of the excellence of the local rescue services.

Stalin'. Churchill made no comment. Continuing with his remarks, he told Roosevelt that he was 'glad to be able to record that, although the British Empire had now entered the sixth year of the war', its effort in Europe, counted in terms of divisions in the field, 'was about equal' to that of the United States.[1] 'This was as it should be,' and he was proud that Britain could claim 'equal partnership with their great Ally.' The 'British Empire effort', he noted however, 'had now reached its peak, whereas that of their Ally was ever-increasing'. There was 'complete confidence' in Eisenhower, whose relations with Montgomery 'were of the best'. In Italy, the Fifth Army, commanded by the American General, Mark Clark, was expected to make a thrust 'that very day'. He had been anxious lest, in Italy, Alexander 'might be shorn of certain essentials for the vigorous prosecution of his campaign', but now he understood that the Combined Chiefs of Staff had agreed 'that there should be no withdrawals' from Alexander's army until either Kesselring's army had been destroyed 'or was on the run out of Italy'.

General Marshall having confirmed this undertaking, Churchill then spoke of what should be done after the Germans had been driven from Italy: 'we should have to look,' he said, '"for fresh fields and pastures new".[2] It would never do for our armies to remain idle,' and he went on to tell the conference:

He had always been attracted by a right-handed movement, with the purpose of giving Germany a stab in the Adriatic armpit. Our objective should be Vienna. If German resistance collapsed, we should, of course, be able to reach Vienna more quickly and more easily. If not, to assist this movement, he had given considerable thought to an operation for the capture of Istria, which would include the occupation of Trieste and Fiume. He had been relieved to learn that the United States Chiefs of Staff were willing to leave in the Mediterranean certain LSTs now engaged in 'Dragoon', to provide an amphibious lift for the Adriatic operation, if this was found desirable and necessary.

An added reason for this right-handed movement was the rapid encroachment of the Russians into the Balkans and the consequent dangerous spread of Russian influence in this area.

Churchill then turned to the Far East, congratulating General Stilwell for his 'brilliant operation' which had resulted in the capture of Myitkina, in keeping open the air line to China, and in rendering India 'secure from attack'. But 'in spite of all these successes', he said, it was 'most undesirable that the fighting in the jungles of Burma

---

[1] 'From the American papers', Jock Colville noted a week later, 'one would scarcely suppose any British troops were fighting'. Colville diary, 20 September 1944: Colville papers.
[2] 'Tomorrow to fresh woods, and pastures new': Milton, *Lycidas*, line 193 (last line).

should go on indefinitely'. That was why the British Chiefs of Staff had put forward plan 'Dracula'. The 'present situation in Europe', however, 'favourable though it was, did not permit a decision being taken now to withdraw forces'.

Churchill could offer, he said, in the naval sphere, 'the British Main Fleet to take part in the major operations against Japan under United States Supreme Command'. It was a Fleet so built up as to be 'independent for a considerable time of shore based resources'.

Replying, Roosevelt spoke of the 'formidable obstacle' which, he believed, the Germans would set up on the right bank of the Rhine. 'The Germans could not yet be counted out.' The operations in the Far East 'would to some extent depend on how the situation developed in Europe'. If the battle 'went well' with Alexander, Roosevelt added, 'we should reach the Piave reasonably soon', and he told Churchill: 'All forces in Italy should be engaged to the maximum intensity.' [1] To Maitland Wilson and Alexander, Churchill telegraphed that day: 'Everything has opened here very well so far as your affairs are concerned.' There was to be 'no weakening' of Alexander's army, Churchill explained, until after Kesselring had been 'disposed of', an event, Churchill added, 'which "Boniface" indicates as probable'. The Americans had also agreed, Churchill reported, to let Alexander use the landing craft he required 'for any amphibious work in the Northern Adriatic that may be found practicable'. His telegram continued:

Pray therefore address yourselves to this greatly improved situation in a spirit of audacious enterprise. The Americans talk without any hesitation of our pushing on to Vienna, if the war lasts long enough. I am greatly relieved at the reception all our ideas have met here. We must turn these advantages to the best account. [2]

Replying to Churchill's telegram, Maitland Wilson proposed an advance during the winter with 'a strong force' into Istria and to Gorizia, 'with a view to further advance in the spring in direction of axis Ljubljana–Maribor'. For such an advance, as well as for the occupation of the remainder of northern Italy, Alexander would acquire 'all the forces now at his disposal'. As, beyond Ljubljana, a force of ten divisions could be employed, all the formations 'now at Alexander's disposal' would still be required. To take away the 5th United

---

[1] 'Minutes of a meeting held at the Citadel, Quebec, on Wednesday, 13th September, 1944, at 11.45 p.m.', COS (Octagon) 1st Plenary Meeting: Cabinet papers, 120/144.
[2] 'Special Unnumbered Signal', 'through Special Channel', 'Personal and Top Secret', 13 September 1944: Cabinet papers, 120/156.

States Army, Wilson warned, 'would cause serious dislocation in Italy which should be avoided if possible'.[1]

'The Conference has opened in a blaze of friendship,' Churchill telegraphed to Attlee and the War Cabinet that evening. 'The Staffs are in almost complete agreement already. There is to be no weakening of Alexander's army till Kesselring has bolted beyond the Alps or been destroyed. We are to have all the LSTs in the Mediterranean to work up in the Northern Adriatic in any amphibious plan which can be made for Istria, Trieste, etc. The idea of our going to Vienna, if the war lasts long enough and if other people do not get there first, is fully accepted here.'[2]

As the first plenary meeting had been drawing to its close, Roosevelt had observed 'that there were certain groups in the United States, and he had no doubt that similar groups existed in Great Britain, who evinced a kindly attitude towards the Germans'. Their theory was, Roosevelt added, that 'evil could be eradicated from the German make-up and the nation could be rejuvenated by a kindly attitude of approach to them'. Such sentiments, Churchill replied, 'would never be tolerated in Great Britain. The British people would demand a tough policy against the Germans. The German working-man should be allowed the means to earn an honest livelihood by his work but no more. The more virulent elements, such as the Gestapo and the young fanatics, should be deported to work in rehabilitating the devastated areas of Europe.'[3]

At dinner at the Citadel on September 13, Henry Morgenthau, Roosevelt's Secretary of the Treasury, spoke of drastic action against Germany once the war was won. The Germans would not be allowed ships, nor the shipyards in which to build them. The whole industrial region of the Ruhr would be closed down, 'to help British exports', Morgenthau explained, 'especially steel'. Lord Moran, who was present, recorded Churchill's reaction:

'I'm all for disarming Germany,' he said, 'but we ought not to prevent her living decently. There are bonds between the working classes of all countries, and the English people will not stand for the policy you are advocating.'
I thought he had done when he growled:
'I agree with Burke. You cannot indict a whole nation.'

[1] 'Special Unnumbered Signal', 'Top Secret', 13 September 1944: Cabinet papers, 120/157.
[2] 'Gunfire' No. 112, 'Personal and Top Secret', sent at 10.37 p.m., 13 September 1944: Cabinet papers, 120/152.
[3] 'Minutes of a meeting, held at the Citadel, Quebec, on Wednesday, 13th September, 1944, at 11.45 p.m.', COS (Octagon) 1st Plenary Meeting: Cabinet papers, 120/144.

If the PM was vague about what ought to be done with Germany, he was at least quite clear what should not be done. He kept saying:

'At any rate, what is to be done should be done quickly. Kill the criminals, but don't carry on the business for years.'

During this discussion, as Moran noted, Morgenthau asked Churchill 'how he could prevent Britain starving when her exports had fallen so low that she would be unable to pay for imports'. Moran added:

The PM had no satisfactory answer. His thoughts seemed to go back to the House of Commons and what he knew of the English people. In five years' time, when passions would have died down, people, he said, would not stand for repressive measures. He harped on the necessity for disarmament. At that point one of the Americans intervened: he thought that Germany should be made to return to a pastoral state, she ought to have a lower standard of living. During all this wild talk only the PM seemed to have his feet on the ground. The President mostly listened. . . .

Roosevelt did comment, in support of the destruction of German industry for all time (what was soon to become known as the 'Morgenthau Plan'), that a factory which made steel furniture could be turned overnight to war production. Of the British guests at the dinner, only Lord Cherwell supported Morgenthau. But his influence on Churchill was considerable. 'I explained to Winston,' he later told Moran, 'that the plan would save Britain from bankruptcy by eliminating a dangerous competitor. Somebody must suffer for the war, and it was surely right that Germany and not Britain should foot the bill. Winston had not thought of it in that way,' Cherwell added, 'and he said no more about a cruel threat to the German people.'[1]

It was proposed, Churchill explained to Attlee and the War Cabinet, 'that the Ruhr and the Saar steel industries shall be completely dismantled. The Russians will claim the bulk of machinery to repair their own plants. In addition some International Trusteeship and form of control would keep these potential centres of rearmament completely out of action for many years to come.' The consequences of this, Churchill noted, 'will be to emphasise the pastoral character of German life and the goods hitherto supplied from these German centres must to a large extent be provided by Great Britain. This may amount to 300 or 400 million pounds a year.' Churchill added: 'I was at first taken aback at this but I consider that the disarmament argument is decisive and the beneficial consequences to us follow naturally.'[2]

*   *   *

[1] Moran diary, 13 September 1944: Moran, *op. cit.*, pages 177–8.
[2] 'Gunfire' No. 166, 'Personal and Top Secret', 15 September 1944: Cabinet papers, 120/153.

While Churchill was at Quebec, news reached him of an un-expectedly rapid Russian advance into Bulgaria. 'This Russian move,' Eden telegraphed from London on September 12, 'has created an entirely new situation since even if they do not penetrate into Greek territory their presence in the Balkans is bound to produce strong political reactions.' If British troops did not 'make their appearance at an early date in the Balkans', Eden warned, 'the influence of Great Britain will suffer seriously. From the political point of view I feel it is highly desirable that the British Force should enter as soon as possible to counter-balance the presence of Russian troops in Bulgaria, to check any tendency by the latter to penetrate into Greece and to forestall a possible Russian attempt to build up Bulgaria under a Government subservient to them at the expense of Greece.'

Eden wanted Churchill to authorize Maitland Wilson to examine the possibility of launching operation 'Manna' as soon as possible. 'It is essential,' Eden added, 'that we should leave the Russians in no doubt about the importance we attach to Greece and I think the time has certainly come to warn them in general terms of our determination to send a British force in.'[1]

Churchill replied that he was 'in general agreement', and that he thought 'this has already occurred to the President'. There was, Churchill added, 'a general feeling among the Staffs that we ought to have a showdown with the bear pretty soon, and we are in a much better position to do this than we were two months ago. But these are profound matters.'[2]

On the morning of September 13, Churchill had joined a meeting of the Chiefs of Staff to discuss the Greek situation. He was 'inclined to agree with the Foreign Secretary's views', Churchill said, 'namely, that the time had come to get our foot in the door in Greece'. It was, however, 'a prickly problem', which he would like to discuss with Eden when the Foreign Secretary arrived on the following day, 'before taking any decision'.[3]

On September 13, with the Chiefs of Staff's approval, Churchill telegraphed to Maitland Wilson that Eden was 'very keen' that British forces should land in the Peloponnese, from which the German troops had already been evacuated. Wilson should therefore 'with the utmost urgency' make a plan for a landing 'so that we can decide whether to do it or not'. Churchill's telegram ended: 'You will observe that I

[1] 'Cordite' No. 157, 12 September 1944: Air Ministry papers, 20/2710.
[2] 'Gunfire' No. 101, 'Personal and Top Secret', 13 September 1944: Cabinet papers, 120/152.
[3] Chiefs of Staff Committee (Octagon), 12th Meeting, 9 a.m., 13 September 1944: Cabinet papers, 120/144.

have turned round in my view because I am alarmed at the delay now that the Russians have come so much nearer.' [1]

Not only was the Red Army already in Bulgaria, but armistice negotiations between the Soviet Union and Bulgaria were about to begin.

Within forty-eight hours Wilson had sent his plan to Quebec, where Churchill, having noted that it 'meets all our requirements', told the Chiefs of Staff that Wilson should be authorized to go ahead as soon as possible. [2]

On September 14, Anthony Eden reached Quebec from London, having come by air. 'W looks much better,' he noted in his diary. [3] That night there was, in Colville's words, 'a shockingly bad film chosen by the President', and he added: 'The PM walked out half way through which, on the merits of the film, was understandable, but which seemed bad manners to the President.'

That night Churchill told Colville about some of the post-war financial advantages which the Americans had promised Britain during that day's discussions. 'Beyond the dreams of avarice,' Colville commented. 'Beyond the dreams of justice,' replied Churchill. [4]

Accompanying Churchill to 'Octagon' were three of his personal secretaries, Kathleen Hill, Elizabeth Layton and Marian Holmes, who noted in her diary that night, as work resumed: 'PM has certainly recovered from all the temperature alarums and excursions. He had an insatiable appetite for work. He kept saying "Come on. What's the matter with you? Gimme more." In the end I said, "There IS no more." Bed 2 a.m.' [5]

The discussions at Quebec covered many aspects of post-war policy. Churchill hoped, as he told Roosevelt on September 14, 'that the President would agree that during the war with Japan we should continue to get food, shipping etc. from the United States to cover our reasonable needs'. Roosevelt, as the record of this conversation noted, 'indicated assent'. It was 'essential', Churchill added, 'that the United States should not attach any conditions to supplies delivered to Britain on Lend-Lease which would jeopardize the recovery of her export trade'. In reply, Roosevelt said that he thought Churchill's proposal 'would be proper'. [6]

---

[1] 'Gunfire' No. 113, Prime Minister's Personal Telegram, T.1771/4, 'Personal and Top Secret', 13 September 1944: Churchill papers, 20/171.
[2] Prime Minister's Personal Minute, M (Octagon) 10/4, 'Top Secret', 'Most Urgent', 16 September 1944: Churchill papers, 20/153.
[3] Eden diary, 14 September 1944: Eden memoirs, *The Reckoning, op. cit.*, page 475.
[4] Colville diary, 14 September 1944: Colville papers.
[5] Marian Holmes diary, 14 September 1944: Marian Walker Spicer papers.
[6] 'Gunfire' No. 168, 15 September 1944: Cabinet papers, 120/153.

The 'Morgenthau Plan' was agreed to by Churchill and Roosevelt on September 15, when both men signed a programme 'for eliminating the war-making industries in the Ruhr and in the Saar' and 'looking forward to converting Germany into a country primarily agricultural and pastoral in its character'.[1] Eden later told Churchill that he and Cordell Hull were both 'horrified' when they found out what Churchill and Roosevelt had initialled, Eden telling Churchill 'that the War Cabinet would *never* agree to such a proposal'.[2] In the event, it was the State Department which rejected it.

Also discussed at Quebec was the nature of civilian government in France, and the part to be played in it by the French National Committee under de Gaulle. On September 15 Eden noted in his diary how he had tried during the day 'to get President and PM to recognise French National Committee as Provisional Government. A pretty hopeless discussion, each going off in turn on a tirade against de Gaulle. W did however go so far as to say that he would rather have a de Gaulle France than a Communist France, a distinct advance!'[3]

On the evening of September 15, Churchill told a Staff conference, at which Eden was present, that he and Roosevelt had discussed the allocation of zones of occupation in Germany 'between ourselves and the Americans'. Roosevelt's 'main anxiety', Churchill explained, was to arrange the zones so that the American area was not anywhere in direct contact with French territory, and so that the American lines of communication did not have to pass through France.

At this same meeting, it was also agreed, at Eden's request, that British forces 'should be reserved to support the ultimate entry of the Greek Government into Athens as soon as the strength of the German forces in that area had been sufficiently reduced to make that operation practicable'.[4]

The final plenary session of 'Octagon' was held at midday on September 16. 'The President looked very frail,' noted Admiral Cunningham, 'and hardly to be taking in what was going on.'[5] On the question of Italy and Istria, General Marshall and Admiral Leahy assured Churchill that Alexander 'would be allowed to invade and dominate the valley of the Po', but Admiral King stressed that as far as a landing on Istria was concerned, Britain must make up its mind

[1] 'Gunfire' No. 169 (to the War Cabinet), 15 September 1944: Cabinet papers, 120/153.
[2] Sir John Colville, notes for the author, March 1986.
[3] Eden diary, 15 September 1944: Eden memoirs, *The Reckoning, op. cit.*, page 477.
[4] Staff Conference, Chiefs of Staff Committee (Octagon), 17th Meeting, 6 p.m., 15 September 1944: Cabinet papers, 120/144.
[5] Cunningham diary, 16 September 1944: Cunningham papers.

'by October 15' as the landing craft would also be wanted for the assault on Rangoon in March 1945.[1] Meanwhile, although one Indian division would have to be sent from Italy to Mountbatten's Burma operation at the end of October, all American troops in Italy would remain in Italy until Kesselring was beaten. 'This is a matter of five divisions, of whose destination we were previously not sure,' Churchill later explained to Alexander, as well as landing craft 'for any Adriatic plan you may have in mind,' and he added: 'I really have done my best.'[2]

On future operations in the Balkans, the Combined Chiefs of Staff proposed, and both Churchill and Roosevelt accepted, that as long as the battle in Italy continued, there would be 'no forces available to employ in the Balkans', except the small force of two British brigades from Egypt 'which is being held ready to occupy the Athens area and so pave the way for commencement of relief and establishment of law and order and the Greek Government', and 'the existing small land forces in the Adriatic being used for Commando type operations'. These were almost the identical words of Maitland Wilson's telegram of a week earlier.

During the second plenary, Churchill had spoken of a possible swift outcome of the war against Japan. He thought it 'quite possible', he said, 'that the heavy sustained and ever-increasing air bombardment of the Japanese cities might cause Japan to throw up the sponge. People stood up to heavy bombardment just so long as they still had the hope that sooner or later it would come to an end. There could be no such hope for Japan, and all they could look forward to was an ever-increasing weight of explosive on their centres of population.'

Discussing the 'Dracula' operation against Rangoon, Churchill told Roosevelt that while 'he accepted the obligation of securing the air route and attaining overland communications with China', operation 'Capital', any tendency 'to over-insure this operation would have the effect of ruling out "Dracula" ', an operation, he said, 'which both he and the British Chiefs of Staff were particularly set on carrying out before the monsoon of 1945'.[3]

That afternoon Churchill and Roosevelt both received honorary degrees from McGill University, 'but instead of their having to go to

---

[1] 'Minutes of Meeting held at the Citadel, Quebec, on Saturday 16th September 1944, at 12 noon', Chiefs of Staff (Octagon) 2nd Plenary Meeting, 'Top Secret': Cabinet papers, 119/10.

[2] Prime Minister's Personal Telegram, T.1830/4, OZ 5610, 'Personal and Top Secret', 27 September 1944: Churchill papers, 20/172.

[3] 'Minutes of Meeting held at the Citadel, Quebec, on Saturday 16th September, 1944, at 12 noon', Chiefs of Staff (Octagon) 2nd Plenary Meeting, 'Top Secret': Cabinet papers, 119/10.

Montreal for the ceremony', Clementine Churchill noted, 'the dig-
nitaries of the University kindly came here'.[1] Churchill, on receiving
his honorary degree, spoke of his friendship with Roosevelt, a
friendship, he said, which had grown 'under the hammer blows of
war'.[2]

The short degree ceremony was followed by a session with the photographers and journalists, to whom Churchill also spoke, noting that as
a result of the earlier conference in Quebec, decisions had been taken
which 'are now engraved upon the monuments of history'. Out of that
first Quebec conference, he said, had come 'arrangements by which
the vast armies were hurled across the sea, forced their way on shore in
the teeth of the enemy's fire and fortification, broke up his armed
strength and liberated, almost as if by enchantment, the dear and
beautiful land of France, so long held under the corroding heel of the
Hun'.

Churchill then told the assembled journalists:

A curious feature in this conference has struck me. I read some of the
papers when I am over here, these great big papers about an inch thick—
(laughter)—very different from the little sheets which we get in Great
Britain. I read these papers, and I see from time to time suggestions that the
British wish to shirk their obligations in the Japanese war, and to throw the
whole burden onto the United States.

And that astonished me very much, because as a matter of fact, the conference has been marked by exactly the opposite tendency. If there was
any point of difference which had to be adjusted, it was that we undoubtedly
felt that the United States meant to keep too much of it to themselves—
(laughter) and or some of them did—some of the respresentatives.

But I am glad to say we have arrived at a thoroughly amicable agreement,
and that Great Britain with her fleet and her air forces and, according to
whatever plans are made, her military forces, all that can be carried by the
shipping of the world to the scene of action will be represented in the main
struggle with Japan.

And we shall go on to the end.

You can't have all the good things to yourselves. You must share.
(laughter)

Churchill then spoke of the reasons, not only for this conference,
but for conferences in general, and for his own wish to meet as often
as possible with Roosevelt:

[1] Letter of 17 September 1944: Spencer-Churchill papers. Of Lord Moran, Clementine
Churchill wrote, in this same letter: 'He is a melancholy old creature, very critical of everybody'.
Three days later Jock Colville described Moran as 'so critical that he runs down everybody in
the party, especially the PM, and so indiscreet that he does so indiscriminately'. Colville diary,
20 September 1944: Colville papers.

[2] 'Informal Remarks. . . .', 3.30 p.m., 16 September 1944: Premier papers, 4/75/2, Part 1,
folio 371.

... when I have the rare and fortunate chance to meet the President of the United States, we are not limited in our discussions by any sphere. We talk over the whole position in every aspect—the military, economic, diplomatic, financial. All—all is examined. And obviously that should be so. And the fact that we have worked so long together, and the fact that we have got to know each other so well under the hard stresses of war, makes the solution of problems so much simpler, so swift and so easy it is.

What an ineffectual method of conveying human thought correspondence is—(laughter)—telegraphed with all its rapidity, all the facilities of our—of modern intercommunication. They are simply dead, blank walls compared to personal—personal contacts. And that applies not only to the President and the Prime Minister of Great Britain, it applies to our principal officers who at every stage enter in the closest association, and have established friendships which have greatly aided the tasks and the toil of our fighting troops.[1]

Following the Press Conference, Roosevelt left Quebec by train for Hyde Park, Churchill remaining in Quebec for one more day. 'Very busy for PM all day,' Marian Holmes noted in her diary, and she added: 'Felt somewhat weary by the afternoon and was a bit slow when the PM asked me to open a letter for him. "Go on—don't eat it—open it." He was in a marvellous good humour and asked if I were enjoying myself out of office hours.'[2]

On September 17, Churchill left Quebec by train. At the station, a crowd gathered around the observation car and sang 'Auld Lang Syne'. That same day, in Europe, the 1st Allied Airborne Army landed in Holland. One division, the British First Airborne, landed at Arnhem.

Reaching Hyde Park on the morning of September 18, Churchill stayed with the President for two days. While they talked, Eden informed Churchill by telegram that Soviet aid was at last reaching Warsaw, the first Soviet flight having been made on September 14.[3] At the same time, 110 aircraft of the American Air Force, having dropped supplies on Warsaw from bases in Britain, landed in Russia to refuel, only two of these aircraft being lost.[4] This Soviet action came far too late, however, to enable the Polish insurgents to continue the battle with any hope of success, although, for two weeks more, they struggled on against the full ferocity of German bombardment and reprisals.

---

[1] 'Press and Radio Conference No. 968, Held on the Parapet at the Citadel in Quebec, Canada, September 16th, 1944, at about 3.45 p.m.', 'Confidential': Premier papers, 4/75/2, part 1, folios 374–89.

[2] Marian Holmes diary, 16 September 1944: Marian Walker Spicer papers.

[3] 'Cordite' No. 347, 'Top Secret', 18 September 1944: Air Ministry papers, 20/2710.

[4] That same week, 40 British and 34 United States bombers had been lost in bombing raids over Germany.

Among those whom Roosevelt had invited to Hyde Park was Harry Hopkins. But it soon became clear that Hopkins was no longer Roosevelt's confidant. For this reason, indeed, he had not been invited to Quebec, much to Churchill's distress. 'He seems to have quite dropped out of the picture,' Clementine Churchill wrote to her daughter Mary on September 18. 'I found it sad and rather embarrassing,' and she added:

We cannot quite make out whether Harry's old place in the President's confidence is vacant, or whether Admiral Leahy is gradually moulding into it. One must hope that this is so, because the President, with all his genius does not—indeed cannot (partly because of his health and partly because of his make-up)—function round the clock, like your Father. I should not think that his mind was pinpointed on the war for more than four hours a day, which is not really enough when one is a supreme war lord.[1]

On the evening of September 18, Churchill, Roosevelt and Hopkins discussed the terms of a proposed joint declaration regarding Italy. It was agreed that the Allies would hand over 'an increasing measure of control' to the Italian administration. The 'partial ban' on contact between British and Italian diplomats throughout the world would be ended. Plans would be made to allow 'a material increase in the flow of supplies to Italy'.[2]

While Churchill was in Quebec and at Hyde Park, the German long-range V2 rockets had continued to fall on London. In all, twenty-six fell on southern England in the week ending September 18, killing fifty-six civilians, seventeen by a single V2 which fell on Southgate. Heavy cross-Channel shelling of Dover and Folkestone by the German gun batteries near Calais had led to a further twenty-two civilian deaths [3] Throughout these days the 'Secrecy ban' remained in force.[4]

While Churchill was at Hyde Park, he and Roosevelt had a conversation about the atom bomb. Both men now knew that a bomb, the equivalent to between 20,000 and 30,000 tons of TNT, would 'almost certainly' be ready by August 1945.[5] Indeed, such a bomb might have three or four times such an explosive power. British scientists

---

[1] Clementine Churchill, letter of 18 September 1944: Spencer-Churchill papers.
[2] Prime Minister's Personal Telegram, T.1785/4 (to Sir Noel Charles and Harold Macmillan), 18 September 1944: Churchill papers, 20/184.
[3] War Cabinet No. 123 of 1944, 18 September 1944: Cabinet papers, 65/43.
[4] It was still in force on 26 September 1944: Chiefs of Staff Telegram, COS (W) No. 348, OZ5567 to Washington, 26 September 1944: Cabinet papers, 105/61.
[5] Lord Cherwell, 'Events Leading up to the Use of the Atomic Bomb, 1945', 'Secret', 28 January 1953: Churchill papers, 4/379. That same week, it took 2,600 sorties by Bomber Command to drop 9,360 tons of bombs.

and technicians, Churchill had earlier been told, were 'co-operating in the design and erection of the American plants'.[1]

Churchill and Roosevelt agreed, and initialled an aide-mémoire to that effect, that the suggestion 'that the world should be informed regarding Tube Alloys, with a view to an international agreement regarding its control and use, is not accepted'. The matter should continue to be regarded as of 'the utmost secrecy', but, 'when a "bomb" is finally available, it might perhaps, after mature considera- tion be used against the Japanese, who should be warned that this bombardment will be repeated until they surrender'.

Churchill and Roosevelt also agreed that 'full collaboration' be- tween Britain and the United States 'in developing Tube Alloys for military and commercial purposes should continue after the defeat of Japan unless and until terminated by joint agreement'.[2]

'Octagon' was at an end. 'This Conference,' Churchill telegraphed to the Australian Prime Minister, 'has been a blaze of friendship and unity. . . .'[3]

[1] 'Tube Alloy Project', 'Summary of Present Position and Future Possibilities', 'Most Secret', 20 March 1944: Premier papers, 139/2, folio 144.

[2] 'Tube Alloys', 'Top Secret', 19 September 1944: Premier papers, 3/139/8A, folio 310. The original of this agreement, initialled by Churchill and Roosevelt, was put into the safe in the underground Cabinet War Rooms.

[3] Prime Minister's Personal Telegram, T.1778/4, 'Winch' No. 7, 18 September 1944: Churchill papers, 20/186.

52

Between Quebec and Moscow

CHURCHILL worked at Hyde Park for most of 19 September 1944: 'had to read a minute out to the PM while he was still reclining in his bath', noted Marian Holmes. 'He told me to initial it for him.' That evening, he was ready to depart. 'Leaving Hyde Park was an experience,' Marian Holmes added. 'The PM sat with the President in his car which was surrounded by Cadillac autos full of bodyguards and G-men. When we drove through Poughkeepsie, they jumped on the running boards and made a terrific show. All traffic on the roads was brought to a standstill by order of the State Police....'

At Poughkeepsie, the train was waiting to take Churchill overnight to New York. 'On the train,' noted Marian Holmes, 'the PM dictated something so funny that it reduced Mr Martin, Cdr Thompson and me to tears of laughter.' [1]

Reaching New York, Churchill embarked on the *Queen Mary* on the morning of September 20. At lunch on board, Colville noted that Churchill was 'in the best of humours and form. He only clouded over once, when he spoke of de Gaulle and said that of recent years "my illusions about the French have been greatly corroded".' [2] As to 'Octagon' itself, he commented, when Moran asked him if he had found it less tiring than the Cairo Conference: 'what is this conference? Two talks with the Chiefs of Staff; the rest was waiting to put in a word with the President.' [3]

Returning across the Atlantic to Britain, Churchill was in mellow mood. 'PM in excellent form,' noted Admiral Cunningham, '& most interesting about his time at the Admiralty in the last war.' [4]

The Enigma decrypts having revealed the presence of German submarines on the *Queen Mary*'s original course, she was routed further

---

[1] Marian Holmes diary, 19 September 1944: Marian Walker Spicer papers.
[2] Colville diary, 20 September 1944: Colville papers.
[3] Moran notes, 20 September 1944: Moran, *op. cit.*, pages 183–4.
[4] Cunningham diary, 21 September 1944: Cunningham papers.

to the south, back to the Gulf Stream, where once again, as on the outward journey, the weather was hot and sticky.[1] Among the letters which Churchill read during the return voyage was one from the socialist writer and philosopher Harold Laski, suggesting the setting up of a 'Churchill Fund' after the war. Half the fund was to be for the purchase of books and manuscripts for the British Museum, half for the endowment of the Royal Society. 'As I look at the Europe Hitler has devastated,' Laski added, 'I know very intimately that, as an Englishman of Jewish origin, I owe you the gift of life itself.'[2] On September 21 Churchill replied that, 'if I had any choice in such a matter, I should prefer a children's park and playground on the south side of the river in some place where all the houses have been blown down'. But these, he reflected, 'are matters for years which I shall not see'. As to the reason for Laski's letter, 'I value,' Churchill wrote, 'the thought which inspired you to send it.'[3]

While Churchill was returning to Britain, the Chiefs of Staff Committee, meeting in London, discussed British policy to Greece. During their meeting, Eden informed them that Churchill 'had now agreed to this proposal that we should remind the Soviet Government of our close interest in Greek affairs and warn them in general terms of our determination to send a British force to that country to restore law and order, so as to pave the way for the provision of relief and to assist the Greek Government to re-establish their authority'.[4]

Elsewhere in the Balkans Britain was to pursue a far less active policy; in connection with Soviet intentions in Bulgaria, Churchill telegraphed to Eden on September 21: 'You should, I think, be careful not to oppose the Russians' wish to let Bulgarian divisions fight against Germans in suitable theatres. We certainly should not repulse any form of effective aid. There is no need for us to recognize them as co-belligerents, for the Russian relation to the Bulgarians has always been different from ours.'[5]

In a third area of the Balkans, Yugoslavia, Churchill telegraphed to Eden that day about a 'stiff telegram' to Tito: 'We have however

---

[1] Three weeks later, from Moscow, Churchill wrote to Brigadier Whitby, to thank him 'for your kindness in so readily accompanying me on my journey' and he added: 'Our latest travels are no less pleasant and, I hope, profitable, and I am glad to say that it is possible to travel from London to Moscow without at any point touching the Gulf Stream.' (Letter of 16 October 1944, 'Moscow': Churchill papers, 20/138.)

[2] 'Private', 2 September 1944: Churchill papers, 20/143.

[3] Letter of 21 September 1944: Churchill papers, 20/138.

[4] Chiefs of Staff Committee No. 314 (Operations) of 1944, 21 September 1944: Cabinet papers, 79/81. Those present were Eden (in the Chair), the three Vice Chiefs of Staff, and three Foreign Office officials, Sir Orme Sargent, Sir William Strang and Douglas Howard.

[5] 'Gunfire' No. 295, 'Personal and Top Secret', 12.16 p.m., 21 September 1944: Cabinet papers, 120/153.

to be careful to give him no excuse to throw himself into the hands of the Russians.' This had now become 'not only possible but probable' owing to the rapid Soviet advances into Roumania and Bulgaria. The position in Yugoslavia, Churchill agreed, could only be dealt with as Eden himself had proposed, 'namely by conversation in Moscow', and Churchill added: 'We must ask Russians plainly what their policy is.'[1]

On this return journey, as on the outward one, Churchill was vexed by the War Cabinet's attitude towards financial benefits for soldiers who would have to serve in Japan after the war in Europe. 'I attach the greatest importance,' he telegraphed to Attlee on September 21, 'to being able to assure the soldiers who go away from this country to what will be to them a new war on the other side of the world while all the rest come home to take jobs of Peace, that they will have special unprecedented treatment on their return and will not be flung on to Dole. Indeed I feel this assurance is essential to peace of mind of these men.' As to the money involved, Churchill noted, the financial burden would be 'not nearly so heavy as would be the cost of a serious breakdown in the willingness of the men to go to the Far East'. The matter could not be left, as the War Cabinet now proposed, until the end of the war against Germany. The real need, Churchill added, 'is to give assurance and comfort now to men who will be going forth'.[2]

Churchill's main task during the voyage was to prepare the speech which he intended to deliver on his return to Britain, and which he dictated in sections to Kathleen Hill and Marian Holmes. 'PM dictated 2,000 words of speech,' Marian Holmes noted in her diary on September 21. 'When I told him he had repeated himself, he said "Alright, alright. Don't break your heart about it—I can always cross it out" rather snappily.'[3]

That night, his work done, Churchill challenged Jock Colville to bezique, 'and by insisting', Colville noted, 'on continuing playing till 3 a.m.'. He also told Colville that he would only ask for a six months extension of Parliament's life in November 'so as to take the wind from the Labour sails'.[4] On the following night there was more speech

[1] 'Gunfire' No. 298, 'Personal and Top Secret', 12.46 p.m., 21 September 1944: Cabinet papers, 120/153.

[2] 'Gunfire' No. 294, 'Personal and Top Secret', 21 September 1944: Cabinet papers: 120/153.

[3] Marian Holmes diary, 22 September 1944: Marian Walker Spicer papers.

[4] Colville diary, 21 September 1944: Colville papers. 'It was important,' Churchill told the War Cabinet on his return, 'that the Government should not give the impression that they were clinging to office.' War Cabinet No. 128 of 1944, 27 September 1944: Cabinet papers, 65/43.

preparation. 'Work with a vengeance,' Marian Holmes noted in her diary. 'PM dictated a further 2,000 words of speech. I got the best view of his behind that I have ever had. He stepped out of bed still dictating and altogether oblivious of his all-too-short bed jacket. Anyway, he was in a kind and conciliatory mood and I felt the waves of approval. PM went to a film. When he came back he popped his head in to the "office", asked if there was any news and how was the speech going. Said it was nearly finished.'[1] Churchill then played Bezique with Jock Colville until 3 a.m.[2]

'This is our last night at sea,' Lord Moran noted after dinner on September 24. 'Winston seems in better heart—no doubt the rest has done him good—and we were soon back in the Boer War.'[3] Churchill had 'regained some of his old spontaneous form', wrote Jock Colville that night, 'and did not depend on reminiscences as much as he usually does now'. Churchill told Colville that when he was Home Secretary in 1910, 'his nerves were in a very bad state and he was assailed by worries in a way he never has been in the war. He then discovered that the best remedy was to write down on a piece of paper all the various matters which are troubling one; from which it will appear that some are purely trivial, some are irremediable, and there are thus only one or two on which one need concentrate one's energies.'

That night, playing bezique with Churchill until 2.30 a.m., Colville noted that the Prime Minister 'was in v mellow mood'.[4]

On the morning of September 26 the *Queen Mary* approached Fishguard harbour. 'I have not been able to signal you before,' Churchill telegraphed to Roosevelt, 'as we were among U-boats and condemned to wireless silence.'[5] Fog having made it impossible to dock at Fishguard, the *Queen Mary* continued through the Irish Channel to the Clyde, where it moored off Greenock. Before leaving by tender for the shore, Churchill made a short speech to the American and other troops on board, then left the ship for his train. His return coincided with bad news: the First Airborne division had been virtually wiped out at Arnhem. Of more than 9,000 men parachuted in eight days earlier, only 2,163 returned. To Field Marshal Smuts, who had telegraphed to Churchill to commiserate on the disaster, Churchill replied:

[1] Marian Holmes diary, 23 September 1944: Marian Walker Spicer papers.
[2] Colville diary, 22 September 1944: Colville papers.
[3] Moran notes, 24 September 1944: Moran, *op. cit.*, pages 188–9.
[4] Colville diary, 24 September 1944: Colville papers.
[5] 'Gunfire' No. 325, Prime Minister's Personal Telegram, T.1816/4, 'Top Secret', 'Hush', 25 September 1944: Churchill papers, 20/172.

I think you have got Arnhem a little out of focus. The battle was a decided victory, but the leading division asking, quite rightly, for more had a chop. I have not sustained any feeling of disappointment over this, and am glad our commanders are capable of running these kinds of risks. I like the situation on the western front, especially as enormous United States reinforcements are pouring in and we hope to have Antwerp before long.[1]

John Peck had flown to Greenock to meet Churchill with the latest pouch of telegrams and documents. 'Another pouch meets you at Rugby first thing in morning,' John Martin was informed by telegram as the *Queen Mary* reached Greenock.[2]

At ten o'clock on the morning of September 26 Churchill's train reached London, where it was met by members of the Government and the Chiefs of Staff. Churchill arrived, noted Brooke, 'looking very fit and cheerful'.[3] An hour and a half later he was in his place in the House of Commons for Prime Minister's Questions, during the course of which he paid tribute 'to the heroism and tenacity of the Polish Home Army and population of Warsaw, who, after five years of oppression, have yet fought for nearly two months to contribute all in their power to the expulsion of the Germans from the capital of Poland'.[4] Churchill also told the House of Commons that the British Government were 'resolved to do their utmost to prevent Nazi criminals finding refuge in neutral territory from the consequences of their crimes'.[5]

On September 27 Churchill worked on a speech to the House of Commons for the following day. He would take the occasion, he telegraphed to Stalin, to say 'what I have said before', that it was the Russian Army 'that tore the guts out of the German military machine, and is at the present moment holding by far the larger portion of the enemy on its front'. Churchill's telegram continued:

I have just returned from long talks with the President, and I can assure you of our intense conviction that on the agreement of our three nations, Britain, United States of America, and USSR, stand the hopes of the world. I was very sorry to learn that you had not been feeling well lately, and that your doctors did not like your taking long journeys by air. The President had

---

[1] Prime Minister's Personal Telegram, T.1912/4, No. 963 to South Africa, 'Top Secret and Personal', 9 October 1944: Churchill papers, 20/173.
[2] 'Cordite' No. 421, 25 September 1944: Premier papers, 4/72/2, Part 2, folio 538.
[3] Brooke diary, 26 September 1944: Bryant, *op. cit.*, volume 2, page 289.
[4] *Hansard*, 26 September 1944, column 26.
[5] *Hansard*, 26 September 1944, column 36.

the idea that The Hague would be a good place for us to meet. We have not got it yet, but it may be the course of the war, even before Christmas, may alter the picture along the Baltic shore to such an extent that your journey would not be tiring or difficult. However, we shall have much hard fighting to do before such plans can be made.

It was Roosevelt's intention, Churchill told Stalin, that 'win or lose' he would visit France and the Low Countries 'immediately after the election' in November. He and Roosevelt both desired 'most earnestly', Churchill added, the intervention of Soviet Russia in the Japanese war, 'as promised by you at Teheran', as soon the German army was 'beaten and destroyed'. Churchill's telegram continued:

The opening of a Russian military front against Japan would force them to burn and bleed, especially in the air, in a manner which would vastly accelerate their defeat. From all I have learnt about the internal state of Japan and the sense of hopelessness weighing on their people, I believe it might well be that once the Nazis are shattered a triple summons to Japan to surrender, coming from our three Great Powers, might be decisive. Of course, we must go into all these plans together. I will gladly come to Moscow in October if I can get away from here. If I cannot, Eden will be very ready to take my place.[1]

'It may be necessary for me to go to Moscow with Mr Eden,' Churchill minuted to Portal on September 27, in asking him for 'a report and a clear plan' of the journey by air, via Cairo, and across the Caucasus.[2]

On September 28 Churchill gave his House of Commons speech on the war situation, first talking for an hour on the military situation and then, after a break for luncheon, for a further hour on foreign affairs. Harold Nicolson, who was present, noted in his diary: 'He is in fine form at the start, finding his words easily, thumping upon the box. But after three quarters of an hour his voice gets husky and his delivery hesitant.' Nicolson, who had wondered how Churchill would treat the Arnhem set-back, noted how he 'solved this difficulty with mastery', speaking 'with emotion' of the men of the First Airborne Division: ' "Not in vain" is the boast of those who returned to us. "Not in vain" is the epitaph of those who fell.'[3]

---

[1] Prime Minister's Personal Telegram, T.1828A/4, No. 3217, Foreign Office to Moscow, 'Top Secret and Personal', 'Decypher Yourself', 27 September 1944: Churchill papers, 20/172.

[2] Prime Minister's Personal Minute, M.976/4, 'For your eyes alone', 'Most Secret', 27 September 1944: Churchill papers, 20/153.

[3] Nicolson diary, 28 September 1944: Nigel Nicolson (editor), *op. cit.*, page 402.

Of the battle of Normandy, 'the greatest and most decisive single battle of the whole war', Churchill told the House of Commons: 'Never has the exploitation of victory been carried to a higher perfection.' In Italy, General Alexander 'has now definitely broken into the basin of the Po', and would strive for the 'destruction or rout' of Kesselring's army, but further than that 'it is not desirable to peer at the present moment'.

In trying to do justice, Churchill told the House of Commons, to the British and American achievements, 'we must never forget, as I reminded the House before we separated, the measureless services which Russia has rendered to the common cause, through long years of suffering, by tearing out the life of the German military monster'. Russia, Churchill added, was 'holding and beating far larger hostile forces than those which face the Allies in the West, and has through long years, at enormous loss, borne the brunt of the struggle on land'.

There was, Churchill stressed, 'honour for all' in the fighting fronts. Of the war in Burma he told the House of Commons that he had been 'somewhat concerned to observe', during the reading of the American press in which he had 'indulged' while in the United States, 'that widespread mis-conception exists in the public mind, so far as that is reflected by the newspapers, about the scale of our effort in Burma and the results to date of Admiral Mountbatten's campaign'. Many important American newspapers had seemed to give the impression 'that the British campaign of 1944 in Burma had been a failure, or at least a stalemate, that nothing much had been done . . .'. Such was not the case, Churchill declared. The 14th British Imperial Army of more than a quarter of a million men, under Mountbatten's command, had 'by its aggressive operation guarded the base of the American air line to China and protected India against the horrors of a Japanese invasion'.

Churchill then told the House of Commons:

. . . the campaign of Admiral Mountbatten on the Burma frontier consti-tutes—and this is a startling fact—the largest and most important ground fighting that has yet taken place against the armies of Japan. Far from being an insignificant or disappointing stalemate, it constitutes the greatest collision which has yet taken place on land with Japan, and has resulted in the slaughter of between 50,000 and 60,000 Japanese and the capture of several hundred prisoners. The Japanese Army has recoiled before our troops in deep depression and heavily mauled. We have often, too, found circles of their corpses in the jungle where each one had committed suicide in suc-cession, the officer, who had supervised the proceedings, blowing out his own brains last of all. We did not ask them to come there, and it is entirely their own choice that they find themselves in this difficult position.[1]

[1] *Hansard*, 28 September 1944, columns 471–87.

'I can assure the House,' Churchill added, 'that the war against the Japanese and other diseases of the jungle will be pressed forward with the utmost energy.'

After a break for luncheon, Churchill spoke again for an hour, on foreign affairs: 'when Winston resumes', Harold Nicolson noted in his diary, 'he has not entirely recovered his first brio. He lags a bit, and appears to be tired and bored.' [1] During this second part of his speech, Churchill warned against 'violent words' and 'intemperate language' about the relations between Russia and Poland, words which might 'mar the hopes we cherish of an honourable and satisfactory solution and settlement'. 'We recognize our special responsibilities towards Poland,' he said, 'and I am confident that I can trust the House not to engage in language which would make our task harder.' Britain's 'prime and overwhelming duty', he stressed, was to bring about 'the speediest possible destruction of the Nazi power'. Churchill added:

I cannot conceive that it is not possible to make a good solution whereby Russia gets the security which she is entitled to have, and which I have resolved that we shall do our utmost to secure for her, on her Western frontier, and, at the same time, the Polish nation have restored to them that national sovereignty and independence, for which, across centuries of oppression and struggle, they have never ceased to strive.

He hoped to have a tripartite conference 'as soon as the military situation renders that possible', Churchill told the House. The 'future of the whole world', he commented, 'and certainly the future of Europe, perhaps for several generations, depends upon the cordial, trustful and comprehending association of the British Empire, the United States and Soviet Russia, and no pains must be spared and no patience grudged which are necessary to bring that supreme hope to fruition.' [2]

Churchill was now anxious to go to Russia as soon as possible. On the day after his House of Commons speech he telegraphed to Roosevelt that he had 'two great objects' in mind in going to see Stalin, 'first, to clinch his coming in against Japan, and, secondly, to try to effect an amicable settlement with Poland'. There were 'other points

---

[1] Nicolson diary, 28 September 1944: Nigel Nicolson (editor), *op. cit.*, page 402.
[2] *Hansard*, 28 September 1944, columns 487–99. Churchill's speech also contained a friendly reference to the Belgians. This reference had been suggested by Eden (Minute PM 44/621 of 27 September 1944) and incorporated by Churchill from a Foreign Office draft, without alteration. (Churchill papers, 9/201.)

too', concerning Yugoslavia and Greece, 'which we would also discuss'. Churchill added: 'I feel certain that personal contact is essential'. All hope of Stalin leaving Russia, however, had now to be abandoned. 'In a conversation with Clark Kerr and Harriman the other night,' Churchill told Roosevelt, 'UJ was most expansive and friendly. He however "grumbled about his own health". He said he never kept well except in Moscow, and even his visits to the front did him harm. His doctors were averse to his flying, and it took him a fortnight to recover from Teheran, etc.'.

In these circumstances, Churchill added, 'Anthony and I are seriously thinking of flying there very soon. The route is shorter now.'[1]

On the day of this telegram, General Sosnkowski was relieved of his post as Commander-in-Chief of the Polish Army, and succeeded by General Bor-Komorowski, commander of the Polish Home Army. The removal of Sosnkowski had long been one of Stalin's persistent demands. But the appointment of Bor-Komorowski led to an immediate protest from the Chairman of the Polish National Committee in Lublin, Stalin's nominee.

At Mikolajczyk's request, Churchill and Attlee saw him that same day, September 29. 'If his speech contained notes of sympathy for Russia,' Churchill explained to Mikolajczyk, 'this was because he wished to create a favourable atmosphere for future talks, on the success of which he had set his heart.'[2]

On October 1 Churchill received a telegram from Stalin, welcoming his wish to visit Moscow in October.[3] 'This is encouraging,' Eden noted in his diary, 'but we shall have tough battle over Polish business. Talk to W about it twice on telephone. He was highly excited and we plan for Saturday night.'[4] On the morning of Monday October 2 Churchill went to Northolt to inspect the aircraft which would be taking him to Moscow.[5] That night, the Warsaw insurgents ended their resistance, after sixty-three days' continuous and savage fighting. More than 17,000 of the 40,000 Polish fighters had been killed. An estimated 10,000 German troops had also perished.

'All good luck on the road,' Sir Archibald Clark Kerr telegraphed to Churchill on October 2. 'The Russians and I are delighted that you have decided to come here and that Anthony will be with you. The

---

[1] Prime Minister's Personal Telegram, T.1840/4, Prime Minister to President, No. 789, 'Personal and Most Specially Secret', 29 September 1944: Churchill papers, 20/172.

[2] 'Conversation . . .', 29 September 1944: *Documents on Polish–Soviet Relations, 1939–1945*, volume 2, document No. 232, pages 395–8.

[3] Telegram of 30 September 1944: Churchill papers, 20/172.

[4] Eden diary, 1 October 1944: Eden memoirs, *The Reckoning, op. cit.*, page 479.

[5] Private Office Diary, 2 October 1944: Thompson papers.

iron stands hot for the striking.'[1] But there was a setback that day in Churchill's plans, a warning from Maitland Wilson that it was going to be 'a tight fit to get the Istria operation launched and carried through' if the target date for the assault on Rangoon was to remain 15 March 1945, and Wilson's United States landing craft were required for it.[2]

That evening, after dinner, Churchill raised the issue with the Chiefs of Staff. Operations in Italy, Brooke noted in his diary, were 'lagging behind and do not admit of the withdrawal of forces. I, therefore, advised against trying to stage Rangoon operation before next monsoon, and PM agreed. It was very disappointing, but I think the correct decision.'[3] He was 'concerned', Churchill told the Staff Conference, 'at the weakening of our effort in Europe' which the release of forces for 'Dracula' would entail. Brooke then told the meeting that three of the divisions needed for 'Dracula', the 6th Airborne, the 3rd Division and the 52nd Division, which he had previously hoped could be released from Montgomery's forces, would be needed by Montgomery to ensure 'the full development of the offensive in France'. In these circumstances, Churchill commented, 'he thought it would be wrong to weaken our effort in France which was and must remain the main theatre of operations until Germany was defeated'. He therefore 'reluctantly' concluded that 'Dracula' must be postponed until after the 1945 monsoon, and that 'all our strength' in South East Asia Command should be devoted to the 'vigorous execution' of operation 'Capital', the campaign to drive from northern Burma to China.

Eden, Cunningham, Portal and Laycock each agreed, Laycock stating that his recent visit to France 'had convinced him that operations for the opening of Antwerp presented difficulties and would require all available resources'.[4]

The Rangoon attack was now postponed until November 1945. 'I am very sorry indeed,' Churchill telegraphed to Mountbatten, 'that we have not been able to carry out this operation, on which I had set my heart, but the German resistance both in France and Italy has turned out to be far more formidable than we had hoped. We must clean them out first.'[5]

*   *   *

[1] No. 2644 from Moscow, 'Personal, Private, Top Secret', 2 October 1944: Cabinet papers, 120/158.

[2] 'Top Secret and Personal', 2 October 1944: Churchill papers, 20/172.

[3] Brooke diary, 2 October 1944: Bryant, op. cit., volume 2, page 290.

[4] Staff Conference, Chiefs of Staff Committee No. 324 (Operations) of 1944, 10 p.m., 2 October 1944: Cabinet papers, 79/81. Those present were Churchill (in the Chair), Eden, Brooke, Portal, Cunningham, Ismay and Laycock.

[5] Prime Minister's Personal Telegram, T.1892/4, 'Personal and Top Secret', 5 October 1944: Churchill papers, 20/172.

On October 3 Churchill took his wife to the theatre, to see Shaw's *Arms and the Man,* a brief respite amid the preparations for his flight to Moscow. The route itself was causing some concern. The flight over the Caucasus meant going above 8,000 feet, which no longer seemed as advisable medically as it had been two years earlier. 'It is not good for me to go much above 8,000 feet,' Churchill telegraphed to Stalin on October 4, 'though I can, if necessary, do it for an hour or so'. It would be 'less of a risk' medically if he could fly across the Aegean and Black Sea, refuelling somewhere in the Crimea.[1] 'What energy and gallantry of the PM. . . .' Oliver Harvey noted in his diary.[2]

In a telegram to Roosevelt on October 4, Churchill set out once more the purpose of his visit. The 'bulk of our visit', he explained, 'will be about the Poles, but you and I think so much alike about this that I do not need any special guidance as to your views'. He and Eden would also try 'to elicit the time it will take after the German downfall for a superior Russian Army to be gathered opposite the Japanese. . . .' The role of the Great Powers in the post war World Organization 'will certainly come up': if Roosevelt had any 'wishes about this matter', Churchill ended, he should let him know, and also instruct Averell Harriman accordingly.

He was 'very glad', Churchill told Roosevelt, that Harriman should 'sit in' at all the principal conferences, 'but you would not, I am sure, wish this to preclude private tête-à-têtes between me and UJ, or Anthony and Molotov, as it is often under such conditions that the best progress is made'. Churchill's telegram ended: 'You can rely on me to keep you constantly informed of everything that affects our joint interests, apart from the reports which Averell will send.'[3]

Should Stalin raise the 'question of voting' among the Great Powers, Churchill telegraphed to Roosevelt on the following day, 'as he very likely will do, I will tell him there is no hurry about this and that I am sure we can get it settled when we are all three together'.[4]

On 26 September 1944 an agreement had been signed at Caserta,

---

[1] Prime Minister's Personal Telegram, T.1879/4, 'Private, Personal and Top Secret', 4 October 1944: Churchill papers, 20/172.

[2] Harvey diary, 4 October 1944: John Harvey (editor), *op. cit.,* page 358.

[3] Prime Minister's Personal Telegram, T.1872/4, Prime Minister to President, No. 790, 'Personal, Private and Top Secret', 4 October 1944: Churchill papers, 20/172.

[4] Prime Minister's Personal Telegram, T.1891/4, Prime Minister to President, No. 791, 'Personal and Top Secret', 5 October 1944: Churchill papers, 20/172.

in Italy, between British and Greek representatives, whereby all the guerilla forces in Greece agreed to place themselves under the orders of the Greek Government, who in turn put themselves under the command of General Scobie. Under this Caserta Agreement, the Greek guerilla leaders agreed that none of their men would take the law into their own hands in the event of a German withdrawal from Greece, and that any military action against the Germans in Athens would be taken only on the direct orders of General Scobie. By the morning of October 4, Scobie had launched the long-awaited operation 'Manna', the first Allied landings on the Greek mainland since the German victory there three and a half years earlier.

On the evening of October 4 Churchill again took his wife to the New Theatre, to see the Old Vic Company in *Richard III*, with Laurence Olivier as Richard and Sybil Thorndike as Margaret of Anjou. On his return to the Annexe, he learned that the preliminary phase of operation 'Manna' had been successful. 'Patras completely occupied 0500 hrs this morning,' Maitland Wilson telegraphed.[1] The Peloponnese part of 'Manna' was over: Athens, and possibly Salonica, remained. That same day, Russian forces in the Balkans linked up with units of Tito's National Army of Liberation. In Poland, Warsaw was still under German rule, with tens of thousands of Poles deported to concentration camps and labour camps in a mass reprisal. 'In the battle for Warsaw,' Churchill told the House of Commons on October 5, 'terrible damage has been inflicted upon that noble city, and its heroic population has undergone sufferings and privations unsurpassed even among the miseries of this war.' The 'final fall' of Warsaw, he declared, 'at a time when Allied Armies are everywhere victorious, and when the final defeat of Germany is in sight, must come as a very bitter blow to all Poles. At such a moment, I wish to express our respect to all those Poles who fell, fought or suffered at Warsaw and our sympathy with the Polish nation in this further grievous loss. Our confidence that the days of their tribulation are rapidly drawing to an end is unshakable. When the final Allied victory is achieved, the epic of Warsaw will not be forgotten. It will remain a deathless memory for the Poles, and for the friends of freedom all over the world.'[2]

Listening to Churchill's remarks were Mikolajczyk and Raczynski, both of whom came up to him in the Lobby and thanked him for his words. 'The words produced by the FO were good,' Colville noted, 'the delivery, due to the PM being too long in his bath and having to rush, was poor.'[3]

[1] ACIC/119, 'Top Secret', received 11.45 p.m., 4 October 1944: Churchill papers, 20/122.
[2] *Hansard*, 5 October 1944, column 1140.
[3] Colville diary, 5 October 1944: Colville papers.

Churchill proposed to leave for Moscow on October 7. Before going, he gave instructions for an aircraft to be kept ready so that, if Stalin agreed to reopen negotiations with the London Poles, Mikolajczyk and his colleagues would be able, as Churchill wrote to Mikolajczyk, 'to fly *at once* to join us in Moscow'. Churchill added: 'I am sure that this is the only way in which we can break the present deadlock and render a solution of outstanding Polish problems possible.' [1]

That afternoon, Jock Colville noted in his diary, 'the PM, while signing photographs (including one for Stalin) and books, began reading Vol. I of *Marlborough* aloud to me and continued about Sir Winston Churchill's home-life and passion for heraldry for nearly an hour.[2] At the end he said that as I had been subjected to this ordeal he would give me a copy for Christmas. He then worked till dinner, seeing various people and every now and then telling me I ought to read the leading article in today's *Manchester Guardian*.' [3]

'Eden and I are off to Ursus Major,' Churchill telegraphed to Smuts, 'and will soon be on the wing. I think it vital to get there now and certainly Uncle Joe has shown himself more forthcoming than ever before. We must strike while the iron is hot.' Churchill added: 'He holds to his promise about the Far East.' [4]

Churchill's immediate problem about the Far East concerned, not Stalin, but the availability of British forces for 'Dracula'. On October 5 the Chiefs of Staff had telegraphed to the Joint Staff Mission in Washington, stressing that as a result of the worsening military situation, 'our penetration into Germany is going to be resisted strongly', and that there was 'very hard fighting still in front of the Allied armies'. Eisenhower had already told them, they added, in relation to the troops that were to have been available that winter for the campaign in Burma, that the 6th Airborne Division was 'almost certain to be required for further airborne operations on the Rhine', that the 3rd

[1] 'Top Secret', 7 October 1944: Churchill papers, 20/138.

[2] Of the first Sir Winston Churchill, the first Duke of Marlborough's father, his descendant wrote: 'he presented in those years the curious figure of a cavalry captain, fresh from the wars, turned perforce recluse and bookworm. Time must have hung heavy on his hands. He had no estates to manage, no profession to pursue. He could not afford to travel; but in the teaching of his children he may well have found alike occupation and solace. Or, again, he may have loafed and brooded, leaving his children to play in the lanes and gardens of that tranquil countryside.' (Winston S. Churchill, *Marlborough, His Life and Times*, volume 1, London 1933, pages 28–9.)

[3] Colville diary, 7 October 1944: Colville papers. Writing of Churchill's intervention in the House of Commons debate, the *Manchester Guardian* said that it was 'characteristic of Mr Churchill, the great Parliamentarian', that a party split should be 'finally exposed' in the Commons 'before it could disrupt the Cabinet', and it referred to Churchill's handling of the issue as 'a striking exhibition of Mr Churchill's political resource and capacity for leadership' ('Crisis Forestalled', *Manchester Guardian*, 7 October 1944).

[4] Prime Minister's Personal Telegram, T.1912/4, No. 963 to South Africa, 'Top Secret and Personal', sent on 9 October 1944: Churchill papers, 20/173.

Division was about to be 'heavily engaged in operations from which it cannot be withdrawn', and that the 52nd Division was 'certain to be required' for operations either in north-west Europe or in Italy. In view of this, and of the airborne signals and administrative units needed for the continuing struggle in north-west Europe, 'we are forced with reluctance', the Chiefs of Staff declared, 'to the conclusion that we should be departing from first principles if we jeopardized the operations against Germany for the sake of "Dracula" in March 1945'.[1]

Such was the message from Brooke, Portal and Cunningham to Marshall, Arnold and King. On the following day, October 6, the three British Chiefs of Staff met again, with Brooke presiding, to discuss the possibilities of an amphibious assault at the head of the Adriatic, now given the code name 'Sunstar'. At this meeting, General Gammell spoke of two 'serious disadvantages' in the Adriatic plan, first, the distance from Alexander's land front, and second, the need to employ one airborne division, two assault divisions, and one follow-up division, in order to 'seize and hold' the bridgehead. It would be 'very difficult if not impossible', Gammel had concluded, for Alexander to provide these forces.[2]

At 11.20 that evening of October 7, Churchill, accompanied by General Ismay, Lord Moran, John Martin and Commander Thompson, left London for Northolt, to join the York in which he was to travel, first to Italy, and then to Moscow. That night Churchill sent his wife a note of apology for an episode on the previous day. 'I have been fretting over our interchange at luncheon yesterday,' he wrote. 'I am sure that no one thought of it as more than my making my own position clear, and that it all passed on the ripple of a most successful party. Anyhow forgive me for anything that seemed disrespectful to you & let yr morning thought dwell kindly on yr penitent apologetic & ever loving W.'[3]

At the King's request, Eden and Brooke set off that same night in separate aircraft. The three men met the next morning in Naples, for breakfast at the Villa Rivalta. Churchill then had a short conference with Alexander and Wilson, who 'left us in no doubt', General Ismay

[1] Chiefs of Staff Telegram, COS (W) 371, OZ5790, 5 October 1944: Cabinet papers, 105/61.
[2] Chiefs of Staff Committee No. 330 (Operations) of 1944, 6 October 1944: Cabinet papers, 79/81.
[3] Letter dated 7 October 1944, 1 a.m.: Spencer-Churchill papers.

later recalled, 'that the withdrawals from the armies in Italy for the Riviera landings had emasculated their campaign'.[1]

The meeting began with a survey by Alexander of the situation on the Italian front. 'He recalled the many withdrawals of troops which had taken place in the course of the last year,' the minutes recorded, 'which had resulted in his having twenty divisions against the Germans' twenty-eight. All his divisions had now been committed to the battle, and we had had some 30,000 casualties in six weeks.' These losses were not being fully made up, 'and with the exception of a Brazilian Division and a Division of negroes, he had not received any fresh formations'. Some of his battalions had had to be reduced to three-Company strength. General Clark was also short of men, 'and he was also anxious about the supply of ammunition'.

The Allied front in Italy, Alexander warned, 'was being allowed to wither away'. The result of all this 'was that he had not had the strength to secure a decisive victory, though he had caused the enemy 42,000 casualties, including 10,000 prisoners. His army was now in a very awkward position, being in a tired state, and being located halfway across the mountains with a bad L. of C.[2] The weather had now broken, and even if we got into the Po Valley, we should find the country very unsuitable for our type of operations at this time of year.' The Allied superiority lay in armour and in air power, in both of which 'we would be much handicapped' in the winter. The Germans also were tired, 'but they had the easier job of defending in country which suited their type of mobility, which depended on horse-drawn transport'.

Alexander ended his survey: 'The Italian campaign had been wrecked by bad strategy. Three more divisions might restore the position. He suggested that three American divisions might be sent into Italy, as he understood that it would be difficult to receive them in France.'

Brooke, in answer to Alexander's suggestion, doubted whether any American divisions could be diverted. General Eisenhower, he said, 'could accept all the formations which could be shipped with the shipping available'.

Churchill, speaking next, suggested that 'if the present offensive was stopped in the Apennines, the effort might be switched to Istria'. An operation against Istria 'would not be like Anzio, as we should have the support of the Partisans, and of the favourable developments on the Russian front near Belgrade and in Hungary'.

The earliest possible date for a landing on Istria, commented

[1] Ismay memoirs, *op. cit.*, page 376.
[2] Lines of Communication.

Maitland Wilson, was late November. This date was governed by the release of landing craft from the south of France.

Alexander now spoke of the possibility of withdrawing divisions from his own Italian front, once the front was stabilised either in the Po Valley or in its present position, and preparing these divisions for an amphibious operation. Alexander added: 'He would hand over the whole of the Italian front to the 5th Army, and would prepare the 8th Army to go in either at Split or into Istria. This would once more give him the two-handed punch which he regarded as one of the essentials for a successful operation.'

Alexander added that everything depended 'on the timing of the blow'. The Germans, he explained, had three divisions in or near Istria, and five others within reach in Dalmatia and Yugoslavia. 'We should therefore have to prepare a strong operation,' Alexander concluded.

Brooke pointed out that 'we should have much difficulty in overcoming the American objections to operations across the Adriatic. The Americans had been quite willing to leave their divisions in Italy for the purpose of defeating Kesselring on the main front. If we suggested withdrawing formations, for what the Americans would term a "Balkan Venture", they would say that they ought rather to be sent to the main front in France. They would say the same about the landing craft, which they were anxious to remove to the Pacific.'

To answer possible American criticisms, Churchill suggested that the amphibious operation might be launched not against Istria, but against the north-east corner of Italy, 'behind Kesselring', but to this Sir John Cunningham noted 'that there were no suitable beaches between Ancona and Trieste'. Moreover, 'the water was heavily mined, and was shallow, and there were a large number of lagoons which would make the penetration inland very difficult'.

It was 'most important', commented Brooke, that a plan should be put forward to the Combined Chiefs of Staff by October 10, to enable it to become 'an approved operation'. Only in this way could the retention of the troops and landing craft be 'justified' to the American Chiefs of Staff. The 'simplest plan', said Brooke, 'would be to put forward Istria as the operation, and to say that owing to the uncertainties in the Balkans and in Hungary, it might be found better nearer the date to strike for the Istrian ports via the Dalmatian coast'.

Churchill shared Brooke's assessment of the American reaction. The Americans, he said, 'were afraid of being "sucked into the Ljubljana Gap". They might also say that if troops could be withdrawn from the Italian front to go to Istria, they might also be drawn from there in order to go to "Dracula".' This would also apply to the tank landing craft. It would be 'best', Churchill thought, for him 'to telegraph to the President, and to say that he had been grieved to find, on examining the position on the spot, that success had been missed for the lack of two divisions for "Dracula", and he had been told that all the divisions were earmarked for France. He could ask him to consider whether two could not be diverted to beating Kesselring.'

As the meeting came to an end, it was agreed that Wilson would put forward a plan to the Chiefs of Staff 'for an amphibious operation directed against the Istrian Peninsula, either as a direct assault or as an advance from the Dalmatian coast with target date February'.[1] Churchill strongly favoured a decision for action, either in the Adriatic, or in Burma, reminding Ismay three days later, while they were in Moscow, of 'our desire to do an amphibious operation before Christmas in the armpit of the Adriatic', but pointing out that it was for the sake of further action by Alexander's army that Mountbatten's operation 'Dracula' had been put off until November.

As a result of the Naples meeting, Churchill told Ismay it had become clear that Wilson and Alexander 'can do nothing in the Italian theatre worth speaking of'. One possibility, Churchill suggested, was to give up altogether this idea of doing 'anything worthwhile' in Italy or the Adriatic, and 'try to produce' a March offensive in Burma, using the tank landing craft 'from the Adriatic venture'. Churchill commented: 'We ought to have action at one place or another.' For this reason, Mountbatten 'should be summoned to meet us at Cairo from Sunday on'. Churchill added: 'It is not much of a flight.'[2]

'Plans are difficult to make,' Brooke wrote in his diary, 'Alex is getting stuck in the Apennines with tired forces and cannot spare any for amphibious operations. At the same time Hungary is suing for peace, Russians are advancing into Yugoslavia and Tito's partisans making ground.' It was, therefore, 'hard to estimate', Brooke added, 'what the situation will be when Alex can find forces, namely in February'.[3]

In the hope of strengthening Alexander's forces, Churchill telegraphed direct to Roosevelt. 'Could you not deflect,' he asked, 'two, or better still three, American divisions to the Italian front, which would enable them to join Mark Clark's Fifth Army and add the necessary strength to Alexander? They would have to be there in three or four

---

[1] 'Minutes of Meeting held at SACMED's villa, Naples, on Sunday, 8 October, at 9.15 a.m.', 'Top Secret', Moscow, 9 October 1944: Cabinet papers, 120/159.

[2] Prime Minister's Personal Minute, M(Tol) 1/4, 11 October 1944: Cabinet papers, 120/158.

[3] Brooke diary, 8 October 1944: Bryant, *op. cit.*, volume 2, page 295.

weeks. I consider the fact that we shall be sending Eisenhower these extra two divisions gives me a case for your generous consideration.' [1]

Roosevelt's reply, sent six days later, was a full and final negative. 'Diversion of any forces to Italy,' he wrote, 'would withhold from France vitally needed fresh troops, while committing such forces to the high attrition of an indecisive winter campaign in Northern Italy. I appreciate the hard and difficult task which our armies in Italy have faced and will face, but we cannot withhold from the main effort forces which are needed in the Battle of Germany.' [2]

Churchill remained at the Villa Rivalta for less than four hours. After the conference with the generals, he took a bath, before a second short conference, this time with George Papandreou, the Prime Minister of Greece, on whose soil, at Patras, British troops were now ashore. Harold Macmillan, who was present, noted in his diary that the conversation with Papandreou 'was entirely confined to a monologue by Winston in praise of monarchy in general and King George of Greece in particular. M. Papandreou looked very uncomfortable—but not more so than the rest of us. When the homily was over, the party left for the airfield.' [3]

From Naples, Churchill flew to Cairo, arriving in time for dinner with Lord Moyne. 'The electric light went out just as we started,' Oliver Harvey wrote in his diary, 'but it came on again. PM in his boiler suit.' [4] As Churchill's plane had landed badly, damaging its undercarriage, he had to fly on that night in Brooke's plane, leaving Cairo just after midnight. That night, Jock Colville, who had remained in London, wrote in his diary:

The PM's visit to Moscow, which is really very dangerous to his health, is, he assured me yesterday, entirely because he wants to discourage any idea that the UK and the USA are very close (as exemplified by the Quebec Conference) to the exclusion of Russia. His visit will make it quite clear that our counsels with Russia are close too, and that there is no tendency to leave her in the cold. [5]

Shortly after midday on October 9, Churchill, Eden and Brooke landed in Moscow, but at the wrong aerodrome. They took off again, landing half an hour later, where Maisky and Vyshinski and a guard of honour were awaiting them. [6] 'Tolstoy' had begun.

[1] Prime Minister's Personal Telegram, T.1914/4, Prime Minister to President No. 793, 'Hearty' No. 18, 'Personal and Top Secret', 10 October 1944: Cabinet papers, 120/164.

[2] President to Prime Minister No. 630, 16 October 1944, sent as 'Drastic' No. 129, from Foreign Office to Tolstoy, 17 October 1944: Churchill papers 20/173.

[3] Macmillan diary, 8 October 1944: *War Diaries, op. cit.*, page 544.

[4] Harvey diary, 8 October 1944: John Harvey (editor), *op. cit.*, page 359.

[5] Colville diary, 8 October 1944: Colville papers.

[6] ' "Tolstoy" ', 'Air Transport Command Arrangements', Aide Memoire by Joan Bright, 7 November 1944: Joan Bright Astley papers.

53
Moscow, October 1944:
'Powerless in the face of Russia'

FROM Moscow airport, on 9 October 1944, Churchill was driven to
Molotov's dacha, which was situated forty-five minutes by car
from the centre of the city, and had been assigned to Churchill as his
residence for the duration of his visit. 'Mr Churchill arrived, suddenly
and unexpectedly early,' recalled Joan Bright, whose responsibility it
had been to arrange the accommodation for the British delegates; 'we
held our thumbs and prayed.' Her account continued:

He came into the hall, followed by Mr Molotov, said 'Hello' to Marian
Holmes, one of his stenographers who had flown out with us, and asked:
'Where is my red box?'
'Your luggage is not here yet,' said his private secretary John Martin,
firmly.
'Never mind; I will have a bath, put on my vest and get into bed,' and the
great man climbed the stairs.
Five minutes later a distracted Inspector Hughes, his detective, rushed
down the stairs. 'The Prime Minister,' he said, 'doesn't know which is the
hot tap and the bath is filling with cold water!' He had turned on a tap
marked with sticking-plaster 'Hot', had not, because it ran cold at first,
believed what it said, had turned it off, turned on the other, and lost confidence.[1]

That evening, Churchill dined at the Molotov villa with Eden and
Sir Archibald Clark Kerr, before driving in to Moscow, and to the
British Embassy. From the Embassy, he was driven to the Kremlin,
for his first meeting with Stalin. The others present were Molotov,
Eden and Clark Kerr, and the two interpreters, Pavlov and Birse.

As Birse's minutes of the meeting recorded, this first session of
'Tolstoy' began with Churchill giving Stalin a signed photograph.
Churchill then told the Soviet leader that he hoped they might 'clear

[1] Joan Bright Astley, *The Inner Circle, A view of the war at the top*, London 1971, pages 161–2.

away many questions about which they had been writing to each other for a long time'. As time had passed, many issues had arisen, 'but they were out of all proportion to the greatness of the common struggle'. By talking to each other, he and Stalin 'could avoid innumerable telegrams and letters, and they could give the Ambassador a holiday'.

The conversation continued, as the minutes recorded:

MARSHAL STALIN replied that he was ready to discuss anything.

THE PRIME MINISTER suggested beginning with the most tiresome question—Poland. He said that they should have a common policy in regard to Poland. At present each had a game-cock in his hand.

MARSHAL STALIN said (with a laugh) that it was difficult to do without cocks. They gave the morning signal.

THE PRIME MINISTER remarked that the question of the frontier was settled as agreed. He would like presently to check up on the frontier with a map.

MARSHAL STALIN remarked that if the frontier was agreed on the Curzon Line it would help their discussion.

At the 'armistice table', Churchill told Stalin, 'the Prime Minister would support the frontier line as fixed at Teheran', and he was 'sure' that the United States would do the same. That decision had been endorsed by the British War Cabinet, 'and he felt it would be approved by his country. He would say it was right, fair and necessary for the safety and future of Russia.' If General Sosnkowski objected, Churchill told Stalin, 'it would not matter', because Britain and the United States 'thought it right and fair'. Churchill added: 'He and Mr Eden had for months been trying to get Sosnkowski sacked. He had now been sacked and as for General Bor, the Germans were looking after him.'[1]

The Poles, said Stalin, were now without a Commander-in-Chief, to which Churchill replied 'that some colourless man had been left. He could not remember his name.'

Churchill then asked Stalin if he thought it would be 'worthwhile' to bring Mikolajczyk and Romer to Moscow. 'He had them tied up in an aircraft,' he said, 'and it would take only 36 hours to Moscow.' Did they have authority to settle questions with the Polish Committee for National Liberation? Stalin asked. He was not sure, Churchill replied, but he thought they would 'not be anxious to go to bed with

---

[1] Following the German suppression of the Warsaw uprising, General Bor-Komorowski surrendered to SS General Bach-Zelewski. Bor-Komorowski survived the war, to become Commander-in-Chief of the Polish Armed Forces (in the West) from May 1945 to November 1946 and then Prime Minister of the Polish Government in Exile (in London), from 1947 to 1949. He died in 1966.

the Committee'. If however they were in Moscow, 'they could, with British and Russian agreement, be forced to settle'.

Mikolajczyk would 'have to make contact' with the Committee, Stalin commented, and went on to stress that the Committee 'now had an army at its disposal and represented a force'. Churchill then 'pointed out' to Stalin, as the interpreters' notes recorded, 'that the other side also thought they had an army, part of which had held out in Warsaw. They also had a brave Army Corps in Italy, where they lost seven or eight thousand men. Then there was the armoured division, one brigade of which was in France. The Polish division which had gone to Switzerland when France fell was coming out in driblets. They were well equipped and they had many friends in England. They were good and brave men.'

The 'difficulty about the Poles', Churchill added, 'was that they had unwise political leaders. Where there were two Poles there was one quarrel,' whereupon Stalin remarked that 'where there was one Pole he would begin to quarrel with himself through sheer boredom'.

It was then agreed, as the first agreement of the 'Tolstoy' conference, that the British, as Churchill phrased it, 'would bring pressure to bear on their Poles', while the Poles in the East 'were already in agreement with the Soviet Government'. The minutes added: 'Marshal Stalin agreed to this.'

The conversation then turned to the German 'satellites'. 'He hoped the Russians would soon be in Budapest,' Churchill commented, and he went on to tell the Soviet leader:

... there were two countries in which the British had particular interest. One was Greece. He was not worrying much about Roumania. That was very much a Russian affair and the terms which the Soviet Government had proposed were reasonable and showed much statecraft in the interests of general peace in the future. But in Greece it was different. Britain must be the leading Mediterranean Power and he hoped Marshal Stalin would let him have the first say about Greece in the same way as Marshal Stalin about Roumania. Of course, the British Government would keep in touch with the Soviet Government.

Stalin replied with understanding for Britain's position with regard to Greece. It was a 'serious matter for Britain', he said, 'when the Mediterranean route was not in her hands'. He 'agreed with the Prime Minister', as the minute recorded, 'that Britain should have the first say in Greece'. The minutes continued:

PRIME MINISTER said it was better to express these things in diplomatic terms and not to use the phrase 'dividing into spheres', because the Americans might be shocked. But as long as he and Marshal Stalin understood each other he could explain matters to the President.

The President, Stalin commented, wanted Averell Harriman 'to attend their talks as an observer', and that 'the decisions reached between them should be of a preliminary nature'. Churchill agreed. He and the President 'had no secrets'. He had told him that he would welcome Harriman 'to a good number of their talks'. But, Churchill told Stalin, 'he did not want to prevent intimate talk between Marshal Stalin and himself'.

Stalin then told Churchill that Roosevelt seemed to him 'to demand too many rights for the USA, leaving too little for the Soviet Union and Great Britain who after all had a treaty of common assistance'. He had no objection, however, to Harriman attending 'the formal talks'.

There then occurred an episode which was significantly to influence the subsequent political balance in eastern Europe and the Balkans. The Prime Minister, as Major Birse's original minutes noted, 'then produced what he called a "naughty document" showing a list of Balkan countries and the proportion of interest in them of the Great Powers. He said that the Americans would be shocked if they saw how crudely he had put it. Marshal Stalin was a realist. He himself was not sentimental while Mr Eden was a bad man. He had not consulted his Cabinet or Parliament.'[1]

According to Churchill's own recollection of this moment in the conversation, as recorded eight years later, he had said to Stalin: 'Let us settle about our affairs in the Balkans. Your armies are in Roumania and Bulgaria. We have interests, missions, and agents there. Don't let us get at cross-purposes in small ways. So far as Britain and Russia are concerned, how would it do for you to have ninety per cent predominance in Roumania, for us to have ninety per cent of the say in Greece, and go fifty-fifty about Yugoslavia?'

While this was being translated, Churchill, as he later recalled, wrote out on a 'half-sheet of paper' his own concept of these percentages. The note read:

---

[1] 'Record of Meeting at the Kremlin, Moscow, October 9th, 1944 at 10 p.m.': Foreign Office papers, 800/302, folios 227–35. This passage in Birse's notes was omitted from the official secret record of the discussion. 'I have sidelined certain passages,' Ian Jacob informed Sir Edward Bridges on October 26, 'which seem most inappropriate for a record of this importance,' and he advised that these passages 'might be cut out'. Stalin and Roosevelt, added Jacob, 'would probably prefer' to have no record at all, as these notes of Birse would 'give the impression to historians that these very important discussions were conducted in a most unfitting manner'. Bridges noted: 'Please delete as proposed,' and the passage was struck out. (Jacob note, 26 October 1944 and Bridges note, 8 November 1944: Cabinet papers, 120/158.)

Roumania

Russia	90%
The others	10%

Greece

Great Britain	90%
(in accord with USA)	
Russia	10%
Yugoslavia	50–50%
Hungary	50–50%

Bulgaria

Russia	75%
The others	25%

Churchill then pushed this piece of paper across the table to Stalin. 'There was a slight pause,' Churchill later recalled. 'Then he took his blue pencil and made a large tick upon it, and passed it back to us.' Churchill's recollection continued:

After this there was a long silence. The pencilled paper lay in the centre of the table. At length I said, 'Might it not be thought rather cynical if it seemed we had disposed of these issues, so fateful to millions of people, in such an offhand manner? Let us burn the paper.' 'No you keep it,' said Stalin.[1]

The discussion then turned, as Birse's notes show, to the Bulgarian split of 75% to Russia and 25% to Britain, with Churchill telling Stalin 'that Britain had been much offended by Bulgaria. In the last war the Bulgarians had beaten back and had cruelly attacked the Roumanians. In this war they had done the same to the Yugoslavs and Greece.'

Stalin then 'recalled' the time of the Treaty of Brest Litovsk in 1918, 'where the Bulgarians had been on the German side'. Three Bulgarian divisions 'had fought against the Russians in the last war'.

Bulgaria, Churchill admitted, 'owed more to Russia than to any other country'. In Roumania, where the Soviet–British split was 90–10, Britain had been 'a spectator'. In Bulgaria, however, she had to be 'a little more than a spectator'.

Turning to the question of the Straits, Stalin told Churchill that he did not want Turkey 'to abuse her sovereignty and to grip Russian trade by the throat'. Turning to which, Churchill replied that he was 'in favour of Russia's having free access to the Mediterranean for her merchant ships and ships of war'. Britain hoped on this issue 'to work in a friendly way with the Soviet Union, but wanted to bring Turkey along by gentle steps, not to frighten her'. This, Stalin said, he 'understood'.

[1] Winston S. Churchill, *The Second World War*, volume 6, London 1954, page 198.

As far as the Straits were concerned, Churchill told Stalin, the Russians should 'take the initiative' and tell Britain and the United States what was in their mind, and he went on to tell the Soviet leader that he thought Russia 'had a right, and moral claim'.

Speaking of Greece and Yugoslavia, Churchill suggested that something should be done 'to prevent the risk of civil war between the political ideologies in these two countries. They could not allow a lot of little wars after the Great World War. They should be stopped by the authority of the three Great Powers.' The minutes added: 'Marshal Stalin agreed.'

Churchill then said that 'he wanted to talk about kings'. In 'no case', he said, would Britain try to 'force' a king on Italy, Greece or Yugoslavia. At the same time, he argued, 'the people ought to be left to decide matters by a free plebiscite in time of tranquillity. They could then say whether they wanted a republic or a monarchy. The people should have a fair chance of freedom of expression.' Northern Italy, Churchill pointed out, 'was not yet in the power of the Anglo-American armies', and he went on to tell Stalin that while Britain 'did not care for the Italian king', above all she did not want a civil war in Italy after the Allied troops had been withdrawn, or even before their withdrawal. Churchill added:

They would like the Soviet Union to soft-pedal the Communists in Italy and not to stir them up. Pure democracy would settle what the people wanted, but he did not want to have disturbances in Turin or Milan and clashes between the troops and the people. The Italians were in a miserable condition. He did not think much of them as a people, but they had a good many votes in New York State. This was off the record. The Prime Minister went on to say that he did not want to have trouble in Italy before the United States left it. The President was their best friend. They would never have such a good one. That was why he petted the Italians, though he did not like them much.

It was 'difficult', Stalin replied, 'to influence the Italian Communists'. If Ercoli was in Moscow he might influence him, but he was in Italy, where the circumstances were different. 'He could send Marshal Stalin to the devil.' Ercoli, added Stalin, 'could say he was an Italian and tell Marshal Stalin to mind his own business'. Ercoli was, however, Stalin commented, 'a wise man, not an extremist, and would not start an adventure in Italy'.[1]

Then, as Birse's notes recorded, Churchill asked Stalin 'to tell him something, as he had been talking the whole time'. Stalin then 'reverted to the Balkans, and asked for the figures about Bulgaria on

[1] 'Ercoli' was the *nom de guerre* of Palmiro Togliatti, leader of the Italian Communist Party.

the "naughty document" to be amended'. It was for Eden and Molotov to 'go into details', was Churchill's only comment, and this was agreed. The conversation then turned to the post-war future of Germany. He was 'all for hard terms', said Churchill. But in the United States opinions were divided. 'The President was for hard terms,' Churchill reported, 'others were for soft.' The problem in Churchill's view was, 'how to prevent Germany getting on her feet in the lifetime of our grandchildren'. The conversation continued, as the minutes recorded:

MARSHAL STALIN thought the Versailles peace was inadequate. It had not removed the possibility of revenge. Hard measures would stir a desire for revenge. The problem was to create such a peace that the possibility of revenge would be denied to Germany. Her heavy industry would have to be destroyed. The State would have to be split up. How that was to be done would have to be discussed. Her heavy industry would have to be reduced to a minimum.

THE PRIME MINISTER suggested it should apply to the electrical and chemical industries also.

MARSHAL STALIN agreed that it should apply to all industry producing war material. Germany should be deprived of the possibility of revenge. Otherwise every twenty-five or thirty years there would be a new world war which would exterminate the young generation. If approached from that angle the harshest measures would prove to be the most humane. Eight to ten million Germans had been lost after every war. Reprisals in Germany might affect only one and a half million Germans. As regards concrete proposals, Mr Eden and M. Molotov should get together.

Molotov then asked Churchill his opinion of the Morgenthau Plan. As the minutes recorded:

THE PRIME MINISTER said that the President and Mr Morgenthau were not very happy about its reception. The Prime Minister went on to say that as he had declared in Teheran, Great Britain would not agree to mass execution of Germans, because one day British public opinion would cry out. But it was necessary to kill as many as possible in the field. The others should be made to work to repair the damage done to other countries. They might use the Gestapo on such work and the Hitler Youth should be re-educated to learn that it was more difficult to build than to destroy.

MARSHAL STALIN thought that a long occupation of Germany would be necessary.

THE PRIME MINISTER did not think that the Americans would stay very long.

When Stalin suggested that France 'should provide some forces', Churchill agreed. Stalin then suggested the use of the small countries, to which Churchill replied that he thought 'United Poland could be employed'. The conversation continued:

MARSHAL STALIN said Silesia would go to the Poles and part of East Prussia. The Soviet Union would take Koenigsberg and the Poles would be very interested in the occupation of Germany.

THE PRIME MINISTER thought the population might be moved from Silesia and East Prussia to Germany. If seven million had been killed in the war there would be plenty of room for them. He suggested that M. Molotov and Mr Eden, with Mr Harriman, should talk this over and get a picture of the general proposals for Marshal Stalin and himself to think about, and thus when the end came they would not be without something unprobed.

It was agreed that Molotov, Eden and Harriman should discuss the future of Germany and report back to Churchill and Stalin.

As the conversation came to an end, Churchill said that he would 'like Marshal Stalin to know' that the British had 'as many divisions fighting against Germany in Italy and France as the United States', and 'nearly as many' fighting Japan. Altogether, he pointed out, Britain had sixty divisions of 40,000 men each at war with Germany and Japan: nearly two and a half million men.[1]

It was well after midnight when Churchill returned with Eden and Clark Kerr to the British Embassy. There he learned that the London Poles had expressed reluctance at coming to Moscow. Churchill at once telegraphed to Mikolajczyk, making it clear that refusal to come to take part in the conversations 'will amount to a definite rejection of our advice and will relieve us from further responsibility as far as your Government is concerned'.[2] This telegram crossed with one from Mikolajczyk, to say that he was prepared to come. 'I am now expecting you,' Churchill replied.[3]

Shortly after two in the morning, Churchill left the British Embassy for his distant dacha, not getting there until just over an hour later. It was 3.10 in the morning. 'I gave him some papers,' noted Marian Holmes, 'but he said he couldn't work.'[4] Churchill had been travelling and working continuously for more than sixty hours. Finally he was in a motionless bed, and slept soundly.

On the following morning, October 10, Churchill worked in bed. Shortly after midday he again left the dacha by car, to return to Moscow, and to the Kremlin, where Stalin was the host at a luncheon

---

[1] 'Record of Meeting at the Kremlin, Moscow, October 9th at 10 p.m.': Foreign Office papers, 800/302, folios 227–35. The polished version, with all reference to the 'naughty document' removed, is in Premier papers, 3/434/4.

[2] 'Hearty' No. 17, 'Personal and Top Secret', 10 October 1944: Churchill papers, 20/181.

[3] 'Hearty' No. 18, 10 October 1944, Churchill papers, 20/181.

[4] Marian Holmes diary, 9 October 1944: Marian Walker Spicer papers.

party. Among those present were Averell Harriman, and General Deane, the Head of the United States military mission. The party continued for nearly four hours, after which Churchill returned to the British Embassy, after having announced on the Kremlin doorstep: 'I'm going back to the Embassy for my Young Lady.'

Churchill then returned from the Embassy to the dacha. 'Now get in the car' were his words to Elizabeth Layton as he prepared to leave, and he added: 'I think I'll dictate in the dark.'[1] It was 'a simply marvellous car,' Elizabeth Layton noted, 'and we were both wrapped up in huge Russian fur rugs. There were guards all along the 23-mile route, who saluted as we passed. He dictated a fairly short thing for Joe, and most of the rest of the way he just chatted.'[2] What, Churchill asked her, did she think 'of the people in the streets—did they look suspicious, were they undernourished etc.'.[3]

As soon as he had returned to the dacha, Churchill sent Roosevelt an account of the previous evening's conversation. It was sent in his and Stalin's joint name, and had been shown in draft to Harriman during the lunch. The telegram, which spoke of the 'extraordinary atmosphere of goodwill', informed Roosevelt that the two leaders had agreed that all discussion of the post-war World Organization should wait until 'we three can meet together'. The telegram continued:

We have to consider the best way of reaching an agreed policy about the Balkan countries, including Hungary and Turkey. We have arranged for Mr Harriman to sit in as an observer at all meetings where business of importance is to be transacted, and for General Deane to be present whenever military topics are raised. We have arranged for technical contacts between our high officers and General Deane on military aspects, and for any meetings which may be necessary later in our presence and that of the two Foreign Secretaries, together with Mr Harriman. We shall keep you fully informed ourselves about the progress we make.[4]

Churchill and Stalin made no reference in this telegram to the sort of agreement they had in mind for the Balkan countries, Hungary or Turkey, nor had Harriman been present when Churchill had jotted down the 'percentages'. After the luncheon, Eden and Molotov met to follow this up. 'Stalin had admitted that Greece was primarily a British concern,' Eden later recalled, 'but Molotov showed a disposition to haggle over the percentages for the other countries.[5]

---

[1] Elizabeth Layton, letter of 10 October 1944: Nel papers.
[2] Elizabeth Layton, 'Short Account of Visit to Moscow', 15 November 1944: Nel papers.
[3] Elizabeth Layton, letter of 10 October 1944: Nel papers.
[4] 'Hearty' No. 20, 'Top Secret', Prime Minister's Personal Telegram, T.1916/4, Prime Minister to President, No. 794, 10 October 1944: Cabinet papers, 120/158.
[5] Eden memoirs, *The Reckoning, op. cit.*, page 482.

The actual 'haggling' between Eden and Molotov was recorded in the minutes:

Mr EDEN said he did not know much about these percentages. All he wanted was a greater share than we already had in Roumania. In Roumania we had 10 per cent which was almost nothing.

M. MOLOTOV pointed out that the idea of percentages arose from the meeting on the previous day, and it was worthy of consideration. Could they not agree on the following: Bulgaria, Hungary and Yugoslavia 75/25 per cent each?

Mr EDEN said that would be worse than on the previous day.

M. MOLOTOV then suggested 90/10 for Bulgaria; 50/50 for Yugoslavia and Hungary subject to an amendment.

Mr EDEN pointed out that they had not agreed about Bulgaria.

M. MOLOTOV remarked that he thought 90/10 was an ultimatum and meant the unconditional surrender of Moscow. However something would have to be done which would be acceptable to all three.

Mr EDEN said he was ready to meet M. Molotov's wishes with regard to Hungary, but he asked for M. Molotov's help to get some participation in Bulgaria after the Germans had been beaten. Possibly some other formula would be accepted. For instance we and the Americans might each have an officer on the Control Commission who would not be as important as the Soviet representative.

M. MOLOTOV then suggested 75/25 for Hungary

M. MOLOTOV continued that they had not finished with Bulgaria. If Hungary was 75/25, then Bulgaria should be 75/25 and Yugoslavia 60/40. This was the limit to which he could go.

Mr EDEN said he could not make this suggestion to the Prime Minister who was greatly interested in Yugoslavia. He had been at pains to champion Tito and to furnish arms. Any change in Yugoslavian percentages would upset him. Mr Eden then suggested Hungary 75/25; Bulgaria 80/20; Yugoslavia 50/50.

M. MOLOTOV was ready to agree to 50/50 for Yugoslavia if Bulgaria were 90/10. If the figure for Bulgaria had to be amended then Yugoslavia would also have to be changed.

Mr EDEN pointed out that with regard to Hungary we had made a concession.

M. MOLOTOV repeated that Hungary bordered on Russia and not on Britain. The Russians had suffered losses in Hungary. Marshal Stalin had mentioned this to the Prime Minister. What did 60/40 for Yugoslavia mean? It meant the coast where Russia would have less interest and would not interfere, but they were to have a greater influence in the centre.

He 'did not care so much about the figures', Eden told Molotov. 'He understood Russia's interest in Bulgaria and Britain accepted it.' But Britain asked for something more there than in Roumania. As to Yugoslavia, and whether Tito and the Yugoslav Government in

London would 'come together', Eden 'preferred to have a common policy'. It was 'desirable', he said, 'that the Allies should pursue the same ideas'.[1]

Eden then drove from Moscow to Churchill's dacha for dinner. Churchill was 'rather upset by my report', he noted in his diary. 'I think he thought I had dispelled the good atmosphere he had created the night before. But I explained this was the real battle and I could not and would not give way.'[2]

Churchill's concept of the meaning of the 'percentages' was set out on October 11 in a letter which he wrote to Stalin, but did not send:

These percentages which I have put down are no more than a method by which in our thoughts we can see how near we are together, and then decide upon the necessary steps to bring us into full agreement. As I said, they would be considered crude, and even callous, if they were exposed to the scrutiny of the Foreign Offices and diplomats all over the world. Therefore they could not be the basis of any public document, certainly not at the present time. They might however be a good guide for the conduct of our affairs.

Churchill then wrote of his own hopes for the Balkans:

If we manage these affairs well we shall perhaps prevent several civil wars and much bloodshed and strife in the small countries concerned. Our broad principle should be to let every country have the form of government which its people desire. We certainly do not wish to force on any Balkan State monarchic or republican institutions. We have however established certain relations of faithfulness with the Kings of Greece and Yugoslavia. They have sought our shelter from the Nazi foe, and we think that when normal tranquillity is re-established and the enemy has been driven out the peoples of these countries should have a free and fair chance of choosing. It might even be that Commissioners of the three Great Powers should be stationed there at the time of the elections so as to see that the people have a genuine free choice.

No ideology should be imposed on any small States, Churchill asserted. 'Let them work out their own fortunes during the years that lie ahead.' There were fears in every country in western Europe of 'an aggressive, proselytising Communism'. Hitler had tried to exploit these fears. But, Churchill ended:

We have the feeling that, viewed from afar and on a grand scale, the differences between our systems will tend to get smaller, and the great common ground which we share of making life richer and happier for the

[1] 'Record of Meeting at the Kremlin, Moscow, on 10th October, 1944 at 7 p.m.', 'Records of Meetings at the Kremlin, Moscow, October 9–October 17, 1944', 'Secret': Premier papers, 3/434/2.

[2] Eden diary, 10 October 1944: Eden memoirs, *The Reckoning*, *op. cit.*, page 483.

mass of the people is growing every year. Probably if there were peace for fifty years the differences which now might cause such grave troubles to the world would become matters for academic discussion.

At this point, Mr Stalin, I want to impress upon you the great desire there is in the heart of Britain for a long, stable friendship and co-operation between our two countries, and that with the United States we shall be able to keep the world engine on the rails.[1]

Before sending this letter, Churchill read it to Harriman, who later wrote: 'I told him that I was certain both Roosevelt and Hull would repudiate the letter, if it were sent.' At that moment, Harriman recalled, Eden came into the room. Churchill said to him: 'Anthony, Averell doesn't think we should send this letter to Stalin.'[2]

Although never sent to Stalin, Churchill's letter reflected his realization not only that the idea of 'percentages' in the Balkans could easily be misunderstood, or misused, but, more urgently, that the situation in the Balkans could soon deteriorate beyond control. To Roosevelt he telegraphed that same day:

It is absolutely necessary we should try to get a common mind about the Balkans, so that we may prevent civil war breaking out in several countries, when probably you and I would be in sympathy with one side and UJ with the other. I shall keep you informed of all this, and nothing will be settled except preliminary agreements between Britain and Russia, subject to further discussion and melting down with you. On this basis I am sure you will not mind our trying to have a full meeting of minds with the Russians.[3]

Churchill slept until eleven o'clock on the morning of October 11. 'He then worked from bed,' noted Marian Holmes, and she added: 'He claimed I was sitting in his light. "That's right. Take away the only bit of light I got." I moved my chair further away. "DON'T GO RIGHT AWAY! Now sit there and be good!" with a beautiful smile!'[4]

'General atmosphere here is most friendly,' Churchill telegraphed to his wife that morning, 'but there are many vexatious points to settle,' and he added: 'I am very well and weather today is brilliant. Love to all.'[5]

During October 11 Churchill learned from Eden that in Albania the future of King Zog was now seriously in doubt, as the local

[1] Unsent letter of 11 October 1944: Winston S. Churchill, *The Second World War*, volume 6, London 1954, pages 201–3.

[2] Abel and Harriman, *op. cit.*, page 358.

[3] 'Hearty' No. 27, Prime Minister's Personal Telegram, T.1919/4, Prime Minister to President, No. 795, 'Personal, Private and Top Secret', 11 October 1944: Cabinet papers, 120/158.

[4] Marian Holmes diary, 11 October 1944: Marian Walker Spicer papers.

[5] 'Hearty' No. 36, Telegram No. 2794 from Moscow to the Foreign Office, 11 October 1944: Premier papers, 4/76/1, folio 219.

communist partisans, the FNC, refused to allow the King to return from the exile into which he had gone at the time of the Italian invasion of Albania in 1939. 'Another King gone down the drain!' Churchill minuted to Eden on October 11, and he added, in a reference to his 'percentages' discussion with Stalin:

We did not mention Albania the other night, but personally I think we should insist upon a fifty-fifty arrangement with the Soviets. Of course if none of the Kings are allowed to go back into any of their countries and strike a blow on the Allied side, the establishment of Soviet-controlled Republics will be the universal pattern. There is not much hope in the policy of setting up the F.N.C. Government and waiting for it to be overthrown by revolution after it has made itself sufficiently odious. As for 'no significant group wanting the King back', there are very few countries in which anybody wants anyone back.[1]

Eden and Molotov now met again, to try to resolve their 'percentages' haggle of the previous evening. The Soviet Union had decided to defer to the British view. 'Could it be agreed,' Molotov asked, 'that if the Soviet Government accepted 80/20 for Hungary and Bulgaria, and 50/50 for Yugoslavia, they could go on to the next questions?' This was precisely what Eden had asked for. Armistice negotiations with Hungary, Molotov told Eden, could begin on the following day. 'Did the British and American Governments agree?' That question, said Eden, 'fundamentally concerned the Soviet Government. As regards the British, they agreed.'[2]

Churchill had worked from bed from eleven that morning until two in the afternoon. Then, after a hurried lunch, he drove into Moscow for a reception to the Diplomatic Corps given by Molotov. Following this reception, he went to a town house which had been put at his disposal for the duration of his Moscow visit, and there he had his early evening sleep.[3] Then, at nine o'clock, he went to the British Embassy for a dinner at which Stalin, Molotov, Vyshinski, the pre-war Foreign Minister, Litvinov, and Lazar Kaganovitch, the Commissar for Railways and Communications, were present. At one moment in the conversation, Birse later recalled, Churchill asked Kaganovitch 'what he had done to make the transport system in Russia efficient. Kaganovitch answered that when an engine driver failed to do his job—Kaganovitch then drew his finger across his throat.'[4] Dinner was interrupted by the noise and sight of fireworks,

---

[1] Prime Minister's Personal Minute, M(Tol) 5/4: Churchill papers, 20/153.

[2] 'Record of Meeting at the Kremlin, Moscow, on the 11th October, 1944, at 3 p.m.', 'Records of Meetings at the Kremlin, Moscow, October 9–October 17, 1944': Premier papers, 3/434/2.

[3] The house was No. 6, Ostrovskaya Street.

[4] 'Moscow, October 1944' letter of 12 June 1947: Churchill papers, 4/391A.

let off to celebrate the news of the capture of the Hungarian city of Szeged by the Red Army. 'The curtains were drawn back,' John Martin wrote to his wife, 'and we all crowded to the windows to watch the star-shells bursting over the Kremlin, a fantastic display. . . .'[1]

Among the topics discussed over dinner was the next British General Election. Churchill later recalled that 'Stalin said he had "no doubt" about the result: "the Conservatives would win".'[2]

After dinner Churchill spent a few minutes among a large party of Russian, British and American guests who had been waiting outside the dining room: he then withdrew, with Stalin, Molotov and Eden, for a private conference, in which they were later joined by the British Ambassador. During the conversation, Eden telegraphed to Sir Orme Sargent at the Foreign Office, 'Marshal Stalin was at great pains to assure the Prime Minister that failure to relieve Warsaw had not been due to any lack of efforts by the Red Army. Failure was due entirely to the enemy's strength and the difficulties of the terrain.' Stalin told Churchill and Eden that he 'could not admit this failure before the world. Exactly the same situation had arisen at Kiev which in the end had only been liberated by outflanking movement.'

Churchill replied that 'he accepted this view absolutely' and he went on to assure Stalin 'that serious persons in the United Kingdom had not credited the reports that failure had been deliberate. Criticism had only referred to the apparent unwillingness of the Soviet Government to send aircraft.'

Eden's telegram to Orme Sargent continued:

The Prime Minister and I then sought to impress on Marshal Stalin how essential it was in the interests of Anglo-Soviet relations that the Polish question should now be settled on a basis which would seem reasonable to the British people. The Prime Minister emphasised how we had entered the war for the sake of Poland although we had no sordid or material interests in that country. The British people would not understand that she should be let down. The London Poles and the Lublin Poles must now be told that they must agree together. If they refused or were unable to agree, then the British and Soviet Governments, the two Great Allies, must themselves impose a reasonable settlement.[3]

Speaking of Italy, Churchill told Stalin that his attitude to the Italians had been changed by the welcome which the Italian people had given him on his recent visit. When Stalin replied that the same

---

[1] John Martin, letter of 12 October 1944: Martin papers.
[2] Winston S. Churchill, *The Second World War*, volume 6, London 1954, page 200.
[3] 'Hearty' No. 51, No. 2819 from Moscow to the Foreign Office, 'Top Secret', 12 October 1944: Churchill papers, 20/145.

crowd had supported Mussolini, Churchill was 'not pleased', as Eden later recalled. As to Yugoslavia, Stalin reported Tito's view that the Croats and Slovenes 'would refuse to join in any government under King Peter'. His own impression, Stalin commented, was that Peter was 'ineffective'. Eden recalled:

I replied that I was sure the King had courage and I thought that he had intelligence. Mr Churchill interjected that the King was very young. 'How old is he?' asked Stalin. 'Twenty-one,' I answered. 'Twenty-one!' exclaimed Stalin with a burst of pride, 'Peter the Great was ruler of Russia at seventeen.' [1]

During their talk in Moscow, as earlier at Teheran, Churchill had readily conceded Stalin's request for a warm-water port on the Baltic. He was now prepared to see Soviet warships given the peace-time right to go through the Dardanelles and into the Mediterranean, contrary to the pre-war Montreux Convention, which gave Turkey the right to prevent the passage of warships. Eden was doubtful of the wisdom of this concession to Russia, but Churchill defended his decision, minuting to Eden on the following day, with a reference to his continuing suspicions of de Gaulle:

... we have no need to fear the movement of a Russian fleet through the Straits. Even if it were to join de Gaulle, a British fleet and air bases in the Mediterranean will be capable of dealing with either or both. All Russian ships who are on the sea, warships or merchant, are hostages to the stronger naval Power. On the other hand, I think it is like breeding pestilence to try to keep a nation like Russia from free access to the broad waters. [2]

It was not until four o'clock in the early hours of October 12 that Churchill's discussion with Stalin ended. It was then so late that Churchill spent what was left of the night at his town guest house; and on the following morning worked in bed until lunchtime. In a telegram to the War Cabinet that morning, he explained his intentions in having set out the 'percentages' for the Balkans. It was not intended, he stressed, 'to be more than a guide', nor did it attempt 'to set up a rigid system of more than spheres of influence'. It might, however, 'help the United States' to see how its two principal Allies 'feel about these regions when the picture is presented as a whole'. The telegram continued:

Thus it is seen that quite naturally Soviet Russia has vital interests in the countries bordering on the Black Sea by one of whom, Roumania, she has been most wantonly attacked with twenty-six divisions, and with the other of whom, Bulgaria, she has ancient ties. Great Britain feels it right to show

[1] Eden memoirs, *The Reckoning, op. cit.*, page 485.
[2] Prime Minister's Personal Minute, M(Tol) 6/4, 12 October 1944: Churchill papers, 20/153.

particular respect to Russian views about these two countries, and to the Soviet desire to take the lead in a practical way in guiding them in the name of the common cause.

Similarly, Great Britain has a long tradition of friendship with Greece, and a direct interest as a Mediterranean Power in her future. In this war Great Britain lost 30,000 men in trying to resist the German-Italian invasion of Greece, and wishes to play a leading part in guiding Greece out of her present troubles . . .

It was 'understood', Churchill added, that Britain would 'take the lead in a military sense' and try to help the Royal Greek Government to establish itself in Athens 'upon as broad and united a basis as possible'. The Soviet Union, he noted, 'would be ready to concede this position and function to Great Britain in the same sort of way as Britain would recognize the intimate relationship between Russia and Roumania'.

Turning to Hungary, Churchill informed the War Cabinet that as it was the Soviet armies which were 'obtaining control' of Hungary, 'It would be natural that a major share of influence should rest with them, subject of course to agreement with Great Britain and probably the United States, who, though not actually operating in Hungary, must view it as a Central European and not a Balkan State.'

Churchill also explained in this telegram the meaning of 'the numerical symbol 50–50' in the case of Yugoslavia. This, he said, 'is intended to be the foundation of joint action and an agreed policy between the two Powers now closely involved, so as to favour the creation of a united Yugoslavia after all elements there have been joined together to the utmost in driving out the Nazi invaders'. It was intended to prevent, for instance, 'armed strife between the Croats and Slovenes on the one side and powerful and numerous elements in Serbia on the other, and also to produce a joint and friendly policy towards Marshal Tito, while ensuring that weapons furnished to him are used against the common Nazi foe rather than for internal purposes'. Such a policy, Churchill believed, 'pursued in common by Britain and Soviet Russia, without any thought of special advantages to themselves, would be of real benefit'.

In ending this telegram, Churchill stressed that what he described as the 'broad disclosure of Soviet and British feelings' in Roumania, Greece, Hungary and Yugoslavia was 'only an interim guide for the immediate war-time future' and would be 'surveyed' by the Great Powers when they met at the armistice or peace table 'to make a general settlement of Europe'.[1]

[1] No copy of this telegram has survived in the Cabinet Office papers ('Hearty' series). Churchill printed the text in full in Winston S. Churchill, *The Second World War*, volume 6, London 1954,

'Everything is most friendly here, but the Balkans are in a sad tangle'; thus, in a telegram to Harry Hopkins on October 12, Churchill began his explanation of why Averell Harriman had been excluded from these 'percentage' discussions. 'We have so many bones to pick about the Balkans at the present time,' he wrote, 'that we would rather carry the matter a little further à deux in order to be able to talk more bluntly than at a larger gathering.' Churchill went on, however, to explain the Soviet attitude towards Bulgaria, Hungary, Roumania and Greece. They were willing, he said, 'to indict Bulgaria for her many offences, but only in the spirit of a loving parent—"This hurts me more than it does you".' Churchill added, of the three other countries involved:

They are taking great interest in Hungary, which, they mentioned erroneously, was their neighbour. They claim fullest responsibility in Roumania, but are prepared largely to disinterest themselves in Greece. All these matters are being flogged out by Mr Eden and Molotov.

Averell Harriman would, Churchill added, be 'sitting in' on the military discussions, the future of Germany talks, and the 'Polish conversations' as soon as they began.[1]

Churchill remained in his town guest house throughout the morning of October 12. His luncheon visitor was Anthony Eden, who noted in his diary 'an interminable meal of tepid meats and the inevitable cold sucking pig, with soup arriving somewhat near the end'. During their lunch, Eden wrote, Churchill 'held forth about Kings, inveighed against Papandreou, said he would take no more interest in Greece, complained that we were dropping Zog in Albania, etc. I argued that it was impossible to regard kings in most of these Balkan lands as other than coming and going like a Labour Government at home.'

Eden and Churchill also discussed the long unresolved question of whether or not to recognize de Gaulle's Committee of National Liberation as the civilian Government of France. Churchill still resisted giving de Gaulle the supreme authority. 'More argument about France, which didn't advance matters much,' Eden noted, and he added: 'the drip drip of water on a stone.'[2]

---

pages 203–4. It was in fact 'Hearty' No. 62, telegram No. 2842 from Moscow, sent at 5.25 a.m. and received in London at 8 a.m. on 13 October 1944, and sent on to Downing Street at 9.15 a.m. that same morning (information in Cabinet papers, 120/164).

[1] 'Hearty' No. 50, Prime Minister's Personal Telegram, T.1920/4, 'Personal and Top Secret', 12 October 1944: Churchill papers, 20/173.

[2] Eden diary, 12 October 1944: Eden memoirs, The Reckoning, op. cit., page 485.

Eden later reflected: 'My pessimism was exaggerated for no one was wiser than Mr Churchill in giving weight to arguments which he had resisted at the time if, on later reflection, he judged them sound.' [1]

'There is no doubt,' Churchill wrote in his telegram to Roosevelt on October 14, 'that the French had been co-operating with Supreme Headquarters and that their provisional Government has the support of the majority of the French people. I suggest therefore that we can now safely recognize General de Gaulle's administration as the provisional Government of France.' [2]

That evening Churchill prepared to drive out of Moscow to his dacha. Before setting off, he telegraphed to Clementine Churchill, using the coded heading 'Following from Colonel Kent to Mrs Kent':

Everything is going well here and there is great cordiality. Life is however the same and I did not get to bed till 4 a.m. this morning. I have a house in Moscow as well as in the country both splendidly served. I am just off to the country house, 45 minutes away, as we are going to have a quiet night tonight. Love to all. [3]

That night Churchill dined at his dacha with Averell Harriman and his daughter Kathleen.

During the evening, Churchill wrote to Stalin to suggest a time for their military conversations. 'We should like to hear any account you may care to give us,' Churchill wrote, 'of your future projects on the Eastern Front, which have of course a vital influence on our Anglo-American offensives both in the West and in the South.' Churchill added: 'Mr Harriman is with me as I write, and is in accord with the above.' [4]

Churchill and Harriman spent the last hours of the evening playing bezique. Then, in the early hours of October 13, Churchill wrote to his wife of his bezique victory—'four games, two Rubicons', and he added:

This is just a line to tell you how I love you & how sorry I am you are not here. I told Kathleen to tell you all the nice things she has heard about you. I do hope that you are happy w yr & *my* Maria. Give her my dearest love.

It is wonderful to get the London papers the same day at about 6 pm. But the couriers also bring heavy bags & in between meals of 12 or 14 courses & conferences of various kinds. I am hard at it. I am vy well except for a little Indig.

[1] Eden memoirs, *The Reckoning*, *op. cit.*, page 485.

[2] 'Hearty' No. 100, Prime Minister's Personal Telegram, T.1927/4, 'Personal and Top Secret', 14 October 1944: Churchill papers, 20/173.

[3] 'Hearty' No. 62, No. 2842 from Moscow to Foreign Office, sent from Moscow at 5.25 a.m., 13 October 1944: Premier papers, 4/76/1, folio 218.

[4] Letter beginning 'My dear Marshal Stalin', 12 October 1944: Cabinet papers, 120/158.

The affairs go well. We have settled a lot of things about the Balkans & prevented hosts of squabbles that were maturing. The two sets of Poles have arrived & are being kept for the night in two separate cages. Tomorrow we see them—in succession. We shall try our utmost. I have had vy nice talks with the Old Bear. I like him the more I see him. *Now* they respect us here & I am sure they wish to work w us. I have to keep the President in constant touch & this is the delicate side.

'Darling,' Churchill ended, 'you can write anything but war secrets & it reaches me in a few hours. So do send me a letter from yr dear hand.'[1]

On the morning of October 13 Churchill worked all morning in bed, getting up only after luncheon, to drive into Moscow for the opening conference with the Poles, who had arrived from London on the previous evening. There were three of them: Prime Minister Mikolajczyk, Foreign Minister Romer and Professor Stanislaw Grabski, Chairman of the Polish National Council. Churchill was accompanied by Eden and Clark Kerr, Stalin by Molotov and Gousev. Averell Harriman was also present. The conversation, which lasted for two and a half hours, took place at the Spiridonovka Palace, a pre-revolutionary town house built in mock Gothic style, the walls of its conference hall—once a ballroom—covered in white marble.[2] As the delegates assembled, Stalin told Churchill that Soviet forces had captured Riga, and that several German divisions had been cut off in Hungary.

During the course of the discussion, Mikolajczyk pointed out that the Polish Government—his Government—was recognized by Britain and the United States, while the Committee of National Liberation, then in Lublin, was recognized by the Soviet Union. He now proposed a new Government 'of the representatives of both parties'. 'If you want to have relations with the Soviet Government,' Stalin replied, 'you can only do it by recognizing the Curzon Line as the principle.' This the London Poles had hitherto refused to do. The Soviet Union's wartime 'sacrifices', Churchill reiterated, 'and its efforts towards liberating Poland', entitled it to a western frontier along the Curzon Line. Poland would receive 'an equal balance' of territory in the west, 'including a good sea coast, an excellent port in Danzig and valuable raw materials in Silesia'.

[1] Letter of 13 October 1944, 'Moscow': Spencer-Churchill papers.
[2] I am grateful to Professor Oleg Rzheshevsky, of the Soviet Academy of Sciences, for arranging for me to visit this magnificent building in August 1985.

Mikolajczyk would not be swayed from his opposition to the Curzon Line. 'You would form a very bad opinion of me,' he told the Conference, 'were I to agree to ceding 40% of the territory of Poland and five million Poles.' When Stalin replied that it was 'Ukrainian territory and a non-Polish population' which was in question, Mikolajczyk admitted that the total population of the area was eleven million: that is, that the Poles were in a minority. Churchill then appealed once more to Mikolajczyk to accept the Curzon Line, telling the Polish Prime Minister:

I do not think that in this state of affairs it would be in the interest of the Polish Government to estrange themselves from the British Government. In the course of this war we were a hair's breadth from defeat; a sword hung over our heads. We have therefore the right to ask the Poles for a great gesture in the interest of European peace. (He turns to Premier Mikolajczyk.) I hope that you will not hold against me these unpleasant but frank words which I have spoken with the best of intentions.

Mikolajczyk: I have already heard so many unpleasant things in the course of this war that one more will not let me lose my balance.

The discussion then turned to Poland's western frontiers. 'Danzig', Churchill told Mikolajczyk, 'is certainly not worth less to Poland than Lvov', to which Stalin added that 'we, Russians, also speak of including into Poland not only Danzig, but also Stettin'. 'Of course', was Churchill's comment, and he then proposed a compromise formula: 'acceptance of the Curzon Line as the *de facto* eastern frontier of Poland with the right of a final discussion of the matter at the Peace Conference'.

Stalin then declared: 'I want to state categorically that the Soviet Government cannot accept Premier Churchill's formula concerning the Curzon Line,' whereupon Churchill, as the minutes of the meeting recorded, 'makes a gesture of disappointment and helplessness'. Stalin was insistent. There could be no future discussions of the Curzon Line. It 'must be accepted' as the Polish–Soviet frontier. 'One cannot keep changing the frontier, for the social and economic organizations are different here and different in Poland. We have collective farms. . . .' The Curzon Line, Stalin told Mikolajczyk, 'gives you Bialystok, Lomza and Przemysl'.[1]

As the discussion came to an end, Churchill appealed to Mikolajczyk, as Eden reported to the Foreign Office, 'to recognise the fact that His Majesty's Government fully supported Soviet attitude in regard to Poland's eastern frontier not because Soviet Russia is strong but because she is right and because a solution on this basis provides

[1] 'Proceedings of the Moscow Conference on Polish Affairs. First meeting. . . .', 13 October 1944: *Documents on Polish-Soviet Relations, 1939–1945*, volume 2, document 237, pages 405–15.

the best guarantee for future Poland which His Majesty's Government are anxious to see prosperous'. For this reason, Churchill 'urged' Mikolajczyk both 'to enter into friendly contact with the Polish Committee and work out with them a solution of their internal problems' and to accept the Curzon Line 'as a *de facto* boundary line with the right to discuss subsequent adjustments when frontier was finally settled at the Peace Conference'. The last word was Stalin's; the Curzon Line, he said, 'must in any case form basis of final frontier settlement'.[1]

The conference was at an end; Churchill returned to his town house to dine with Eden, Harriman and Clark Kerr. All four men then returned to the Spiridonovka Palace for a conference with the Lublin Poles. This conference also lasted for two and a half hours. Churchill later recalled:

> It was soon plain that the Lublin Poles were mere pawns of Russia. They had learned and rehearsed their part so carefully that even their masters evidently felt they were overdoing it. For instance, M. Bierut, the leader, spoke in these terms: 'We are here to demand on behalf of Poland that Lvov shall belong to Russia. This is the will of the Polish people.' When this had been translated from Polish into English and Russian I looked at Stalin and saw an understanding twinkle in his expressive eyes, as much as to say, 'What about that for our Soviet teaching!' The lengthy contribution of another Lublin leader, Osobka-Morawski, was equally depressing.[2]

'They seemed creepy to me,' Eden later recalled of the Lublin Committee representatives. ' "The rat and the weasel", I murmured to the Prime Minister in reference to two of them, Bierut and Osobka-Morawski, who were fulsome, not to say servile, to the Russians.'[3]

The British Government's aims and interests, Churchill told Bierut and Morawski, 'were to achieve unison of all Poles against the Germans and to ensure a future home worthy of Polish people'. He was 'distressed' at the quarrels 'which had grown up among Poles at this stage of the war. The world was growing tired of such quarrels.' By reason of 'their consistent support' of Poles and the Polish Government since September 1939, Churchill added, 'His Majesty's Government were entitled to call upon all Poles to play their part in reaching a friendly settlement.'

Bierut, 'supported by M. Morawski', as Eden telegraphed to London, then 'embarked upon a long catalogue of grievances against Mikolajczyk'. Eden's telegram continued: 'M. Bierut and M. Morawski did not make a good impression. The Prime Minister chided

[1] 'Hearty' No. 106, sent at 10.55 p.m., 14 October 1944: Cabinet papers, 120/158.
[2] Winston S. Churchill, *The Second World War*, volume 6, London 1954, page 205.
[3] Eden memoirs, *The Reckoning*, op. cit., page 486.

them and made repeated appeals to adopt a less cantankerous and more friendly and constructive attitude. Marshal Stalin supported the Prime Minister's appeal for unity and agreed that the constitutional issue must not form an obstacle to a settlement.' Eden added that Stalin 'gave the impression of being chiefly concerned to secure acceptance of Curzon Line which the Representatives readily conceded, and of caring little about the Committee's domestic ambition'.[1]

Two days later Churchill sent an account of these Polish discussions to the King, informing him that:

The day before yesterday was 'all Poles day'. Our lot from London are, as Your Majesty knows, a decent but feeble lot of fools but the delegates from Lublin seem to be the greatest villains imaginable. They could hardly have been under any illusions as to our opinion of them. They appeared to me to be purely tools and recited their parts with well-drilled accuracy. I cross-examined them fairly sharply and on several points Marshal Stalin backed me up.

'We shall be wrestling with our Poles all today,' Churchill added, 'and there are some hopes that we may get a settlement. If not we shall have to hush the matter up and spin it out until after the presidential election.'[2]

That evening, the sky above Moscow was again lit by fireworks, this time to celebrate the entry of the Red Army into Riga.

Half an hour after midnight, Churchill, Eden, Harriman and Clark Kerr returned to Churchill's town house. After a short talk together, all but Harriman left; he stayed, talking and playing bezique with the Prime Minister, until about a quarter to three, when Churchill went to bed.

---

[1] 'Hearty' No. 107, No. 2908 from Moscow to Foreign Office, 'Top Secret', sent at 9.45 p.m., 14 October 1944: Cabinet papers, 120/165.
[2] 'Hearty' No. 114, No. 2935 from Moscow to the Foreign Office, 'Top Secret', 15 October 1944: Cabinet papers, 120/165.

54

'Hunter with bow against a bear'

O N the morning of 14 October 1944, in his Moscow town house, Churchill 'wandered into the office', Marian Holmes noted, 'very sleepy-eyed in his dressing gown'. Her account continued: 'Followed him back to his bedroom with some telegrams. He asked if I would be going to the ballet tonight. Said I hoped so. He said "of course you *must* go". Poured him another cup of tea. He said "That's right. The hand that rocks the cradle ought to be able to pour me a cup of tea." He had been eating chicken with his fingers. Sawyers brought him a finger bowl. "What's this?" "To wash your hands, Sir." "Good heavens! I'm going to wash me whole body in a minute."' [1]

Shortly before noon on October 14, Churchill went to the British Embassy to discuss the situation with the London Poles. He again urged them to accept the Curzon Line, telling them, as Eden telegraphed to London, that in his opinion 'the crux of the situation was the Curzon Line. If the Poles could accept that as a basis for a settlement of the eastern frontier other issues such as constitutional problems and the composition of the new Polish Government would be resolved since Marshal Stalin clearly regarded these as subsidiary and would be able to persuade the Lublin Poles to adopt a reasonable attitude.'

Churchill then 'strongly urged' Mikolajczyk 'to take the responsibility of making a courageous decision'. This was Mikolajczyk's 'last chance of retrieving the situation'. Churchill added:

The three Great Powers who had expended their blood and treasure in order to liberate Poland for the second time in a generation were entitled to insist that a matter of domestic concern to the Poles should not be allowed to become the cause of friction among them. If Mr Mikolajczyk accepted the Curzon Line and returned to Poland he would enjoy our full support and a British Ambassador would be accredited to him. If he refused, the Prime

[1] Marian Holmes diary, 14 October 1944: Marian Walker Spicer papers.

Minister would be obliged to declare to Parliament that the present talks with the Soviet Government had broken down through Mr Mikolajczyk's fault and that in consequence His Majesty's Government could do no more for him.[1]

Churchill then told the three Poles, as the Polish record of the discussion noted:

Our relations with Russia are much better than they have ever been. I talked to General Anders the other day to whom I took great liking. He entertains the hope that after the defeat of Germany the Russians will be beaten. This is crazy, you cannot defeat the Russians.

I beg you to settle upon the frontier question. You must take responsibilities. If you reach a formula with me I'll go to Stalin at 4 p.m.

What is there else beside the frontier question? It means compensation in the west and the disentanglement of populations. If you agree on the frontier then the Russians will withdraw the support from the Committee. When I criticized the Lublin Poles last night Stalin on many occasions supported me. You are really dealing with Russia. The word 'basis' is very helpful; we were nearly at it in January. If you do not agree now that means that you are going to use again the 'Liberum Veto' which shattered the independence of Poland. What does it matter supposing you lose the support of some of the Poles? Think what you will gain in return! Ambassadors will come. The British Ambassador will be with you. The Americans will have an Ambassador, the greatest military power in the world. You must do this. If you miss this moment everything will be lost.

In reply, Mikolajczyk said that he and his Government could not decide 'to deprive ourselves of Polish territory', nor to agree to join the Lublin Committee. 'Should I sign a death sentence against myself,' he asked. Churchill's patience was nearly exhausted, as the Polish Government's minutes recorded:

Churchill (angrily): I wash my hands off; as far as I am concerned we shall give the business up. Because of quarrels between Poles we are not going to wreck the peace of Europe. In your obstinacy you do not see what is at stake. It is not in friendship that we shall part. We shall tell the world how unreasonable you are. You will start another war in which 25 million lives will be lost. But you don't care.

Mikolajczyk tried to argue that agreement on the Curzon Line by the Lublin Committee 'does not change anything', but Churchill was emphatic that it was the last chance for an independent Poland. 'Unless you accept the frontier,' he warned, 'you are out of business forever. The Russians will sweep through your country and your people will be liquidated. You are on the verge of annihilation.'

Once there was an 'understanding' on the Curzon Line, Eden inter-

---

[1] 'Hearty' No. 122, No. 2943 from Moscow to the Foreign Office, 'Top Secret', sent at 8.36 a.m., 16 October 1944: Cabinet papers, 120/165.

vened, 'on all the other things you will get agreement from the Russians. You will get a guarantee from us.' The conversation continued, still heated:

Churchill: Poland will be guaranteed by the three Great Powers and certainly by us. The American Constitution makes it difficult for the President to commit the US. In any case you are not giving up anything because the Russians are there already.

Mikolajczyk: We are losing everything.

Churchill: The Pripet marshes and 5 million people. The Ukrainians are not your people. You are saving your own people and enabling us to act with vigour.

Mikolajczyk: If we are going to lose independence, must we sign this?

Churchill: You have only one thing to do. It makes the greatest difference if you agree.

Mikolajczyk: Would it not be possible to proclaim that the three Great Powers have decided on the frontiers of Poland without our presence?

Churchill: We will be sick and tired of you if you go on arguing.

If Mikolajczyk would accept the Curzon Line, Churchill said, he might be able to get 'better than fifty fifty' for the composition of the Polish Government 'consolidation' with the Lublin Committee. 'I think I ought to get 60:40.' It was the Polish Government's 'fault', Churchill declared, 'that the Lublin Poles have come into existence', and he added: 'With regard to the frontiers, think what you get in Silesia.' But Mikolajczyk was reluctant to concede any point of the argument. As the record noted:

Mikolajczyk explains that the eastern territories do not contain mere marshes and non-arable land. On the contrary. The province of Tarnopol, for instance, has the most fertile soil among all the provinces. On the other hand, Eastern Prussia is a poor country, full of lakes and marshes.

Churchill: If you accept the frontier the USA will take a great interest in the rehabilitation of Poland and may grant you a big loan after this war possibly without interest. As to ourselves we shall be poor after this war. At any rate I will try to get for you the best possible solution.

Churchill left the room to prepare a draft declaration, which the Poles could accept, and which he could then take to Stalin. The declaration would commit the Polish Government to the Curzon Line, but would not make explicit the territorial compensation. 'Publication at present of what it is intended to take away from the Germans in the East,' Churchill explained on his return, 'would arouse the German fury and this would cost many human lives. On the other hand if the agreement between Poland and Russia is not reached now, it would also cause victims in human beings.'

Churchill then read the draft of his declaration, telling the Poles that he intended to say to Stalin: 'If I can procure the agreement of the Polish Government to this, will you back it up and support it in the letter and in the spirit?' Churchill continued, as the Polish minute recorded:

If Stalin's answer is negative or unsatisfactory, and I doubt if it would be, you'll lose nothing, on the contrary you'll go back to London strengthened and will continue to have our support. If, on the other hand, Stalin thinks that it is all right, then I would put off the meeting with the Lublin Poles in the presence of Eden, Molotov and the representatives of the USA. You are bound to accept the decision of the Great Powers.

Mikolajczyk says that he cannot agree to the word 'accept'.

Churchill (angrily and with a gesture of impatience): I take no interest in you.

Mikolajczyk once again explains the reasons why he cannot express his consent to Churchill's formula.

Churchill: Everything is in the word 'accept'.

When Romer asked Churchill directly whether, if he were in their position, he would agree to the frontiers on which Stalin was so emphatic, Churchill replied: 'I certainly would.' If he agreed to those frontiers, Churchill added, he would 'be blessed by future generations if I were in your situation', and he went on to ask the Poles: 'Look, what is the alternative? You are threatened with virtual extinction, you will be effaced as a nation.'

At that moment Professor Grabski took the seat near Churchill and expounded to him in French his opinion on the solution of the Russo-Polish conflict. For thirty years, he told Churchill, he had been struggling for friendly relations between Poland and Russia. The minutes of the meeting continued:

Grabski explains the importance to Poland of Lvov and of the oil fields in particular and concludes with the expression of the view that the public opinion of Poland would not be able to understand and to agree to that paradox that Poland, who first opposed German aggression, would be diminished in her territory after the war.

Churchill (ironically). 'Rien ne peut empêcher la Pologne de déclarer la guerre à la Russie lorsque celle-ci sera dépourvue du soutien des autres Puissances. . . . Qu'est-ce que c'est l'opinion publique? Le droit d'être écrasé! . . . Je veux sauver la fleur de la nation polonaise.'[1]

Mr Churchill before he leaves addresses Mikolajczyk with sympathy and mentioning the Committee says: 'I don't envy you. I took a considerable dislike to them.'

It was nearly two o'clock in the afternoon. The discussion had been

[1] 'Nothing can prevent Poland from declaring war on Russia' when Poland will be deprived of the help of the other Powers. . . . What is public opinion? The right to be crushed! . . . I wish to save the flower of the Polish nation.'

going on for more than two hours. The Polish delegation now retired to a room in the British Embassy to discuss the British draft. 'Ultimately,' the minutes recorded, 'it was agreed that the Polish side could not express their consent for the acceptance of the Curzon Line. . . .'[1]

Churchill returned to his town house for lunch with Eden. At three o'clock Mikolajczyk arrived, and for forty minutes tried to explain why the Curzon Line was unacceptable. Churchill replied, in what the Polish minutes of the conversation called 'a very violent manner':

You are no Government if you are incapable of taking any decision. You are callous people who want to wreck Europe. I shall leave you to your own troubles. You have no sense of responsibility when you want to abandon your people at home, to whose sufferings you are indifferent. You do not care about the future of Europe, you have only your own miserable interests in mind. I will have to call on the other Poles and this Lublin Government may function very well. It will be *the Government*. It is a criminal attempt to wreck, by your 'Liberum Veto', agreement between the Allies. It is cowardice on your part.

To Mikolajczyk's suggestion that Churchill could present his declaration 'as his own proposal', regarding which the Polish Government would confine itself to a purely formal protest, Churchill 'retorted': 'I am not going to worry Stalin. If you want to conquer Russia we shall leave you to do it. I feel as if I were in a lunatic asylum. I don't know whether the British Government will continue to recognize you.'

Churchill then declared 'with passion' that Britain was 'powerless in the face of Russia'. To Mikolajczyk's remark that the Polish Government had to reserve for itself the right to defend the interests of Poland at the Peace Conference, Churchill replied:

You are not going to be in a better position at the Peace Conference, I cannot speak for the American Government. The USA is not represented here.

In the last war more Poles fought against us than for us. In this war what is your contribution to the Allied effort? What did you throw into the common pool? You may withdraw your divisions if you like. You are absolutely incapable of facing facts. Never in my life have I seen such people.

As the Polish record of the meeting recorded, Churchill then quoted General Anders' words, 'after having beaten the Germans we shall beat the Muscovites' and said with emphasis: 'You hate the Russians, I know you hate them.'

In spite of Romer's remark that the fact of the Polish delegation staying in Moscow gave the 'direct lie' to the assertion of Polish hatred

[1] 'Notes on Conversation between M. Mikolajczyk and Mr Churchill. . . .', 14 October 1944: *Documents on Polish-Soviet Relations, 1939–1945*, volume 2, document 239, pages 416–22.

towards the Russians and to the alleged unwillingness of the Poles to come to an understanding with the Russians, Churchill kept 'stubbornly' repeating: 'You hate the Russians.'

At one point, in desperation, Churchill told Mikolajczyk that if the Polish delegation was not prepared to accept the Curzon Line, then its return to London 'would serve no purpose', to which Mikolajczyk commented that he 'fully realized that the Polish Government would not be able to continue to reside in London'.

It was 4.20 in the afternoon. The conversation, or rather the recriminations, were interrupted, perhaps fortunately, by John Martin, who announced that Stalin would receive Churchill in ten minutes time. 'Mr Churchill went out in a hurry,' the Polish record continued, 'hardly bidding anyone goodbye. . . .'[1]

Churchill spent an hour with Stalin alone except for their interpreters. In a bold attempt to break the deadlock, and to preserve Polish independence, he put to Stalin a draft formula for an all-Party Polish Government, made up of London Poles and Lublin Poles in equal number, as well as Polish acceptance of the Curzon Line, in return for territorial compensation at Germany's expense. It was Churchill's intention, Eden informed Cadogan, to ask Stalin 'whether, if the Polish Government assented to a declaration on these lines, Marshal Stalin would be ready to participate in it'.

Churchill put this proposal to Stalin, and Stalin, so Eden reported, 'agreed in principle to a solution on the lines proposed'.[2] All now depended upon Churchill being able to persuade Mikolajczyk to accept the Curzon Line.

Shortly after six o'clock that evening, Churchill went to a concert at the Bolshoi Theatre, 'a special performance of the ballet', Churchill informed the King, 'which was very fine'. He himself had received 'a prolonged ovation from an enormous audience'. Presently, Churchill added, 'when Marshal Stalin came into the box for the first time in this war', and stood beside Churchill, 'there was an almost passionate demonstration'.[3]

Kathleen Harriman, who had been among the first to arrive in the

[1] 'Notes on a conversation concerning the Curzon Line. . . .', 14 October 1944: *Documents on Polish-Soviet Relations, 1939–1945*, volume 2, document 241, pages 423–4.
[2] 'Hearty' No. 122, Telegram No. 2943 from Moscow to the Foreign Office, 'Top Secret', sent at 8.36 a.m., 16 October 1944: Cabinet papers, 120/158.
[3] 'Hearty' No. 114, No. 2935 from Moscow, 15 October 1944: Cabinet papers, 120/165.

royal box, with her father, described the scene in a letter to Pamela Churchill:

The PM arrived later, with UJ coming in some minutes afterward, so the audience didn't realize they were there till the lights went on after the first act. A cheer went up (something I've never seen happen here) and UJ ducked out so that the PM could have all the applause for himself, which was a very nice gesture. But the PM sent Vyshinski out to get UJ back and they stood together while the applause went on for many minutes. It was most, most impressive, the sound like a cloudburst on a tin roof. It came from below and above on all sides and the people down in the audience said they were thrilled at seeing the two men standing together. Perhaps this may sound odd to you but that night was the first time probably that most of the audience had seen either man. Stalin hasn't been to the theatre since the war started and for him to go with a foreigner was even more amazing.

The performance began with the first act of *Giselle*, followed after an interval by two hours' singing and dancing by the Red Army Choir. 'I noticed the PM thoroughly enjoying the martial songs,' noted Marian Holmes, 'and beating time to them with his hands. Stalin didn't change his personal expression at all. . . .'[1] Between the two acts there was a dinner, at which the mood was a lighthearted one. When someone spoke of the Big Three as the 'Holy Trinity', Stalin remarked: 'If that is so, Churchill must be the Holy Ghost. He flies around so much.'[2]

Eden, who was with Churchill during this short meal, later recalled:

Towards the end of an interval for refreshment the Prime Minister and I were shown where we could wash our hands. Here Mr Churchill suddenly became excited by a thought which came to him to help in the Polish dilemma and he began to expound it eagerly to me. After repeated efforts I had at last to stop him with a reminder that the audience must have been waiting quite a while. When we returned to the box the Russians, scrupulous hosts as ever, made no comment.

However, three nights later Stalin asked us both up to his flat for supper. As we came into the little entrance hall, he nodded to a door in the corner saying: 'That's where you can wash your hands if you want to, the place as I understand it where you English like to conduct your political discussions.'[3]

Listening to the BBC radio news on the following day, Clementine Churchill wrote to her husband of how 'there was a vivid description of your visit to the Moscow Opera House in company with "the old

[1] Marian Holmes diary, 14 October 1944: Marian Walker Spicer papers.
[2] Abel and Harriman, *op. cit.*, page 362.
[3] Eden memoirs, *The Reckoning, op. cit.*, page 487.

Bear". I wish I could have witnessed this hard-won recognition of your continuing & persistent work.'[1]

From the Bolshoi Theatre, Churchill returned for a few minutes to his town house, before going on to the Kremlin for a conference on military subjects. The meeting was held, with Stalin present, in Molotov's study, and began with Brooke describing the military situation on the French, Italian and Burmese fronts. Brooke was followed by Major-General Deane, who described the Pacific war, and General Antonov, the Deputy Chief of the General Staff of the Red Army, who described the situation on the Russian front. General Deane then asked Stalin three questions, on behalf of the American Chief of Staff: 'how soon after the defeat of Germany would Russia declare war on Japan, how long would the Soviet far eastern forces need before they could take the offensive, and how much of the capacity of the Trans-Siberian railway could be devoted to the build up and support of an American strategic air force?'[2] 'Young man,' Churchill said to Deane, 'I admire your nerve in asking Stalin those last three questions. I have no idea that you will get an answer, but there was certainly no harm in asking.'[3]

At one moment in the military discussion, Stalin gave an assurance, as Churchill reported to Attlee two days later, that the operations of the Russian armies would be pressed 'vigorously and continuously into Germany, and that we need not have the slightest anxiety that the Germans would be able to withdraw any troops from their Eastern Front'.[4] For his part, Churchill assured Stalin that if the Germans were to withdraw into Switzerland, 'we should, of course, follow them'.

The discussion then turned to the Italian front and the Balkans. The Russians, said Stalin, 'did not propose to advance westward into Yugoslavia. They would prefer to join hands with General Alexander's forces in Austria.' He 'could not tell', Churchill commented, 'how soon General Alexander would be in Vienna, though he would push forward as quickly as possible'.[5]

From this military meeting, which ended shortly after midnight,

---

[1] Letter of 15 October 1944: Spencer-Churchill papers.

[2] 'Tolstoy', 'First Military Meeting', 'Minutes of a Meeting held in the Kremlin at 10 p.m. on Saturday, 14th October', 15 October 1944: Premier papers, 3/434/5, also Cabinet papers, 127/34. The British present were Churchill, Brooke, Ismay and Lieutenant General Burrows (head of No. 30 Military Mission); the Americans present were Harriman and Deane; the Russians, Stalin, Molotov, Army General Antonov and Lieutenant-General Shevchenko (Chief of Staff of the Soviet Army in the Far East).

[3] Abel and Harriman, *op. cit.*, page 363.

[4] 'Hearty' No. 132, No. 2954 from Moscow to the Foreign Office, 'Top Secret', 16 October 1944: Cabinet papers, 120/165.

[5] 'Tolstoy', 'First Military Meeting', 'Minutes of a Meeting held in the Kremlin at 10 p.m. on Saturday, 14 October, 1944', 15 October 1944: Cabinet papers, 127/34.

Churchill returned to his town guest house, where he talked 'for some time' with Harriman, before going to bed.[1]

When Churchill awoke on the morning of October 15, he was in considerable discomfort, the victim of a violent attack of diarrhoea. 'Russian specialists were called in,' noted Marian Holmes.[2] That morning Churchill remained in bed until shortly after midday, when Mikolajczyk and Romer arrived to discuss the proposal which Churchill had put to Stalin. Oliver Harvey, who was present throughout the discussion, recorded in his diary, referring to Mikolajczyk as 'Mick':

We first went through the document which PM had shown Stalin guaranteeing to Poland E. Prussia, Danzig, Oppeln and up to Oder in West in return for acceptance of Curzon Line in East, together with a united Polish Government in Lublin, with which both HMG and Soviet Government would deal. This document the PM now wished to be authorized to give to Stalin as having been accepted by the Poles.

Poles first asked for Stettin. PM was ready to give this, but AE demurred because of British opinion and effect on Germany. But the final blow came when Mick said he could not agree to PM giving the document to Stalin unless it gave the Poles Lvov too. PM blew up and rated Mick most soundly as unrealistic, as sacrificing his people and his country for a single town, as irresponsibly sowing the seeds of future wars.

Nothing would move Mick who sat impassive while the PM raged. From time to time things were calmer but then the storm blew up again until the PM lost his temper. Up and down the room he paced, threatening and cursing 'I will have nothing more to do with you.' 'I don't care where you go.' 'You only deserve to be in your Pripet marshes.' 'I shall indict you.' All through this Mick remained firm and impassive. He said he could agree to nothing which did not include Lvov.[3]

'The Prime Minister and I emphasised with all the force at our disposal,' Eden telegraphed to the Foreign Office, 'that the amendment would render the draft completely unacceptable to the Soviet Government,' nor, said Churchill, could he undertake to give Stalin 'any revised draft in which it was embodied'. Churchill did offer, however, 'to make an appeal to Marshal Stalin in the interests of Anglo-Soviet relations and the effect of such a gesture upon world opinion towards the USSR, to agree to the retention of Lvov, by

---

[1] Private Office diary, 14 October 1944.
[2] Marian Holmes diary, 14 October 1944: Marian Walker Spicer papers.
[3] Harvey diary, 15 October 1944: John Harvey (editor), *The War Diaries of Oliver Harvey*, London 1978, pages 361–2.

Poland. He could however only do so if he were authorised to hand him the document without reference to Lvov in the event of the appeal having failed.'

The Polish Prime Minister declined, however, Eden reported, 'to give such an authority'.[1] 'Finally,' noted Oliver Harvey, 'the PM left the room, and we showed the Poles to their car.'

'A painful scene to witness,' wrote Oliver Harvey, 'the PM so right and the Poles so foolish—like Bourbons expecting everything to come back to them.'[2]

That afternoon Churchill developed a fever, and was forced to spend the rest of the day in bed. He was therefore unable to attend the second Military Meeting, where he was represented by Eden. Also present was Ismay, who, in a telegram to Attlee, described how Stalin made it clear that the Russians intended to enter the war against Japan 'as soon after the defeat of Germany as they can collect the necessary forces in the Far East, and when adequate stocks of materials have been accumulated'.[3] Stalin added that he was 'not anxious about the effect which these preparations would have on the Japanese. In fact, he expressed the hope that the Japanese would make a "premature attack" as this would provide an incentive to the Russians to fight their best.' Ismay added that Stalin 'has evidently some claims against the Japanese'. The Russians, Stalin explained, 'would have to know what they were fighting for'.[4]

As Churchill's temperature rose above 100°, Cairo was alerted, and three doctors including Brigadier Bedford were instructed by Lord Moran to fly to Moscow that evening, together with two nurses.[5] There was welcome news for Churchill, however, in one of the messages which was brought to his bedside, a telegram from General Maitland Wilson reporting that the Germans had evacuated Athens 'night 13th/14th October', and that a detachment of the Second Special Air

---

[1] 'Hearty' No. 122, No. 2943 from Moscow to the Foreign office, 'Top Secret', sent at 8.36 a.m., 16 October 1944: Cabinet papers, 120/158.

[2] Harvey diary, 15 October 1944: John Harvey (editor), *op. cit.*, page 361.

[3] Stalin spoke of 'several months'. The impression, Ismay noted, was that this would be a period of three to four months. The war against Germany ended, for the Soviet Union, on 9 May 1945. The Soviet declaration of war on Japan was made on 8 August 1945. Japan surrendered on 15 August 1945.

[4] As a result of the war with Japan, Russia acquired the southern Sakhalin islands.

[5] 'Top Secret', 'Immediate', 15 October 1944: Cabinet papers, 120/160. The doctors were Brigadier Bedford, Colonel Findlay and Lieutenant-Colonel Scadding. The nurses were Miss K. Macleod and Miss J. E. Marsdon.

Service Brigade with 'Jellicoe patrols'[1] had entered the Greek capital from the west, and Commandos together with Greek troops from the south, on October 14. The main body of 'Manna', Wilson added, 'moves in today by sea and air'.

Wilson told Churchill that Athens was reported 'quiet' but with the EAM 'showing truculence'. This, he said, 'should disappear with arrival of more British troops enabling population to overcome their fears'. In Patras, where an EAM procession had been 'gazed at in silence', the British troops had been received 'with acclamation'.[2]

Still feeling ill, Churchill remained in bed throughout the evening of October 15. That night, shortly before 11 o'clock, he called for Elizabeth Layton and asked her, as she wrote in her diary, 'if I'd like to read to him!!!!' Her account continued:

> He very seldom reads a book these days, but he has one at present called *Primer of the Coming World* by Leopold Schwarzschild, all about finance capitalists, the influence of capitalism on wars, the prospects of preventing Germany from starting another war, and so forth. And believe me, I sat there for an hour and a quarter and let off this stuff, enunciating with meticulous care. Every now and then he would say 'What was that', but I knew he really heard and it was only to show that he hadn't gone to sleep—for he sat there in bed with a black bandage over his eyes to enable him to concentrate better. God's teeth, it was quite a strain, but certainly an experience that I'm glad to have had![3]

Waking up on the morning of October 16 with his temperature returned to normal, Churchill at once countermanded Lord Moran's orders for the despatch of doctors and nurses from Cairo.[4] That morning, Churchill telegraphed to Papandreou: 'The liberation of Athens, the city in which democracy was born, is a fitting symbol of resurgence of security throughout oppressed Europe.'[5] Eight hours later Churchill learnt from Maitland Wilson that the headquarters of the Special Air Service brigade, together with two battalions of British troops, had reached Athens, and had taken over from Jellicoe. 'British troops had received an enthusiastic welcome,' Wilson added. 'City well under control with only a few disturbances in outlying districts.'

---

[1] George Jellicoe (2nd Earl), commanding the First Special Air Service Regiment, had earlier been parachuted into Rhodes, in September 1943, in an unsuccessful attempt to persuade the Italian garrison to join the Allies.

[2] 'Drastic' No. 114, 'Top Secret and Personal', 15 October 1944: Churchill papers, 20/173.

[3] Elizabeth Layton, letter of 30 October 1944: Nel papers.

[4] 'Top Secret', 16 October 1944: Cabinet papers, 120/160. 'I had a touch of fever on Sunday night', Churchill telegraphed to his wife on October 17, 'but it came from the tummy and not from the chest, and I am now quite well again'. ('Hearty' No. 157, 'Top Secret', Telegram No. 3005 from Moscow to the Foreign Office, 17 October 1944: Premier papers, 4/76/1, folio 179.)

[5] 'Hearty' No. 126, Prime Minister's Personal Telegram, T.1931/4, 16 October 1944: Churchill papers, 20/173.

The seaborne 'Manna' force, delayed by an 'unexpected minefield', would arrive that same day.[1]

With Churchill too ill to leave his bed on October 15, it was Eden who saw Stalin and Molotov that evening, to try to reach a compromise over the future of Lvov. But in a telegram describing his meeting, Eden reported that when he had asked Stalin if he could 'help me' over Lvov, Stalin 'immediately replied that he was very sorry but this was impossible. The Poles could not get away with that. He could not betray the Ukrainians. He was an old man and could not be expected to go to his grave under the stigma of one who had betrayed the Ukrainians.'[2]

Churchill felt well enough on October 16 to re-enter the Polish discussions, trying once more, with Eden, to find a formula on the Curzon Line acceptable to both Stalin and Mikolajczyk. 'I pray for results with the Poles,' Clementine Churchill had written on the night of October 15.[3] Her prayers seemed answered during the morning of October 16, when the Poles seemed to agree, in conversation with Eden at the British Embassy, that they would accept the Curzon Line provided that it could be described, as Oliver Harvey noted, 'not as a frontier but as a demarcation line'.

At three o'clock that afternoon Eden and Harvey took Mikolajczyk and Romer to see Churchill, who was, Harvey wrote, 'much more kindly to the Poles'. Churchill promised to put the new formula to Stalin with 'demarcation' line and not a 'frontier' line, 'and to do his best'.[4]

At five o'clock Churchill and Eden went to see Stalin at the Kremlin. The only other person present was Stalin's interpreter, Pavlov. In two and a quarter hours Churchill tried to persuade Stalin to accept the 'demarcation line' formula, but his advocacy was in vain. 'The Prime Minister used all possible arguments,' Eden reported to the Foreign Office, 'but was unable to move him.'[5] Stalin not only wanted the Curzon Line to be the new Soviet frontier with Poland, but to be described as such. Until this was accepted, he would not allow the formation of a united Polish Government made up of London Poles and Lublin Poles in coalition. He and Molotov, Stalin told Churchill in the course of the conversation, were 'the only two of

[1] 'Drastic' No. 122, 'Top Secret and Personal', 16 October 1944: Churchill papers, 20/173.
[2] 'Hearty' No. 124, No. 2945 from Moscow to the Foreign Office, 'Top Secret', sent at 6.56 a.m., 16 October 1944: Cabinet papers, 120/158. During the discussion about Lvov, Stalin told Eden: 'That Mr Mikolajczyk was so obstinate that he thought he must be of Finnish origin.'
[3] Letter of 15 October 1944: Spencer-Churchill papers.
[4] Harvey diary, 16 October 1944: John Harvey (editor), op. cit., page 362.
[5] 'Hearty' No. 170, No. 3029 from Moscow to the Foreign Office, 'Top Secret', sent at 11.42 a.m., 18 October 1944: Cabinet papers, 120/158.

those he worked with' who were favourable to dealing 'softly' with Mikolajczyk. 'I am sure,' Churchill reported to Attlee, 'there are strong pressures in the background, both party and military.' Churchill's account of his discussion with Stalin continued:

In one way and another I have uncovered to him all the dangers we see from the festering sore of Soviet-Polish affairs, and I regret it desirable to proceed with attempt to form a united Polish Government without frontier question being agreed. Had this been settled he was quite willing that Mikolajczyk should head the new Government. I myself consider difficulties not less obstinate would arise in discussion for a merger of the Polish Government with Lublin Poles, whose representatives made worst possible impression on Foreign Secretary and me and whom I consider, as I told Stalin, 'only an expression of Soviet will'. They have no doubt also the ambition of ruling Poland and are thus a kind of inverted Quislings.[1]

That night Churchill saw Mikolajczyk once more, their sixth meeting in three days, and urged him to agree to the word 'frontier'. But Mikolajczyk would not do so, and, as Churchill had explained to Stalin that afternoon, almost certainly could not do so without being 'repudiated by his own people'.

One more day of negotiations remained, and on the morning of October 17, Mikolajczyk told Eden he was willing to discuss the matter with the leaders of the Lublin Poles. Churchill, meanwhile, urged Maitland Wilson not to proceed with the appointment of a new Polish Commander-in-Chief, in succession to General Sosnkowski. 'The appointment of General Anders for instance,' Churchill telegraphed to Wilson, 'would be fatal to any hopes of Polish-Russian agreement.'[2] In a letter to Stalin that morning, Churchill put the case for Mikolajczyk. 'I am more than ever convinced,' Churchill wrote, 'of his desire to reach an understanding with you and with the National Committee, despite the very real difficulties that confront him.' Churchill asked Stalin to see Mikolajczyk, who wished 'to tell you what his plans now are and to seek your advice', and he added: 'The conversations which I have had with him since I saw you lead me to press this request most strongly upon you.'

Churchill ended his letter on a personal note, telling Stalin 'what a great pleasure it has been to me to find ourselves talking on the difficult and often unavoidably painful topics of State policy with so much ease and mutual understanding'.[3]

---

[1] 'Hearty' No. 167, Telegram No. 3023 from Moscow to the Foreign Office, 'Personal and Top Secret', 17 October 1944: Cabinet papers, 120/165.

[2] 'Hearty' No. 158, Prime Minister's Personal Telegram, T.1935/4, 'Personal and Top Secret', 17 October 1944: Churchill papers, 20/173.

[3] Letter of 17 October 1944: Churchill papers, 20/138.

Stalin did see Mikolajczyk, as Churchill asked, 'and had $1\frac{1}{4}$ hours very friendly talk', Churchill telegraphed to Roosevelt four days later. Churchill's telegram continued: 'Stalin promised to help him and Mik promised to form and conduct a Government thoroughly friendly to the Russians. He explained his plan but Stalin made it clear that the Lublin Poles must have the majority.'[1]

On October 17 Churchill and Stalin held their final conference. It lasted from ten in the evening until four in the morning. Eden, Clark Kerr and Molotov were also present. Shortly before the meeting began, news had reached Moscow that Admiral Horthy had been arrested by the Germans as a precaution now that the whole German front in Hungary was disintegrating. Churchill told Stalin that he hoped the Ljubljana Gap could be reached 'as fast as possible', but added that he did not think the war would be over before the spring.

Churchill then told Stalin 'that he hoped the Marshal understood what powerful blows were being delivered by our Air forces in the West. We were destroying whole cities: they were advance bases for the Army.' On Duisburg, 10,000 tons of bombs had been dropped in twelve hours. That, said Stalin, 'was good'.

Churchill then 'recalled', as the minutes of the meeting noted, that Britain was sending back to Russia 11,000 'Soviet ex-prisoners of war'. These were Russians captured in the west as German military units surrendered. Many of these Russians, said Stalin, 'had been made to fight for the Germans while others had done so willingly', whereupon Churchill 'pointed out the difficulty for the British authorities in separating the two'.

The discussion turned finally to the future of Germany. 'Prussia was the root of the evil,' said Churchill, 'and the Prussian military caste.' Prussia should therefore be isolated, and Allied control set up over the Ruhr and Saar. 'First,' said Churchill, 'it was necessary to take away all the machinery and machine tools that Russia, Belgium, Holland and France needed. He would support Marshal Stalin in repairing the damage to Russia's Western provinces which had suffered so much. It was only fair. The same applied to the smaller Allies. This was the policy which Mr Morgenthau had laid before the President—to put the Ruhr and Saar out of action.'

Churchill then turned to Britain's own economic problems, asking Stalin:

Why should not the British make the things needed by Europe in fair competition with other countries? After this war Great Britain would be the

---

[1] 'Hearty' No. 264, Prime Minister's Personal Telegram, T.1946/4, 21 October 1944: Churchill papers, 20/173.

only great debtor nation. Foreign securities amounting to £400,000,000 had been sold. Sterling debts now amounted to £3,000 million. She would have to make every effort to increase her exports to buy food. Russia's intention to take away German machinery was in harmony with Great Britain's interest in filling in the gap left by Germany. This was only justice.

Stalin agreed: he would, he said, 'support any steps taken by Britain to receive compensation for the losses she had suffered'.

Churchill then told Stalin that he would support Russia 'in getting the machine tools required by the Ukraine and other ravaged regions', and he added: 'He would not trust Germany with the development of her metallurgy, chemical or electrical industries. He would stop those altogether for as long as he had a word to say, and he hoped for a generation at least. The Ruhr and the Saar, Churchill declared, 'would be put permanently out of action.'

The discussion then turned to naval matters. Great Britain, commented Stalin, 'could use some of Germany's ships', to which Churchill replied 'that Russia could do the same, but in the future air would be stronger than the fleet'. The discussion continued:

MARSHAL STALIN said that Great Powers could not be without navies. Germany's mistake was that she had no fleet. She had no fuel in Europe and was short of food, and a fleet was necessary to convoy fuel and food. Germany had not understood this.

THE PRIME MINISTER said that Great Britain intended to maintain a strong fleet and a strong air component. She would welcome the appearance of a strong Russian fleet on all the seas. She would create no obstacles to Russia's having a fleet. After the last war Rathenau had told the Germans that being deprived of their army and navy would not matter; he promised to arrange factories and make new weapons and Germany would build up her strength again more quickly than the others. Brüning carried on this policy, but no one dared go into production until Hitler appeared. Hitler did not invent this theme, Rathenau and Brüning had thought of it. Hitler only pulled the lever. It should not happen again. Industrial armament was the important thing. To begin with, the machine tools must be taken away.

MARSHAL STALIN agreed and added that all metallurgical works should be destroyed. They were difficult to restore. Germany produced four times more pig iron than England.

A map of Germany was then produced. Churchill suggested that Bavaria and Austria 'should go together with Vienna as the capital' and form a separate State 'with Wurtemberg and Baden'. There would then be three States in Germany, Bavaria and Austria 'soft treatment', Prussia 'hard treatment', and the industrial area on the Rhine—'under international control'. Saxony, 'when stripped', might go to Prussia.

Stalin then made his contribution to the proposed future borders of central Europe, telling Churchill:

Hungary would have to remain a separate State. Neither the Hungarians nor the Slavs should ever form part of any German State. They were too weak and Germany was too advanced. Germany would quickly dominate them. The small nations in Europe should be made to police Germany. The Poles would be glad to take a hand in the occupation. The Poles deserved to get territory on their Western borders. They had suffered much for over a century.

Churchill then turned to the idea of the three States of central Europe, Poland, Czechoslovakia and Hungary, forming what he called 'a separate grouping', and he went on to explain to Stalin what he had in mind, and why:

THE PRIME MINISTER explained that it would be more than an entente, it would be a 'Zollverein'. The evil in Europe was that travelling across it one used many different currencies, passed a dozen frontiers, many customs barriers, and all this was a great obstacle to trade. He wanted to see Europe prosperous and some of the old glory return to her. In this way perhaps hatred would die. He thought this might be achieved by groupings for commercial and trade purposes.

Neither Stalin nor Molotov were impressed by Churchill's vision, as the minutes recorded:

MARSHAL STALIN suggested that this question might come up later, but that the immediate point was that after this war all States would be very nationalistic. The Hungarians, Czechs and Poles would first want to build up their national life and not restrict their own rights by combining with others. The feeling to live independently would be the strongest. Later, economic feelings would prevail, but in the first period they would be purely nationalistic and therefore groupings would be unwelcome. The fact that Hitler's regime had developed nationalism could be seen in the example of Yugoslavia where Croats, Montenegrins, Slovenes, &c. all wanted something of their own. It was a symptom.

M. MOLOTOV said that after the last war many new small States had been formed. Many of them had failed. It would be dangerous to go to the other extreme after this war and to force States to form groups. It would be impossible for Czechs and Hungarians to unite and to find a common language immediately after this war. Nor could the Czechs and Poles do so. They all had a great desire for an independent life. Their independence had been of short duration.

The discussion then turned to the German air force. Germany, suggested Churchill, 'should be deprived of all her aviation'. To this Stalin agreed, adding 'that neither civil nor military flying should be allowed', and that 'all training schools for pilots should be forbidden'.[1]

The last formal meeting of 'Tolstoy' was at an end. Reflecting on what had been said and done, Churchill telegraphed that night to Attlee: 'There is no doubt that in our narrow circle we have talked with an ease, freedom and beau geste never before attained between our two countries. Stalin has made several expressions of personal regard which I feel sure were sincere. But I repeat my conviction that he is by no means alone. "Behind the horseman sits dull care."'[2]

During this final conference, Churchill succeeded in persuading Stalin to accept a formula for the Curzon Line to which he hoped Mikolajczyk could agree. The Curzon Line was no longer to be 'the frontier', as Stalin had originally insisted, but rather the 'basis for frontier'. This seemed nearer to Mikolajczyk's formula, 'line of demarcation'. Churchill now hoped to persuade Mikolajczyk to agree to Stalin's form of words. It seemed, however, he warned Attlee, 'Neither side will give way.'[3]

Not all the talk that evening was political. 'Stalin's sense of humour,' Churchill told Lord Moran on the following morning, 'is his strongest characteristic.' Churchill had spoken of the British intervention against the Bolsheviks in 1919, when he had been Secretary of State for War, and Stalin a member of the Bolshevik leadership. 'I said, "I'm glad now that I did not kill you. I hope you are glad that you did not kill me?"' Stalin agreed 'readily', and went on to quote a Russian proverb: 'A man's eyes should be torn out if he can only see the past.'

At three in the morning Churchill and Eden had made a move to go, but Stalin had not let them and kept them another hour. 'All the time,' Churchill told Moran, 'he got more animated and expansive.'[4] Among the topics discussed was Switzerland. 'I was astonished,' Churchill wrote to Eden six weeks later, 'at U.J.'s savageness against her and, much though I respect that great and good man, I was entirely uninfluenced by his attitude. He called them "swine", and he does not use that sort of language without meaning it. I am sure we ought to stand by Switzerland, and we ought to explain to U.J. why it is we do so.' The moment for sending such a message, Churchill

---

[1] 'Record of Meeting held at the Kremlin on the 17th October 1944, at 10 p.m.': Premier papers, 3/434/4.

[2] The quotation is from Horace, Odes III, i, 40: 'Post equitem sedet atra cura.'

[3] 'Hearty' No. 167, No. 3023 from Moscow to the Foreign Office, 'Personal and Top Secret', 17 October 1944: Cabinet papers, 120/165.

[4] Moran diary, 18 October 1944: Moran, op. cit., pages 204–5.

added, 'should be carefully chosen. Personally, I stand by the only decent neutrals in the world.'[1]

Reporting to Attlee on his final discussions with Stalin, Churchill wrote with confidence of the 'percentages' agreement, telling the Deputy Prime Minister:

The arrangements made about the Balkans are I am sure the best that are possible. Coupled with our successful military action we should now be able to save Greece, and I have no doubt that agreement to pursue a 50–50 joint policy in Yugoslavia will be the best solution for our difficulties in view of Tito's behaviour and changes in local situation resulting from arrival of Russian and Bulgarian forces under Russian Command to help Tito's eastern flank. The Russians are insistent on their ascendancy in Roumania and Bulgaria as Black Sea countries.

As to Poland, Churchill warned, 'forcing the Curzon Line' upon the Poles, 'although Parliament is well aware that this is our policy, will excite criticism'.[2] One problem for Churchill was a discussion which Stalin and Roosevelt had apparently had at Teheran, without Churchill having been informed. As Churchill telegraphed to Roosevelt on October 18:

. . . Molotov stated at our opening meeting with the London Poles that you had expressed agreement with the Curzon Line at Teheran. I informed Stalin afterwards that neither I nor Eden could confirm this statement. Stalin thereupon said that he had had a private conversation with you, not at the table, when you had concurred in the policy of the Curzon Line, though you had expressed a hope about Lvov being retained by the Poles, I could not of course deal with this assertion. Several times in the course of my long talks with him, he emphasised his earnest desire for your return at the election and of the advantage to Russia and to the world which that would be. Therefore you may be sure that no indiscretion will occur from the Russian side.

Both the London Poles and the Lublin Poles would, Churchill told Roosevelt, 'now return home to consult their colleagues on outstanding points'. Britain's position was that it would 'support the Curzon

---

[1] Prime Minister's Personal Minute, M.1181/4, 3 December 1944: Churchill papers, 20/153. Churchill explained in this minute the reason for his regard for Switzerland, telling Eden: 'Of all the neutrals, Switzerland has the greatest right to distinction. She has been the sole international force linking the hideously sundered nations and ourselves. What does it matter whether she has been able to give us the commercial advantages we desire or has given too many to the Germans, to keep herself alive? She has been a democratic State, standing for freedom in self defence among her mountains, and in thought, in spite of race, largely on our side.'

[2] 'Hearty' No. 167, No. 3023 from Moscow to the Foreign Office, 'Personal and Top Secret', sent at 8.35 a.m., 18 October 1944: Cabinet papers, 120/165.

Line and its compensations' at the Armistice or Peace Conference, 'which alone can give a final and legal validity to all territorial changes'.

Churchill also sent Roosevelt a note about the 'considerable advantages which had been gained 'in other directions' as a result of the Moscow discussions. 'You have already been informed,' he wrote, 'about the obvious resolve of the Soviet Government to attack Japan on the overthrow of Hitler, of their detailed study of the problem and of their readiness to begin Inter-Allied preparations on a large scale. When we are vexed with other matters we must remember the supreme value of this in shortening the whole struggle.'[1]

This information about Russia entering the war against Japan had also been telegraphed to the Chiefs of Staff Committee by General Ismay.[2] Churchill was appalled when he saw a copy of this telegram, minuting to Ismay:

I think it very wrong to publish and circulate all this to widening circles. There was no need for the Chiefs of Staff Committee in London to know anything about it till our return. You should have informed me before taking such a serious step. I dread your Roneo newspapers dealing with such deadly secrets.

Action: You should telegraph to London forbidding all circulation and ask that a list of names be prepared of those who have had access to this knowledge. You should suppress, recall and destroy all copies wherever possible. Let me have a list of every single copy that has been struck. Make sure that none remain on the machine and that the stencil has been destroyed by fire.

I shudder to think what Stalin would feel if he saw this document, the consequences of leakage might involve an immediate attack by Japan on Russia, even while the German war was going on.[3]

In sending this minute to General Hollis, Ian Jacob commented: 'We have just had one of the Old Man's secrecy flaps, so General Ismay thinks it would be advisable to do nothing with the Moscow documents until he returns.' It would be 'easier to proceed', Jacob added, 'when the heat had died down'.[4]

---

[1] 'Hearty' No. 174, Prime Minister's Personal Telegram, T.1937/4, 18 October 1944: Churchill papers, 20/173.

[2] 'Hearty' No. 166, 17 October 1944: Cabinet papers, 20/165.

[3] Prime Minister's Personal Minute, D(Tol)2/4, 'Most Secret', 18 October 1944: Cabinet papers, 120/158.

[4] 'Top Secret and Personal', 17 October 1944: Cabinet papers 127/34. An enquiry into the circulation of top secret documents revealed that, 'excluding Buckingham Palace and 10 Downing Street', a total of ninety-nine people either saw, or knew of, a typical top secret telegram. These included twenty-four at the Admiralty, seventeen at the War Office, nine in the Defence Office, seven in the Air Ministry, seven in Combined Operations, and five in the Deputy Prime Minister's office (including Attlee himself). Another Top Secret telegram involving Foreign policy had been seen in addition by nine members of the Foreign Office.

The 'Tolstoy' conference was almost at an end, after nine days of discussions, dominated by Poland. 'Hours and hours have been spent,' Jacob wrote to Hollis on October 17, 'trying to dragoon the Poles, but I do not think there has been any satisfactory settlement. The stumbling block is Lvov, upon which both the Russian and the Poles are adamant.'[1]

On October 18 Churchill went to the British Embassy where he gave a Press Conference for the American, British and Russian correspondents. Both Elizabeth Layton and Marian Holmes were there to take down the proceedings in shorthand. 'We sat behind the PM and Mr Eden,' noted Marian Holmes, 'before an audience of correspondents. PM spoke for three-quarters of an hour. Afterwards he said to us "You didn't take down all that tripe, did you?"'[2]

Churchill's last official appointment in Moscow, at seven o'clock that evening, was with Mikolajczyk, to discuss Stalin's own compromise formula in the Curzon Line. As Churchill reported to Roosevelt on the following day, however, Mikolajczyk said that if he accepted Stalin's formula his supporters would repudiate it. This impasse was the final blow to Churchill's hopes of reaching an agreement while he was still in Moscow, all the more so as Stalin had told him that, once such a Government of National Unity was set up on Polish soil, 'he agreed that M. Mikolajczyk should be Prime Minister', but that without agreement on the frontier, it was 'not worthwhile proceeding' with the establishment of a Polish Government of National Unity.[3]

Some small glimmer of hope still remained that the Polish Government in London might accept the conditions on which Stalin was so emphatic. As Churchill later reported to Roosevelt, Mikolajczyk now agreed 'to urge upon his London colleagues the Curzon Line, including Lvov, for the Russians'. Churchill added: 'I am

---

[1] 'Top Secret and Personal', 17 October 1944: Cabinet papers, 127/34.

[2] Marian Holmes diary, 18 October 1944: Marian Walker Spicer papers. At one moment during the Press Conference Churchill told the journalists: 'I remember my old friend Mr Asquith saying on one occasion "there is a lot of ruin in any nation", and there is indeed a lot of ruin in the German nation.' (Press Conference notes, 18 October 1944: Churchill papers, 9/201.)

[3] 'Hearty' No. 175, Prime Minister's Personal Telegram (to President Roosevelt), T.1938/4, 'Personal and Top Secret', 18 October 1944: Churchill papers, 20/173. In a telegram to Cadogan, Eden confirmed that 'Marshal Stalin gave the Prime Minister "his word" (in these terms) that he was favourable to appointment of Mikolajczyk as Prime Minister. He only did not want it expressed in that particular way.' ('Hearty' No. 200, No. 3073 from Moscow to the Foreign Office, 'Top Secret', sent at 2.50 a.m., 19 October 1944: Cabinet papers, 125/158.)

hopeful that even in the next fortnight we may get a settlement. If so I will cable you the exact form. . . .'[1]

At eight o'clock that evening, Churchill went to the Kremlin for the farewell dinner, at which Stalin, Molotov and Voroshilov were present. 'The party lasted till 2 a.m.,' Churchill's secretariat noted.[2] During dinner, news reached Moscow that the Red Army had entered Czechoslovakia. Once more, the city was illuminated by multi-coloured rockets, and reverberated to the boom of guns.

It was 2.30 in the morning before Churchill and Eden reached their respective beds. 'I am very tired and must take a few days rest on my way back,' Eden had telegraphed that night to the Chief Whip, James Stuart, and he added: 'The Prime Minister is in good form.'[3]

On the morning of October 19 Churchill was ready to leave Moscow. Before setting off for the airport, he received two gifts from Stalin, together with the following letter:

Dear Mr Churchill,
On the day of your departure from Moscow, I beg you to accept from me in memory of your stay in the Soviet capital these modest presents—for Mrs Churchill a vase 'Steersman in a boat', and for yourself a vase 'Hunter with bow against a bear'.

Again I wish you health and good spirits.

J. Stalin[4]

Churchill replied at once:

My dear Marshal Stalin,
I have just received the two beautiful vases which you have given to me and my Wife as a souvenir of this memorable visit to Moscow. We shall treasure them among our most cherished possessions.

I have had to work very hard here this time and also have received an Air Courier every day entailing decisions about our own affairs. Consequently I have not been able to see any of the City of Moscow, with all its historic memories. But in spite of this, the visit has been from beginning to end a real pleasure to me on account of the warm welcome we have received, and most particularly because of our very pleasant talks together.

My hopes for the future alliance of our peoples never stood so high. I hope you may long be spared to repair the ravages of war and lead All The Russians out of the years of storm into glorious sunshine.

Your friend and war-time comrade,

Winston S. Churchill[5]

[1] Prime Minister's Personal Telegram, T.1946/4, Prime Minister to Presdident No. 801, 'Hearty' No. 264, 21 October 1944: Cabinet papers, 120/165.
[2] 'Diary of a Visit to Moscow', 18 October 1944.
[3] No. 3076 from Moscow, sent at 3.24 a.m., 19 October 1944: Cabinet papers, 120/165.
[4] Letter of 19 October 1944 (original in Russian, translation as given to Churchill in Moscow): Churchill papers, 2/497.
[5] Letter of 19 October 1944: Churchill papers, 2/497.

To stress the unity of the Allies, and the importance of his visitor, Stalin had gone to Moscow airport to see Churchill off. Churchill had not yet arrived, and Stalin waited in the rain. As soon as Churchill reached the airport, there were brief speeches. 'We have worked very hard,' Churchill told those who had gathered to see them off. 'We have been a council of workmen and soldiers.' The 'generous hospitality and cordial friendship' with which he and Eden had been 'welcomed and sustained' had left them 'with the most pleasant memories of these crowded and serious days'.[1]

There was also a more private moment, when, as Churchill later told Eden, 'I asked Stalin, through Birse, on the departure airfield, whether I could tell Pavlov that he would receive a decoration. Therefore I am committed, and I think an honorary C.B.E. would be warmly accepted and give pleasure to all around. One must remember that Pavlov had been privy to the most deadly secrets of State.' Churchill added, in his note to Eden: 'Should the Soviet Government wish to give Birse some equal trinket, I think we should certainly accept without prejudice to general principles.'[2]

As Churchill's 'Commando' was ready to leave, he invited Stalin to come on board to see it. The Marshal accepted. Molotov also entered, with Eden, to see the Prime Minister's travelling comforts. 'I felt very proud to be in the same plane with all of them at once,' Elizabeth Layton noted. 'Joe had his new uniform on with red tabs and collar and a little gold lace, not much—and he certainly looked impressive. He is much shorter than you would think, but has a very special dignity about him.'[3]

Stalin and Molotov then left the aircraft, and stood on the runway, Stalin waving his handkerchief, as the plane slowly taxied off.[4]

From Moscow, Churchill's aircraft flew south to the Crimea, landing at Sarabuz airfield at 3.30 in the afternoon, after a flight of nearly five hours. From Sarabuz he drove 'along an exceedingly rough road', as John Martin noted, to Simferpol.[5] Churchill slept, while Eden, Brooke and Ismay drove into the countryside in the direction of Yalta. Dinner that night was at seven o'clock, Churchill's hosts being the Chairman of the Crimean Soviet, Mr Kabanov, and Lieutenant-General Yermetchenko, commander of the local ground and air forces. 'Things were getting on very nicely,' Elizabeth Layton noted, 'when

[1] Speech of 19 October 1944: Nel papers.
[2] Prime Minister's Personal Minute, M.1127/4, 20 November 1944: Churchill papers, 20/153.
[3] Elizabeth Layton, 'Short Account of Visit to Moscow', 15 November 1944: Nel papers.
[4] Elizabeth Layton, letter of 19 October 1944: Nel papers.
[5] John Martin, letter of 20 December 1944: Martin papers. Simferopol was given the code name 'Agrippa'; Sarabuz airfield, 'Stardust'.

Master got to his feet and with a very distinct twinkle in his eye proposed the health of—Miss Layton, the only lady present! They all roared with laughter and goodwill, and were perfectly sweet and drank it with quite a show of enthusiasm, then the Russian General seized a huge bowl of flowers on the table, vase and all, and dumped it in my lap saying in Russian "The lady must have a bouquet". Someone called *speech*, so blushing furiously and feeling like a natural I arose and said hastily "Thank you very much everyone, I feel very honoured", and sat down covered in confusion but extremely happy.'[1]

Returning after dinner to Sarabuz, the British team took off at about 12.45 a.m. for Cairo. 'Tolstoy' was at an end.

---

[1] Elizabeth Layton, 'Short Account of Visit to Moscow', 15 November 1944: Nel papers. Churchill was much amused by the action of the Russian General, or possibly it was an Admiral. 'One night,' Miss Layton noted a few weeks later, 'it was very late, and I'd been sitting and sitting, when suddenly he turned on me with a huge beam and said, apropos of nothing, "I've never seen anyone react as quickly as that Admiral did when we drank your health. He'd been sitting there like a mummy all evening saying nothing, dumb as a post, and then like a flash he jumped up and dumped the bowl of flowers on your knee."' (Elizabeth Layton, letter of 5 December 1944: Nel papers.)

55

The Aftermath of 'Tolstoy'

A T eight on the morning of 20 October 1944, Churchill, Eden and Brooke reached Cairo from the Crimea. Churchill rested that morning at Lord Moyne's villa, then lunched with Eden. At three o'clock that afternoon, joined by Mountbatten who had flown back from India, Churchill held a conference on Far Eastern strategy. 'The conference went well,' Brooke noted in his diary, 'and we got the PM to agree to plans connected with freeing Arakan of Japs.'[1] A new factor in Allied policy in the Far East was introduced by the United States Chiefs of Staff, in a memorandum sent from Washington that same day, stating that in view of 'the impossibility of launching an amphibious operation in the Trieste area this year', United States landing craft would be withdrawn from the Mediterranean, beginning 'about November 1st'.[2]

At six o'clock on the evening of October 20 there was a second conference, about Syria and the Lebanon and the 'undesirability' of letting French troops be sent there. It was discovered, Oliver Harvey wrote in his diary, that the British Army was using Syria 'as a training ground' and building semi-permanent barracks there. 'This annoyed even PM,' Harvey noted, 'who said it was gross waste of money to build in other people's countries, apart from feeding French suspicion of our intentions.' Harvey added: 'PM let out about Arabs and Jews— "The Arabs have done nothing for us except to revolt in Iraq."' Churchill also told the conference that he did not want to upset the Arabs in Syria 'because of the pill—Zionism—which he knew they would have to swallow in Palestine'.[3]

[1] Brooke diary, 20 October 1944: Bryant, *op. cit.*, volume 2, page 312. On his return to London, Brooke gave the Chiefs of Staff Committee an account of this discussion. Mountbatten, he said, had wanted an amphibious lift for one division for pre-monsoon operations, and could get most of these 'from local resources'. (Chiefs of Staff Committee No. 345 (Operations) of 1944, 11 a.m., 23 October 1944: Cabinet papers, 79/82.)

[2] United States Chiefs of Staff paper, CCS 714, 20 October 1944, sent to London as JSM 311, IZ 7985, 10.35 p.m., 20 October 1944: Cabinet papers, 105/47.

[3] Harvey diary, 20 October 1944: John Harvey (editor), *op. cit.*, pages 363–4.

During the day, Churchill sent Stalin a telegram of thanks and of personal reflection. 'Eden and I,' it began, 'have come away from the Soviet Union refreshed and fortified by the discussions which we had with you, Marshal Stalin, and with your colleagues.' Churchill added: 'This memorable meeting in Moscow has shown that there are no matters that cannot be adjusted between us when we meet together in frank and intimate discussion. Russian hospitality which is renowned excelled itself on the occasion of our visit. Both in Moscow and in the Crimea, where we spent some enjoyable hours, there was the highest consideration for the comfort of myself and our mission. I am most grateful to you and to all those who were responsible for these arrangements. May we soon meet again.' [1]

Churchill's thoughts had turned to home. 'Hope Sarah and Mary will be at Chequers,' he telegraphed to his wife that afternoon, and he added: 'would like to see Brendan there Sunday night.' [2]

That night, at dinner, 'PM was in great form,' Brooke noted, 'and produced several gems.' [3] But there was sadness to follow, in the form of a telegram announcing that Oliver Lyttelton's son Julian, with whom Churchill had dined in Italy, had been killed in action. [4] 'We have just heard with profound grief and sympathy of the death of your gallant son,' Churchill and Eden telegraphed jointly. 'We think constantly of you both.' [5] 'My dear Winston,' Lyttelton replied, 'Thank you so very much for your telegram. He died as a soldier should and in that spirit we must press on and not look back. But the wound is deep.' [6]

On the morning of October 21 Churchill flew from Cairo to Naples, making a detour over Benghazi to avoid flying across Crete, which was still held by the Germans. 'PM very particular about the temperature of the aircraft,' Brooke noted in his diary, 'and walks about with a small thermometer. He is complaining of a cold. I pray to Heaven that it does not develop into anything before we get home.' [7] 'The PM has a cabin at the end of the plane,' noted Marian Holmes. 'I had to move very near him when he dictated as I could hardly hear a word for the noise of the engine. Set up my gear in the bunks area and managed to type, assisted by liquid refreshment from the

[1] 'Hearty' No. 253, Prime Minister's Personal Telegram, T.1943/4, 'Personal and Secret', 20 October 1944: Cabinet papers, 120/858.

[2] 'Hearty' No. 258, 'For Mrs Kent from Colonel Kent', 21 October 1944: Cabinet papers, 120/165.

[3] Brooke diary, 20 October 1944: Bryant, op. cit., volume 2, page 313.

[4] 'Drastic' No. 183, 20 October 1944: Churchill papers, 20/144.

[5] 'Hearty' No. 261, 21 October 1944: Churchill papers, 20/144.

[6] Letter of 24 October 1944: Churchill papers, 20/144.

[7] Brooke diary, 21 October 1944: Bryant, op. cit., volume 2, page 313.

steward. I was preparing to have lunch quietly with Sawyers when the PM sent for me to have lunch with them. A very good luncheon. PM yelled across the table, "Miss Holmes, have some of this brandy." I declined, thinking I'd never be able to do any more work for drowsiness. PM was insistent but finally capitulated after saying to Lord Moran, "I think you had better prescribe some for her." [1]

After a seven-hour flight, Churchill's York reached Naples, where he drove once more to the Villa Rivalta. There followed a conference on the possibility of carrying out a limited Istria operation by a landing on the Dalmatian coast. At dinner at the Villa Rivalta that night, Maitland Wilson's guests included Churchill, Brooke, Alexander, Mark Clark and Macmillan. 'PM in the very best form,' Brooke wrote in his diary, 'but unfortunately kept us up till 1 a.m. local time but 3 a.m. Cairo time, which was the time we had got up by.' [2]

During his day in Naples, Churchill received from Alexander an appeal for more beer for the British troops in Italy. Churchill took the matter seriously, minuting to the Secretary of State for War two days later:

The Americans are said to have four bottles a week, and the British rarely get one. You should make an immediate effort, and come to me for support in case other Departments are involved. Let me have a plan with time schedule for this beer. The question of importing ingredients should also be considered. The priority in issue is to go to the fighting troops at the front, and only work back to the rear as and when supplies open out.

The question of soldiers' leave, Churchill told Grigg, 'is also pressed strongly', and he urged him to try to work out 'a 1,000 a month plan'. If only a small proportion of the troops could have leave, Churchill stressed, 'it would be much appreciated'. Could not the men come back 'across France'? he asked. 'I am aware that Marseilles is greatly congested but are there not other routes?' [3]

On the morning of Sunday October 22 Churchill left Naples for London, reaching Northolt at 5.30 in the afternoon, after a flight of six and three quarter hours. Having been met at Northolt by his wife, Churchill drove at once to Chequers, where the only guests were his brother Jack, his daughters Sarah and Diana, his son-in-law Duncan Sandys, and Brendan Bracken. That night, Jock Colville was the duty Secretary, remaining with the guests after dinner to see a film, 'The Hitler Gang,' in which the leading Nazis, Colville noted, 'were represented in a most lifelike way.' After the film, Colville added:

[1] Marian Holmes diary, 21 October 1944: Marian Walker Spicer papers.
[2] Brooke diary, 21 October 1944: Bryant, *op. cit.*, volume 2, pages 313–14.
[3] Prime Minister's Personal Minute, M.1020/4, 23 October 1944: Churchill papers, 20/153.

... the PM cleared his box and then went into the Great Hall where Brendan and Duncan told him he ought to take more interest in the home front. There followed a violent discussion, though very good natured, during which the PM said that if a majority of the Tories went into the Lobby against him during the coming debate on Town and Country Planning (The Tories oppose the Government plan for compensating owners of requisitioned land on the basis of 1939 prices), he would resign the leadership of the Conservative Party.[1]

The Conservative revolt over the new Bill forced Churchill to intervene, as he so seldom did, in an entirely Party political matter, writing to Lord Cranborne that while it would be for the 'Parliaments of the future' to fix the 'permanent principles' of compensation, 'I am sure however of this—that nothing will be more detrimental to Conservatism in its highest and most enduring state than for our Party to forget all the great issues still at stake for the sake of wrangles about occupying and investing owners while leaving so many other cases of overwhelming hardship untouched and untouchable.'[2] In the Division, more than fifty Conservative MPs voted against the Bill.

Just as, on reaching Cairo, Churchill had learned of the death of Oliver Lyttelton's son Julian, so, on reaching Chequers, he learned that Lord Kemsley's son had also been killed in action in Italy. 'A telegram must be sent to Lord Kemsley with my deep sympathy,' he minuted to his Private Office.[3] 'It was so good of you to think of me at this time,' Kemsley replied. 'I and my family will treasure the telegram from you personally, from you as our Prime Minister now, and from you as a soldier.'[4]

Churchill's travels, to Italy, and to Quebec, and to Moscow, did not seem to have diminished his zeal: 'he looks none the worse for his journeys', John Martin wrote to Randolph Churchill, 'and seems to me to have returned from Moscow fitter and in better spirits than he has been for a long time'.[5] 'PM in robust form,' Admiral Cunningham noted in his diary on October 23, so robust indeed that when the meeting was over the First Lord had 'hinted at leaving the Government & campaigning politically on behalf of the Navy'. 'I

---

[1] Colville diary, 22 October 1944: Colville papers.
[2] Letter of 24 October 1944: Churchill papers, 20/138.
[3] Minute of 22 October 1944: Churchill papers, 20/142.
[4] Letter of 1 November 1944: Churchill papers, 20/142. Kemsley's son had been killed in the same engagement as Lyttelton's son, at Monte Battaglia, south of Bologna. The battle was described by Maurice Watts in a despatch to the *Sunday Times* on 29 October 1944 ('Guards Held Hill In Storms & Shellfire').
[5] Letter of 25 October 1944: Churchill papers, 20/150.

think the PM says these things to try & annoy us,' Cunningham commented.[1] Churchill's own thoughts that day were on the much delayed meeting of the Big Three.[2] In a telegram to Roosevelt he suggested Athens or Cyprus as possible locations.[3] Roosevelt, in a telegram to Stalin on the following day, suggested Malta, Athens or Cyprus, 'if my getting into the Black Sea on a ship should be impracticable or too difficult'.

Roosevelt sent Churchill a copy of this message.[4] 'I like it all,' was Churchill's four word reply.[5] It was clear to Churchill that the Three Power meeting ought to take place as soon as possible after the Presidential Elections in November. To Eden, who had raised the question of treatment of War Criminals after the war, Churchill minuted on October 24 that in view of the opinion which Stalin had expressed 'the other night', he felt 'that we should let this matter lie until there is a triple meeting'.[6]

The opinion which Stalin had expressed on 'major war criminals', Churchill had informed Roosevelt, Attlee and the King three days earlier, was 'unexpectedly ultra-respectable'. There must be 'no executions without trial', Stalin had said, 'otherwise the world would say we were afraid to try them'. When Churchill pointed out 'the difficulties in international law' in such trials, Stalin had replied that 'if there were no trials there must be no death sentences, but only lifelong confinements'.[7]

Stalin's behaviour at the Moscow meetings had impressed Churchill in another area, that of Japan, and he was therefore annoyed to read a Foreign Office estimate of Russian aims in the Far East, which warned of possible Soviet delays in entering the war against Japan, and of the danger, after Japan's defeat, of Russia becoming a naval power in the northern Pacific.[8] Churchill had been impressed, he told Eden and the Chiefs of Staff Committee, by the way in which Stalin had opened the second military meeting with the words: 'You asked

---

[1] Cunningham diary, 23 October 1944: Cunningham papers.

[2] Churchill did not approve of this phrase, minuting to Eden in the first week of 1945: 'I have never sanctioned any expressions like "A meeting of the Big Three" or "The Three Great Men". "The Meeting of the Heads of Governments" is the proper term to use.' (Prime Minister's Personal Minute, M.28/5, 6 January 1945: Cabinet papers, 120/170.)

[3] Prime Minister's Personal Telegram, T.1957/4, Prime Minister to President, No. 804, 'Personal and Top Secret', 23 October 1944: Cabinet papers, 120/170.

[4] President to Prime Minister, No. 635, 'Personal and Top Secret', 24 October 1944: Cabinet papers, 120/170.

[5] Prime Minister's Personal Telegram, T.1966/4, Prime Minister to President, No. 808, 'Personal and Top Secret', 25 October 1944: Cabinet papers, 120/170.

[6] Prime Minister's Personal Minute, M.1029/4, 24 October 1944: Churchill papers, 20/153.

[7] 'Hearty' No. 264, Prime Minister's Personal Telegram, T.1946/4, Prime Minister to President, No. 801, 21 October 1944: Cabinet papers, 120/170.

[8] Foreign Office memorandum dated 5 October 1944.

when will the Soviet Government march against Japan? That will be on the day that the German Armies are destroyed.' Churchill commented: 'I heard this with my own ears, and considered it the most important statement at the Conference.' Since then, he noted, there had been a 'great advance into details of preparation', knowledge of which was not available to the Foreign Office. Nor, Churchill added, was it known to the Japanese. 'Here I must point', he wrote, 'to the astonishing ignorance of the Japanese about the true position, as evidenced even in the most recent Boniface that I have seen'. As to the fears as to Russia's post-war naval power in the Far East, Churchill minuted that the Chiefs of Staff Committee 'should be asked to consider what harm there would be to British interests in Russia having a warm water base or bases in the Northern Pacific, and what danger to us would arise from a fleet vastly inferior to that of either the United States or Great Britain having access to the sea'. Would not the Russian ships and commerce, Churchill asked, be 'hostages to the stronger naval Powers?'

It would be 'absolutely necessary', Churchill continued, 'to offer Russia substantial war objectives in the Far East, and I do not see what injury we should suffer if she had—in one form or another—all effective rights at Port Arthur. Any claim by Russia for indemnity at the expense of China, would be favourable to our resolve about Hong Kong.' Britain should not show herself 'in any way hostile' to the 'restoration' of Russia's position in the Far East, nor commit herself 'in any way to any United States wish to oppose it at this stage'.[1]

On October 27 Churchill gave the House of Commons an account of the Moscow talks. '10.15 summoned to PM's bedside,' Sir Alexander Cadogan noted in his diary, 'and went through the speech with him. He was due to make it at 11, and didn't upheave himself out of bed till 10.40.'[2]

'The present stage of the war is dour and hard,' Churchill began, 'and the fighting must be expected on all fronts to increase in scale and in intensity,' and he went on: 'We believe that we are in the last lap, but this is a race in which failure to exert the fullest effort to the end may protract that end to periods almost unendurable to those who now have the race in their hands after struggling so far.'

Of the 'different views' of Britain, the United States and the Soviet Union, Churchill declared: 'The marvel is that all has hitherto been kept so solid, sure and sound between us,' and his own travels had

---

[1] Prime Minister's Personal Minute, M.1025/4, 'Most Secret', 23 October 1944: Churchill papers, 20/153.
[2] Cadogan diary, 27 October 1944: David Dilks (editor), op. cit., page 675.

been an attempt to give this process 'constant care and attention'. He had not hesitated, he said, 'to travel from court to court like a wandering minstrel, always with the same song to sing, or the same set of songs'. His aim was the unity of the Allied powers. 'Let all hope die in German breasts that there will be the slightest division or weakening among the forces which are closing in upon them, and will crush the life out of their resistance.' As for any Anglo-Soviet 'divergence of policy or doctrine' in Greece, Roumania, Bulgaria, Yugoslavia and, 'beyond the Balkans', Hungary, Churchill told the House of Commons, Britain and Russia 'have reached a very good working agreement about all these countries, singly and in combination, with the object of concentrating all their efforts, and concerting them with ours against the common foe, and of providing, as far as possible, for a peaceful settlement after the war is over'.[1]

Later that day Harold Nicolson reported on Churchill's speech to his sons. 'He did it with the utmost ingenuity, calm and skill,' he told them. 'In fact, he is quite himself again.' Nicolson added:

A few months ago he seemed ill and tired and he did not find his words as easily as usual. But today he was superb. Cherubic, pink, solid and vociferous. After he had made his speech he came into the smoking-room. He went to the bar. 'Collins,' he said to the barman, 'I should like a whisky-and-soda-single.' He sat down in an armchair. He then struggled out of his arm-chair and walked again to the bar. 'Collins,' he said, 'delete the word "single" and insert the word "double".' Then, grinning at us like a schoolboy, he resumed his seat.[2]

That day, having learned with indignation that Stanley Baldwin had been insulted in public, and stones thrown at his car, Churchill lunched with the former Prime Minister who has also been his adversary. In the evening, on the way to Chequers, he called in to see Subaltern Mary Churchill at her anti-aircraft battery in Hyde Park.[3]

During the day, Churchill learned that the battle for Leyte Gulf in the Philippines, four days earlier, had resulted in a decisive American victory over the Japanese fleet. Three Japanese battleships, four aircraft carriers, ten cruisers, nine destroyers and one submarine had been sunk, and the island of Leyte laid open to an American landing, at a cost to the United States of only three aircraft carriers, three destroyers, and one submarine. 'Pray accept my most sincere congratulations,' Churchill telegraphed to Roosevelt as soon as the news of the victory reached him, 'which I tender on behalf of His Majesty's government, on the brilliant and massive victory gained by the sea

[1] Hansard, 27 October 1944, columns 490–8.
[2] Harold Nicolson, letter of 27 October 1944: Nigel Nicolson (editor), op. cit., page 408.
[3] Private Office Diary, 27 October 1944.

and air forces of the United States over the Japanese in the recent heavy battles.' Churchill added: 'We are very glad to know that an Australian Cruiser Squadron had the honour of sharing in this memorable event.' [1]

Churchill's health and good humour had both returned in full measure. To Eden, who was in Athens, and who asked if he could stay two days longer, Churchill telegraphed on October 29: 'Go ahead and don't worry. Make a good job of it. All is peaceful here.' [2] 'He was in good mood,' Brooke noted after a Staff Conference at ten in the evening on October 30, 'and we got through surveys of the French front, Italian front and Burma front by midnight.' [3] In the past week, Churchill told the Staff Conference, Alexander's forces had advanced despite the bad weather. When he had met Alexander in Italy, 'he had pressed him to do the utmost possible to capture Bologna'. He thought it 'most important' that Alexander 'should not be deprived of the air forces required to support his operations'. As to Maitland Wilson's suggested programme of operations, whereby he would advance on Trieste and Fiume in February 1945, that, Churchill thought, 'was much too late', and he went on to tell the Staff Conference: 'By that time these ports might well be in the hands of the Partisans.' [4]

In the aftermath of the Moscow conference, Churchill sought to carry out and to defend the agreements which had been reached. One Soviet request, which he and Eden had accepted, was for the transfer back to Russia of Russians who had served in the German army, and were now being captured in large numbers on the western front. The Russians were now asking for these prisoners to be sent back, but the British Embassy in Moscow had raised a number of questions as to procedure. [5] Reading this, during Eden's absence in Greece, Churchill minuted to the Foreign Office: 'Are we not making un-

[1] Prime Minister's Personal Telegram, T.1903/4, Prime Minister to President, No. 812, 27 October 1944. Churchill papers, 20/173.

[2] Prime Minister's Personal Telegram, T.2001/4, 'Personal and Top Secret', 29 October 1944: Churchill papers, 20/174.

[3] Brooke diary, 30 October 1944: Bryant, *op. cit.*, volume 2, page 319.

[4] Staff Conference, Chiefs of Staff Committee No. 353 (Operations) of 1944, 10 p.m., 30 October 1944: Cabinet papers, 79/82. Tito's partisans were indeed to forestall Alexander's forces in both ports.

[5] Prime Minister's Personal Telegram, T.1837/4, Moscow Telegram No. 3150, 4 October 1944: Premier papers, 3/364/8, folio 255.

necessary difficulties? It seems to me we work up fights about matters already conceded in principle,' enabling the 'lower grades' of Soviet officials to obtain 'an undue prominence' in these disputes. 'I thought,' Churchill ended, 'we had arranged to send all the Russians back to Russia.' [1]

Field Marshal Smuts had also expressed doubts about one of the Moscow decisions. He was concerned that, once the Curzon Line had been fixed as Poland's eastern border, several million Poles living east of the Line would be moved into those eastern regions of Germany with which Poland was to be compensated. On October 30 Churchill telegraphed to Smuts:

It is of course intended to move all Germans out of the ceded territories back into Germany. The disentanglement of populations is an essential feature in all changes. Look what a success it has been between Turkey and Greece. The number affected by the Polish changes is under 6 millions. The Germans have lost at least 7 millions so far and probably there will be large additions to this before the end of the War. I do not therefore see why there should not be room for the repatriates in the German home lands from which, however divided, only a small proportion of territory is taken. Moreover they have at the present time about 12 million foreign workers or slaves and seem to be able to feed them all right. [2]

Churchill's confident assertions, whether about the lack of any Soviet naval threat in the Pacific, or the need to return captured Russians without question, or the logic of events that would follow the establishment of the Curzon Line, depended to a large extent upon the willingness of the Soviet Union to abide by agreements reached, and not to seek extra or underhand advantage. On October 30, however, an ominous warning of possible future Soviet duplicity reached the War Cabinet, in the form of a Soviet Note about Polish representation at the forthcoming conference on the European Inland Transport Organisation. The Soviet Note stated that the Lublin Committee, given 'the importance of the subject matter to Poland, and the inadequacy of the "émigré Government" in London', insisted that it should be invited to the conference, to which it would be prepared to send representatives. The Soviet Government added that it regarded this claim as 'well founded and reasonable', and that unless invitations were issued to the Lublin Government, the Soviet Government itself would not take part in the conference.

Churchill was angered by this Soviet initiative, telling the War Cabinet 'that we could not be manoeuvred in this way into recog-

[1] Prime Minister's Personal Minute, M.1037/4, 30 October 1944.
[2] Prime Minister's Personal Telegram, T.2010/4, 30 October 1944: Churchill papers, 20/184.

nizing the Lublin Government as the Government of Poland', and suggesting that Britain should reply 'that we were hoping that M. Mikolajczyk would return to Moscow before long, and that we deprecated a decision being taken meanwhile'. Britain should also, if possible, 'bring out that we thought the word "émigré" a prejudicial term in relation to the Polish Government in London'.[1]

Churchill now made one last effort to persuade the Polish Government to return to Moscow and to reach an agreement with Stalin. 'There is danger in delay,' he told Mikolajczyk, Raczynski and Romer on November 2, 'as the friendly atmosphere created in Moscow may vanish.' Poland would get Britain's 'full support', Churchill said, if the negotiations failed 'because of an issue on which you could reckon on our full support. We cannot support you on the question of eastern frontiers.'

Mikolajczyk spoke, as Romer's notes of the meeting recorded, of the 'recent evidence' of Soviet behaviour in Roumania and Persia.[2] This was 'not encouraging', he said, as far as Poland's future was concerned. To these two examples Churchill replied:

Better mind your own business. So far as Roumania is concerned, that is quite a different matter, for it is a question of one of the States which until recently were German satellites and provoked Russia. We have a good chance of keeping Greece under our control. Now, what can we do for a Polish Government which is unable to bring itself to a decision—yes or no? It would be much better if you had said that you would never agree to a solution which would not leave Lvov with Poland. Then I would wash my hands of this. You have carried things to extremes.

Why, asked Mikolajczyk, should Poland 'alone among the United Nations' make territorial sacrifices, 'and that at once'? Churchill replied, 'trying to control himself' as the Polish minutes of the meeting noted:

Well, if so, let the Lublin Poles remain in control of Polish affairs, which you are unwilling to take from them. 'Dirty, filthy brutes, Quisling Poles' will lead your country. You can continue to stay here, but Russia will refuse to speak to you any more. Is she not the third Great Power of the world? So far as I am concerned I have done everything possible, I tried to persuade Stalin and I convinced him of the necessity of coming to terms with Poland. Today you might have been again in Moscow, with success at hand and, instead, you stay here, quite helpless.

'I am very sorry.'

[1] War Cabinet No. 142 of 1944, 30 October 1944, Confidential Annex: Cabinet papers, 65/48.

[2] The Russians had just asked for exclusive oil concessions in part of northern Persia, where they had for some time been encouraging a separatist movement. On 18 November 1944 Sir Alexander Cadogan protested formally to a Soviet Embassy official, Counsellor Konkin, about Russia's involvement in these separatist activities.

Churchill now proposed that the Poles should say that they recognize the Curzon Line 'on the condition' that Poland's independence would be 'respected and guaranteed by a Treaty'. For any such discussions, Mikolajczyk replied, he would want an 'assurance' that they would also deal with the Polish territories situated to the east of the Curzon Line. Churchill was indignant. 'This is nonsense, a pure utopia!' he replied, and he went on:

You surely remember all my hard struggles with Stalin in order to render your visit to Moscow possible. Your present endeavours will vanish into thin air; you will lose control over the further turn of events. I shall be obliged to tell Stalin that the Polish government is unable to take any decision. You return to the old traditions of the Liberum Veto. So far as I am concerned I shall let this remain as it is and shall not proceed any further with you. What might be Poland's prospects in future? Think only of the terrible massacre which awaits your underground movement.

While these discussions continued in London without agreement, Churchill pointed out, 'the Lublin Poles are acting and in spite of everything gaining the upper hand'. The British, Mikolajczyk argued, wanted Poland to accept the Curzon Line but could offer 'no guarantees' about the future Government of Poland, to which Churchill exploded:

I am fed up. When leaving Moscow you were saying that you would possibly stay 48 hours only in London. Today, after a fortnight, you have not made a step forward. You are only able to bargain about one thing—the Curzon Line. As far back as January you rejected it and here are the consequences of this step. Do you really think that the Soviet troops will stay where they are in Poland and are unable to advance any further?

Quite to the contrary, Mikolajczyk replied, 'we foresee a further advance of Soviet troops'. For this reason the London Poles were suspicious of any Soviet plan. But Churchill was conscious of even greater dangers in prevarication.

'The consequence of your line of conduct,' he told the Polish Prime Minister, 'will unavoidably be the setting up of a rival Polish Government in Poland. I do not blame you, but you are a helpless man, unable to say either yes or no. I told Stalin in Moscow that I could not accept a 75%:25% proportion in the Committee's favour and insisted on at least a 50%:50% proportion.'

The Poles had pressed Britain for guarantees, which Cadogan had set out in a letter which he now sought to explain to the Poles. In the event of aggression by Russia, Cadogan told the Poles, the British guarantee 'will not operate'. In such a case, however, 'Soviet aggression would be a patent violation of an international obligation contracted not only towards Poland but also towards Great Britain.' This 'in itself', Cadogan said, was 'a kind of security'. Churchill then told the Poles:

What are you waiting for, having lost your bearings? It looks as if you were stricken with paralysis. You are playing for time and with this end in view you continually put to us ever new questions. We are taking much trouble to reply to them and with what result? I cannot conceal that it was not so easy for me to persuade my colleagues of the necessity of giving you satisfaction and this results in your putting further questions to us because you don't care. I have had enough of this and I withdraw my promises.

This acrimonious discussion continued for nearly two and a half hours. 'If you don't go to Moscow tomorrow night,' Churchill angrily declared as the discussion became chaotic, 'I shall consider everything finished and I shall inform Stalin of this by telegram. I withdraw our letter with guarantees.' The 'whole conversation', noted Romer, 'was carried out by Churchill, who looked very fit, in a rather unpleasant and pressing manner, although he was trying to control himself in order not to lose his temper'.[1] The official British minutes of the meeting recorded Churchill's final words: 'The Prime Minister said he was prepared to give the Polish Government forty-eight hours, but if at the end of that time there was no decision, he would have so to inform Marshal Stalin.'[2]

'PM knocked them about badly,' noted Cadogan, '—and rightly. Finally gave them 48 hours in which to say "Yes" or "No". Think that's right.'[3] Twenty-four hours later, the Polish Cabinet decided that it could not, 'at present', accept Stalin's conditions or Britain's guarantees.[4]

In western Europe, the advance of the liberating armies was slowing down. In preparation for an assault on the strongly-held Dutch island of Walcheren, the Chiefs of Staff discussed bombing the island's defences at Flushing. 'PM objecting,' Brooke noted, 'from humanitarian reasons and Ike pressing for it to save casualties in the infantry attack—PM agreed.'[5] According to the minutes of this Staff Confer-

[1] 'M. Romer's note on a conversation. . . .', 2 November 1944: *Documents on Polish Soviet Relations, 1939–1945*, volume 2, document No. 257, pages 450–57.

[2] Anthony Eden to Sir Owen O'Malley, No. 504, 'Top Secret', C.15255/8/G, 6 November 1944: Foreign Office papers, 954/20, folio 346.

[3] Cadogan diary, 2 November 1944: David Dilks (editor), *op. cit.*, page 677.

[4] Polish Government, decisions of the Cabinet, 3 November 1944: *Documents on Polish-Soviet Relations 1939–1945*, volume 2, 1943–1945, London 1967, document No. 259, page 457.

[5] Brooke diary, 31 October 1944: Bryant, *op. cit.*, volume 2, page 319.

ence, Churchill explained to Brooke, Portal and Cunningham 'that his veto was intended to apply to bombing of the actual town' of Flushing. 'There was no objection,' he added, 'to attacking batteries in the neighbourhood.'[1]

In Italy, Alexander's armies were unable to push forward as far or as fast as they had hoped. On October 31 Alexander sent Churchill the casualty figures from the previous two months: 3,968 killed, 16,590 wounded and 2,497 missing.[2] Speaking in the House of Commons on October 31, Churchill said that, in asking for the extension of the life of the Parliament for another year, he could not predict, 'still less guarantee', the end of the German war before the end of the spring 'or even before we reach the early summer'. If the German war were to end 'in March, April or May', and some or all of the Parties wished to withdraw from the Coalition, it would, he said, be a matter of regret to a great many people, 'but it would not be a matter of re-proach or bitterness between us in this Government or in this House once Germany has been defeated'. The dissolution of Parliament which would then take place would 'necessarily mark the close of the present Administration'. Elections would have to be held, and the Conservative Party, with its majority of more than a hundred, would have to make the arrangements for that Election. Time would be needed to ensure that all soldiers, sailors and airmen had 'a full op-portunity of recording their votes'. But unless all political parties resolved to maintain the Coalition until the defeat of Japan, 'we must look to the termination of the war against Nazism as a pointer which will fix the date of the General Election'. He himself, Churchill told the House of Commons, had a 'clear view' that it would be wrong to continue the present Parliament 'beyond the period of the German war'. Churchill then set out his thoughts in the wider issue of votes and power:

The foundation of all democracy is that the people have the right to vote. To deprive them of that right is to make a mockery of all the high-sounding phrases which are so often used. At the bottom of all the tributes paid to democracy, is the little man, walking into the little booth, with a little pencil, making a little cross on a little bit of paper—no amount of rhetoric or voluminous discussion can possibly palliate the overwhelming importance of that point. The people have the right to choose representatives in accordance with their wishes and feelings, and I cannot think of anything more odious than for a Prime Minister to attempt to carry on with a Parliament so aged, and to try to grapple with the perplexing and tremendous problems of war

[1] Staff Conference, Chiefs of Staff Committee, 353rd Meeting (Operations) of 1944, 30 October 1944: Cabinet papers, 79/82.
[2] MA/1763, IZ 8255, 31 October 1944: Churchill papers, 20/174.

und peace, and of the transition from war to peace, without being refreshed by contact with the people or without being relieved of any special burdens in that respect.[1]

Harold Nicolson noted in his diary: 'I have never admired Winston's moral attitude more than I did this morning.'[2]

On November 2 Roosevelt told Churchill, in regard to the next meeting of the Big Three, that Stalin's doctors again did not wish him to make any 'big trips'. Roosevelt therefore suggested the Piraeus, Salonica or Constantinople for their meeting place.[3] Health conditions in Black Sea ports such as Odessa, Roosevelt had been told by his own doctor, 'are very bad, and we must think of the health of our staff and our ship's crews as well as ourselves'.[4] A conference on warships was Roosevelt's preference. Churchill, Ismay and Cunningham discussed this on November 3. Cunningham had already deprecated the Black Sea or Aegean 'on account of mines & weather'. He then suggested Alexandria.[5]

Not Alexandria, however, but Jerusalem, was Churchill's choice. In Jerusalem, he explained to Roosevelt, 'there are first-class hotels, Government houses, etc., and every means can be taken to ensure security. The warships could probably lie at Haifa unless the weather turned very rough, in which case they could go to Port Said or Alexandria. Stalin could come by special train, with every form of protection, from Moscow to Jerusalem.' Churchill added: 'I am having the timetables of the journeys studied and will telegraph to you about them.'[6]

Churchill felt strongly, as he told Roosevelt, that they should put the Jerusalem proposition to Stalin 'and to throw on him the onus of refusing'. 'After all,' Churchill commented, 'we are respectable people too.' In the event of Stalin not coming, 'I earnestly hope,' Churchill wrote, 'you will pay your long-promised and deferred visit to Great Britain and then visit your Armies in France. The right thing would be to have the Conference between us in Britain. I have trenched so

[1] *Hansard*, 31 October 1944, columns 662–8.
[2] Harold Nicolson diary, 31 October 1944: Nigel Nicolson (editor), *op. cit.*, page 409.
[3] British patrols, part of operation 'Manna', landed at Salonica on 5 November 1944.
[4] President to Prime Minister, No. 641, 'Personal and Top Secret', 2 November 1944: Cabinet papers, 120/170.
[5] Cunningham diary, 3 November 1944: Cunningham papers.
[6] In November 1944 there was a direct railway link between Moscow–Tiflis, Tiflis–Angora, Angora–Adana, Adana–Beirut, Beirut–Haifa, Haifa–Jerusalem (also Haifa–Alexandria).

often on your hospitality. We could no doubt get Molotov to deputize for Stalin. He counts for a lot.'[1]

Churchill's suggestion that the Big Three should meet in Jerusalem did not come out of the blue. That same day, at Chequers, he had lunched with Dr Chaim Weizmann, the Zionist leader whom he had first met in Manchester nearly forty years before. Weizmann wanted Churchill to make a public statement about the setting up of a Jewish State in Palestine. He could make 'no pronouncement just now', Churchill told Weizmann, nor would he be able to say anything 'until the end of the German war, which might take from three to six months'.[2] He went on to warn Weizmann that he had 'little support in the Conservative Party' for the idea of a Jewish State. When Weizmann replied that he had heard that opinion in the Conservative Party 'was veering round on the Palestine problem', Churchill replied that 'it might be so, but it was a slow process, and he would have to speak to them on the subject'.

Churchill then told Weizmann that he had been rather struck by the 'opposition' to Zionism among certain Jews in America, and mentioned the name of Bernard Baruch. In reply, Weizmann said that there might be a few 'rich and powerful Jews' who were still 'against them', but that these Jews 'did not know very much about the subject'. He would like to repeat to Churchill what he had once said to Balfour: 'namely, that he met the wrong type of Jews'. Smiling at this, Churchill reiterated that still there were some Jews who were opposed to Zionism, and he again mentioned Baruch. Those Jews who were against Zionism, Weizmann remarked, had also been those 'who were against Roosevelt and Churchill', to which Churchill commented 'that Dr Weizmann was right and he knew it'.

Churchill then told Weizmann that if 'people of this kind' started talking in the same way as the military did, 'it only hardened his heart'. But he would still like to have 'as much support as he could get'.

Weizmann then asked Churchill what truth there was in the rumours which they had heard about a partition scheme for Palestine which would give the Jews 'merely a beach-head—or a bathing beach—in Tel Aviv'. Such rumours, Churchill said, were 'a pack of lies'. He had seen Sir Harold MacMichael's successor as High Commissioner for Palestine, Lord Gort, and had told Gort 'how he felt' in the matter. As to the details of any partition, Churchill commented, 'he, too, was for the inclusion of the Negev' in any

[1] Prime Minister's Personal Telegram, T.2055/4, Prime Minister to President, No. 814, 'Personal and Top Secret', 4 November 1944: Churchill papers, 20/174.
[2] It took six months, almost to the day.

Jewish State, as was Weizmann. If the Jews could get 'the whole of Palestine', he added, 'it would be a good thing'. But if it came to a choice between no State at all, and partition, 'then they should take partition'.

American Jews, Churchill told Weizmann, 'must give active support, and not merely criticism'. If he and Roosevelt were to meet at the conference table, 'they would get what they wanted' for the Jews of Palestine.

When Weizmann, referring to 'the Arab problem', indicated the kind of speech that Churchill might make to the Arabs, Churchill replied that 'he had already spoken in that way, but that Roosevelt and he would do it again'. Churchill then referred 'to the terrorism in Palestine', the recent murder by Jewish extremists of British soldiers, but, as Weizmann's record of the discussion commented, Churchill 'had not laboured the point'. He had gone on, instead, to say 'that Dr Weizmann should see Lord Moyne in Cairo', and he added: 'Lord Moyne had changed and developed in the past two years.'

In all these matters, Churchill promised, Weizmann 'would be consulted', and he went on to ask the Zionist leader 'whether it was their intention to bring in large numbers of Jews into Palestine?' Weizmann replied in the affirmative, telling Churchill that they had in mind something like '100,000 or more Jews a year for some 15 years'. Churchill asked whether that meant 'something like one-and-a-half million Jews?' to which Weizmann replied that this was so 'in the beginning'.

Weizmann then spoke of 'the large numbers of Jewish children in Europe who would have to be brought to Palestine', at which Churchill commented 'that it would be for the Governments to worry about the children'. Churchill then mentioned financial aid, whereupon Weizmann told him 'that if the political field were clear then the financial problem would become one of secondary importance'.

The luncheon was over. It had been, noted Weizmann, 'a long and most friendly conversation. Churchill then took Weizmann to his study, and repeated his three themes: nothing would happen until the end of the war, he was in 'close touch' with the Americans on the subject, and 'Dr Weizmann would be consulted'. He seemed worried, Weizmann noted, that America 'was more or less academic in its attitude, and that he, Churchill, 'was not supported in the Conservative Party'. Nor, Weizmann noted, did Churchill 'think much of the Arabs and their attitude to the war'.

Weizmann wanted to show Churchill a map, in order to make his points against partition, but Churchill countered by saying 'that he did not want to study maps with Dr Weizmann'.

At one stage in the conversation Churchill mentioned that he had a committee sitting on the Palestine problem, on which were 'all their friends': Sir Archibald Sinclair, 'and the Labour people'.[1]

The discussion was at an end. For security reasons, Churchill had been unable to mention to Weizmann his thought of having the next Big Three conference in Jerusalem. Nor could he refer to his earlier proposal that Weizmann himself should succeed Sir Harold Mac-Michael as High Commissioner in Palestine. Weizmann, for his part, had made no mention of the Jewish Agency's earlier request to bomb Auschwitz and the railway lines leading to it: his concern had been to press for a British commitment to Jewish Statehood.[2]

One practical suggestion made by Churchill at this lunchtime talk on November 4 was that Weizmann should go to Cairo to see Lord Moyne. But twenty-four hours later, Moyne was dead, shot down together with his driver by Jewish terrorists, members of the Stern Gang, outside his house in Cairo. Churchill was shocked and shaken by the murder of one of his oldest friends, who, as Walter Guinness, had been his Financial Secretary at the Treasury twenty years before. On learning of his friend's death, Churchill telephoned Moyne's daughter to say that her father 'had died like a soldier'.[3]

Churchill, who reported the news of Moyne's murder to the War Cabinet on the afternoon of November 6, suggested that the Colonial Secretary, Oliver Stanley, 'should see Dr Weizmann and impress upon him that it was incumbent on the Jewish Agency to do all in their power to suppress these terrorist activities'.[4] 'The State has been deprived of a devoted servant,' Churchill telegraphed to MacKenzie King, 'and I have lost a valued friend.'[5]

---

[1] 'Short Minutes of Meeting held on November 4th 1944 between the PM, W. S. Churchill and Dr Weizmann at Chequers': Weizmann papers.

[2] For his part, Churchill had not been shown the two telegrams sent to him in Moscow, one on October 19 from Yitzhak Gruenbaum, President of the Rescue Committee of the Jewish Agency, about the 'threatened slaughter of Hungarian Jewry' in and around Budapest, the other on October 16 from Dr Weizmann to John Martin, urging, as a precondition of peace negotiations with Hungary, that 'all steps be taken by Hungarians to protect Jews from German attempts to exterminate them'. 'I do not propose,' John Martin wrote to C. H. Thornley at the Colonial Office about the Gruenbaum telegram, 'to trouble the Prime Minister personally with this' (Letter of 30 October 1944). Earlier Martin had written to Pierson Dixon about Weizmann's telegram: 'It has not been shown to the Prime Minister' (letter of 17 October 1944): Premier papers, 4/51/10, folios 1302–13.

[3] Letter of 2 April 1976 from Lord Moyne's secretary, Dorothy Osmond, to the 2nd Viscount Moyne.

[4] War Cabinet No. 146 of 1944, 6 November 1944: Cabinet papers, 65/44.

[5] Prime Minister's Personal Telegram, T.2116/4, 7 November 1944: Churchill papers, 20/144. Churchill had known Lord Moyne, formerly Walter Guinness, for many years. They had sat in

Speaking in the House of Commons of his 'grief' at Moyne's death, Churchill noted that during the past year Moyne had 'devoted himself to the solution of the Zionist problem', and he added: 'I can assure the House that the Jews in Palestine have rarely lost a better or more well-informed friend.' [1]

Churchill now prepared a formal statement for Parliament on Moyne's murder. As he did so, he was pressed by the Colonial Secretary, Oliver Stanley, either to suspend Jewish immigration to Palestine altogether, or to threaten to suspend it unless all terrorism ceased. Churchill was reluctant to take this course, minuting to Oliver Stanley a few hours before he was due to speak in the House of Commons:

Will not suspension of immigration or a threat of suspension simply play into the hands of the extremists? At present the Jews generally seem to have been shocked by Lord Moyne's death into a mood in which they are more likely to listen to Dr Weizmann's counsels of moderation. The proposed announcement would come as a shock of a different kind and, so far from increasing their penitence, may well provide a not unwelcome diversion and excite bitter outcry against the Government. Dr Weizmann will no doubt join in the protests (saying that the whole community are being punished for the acts of a small minority), but the initiative in such a situation will pass to the extremists. Thus those responsible for the murder will be themselves the gainers. It may well unite the whole forces of Zionism and even Jewry throughout the world against us instead of against the terrorist bands.

Certainly the situation calls for signal action; but should it not be more clearly directed against that section of the community with whom the responsibility lies—e.g. by enforcing even more drastic penalties in the case of those found in possession of firearms or belonging to proscribed societies? In particular, might not action be taken against the nominally respectable leaders of the party, whose extremist wing are the authors of these political crimes? If their national status is non-Palestinian, they might be deported: if Palestinian they should be banished.

The rules on immigration remained unchanged; indeed, an increasing number of Jewish survivors of the atrocities in eastern Roumania were, at that very moment, being allowed to proceed by train from Istanbul to Palestine. But although Churchill would allow no punitive measures against the Jewish community, he did speak strongly, in the statement, of the impact of 'this shameful crime' on those who, like himself, had 'in the past' been, as he phrased it, 'con-

---

Parliament together since 1907, and in Cabinet together from 1924 to 1929. In the ten years before his murder, he had been a member of Churchill's Other Club, whose members dined together once every two weeks while Parliament was in session. In 1928 his elder son had married Clementine Churchill's cousin, Diana Mitford (who later married Oswald Mosley).

[1] *Hansard*, 7 November 1944, columns 1269–70.

sistent friends of the Jews and architects of their future'. Churchill continued, in solemn tones:

It our dreams for Zionism are to end in the smoke of assassins' pistols and our labours for its future to produce only a new set of gangsters worthy of Nazi Germany, many like myself will have to reconsider the position we have maintained so consistently and so long in the past. If there is to be any hope of a peaceful and successful future for Zionism, these wicked activities must cease, and those responsible for them must be destroyed root and branch.

The 'primary responsibility' for destroying the terrorists, Churchill stressed, 'lay with the British authorities in Palestine, who had already, two weeks before Moyne's murder, arrested and deported 251 Jews suspected of terrorist activities'.[1] But although the primary responsibility was 'that of the Government', Churchill added, 'full success' depended upon the 'wholehearted co-operation of the entire Jewish community', a co-operation which the British Government 'is entitled to demand and to receive'. Churchill continued: 'I have received a letter from Dr Weizmann, President of the World Zionist Organization—a very old friend of mine—who has arrived in Palestine, in which he assures me that Palestine Jewry will go to the utmost limit of its power to cut out this evil from its midst.'

The murderers of Lord Moyne, and the terrorist groups who supported them, had already been denounced by the Jewish Agency for Palestine, whose Executive, Churchill noted, had called upon the Jewish community of Palestine 'to cast out the members of this destructive band, deprive them of all refuge and shelter, to resist their threats, and to render all necessary assistance to the authorities in the prevention of terrorist acts, and in the eradication of the terrorist organization'. These were 'strong words', Churchill told the House of Commons, 'but we must wait for these words to be translated into deeds. We must wait to see that, not only the leaders, but every man, woman and child of the Jewish community does his or her best to bring this terrorism to a speedy end.'[2]

The murderers of Lord Moyne were tried in Egypt. Churchill followed the case closely. 'Everyone would be in favour of these two assassins having a fair trial,' he minuted to Eden, 'but if they are found guilty of having murdered Walter Moyne and are not put to death with all proper despatch by the Egyptian Government, I cannot

[1] Following a Jewish terrorist attempt to assassinate Sir Harold MacMichael in August 1944, the Jewish Agency's defence force, the Hagana, had co-operated with the British in securing the arrest of 300 Jewish terrorists, members of the Etzel (Irgun) and Lehi terrorist groups. This co-operation was known as the 'Season'. Those arrested had been held in detention camps at Latrun and Acco. On 19 October 1944, 251 of those arrested had been deported to Eritrea and the Sudan.

[2] *Hansard*, 17 November 1944, columns 2242–3.

measure the storm that will arise. I think you ought to warn Killearn so that he may not underrate the danger of which I speak.' [1]

Both Moyne's murderers were found guilty. When nearly two months later, Churchill discovered that they had not yet been executed, he telegraphed to Lord Killearn, British Ambassador in Cairo:

I hope you will realize that unless the sentences duly passed upon the assassins of Lord Moyne are executed, it will cause a marked breach between Great Britain and the Egyptian Government. Such a gross interference with the course of justice will not be compatible with the friendly relations we have established. As they may be under pressure from Zionist and American Jewry, I think it right to let you know my personal views on the matter. You will no doubt use the utmost discretion and propriety in anything you may do. I have no reason of course to believe that the law will not be allowed to take its course and only send you this for greater assurance. [2]

'It is of the utmost importance,' Churchill telegraphed to Lord Killearn again, from the Crimea, on February 12, 'that both assassins should be executed,' and he instructed Killearn to make 'an instant complaint' at the delay. [3]

On November 4 Field Marshal Dill died in Washington. 'For some months,' the Joint Staff Mission stated in a public announcement, 'the Field Marshal had been fighting a refractory type of anaemia for which no specific treatment is yet known to medical science.' In spite of repeated blood transfusions, 'in the long run the strain of this disorder proved too great for his constitution'. [4] 'He would surely have lived far beyond his sixty-three years,' Churchill later wrote, 'but for his selfless devotion to duty; but even when a very sick man he would not give in.' [5]

To succeed Dill as Head of the British Joint Staff Mission, General Marshall had proposed Ismay, but Churchill could not spare Ismay, the man who more than any other was privy to all his and all the war's secrets, and who acted as the perfect conduit of business between Churchill and the Chiefs of Staff. It was to Ismay himself that Churchill wrote, on November 3, 'can we find anyone of equal status

---

[1] Prime Minister's Personal Minute, M.1185/4, 3 December 1944: Churchill's papers, 20/153.
[2] Prime Minister's Personal Telegram, T.149/5, 'Personal and Top Secret', 28 January 1945: Churchill papers, 20/211.
[3] 'Jason' No. 373, 12 February 1945: Churchill papers, 20/223. The two men, Eliahu Hakim and Eliahu Bet-Zuri, both in their early twenties, were hanged in Cairo on 22 March 1945.
[4] Joint Staff Mission telegrams, JSM 346, IZ 8410, 4 November 1944: Cabinet papers, 105/47.
[5] Winston S. Churchill, *The Second World War*, volume 6, London 1954, page 230.

and personal influence' to Dill, and he added: 'If so, it would be very useful, but it is no use merely filling an empty chair with someone who will have neither influence nor access.' [1]

The matter was urgent: the link between Churchill and the British Chiefs of Staff in London, and the United States Chiefs of Staff in Washington, was one which required daily exertions. 'I see no other officer of sufficient status to fill this gap,' Churchill minuted to Sir James Grigg and General Brooke, 'except General Maitland Wilson. He would head our delegation and would I believe, by his personality and record, obtain access to the President and intimacy with General Marshall.'

Churchill also noted that Wilson's Mediterranean Command had changed considerably in scope since its formation ten months earlier. 'The Levant is quiet,' he told Grigg and Brooke in his minute of November 3, 'Greece is in rapid process of liberation; the Germans in the islands will fall in like rotten plums.' The Riviera front had been 'taken over' by the Americans. The French were in 'full charge' in Tunisia and Algeria. There remained 'only the great campaign in Italy, which is in General Alexander's province, and any movement we may make across the Adriatic, which again is an off-shoot of the Italian campaign'. [2]

Churchill's first idea, as he later telegraphed to Alexander, had been that Alexander herself should 'manage both the front and the Supreme Command'. But Brooke had considered this 'a faulty arrangement on account of being so much political business to be dealt with from Caserta', and Churchill had been 'impressed with this view'. As a result Mark Clark was to be given command of an Army Group which, as Churchill commented, was 'four-fifths British-controlled', a 'strong order', he reflected. 'On the other hand,' Churchill added, 'we shall get more from America by this arrangement.' [3]

Amid these decisions of command, all was not well on the battle fronts. In Belgium and Holland 'very hard fighting', as Churchill reported to Stalin on November 5, had led to more than 40,000 British casualties. In Italy, 'tremendous torrential rain' had broken 'a vast number of bridges', and all movement was at a standstill.

As for political decision about Poland, Churchill wrote, 'you may

---

[1] Prime Minister's Personal Minute, D.263/4, 3 November 1944: Cabinet papers, 127/35.

[2] Prime Minister's Personal Minute, M.1061/4, 'Top Secret', 3 November 1944: Cabinet papers, 127/35.

[3] Prime Minister's Personal Telegram, T.2099/4, 'Personal, Private and Top Secret', 'Guard', 'Through "C"', 8 November 1944: Churchill papers, 20/174. On 25 November 1944 General Sir Henry Maitland Wilson was appointed head of the British Joint Staff Mission in Washington, Alexander was appointed both Field Marshal and Supreme Allied Commander, Mediterranean Area, and Mark Clark Commander-in-Chief, Allied Armies in Italy. Alexander's promotion to Field Marshal was backdated to 4 June 1944.

be sure I have not been idle'. At the same time, the Poles 'are still talking to the United States'. Churchill added: 'It will be a great blessing when the election in the United States is over.'[1]

During the early days of November, the 'percentages agreement' which Churchill had made with Stalin in Moscow came twice into effect. The first time, on November 2, was when the British Political Representative in Roumania, John Le Rougetel, reported a protest by the head of the British Military Mission there, Air Vice-Marshal Stevenson, about action taken by Russia, without consultation with the British Military Mission.[2] On reading of this protest, Churchill minuted at once to Eden:

Le Rougetel evidently does not understand that we have only a 10 per cent interest in Roumania and are little more than spectators. With energy and zeal he is throwing himself into a position far in excess of any we can presume to claim. You had better be careful about this or we shall get re-taliation in Greece, which we still hope to save.[3]

It was in Greece that the second application of the percentages agreement arose, and did so almost at once, when the British authorities in Athens were worried about action which Papandreou wished to take against the Greek Communists, whose anti-Government activities were intensifying. On November 7 Churchill minuted to Eden:

In my opinion, having paid the price we have to Russia for freedom of action in Greece, we should not hesitate to use British troops to support the Royal Hellenic Government under M. Papandreou.

This implies that British troops should certainly intervene to check acts of lawlessness. Surely M. Papandreou can close down E.A.M. newspapers if they call a newspaper strike.

I hope the Greek Brigade will soon arrive, and will not hesitate to shoot when necessary. . . .

Another eight or ten thousand 'foot soldiers', Churchill added, should be sent to 'hold the capital and Salonica' for Papandreou's Government. 'Later on,' Churchill wrote, 'we must consider extending the Greek authority.' He fully expected a 'clash' with the Greek communists, and felt strongly that 'we must not shrink from it, provided the ground is well chosen'.[4]

Britain's rights in Greece derived firmly, in Churchill's mind, from

[1] Prime Minister's Personal Telegram, T.2064/4, 'Personal and Most Secret', 5 November 1944: Churchill papers, 20/174.
[2] Telegrams No. RAC 192 and 193/112 of 2 November 1944.
[3] Prime Minister's Personal Minute, M.1070/4, 4 November 1944: Churchill papers, 20/153.
[4] Prime Minister's Personal Minute, M.1082/4, 7 November 1944: Churchill papers, 20/153.

his Moscow talks. 'As long as the Russians leave us a free hand in Greece,' Churchill reiterated to Eden on November 7, 'we cannot do more than be spectators in Roumania.' This, he added, 'was in accordance with our agreement', and he went on to tell Eden, of the British Political and Military Missions in Bucharest: 'I do not think our people out there have the slightest idea of the very small stake we have elected to take in the affairs of Roumania.'[1]

Indications that the Greek Communists intended 'to seize power by force', Churchill telegraphed to Maitland Wilson and Reginald Leeper in November 8, made the 'immediate dispatch' of reinforcements urgent.[2] 'British troops,' he and Eden telegraphed to Leeper later that same day, 'should certainly be used to support law and order, even by shooting if necessary.' Papandreou should be urged to 'deal firmly' with the newspaper situation. It was 'intolerable' that Communists 'should have monopoly of newspaper production'.[3] 'I am all for disarming EAM and ELAS as painlessly as possible,' Churchill minuted to Eden on the following day.[4] As for a possible appeal to Russia to put pressure on the Communists, Churchill deprecated this, telegraphing to Macmillan in Caserta: 'The Russians have agreed to leave Greek affairs in our hands, and it would be a confession of failure to ask for their help.' Nor was it certain that the Russians would agree to make a statement 'sufficiently definite to be effective'.[5]

In Churchill's view, the Moscow percentages agreement had been more than an indication of respective areas of authority as the German troops withdrew from the Balkans. It was also part of a design for forestalling Soviet interference in those Adriatic and Mediterranean lands which lay beyond the immediate reach of the Red Army. 'At this time,' Churchill minuted to Eden on November 10, 'every country that is liberated or converted by our victories is seething with communism. All are linked together and only our influence with Russia prevents their actively stimulating this movement, deadly as I conceive it to peace and also to the freedom of mankind.'[6]

*   *   *

[1] Prime Minister's Personal Minute, M.1083/4, 7 November 1944: Churchill papers, 20/153.

[2] Prime Minister's Personal Telegram, T.2078/4, 'Private and Top Secret', 8 November 1944: Churchill papers, 20/174.

[3] Prime Minister's Personal Telegram, T.2079/4, 'Most Immediate', 'Top Secret', 8 November 1944: Churchill papers, 20/174.

[4] Prime Minister's Personal Minute, M.1090/4, 9 November 1944: Churchill papers, 20/153.

[5] Prime Minister's Personal Telegram, T.2134/4, No. 1957 to Caserta, 'Top Secret', 19 November 1944: Churchill papers, 20/175.

[6] Prime Minister's Personal Minute, M.1101/4, 10 November 1944: Churchill papers, 20/153.

In the United States, on November 7, Roosevelt was re-elected to a fourth term as President. 'I always said that a great people could be trusted to stand by the pilot who weathered the storm,' Churchill telegraphed to Roosevelt on the following day, and he added: 'It is an indescribable relief to me that our comradeship will continue and will help to bring the world out of misery.'[1]

On November 9 Churchill spoke at the Mansion House, at the Lord Mayor's annual luncheon. Among those present was the French Governor of Paris and the Belgian Burgomaster of Brussels, 'living representatives', Churchill remarked, 'to bring home to us the splendid events which have so recently taken place'. Now the Allies stood 'on the threshold of Germany'. But 'supreme efforts' had still to be made. 'It is always in the last lap that races are either gained or lost. The effort must be forthcoming. This is no moment to slacken.'[2] 'Greatly enjoyed broadcast of your speech,' Randolph Churchill telegraphed from a partisan base in Croatia. 'It was one of your best. I was particularly glad that your voice was so clear and vigorous.'[3] 'PM called me whilst I was having dinner,' noted Marian Holmes. 'Finished quickly. He was dining in bed and was solicitous about whether I had finished my own dinner properly. He listened to a broadcast of his Mansion House speech. He said "It went down very well but it was very hesitant. I nearly bitched it." He did a lot of work.'[4]

On the following afternoon, Churchill set off once more on his travels, flying, for the first time since 1939, from London to Paris, where he, his wife, and his daughter Mary were met at the airport by General de Gaulle.

That night Churchill was de Gaulle's guest at the Quai d'Orsay, where he and his wife were given the rooms in which the King and Queen had stayed on their last pre-war visit. In the next suite of rooms was Eden, who later recalled going into Churchill's suite on the morning of November 11. The bedroom was empty, 'but through the open bathroom door I heard splashing and then a voice called out: "Come in, come in, that is if you can bear to see me in a gold bath when you only have a silver one." '[5] The gold bath, it appeared, had been intended for the use of General Goering.[6]

---

[1] Prime Minister's Personal Telegram, T.2086/4 Prime Minister to President, No. 816, 'Personal and Top Secret', 8 November 1944: Churchill papers, 20/174.

[2] Speech of 9 November 1944: BBC Written Archive.

[3] No. 1012 from Bari, 11 November 1944: Churchill papers, 20/150.

[4] Marian Holmes diary, 9 November 1944: Marian Walker Spicer papers.

[5] Eden memoirs, *The Reckoning, op. cit.*, page 493.

[6] Cadogan diaries, 11 November 1944, editorial note: David Dilks (editor), *op. cit.*, pages 679–90.

November 11, the day of the armistice in 1918, found the Paris of 1944 in a fever of excitement. That morning Churchill and de Gaulle drove together to the Arc de Triomphe, where both men laid a wreath to the Unknown Soldier. They then walked together down the Champs-Elysées, to a reviewing stand, where they took the salute at an hour-long march-past.[1] 'Enormous, enthusiastic and good-humoured crowd,' Cadogan wrote in his diary, 'who, most of the time, chanted Chur-chill!'[2] 'He had a wonderful reception,' Brooke noted, 'and the Paris crowd went quite mad over him. . . .'[3]

From the Champs-Elysées, Churchill and de Gaulle drove to the Clemenceau statue, where they 'laid a wreath, and then on to Les Invalides, to lay another wreath at the tomb of Marshal Foch, in the presence of Foch's widow, and then to the Hotel de Ville, after which Churchill was de Gaulle's guest at a luncheon in the Ministry of War.

'I certainly had a wonderful reception from about half a million French in the Champs-Elysées,' Churchill telegraphed to Roosevelt four days later, 'and also from the partly Opposition centre at the Hotel de Ville. I reestablished friendly private relations with de Gaulle, who is better since he lost a large part of his inferiority complex.' Churchill added:

I thought very well of Bidault. He looks like a younger and better looking Reynaud, especially in speech and smiling. He made a very favourable impression on all of us and there is no doubt that he has a strong share in the power.[4]

Giraud was at the banquet apparently quite content. What a change in fortunes since Casablanca.

'I had a considerable feeling of stability', Churchill added, 'in spite of communist threats, and that we could safely take them more into our

[1] It was sixty years since Churchill had first seen the Champs-Elysées. In 1930, in *My Early Life*, he had recalled the sight, at the Place de la Concorde, of the statues of 'Alsace' and 'Lorraine' draped in black, as mourning for their annexation by Germany in 1871. One of his favourite quotations referred to the loss of these two Provinces, Gambetta's exhortation: 'Think of it always, speak of it never.'

[2] Cadogan diary, 11 November 1944: David Dilks (editor), *op. cit.*, page 679.

[3] Brooke diary, 11 November 1944: Bryant, *op. cit.*, volume 2, page 326. Brooke rendered the Partisans' cry as 'Churcheel! Churcheel!'

[4] Since joining the Free French in Algiers in 1943, Georges Bidault (born 1899) had been de Gaulle's political link with the non-Communist resistance inside France. In 1946 he helped to found the MRP (Movement Républicaine Populaire), a Catholic party slightly to the left of the French political centre, and, after the elections of June 1946, the largest political group in the Constituent Assembly. From October 1949 to June 1950 Bidault was Prime Minister of a coalition Government. Moving to the right, from 1961 he supported the militant OAS (Organisation de L'Armée Secréte). In 1963, after de Gaulle had ordered his arrest on a charge of treason, he fled to Brazil, where he remained in exile until 1968, when charges against him were dropped. He died in 1976.

confidence. I hope you will not consider that I am putting on French clothes when I say this.'

During the luncheon, Churchill asked de Gaulle a number of questions, 'which made me feel', Churchill told Roosevelt, 'how very little they were informed about anything that had been decided or was taking place'. De Gaulle had pressed Churchill 'very strongly' about France being given a share in the imminent occupation of Germany, 'not merely as sub-participation under British or American command, but as a French command'. Churchill's report of these discussions continued:

I expressed my sympathy with this, knowing well that there will be a time not many years distant when the American armies will go home and when the British will have great difficulty in maintaining large forces overseas, so contrary to our mode of life and disproportionate to our resources, and I urged them to study the type of army fitted for that purpose.

'One must always realize,' Churchill added, 'that before five years are out a French army must be made to take on the main task of holding down Germany.'[1] The question of a French zone in Germany, Roosevelt replied, should be discussed first with Stalin. But he did now tell Churchill: 'You know of course that after Germany's collapse I must bring American troops home as rapidly as transportation problems will permit.'[2]

Churchill also telegraphed to Stalin about his discussion with de Gaulle, saying that Britain 'would certainly favour the French taking over as large a part as their capacity allowed' but that this must be settled 'at an inter-Allied table'. While in Paris, Churchill added, 'I felt in the presence of an organized Government, broadly based and of rapidly growing strength, and I am certain that we should be most unwise to do anything to weaken it in the eyes of France at this difficult, critical time.'[3] To help de Gaulle internally, Churchill instructed Ismay to send 2,000 rifles and 100 Sten guns 'as fast as possible' to the French Minister of the Interior, 'for the purpose of arming the police'.[4]

After the luncheon, Churchill and de Gaulle both spoke to the assembled guests. It was a 'fundamental principle of British policy',

[1] Prime Minister's Personal Telegram, T.2122/4, Prime Minister to President, No. 822, 'Personal and Top Secret', 15 November 1944: Cabinet papers, 120/170.
[2] President to Prime Minister, No. 649, 'Personal and Top Secret', 19 November 1944: Cabinet papers, 20/170.
[3] Prime Minister's Personal Telegram, T.2127/4, No. 4298 to Moscow, 'Personal and Top Secret', 16 November 1944: Churchill papers, 20/175.
[4] Prime Minister's Personal Minute, D.268/4, 'Action this Day', 15 November 1944: Churchill papers, 20/153.

Churchill declared, 'that the alliance with France should be un-shakable, constant, and effective' and he went on to tell his listeners: 'This morning I was able to see that the French people wanted to march hand in hand with the British people.' It was, he said, 'a privi-lege' for him to be at de Gaulle's side. 'In spite of all the critics, we still believe in the defeat of the enemy.' [1]

That night Churchill dined with de Gaulle at his house in Neuilly. On the following day, while still in Paris, he learned that the *Tirpitz* had been sunk in Tromso Fjord by the Royal Air Force. 'Let us re-joice together,' he telegraphed to Stalin. [2] 'It is a great relief to us,' he told Roosevelt, 'to have this brute where we have long wanted her.' [3]

It was while he was in Paris on November 12, that Churchill studied a file which Ismay had submitted to him, on 'Tube Alloys', the code name for the atom bomb, the British side of research work on which had remained under the ministerial direction of Sir John Anderson. Hitherto, even the Chiefs of Staff had known only 'vaguely' about the bomb, Ismay had explained to Churchill in a note of November 8, but as a result of Intelligence information about Germany's own efforts to develop the bomb, Sir Charles Portal had recently been asked to bomb 'a certain objective' in Germany. The Chiefs of Staff now asked to be put 'into the picture', Ismay explained to Churchill. [4] 'Yes', Churchill minuted on November 12, adding that Lord Cherwell 'should also be present' when Anderson gave the Chiefs of Staff the details. [5] These details were minimal however, so much so that within six weeks Brooke, Portal and Cunningham had asked Anderson if they could be told more. 'May I have your authority to put the Chiefs of Staff fully into the picture,' Anderson asked Churchill. [6] Ismay again put the request to Churchill, who replied that Anderson now had permission 'to inform the Chiefs of Staff and nobody else' about the 'development and possibilities' of the atom bomb. [7] 'There is surely no necessity,' however, Churchill told Anderson, 'for them to go into technical details which are a life-study in themselves.' Ismay should 'also be informed' of fuller details, Churchill minuted, 'but I

[1] Speech of 11 November 1944: Churchill papers, 9/204.

[2] Prime Minister's Personal Telegram, T.2117/4, No. 4255 to Moscow, 'Top Secret', 12 November 1944: Cabinet papers, 120/858.

[3] Prime Minister's Personal Telegram, T.2122/4, No. 822 from Prime Minister to President, 'Personal and Top Secret', 15 November 1944: Churchill papers, 20/175.

[4] 'Top Secret', 8 November 1944: Cabinet papers, 127/37.

[5] Prime Minister's Personal Minute, unnumbered and unregistered, 12 November 1944: Cabi-net papers, 127/37.

[6] Minute of 19 January 1945: Cabinet papers, 127/37.

[7] Note by Ismay, marked 'Oral, 25/1/45': Cabinet papers, 127/37.

am entirely opposed to any other person in the Defence system who does not already know, being made a party'.[1]

During the afternoon of November 12, at the Hotel de Ville, Churchill was made an honorary citizen of Paris, and presented with a German flag which had flown on the Hotel de Ville during the occupation. Churchill responded in 'an extempore speech of about $\frac{1}{4}$ hour—in *French*!', Cadogan noted in his diary, and he added: 'Don't know what it conveyed to the natives, but it was very forceful, and tearful, with a lot of table-thumping!'[2]

In his speech, made in the presence of many Resistance leaders who were hostile, some deeply hostile, to de Gaulle, Churchill described his own former adversary as the 'incontestable leader' of France. 'From time to time I have had lively arguments with him about matters relating to this difficult war,' he declared, 'but I am absolutely sure that you ought to rally round your leader and do your utmost to make France united and indivisible.'[3]

The welcome he had received from the people of Paris, Churchill wrote that day to Louis Marin, a pre-war painter friend, had shown him 'that the sufferings of these four years have served only to strengthen the friendship between our two peoples'.[4] That night, after dining at the British Embassy, Churchill drove to the Gare de Lyon, where he boarded the Presidential train, and travelled with de Gaulle eastward through the night, reaching Besançon after breakfast on November 13. There, they were met by General de Lattre de Tassigny, and drove some sixty miles through thick snow to de Lattre's advanced headquarters, at the village of Maiche. De Lattre, as General Brooke noted in his diary, 'had hoped to take us forward to an observation-post from which we could have seen the beginning of the battle which was to start today. But it was snowing far too heavily to see anything. There was already quite a foot of snow and the attack had had to be put off.' Brooke's account continued: 'The PM's car punctured twice and we got temporarily stuck in the rut at the side of the road. However we finally arrived at Maiche. The PM was very cold and miserable looking and I hope will not be any the worse for it.'

De Lattre was then Churchill's host at luncheon. Once more, Brooke was a witness to the Prime Minister's discomfort:

[1] Prime Minister's Personal Minute, M.97/5, 'Top Secret', 21 January 1945: Cabinet papers, 127/37.

[2] Cadogan diary, 12 November 1944: David Dilks (editor), *op. cit.*, page 680.

[3] Speech of 12 November 1944: Churchill papers, 9/166

[4] Letter of 12 November 1944: Churchill papers, 20/138.

He arrived completely frozen and almost rolled up on himself like a hedgehog. He was placed in a chair with a hot-water-bottle at his feet and one in the back of his chair; at the same time good brandy was poured down his throat to warm him internally. The results were wonderful, he thawed out rapidly and when the time came produced one of those indescribably funny French speeches which brought the house down.[1]

From the lunch, Churchill and de Gaulle drove back towards Besançon. At Valdhahon, with snow still falling heavily and darkness coming on, a march past had been arranged. Commander Thompson, who had accompanied Churchill throughout this visit, later recalled:

It was even colder by then and the roads were deep in slush. We got warmed up a bit in a canteen with coffee and then watched march past which finished in almost complete darkness, the final unit being tanks which had to have their head lamps on!

When this was over I hoped to get W.S.C. warmed up again and into the car but no, a scout car or something of the sort drew up opposite us and a man leapt on to it and shouted 'Alors, on va chanter'. A band struck up somewhere in the darkness and equally obscured was what must have been a large choir of poilus who sang several songs!!

After this he got under weigh and returned to the train.[2]

That night Churchill dined with de Gaulle in the Presidential train, as it began the overnight journey westward. 'Winston was in excellent form,' Brooke noted, 'and even de Gaulle unbent a little.'[3]

The Presidential train reached Paris at six o'clock on the morning of November 14. De Gaulle's coaches were then taken off, and Churchill's sent on to Rheims. There Eisenhower was waiting to take Churchill to his Advance Headquarters to learn of the course of operations and the dispositions at the front. Brooke, who was present, noted that Eisenhower 'seemed fairly vague as to what was really going on'.[4]

During their discussion, Eisenhower mentioned to Churchill the possibility that, should he reach the river Rhine opposite the industrial cities of the Ruhr 'in the course of the present operations', the American long-range artillery would be able 'to dominate and destroy at least half of that area'. Churchill at once saw a chance to contribute to the attack, remembering the heavy batteries which, in 1918, as

---

[1] Brooke recollections: Bryant, *op. cit.*, volume 2, page 331.

[2] 'Visit by the Prime Minister to the Vosges in November 1944 (Notes by Commander Thompson)', 15 December 1952: Churchill papers, 4/357.

[3] Brooke diary, 13 November 1944: Bryant, *op. cit.*, volume 2, page 330.

[4] Brooke diary, 14 November 1944: Bryant, *op. cit.*, volume 2, pages 331–2.

Secretary of State for War, he had caused to be retained.[1] As he minuted to the Chiefs of Staff Committee two days later:

Cannot some of our heavy batteries erected in the Dover area be of use for this, especially those on railway mountings? A range of 30,000 yards is achieved by the medium American guns up to 240 mm. But might not the intervention of our 12" and 13.5", and even 15", be accepted? What are the ranges of the principal guns that can be mounted on railway mountings? I am afraid our 18" howitzers would be judged too short-range.

Anyhow, let the whole matter be examined with care and a plan made out that can be offered to General Eisenhower for transporting, probably through the Port of Antwerp when it is open, about 20 of these long-range very heavy guns. Every dog has his day, and I have kept these for a quarter of a century in the hope that they would have their chance.[2]

After luncheon with Eisenhower, Churchill and Brooke flew back to England. 'Much was achieved in these two days in Paris,' Churchill wrote to Duff Cooper after his return. 'I feel that we have now re-established the Entente in full vigour. the unrestrained welcome on all sides showed, if proof were needed, that the trials of these last four years have served only to strengthen its hold on the minds and hearts of the French people.'[3] 'It must be wonderful,' Churchill telegraphed to de Lattre de Tassigny on November 25, after the liberation of Strasbourg, 'to be a Frenchman twenty years old with good weapons in his hands and France to avenge and save.'[4]

---

[1] On 9 May 1945 Churchill wrote to Eisenhower: 'The heavy cannon I preserved from the last War fired constantly from the heights of Dover in this War.' (Prime Minister's Personal Telegram, T.844/5, OZ 2967, 9 May 1945: Churchill papers, 20/218.)

[2] Prime Minister's Personal Minute, D.269/4, 16 November 1944: Churchill papers, 20/153. At a Staff Conference on November 17, Brooke pointed out that the bad state of the railways in France would make it difficult to move the howitzers by rail. If the advance were held up by the Rhine, however, the howitzers would 'be of value', especially once the railways had been restored (Staff Conference, Chiefs of Staff Committee No. 373, Operations, of 1944, 17 November 1944: Cabinet Papers, 79/83).

[3] Letter of 17 November 1944: Churchill papers, 20/138.

[4] Prime Minister's Personal Telegram, T.2178/4, 'Personal and Top Secret', 25 November 1944: Churchill papers, 20/175.

56

'My relations with Stalin are so good . . .'

O N his return from Paris on 15 November 1944 Churchill learned that Roosevelt had decided to postpone 'a meeting of the three of us' until after the Inauguration on January 20. The location of a meeting now, Roosevelt wrote, was 'very difficult', there was no chance 'that Uncle Joe would agree to Jerusalem, Egypt or Malta'. At the end of January or early February, however, there was 'a real chance' that he could get rail transportation to the head of the Adriatic, and be willing from there to come to Rome or the Riviera.[1] Churchill was distressed by this reply, as well as by Roosevelt's insistence that he did not wish the French to be present at the Big Three meeting. 'I had thought they might come in towards the end,' Churchill replied, 'in view of their vital interests in the arrangements made for policing Germany as well as in all questions affecting the Rhine frontiers.' Churchill also took up a phrase in a telegram from Roosevelt, sent on November 18, about post-war Europe:

Para. 2 of your 649 causes me alarm. If after Germany's collapse you 'must bring the American troops home as rapidly as transportation problems will permit' and if the French are to have no equipped post-war Army or time to make one, or to give it battle experience, how will it be possible to hold down Western Germany beyond the present Russian occupation line? We certainly could not undertake the task without your aid and that of the French. All would therefore rapidly disintegrate as it did last time. I hope however that my fears are groundless. I put my faith in you.

Churchill's hopes of a Big Three meeting in November or early December had been dashed. Even if a meeting could be arranged by the end of January, he warned Roosevelt, 'the two and a half inter-

[1] President to Prime Minister, No. 648, 'Personal and Top Secret', 14 November 1944: Churchill papers, 20/175.

vening months will be a serious hiatus'. There were 'many important matters awaiting settlement', among them the post-war treatment of Germany and the future world organization, relations with France, the position in the Balkans, as well as the Polish question, all of which 'ought not to be left to moulder'.[1]

Churchill's one area of satisfaction with regard to Soviet policy was Greece, and the apparent smooth working there of the Moscow 'percentages'. On November 19 he read of George Papandreou's opinion that the 'aloofness' of Russia and the active British presence in Greece had combined to produce a 'damping effect' on the Greek Communists.[2] 'This "aloofness" of Russia,' he minuted to Eden, 'shows the way in which they are keeping to the general lay-out we fixed at Moscow.'[3] 'This is good,' Churchill minuted to Eden four days later, 'and shows how Stalin is playing the game.'[4]

On November 20 the Yugoslav Prime Minister, Subasic, following his agreement with Tito on the establishment of a joint government, began a four-day visit to Moscow. De Gaulle had also asked 'to establish contact', as Stalin informed Churchill, 'with the leaders of the Soviet Government', and the Russians had replied 'agreeing to this'.[5] Churchill watched these movements with care, reminding Maitland Wilson on November 20, about Tito: 'We have agreed with the Russians to pursue a joint policy towards him and Yugoslavia fifty-fifty.' Such an agreement meant that there was nothing to prevent the landing of 'British light forces' on the Yugoslav coast.[6] Tito had no objection to this, Wilson had explained, even though he preferred British equipment rather than British troops. Wilson added that Tito was 'in favour of an Allied landing on Istrian peninsula'.[7]

Churchill did not approve of Tito's independent tone, which was at variance with the Moscow agreement. Partisan commanders had also raised difficulties over the landing of British troops on the Dalmatian coast, especially at Split and Zadar. 'Pray let me have notes on which to send a message to Tito,' Churchill minuted to the Foreign Office, Brooke and Brigadier Maclean four days later. 'For instance, we shall land anywhere we like, whatever we like and as much of it as we

[1] Prime Minister's Personal Telegram, T.2137/4, Prime Minister to President, No. 825, 'Personal and Top Secret', 19 November 1944: Churchill papers, 20/175.

[2] Telegram No. 270 from Athens.

[3] Prime Minister's Personal Minute, M.1111/4, 19 November 1944: Churchill papers, 20/153.

[4] Prime Minister's Personal Minute, M.1135/4, 23 November 1944: Churchill papers, 20/153.

[5] 'Secret and Personal', 20 November 1944: Churchill papers, 20/175.

[6] Prime Minister's Personal Telegram, T.2141/4, OZ 6800, 'Private and Top Secret', 20 November: Churchill papers, 20/175.

[7] 'Top Secret', 'Personal', 'Unnumbered', 19 November 1944: Churchill papers, 20/175.

choose.'[1] In a letter to Randolph, who was with Tito's partisans in Croatia, Churchill explained that same day:

I have been much disappointed with Tito, who has not responded to the generous manner in which I have approached and dealt with him. However my relations with Stalin are so good that I cannot think the two great Powers will be drawn into any great quarrel over Yugoslavia. We have agreed to pursue a joint policy, fifty-fifty, towards Yugoslavia of which the foundation is, 'No needless slaughter of anyone but Huns.'[2]

Churchill's hopes of a British initiative against Istria had been raised twice during October, first on October 9, when Maitland Wilson had telegraphed to the Chiefs of Staff to say that, as Alexander's forces could make no further significant progress in Italy over 'a series of water obstacles and waterlogged country in unfavourable weather', a plan should be made to capture Trieste. This could be done, Wilson proposed, using three fresh divisions, 'at the earliest possible moment and at any rate before the end of December'. Wilson suggested either a seaborne and airborne assault against Trieste itself, or a landing on the Adriatic coast south of Fiume, and then a landward advance to Trieste, in conjunction with Tito's partisans, if they had gained control by then of the eastern Adriatic.[3]

In his second telegram, sent to the Chiefs of Staff on October 24, Wilson argued in favour of a plan to capture Fiume and Trieste, followed by the landing there of six divisions 'and possibly more' which would advance northwards, cutting off the German communications in Italy from their forces in south-east Austria and the Balkans, 'and in conjunction with the pressure by the formations remaining in Italy, squeeze and destroy' the German forces. Every effort would then be made, Wilson proposed, by both air and partisan action, to block the German escape routes from Italy 'through the Alpine passes to the north'. Wilson ended his telegram of October 24 with a request for 'urgent approval' of an amphibious landing on the Dalmatian coast.[4] His suggestion had been opposed however, both by the British and the United States Chiefs of Staff. On October 31 the British Chiefs of Staff had telegraphed to Washington: 'The first and immediate requirement is the capture of Bologna. There must be no question of withdrawing for other purposes the air support which is necessary for Alexander's operations.' The most that the British Chiefs were prepared to consider in the Adriatic was the introduction through

---

[1] Prime Minister's Personal Minute, M.1133/4, 23 November 1944: Churchill papers, 20/153.

[2] Letter of 23 November 1944: Churchill papers, 20/142.

[3] MEDCOS No. 201, IZ 7752, 9 October 1944: Cabinet papers, 105/154.

[4] MEDCOS No. 205, IZ 8104, 24 October 1944: Cabinet papers, 105/154.

liberated Adriatic ports 'of substantially increased light forces to co-operate with the partisans in harassing and destroying the enemy fighting to withdraw'. The emphasis was on 'light forces'.[1]

On November 17 the United States Chiefs of Staff made it clear that in their view the February 1945 date in Wilson's proposal 'would be too late to execute any major operations across the Adriatic into the Balkans unless the war is prolonged into the spring and summer of 1945'. At the same time, 'we question seriously', they wrote, 'that, under any circumstances, General Wilson has the capability of carrying out a large scale operation in the Balkans by February'. To try to develop the Dalmatian ports, as Wilson proposed, would, the United States Chiefs of Staff added, be 'time-consuming and costly'.[2]

In London, the Joint Planning Staff supported the United States Chiefs of Staff, informing Churchill on November 19 that the transfer of major forces to the Balkans 'would fail to attain any military objectives to the north and north-east of the Adriatic in time to be of assistance to the general war effort', unless the German war were to continue 'until the late spring or early summer of 1945'.[3] This view was upheld by the Chiefs of Staff, who proposed a directive to Maitland Wilson, which Churchill accepted, that his proposal was 'not favourably considered at this time', that he should restrict his Balkan activities to the introduction, as hitherto, of 'light forces through liberated Dalmatian ports in order to harass, and exert pressure and attrition on the Germans withdrawing from the Balkans'.[4]

Maitland Wilson was about to be sent to Washington as Dill's successor. 'I can find only one officer with the necessary credentials,' Churchill telegraphed to Wilson on November 21, 'namely yourself'. These words had been written by the Chiefs of Staff.[5] Churchill added: 'My York will come out at once. I hope you will bring Macmillan with you.'[6] 'You have done splendid work in the Mediterranean,' Churchill telegraphed two days later, after Wilson, in accepting the move, had expressed his sadness at leaving the Mediterranean. Churchill added: 'It may well be that the most important operations are over in that theatre. Anyhow, we need you in Washington.' He

[1] Chiefs of Staff Committee Telegram, COS(W)405, OZ 6383, 31 October 1944: Cabinet papers, 105/62.

[2] United States Chiefs of Staff Paper, COS 677/3, sent to London by the Joint Staff Mission as JSM 375, IZ 8757, 17 November 1944: Cabinet papers, 105/47.

[3] Joint Planning Staff Paper No. 294 (Final) of 1944, 'Top Secret', 19 November 1944: Cabinet papers, 79/83.

[4] Minute 'from General Ismay to the Prime Minister', 'Mediterranean Operations', 20 November 1944, Joint Planning Staff Paper, No. 294 (Final) of 1944, Annex I: Cabinet papers, 79/83.

[5] Chiefs of Staff, draft telegram, 'Top Secret', 21 November 1944: Cabinet papers, 127/35.

[6] Prime Minister's Personal Telegram, T.2159/4, 'Special Unnumbered Signal', 'Personal', 'Guard', 21 November 1944: Cabinet papers, 127/35.

hoped to see Wilson soon in England. 'Perhaps you would spare me a night at Chequers, either Saturday or Sunday, in accordance with your domestic convenience.' [1]

Churchill's York flew to Caserta to bring Wilson and Macmillan back to London. 'Especial care must be taken about their journey across the waist of France,' Churchill minuted to Ismay. 'I doubt if there can be any truth in this German statement that they had a fighter out there. Nevertheless it would be a terrible disaster if we lost these two men. Perhaps they ought to come in separate aeroplanes.' [2]

On Sunday November 26, Maitland Wilson dined with Churchill at Chequers, and stayed overnight, as did Ismay. [3] Macmillan had flown back by a different route. 'I think,' he wrote after seeing Wilson in London on November 27, 'that "Jumbo" is really rather pleased to hand over the Mediterranean command. He is going to be made a Field Marshal when he arrives in Washington—so that will help.' [4]

Since November 8, the Air Ministry had been trying each day to obtain the Soviet Government's permission for special operations to Poland to fly over Russian-occupied territory on their way to their dropping zones, rather than over German-occupied territory. This request had been repeatedly refused. 'To continue to ask our crews to run the gamut of German night fighter defences in the Vienna-Cracow area,' Slessor signalled to Portal on November 20, 'where they could reach their targets just as easily while flying in safety behind Russian lines is a grave reflection on the status of the Russians as Allies.' [5] Slessor suggested that Churchill might intervene with Stalin. But no such intervention took place.

On the following day, November 21, the British Military Mission in Moscow were told that, as the 'great majority' of Allied supplies to Poland 'falls into the hands of the Germans or so-called Partisans who are, in fact, fighting against the Red Army', the Soviet General Staff could not agree to the proposed route over Soviet-controlled territory. The Mission noted that the only Partisans whom the Soviets con-

[1] 'Through Special Channel', 'Personal and Top Secret', 23 November 1944: Cabinet papers, 127/35.
[2] Prime Minister's Personal Minute, D.274/4, 'Top Secret', 21 November 1944: Cabinet papers, 127/35.
[3] Prime Minister's War Diary, 26 November 1944.
[4] Macmillan diary, 27 November 1944: *War Diaries, op. cit.*, page 592.
[5] JCS 852, IZ 8832, 'Personal', 20 November 1944: Air Ministry papers, 20/2710.

29. With General Alexander in the war zone, Italy, 26 August 1944.

30. The war zone, Italy, 26 August 1944. Churchill later wrote: 'The whole front of the Eighth Army offensive was visible. But apart from the smoke puffs of shells bursting seven or eight thousand yards away in a scattered fashion there was nothing to see' (pages 914–15)

31. Churchill in the war zone, Italy, 26 August 1944. Alexander later recalled: 'He absolutely loved it. It fascinated him—the real warrior at heart' (page 915)

32. Churchill leaving Moscow, 19 October 1944, after his second wartime visit. Left to right: John Martin, Andrei Vyshinski (behind Churchill), Pavlov (Stalin's interpreter), and Molotov (in fur hat). The meeting had been given the codename 'Tolstoy' (pages 989–1033)

33. With General de Gaulle in Paris, Armistice Day, 11 November 1944. Behind Churchill's right shoulder is Sir Alexander Cadogan. 'In spite of all the critics,' Churchill told the French crowd, 'we still believe in the defeat of the enemy' (pages 1059–60)

34. With Marshal Tito, Naples, 12 August 1944. The 'right solution for Yugoslavia', Churchill told Tito, was 'a democratic system based on peasants. . . .' (page 890)

35. Churchill leaving HMS *Ajax*, Athens, 26 December 1944, preceded by Marian Holmes, who is carrying her typewriter. Left, in dark headgear between two white Naval hats, Lord Moran. Close behind Churchill, Jock Colville

36. Yalta, February 1945. Churchill with Stalin. Churchill's comment: 'The only bond of the victors is their common hate' (pages 1171–96)

37. Yalta, February 1945. Churchill with Roosevelt. 'The President is be-having very badly,' Churchill remarked: 'He won't take any interest in what we are trying to do' (page 1210). Two months later, Roosevelt was dead.

38. With King Ibn Saud of Saudi Arabia, Fayyum Oasis, Egypt, 17 Feb-ruary 1945. Far right, Lieutenant-Commander C. R. ('Tommy') Thompson. Churchill told Ibn Saud: '. . . my religion prescribed as an absolute sacred rite smoking cigars and drinking alcohol before, after, and if need be during, all meals and the intervals between them' (page 1225)

39. At the memorial service for David Lloyd George (Earl Lloyd George of Dwyfor), Westminster Abbey, 10 April 1945. On the left: Field Marshal Smuts, Anthony Eden and Peter Fraser (Prime Minister of New Zealand). Far right, Clement Attlee. Churchill said, of Lloyd George: 'There was no man so gifted, so eloquent, so forceful, who knew the life of the people so well' (page 1270)

40. Churchill at 10 Downing Street on 8 May 1945, a few moments before his Victory broadcast. Churchill told the British people: '. . . almost the whole world was combined against the evil-doers, who are now prostrate before us' (page 1344)

sidered to be fighting in support of the Allies 'are those known to and supplied by the Red Army'. The refusal to allow the British to help the Warsaw Poles, the Mission added, 'is obviously prompted by political reasons'.[1]

The British had no means to overcome the Soviet refusal, and, as the weeks passed, and Polish resistance was crushed, the 'military advantages' of sending supplies by air to Poland, Eden minuted to Churchill, had become small. 'On the other hand,' Eden added, 'I am reluctant to abandon the Polish Underground Army and so possibly to arouse serious discontent among the Polish forces serving with us. There would also be considerable criticism in Parliament and in the country when it became known that we had suspended help to Poland and acquiesced in the Soviet attitude without question.'[2]

Eden had already given his support to a Foreign Office initiative for the creation of a 'Western bloc' of powers, as one of the essential features of the post-war world. Churchill was reluctant to press for this too soon. 'There has been some talk in the Press,' he telegraphed to Stalin on November 23, 'about a Western bloc. I have not given my agreement to any such plan. I trust first of all to our triple agreement embodied in a world organization to ensure and compel peace upon the tortured world.'[3] It was only 'after and subordinate to' any such world structure that 'European arrangements for better comradeship' would be set on foot, 'and in these matters we shall have no secrets from you . . .'.

In his telegram to Stalin, Churchill commented on the severe fighting in the battle in the west, and on the effects of the equally severe weather. If the German armies were beaten west of the Rhine in the next week or ten days, 'we can go on in spite of the weather'. Otherwise, there might be 'some lull during the severity of the winter'. Then, when winter had passed, 'one more major onslaught should break the organized German resistance in the West'.

Churchill ended his telegram with a reference to political as well as military problems. 'Please do not fail to let me know,' he wrote, 'if anything troublesome occurs so that we can smooth it away and keep the closing grip on Nazidom at its most intense degree.'[4]

Although Churchill had agreed to change the sentence 'I have not

---

[1] Air 945, 'Top Secret', 21 November 1944: Air Ministry papers, 20/2710.

[2] Foreign Secretary's Minute, PM/44/763, 13 December 1944: Air Ministry papers, 20/2710.

[3] Such was Churchill's original sentence, dictated on 23 November 1944. It was changed, at Eden's urging, to: 'I have not yet considered this' (Prime Minister's Personal Telegram, T.2183/4, 25 November 1944: Churchill's papers, 20/184).

[4] Prime Minister's Personal Telegram, T.2165/4, 'Personal and Top Secret', 23 November 1944: Churchill papers, 20/175.

given my agreement to any such plan' to 'I have not yet considered this', he remained sceptical about the idea of a Western bloc, minuting to Eden on November 25:

I think we should have a talk in the Cabinet pretty soon about the Western bloc. Until a really strong French Army is again in being, which may well be more than five years away or even ten, there is nothing in these countries but hopeless weakness. The Belgians are extremely weak, and their behaviour before the war was shocking. The Dutch were entirely selfish and fought only when they were attacked, and then for a few hours. Denmark is helpless and defenceless, and Norway practically so.

That England should undertake to defend these countries, together with any help they may afford, before the French have the second Army in Europe, seems to me contrary to all wisdom and even common prudence. It may well be that the Continent will be able to fire at us and we at the Continent; and that our island position is damaged to that extent. But with a strong Air Force and adequate naval power the Channel is a tremendous obstacle to invasion by armies and tanks.

I cannot tell whether Parliament will be agreeable to the gigantic expense and burden of maintaining a large army for Continental obligations. Even if they would, I should think it wiser to put the bulk of the money into the Air, which must be our chief defence with the Navy as an important assistant.

The situation would change if the French became notably friendly to us and prepared to act as a barrier against the only other Power which after the extirpation of German military strength can threaten Western Europe, namely Russia, and if at the same time they built up an army comparable to that of 1914. But a second condition would also be necessary, as the French quite possibly may decide to work with Russia. This condition is the building up of the World Organization.

Eden had insisted on the World Organization being described in Churchill's telegram to Stalin as a 'mainstay', but he had agreed to this, he said, 'only for the moment, as I consider it must be an overall shield and canopy'. His minute continued:

I do not know how these ideas of what is called a 'Western bloc' got around in Foreign Office and other influential circles. They would certainly require the mature deliberation not only of the Cabinet but of Parliament before any effect could be given to them. The foreigners will also ask immediately 'How large an army are you going to contribute?' I cannot imagine that even if we went on with taxes at the present rate, which I am sure would be ruinous for economic revival, we could maintain an Expeditionary Army of 50 or 60 divisions, which is the least required to play in the Continental war game.[1]

The question of the Western bloc was discussed in the War Cabinet

---

[1] Prime Minister's Personal Minute, M.1144/4, 25 November 1944: Cabinet papers, 20/153.

on November 27. He was 'very doubtful himself', Churchill told his colleagues, 'as to the soundness or practicability' of such a bloc. The 'only real safeguard', he felt, was agreement between 'the three Great Powers', within the framework of the World Organization. His personal feeling, Churchill added, was that Russia 'was ready and anxious to work in with us. No immediate threat of war lay ahead of us once the present war was over, and we should be careful of assuming commitments, consequent on the formation of a Western bloc, that might impose a very heavy military burden upon us.'[1]

Churchill's reluctance to see a division of post-war Europe into hostile and fragmented blocks affected his attitude to anti-Communist as well as to Communist regimes. In the last week of November, Eden pressed him to agree to a message to General Franco, stating that Spain must not expect the future world organisation to align Spain and Britain against Russia. 'I shall try my best to write your insulting letter to Franco over the weekend,' Churchill replied, 'but I cannot give any guarantee.' Churchill added: 'The relations between England and Spain have undergone many vicissitudes and variations since the destruction of the Spanish Armada, and I cannot feel that a few hours more consideration on my part of the letter for which I am to be responsible are likely markedly to affect the scroll of history.'[2]

The return of Fitzroy Maclean to Yugoslavia that November had given Churchill an opportunity of sending his son, a personal letter. Randolph was then with his friend Freddie Birkenhead, the second Earl, and son of Churchill's friend 'FE', who had died in 1930. Churchill wrote:

Dearest Randolph,

Fitzroy is bringing you this letter, and I am very glad to hear that you and he will probably meet in Belgrade. It is nice for me to think that Freddie is with you, so that you will have good company even if comfort, victuals and liquor are scarce.

---

[1] War Cabinet No. 156 of 1944, 27 November 1944, Confidential Annex: Cabinet papers, 65/48.

[2] Prime Minister's Personal Minute, M.1172/4, 2 December 1944: Premier papers, 4/21/2, folio 151. The letter as eventually sent to Franco read: 'I should be seriously misleading you if I did not at once remove any misconception that His Majesty's Government are prepared to consider any grouping of powers in Western Europe or elsewhere on the basis of hostility towards or of the alleged necessity of defence against our Russian allies. The policy of His Majesty's Government remains firmly based upon the framework of the future world organisation as essential not only to their own interests, but also to the future peace and prosperity of Europe as a whole.' (Letter of 20 December 1944: Churchill papers, 20/138.)

You will have seen how things are going here, and how we all seem set for an Election as soon as the Germans are beaten. Unless some change intervenes in the situation, polling day will be about two months from the official collapse of the Germans. I am expecting of course you and Fitzroy to defend your seats with vigour in these two months. All necessary permissions will be given to Members and candidates subject only to battle exigences.

I have only seen Winston once all these months, but he seems very lively and very well, and I am informed that the train is still running. Considering all the railways that have been cut and the general breakdown of communications over large areas, this peculiarly threatened sector seems to have done well, especially as I am assured there has been a good deal of traffic.

I have been considering the state of your income in view of the provision you make for Pamela, and I thought in all the circumstances I might execute a 7-year Deed securing you an additional £500 a year free of Income Tax. This will cost me £1,000 a year. But London can take it. I am therefore about to execute this Deed. Seven years will more than see me out, but if I should survive so long, we shall have to consider the matter afresh from the point of view of your conduct and my resources. As you were so angry when I made a similar arrangement for Pamela because you were not told beforehand, I shall be glad to have a telegram from you approving of this particular transaction. . . .

I gather you have been lurking to the south-west of Zagreb, and I should always be glad to have news of you by any sure hand.

You will learn from the news and the broadcasts that I have put Duncan into the forefront of the housing battle. I am sure that he is capable of facing the extremely difficult emergency tasks imposed upon him. On the home front housing is the sector most threatened at the present time, and of course I am using any spare life and strength I have to see it is made good. I am sure I could not find anyone better or so good. I know you will be pleased.

I had a hope that the difficulties of your commissariat would enforce abstention from the endless cigarette. If you can get rid of your husky voice and get back the timbre which your aged father still possesses, it might affect the whole future of your political life. It may be that abandoning cigarettes may not be the remedy, but it is in my bones that it is worth trying. Your sisters told me that it was in the Liverpool election that, with a very sore throat and against the doctor's warnings, you bellowed for a considerable time in the market-place. Weigh these counsels of a friend, even if you are unwilling to receive them from a father.

All your sisters send their love, and I hope some have written by Fitzroy, though they only knew this morning. Mary has been promoted to Junior Commander with 3 pips, equal to Captain. She is back at the Hyde Park Battery commanding 230 women. Not so bad at 21! The Battery is to go to the front almost immediately, and will be under a somewhat stiffer rocket fire than we endure with composure here. Mary is of course very elated at the honour of going to the front, and at the same time bearing up against her responsibilities. So far we are proceeding on the voluntary basis in regard to young women sent into the fight. If we do not get enough that way, they will have to be directed. Many of them have troubles at home with their papas and mammas. When Mary sounded her girls as to whether they wished to go overseas, the almost universal reply was, 'Not half!' I hope the Battery will produce a record in volunteering. The Battery, I must explain, has eight guns of which only four are in Hyde Park, and Mary journeys from one to the other to discharge her manifold duties. We are well back in the Stone Age now though, as Stalin pointed out to me, we have not yet reached cannibalism.

God protect us all, especially the young who are retrieving the follies of the past and will, I pray, ward off the worst follies that threaten us in the future.[1]

On November 22 Roosevelt had proposed to Churchill a 'joint statement' aimed at helping to 'break down German morale'. The statement was to make it clear, as Churchill told the War Cabinet two days later, 'that we did not seek to devastate Germany or destroy the German people but only to eliminate Nazi control'.[2] According to Roosevelt the declaration would emphasize 'that this war does not seek to devastate Germany or eliminate the German people', who should therefore join 'all the other people in Europe and Africa and America and Asia in this great effort for decency and peace among human beings'.[3] Churchill saw no point in such an Anglo-American appeal, replying to Roosevelt, with the approval of the Chiefs of Staff and the War Cabinet, on November 24:

I do not think that the Germans are very much afraid of the treatment they will get from the British and American armies or governments. What they are afraid of is a Russian occupation, and a large proportion of their people being taken off to toil to death in Russia or, as they say, Siberia. Nothing that we can say will eradicate this deep-seated fear.

Moreover UJ certainly contemplates demanding two or three million Nazi youth, Gestapo men, etc., doing prolonged reparation work, and it is hard to say that he is wrong.

'If I were a German soldier or General,' Churchill told Roosevelt, 'I should regard any such statement at this juncture, when the battle for Cologne is at its height, as a confession of weakness on our part and as proof positive of the advantages of further desperate resistance. The

[1] Letter of 23 November 1944: Churchill papers, 1/381.
[2] War Cabinet No. 155 of 1944, 24 November 1944: Cabinet papers, 65/44.
[3] President to Prime Minister, No. 655, 'Personal and Top Secret', 22 November 1944: Churchill papers, 20/175.

Chiefs of the Staff and Ministry of Information both independently agree with me that this might well be the consequence of any such announcement now.' He saw no alternative, Churchill added, than to follow the attitude of General Grant, 'to fight it out on this line, if it takes all summer'.

In his telegram to Roosevelt on November 24, Churchill pointed out that 'we did not, as you probably know, entirely like the lay-out of this great battle', and he went on to explain, with the approval of the Chiefs of Staff, that he and his advisers 'thought that there was a danger of our not being strong enough to break through at the decisive point, on account of the very wide front of the attack and the numerous points of penetration which were sought'. However, Churchill added, the 'brilliant French success' in the south and the break-through of the 7th American Army towards Strasbourg 'are tremendous facts which must be added to the intense pressure of the American 1st and 9th Armies. Even if we do not conquer at the strongest point towards Cologne, enough has been already gained to make the battle an undoubted victory.'

'Words, I am sure, play no part now,' Churchill added, 'and we can, it seems to me, speak no words to which the Russians, who are still holding on their front double the number of divisions opposite us, are not parties.' To make the 'great Governments' responsible for anything 'which would look like appeasement', Churchill warned, 'would worsen our chances, confess our errors and stiffen the enemy resistance'. Churchill's telegram ended: 'Please however do not hesitate to correct me if you think I am wrong. I remain set where you put me on unconditional surrender.'[1]

The proposed declaration to the German people was not the only issue in dispute between Churchill and Roosevelt, or between Britain and the United States. As Jock Colville noted in his diary on November 25:

Winant came with a letter containing a telegram from the President about Civil Aviation. It was pure blackmail, threatening that if we did not give way to certain unreasonable American demands, their attitude about Lease Lend supplies would change. Winant was shame-faced about presenting it and didn't want to stay to lunch, but the PM said that even a declaration of war should not prevent them having a good lunch. The rest of the weekend was largely devoted to concerting, by telephone with Beaverbrook, a long reply. The Americans are also being tough, and even threatening, about a number of other things and the PM is disturbed at having to oppose them over so many issues. The President wanted to make a declaration to the Germans about our good intentions: it was a silly idea, ambrosia for Goebbels,

---

[1] Prime Minister's Personal Telegram, T.2171, Prime Minister to President, No. 828, 'Personal and Top Secret', 24 November 1944: Churchill papers, 20/175.

and the PM turned it down flat. And there is a sharp wrangle about our imports of Argentine meat, the Americans being anxious to bring economic pressure on the Argentine.

During November 25 Churchill did much of his work from bed. 'I took over from Elizabeth,' noted Marian Holmes. 'He asked for a document and said testily "I believe that silly woman has taken it downstairs". I searched around and discovered it under a pile of papers and handed it to him. "Oh thank you. If you had been downstairs, I would have called you a silly woman. But I didn't mean it"—all with beatific grin.'[1]

That evening, Churchill, his wife, and their daughter Sarah, Marian Holmes, Elizabeth Layton, and others of the Chequers entourage, watched *Henry V* in Technicolor. 'The PM went into ecstasies about it,' Colville noted.[2]

On November 26 Churchill continued his work at Chequers. 'PM was concerned,' noted Marian Holmes, 'when he discovered Elizabeth and me working in the Hawtrey Room without a coal fire. "Oh, you poor things. You must light a fire and get your coats. It's just as well I came in." He then lit the fire himself and piled it high with logs.' That evening work continued without the usual break for an after-dinner film.[3]

On November 24 Mikolajczyk resigned as Prime Minister of Poland, having been unable to convince his Government to continue negotiations with Russia, even on the basis, as now envisaged by Roosevelt, that Lvov and the east Galician oilfields would remain in Poland. At three talks with Roosevelt, the last on November 18, Averell Harriman noted that 'The President developed the fantastic idea that Stalin might agree to have the city, which was a Polish island in a sea of Ukrainian peasants, governed by an international committee, leaving it for future plebiscites to decide the outcome.'[4] Roosevelt's hopes of a compromise over Lvov were dashed however, even as they were voiced. 'For all but his own Peasant Party,' Mikolajczyk told Averell Harriman, 'even Lvov was not enough.'[5]

Mikolajczyk was succeeded as Polish Prime Minister by Tomasz Arciszewski, a socialist, and a member of the Polish underground who

[1] Marian Holmes diary, 25 November 1944: Marian Walker Spicer papers.
[2] Colville diary, 25 November 1944: Colville papers.
[3] Marian Holmes diary, 26 November 1944: Marian Walker Spicer papers.
[4] Averell Harriman, notes: Abel and Harriman, *op. cit.*, page 369.
[5] Abel and Harriman, *op. cit.*, page 373.

had been smuggled out of German-occupied Poland four months earlier. From Moscow, Clark Kerr warned of a 'head-on collision' with
the Soviet Union if Britain were to recognize Mikolajczyk's successor
as Prime Minister, and suggested the time had come for Britain to
make a formal break with the London Poles. Churchill was not convinced. 'My idea was that we should just leave them alone,' he
minuted to Eden. As to Clark Kerr's suggestion that recognition
should now be withheld, Churchill told Eden:

> One does not cease to recognise a State every time the Prime Minister
> changes. I presume our contact with the Polish President continues, as will, I
> imagine, similar contacts of the United States and all the other United
> Nations. I was only proposing at this moment to leave them severely alone. I
> do not see that this should produce a 'head-on collision' with Stalin, or what
> wicked thing we have done that he should be suddenly angry with us. We
> certainly cannot forget that we have 100,000 Poles fighting with us very
> bravely, both in Italy and in France. These men's legal attachment is to the
> President of Poland. They are certainly not likely to give any allegiance to
> the Lublin Government, whoever recognises the latter.

Before there was a 'head-on collision' with Stalin, Churchill commented, 'he presumably would blow his whistle, as at present our
relations are most friendly'.[1]

At the War Cabinet on November 27, Churchill stressed that there
would be 'no question of breaking off relations with the Polish
Government in London', since Britain 'recognized it as the spokesman
of Poland'. But at the same time 'we should adopt an attitude of
complete detachment and of frigidity and leave them to look after
their own affairs. The less Britain had to do with them in the way of
active relations, the better.'[2]

Early in December, Stalin telegraphed to Churchill that the London
Poles, 'the Polish émigré Government', as he described them, was
made up of people 'who have lost touch with the national soil and
have no contact with the Polish people'. 'I think,' Stalin added, 'that
now our task consists in backing up the Polish National Committee at
Lublin and all those who are willing and able to work with them.'[3]

Churchill refused to accept Stalin's view. The Lublin Committee,
he telegraphed to Roosevelt a week later, was not regarded by Britain
'as in any way representative of Polish opinion'. Britain would
maintain its recognition of the 'London Government', which was, he
added, 'the legal Government of Poland and the authority to which

---

[1] Prime Minister's Personal Minute, M.1155/4, 26 November 1944: Churchill papers, 20/153.
[2] War Cabinet No. 156 of 1944, 27 November 1944, Confidential Annex: Cabinet papers, 65/48.
[3] 'Personal and Top Secret', 8 December 1944: Churchill papers, 20/177.

the large Polish forces fighting under British command owe allegiance'.[1]

Within a month, the Lublin Committee announced that it had become the Provisional Government of Poland. No one from the Polish Government in London was invited to join it.

The morning of November 29 saw the Opening of Parliament. Churchill was not present. Instead, he spent the morning in bed, writing his speech.[2] He was up for a small luncheon party, at which Lady Mountbatten and Mrs Neville Chamberlain were among the guests, and then went to the House of Commons to listen to the first hour of the debate on the Loyal Address. Shortly after three o'clock he rose to speak. Harold Nicolson, who entered the Chamber at that moment, wrote to his sons:

When he came back from his Italian visit, we had all been horrified by his apparent exhaustion. But Moscow did him good, and the snow-drifts of the Vosges did him even more good. He is, or seems, as fit as he ever was, even in his best days. It is incredible that he should be seventy, all but a day. He made a lovely speech. He spoke of tradition as the flywheel of the State. He spoke of the need of youth—'Youth, youth, youth, and renovation, energy, boundless energy'—and as he said these words, he bent his knees and pounded the air like a pugilist—'and of controversy, health-giving controversy'. 'I am not afraid of it in this country,' he said, and then he took off his glasses and grinned round at the Conservative benches. 'We are a decent lot,' he said, beaming upon them. Then he swung round and leant forward over the box right into the faces of the Labour people: 'All of us,' he added, 'the whole nation.'

'It read so mildly in the newspapers the next morning,' Nicolson added. 'Yet in fact it was a perfect illustration of the Parliamentary art.'[3]

Churchill spoke of the course of the war, and of domestic policies. 'Housing is the most threatened sector in the home front,' he said. 'I have for some time been disquieted by the situation.' A Cabinet Committee had been set up to examine what should be done. 'I have reserved to myself,' Churchill pointed out, 'the right to take the Chair when and if at any time I think it is necessary or desirable.'

Churchill did not speak on foreign affairs. 'I have a list of twenty-five

[1] Prime Minister's Personal Telegram, T.2375/4, Prime Minister to President, No. 854, 'Personal and Top Secret', 16 December 1944: Churchill papers, 20/177.
[2] Private Office diary, 29 November 1944.
[3] Harold Nicolson letter, 29 November 1944: Nigel Nicolson (editor), op. cit., page 413.

countries,' he said, 'on which I am prepared to give information about their tangled politics and their relations to ourselves, but the House may rest assured that I have no intention of doing so. . . .' The 'united Powers of the Grand Alliance', he added, 'were never more closely and intimately and comprehensively united than they are at this time'.[1]

That evening, Churchill told a Staff Conference, at which Maitland Wilson was also present, that he was 'increasingly concerned' at the situation in Italy, where Bologna still remained in German hands. 'It was true,' he said, 'that our forces were at present containing a large number of German divisions,' but he found it hard to understand why Kesselring did not withdraw to the line of the Adige. 'If he decided to do this we could not stop him, and he would be able to reduce the number of divisions facing us in Italy. Thus our present success in Italy largely resulted from an error of the enemy's. We could not count on this situation continuing, and he wished to know what plans existed to meet any change in the situation.'

Brooke 'agreed' with Churchill's description of the situation, and suggested three possible courses of action once the Germans withdrew to the line of the Adige: it might be 'best to open major operations across the Adriatic', or to reopen an offensive in Italy 'and try to drive through to the North', or, thirdly, 'it was conceivable', Brooke said, 'that it would be correct strategy, when the time came, to remove forces from Italy to join in the battle in Western Europe'.

No Adriatic operation could now be undertaken, commented Maitland Wilson, 'before about April'. Wilson added that, as far as the intended attack on Bologna by the Americans was concerned, it was 'important for the Americans to capture Bologna as soon as possible, since, with the approach of winter, they were faced with the prospect, otherwise, of wintering in the mountains. The Americans' ammunition situation was not satisfactory.' The 5th Army, Wilson warned, 'had sufficient ammunition to allow for intensive operations over a period of only 15 days'.

At Maitland Wilson's suggestion, it was agreed that until a new strategy could be devised, consequent upon a German withdrawal, the strategic role of the Istrian peninsula was to be one of deception

---

[1] *Hansard*, 29 November 1944: columns 24–38. Eden had wanted Churchill to say: 'His Majesty's Government still hopes that a friendly arrangement between Poland and Russia can be arrived at which leaves Poland sovereign and independent. Marshal Stalin has declared that this is the policy of the Soviet Government and His Majesty's Government are convinced of his sincerity in the matter and of his determination to adhere to this policy.' In a covering note to Churchill, Eden explained that he thought 'Max is right' in a *Daily Express* leading article that morning 'when he indicated that there are some who want to use this Polish domestic crisis as a means for creating further suspicion of Russia'. (Minute PM44/729, 'Immediate', 29 November 1944: Churchill papers, 9/202.) Churchill did not use Eden's extra sentences.

whereby, by a series of 'feint attacks' and other measures, the Germans would be led to believe 'that we intended to attack the Peninsula'.[1]

On November 30, Churchill celebrated his seventieth birthday. 'We couldn't think of a present from the Private Office,' John Martin wrote to his wife, 'having turned down the idea of a cat, and ended up sending only a message.'[2] 'Ever so many happy returns of the day,' Roosevelt telegraphed, and he added: 'I shall never forget the party with you and Uncle Joe a year ago and we must have more of them that are even better.'[3] From Pretoria came a telegram from Field Marshal Smuts. 'My thoughts today are much with you my friend,' Smuts wrote, 'the one in all the world to whom so many owe so much. May God continue to bless you with strength of body as he has blessed you with strength of soul.'[4] Jock Colville noted in his diary:

The PM's seventieth birthday brought such a spate of letters and telegrams as never was seen. Everybody, from the Shah of Persia to Harry Lauder, from Queen Mary to Rosa Lewis, sent their good wishes. With Leslie on leave, John Peck retiring early with a headache and Tony Bevir away, I found the combination of ordinary work and the birthday almost unmanageable. Meanwhile the PM's box is in a frightful state, with scores of urgent papers demanding a decision. He has frittered away his time in the last week and has seemed unable or unwilling or too tired to give his attention to complex matters. He has been reading the first paragraph or so and referring papers to people without seeing what is really required of him. Result: chaos.[5]

That night there was a family birthday party at the Annexe. Churchill's wife and three daughters were there, his brother Jack, Clementine's sister Nellie and her cousin Moppet, Duncan Sandys, Beaverbrook, Bracken and Eden. 'When we were all assembled,' Mary Churchill wrote in her diary, 'the candles were lit on the cake—70 of them—Papa looked so pleased and well. . . .' After dinner, Beaverbrook proposed Churchill's health. 'Papa's reply made me weep,' Mary

---

[1] Staff Conference, Chiefs of Staff Committee No. 385 (Operations) of 1944, 6.30 p.m., 29 November 1944: Cabinet papers, 79/83.

[2] John Martin, letter of 30 November 1944: Martin papers.

[3] President to Prime Minister, No. 662, 'Personal and Secret', 30 November 1944: Churchill papers, 20/139.

[4] 'Most Immediate', 30 November 1944: Churchill papers, 2/517.

[5] Colville diary, 30 November 1944: Colville diary. Anthony Bevir, who had been badly gassed in the First World War, had charge of all patronage matters at 10 Downing Street (apart from the Honours' List and appointment of Lord Lieutenants). Jock Colville writes: 'He held this post for twenty-five years, took large quantities of snuff, occasionally lost the office keys and was always at hand to give wise and practical advice to anybody who applied to him. He was among the kindest of men.' (John Colville, *The Fringes of Power, Downing Street Diaries 1939–1955*, London 1985, page 733.)

Churchill wrote. 'He said we were "the dearest there are"—he said he had been comforted and supported by our love,' and then, 'very slowly—almost solemnly he clinked glasses with each one of us. . . .'[1]

From Yugoslavia, Randolph Churchill reported to his father on how, at a dinner attended by 'all the Croatian generals', as well as the American and Russian Missions, 'Old Doctor Mandić who belonged to the Yugoslav Committee in the last war proposed your health and it was drunk with great enthusiasm'.[2]

[1] Mary Churchill diary, 30 November 1944: Mary Soames, *Clementine Churchill*, *op. cit.*, page 362.

[2] Letter of 30 November 1944 from Topusko: Churchill papers, 1/381. Ante Mandić was born in Trieste in 1881. A prominent South Slav propagandist in Petrograd in 1915–16, in 1917 he worked for the Yugoslav Committee in London, urging the creation of a post-war unitary state of Serbs, Croats and Slovenes. In 1937 he took part in talks in Belgrade which sought to improve the status of the Croats. In November 1943 he was a delegate to the Anti-Fascist National Liberation Committee's 'Jajce Congress'. He died in 1959.

57
December 1944: Disputes over Greece, Italy, Poland . . .

O N 1 December 1944, Churchill drove to Chequers via Harrow, where he joined in the school concert of songs, singing once more the songs of his own youth. Afterwards there was a sherry party, where, Jock Colville noted, 'the PM talked long and charmingly to the School Monitors, much as he did to the Midshipmen on the KGV last January, enthralling but never patronizing'.[1]

In a telegram to Field Marshal Smuts that night, sent from Chequers, Churchill declared: 'Of all the messages which reached me on my birthday, none was more movingly phrased or gave me more encouragement than yours, my old and trusted friend.' Reflecting on the war in Europe, in Italy and in the Far East, Churchill commented first on the 'strategic reverse' on the western front:

Before this offensive was launched we placed on record our view that it was a mistake to attack against the whole front and that a far greater mass should have been gathered at the point of desired penetration. Montgomery's comments and predictions beforehand have in every way been borne out. I imagine some readjustments will be made giving back to Montgomery some of the scope taken from him after the victory he gained in Normandy. You must remember however that our armies are only about one-half the size of the American and will soon be little more than one-third. All is friendly and loyal in the military sphere in spite of the disappointment sustained. We must now re-group and reinforce the armies for a spring offensive. There is at least one full-scale battle to fight before we get to the Rhine in the north, which is the decisive axis of advance. I am trying meanwhile to have Holland cleaned up behind us.

'But it is not so easy as it used to be,' Churchill commented, 'for me to get things done.'

Of the offensive in Italy, Churchill told Smuts:

[1] Colville diary, 1 December 1944: Colville papers. It was by 'broadening the intake', Churchill told the assembled school, 'by the schools becoming more and more based upon aspiring youth in every class in the nation, and coming from every part of the island—it is by that that you will preserve these great Public Schools, and make them a possession of all our fellow countrymen, and of lads from every part of the land'. (Remarks of 1 December 1944: Churchill papers, 2/336.)

Our armies in Italy were delayed by 'Anvil' and greatly weakened for its sake. Consequently we cleared the Apennines only to find the valley of the Po a bog. Thus both in the mountains and on the plains our immense armour superiority has been unable to make itself felt, and now the bad weather in Italy, as on the Western Front, greatly diminishes the tactical air-power in which we have so great a predominance. Hitherto in Italy we have held twenty-eight German divisions, and therefore no reproach can be made against our activities. On the contrary, General Marshall is astonished we have done so well. This is only however because the Germans have delayed a withdrawal through the Brenner and Ljubljana, presumably in order to bring their forces home from the Balkans. We cannot look for any very satisfactory events in Northern Italy at present, though we are still attacking. . . .

As to the campaign in Burma, affected by recent reverses to Chiang Kai Shek's advance in China, Churchill wrote, of Mountbatten's 'already unappetising operations':

We seem condemned to wallow at half-speed through these jungles, and I cannot so far procure agreement for a far-flung amphibious strategical movement across the Bay of Bengal. Everything has to be chewed up by the Combined Staffs and 'Safety first' overloads every plan. The Americans are having hard fighting at Leyte, but their advance in the Pacific has been admirable during the year, and I hope our Fleet will join them in growing strength in 1945. As old Fisher said, 'The Royal Navy always travels first class,' and you can imagine the enormous demands in man-power, ancillary vessels, and preparations of all kinds which the Admiralty blithely put forward.

Of the year to come, military events apart, Churchill told Smuts:

Meanwhile there approaches the shadow of the General Election, which before many months have passed will certainly break up the most capable Government England has had or is likely to have. Generally we have a jolly year before us. Our financial future fills in any spaces in the horizon not already overcast with clouds. However, I am sure we shall master all these troubles as they come upon us, singly or in company, even though the tonic element of mortal danger is lacking.[1]

The 'percentages' agreement of October 1944 had been intended as a realistic delineation of areas of influence and exclusion. The 'fifty-fifty' figure for Yugoslavia had seemed to give Britain a real position with Tito, and in Yugoslavia. But, as Churchill's telegram to Smuts had made clear, the Yugoslav 'percentage' was not working: 'Tito has turned very nasty,' he wrote, 'and is of course thinking now only of grabbing Trieste, Istria, Fiume, etc. for a virtually Communised Yugoslavia. I am having great difficulty in getting the right-handed

---

[1] Prime Minister's Personal Telegram, T.2235/4, No. 1122 to South Africa, 'Top Secret and Personal', 3 December 1944: Churchill papers, 20/176.

move, to which you know I am attracted, under way in time to influence events. Everything is very ponderous.'[1]

In the last week of November Churchill learnt from Maitland Wilson that Tito had asked for all British forces in the Dubrovnik area, where they were helping the partisans in military operations against the Germans, to be withdrawn. British ships at Split and Sibenik had been refused docking and berthing facilities. On December 3 Churchill set out these grievances in a telegram to Tito. 'I am sending a copy of this telegram to Stalin,' he warned, and went on to tell the Yugoslav leader:

As you know we have made an arrangement with the Marshal and the Soviet Government to pursue as far as possible a joint policy towards Yugoslavia, and that our influence there should be held on equal balance. But you seem to be treating us in an increasingly invidious fashion. It may be you have fears that your ambitions about occupying Italian territories in the North of the Adriatic lead you to view with suspicion and dislike every military operation on your coast we make against the Germans. I have already assured you that all territorial questions will be reserved for the peace conference, when they will be judged irrespective of war time occupations, and certainly such issues ought not to hamper military operations now.[2]

Even as Churchill sent off this rebuke to Tito, the cornerstone of his own Balkan policy was in danger of being wrenched away. George Papandreou, the Prime Minister of Greece, ruling in an Athens protected by British as well as Greek military units, had failed to obtain Communist agreement to the demobilisation of guerilla forces, despite the initial willingness of the EAM Ministers to do so. 'He really does require some stiffening,' Churchill had minuted to Eden on November 28, and he added:

When you think what we have done for him in troops, in operations, in food, in currency and in cash, one begins to ask oneself the question, 'Are we getting any good out of this old fool at all' and would it not be better to let them adjust their political difficulties in their own way and without our being involved? If he is not going to put up the slightest resistance to EAM and if no one else appears who will, the usefulness of our remaining in Athens is called in question. I think it would be good for me to send him a rough telegram such as I have planned. Everything is degenerating in the Greek

---

[1] Prime Minister's Personal Telegram, T.2235/4, No. 1122 to South Africa, 'Top Secret and Personal', 3 December 1944: Churchill papers, 20/176.

[2] Prime Minister's Personal Telegram, T.2246/4, No. 989 to Bari, repeated as No. 4556 to Moscow, 'Personal and Top Secret', 3 December 1944: Churchill papers, 20/176. Churchill did indeed send a copy of this telegram to Stalin, who replied: 'I confirm your statement that the Soviet and British Governments agreed in Moscow to pursue as far as possible a joint policy towards Yugoslavia.' 'Personal and Top Secret', 14 December 1944: Churchill papers, 20/177.

Government, and we must make up our minds whether we will assert our will by armed force, or clear out altogether.[1]

Churchill was determined, however, to make the percentages agreement work as it had been intended, and, with civil war imminent in Greece, decided that the moment had come to assert Britain's will. 'It is important to let it be known,' he informed Eden on November 30, 'that if there is a civil war in Greece we shall be on the side of the Government we have set up in Athens, and that above all we shall not hesitate to shoot.'[2]

On December 1, in Athens, the six Left Wing and Communist Ministers associated with EAM resigned, and EAM announced a general strike for the following day. Papandreou's remaining Ministers then passed a decree dissolving ELAS, the Communist military wing, whereupon the Communist Party moved its headquarters from the capital. General Scobie, commanding the British forces in Greece, at once proposed disarming both leftist and rightist forces in the capital. Maitland Wilson approved Scobie's action, and Wilson's approval was itself endorsed by Churchill and the Chiefs of Staff. But on December 2 Scobie reported that he would have insufficient troops for the task because Supreme Allied Headquarters, Mediterranean, were refusing to send him even a relief battalion to replace the 2nd Parachute Brigade until three to five days after December 5. Scobie appealed to Leeper to 'intervene urgently with the Chief of Imperial General Staff'.[3] On receiving Leeper's telegram, Churchill telegraphed at once to Wilson and Alexander: 'A disaster in Greece through lack of a few battalions would be grievous and have reactions on a very large scale.' The battle in Italy, which was already short of troops because of the South of France landings, could not take priority. 'A disaster in Athens,' Churchill warned, 'would not be offset by the capture of Bologna.'[4]

On December 3, a Communist demonstration in Athens clashed with the Greek police. One policeman and eleven demonstrators were killed, and sixty demonstrators injured. Churchill, noted Jock Colville on the following day, was becoming 'more and more vehement in his denunciation of communism, and in particular of ELAS and EAM in Greece, so that before lunch today Mrs C had to send him a note begging him to restrain his comments'.[5] The note read:

[1] Prime Minister's Personal Minute, M.1161/4, 28 November 1944: Churchill papers, 20/153.
[2] Prime Minister's Personal Minute, M.1166/4, 30 November 1944: Churchill papers, 20/153.
[3] No. 416 from Athens, 2 December 1944.
[4] Prime Minister's Personal Telegram, T.2241/4, 'Guard', 3 December 1944: Churchill papers, 20/176.
[5] Colville diary, 4 December 1944: Colville papers.

My darling Winston,

Please do not before ascertaining full facts repeat to anyone you meet today what you said to me this morning i.e. that the Communists in Athens
had shown their usual cowardice in putting the women & children in front
to be shot at—Because altho' Communists are dangerous, indeed perhaps
sinister people, they seem in this War on the Continent to have shown personal courage.

I write this only because I may not see you till tomorrow & I am anxious
(perhaps over-anxious).

Your loving & devoted

Clementine Churchill ended her letter with a postscript: 'Tout savoir,
c'est tout comprendre, tout comprendre c'est tout pardonner.' [1]

Churchill was now determined to see British military force used, and
used effectively, in the Greek capital. 'Your first task,' he telegraphed to
Wilson and Alexander, 'with overriding priority, is victory in Athens.' [2]
'Matters are extremely urgent,' he telegraphed to Wilson at midnight,
'and it is your responsibility to make sure that Scobie has all possible
forces in his hands. I am giving him orders direct. . . .' [3]

To draft these orders, Churchill had enlisted Eden's help. The two
men had spent much of the day together, following from hour to hour
the telegrams from Athens which told of growing Communist violence
in the streets, the seizure by the Communists of most of the police
stations in the city, and the murder of many policemen. Both men
were agreed that Scobie would have to take military action. At two
o'clock in the morning, seeing how tired Eden was, Churchill said to
him: 'If you like to go to bed, leave it to me.' [4] Churchill then worked
on the telegram, helped by Jock Colville and Pierson Dixon.

Scobie's orders, as finally sent from Downing Street at 4.50 in the
morning of December 5, were unambiguous:

You are responsible for maintaining order in Athens and for neutralising
or destroying all EAM ELAS bands approaching the city. You may make
any regulations you like for the strict control of the streets or for the rounding
up of any number of truculent persons. Naturally ELAS will try to put
women and children in the van where shooting may occur. You must be
clever about this and avoid mistakes. But do not hesitate to fire at any armed
male in Athens who assails the British authority or Greek authority with
which we are working. It would be well of course if your command were
reinforced by the authority of some Greek Government, and Papandreou is

[1] Letter of 4 December 1944: Spencer-Churchill papers.
[2] Prime Minister's Personal Telegram, T.2242/A, OZ 7082, 'Private and Top Secret', 4 December 1944: Churchill papers, 20/176.
[3] Prime Minister's Personal Telegram, T.2254/4, OZ 7103, 'Private and Top Secret', 4 December 1944: Churchill papers, 20/176.
[4] Winston S. Churchill, *The Second World War*, volume six, London 1954. page 252.

being told by Leeper to stop and help. Do not however hesitate to act as if you were in a conquered city where a local rebellion is in progress.

There was also the question of Communist forces which were approaching Athens from the countryside. With regard to these, Churchill told Scobie, 'you should surely be able with your armour to give some of them a lesson which will make the others unlikely to try'. Churchill's telegram ended: 'You may count upon my support in all reasonable and sensible action taken on this basis. We have to hold and dominate Athens. It would be a great thing for you to succeed in this without bloodshed if possible, but also with bloodshed if necessary.'[1]

Britain would not hesitate, Churchill told the House of Commons on December 5, to use 'the considerable British army now in Greece, and being reinforced', to see 'that law and order are maintained'. 'Whether the Greek people form themselves into a monarchy or a republic,' Churchill declared, 'is for their decision. Whether they form a Government of the right or left is their decision. These are entirely matters for them.' But, he warned, no Government could have 'a sure foundation' so long as there were private armies 'owing allegiance to a group, a party or an ideology instead of to the State and nation'.

Should not the British Government adopt a 'conciliatory policy', asked the Labour MP and Privy Councillor, F. W. Pethick-Lawrence. 'Oh, yes certainly, a conciliatory policy,' Churchill replied, 'but that should not include running away from, or lying down under, the threat of armed revolution and violence.'[2]

'You must force Papandreou to stand to his duty,' Churchill had telegraphed to Leeper shortly before his Scobie telegram, 'and assure him he will be supported by all our forces if he does so.'[3] In an attempt to forestall a military coup against Papandreou, General Scobie had ordered the ELAS troops to be clear of the Athens area by midnight on December 6. Churchill was worried, not that Scobie would fail, but whether Papandreou's Government might not have 'the ability and determination' to carry out the order.[4]

On December 6 Churchill worked late at the Annexe. 'The PM was exceptionally tired tonight,' noted Marian Holmes, 'but in great humour. The Greek and American troubles weigh very heavily upon him. He dropped his gold pen and said "Miss Holmes I am sure you

[1] Prime Minister's Personal Telegram, T.2255/4, 'Personal and Top Secret', despatched 4.50 a.m., 5 December 1944: Churchill papers, 20/176.

[2] *Hansard*, 5 December 1944, columns 356–65.

[3] Prime Minister's Personal Telegram, T.2256/4, No. 357 to Athens, 'Personal and Top Secret', despatched at 3.20 a.m., 5 December 1944: Churchill papers, 20/176.

[4] Prime Minister's Personal Telegram, T.2260/4, IZ 9227, ACIC/146, 'Guard', 5 December 1944: Churchill papers, 20/171.

would help an old man weighed down with age by picking it up for me". I wonder how long he will last. About P.G.W. "Let him go to hell—as soon as there's a vacant passage."' [1]

These 'American troubles' were set out in two telegrams to Roosevelt which Churchill dictated that night to Marian Holmes. In the first, Churchill referred bitterly to the reasons underlying the failure of the campaign in Italy. 'We have secured weighty advantages from "Dragoon" for the battle on the main front,' he wrote, 'but the reason why the 15th Group of Armies has not been able to inflict a decisive defeat on Kesselring is that, owing to the delay caused by the weakening of our forces for the sake of "Dragoon", we did not get through the Appennines till the Valley of the Po had become waterlogged. Thus neither in the mountains nor on the plains have we been able to use our superiority in armour.'

Churchill then set out what he believed the Allies now had to face 'in varying degrees of probability'. He saw five dismal prospects:

(a) A considerable delay in reaching, still more in forcing, the Rhine on the shortest road to Berlin.
(b) A marked degree of frustration in Italy.
(c) The escape home of a large part of the German forces from the Balkan Peninsula.
(d) Frustration in Burma.
(e) Elimination of China as a combatant.

'When we contrast these realities,' Churchill added, 'with the rosy expectations of our peoples in spite of our joint efforts to dampen them down the question very definitely arises: "What are we going to do about it?"' The answer could only be reached, in Churchill's view, by a meeting at the highest level. Hence Churchill's disappointment with Roosevelt, which he explained at the end of the telegram:

My anxiety is increased by the destruction of all hopes of an early meeting between the three of us and the indefinite postponement of another meeting of you and me with our Staffs. Our British plans are dependent on yours, our Anglo-American problems at least must be surveyed as a whole, and the telegraph and the telephone more often than not only darken counsel. Therefore I feel that if you are unable to come yourself before February, I am bound to ask you whether you could not send your Chiefs of Staff over here as soon as possible, where they would be close to your main armies and to General Eisenhower and where the whole stormy scene can be calmly and

---

[1] Marian Holmes diary, 6 December 1944: Marian Walker Spicer papers. PGW was P. G. Wodehouse, author of the Jeeves stories, who had been interned in Germany since May 1940, during which time he had made five broadcasts to America. As a result of these broadcasts, he was much vilified, but no charges were ever brought against him. After the war he lived in the United States. He was knighted in 1975, and died six weeks later, at the age of 93.

patiently studied with a view to action as closely concerted as that which signalised our campaign of 1944.[1]

Trouble had also arisen with the United States over Italy, where reports reaching London suggested that Count Sforza, whom Churchill regarded as untrustworthy, was said to be about to become, either Italian Ambassador to the United States, Italian Minister of Foreign Affairs, or even Prime Minister. In sentences which were widely interpreted as critical both of British influence in Italy and British intervention in Greece, the State Department issued a statement on December 5 which read: 'we expect the Italians to work out their problems of government along democratic lines without influence from outside. This policy would apply to an even more pronounced degree with regard to governments of the United Nations in their liberated territories.'[2]

Churchill's second telegram to Roosevelt on December 6 was to protest against this State Department statement. As he told Roosevelt: 'In view of the State Department's communiqué on Italy issued yesterday, there will no doubt be a debate in Parliament. I shall be called upon to reply to its strictures by implication upon His Majesty's Government's policy and action not only in Italy but in Greece and possibly in Belgium. This I am quite prepared to do and I hope you will realise that I must have all liberty in this matter.'

The reference to Belgium concerned American Press criticism of a British military alert during anti-Government demonstrations in Brussels. It was in fact Eisenhower who had ordered the troops to intervene.

Of Sforza, Churchill wrote in this second telegram to Roosevelt: 'It has never been our policy and we have no power, to veto the appointment of particular Italian ministers to particular positions. But it is certain that were Count Sforza to obtain the Premiership or the Foreign Secretaryship, the relations between the British Government and the Italian Government would suffer very much from our complete want of confidence in him.'

Churchill then raised with Roosevelt the wider issue of United States criticisms of Britain:

I was much astonished at the acerbity of the State Department's communiqué to the public, and I shall do my best in my reply to avoid imitating it. I feel however entitled to remind you that on every single occasion in the course of this war I have loyally tried to support any statements to which

[1] Prime Minister's Personal Telegram, T.2262/4, Prime Minister to President, No. 844, 6 December 1944: Churchill papers, 20/184.

[2] *Foreign Relations of the United States, 1944*, volume 3, page 1162 (quoted in Kimball, *op. cit.*, volume 3, page 436).

you were personally committed; for instance, in the Darlan affair I made the greatest possible exertions as you may remember to sustain the action of the United States Government and Commander, which was and still is much criticized in quarters ever ready to be critical. Also, in the matter of the division of the Italian Fleet I not only did all in my power to avoid the slightest appearance of difference between us, though the difference was considerable, but His Majesty's Government have actually supplied fourteen out of the fifteen warships lent to the Russians to make up for their one third of the Italian Fleet to which you had referred. Finally, it was I who proposed to you the bulk of the mitigations which were introduced into our relationship with Italy as the result of our talks at Quebec and Hyde Park.

In all these circumstances I was much hurt that a difference about Count Sforza should have been made the occasion for an attempt on the part of the State Department to administer a public rebuke to His Majesty's Government. In the very dangerous situation in which the war is now it will be most unfortunate if we have to reveal in public controversy the natural differences which arise inevitably in the movement of so great an alliance I do not remember anything that the State Department has ever said about Russia or about any other allied state comparable to this document with which Mr Stettinius had inaugurated his assumption of office. I am sure such things have never been said by the State Department about Russia even when very harsh communications have been received and harsher deeds done.[1]

On the evening of December 7, it was not Italy however, but Greece, which dominated the discussions of the War Cabinet, when Churchill reported that thirty or forty Greeks had been killed and about a hundred wounded. 'We had on the other hand,' he added, '1,800 prisoners.' Reinforcements were on their way to Athens, and both Alexander and Macmillan were expected there shortly. 'The great thing,' Churchill stressed, 'was to establish order in and around the capital.' Once that had been done, negotiations could begin for 'a purely Greek Government' to assume responsibility. When that had been achieved, Britain's task would be done, 'and it was to be hoped that we might be able to leave Greece to herself'.[2]

Eden, speaking of the danger of Soviet support for a 'Yugoslav–Bulgarian combination', and of Bulgaria's territorial claims against Greece, wanted to 'talk the matter over with the Russians' without delay, making clear to them Britain's strong opposition. Churchill deprecated any such protest, stressing 'the importance of our avoiding a clash with the Russians over this matter', and he added:

There could be little question under present circumstances that Communist

[1] Prime Minister's Personal Telegram, T.2263/4, Prime Minister to President, No. 845, 6 December 1944: Churchill papers, 20/184. Stettinius had replaced the ailing Cordell Hull on 1 December 1944.

[2] War Cabinet No. 162 of 1944, 7 p.m., 7 December 1944, Confidential Annex: Cabinet papers, 65/48.

influence, under Russian patronage, was in due course, even without specific action by Russia, likely to establish itself throughout the Balkan peninsula, save possibly in Greece. He thought in any event that there would be advantage in awaiting the restoration of stability in Athens before any conversations were initiated.[1]

Churchill's action in sending British troops to Athens in support of Papandreou's Government had led to an outburst of criticism in Britain, especially by those who regarded EAM–ELAS as representing a legitimate left-wing movement which could not be pushed out of the governance of Greece. 'The general public,' Jock Colville noted in his diary on December 7, 'have no idea of the true nature of ELAS, which they believe to be a heroic left-wing Resistance Movement.'[2] In the House of Commons, the Government's Greek policy was challenged in debate, with Sir Richard Acland, Emanuel Shinwell and Aneurin Bevan leading the attack. Churchill demanded that the vote be a Vote of Confidence, and spoke forcefully, even angrily, in defence of his actions, on the morning of December 8:

One must have some respect for democracy and not use the word too lightly. The last thing which resembles democracy is mob law, with bands of gangsters, armed with deadly weapons, forcing their way into great cities, seizing the police stations and key points of government, endeavouring to introduce a totalitarian regime with an iron hand, and clamouring, as they can nowadays if they get the power—

Churchill was interrupted at this point by William Gallacher, the Communist MP for Western Fife, who called out: 'That is not fair.' 'I am sorry,' Churchill said, 'to be causing so much distress'—at which there was a further interruption. Patiently, Churchill continued:

I have plenty of time, and if any outcries are wrung from hon. Members opposite I can always take a little longer over what I have to say, though I should regret to do so. I say that the last thing that represents democracy is mob law and the attempt to introduce a totalitarian regime which clamours to shoot everyone who is politically inconvenient as part of a purge of those who are said to have collaborated with the Germans during the occupation. Do not let us rate democracy so low, do not let us rate democracy as if it were merely grabbing power and shooting those who do not agree with you. That is the antithesis of democracy. That is not what democracy is based on.

Once more Gallacher interrupted. 'That is not what has happened,' he called out, to which Churchill replied: 'The hon. Member should not get so excited because he is going to have much the worse of the

[1] War Cabinet No. 162 of 1944, 7 December 1944: Confidential Annex: Cabinet papers, 65/48.
[2] Colville diary, 7 December 1844: Colville papers.

argument and much the worse of the Division. I was eleven years a fairly solitary figure in this House and pursued my way in patience, and so there may be hope for the hon. Member.'

Churchill then continued with his speech, telling the House of Commons:

Democracy, I say, is not based on violence or terrorism, but on reason, on fair play, on freedom, on respecting other people's rights as well as their ambitions. Democracy is no harlot to be picked up in the street by a man with a tommy gun. I trust the people, the mass of the people, in almost any country, but I like to make sure that it is the people and not a gang or bandits from the mountains or from the countryside who think that by violence they can overturn constituted authority, in some cases ancient Parliaments, Governments and States. That is my general description of the foundation upon which we should approach the various special instances on which I am going to dwell.

During the war, of course, we have had to arm anyone who could shoot a Hun. Apart from their character, political convictions, past records and so forth, if they were out to shoot a Hun we accepted them as friends and tried to enable them to fulfil their healthy instincts.

'Now you are paying for it,' called out John MacGovern, Independent Labour Party MP for Glasgow Shettleston, who in 1934 had led the Hunger March from Glasgow to London. Churchill replied:

We are paying for it in having this Debate to-day, which personally I have found rather enjoyable, so far. We are paying for it also with our treasure and our blood. We are not paying for it with our honour or by defeat. But when countries are liberated it does not follow that those who have received our weapons should use them in order to engross to themselves by violence and murder and bloodshed all those powers and traditions and continuity which many countries have slowly developed and to which quite a large proportion of their people, I believe the great majority, are firmly attached. If what is called in this Amendment the action of 'the friends of democracy' is to be interpreted as carefully planned *coups d'état* by murder gangs and by the iron rule of ruffians seeking to climb into the seats of power, without a vote ever having been cast in their favour—if that is to masquerade as democracy I think the House will unite in condemning it as a mockery.

Speaking of those whom Britain had armed to fight the Germans, 'the men who went out into the hills and were given rifles or machine guns by the British Government', Churchill warned that if people claimed that they, for that reason, 'by fee simple', had acquired the right 'to govern vast complex communities such as Belgium or Holland—it may be Holland next—or Greece, I say I repulse that claim'.

Vigorously, Churchill asserted Britain's responsibilities in liberated Europe:

We march along an onerous and painful path. Poor old England! (Perhaps I ought to say 'Poor old Britain!') We have to assume the burden of the most thankless tasks, and in undertaking them to be scoffed at, criticised, and opposed from every quarter; but at least we know where we are making for, know the end of the road, know what is our objective. It is that these countries shall be freed from the German armed power, and under conditions of normal tranquillity shall have a free universal vote to decide the Government of their country—except a Fascist regime—and whether that Government shall be of the Left or of the Right.

There is our aim—and we are told that we seek to disarm the friends of democracy. We are told that because we do not allow gangs of heavily armed guerrillas to descend from the mountains and install themselves, with all the bloody terror and vigour of which they are capable, in power in great capitals, we are traitors to democracy. I repulse that claim too. I shall call upon the House as a matter of confidence in His Majesty's Government, and of confidence in the spirit with which we have marched from one peril to another till victory is in sight, to reject such pretentions with the scorn that they deserve. . . .

Churchill ended his speech by offering to resign:

If I am blamed for this action I will gladly accept my dismissal at the hands of the House; but if I am not so dismissed—make no mistake about it—we shall persist in this policy of clearing Athens and the Athens region of all who are rebels against the authority of the constitutional Government of Greece—of mutineers against the orders of the Supreme Commander in the Mediterranean under whom all the guerrillas have undertaken to serve. I hope I have made the position clear, both generally as it affects the world and the war and as it affects the Government.[1]

The debate continued, with Eden summing it up for the Government. Of Churchill's speech, Harold Nicolson wrote to his sons: 'Winston was in one of his boyish moods, and allowed himself to be interrupted all the time. In fact, he seemed to me to be in rather higher spirits than the occasion warranted. I don't think he quite caught the mood of the House, which at its best was one of distressed perplexity, and at its worst one of sheer red fury.'[2]

When the Vote of Confidence was taken, 279 MPs voted for the Government, and 30 against. 'Do not be misled by our majority yesterday,' Churchill telegraphed to Harry Hopkins on December 9. 'I could have had another eighty by sending out a three-line whip instead of only two. On Fridays, with the bad communications prevailing here, Members long to get away for the week-end. Who would not?'[3]

---

[1] *Hansard*, 8 December 1944, columns 934–47.

[2] Harold Nicolson, letter of 8 December 1944: Nigel Nicolson (editor), *op. cit.*, page 410.

[3] Prime Minister's Personal Telegram, T.2309/4, 'Personal, Private and Top Secret', 9 December 1944: Churchill papers, 20/177.

On December 9 Churchill telegraphed to Leeper in Athens:

Do not be at all disquieted by criticisms made from various quarters in the House of Commons. No one knows better than I the difficulties you have had to contend with. I do not yield to passing clamour, and will always stand with those who execute their instructions with courage and precision. In Athens as everywhere else our maxim is 'No peace without victory'.[1]

Soon after the Debate, Lord Halifax telegraphed to Churchill that both James Forrestal, the Secretary of the Navy since May 1944, and Harry Hopkins, had telephoned him to express, as Halifax reported, 'enthusiastic approval of your speech on Greece, which they both think will have done immense good'.[2]

Harold Macmillan, who had been present in the House of Commons when Churchill spoke, noted in his diary: 'His speech was a superb Parliamentary performance and its courage magnificent. It was not, however, a very profound speech—that is, I think it oversimplified the problem. Perhaps that was necessary, and in any case Anthony's brilliant "wind-up" was complementary to the PM's introduction and filled in many points of detail . . .' That night, Churchill asked Macmillan to join him at the Annexe where, Macmillan wrote, 'I found him alone. He had slept after the debate, dined about 9 p.m., and was in a very exhausted and rather petulant mood.' After some 'general talk' on the debate, Macmillan wrote, 'he made a sudden attack on me for "deserting my post". He almost hinted that my absence from Rome and Athens was poltroonery. Of course, he is old and worried. I told him firmly that I came to England on his orders. . . .' Macmillan added: 'He rambled on in rather a sad and depressed way. The debate had obviously tired him very much, and I think he realised the dangers inherent in the Greek policy on which we are now embarked. He has won the debate but not the battle of Athens.'[3]

In Palestine, the British Government and the Jewish Agency had been cooperating, in the wake of Lord Moyne's murder, to try to find and to arrest members of the terrorist group responsible. Even this effort seemed, however, to be likely to be set back as a result of the Greek imbroglio, and the yet further depleted Italian campaign. 'There can be no question,' Churchill had minuted on December 4 to

---

[1] Prime Minister's Personal Telegram, T.2310/4, Foreign Office No. 413 to Athens, 'Personal and Top Secret', 10 December 1944: Churchill papers, 20/177.
[2] No. 6566 from Washington, 8 December 1944: Churchill papers, 20/176.
[3] Macmillan diary, 8 December 1944: *War Diaries, op. cit.*, pages 599–600.

Ismay, for the Chiefs of Staff Committee, 'of delaying the movement of the 5th Division to Italy. All strong offensive activities by us against illegally-armed Jews must await the clearing up of the Athens situation. We do not want two of this kind on at once. Pray consider this view at your meeting this morning.' [1]

There had 'never been any intention', the Chiefs of Staff replied, 'of delaying the move of the 5th Division to Italy'. [2]

On December 8 Maitland Wilson sent Churchill an account of the situation in Greece, as reported by Scobie. In the Athens–Piraeus area fighting had continued throughout the previous day, but progress had been limited 'owing to widespread sniping and increased rebel activities'. In the port area British troops had been 'forced to withdraw' in face of strong opposition. In Salonica the general situation was 'tense' and ELAS 'more in evidence' in the town. [3]

Wilson's telegram was sent as the first in a new series codename 'Greek'. 'Your "Greek" fills me with concern,' Churchill telegraphed to Wilson in the early hours of December 9, and he added:

You should send further reinforcements to Athens without the slightest delay. The prolongation of the fight has many dangers. I warned you of the paramount political importance of this conflict. At least two more Brigades should hurry to the scene.

In addition to the above, why does not the Navy help all the time instead of only landing a small number in a crisis? [4]

'You seem to be having rather a stiff time,' Churchill telegraphed to Scobie half an hour later. 'Have you enough troops? Do not hesitate to ask for them from the Supreme Commander who keeps me informed of everything.' Churchill also wanted to know how long Scobie thought it would take 'to clear Athens and the Piraeus and the district immediately around? Is it a matter of days or weeks?' [5]

During December 9 Churchill received a full report from Scobie, sent through General Wilson. 'Signs of increased rebel movement

---

[1] Prime Minister's Personal Minute, D.298/4, 4 December 1944: Chiefs of Staff Committee No. 389 (Operations) of 1944, Enclosure to Annex II: Cabinet papers, 79/83.

[2] Chiefs of Staff Committee No. 389 (Operations) of 1944, 11 a.m., 4 December 1944: Cabinet papers, 79/83.

[3] 'Greek' No. 1, IZ 9288, 8 December 1944: Churchill papers, 20/176. On 2 January 1945 Churchill telegraphed to the British Consul General in Salonica, Thomas Rapp (who had been interned in Germany from 1941 to 1943): 'All your messages from Salonica are being carefully read by me and I compliment you upon their clarity and interest as well as upon your own firmness of bearing in circumstances of exceptional perplexity.' (Prime Minister's Personal Telegram, T.8 of 1945, No. 5 to Salonica, 2 January 1945: Churchill papers, 20/210.)

[4] War Office telegram No. 50355, 'Personal and Top Secret', 'Guard', despatched 3.55 a.m., 9 December 1944: Churchill papers, 20/176.

[5] War Office telegram No. 50402, 'Personal and Top Secret', 'Guard', despatched 4.30 a.m., 9 December 1944: Churchill papers, 20/176.

towards city,' Scobie warned. Inside Athens, however, several strong points had been 'cleaned up' and machine guns 'eliminated by tanks'. Approximate 'rebel' casualties were fourteen killed and 250 taken prisoner. As well as Athens, British troops were present in several towns, including Salonica, as well as on Corfu and, at last, Crete. An additional Spitfire squadron had flown in from Italy on the previous day.[1] Some three hours later Scobie telegraphed direct to Churchill. 'Task is not an easy one,' he wrote, 'as we are up against a highly organized unscrupulous and determined organization. We held firmly the vital points in the centre of Athens and are gradually extending our grip. Everyone in great spirits and much heartened by your speech yesterday.'

Scobie's telegram went on to set out the main difficulties of the British position:

Troops are insufficient to clear Athens–Piraeus under present conditions without resorting to shelling and bombing in built up areas regardless of damage or civilian casualties. This is an immense city area and the cleaning of numerous pockets of well established resistance is a slow and arduous task. Having cleared such areas it is not possible to keep them free from infiltration by small bodies of rebels most of whom are in civilian clothes including some women. Rebels make free use of churches as strong points and only solution is to starve them out.

Scobie added, ominously: 'Am concerned at activities of Russian Military Mission under Colonel Popoff.'[2]

Churchill was not worried, however, at Russian activities: no word of criticism of Britain's policy had come from Moscow, nor had any public criticism appeared in the Soviet Press. When, later that week, the British Embassy in Bucharest complained about further Soviet activities in Roumania, Churchill minuted to Eden:

Considering the way the Russians have so far backed us up over what is happening in Greece, which must throw great strain on their sentiments and organization, we really must not press our hand too far in Roumania. Remember the percentages we wrote out on paper. I think we have had pretty good treatment from Stalin in Greece, much better in fact than we have had from the Americans. It is an awful thing that one cannot have it both ways, but you and I took great responsibility and we cannot overplay our hand in Roumania least of all at a time like this. Without letting it appear in telegrams, you ought to make your will felt.[3]

*   *   *

[1] 'Greek' No. 3, IZ 9321, 9 December 1944: Churchill papers, 20/177.

[2] Air Force Headquarters Middle East, Telegram F.65755, IZ 9320, 9 December 1944: Churchill papers, 20/177. Colonel Grigory Popoff (also spelt Popov) had flown from the Soviet Union to Vis, then to Bari, and then to Athens.

[3] Prime Minister's Personal Minute, M.1207/4, 'Personal, Private and Confidential', 11 December 1944: Churchill papers, 20/153.

On the afternoon of December 9, the London evening newspapers reported that ELAS had offered to make peace. Similar reports reached Churchill from Cairo.[1] 'Naturally we should be glad to have this matter settled,' Churchill telegraphed at once to General Scobie, 'but you should make quite sure, so far as your influence goes, that we do not give away for the sake of kindness what has been won or can still be won by our troops.' It was 'difficult', Churchill added, 'to see how EAM leaders, with their hands wet with Greek and British blood, should resume their places in the Cabinet. This might however be got over. The great thing is to proceed with caution and to consult us upon the terms when they are made.' Britain's 'clear objective', Churchill stressed, was 'the defeat of EAM. The ending of the fighting is subsidiary to this.' He was ordering 'large reinforcements' to Athens. 'Firmness and sobriety are what are needed now and not eager embraces, while the real quarrel is unsettled.'[2]

In Washington, the new Secretary of State, Edward Stettinius, had defended his disapproval of Britain's policy in Greece. On December 9 Churchill telegraphed to Hopkins, hoping through him to influence Roosevelt:

I hope you will tell our great friend that the establishment of law and order in and around Athens is essential to all future measures of magnanimity and consolation towards Greece. After this has been established will be the time for talking. My guiding principle is 'no peace without victory'. It is a great disappointment to me to have been set upon in this way by ELAS when we came loaded with good gifts and anxious only to form a united Greece which could establish its own destiny. But we have been set upon, and we intend to defend ourselves. I consider we have a right to the President's support in the policy we are following. If it can be said in the streets of Athens that the United States are against us, then more British blood will be shed and much more Greek.

'It grieves me very much,' Churchill added, 'to see signs of our drifting apart at a time when unity becomes ever more important, as danger recedes and faction arises.'[3]

On December 9, United States hostility to Britain's action in Greece reached a climax when Admiral King cancelled the order whereby American landing craft were helping British troops in Greece, as Britain had requested. Two of these landing craft were due to sail for Athens on the following day, and seven were already engaged in their

---

[1] Air Force Headquarters Middle East, telegram F.65755, IZ 9320, 'Emergency', 9 December 1944: Churchill papers, 20/177.

[2] Prime Minister's Personal Telegram, T.2297/4, War Office telegram, 50458, 'Personal and Top Secret', 'Guard', despatched 4.45 p.m., 9 December 1944: Churchill papers, 20/176.

[3] Prime Minister's Personal Telegram, T.2309/4, 'Personal, Private and Top Secret', 9 December 1944: Churchill papers 20/177.

essential task. Their orders were, as Maitland Wilson telegraphed to London that morning, 'to cease forthwith conveying troops, stores and supplies to Greece'. This, Wilson warned, 'would gravely endanger the security of the forces now in Greece, and delay the introduction of relief vehicles and supplies'.[1] A further telegram from Admiral Somerville reported a conversation between Somerville and the Chief of the United States Navy Staff, Admiral Cook, who 'had stated that the war in Greece was one in which the US were not participating'.[2]

Churchill at once drafted a strong telegram of protest, but decided not to send it. Admiral King's orders, Churchill had written, 'might produce a disaster of the first magnitude, which might endanger all the relations between Great Britain and the United States and by so doing affect the progress of the main war against Germany and thereafter against Japan'. Churchill's final paragraph was to have read:

I am sure that you have never seen these orders and that you will have them stamped upon at the earliest moment. If this were not so, I am sure you would have let me know in good time. I shall be forced when the House of Commons meets on Tuesday to make full explanation and I would like to be able to assure them that there is no fundamental breach between Britain and the United States.[3]

Instead of sending this telegram, Churchill telephoned Hopkins on December 10, to tell him direct, as Churchill noted, 'of the dangerous character of the alleged American orders to withdraw all American ships and to cut our communications from Italy to Greece'. Hopkins promised Churchill that he would 'bring this matter to the notice of the President tomorrow morning'.

According to Churchill's note of his decision to telephone, he 'thought in view of our command of the Mediterranean, there was less risk in telephoning by the only channel open than in leaving matters in their present condition'. Churchill added: 'It is very unlikely that we shall be listened in to, but even if we are what can they do that would be worse than the American ships being cut out of the traffic and an open breach between Britain and the United States becoming known?'[4]

[1] MEDCOS No. 215, IZ 9319, 'Emergency', sent at 2.45 p.m., 19 December 1944: Premier papers, 3/212/5, folio 337.

[2] FMD No. 281, Chiefs of Staff Committee No. 396 of 1944, 11 December 1944, documents submitted with Item 10: Cabinet papers, 79/84.

[3] 'Personal and Top Secret', 'Prime Minister to President', Unsent draft, 10 December 1944: Premier papers, 3/212/5, folios 328/9.

[4] 'Note', 'Dictated by PM', 10 December 1944: Premier papers, 3/212/5, folio 315.

Hopkins saw Admiral King, who 'agreed to cancel his order', as Halifax at once informed Churchill. Hopkins also told Halifax that King 'had apparently issued the order on his own'. As to the cancellation of the order, 'the President has not been in on it', Halifax reported, 'though Harry will probably tell him what had passed'. Halifax added that Hopkins was 'anxious to avoid further trouble'.[1]

Further troubles were soon to come, and arose from the error of a Private Secretary seven days earlier, in sending the telegram to General Scobie, instructing him to act in Athens as though he were in 'a conquered city'. Churchill had intended this telegram to be prefaced with the codeword 'Guard'. 'As the Combined HQ at Caserta contained both British and American officers,' Jock Colville later explained, 'we had a convention that any telegrams which we did not wish the Americans to read, because they were concerned with purely British matters, should be headed "Guard".'[2]

Owing, however, as Colville later explained, to the fact that 'we were all very tired', and that, at five in the morning, Churchill 'insisted that the telegram should be sent off straightway', Colville 'sent it over to the Foreign Office but omitted to put the word "Guard" on top!'[3]

As a result of this simple error, Churchill's telegram passed to the Americans, was leaked and on December 11 was published in the *Washington Post* by the columnist Drew Pearson.[4] The Americans were outraged. Churchill, in a telegram to Roosevelt, sought to explain the various occasions on which the United States had earlier expressed its support for what Britain was now doing in Greece. He decided to send this telegram, not to Roosevelt, but to Hopkins. 'I must frankly confess,' he told Hopkins in a covering letter, 'I never knew EAM would be so powerful. I only wish they had fought one tenth as well against the Germans. We have got many troops coming in now but I certainly do not want to fight another war against ELAS.'

Churchill went on to tell Hopkins that if he could get 'any word of approval spoken by the United States in favour of the Allied intervention in Athens by British troops, you may save many British and Greek lives and set free soldiers who are needed elsewhere'.[5]

That night Churchill received a report from Alexander, who had reached Athens with Macmillan in the early afternoon. 'The military

[1] Washington Telegram No. 6586 to Foreign Office, 'Personal and Secret', 10 December 1944: Premier papers, 3/212/5, folio 313.
[2] Colville note, attached to diary entry for 4 December 1944: Colville papers.
[3] Colville letter of 8 August 1952 (to Denis Kelly): Churchill papers, 4/360.
[4] Drew Pearson regularly printed secret documents which he had obtained from a source in either the White House or the State Department.
[5] 'Private', 11 December 1944: Premier papers, 3/212/5, folio 325.

situation,' Alexander reported, 'is more serious than I had thought from information which we had in London. The initiative is not wholly with us. The British forces are in fact beleaguered in the heart of the city.' The airfield itself was 'not too secure', nor was the port of Piraeus fully controlled by the British. Stores could not be unloaded there, and there were only six days' rations and three days' ammunition available 'at present rate of expenditure' for the troops in the central area of Athens.

Alexander said that he was arranging for 'strong reinforcements'. He also advised that 'stern measures after proper warning' were needed 'to clear Piraeus and Athens'. He also urged that the King of Greece immediately appoint Archbishop Damaskinos as Regent. 'In this way,' he explained, 'a proper measure of responsibility can be restored to the head of the Greek State, and the most powerful cry against us, foreign intervention, effectively answered.'[1]

At the War Cabinet on December 12, it was agreed that Alexander should be told, as Churchill suggested, 'that the War Cabinet would support him in the military measures which he considered necessary'.[2] But, as Churchill explained to Alexander, Leeper and Macmillan, the King of Greece, while willing that Archbishop Damaskinos should replace Papandreou as Prime Minister, refused to accept him as Regent.[3] Yet it was only by appointing Damaskinos as Regent, Macmillan and Leeper urged, that 'confidence' could be restored. 'At the moment, fear dominates political scene.'[4] President Roosevelt also favoured a Regency and, as he telegraphed to Churchill, a declaration by the King of Greece 'of his intention not to return unless called for by popular plebiscite'. 'This might be particularly effective,' Roosevelt added, 'if accompanied by an assurance that elections will be held at some fixed date, no matter how far in the future, when the people would have full opportunity to express themselves.' Roosevelt's telegram continued: 'Meanwhile, might it not be possible to secure general agreement on the disarmament and dissolution of all the armed groups now in the country, including the Mountain Brigade and the Sacred Battalion, leaving your troops to preserve law and order alone until the Greek national forces can be reconstituted on a non-partisan basis and adequately equipped.'

[1] Athens telegram No. 563 to Foreign Office, 'Personal', 'Most Immediate', 11 December 1944 (received 12.40 a.m., 12 December 1944): Foreign Office papers, 954/11, folios 347–8.

[2] War Cabinets No. 165 and 166 of 1944, 12 December 1944 (3 p.m. and 5.30 p.m.), Confidential Annex: Cabinet papers, 65/48. At nine o'clock that morning, Alexander had formally 'assumed command in the Mediterranean theatre' (MEDCOS 218, IZ 9397, Field Marshal Alexander to the Chiefs of Staff, 12 December 1944: Cabinet papers, 105/154).

[3] Prime Minister's Personal Telegram, T.2351/4, 'Top Secret', 12 December 1944: Churchill papers, 20/177.

[4] Athens No. 587 to Foreign Office, 'Personal', 13 December 1944: Churchill papers, 20/177.

In this telegram, Roosevelt made it clear that while he was anxious 'to be of the greatest help to you in this trying situation', there were 'limitations' imposed in part by the 'traditional policies' of the United States, and in part by the 'mounting adverse reaction of public opinion in this country'.

United States opinion, hostile to the Greek King and hostile to the Government of Papandreou, regarded a Regency with suspicion, seeing in it a British device to preserve the monarchy. Britain's purpose in pressing for a Regency was, however, to ensure that power did not immediately revert to the exiled King, who had previously supported the Metaxas dictatorship.[1]

At the War Cabinet on December 13, Eden made it clear that Damaskinos would refuse to be Prime Minister and Eden was asked, with Churchill, to press the King once more to agree to a Regency.[2] Churchill and Eden saw the King on December 14, but he declined to appoint Damaskinos as Regent.[3] On the following morning the King wrote to Churchill: 'What would be the position if, after the announcement of the Regency, the Guerillas were to persist in their refusal to disarm or were to put forward new terms? And what would be my own responsibility if I were now to surrender my authority to a Regent who would be able to take decisions in my name, without my being sure that the large but unarmed majority of my people would not be handed over tomorrow to the tender mercies of an armed minority?'[4]

'I know of nothing to the credit of the Archbishop,' Churchill informed Roosevelt on December 14, 'except that our people on the spot think he might stop a gap or bridge a gully.' The policy of setting up a Regency was supported by the War Cabinet irrespective of party. Referring to a speech by Ernest Bevin at the Trades Union Congress on December 13, in which the Minister of Labour had defended the Cabinet's decision to intervene in Greece, Churchill told Roosevelt:

I hope that the British reinforcements now coming steadily into Attica may make a more healthy situation in Athens. You will realize how very serious it would be if we withdrew, as we easily could, and the result was a frightful massacre, and an extreme left wing regime under Communist inspiration installed itself, as it would, in Athens. My cabinet colleagues here of

[1] President to Prime Minister, No. 673, 'Personal and Top Secret', 13 December 1944: Churchill papers, 20/177.
[2] War Cabinet No. 167 of 1944, 13 December 1944, Confidential Annex: Cabinet papers, 65/48.
[3] Eden memoirs, *The Reckoning, op. cit.*, page 498.
[4] Letter of 14 December 1944, sent by Churchill to Roosevelt as Prime Minister's Personal Telegram, T.2359/4, Prime Minister to President No. 852, 'Personal and Top Secret', 14 December 1944: Churchill papers, 20/177.

all parties are not prepared to act in a manner so dishonourable to our record and name. Ernest Bevin's speech to the Labour Conference won universal respect.

Stern fighting lies ahead, and even danger to our troops in the centre of Athens. The fact that you are supposed to be against us, in accordance with the last sentence of Stettinius' press release, as I feared has added to our difficulties and burdens. I think it probable that I shall broadcast to the world on Sunday night and make manifest the purity and disinterestedness of our motives throughout and also of our resolves.

Meanwhile I send you a letter I have received from the King of Greece, to whom we have suggested the policy of making the Archbishop of Athens Regent. The King refuses to allow this. Therefore an act of constitutional violence will be entailed if we finally decide upon this course.[1]

In one area of the Greek intervention, the Russian attitude, Alexander was able to set Churchill's mind at rest that day. 'I met Colonel Popoff of the Russian Military Mission today,' he telegraphed, 'and walked him down the street in friendly and animated conversation for the benefit of the Greeks who I hope will be duly impressed.'[2] Although Communists were at 'the root of the business' in Greece, Churchill later telegraphed to Mackenzie King, 'Stalin has not so far made any public reflection on our actions.'[3] The Canadian Government had not been too anxious to support the British move, so much so that Mackenzie King threatened to publicize the disagreement. Churchill telegraphed at once to Ottawa:

I was surprised and grieved at the suggestion that you might find it necessary to issue a public statement that Canadian troops shall not be used in Greece. Such a statement could only increase our difficulties and postpone a settlement of the present troubles in that country. It would be generally regarded throughout the world as a dissociation of Canada from the policy of His Majesty's Government and a marked reflection on our credit and honour. We went into Greece at the invitation of the Greek Prime Minister and with the knowledge of a Greek Government composed of all parties, including EAM and Communists. We went in, with the approval of the United States and the assent of Russia, to bring to the Greek people food and order. We cannot abandon this task without loss and a blow to British prestige. It is on such occasions as this that the British Commonwealth should stand together.

On the specific question of Canadian troops being sent to join Scobie's forces, Churchill told Mackenzie King:

[1] Prime Minister's Personal Telegram, T.2358/4, Prime Minister to President, No. 851, 'Personal and Top Secret', No. 10555 from Foreign Office to Washington, 14 December 1944: Foreign Office papers, 954/11, folio 363.

[2] 'Top Secret', sent through Bari at 11.30 p.m., 12 December 1944: Foreign Office papers, 954/11, folios 351–2.

[3] Prime Minister's Personal Telegram, T.2388/4, No. 219 to Ottawa, 'Top Secret and Personal', 18 December 1944: Churchill papers, 20/177.

We have never in fact had any intention of proposing that Canadian troops should be sent to Greece. Specific orders to this effect have been sent to Field-Marshal Alexander and your mind may therefore be quite at ease on that point. But a public statement at the present juncture by the Canadian Government that they had asked for such an assurance would be disastrous. The United States landing craft and aircraft are continuing their assistance to the British troops after the point had been decided at Washington. It would be a great pity for Canada to take isolated action and for the Empire to be wounded in this fashion.[1]

The King of Greece still refused to appoint Archbishop Damaskinos as Regent, despite a second appeal by Churchill and Eden on December 16. 'I have heard mixed accounts of the Archbishop,' Churchill telegraphed to Alexander on the following day, 'who is said to be in touch with EAM and to have keen personal ambitions. We have not yet decided whether or in what way to overcome the King's resistance.' Churchill added: 'Personally I feel that our military predominance should be plainly established before we make terms, and in any case I should not like to make terms on grounds of weakness rather than of strength. Of course if you tell me it is impossible for us to be in control of Attica within a reasonable time the situation presents difficulties, but not such as should daunt us after all the others we have overcome.'[2]

British reinforcements to Greece continued. By the 'middle of next week', Churchill telegraphed to Roosevelt on December 17, Britain would be 'far superior in numbers' in Athens and the Piraeus. Securing those two towns was the 'immediate task'. ELAS might then 'agree to depart', and this would 'give us a firm basis from which to negotiate the best settlement possible between the warring Greek factions'. Churchill added:

I am sure you would not wish us to cast down our painful and thankless task at this time. We embarked upon it with your full consent (see my No. 755 and your reply).[3] We desire nothing from Greece but to do our duty by the common cause. In the midst of our task of bringing food and relief and maintaining the rudiments of order for a Government which has no armed forces, we have become involved in a furious, though not as yet very bloody, struggle. I have felt it much that you were unable to give a word of explanation for our action but I understand your difficulties.

---

[1] Prime Minister's Personal Telegram, T.2374/4, No. 217 to Ottawa, 'Secret and Personal', 16 December 1944: Premier papers, 3/212/6, folios 351–2.

[2] Prime Minister's Personal Telegram, T.2376/4, 'Personal, Private and Top Secret', 'Guard', 'Despatch through "C",' 'To be decyphered only by the Field Marshal's Confidential Officer', 'No circulation to Anyone', 'Eyes Only', 17 December 1944: Premier papers, 3/212/6, folios 835–7. These extra security instructions arose out of the leakage of the Scobie telegram, and were to be put on a number of Churchill's subsequent telegrams to Alexander.

[3] No. 755 of 17 August 1944 (see page 906 n. 2), in which Churchill had stressed the need to

At the Labour Party Conference, Churchill noted, Ernest Bevin had spoken in support of the Government's Greek policy, which the Conference had endorsed by 2,455,000 votes to 137,000. Churchill added: 'I could at any time obtain, I believe, a ten to one majority in the House of Commons.'

Churchill confided in Roosevelt his own doubts about the appointment of Damaskinos as Regent, a course 'strongly recommended' by both Macmillan and Leeper. A one-man Regency, Churchill explained, was 'obnoxious' to the Papandreou Government, though they 'might' be persuaded to advocate a regency of three: Archbishop Damaskinos, General Plastiras, the most prominent and most irreconcilable republican figure in Greece, and Philippos Dragoumis, a senior politician and friend of the King. As to having the Archbishop as sole regent, Churchill warned Roosevelt, 'There is suspicion that the Archbishop is ambitious of obtaining chief political power and that, supported by EAM, he will use it ruthlessly against existing ministers. Whether this be true or not I cannot say. The facts are changing from hour to hour. I do not feel at all sure that in setting up a one-man regency we might not be imposing a dictatorship in Greece.'[1]

On December 17 Alexander sent Churchill a word of warning. He expected to be able 'to hold our present positions' in Athens, 'but not perhaps defeat the rebels there yet'. It might even be necessary to send for another infantry division, which could only come from the Italian front, 'with serious results on the battle there'. Nor could such a division be operative in Greece 'before some three weeks'.[2] 'We are waiting here till scene clears a little more,' Churchill replied, 'after which we shall give all the necessary directions,' and he cautioned Alexander, who had now taken up his command as Wilson's successor in Italy: 'I trust I may have from you your full help, even though I know that your heart is in the North.'[3]

---

prepare a British force 'not exceeding 10,000 men' which could be sent to Athens to forestall the establishment of 'a tyrannical Communist government', and No. 608 of 26 August 1944 in which Roosevelt replied: 'I have no objection to your making preparations to have in readiness a sufficient British force to preserve order in Greece when German forces evacuate that country.' There was 'also no objection', Roosevelt wrote, 'to the use by General Wilson of American transport airplanes that are available to him at the time and that can be spared from other operations'.

[1] Prime Minister's Personal Telegram, T.2379/4, Prime Minister to President, No. 855, 'Personal and Top Secret', 'Private and Confidential', 17 December 1944: Churchill papers, 20/177.

[2] 'Special unnumbered signal', 'Guard', 'Top Secret', 18 December 1944: Churchill papers, 20/177.

[3] Prime Minister's Personal Telegram, T.2397/4, 'Personal and Top Secret', 'Guard', 19 December 1944: Churchill papers, 20/177.

Churchill was more confident of success than Alexander. 'Give us a few more days,' he minuted to Eden, 'and we may well have a solid foundation on which to act.'[1] To Harold Macmillan, Churchill had sent a telegram of 'sympathy for you and Leeper in the tangled and exciting situation in which you are placed'. British policy, Churchill explained, was to avoid raising the constitutional crisis with the Greek King 'till we see whether we can obtain military predominance in the next few days'. Churchill added: 'You need not worry about my personal position or that of the Government being in danger. We can, I think, at any time have a ten to one vote in the House of Commons and I am confident I can explain matters in a broadcast to the country tonight. But even if these good and solid conditions did not exist here, they would make no difference to the decisions which we should take.'

'At the moment,' Churchill commented, 'the Greek question is somewhat obscured by the Polish, in which far graver issues are involved.'[2]

On 14 December 1944, in the House of Commons, Churchill spoke about Poland, telling Members of Parliament of his and Eden's disappointment that no agreement had been reached between Poland and Russia. 'We have never weakened in any way,' he declared, 'in our resolve that Poland shall be restored and stand erect as a sovereign, independent nation, free to model her social institutions or any other institutions in any way her people choose, provided, I must say, that these are not on Fascist lines, and provided that Poland stands loyally as a barrier and friend of Russia against German aggression from the West.'

Turning to the wider task of the United Nations, through whose World Organization a Polish settlement might pass, Churchill then spoke of how 'another great war, especially an ideological war, fought as it would be not only on frontiers but in the heart of every land with weapons far more destructive than men have wielded, would spell the doom, perhaps for many centuries, of such civilisation as we have been able to erect since history began to be written'. On many issues, 'strong, authoritative, if provisional decisions' were now required, not only on the Russo-Polish question, 'but on a host of vital matters, political, international, military and economic'. For this reason, a meeting of the 'three Great Powers' was needed 'at the earliest possible moment', and Churchill added:

[1] Prime Minister's Personal Minute, M.1231/4, 19 December 1944: Churchill papers, 20/153.
[2] 'Prime Minister's Personal Telegram, T. 2380/4, 'Personal, Private and Top Secret', 'Guard', 17 December 1944: Premier papers, 3/212/13, folio 807.

So far as I and my right hon. Friend the Foreign Secretary are concerned, we can only repeat what has been said so often, that we will proceed to any place at any time, under any conditions, where we can meet the heads of our two chief Allies, and we should welcome, above all, a meeting in this island, a meeting in Great Britain, which has waged war from the very outset and has risked, without flinching, national annihilation in the cause of freedom.[1]

Turning to the Polish question, in a telegram to Roosevelt on the following day, Churchill spoke of the 'fatalistic' mood among the London Poles, 'waiting for something to turn up'. But 'with Poles', he added, 'these moods do not last'. As for the Lublin Committee, 'we do not regard it as in any way representative of Polish opinion', Churchill wrote, 'and whatever developments there may be in the Soviet Government's attitude we do not, at present, intend to recognize it'. Churchill ended his telegram: 'We shall maintain our recognition of the London Government, which is the legal government of Poland and the authority to which the large Polish forces fighting under British command owe allegiance. We hope that we can keep in step and consult beforehand on all this.'[2]

The Enigma decrypts since mid-November had suggested some unusual German preparations in the north-European war zone. On December 3, Churchill had asked the Joint Intelligence Committee if there was 'any further news'.[3] He was told that nothing was amiss. That same day, Montgomery's chief Intelligence Officer, Brigadier Williams, commented on the most recent decrypt that the German's 'bruited sweep to Antwerp is clearly beyond his powers'.[4]

On December 12, Churchill invited Eisenhower to explain his future operations against Germany. At a meeting, held in Churchill's Map Room, 'Ike set out the situation,' noted Admiral Cunningham in his diary, 'and his future plans, which certainly were a bit woolly, but seemed to indicate that Germany was to be attacked by simultaneous thrusts across the Rhine in May, one north of the Ruhr and the other from Mainz–Frankfurt towards Kassel.'[5]

---

[1] *Hansard*, 15 December 1944, columns 1478–89.

[2] Prime Minister's Personal Telegram, T.2375/4, Prime Minister to President, No. 854, 'Personal and Top Secret', 16 December 1944: Churchill papers, 20/177.

[3] Prime Minister's Personal Minute, D. 293/4, 3 December 1944: Cabinet papers, 121/413, and exchanges between General Hollis and the Secretary of the Joint Intelligence Committee of 4 and 5 December 1944.

[4] 21st Army Group Intelligence Summary, 3 December 1944: War Office papers, 171/134, No. 168.

[5] Cunningham diary, 12 December 1944: Cunningham papers.

Most of the German divisions, Eisenhower told the Staff Conference of December 12, 'were weak either in armour or personnel, a large proportion of whom were badly trained'. General Patton 'was of the opinion', Eisenhower added, 'that the army opposite him was on the verge of cracking'.[1]

Brooke, who spoke after Eisenhower, argued 'vehemently', as Cunningham noted in his diary, 'for a really strong thrust north of the Ruhr', the thrust to Frankfurt 'to be subsidiary'.[2]

There was 'a dangerous dispersal of forces', Brooke told Eisenhower, on the existing plan. The 'main thrust', wherever made, should be 'as strong as possible'. To have, as Eisenhower wished, two major thrusts of approximately equal forces, one in the north, the other in the south, created 'a serious danger that neither would succeed'. In Brooke's view, the main attack should be north of the Ruhr, with 55 of the 80 divisions available being allocated to it. At the Quebec Conference, Brooke pointed out, the Combined Chiefs of Staff 'had drawn General Eisenhower's attention to keeping his left flank strong'. The 'failure to reach the Rhine' was due 'in large part to a shift of the emphasis to the centre and right'.

Replying to this, Eisenhower 'agreed that he had not fully accomplished the tasks given in his directives'. Divisions had been 'starved of resources' and a 'calculated risk' had been taken in the airborne operations at Arnhem.[3]

Churchill made no comment. The Staff Conference at an end, 'We all dined with the PM,' Cunningham noted in his diary, 'and discussed many things. Ike in reply to a small speech by the PM said that after the war he was going to resign and devote himself to the promoting of good US—British relations.'

The after-dinner talk did not end until 1.30 in the morning. As the Chiefs of Staff were leaving, Churchill called Cunningham into the Cabinet Room, asked if he was Scottish, and then asked if he would like to be a Knight of the Thistle. This Cunningham accepted.

'After a cup of soup,' Cunningham added, 'he then proceeded to sit down to a pile of papers, in spite of my remonstrance as he was obviously dead tired.'[4]

*   *   *

[1] Staff Conference, Chiefs of Staff Committee No. 399 (Operations) of 1944, 12 December 1944: Cabinet papers, 79/84.
[2] Cunningham diary, 12 December 1944: Cunningham papers.
[3] Staff Conference, Chiefs of Staff Committee No. 399 (Operations) of 1944, 12 December 1944: Cabinet papers, 79/84.
[4] Cunningham diary, 12 December 1944: Cunningham papers. It was Churchill's habit before going to bed to drink a cup of soup made from soup cubes sold by Fortnum and Mason, and said to contain a mild sleeping draught.

Undeterred by British doubts about his two-thrusted attack to-wards the Rhine, Eisenhower struck both at Aachen in the north and through Alsace in the south. 'In spite of appalling weather conditions,' Churchill telegraphed to Smuts ten days later, 'our friends however pushed on confidently, and were very much spread from north to south when the enemy began his counterstroke.' [1]

This German counterstroke was launched on December 14, at the weak centre of Eisenhower's forces, through the high ground of the Ardennes. [2]

For six months these same Germans had been in retreat, fighting every mile, but being driven continuously eastward towards Germany. Now they were moving forward again.

At a series of meetings of the Chiefs of Staff Committee in the im-mediate aftermath of the German counter-attack, Churchill heard first of the unexpected force of the German thrust, deep into the Ardennes, and then of Eisenhower's confidence in halting it. On December 20, Brooke asked Churchill to telephone Eisenhower, with the proposal that Montgomery should command all Allied forces north of the breakthrough, and Bradley all those in the south. 'Ike agreed,' Brooke noted in his diary. [3] Eisenhower had also imposed a temporary news blackout. 'We, of course,' Churchill told the House of Commons, 'sup-port him.' [4]

At a Staff Conference that evening, Churchill spoke of how, since his meeting with Roosevelt at Quebec in September, events 'had been the cause of much disappointment'. On the western front, and in Italy, 'the Germans were holding fast; and in Burma our campaign, which was developing so favourably, was being seriously affected by the necessity to withdraw Chinese Divisions for the defence of the vital areas of China. The scene was one of frustration and disillusion. It might be that the present battle on the Western Front would furnish the opportunity for a decisive victory, but on the other hand one

[1] Prime Minister's Personal Telegram, T.2412/4, 'Personal and Top Secret', 'Decypher your-self', Dominions Office No. 1166 to South Africa, 'No Circulation. (PM's instructions)', 22 December 1944: Churchill papers, 20/178.

[2] There had been a number of Enigma indications of a movement of German troops westward across the Rhine and their subsequent concentration on the western side. There had also been indications of an impending large-scale air attack. These indications, arriving over a prolonged period, were not however satisfactorily brought together, partly because the German troop movements thus revealed were seen as an attempt to meet an impending Allied attack, and partly because those who interpreted them did not feel that the Germans were any longer capable of a serious counter-attack.

[3] Brooke diary, 20 December 1944: Bryant, op. cit., volume 2, page 357. The announcement that this had been done was issued on 5 January 1945.

[4] Hansard, 19 December 1944, column 1616.

could not yet tell whether the Germans might not succeed in disrupting our offensive plans and prolonging the war.'

Churchill proposed an immediate public announcement 'that we
were still capable of vigorous action'. Such an announcement, he
believed, 'would stimulate feeling in America, would encourage our
own troops, and would contribute to an earlier victory'. Churchill
went on to tell the Staff Conference:

An intense effort would be necessary to achieve what he had in mind.
There must be no more reduction of formations, and, indeed, divisions should
be recreated. Conventional methods must be scrapped, lower standards
accepted, and we must emulate in this crisis of the war the exertions of the
Germans. Figures which had been presented to him by Lord Cherwell showed
that more than two million men now in the Army were outside divisional
and brigade organisations. This was a state of affairs which could not be
allowed to persist, and somehow or other a higher percentage of the Army
must be brought into fighting formations.

Churchill then proposed raising the upper age limits of the infantry
from thirty-five to thirty-eight and also calling for volunteers from the
Home Guard. 'Every kind of expedient had been adopted by the
Germans,' he pointed out, 'and we too must descend to makeshifts.' A
further 250,000 men should be added to the fighting strength of the
British Army on the western front. The 'time had now come', Churchill
reiterated, 'for extreme measures'.[1]

A quarter of a million extra 'fighting men' were now called for,
Churchill announced in a public statement on December 22, to enable
the Allied armies to regain the initiative in the West. These men were
to be found not only by combing out existing Service units, but by 'a
new call up from civil life'.[2] In issuing this statement, Churchill
telegraphed to Eisenhower: 'I am putting this out as a mark of our
confidence in you.'[3]

It was towards British policy in Greece that criticism now grew,
with Churchill answering questions almost daily in the House of
Commons, and the newspapers increasingly uneasy about Britain's
support for the King and Papandreou. The Chief Whip, James Stuart,

[1] Staff Conference, Chiefs of Staff Committee No. 406 (Operations) of 1944, 10.30 p.m., 19
December 1944: Cabinet papers, 79/84. Those present were Churchill (in the Chair), Sir James
Grigg (Secretary of State for War), Lord Cherwell (Paymaster General), Lieutenant-General
Sir Ronald M. Weeks (War Office) and Major-General J. S. Steele (War Office).
[2] *The Times*, 23 December 1944.
[3] Prime Minister's Personal Telegram, T.2414/4, OZ 7508, 'Private', 22 December 1944:
Churchill papers, 20/178. It was of 'the utmost importance', Churchill told the War Cabinet on
2 January 1945 at which the raising of the 250,000 extra men was reported, 'that all men who
wore The King's Uniform should have arms and should be trained to use them against the
enemy in an emergency, even if they were normally employed in a sedentary or non-combatant
role' (War Cabinet No. 1 of 1945, 2 January 1945: Cabinet papers, 65/49).

told Colville that it was 'the first time' he had seen the House of Commons 'really irritated and impatient', with Churchill.[1] From Athens, Macmillan urged further pressure on the King to appoint Archbishop Damaskinos as Regent, pointing out that this would lessen both British and American criticisms of the Government's Greek policy.[2] 'You should not,' Churchill replied, 'have brought arguments about relieving the political situation at home and about the strength of press and political criticism into a discussion of the Greek question. You cannot judge from where you are whether the position of His Majesty's Government is injured.'[3] Macmillan commented in his diary that the 'real reason' for Churchill's anger was that he 'is beginning to realize what a troublesome affair this is going to be. It may well threaten the present Government and delay the whole progress of the war.' In spite of Churchill's strictures, Macmillan added, 'he will be very grateful if we can get him out of it'.[4]

Leeper, like Macmillan, saw danger in a Right Wing ascendancy, and pressed for it to be made clear to the Greek Government that it could not automatically be supported by Britain after 'our victory over the insurgents'.[5] 'This has certainly not occurred yet,' Churchill commented, and he told Eden: 'We can easily at any time, when we are victors, compel obedience from the Right Wing by threatening to withdraw our forces.' Once the Right Wing had become 'the victors', Churchill minuted, 'I am sure we can put a screw on', to any extent, and with 'great acceptance' in the House of Commons. Churchill added: 'Everything convinces me that these two, Macmillan and Leeper, require strong sedatives and icebags on their heads.'[6]

On December 18 *The Times* published the text of the Caserta agreement of September 24, which had been made public in Athens by General Scobie two days earlier. The agreement had been signed by Maitland Wilson and Macmillan for Britain, by Papandreou for the Greek Government, General Zervas for the nationalist partisans, EDES, and by General Saraphis, leader of the communist ELAS forces. According to clause one of the agreement, all guerilla forces operating in Greece 'place themselves under the orders of the Greek Government of National Unity'. Under clause two, the Greek Government places these forces 'under the orders of General Scobie'.

[1] Colville diary, 19 December 1944: Colville papers.
[2] Athens telegrams to the Foreign Office, No. 634 and 636: Foreign Office papers, 954/11, folio 373.
[3] Prime Minister's Personal Telegram, T.2386/4, No. 507 to Athens, 'Personal Private and Top Secret', 'Guard', 19 December 1944: Foreign Office papers, 954/11, folio 374.
[4] Macmillan diary, 19 December 1944: *War Diaries, op. cit.*, page 612.
[5] Athens telegram to the Foreign Office, No. 655.
[6] Prime Minister's Personal Minute, M. 1231/4, 19 December 1944: Churchill papers, 20/153.

In Athens, read clause four, 'no action is to be taken save under the direct orders of General Scobie'.[1]

'I think our case is so good,' Churchill minuted to Eden later that day, 'especially after having read the Caserta agreement, that I should welcome something more being said on this subject,' and he suggested doing so himself on the Adjournment for the Recess.[2] To Macmillan and Leeper, Churchill telegraphed on December 19 that more troops were on their way. 'A whole division has yet to come into play,' he informed them, 'together with armour and artillery, and furthermore there are still two brigades of the 46th Division which can be moved.' Churchill added: 'Do not imagine you can settle these bitter Greek struggles with a diplomatic wave of the wand. The Government here is composed of men who have been through a lot and are not likely to be perturbed by newspaper buzzings or superficial demonstrations. This is a time when we can afford to wait, and then we may recall Talleyrand's maxim for a diplomatist "surtout pas trop de zèle".'

Churchill's telegram ended: 'We have been through much rougher times than this. Also, you may be interested to know that there is a very heavy German counter-offensive on the western front in which considerable issues are involved.'[3]

On December 20 General Scobie warned the civilians of Athens to avoid areas from which ELAS guns were firing, as he intended to bomb them. 'Poor Winston,' Macmillan wrote in his diary on the following day. 'What with Greece, Poland and the German breakthrough on the Western Front, this is going to be a grim Christmas.'[4]

On the afternoon of December 22 Churchill and Eden saw the King of Greece. As Eden telegraphed to Leeper, the King reported, albeit in somewhat evasive terms, that the 'general trend' of the Ministers in Athens was against a Regency. His own 'position as King, and his responsibilities', the King explained, 'were not personal ones but hereditary'. Only the Crown Prince could act as Regent. Were the King to appoint the Archbishop, he would therefore be performing 'an unconstitutional act'.

Churchill then asked the King 'whether it was correct' that he would not go back until the Greek people 'had expressed themselves

[1] *The Times*, 18 December 1944.

[2] Prime Minister's Personal Minute, M.1225/4, 18 December 1944: Premier papers, 3/212/13, folio 761.

[3] Prime Minister's Personal Telegram, T.2396/4, 'Personal and Top Secret', 19 December 1944: Premier papers, 3/212/13, folios 768–770.

[4] Macmillan diary, 21 December 1944: *War Diaries, op. cit.*, page 613.

by a plebiscite', to which the King replied that 'this was the position'. He would not return 'until the people had expressed their will'. This, said Churchill, was 'important'.[1]

At a meeting of the War Cabinet that afternoon, Eden and others pressed Churchill to urge the King of Greece to reconsider his opposition to a Regency. So many hopes now seemed to centre upon the ability of Archbishop Damaskinos to reconcile the Left and Right Wing forces. But Churchill was convinced, as he told the War Cabinet, that Damaskinos would prove to be 'a dictator of the Left', telling the War Cabinet, as Alexander Cadogan noted, 'I won't install a Dictator.'[2] 'W has his knife into the Archbishop,' Eden wrote, 'and is convinced that he is both a Quisling and a Communist. In fact, as Alec puts it neatly, he has taken the place of de Gaulle. Brendan was maddening and supported W, knowing absolutely nothing of the matter, and attacked Leeper. . . .'[3] During the meeting, as Oliver Harvey noted, Churchill said, of Britain's representatives in Athens, 'we had got two fuzzy-wuzzies there—meaning Macmillan and Leeper'.[4]

Macmillan had sympathized with the combination of problems with which Churchill was confronted. On December 21, Jock Colville noted in his diary:

I met Alec Cadogan in the park. He said the PM was creating a deplorable impression in Cabinet now because he would not read his papers and would talk on and on. It is v. distressing and unless he will delegate much of his work I see little hope of a change. Obviously he is hopelessly overtired and at seventy his powers of recuperation may not be very good.

There were 'signs', Colville added, 'of an impending quarrel between the PM and Eden about the Regency in Greece'.[5]

Churchill did not however take up as uncompromising a position as at first appeared. 'I have personally grave doubts about the Archbishop, who might quite conceivably make himself into a dictator supported by the Left Wing,' he telegraphed to Alexander on December 22. 'However,' Churchill added, 'these doubts may be removed in the next few days, and I am hopeful that in these days we shall achieve the mastery in Attica and cleanse Athens.' He continued: 'We can achieve no political solution while negotiating from a basis of weakness and frustration. The political field in the present circum-

---

[1] Telegram No. 308 to Athens, 'Top Secret', 22 December 1944: Foreign Office papers, 954/11, folios 377–8.
[2] Cadogan diary, 21 December 1944: David Dilks (editor), *op. cit.*, page 689.
[3] Eden diary, 21 December 1944: Eden memoirs, *The Reckoning, op. cit.*, page 499.
[4] Harvey diary, 21 December 1944: John Harvey (editor), *op. cit.*, pages 369–70.
[5] Colville diary, 21 December 1944: Colville papers.

stances can only be entered by the gate of success.'[1] That afternoon Churchill telegraphed to Smuts:

I have had endless trouble about Greece where we have indeed been wounded in the house of our friends. Communist and Left Wing forces all over the world have stirred in sympathy with this new chance and the American Press reporting back has to some extent undermined our prestige and authority in Greece. There would be no chance of our basing a British policy upon the return of the King. We must at all costs avoid appearing to be forcing him on them by our bayonets.

Churchill's telegram continued:

I am very doubtful about the Regency which may well take the form of a dictatorship. I do not know enough about the Archbishop to tell whether it would be a dictatorship of the Left. It is certainly supported by all Leftist forces and by our people on the spot. Alexander of course has his heart in the north and hates the whole Greek business. If, however, as is quite likely, the powers of evil prevail in Greece, we must look forward to a quasi Bolshevized Russian-led Balkans Peninsula and this may spread to Hungary and Italy. I therefore foresee great dangers to the world in these quarters but have not the power without causing great stresses in the Government and quarrelling with the United States to do anything effective.

He was hoping, Churchill added, that military operations inland from Athens 'may be better in the next few days, and so induce a healthier atmosphere'. In the meantime, reinforcements were coming in, 'and of course we are greatly superior in numbers to ELAS'.

Churchill's telegram ended: 'It is not, however, a very pleasant situation.'[2]

That Friday evening, talking to John Martin and Jock Colville after dinner, Churchill spoke of his 'intention', as Colville noted in his diary, 'of flying to Athens to settle the matter'. He also spoke of 'the fact that the English people throughout their history always turned on those who they thought had served them well in hard times (e.g. Marlborough, Wellington, Lloyd George)'. So long did he talk, Colville added, 'that he became too tired, and it became too late, to go down to Chequers . . .'.[3]

That night Churchill slept at the Annexe, in spite of the fact that his valet Sawyers and the luggage had already gone down to Chequers for the long Christmas weekend. On the following day, Saturday

---

[1] Prime Minister's Personal Telegram, T.2410/4, 'Through Special Channel', 'Personal, Private and Top Secret', 'Guard', 22 December 1944: Churchill papers, 20/178.

[2] Prime Minister's Personal Telegram, T.2412/4, No. 1166 to South Africa, 'Personal and Top Secret', 'Decypher yourself', 'No circulation, PM's instructions', 22 December 1944: Churchill papers, 20/178.

[3] Colville diary, 22 December 1944: Colville papers.

December 23, Churchill worked in bed at the Annexe until five in the afternoon. In Athens, General Scobie worked to secure an agreement between the warring factions, based upon the willingness of EAM to join, as Eden wrote to Churchill, 'a broad-based Cabinet'. The question was, after EAM had accepted these terms, who would be Prime Minister. It was 'hardly conceivable' that Papandreou would agree to preside over such a coalition. Hence the need for a Regent.[1]

Churchill remained hesitant as to the wisdom of installing the Archbishop as Regent. During December 23 he dictated a telegram to Alexander, which, in the event, was cancelled. In it, however, he revealed the basis of his hesitations about Damaskinos:

It would be a very serious thing to throw over a constitutional sovereign, acting within the constitution and on the sincere advice of his Ministers, in order to instal under British overpersuasion a clerical dictator of whom we know very little except that he gained office by posing as a German tool and then added to his reputation by double-crossing them.

Churchill's telegram continued:

I do not like setting up dictators as a result of using British troops in action. I am a believer in constitutional processes. Of course if the Greeks agree among themselves that the Archbishop is the best man to head the new Government as Prime Minister it might be a very good solution; but to make him dictator of Greece to get round an awkward political corner is entirely contrary to the guiding principles on which I act.

'I am hoping,' Churchill added, 'that in these next few days our troops will gain a decided mastery of ELAS.' Then, 'once victory is secured', the spirit 'that should guide you', Churchill advised, 'is the invocation of Lord Chatham to the English: "Be one people." '[2]

That afternoon Churchill drove down to Chequers, where a family gathering was expecting what would surely be the last Christmas of the war. Churchill, who on the outbreak of war had not reached his sixty-fifth birthday, was now seventy. The strains of war had been massive, including two mild heart attacks and a severe, nearly fatal, bout of pneumonia.

But on reaching Chequers, Churchill told his wife that he would not be staying for the Christmas celebrations; that he would be flying to Athens.

Early that evening Clementine Churchill's sister, Nellie Romilly, reached Chequers for the family gathering. There, as Churchill's daughter Mary has recalled, 'she found Winston sitting in the Great

---

[1] Eden minute of 23 December 1944: Eden memoirs, *The Reckoning, op. cit.*, page 500.
[2] 'Guard', 'Through "C" ,' 'Cancelled' 23 December 1944: Premier papers, 3/212/13, folios 700-1.

Hall. He welcomed her, and then, under the seal of secrecy, told her that he was off the next day to Athens; he begged her to go and find Clementine, who was upstairs and "very upset". Nellie went to her sister's bedroom and found her in floods of tears. It was so rare for Clementine to give way; she was accustomed to sudden changes of plan, and had, in these last years especially, developed a strict sense of priorities. Somehow this sudden departure of Winston laid her low.'[1]

That night, after dinner, Churchill asked Jock Colville to make the preliminary arrangements for flying to Greece. Colville did so, but, as he noted in his diary, 'did not think seriously' that Churchill would make the journey.[2] Churchill was, however, in earnest, and worried only lest 'the weather might bugger us up'.[3] On the morning of December 24 he telephoned to Eden, who said that he would go instead of Churchill. It was eventually agreed that they would go together. Weather permitting, they would leave that night, Christmas Eve. 'Two of your friends', Churchill telegraphed to Alexander, 'of whom I am one, hope to be in Athens tomorrow, Monday night, or early Tuesday morning.' Macmillan, Leeper and Scobie should each be told. 'Otherwise tell no-one.'[4]

Among the luncheon guests at Chequers on December 24 was Lord Cranborne, who argued against the proposed mission, and almost, as Colville noted, 'dissuaded' him.[5] But the hesitation was short-lived. At half past five that afternoon Churchill telephoned Eden to say that 'the weather was good and we must be off tonight'.[6] 'I am sending you out an important envoy,' Churchill telegraphed to Macmillan and Leeper. 'Make sure you have competent and trustworthy interpreters available for discussions.'[7]

Jock Colville, who was making the final arrangements for the journey, noted in his diary:

A chaotic evening ensued, with the PM telling the King, Attlee, Bevin, Beaverbrook on one telephone and me warning the CAS, Admiralty, Tommy, etc. etc. on the other. Mrs C. was greatly distressed but resigned herself to the inevitable. I had had my uniform sent down from London and at 11.30

[1] Mary Soames, *Clementine Churchill, op. cit.*, pages 363–4.

[2] Colville diary, 23 December 1944: Colville papers.

[3] Marian Holmes diary, 23 December 1944: Marian Walker Spicer papers. After making this comment Churchill turned to Miss Holmes with the words, 'Sorry, that wasn't meant for your ears.'

[4] Prime Minister's Personal Telegram, T.2424/4, 'Through "C"',' 'Personal, Private and Top Secret', 'For Him Alone', 'Guard', 24 December 1944: Cabinet papers, 120/167.

[5] Colville diary, 24 December 1944: Colville papers.

[6] Eden diary, 20 December 1944: Eden memoirs, *The Reckoning, op. cit.*, page 501.

[7] Prime Minister's Personal Telegram, T.2426/4, No. 556 from Foreign Office to Athens, 'Decypher yourself', 'Top Secret', 24 December 1944: Churchill papers, 20/178.

p.m. we were all dressed and ready to depart, though it was difficult to drag the PM from the sofa in the Great Hall where he was reading telegrams, dictating manuscript comments, and carrying on a conversation with Mrs Romilly (who was most outrageously reading the telegrams too) all at the same time.[1]

One of those telegrams was a refusal by Tito's partisans to agree to a British request to pack airborne supplies to Greece.[2] If Yugoslav troops did not participate, Churchill telegraphed to Bill Deakin, who was then in Bari, 'a complete shut-down will be established on all supplies to Yugoslavia . . .'.[3]

Outside the secret circle, there was a feeling that events in Greece were improving. 'The news from Greece is encouraging,' Sir Archibald Sinclair wrote to Churchill on December 24. 'I hope your Christmas will be all the happier!'[4]

At half past eleven that evening, 'after some turmoil' as his Private Office diary recorded, Churchill left Chequers for Northolt, on the first stage of his Christmas journey.[5] Lord Cherwell and Duncan Sandys drove with him, to see him off. Also travelling to Athens were Lord Moran, Jock Colville, Commander Thompson, Elizabeth Layton and Marian Holmes.[6] From the Foreign Office came Pierson Dixon, who later recalled the scene in the 'VIP waiting room':

There were so many senior Air Force officers in the room that when they came in I didn't at first recognize the PM and Jock Colville, one in Air Commodore's, the other in Pilot Officer's uniform. The PM waved us all in the aircraft at once—his new C54, a huge and luxurious thing, bigger and quieter than a York, but alas American. We took off at 01.05. A conversation in the saloon, over turtle soup, ham sandwiches and whisky, about Greece and what we should do. The PM chided me for having let him send off his now famous telegram to Scobie 'in the early hours of Tuesday morning', which Drew Pearson got hold of and published. 'Of all the telegrams I have written in this war it is the one I least liked after I had written it and the only one that has ever been published.'[7]

The C.54 Skymaster had only completed its trials the previous day.[8] 'She is the most luxurious craft imaginable,' Marian Holmes and

[1] Colville diary, 24 December 1944: Colville papers.
[2] Cairo telegram No. 559, 23 December 1944.
[3] Prime Minister's Personal Telegram, T.2429/4, 24 December 1944: Churchill's papers, 20/184.
[4] Letter of 24 December 1944, marked by Jock Colville 'seen by PM': Premier papers, 3/212/13, folio 695.
[5] Private Office diary, 24 December 1944.
[6] 'The PM's two most attractive typists' was Colville's description of Miss Layton and Miss Holmes (Colville diary, 25 December 1944: Colville papers).
[7] Pierson Dixon memoirs, Piers Dixon, op. cit., page 118.
[8] Private Office diary, 24 December 1944.

Elizabeth Layton noted in their joint diary of the journey, 'there are bunks for 8 besides the PM and a dining saloon and 6 of the bunks turn into 3 Pullman seats during the day, for the lower members of the staff.' The whole aircraft, they added, 'is most sumptuously fitted up, swivel chairs and satin curtains, carpets, etc.'.[1]

During the journey to Naples, the Skymaster had to go up to 13,500 feet to avoid the worst of a snowstorm. 'It was cold and very difficult to breathe,' Dixon recalled, 'very like the conditions when crossing the Atlantic after Quebec.'[2] 'We had to climb to 13,500 feet over France,' Colville wrote to John Martin, 'and as no-one but the PM was awoken for oxygen, we all arose with splitting headaches.'[3]

At Pomigliano airfield outside Naples, where the Skymaster landed to refuel, Churchill was met by Air Chief Marshal Slessor, Admiral Sir John Cunningham and General Harding. Breakfast was provided in a 'seriously blitzed block of buildings on the airfield'.[4] From Pomigliano, Churchill telegraphed to his wife: 'Love and many thoughts for you all at luncheon today. I am sorry indeed not to see the tree. Very good passage so far and we can go the whole way in the big plane.'[5] At 10.45 the Skymaster was airborne again, flying over Taranto, across the southern Adriatic, eastward along the Gulf of Corinth, and on to Athens.

During the flight, Churchill dictated a telegram to Roosevelt, describing his mission. 'Anthony and I,' he wrote, 'are going out to see what we can do to square this Greek entanglement.' The 'basis of action', Churchill explained, was that the King of Greece would not return 'until a plebiscite in his favour has been taken'. Churchill added: 'For the rest, we cannot abandon those who have taken up arms in our cause, and must if necessary fight it out with them. It must always be understood that we seek nothing from Greece, in territory or advantages. We have given much and will give more if it is in our power. I count on you to help us in this time of unusual difficulty.'[6]

At Athens, Alexander, Scobie, Macmillan and Leeper were waiting at Kalamaki airfield, as the Skymaster landed without incident. It was two in the afternoon on Christmas Day. One of the most bizarre and dramatic episodes of Churchill's life had begun.

---

[1] 'Operation "Freehold",' diary kept by Marian Holmes and Elizabeth Layton: Nel papers.
[2] Pierson Dixon memoirs: Piers Dixon, *op. cit.*, page 118.
[3] Jock Colville, letter of 26 December 1944: Spencer-Churchill papers.
[4] Private Office diary, 25 December 1944.
[5] 'Mason' No. 2, 'Emergency', 'Following for Mrs Kent from Colonel Kent', 8.45 a.m., 24 December 1944: Cabinet papers, 120/169.
[6] Prime Minister's Personal Telegram, T.2430/4, Prime Minister to President, No. 858, 'Personal and Top Secret', 'Eyes Only', 25 December 1944: Churchill papers, 20/178.

58

Christmas 1944: Athens Amid Gunfire

<hr>

AS soon as the Skymaster had landed at Kalamaki airfield in the early afternoon of 25 December 1944, it was surrounded by British soldiers, Alexander, Scobie, Macmillan and Leeper then went on board, where a conference began at once. The wind was 'howling round', Elizabeth Layton noted, while the aircraft 'slowly got colder and colder'.[1]

The aircraft conference began with a report from Alexander which, as Churchill telegraphed that night to Attlee, 'gave an encouraging account of present military situation, which had been grave a fortnight ago but was now much better'. Alexander had formed 'the decided view', however, 'that behind the ELAS units there was a stubborn core of resistance', Communist in character, which was stronger than we had thought and would be very difficult to eradicate. If we were successful in pushing the ELAS force outside the boundaries of Athens we should still be faced with a tremendous task if we tried to eliminate them altogether.[2]

At the time when Scobie had been sent his instructions on December 5, Churchill commented, 'the calculation was that a volley from British troops was what was required to re-establish order. This calculation had been disproved.' The British Government had no intention 'of becoming indefinitely involved in Greek civil strife', but they could not on the other hand leave Greece 'except with honour and with due protection for those Greeks who had helped us'. There would have to be a National Greek Army under the Greek Government. The King, however, was 'entirely unwilling to agree to appoint a Regent'.

Macmillan then commented that a regency 'was the one possible

<hr>

[1] Elizabeth Layton, diary of the Athens Conference: Nel papers.
[2] 'Mason' No. 5, 'Most Immediate', sent by Naval Cypher, 2.47 a.m., 26 December 1944, received in London, 3.17 a.m., 26 December 1944: Cabinet papers, 120/167.

idea which might have helped to solve the situation'. It no longer seemed so helpful. He, Leeper and Alexander had therefore considered 'whether it might not help to summon a conference of all the political leaders, which ELAS would be invited to attend'. Such a conference, said Eden, 'might be useful. ELAS should certainly be invited to join it, if only with the object of splitting the good from the bad in ELAS.' [1]

After two hours, a procedure had been agreed upon. It would be announced that Churchill and Eden had arrived, and they would hold a conference of those 'generally representative of Greek political opinion', Macmillan's formula.[2] Churchill then 'dictated a Press Communiqué to Elizabeth', Marian Holmes noted in her diary, 'who had difficulty typing it out with fingers numb with cold'.[3]

Churchill's cabin in the aircraft, Elizabeth Layton noted, 'was bumping up and down in the wind. He looked flushed and uncomfortable, and was wrapped in several coats.' During the dictation Churchill 'stopped once to say "That was a cannon—did you hear it?".' Elizabeth Layton added: 'I suddenly began to feel frightened. What would happen if he caught cold in this bitter wind? Where was there we could go?'[4]

At four o'clock, with the communiqué typed out, Churchill left the Skymaster to drive by armoured car to the Naval College at Phaleron. 'The last man who sat where you are sitting,' the driver told Jock Colville, 'died yesterday morning.' There was however no sniping on the journey, 'although at one point', Colville wrote, 'we passed a place which ELAS had been mortaring during the morning'.[5]

It was just after sunset when Churchill reached Phaleron Bay, and boarded HMS *Ajax*, flagship of the Eastern Mediterranean Fleet, whose Captain, John Cuthbert, welcomed him aboard. Churchill at once sent off a second telegram to his wife: 'Arrived Athens air field safely and drove to Piraeus. Now on board *Ajax*. Alexander and the others are here and we are all making plans for a conference.'[6]

Shortly after Churchill had reached *Ajax*, Macmillan, Leeper and Scobie arrived on board, bringing with them Papándreou and the Archbishop. Churchill saw Papandreou first, at seven o'clock that

[1] 'Record of a Meeting held on board the Prime Minister's aeroplane at Kalamaki airfield, Athens, on Christmas Day, 1944', 'Secret', Athens, 25 December 1944: Foreign Office papers, 954/11, folios 394–5.

[2] Macmillan diary, 25 December 1944: *War Diaries, op. cit.*, page 616.

[3] Marian Holmes diary, 25 December 1944: Marian Walker Spicer papers.

[4] Elizabeth Layton, diary of the Athens Conference: Nel papers.

[5] John Colville, letter of 26 December 1944: Spencer-Churchill papers.

[6] 'Mason' No. 3, 'Top Secret', 'Following for Mrs Kent from Colonel Kent', sent at 6.31 p.m., 25 December 1944: Cabinet papers, 120/169.

evening, urging him to agree to a conference on the following day of all the Greek factions, including ELAS. Papandreou agreed.

While Papandreou was with Churchill in the Admiral's cabin, the Archbishop was waiting in another cabin with Jock Colville and Tommy Thompson. As soon as a message reached them that Papandreou had gone, Colville escorted the Archbishop towards the Admiral's cabin. It was Christmas Day. The ship's company was in the midst of much revelry, including a fancy dress parade. As Colville was leading the Archbishop along, they ran into a party from the Lower Deck, 'led', as Colville later wrote, 'by a man in a curly-brimmed bowler hat, a large white hunting stock and tie pin, in the shape of a gold fox, and a false nose. He had a glass of gin in each hand and was leading a number of other people similarly dressed. They obviously thought the Archbishop was a rival "funny party" but the Admiral intervened in time to prevent disaster.' [1]

Churchill then saw the Archbishop, his 'Dictator of the Left'. No sooner had they finished their first conversation than the attitudes of Churchill and Eden towards the Archbishop were reversed. As Colville explained to John Martin: 'The Archbishop impressed the Prime Minister as much as he had the rest of us and we are now in the curious topsy-turvy position of the Prime Minister feeling strongly pro-Damaskinos (he even thinks he would make a good Regent).' Eden, added Colville, 'is inclined the other way'. [2]

At their ship-board meeting, Churchill asked Archbishop Damaskinos if he would preside over the forthcoming conference, and the Archbishop agreed. The Archbishop's 'bitterness over the atrocities committed by ELAS', Eden recalled, 'soon converted Mr Churchill from his former distrust'. [3] This was true; as Churchill reported to Attlee that night, the Archbishop had spoken during their meeting 'with great bitterness against the atrocities of ELAS and the dark, sinister hand behind EAM. Listening to him, it was impossible to doubt that he greatly feared the Communist, or Trotskyite as he called it, combination in Greek affairs.' The Archbishop also told them, Churchill added, 'that he had issued an encyclical to-day condemning the ELAS crowd for taking eight thousand hostages, middle-class people, many of them Egyptians, and shooting a few every day, and that he had said that he would report these matters to the Press of the world if the women were not released. After some wrangling he understood that the women would be released.' The Archbishop, Churchill told Attlee, was, at Churchill's request, sending him proposals 'for the agenda of the conference' on the following day, and he commented:

[1] Letter of 8 August 1952 (Jock Colville to Denis Kelly): Churchill papers, 4/360.
[2] Colville, letter of 26 December 1944: Spencer-Churchill papers.
[3] Eden memoirs, *The Reckoning*, op. cit., page 501.

I cannot foretell what may come out of it. It may be of course that ELAS will refuse the invitation. If they do so they will be shown before the world as making an unbridled bid for power. If they do accept I do not rate the chance of forming a united Government high. I was impressed, especially from what the Archbishop said, by the intensity of hatred for Communists in the country. We had no doubt of this before we came here. Present position is confirmed by all we have heard so far. There is no doubt how the people of Athens would vote if they had a chance, and we must keep the possibility of getting them that chance steadily in view.[1]

While Churchill and the Archbishop had been in conference to-gether, a telegram reached *Ajax* from Roosevelt. 'Eleanor joins with me,' it read, 'in a Happy Christmas to you and Clemmie and the children and an old fashioned Good Luck for all of you in the New Year. Bless you all.'[2]

During the afternoon, a telegram had also reached *Ajax* from Montgomery, reporting that in the Ardennes, following the German success in driving back the American forces along a seventy-mile front, and isolating the garrison at Bastogne, the 5th Panzer Army was 'still attacking'. Montgomery added: 'I cannot pass over to any large offensive action just at present, as I am very stretched and the American divisions are all weak and below establishment.' He was confident, however, that he could 'hold firm' on his existing line, assuring Churchill: 'I do not think the enemy will be able to break it or to get over the Meuse north of Givet.'[3]

From a 'summary of operations' reaching Athens from London twenty minutes after Montgomery's telegram, Churchill learned that the Third United States Army was advancing towards besieged Bastogne, although 'against stiffening resistance'. The garrison at Bastogne, the summary added, 'now holds more ground west of the town and has resisted enemy attacks'.[4]

That night Churchill slept aboard *Ajax*.

On the morning of December 26, with the sun shining brightly, Jock Colville persuaded Churchill 'to get up and go out on the quarterdeck'. Colville wrote:

From the Bridge one can see the smoke of battle in the street fighting

---

[1] 'Mason' No. 5, *op. cit.*: Cabinet papers, 120/167.

[2] 'Label' No. 1, President to Prime Minister, No. 678, 'Personal and Top Secret', 25 December 1985: Cabinet papers 120/162.

[3] 'Label' No. 2, M/393, sent at 10.25 p.m., 24 December 1944, received in Athens, 4.40 p.m., 25 December 1944: Cabinet papers, 120/162.

[4] 'Label' No. 3, 'Summary of Operations', sent 2.15 p.m., received 5 p.m., 25 December 1944: Cabinet papers, 120/162.

west of the Piraeus, and there is a constant noise of shell-fire and machine-guns. We had a splendid view of Beaufighters strafing an ELAS stronghold on the side of one of the hills surrounding Athens. Four of them went round and round diving with all their cannons blazing and then joining in behind the tail of the preceding aircraft to continue the process. As ELAS seem to be deficient of flak, however well provided they may be with other weapons, the Beaufighters seem to be having a very pleasant time.[1]

Churchill remained on board *Ajax* until after lunch. 'I was taking dictation from the PM,' Marian Holmes wrote in her diary, 'when shells rocked the boat. "There—you bloody well missed us!" he cried, "Come on—try again!"'[2]

Just before Churchill left the ship, it was again straddled by shells, and another fell quite close as they reached the shore. Here, Churchill later recalled, an armoured car and military escort awaited them. Churchill's account continued:

I said to my Private Secretary, Jock Colville, 'Where is your pistol?' and when he said that he had not got one I scolded him, for I certainly had my own. In a few moments, while we were crowding into our steel box, he said, 'I have got a tommy gun.' 'Where did you get it from?' I asked. 'I borrowed it from the driver,' he replied. 'What is he going to do?' I asked. 'He will be busy driving.' 'But there will be no trouble unless we are stopped,' I answered, 'and what is he going to do then?' Jock had no reply. A black mark![3]

Churchill then drove to the British Embassy, where, as Lord Moran noted, an officer appeared who 'wanted to get the Prime Minister into the Embassy as soon as he could, but the Prime Minister stood gazing up at the windows of the houses opposite and gave the "V" sign to the Greeks looking out'.

With the arrival of the Archbishop, Churchill went into the small garden at the back of the Embassy, 'to pose for photographs', as Moran wrote, 'whereupon an officer spoke to two soldiers who proceeded to cover the upper windows of the adjoining buildings with their tommy guns'.[4]

Going back inside the Embassy, Churchill then held his second talk with the Archbishop, to whom he declared that 'if all else failed and it proved impossible to reach agreement at the Conference, it would be necessary to consider what steps should be taken to establish order

---

[1] Colville letter of 26 December 1944: Spencer-Churchill papers.

[2] Marian Holmes diary, 'Athens: Christmas 1944: Operation "Freehold"': Marian Walker Spicer papers.

[3] Winston S. Churchill, *The Second World War*, volume 6, London 1954, page 274.

[4] 'A Conference at Athens', notes by Lord Moran sent to Churchill on 30 December 1944: Premier papers, 4/76/3.

and security in Athens after the British and Greek troops had cleared ELAS out and away'. Would it be possible, Churchill went on to ask the Archbishop, 'to establish a governing Committee, or Council of State, consisting of the best men available, and to seek the authority of the four Great Powers—Great Britain, the United States, the USSR and France—as the foundation of action?' The four Great Powers would have to be asked to agree to appoint a Four Power Commission in Athens, under the authority of which the Council of State 'would carry out the functions of government'.

When both the city of Athens and the Piraeus had been 'cleared', Churchill told the Archbishop, the Council of State 'would find it necessary to reinforce itself by a plebiscite or mandate of some kind based on universal suffrage in the city and on the secret ballot'. Whatever arrangements were made, Churchill added, 'it might not be advisable to establish too close an association with the Communists'.

Damaskinos expressed his 'full agreement' with what Churchill had said, adding 'that, indeed, collaboration with the Communists in any form would be fatal to the welfare of the country and would alienate the majority of the Greek people'.[1]

'The point of this meeting,' Pierson Dixon noted in his diary, 'was to enable the chief actors in the Conference to rehearse their parts and decide the order of speaking. It was agreed that the Archbishop should open and then invite the PM and the rest to speak—the idea being to advertise the Greek character of the Conference.'[2]

While he was at the Embassy, awaiting news of whether the ELAS delegates would agree to attend the conference, Churchill made what Colville described as a 'stirring speech' to the Embassy staff, to thank them for 'their excellent work in arduous conditions'. This speech, Colville told Martin, 'gave enormous pleasure both to Leeper and to the Staff'.[3] 'I addressed all the plucky women on Embassy staff who have been in continued danger and discomfort for so many weeks,' Churchill telegraphed to his wife, 'but are in gayest of moods. Mrs Leeper is an inspiration to them.'[4]

Shortly after five o'clock, Churchill and Eden left the British Embassy in two armoured cars to drive to the Greek Foreign Ministry. Among those awaiting them were the French and American observers, and Colonel Popoff, the Soviet representative in Athens. In his letter to John Martin, Jock Colville described the proceedings:

---

[1] 'Record of a Meeting at the British Embassy, Athens, at 4.30 p.m. on 26th December 1944': Foreign Office papers, 954/11, folios 395–6.

[2] Pierson Dixon diary, 26 December 1944: Piers Dixon, *op. cit.*, page 120.

[3] Colville letter of 26 December 1944: Spencer-Churchill papers.

[4] 'Mason' No. 8, 'Top Secret', 'Hush', 26 December 1944: Churchill papers, 20/182.

It looked as if ELAS would not turn up for the meeting and the Archbishop had made his opening speech and the PM was half way through his, when there were noises off and three shabby desperados, who had been searched and almost stripped before being allowed to enter, came into the dimly-lit Conference Room. All the British delegation, the American, the Russian and the Frenchman, rose to their feet, but the Greek Government remained firmly seated. The PM was only prevented from rushing to shake the ELAS people by the hand by Field Marshal Alexander's bodily intervention.[1]

There were three ELAS delegates, Partsalides, Siantos, and General Mandakas, who had been persuaded, but only after some argument, to leave his Mauser rifle and considerable quantities of ammunition in a locked room outside the conference chamber.[2] Colville's account continued: 'The proceedings then began all over again and, with the sound of rocket-firing Beaufighters, and bursting mortar shells without, the light of a few Hurricane lamps within and the spectacle of what was surely the oddest galaxy of stars ever assembled in one place, one had continually to rub one's eyes and be sure one was not dreaming.'[3]

It was all 'intensely dramatic', Churchill wrote to his wife, 'All those haggard Greek faces round the table and the Archbishop with his enormous hat, making him, I should think, seven feet high, whom we got to preside.' Of the ELAS delegates, Churchill wrote: 'They certainly look a much better lot than the Lublin illegitimates,' and he added: 'Thanks were proposed with many compliments to us for coming by the Greek Govt, and supported by ELAS representatives, who added ref to G.B. quote Our Great Ally unquote—all this with guns firing at each other not so far away.'[4]

After the Archbishop had repeated, and completed, his speech of welcome, Churchill began his speech again, addressing his remarks, Colville noted, largely in the direction of the three ELAS delegates.[5] 'Mr Eden and I,' Churchill said, 'have come all this way, although great battles are raging in Belgium and on the German frontier, to make this effort to rescue Greece from a miserable fate and raise her to a point of great fame and repute.' It was Britain's intention, Churchill said, to 'leave you Greeks to your own discussions', under the chairmanship of the Archbishop, 'this most eminent and venerable

---

[1] Colville letter of 26 December 1944: Spencer-Churchill papers.

[2] 'Description of the Conference of Greek Parties convened by the Prime Minister on Tuesday, December 26, 1944' (by Jock Colville): Churchill papers.

[3] Colville letter of 26 December 1944: Spencer-Churchill papers.

[4] 'Mason' No. 8, *op. cit.* The sentence about the 'Lublin illegitimates' was omitted when 'Mason' No. 8 was circulated to several Ministers, as well as to the Foreign Office, the Defence Office and the Chiefs of Staff. (Note by John Martin, undated: Cabinet papers, 120/169.)

[5] 'Description of the Conference. . . .' *op. cit.*

citizen, and we shall not trouble you unless you send for us again. We may wait a little while, but we have many other tasks to perform in this world of terrible storm.' 'Whether Greece was a monarchy or a republic,' he said, 'is a matter for Greeks and Greeks alone to decide. All we wish you is good, and good for all.' Churchill added:

My hope is however that the conference which begins here this afternoon in Athens will restore Greece once again to her fame and power among the Allies and the peace-loving peoples of the world, will secure the Greek frontiers from any danger from the north, and will enable every Greek to make the best of himself and the best of his country before the eyes of the whole world. For all eyes are turned upon this table at this moment, and we British trust that whatever has happened in the heat of fighting, whatever misunderstandings there may have been, we shall preserve that old friendship between Greece and Great Britain which played so notable a part in the establishment of Greek independence.[1]

In his official note on the conference, Jock Colville wrote:

Gradually, as Mr Churchill proceeded, the three rebel leaders lost their look of intimidation and seemed to abandon their suspicion of an intended 'coup de main'. Perhaps it was wholesome that whenever they raised their eyes from the table they looked straight into the glittering spectacles, spotless uniform and impeccable bearing of Colonel Popoff, whose appearance was every inch that of an officer and a gentleman.

While the Prime Minister was speaking, the sound of gunfire went on ceaselessly without, and at one moment the roar of descending rockets, launched by Beaufighters at some nearby enemy position, almost drowned his words.[2]

When Churchill had finished speaking, Alexander, for whom the Greek imbroglio was an unwelcome distraction from the battle in Italy, told the assembled disputants how much he disliked his soldiers fighting Greeks. 'At this point,' Pierson Dixon noted, 'the three ELAS men turned their eyes on the Field Marshal, and only cast them down again when he said at the end, "Instead of me pouring men into Greece, you ought to be pouring men into Italy to join my victorious armies against the enemy."'[3] Alexander's speech, Colville noted, 'clearly left its effect on his audience'.[4]

The Archbishop then asked if any of the Greek representatives had any questions to ask. 'There was an awkward pause,' Colville wrote, 'and it was evident that a difference of opinion existed in the ELAS

---

[1] 'Conference at the Ministry of Foreign Affairs, Athens, on 26th December, 1944, at 5.30 p.m.': Foreign Office papers, 954/11, folios 396–8.

[2] 'Description of the Conference . . .,' op. cit.

[3] Pierson Dixon diary, 26 December 1944: Piers Dixon, op. cit., page 123.

[4] 'Description of the Conference . . .,' op. cit.

ranks.' While Pierson Dixon noted how the three ELAS representatives 'consulted furtively, looked up, found the steady eye of the Soviet Colonel upon them, and cast their eyes down again'. Then, just as Churchill was suggesting that the British delegates should depart, and leave the Greeks 'to their own deliberation', an 'aged Royalist', Maximos, then made 'a short and highly coloured speech of welcome'. Maximos was followed by Papandreou, who spoke at greater length and 'with evident shyness and embarrassment'. One of the three ELAS delegates, Partsalides, then paid 'a glowing tribute' to Churchill but, carried away by his excitement, went on to claim, as Pierson Dixon noted, 'that ELAS was the soul of Greece'.[1] 'Now is the time,' Churchill interjected, 'for the Greeks to be left to discuss these matters among themselves.'[2] At this, Pierson Dixon noted, Churchill rose 'heavily' to his feet and said to the assembled Greeks: 'I should like to go now. We have begun the work. See that you finish it.'[3]

'Everyone rose,' Lord Moran later recalled. 'The PM passed down the side of the long table, shaking hands with the members of the Greek Government, until he came to the Communists, when he paused. He had vowed that he would not shake hands with these villains. What was he going to do? "Who," he asked, "will introduce these gentlemen to me?" He then shook hands with each of them in turn. And now for the first time the expressionless features of ELAS came to life, and a look of pleasure crossed their faces. They wrung Mr Churchill's hand with slight, stiff bows.'[4] It was clear from their response, Churchill told his wife, 'that they were gratified'.

Jock Colville, who had risen to go with the rest of the British and foreign participants, recorded:

. . . headed by the Prime Minister, the British representatives walked out of the room, shaking hands as they left with members of the Greek Government and lastly with the delegates of ELAS, whose bows could not have been lower, handshakes warmer nor protestations more friendly had they been ambassadors of a party under the deepest obligation to Great Britain.

On the steps of the Ministry of Foreign Affairs, while Mr Churchill was entering his armoured car, there was a further alarm, and indeed excursion, as various Greeks, headed by the 84-year-old Liberal leader, Monsieur

[1] Pierson Dixon diary, 26 December 1944: Piers Dixon, op. cit., page 123.

[2] 'Conference at the Ministry of Foreign Affairs, Athens, on 26th December 1944, at 5.30 p.m.': Foreign Office papers, 954/11, folios 396–8.

[3] Pierson Dixon diary, 26 December 1944: Piers Dixon, op. cit., page 124. According to Leeper's telegraphic report, Churchill's final words were: 'We should like to go now. We have begun the work, make sure you finish it.' (Telegram No. 720, Athens to Foreign Office, War Cabinet Distribution, sent 12.15 a.m., 27 December 1944: Cabinet papers, 120/167.)

[4] 'A Conference at Athens', notes sent by Lord Moran to Churchill on 30 December 1944: Premier papers, 4/76/3.

Sophoulis, made a desperate effort to flee from the Conference chamber. They were however firmly held and persuaded to return to their places at the council table.[1]

The Greeks at the Conference, Churchill telegraphed to his wife, 'are the very top ones', and he added: 'We have now left them together as it was a Greek show. It may break up at any moment. We shall wait for a day or two if necessary to see. At least we have done our best.' Churchill added, on a personal note: 'I do hope the Christmas tree was a success. Fondest love to you and all. Please show any parts of this telegram which are relevant to intimate colleagues.'[2]

From the conference hall, Churchill returned to *Ajax*, which had moved a mile further offshore to avoid the continuing if spasmodic mortar fire. From *Ajax* he sent Brendan Bracken instructions to publicize the full texts of all the conference speeches, except for Alexander's final sentence. Churchill added: 'Do not fail to point out that our military state is improving daily and that we did not convene conference because we in any way shrank from discharging task which we are in honour bound to fulfil.'[3]

That afternoon Churchill was briefly on the bridge with Captain Cuthbert. As further shells fell in the sea around them, Cuthbert asked Churchill if he could return the fire. 'The PM replied,' noted Marian Holmes, '"I have come to Greece on a mission of peace, Captain. I bear the olive branch between my teeth. But far be it for me to interfere with military necessity. RETURN FIRE!"'[4]

'Master was just a darling,' Elizabeth Layton wrote home. 'Never, never before has there been such a small and such a *very* happy party. We were under shell-fire and gunfire and all day long one could hear the cannons roll.'[5]

From Montgomery had come news of heavy German pressure on the western flank of the 1st Army during the previous day, and of a renewed but successful Allied withdrawal. In the air, however, December 25 had been what Montgomery described as a 'very good day', with many German attempts to develop new attacks being 'smashed up'.[6]

---

[1] 'Description of the Conference. . . .' *op. cit.*

[2] 'Mason' No. 8, 26 December 1944: Cabinet papers, 120/169. The 'intimate colleagues' to whom 'Mason' No. 8 was circulated were Attlee, Anderson, Bevin, Lyttelton, Morrison, Cranborne, Woolton, Beaverbrook, Bracken, the Foreign Office, Sir Edward Bridges, the Defence Office and the Chiefs of Staff. (Note by John Martin, undated, Cabinet papers, 120/169.)

[3] 'Mason' No. 9, 'Top Secret', sent at 0.29 a.m., 27 December 1944: Churchill papers, 20/182.

[4] Marian Holmes diary, 'Athens: Christmas 1944: Operation "Freehold"': Marian Walker Spicer papers.

[5] Elizabeth Layton, letter of 6 January 1945: Nel papers.

[6] 'Label' No. 7, M/395, sent at 10.05 p.m., 25 December 1944, received in Athens during 26 December 1944: Cabinet papers, 120/168.

That night Churchill dined on *Ajax* with Alexander and Macmillan. During dinner they were joined by Eden and Dixon, who noted in his diary how on reaching the cruiser:

> ... found the PM, Field Marshal and the rest at the height of a cheerful dinner, which we joined. The conversation was mostly of strategy, until the PM settled down after dinner in front of the Admiral's electric fire, and embarked on a long discussion about our difficulties in Greece. Alex explained why we could not clear Athens faster, pointing out the peculiar complications of street warfare. Of course, said Alex, we could go quicker if we stormed our way through the streets with tanks and 'Rotterdamed' whole quarters by air bombardment—as the Germans and Russians in a similar situation would probably do. But, apart from other disadvantages of such a policy, the troops would refuse to do it. Alex enquired when Parliament reassembled and, when told January 16th, said that he could promise to have cleared Athens by that date.
>
> Leaving at 1 a.m., Alex said that he must go now or he would be keeping the PM up. AE had already gone to bed, and I followed soon, after talking with the PM and telling him how much the Embassy staff had valued the speech he made them this afternoon.[1]

Throughout the night, Colville noted in his diary, depth charges were exploded 'by way of precaution'.[2]

At noon on December 27 Churchill went ashore, and, after calling at the Embassy, asked General Scobie to take him for a review of the British military position. As they were about to set off, Colville noted, 'a burst of machine gun fire, coming from well over a mile away, struck the wall of a house some 30 feet over his head. Several bursts were fired and a woman in the street was killed.'[3]

After visiting the British troop positions, Churchill returned to the British Embassy. Pierson Dixon, who was present, noted in his diary: 'We had a cheerful lunch with the PM in the Embassy drawing-room, in our overcoats, in a draughty corner thought the safest part of the room from sniping.'[4] After lunch Churchill saw the American Ambassador, MacVeagh, and, as Colville noted, 'gave him a piece of his mind about the very inadequate support the USA have given us in this affair'.[5] A Regency under the Archbishop,

---

[1] Pierson Dixon diary, 26 December 1944: Piers Dixon, *op. cit.*, page 125.

[2] Colville diary, 27 December 1944: Colville papers.

[3] Colville diary, 27 December 1944: Colville papers.

[4] Pierson Dixon diary, 27 December 1944: Piers Dixon, *op. cit.*, page 126.

[5] Colville diary, 27 December 1944: Colville papers. Good news reached Churchill from western Europe that afternoon. 'I am now planning to pass to the offensive,' Montgomery had telegraphed on the previous evening. 'Reconnaissance and plans for the operation begin today.' At Bastogne, Montgomery added, the Third Army had joined up with the garrison, 'which is good'. ('Label' No. 13, M/397, sent at 11 p.m., 26 December 1944, received in Athens, 27 December 1944: Cabinet papers, 120/168.)

Churchill told MacVeagh, was 'the only course open' at that moment.[1]

At 3.30 in the afternoon there was a Press Conference in the Embassy, attended, as Elizabeth Layton noted, by about thirty correspondents, 'tough looking creatures, most of them. Some were British and some American, some pro-ELAS and some pro-us; some had on badges of those who were neutral.' Her account continued:

I had to sit with my ear almost on Master's shoulder—the room was so full of buzz, and it was essential to hear. Mr Eden and all the Macmillan and Scobie gang were present, and I fancy the PSs were in the background somewhere. Master spoke very fast, and it was all I could do to write him down; frequently he was half interrupted by the booming of cannon, and once there was such a prolonged roll of explosions that I lost what he said.[2]

'We seek nothing from Greece,' Churchill told the journalists in his opening remarks. 'We look for no selfish advantages. We want no territory. We do not require bases or anything like that. As for money we would rather give it than take it. There is nothing we want of any kind from Greece except her friendship.' As to the outcome of the discussions going on between the Greek groupings, 'I am hoping,' Churchill said, 'that we shall see our way clear tonight.'

Churchill then answered several questions. Would there be an amnesty for the ELAS leaders? 'Obviously,' he replied, 'if there is a cessation of fighting there ought not to be a proscription either way.' What would happen if no agreement was reached? 'If no agreement is reached the guns will go on firing as they are now, the troops will clear this area, we shall establish security and peace and order in Attica.' Churchill continued: 'We are absolutely determined that the whole of this built up area must be cleared of armed persons not under the control of any recognized Government and that a sufficient area all around must be cleared. We shall use whatever force is necessary to obtain that object. Then we will hope that some good sense will come to this tortured people, that they will see that there is some purpose in working together.'

In a 'not very long time', Churchill told the Press Conference, Roosevelt, Stalin and he would meet, with their advisers, and if no 'satisfactory and trustworthy democratic foundation' had yet been agreed upon, 'you may have to have, for the time being, an international trust of some kind or other. We cannot afford to see whole peoples drifting into anarchy.'

What was the King's attitude? 'Of one thing I am sure, that he will

---

[1] 'Note on a discussion between the Prime Minister and the United States Ambassador at 3 p.m. on the 27th December 1944, at the British Embassy, Athens': Foreign Office papers, 954/11, folio 399.

[2] Elizabeth Layton, diary of the Athens Conference: Nel papers.

not come back here unless a plebiscite of his people desires his return.'[1]

The Press Conference was at an end. Elizabeth Layton hurried to the Embassy cellar where she dictated her shorthand outlines to a member of the Embassy staff, who typed it out, 'pages and pages of foolscap', she noted. Halfway through this dictation, Jock Colville descended to the cellar with the message, 'Go up to the PM—which I did.' Her account continued:

He was sitting in a corner of the room adjoining the conference chamber. It was very dimly lit—some lamps and I believe one electric light—and very cold. He had on his greatcoat and some rugs over his knees. The Archbishop sat beside him, robed all in black with a high black 'chef's' hat and the great silver ornament (it looked like an eagle) round his neck. He had a long beard and glasses, and seemed to be a deep old chap.[2]

The Archbishop had just reported to Churchill on the failure of the discussions with the ELAS leaders, who had, as he later told the War Cabinet, 'adopted a very uncompromising attitude'. The terms they had demanded 'would enable them to wreck any Government': the offices for which they had asked 'were the same as those which had been asked for in the Polish Government by the Lublin Poles'.[3] Churchill therefore agreed to ask the King to appoint the Archbishop as Regent of Greece, and to entrust the Archbishop in the meanwhile with forming a Government from which the Communists would be excluded.[4]

The British Government's position, Churchill told the Archbishop, 'would not be affected by public criticism'. On his return to London, he would urge the King to set up a Regency for a year, 'or until a plebiscite could be held under normal conditions of tranquillity, whichever period should be the less'. British military operations would meanwhile continue, Churchill told the Archbishop, 'with full vigour until ELAS accepted General Scobie's terms or the Athens area were freed'; but he 'made it clear', as the minutes of the meeting recorded, 'that we could not commit ourselves to military operations after the clearing of Attica, although we would try to keep British forces in Greece until the Greek National Army had been formed'.[5]

Two of the ELAS delegates, Siantos and Partsalides, had asked

[1] Press Conference of 27 December 1944, Athens: Telegram No. 737 from Athens to the Foreign Office, sent at 11.15 p.m., 27 December 1944: Cabinet papers, 120/167.
[2] Elizabeth Layton, diary of the Athens Conference: Nel papers.
[3] War Cabinet No. 175 of 1944, 29 December 1944, Confidential Annex: Cabinet papers, 65/48.
[4] Pierson Dixon, 27 December 1944: Piers Dixon, op.cit., page 127.
[5] 'Record of a Meeting at the British Embassy, Athens, 5.30 pm, 27th December 1944': Foreign Office papers, 954/11, folios 400–1.

Churchill for a private meeting. But the Archbishop, as the British notes recorded, was 'strongly against' any such meeting.[1] 'Considering the responsibilities with which we are about to see him saddled,' Eden telegraphed to Cadogan, 'it would be wrong to ignore his advice and thus queer his pitch.'[2]

The letter which Elizabeth Layton took down was Churchill's reply to the ELAS leaders. 'Although personally I should have been willing to comply,' Churchill wrote, 'I feel that the Conference being wholly Greek in character,' he could not see them. His letter continued, however: 'Let me add my fervent hope that the discussions which have taken place and contacts which have been made will result in a speedy end to the melancholy conflict proceeding between men of one country.'[3] Churchill was not altogether happy with his decision not to see the ELAS leaders. As Macmillan noted in his diary that night:

Winston was very inclined to see them, but I persuaded him (and Anthony agreed) that if we were going to put our money on the Archbishop, we must let him play the hand as he thought best. Winston partly wanted to see them as a good journalist, and partly because he has an innocence which is very charming but sometimes dangerous. He believed he could win them over. But I felt he would much more probably be deceived and betrayed.[4]

During the discussion with the Archbishop that afternoon, Churchill stressed that Britain could not commit itself to military operations after the 'clearing' of Attica, 'although we could try to keep British forces here until the Greek National Army had been formed'.[5]

At seven o'clock that evening, Churchill and Alexander left the Embassy for Phaleron, where they boarded the barge to take them to *Ajax*. Elizabeth Layton reached the barge when Churchill was already seated in the cabin. 'I went to the further corner of the cabin,' she noted, 'but he said, "No, come and sit by me."' A 'huge rug' was then brought, 'and Master and I shared it!!!!', much to Alexander's amusement.[6]

At about 11.30 that night Macmillan went to see Churchill on *Ajax*. 'Winston is more and more delighted with the Archbishop,' he

[1] 'Discussion with Archbishop', Telegram No. 741 from Athens to the Foreign Office, signed by Eden, 28 December 1944: Cabinet papers, 120/167.

[2] Telegram No. 741 from Athens to the Foreign Office, sent at 9.12 a.m., 28 December 1944: Cabinet papers, 120/167.

[3] Letter of 27 December 1944, Telegram No. 742 from Athens to the Foreign Office, 28 December 1944: Cabinet papers, 120/167.

[4] Macmillan diary, 27 December 1944: *War Diaries, op.cit.*, page 620.

[5] 'Discussion with Archbishop', 27 December 1944: *War Diaries, op.cit.*, page 627.

[6] Elizabeth Layton, diary of the Athens Conference: Nel papers.

wrote, 'but is still worrying about his refusal to grant a private interview to the ELAS delegates.' [1] That night Churchill telegraphed to the Chiefs of Staff Committee:

It is clear to me that great evils will follow here in Athens, affecting our position all over the world, if we cannot clear up situation quickly—i.e. in two or three weeks. This would entail, according to Alexander, the moving in of the two brigades of the 46th Division, which are already under orders and standing by. On the other hand, the military situation in Western Apennines is such that any serious weakening of the reserves of Fifteenth Army Group might be attended with danger.

Churchill proposed moving a brigade of the Fifth Division from Palestine to Greece. 'This of course would mean,' he pointed out, 'that no violent action could be taken in Palestine, irritating the Jews, such as the search for arms on a large scale, until the situation is easier all round.' [2]

While on board *Ajax*, Churchill asked Colville to telegraph to John Martin in London, to ask that the names of fifteen ladies on the staff of Leeper and Scobie should be included in the New Year's Honours List for the British Empire Medal. Churchill asked Martin to approach the King's Private Secretary, 'to explain that these ladies have been living for three weeks under the constant fire of the enemy, in spite of which they have carried out their duty with utmost credit and tireless devotion to duty. The Prime Minister therefore very much hopes that His Majesty will consent to inclusion of these names even at this late date.' [3]

That night, Churchill sent his wife an account of the day's events. 'Today, Wednesday, has been an exciting and not altogether fruitless day,' he telegraphed. 'The hatreds between these Greeks are terrible. When one side have all the weapons which we gave them to fight the Germans with and the other, though many times as numerous, have none, it is evident that a frightful massacre would take place if we withdrew.' [4]

---

[1] Macmillan diary, 27 December 1944: *War Diaries, op. cit.*, page 620.

[2] 'Mason' No. 18, 28 December 1944: Churchill papers, 20/182.

[3] 'Mason' No. 13, 'Top Secret', 'Most Immediate', by Naval Cypher, sent at 5.04 p.m., received at 6.24 p.m., 27 December 1944: Cabinet papers, 120/162. One of the ladies in Churchill's list, Miss Lucy Manley, is listed in the *London Gazette* of 5 January 1945 as having been made an MBE 'for services in Greece and tireless devotion to duty under fire'.

[4] 'Mason' No. 23, 'Top Secret', sent at 2.41 a.m., 28 December 1944: Premier papers, 3/208, folio 20. The Chiefs of Staff approved of Churchill's suggestion. 'We entirely agree,' they replied, 'that the troops necessary to clear up the situation in Athens within the next two or three weeks should be provided.' ('Label' No. 31, 28 December 1944: Cabinet papers, 120/168.)

On the morning of December 28 there were 'some afterthoughts', as Pierson Dixon noted, about 'our refusal' to see the two ELAS leaders who had written to Churchill on the previous afternoon. 'This was talked over till the hour of departure at noon,' Dixon added, 'with Rex and Harold Macmillan, who were summoned aboard.' Rex Leeper, on reaching the cruiser, had enquired anxiously, 'What has happened? Is there a change of policy?' [1] Macmillan noted in his diary:

We found Winston still fussing about the ELAS delegates. He thought he would stay another day and summon a further meeting of the conference. He did not like the idea of going home without a peace, or at least a truce, arranged. I argued strongly in favour of his immediate return *to secure the regency*. This would be a service to Greece which only could be performed in London (since the King was the stumbling-block and the King was in London), and which only he (Winston) could carry to a successful conclusion.

Finally, to clinch the matter, it was decided to issue a communiqué— which would commit H.M.G. publicly to the regency. [2]

Churchill's Greek mission was at an end. Before leaving *Ajax*, he telegraphed to Roosevelt, explaining that the final decision was to press the King of Greece to appoint the Archbishop as Regent, after which the Archbishop would try to form a government 'of ten or less of the "best will"'. [3]

'I have seen the Archbishop several times,' Churchill explained, 'and he made a very good impression on me by the sense of power and decision which he conveyed as well as by his shrewd political judgments. You will not expect me to speak here on his spiritual qualities for I really have not had sufficient opportunity to measure these.' Of the Archbishop's political views, Churchill commented: 'I do not consider Archbishop is at all Left Wing in Communist sense. On the contrary he seems to be an extremely determined man bent on establishing a small strong executive in Greece to prevent the continuance of Civil War.'

Once they had returned to England, Churchill told Roosevelt, he and Eden 'shall advise our colleagues who are already inclined to this course, that we should put the strongest pressure on Greek King to accept advice of his Prime Minister, Monsieur Papandreou', and agree to a Regency. Unfortunately, Churchill noted, Papandreou 'changes

---

[1] Pierson Dixon diary, 28 December 1944: Piers Dixon, *op. cit.*, page 127.

[2] Macmillan diary, 28 December 1944: *War Diaries, op. cit.*, page 629.

[3] In the first week of January 1945 a Government was formed by General Nikolaos Plastiras, with the Communists excluded. 'He was very sensible', Macmillan noted after his first meeting with Plastiras, 'and seemed to understand that he must help us politically, just as we were helping him militarily'. (Macmillan diary, 5 January 1945: *War Diaries, op.cit.*, page 639.)

his mind about three times a day', but had now agreed to urge the King to agree to a Regency. This Regency, Churchill told Roosevelt, 'should be only for a year, or till a plebiscite can be formed under conditions of what is called "normal tranquillity" ', and he added:

Mr President, we have lost over one thousand men, and though the greater part of Athens is now clear it is a painful sight to see this city with street-fighting raging now here, now there, and the poor people all pinched and only kept alive in many cases by rations we are carrying, often at loss of life, to them at the various depots. Anything that you can say to strengthen this new lay-out as the time comes will be most valuable, and may bring about acceptance by ELAS of the terms of truce set forth by General Scobie. For the rest we are reinforcing as is necessary and military conflict will go on. The vast majority of the people long for a settlement that will free them from the Communist terror.[1]

One of the last telegrams which Churchill received before leaving Athens was from Montgomery. The German 5th Panzer Army, Montgomery reported, 'has been forced to give up its attempts to swing towards Namur'.[2]

At 12.45, after addressing the ship's company, Churchill left *Ajax* by barge for Phaleron, and then drove in a procession of jeeps and armoured cars to Kalamaki airport. There, after making a short speech to the British air force personnel, he boarded the Skymaster. But the Greek episode was not yet over. As Pierson Dixon recorded:

We were sitting in Skymaster, with our safety-belts buckled ('Even the most eminent persons are subject to the laws of gravity,' said the PM, fastening his) and were taxi-ing up to the take-off, when the PM called out, 'Stop the aircraft.' He had just read an amendment to the final Communiqué saying that Macmillan and Alexander (as well as the PM and S of S) had left. This, we all felt, might give the impression that we were abandoning Greece to her fate.

There was a great upset and the aircraft was stopped. I climbed down out of the nose by a flexible steel ladder, ran between the propellers and under the fuselage, and, waving the peccant document, was met by Harold Caccia, to whom I explained the point. I then ran back under the aeroplane and climbed up.[3]

At 2.30 p.m., the Skymaster at last took off, flying back across the snow-capped mountains of the Peloponnese. Landing at Pomigliano at 4.10 p.m., Churchill and Alexander were met by Slessor, Cun-

---

[1] 'Mason' No. 19, Prime Minister's Personal Telegram, T.2436/4, Prime Minister to President, No. 859, 'Personal and Top Secret', 28 December 1944: Churchill papers, 20/178.

[2] 'Label' No. 24, M/400, sent at 11 p.m., 27 December 1944, received in Athens at 11.25 a.m., 28 December 1944: Cabinet papers, 120/168.

[3] Pierson Dixon diary, 28 December 1944: Piers Dixon, *op. cit.*, page 128.

ningham and Harding, and drove straight to Alexander's villa. Churchill had intended to fly back to London that night, but as there were reports of fog over southern England, he decided to stay in Naples. 'I have been moved and thrilled to read of all that has happened while you were in Athens,' 'Mrs Kent' telegraphed to 'Colonel Kent' on December 28. 'I am so grateful that you are well and long for your return. All my love, Clemmie.' [1]

'Delighted to receive your messages,' Churchill replied. 'I was feeling lonely. Hope to be with you at dinner tomorrow. Tender love.' [2]

'Unless we are very unfortunate with the weather,' Jock Colville telegraphed to John Martin that evening, 'the Prime Minister will be back in time for lunch with the King at one p.m. on Saturday at Buckingham Palace and would much like to do so.' [3]

'The news is better,' Harold Nicolson, in London, noted in his diary that night. 'Winston has left Athens, having been shot at by a sniper and used the expression "Cheek!" In the Ardennes and Belgium we seem to have held Rundstedt some seven miles from the Meuse.' [4]

'Arising long before dawn,' noted Churchill's Private Office, 'the party left the Field Marshal's villa sharp at 7 a.m. and was airborne at 8.' [5] 'You see,' Churchill remarked to Marian Holmes at the airport, 'I am on time for the first time this year,' and she added: 'It was Friday, 29th December 1944.' [6] 'W unexpectedly punctual,' Eden noted in his diary, 'and pleased with his prowess.' [7]

The return flight followed the Italian coast past Ostia and the Tiber, then crossed over the northern tip of Corsica, over Toulon, and across France towards Cherbourg. About two hours after take-off, Elizabeth Layton noted in her diary, 'I went along to the tail of the plane where he was in bed and working. I sat on the typewriter box and tried not to fall off when the plane jerked, which it did quite frequently. He just worked in exactly the usual way, me passing the ash-tray every few

[1] 'Label' No. 30, 'Personal and Private', 'Top Secret', 28 December 1944: Premier papers, 3/208, folio 21.
[2] 'Mason' No. 28, 'For Mrs Kent from Colonel Kent', sent at 1.15 a.m. 29 December 1944: Cabinet papers, 120/169.
[3] 'Mason' No. 27, sent at 8.10 p.m., 28 December 1944: Cabinet papers, 120/169.
[4] Harold Nicolson diary, 28 December 1944: Nigel Nicolson (editor), op. cit., page 422.
[5] Private Office diary, 29 December 1944.
[6] Marian Holmes diary, 'Athens: Christmas 1944: Operation "Freehold"': Marian Walker Spicer papers.
[7] Eden diary, 29 December 1944: Eden memoirs, The Reckoning, op. cit., page 502.

minutes. Every now and then he would look out and say "Oh, now we're crossing the coast of France" or some other trifle.' Elizabeth Layton added: 'One just sat and felt quite, quite ordinary; and yet one was with the greatest man in the whole world, flying at 6,000 feet above the Mediterranean, crossing over Corsica and Toulon and Toulouse, taking down ordinary dictation and feeling as much at home as on the office stool.' [1]

On seeing Mont St Michel, Colville noted, 'I started a hare by pointing out that the Channel Islands were still in German hands; but we were assured our course went far east of them.' Because of thick fog over London, the Skymaster flew on to Bovingdon airfield north of London, where it landed at 3.30 in the afternoon. Clementine Churchill, Jack Churchill, John Martin, John Peck and Lady Moran were there to meet them. [2]

Two and a half hours later, Churchill and Eden gave the War Cabinet an account of their Greek visit, after which they had two long sessions with the King of Greece, the first at 10.30 p.m., the second at 1.30 a.m. 'W was firm and steady,' Eden noted. [3] 'This has been a very painful task to me,' Churchill telegraphed to Roosevelt. 'I had to tell the King that if he did not agree the matter would be settled without him and that we should recognise the new government instead of him.' [4]

The discussion ended at 4.00 a.m., when the King agreed to appoint Archbishop Damaskinos as Regent of Greece. Half an hour later, twenty-two hours since he had been wakened in Naples, Churchill went to bed. [5] His Greek journey had not achieved peace between Left and Right, but it had produced a Government more capable than the last to seek the entry of Greece into the post-war world. 'If we had not intervened,' he told the War Cabinet on the afternoon of his return, 'there would have been a massacre.' He was 'glad also to feel,' Churchill told the War Cabinet, 'that no harm had been done by his not having paid his visit sooner.' The Archbishop had made 'a most favourable impression. He was shrewd, able and forthcoming'; there was 'little doubt' that once he had secured power he would be ready to use it. The present state of anarchy in Athens, Churchill added, showed 'how much a strong hand was needed': the Archbishop 'was definitely anti Communist . . .'. [6]

[1] Elizabeth Layton, diary of the Athens Conference: Nel papers.
[2] Colville diary, 29 December 1944: Colville papers.
[3] Eden diary, 29 December 1944: Eden memoirs, *The Reckoning*, *op. cit.*, page 502.
[4] Prime Minister's Personal Telegram, T.2249/4, 30 December 1944: Churchill papers, 20/184.
[5] Private Office diary, 29 December 1944.
[6] War Cabinet No. 175 of 1944, 6 p.m., 29 December 1944, Confidential Annex: Cabinet papers, 65/48.

'One might well ask,' Pierson Dixon confided to his diary on 1 January 1945, 'was this journey really necessary?' Brendan Bracken's caustic comment on the visit, Dixon wrote, had been, 'that Winston and Anthony were "like two housemaids answering every bell"'. Pierson Dixon thought that one effect of the visit had been on ELAS; it had 'sent their sense of importance soaring', leading them 'to raise their terms astronomically'. But for one reason, if no other, Pierson Dixon thought the visit had indeed been necessary. It was necessary, he wrote in his diary, if only because Eden and Churchill had disagreed about the Greek policy 'and the PM would not agree to follow Anthony's ideas unless he went out and saw things for himself'.[1]

'Your visit to Athens,' Macmillan telegraphed to Churchill from Italy on January 1, 'has given us a wonderful new start. It would please you to know of the admiration for your courage and unremitting labours which I hear amongst all ranks of both British and Americans.'[2]

For Churchill, the Greek visit confirmed his sense of the need for vigilance in maintaining the balance between the Communist and non-Communist forces struggling for power in the Balkans. The Tito–Subasic agreement on the composition of the future Yugoslav Government, he minuted to Eden on January 1, was 'hopelessly one-sided and can mean nothing but the dictatorship of Tito, that well-drilled Communist'.[3] In a minute to the Chiefs of Staffs that same day, opposing the evacuation of British troops from Patras, he wrote: 'We are playing a winning hand in Greece if we do not throw our advantages away.'[4]

---

[1] Pierson Dixon diary, 1 January 1945: Piers Dixon, *op. cit.*, page 129.
[2] Rome Telegram No. 4 of 1 January 1945: Churchill papers, 20/210.
[3] Prime Minister's Personal Minute, M.4 of 1945, 1 January 1945: Churchill papers, 20/209.
[4] Prime Minister's Personal Minute, D 4 of 1945, 1 January 1945: Churchill papers, 20/209. A week later, Churchill and Eden minuted jointly to Alexander and Macmillan: 'Although we must clearly face the possibility of continued resistance, it is essential that no opportunity should be missed of drawing away moderate elements from EAM and ELAS. In this way the Communist extremists might find themselves compelled to come to terms with the Greek Government rather than risk losing the bulk of their followers.' (Prime Minister's Personal Telegram, T.61/5, No. 89 to Athens, 'Top Secret', 8 January 1945: Churchill papers, 20/210.)

59

1945: 'This "New, disgusting year"...'

ON his return to Britain on 29 December 1944, Churchill began to work for as early a meeting as possible between himself, Roosevelt and Stalin. More than any other single problem, the future of Poland called out most urgently for decision. Churchill had already been asked by Eden to help assuage the fears among many Polish soldiers in Italy and western Europe, not only that post-war Poland would not be a place where they could live, but that nowhere else might be open to them. 'Surely,' he had minuted to Eden on December 28, 'it would be possible to reassure these men who have fought in the Polish Divisions that whatever else happens to them the British Empire will find them a home.'[1]

Stalin was now threatening to recognize the Lublin Committee as the Government of Poland. 'I think,' he telegraphed to Churchill, 'we cannot allow the Polish people to say that we are sacrificing the interests of Poland in favour of the interests of a handful of Polish emigrants in London.'[2] Churchill received this telegram on December 29. That same day he sent Roosevelt details of a possible Big Three meeting place: the Soviet Black Sea resort of Yalta.

'If this place is chosen,' Churchill wrote, 'it would be well to have a few destroyers on which we can live if necessary.' They should aim, in his view, to meet at the end of January. 'I daresay Stalin will make good arrangements ashore.'[3]

---

[1] Prime Minister's Personal Minute, M.1248/4, 28 December 1944: Churchill papers, 20/153.

[2] 'Personal and Top Secret', sent from Moscow 27 December 1944, received in London 29 December 1944: Churchill papers, 20/178 (sent by Roosevelt to Churchill as Prime Minister's Personal Telegram, T.2444/4, Prime Minister to President, No. 681, 29 December 1944: Churchill papers, 20/178).

[3] Prime Minister's Personal Telegram, T.2440/4, Prime Minister to President, No. 861, 'Personal and Top Secret', 29 December 1944: Churchill papers, 20/178. Two of Churchill's advisers were sceptical about Yalta as the meeting place. Admiral Cunningham was afraid that

Roosevelt was agreeable to going to Yalta, but concerned about the flight from Italy, across the high mountains of the Balkans. One possibility was to go by sea to Malta, and to fly from there. 'We shall be delighted if you will come to Malta,' Churchill telegraphed on 1 January 1945. 'I shall be waiting on the quay,' and he added: 'No more let us falter! From Malta to Yalta! Let nobody alter!' [1] Churchill proposed for the new conference the code name 'Argonaut', and Roosevelt agreed. 'You and I,' he noted, 'are direct descendants.' [2] As for the preliminary Conference at Malta, on which Eden was particularly emphatic, Churchill telegraphed to Roosevelt ten days later:

Eden has particularly asked me to suggest that Stettinius might come on forty-eight hours earlier to Malta with the United States Chiefs of Staff, so that he (Eden) can run over the agenda with him beforehand.[3] Even though Molotov were not invited, I am sure this would be found very useful. I do not see any other way of realizing our hopes about World Organization in five or six days. Even the Almighty took seven. Pray forgive my pertinacity.[4]

Churchill had intended to return to London later that day, having spent the Saturday night and all Sunday with his family at Chequers.[5] His Private Office diary of Monday, January 1 recorded:

The Prime Minister worked on his box during the morning and lunched in bed. He continued working until 6, when he slept until dinner time. At 9.15 he started for London and at 9.20 returned to the house owing to the unsatisfactory state of the roads and the weather. He read a book and listened to the gramophone until 1.15.[6]

'You know I can't give you the excitement of Athens every day,' Churchill commented to Marian Holmes that Tuesday.[7]

---

with the use of battleships as headquarters in the stormy winter waters of the Black Sea, Roosevelt and Churchill might be cut off from each other for two or three days at a time. Ismay felt that even if Stalin were to find his guests 'suitable accommodation' ashore, 'the risks would have to be taken of all our conversations being tapped by the Russians'. When Ismay read out these two points to Churchill, however, he noted that the Prime Minister 'did not altogether agree'. ('Top Secret', 30 December 1944: Cabinet papers, 120/170.)

[1] Prime Minister's Personal Telegram, T.4 of 1945, Prime Minister to President, No. 871, 'Personal and Top Secret', 1 January 1945: Churchill papers, 20/210.

[2] President to Prime Minister No. 690, 'Personal and Top Secret', 3 January 1945: Churchill papers, 20/210.

[3] On 27 November 1944 Cordell Hull had resigned as Secretary of State. He had been succeeded by Edward Stettinius.

[4] Prime Minister's Personal Telegram, T.69/5, Prime Minister to President, No. 884, 'Personal and Top Secret', 10 January 1945: Churchill papers, 20/210.

[5] Private Office diary for Saturday 30 December 1944 and Sunday 31 December 1944.

[6] Private Office diary, 1 January 1945. On 7 January 1945 John Martin sent Churchill a note of 'the steady increase in the number of personal telegrams (in and out) registered in the Private Office'. These were, 1941 (April to December), 1,092; 1942, 1,779; 1943, 2,096 and 1944, 2,468. (Premier papers, 4/69/2.)

[7] Marian Holmes diary, 2 January 1945: Marian Walker Spicer papers.

In the Ardennes, the first week of January saw the American First Army recapture most of the villages lost in the surprise German offensive, and launch their own first counter-offensive.

At a Staff Conference which met at noon on January 2, and at which Maitland Wilson was present, Churchill was 'pleased to note' the action that was being taken to provide arms and equipment for the French. The 'importance' of arming and equipping the Greek National Forces, he added, 'should not, however, be lost sight of'. Brooke then explained that 'good progress' was being made with the arming of 40,000 Greeks, but it was 'difficult to see how we could make sufficient arms and equipment available for four mountain divisions'.

When the discussion turned to Alexander's possible operations from Italy towards Austria, Brooke warned that a force of eight Allied divisions, operating on the left flank of the Russian advance into Austria, 'could probably be contained by comparatively small German forces operating in this difficult and mountainous country'. Brooke added that it might be 'better strategy' to move divisions from Italy to the western front, 'where our maximum strength was needed'.

Churchill agreed that 'in certain circumstances', such a course of action 'might have to be considered'. He would not, however, 'be prepared to see the Italian front denuded of American divisions, leaving there a large British army to conduct static operations'.[1]

On January 3, only five days after his return from Greece, Churchill left England once more, flying with Brooke from Northolt to Eisenhower's headquarters at St Germain, near the Palace of Versailles. 'He spurned the company both of the Defence Office and the Private Office,' Colville noted in his diary, 'and took with him a strange trio, Commander Thompson, Kinna and Sawyers.'[2] During the afternoon, Churchill and Eisenhower were joined by de Gaulle. To shorten the front as the counter-offensive began in the Ardennes, Eisenhower had given the order to evacuate Strasbourg, captured earlier by the French, and to pull back in the whole sector from the Rhine to the Vosges. This meant leaving Strasbourg open to the enemy. There was understandable consternation in French political and military circles. What vengeance would fall upon the citizens of Strasbourg, who had rallied so passionately to their deliverers![3] On January 2 Duff Cooper had telegraphed to Churchill from Paris of the 'dire political conse-

---

[1] Staff Conference, Chiefs of Staff Committee No. 3 of 1945, 12 noon, 2 January 1945: Cabinet papers, 79/28.

[2] Colville diary, 3 January 1945: Colville papers.

[3] Winston S. Churchill, *The Second World War*, volume 6, London 1954, page 245.

quences' that would follow the evacuation of the city, 'to the discredit of the Americans'.[1] Churchill later recalled:

I chanced to be at Eisenhower's headquarters at St Germain at this juncture, and he and Bedell Smith listened attentively to my appeal. The enemy did indeed spring into action on the Army Group's front, especially in the Colmar pocket, but were repulsed. Eisenhower cancelled his instructions, and the military necessity which might have made the evacuation of Strasbourg imperative never arose. De Gaulle expressed his gratitude.[2]

That evening Churchill dined with Eisenhower and his senior Staff officers, returning to his room at Eisenhower's headquarters at 1.30 in the morning.[3] 'He then dragged me into his bedroom for a further talk,' Brooke noted in his diary. 'He said that he was beginning to see that any operation from Italy towards Vienna had little prospects.'[4]

On January 4 Churchill left Versailles in Eisenhower's special train, for the overnight journey to Montgomery's headquarters. He had intended to travel by air, but because of snow had to go the much slower way. To Patrick Kinna, who accompanied him on the train, he dictated a series of minutes and telegrams, before going to bed at 1.45 a.m. One of his minutes was to Eden, who was anxious that, before the Big Three met at Yalta, there should be a clear British policy on the future of Germany. Stalin, noted Eden in his diary that day, was 'the only one of the three who has a clear view of what he wants and is a tough negotiator. PM is all emotion in these matters, FDR vague and jealous of others.'[5] But Churchill was not to be drawn into any detailed proposals for 'putting poor Germany on her legs again' in order to prevent there being 'a poisoned community in the heart of Europe'. As he wrote to Eden:

It is a mistake to try to write out on little pieces of paper what the vast emotions of an outraged and quivering world will be either immediately after the struggle is over or when the inevitable cold fit follows the hot. These awe-inspiring tides of feeling dominate most people's minds, and independent figures tend to become not only lonely but futile. Guidance in these mundane matters is granted to us only step by step, or at the utmost a step or two ahead. There is therefore wisdom in reserving one's decisions as long as possible and until all the facts and forces that will be potent at the moment are revealed. Perhaps our approaching triple discussions will throw more light upon the problem.[6]

---

[1] Paris Telegram No. 11, 'Top Secret', 2 January 1945: Churchill papers, 20/210.
[2] Winston S. Churchill, *The Second World War*, volume 6, London 1954, page 245.
[3] Private Office diary, 3 January 1945.
[4] Brooke diary, 3 January 1945: Bryant, *op.cit.*, volume 2, page 374.
[5] Eden diary, 4 January 1945: Eden memoirs, *The Reckoning*, *op.cit.*, page 504.
[6] Prime Minister's Personal Minute, M.22/5, 'Personal and Private', 4 January 1945: Churchill papers, 20/209.

On the following day, Colville noted that Churchill was 'incensed with Stafford Cripps for making a speech about brotherly feelings for the Germans. He says he might agree with such sentiments when victory is won, but not with a great battle raging and the Huns shooting captured soldiers in cold blood.'[1]

Through the night Churchill's train travelled across France and Belgium, through Amiens, Arras, Lille and Brussels, reaching Ghent on the morning of January 5, where he spent the morning with Montgomery, before driving through Louvain to Brussels airfield, for the flight back to England.[2]

In the Far East, Mountbatten's forces entered the Burmese port of Akyab. In Athens and the Piraeus, the fighting between ELAS and the Government came to an end. From Moscow, the Soviet Government announced that it recognized the Lublin Committee as the Provisional Government of Poland. 'Naturally I and my War Cabinet colleagues are distressed at the course events are taking,' Churchill telegraphed at once to Stalin, and he added: 'I am quite clear that much the best thing is for us three to meet together and talk all these matters over, not only as isolated problems but in relation to the whole world situation both of the war and the transition to peace.' Meanwhile, 'our attitude as you know it remains unchanged'.

He was 'looking forward very much', Churchill told Stalin, 'to this momentous meeting' at Yalta, and he ended: 'I reciprocate your cordial wishes for the New Year. May it shorten the agony of the great nations we serve and bring about a lasting peace on our joint guarantee.'[3]

Following up Eden's suggestion of an Anglo-American Conference before the Big Three met at Yalta, Churchill now proposed that he and Roosevelt spend two or three nights at Malta 'and let the Staffs have a talk together unostentatiously'. Eisenhower and Alexander could both be asked to attend. 'We think it very important,' Churchill explained, 'that there should be some conversation on matters which do not affect the Russians—e.g. Japan—and also about the future use of the Italian armies.' 'You have but to say the word,' Churchill ended, 'and we can arrange everything.'[4]

[1] Colville diary, 5 January 1945: Colville papers. Eisenhower had told Churchill during his visit to St Germain that the Germans had shot 130 prisoners-of-war (Colville diary, 5 January 1945: Colville papers).

[2] Private Office diary, 5 January 1945.

[3] Prime Minister's Personal Telegram, T.32/5, No. 77 to Moscow, 'Most Immediate', 'Top Secret', 5 January 1945: Churchill papers, 20/210.

[4] Prime Minister's Personal Telegram, T.31/5, Prime Minister to President, No. 874, 'Personal and Top Secret', 5 January 1945: Churchill papers, 20/210. The proposed Combined Chiefs of Staff conference was codenamed 'Cricket', the Yalta conference 'Magneto', in all telegrams during January.

Reporting on his visit to Eisenhower and Montgomery, Churchill assured Roosevelt that he had not found 'a trace of discord' at either headquarters, but, he added, 'there is this brutal fact: we need more fighting troops to make things move', and he ended his telegram:

I have a feeling this is a time for an intense new impulse, both of friendship and exertion, to be drawn from our bosoms and to the last scrap of our resources. Do not hesitate to tell me of anything you think we can do.[1]

Plans for a new offensive in the West depended, Eisenhower had explained to Churchill, upon knowing the date of the renewed Soviet offensive in the East. Brooke had already pointed out, at a Staff Conference four days earlier, that a 'notable development' in the war in Europe was 'the relatively high proportion of German divisions engaged in the West and South, as compared with the Eastern front'.[2] The American and British liaison officers in Moscow had failed, however, to obtain information from the Soviet Chiefs of Staff as to when the next Soviet offensive would be launched. With Churchill's approval, Eisenhower had asked his Deputy, Air Marshal Tedder, to go to Moscow for the specific purpose of finding out when the Red Army would move forward again. But the bad weather that had forced Churchill to travel across north-western France by train had also prevented Tedder from flying to Moscow, and on January 6, with Tedder apparently still weather-bound in Cairo, Churchill telegraphed direct to Stalin:

In case he has not reached you yet, I shall be grateful if you can tell me whether we can count on a major Russian offensive on the Vistula front, or elsewhere, during January, with any other points you may care to mention. I shall not pass this most secret information to anyone except Field-Marshal Brooke and General Eisenhower, and only under conditions of the utmost secrecy. I regard the matter as urgent.

The battle in the west was 'very heavy', Churchill explained, 'and at any time large decisions may be called for from the Supreme Command. You know yourself from your own experience how very anxious the position is when a very broad front has to be defended after the temporary loss of the initiative.' Eisenhower needed to know what Stalin planned to do, as 'this obviously affects all his and our major decisions'.[3]

---

[1] Prime Minister's Personal Telegram, T.41/5, Prime Minister to President, No. 877, 'Personal and Top Secret', 6 January 1945: Churchill papers, 20/210.
[2] Staff Conference, Chiefs of Staff Committee No. 3 of 1945, 12 noon, 2 January 1945: Cabinet papers, 79/28.
[3] Prime Minister's Personal Telegram, T.39/5, No. 100 to Moscow, 'Personal and Operational Secrecy', 6 January 1945: Churchill papers, 20/210.

The Soviet Union was indeed planning a new offensive, Stalin replied within a few hours of receiving Churchill's telegram. Although the weather was unfavourable, 'taking into account the position of our Allies on the Western Front', the Soviet Supreme Command had decided to 'accelerate' its preparations, and 'regardless of the weather', to begin large-scale offensive operations against the Germans along the whole Central Front 'not later than the second half of January'.[1]

'I am most grateful to you for your thrilling message,' Churchill replied. 'I have sent it over to General Eisenhower for his eyes only. May all good fortune rest upon your noble venture.' Stalin's news would be a 'great encouragement' to Eisenhower, Churchill added, 'because it gives him the assurance that the German reinforcements will have to be split between both our flaming fronts'.[2]

Churchill sent Commander Thompson to Eisenhower's head-quarters, with a copy of Stalin's telegram. In a covering note beginning 'My dear Ike', Churchill asked that Eisenhower should 'keep the matter entirely to yourself and Bedell, and not let it get in the hands of the Staffs. Once you know where you are, you can act without explaining why. I would indeed be glad if you put it in the fire.' The official reports, Churchill added, 'will no doubt come along later when Tedder comes through, and when all can be made official. This is off the record, between you and me.'[3]

Eisenhower replied by telegram on the following day: 'I have burnt it and have communicated its contents to *no* one except to individual you suggest. Your news is most encouraging.'[4]

The prospect of renewed offensives in the east and west did not give Churchill peace of mind. Instead it accentuated the post-war worries that already loomed. 'John Peck thinks the prospect of the end of the war and the problems it will bring with it are depressing the PM,' Jock Colville noted in his diary on January 8. Churchill's 'prevalent feelings' were shown, Colville added, in a letter to someone to whom he had sent best wishes for this 'New, disgusting year'.[5]

In a telegram to Roosevelt on January 8, after stressing the 'high importance' of a meeting of the Combined Chiefs of Staff 'before we arrive at Yalta', Churchill added, of the Yalta meeting itself: 'this may well be a fateful Conference, coming at a moment when the Great Allies are so divided and the shadow of the war lengthens out

---

[1] 'Personal and Most Secret', 7 January 1945: Churchill papers, 20/210.
[2] Prime Minister's Personal Telegram, T.60/5, No. 127 to Moscow, 'Top Secret', 'Decypher Yourself', 9 January 1945: Churchill papers, 20/210.
[3] 'Private and Top Secret', 9 January 1945: Churchill papers, 20/193.
[4] S.74440, 'Emergency', 10 January 1945: Churchill papers, 20/210.
[5] Colville diary, 8 January 1945: Colville papers.

before us. At the present time I think the end of this war may well prove to be more disappointing than was the last.'[1]

In Greece, however, as the Chiefs of Staff noted on January 9, although Scobie had, 'by dint of severe fighting', succeeded in 'clearing' Athens and the Piraeus, and was 'pursuing' the ELAS forces 'out of Athens', Patras was 'by no means secured', with the result that Alexander had ordered two brigades of the 46th Division to concentrate there, and put the 3rd Brigade, which was still in Italy, 'available to call forward to Athens when required'.[2]

In the Far East, on January 9, American forces landed on Luzon, in the Philippines, with 100,000 men put safely ashore on the first day. In northern Burma, the Fourteenth Army was opening the overland route to China. In the Ardennes, the United States Third Army launched a new counter-attack from the south of the salient. In Italy, Churchill learned from General McCreery that the Fourth Hussars, Churchill's own regiment, had, with 'great skill and enterprise', beaten back a strong German attack.[3]

In France, Montgomery had given what Jock Colville described as a 'triumphant, jingoistic and exceedingly self-satisfied' talk to the Press, which had given 'wide offence'.[4] 'You thus have a picture,' Montgomery had said, 'of British troops fighting on both sides of American forces who have suffered a hard blow. This is a fine allied picture.'[5] 'In contradistinction to the rather crestfallen American command,' Montgomery later admitted, 'I appeared, to the sensitive, to be triumphant—not over the Germans but over the Americans.'[6]

To 'soothe the Americans', Colville wrote, Churchill had countered on January 9 by means of a public telegram of congratulations to General Bradley.[7] Churchill's distress at the effect of Montgomery's remarks was considerable. As he minuted to the Chiefs of Staff Committee:

I fear great offence has been given to the American Generals, not so much by Montgomery's speech but by the manner in which some of our papers seem to appropriate the whole credit for saving the battle to him. Personally I thought his speech most unfortunate. It had a patronizing tone and completely overlooked the fact that the United States have lost perhaps 80,000

[1] Prime Minister's Personal Telegram, T.54/5, Prime Minister to President, No. 880, 'Personal and Top Secret', 8 January 1945: Churchill papers, 20/210.

[2] Chiefs of Staff telegram, COS(W)569 to the Joint Staff Mission, Washington, approved at Chiefs of Staff Committee No. 9 of 1945, 9 January 1945: Cabinet papers, 79/29.

[3] 'Secret', 8 January 1945: Churchill papers, 20/198.

[4] Colville diary, 9 January 1945: Colville papers.

[5] Notes of a Press conference held on 7 January 1945: *The Memoirs of Field-Marshal the Viscount Montgomery of Alamein KG*, London 1958, pages 311–14.

[6] Montgomery, *supra*, page 314.

[7] Colville diary, 9 January 1945: Colville papers.

men and we but 2,000 or 3,000. Through no fault of ours we have been very little engaged in this battle, which has been a great American struggle with glory as well as disaster. Eisenhower told me that the anger of his Generals was such that he would hardly dare to order any of them to serve under Montgomery. This of course may cool down, but also it may seriously complicate his being given the leadership of the northern thrust.[1]

There was also a domestic policy dispute, between Eden and Lord Cherwell, with which Churchill was directly and unpleasantly involved. Jock Colville noted in his diary on January 9:

About midnight, while Lord Beaverbrook and Brendan were closeted in the PM's bedroom, having come no doubt on some nefarious intrigue (anti-Bevin, whom the PM cherishes above all Labour Ministers, I suspect), Anthony Eden rang up in a storm of rage. It was about a minute from Lord Cherwell, forwarded by the PM to the FO, in which Eden's assertions about the starvation confronting Europe were flatly denied.

Eden told me he would resign if inexpert, academic opinions were sought on subjects to which he had given so much thought. I put him through to the PM, to whom he ranted in a way in which neither the PM nor I (who was listening in) had ever heard him before. The PM handled the storm in a very adept and paternal way, said he would take the Prof's paper back and go into it himself, protested at Anthony vexing himself with such matters at the end of a long, weary day, and said there was only one thing he could and would not allow: the feeding of Europe at the expense of an already hard-rationed England.[2]

On the following day Churchill wrote to Eden:

I am of course sorry if I have offended you by sending you on a minute written by the Professor for my personal information. I very often have lengthy and complicated reports of this kind vetted for me by other people so that I may weigh the pros and cons. Otherwise I do not think I could get through my work. I will try however as much as possible to give you my own conclusion in my own words after I have made all the necessary inquiries.

'I must make it quite clear,' Churchill added, 'that you have no reason to be vexed with the Professor, who merely at my directions wrote out

[1] Prime Minister's Personal Minute, D.20/5, 10 January 1945: Churchill papers, 20/209. On 12 January 1945 the United States Office of War Information announced the United States battle casualties on all fronts since the outbreak of war in December 1941. The figures were, 138,393 killed, 370,647 wounded, 73,594 missing presumed killed, and 63,764 prisoners-of-war. Four days later Churchill circulated a table showing British and Commonwealth casualties from 3 September 1939 to 30 November 1944. There were, of those known to have been killed, 199,497 United Kingdom; 28,040 Canadian; 18,015 Australian; 17,415 Indian; 8,919 New Zealand; 5,783 South Africa and 4,493 Colonial troops. The total number of prisoners-of-war was 294,438, of whom 161,020 were from the United Kingdom. (*Hansard*, 16 January 1945, columns 65–6.)

[2] Colville diary, 9 January 1945: Colville papers.

his opinion for me and would never have intervened in this matter at all if I had not asked his advice, as I think I am entitled to do.' [1]

On January 11 the Red Army opened its offensive against the German forces defending Warsaw. That day, King Peter of Yugoslavia issued a statement denouncing the Tito-Subasic agreements of 1 November and 7 December 1944. 'He thinks,' Churchill telegraphed to Stalin, 'that if he keeps himself free of all that is going to happen in Yugoslavia in the next few years, a day will dawn for him.' As a result of King Peter's statement, Churchill told Stalin, Britain would 'favour the idea' of recognizing a Tito-Subasic Government, 'set up under the Regency', as the Royal Yugoslavian Government, and would propose sending a British Ambassador to Belgrade—which had recently been liberated—and receiving a Yugoslav Ambassador in London.[2] 'I hope you will think this is a good way out of the difficulty,' Churchill added, 'until there is a free and fair expression of the people's will.' [3]

'You know my views on this matter so well,' Churchill telegraphed to Roosevelt two days later, 'that I do not have to report that we should insist so far as is possible on full and fair elections deciding the future régime of the Yugoslav people or peoples.' [4] In the Foreign Office draft of this telegram had appeared the sentence, 'By taking this action King Peter may well have burnt his boats.' Churchill minuted to Eden: '"Burn his boats" does not seem to bear any relation to what he has in fact done. Invaders who land on enemy soil have been known to burn their boats in order that their army may not be able to run away home and will have to stay in the invaded country and fight it out. . . . Far from wishing to "burn his boats" and leave himself stranded on a foreign shore, King Peter now hopes to get hold of a boat which some day or other may carry him back to his native shore. I wondered whether the expression "cooked his goose" might not have fitted the context, but on the whole I thought and still think it better to leave out the sentence altogether. Forgive my chaff and pedantry.' [5]

Churchill, in spite of what were thought to be his monarchist in-

[1] 'Private', 10 January 1945: Churchill papers, 20/193.
[2] The Tito-Subasic agreement envisaged Marshal Tito as Prime Minister and Dr Subasic as Foreign Minister.
[3] Prime Minister's Personal Telegram, T.79/5, 12 January 1945: Churchill papers, 20/225.
[4] Prime Minister's Personal Telegram, T.90/5, Prime Minister to President, No. 888, 'Personal and Top Secret', 14 January 1945: Churchill papers, 20/210.
[5] Prime Minister's Personal Minute, M.65/5, 14 January 1945: Churchill papers, 20/209.

clinations, had now distanced himself from two Balkan Kings, George of Greece and Peter of Yugoslavia, both of whom had opposed or rejected the compromise proposals which Churchill had urged upon them, if they were to retain their thrones. In Greece, a truce between the British forces and ELAS was signed on January 12, with the 'cease fire' to come into force one minute after midnight two days later. 'Naturally,' Churchill telegraphed to his American friend Bernard Baruch on January 12, 'I felt the sudden way in which very large sections of the American press, which has hitherto appreciated my ceaseless efforts to keep our two countries in harmony, turned upon me over the Greek affair,' and he added: 'How stultified they must feel today when, after infinite toils and many hazards, every ideal in the Atlantic Charter is being secured for Greece, and when the gratitude of her people for their deliverance from a dictatorship of a Communist gang is expressed on every side.'

American criticism of his Greek policy led Churchill to draw a wider lesson. 'We have only to stand together,' he told Baruch, 'and fight down harsh, premature judgments of each other's solutions of war problems, to bring the whole world out of its miseries and secure our children from a renewal of these torments.'[1]

That day, January 12, the Red Army launched its offensive in southern Poland. Two days later they had cut the Kielce to Cracow railway line, and captured the western Galician town of Pinczow. By January 15 they were only forty miles from Cracow. 'The Germans are resisting, furiously,' Stalin telegraphed to Churchill, 'but are being forced to retreat. I hope this will facilitate and hasten the offensive on the Western front planned by General Eisenhower.'[2]

Over southern Britain, the V2 rockets, increasing in volume, had begun to take a heavy toll. On January 15 Churchill told the Chiefs of Staff Committee, in a parody of John Bright: 'The Angel of Death is abroad in the land, only you can't always hear the flutter of its wings.'[3]

On Saturday January 13 Churchill drove down to Chequers, where the final plans were to be made for Yalta. That night Leslie Rowan was on duty from the Private Office, and Marian Holmes the secretary

---

[1] Prime Minister's Personal Telegram, T.86/5, 'Personal and Top Secret' (Via Harry Hopkins) No. 409 to Washington, 12 January 1945: Churchill papers, 20/210.

[2] 'Personal and Most Secret', 15 January 1945: Churchill papers, 20/210.

[3] Cunningham diary, 15 January 1945: Cunningham papers. On 23 February 1855, during the Crimean War, John Bright told the House of Commons: 'The angel of death has been abroad throughout the land; you may almost hear the beating of his wings.'

for the late dictation. In her diary she noted how, when Churchill asked her if she wanted to go to Yalta she had hesitated, knowing that her colleague Jo Sturdee wanted so much to be on this particular journey. Marian Holmes' diary continued:

PM said 'Would you like to come?' 'I'd love to.' I can hardly believe it. PM then turned everyone out of the room and dictated 5,000 words of speech to me which I took down also in shorthand. When he finished he said I must on no account type it out tonight. He was extremely amiable and went off to bed. By this time, Mr Rowan had fallen fast asleep on a sofa in the Great Hall. Awakened him. Told him that much as I would of course love to go to Yalta, I would not wish to go if it meant displacing Jo. He promised it wouldn't mean this and said 'What the Boss says, goes!' and 'Orders is orders'. . . .[1]

On the following morning, when Marian Holmes was again taking dictation, Churchill said to her: 'You wouldn't like my job, so many different things come up which have to be settled in two or three minutes.'[2]

In making plans for Yalta, Churchill hoped that Britain and the United States would be able to present a united policy over as many issues as possible. One region which needed an agreed policy was Persia. On January 15 Churchill telegraphed to Roosevelt about 'the various forms of pressure' which Russia had been exerting on Persia, pressure which seemed to Britain to be 'a departure' from the Declaration about Persia signed at Teheran in December 1943, pledging Britain, the United States and the Soviet Union to maintain Persian 'independence, sovereignty and territorial integrity'.[3] Churchill told Roosevelt:

This may be something of a test case. Persia is a country where we, yourselves and the Russians are all involved; and we have given a joint undertaking to treat the Persians decently. If the Russians are now able not only to

[1] Marian Holmes diary, 13 January 1945: Marian Walker Spicer papers.
[2] Marian Holmes diary, 14 January 1945: Marian Walker Spicer papers. 'He was well aware that his staff worked long and unorthodox hours for him', Marian Holmes later recalled. 'He required the highest standard of quick efficiency and could be impatient if anything less were forthcoming. But in all his moods—totally absorbed in the serious matter of the moment, agonized over some piece of wartime bad news, suffused with compassion, sentimental and in tears, truculent, bitingly sarcastic, mischievous or hilariously funny—he was at all times splendidly entertaining, humane and lovable.' (Marian Spicer recollections: letter to the author, 12 February 1985.)
[3] Cunningham diary, 15 January 1945: Cunningham papers.

save their face by securing the fall of the Persian Prime Minister who opposed them, but also to secure what they want by their use of the big stick, Persia is not the only place where the bad effect will be felt.[1]

This telegram to Roosevelt, like the telegram on the previous day about Yugoslavia, had been drafted by the Foreign Office. On January 16 Jock Colville noted in his diary:

Looking at the messages and letters that go out from this office under the PM's signature, I often think how difficult it will be for future historians to know what is 'genuine Churchill' and what is 'school of'. We are all fairly good imitators of his epistolary style now, and though his speeches are of course all original, as are most of his minutes, only a few of his letters and messages are. But I defy anyone to trace a bar sinister in my message to Papandreou signed to-day or in recent letters I have composed for the PM's signature to M. Lebrun, Mrs Philip Guedalla, Mrs Wendel Willkie, Mrs Deneys Reitz, etc.[2]

As far as Churchill's speeches are concerned, there is no such problem, as Colville had indicated. Indeed, in that same diary entry he noted: 'The PM has something of a sore throat and so, after taking questions (the House reassembled to-day), he retired to bed and spent the day there, composing his speech on the war for next Thursday and emptying his box.'[3] Colville also noted, on the following day, one of Churchill's marvellous phrases. Speaking to the new South African High Commissioner, Heaton Nicholls, Churchill remarked: 'Smuts and I are like two old love-birds moulting together on a perch but still able to peck.'[4]

On January 17 the Red Army entered Warsaw, and on January 18 the Lublin Committee, now recognized by Russia, but not by Britain or the United States, as the Polish Provisional Government, entered the Polish capital. That day, Churchill made the speech in the House of Commons which he had been preparing for several days: 'rhetorically', Colville noted, 'it was the best effort I have heard him make

[1] Prime Minister's Personal Telegram, T.97/5, Prime Minister to President, No. 890, 'Personal and Top Secret', 15 January 1945: Churchill papers, 20/210.

[2] Colville diary, 16 January 1945: Colville papers. In studying his correspondence, Churchill usually indicated which replies should be drafted for him. His own archives, and the official archives of his premiership, contain many of these drafts, their different versions, and the correspondence about them. They also contain Churchill's own detailed minutes and instructions indicating what he would like the drafts to contain. Nevertheless, Colville's strictures are valid; it is not always possible to say for certain which are 'genuine Churchill' letters.

[3] Colville diary, 16 January 1945: Colville papers.

[4] Colville diary, 17 January 1945: Colville papers.

since 1941 or even 1940'.[1] Harold Nicolson, who was present, wrote to his sons:

> Winston opened the two-day debate on Greece and the general war situation. He started by telling us that he had a bad cold in the head—and in fact he was pink about the nostrils and somewhat hoarse—but he spoke for two hours with immense vivacity, persuasiveness and humour. He made a terrific attack on *The Times*, which was greeted with cheers such as I have not heard since that unhappy Munich morning.[2]
>
> He had a good reference to 'unconditional surrender'. Without actually repudiating that regrettable phrase, he made it clear that it signified only 'total victory', *la victoire intégrale*. He rebuffed all assertions that it was our intention to exterminate or trample on the German people. 'Not at all,' he said—and then he took off his glasses and turned aside to face the Speaker. He struck his breast like an orang-outang. 'We remain bound,' he shouted, 'by our customs and our own nature.' Very effective.[3]

During the course of his speech, Churchill spoke of his visit to Athens, and of his conference there with those 'severed by mortal hatred—mortal and living hatred'. The Archbishop, now the Regent, 'struck me as being a very remarkable man, with his headgear, towering up, morally as well as physically, above the chaotic scene'. After Churchill's departure, the Archbishop had called on General Plastiras to form a Government of the Liberal, Socialist, Left Wing, Democratic and Republican parties, 'in fact', Churchill commented, 'as we are assured, with all the modern virtues, but, undoubtedly, violently against the Communists'. As he flew to Athens, he said, he had thought of the possibility of making 'a Government of all parties, and of everyone being persuaded to fall upon each other's necks, or, at any rate, to work together in a sensible manner'. This, however, had proved impossible, and Churchill continued:

> . . . the House must not suppose that, in these foreign lands, matters are settled as they would be here in England. Even here it is hard enough to keep a Coalition together, even between men who, although divided by party, have a supreme object and so much else in common. But imagine what the difficulties are in countries racked by civil war, past or impending, and where clusters of

---

[1] Colville diary, 18 January 1945: Colville papers.

[2] Nicolson was referring to the cheers which greeted Neville Chamberlain when he told the House of Commons that he would be going to meet Hitler at Munich. Churchill's attack on *The Times* reflected his long-standing dislike of the 'appeasement' policy pursued between 1933 and 1939 by the pre-war editor, Geoffrey Dawson. On 23 May 1937 Dawson had written privately, to Lord Lothian: 'I should like to get going with the Germans. I simply cannot understand why they should apparently be so much annoyed with *The Times* at this moment. I spend my nights in taking out anything which I think will hurt their susceptibilities and in dropping in little things which are intended to soothe them' (Lord Lothian papers).

[3] Harold Nicolson, letter of 18 January 1945: Nigel Nicolson (editor), *op. cit.*, page 430.

petty parties have each their own set of appetites, misdeeds and revenges.

If I had driven the wife of the Deputy Prime Minister out to die in the snow, if the Minister of Labour had kept the Foreign Secretary in exile for a great many years, if the Chancellor of the Exchequer had shot at and wounded the Secretary of State for War, or the head of one or other of the great spending Departments, if we, who sit here together, had back-bitten and double-crossed each other while pretending to work together, and had all put our own group or party first and the country nowhere, and had all set ideologies, slogans or labels in front of comprehension, comradeship and duty, we should certainly, to put it at the mildest, have come to a General Election much sooner than is now likely.

When men have wished very much to kill each other, and have feared very much that they will be killed quite soon, it is not possible for them next day to work together as friends with colleagues against whom they have nursed such intentions or from whom they have derived such fears. We must recognize the difference between our affairs and those which prevailed in Athens, especially while the firing was continuous all round us. That cannot possibly be overlooked.

As to the Greek Communists, 'I must admit,' Churchill said, 'that I judged them on their form against the Germans.' It was not against the Germans, he added, that they were trying to fight 'to any great extent. They were simply taking our arms, lying low and awaiting the moment when they could seize power in the capital by force, or intrigue, and make Greece a Communist State with the totalitarian liquidation of all opponents.' Not only had he been wrong in not recognizing the aims of 'the Communist-directed ELAS', he had also made a mistake in 'underrating' them as a fighting force. 'If I am accused of this mistake, I can only say with M. Clemenceau on a celebrated occasion: "Perhaps I have made a number of other mistakes of which you have not heard."'

Churchill then spoke of the principles for which Britain was striving on behalf of the liberated countries, and the 'repentant satellite countries'. This principle was, 'Government of the people, by the people, for the people, set up on a basis of free and universal suffrage elections, with secrecy of the ballot and no intimidation.' Churchill stressed:

That is and has always been the policy of this Government in all countries. That is our only aim, our only interest, and our only care. It is to that goal that we try to make our way across all the difficulties, obstacles and perils of the long road. Trust the people, make sure they have a fair chance to decide their destiny without being terrorised from either quarter or regimented. There is our policy for Italy, for Yugoslavia and for Greece. What other interests have we than that? For that we shall strive, and for that alone.[1]

[1] In a passage which Churchill dictated for his speech, but then deleted, he intended to say: 'I

Churchill made no reference to Poland. But he did comment that Bulgaria and Roumania had recently passed 'under the control of the Soviet military authorities', and that 'Russian-controlled armies' were 'in contact' with Yugoslavia, telling the House of Commons:

As we feared that there might be misunderstandings and contrary policies between us and the Soviet Government about Yugoslavia, which can easily arise when armies enter a country which is in great disorder, the Foreign Secretary and I reached at Moscow an understanding with Marshal Stalin by which our two countries pursue a joint policy in these regions, after constant discussions. This agreement raised no question of divisions of territory or spheres of interest after the war. It aimed only at the avoidance, during these critical days, of friction between the great Allies.

Britain had now reached the sixty-fifth month of the war, and its weight, Churchill noted, 'hangs heavy upon us. No one knows what stresses are wrought in these times by this long persistence of strain, quite above the ordinary normal life of human society.' Churchill continued:

Let us be of good cheer. Both in the West and in the East overwhelming forces are ranged on our side. Military victory may be distant, it will certainly be costly, but it is no longer in doubt. The physical and scientific force which our foes hurled upon us in the early years has changed sides and the British Commonwealth, the United States and the Soviet Union undoubtedly possess the power to beat down to the ground in dust and ashes the prodigious might of the war-making nations and the conspiracies which assailed us. But, as the sense of mortal peril has passed from our side to that of our cruel foes, they gain the stimulus of despair and we tend to lose the bond of combined self-preservation, or are in danger of losing it.

There is, therefore, demanded of us a moral and intellectual impulse to unity and a clear conception and definition of joint purpose sufficient to overbear the fleeting reinforcement which our enemies will derive from the realization of their forlorn condition. Can we produce that complete unity and that new impulse in time to achieve decisive military victory with the least possible prolongation of the world's misery, or must we fall into jabber, babble and discord while victory is still unattained? It seems to me to be the supreme question alike of the hour and of the age.

Speaking of the phrase and policy of 'unconditional surrender', Churchill told the House of Commons:

---

think that on the whole a monarchy is a valuable element in these Balkan countries. It separates pomp from power. It gives a certain sense of continuity and it tends to keep the summit of the State free from unbridled dictatorship. But that is only my personal view and I will not allow it to affect the march of events or stand against the wishes, [however ephemeral], of the peoples.' The phrase in square brackets was deleted by Churchill before he deleted the whole paragraph. (Churchill papers, 9/205).

I read somewhere that when the ancient Athenians, on one occasion, over-powered a tribe in the Peloponnesus which had wrought them great injury by base, treacherous means, and when they had the hostile army herded on a beach naked for slaughter, they forgave them and set them free, and they said:

'This was not done because they were men; it was done because of the nature of Man.'

Similarly, in this temper we may now say to our foes, 'We demand un-conditional surrender, but you well know how strict are the moral limits within which our action is confined. We are no extirpators of nations, or butchers of peoples. We make no bargain with you. We accord you nothing as a right. Abandon your resistance unconditionally. We remain bound by our customs and our nature.'

Although the war still contained many dangers, among them 'the jet-propelled fighter aircraft', the V-rockets, and 'above all', the renewed U-boat menace, Churchill commented that he had 'never at any time' been able to present the House with a more confident state-ment about the 'ever-growing might and ascendancy' of the United Nations, or of the 'military solidarity' of the three great Allies. As for the 'essentially minor' political misunderstandings and difficulties that confronted them, Roosevelt had just announced a meeting of the Big Three 'somewhere or other, and quite soon', and Churchill added, 'the Foreign Secretary and I, with our military and technical advisers, will be present without fail at the rendezvous. . . .' [1]

Among those who were in the House of Commons when Churchill spoke was Oliver Lyttelton. 'How wonderful and inspiring,' he wrote, adding that the speech 'ranks in my mind with the Darlan one as a perfect Parliamentary effort', with 'all the stops from Vox Humana to the Grand Swell pulled out'. [2]

One note of protest was struck, from the Italians. Churchill's remark 'about needing Italy no more than Spain', Sir Noel Charles tele-graphed from Rome, 'has *hurt*'. The Ambassador went on to explain that 'in her own eyes Italy deserved sympathy and credit for trying at great sacrifice to redeem her recent past while Spain is still Fascist and unregenerate'. [3] Reading this complaint, Churchill remembered Italy's attack on France in May 1940, minuting to Eden: 'Spain did not stab us in the back—a trifle no doubt, but not overlooked by WSC.' [4]

*   *   *

[1] *Hansard*, 18 January 1945, columns 396–428.
[2] Letter of 18 January 1945: Churchill papers, 9/205. The 'Darlan' speech was Churchill's Secret Session speech of 10 December 1942, quoted on pages 274–8 of this volume.
[3] No. 150 from Rome, 20 January 1945: Churchill papers, 9/205.
[4] Note of 21 January 1945: Churchill papers, 9/205.

As Yalta drew nearer, Soviet activity in the newly occupied eastern regions intensified. On January 18 Churchill read British diplomatic reports from Roumania, protesting against the deportation of German-speaking Saxons from Roumania, an ethnic German minority that had lived in Roumania for many centuries.[1] 'Why are we making a fuss about the Russian deportations in Roumania of Saxons and others?' he minuted to Eden. 'It is understood that the Russians were to work their will in this sphere. Anyhow we cannot prevent them.'[2]

On the following day Churchill read a further criticism of these and other deportations, in a Foreign Office enquiry to the British Embassy in Bulgaria.[3] He at once minuted again, to Eden:

We seem to be taking a very active line against the deportation of the Austrians, Saxons and other German or quasi-German elements from Roumania to Russia for labour purposes. Considering all that Russia has suffered, and the wanton attacks made upon her by Roumania, and the vast armies the Russians are using at the front at the present time, and the terrible condition of people in many parts of Europe, I cannot see that the Russians are wrong in making 100 or 150 thousand of these people work their passage. Also we must bear in mind what we promised about leaving Roumania's fate to a large extent in Russian hands. I cannot myself consider that it is wrong of the Russians to take Roumanians of any origin they like to work in the Russian coalfields, in view of all that has passed.[4]

Following the extension by Britain and the United States of full recognition to de Gaulle's Government as the Government of France, Churchill was confronted in the middle of January 1945 by de Gaulle's request that France should participate in the Yalta discussions. On January 19 Churchill wrote to Eden, in a letter 'not for official circulation', of his strong opposition to this request. De Gaulle would, Churchill wrote, 'be forever intriguing and playing off two against the

---

[1] These 'Saxons' were Germans from the Rhineland and Luxembourg who, in the twelfth century, had been settled in by the King of Hungary and Croatia in colonies to guard the passes through the Transylvanian Alps. Alan Palmer writes: 'They enjoyed extensive self-government and were favoured by the rulers right down until the Reformation, when they became the main Lutheran outpost in Eastern Europe. In 1918–19 they hurriedly made their own, quite favourable, settlement with the Roumanian peace delegation at Paris. Roumania's Minority Treaty safeguarded the communal rights of the Saxons in Transylvania.' (Letter to the author, 5 June 1985.)

[2] Prime Minister's Personal Minute, M.84/5, 18 January 1945: Foreign Office papers, 954/23, folio 382.

[3] Foreign Office Telegram No. 68, to Sofia.

[4] Prime Minister's Personal Minute, M.90/5, 19 January 1945: Churchill papers, 20/209.

third'. As to the French war effort, 'France contributes a very small fighting stake to the pool at present. It is not French blood that is being shed to any extent in any quarter of the globe.' Churchill added that Canada had 'more right than France' to be considered the 'Fourth Power'. In the recent fighting around Colmar, 80,000 Frenchmen had faced 12,000 Germans 'and made no headway', nor would an extra 50,000 ex-Maquis Frenchmen agree to be employed in the existing divisions, but insisted upon being kept in their own formations, 'with a view no doubt to political power', nor had de Gaulle 'and his harassed Government' felt able to 'come to grips' with the ex-Maquis fighters on this subject. 'Really France has enough to do this winter and spring in trying to keep body and soul together, and cannot masquerade as a Great Power for the purpose of war,' Churchill's letter continued; she had been treated 'very well' by being admitted so early to the European Advisory Commission 'and other Allied bodies'. Churchill ended: 'I cannot think of anything more unpleasant and impossible than having this menacing and hostile man in our midst, always trying to make himself a reputation in France by claiming a position far above what France occupies, and making faces at the Allies who are doing the work.' [1]

'The whole character of our discussions will be destroyed,' Churchill minuted to Eden six days later, 'if de Gaulle were present, and of course he would come, even though only invited on shipping', as had now been proposed 'and make a grievance on the rest'. [2]

On January 20 Hungary signed an armistice with the Allies. That same day, the Red Army entered the German provinces of Silesia and East Prussia. Clement Attlee, meanwhile, had decided to send Churchill a formal protest about the conduct of Government business. As Colville noted in his diary:

Attlee has written a very blunt letter to the PM, protesting:
(1) against the PM's lengthy disquisitions in Cabinet on papers which he has not read and on subjects which he has not taken the trouble to master.
(2) against the PM's undue attentiveness to Brendan and Lord Beaverbrook, whose views, often entirely ignorant, are apt to be thrown into the scale against the considered opinion of a Cabinet Committee when that Committee brings its views to the War Cabinet.

This, Colville commented, had happened 'several times' recently, and he added:

[1] 'Private and Personal', 'Not for Official Circulation', 19 January 1945: Churchill papers, 20/193.
[2] Prime Minister's Personal Minute, M.113/5, 25 January 1945: Churchill papers, 20/209.

Greatly as I love and admire the PM I am afraid there is much in what Attlee says, and I rather admire his courage in saying it. Many Conservatives, and officials such as Cadogan and Bridges, feel the same. However the PM exploded over Attlee's letter, drafted and redrafted a sarcastic reply, said it was a socialist conspiracy, harped on nothing but the inadequate representation of the Tories in the Cabinet, in spite of their numerical weight in the House (which is beside the point), and, worst of all, finally read Attlee's very personal letter—poorly typed by his own hand so that none of his staff should see it—to Beaverbrook on the telephone, having first of all discussed it with Mrs Churchill. As John Martin said, 'that is the part of the PM which I do not like'.

However, what of it? The Russians sweep gaily on, past Lodz, past Cracow, over the Silesian border. The war, once again, enters a fast-moving, thrilling phase and hopes rise high.

After dinner there was a film in an Air Ministry room on the ground floor in King Charles St. The PM bid us all cast care aside and 'not bother about Atler or Hitlee', and so all the typists, drivers, servants, etc. saw first of all a first class newsreel of the Luftwaffe attack on our airfields in Holland on New Year's Day and then Bette Davis in 'Dark Victory', a brilliantly acted film and one of the few I have seen end as a tragedy.[1]

On the following day, January 21, Colville walked in St James's Park with Clementine Churchill, 'who says', Colville noted in his diary, 'she thinks Attlee's letter of yesterday both true and wholesome'. The 'last straw' to Churchill, Colville added, was when Beaverbrook, against whom the letter was 'partly aimed', said, after seeing it that day, that 'he thought it a very good letter'.[2] Churchill, 'still sorely piqued', Colville wrote, 'but probably in his heart of hearts not unmoved by the arguments', sent Attlee a short, succinct reply:

My dear Lord President,
    I have to thank you for your Private and Personal letter of January 19. You may be sure I shall always endeavour to profit by your counsels.

Yours sincerely
WSC[3]

From one of Churchill's earlier soldiering companions-in-arms, Richard Molyneux, there came, on January 22, a letter recalling the day in 1897 when Churchill had given a piece of his own skin in order to heal Molyneux's wound. 'I never mention and always conceal it,' Molyneux wrote, 'for fear people might think I was bucking.'[4] 'Thank

---

[1] Colville diary, 20 January 1945: Colville papers.
[2] Colville diary, 21 January 1945: Colville papers.
[3] Letter of 22 January 1945: Churchill papers, 20/193.
[4] Letter of 22 January 1945: Churchill papers, 20/198.

you so much, dear Dick,' Churchill replied. 'I often think of those old days, and I should like to feel that you showed the bit of pelt. I have frequently shown the gap from which it was taken.' [1]

On January 22 the Red Army reached the river Oder. Soviet troops now stood, as liberators, in all the territory to be annexed from Germany, and to be given to Poland and Russia, under the agreements reached by the Big Three at Teheran. [2] 'The Russians are within 165 miles of Berlin,' Colville noted, 'and still advancing.' [3] On the following night, before going to bed, Churchill said to Colville: 'Make no mistake, all the Balkans, except Greece, are going to be bolshevized; and there is nothing I can do to prevent it. There is nothing I can do for poor Poland either.' [4]

Churchill still hoped to see some British military action towards the Ljubljana gap. It was 'with great regret', he told a Staff Conference on January 23, that he had 'given up hope of a British right-handed thrust into the armpit of the Adriatic', and agreed that it 'would be right in principle to transfer forces from Italy to the Western front'. But the Chiefs of Staff now proposed moving only three divisions from Italy, which would take two and a half months to be in their place on the western front. Given the small size of this force, and the long time span before it could see action, Churchill argued that the 'gain to the Western front was a small reward for having to give up all hopes of offensive action in Italy and the Adriatic'.

Replying, Brooke spoke of 'two alternatives' for the British troops in Italy, should Churchill's wishes be practicable. They could fight in Yugoslavia 'in an attempt to cut off the German forces retiring through that country', or they could fight 'on the left flank of the Russians advancing towards Vienna'. But, Brooke added, 'the prospect of operating in Yugoslavia was not attractive and it was doubtful if we should be able to cut off any considerable portion of the Germans retiring through that country. If we joined the Russians it was practically certain that our forces would not be allowed to march on Vienna and that our six divisions would be employed on the Russian left flank somewhere south of Vienna.'

[1] Telegram of 28 January 1945: Churchill papers, 20/198. Molyneux died in 1954.
[2] Russia was to receive the northern half of East Prussia, including the port of Königsberg (now Kaliningrad); Poland was to receive the southern half of East Prussia, and the eastern Provinces of Germany proper, including all of German Silesia (with its principal city Breslau, now Wroclaw).
[3] Colville diary, 22 January 1945: Colville papers.
[4] Colville diary, 23 January 1945: Colville papers.

Churchill deferred to Brooke's arguments, stating 'that he would give the matter further consideration'.[1]

Poland's prospects seemed as bleak as those of the Balkans, although there still seemed a remote possibility that Mikolajczyk, who had conducted such long and obstinate negotiations with Stalin and Churchill in 1944, might still, as Leader of the Peasant Party, be able to effect some compromise in the composition of the Polish Provisional Government, now exclusively made up as Stalin wished, of members of the Lublin Committee. 'Yes, let us stick to Mikolajczyk,' Churchill minuted to Eden on January 25. 'It may all come back to him.'[2] When, that same day, Mikolajczyk's successor as Prime Minister, Arciszewski, asked to be received officially by Eden, together with Adam Tarnowski, his Foreign Minister, Churchill minuted again: 'I am anchored alongside Mikolajczyk, and I should like to be able to tell Stalin that we have not seen Arciszewski and Co. although we have recognized them officially.'[3]

At the War Cabinet five days later, Churchill explained what he had in mind. It must be expected, he said, 'now that the Germans had been practically driven out of the whole of Poland, that the Lublin Committee, with the Russian Government behind them, would grow very rapidly in power'. Churchill told the War Cabinet that he expected 'that the Soviet representatives at the forthcoming meetings of Heads of Governments would demand the recognition of the Lublin Committee as the Government of Poland. We must bear in mind that recognition was the one counter which remained in our hands, and that we should not give it up save in return for something worth having.' In general, Churchill concluded, 'our attitude would be, if the War Cabinet approved, to continue to advise the Poles to compromise as regards the Eastern frontier, and to remain adamant on the question of ensuring a free, sovereign and independent Poland, coupled with arrangements for free elections'.[4]

The plans to meet at Yalta were proceeding. 'Ironically,' as Averell Harriman has recalled, 'the ailing Roosevelt had decided to travel all the way to the Crimea—4,883 miles by sea from Newport News, Virginia, to Malta, and then 1,375 miles by air from Luqa Airfield, Malta, to the snowy runway at Saki—because Stalin, on the advice of his doctors, refused to leave the Soviet Union.'[5] Churchill, at seventy

---

[1] Staff Conference, Chiefs of Staff Committee No. 25 of 1945, 23 January 1945: Cabinet papers, 79/28.

[2] Prime Minister's Personal Minute, M.111/5, 25 January 1945: Churchill papers, 20/209.

[3] Prime Minister's Personal Minute, M.112/5, 25 January 1945: Churchill papers, 20/209.

[4] War Cabinet No. 11 of 1945, 26 January 1945, Confidential Annex: Cabinet papers, 65/51.

[5] Abel and Harriman, *op. cit.*, page 390. Saki was given the code name 'Albatros'.

the oldest of the Big Three, had likewise to make a long and arduous journey. On January 24 Harry Hopkins, who was in London, sent Roosevelt a telegram about Churchill's attitude to the location of Yalta: 'if we had spent ten years on research', Churchill had told Hopkins, 'we could not have found a worse place in the world'.[1] Churchill felt that he could survive it, however, by bringing 'an adequate supply' of whisky. He claims it is 'good for typhus', Hopkins reported in this same telegram, 'and deadly on lice which thrive in those parts'.[2]

January 24 was, as Churchill reminded Colville, the fiftieth anniversary of the death of his father, Lord Randolph Churchill. From a prisoner-of-war camp in Germany that day came a poignant family message, from his second cousin, Lieutenant Jack Leslie, son of Sir Shane Leslie. Jack Leslie, who had been taken prisoner at Calais in 1940, wrote to his kinsman at 10 Downing Street: 'so many of us would be more than grateful if you could by any chance arrange the repatriation of prisoners captured in 1940. We are fully aware that our trivial discomforts are as nothing compared to the suffering world. Yet we feel a change would favour many both mentally & physically.'[3]

At Moscow in October 1944, Eden had already given his assent in general terms to the repatriation to Russia of Russians who had been captured on the western front, many of whom, since 1941, had been serving in the German army. Eden had agreed to this repatriation in part because of the large number of British prisoners-of-war held in camps which were at that very moment being liberated by the Red Army, and whose rapid and unimpeded return to Britain seemed to be both a British responsibility and a priority.

To Churchill, who had originally intended to travel from Alexandria to Yalta on board the pre-war liner, the SS *Franconia*, Ismay minuted on 1 January 1945: 'Marshal Stalin is pressing for the repatriation of Soviet Nationals taken prisoner by us on the Western Front, and it is proposed to put one or two thousand of these into the *Franconia*, if you approve. I am assured that they can be completely segregated from our Party, and that they will be reasonably sanitary. They will, of course, be disembarked directly we get to our destination so that they will in any case not be in your way.'[4]

At a meeting of the War Cabinet on January 31, after Churchill

---

[1] Telegram of 24 January 1945: Robert E. Sherwood, *The White House Papers of Harry L. Hopkins*, London 1949, volume 2, page 839.

[2] Kimball, *op. cit.*, volume 3, page 518.

[3] 'Kriegsgefangenenpost, Postkarte', 24 January 1945: Churchill papers, 1/386.

[4] 'Top Secret', 'Argonaut', 1 January 1945: Cabinet papers, 120/170. Churchill replied: 'I see no harm in this provided the place can be properly cleared up after they have left.' (Prime Minister's Personal Minute, D.8/5, 2 January 1945: Cabinet papers, 120/170.)

had left for Yalta, there was a discussion about a Soviet proposal that any reciprocal agreement to cover the repatriation of prisoners-of-war 'should be extended to all liberated Soviet and British subjects'. The 'general view' of the War Cabinet was to accept this Soviet proposal.[1] This meant that any Soviet citizen who was liberated in western Europe should be 'repatriated' to Russia, not merely those who had fought in the German ranks, or aided in some way the German policy of persecution.[2]

On January 25 a Joint Intelligence Committee Report, sent to Churchill and the Chiefs of Staff, stated that the war could be shortened 'decisively' if the British and American strategic bomber force could give 'assistance to the Russians during the next few weeks'. According to this report, the 'degree of success' attained by the new Russian offensive was likely to have 'a decisive effect on the length of the war'. Because of this, the Committee believed that 'the assistance which might be given to the Russians during the next few weeks by the British and American strategic bomber force' justified an 'urgent review' of the current bomber targets.

The existing targets were, in order of priority, Germany's synthetic oil production factories and oil storage depots, and tank factories. These priorities would remain, but added to them would be two others: the 'devastation of Berlin', and an attack on German 'rail communications' in order to delay the German reinforcements which were being sent to the River Oder battle, some from as far away as Italy, Hungary and even Norway.

The Joint Intelligence Committee report pointed out that a heavy flow of refugees from Berlin, coinciding with 'the trekking westwards' of Germans fleeing from eastern Germany, 'would be bound to create great confusion, interfere with the orderly movement of troops to the front and hamper the German military and administrative machine'. There might even be a 'political value', the report said, 'in demonstrating to the Russians, in the best way open to us, a desire on the part of the British and Americans to assist them in the present battle'.[3]

[1] War Cabinet No. 13 of 1945, 31 January 1945: Cabinet papers, 65/49.

[2] At this War Cabinet, Clement Attlee was in the Chair. The other War Cabinet ministers present were Sir John Anderson, Ernest Bevin, Oliver Lyttelton, Herbert Morrison and Lord Woolton. Thirteen other Ministers were present, as well as Sir Orme Sargent, Deputy Under-Secretary of State for Foreign Affairs.

[3] Joint Intelligence Committee Report, No. 31 (Operations) (Revised Final) of 1945, 'Top Secret', 25 January 1945: Cabinet papers, 79/29.

Asked that same day to comment on this report, Sir Arthur Harris suggested simultaneous attacks on Berlin, Leipzig and Dresden, as focal points of the German system of communications in front of the Red Army.[1] That night, in conversation, Churchill had asked Sinclair 'whether Berlin, and no doubt other large cities in East Germany, should not now be considered especially attractive targets'. On the following day Churchill added: 'Pray report to me tomorrow what is going to be done.'[2]

In passing on Churchill's request to his Staff on January 26, Sinclair told them that the Prime Minister wished to know what plans the Air Ministry had for 'blasting the Germans in their retreat from Breslau'.[3] On the following day Portal informed Sinclair in answer to Churchill's question, that in the view of the Air Staff, the Air Ministry 'should use available effort in one big attack on Berlin and attacks on Dresden, Leipzig, Chemnitz, or any other cities where a severe blitz will not only cause confusion in the evacuation from the East, but will also hamper the movement of troops from the West'.[4]

On January 27, Soviet forces completed the clearing of Lithuania, drove the Germans from Memel on the Baltic, and crossed the River Vistula near Torun, once one of the most westerly towns of Tsarist Russia. 'We are spellbound by your glorious victories over the common foe,' Churchill telegraphed to Stalin on January 27, 'and by the mighty forces you have brought into the line against them. Accept our warmest thanks and congratulations on historic deeds.'[5]

On January 27 Churchill and his wife went to Hyde Park Gate, in Kensington, to look at a house they were interested in as a possible London residence once the war was ended. 'Yesterday afternoon I took Papa to see the little house I covet,' Clementine Churchill wrote to their daughter Mary. 'He is mad about it, so now I must be careful not to run him into something which is more than he can afford.'[6]

On the eve of his departure, Churchill was asked by Eden about a possible revision of the Straits Convention in Russia's favour.

[1] Note by Sir Norman Bottomley (for Sir Charles Portal) on a conversation with Sir Arthur Harris, 26 January 1945: Sir Charles Webster and Noble Frankland, *The Strategic Air Offensive against Germany, 1939–1945*, volume 3, Part 5, London 1961, page 100.

[2] Prime Minister's Personal Minute, M.115/5, 26 January 1945: Churchill papers, 20/209.

[3] Minute by Air Chief Marshal Sir Wilfrid Freeman, 26 January 1945: Webster and Frankland, *op. cit.*, page 101.

[4] Letter from Sir Norman Bottomley to Sir Arthur Harris, 27 January 1945: Webster and Frankland, *op. cit.*, page 103.

[5] Prime Minister's Personal Telegram, T.144/5, 27 January 1945: Churchill papers, 20/225.

[6] Letter of 28 January 1945: Lady Soames, *Clementine Churchill*, London 1979, page 380.

Churchill minuted on January 28 that while, 'naturally, one does not wish to give away things that are not asked for', nevertheless, he would not be prepared 'to resist a Russian demand for freedom of the Straits'. Churchill also noted, in connection with Russia's possible entry into the war against Japan, that a 'speedy termination of the Japanese war, such as might be procured by the mere fact of a Russian declaration against Japan, would undoubtedly save us many thousands of millions of pounds', and he added: 'The Staffs see no particular harm in the presence of Russia as a Pacific power.' [1]

[1] Prime Minister's Personal Minute, M.127/5, 'Top Secret', 28 January 1945: Cabinet papers, 120/714.

60

Maltese Prelude

ON 29 January 1945, the British 'Argonauts' were ready to leave on the first stage of the long journey to Yalta. At 9.30 in the morning the first aircraft left Northolt for Malta. In it were General Brooke, Anthony Eden, Cadogan, and Pierson Dixon. Churchill followed at 9.30 that evening in the Skymaster. With him were his daughter Sarah, Lord Moran, Sir Edward Bridges, John Martin, Leslie Rowan and Commander Thompson.[1] The flight was not a success, as Sarah wrote to her mother:

We had a delicious dinner, but as usual, at first the plane was cold—so everything was turned on and Papa sat huddled in his great coat. Then it began to get hot and in a minute we were all as pink as tomatoes screaming for air. More re-adjustments; but Papa looked like a poor hot pink baby about to cry! He took his temperature—and it was up and, 'Oh Lord!' I thought, 'there we go again.' It was about one o'clock before we settled in for the night but nobody slept much, if at all.

We landed at 4.30. Tommy tumbled out of his bunk where he had been lying half dressed and tottered forth bleary-eyed to check with the airfield station master that we had cancelled the reception. Had? Well, to his horror, everything but massed bands greeted him. The tarmac was literally laced with gold braid: something had obviously gone wrong, and some very angry scrambled eggs rumbled off back to their beds!

Churchill's temperature had risen during the night to just over 102°. By morning it was still 100°. Churchill remained in bed on the Skymaster as it sat on the tarmac. Sarah Churchill's account continued:

What to do—he was miserable and convinced he was in for something. Sawyers—he is a miracle of devotion—muttered to me: 'He's always like this after Lord Moran's pills!' I meditated on this profound statement and passed it on to Papa, who grunted and said 'True!' So I followed up with: 'I'm sure it will soon go—it is a pretty powerful drug, and when we get out of this hot

[1] John Martin diary, 29 January 1945: Martin papers.

plane I'm sure you'll feel better.' It was touch and go between the ship and the hospital for a few hours. The hospital was laid on—the ship was cancelled—the hospital was cancelled, and the ship laid on.[1]

At 10.30 that morning, after six hours in bed on the Skymaster at Luqa airfield, Churchill felt well enough to leave the aircraft and drive to the cruiser HMS *Orion*, where he went straight to bed. 'Lovely passage but a little fever which is I think departing,' he telegraphed to Clementine Churchill that morning, his telegram headed: 'For Mrs Kent from Colonel Kent.'[2]

Churchill still had two more days at Malta, before flying on to the Crimea. 'I hope you will rest well these two spare days,' Clementine Churchill wrote on January 30, 'so as to be fresh for the ordeals of the Conference.'[3] On board *Orion*, Churchill remained in bed. 'Temperature has returned to normal,' John Martin telegraphed to the Private Office that afternoon, 'and Colonel Kent is in good heart.'[4]

As Churchill lay in bed, both Brooke and Alexander went to see him.[5] Their purpose was to put to him the conclusions reached that morning at a meeting of the Chiefs of Staff Committee, held in Malta.

With the advance of the Russian armies in the East, the Chiefs of Staffs agreed, 'operations across the Adriatic through Yugoslavia were unlikely to pay a substantial dividend'.[6] But Eisenhower's forces in western Europe were 'barely adequate to enable him to stage an offensive of sufficient power'. Therefore the Chiefs of Staff felt 'impelled' to propose the reinforcement of Eisenhower's forces by divisions drawn from Italy. Three divisions should go to Eisenhower 'forthwith' and three more 'as soon as the situation in Greece allowed'.[7]

This conclusion, which Churchill accepted that same afternoon, constituted the final reversal of his earlier persistent hopes for preserving some form of democracy in the Balkans and central Europe. But it was dictated by a new military situation which he quickly grasped. 'He said that he was now entirely with us,' Brooke noted in his diary, 'and that I could now go ahead and discuss it with the Americans.' This, Brooke added, 'is a godsend'.[8]

That night, Eden, Cadogan and Harriman were among Churchill's

---

[1] Letter of 31 January 1945: Sarah Churchill, *Keep on Dancing*, London 1981, page 72.
[2] 'Jason' No. 5, 11.47 a.m., 30 January 1945: Premier papers 4/78/1, Part 2, folio 543.
[3] Letter of 30 January 1945: Spencer-Churchill papers.
[4] 'Jason' No. 14, 5.25 p.m., 30 January 1945: Premier papers, 4/77/1B, folio 221.
[5] Private Office diary, 30 January 1945.
[6] Both Budapest and Belgrade had been liberated by Soviet forces.
[7] War Cabinet, Chiefs of Staff Committee (Argonaut) 1st Meeting, 30 January 1945: Cabinet papers, 120/170.
[8] Brooke diary, 30 January 1945: Bryant, *op. cit.*, volume 2, pages 391–2.

dinner guests.[1] Churchill seemed fully recovered, 'cheerful and eating and drinking everything within reach', Cadogan noted in his diary.[2] 'We had some quite good preliminary talk on our conference problems,' Eden noted in his diary.[3]

After Eden and Cadogan had left, Harriman remained, 'playing bezique with the Prime Minister until shortly after midnight.'[4]

At Malta on January 31, the Combined Chiefs of Staff met to discuss the previous day's decision. It was agreed, as Ismay told Churchill, and later reported in writing, that five divisions would be withdrawn from the Mediterranean front to the Western front. 'To our surprise,' Ismay added, 'the United States Chiefs of Staff suggested that, for political and military reasons, the divisions to be withdrawn from the Mediterranean should be British and Canadian, leaving the United States 5th Army intact. The Chiefs of Staff felt that you would welcome this arrangement and accepted it. This means that the first three divisions to be withdrawn will be two Canadian and one British '[5]

Also on January 31, Portal told Brooke and Cunningham that the Air Staff would shortly be submitting an appreciation 'of the assistance to the Russian advance which might be effected by the strategic bomber force'. Portal also spoke of rearranging the Anglo-American bombing priorities in such a way as to make it possible both to attack Berlin, and German tank factories, 'in relation to the present Russian offensive'. Sir Charles Portal commented that if the forces employed on bombing communications could be reduced, it would be possible both to attack German tank factories, 'and also to make heavy attacks in the four cities, Berlin, Dresden, Leipzig and Chemnitz', where the 'resulting confusion' was 'most likely to hamper enemy efforts to transfer forces between the Western and Eastern fronts'.[6]

On February 1, from Malta, both Sarah Churchill and her father wrote long letters home. Churchill was clearly on the mend: 'All

---

[1] Also present were Lord Moran, John Martin, Sarah Churchill, Commander Thompson, and the Captain of the *Orion*, Captain Gornall.

[2] Cadogan diary, 31 January 1945 (for 30 January 1945): David Dilks (editor), *op. cit.*, page 700.

[3] Eden diary, 30 January 1945: Eden memoirs, *The Reckoning, op. cit.*, page 510.

[4] Private Office diary, 30 January 1945.

[5] 'Notes of Combined Chiefs of Staff Meeting on 31st January, 1945', 'Top Secret', 31 January 1945: Premier papers, 3/51/10, folios 87–91. John Martin noted on this document on 1 February 1945: 'This is for record only, Gen. Ismay having reported orally to PM.'

[6] Chiefs of Staff Committee (Argonaut) No. 2, 31 January 1945: Cabinet papers, 120/170.

yesterday,' Sarah told her mother, 'he was in the best of spirits. To quote his own words as we drove to dinner at the palace, "My temperature is down—my tummy ache gone—my functions have resumed their norm: in fact I'm in the best of form!"' Sarah ended her account: 'much love darling—try not to worry—these three days are being very useful. He is getting some rest and it gives the Americans and our English time to put in some good ground work.' [1]

That same day, February 1, Eden, Stettinius and their advisers examined sixteen topics of foreign policy, each of them liable to lead to controversy with the Russians, which were to be discussed at Yalta. [2] Also on February 1, the British Chiefs of Staff discussed every facet of future strategy for the war in Europe and in the Far East, Alexander telling the Chiefs of Staff, during the discussion on an American proposal to transfer air forces from the Mediterranean theatre to north-west Europe, that 'it was also important that the remaining air forces should not be so weak that they could not effectively attack the enemy if he decided to withdraw'. [3]

For Churchill, on board HMS *Orion*, it was a time for reflection and foreboding. He had been reading, and had nearly finished, a book by Beverley Nichols, *Verdict on India*, given to him by Jock Colville, and he wrote to his wife:

I think you would do well to read it. It is written with some distinction and a great deal of thought. It certainly shows the Hindu in his true character and the sorry plight to which we have reduced ourselves by losing confidence in our mission. Reading about India has depressed me for I see such ugly storms looming up there which, even in my short flight, may overtake us. I have had for some time a feeling of despair about the British connection with India, and still more about what will happen if it is suddenly broken. Meanwhile we are holding on to this vast Empire, from which we get nothing, amid the increasing criticism and abuse of the world and our own people and increasing hatred of the Indian population, who receive constant and deadly propaganda to which we can make no reply.

However out of my shadows has come a renewed resolve to go fighting on as long as possible and to make sure the Flag is not let down while I am at the wheel. I agree with the book and also with its conclusion—Pakistan.

---

[1] Letter of 1 February 1945: Spencer-Churchill papers.

[2] The sixteen topics were: Zones of Occupation in Germany, Zones of Occupation in Austria, Poland, Persia, Warm water Port for Russia (Straits and the Far East), China, Emergency High Commission For Europe, Germany, Dumbarton Oaks (World Organization, voting of the Big Powers), Polish–German Frontier, Austro–Yugoslav Frontier, Conduct of the Russians in Eastern Europe, Civil Supplies, Prisoners of War, Anglo–American Warning to Germany about Allied Prisoners of War, and Treatment of Major War Criminals: Foreign Secretaries Meeting (Argonaut), 1st Meeting, 1 February 1945: Cabinet papers, 120/170.

[3] Chiefs of Staff (Argonaut), 3rd Meeting, Malta, 10.30 a.m., 1 February 1945: Cabinet papers, 120/170.

Churchill also wrote to his wife about 'the little band of insulters who have been so forward about Greece', and about how, every day, came 'proofs of how right we were'. Churchill added:

The bitter misunderstandings which have arisen in the United States, and in degenerate circles at home, are only a foretaste of the furies which will be loosed about every stage of the peace settlement. I am sure in Greece I found one of the best opportunities for wise action that this war has tossed to me from its dark waves.

The future of Germany was to be one of the main topics for discussion at Yalta. Churchill told his wife in his letter of February 1:

I am free to confess to you that my heart is saddened by the tales of the masses of German women and children flying along the roads everywhere in 40-mile long columns to the West before the advancing Armies. I am clearly convinced that they deserve it; but that does not remove it from one's gaze. The misery of the whole world appals me and I fear increasingly that new struggles may arise out of those we are successfully ending.

Churchill ended his letter on a personal note. 'Tender love my darling. I miss you much. I am lonely amid this throng. Your ever-loving husband, W.'[1]

At about 9.30 on the morning of February 2 President Roosevelt arrived at Malta in the cruiser *Quincy*. As the ship steamed slowly past HMS *Orion*, the two leaders waved to each other across the water. Two hours later Churchill felt well enough to go aboard the *Quincy*, to greet Roosevelt, and to stay for luncheon. 'My friend has arrived in best of health and spirits,' Churchill telegraphed to his wife. 'Everything going very well. Lovely warm sunshine,' and he added: 'We are on the wing at dawn.'[2] No one else who saw the President that day described him as 'in best of health'. 'What a change in the President,' noted Marian Holmes, 'since we saw him in Hyde Park last October. He seems to have lost so much weight, has dark circles under his eyes, looks altogether frail and as if he is hardly in this world at all.'[3]

As Churchill and Roosevelt began their luncheon, the Combined Chiefs of Staff met to co-ordinate their strategic plans, for presentation to Churchill and Roosevelt that evening.[4] Eden, who was at the luncheon, noted in his diary that Roosevelt 'looked considerably older since Quebec; he gives the impression of failing powers'. Eden added,

[1] Letter of 1 February 1945: Spencer-Churchill papers.
[2] 'Jason' No. 63, 4.02 p.m., 2 February 1945: Premier papers, 4/78/1, Part II, folio 514.
[3] Marian Holmes diary, 2 February 1945: Marian Walker Spicer papers.
[4] Combined Chiefs of Staff, 185th Meeting, Malta, 2 February 1945: Churchill papers, 23/15.

'Pleasant, but no business whatsoever done. So a dinner was arranged specifically for this purpose.'[1]

After luncheon, Churchill returned to *Orion* to rest. That afternoon, Randolph Churchill arrived from Bari.

Grim news reached the gathering of 'Argonauts' on February 2: a York, flying from Britain with yet more participants for the conference, had crashed in the sea off the island of Lampedusa. Of the twenty passengers, only seven were saved. Among the dead was Brooke's ADC and confidant, 'Barney' Charlesworth.[2] Also killed were three Foreign Office officials, Peter Loxley, Armin Dew and John Chaplin, as well as Eden's detective, Inspector Battley, and one of the more recent recruits to Churchill's Map Room Staff, Lieutenant-Colonel Bill Newey.[3]

At 6 o'clock that evening, Churchill returned to the *Quincy*, where he and Roosevelt attended a meeting of the Combined Chiefs of Staff, and listened to the results of their three days of discussion dominated by Eisenhower's plans to reach and to cross the Rhine. One of those present, General Ismay, later recalled: 'Roosevelt looked a very sick man'.[4]

Two days earlier, at the Combined Chiefs of Staff meeting on January 30, Bedell Smith had urged two simultaneous thrusts across the Rhine, one in the north and one in the south of the Allied line. Brooke argued, however, that there was 'not sufficient strength for two major operations', and pressed for a decision to do the northern one alone, as being the 'most promising'.[5] Brooke's argument was accepted by Eisenhower on the following day; in their report to Churchill and Roosevelt, the Combined Chiefs of Staff reported Eisenhower's assurance 'that he will seize the Rhine crossings in the North just as soon as this is a feasible operation and without waiting to close the Rhine throughout its length'.[6]

Among the strategic decisions presented by the Combined Chiefs of Staff was the decision to withdraw three divisions from Italy, followed by three more, to help Eisenhower's advance. As he had done earlier with Brooke, Churchill again gave his approval for this decision. 'He was anxious,' he told the meeting, 'that the British contribution to the

---

[1] Eden diary, 2 February 1945: Eden memoirs, *The Reckoning*, *op. cit.*, page 512.

[2] Brooke diary, 2 February 1945: Bryant, *op. cit.*, volume 2, page 400. The loss of Charlesworth, Brooke later recalled, 'was one of the worst blows I had during the war'.

[3] Pierson Dixon diary, 2 February 1945: Piers Dixon, *op. cit.*, page 136; and Colville diary, 2 February 1945: Colville papers.

[4] Ismay memoirs, *op. cit.*, page 385.

[5] Combined Chiefs of Staff, 182nd Meeting, noon, 30 January 1945: Cabinet papers, 120/170.

[6] Report to the President and the Prime Minister of the Agreed Summary of Conclusions reached by the Combined Chiefs of Staff at the '"Argonaut" Conference', 2 February 1945: Cabinet papers, 120/170.

heavy fighting which would be taking place in North-West Europe should be as great as possible.' To his question whether there should be 'plenty of divisions available' in reserve, 'so that tired divisions could be replaced', Brooke replied that this had been allowed for with ten reserve divisions. Others could also be taken 'from the less active parts of the front'.

Churchill also approved the decision of the Combined Chiefs of Staff, not to make 'any significant withdrawal' of amphibious assault forces from Italy. He 'attached great importance', he said, 'to a rapid follow-up of any withdrawal or of any surrender of the German forces in Italy. He felt it was essential that we should occupy as much of Austria as possible, as it was undesirable that more of western Europe than necessary should be occupied by the Russians.'

There was no dissent.[1] That night Churchill returned to the *Quincy* for dinner, for the discussion with Roosevelt on at least some of the matters to be decided between them before they met Stalin. This dinner, however, as Eden noted, 'was no more successful than the luncheon', and he added:

Impossible even to get near business. I spoke pretty sharply to Harry about it, when he came in later, pointing out that we were going into a decisive conference and had so far neither agreed what we would discuss nor how to handle matters with a Bear who would certainly know his mind.[2]

At eleven o'clock Churchill and Eden returned to the *Orion*, where they remained for an hour and a half, 'spending most of the time', Churchill's Private Office diary recorded, 'in conversation with Major Randolph'.[3] Randolph, as his father later noted, was 'furious' at not having been asked to join the Yalta party. 'However,' Churchill wrote, 'he beat up Anthony and took it out of him.'[4]

Churchill also found time that night for a brief visit to the Wardroom, 'where he stood at the bar', Marian Holmes noted, 'and had a drink with all the officers crowding round him. He is simply wonderful,' she added, 'at these impromptu chats. He talked about the delay caused by a certain late arrival, "There was I—waiting at the Church . . . ."'[5] He talked to the ship's officers, Elizabeth Layton

---

[1] 'Argonaut' Conference, 1st Plenary Session between the United States and Great Britain, 6 p.m., 2 February 1945: Cabinet papers, 120/170.

[2] Eden diary, 2 February 1945: Eden memoirs, *The Reckoning, op. cit.*, page 511.

[3] Private Office diary, 2 February 1945. Churchill's conversation with his son 'lasted so long', John Martin wrote to Jock Colville, 'that, after we had drunk all the whisky we thought proper, and then all the beer, and then all the cocoa, I was about to turn to Horlicks Malted Milk when the signal was at last given'. (Letter of 5 February 1945: Martin papers.)

[4] 'Notes on Volume VI': Churchill papers, 4/362. Churchill dictated these notes in 1951, when he was beginning work on Volume Six of his War Memoirs.

[5] Marian Holmes diary, 2 February 1945: Marian Walker Spicer papers.

wrote, 'in his most wonderfully amusing way, and finished up by saying, "I hope you've looked after my two young ladies. They go everywhere with me and don't mind putting up with my bad temper."' [1]

At 12.30 that night Churchill and Eden drove to the airport. 'The Russians were told we were bringing 35 people apiece,' Sarah Churchill wrote to her mother, '—the total complement of souls is now 535!' [2] So the transport planes took off, at ten-minute intervals, on the 1,400 mile flight. Three hours after reaching the airfield, Churchill, too, flew eastward to the Crimea. 'The only hope for the world is the agreement of the Great Powers,' he had minuted to Eden eight days earlier. 'If they quarrel, our children are undone.' [3]

[1] Elizabeth Layton, diary for 2 February 1945: Nel papers.
[2] Letter of 1 February 1945: Spencer-Churchill papers.
[3] Prime Minister's Personal Minute, M. 110/5, 25 January 1945: Churchill papers, 20/209.

61

Yalta: 'The only bond of the victors is their common hate'

I T was 3.30 in the morning of 3 February 1945 when Churchill's plane left Luqa airfield, Malta, flying eastward to the Crimea, where, after a seven-hour flight, it landed, just after midday, local time, at Saki. At the airfield, which Roosevelt had reached shortly before him, Churchill was met by Molotov and Vyshinski. He then walked over to Roosevelt's aircraft, the 'Sacred Cow', stood while Roosevelt was helped out by his bodyguard, and 'deposited into a jeep', as Cadogan noted. Churchill later recalled, of Roosevelt and that moment: 'He was a tragic figure. You have only to look at the photographs. He could not get out of the open motor car, and I walked at his side while he inspected the guard.' [1]

Churchill and Roosevelt then went, Roosevelt in the jeep, Churchill walking beside it, to another part of the airfield, where they inspected a Guard of Honour. Cadogan recorded the scene in his diary:

The PM walked by the side of the President, as in her old age an Indian attendant accompanied Queen Victoria's phaeton. They were preceded by a crowd of camera-men, walking backwards as they took snapshots. The President looked old and thin and drawn; he had a cape or shawl over his shoulders and appeared shrunken; he sat looking straight ahead with his mouth open, as if he were not taking things in. Everyone was shocked by his appearance and gabbled about it afterwards.

From Saki airfield, Churchill set off by car to Yalta. Sarah Churchill, in a letter to her mother on the following day, described the subsequent journey, on which Roosevelt, at Harriman's suggestion, had already preceded them:

[1] 'Notes on Volume VI', dictated by Churchill in 1950: Churchill papers, 4/362.

Averell must be mad to make his poor President endure that endless and very boring drive. It was not as bad as painted, but tedious. One had to travel so slowly because for the first two hours the roads were so bad, and it wasted a whole day—and will waste another precious one on the way back!

I drove with Papa which was lovely, but we had a sticky start—20 miles an hour over bumpy slushy road, through a countryside as bleak as the soul in despair! After what seemed an eternity Papa asked how long we had been going and I replied 'about an hour'. 'Christ' said Papa 'five more of this' and gloom and muttered bad language set in!

After $2\frac{1}{2}$ hours we reached the mountains and the country-side improved. Oh, I have to tell you—the whole 100 miles of the road was lined every 200 yards with Red Army men and girls, who sprang to proud salutes. They were magnificent looking, and this display went on long after darkness had fallen. On, on through this bleak country peopled by a few grim-faced peasants.

We passed the President's convoy—they stopped for some coffee and sandwiches—we persevered because we had heard about a rest house ahead—most necessary for more reasons than resting. On, on, bearing all with fortitude, patience and a bottle of very good brandy! Still no rest house, so we stopped and ate a very stale ham sandwich and drank a little soup plus a swig of brandy!

And then off again. The call of nature was pretty desperate by now! I scanned the horizon—cars in front—press photographers behind!! Obviously no future in that! At last when hope had barely died, the convoy stopped. We were at the rest house. Papa and I clambered out for what we thought would be a short pause. We were led into a small room—groaning with food and wine—and a smiling Molotov.

A 'most magnificent luncheon', Churchill later recalled, had been prepared 'for me and the President, or anyone else. Champagne, caviare, every luxury. Alas, we had eaten a good deal before, but still there was a very pleasant hour or two of talk and gourmandizing. Then we started off to finish the journey to Yalta, another three or four hours.' [1] 'The PM was very concerned about what kind of journey we'd had,' noted Marian Holmes. '"What a hole I've brought you to!" he said.' [2]

That night, at the Vorontsov villa which was to be his home for the next eight days, Churchill dined with his daughter Sarah, and Anthony Eden. After dinner, Field Marshal Alexander came for a short talk. 'The Prime Minister went to bed early,' his Private Office noted, 'complaining that there was no news.' [3]

Not surprisingly, after his fourteen hours of travel on the previous

[1] 'Notes on Volume VI': Churchill papers, 4/362.
[2] Marian Holmes diary, 3 February 1945: Marian Walker Spicer papers.
[3] Private Office diary, 3 February 1945.

day, Churchill woke late on the morning of February 4, and worked in bed until lunchtime. 'Arrived safely after good journey and long drive,' he telegraphed to his wife at midday. 'Bright sunshine and no snow. UJ is coming to see me at 3 o'clock. All well. Sarah sends her love.' [1]

Churchill lunched on February 4 with Eden. At three in the afternoon he was visited by Stalin, who was accompanied by Pavlov, to whom Churchill presented the insignia of the CBE. [2]

Stalin told Churchill of the continuing Russian advance: 'pockets of Germans were being mopped up'. Churchill then told Stalin of the Anglo-American plans for an offensive in the West. Montgomery, in command of the 21st Army Group and the 9th United States Army, was preparing a thrust in the direction of Düsseldorf, which was due to start in four days' time.

Stalin felt that a combined attack from the East and the West 'might hasten the internal collapse of Germany', which was now short of bread and coal. When Churchill asked what Stalin would do if Hitler moved South, 'say to Dresden', Stalin answered: 'the Red Army would follow him, and the intention was to give the Germans no rest'.

Churchill took Stalin to see the Map Room which Captain Pim, who had reached Yalta several days earlier, had set up in the Vorontsov Villa. After Churchill had explained on the map the military situation on the western front, Alexander explained the situation in Italy. Stalin then suggested that, as a German offensive on the Italian front was 'improbable', the bulk of the British forces should be transferred from Italy 'to Yugoslavia and Hungary in the direction of Vienna, where they could join up with the Red Army, thereby out-flanking the German positions south of the Alps'. Such a move, Stalin 'admitted', would require a considerable force, to which Churchill commented 'that the Red Army might not give us time to complete it'. [3]

Stalin remained at the Vorontsov Villa for about three quarters of an hour. Then, an hour after Stalin had left, Churchill went by car to the Livadia Palace, where Roosevelt was staying, for the first plenary meeting. The drive, which took some twenty-five minutes, was to become a regular feature of Churchill's Yalta existence. The meeting began at five o'clock. 'We had the world at our feet,' Churchill later

---

[1] 'Jason' No. 109, 'Personal and Private', 12.30 p.m., 4 February 1945: Premier papers, 4/78/1, Part 2, folio 501.

[2] The only other presentations made by Churchill in place of the Sovereign during the Second World War were to Alexander and Montgomery.

[3] 'Argonaut', 1st Military Meeting, Vorontsov Palace, 4 February 1945: Cabinet papers, 120/170.

reflected. 'Twenty-five million men marching at our orders by land and sea. We seemed to be friends.'[1]

Roosevelt, invited by Stalin to open the proceedings, expressed 'his warmest admiration for the great achievements of the Russian armies against the common enemy'. Taking up Stalin's suggestion at their meeting two hours earlier, a suggestion which Churchill, the British Chiefs of Staff and the Combined Chiefs of Staff had rejected on January 31, Churchill now proposed that the Staffs might look into whether the Allied forces in Italy 'should attempt a blow at the head of the Adriatic and through the Ljubljana Gap in order to join up with the Russian left flank'. Speaking of Montgomery's plan to drive forward on February 8 towards Düsseldorf and the Rhine, Churchill said that any Russian expert advice on river crossings, especially when impeded by ice, 'would be very gratefully received'.

On the Eastern Front, Stalin pointed out the Russians had put 180 Divisions against 80 German divisions, 'a preponderance of over two to one', and asked, 'How did we stand as regards preponderance of troops in the West?' Churchill, answering, explained that neither in France nor Italy did the Anglo-American forces have 'any large preponderance' in infantry, 'although we had an overwhelming preponderance in the air, and also in tanks at those points at which we had decided to concentrate force'. On the Western Front, noted General Marshall, the Germans had 79 Divisions as against 78 Allied Divisions.

What, Stalin asked, were Churchill's and Roosevelt's wishes 'in regard to the Red Army'? 'Put very shortly,' Churchill replied, 'we would like the continuance of the Russian offensive....' He had regarded the launching of the January offensive as 'a moral duty', Stalin commented. Nothing in the Teheran decisions had bound Russia to a winter offensive. 'It had been their duty to the Allies.' If the weather permitted, it would be continued until the end of March, as Air Chief Marshal Tedder had requested in Moscow.

'We had been sure,' said Churchill, 'that everything that could be done would be done.' The three Staffs should now review the co-ordination of Allied military plans. 'If such consultation did not take place,' Churchill warned, 'history might be critical if the offensives in the East and West should appear to be disconnected. The blows struck from the East and West should be concerted blows, and if possible the ideal was that they should be struck at the same time.'

As this first meeting of the Big Three at Yalta came to an end, Churchill pointed out that a new type of German U-boat, 'ahead of us in certain technical ways', had sunk about twelve ships in waters

---

[1] Notes dictated by Churchill while writing volume six of his war memoirs, December 1950: Churchill papers, 4/361.

close to the British Isles. These U-boats were being built at Bremen, Hamburg and Danzig. He would 'ask the Russians to take Danzig', since thirty percent of the new U-boats were built in this area. It was then explained that the Russian forces were not yet near enough to shell the assembly lines, 'but that they hoped to approach the town before very long'.[1]

Commenting in his diary on this first reunion of the Big Three since Teheran, Admiral Cunningham noted: 'The President, who is undoubtedly in bad shape & finding difficulty in concentrating did not rise to the occasion but the PM did brilliantly.' Cunningham added: 'Stalin was good & clear in his points, the PM also very good but the President does not appear to know what he is talking about and clings to one idea.'[2]

Five years later Churchill recalled 'the President's feeble health. He was transparent.'[3] Roosevelt was indeed a very sick man. Lord Halifax told Churchill two months later that Harry Hopkins had doubted if, at Yalta, the President 'had heard more than half of what went on round the table. . . .'[4]

'Military session was a success,' Eden noted in his diary, 'Russians being obviously pleased to learn of our plans.'[5] 'The subsequent dinner party did not go so well,' John Martin wrote to Jock Colville. 'UJ. as a republican, refused to drink the King's health, and a jest by the President about the name "Uncle Joe" did not go down.'[6] Angrily, Stalin had asked: 'When can I leave this table?', but, as Churchill later recalled, James Byrnes then countered: 'After all you do not mind talking about Uncle Sam, so why should Uncle Joe be so bad?' On this, Churchill recalled, Stalin 'subsided'.[7]

'President vague and loose and ineffective,' noted Eden in his diary. 'W, understanding that business was flagging, made desperate efforts and too long speeches to get things going again. Stalin's attitude to small countries struck me as grim, not to say sinister. We were too many and there was no steady flow and brisk exchanges

---

[1] 'Argonaut', 2nd Military Meeting, Combined Chiefs of Staff, 'Anglo-Soviet-United States Conversations at Yalta, February 1945, Livadia, Yalta, 5 p.m., 4 February 1945': Cabinet papers, 120/170.

[2] Cunningham diary, 4 February 1945: Cunningham papers.

[3] 'Notes on Volume VI' written in December 1950: Churchill papers, 4/362.

[4] Washington Telegram, No. 2572, 'Personal and Top Secret', 15 April 1945: Churchill papers, 20/214.

[5] Eden diary, 4 February 1945: Eden memoirs, *The Reckoning*, op. cit., page 512.

[6] 'Private', 4 February 1945: Martin papers.

[7] 'Notes on Volume VI', written in December 1950: Churchill papers, 4/362. Of Byrnes, Roosevelt's recently approved Assistant Secretary of State (later Secretary of State), Churchill noted: 'Pretty light weight at that moment.'

as at Teheran. I was greatly relieved when whole business was over.'[1]

At one moment in the dinner, Churchill told Brooke on the following day, Stalin made 'an excellent speech' proposing Churchill's health, 'stating that Churchill alone had stood up to the might of Germany at the critical moment and supported Russia when she was attacked, a thing he would never forget!'[2] During his own remarks that evening, Churchill later recalled, 'I rubbed it into both of them that I was the only one dependent from day to day upon the vote of a representative elected on a universal suffrage. They were both dictators.'[3]

One of those present during these exchanges was Roosevelt's adviser Charles E. Bohlen, who later recalled that when Roosevelt agreed with Stalin that peace should be made by the Great Powers and not by the small powers, Churchill commented: 'The eagle should permit the small birds to sing and care not wherefore they sang.'[4]

As the Big Three began their discussions at Yalta, their Air and Intelligence Staffs were working together to co-ordinate emergency Air policy. On February 1 three German infantry divisions from the Western front had been identified on the central sector of the Eastern front. 'Reports indicate that further divisions may be on their way,' the British Chiefs of Staff were told, 'including the armoured divisions of Six Panzer Army.'[5] On the following day, in London, the Vice Chiefs of Staff had met to examine the strategic bombing offensive 'in relation to the present Russian offensive'. They had then agreed to set a new priority for 'communications targets' south and east of Berlin. The first priority was to bomb 'rail assembly areas and bottlenecks for eastward movements'. The second was to bomb targets in relation to the impending Anglo-American operations on the western front. The third was 'communication targets in cities such as Berlin, Dresden etc.'.[6]

These three suggestions had been telegraphed to Yalta that night. The telegram suggested, as a matter of urgency, that attacks on communication targets should be 'concentrated more closely' on several critical areas including 'specially vulnerable bottlenecks' affecting the assembly and entrainment of German troops to the east.

[1] Eden diary, 4 February 1945: Eden memoirs, *The Reckoning*, op. cit., page 512.

[2] Brooke diary, 5 February 1945: Bryant, op. cit., volume 2, page 407.

[3] 'Notes on Volume VI', written in December 1950: Churchill papers, 4/362.

[4] Charles E. Bohlen, *Witness of History*, New York 1973, page 181.

[5] Chiefs of Staff Weekly Resume No. 283, up to 7 a.m. on 1 February 1945.

[6] Chiefs of Staff Committee No. 35 of 1945, 2 February 1945, item No. 9, sent to Yalta as 'Fleece' No. 75: Cabinet papers, 79/29.

Also identified as priority targets were 'focal points in the evacuation areas behind the Eastern front, namely Berlin, Leipzig, Dresden, and Chemnitz, or similar cities'.[1]

This telegraphic advice was reinforced in its urgency on February 3, by the Deputy Chief of Staff of the Red Army, General Antonov, who, in a note to the British and United States Chiefs of Staff at Yalta, explained that Soviet wishes were 'to prevent the enemy from transferring his troops to the East from the Western front, Norway and Italy, by air attacks against communications'.[2]

Antonov's request for Anglo-American air support had been presented to the Big Three at their meeting on the afternoon of February 4, when he had told the meeting that the Germans were transferring to the eastern front a total of eight divisions from the interior of Germany, eight from Italy, three from Norway and twelve from the western front, in addition to six already transferred. It was this exaggerated assessment—only four divisions were transferred from Italy, for example—which had led Stalin to ask what Churchill and Roosevelt's wishes were 'in regard to the Red Army', to which Churchill had replied that they would like the Russian offensive to continue.[3] The urgency of the need to take some substantial air action to help that offensive continue was made clear by a sentence in the Cabinet War Room Record that day, pointing out that 'between the Oder bend north west of Glogau and the Carpathians all Russian attacks failed in the face of strengthened German resistance'.[4] On the following day, in a memorandum for the Combined Chiefs of Staff, the British Chiefs of Staff agreed 'to do what is possible to assist the advance of the Soviet Army'.[5] That same day, at a meeting of the joint British, United States and Russian Chiefs of Staff, Antonov went so far as to warn the western Generals that if the Allies 'were unable to take full advantage of their air superiority they did not have sufficient superiority on the ground to overcome enemy opposition'.

The British and American Chiefs of Staff at once agreed to deflect some of their bomber forces from the attack on Germany's oil reserves and supplies, then the current priority, to an attack on the German army's lines of communication in the Berlin-Dresden-Leipzig region. They also agreed, at Antonov's suggestion, that these three specific

---

[1] 'Fleece' No. 75: Cabinet papers 120/175.

[2] Note of 3 February 1945: Cabinet papers, 120/170.

[3] 'Argonaut', '1st Military Meeting', 4 February 1945: Cabinet papers, 120/170.

[4] Cabinet War Room Record, No. 1981, for the 24 hours ending 7 a.m., 4 February 1945', 'Secret': Cabinet papers, 100/13.

[5] Combined Chiefs of Staff Paper No. 778 (Argonaut), 'Liaison with the Soviet High Command over Anglo-American Strategic Bombing in Eastern Germany', 'Memorandum by the British Chiefs of Staff', 5 February 1945: Cabinet papers, 120/170.

cities should be 'allotted to the Allied air forces', leaving Russian bombers to attack targets further east.[1]

During this military meeting it became clear that it was not only on the eastern front, but also on the western front, that the Allies, as General Marshall stated, 'had no superiority on the ground in numbers, and were, therefore, dependent upon the Air to give them the necessary preponderance'.

At the end of the meeting there was some discussion about the date of the end of the war with Germany. 'The first of July,' declared Antonov, 'should be a reasonably certain date if all our efforts were applied to this end.'[2]

On the morning of February 5 Churchill remained in bed until after luncheon. 'There is a sliding door into the PM's bedroom which is noisy and difficult to open and shut,' Marian Holmes noted in her diary. 'After filling his pen, I returned, opened the door just a few inches and squeezed myself through. The PM burst out laughing and said I looked like a lizard.'[3]

Shortly before four o'clock, Churchill drove once more to the Livadia Palace, for the first Political Plenary. At Roosevelt's suggestion, the subject was to be the future of Germany. Stalin, recalling Roosevelt's proposal at Teheran to divide Germany into five parts, said that he 'associated himself' with this view. In Roosevelt's absence from the Moscow talks, Stalin added, no decision had been taken: the time had now come 'to take a definite decision'. Churchill, while stating that 'in principle' all three were agreed on the dismemberment of Germany, spoke words of caution. The 'actual method', he said, 'was much too complicated to settle here in five or six days'. It would require, he said, 'a very searching examination of the historical, ethnographical and economic facts and would need prolonged consideration by a special committee, which would have to go into the different proposals put forward and advise on them'.[4]

Stalin had not expected Churchill to oppose an immediate decision for the dismemberment of Germany. As Pierson Dixon jotted down in

[1] '"Argonaut" Conference', 'Minutes of the first tripartite military meeting held in the Soviet Headquarters, Yalta, on Monday 5th February, 1945, at 1200': Cabinet papers, 120/170.

[2] 'Rough Notes of Tripartite Military Conference, Monday, 5 February, 1945', 'Top Secret' (sent by Ismay to Churchill, and seen by Churchill on 7 February 1945): Cabinet papers, 120/170.

[3] Marian Holmes diary, 5 February 1945: Marian Walker Spicer papers.

[4] 'Argonaut', 1st Plenary Meeting (Political), 4.15 p.m., 5 February 1945: Cabinet papers 120/170.

a note for Eden, 'I think that the Marshal did not like the suggestion of the PM that dismemberment should come *at a second stage.*' [1]

The next question raised by Stalin was whether, if some group in Germany 'declared that they had overthrown Hitler, we should be prepared to negotiate with such a Government'. To this Churchill replied:

If Hitler or Himmler were to come forward and offer unconditional surrender, it was clear that our answer should be that we would not negotiate with any of the war criminals. If those were the only people the Germans could produce, we should have to go on with the war. It was more probable that Hitler and his associates would have been killed or would have disappeared, and that another set of people would offer unconditional surrender. In that case the three great Powers must immediately consult and decide whether such people were worth dealing with or not. If it was decided that they were, the terms of surrender which had been worked out would be laid before them; if not, the war would be continued and the whole country occupied by strict military government.

Stalin then returned to the question of dismemberment, asking whether it could be mentioned to 'any new group' in Germany which emerged and asked for peace. Churchill again set his voice against dismemberment. Any such group of Germans, he said, 'would surrender unconditionally'. There was therefore no need to discuss the future of Germany with them. Unconditional surrender would give the Allies the opportunity to discuss such matters 'at their leisure'. By the terms of the surrender, 'they would reserve all their rights over German land, liberties and even lives'.

Roosevelt now entered the discussion. If dismemberment were to become a matter of public discussion, he said, 'there would be a hundred different plans'. He therefore urged that the three Foreign Secretaries should produce 'a definite plan for dismemberment' within thirty days. Churchill deferred to Roosevelt's request, which ensured that no decision to break up Germany into five separate States would be taken at Yalta. He agreed, Churchill said, 'to the most rapid examination possible of the best method of studying the question, but he did not believe it was possible at this Conference to discuss the actual method of putting dismemberment into practice'.

The next topic for discussion was whether the French Government should have its own Zone of Occupation in Germany. 'He personally,' Churchill said, 'was in favour of it, and he would gladly give them

[1] Pierson Dixon note, 5 February 1945: Piers Dixon, *op. cit.*, page 139. Churchill's own view of the territorial future of Germany was, he explained to the War Cabinet six weeks later, the isolating of Prussia, and the creation 'of a South German State including Austria and the South German kingdoms, which could receive more lenient treatment than Prussia'. (War Cabinet No. 35 of 1945, 22 March 1944, Confidential Annex: Cabinet papers, 65/51.)

part of the British zone.' The British Government, he pointed out, 'would find it a great burden to occupy a large area for a long time and would be very glad if the French would take part of the burden. No other Power would have a zone to itself, but it might be convenient if the Dutch and the Belgians were to relieve us of part of our burden in our own zone.'

Stalin asked whether, if the French had a zone to themselves, they would therefore be admitted 'as a fourth Power' in the Control Commission which was to be set up for Germany, 'which had hitherto been considered a three-Power body'. Churchill replied that France should become a member of the Control Commission 'and as the French army grew, France would be able to take more responsibility'. Roosevelt then stated, 'that the United States would take all reasonable steps to preserve peace, but not at the expense of keeping a large army indefinitely in Europe 3,000 miles away from home. That was why the American occupation was limited to two years.'

Churchill was worried, he said, by what would happen 'if the Germans were to rise again'. Without French help, the British 'might be in difficulties'. But both Roosevelt and Stalin, while agreeing to a French zone of occupation in Germany, opposed French participation in the Control Commission. Churchill argued forcefully against them. Great Britain would need 'a strong French army to contain Germany in the West', he said, and he went on to warn the conference:

The prolonged control of Germany without French participation would be very difficult. The Americans were free to go away from Europe but the French would always remain next door to Germany; and the security of Great Britain demanded that France should have a strong army and should be in a position to prevent rocket sites &c., being built on the French coast.

Churchill then proposed, as a compromise, that France should be offered a zone in Germany now, but that her 'status' should be the subject of 'separate discussions'. Roosevelt replied that a zone was all right, but that 'anything further should be postponed for the time being'. Stalin agreed.[1]

Reporting five days later to Attlee and the War Cabinet on these discussions about France, Churchill noted: 'So far here we have been the only ones to speak a friendly word for France. Nevertheless I am quite sure that presence of De Gaulle and his representative at this Crimean meeting would have wrecked all possible progress, already difficult enough.' The Russians were 'as determined as the Americans', Churchill added, 'to keep France, and especially De Gaulle, out of

[1] 'Argonaut', 1st Plenary Meeting (Political), 4.15 p.m., 5 February 1945: Cabinet papers, 120/170.

the so-called Big Three. I was surprised at the anti-French attitude of the Russians. Both great powers are resisting our attempts to allow the French a seat on the Allied Control Commission for Germany, which is of course absolutely necessary if the French have a zone.'[1]

The next question was that of Reparations. Here Maisky spoke of removing substantial industrial plant from Germany to Russia. Germany should be left with only twenty percent of her heavy industries, 'which would suffice to deal with Germany's real economic needs'. Then there should be money payments, over a period of ten years, based on the 'proportionate contribution' each country had made towards winning the war, and the proportionate value of the 'direct material losses' each country had sustained. The Russian share, Maisky said, was a suggested ten thousand million dollars, over the ten year period.

Churchill then spoke of what had happened after the First World War, the experience of which, in regard to Reparations, 'had been very disappointing'. The total sum extracted had been about one thousand million pounds—then the equivalent of five thousand million dollars—for all the victor countries combined, 'but even this sum would not have been extracted had not America, and to a lesser extent Great Britain, lent much larger sums to Germany on which she had defaulted'. If he could see any way in which the British economy 'could be substantially benefited by reparations from Germany, he would be very glad to follow it. But once bit twice shy: and he felt grave doubts on the matter.' 'There was a further consideration,' Churchill said, which he expressed in the form of questions: 'What would happen if Germany was reduced to a position of starvation? Did we intend to stand by and do nothing and say it served her right? Or did we intend to provide enough food to keep the Germans alive and if so who would pay for it?'

'If you wanted your horse to pull your wagon,' Churchill concluded, 'you had to give him some hay.'

It was Maisky who answered Churchill's points. Germany was 'not entitled', he said, 'to live in a higher standard of living than the Middle European standard' after the war. The Russians had calculated that Germany 'would be able to live on the Middle European standard after making the reparation payments now claimed'. Germany's economy, he said, would secure for the Germans 'a modest but a decent standard of living'.

The question, Churchill proposed, should be examined by a commission, which, he said, 'should sit in secret and should be attended by no publicity', and report in a month's time. But it 'must

[1] 'Jason' No. 321, 10 February 1945: Cabinet papers, 120/180.

not be taken that His Majesty's Government were prepared to accept the reparation plan which had been so ably expounded but which had not previously been brought to their notice'.

Stalin then spoke of the relative national claims to any reparations amount which might be agreed upon. The three Great Powers, 'who had shared the burden of the war', were entitled to receive the maximum sum which any country could receive. He did not include France with the three Great Powers, he said, 'because she had suffered far less damage. Indeed, she had suffered less than Yugoslavia and Holland. Again, while he greatly respected France, the French had done nothing by way of sacrifice or action comparable to the sacrifices or achievements of the three Great Powers.' At the 'present time', Stalin said, 'France had eight divisions in the war and some naval forces. Yugoslavia had twelve divisions in the war and the Lublin Poles had ten divisions.'

Churchill's comment on this was that the Great Powers must not let it be thought that they were only looking after their own interests 'and were leaving other nations altogether in the cold'. Roosevelt then accepted Stalin's suggestion that the Reparations Commission should meet in Moscow, to which Churchill also gave his assent.[1]

Churchill returned to the Vorontsov Villa at about 8.30 p.m. One problem during the day had been a certain lack of news from the Private Office in London: 'it has gone to my heart', Martin wrote to Colville, 'to hear Colonel Kent calling again and again for news and being offered only caviar'.[2]

That night, Churchill dined with his daughter Sarah and Eden. Before he went to sleep, Churchill said to his daughter: 'I do not suppose that at any moment in history has the agony of the world been so great or widespread. To-night the sun goes down on more suffering than ever before in the World.'[3]

'Papa is well and in good spirits and steady strength.' Such was Sarah Churchill's report to her mother on the morning of February 6, and she added: 'You know whatever material difficulties of this place our paws are well buttered here. Wow.'[4]

On February 6 Churchill lunched with Roosevelt, 'quite agreeable

---

[1] 'Argonaut', 1st Plenary Meeting (Political), 4.15 p.m., 5 February 1945: Cabinet papers, 120/170.
[2] 'Vorontsov Villa', Letter of 5 February 1945: Martin papers.
[3] Letter No. 1 of 6 February 1945: Sarah Churchill, *Keep on Dancing, op. cit.*, pages 75–6.
[4] Letter No. 2 of 6 February 1942: Spencer-Churchill papers.

and amusing', as Cadogan who was present described it in a letter to his wife, 'but not awfully useful'. Roosevelt, he noted, 'has certainly aged'.[1] After lunch, the second political plenary began. Returning to the discussion of the French zone of occupation in Germany, Churchill stressed that in view of Roosevelt's statement on the previous day 'about the withdrawal of United States forces from Europe two years after the end of the war', the position of France became 'of very great importance'. Britain was not strong enough to do her part in the west against Germany 'unless there was a strong French army'.

The discussion turned to the future World Organization, and the voting in its Security Council. While the 'achievement of world peace on a lasting foundation' depended, Churchill said, in the last resort 'on the friendship and collaboration of the three Great Powers', the British Government felt that they would not be doing justice to their true intentions 'if no provision was made for a full statement of griev- ances by the many smaller nations of the world'. The three Great Powers were not seeking 'to rule the world'. Their desire was 'to serve the world' and to preserve it from any renewal 'of the frightful horrors which had fallen on the mass of its inhabitants'. The Great Powers should therefore, within the world organization, 'make a proud submission to the general community of the world', allowing, as the Americans had proposed, 'any State involved in a conflict to present its own case' but not to vote on it, if the country concerned were also a member of the Security Council. The case Churchill wished to take was that of Hong Kong. 'If His Majesty's Government agreed to the President's proposals,' he said, 'China might ask His Majesty's Government to return Hong Kong.' His Majesty's Government would have the right to state their case fully against any case made by the Chinese. It would be open to China 'to make her full case', and it would be open to the Security Council to 'decide on any of those questions without Her Majesty's Government being allowed to vote'. The British Government 'accepted' this position. There should be no Great Power veto on matters concerning itself. Of course, he added, 'there was no question of their being compelled by the Security Council to give Hong Kong back to China if they did not think that this was the right step for them to take. On the other hand they felt it would be wrong that China should not have a chance of stating her case fully. . . .'

The discussion turned, for the first time at Yalta, to Poland, the

[1] Letter of 7 February 1945: David Dilks (editor), *op. cit.*, page 705.

issue which was to take up more time at the Big Three discussions than any other. 'Coming from America,' said Roosevelt, 'he took a distant point of view of the Polish question.' The five or six million Poles in the United States were 'mostly of the second generation'. His position, 'and that of most Poles in the United States', was, 'as he had said at Teheran', in general in favour of the Curzon Line. But it would 'make it easier for him' if the Soviet Government would alter the Curzon Line at its southern end, leaving Lvov and some of the oil-bearing areas to Poland, to counterbalance 'the loss of Königsberg'. This, the main port of East Prussia, was to go, not to Poland with much of the rest of East Prussia, but to the Soviet Union.

Churchill, who spoke next, said that he believed that Russia's claim to the Curzon Line, including Lvov, 'was founded not on force but on right'. Nevertheless, if Russia were to make the territorial concession suggested by Roosevelt, 'he need not say how much we should both admire and acclaim the Soviet action'. He was 'more interested', he said, 'to see a strong, free, independent Poland than he was in a particular national boundary'. He wanted the Poles to be in a position 'to live freely and to live their own lives in their own way'. It was because he put his 'trust' in Stalin's declarations as to the 'sovereignty, independence and freedom' of Poland, Churchill said, 'that he did not consider the frontier question to be one of supreme importance'. It was to enable Poland to be 'free and sovereign', he said, that Britain had gone to war. 'Everyone knew what a terrible risk we had taken when we had gone to war in 1939 although so ill-armed. This action had nearly cost us our life, not only as an Empire but as a nation.'

Freedom for Poland, Churchill added, could not be made to cover 'any hostile design by Poland or by any Polish group—possibly in intrigue with Germany, against Russia'. Subject to this reservation, it was Britain's 'earnest desire' that Poland 'should be mistress in her own house and captain of her own soul'.

Churchill then proposed that the three Great Powers create, at Yalta, 'a government or governing instrument of Poland', which would continue 'pending full and free elections', and which could be recognized by all the Great Powers, and by the other States 'which had withdrawn recognition from the London Government of Poland'. This new Government would be charged with preparing the way 'for a free vote of the Polish people on their future Constitution and Administration'.

The Conference then adjourned for ten minutes. When it re-assembled, Stalin spoke emphatically about the need for the Curzon Line as Russia's western frontier. It had been devised, not by Russia, but by Curzon and Clemenceau. 'The Ukrainians when they come to

Moscow would say that Stalin and Molotov were less reliable defenders of Russia than Curzon or Clemenceau.' He could not take up such a position, Stalin added, 'and return to Moscow with an open face'. But Poland's compensation could go beyond the river Neisse near Breslau, to another river of the same name 'further west'. It was the western of these two rivers, he said, that he 'had in mind' and he asked the Conference to support his proposal.

As to the creation of the Government of Poland, Stalin said, that could not be done without the 'participation and consent' of the Poles themselves. The members of the Lublin Government, he said, 'or Warsaw Government as it should now be called', did not want 'anything to do' with the Polish Government in London. They were prepared to take into their Government two of the London Poles, General Zeligowski and Professor Grabski. But they 'would not hear' of Mikolajczyk becoming Prime Minister. Stalin was prepared, however, he said, 'to support any attempt to create unity, if that attempt had any likelihood of success'. If Churchill and Roosevelt liked to ask members of the Lublin Government to come down to talk to them, or would like to meet them in Moscow, 'that could be arranged'. But he 'thought it necessary to say frankly that the Warsaw Government had, at any rate, as much democratic basis in Poland as General de Gaulle had in France'.

Stalin also spoke angrily of the 'agents in Poland of the London Government', telling the Conference: 'So far, these agents of the London Government had killed 212 Russian troops. They had also raided supply dumps in order to get arms.'

Roosevelt then suggested that the Conference adjourn until the following day. But Churchill asked first to 'put it on record' that the British and Soviet Governments had 'different sources of information' in Poland, and had received 'different accounts of what had happened'. Churchill told the Conference that according to information at Britain's disposal, 'the Lublin Government could not be regarded as representing more than one-third of the Polish people if they were free to express their opinion. This, of course, was based on the best information which we could obtain and we might be mistaken in certain particulars.' Stalin knew, Churchill continued, that 'we had been greatly disturbed at the fear that the Polish Underground Army might come into collision with the representatives of the Lublin Government. We had greatly feared that these collisions would lead to bitterness and bloodshed which would result in arrests and deportations and it was for this reason that we had been so anxious for a joint arrangement. We greatly feared the effect which all this would have on the Polish question which was already difficult enough.'

It was recognized, Churchill said, that 'whoever attacked the Red Army must be punished'. But he could not feel that the Lublin Government 'had a right to say that they represented the Polish nation according to the facts at his disposal'.

Stalin made no comment. But Roosevelt remarked, somewhat testily, that 'Poland had been a source of trouble for over 500 years'. Churchill did not let this remark go unanswered: 'we must do what we could', he replied, 'to put an end to these troubles'.[1]

The second political plenary was at an end. That evening Churchill dined with Eden at the Vorontsov Villa. After dinner, Averell Harriman brought them a draft letter from Roosevelt to Stalin, about Poland. 'It was on the right lines,' Eden noted in his diary, 'but not quite stiff enough. I suggested some amendments which Winston and A.H. approved and he took draft back.'[2]

Roosevelt accepted Eden's amendments, and sent the letter to Stalin. 'I have had to make it clear to you,' the letter read, 'that we cannot recognize the Lublin Government as now composed'; and he proposed inviting to Yalta the two leaders of the Lublin Government, Bierut and Morawski, and any two of a list of five other Poles representing 'the other elements of the Polish people'.[3] 'If,' Roosevelt's letter continued, 'as a result of the presence of these Polish leaders here, we could jointly agree with them on a provisional Government in Poland which should no doubt include M. Mikolajczyk, M. Romer and M. Grabski, the United States Government, and I am sure the British Government as well, would then be prepared to examine with you conditions in which they would dissociate themselves from the London Government and transfer their recognition to the new provisional Government.'[4]

That night Churchill sent a message to Attlee. 'We are having a hard time here,' he reported. 'Poland will be very difficult. Conference is prolonged at least till the end of the eleventh. Stalin himself proposed this. All personal relations are excellent.'[5]

---

[1] 'Argonaut', '2nd Plenary Meeting (Political)', 4 p.m., 6 February 1945: Cabinet papers, 120/170.

[2] Eden diary, 6 February 1945: Eden memoirs, *The Reckoning, op. cit.*, page 518.

[3] This list consisted of Bishop Sapieha of Cracow, Vincente Witos, Zygmunt Zurlowski (the Trade Union leader and Socialist), Professor Franciszek Bujak (Professor of Chemistry at Lvov University) and Professor Stanislaw Kutrzeba (an historian from Cracow, and President of the Polish Academy of Sciences). On 23 February 1945, the Polish Provisional Government rejected all but Professor Kutrzeba for coalition talks in Moscow.

[4] Letter of 6 February 1945 ('My dear Marshal Stalin'): *Correspondence Between the Chairman of the Council of Ministers of the USSR and the Presidents of the USA and the Prime Ministers of Great Britain During the Great Patriotic War of 1941–1945*, volume 2, Moscow 1957, pages 177–9, document No. 266.

[5] 'Jason' No. 178, despatched at 2.40 a.m., 7 February 1945: Churchill papers, 20/223.

Once more, on February 7, Churchill worked in bed and lunched in bed before driving from the Vorontsov Villa to the Livadia Palace, for the third political plenary, which began at four o'clock that afternoon. Sarah, who drove with her father, wrote home:

It was a lovely day again—the sun did its best for the scene—it tried hard to warm the granite peaks—it shone so hard on the sea that the reflection made one blink, Papa and I looked stolidly out on the scene and presently he said 'The Riviera of Hades'! That my darling Mummie describes it beautifully! I retire!

The third political plenary began with a report by Molotov on the meeting that morning of the three Foreign Secretaries. Churchill raised only one point of dissent, still arguing that France should have a place on the Control Commission for Germany, as well as a zone of occupation. 'There must be uniformity in the treatment of Germany by the four Allies as far as possible,' he said. 'Otherwise there would be endless petty disputes and many Germans would want to go from one part to another, and one part would be held up as a model to the others, and so on.' Churchill then asked, 'Why not therefore settle the question here before parting?' Roosevelt said that they should 'let it rest for several weeks'; Churchill replied 'that once they separated, he did not know what would happen, as correspondence on a matter such as this might drag on for months'.

Stalin supported Roosevelt: they had, he said, 'settled many questions by correspondence'.

Hitherto, the Soviet Union had rejected America's proposals for the World Organization and its Security Council. They had also demanded sixteen membership votes in the Assembly, for all sixteen of their Republics. At this third political plenary, Molotov surprised Churchill and Roosevelt by accepting the American organizational plan, and offering to reduce their sixteen votes to three, 'or at any rate four': the Ukraine, White Russia and Lithuania, in addition to the Russian Republic.

Churchill supported Molotov's suggestion. As he telegraphed that night to Attlee and the War Cabinet, Britain was asking 'a great deal' of the United Nations Assembly in having four or five members —in fact five, Canada, Australia, South Africa, New Zealand—'six' if India was included, in addition to Britain, 'when Russia has only one'. Churchill added:

I should like to be able to make a friendly gesture to Russia in this matter in view of other important concessions by them which are achieved or pending. It is not much to ask that they should have two besides their chief, and we will be in a strong position in my judgment, because we shall not be the only multiple-voter in the field.[1]

Churchill's advocacy of Russia's two or three extra voting places at the World Organization's Assembly made a strong impression on the Conference. After Churchill had spoken, Roosevelt proposed a meeting 'as early as possible, say, at the end of March', to invite the nations of the world to set up the actual organization of the United Nations. Churchill, while approving Molotov's two suggestions, which constituted 'a remarkable advance' towards general agreement, saw difficulties in holding the organization meeting 'as early as March', as Roosevelt had suggested. 'At this date,' he said, 'the critical battle against Germany might well be at its height.'[2] Churchill's comment, Eden noted in his diary, was 'not unnaturally resented by the Americans, since we had long ago agreed to such a meeting'.[3]

It was finally agreed that the Foreign Secretaries should recommend the 'time and place' at which the organization conference should be held, with no reference to Churchill's doubts about too early a date.

The third political plenary now turned its attention to Poland. Roosevelt, who began the discussion, said he wished to 'emphasize the very great importance' he attached to 'the Polish Government question'. It was 'quite within the province' of the Big Three to set up an 'interim Government' for Poland 'which would see them through until they had a chance to set up a Government of their own'. To do something like that 'would come like a breath of fresh air in the murk that existed at the moment on the Polish question'.

Stalin, replying, said that he had received Roosevelt's letter about an hour and a half previously. Molotov would read out the new Soviet proposals: the Curzon Line to be Poland's eastern frontier; the River Oder and the Western Neisse to be Poland's western frontier; it was considered 'desirable' to add to the 'Polish Provisional Government' what the Soviet document called 'some democratic leaders from Polish émigré circles'; this enlarged Provisional Polish Government 'should be recognized by the Allied Governments'; and this Government, enlarged as Roosevelt had suggested, 'should as soon as possible call the population of Poland to the polls for the establishment by general vote of permanent organs of the Polish Government'.

This suggestion, Roosevelt replied, showed that they were making 'definite progress'. But he 'did not like the word "émigré"'. Nor did Churchill, telling the Conference 'that he shared the President's

[1] 'Jason' No. 220, 8 February 1945: Churchill papers, 20/223.
[2] 'Argonaut', '3rd Plenary Meeting (Political)', 'Record of a Meeting held at the Livadia Palace, Yalta, at 4 p.m. on 7th February, 1945': Cabinet papers, 120/170.
[3] Eden diary, 7 February 1945: Eden memoirs, *The Reckoning, op. cit.*, page 517.

dislike of the word *émigré*. It was a term which originated with the French who were driven out after the French Revolution and was properly applied only to those who had been driven out of their own country by their own people. But the Poles abroad had been driven out of their country by the Germans and he suggested that the words "Poles abroad" should be substituted for *émigré*.'

Stalin agreed. Churchill then raised the question of the Western Neisse river, which Molotov, and earlier Stalin, had said could become the western frontier of Poland. Churchill commented:

... he had in previous talks always qualified the moving of the Polish frontier westwards by saying that the Poles should be free to take territory in the West, but not more than they wished or could properly manage. It would be a great pity to stuff the Polish goose so full of German food that it died of indigestion.

He was conscious of a large body of opinion in Great Britain which was frankly shocked at the idea of moving millions of people by force. He himself was not shocked, but it was certainly a view which would come very much to the fore in Great Britain. A great success had been achieved in disentangling the Greek and Turkish populations after the last war and the two countries had enjoyed good relations ever since; but in that case under a couple of millions of people had been moved. If Poland took East Prussia and Silesia as far as the Oder, it would mean moving six million Germans back to Germany. That might be managed, subject to the moral question, which he had to settle with his own people.

No Germans were to be found in these areas, Stalin observed, 'as they had all run away'. He was 'not afraid' of the problem of transferring populations, Churchill continued, 'so long as it was proportionate to what the Poles could manage and to what could be put into Germany'.[1]

The third political plenary was over. That night Churchill telegraphed to Attlee:

It is our plan to fight hard for a Government in Poland which we and United States can recognize and to which we can attract the recognition of all the United Nations. In return for this we require real substantial and effective representation from the Polish element with whom we have at present been associated, especially Mikolajczyk, Grabski, and Romer, as well as from a number of Poles still in Poland, Witos, Sapieha, etc., whom the Americans have listed.

If it can be so arranged that eight or ten of these are included in the Lublin Government it would be to our advantage to recognize this Government at once. We could then get ambassadors and missions into Poland, and find out at least to some extent what is happening there and

[1] 'Argonaut', '3rd Plenary Meeting (Political)', 'Record of a Meeting held at the Livadia Palace, Yalta, at 4 p.m. on 7th February, 1945': Cabinet papers, 120/170.

whether the foundations can be laid for the free, fair, and unfettered election, which alone can give life and being to a Polish Government.[1]

That night Churchill dined with his daughter Sarah, Eden and Alexander. 'This has been a much better day,' Churchill telegraphed to his wife in the early hours of February 8, and he added: 'Sarah is a great comfort.'[2]

That night, Marian Holmes heard Churchill singing: his song— 'There is a happy land, far, far away.'[3]

On the morning of February 8, as had become his habit at Yalta, Churchill remained in bed until after luncheon. During the morning, Sarah Churchill sent her mother an account of Yalta life so far:

Papa is bearing up very well—despite the strain of getting through so much in really so short a time, and the accompanying patience and toil that a million complexities call for. Physically, however, this conference does not seem as hard as the one last year. They do not meet till 4 in the afternoon, when they have a whacking session of 4 to 5 hours and then they part, returning to their separate lairs. We dine quietly here—generally just Papa and Anthony and me—which of course is heaven. The pouch arrives unfortunately at about midnight—which prevents him getting to bed much before two, though I do my best. He has been sleeping well though— without any little pink pills. Morning presents a certain problem as he wakes rather late, and there isn't time for breakfast and lunch and work and a little sleep before the 'do' at 4—so now he has just orange juice when he is called and 'brunch' at 11.30—then nothing till 9 o'clock! This seems a very long time, but he really is very sensible and says that is what he likes best; so I feel the thing is to try it, and see how it works. . . .[4]

Among the telegrams which Churchill sent that morning was one to Montgomery, whose new offensive, operation 'Veritable', aimed at securing possession of all ground west of the Rhine, began that day. 'All our thoughts are with you and your splendid troops,' Churchill wrote. 'Strike hard for victory in the West. Keep me informed through CIGS. All confidence and every good wish.'[5]

The fourth political plenary began at the Livadia Palace at 4.30 that afternoon. During the discussion about which States should be

[1] 'Jason' No. 220, 8 February 1945: Churchill papers, 20/223.

[2] 'Jason' No. 218, 2.40 a.m., 8 February 1945: Premier papers, 4/78/1, Part II, folio 667.

[3] Marian Holmes diary, 8 February 1945 (referring to the night of 7 February 1945): Marian Walker Spicer papers.

[4] Sarah Churchill, letter of 8 February 1945: *Keep on Dancing*, *op. cit.*, page 76.

[5] 'Jason' No. 213, Prime Minister's Personal Telegram, T.184/5, 8 February 1945: Churchill papers, 20/11.

invited to the United Nations Conference, the date of which was now fixed for April 25, Stalin stressed that only States which had already declared war on Germany should be invited. If Turkey 'was now ready to make a death-bed repentance and declare war', Churchill remarked, she should receive an invitation. Stalin agreed.[1]

In turning to Poland, Roosevelt 'saw little justification' in a line as far west as the Western Neisse, because of the difficulties involved 'in large transfers of population'. Molotov then asked, in regard to the proposed Polish Government of National Unity, if, once it had been formed, 'the Polish Government in London would cease to be recognized'. Both Churchill and Roosevelt agreed 'that this would be so'. If and when a stage was reached, Churchill told Stalin, when Britain could recognize the Polish Government of National Unity, 'it would follow that we should withdraw recognition from the London Government of Poland and accredit an Ambassador to the new Government'.[2]

The Conference then adjourned for a short interval. 'Sawyers and I have had a wonderful idea (we hope),' Sarah Churchill had written that morning to her mother. 'We are going to send him over some chicken soup in a thermos—and when they break for a few minutes for tea—he could have his chicken soup! If he doesn't have a whisky and soda!'[3]

When the fourth political plenary resumed, Molotov stressed that the Polish Provisional Government 'existed and was now in Warsaw'. Now the discussion should be how to extend it, 'that new members should join it'. The possibility 'could not be excluded', he said, that the Provisional Government 'would refuse to talk at all with some people, for instance with M. Mikolajczyk ...'.

Churchill now embarked upon one of the most difficult speeches, and advocacies, of his career. 'They were at a crucial point of this Conference,' he warned. 'This was the question for the settlement of which the whole world was waiting.' If they left Yalta still recognizing different Polish Governments, 'it would be accepted all over the world that fundamental differences existed between Russia and their British and American allies'. The consequences of this 'would be most lamentable'. Failure to agree on a Polish Government 'would stamp this conference with the seal of failure'. Molotov had said that the Lublin Government 'had been enthusiastically acclaimed by the majority of the Polish people'. According to the British Government's information, Churchill declared, the Lublin Government 'did not

[1] Turkey declared war on Germany on 23 February 1945, with effect from 1 March 1945.
[2] 'Argonaut', '4th Plenary Meeting (Political), 4.30 p.m., 8 February 1945: Cabinet papers, 120/170.
[3] Sarah Churchill, letter of 8 February 1945: Spencer-Churchill papers.

commend itself to the great majority of the Polish people'. If the Yalta conference 'were to brush aside the existing London Government', he said, 'and lend all its weight to the Lublin Government, there would be a world outcry'. As far as could be foreseen, the Poles outside of Poland 'would make a virtually united protest'. There was 'under British command' a Polish army of 150,000 men 'gathered from among all those who had been able to come together from outside Poland'. This army, Churchill added, 'had fought, and was still fighting, very bravely'. He did not believe that this army would be 'at all reconciled' to the Lublin Government.

Speaking of the London Government, Churchill told the Conference:

As Marshal Stalin and M. Molotov well knew, he himself did not agree with the London Government's actions, which had been foolish at every stage. But the formal act of transferring recognition from those whom they had hitherto recognized to this new Government would cause the gravest criticism. It would be said that His Majesty's Government had given way completely on the Eastern frontier (as they in fact had) and had accepted and championed the Soviet view. It would also be said that they had broken altogether with the lawful Government of Poland, which they had recognized for these five years of war; and that they had no knowledge of what was actually proceeding in Poland. They could not enter the country. They could not see and hear what opinion was. It would be said that they could only accept what the Lublin Government proclaimed about the opinion of the Polish people, and His Majesty's Government would be charged in Parliament with having forsaken altogether the cause of Poland. The debates which would follow would be most painful and embarrassing to the unity of the Allies. . . .

All Britain's worries about how 'truly representative' the Lublin Government was could be 'removed', he said, 'if a free and unfettered general election were held in Poland by ballot and with universal suffrage and free candidatures. Once such an election had been held, His Majesty's Government would salute the Government that emerged without regard to the Polish Government in London. It was the interval before that election that was causing them so much anxiety.'

Roosevelt, speaking as one of the 'inhabitants of another hemisphere', urged as 'the great objective' of the Americans that there should be 'an early election in Poland'. Stalin, returning to Churchill's remarks, asserted the popularity of the Lublin Government, and its leaders, Bierut, Osobka-Morawski and Zymierski. He 'did not believe they were geniuses', Stalin admitted. 'The London Government might contain cleverer people, but they were not liked in Poland because they had not been there at the time when the population was suffering under the Hitlerite occupation. That feeling was primitive perhaps, but it certainly did exist.'

Turning to the question of elections, Stalin referred to one of the Anglo-American dilemmas of the pre D-Day months, the recognition of de Gaulle's 'Government', telling the Conference:

It would naturally be better to have a Government based on free elections, but the war had so far prevented that. The day was, however, near when elections could be held; but until then they must deal with the Provisional Government as they had dealt, for instance, with General de Gaulle's Government in France which also was not elected. He did not know himself whether Bierut or General de Gaulle enjoyed greater authority, but it had been possible to make a treaty with General de Gaulle and therefore why should it not be possible to do so with an enlarged Polish Government which would be no less democratic than the Government of General de Gaulle. It was not reasonable to demand more from Poland than from France. Up to the present time the French Government had carried out no reform which created enthusiasm in France, whereas the Polish Government had enacted a land reform which had aroused great enthusiasm. If they approached the matter without prejudice they would be able to find a common basis. The situation was not as tragic as the Prime Minister thought and the question could be settled if too much importance was not attached to secondary matters and if they concentrated on essentials.

Roosevelt then asked how 'soon' it would be possible to hold elections, to which Stalin replied, disarmingly, that he 'thought it should be possible to hold them within a month unless there was some catastrophe on the front, which he thought was improbable'. A 'free election', Churchill commented, 'would, of course, set His Majesty's Government's mind at rest'. They would feel that they could 'wholeheartedly support' a freely elected Government, 'which would supersede everything else'. If it were possible 'to ascertain the will of the Polish people in so short a time, or even within two months, it would create an entirely different situation for His Majesty's Government and no one would oppose it'.

The Polish discussion was over, for the moment. Briefly, the Conference turned to Yugoslavia, where Churchill said that from the moment that the King had made difficulties about the Tito-Subasic agreement, 'he had made it clear publicly that he would be by-passed if he withheld his assent'. The discussion then ended, with the following brief, prophetic exchange:

MARSHAL STALIN observed that Tito was now also popular and that if anybody gave him advice he sometimes kicked.

THE PRIME MINISTER suggested that Marshal Stalin might take the risk.

Turning momentarily to Greece, Stalin said he had heard 'many rumours'. He had 'no intention of criticizing', he hastened to add, 'but would like to know what was happening'. Churchill replied that he hoped that peace would come soon, 'on the basis of an amnesty except for acts contrary to the laws of war. He doubted whether a Government could be formed which contained all parties, because they hated each other so much that they could hardly keep their hands off their opponents.' Perhaps, Stalin suggested, 'they had not yet got used to discussions'.

Churchill then told the Conference that the British 'had had rather a rough time in Greece'. He was 'much obliged' to Stalin 'for his attitude to this matter'. All he wanted, Stalin repeated, was information, 'he did not wish to interfere'.[1]

The fourth political plenary was over. There were, it seemed, to be early elections in Poland, and there was to be no Soviet interference in Greece. 'The atmosphere of the meeting was good,' Pierson Dixon noted in his diary, 'much more cordial than any yet.'[2]

That night, at the Yusupov Palace, Stalin was host to more than thirty guests, with Churchill and Roosevelt as his guests of honour. 'Stalin was in the very best of form,' Brooke noted in his diary, 'and was full of fun and good humour, apparently thoroughly enjoying himself.' The standard of the speeches, Brooke added, 'was remarkably low and mostly consisted of insincere, slimy sort of slush!'[3] Churchill's contribution to this stage of the proceedings began:

It is no exaggeration or compliment of a florid kind when I say that we regard Marshal Stalin's life as most precious to the hopes and hearts of all of us. There have been many conquerors in history, but few of them have been statesmen, and most of them threw away the fruits of victory in the troubles which followed their wars. I earnestly hope that the Marshal may be spared to the people of the Soviet Union and to help us all to move forward to a less unhappy time than that through which we have recently come. I walk through this world with greater courage and hope when I find myself in a relation of friendship and intimacy with this great man, whose fame has gone out not only over all Russia but the world.

Churchill also had solemn words for the festive gathering, telling the assembled quests: 'I must say that never in this war have I felt the responsibility weigh so heavily on me, even in the darkest hours, as now during this Conference,' and he went on to sound a note of realism, and foreboding:

Do not let us under-estimate the difficulties. Nations, comrades in arms, have in the past drifted apart within five or ten years of war. Thus toiling

---

[1] 'Argonaut', '4th Plenary Meeting (Political)', 4.30 p.m., 8 February 1944: Cabinet papers, 120/170.

[2] Pierson Dixon diary, 8 February 1945: Piers Dixon, *op. cit.*, page 144.

[3] Brooke diary, 8 February 1945: Bryant, *op. cit.*, volume 2, pages 410–11.

millions have followed a vicious circle, falling into the pit, and then by their sacrifices raising themselves up again. We now have a chance of avoiding the errors of previous generations and of making a sure peace.

People cry out for peace and joy. Will the families be reunited? Will the warriors come home? Will the shattered dwellings be rebuilt? Will the toiler see his home?

To defend one's country is glorious, but there are greater conquests before us. Before us lies the realisation of the dream of the poor—that they shall live in peace, protected by our invincible power from aggression and evil. My hope is in the illustrious President of the United States and in Marshal Stalin, in whom we shall find the champions of peace, who after smiting the foe will lead us to carry on the task against poverty, confusion, chaos, and oppression. That is my hope, and, speaking for England, we shall not be behindhand in our efforts. We shall not weaken in supporting your exertions.

The Marshal spoke of the future. This is the most important of all. Otherwise the oceans of bloodshed will have been useless and outrageous. I propose the toast to the broad sunlight of the victorious peace.

During their talk together, Stalin told Churchill of the negotiations which led up to the Nazi-Soviet pact of August 1939. 'Ribbentrop told the Russians,' Stalin recalled, 'that the British and Americans were only merchants, and would never fight.' [1]

The final toast of the evening was proposed by Stalin, and was to the interpreters. Churchill seconded it with the words: 'Interpreters of the world, unite! You have nothing to lose but your audiences': a parody of Karl Marx which, noted Portal, 'went with a bang'. [2]

'PM has just returned from his dinner,' noted Marian Holmes. 'He is next door singing "The Glory Song".' [3]

That night Churchill sent Attlee and the War Cabinet an account of the various Anglo-American discussions that had been going on at Yalta, in parallel with the main discussions. 'The Americans tell us repeatedly,' Churchill wrote, 'that they are resolved to see us through after the war till we can get into a normal position, and Stettinius says they will pile ships to us beyond any tonnage we have ever possessed in our history. This shows the good spirit prevailing.'

Churchill added a touch of local colour:

This place has turned out very well so far, in spite of our gloomy warning and forebodings. It is a sheltered strip of austere Riviera with winding corniche roads and the villas and palaces more or less undamaged of an extinct imperialism and nobility. In these we squat on furniture carried with extraordin-

---

[1] War Cabinet Paper No. 111 of 1945, 'Crimea Conference', 'Top Secret', 18 February 1945, speeches of 8 February 1945: Churchill papers, 23/14.

[2] Portal notes: Denis Richards, *Portal of Hungerford*, London 1977, page 288.

[3] Marian Holmes diary, 8 February 1945: Marian Walker Spicer papers.

ary effort from Moscow and with plumbing and road-making done regardless of cost in a few days by our hosts, whose prodigality excels belief.[1]

In recalling this 'prodigality' five years later, Churchill noted 'the terrific efforts made by the Soviets for our comfort. For instance, there was a glass tank with many plants growing, and Peter Portal made a chance comment that there were no fish in it. A whole consignment of living goldfish were flown from God knows where and appeared two days later.'[2]

The courtesy and consideration of the Russians in all domestic arrangements could not mask the divergent moods and intentions of the Allies. 'The only bond of the victors is their common hate,' Churchill minuted to Eden on February 8, in connection with the proposed dismemberment of Germany, and he added: 'To make Britain safe she must become responsible for the safety of a cluster of feeble States.'[3]

---

[1] 'Jason' No. 220, 8 February 1945: Churchill papers, 20/223.
[2] 'Notes on Volume VI': Churchill papers, 4/362.
[3] Prime Minister's Personal Minute, M(Arg) 7/5, 8 February 1945: Churchill papers, 20/209.

62

Yalta: 'The weight of responsibility'

'PM seems well,' Cadogan noted in his diary on 9 February 1945, 'though drinking buckets of Caucasian champagne which would undermine the health of any ordinary man.'[1] 'Papa's eyes are sore,' Sarah Churchill wrote to her mother that morning, 'and are bothering him quite a bit. Charles thinks he should see another eye-man when he gets back. . . .'[2] At noon Churchill attended a plenary session at which the Combined Chiefs of Staff presented the result of their own discussions since Malta. The meeting was held, as were all plenaries, at the Livadia Palace, so that Roosevelt could attend without problems. Roosevelt was 'not in very good shape', noted Admiral Cunningham.[3]

During the discussion on February 9, Churchill suggested a Four Power ultimatum, in which China would be the fourth Power, 'calling upon Japan to surrender unconditionally, or else be subjected to the overwhelming weight of all the forces of the Four Powers'. If she accepted this ultimatum, some 'mitigation' might be extended to her. There was 'no doubt', he said, 'that some mitigation would be worthwhile if it led to the saving of a year or a year and a half of a war in which so much blood and treasure would be poured out'. Whatever the decision, Churchill added, 'Great Britain would see the matter through to the end.'

Roosevelt felt, however, that the Japanese 'would be unlikely to wake up to the true state of affairs until all of their islands had felt the full weight of air attack'.[4]

[1] Cadogan diary, 9 February 1945: David Dilks (editor), *op. cit.*, page 707.
[2] Sarah Churchill, letter of 9 February 1945: *Keep on Dancing, op. cit.*, pages 76–7.
[3] Cunningham diary, 9 February 1945: Cunningham papers.
[4] '"Argonaut" Conference', 'Minutes of 2nd Plenary Session between the United States and Great Britain', Livadia Palace, Yalta, 12 noon, 9 February 1945: Cabinet papers, 120/170. The Americans present were Roosevelt, Leahy, Marshall, King and Major-General L. S. Kuter

Churchill lunched that day with Roosevelt, before going to the fifth political plenary, which began at 4 p.m. The Polish question was the first item on the agenda. Molotov proposed amendments to an American formula, which had been presented by Stettinius at a meeting of Foreign Ministers that morning, to set up in Poland a 'Provisional Government of National Unity'. The basis of the American proposal and the Russian amendments was the establishment of a Provisional Government 'reorganized', as the Russians were prepared to accept, 'on a wider democratic basis with the inclusion of democratic leaders from Poland itself and also from those living abroad'. This 'Government of National Unity', as the American proposal described it, 'would be pledged to the holding of free and unfettered elections as soon as practicable on the basis of universal suffrage and secret ballot. . . .' This formulation was acceptable to the Russians.[1]

Churchill then asked for a break in the Polish discussions. He sensed, he told the Conference, 'a desire to put foot in stirrup and be off', and he added: 'We could not afford to allow the settlement of these important matters to be hurried and the fruits of the Conference lost for lack of another twenty-four hours. A great prize was in view and decisions taken must be unhurried. These might well be among the most important days in the lives of those present.'

These were solemn words, deeply felt. Poland's future was a test case, in some ways *the* test case, of the future relationship of the Great Powers. It was agreed to move on to other matters, so that some thought could be given to the American formula and the Soviet amendment. On reparations, Stettinius presented a formula, agreed to by the Soviet Union, and to be discussed by the Reparations Commission, whereby a total sum of twenty billion dollars would be demanded, 'and that 50 per cent of it should go to the Soviet Union'. To this Eden commented 'that he would be obliged to await instructions from his Government'. Churchill made no comment.

Turning to the World Organization, Stettinius read out the agreement of the Foreign Ministers that the five Governments which

---

(representing General Arnold). The British present were Churchill, Brooke, Portal, Cunningham, Maitland Wilson, Ismay and Admiral Sir James Somerville. Secretariat: Major-General E. I. C. Jacob and Brigadier General A. K. McFarland.

[1] On the morning of February 10, Eden informed Churchill that the Americans, 'without even giving Russia time to make any comment on last night's Polish discussion', offered to withdraw the 'tail piece', provided Roosevelt 'could say publicly something of the kind'. Eden added: 'Americans gave us no warning and I don't propose to agree to their action.' To this, Churchill commented: 'Certainly do not agree.' (Foreign Ofice papers, 954/20, folio 424, note by Pierson Dixon and folio 425, note by Eden and report of comment by Churchill.)

would have permanent seats on the Security Council should, before the United Nations Conference, 'consult each other' on the subjects of 'territorial trusteeship and dependent areas'.[1] It was also agreed that these subjects 'should be discussed' at the United Nations conference itself, now fixed for the last week of April.

Churchill entered the discussion with a caveat. He 'could not agree', he said, 'at any rate without consultation with the Dominions, to any British territory being made the subject of a system under which it would be open to other Powers to make criticisms of the work which we had done in our Colonies, and which called upon us to justify our standard of administration'. His objection would be met, Churchill added, if it was 'made clear' that the proposed system of territorial trusteeship, intended, as Stettinius had just explained, 'to deal with the territorial trusteeship', would not 'in any way' affect the integrity of the British Commonwealth and Empire.

On Yugoslavia, Stettinius and Molotov stressed the need for agreement to be reached on the execution of the Tito-Subasic agreement 'before the termination of the Crimea Conference'. The agreement had been signed on January 11. It was now February 9. Nevertheless, 'the agreement had not been put into operation', and the British representatives 'had now suggested two amendments'. It was not a question of 'amendments', Eden said, but of 'assurances' which Subasic would ask from Tito. If Tito gave these assurances, the agreement 'would come into force at once'.

The two assurances concerned the inclusion in the Anti-Fascist Assembly of National Liberation of all the members of the pre-war Parliament 'other than those who had compromised themselves', and that the legislation of the National Liberation Assembly should ultimately be 'confirmed by the Constituent Assembly'. Stalin accepted this, whereupon Churchill commented that he 'knew that he could then rely on Marshal Stalin's goodwill' in asking Tito to give these additional assurances. Stalin replied 'that when he made a statement he would carry it out'.

After a short interval, the discussion on Poland resumed. Molotov now asked the Conference to delete from the American draft the proposal that the Ambassadors of the three Great Powers in Warsaw should be responsible for 'observing and reporting' to their respective Governments 'on the carrying out of the pledge in regard to free and

[1] The five Governments were Britain, China, France, the Soviet Union and the United States.

unfettered elections'. Speaking for 'some six million Poles' in the United States, emigrants and the children and grandchildren of emigrants, Roosevelt then asked 'for some assurance that the elections really would be honest and free'. Churchill also spoke in favour of the American proposal for diplomatic observers, telling Stalin:

His Majesty's Government were at a great disadvantage in discussing Polish affairs because they really knew little of what was actually going on, yet they had to take decisions of great responsibility. But they did know of the bitter feelings among the Poles and the very fierce language which had been used by M. Osobka-Morawski. He had been informed that the Lublin Government had openly declared its intention to try as traitors all members of the Polish Home Army and Underground Movement. That caused him very great anxiety and distress, and was a matter of great perplexity to him in forming his views.

Of course, he put first the non-hampering of the operations of the Red Army. But he would like Marshal Stalin, with his patience and kindness, to consider the difficulty of the British position. The British Government did not know what was going on inside Poland, except through dropping brave men by parachute and bringing members of the Underground Movement out. They had no other means of knowing, and did not like getting their information in that way. How could this be remedied without in any way hampering the movements of the Red Army? Could any facilities be granted to the British (and no doubt the United States would wish to participate in anything that was granted) in order to see how these Polish quarrels were being settled?

Churchill went on to point out that Marshal Tito had said that 'when elections took place in Yugoslavia he would not object to Russian, British and American observers being present to report impartially to the world that they had been carried out fairly'. So far as Greece was concerned, 'His Majesty's Government would greatly welcome it, when the elections were held as soon as possible, if American, Russian and British observers were there to make sure that the business was conducted as the people wished.' The same question would arise in Italy, where, when Northern Italy was 'delivered', there would have to be an election before forming a constituent assembly or Parliament. The British formula in Italy, Churchill declared, 'was the same. Russian, American and British observers should be present to assure the world that everything had been done in a fair way.' Even in Egypt, when Nahas Pasha had quarrelled with the King, there had been an election, and Nahas Pasha had been 'turned out'.

Stalin was not impressed by this last point. He 'did not much believe' in Egyptian elections, he said, 'as there was a great deal of corruption there'. He also wondered what the percentage of literacy in Egypt was. Churchill replied at once that 'he did not mean to compare Poland and Egypt, but merely to point out the importance of carrying out elections fairly. For instance would Mikolajczyk be able to go back to Poland 'and organize his party for the elections?' He 'must be able to tell the House of Commons' that the elections in Poland 'would be free', and that there would be 'effective guarantees that they were freely and fairly carried out'.

Under persistent questioning from Churchill, Stalin agreed, not only that Mikolajczyk would be able to take part in the elections, together with other candidates from his Peasant Party, but also that the existing Polish Government 'should include a Peasant Party representative'. They would 'leave it at that', Churchill commented, adding that he hoped nothing he had said 'had given offence, since nothing had been further from his heart'.

Churchill then spoke of the Curzon Line. He 'wanted to be able' to carry the eastern frontier question through Parliament, he told Stalin, and thought that this would be possible 'if Parliament was satisfied that the Poles had been able to decide for themselves what they really wanted'. There were 'some good people' among the Poles, Stalin commented, they were 'good fighters' and there had been 'good scientists, musicians etc. among them. But they were very quarrelsome'; to which Churchill replied: 'all he wanted was to ensure that all sides got a fair hearing'.

The elections in Poland, Roosevelt remarked, had to be 'above criticism—like Caesar's wife'. He did not want anybody 'to be in a position to question the purity of the elections. It was a question of good politics rather than of principle.' The question of observers, Molotov declared, was better discussed with the Poles, or they 'would feel that they were not trusted'.

The discussion on Poland rested, leaving a few moments for discussion on other matters. Speaking of Greece, Stalin remarked that he had 'complete confidence' in British policy there. Turning to the question of War Criminals, Churchill said they should draw up a list of the 'grand criminals', with power to add to the list. Such a list would separate the criminals 'from their people'. He 'personally' was inclined, he said, 'that they should be shot as soon as they were caught and their identity established'. Stalin asked about Hess. He 'would catch up with the others', Churchill replied.[1]

[1] Having been interned in Britain since his flight from Germany in May 1941, Hess was sentenced to life imprisonment as a major war criminal in September 1946 at the Nuremberg Trials. Imprisoned at Spandau Prison, West Berlin, he was from 1966 the sole detainee. Several British, American and French proposals for his release were rejected by the Soviet authorities who, by treaty, have joint rights with their former allies. In 1984 the still imprisoned Hess was ninety years old.

Was it Stalin's view, Churchill asked, 'that grand criminals should be tried before being shot', in other words, that it should be 'a judicial rather than a political act'. Stalin replied that 'that was so'. But Roosevelt commented that 'it should not be too judicial. He wanted to keep out newspapers and photographers until the criminals were dead.'

The fifth political plenary was nearly at an end. Asked by Stalin whether the offensive on the Western Front had begun, Churchill gave details of Montgomery's operation, which had begun on the previous morning, to drive south from Nijmegen along the western bank of the Rhine. The plenary then ended. Returning to the Vorontsov Villa, Churchill sent Stalin 'the latest news from London' regarding Montgomery's battle, as well as a memorandum setting out 'the latest position' in Greece, and he added: 'I trust these notes may be of interest to you.' [1]

The message from Montgomery, sent from London at six that evening, was that his new offensive south-east of Nijmegen was 'keeping up its momentum' on the upper end of the Siegfried Line, where British and Canadian troops had advanced four and a half miles, and were 'well into the first of the three Siegfried lines'. Seven towns and villages had been captured, and 1,800 prisoners taken. In the south, on the west Rhine below Strasbourg, German resistance had ended. [2]

The note on Greece had been sent to Churchill from Eden. [3] It told of the continuing negotiations between ELAS delegates, and of the resumption of British food supplies to Greece, through Salonica, Piraeus and Patras, where order had now been restored. [4]

That night Churchill dined at his villa with General Marshall, Brooke and Alexander. 'We never got up from the table till 12.30 a.m.,' Brooke noted in his diary, 'and then only to go into the Map

---

[1] 'Secret', Villa Vorontsov, 9 February 1945: Premier papers, 3/213/6, folio 177. Leslie Rowan later recalled: 'One of the small but quite important things which impressed the Russians when we were at Yalta, was the daily service of official papers which we received from London. These were sent by Mosquito which left London at about midnight and reached the Crimea in the course of the morning and then came by car to Yalta itself. This meant that official papers could be in the Prime Minister's hands in the afternoon of the day following that on which they were dealt with in London. It also meant that we had the London newspapers at tea-time on the day of their issue as the early editions were sent by the official bag. So far as I can recall this service never failed and it created quite an impression.' (Letter to Bill Deakin, 19 March 1952: Churchill papers, War Memoirs correspondence.)

[2] 'London, 6 p.m., 9.2.45', sent from the Map Room, Vorontsov Villa: Premier papers, 3/213/6, folio 178.

[3] Foreign Secretary's Minute, PM(A) 14, 9 February 1945: Premier papers, 3/213/6, folio 181.

[4] 'Note on Greece', initialled 'WSC, 9.2.45': Premier papers, 3/213/6, folios 179–80.

Room for half an hour. Finally Marshall left, Winston disappeared, and I was left alone with Alex.'[1]

'Have been very hard pressed these last few days,' Churchill telegraphed to 'Mrs Kent' on February 10. 'All is well and I hope for substantial results.' His eyes had been giving him trouble, Churchill added, 'but otherwise I am very well and most comfortable'.[2] 'PM a bit irate,' noted Marian Holmes. 'Bothered about the sun shining in his eyes,' and she added: 'A lot of fuss and bother about fixing the curtain "Down a little. No that's too much. A little higher." He mellowed a bit. When I couldn't hear a word and asked him, instead of blowing me up he said, "It's no wonder you can't hear me," with a sweet smile. Sir Alexander Cadogan came in and I nipped out of the room. PM said, "Stay not far away." When I returned, again there were problems with the window blind. Commander T. squeezed himself round that awkward sliding door, making a grimace. PM said mischievously, "I trust there are no serious consequences."'[3]

Churchill remained in bed on February 10 until the mid-afternoon, when, at 3 p.m., he went to the Yusupov Villa for a private meeting with Stalin. Before leaving, he telegraphed to Attlee, for the War Cabinet, that the only remaining point about Poland was the 'arrangement for supervising voting, and also for informing ourselves properly about what is going on in Poland'. All the 'reality' in the Polish business 'depends on this point', Churchill added, 'which will be fought out today'.[4]

At his meeting with Stalin on February 10, Poland was the first item to be discussed. After Churchill had stressed the 'disadvantage' to Britain of not having representatives in Poland 'who could keep us informed of what was going on', Stalin replied that after the recognition of the new Polish Government, 'it would be open' to Britain to send an Ambassador to Warsaw. Churchill asked whether the Ambassador would have 'freedom of movement' within Poland. As far as the Red Army command was concerned, Stalin replied, 'there could be no interference' with the Ambassador's movements, and he 'promised to give the necessary instructions'. There was however 'also the Polish Government', with whom Britain would have to make its 'own arrangements'.

[1] Brooke diary, 9 February 1945: Bryant, *op. cit.*, volume 2, page 411.
[2] 'Jason' No. 317, 10 February 1945: Premier papers, 4/78/1, Part 2, folio 591.
[3] Marian Holmes diary, 10 February 1945: Marian Walker Spicer papers.
[4] 'Jason' No. 321, 10 February 1945: Churchill papers, 20/223.

The discussion then turned to the issue of the repatriation of Russians who had been captured fighting in the ranks of the German army. Earlier that day, Churchill had been shown a minute, written by Patrick Dean for the Foreign Office, on the agreement which had been reached on the previous day between Britain, the United States and the Soviet Union about the repatriation of prisoners-of-war. British and American prisoners-of-war were to be repatriated to Britain and the United States, and Soviet citizens captured in the German ranks were to be repatriated to Russia. Churchill commented: 'I agree, but what has gone wrong with the Foreign Office typewriter?' [1]

The minutes of the discussion of February 10 recorded:

THE PRIME MINISTER spoke of the embarrassment caused us by the large number of Russian prisoners in the west. We had about 100,000 of them, 11,000 had already been transported home, and 7,000 more would leave this month. He wanted to know the Marshal's wishes about the rest.

MARSHAL STALIN hoped they could be sent to Russia as quickly as possible. He asked that they should not be ill-treated and that they should be segregated from the Germans. The Soviet Government looked upon all of them as Soviet citizens. He asked that there should be no attempt to induce any of them to refuse repatriation. Those who had agreed to fight for the Germans could be dealt with on their return to Russia.

THE PRIME MINISTER explained that we were anxious that these prisoners should be repatriated, and the only difficulty arose from a lack of shipping space. As regards segregating them from the Germans, this was difficult in the first instance, but as soon as they were sorted out, they would be kept separate.

THE PRIME MINISTER asked how many British prisoners the Red Army had released during its advance. He begged for good treatment for them: every mother in England was anxious about the fate of her prisoner sons.

MARSHAL STALIN replied that very few British prisoners had been released by the Red Army so far. There might be more as the Russians advanced deeper into Germany. So far the few British pilots, &c. had been handed over to British liaison officers in Roumania or Bulgaria.

THE PRIME MINISTER said we wanted to send liaison officers to the Red Army to look after our men. Until that could be arranged he proposed that No. 30 Mission should perform the necessary liaison duties. [2]

MARSHAL STALIN agreed.

Thus was decided what was later to become one of the more controversial issues of the Yalta agreements, the return to the Soviet

---

[1] Prime Minister's Personal Minute, M(Arg) 8/5, 10 February 1945: Churchill papers, 20/20.

[2] No. 30 Mission was the British Military Mission in Moscow.

Union of men, some of whom had fought actively in the German ranks and some of whom had not, but the majority of whom, in spite of Stalin's assurances, were subjected on their return to the most rigorous punishment.[1]

The Churchill–Stalin conversation then returned to reparations, with Churchill telling Stalin that he thought 'it would be impossible' to collect from Germany the high figure which Russia proposed. 'For ourselves,' Churchill said, 'we did not want German labour. We might take over part of German trade and certain raw materials, like potash, timber &c. But we did not want manufactured goods, which would only mean unemployment for us.' Stalin then suggested that 'Britain should take over shares in German undertakings', to which Churchill made no reply, except to point out 'that by removing factories and equipment from Germany, Russia would be doing us a service, for it would put an end to German exports which could then be replaced by British exports'.

Churchill then asked Stalin what were Russia's 'wishes' with regard to the Far East, to which Stalin replied 'that the Russians wanted a naval base such as Port Arthur'. The Americans had already said that they 'would prefer the ports to be internationalised', but the Russians 'wanted their interests safeguarded'. Churchill had no criticism of the Russian desire, assuring Stalin that Britain 'would welcome the appearance of Russian ships in the Pacific' and adding that he was 'in favour of Russia's losses of 30 or 40 years ago being made good'.

Stalin then raised the question of the Montreux Convention, signed in 1936, which had given Turkey control over the passage of warships between the Black Sea and the Aegean. It was 'intolerable', he told Churchill, that Russia should be 'at the mercy of the Turks, not only in war but in peace, and for Russia to have to beg the Turks to let her ships go through the Straits'. Churchill replied that he would support the Russian request for a revision of the Montreux Convention.[2]

From the Yusupov Villa Churchill and Stalin proceeded to the

---

[1] One author, Nikolai Tolstoy, has estimated that some 20% of all those repatriated to Russia, including those under the Yalta repatriation agreement, were sentenced either to death, or to 25 years penal servitude in labour camps; that up to 20% were given labour camp sentences of between five and ten years; that perhaps 15% were sent as conscript labourers to the various areas devastated by the war; and that up to 20% were allowed to return home. (Nikolai Tolstoy, *Victims of Yalta*, London 1977, page 409.)

[2] 'Argonaut', 6th Plenary Meeting (Political), 3 p.m., 10 February 1945: Cabinet papers, 120/170. The six people present at this meeting were Churchill, Stalin, Eden, Molotov and the two interpreters, Birse and Pavlov.

Livadia Palace for the final working meeting of the Big Three, which began at 4.45. It was Molotov who, in deference to the earlier insistence by Churchill and Roosevelt, proposed that Britain and America would establish diplomatic relations with the Polish Provisional Government of National Unity once it was formed, and would exchange ambassadors 'by whose reports the respective Governments will be kept informed about the situation in Poland'. This was immediately agreed.

Speaking of Poland's western frontier, Churchill said that the British delegation 'had had a telegram from the War Cabinet strongly deprecating any reference to a frontier as far west as the Western Neisse, because the problem of moving the population was bigger than could be managed'. On the eastern frontier, Churchill added, 'they were all agreed'. But Roosevelt informed the Conference that it would be 'easier for him' if neither frontier were mentioned, 'as he had no right to agree on questions of that kind which were really a matter for the Senate'. Molotov felt it would be 'useful', however, if the Curzon Line could be mentioned, and this was eventually agreed. The western frontier would be defined in line with wording suggested by Churchill, that Poland should receive 'substantial' accessions of territory in 'the north and west', the final line to await the Peace Conference.

The Polish discussions were at an end: free elections, British and American diplomats to observe them, and the Curzon Line to be Poland's frontier in the east, with substantial territorial compensation in the west: such was now the declared policy of Britain, the United States and the Soviet Union.

The next issue at this final political plenary was reparations. When Churchill said that the British delegation had been instructed by their Government 'not to mention figures', and Roosevelt added 'that no mention should be made of money', Stalin remarked caustically: 'Perhaps the Conference would prefer that the Russians should have no reparations at all. If so, they had better say so.' Under further sharp questioning from Stalin, Churchill stated that the 'principle' of reparations was accepted, whereupon Stalin agreed to allow the actual amount to be paid, in cash or kind, to be decided by the Reparations Commission, which would sit in Moscow, and would, as Roosevelt at once agreed, take 20 billion dollars 'as the basis for discussion' of the amount of reparations 'to be extracted' from Germany. Churchill, dissenting, said that the British Government 'could not commit themselves to a figure of 20 billion dollars, or to any other figure until the problem had been examined'. He then read out a telegram from the War Cabinet in London:

We consider it quite inadmissible to state any figure for German deliveries until the possibilities have been properly investigated on the spot. We consider 20 billion dollars (equals 500 million pounds a year) as far too great. It is roughly the equivalent of Germany's pre-war gross exports (i.e., not allowing for any imports) in an average year. It is not to be thought that this should be paid by a Germany which has been bombed, defeated, perhaps dismembered and unable to pay for imports. True, some of it will be her capital assets, but that will make it so much the harder for her to pay the rest. We also attach particular importance to some mention being made of payments for German imports. Unless this has a priority at least equal to that of reparation, we shall find ourselves paying for the imports necessary to keep Germany alive while others obtain the reparation.

This, Churchill commented, 'was a very severe telegram'.

Stalin then deferred to the British view. On the assumption that 'the expert who had written this telegram' was correct, 'a smaller sum could be fixed'. The amount itself, he suggested, should be decided by the Reparations Commission. To this both Churchill and Roosevelt gave their assent.

Also in further deference to Churchill's strongly expressed views, first Roosevelt and then Stalin agreed that France should not only have a zone of occupation in Germany, but should also become a member of the Allied Control Commission for Germany. Stalin then raised the question of the Montreux Convention, which was 'now out of date'. It was 'impossible', he said, 'to put up with a situation in which a small State like Turkey could keep a hand on the throat of a large country like Russia'. Churchill, without referring to his meeting with Stalin earlier that afternoon, said that Stalin 'had mentioned this matter' to Eden and himself when they had last been in Moscow. Then, as now, they viewed Stalin's proposal 'with sympathy', if, Churchill added, when the time came to change the Convention, 'some undertaking' could be given to Turkey which would make it 'easier for her and for everybody else'. Stalin at once agreed that it 'should be possible' to give Turkey 'an assurance of this kind'.

Turkey was the last substantive issue discussed: the Big Three were not to meet again except to give their approval to the formal statements on which they had already agreed.[1]

---

[1] Also confirmed at Yalta, in absolute secrecy, was the future entry of the Soviet Union into the war against Japan, as soon as possible after Germany had been defeated. A month later, Churchill was sent one of several circulated copies of this agreement. 'I am shocked,' he minuted to Eden, 'to see that there have been eight copies of this secret document. How many are there altogether? They ought not to be circulated except in a locked box. There is no need whatever to inform the Dominions or to show the document to anyone who is not now cognisant of it.' (Prime Minister's Personal Minute, M.191/5, 10 March 1945: Churchill papers, 20/209.)

That night Churchill gave a dinner party at the Vorontsov Villa, at which the guests of honour were Roosevelt and Stalin. Waiting to greet his guests, Churchill sat in a chair at the entrance to the Villa, 'eyeing the Russian soldiery', Marian Holmes noted. Her account continued: 'At 2 minutes past 9, the entrance doors opened and President Roosevelt was wheeled in. The PM greeted him and the President said in a deep, loud voice "Sorree I'm late. I couldn't get something done up." Stalin's entrance was ruined as he came hard on the heels of the President. Stalin remained a little in the background. The PM said courteously "May I escort you" and led the Marshal into the banqueting room.'[1]

At dinner, when proposing Stalin's health, Churchill told his guests:

There was a time when the Marshal was not so kindly towards us, and I remember that I said a few rude things about him, but our common dangers and common loyalties have wiped all that out. The fire of war has burnt up the misunderstandings of the past. We feel we have a friend whom we can trust, and I hope he will continue to feel the same about us. I pray he may live to see his beloved Russia not only glorious in war, but also happy in peace.[2]

During the dinner conversation, as Churchill recalled five years later, 'I said to Stalin: "We are going to have an Election quite soon in England and I shall have to speak very harshly about the Communists." He said: "The Communists are good boys." I said: "We are against them, and we shall have to make our case. You know we have two parties in England." "One party is much better," said Stalin.'[3]

After dinner Churchill took his guests into the Map Room, later referring to that moment as 'the zenith of the Map Room's career'. As Captain Pim, who together with Lieutenant-Colonel J. A. T. Miller had supervised the preparation of the maps that evening, later recalled that Churchill's guests remained in the Map Room for half an hour, 'discussing world strategy'. Pim's account continued:

That day the Soviet forces were only 38 miles from Berlin on the river Oder and the British and Canadians were storming their way to the banks of the Rhine. In Luzon the US forces had captured Manila after a wonderfully swift campaign.

[1] Marian Holmes diary, 10 February 1945: Marian Walker Spicer papers.
[2] 'Speeches at Dinner at Vorontsov Villa on 10th February 1945': War Cabinet Paper No. 111 of 1945, 'Top Secret', 18 February 1945: Churchill papers, 23/14.
[3] 'Notes on Volume VI': Churchill papers, 4/362.

The Prime Minister told the President and the Marshal the story of Anne of Cleves. This had arisen out of the fact that Allied forces had that day captured Cleves and he then, referring to the great offensive which in the course of the next few weeks was to push the Allied forces up to the western bank of the Rhine, reminded them of that well-known song of the last war 'When we've wound up the watch on the Rhine' and favoured them with a few bars.

One of the Marshal's sallies did not commend itself to Mr Churchill. It must have suggested that the British might wish to make an earlier armistice than the Russians—and the Prime Minister looked hurt and in a corner of the Map Room, with his hands in his pockets, gave us a few lines of his favourite song 'Keep right on to the end of the road'. Stalin looked extremely puzzled. The President said with a broad grin to the Russian interpreter, 'Tell your Chief that this singing by the Prime Minister is Britain's secret weapon.' [1]

Among the documents to which Churchill, Roosevelt and Stalin were about to put their signatures was one entitled 'Declaration on Liberated Europe'. This pledged the three Powers to give such help as they could to the peoples of liberated Europe 'to solve by democratic means their pressing political and economic problems', during what the Declaration called 'the temporary period of instability'. As stated in this Three Power Declaration:

The establishment of order in Europe and the re-building of national economic life must be achieved by processes which will enable the liberated peoples to destroy the last vestiges of Nazism and Fascism and to create democratic institutions of their own choice.

This is a principle of the Atlantic Charter—the right of all peoples to choose the form of Government under which they will live—the restoration of sovereign rights and self-Government to those peoples who have been forcibly deprived of them by the aggressor nations.

The Declaration went on to state that the Three Powers would 'jointly assist' the peoples in any European country 'to form interim Governmental authorities broadly representative of all democratic elements in the population and pledged to the earliest possible establishment through free elections of Governments responsive to the will of the people', and to facilitate 'where necessary' the holding of such elections.

The text of this Declaration was telegraphed to the Cabinet in London on the afternoon of February 11, as part of the official summary of the Yalta discussions. [2]

*   *   *

---

[1] Pim recollections: Pim papers.
[2] 'Jason' No. 347, 3.20 p.m., 11 February 1945: Premier papers, 3/51/10, folios 44–52.

During the afternoon meeting on February 10, Roosevelt had suddenly announced that he would be leaving on the following day. 'The President is behaving very badly,' Churchill remarked to Lord Moran at breakfast on February 11. 'He won't take any interest in what we are trying to do.'[1] 'The President in particular,' noted Cadogan, 'is very woolly and wobbly.'[2] Roosevelt was indeed extremely ill.

At noon on February 11 the Big Three met for the eighth and last political plenary, to approve the communiqué on which their respective civil servants had worked through the night. 'The atmosphere was very cheerful,' Pierson Dixon wrote in his diary, 'Stalin saying "OK", and the PM and the President "Horosho" as point after point was approved.'[3] Dixon added: 'The President was clearly in a hurry to get off, and proposed that the Foreign Secretaries should be left to lick the communiqué into final shape and draw up the Protocol of Conclusions.'[4]

For a brief moment, Churchill and Stalin clashed again on Poland, as Stalin asked whether Britain accepted the Polish decisions. The minutes of the meeting recorded the following brief exchange:

THE PRIME MINISTER said that he was content with this section, although he would be strongly criticised for it at home on the grounds that we had yielded completely to the Russian view.

MARSHAL STALIN asked whether the Prime Minister agreed with this section.

THE PRIME MINISTER said that he did, but he would certainly be strongly criticised.[5]

These were the last serious words exchanged at Yalta.

The secret discussions were at an end. Immediately following them, the three leaders issued a statement of what had been decided. The statement was in eight sections, the first, on the defeat of Germany, declaring that 'new and more powerful blows' were about to be launched 'into the heart of Germany', and that the German people 'will only make the cost of their defeat heavier by attempting to continue a hopeless resistance'. The second section set out the arrangements for the post-war occupation and control of Germany by the Three Powers. 'It is not our purpose to destroy the people of Germany,' this section ended, 'but only when Nazism and militarism have

[1] Moran notes, 11 February 1945: Moran, *op. cit.*, page 231.
[2] Cadogan diary, 11 February 1945: David Dilks (editor), *op. cit.*, pages 708–9.
[3] 'Horosho', the Russian word for 'good' or 'OK', written in cyrillic as: 'хорошо'.
[4] Pierson Dixon diary, 11 February 1945: Piers Dixon, *op. cit.*, page 146.
[5] 'Argonaut', '8th Plenary Meeting (Political)', 12 noon, 11 February 1945: Cabinet papers, 120/170.

been extirpated will there be hope for a decent life for Germans and a place for them in the comity of nations.'

Section three was about reparations: it was 'just' that Germany be obliged to make compensation 'to the greatest extent possible' for the damage in kind which she had caused. The next section was about the forthcoming United Nations Conference, which 'should be called to meet' at San Francisco on April 25 to 'prepare the Charter' of the United Nations Organization. Both China and France would be invited 'to sponsor invitations' to the Conference, jointly with the United States, Great Britain and the Soviet Union.

There followed, as section five, the Declaration on Liberated Europe, followed in its turn by what was to prove the most testing aspect of the Yalta agreements, Poland. As a result of Poland's 'complete liberation by the Red Army', the agreement began, there was need for the establishment of a Polish Provisional Government 'which can be more broadly based than was possible before the recent liberation of Western Poland. The Provisional Government which is now functioning in Poland should, therefore, be reorganised on a broader democratic basis with the inclusion of democratic leaders from Poland itself and from Poles abroad.' This new Government would then be called 'the Polish Provisional Government of National Unity'.

Molotov, Harriman and Clark Kerr were then authorized as a Commission 'to consult in the first instance in Moscow with members of present Provisional Government and with other Polish democratic leaders from within Poland and from abroad, with a view to reorganisation of the present Government along the above lines'. This Polish Provisional Government of National Unity 'shall be pledged to the holding of free and unfettered elections as soon as possible on the basis of universal suffrage and secret ballot'. In these elections 'all democratic and anti-Nazi parties shall have the right to take part and to put forward candidates'.

When a Polish Provisional Government of National Unity had been 'properly formed in conformity with the above', the Government of the Soviet Union, 'which now maintains diplomatic relations with the present Provisional Government of Poland, and the Government of the United Kingdom and the Government of the United States will establish diplomatic relations with the new Polish Provisional Government of National Unity, and will exchange Ambassadors by whose reports the respective Governments will be kept informed about the situation in Poland'.

The agreement on Poland ended with reference to Poland's future frontiers. 'The Three Heads of Government,' it read, 'consider that the Eastern frontier of Poland should follow the Curzon Line with digressions from it in some regions of 5 to 8 kilometres in favour of Poland. They recognise that Poland must receive substantial accessions of territory in the North and West. They feel that the opinion of the new Polish Provisional Government of National Unity should be sought in due course on the extent of these accessions and that the final delimitations of the Western frontier of Poland should thereafter await the Peace Conference.'

A brief seventh section, on Yugoslavia, reommended to Tito and Subasic that the agreement between them 'should be put into effect immediately, and that a new Government should be formed on the basis of that agreement', with Tito's anti-Fascist Assembly of Liberation, AVNOJ, being extended 'to include members of the last Yugoslav Parliament (Skupshtina) who have not compromised themselves by collaboration with the enemy, thus forming a body to be known as a temporary Parliament'.

Section eight set out the decision of the Foreign Secretaries to set up a 'permanent machinery' for regular consultation, 'probably about every three or four months'. The ninth and final section, headed 'Unity for Peace as for War', declared that only with 'continuing and growing co-operation and understanding among our three countries and among all the peace-loving nations can the highest aspiration of humanity be realised—a secure and lasting peace which will, in the words of the Atlantic Charter "afford assurance that all the men in all the lands may live out their lives in freedom from fear and want".'

This statement of February 11 was signed by Churchill, Roosevelt and Stalin.[1] At 4.30 that afternoon Churchill left the Livadia Palace for the drive to the Vorontsov Villa. He had intended to leave Yalta on the following morning, 'easily, orderly and quietly', as Sarah Churchill wrote to her mother. At his own villa, however:

. . . Papa, having said goodbye to everyone, suddenly felt lonely I think. 'Why do we stay here? Why don't we go tonight—I see no reason to stay here a minute longer—we're off!' He sprang out of the car and whirling into the Private Office announced: 'I don't know about you—but I'm off! I leave in 50 minutes!'

After a second's stunned silence, everyone was galvanized into activity. Trunks and large mysterious paper parcels given to us by the Russians—whoopee—filled the hall. Laundry arrived back clean but damp. Naturally 50 minutes gave us time to change our minds six more times. 'We will spend the night here after all and leave tomorrow lunchtime—We will

[1] 'Report of Crimea Conference', text sent by telegram to London as 'Jason' No. 347, 3.20 p.m., 11 February 1945: Premier papers, 3/51/10, folios 44–52.

fly—We will leave tonight and go by sea—We will go to Athens—Alexandria—Cairo—Constantinople—We will not go to any of them—We will stay on board and read the newspapers! Where is the pouch? Why hasn't it arrived?'

Sawyers, tears in his eyes, surrounded by half-packed suitcases, beat his breast and said: 'They can't do this to me!' He put a sponge-bag in and then took it out. He carefully laid out the Lord Warden of the Cinque Ports suit, then changed it for the Royal Yacht Squadron suit. Papa, genial and sprightly like a boy out of school, his homework done, walked from room to room saying: 'Come on, come on!'

Believe it or not, 1 hour and 20 minutes later, about 5.30, saw a cavalcade of cars groaning with bulging suitcases winding its way to Sebastopol! And quick though we had been, we were last! The President left an hour before us—but on an orderly plan laid days ago. Stalin, like some genie, just disappeared.

'I really think Papa is well,' Sarah wrote, and she added: 'Though there have been some tough problems, he says he has felt the weight of responsibility more than ever before, this Conference does not seem to have been anything like the strain of Teheran and Cairo last year.'

From Yalta, Churchill and his daughter drove south-westward along the rugged coast, then north-westward over the mountains. As Sarah wrote to her mother:

We crept right up to the base of the granite peaks. Once, near the top, we got out and looked. 400 to 500 feet sheer precipice of rock rose above us,—so straight, it seemed to lean over like the beetling brows of a giant. I call it granite, only because that is what it looks like—grey and indestructible—but as a matter of fact I believe it's limestone! All the way we had our sentinels, and once when we passed through a small village, although by then it was dark and they could not possibly see—they gave a cheer.[1]

On reaching the *Franconia*, which was anchored off Sebastopol, Churchill was greeted by the ship's Captain, Harry Grattidge. 'I thought he looked tired,' Grattidge noted in his diary, 'but his first question was whether the Courier had arrived so that he could get to work.'[2]

That night, from the decks of the *Franconia*, Churchill and his daughter looked out over the ruins of the once great city, so savagely

---

[1] Sarah Churchill, letter of 12 February 1945: *Keep on Dancing, op. cit.*, pages 77–8.

[2] Captain Grattidge diary, 'Franconia and the Crimea Conference', entry for 11 February 1945: Westminster College Library, Fulton, Missouri (I am grateful to Joan Astley for a copy of this diary). Grattidge, who joined Cunard in 1914, retired in 1953. In 1958 he published his memoirs, *Captains and Queens*. For the duration of the Crimean Conference the *Franconia* had been given the code name 'Disraeli' and Sebastopol the code name 'Buchan'.

bombarded in the fighting of the previous year. Sarah told her mother:

Sebastopol at night was a revelation. You remember I told you of the devastation, of not a house in view standing or unbroken, and how one wondered where or how they lived? Well, at night one discovers. From nearly every ruin, wherever four walls of one room still stand, from behind boards that fill gaps, from basements, from piles of stones even, shafts and specks of lights shine and twinkle. It is incredible! They are incredible! [1]

That night Alexander was Churchill's guest at dinner.

At ten o'clock on the following morning, February 12, the Russian Admiral Commanding the Black Sea Fleet and his Staff 'called to see the PM', Captain Grattidge noted in his diary, 'but he was asleep'.[2] At 1.30 in the afternoon Eden arrived on board, together with Cadogan, who noted in his diary: 'I joined Winston at a terrific lunch—dressed crab, roast beef, apple pie, washed down with excellent Liebfraumilch, and gorgonzola and port!'[3] At 1.45 the luncheon party was joined by Molotov, and the Soviet Black Sea Fleet Commander.

After lunch, Churchill was driven to Sebastopol, where he saw the tomb of the Crimean War commander, Lord Raglan, and was, as he recalled five years later, 'greatly struck by the extraordinary care and respect with which it has been treated by the Russians. It might have been one of their own heroes. Even the Germans had not molested it.' 'The Russians in Sebastopol came out to greet him,' Major Birse later recalled, 'and as much as they were allowed, followed him through the streets. Our party were not permitted to stray far from the road on to the battlefield owing to the danger of unexploded mines. Mr Churchill visited also the memorial to the British who fell in the Crimean War and a panorama of the old battle. Sebastopol, as we saw it, was damaged to an extent only slightly less than Stalingrad.'[4]

From Sebastopol, the British visitors were driven to the battlefield of Balaclava. 'We were conducted there by Russian generals,' Churchill later recalled, 'they did not know much about it, and thought it was a great Russian victory, so all went off pleasantly.'

At the Balaclava battlefield, a British Officer, Brigadier Peake, pointed out, as Churchill recalled, 'the wonderful valley down which the Light Brigade charged, and the ridge which the Highland Regiments defended'. Churchill was then taken to the port which had

[1] Sarah Churchill, letter of 12 February 1945: Spencer-Churchill papers.
[2] Captain Grattidge diary, 'Franconia and the Crimea Conference', entry for 12 February 1945: Westminster College (Fulton, Missouri) archive.
[3] Cadogan diary, 12 February 1945: David Dilks (editor), *op. cit.*, pages 709–10.
[4] 'Yalta, January 1945', letter of 12 June 1947: Churchill papers, 4/391A.

been the British base during the Crimean War. 'I was struck,' he recalled, 'by the large number of prisoners of war, slaves, Roumanians, etc., who were toiling there, no harder than they could make them.' [1]

With Churchill during his travels on February 12 was the Commander of the Soviet Black Sea Fleet, who had 'orders from Moscow', as Churchill later recalled, 'to be in attendance on me whenever I came ashore'. Churchill added:

We were a little shy and very tactful with our host. But we need not have worried. As Peake pointed to the line on which the Light Brigade had been drawn up the Russian admiral pointed in almost the same direction and exclaimed, 'The German tanks came at us from over there.' A little later Peake explained the Russian dispositions, and pointed to the hills where their infantry had stood, whereupon the Russian admiral intervened with obvious pride: 'That is where a Russian battery fought and died to the last man.' I thought it right at this juncture to explain that we were studying a different war, 'a war of dynasties, not of peoples'. Our host gave no sign of comprehension, but seemed perfectly satisfied. So all passed off very pleasantly. [2]

Returning to Sebastopol and the *Franconia*, Churchill 'defeated us', Captain Grattidge noted, 'by wanting to get his clothes de-loused'. [3]

That night Churchill dined on board the *Franconia* with Eden, Alexander and Sarah. 'Some good talk at dinner,' Eden noted, 'but also much order, counter-order and disorder of plans. Eventually decided on at least another day of rest here, which is good.' [4]

In London that evening the War Cabinet met to discuss the Yalta conclusions, with Attlee telling his colleagues that the results, 'which, in the face of great difficulties, had been achieved by the Prime Minister and the Foreign Secretary, were highly satisfactory'. As regards the dismemberment of Germany, he noted, while the principle had been agreed, 'ample elbow-room had been obtained'. Agreement had also been reached 'on the very difficult matter of Poland'. In the granting of founder membership of the World Organization to the Ukraine and White Russia, 'the Americans were wholly with us'. [5] It was then agreed, at Attlee's suggestion, to send Churchill and Eden a telegram of congratulation. 'War Cabinet send their warmest congratulations to you and to the Foreign Secretary,' the telegram read, 'on the skill and success with which you have conducted discussions at Crimean Conference and on the most satisfactory result you have achieved, and wish you a safe journey home.' [6]

[1] 'Notes on Volume VI', written in December 1950: Churchill papers, 3/362.
[2] Winston S. Churchill, *The Second World War*, volume 6, London 1954, page 346.
[3] Captain Grattidge diary, 12 February 1945: Westminster College (Fulton, Missouri) archive.
[4] Eden diary, 12 February 1945: Eden memoirs, *The Reckoning, op. cit.*, page 518.
[5] War Cabinet No. 18 of 1945, 12 February 1945, Confidential Annex: Cabinet papers, 65/51.
[6] 'Fleece' No. 412, despatched 8.05 p.m., 12 February 1945: Cabinet papers, 65/51.

'Read the full and interesting records of the Plenary Conferences at the Crimea,' Jock Colville noted in his diary three days later. 'We seem to have won most of our points and the PM has won another great personal success. He was tireless in pressing for this Conference, in spite of Roosevelt's apathy, and deserves most of the credit for what has been achieved.' [1]

The 'achievements' of Yalta have been much debated. But at the time, and for many of Churchill's friends and associates, as for Colville, those achievements were considerable. '*The Times* in its first leader,' Brendan Bracken telegraphed to Churchill on February 13, 'uses such glowing language about you that I might have written the article myself.' [2]

For the Polish Government in London, there were disturbing aspects in the Yalta communiqué. 'There was, for example,' Count Raczynski told Richard Law and Sir Orme Sargent on February 12, 'no mention of the number of Poles from inside Poland and from London who were to be included in the new Government.' The Moscow discussions in October, Raczynski pointed out, had been conducted on the hypothesis that any new Government 'would contain a fifty-fifty representation of London Poles and Lublin Poles'. But Sargent pointed out 'that at Moscow the conditions were very much more favourable to the London Government than they were today, inasmuch as then M. Mikolajczyk was still Prime Minister and the Russians had not recognised the Lublin Committee as a Government. It was hardly likely that they would be prepared to accept the fifty-fifty proportion today.'

The communiqué spoke of the Provisional Government which was now functioning in Poland being recognized. That, Raczynski pointed out, 'would imply to the members of the London Government that it was the Lublin Government which was the real thing'.

Raczynski then referred to the passage in the communiqué which guaranteed the right of different parties to participate, and to put forward candidates, provided they were democratic and anti-Nazi. 'The Russian idea of a democratic and anti-Nazi party,' Raczynski remarked, 'was in the highest degree selective and, unless the position was carefully watched, any party that was not a puppet of the Russians would be labelled by them as undemocratic and pro-Nazi.'

---

[1] Colville diary, 15 February 1945: Colville papers.
[2] 'Fleece' No. 426, 13 February 1945: Premier papers, 4/78/1, folio 332. *The Times*, in its leading article of 13 February 1945, spoke of the 'remarkable harmony of policy' that had been attained 'over a wide and most controversial range'. Credit 'in a very high degree' it declared 'belonged to the Prime Minister, who has laboured unceasingly and insistently to overcome the obstacles delaying this particular meeting with full knowledge of its unexampled significance both for his own country and for the world'.

Richard Law and Orme Sargent told Raczynski that, in their view, the alternative to an agreement of this kind 'could only be that the London Government would remain in permanent exile from Poland and that the Lublin Government would establish its position more and more strongly inside Poland'. By the agreement which had been reached, they added, 'the Russians were pledged once again to the independence of Poland, but what was even more important was the association of ourselves and the United States with the Russians in that pledge. We, the Americans and ourselves, were now in the position, in which we had never been before, that the Russians formally recognised our interest in the political future of Poland and our responsibility for securing the independence of Poland.'

Raczynski was 'not greatly comforted by this', noted Richard Law. But he had ended the conversation by telling the Ambassador 'that whether his pessimistic predictions were fulfilled or not there was really no alternative to the suggested procedure'.[1]

Churchill spent February 13 on board the *Franconia*, off Sebastopol, working in bed all morning. 'We are taking another day's rest here,' he telegraphed to his wife, 'on this most comfortable ship with its *Queen Mary* Staff.'[2] That day, Churchill lunched on board the *Franconia* with Alexander, Eden and Cadogan. 'We rose from the luncheon table at 4.10 p.m.,' Cadogan wrote to his wife.[3]

Life on board ship had its drawbacks for Churchill. 'The PM complained about certain noises,' Captain Grattidge noted in his diary, 'so we have closed down the Card Room and everything where the slightest noise is detected.'[4]

That evening Churchill made a short speech to the ship's company, telling them over the ship's broadcast system what a 'great rest and pleasure' it had been for him to spend two days on board 'after the hard work we have had to do'.[5] That night he dined with Eden, Clark Kerr, Alexander and Ismay. 'Here at Sebastopol,' John Martin wrote home on February 13, 'we have the morning London newspapers at 6 p.m. the same day.'[6]

[1] 'Record of Conversation between Polish Ambassador and Minister of State, 12th February 1945', 'Top Secret', Foreign Office reference N 1648/6/G: Premier papers, 3/356/3, folio 35.
[2] 'Jason' No. 389, 9.13 a.m., 13 February 1945: Premier papers, 4/78/1, Part 2, folio 701.
[3] Letter of 13 February 1945: David Dilks (editor), *op. cit.*, pages 710–11.
[4] Captain Grattidge diary, 13 February 1945: Westminster College (Fulton, Missouri) archive.
[5] 'Prime Minister's Speech to the Crew, on board S.S. *Franconia*, 13th February, 1945': Roger Jones collection.
[6] Letter of 13 February 1945: Martin papers.

Churchill spent the night of February 13 on board the *Franconia*. The 'success' of Yalta, Lord Beaverbrook wrote to him on the following day, 'followed so swiftly on the heels of the Greek triumph, that you now appear to your countrymen to be the greatest statesman as well as the greatest warrior'. The Crimea Conference, Beaverbrook added, 'which gave rise to such anxieties before the event, is now the subject-matter for a fascinating chapter—if you will give us a bit of clover—perhaps the most engrossing chapter since the early days of the war'.[1]

---

[1] Letter of 14 February 1945: Premier papers, 4/77/1B, folio 359.

63

'The shadows of victory'

O N the night of 13 February 1945, while Churchill slept on board the *Franconia* off Sebastopol, British bombers struck at the city of Dresden, dropping 1,471 tons of high explosive bombs, and 1,175 tons of incendiaries. A few hours later American bombers carried out a daylight raid over the same city, dropping 689 tons of bombs on the still-burning ruins. The raid was a direct result of the agreement reached at Yalta by the British, United States and Soviet Chiefs of Staff, to make emergency use of Anglo-American air power in order to disrupt German reinforcements moving eastward to the Russian front.

On the morning of February 14, United States bombers also dropped 642 tons of bombs on Chemnitz and 725 tons on Magdeburg. That morning, Churchill received a telegram from the War Cabinet Office, reporting on eleven aspects of the previous day's military events. On the western front, he learned, six thousand German soldiers had been captured. In north Russia, a British convoy of twenty-eight ships had arrived without loss. In central Burma, a series of Japanese attacks had been beaten back. In central Europe, Budapest had been entered by Russian troops, and tens of thousands of German soldiers killed in the battle. In the air, and this was the tenth item in the list of eleven, Bomber Command had despatched a total of 1,252 aircraft over Germany, of which 805 had gone to Dresden, 368 to the Böhlen Synthetic oil factory, 71 to Magdeburg and 8 to the Misburg oil refinery. The telegram gave no estimate of casualties and no description of damage.

The eleventh and final item in this War Cabinet Office telegram concerned the continuing V2 rocket attacks on Britain. In the fifteen hours before daybreak on February 14, fourteen rockets had fallen in the London area, killing twelve civilians at Wood Green, twelve at Romford, twenty-eight at West Ham and three at Bexley.[1] The total

---

[1] 'Fleece' No. 433, 14 February 1945: Premier papers, 4/78/1, folios 323–4.

number of V bomb deaths in the week ending February 15, Churchill later learned, was 180, the highest since the rocket attacks had begun. [1]

That same day, the first report on the Dresden raid was prepared, based on an analysis of aerial photographs. Although it gave no casualty figures, the report noted the 'great material damage' to be seen in the photographs, adding that it was 'apparent, from the many blocks of buildings seen gutted, that fires have already destroyed part of the city'. [2] Interpretation of further photographs taken on February 15 was 'rendered difficult', the Chiefs of Staff Committe learned a week later, 'by the haze from fires still burning more than 36 hours after the last attack'. [3]

On February 14 Churchill left the *Franconia*, and, as Captain Grattidge noted, 'was cheered from all sides'. [4] From Sebastopol he drove north to Saki aerodrome, a journey of three hours. 'On the way,' he recalled five years later, 'we saw a colossal heap of loco-motives—a thousand or more—which had been pitched into a chasm by the Germans before they quitted. Amazing sight.' [5]

At the aerodrome, he inspected a Soviet guard of honour. 'I inspected them, using my usual method,' Churchill later recalled, 'of looking every single man in the eye as I walked along the line. This took a long time as there were at least two hundred—both ranks. This was much commented on favourably in the Russisan press. These were the flower of the Soviet armies. The political troops. Magnificent men, capable of doing anything.' [6]

Churchill then made a short speech of farewell, to 'the redeemed Crimea, cleansed by Russian valour from the foul taint of the Hun', to 'your great leader' Stalin, to the Russian forces, and to Russia's

---

[1] Chiefs of Staff Weekly Résumé No. 285, up to 7 a.m., on 15 February 1945: Cabinet papers, 80/47.

[2] 'Immediate Interpretation Report No. K 3742', 'Confidential', 15 February 1945: Air Ministry papers, 40/803. Five years later, Hilary St George Saunders, the historian of the Royal Air Force, in asking Churchill for recollections of Dresden, told him: 'In February 1945 there was a bomber attack on Dresden. Not less than 100,000 persons were killed. It was the most serious single blow against Germany by Bomber Command.' (Note of a telephone conversation, 11 May 1950: Churchill papers, 4/390A.) Churchill noted: 'I cannot recall anything about it. I thought the Americans did it. Air Chief Marshal Harris would be the person to contact.' (Note of 12 May 1950: Churchill papers, 4/390A.)

[3] Chiefs of Staff Committee, Weekly Résumé No. 286 for the week ending 7 a.m., 22 February 1945: Chief of Staff paper No. 30, of 1945 (also War Cabinet Paper No. 106 of 1945), 'Secret', 22 February 1945: Cabinet papers, 80/47.

[4] Captain Grattidge diary, 14 February 1945: Westminster College (Fulton, Missouri) archive.

[5] 'Notes on Volume VI', written in December 1950: Churchill papers, 4/362.

[6] 'Notes on Volume VI', written in December 1950: Churchill papers, 4/362.

'valiant people'. 'We pray,' he ended, 'that they may never again be subjected to the cruel ordeals from which they have emerged with so much glory.' [1]

From Saki, Churchill flew across the Black Sea and Turkey to Athens. During the flight he asked the pilot to circle the Aegean island of Skyros, on which Rupert Brooke was buried, and on whose death he had written an obituary in *The Times* thirty years before.

The flight from Saki to Athens had taken five hours. On arrival, at 4.30 local time, Churchill was met by Macmillan, Leeper, Scobie, and his son Randolph. He then drove into Athens, where a considerable and cheering crowd awaited him. The truce had held, the city was at peace, and the Archbishop was in control as Regent: the direct result of Churchill's visit to the city on Christmas Day.

Calling upon the Archbishop at his house, Churchill drove with him in an open car to the Old Palace. 'He had driven two or three hundred yards with the Regent,' he later told the War Cabinet, 'through streets where, a month ago, there had been firing and murder, and he had been enormously impressed by the enthusiasm shown.' The joy of these people, he added, 'who had been relieved from fear and war, was incredible'.

Churchill then addressed the vast crowd assembled in Constitution Square, 'the biggest he had ever seen'. [2]

The scene in Constitution Square, Churchill told Leeper two days later, 'was one that I shall never forget'. [3] Harold Macmillan estimated the crowd at about 40,000: 'an upturned sea of faces and a crowd of a size and character beyond anything I have seen'. [4] 'Let right prevail,' Churchill declared. 'Let party hatreds die. Let there be unity, let there be resolute comradeship.' [5] 'I have never seen anything like the size of the crowd or so much enthusiasm,' Churchill telegraphed to his wife. [6]

'The ovation was terrific,' noted Marian Holmes. 'A Greek band played "God Save the King" and the Greek National Anthem. The PM didn't recognise this latter and continued walking along until he

---

[1] Speech of 14 February 1945, Saki airfield: Churchill papers, 9/169.

[2] War Cabinet No. 22 of 1945, 6.30 p.m., 19 February 1945, Confidential Annex: Cabinet papers, 65/61.

[3] 'Jason No. 572' (from Cairo), 18 February 1945: Premier papers, 3/213/5, folio 149. 'Wonderful reception,' Churchill recalled in a series of brief notes written for his memoirs. 'I address forty or fifty thousand. The evening light beautiful. The Parthenon, I think, visible on the left. See speech, impromptu. There was no time to make anything up. Frantic cheers, but not a man or woman upon whom I looked had not lost a dear one in the last two months.' ('Notes on Volume VI', written in December 1950: Churchill papers, 4/362.)

[4] Harold Macmillan, diary, 14 February 1945: *War Diaries, op. cit.*, page 692.

[5] Speech of 14 February 1945: Churchill papers, 9/169.

[6] 'Jason' No. 558 (from Cairo), 16 February 1945: Premier papers, 4/78/1, Part 2, folio 440.

noticed that General Scobie had stopped and was standing smartly to attention.'[1]

From Constitution Square, Churchill drove, again through cheering crowds, to the British Embassy, where there was a dinner in his honour. 'I sat on Winston's right,' Macmillan noted. 'He was in excellent form, having enjoyed the whole thing enormously, and been much touched by the scene.'[2] After the dinner, the Archbishop called to see him. 'His Beatitude said to me that he hoped the ancient claims of Greece to Constantinople might be remembered,' Churchill told Lord Moran. 'I retorted: "Dismiss those dreams from your mind."'[3]

At 11.45 that night Churchill left the British Embassy for the airfield, where he slept in his aircraft.[4] In Churchill's honour, the Acropolis was floodlit, for the first time since the German occupation of Greece in April 1941.[5]

At 7.35 on the morning of February 15, Churchill flew from Athens to Alexandria, a flight of just over three hours. At the airport, amid the usual flight security, an armed escort was waiting. 'There was a slight break at the briefing,' one of the escort, Alan Wright, later recalled, 'where we were not told whom we were to escort, but we heard the officer in charge of the operation enquire if the brandy and cigars had arrived!'[6]

From the airport Churchill drove in a convoy of ten vehicles to the docks, 'where the party', as Alan Wright later recalled, 'embarked on small launches and vanished out to sea'.[7] Their destination was the USS *Quincy*, where Churchill, Sarah and Randolph lunched with Roosevelt. Five years later Churchill recalled Roosevelt's 'placid, frail, aspect'[8]

Alone for a while with Roosevelt and Hopkins, Churchill read out to the two men a proposal for the development of atom bomb research in Britain after the war. This proposal had been put forward by Lord

---

[1] Marian Holmes diary, 14 February 1945: Marian Walker Spicer papers.
[2] Macmillan diary, 14 February 1945: *War Diaries*, *op. cit.*, page 693.
[3] Moran diary, 14 February 1945: Moran, *op. cit.*, page 239.
[4] Private Office diary, 14 February 1945.
[5] Letter from Leslie Rowan to Bill Deakin, 19 March 1952.
[6] Alan W. Wright recollections: letter to the author, 9 June 1985.
[7] Alan W. Wright recollections: letter to the author, 21 May 1985. Of the ten vehicles, Churchill rode in the first, a Buick; Randolph in the second, a Rolls Royce; Lord Moran and Sarah Oliver in the third, a Ford; John Martin, Leslie Rowan, Peter Kinna, Marian Holmes and others in the remaining seven, all army vehicles. ('Operation Argonaut, Transport Arrangements from Aboukir', 'Top Secret', 13 February 1945: Alan W. Wright papers.)
[8] 'Notes on Volume VI', written by Churchill in December 1950: Churchill papers, 4/362.

Cherwell. After the war, Cherwell had written to Churchill three weeks earlier, 'we shall want to do work here on a scale commensurate with our resources; indeed, we should like, even earlier, to do more to pull our weight and shall wish to discuss with the Americans fairly soon what work we can best undertake to this end without impairing our contribution to the production in America for use in this war'.[1] The President 'made no objection of any kind', Churchill informed Anderson and Cherwell. He remarked, Churchill noted, that the possibilities of atomic power 'being used for commercial purposes had receded', and mentioned, on the military side, September 1945 as the date for 'the first important trials'.[2]

The President had decided to leave Egypt that same afternoon. Churchill later recalled 'My joke about UNRRA'—the United Nations Relief and Rehabilitation Agency—'RUNRRA' I called it. They all laughed. 'But I was complaining of not getting more help at this juncture.' Churchill added: 'This was the last time I saw Roosevelt. We parted affectionately. I felt he had a slender contact with life.'[3]

Having said goodbye to Roosevelt, Churchill then flew to Cairo, a flight of 45 minutes, where he drove to the Minister Resident's villa for dinner. Once known as the 'Casey' villa, it was now the home of Lord Moyne's successor, Sir Edward Grigg.

In Cairo on February 16, Churchill worked in bed during the morning and, as he had slight earache, did not get up for lunch. In the afternoon he received the Emperor of Ethiopia, who, he told the War Cabinet three days later, had made a 'far from favourable impression', and had shown 'no particular gratitude' for all that had been done by Britain to restore him to his throne.[4] 'Am now near the Pyramids receiving Potentates,' Churchill telegraphed to his wife.[5]

While Churchill was in Cairo, he received news of the first British discontent at the Yalta decisions on Poland. 'Congratulate Prime Minister and you on great success,' James Stuart telegraphed to Eden from the Chief Whip's Office on February 15, 'but for your guidance must warn you of Conservative anxiety over Poland increased by active lobbying by Poles now in progress here. Attlee and I have cabled Prime Minister advising against debate on motion of confidence which would inevitably be followed by some amendment.' Any 'open

[1] 'TA', 26 January 1945: Premier papers, 3/139/11A, folio 811.

[2] Prime Minister's Personal Minute, M(Arg) 16/5, 'Top Secret', 16 February 1945: Premier papers, 3/139/11A, folio 810.

[3] Notes dictated by Churchill while writing volume six of his war memoirs: Churchill papers, 4/361.

[4] War Cabinet No. 22 of 1945, 19 February 1945, Confidential Annex: Cabinet papers, 65/51.

[5] 'Jason' No. 558, 16 February 1945: Premier papers, 4/78/1, Part 2, folio 440.

display of disunity among Conservatives', Stuart added, would be 'deplorable'.[1]

On receiving Stuart's telegram, Eden discussed it in Cairo with Churchill. The 'fact is', Eden replied, 'that over Poland we have given nothing away and shall judge of whether new Government is satisfactory or not. We fought hard and got almost all I had stipulated for. We have nothing to fear either from anti-Russian and pro-Polish on right or pro-EAMites on left; and can confidently put our actions to a division if they force it on us.' Eden added: 'Indeed a debate with a division in such circumstances would, I believe, be more useful in showing where we stand than a debate with no division. What I should most dislike would be two days of debate with most speeches critical, left about Greece and right about Poland. The world would never understand that the country approve of our work as I am sure it does.'[2]

'I am not at all afraid of a Conservative amendment on the Polish question,' Churchill telegraphed to Attlee and James Stuart on February 16. 'It might even be helpful from the Russian point of view. In any case, I am confident Eden and I can convince the Conservative party.'[3] That night, Churchill and Randolph dined alone.[4]

In a telegram to Stalin on the morning of February 17, five days after leaving Yalta, Churchill expressed his thanks 'for all the hospitality and friendship extended to British Delegation to the Crimea Conference'. The British delegation, he said, 'were deeply impressed by the feats of organisation and of improvisation which enabled the conference to meet in such agreeable and convenient surroundings, and we all take back with us most happy recollections. To this I must add a personal expression of my own thanks and gratitude.' Churchill's telegram continued:

No previous meeting has shown so clearly the results which can be achieved when the three Heads of Government meet together with the firm intention to face difficulties and solve them. You yourself said that co-operation would be less easy when the unifying bond of fight against a common enemy had been removed. I am resolved, as I am sure the President and you are resolved, that the friendship and co-operation so firmly established shall not fade when victory has been won. I pray that you may long be spared to preside over destinies of your country, which has shown its full greatness under your leadership, and I send you my best wishes and heart-felt thanks.[5]

[1] Foreign Office Telegram No. 512 to Athens, 15 February 1945: Foreign Office papers, 945/20, folio 410.
[2] Telegram No. 365 from Cairo, 17 February 1945: Foreign Office papers, 954/20, folio 411.
[3] 'Jason No. 565', 16 February 1945: Cabinet papers, 120/182.
[4] Private Office diary, 16 February 1945.
[5] 'Jason' No. 573, Prime Minister's Personal Telegram, T.197/5, sent at 11.15 a.m., 17 February 1945: Premier papers, 3/51/10, folio 31.

On February 17 Churchill drove into the desert, to the Hotel du Lac on Lake Fayyum, where he met King Abdul Azziz Ibn Saud of Saudi Arabia. One of those present at Fayyum, Laurence Grafftey Smith, the newly appointed Minister to Saudi Arabia, later recalled that Churchill had told him, before the meeting, 'that he was *not* going to mention Palestine' to Ibn Saud.[1] During the conversation, however, as Churchill reported to the War Cabinet two days later, 'He (the Prime Minister) had pleaded the case of the Jews with His Majesty but without, he thought, making a great deal of impression, Ibn Saud quoting the Koran on the other side, but he had not failed to impress upon the King the importance which we attached to this question'.[2]

'As regards Palestine,' Sir Alexander Cadogan noted twelve days later, 'His Majesty explained his anxiety about the situation which was developing in that country; the Prime Minister expressed the hope that he might count on His Majesty's assistance to promote a definite and lasting settlement between the Jews and the Arabs.'[3]

The high point of Churchill's meeting with Ibn Saud was a magnificent banquet. Ten years later Churchill set down his recollections of this luncheon, before which he had been told that the King 'could not allow smoking or drinking alcohol in his presence'. Churchill added:

I was the host and I said that if it was his religion that made him say such things, my religion prescribed as an absolute sacred rite smoking cigars and drinking alcohol before, after, and if need be during, all meals and the intervals between them. Complete surrender. However he had his own cup bearer from Mecca and offered me a glass of water from their sacred well. Most delicious water I have ever drunk in my life. Remarkable figure Ibn Saud. Seventy (?) ladies in his harem and forty (?) living sons. Of the seventy ladies, four wives as prescribed by the Prophet, but one vacancy always kept. He was about seventy. All passed off very well. We were given something to drink. Did not know what it was. It seemed a very nasty cocktail. Found out afterwards it was an aphrodisiac.

Churchill also set down his recollections of the exchange of gifts with Ibn Saud, a story he was often to re-tell with wry amusement:

Tommy bought for me in Cairo for about £100, at the Government expense, a little case of very choice perfumes, which I presented. However Eden and I were given jewelled swords, diamond hilted, and then other

---

[1] Sir Laurence Grafftey Smith, recollections: letter to the author, 11 February 1985.
[2] War Cabinet No. 22 of 1945, 19 February 1945, Confidential Annex: Cabinet papers, 65/51.
[3] 'Meeting between the Prime Minister and King Abdul Azziz ibn Abdurrahman el Feisal Al Saud', note dated 23 February 1945: Churchill papers, 9/206.

presents, robes, etc., and I began to feel we were rather outclassed in gifts. So I said, 'What we bring are but tokens. His Majesty's Government have decided to present you with the finest motor car in the world. Every comfort for peace, and every security against hostile action.'

When I got back to Cairo, via the Pyramids, Sarah opened the enormous portmanteau which Ibn Saud had given for 'your womenfolk'. In this were splendid robes, and at the bottom about £3,000's worth of diamonds and pearls, with the prices attached to them. As the motor car, which I had given without any previous authority, would cost £5,000 or £6,000, Eden and I insisted to the Cabinet that we hand over all the jewels that could be sold, provided that the sale was kept secret. The Cabinet were very much inclined to let us keep them, but we were firm.[1]

Returning from the Fayyum Oasis to the 'Casey' villa, Churchill received King Farouk, to whom he expressed his 'regret' that so much of the population of Egypt 'might be without representation in the new Parliament'. In the account of this two days later, Churchill told the War Cabinet:

He had advised the King to concentrate on good works and, in particular, on improving the condition of the Fellaheen, for while Egypt at the moment was a country of great wealth, the differences between the level of living of the various social classes were more marked than ever before. The President, he understood, had spoken to King Farouk on much the same lines, and he trusted that some good might come out of it.[2]

Later that afternoon, Churchill received the President of Syria, Shukri Quwatli. 'We gave him a little plain, but polite, speaking,' Cadogan noted, 'which I hope will do him good.'[3] British foreign policy to Syria and the Lebanon, Churchill minuted to Eden on the following day, seemed to be 'we neither guarantee the States their independence nor the French their privileges, but we should like to see both objects achieved'.[4] 'The Prime Minister made it clear beyond all possibility of doubt,' Cadogan noted twelve days later, 'that we did not aim at replacing the French in Syria.'[5]

Following his talk with Shukri, however, Churchill 'did not think', as he told the War Cabinet two days later, 'that the French had a hope of maintaining their privileged position in Syria and the Lebanon'. Churchill added, of Syria and the Lebanon:

Those countries would, in their present mood, be ready to fight before

[1] Notes dictated by Churchill while writing volume six of his war memoirs, pre-1954: Churchill papers, 4/361.

[2] War Cabinet No. 22 of 1945, 19 February 1945, Confidential Annex: Cabinet papers, 65/51.

[3] Cadogan diary, 17 February 1945: David Dilks (editor), *op. cit.*, pages 714–15.

[4] Prime Minister's Personal Minute, M.133/5, 18 February 1945: Churchill papers, 20/209.

[5] 'Meeting between the Prime Minister and the Syrian President, his Excellency M. Shukri Quwatli', note dated 23 February 1945: Churchill papers, 9/206.

conceding it, and in dealing with the French they were greatly strengthened by the fact that they were recognized both by Russia and the United States. Our object, of course, was to maintain the independence of Syria and the Lebanon, and while we were quite ready to see the French enjoy a privileged position there, if they were able to persuade the Syria and the Lebanon to grant one, and while we were anxious, in the interests of maintaining general good relations to try to help both parties, we must be at pains to avoid burning our own fingers.[1]

'Most interesting interviews with one Emperor, two Kings and one President,' Churchill telegraphed to his wife on the afternoon of February 17.[2]

Churchill remained in Cairo throughout February 18. 'An idle day', Pierson Dixon noted in his diary,

... with a highly entertaining lunch at the Embassy, at which the PM was at his most amusing in a small company. At the end he declared himself most disinclined for work and said that what he would like to do would be to go down to the Mohammed Ali Club and gamble. He is always in good form at the Cairo Embassy, in which Miles and Jacqueline Killearn contrive to create a very ample and hospitable atmosphere. Some business was talked at lunch. . . .[3]

That night, at midnight, Churchill drove to Cairo West airport. The aircraft was not yet ready for take-off so 'we all sat in the saloon of the aircraft', as Elizabeth Layton wrote home, 'Master in his overcoat and cap (Air Commodore)'. Her account continued:

He and Sarah did most of the talking, and very amusing it was too. Sometimes he would burst into a small snatch of song, and go right through the song too. He was in a grand mood, rather sleepy and very funny and I must admit rather lovable. After a while he looked up and said 'Mr Kinna, do you remember one time when we were leaving Tripoli and I said to you that if we came down in the Desert you wouldn't be much good as a meal?' P.K said he did. So He said 'Well, the same applies now'. But his eye travelled round and he added—'However we shall be all right as we now have Miss Layton and she will keep us all going for 10 days.'[4]

Sarah Churchill later recalled how, whenever she and her father travelled together, he would sing to her, and with her, that favourite song of his from Gilbert and Sullivan, 'A wandering minstrel I, a thing of threads and patches. . . .'[5]

At two o'clock that morning the aircraft was ready, and Churchill airborne, for a non-stop flight of thirteen hours and forty minutes. He had been out of England for three weeks.

[1] War Cabinet No. 22 of 1945, 19 February 1945, Confidential Annex: Cabinet papers, 65/51.
[2] 'Jason' No. 577, 5.21 p.m., 17 February 1945: Premier papers, 4/78/1, Part 2, folio 421.
[3] Pierson Dixon diary, 18 February 1945: Piers Dixon, op. cit., page 152.
[4] Elizabeth Layton letter, 2 March 1945: Nel papers.
[5] Sarah Churchill, recollections: in conversation with the author, 25 May 1981.

Bad weather at Northolt forced Churchill to land at Lyneham, in Wiltshire, nearly four hours' drive from London. 'I was afraid that our sudden and unexpected arrival at Lyneham yesterday,' he wrote to Wing Commander McGinn on February 21, 'must have caused you considerable trouble and inconvenience. The necessary arrangements for our reception and transport to London were nevertheless made with great promptness and efficiency and I was touched by the kindness with which cups of tea and other refreshments were offered to us immediately we landed. Will you please express my warm thanks to all those who had a share in administering to our wants and in speeding us on our journey to London.'[1]

Churchill drove first to Reading, where, in the Manager's Office at the Station Hotel, Clementine Churchill found him 'imbibing whisky and soda', as she told her daughter Mary. 'He is marvellously well,' she added, 'much, much better than when he went off for this most trying and difficult of conferences.'[2]

Four hours after his aeroplane touched down at Lyneham airport, he reached 10 Downing Street, where the War Cabinet was waiting to greet him, to whom he at once gave his impressions.

Speaking of Stalin and Poland, Churchill told the War Cabinet that he was 'quite sure' that Stalin 'meant well to the world and to Poland', nor did he think that there would be 'any resentment on the part of Russia about the arrangements that had been made for free and fair elections in that country'.[3] Eden's view, which he had expressed to Colville on the drive from Lyneham to London, was 'that he thought the Tories had no right to complain about Poland. The PM had not sold the pass. On the contrary the Curzon Line was a boundary proposed as fair by H.M.G. after the last war; we had not committed ourselves to accepting any specific western frontier for Poland; and finally we had only undertaken to recognize a new Polish Government in Poland if and when we were satisfied with its composition.'[4]

This mood of confidence, even of optimism, over Poland's future, and faith in Stalin's promise for free elections, was to come under fierce attack in Parliament. But Cadogan, who had participated in the negotiations, shared the view of his Chief and his Prime Minister, writing to a former Foreign Secretary, Lord Halifax, on February 20: 'The PM and Anthony are well satisfied—if not more—and I think

---

[1] Letter of 21 February 1945: Churchill papers, 20/193.

[2] Letter of 21 February 1945: Mary Soames, *Clementine Churchill, op. cit.*, page 366.

[3] War Cabinet No. 22 of 1945, 6.30 p.m., 19 February 1945, Confidential Annex: Cabinet papers, 65/51.

[4] Colville diary, 19 February 1945: Colville papers.

they are right. Of course Poles in London, and extreme right-wing MPs, criticise and grumble. All I can say is that, in the circumstances, I think we did much better by Poland than I, at least, could have thought possible before we left.'[1] That same day Churchill accepted without amendment a draft message which had been 'composed' by Jock Colville, for despatch to Stalin.[2] It read, as written by Colville and telegraphed to Moscow in Churchill's name: 'The Red Army celebrates its 27th Anniversary amid triumphs which have won the unstinted applause of their Allies and have sealed the doom of German militarism. Future generations will acknowledge their debt to the Red Army as unreservedly as do we who have lived to witness these proud achievements. I ask you, the great leader of a great Army, to salute them from me today, on the threshold of final victory.'[3]

That night, Churchill and his wife dined with the King and Queen at Buckingham Palace.[4] On the following afternoon he received a visit from General Anders. 'Both rather lost their temper at first,' Cadogan noted, 'but calmed down later. It *may* have done some good, and they will meet again in a week. But it lasted 2½ hours.'[5] During the course of their discussion, Anders had made what Churchill called 'the very difficult point' that he and his troops had sworn allegiance to the Polish Government in London. What would happen if that Government declined to release him and his troops from their oath?

In reporting this conversation to the War Cabinet that same afternoon, Churchill said that he had thought it necessary to give Anders 'all proper reassurance'. In the 'immediate future', he said, there was 'an obvious place' for his troops in the occupation of Germany in the British zone. Churchill added 'that if in the last resort all else failed and Polish troops in Western Europe, or elements of them, felt that they could not return to Poland under the conditions, they should have the right to become citizens of the British Empire and to receive the treatment accorded to British soldiers who had rendered equal service'.

The War Cabinet approved Churchill's pledge. It also approved Churchill's suggestion that the 'present Polish Government in London' should be entitled to 'all the privileges which would be available to a Government recognized by us'. This also was accepted.

At this War Cabinet on February 21, Churchill looked back with

---

[1] Letter of 20 February 1945: David Dilks (editor), *op. cit.*, page 719.

[2] Colville diary, 23 February 1945: Colville papers.

[3] Prime Minister's Personal Telegram, T.199/5, 20 February 1945: Churchill papers, 20/211. The telegram, sent through the British Ambassador in Moscow, was delivered on 23 February 1945, the anniversary of the founding of the Red Army in 1918.

[4] Private Office diary, 20 February 1945.

[5] Cadogan diary, 21 February 1945: David Dilks (editor), *op. cit.*, page 719.

mixed feelings at the decisions which had been reached at Yalta just over a week before, telling his colleagues:

> . . . if the terms of the communiqué agreed with Premier Stalin were carried out in good faith, all would be well. If, on the hand, effective reality were not given to those undertakings, our engagement would be altered. It was not the intention of His Majesty's Government to cease to recognise the Polish Government in London as the legitimate Government of Poland until a Government had been set up in Poland on the basis contemplated in the communiqué to tide over the period until free elections could be held in that country.
>
> Once an election of that nature had been held, our responsibilities to Poland were of course discharged. There was no question of failing to honour engagements which we had entered into.
>
> His own feeling was that the Russians would honour the declaration that had been made, but the acid test of the sincerity in this matter in the immediate future would be whether any objection would be raised to M. Mikolajczyk returning to Poland. M. Mikolajczyk was in fact prepared to go back, but if his return was opposed by the Lublin Government, that would be an issue that we must contest.[1]

Acid tests, honour, reality, contests: these were to be the constant, conflicting refrains of the weeks ahead. Churchill was under no illusions as to the weakness of Britain's position in ensuring that the Yalta pledges on Poland were kept. On February 23 the Polish Provisional Government refused to invite to coalition talks in Moscow all but one of the five 'other elements of the Polish people' proposed by Roosevelt at Yalta on 6 February 1945 as possible future members of the Polish Government. Nor did Churchill disguise the weaknesses which had led to the Yalta agreement in the first place. When the Prime Minister of New Zealand, Peter Fraser, raised doubts as to the efficacy of the pledge to Poland, Churchill decided to write him a 'direct answer', rather than have, as he minuted to Lord Cranborne, 'some conventional pap fed out to him'.[2] Churchill told Cranborne: 'People ought to be stirred out of their complacency and given some sense of the forces moving in the world.'

The 'force' of Fraser's criticisms were 'indeed inescapable', Churchill wrote, 'and have throughout been very much in our minds'. But Britain was not, he pointed out, 'in a position to get exactly the solution we should wish', and he went on to explain:

[1] War Cabinet No. 23 of 1945, 21 February 1945, Confidential Annex: Cabinet papers, 65/61.

[2] Prime Minister's Personal Minute, M.145/5, 23 February 1945: Premier papers, 3/356/4, folio 120.

Great Britain and the British Commonwealth are very much weaker militarily than Soviet Russia, and have no means, short of another general war, of enforcing their point of view. Nor can we ignore the position of the United States. We cannot go further in helping Poland than the United States is willing or can be persuaded to go. We have therefore to do the best we can.

The New Zealand Prime Minister had been particularly concerned that moving Poland's frontiers so far to the West would displace many Germans and lead to trouble in the future. Churchill replied:

With regard to boundaries, we have opposed the idea of Poland gaining excessive territories in the West and in particular occupying territory up to the Western Neisse. There does not seem to be much difficulty in 'displacing' the Germans in the areas east of the Oder, as nearly all have already fled before the advance of the Russian Armies. We had not thought of the population transference in terms of more than about six million. As probably this number of Germans have been killed already or will be killed before the end of the war, the necessary living space should not be lacking.

'You speak of laying the seeds of future German hostility,' Churchill wrote, and he commented: 'we intend to destroy the German power in such a fashion and to such an extent that no counterstroke will be possible from her for many years to come'.

Fraser's final worry was about the Commission on Poland, which was to supervise the 'free elections' promised in the Yalta Protocol. 'I freely admit,' Churchill wrote, 'that the Polish proposals can only be judged by the way they work out,' and he ended his reply:

The proof of the pudding is in the eating. We are only committed on the basis of full execution in good faith of the terms of our published communiqué. Personally in spite of my anti-Communist convictions I have good hopes that Russia, or at any rate Stalin, desires to work in harmony with the Western Democracies. The alternative would be despair about the long future of the world. We shall not flinch however from our duty as we conceive it, to the last scrap of our life and strength.[1]

'It seems,' Churchill minuted to his Private Office on February 26, 'that the Ambassadors at Moscow have invited all the important Poles they are interested in thither, not to join the new Polish Government, but for consultation. This is all to the good. Let me have continually the latest telegrams from Moscow as to how the "new" government is going on.'[2]

[1] Prime Minister's Personal Telegram, T.204/5, No. 37 to New Zealand, 'Top Secret and Personal', 24 February 1945: Premier papers, 3/356/4, folios 114–15.
[2] Minute of 26 February 1945: Premier papers, 3/356/3, folio 24. The Ambassadors' Commission in Moscow consisted of two Ambassadors, Clark Kerr and Harriman, and Molotov.

Following Churchill's return from Yalta, there was a short respite from the usual intensity of meetings and dinners with large numbers of guests. On February 21 Churchill and his wife dined alone.[1] They dined alone again on February 22. After dinner that night Churchill worked alone until 1.45 in the morning.[2] On the following morning he worked in bed until noon, when he went to the House of Commons for an hour to address those Ministers not in the War Cabinet on the Yalta Conference. He then lunched alone with his wife, before going, in the early evening, to Chequers.

That evening there were only two dinner guests at Chequers, Sir Edward Bridges and Air Chief Marshal Sir Arthur Harris.[3] Jock Colville, who was the duty Private Secretary that weekend, recorded in his diary the conversation and moods of that Friday night:

The PM was rather depressed, thinking of the possibilities of Russia one day turning against us, saying that Chamberlain had trusted Hitler as he was now trusting Stalin (though he thought in different circumstances), but taking comfort, as far as Russia went, in the German proverb about the trees not growing up to the sky.

With regard to Spaatz, the American Air C-in-C, the PM said: 'He is a man of limited intelligence': Harris replied: 'You pay him too high a compliment.'

At dinner I asked the PM if he had read Beverley Nichols' *Verdict on India* which I had urged him to take to Yalta. He said he had, with great interest. He had been struck by the action of the Government of India in not removing a 'Quit India' sign which had been placed in a prominent place in Delhi and which Nicholls had seen on arrival and on departure a year later. He seemed half to admire and half to resent this attitude. The PM said the Hindus were a foul race 'protected by their mere pulullation from the doom that is their due' and he wished Bert Harris could send some of his surplus bombers to destroy them. As for Lord Wavell, and his Anthology of Poetry, he thought him 'mediocrity *in excelsis*'.

After dinner we saw an amusing film: Bob Hope in 'The Princess and the Pirate'; Then we sat in the Great Hall and listened to the Mikado played, much too slowly, on the gramophone. The PM said it brought back 'the Victorian era, eighty years which will rank in our island history with the Antonine age'. Now, however, 'the shadows of victory' were upon us. In 1940 the issue was clear and he could see distinctly what was to be done. But when Harris had finished his destruction of Germany 'What will lie between the white snows of Russia and the white cliffs of Dover?' Perhaps, however, the Russians would not want to sweep on to the Atlantic or something might stop them as the accident of Ghenghis Khan's death

[1] Private Office diary, 21 February 1945.
[2] Private Office diary, 22 February 1945.
[3] Private Office diary, 23 February 1945.

had stopped the horsed archers of the Mongols, who retired and never came back.

Bert Harris: 'You mean now they will come back?' WSC: 'Who can say? They may not want to. But there is an unspoken fear in many people's hearts.'

After this war, continued the PM, we should be weak, we should have no money and no strength and we should lie between the two great powers of the USA and the USSR. If he lived, we should concentrate on one thing: the air.

Harris replied that it would have to be rockets: 'The bomber is a passing phase and, like the battleship, it has nearly passed.' 'Then,' said the PM, 'you mean we must make our island into a volcano.'

Finale: The PM quoted 'Ye Mariners of England' at length. Bert Harris: 'That was written before the invention of the 12,000 lb bomb.'

The PM: 'Ye Doodle-Bugs of England . . .'.[1]

On Saturday February 24, President Beneš of Czechoslovakia lunched with Churchill at Chequers, together with his Foreign Secretary, Jan Masaryk. Churchill told them, as Jock Colville noted: 'a small lion was walking between a huge Russian bear and a great American elephant, but perhaps it would prove to be the lion who knew the way'.[2]

On February 27 Churchill presented the House of Commons with a survey of the results of the Yalta Conference. 'He makes an extremely good case,' Harold Nicolson noted in his diary, 'for arguing that Poland in her new frontiers will enjoy an independent and prosperous existence. But in his closing words before luncheon he rather destroys all this by saying that we will offer British citizenship to those Polish soldiers who are too frightened to return.'[3]

During his speech, Churchill asked the questions that had been troubling many Members of Parliament:

. . . even more important than the frontiers of Poland, within the limits now disclosed, is the freedom of Poland. The home of the Poles is settled. Are they to be masters in their own house? Are they to be free, as we in Britain and the United States or France are free? Are their sovereignty and their independence to be untrammelled, or are they to become a mere projection of the Soviet State, forced against their will by an armed minority to adopt a Communist or totalitarian system? I am putting the case in

[1] Colville diary, 23 February 1945: Colville papers.
[2] Colville diary, 24 February 1945: Colville papers.
[3] Harold Nicolson diary, 27 February 1945: Nigel Nicolson (editor), *op. cit.*, page 436.

all its bluntness. It is a touchstone far more sensitive and vital than the drawing of frontier lines. Where does Poland stand? Where do we all stand on this?

Churchill went on to tell the House of Commons: 'Most solemn declarations have been made by Marshal Stalin and the Soviet State', at Yalta, 'that the sovereign independence of Poland is to be maintained'. That decision 'is now joined in by both Great Britain and the United States'. There was also the World Organization which would in due course 'assume a measure of responsibility'. It was a question of Soviet good faith, and, as Churchill told the House of Commons:

The impression I brought back from the Crimea, and from all my other contacts, is that Marshal Stalin and the Soviet leaders wish to live in honourable friendship and equality with the Western democracies. I feel also that their word is their bond. I know of no Government which stands to its obligations, even in its own despite, more solidly than the Russian Soviet Government. I decline absolutely to embark here on a discussion about Russian good faith. It is quite evident that these matters touch the whole future of the world. Sombre indeed would be the fortunes of mankind if some awful schism arose between the Western democracies and the Russian Soviet Union.

In 1940 and 1941 the actions Britain had had to take 'seemed plain and simple. If a man is coming across the sea to kill you, you do everything in your power to make sure he dies before finishing his journey. This may be difficult, it may be painful, but at least it is simple.' Four years had passed:

We are now entering a world of imponderables, and at every stage occasions for self-questioning arise. It is a mistake to look too far ahead. Only one link in the chain of destiny can be handled at a time.

I trust the House will feel that hope has been powerfully strengthened by our meeting in the Crimea. The ties that bind the three Great Powers together and their mutual comprehension of each other have grown. The United States has entered deeply and constructively into the life and salvation of Europe. We have all three set our hands to far-reaching engagements at once practical and solemn.

'United,' Churchill declared, 'we have the unchallengeable power to lead the world to prosperity, freedom and happiness. The Great Powers must seek to serve and not to rule.'[1]

Churchill had spoken for nearly two hours, with a short break in the middle of his speech. One phrase was not in his speech. He had

[1] *Hansard*, 27 February 1945, columns 1267–95.

intended to say: 'Soviet Russia seeks not only peace, but peace with honour.' Against this sentence in the draft, Jock Colville had noted: '?Omit. Echo of Munich,' and it had been omitted.[1] Churchill had also prepared a peroration which he likewise omitted. It read:

No one can guarantee the future of the world. There are some who fear it will tear itself to pieces and that an awful lapse in human history may occur. I do not believe it. There must be hope. The alternative is despair, which is madness. The British race has never yielded to counsels of despair.[2]

That evening, in the Smoking Room, he joined Harold Nicolson and Lord de la Warr for a drink. 'He is really very sensible,' Nicolson noted in his diary. 'He says he does not see what else we could possibly do.' Not only were the Russians 'very powerful', Churchill said, 'but they are on the spot; even the massed majesty of the British Empire would not avail to turn them off that spot'. Nicolson's account continued:

... It seemed to him a mistake to assume that the Russians are going to behave badly. Ever since he had been in close relations with Stalin, the latter had kept his word with the utmost loyalty. During the three weeks of the Greek crisis, for instance, a single article in *Pravda* would have tipped the whole balance, but Stalin kept an obstinate silence which was of immense value to us. At the mention of Greece his whole face lit up. He put his hand on my arm. 'I have had great moments in my life,' he said, 'but never such a moment as when faced with that half-million crowd in Constitution Square. You will understand that.'

I ask him whether he thinks it would be indiscreet of me to say that the test of the Crimean resolution will be whether or not Mikolajczyk and Romer are invited to Moscow. He thinks for a moment and then says, 'Yes, that would be a good thing. I could not say that, but you can.' As he goes, he says with his funny schoolboy grin, 'I hope in your speech tomorrow you will not attack me very bitterly. I count you among my firmest friends.'

During the ensuing debate, one of the fiercest critics of the 'abandonment' of Poland was Lord Dunglass who, six years earlier as Neville Chamberlain's Private Secretary, had not only flown to Munich, but been one of the staunchest supporters of the Munich Agreement. 'Winston is as amused as I am,' Nicolson added, 'that the warmongers of the Munich period have now become the appeasers, while the appeasers have become the warmongers.'[3] 'The PM is trying to persuade himself that all is well,' Colville noted in his diary on the

[1] Draft speech of 27 February 1945, and Colville note: Churchill papers, 9/206.
[2] Draft speech of 27 February 1945: Churchill papers, 9/206.
[3] Harold Nicolson, 27 February 1945: Nigel Nicolson (editor), *op. cit.*, page 437.

day of the Yalta debate, 'but in his heart I think he is worried about Poland and not convinced of the strength of our moral position.'[1]

In a speech noted for its passion by all who heard it, one of the leading figures of the Labour Party, Arthur Greenwood, declared: 'The Poles have been allowed to say very little about how their coat is to be cut,' and he added: 'I really do feel that the Poles—all the Poles—might have been consulted in the matter.' The decision on their future 'ought not to have been taken, so to speak, behind their back'.[2]

The Yalta debate in the House of Commons continued during February 28, with twenty-one Conservatives moving an amendment regretting the decision to transfer 'the territory of an Ally'—eastern Poland—'to another Power', and regretting also 'the failure to ensure to those nations which have been liberated from German oppression the full right to choose their own Government free from the influence of any other power'.[3]

'We shall no doubt defeat the amendment by an overwhelming majority,' Churchill telegraphed to Roosevelt during the morning. 'Nevertheless there is a good deal of uneasiness in both Parties that we are letting the Poles down etc.' In these circumstances, Churchill added, it was of 'the utmost importance that as many representative Poles as possible should be invited as soon as possible to the consultations in Moscow and, above all, that Mikolajczyk who is the leading test case should be invited'. The London Polish Government, Churchill warned Roosevelt, 'is of course trying to prevent any Poles leaving here for Moscow or Poland, and is playing for a breakdown'.

Churchill also told Roosevelt that there were 'many stories put about of wholesale deportations by the Russians and of liquidations by the Lublin Poles of elements they do not like, and I have no means of verifying or contradicting these assertions'.[4]

The London Poles had decided to challenge the Yalta agreement, and as a gesture of independence had appointed General Anders to be Commander-in-Chief of the Polish forces. The British Government had not been consulted on this. As the House of Commons debate continued, Churchill telegraphed to Clark Kerr in Moscow:

The London Polish Government wish to prevent all Poles from going to Poland from here, and are putting forth the utmost pressure they can assert. They hope to break down the Crimea policy and bring about if possible a

---

[1] Colville diary, 28 February 1945: Colville papers.

[2] *Hansard*, 27 February 1945, columns 1299–1300.

[3] *Hansard*, 28 February 1945, columns 1421–1520.

[4] Prime Minister's Personal Telegram, T.227/5, Prime Minister to President, No. 901, 'Personal and Top Secret', 28 February 1945: Premier papers, 3/356/9, folios 842–3.

rift between the Soviets and the Western Democracies. They do this regardless of any misfortunes it may bring on their country and with the hopes that they may catch fish from troubled waters.

At the same time, Bierut and Co. have an obvious interest in keeping the whole power in their hands. In fact both extreme sets of Poles will behave as badly as possible. The only way to defeat these most dangerous manoeuvres is to insist upon invitations being sent to the widest circle at the earliest moment. Mikolajczyk is of course a decisive figure. If he were not enabled to come, a very serious position would be created. There never has been any question of Anders going, and I have regarded his appointment as Com-mander-in-Chief as so offensive that I have cancelled an interview which I had promised to accord him.

Churchill urged Clark Kerr to obtain Molotov's agreement to send at once 'three or four trustworthy men' as observers into Poland, in order that Britain should have 'direct sources of information' on what was happening there. As he explained to the Ambassador:

The London Poles have been spreading it about among Members of Par-liament that there have been wholesale deportations and liquidations in Poland. We have no means of denying or disproving this. You should draw Molotov's attention to the course of the Debate yesterday, and particularly to the fact of Greenwood's speech, which was extremely hostile to the Crimea policy about Poland.

We are now discussing an Amendment by twenty-one Tory Members which is most condemnatory. I have no doubt that these moves will be defeated by a very large majority. It would, however, be a mistake to suppose there is not a good deal of uneasiness in the House which will not find expression in the Lobby on a Vote of Confidence.[1]

On February 27, Molotov had agreed to allow Britain and the United States to send diplomatic observers to Poland. But at the same time, he told Clark Kerr and Harriman, who had made the request jointly, that, if only for 'reasons of practical convenience', the visit of the observers 'would have to be cleared' with the Polish Provisional Government.[2]

That night news began to reach London from Roumania 'shewing', as Colville noted in his diary, 'that the Russians are intimidating the King and Government and setting about the establishment of a communist minority government with all the technique familiar to students of the Comintern'.

Churchill was dining with the King at Buckingham Palace when these first 'sinister telegrams', as Colville described them, reached 10

[1] Prime Minister's Personal Telegram, T.236/5, 'Personal and Top Secret', 28 February 1945: Premier papers, 3/356/9, folios 844–6.
[2] Moscow telegram No. 643, 2 March 1945: Churchill papers, 20/212.

Downing Street and the Foreign Office. Eden, telephoning Downing Street, told Colville that 'he viewed these events with great concern because Vyshinski, who was their executor, had come fresh from the understanding and undertakings of Yalta'. When Churchill returned from the Palace, Colville 'spoke to him of the position', but Churchill replied that 'he feared he could do nothing. Russia had let us go our way in Greece; she would insist on imposing her will in Roumania and Bulgaria. But as regards Poland we would have our say.'

That night, as he went to bed shortly after two o'clock, Churchill said to Colville: 'I have not the slightest intention of being cheated over Poland, not even if we go to the verge of war with Russia.'[1]

On March 1 Churchill was in the House of Commons to vote on the Yalta amendment, which was defeated by 396 votes to 25. Churchill was 'overjoyed', Harold Nicolson wrote to his wife, 'by the vote tonight, and behaved like a schoolboy. Anthony was quite different. He said to me, "My God, what a mess Europe is in! What a mess!"'[2]

---

[1] Colville diary, 28 February 1945: Colville papers.

[2] Nicolson letter, 1 March 1945: Nigel Nicolson (editor), *op. cit.*, page 438. That night, in protest against the Polish decisions, a Conservative Junior Minister, George Strauss, Parliamentary Secretary at the Ministry of Town and Country Planning, resigned from the Government.

64

Yalta Betrayed

O N the Western Front, having crossed the Siegfried Line, the Allies were advancing towards the Rhine. In the northern sector, the Siegfried Line and Aachen were already in Allied hands; Cologne, and the Rhine itself the prizes that lay in front of them. On 2 March 1945, determined to cross the Siegfried Line himself, and to go as far forward as possible, Churchill flew to Brussels with Brooke and Ismay. Then, after lunch with his daughter Mary, he flew on to Eindhoven, to dine with Montgomery, before going to Eisenhower's train nearby, at Geldrop, for the night. Once more, he was in the war zone.

On the morning of March 3, accompanied by Brooke and Montgomery, Churchill visited the United States Ninth Army, lunching with General Simpson at Jülich, and driving on to the Siegfried Line. As Brooke later recalled:

On arrival there the column of some twenty to thirty cars halted, we processed solemnly out and lined up along the Line. As the photographers had all rushed up to secure good vantage points, he turned to them and said, 'This is one of the operations connected with this great war which must not be reproduced graphically.' To give them credit they obeyed their orders and, in doing so, missed a chance of publishing the greatest photographic catch of the war! I shall never forget the childish grin of intense satisfaction that spread all over his face as he looked down at the critical moment.[1]

From the Siegfried Line, Churchill drove into Aachen, before returning to Eisenhower's train at Geldrop to dine with Montgomery, and with the Second Army Commander, General Dempsey, and his Corps Commanders, General Ritchie and General Barker.[2]

[1] Brooke recollections: Bryant, *op. cit.*, volume 2, page 423.
[2] Because Churchill was suffering from ear-ache, an otologist was summoned to the train: Lieutenant-Colonel John Stewart, Adviser in Laryngology to the British Liberation Army. 'He had a minor complaint,' Stewart later recalled, 'which necessitated my seeing him morning and evening for treatment. He took a great interest in his progress and constantly asked me if I had established a "bridgehead yet".' (John Stewart, 'War Diary', typescript, pages 184–5.)

Churchill continued his tour on March 4, visiting the First Canadian Army area and lunching with General Crerar. Two days later Churchill told the War Cabinet that he was 'obviously concerned at the failure to present adequately to the public the extent of the contribution made by British arms to the victories on the Western Front'. In spite of Montgomery's undertaking 'to make the facts known to war correspondents at the front, it was still not generally recognized that the major part of General Crerar's Army consisted of British troops'. During his visit to France, Churchill told the War Cabinet, he had also raised with Montgomery and Eisenhower the related question of disclosing the names of units engaged in the fighting. 'Neither had seen any objection to British divisions and regiments being named when once they had become engaged with the enemy.' If a general impression was created, Churchill warned, 'that British units were doing very little fighting (an impression quite contrary to the real state of affairs), this might well have serious results on the British contribution to the peace settlement'.

Two-thirds of Crerar's troops, explained Sir James Grigg, were British: this had already been stated in Parliament.[1]

After lunch with Crerar, Churchill drove to Goch, where an eight-inch gun had just been loaded and made ready to fire. 'Surrounded by Press photographers,' Brooke noted, 'he pulled the lanyard and let her off.' Churchill then drove back to the train, where he dined with Montgomery and General de Guingand. 'Winston fretting,' Brooke noted, 'because he was not allowed nearer the front, and trying to make plans to come back for the operations connected with the crossing of the Rhine!'[2]

Shortly after midnight the train left Geldrop for Rheims. During the morning, advance elements of the United States First Army entered Cologne. Churchill, having reached Rheims at ten in the morning, spent the day at Eisenhower's headquarters, where he followed the latest advances in Eisenhower's map room. During his visit to the British Liberation Army, and to the United States forces, he had dictated three minutes to Eden on Poland and eastern Europe. The first two concerned a telegram from the British Military Mission in Roumania, describing a protest by the Mission at Soviet activities in the capital, where a Soviet-sponsored Government had been established.[3] The Roumanians and Bulgarians, Churchill urged on March 4, 'have been our foes and we cannot run the the same risk for them as we have done for Greece and Poland'. He was 'much concerned'

---

[1] War Cabinet No. 26 of 1945, 6 March 1945: Cabinet papers, 65/49.
[2] Brooke diary, 4 March 1945: Bryant, *op. cit.*, volume 2, page 424.
[3] Military Mission Telegram, RAC 525/165. This new Roumanian Government was headed

lest Stalin should reproach Britain 'for breaking our understanding with him about Roumania at the same time as the strife about Poland comes to a head. We must keep our own word however painful if we are to use that argument to him with effect.' 'I am anxious to go full out about Poland,' Churchill added, 'and this requires concentration at the expense of other matters.' [1]

In the first of his two minutes on March 5, Churchill informed Eden, for immediate action:

We really have no justification for intervening in this extraordinarily vigorous manner for our late Roumanian enemies, thus compromising our position in Poland and jarring upon Russian acquiescence in our long fight in Athens. If we go on like this, we shall be told, not without reason, that we have broken our faith about Roumania after taking advantage of our position in Greece, and this will compromise the stand we have taken at Yalta over Poland.

I consider strict instructions should be sent to all our representatives in Roumania not to develop an anti-Russian political front there. This they are doing with untimely energy without realising what is at stake in other fields. [2]

The chief of these 'other fields' was Poland. That same day, in his third minute to Eden, in connection with his pledge in the House of Commons that any Polish soldiers who wished to remain in Britain could do so, Churchill declared:

I have every intention of working to the utmost for a Poland free to manage its own affairs and to which Polish soldiers in our service will be glad to return. If this fails we must provide for the Poles in arms inside the British Empire, which can easily accommodate such brave and serviceable men. In the first instance no doubt they would be employed upon garrisoning Germany, with proportionate relief of our military burden.

However, there may always be a certain number of individual Poles who will not wish to go back to Poland because of their inveterate hostility to Russia. For these, who will not be many if we are successful, the alternative of British citizenship must be open, even if they are unreasonable in their views about the kind of life open to them in Poland. [3]

That night Churchill dined at Eisenhower's headquarters, with Eisenhower, Bedell Smith, Spaatz, Brooke and Ismay, before sleeping

---

by Paul Groza (born in 1884), a founder member, in 1933, of the most radical of Roumania's peasant movements, the Ploughmen's Front. In 1943 the Ploughmen's Front had been recognised unofficially by the Soviet Union as the chief rural Communist group in Roumania. Under Soviet pressure, King Michael appointed Groza Prime Minister in March 1945. In 1952 he became Head of State. He died in 1958.

[1] Prime Minister's Personal Minute, M.163/5, 4 March 1945: Foreign Office papers, 954/23, folio 387.

[2] Prime Minister's Personal Minute, M.164/5, 'Urgent', 5 March 1945: Foreign Office papers, 954/23, folio 388.

[3] Prime Minister's Personal Minute, M.172/5, 5 March 1945: Churchill papers, 20/209.

in the train for the fourth consecutive night. On the following morning, March 6, he flew back to Britain. 'We are now labouring,' he wrote to a Conservative MP, Sir Irving Albery, 'to make sure that the Yalta Agreement about Poland and free elections is carried out in the spirit as well as in the letter.'[1]

Evidence that Stalin intended to follow neither the spirit nor the letter of the Yalta agreement reached London that same day. At the War Cabinet that evening, Eden reported 'a very unsatisfactory discussion' of three hours between Molotov, Clark Kerr and Harriman, during which it became clear that Molotov 'was going to make a determined effort' to exclude Mikolajczyk from the reorganized Government. Only Moscow's nominees were to be in the Government. Clark Kerr and Harriman had offered Molotov 'the whole of M. Bierut's list of nominees in exchange for our five', but Molotov 'had not been prepared to accept this'.

Churchill was angered by this news. The Government, he said, 'had been fully entitled to take the line we had in the debate in the Crimea Conference, since we were bound to assume the good faith of an Ally in the execution of an agreement so recently signed'. If, however, 'it became clear that the Russians were not going to carry out the conditions to which we had agreed', Churchill told his colleagues, 'it would be necessary to give the full story to Parliament. We could not run any risk of a suggestion that Parliament, in which feeling on this matter was strong in all parties, had been deceived.' Britain 'must make it clear to the Russians that we could not agree to these proposals. We were, however, entitled to expect the full support of the USA in doing so, and must carry them with us; for we could do no more to help the Poles than the United States would help us to.' If Stalin was 'in fact behind these proposals, he might modify his attitude if, after consultation with the US Government, we warned him that, if they were pressed, we should have to explain the position to Parliament and admit with great regret that the Yalta Agreement had failed'.[2]

The excitement of the now almost daily military successes against Germany in the west was soured and even overshadowed by the realisation of Russia's perfidy in the east. On March 7 the Foreign Office telegraphed to Clark Kerr in Moscow the summary of a Polish Government report giving details of 'mass arrests' in the Cracow area, 'including 21 University professors as well as priests, intellectuals etc.'. Two train loads 'of 2,000 persons each', the report added, had been sent from Poland 'to labour camps at Voroshilovgrad'. As many as

[1] Letter of 6 March 1945: Churchill papers, 20/193.
[2] War Cabinet No. 26 of 1945, 6 March 1945, Confidential Annex: Cabinet papers, 65/51.

6,000 former Home Army officers were in a camp near Lublin directed by Soviet officials. 'Prisoners are badly treated,' the telegram asserted, 'and many are removed every few days to an unknown destination.' Home Army men arrested in Bialystok 'are starved, beaten and tortured, and accused of spying for Great Britain and for Polish Government in London as well as of collaboration with the Germans. There are many deaths.'[1] Reading this, Churchill minuted to Eden: 'Surely this should be repeated to Washington & President.'[2]

On the west bank of the Rhine, the Allied forces were destroying what was left of German military resistance. On March 7 Cologne was abandoned by its defenders, while, to the south, units of the United States First Army crossed the Rhine over the railway bridge at Remagen. That day, Churchill was shown a telegram from Roumania, 'reporting that the new Russian-sponsored Roumanian Government may forcibly remove Radescu, the late Prime Minister, from the sanctuary which has been given him by the British Military mission'. This, in spite of his earlier reluctance to become involved in Roumania's troubles, was too much for Churchill: it 'inflamed the PM who saw that our honour was at stake', noted Colville. Later, Churchill spoke to Eden on the telephone. 'The PM and Eden both fear that our willingness to trust our Russian ally may have been vain and they look with despondency to the future,' Colville recorded. 'The PM is prepared to put the issue to the House and the Country with confidence in their support but Eden, though nauseated, still hopes the Russians will not face an open breach with ourselves and the Americans.'[3]

The realization that Stalin had no intention of abiding by the Yalta agreement on Poland was deeply upsetting to Churchill, as were the Soviet moves in Roumania. At work that night, Marian Holmes found him 'exceptionally tired and inclined to shout'. It was not until three in the morning that the work was done. Just before Churchill went to bed he told Jock Colville 'he hoped Miss Holmes had forgiven him "for being in such a bad temper"'.[4]

At the War Cabinet on the following evening, Churchill reported the intention of the British Military and Air representatives in Roumania to open fire if it became necessary 'in the last resort', to prevent General Radescu being taken from the Military Mission. Churchill supported this proposal. If the Roumanian authorities in

---

[1] Foreign Office Telegram No. 1085 to Moscow, 7 March 1945: Premier papers, 3/356/9, folio 822.
[2] Minute of 8 March 1945: Premier papers, 3/356/9, folio 822.
[3] Colville diary, 7 March 1945: Colville papers.
[4] Marian Holmes diary, 7 March 1945: Marian Walker Spicer papers.

Bucharest 'were warned in advance', he said, 'that we were prepared to take this course in the last resort, he thought it unlikely that the attempt would be made to remove M. Radescu by force'.

The War Cabinet supported Churchill. 'The British Military Mission should open fire if necessary, to guard the fugitive.'[1]

Churchill, distressed by events in Roumania and Poland, appealed on March 8 to Roosevelt to help him out of his predicament. 'I feel sure that you will be as distressed as I am by recent events in Roumania,' Churchill's telegram began. The Russians had succeeded in establishing the rule of a Communist minority 'by force and mis-representation'. Britain had been 'hampered' in its protest against these developments, 'by the fact that, in order to have the freedom to save Greece', Eden and he, at Moscow in October, had 'recognized that Russia should have a largely predominant voice' in Roumania and Bulgaria, while Britain 'took the lead' in Greece. 'Stalin adhered very strictly to this understanding during the thirty days' fighting against the Communists and ELAS in the city of Athens,' Churchill explained to Roosevelt, 'in spite of the fact that all this was most disagreeable to him and those around him.'

In Roumania and Bulgaria, Stalin was pursuing 'the opposite course' to that pursued by the British in Greece, when the British 'supreme ultimate objective' was a constitution and government 'erected on the indisputable will' of the people. The recent events in Roumania were 'absolutely contrary to all democratic ideas'. Churchill added: 'Since the October Anglo-Russian conversations in Moscow, Stalin has subscribed on paper to the principles of Yalta which are certainly being trampled down in Roumania. Nevertheless I am most anxious not to press this view to such an extent that Stalin will say "I did not interfere with your action in Greece, why do you not give me the same latitude in Roumania?" This again would lead to comparisons between the aims of his action and those of ours. On this neither side would convince the other.'

Much as Churchill wished to protest against Soviet action in Roumania, he still felt that such a protest would 'prejudice our prospects of reaching a Polish settlement'. He felt, nevertheless, that Stalin 'should be informed of our distress at the developments which led to the setting up by force of a government in Roumania of a Communist minority, since this conflicts with the conclusions of the Declaration on Liberated Europe upon which we were agreed at the Crimea Conference. More especially I am afraid that the advent of this Communist Government may lead to an indiscriminate purge of anti-Communist

---

[1] War Cabinet No. 27 of 1945, 6.30 p.m., 8 March 1945, Confidential Annex: Churchill papers, 65/51.

Roumanians, who will be accused of Fascism much on the lines of what has been happening in Bulgaria.'

Churchill wanted Roosevelt to send a message to Stalin, asking the Soviet leader 'to see to it' that the new Government in Roumania 'does not immediately start a purge of all political elements which are in opposition to their views on the ground that they have been encouraged to do so by the Yalta Declaration'. If Roosevelt would agree to send such a message, Churchill would also send one to Stalin 'supporting it'.

The news from Poland, Churchill continued, was 'also most disappointing', and he went on to tell Roosevelt:

I must let you know that the Government majorities here bear no relation to the strong under-current of opinion among all parties and classes and in our own hearts against a Soviet domination of Poland. Labour men are as keen as Conservatives, and Socialists as keen as Catholics. I have based myself in Parliament on the assumption that the words of the Yalta Declaration will be carried out in the letter and the spirit. Once it is seen that we have been deceived and that the well-known Communist technique is being applied behind closed doors in Poland, either directly by the Russians or through their Lublin puppets, a very grave situation in British public opinion will be reached.

How would the matter go in the United States? I cannot think that you personally or they would be indifferent. Thus just at the time when everything militarily is going so well in Europe and when the Japanese policy is also satisfactorily arranged, there would come an open rift between us and Russia not at all confined, in this country at any rate, to Government opinion, but running deep down through the masses of the people.

Churchill then explained to Roosevelt that, after 'a fairly promising start', including the suggestion on February 27 that Britain and the United States could now send observers into Poland, Molotov was now 'refusing to accept' any interpretation of the Yalta proposals on Poland 'except his own extremely rigid and narrow one'. He was attempting, Churchill wrote, to bar 'practically all our candidates' from the consultations for the formation of a Provisional Government, 'and is taking the line that he must base himself on the views of Bierut and his gang and has withdrawn his offer that we should send observers to Poland'. Churchill continued:

In other words, he clearly wants to make a farce of consultations with the 'non-Lublin' Poles—which means that the new Government in Poland would be merely the present one dressed up to look more respectable to the ignorant and also wants to prevent us from seeing the liquidations and deportations that are going on and all the rest of the game of setting up a totalitarian regime before elections are held and even before a new Government is set up. As to the upshot of all this, if we do not get things right now, it will soon be seen by the world that you and I by putting our signatures to the Crimea settlement have under-written a fraudulent prospectus.

Churchill was 'pledged' to Parliament, he told Roosevelt, to tell them if the 'spirit of the Yalta declaration' could not be carried out in 'the business of setting up a new Polish Government etc.' For this reason, his own personal message to Stalin would have to make clear 'what are the essential things we must have in this business' if he was to avoid telling Parliament 'that we have failed', and he ended his telegram:

I think you will agree with me that far more than the case of Poland is involved. I feel that this is the test case between us and the Russians of the meaning which is to be attached to such terms as democracy, sovereignty, independence, representative Government and free and unfettered elections. I therefore propose to send to Stalin a message on the lines set out below.

'I am sorry to say,' Churchill's message to Stalin began, 'that the discussions in the Moscow Commission on Poland show that M. Molotov has quite a different view from us as to how the Crimea decision on Poland should be put into effect.' Churchill added: 'As you know, nobody here believes that the present Warsaw administration is really representative and criticism of the decision in Parliament took the line that the discussion in Moscow would not result in a really representative government being set up and that, if this was so, all hope of free elections disappeared.'

Churchill also put directly to Stalin the question of the deportations. 'All parties,' he explained, 'were also exercised about the reports that deportations, liquidations and other oppressive measures were being put into practice on a wide scale by the Warsaw administration against those likely to disagree with them.'

Churchill then set out for Stalin the five points at issue, pointing out, first, that there was now no 'prior consultation' on the Moscow Commission on Poland as promised at Yalta.[1] Secondly, Churchill noted, Molotov had raised objections to inviting Mikolajczyk to the Moscow discussions although his presence there 'would certainly be vital'. Thirdly, the Moscow Commission should preside over the Polish discussions 'in an impartial arbitral capacity'. Fourth, the Commission should ensure that no further legal or administrative action was allowed 'of a fundamental character affecting social, constitutional, economic or political conditions in Poland'. Fifth, Churchill told Stalin, the Soviet Government should make arrangements to enable

[1] The three-man Moscow Commission, consisting of Molotov, Clark Kerr and Harriman, had been meeting in Moscow since 23 February 1945.

British and American observers 'to visit Poland and report upon conditions there', arrangements which Molotov himself had 'spontaneously' offered to make earlier in the Commission discussion.

'We must not let Poland become a source of disagreement and misunderstanding between our two peoples,' Churchill ended.[1]

On March 9 this circle of acrimony was broken momentarily when Churchill received, three weeks after he had left Yalta, the Russian products which Stalin had sent to the *Franconia* for him. These included 7 one-kilo tins of caviar, 72 bottles of Russian champagne, 18 bottles of vodka, 9 bottles of liqueur, a 14 pound box of butter, 4 cases of oranges and a case of lemons. 'Please accept my warmest thanks,' Churchill telegraphed that day, 'for this most generous gift which I shall enjoy almost as much as I value the kind thought which prompted you to send it.'[2]

On the day after sending this telegram to Stalin, Churchill sent Roosevelt the information he had seen, prepared by the Polish Government in London, and already sent to Clark Kerr in Moscow, listing the twenty Polish provinces and districts in which members of the Home Army had been arrested, attacked and even murdered on the authority of the Lublin Committee, in many cases immediately after they had fought the Germans in the same regions. 'Of course we cannot guarantee any of this information,' the telegram continued, at Eden's suggestion, 'which comes', Eden's addition stated, 'from the Polish Government agents in Poland who are not likely to minimize these things nor do we know what opportunities they have of checking their information, as they must be living underground'.[3] 'All this,' the telegram ended, 'emphasizes the need for sending our observers into the country.'[4]

On March 8 the State Department had instructed Averell Harriman to 'request the rival groups' in Poland 'to adopt a political truce'. As soon as these instructions were shown to Lord Halifax on March 9, Halifax telegraphed them from Washington to London. Churchill immediately saw danger in the proposal for a political truce. 'The Lublin Poles will assert that complete and perfect unity exists among all parties,' he minuted at once to Eden, 'except with traitors

---

[1] Draft telegram to Stalin, enclosed in Prime Minister to President No. 905, Prime Minister's Personal Telegram, T.260/5, 'Personal and Top Secret', 8 March 1945: Churchill papers, 20/212.

[2] Prime Minister's Personal Telegram, T.264/5, 9 March 1945: Premier papers, 4/77/1B, folios 385–6.

[3] 'Addition suggested by Mr Eden' (note by John Martin): Premier papers, 3/356/9, folio 793.

[4] 'Summary of the more important Information sent from Poland in the period 17th January to 1st March', included in Prime Minister's Personal Telegram, T.274/5, Prime Minister to President, No. 909, 'Personal and Top Secret', 10 March 1945: Churchill papers, 20/225.

and collaborators who wish to restore Fascist conditions and have no claim to be regarded as "democratic".' This would then 'open up a field of argument far less suitable for us than, for instance, the simple question whether Mikolajczyk, Romer and Grabski can be called to Moscow for consultation or whether the democratic Poles we have mentioned in Poland can be found, liberated and sent there', or whether Britain could send in observers.

'I do not understand,' Churchill added, 'how this political truce is to operate or how we are to know that it is operating, considering we are barred from all entry into the country. I fear that all that will happen is that another fortnight will be lost during which the process of procuring agreement among all political groups by the Lublin Government, assisted by the Russian Ogpu, liquidating all personalities hostile to them, will be continued.' [1]

Churchill's minute was read to Eden over the telephone from Chequers. Churchill then spoke to Eden about it, also over the telephone, before dictating a further telegram to Roosevelt.[2] Eden was in 'full agreement' with this telegram, Churchill was informed.[3] In this telegram, Churchill told Roosevelt that he was 'distressed' at the proposal for a political truce, 'which I fear may lead us into great difficulties'. Churchill added: 'I do not know what the answer of the London-Polish Government would be to a request for a political truce. They continue to assert, with a wealth of detail, that their friends in Poland are being arrested, deported and liquidated on a large scale. At the best they would make conditions of an impossible character.'

As to the Lublin Poles, Churchill wrote, 'they may well answer that their government can alone ensure "The maximum amount of political tranquillity inside", that they already represent the great mass of the "Democratic Forces in Poland" and that they cannot join hands with émigré traitors to Poland or fascist collaborationists and landlords, and so on according to the usual technique'.

The prospect of a long delay, Churchill pointed out, 'suits the Soviets very well, so that the process of liquidation of elements unfavourable to them or their puppets may run its full course. This would be furthered by our opening out now into proposals of a very undefined character for a political truce between these Polish parties (whose hatreds would eat into live steel) in the spirit and intent of the Crimea decision, and might well imply the abandonment of all clear-cut requests, such as those suggested in my last telegram to you.'

Feeling in Britain was 'very strong', Churchill reiterated, four Cabi-

---

[1] Minute of 9 March 1945: Premier papers, 3/356/9, folios 810–11.
[2] Note by John Martin, 10 March 1945: Premier papers, 3/356/9, folio 810.
[3] 'Note', 9 March 1945: Premier papers, 3/356/9, folio 809.

net Ministers having abstained from the Divisions and two having 'already resigned'.[1]

'If we two get out of step,' Churchill had written in his original draft, 'the doom of Poland is sealed'; but he deleted this sentence before the telegram was despatched.[2]

On March 11, in a telegram drafted in its entirety by the State Department and Admiral Leahy, Roosevelt set out the difference, as seen at least by the State Department and Leahy, in Churchill's position, and that of the United States. As the telegram sought to explain:

You would prefer that the demand in regard to the Lublin Poles be put squarely to the Soviet Government as such whereas we feel that the chances of achieving our common objective would be immeasurably increased if it were done under the guise of a general political truce. You will recall at Yalta that Stalin made quite a point of the 'terrorist' activities of the underground forces of the London Government against the Red Army and the Lublin Poles. Whether or not these allegations have any foundation in fact is beside the question since it is definitely the position of the Soviet Government. In view of Stalin's attitude we feel we would be inviting certain refusal if we merely demanded that the Lublin Poles alone be forced to cease their persecutions of political opponents. Furthermore, we must be careful not to give the impression that we are proposing a halt in the land reforms. This would furnish the Lublin Poles with an opportunity to charge that they and they alone defend the interests of the peasants against the landlords.

Even on the question of observers, the United States view was 'that more would be accomplished by pressing for low level observers at this point who would certainly see as much if not more than some more spectacular body'.[3]

In a second telegram to Churchill that same day, a telegram sent as drafted by the State Department and Leahy, Roosevelt advised that it would be 'much better' to await the results of the steps taken by Clark Kerr and Harriman 'before either you or I intervene personally with Stalin particularly since there is no question of either of our Governments yielding to Molotov's interpretation. I feel that our personal intervention would best be withheld until every other possibility of bringing the Soviet Government into line has been exhausted. I very much hope, therefore, that you will not send any message to Uncle Joe at

[1] Prime Minister's Personal Telegram, T.266/5, Prime Minister to President, No. 907, 'Personal and Top Secret', 10 March 1945: Churchill papers, 20/212.

[2] 'Prime Minister to President', draft telegram, 10 March 1945: Premier papers, 3/356/9, folios 812–13.

[3] President to Prime Minister, No. 713, 'Personal and Top Secret', 11 March 1945: Churchill papers, 20/212.

this juncture—especially as I feel that certain parts of your proposed text might produce a reaction quite contrary to your intent.'[1]

Churchill deferred to Roosevelt's wish, warning the President two days later that a month had passed since Yalta, 'and no progress of any kind has been made'. Soon he would be pressed in Parliament about developments in Poland, 'and I shall be forced to tell them the truth'. Churchill continued:

At Yalta also we agreed to take the Russian view of the frontier line. Poland has lost her frontier. Is she now to lose her freedom? That is the question which will undoubtedly have to be fought out in Parliament and in public here.

I do not wish to reveal a divergence between the British and the United States Governments, but it would certainly be necessary for me to make it clear that we are in the presence of a great failure and an utter breakdown of what was settled at Yalta, but that we British have not the necessary strength to carry the matter further and that the limits of our capacity to act have been reached.

The moment that Molotov sees that he has beaten us away from the whole process of consultations among Poles to form a new Government he will know that we will put up with anything. On the other hand, I believe that combined dogged pressure and persistence along the lines on which we have been working and of my proposed draft message to Stalin, would very likely succeed.[2]

Roosevelt was in no state to apply that 'dogged pressure'. Yet without American concurrence and common action, the limits of Britain's 'capacity to act' had indeed been reached, not only towards Poland, but throughout Eastern Europe and the Balkans. In Yugoslavia, with the formation of the United Government, and Tito's assumption of the Premiership, Communist predominance seemed complete, and the 'fifty-fifty' percentage a thing of the past. Churchill minuted to Eden on March 11:

My feeling is that henceforward our inclination should be to back Italy against Tito. Tito can be left to himself in his mountains to stew in Balkan juice, which is bitter. But the fact that we are generally favourable to Italian claims at the head of the Adriatic will give us an influence over Italian internal politics as against Communists and wild men which may assist the re-integration of the Italian State. I have lost my relish for Yugoslavia, which State must rest on the basis of the Tito–Subasic Agreement &c. On the other hand, I hope we may still save Italy from the Bolshevik pestilence.[3]

[1] President to Prime Minister, No. 714, 'Personal and Top Secret', 11 March 1945: Churchill papers, 20/212'
[2] Prime Minister's Personal Telegram, T.284/5, Prime Minister to President, No. 910, 13 March 1945: Churchill papers, 20/212.
[3] Prime Minister's Personal Minute, M.196/5, 'Top Secret', 'Private and Confidential', 11 March 1945: Churchill papers, 20/209.

The parameters of British action and influence were being steadily curtailed. In Roumania, where Air Vice-Marshal Stevenson continued to protest against the all-pervasive Soviet influence, there was no means whereby, without United States support, that influence could be effectively challenged. Nor did Churchill regard the position as one which called for a British initiative. 'We must remember', he minuted to Eden on March 13:

(a) Roumania is an ex-enemy State which did great injury to Russia;
(b) That we, for considerations well-known to you, accepted a special degree of predominance of Russia in this theatre;
(c) That the lines of the Southern Russian army communications pass through Roumania;
(d) The weakness of the United States diplomacy.[1]

Not only United States diplomacy, but United States economic policy, was now causing Churchill distress. At the War Cabinet on March 14 it was announced that the United States proposed a halt to all meat exports to Britain during the second quarter of 1945. In view of this, Churchill said, 'we should defer fulfilment of our recent offer to supply 25,000 tons of corned beef to Russia'. At this stage in the war, Churchill added, 'the maintenance of minimum scales of food supply should, if need be, take priority over the needs of military operations'.[2]

On March 15, Churchill spoke at the Conservative Party Conference at Central Hall, Westminster, 'a good fighting speech', noted Henry Channon in his diary, 'which ought to win the next election'.[3] During the course of his speech, Churchill criticized those whom he called the 'stay-at-home' Left Wing intelligentsia, who intended to offer 'a new world' to the soldiers returning from the war: a new world, he said, 'constructed behind their backs by politicians who seek their votes'. These soldiers, he added, 'do not regard themselves as a slum-bred serf population chased into battle from a land of misery and want. They love their country and the scenes of their youth and manhood, and they have shown themselves ready to die not only in defence of its material satisfactions, but for its honour.' A few moments later Churchill declared:

---

[1] Prime Minister's Personal Minute, M.205/5, 'Top Secret', 13 March 1945: Churchill papers, 20/209.
[2] War Cabinet No. 30 of 1945, 14 March 1945: Cabinet papers, 85/44.
[3] Channon diary, 15 March 1945: Robert Rhodes James (editor), *Chips, op. cit.*, page 399.

Let there be no mistake about it; it is no easy, cheap-jack Utopia of airy phrases that lies before us. This is no time for windy platitudes and glittering advertisements. The Conservative Party had far better go down telling the truth and acting in accordance with the verities of our position than gain a span of shabbily-bought office by easy and fickle froth and chatter.

All my experience of the British people, which is a long one, convinces me that never at any moment more than this have they wished and meant to face realities, and woe betide those public men who seek to slide into power down the slippery slope of vain and profligate undertakings.

This is no time for humbug and blandishments, but for grim, stark facts and figures, and for action to meet immediate needs.[1]

'The country's reaction to the PM's speech is favourable,' Henry Channon noted on the following day. 'Even the Labour people half admit that he has won the next election already by his address yesterday.'[2]

Churchill now received a further telegram from Roosevelt about Poland. Once more it had been written in its entirety for him, and sought to rebuke Churchill for claiming that there was a 'divergence' between the two Governments on the Polish question. Even so, the telegram, the third on this subject in four days, again set out the American reluctance to challenge the Russians over the question of the diplomatic observers. The 'demand for freedom of movement and communications', the telegram stated, 'would arouse needless discussion at this stage in the negotiations'.[3]

Churchill's reply to Roosevelt was drafted by the Foreign Office. Sent to Washington on March 16, it re-iterated Churchill's refusal to endorse the truce proposal, which was described as 'actively dangerous'. The telegram continued:

At present all entry into Poland is barred to our representatives. An impenetrable veil has been drawn across the scene. This extends even to the liaison officers, British and American, who were to help in bringing out our rescued prisoners of war. According to our information, the American officers as well as the British who had already reached Lublin have been requested to clear out.

'There is no doubt in my mind,' the telegram continued, as if by Churchill himself, 'that the Soviets fear very much our seeing what is

---

[1] Speech of 15 March 1945: Churchill papers, 9/169.
[2] Channon diary, 15 March 1945: Robert Rhodes James (editor), *Chips, op. cit.*, page 400.
[3] President to Prime Minister, No. 718, 'Top Secret and Personal', 16 March 1945: Premier papers, 3/356/9, folios 758–61.

going on in Poland. It may be that, apart from the Poles, they are being very rough with the Germans. Whatever the reason, we are not to be allowed to see.' This was 'not a position', Churchill's telegram ended, 'that could be defended by us'.[1]

Churchill's earlier and brief indignation about Roumania was now completely overshadowed by Poland, to the extent that he again advocated a conciliatory policy towards Russia, suggesting to Eden 'a soothing policy' as far as protesting against Russia's action in Roumania was concerned. He also suggested giving a 'hint' to the Russians that the dismissal of General Plastiras in Greece, a dismissal which Churchill wished for on other grounds, 'is partly done out of our desire to pursue a policy in Greece which will not be unduly disagreeable to them'. Churchill went on to explain to Eden: 'Thus instead of our going all out against the Russian view (with which I totally disagree) in two theatres, we should work for a *detente* in both and concentrate on Poland. We should certainly market the dismissal of Plastiras in Moscow, and, though we back up the Americans in Roumania, we should quite definitely play second fiddle.'[2]

On March 17 Eden suggested to Churchill that there was a need for a telegram to Roosevelt on future policy towards Italy. The Foreign Office had again drafted a telegram for Churchill to consider, for despatch in the 'Prime Minister' telegraphic series. Churchill, while anxious to come to clear decisions with regard to Italy, was not certain that the proposed telegram was the right method, or its contents quite what he would wish. For Churchill now realised that Roosevelt was not able to follow the intricacies of these critical issues. As he explained in a minute to Eden:

I should be willing to send a letter. I have to be very careful now not to overwhelm him with telegrams about business which I fear may bore him. A letter would be on a different footing, and could be delivered through our Ambassador. You have not mentioned in your draft the question of frontiers, colonies and *fleets*. I should also like to add an indication that we were favourably disposed towards Italy in the Northern Adriatic as against Tito's claims and find out what he thought of that. I know his idea is that Trieste should be an international outlet. It might be an international port in Italian territory.[3]

In the previous two days Churchill had agreed to send three long departmental telegrams to Roosevelt drafted in order to fit the 'Prime

[1] Prime Minister's Personal Telegram, T.294/5, Prime Minister to President, No. 912, 'Personal and Top Secret', 16 March 1945: Churchill papers, 20/212.

[2] Prime Minister's Personal Minute, M.215/5, 'For your eyes alone', 'Top Secret', 'Personal and Private', 17 March 1945: Churchill papers, 20/209.

[3] Prime Minister's Personal Minute, M.216/5, 17 March 1945: Churchill papers, 20/209.

Minister to President' series, the first on Poland, the second on 'the approaching crisis' in post-war food supplies, and the third on a conflict over responsibilities in Indo-China between Mountbatten and Wedemeyer.[1] He knew, however, after a talk on March 13 on Britain's dwindling food reserves with Roosevelt's friend and emissary Judge Samuel Rosenman, just how ill Roosevelt was.[2] In an attempt to make his messages more personal, and less burdensome, on March 18 Churchill dictated for Roosevelt a telegram with words of encouragement, family news, and reflections. The telegram read:

I hope that the rather numerous telegrams I have to send you on so many of our difficult and intertwined affairs are not becoming a bore to you. Our friendship is the rock on which I build for the future of the world so long as I am one of the builders. I always think of those tremendous days when you devised Lend–Lease, when we met at Argentia, when you decided with my heartfelt agreement to launch the invasion of Africa, and when you comforted me for the loss of Tobruk by giving me the 300 Shermans of subsequent Alamein fame. I remember the part our personal relations have played in the advance of the World Cause now nearing its final military goal.

I am sending to Washington and San Francisco most of my Ministerial colleagues on one Mission or another, and I shall on this occasion stay at home to mind the shop. All the time I shall be looking forward to your long-promised visit. Clemmie is off to Russia next week for a Red Cross tour as far as the Urals to which she has been invited by Uncle Joe (if we may venture to describe him thus) but she will be back in time to welcome you and Eleanor. My thoughts are always with you all.

Peace with Germany and Japan on our terms will not bring much rest to you and me (if I am still responsible). As I observed last time, when the war of the giants is over, the wars of the pygmies will begin. There will be a torn, ragged and hungry world to help to its feet; and what will UJ or his successor say to the way we should both like to do it? It was quite a relief to talk party politics the other day. It was like working in wood after working in steel. The advantage of this telegram is that it has nothing to do with shop except that I had a good talk with Rosenman about our daily bread.

[1] Prime Minister's Personal Telegram, T.392/5 of 16 March 1945, T.294/5 of 16 March 1945, and T.297/5 of 17 March 1945. Two days later, Churchill sent a message to General Marshall: 'the Prime Minister feels that it will look very bad in history if we let the French force in Indo-China be cut to pieces by the Japanese through shortage of ammunition, if there is anything we can do to save them. He hopes therefore that we shall be agreed in not standing on punctilio in this emergency.' (Prime Minister's Personal Telegram, to Field Marshal Wilson, Washington, T.303/5, 19 March 1945: Churchill papers, 20/225.)

[2] Publicity had been given to the United States to a figure of 700 million tons as the amount of Britain's food reserves. In a Press Conference given by the Minister of Food, the Minister had not been 'at liberty', Churchill told the War Cabinet on March 22, 'to state the actual figure at which these reserves now stood, viz. only about 6 million tons'. (War Cabinet No. 34 of 1945, 21 March 1945: Cabinet papers, 65/9.) The War Cabinet approved Churchill's suggestion that the correct figure should be made public.

Churchill ended this telegram, as he would normally have ended it had it been a letter: 'All good wishes, Winston.' [1]

Since his return from Yalta, Churchill frequently, as on March 17, dined alone.[2] On March 19, he both lunched and dined with only his wife. That night he stayed up after dinner to talk to James Stuart until 11 p.m., then to Sinclair, and finally to Bracken, who stayed until 3.40 a.m. It was not until 4 a.m. that 'the Prime Minister went to bed', as his Private Office diary recorded.[3] 'He *will* keep up this dreadful 4 o'clock stunt, sometimes 4.30,' Elizabeth Layton wrote home two weeks later, and she added: 'We have all got to a stage now where we don't expect to get to bed before 4.30, and we don't expect to feel anything but dog-beat all day long, day after day. Never mind, nothing is forever.' [4]

Among Churchill's worries in the third week of March was the extent to which Hitler might still be able to prolong the war. 'I should like the Intelligence Committee,' he informed the Chiefs of Staff on March 17, 'to consider the possibility that Hitler, after losing Berlin and Northern Germany, will retire to the mountainous and wooded parts of Southern Germany and endeavour to prolong the fight there.' The 'strange resistance' which the Germans had made at Budapest, and were now making at Lake Balaton, and the retention for 'so long' of Kesselring's army in Italy seemed, Churchill wrote, 'in harmony with such an intention'. Churchill added: 'But of course he is so foolishly obstinate about everything that there may be no meaning behind these moves Nevertheless the possibilities should be examined.' [5]

On March 18 the United States Third Army occupied the town of Bingen on the Rhine. British troops were liberating Holland. That same day Churchill was shown the battlefield casualty figures for western Europe between D-Day and 10 March 1945. There had been

---

[1] Prime Minister's Personal Telegram, T.298/5, Prime Minister to President, No. 914, 'Personal and Private', 18 March 1945: Churchill papers, 20/212.

[2] Private Office diary, 17 March 1945.

[3] Private Office diary, 19 March 1945. Churchill dined also alone with his wife on March 21 shortly before she set off on the long flight to Moscow, via Cairo, on her Red Cross tour of Russia, a tour which continued until mid-May.

[4] Elizabeth Layton, letter of 7 April 1945: Nel papers.

[5] Prime Minister's Personal Minute, D.74/5, 'Top Secret', 17 March 1943: Churchill papers, 20/209.

71,000 American dead, and 33,000 British and Canadian dead. In relation to the size of the forces involved, Churchill noted, the proportion of men killed had been 'very much the same between the two Allies'.[1] That day, Churchill read a complaint from the Dutch Foreign Minister about several hundred Dutch civilian deaths caused in The Hague, during a British bombing raid.[2] While Churchill had been on the Dutch–German border on March 3, visiting the Allied armies, British bombers struck at German V2 Rocket sites in the Hague Wood, dropping both incendiary and high explosive bombs. By accident the bombs had fallen on several residential areas, including the Government centre. As well as the civilian deaths, many public buildings had been destroyed.[3] 'The temper of the civilian population,' a report smuggled out of Holland declared, 'has become violently anti-Ally as a result of this bombardment.'[4] On reading this report, Churchill minuted for the Chiefs of Staff Committee, Sinclair and Portal:

This complaint reflects upon the Air Ministry and Royal Air Force in two ways. First, it shows how feeble have been our efforts to interfere with the rockets, and, secondly, the extraordinarily bad aiming which has led to this slaughter of Dutchmen. The matter requires a thorough explanation. We have had numerous accounts of the pin-point bombing of suspected Gestapo houses in Holland and of other specialised points; but good indications are given in this account of the wood where the rockets are stored, and of the railway lines which, if interrupted, would hamper the supply of rockets. All this ought to have been available from Air Intelligence. Instead of attacking these points with precision and regularity, all that has been done is to scatter bombs about this unfortunate city without the slightest effect on their rocket sites, but much on innocent human lives and the sentiments of a friendly people.[5]

In reply, Sinclair noted 'the difficulty of attack upon these rocket objectives', and he added: 'The Germans are deliberately placing their launching and storage sites in and near built-up areas in Holland.' Nor, Sinclair added, would the bombing of railway lines necessarily avoid losses in Dutch civilian life. Full investigations were nevertheless already in progress, Sinclair added, 'into the reasons for this deplorable event', and he went on to assure Churchill that

[1] Prime Minister's Personal Minute, M.226/5, 18 March 1945: Churchill papers, 20/209.

[2] According to A. Korthals, *Luchtgevaar* ('Danger from the Sky'), Amsterdam 1984, the minimum deaths were 520. At Rotterdam, in 1940, 900 had been killed during the German bombing raid on the city which preceded the Dutch surrender.

[3] Including the Provincial Government buildings, the Law Court, the Military Staff College, the French Embassy, three Roman Catholic Churches and the British Church.

[4] Report transmitted by the Netherlands Foreign Minister, 14 March 1945.

[5] Prime Minister's Personal Minute, D.75/5, 18 March 1945: Churchill papers, 20/209.

bombing attacks upon the rocket sites 'ought not to involve serious risk to Dutch civilian life'.[1] Inside the Air Ministry, Portal had already written to Air Marshal Sir Arthur Coningham, at 2nd Tactical Air Force, about the 'gross errors' involved in this Hague bombardment.[2]

Ten days after his minute to Sinclair about the Hague bombing, Churchill made another incursion into the controversial area of bombing policy, having been shown accounts of the bombing of Dresden on the night of February 13. Churchill's reaction was to raise the whole issue of such bombardments. As he minuted to the Chiefs of Staff Committee, and to Portal:

It seems to me that the moment has come when the question of bombing of German cities simply for the sake of increasing the terror, though under other pretexts, should be reviewed. Otherwise we shall come into control of an utterly ruined land. We shall not, for instance, be able to get housing materials out of Germany for our own needs because some temporary provision would have to be made for the Germans themselves. The destruction of Dresden remains a serious query against the conduct of Allied bombing. I am of the opinion that military objectives must henceforward be more strictly studied in our own interests rather than that of the enemy.

The Foreign Secretary has spoken to me on this subject, and I feel the need for more precise concentration upon military objectives, such as oil and communications behind the immediate battle-zone, rather than on mere acts of terror and wanton destruction, however impressive.[3]

At a meeting of the Chiefs of Staff on March 29, Portal pointed out 'that it had always been the aim of our bombing of large cities to destroy the industries and transportation services centred in those cities and not to terrorise the civilian population of Germany'.[4] Churchill then agreed to withdraw his 'rough' minute, and instructed Portal to redraft it 'in less rough terms'.[5] In Portal's redraft, the word 'terror' did not appear. The new minute still asserted, however, that the time had come to consider a halt to this type of raid. Drafted by Portal, but signed by Churchill, it read:

It seems to me that the moment has come when the question of the so called 'area bombing' of German cities should be reviewed from the point of view of our own interests. If we come into control of an entirely ruined land, there will be a great shortage of accommodation for ourselves and our Allies;

[1] 'Top Secret', 26 March 1945: Air Ministry papers, 19/432.
[2] 'Top Secret', 16 March 1945: Air Ministry papers, 19/432.
[3] Prime Minister's Personal Minute, D.83/5, 'Top Secret', 28 March 1945: Premier papers, 3/12, folio 25.
[4] Chiefs of Staff Committee, No. 80 of 1945, 29 March 1945: Cabinet papers, 79/31.
[5] 'Top Secret' (Portal to Churchill), 30 March 1945: Premier papers, 3/12, folio 23.

and we shall be unable to get housing materials out of Germany for our own needs because some temporary provision would have to be made for the Germans themselves. We must see to it that our attacks do not do more harm to ourselves in the long run than they do to the enemy's immediate war effort. Pray let me have your views.[1]

This minute was issued on April 1. Three days later the Air Staff agreed that 'at this advanced stage of the war' there was 'no great or immediate additional advantage' to be expected from air attack on 'the remaining industrial centres of Germany'.[2]

Churchill assumed that the new policy would be strictly followed. He was therefore puzzled, two and a half weeks later, to read aircraft had been despatched on the night of April 14 to bomb Potsdam.[3] He wrote at once to Sinclair and Portal: 'What was the point of going and blowing down Potsdam?'[4]

In his reply, Portal pointed out that this attack had come about following a report of the Joint Intelligence Committee, describing the evacuation of the German Air Force operational headquarters from Berlin to Potsdam. Another object of the raid, Portal explained, was to destroy 'communications leading West from Berlin through Potsdam'. Portal's reply ended, with a reference to Churchill's earlier protest of March 28: 'In accordance with your decision on the re-commendation of the Chiefs of Staff we have already issued instructions to Bomber Command that area bombing designed solely with the object of destroying industrial areas is to be discontinued.' The attack on Potsdam, however, Portal explained, 'was calculated to hasten the disintegration of enemy resistance'.[5]

In the third week of March a new dispute arose between Britain and the Soviet Union. At Yalta the Soviet Union had agreed to re-patriate all British and American prisoners-of-war liberated by the

[1] Prime Minister's Personal Minute, D.89/5, 'Top Secret', 2 April 1945: Premier papers, 3/12, folio 24. Churchill accepted Portal's redraft in its entirety.

[2] 'Area Bombing, Note by Chief of the Air Staff', 'Top Secret', 4 April 1945: Premier papers 3/12, folios 19–21.

[3] Cabinet War Room Record No. 2051 for the 24 hours ending 7 a.m., 15 April 1945, 'Secret': Premier papers, 3/12, folio 4. The Chiefs of Staff Committee Weekly Résumé No. 294, of the naval military and air situation for 12 April to 19 April 1945, gave details from aerial photographs taken on April 16 of 'severe damage' in the vicinity of the railway centre and locomotive depot, as well as damage at an aircraft component factory. It also reported 'several areas of devastation' in the city, 'where the majority of the buildings have been gutted or destroyed', including the Post Office and the Town Hall (Chiefs of Staff Paper No. 79 of 1945, 'Secret' 19 April 1945: Cabinet papers, 80/48).

[4] Prime Minister's Personal Minute, M/362/5, 19 April 1945: Premier papers, 3/12, folio 3.

[5] 'Top Secret', 20 April 1945: Premier papers, 3/12, folio 2.

Red Army, in return for Russian-born soldiers captured by the western allies as the German units in which these Russians were serving surrendered to British or American forces. Stalin had been insistent at Yalta that no harm should come to those captured Russians while they were still in British or American custody. Learning that many of the British prisoners-of-war still in Russia were being subjected to harsh treatment, Eden wanted Churchill to telegraph to Stalin protesting. But Churchill declined to do so. 'I do not wish to send this telegram to Stalin,' he minuted to Eden on March 21, 'as it would only make a row between us after a month's silence.' Churchill did draft his own telegram to Stalin, however, using language which, as he told Eden, 'gives no excuse for a rough answer'.[1] To Stalin, Churchill telegraphed direct that same day:

> There is no subject on which the British nation is more sensitive than on the fate of our prisoners in German hands and their speedy deliverance from captivity and restoration to their own country. I should be very much obliged if you would give the matter your personal attention, as I am sure you would wish to do your best for our men, as I can promise you we are doing for your men as they come into our control along the Rhine.

'We seem to have a lot of difficulties now,' Churchill commented, 'since we parted at Yalta, but I am quite sure that all these would soon be swept away if only we could meet together.'[2]

On the night of March 22 the United States Third Army crossed the Rhine south of Mainz, into the German heartland. That same night, on the Baltic, Soviet forces completed the isolation of Danzig. On Friday, March 23, Montgomery's 21st Army Group prepared for operation 'Plunder', the crossing of the Lower Rhine at four places, followed by the airborne landing of 14,000 troops on the eastern bank, together with their artillery. As Churchill had told Stalin two days earlier, Montgomery had 'under his orders' for this attack the Canadian Army, the British Second Army and the American Ninth, 'and I hope to have good news to send you before very long'. Churchill commented: 'The field is now set for the next phase, and I am going to Montgomery's headquarters to witness it.'[3]

During his visit at the beginning of March, Churchill had suggested to Montgomery that he would like to visit him again for the 'Battle of the Rhine', and Montgomery's invitation had reached him on March 10, with its added note: 'I shall ask you to write a Chap IX for my

[1] Prime Minister's Personal Minute, M.246/5, 21 March 1945: Churchill papers, 20/209.
[2] Prime Minister's Personal Telegram, T.312/5, 'Personal, Private and Top Secret', 21 March 1945: Churchill papers, 20/213.
[3] Prime Minister's Personal Telegram, T.312/5, 'Personal and Top Secret', 21 March 1945: Churchill papers, 20/225.

book!!'[1] Churchill had replied at once, promising not to bring to the caravan more than himself, Brooke, Tommy Thompson, and his valet, 'four in all'. His letter continued:

However it would be necessary for me to have somewhere 20 or 30 miles further back a train, or perhaps a railway coach, where I can keep a Private Secretary and Mr Kinna, who deals with facilities for scrambling messages. Probably one or two detectives will be there; I do not need them at the front. You must remember I have to keep in touch with events, which sometimes move very quickly indeed. A motor-cyclist or two would keep me in contact with this 'base', which I would drop wherever you say on my way out and pick up on my way back. The nearer to an airfield the better. I shall almost certainly come in a Dakota, as my Skymaster is taking Clemmie on her mission to Russia.

I may add that General Eisenhower suggested to me when I talked my wishes over with him that a tank would be the best way of seeing things, and would give protection in the forward areas from stray airplane attacks. Perhaps this has already occurred to you.[2]

Shortly after two in the afternoon on March 23, Churchill left London by air for Venlo, accompanied by Brooke, Colville, Kinna, Sawyers and Commander Thompson. Their flight path took them over Dungeness, Cap Gris Nez and Brussels, to Venlo, 'where we landed', Colville noted, 'on a heavily bomb-scarred aerodrome'.[3] From the aerodrome they drove to 21 Army Group headquarters at Straelen, on German soil, and were met by Montgomery, who explained his plans for the offensive, to be launched that night. To Stalin, Churchill telegraphed that evening:

I am at Field-Marshal Montgomery's HQ. He has just given orders to launch the main battle to force the Rhine on a broad front centering about Wesel supported by the landing of an Airborne Corps and by about 2,000 guns.

It is hoped to pass the river tonight and tomorrow and establish bridgeheads. A very large reserve of armour is available to exploit the assault once the river is crossed.

I shall send you another message tomorrow. Field-Marshal Montgomery asks me to present his respects to you.[4]

Montgomery made two of his caravans available to Churchill, one for work and the other for sleep. That night, Colville noted, 'I went by jeep to Monty's camp after dinner and took the PM some important telegrams, including a venomous one from Molotov who, on

[1] 'Personal', 10 March 1945: Premier papers, 3/339/11, folios 33–6.
[2] 'Top Secret', 11 March 1945: Premier papers, 3/339/11, folios 25–8.
[3] Colville diary, 23 March 1945: Colville papers.
[4] Prime Minister's Personal Telegram, T.334/5, IZ 2939, 23 March 1945: Churchill papers, 20/213.

the eve of what may be our war-winning operations, had the impudence to say that the Russians were bearing the main brunt of the war.'[1] Brooke, who was with Churchill when he read the Molotov telegram, noted in his diary that it concerned operation 'Crossword', the negotiations which SS General Karl Wolff was, at that very moment, conducting with the British and Americans in Switzerland, for the surrender of the German army in Italy, and the Russian fear 'lest we should make a separate peace on the Western Front without their being in'. Brooke added: 'He dictated a reply, let his secretary out of the caravan, called him back, considered it, started writing another and finally very wisely left it till tomorrow to think over carefully.'[2]

The Russians, Churchill minuted to Eden on the following day, 'may have a legitimate fear of our doing a deal in the west to hold them well back in the east'.[3] 'I suppose it is all right Clemmie going on her journey in these circumstances,' he asked Eden in a second message that day. 'Let me know your unprejudiced opinion whether it would be better to put it off for a few days or weeks, or whether it would be considered as a sign of personal goodwill.' Churchill added: 'I incline to her going as arranged.'[4]

While he was at Montgomery's headquarters, Churchill also received a message from Stalin, about the released British prisoners-of-war. They were, he said, all 'en route for Odessa and the voyage home', and had until then, when under Russian control, been living 'in better conditions than was the case with Soviet prisoners of war in English camps, when the latter in a number of cases suffered persecution and even blows'.[5]

The British offensive began in the early hours of March 24. Churchill, from an Observation Point at Ginberich, overlooking the Rhine, watched that morning as the first group of airborne troops went in, some four or five miles distant. 'Monty attacked last night, and it seemed to go well,' Cadogan, in England, noted in his diary, and he added: 'PM there, of course.'[6]

---

[1] Colville diary, 23 March 1945: Colville papers.

[2] Brooke diary, 23 March 1945: Bryant, *op. cit.*, volume 2, pages 432–3.

[4] Prime Minister's Personal Minute, M.254/5, 'Top Secret', 24 March 1945: Churchill papers, 20/209.

[4] Prime Minister's Personal Minute, M.256/5, 'Personal and Top Secret', 'Scrambled to London', 24 March 1945: Churchill papers, 20/204.

[5] 'Personal and Secret', 23 March 1945: Churchill papers, 20/213.

[6] Cadogan diary, 24 March 1945: David Dilks (editor), *op. cit.*, page 724.

Churchill's own account, written nine years later, described the scene that Saturday morning:

It was full daylight before the subdued but intense roar and rumbling of swarms of aircraft stole upon us. After that in the course of half an hour over 2,000 aircraft streamed overhead in their formations. My view-point had been well chosen. The light was clear enough to enable one to see where the descent on the enemy took place. The aircraft faded from sight, and then almost immediately afterwards returned towards us at a different level. The parachutists were invisible even to the best field-glasses. But now there was a double murmur and roar of reinforcements arriving and of those who had delivered their attacks returning. Soon one saw with a sense of tragedy air-craft in twos and threes coming back askew, asmoke, or even in flames. Also at this time tiny specks came floating to earth. Imagination built on a good deal of experience told a hard and painful tale. It seemed however that nineteen out of every twenty of the aircraft that had started came back in good order, having discharged their mission.[1]

Brooke, who accompanied Churchill to the Observation Point, noted in his diary:

We remained at this viewpoint for about two hours and then embarked in two armoured cars, one each. We went down into Xanten where we turned north and through Marienbaum at the north-east corner of the Hochwald and on to a bit of high ground just south of Calcar. There we had a good view looking out on to the crossing-place of the 51st Division, whose divisional commander was unfortunately killed this morning.[2] We lunched there and then dropped down to 3rd Division HQ in an old castle.

Winston then became a little troublesome and wanted to go messing about on the Rhine crossings and we had some difficulty in keeping him back. However, in the end he behaved well and we came back in our armoured cars to where we had left our own car, and from there on back to the HQ. PM went off for a sleep which he wanted badly; he had been sleeping in the car nearly all the way home, gradually sliding on to my knee.[3]

That night Churchill commented to Colville, who had sur-reptitiously crossed the Rhine, and had nearly been killed by a shell: 'sleep soundly. You might have slept more soundly still.'[4]

There was work to be done before going to bed; at midday on March 24, Churchill's Private Office had sent him a bag of selected materials for his scrutiny, including fifty-eight Foreign Office tele-grams, five War Cabinet papers, the latest Cabinet War Room Record of military, naval and air operations, more than twenty-five letters

[1] Winston S. Churchill, *The Second World War*, volume 6, London 1954, page 362.
[2] Major-General T. G. Rennie.
[3] Brooke diary, 24 March 1945: Bryant, *op. cit.*, volume 2, page 434.
[4] Colville diary, 24 March 1945: Colville papers.

and minutes, and all the British newspapers for that day.[1] One of the documents sent out to Churchill was a minute from Eden, about the worsening situation in Moscow on the Polish question. The Soviet Union had already indicated its displeasure with the Anglo-American policy on Poland by letting it be known that it would not be Molotov, but a less senior official, who would be going to San Francisco. Molotov was still refusing to allow western diplomats to act as observers of the Polish elections, and, Eden told Churchill in his minute of March 24, Clark Kerr was being hampered in his advocacy 'by lack of support from Harriman'.

On March 25 Churchill drove to Eisenhower's headquarters near Rheinburg, where, as he later recalled:

After various interchanges we had a brief lunch, in the course of which Eisenhower said that there was a house about ten miles away on our side of the Rhine, which the Americans had sandbagged, from which a fine view of the river and of the opposite bank could be obtained. He proposed that we should visit it, and conducted us there himself. The Rhine—here about four hundred yards broad—flowed at our feet. There was a smooth flat expanse of meadows on the enemy's side. The officers told us that the far bank was unoccupied so far as they knew, and we gazed and gaped at it for a while. With appropriate precautions we were led into the building. Then the Supreme Commander had to depart on other business and Montgomery and I were about to follow his example when I saw a small launch come close by to moor. So I said to Montgomery, 'Why don't we go across and have a look at the other side?' Somewhat to my surprise he answered, 'Why not?' After he had made some inquiries we started across the river with three or four American commanders and half a dozen armed men. We landed in brilliant sunshine and perfect peace on the German shore, and walked about for half an hour or so unmolested.

As we came back Montgomery said to the captain of the launch, 'Can't we go down the river towards Wesel, where there is something going on?' The captain replied that there was a chain across the river half a mile away to prevent floating mines interfering with our operations, and several of these might be held up by it. Montgomery pressed him hard, but was at length satisfied that the risk was too great. As we landed he said to me, 'Let's go down to the railway bridge at Wesel, where we can see what is going on on the spot.' So we got into his car, and, accompanied by the Americans, who were delighted at the prospect, we went to the big iron-girder railway bridge, which was broken in the middle but whose twisted ironwork offered good perches. The Germans were replying to our fire, and their shells fell in salvos of four about a mile away. Presently they came nearer. Then one salvo came

---

[1] 'Contents of Bag sent Midday, March 24, 1945': Premier papers, 3/339/11, folios 7–9. On the following day the bag included 'Prime Minister's Gas Mask and Shrapnel Helmet', and on March 26 a set of Churchill's four volume *Marlborough* biography (for General Eisenhower). A second set had earlier been sent across for Montgomery.

overhead and plunged in the water on our side of the bridge. The shells seemed to explode on impact with the bottom, and raised great fountains of spray about a hundred yards away. Several other shells fell among the motorcars which were concealed not far behind us, and it was decided we ought to depart.[1]

The decision to 'depart' was not taken with ease, as Brooke later recalled a picture 'as vivid in my mind as it was on that day':

It is that of the US General Simpson, on whose front we were, coming up to Winston and saying, 'Prime Minister, there are snipers in front of you; they are shelling both sides of the bridge and now they have started shelling the road behind you. I cannot accept the responsibility for your being here and must ask you to come away.' The look on Winston's face was just like that of a small boy being called away from his sand-castles on the beach by his nurse! He put both his arms round one of the twisted girders of the bridge and looked over his shoulder at Simpson with pouting mouth and angry eyes. Thank heaven he came away quietly. It was a sad wrench for him; he was enjoying himself immensely.[2]

'I clambered down,' Churchill recalled, 'and joined my adventurous host for our two hours' drive back to his headquarters.'[3] 'We have had a jolly day,' Churchill telegraphed to Eden that evening, 'having crossed the Rhine. Tomorrow we go to the 15th Scottish Division, on the other side.'[4] A few hours earlier he had telegraphed:

We have had a glorious day here, and I hope the consequences will be far-reaching. I am to see Eisenhower tomorrow at his request. I showed Montgomery Molotov's rude message, as of course the venue of the negotiations may easily be changed to this theatre. I well understand the Russian anxiety lest we should accept a military surrender[5] in the West or South, which means that our armies will advance against little or no opposition and will reach the Elbe, or even Berlin, before the Bear.[6]

In his draft of this message to Eden, Churchill had continued, in a section subsequently deleted:

Therefore should military negotiations break out on this front, which is not a secondary front like Italy, it will not be possible to keep the military and the political aspects separate.

[1] Winston S. Churchill, *The Second World War*, volume 6, London 1954, pages 364–5.

[2] Brooke recollections: Bryant, *op. cit.*, volume 2, page 438.

[3] Winston S. Churchill, *The Second World War*, volume 6, page 365.

[4] Prime Minister's Personal Minute, M.262/5, 'Private and Top Secret', 25 March 1945: Churchill papers, 20/209.

[5] In his first draft, Churchill had written 'make a deal'. He later replaced these words with the phrase 'accept a military surrender'.

[6] Prime Minister's Personal Minute, M.255/5, 'Personal and Top Secret', 25 March 1945: Churchill papers, 20/209.

In my view the Russians should be in from the start, both on the military and political, and we should, unless convinced of their goodwill, carry on in accordance with our duty and our obvious advantage. They are claiming to have everything yielded to them at every point and give nothing in return except their military pressure. They ought to be made to feel that we also have our point of view.

Any negotiations on German soil, Churchill added, 'should have full political representatives present as well as military, or alternatively the military must refer to their Governments before reaching any con-clusion'.[1]

That night Colville noted in his diary: 'The PM said he hardly liked to consider dismembering Germany until his doubts about Russia's intentions had been cleared away.'[2]

Among the documents in Churchill's box on March 25 was a proposal to inform de Gaulle of the secret of the atom bomb. Churchill at once minuted to Eden:

1. I certainly do not agree that this secret should be imparted to the French. My agreement with President Roosevelt in writing forbids either party to reveal to anyone else the secret. I believe you under-rate the lead which has been obtained by the United States, in which we participate, through their vast expenditure of money   I believe above four hundred million pounds.

2. [I was shocked at Yalta too when the President in a casual manner spoke of revealing the secret to Stalin on the grounds that de Gaulle, if he heard of it, would certainly double-cross us with Russia.]

3. In all the circumstances our policy should be to keep the matter so far as we can control it in American and British hands and leave the French and Russians to do what they can. The Chancellor[3] said that the Frenchmen whom he had interviewed would never betray the secret to de Gaulle, and he vouched for their good behaviour. But anyhow there is all the difference between having certain paper formulae and having a mighty plant in exist-ence, and perhaps soon in working order. Once you tell them they will ask for the very latest news, and to see the plants. This will speed them up by two years at least. You may be quite sure that any power that gets hold of the secret will try to make the article and that this touches the existence of human society.

4. I am getting rather tired of all the different kinds of things that we must do or not do lest Anglo-French relations suffer. [One thing I am sure that there is nothing that de Gaulle would like better than to have plenty of TA to punish Britain, and nothing he would like less than to arm Communist Russia with the secret.] This matter is out of all relation to anything else that exists in the whole world, and I could not think of any disclosure to third or

---

[1] Draft minute, 'Personal and Top Secret', dictated 24 March 1945: Premier papers, 3/356/9, folios 718–20.

[2] Colville diary, 25 March 1945: Colville papers.

[3] Sir John Anderson, Chancellor of the Exchequer, the Minister responsible for atom bomb research (code name 'TA' or Tube Alloys).

fourth parties at the present time. I do not believe there is anyone in the world who can possibly have reached the position now occupied by us and the United States.

5. As to questions of honour as between us and France. At that time France was represented by Vichy and de Gaulle had no status to speak for her. I have never made the slightest agreement with France or with any Frenchman. I shall certainly continue to urge the President not to make or permit the slightest disclosure to France or Russia. [Even six months will make a difference should it come to a show-down with Russia, or indeed with de Gaulle.]

Before sending this minute to Eden, Churchill showed it to Anderson and Cherwell. The result was the deletion of the three sentences in square brackets.[1]

On March 26 Churchill continued his tour of the 21st Army Group positions, driving with Montgomery to the Rhine, crossing the river by bridge to the village of Bislich, and driving down the east bank for a short while before recrossing in a tank landing vehicle, known as a 'Buffalo'. 'The children looked well fed and healthy,' Colville noted in his diary, 'but the PM told me this afternoon that he thought their faces very strained and that for his part what he had seen of the German civilian population had moved and upset him.'[2] Colville added: 'I think this is his reaction to the apparently sinister designs of Russia who—in addition to obvious moves against the spirit of the Yalta agreement—have now decided not to send Molotov to San Francisco but to send three subordinate officials.'[3]

After a picnic lunch on the west bank of the river, Churchill returned to Montgomery's headquarters. Colville noted in his diary:

We said good-bye to Monty and his staff at 4.15 p.m. (Winston giving him a fine edition of *Marlborough*, a long inscription for his autograph book and a heap of compliments) and took off from much bombed Venlo in a Dakota escorted by twelve Spitfires. The PM worked in the plane, which was alternatively too hot and too cold, and we landed at Northolt after an exciting weekend in glorious weather, much the better in health and temper.[4]

That night, Churchill dined alone with his wife, who wrote to Montgomery two days later:

Winston loved his visit to you. He said he felt quite a reformed character & that if in earlier days he had been about with you I should have had a much easier life! referring I suppose to his chronic unpunctuality & to his

[1] Prime Minister's Personal Minute, M.262/5A, 25 March 1945: Premier papers, 3/139/6, folios 248–50.
[2] Colville diary, 26 March 1945: Colville papers.
[3] Colville diary, 26 March 1945: Colville papers.
[4] Colville diary, 26 March 1945: Colville papers.

habit of changing his mind (in little things) every minute! I was much touched & said I had been able to bear it very well as things are. So then he said perhaps he need not bother to improve? But I said 'please improve becos we have not finished our lives yet'.[1]

Clementine Churchill set off for Moscow, and for a five week journey throughout the Soviet Union, to see the hospitals helped by her Red Cross Fund. 'You are ceaselessly in our thoughts,' Churchill telegraphed to her on March 31, after she had reached Cairo. If she were to be delayed in Cairo, he added, 'the thing to see is the Siwa Oasis where Anthony and Cleopatra spent their honeymoon'.[2]

The amount of money which Clementine Churchill and her Fund had collected, Churchill told Stalin two weeks later, 'is perhaps not great, but it is a love offering not only of the rich but mainly of the pennies of the poor who have been proud to make their small weekly contributions'. Churchill added: 'In the friendship of the masses of our peoples, in the comprehension of their governments and in the mutual respect of their armies the future of the world resides.'[3]

[1] Letter of 28 March 1945: Mary Soames, *Clementine Churchill, op. cit.,* page 367.
[2] 'Personal and Secret', 31 March 1945: Spencer-Churchill papers.
[3] 'Personal and Secret', 14 April 1945: Spencer-Churchill papers.

65
Worsening Relations
with Russia

O N 27 March 1945, the one thousand and fiftieth V2 rocket reached England. It was the last, its launching site being destroyed that day by Allied air attack. That morning Churchill learned that David Lloyd George had died the previous morning. 'I do not think we can do any more Business today,' he told the House of Commons after he had announced the news.[1] That night he prepared his tribute to the man who had been his friend, colleague and Chief more than twenty-five years before.

On March 27, Churchill also gave his approval to two Foreign Office drafts of telegrams to Roosevelt on the worsening relations with the Soviet Union over Poland. On the Moscow Commission, Molotov now refused even to answer when Britain and America put forward names for inclusion in the Polish coalition. It was all 'as plain as a pikestaff', the first telegram to Roosevelt read, that Molotov's tactics were 'to drag the business out while the Lublin Committee consolidate their power', and it continued, as approved and signed by Churchill: 'Surely we must not be manoeuvred into becoming parties to imposing on Poland, and on how much more of Eastern Europe, the Russian version of democracy?'

This first telegram then listed the other Russian actions 'at variance with the spirit of Yalta'; Molotov's 'rude questioning' about the operation 'Crossword' negotiation with SS General Wolff in Switzerland, the 'unsatisfactory proceedings' over the British prisoners-of-war liberated by the Red Army, the 'coup d'état' in Roumania, and the Russian 'refusal' to allow the Yalta Declaration on Liberated Europe to operate. The first telegram continued:

What also do you make of Molotov's withdrawal from San Francisco? It

[1] *Hansard*, 27 March 1945, column 1335.

leaves a bad impression on me. Does it mean that the Russians are going to run out, or are they trying to blackmail us? As we have both understood them, the Dumbarton Oaks proposals, which will form the basis of discussion at San Francisco, are based on the conception of Great Power unity. If no such unity exists on Poland, which is after all a major problem of the post-war settlement—to say nothing of the other matters just mentioned—what, it will legitimately be asked, are the prospects of success of the new World Organisation? And is it not indeed evident that, in the circumstances, we shall be building the whole structure of future world peace on foundations of sand?[1]

This last phrase in Churchill's telegram echoed Eden's comment, in a minute to Churchill three days earlier, sent by pouch to Eisenhower's headquarters on German soil: 'How can we lay foundations of any new world order when Anglo-American relations with Russia are so completely lacking in confidence?' Was there any way, Eden asked, 'by which the Russians can be forced to choose between mending their ways and the loss of Anglo-American friendship?', and he added: 'This is the only method by which we can hope to obtain anything approaching a fair deal for the Poles.'

Eden urged Churchill to send a message to Stalin jointly with Roosevelt.[2] Thus Churchill's second telegram to Roosevelt on March 27, drafted in its entirety by the Foreign Office, contained a proposed message to Stalin, to be sent jointly by the President and Prime Minister. It dealt entirely with Poland, and with Molotov's refusal to allow the Moscow Commission to operate as envisaged at Yalta. 'There ought not to be a veto by one Power on all nominations,' the telegram declared. Molotov's suggestion that Britain and the United States could send observers to Poland had been withdrawn, 'to our surprise'. It was for Stalin to ensure that 'the aim of the Yalta settlement of Poland, viz., the setting up of a representative Government which Britain and the USA can recognize, may be carried out without delay.'[3]

On the day Churchill sent these two telegrams to Roosevelt, General Kazimierz Okulicki, the successor to Bor-Komorowski in command of the Polish Underground Army, a second Underground leader, and the Polish Socialist leader, Kazimierz Puzak, met a Soviet representative, Guards Colonel Pimenov of the NKVD, in the town of Pruszkow, a few miles to the west of Warsaw. Pimenov was to take

---

[1] Prime Minister's Personal Telegram, T.347/5, Prime Minister to President, No. 925, 'Personal and Top Secret', 27 March 1945: Churchill papers, 20/213.
[2] Foreign Secretary's Minute, PM/45/134, 24 March 1945: Premier papers, 3/356/9, folios 722–3.
[3] Prime Minister's Personal Telegram, T.348/5, Prime Minister to President, No. 926, 'Personal and Top Secret', 27 March 1945: Premier papers, 3/356/9, folios 672–3.

them, under promise of safe conduct, to the headquarters of Colonel General Ivanov, of the First White Russian Front Command. On the following day, while still in Pruszkow, the Poles were joined by twelve other Poles, representing the major Polish political parties.[1] Not one of these fifteen Poles was to return from the meeting.[2]

That evening, unaware as yet of what was happening in Pruszkow, Churchill drove to Northolt aerodrome with his wife, to see her off, on her flight to Moscow. Returning to the Annexe, at midnight he began to dictate to Elizabeth Layton his tribute to Lloyd George. 'It took him about two hours,' she wrote to her parents, 'and me one and a half to type out, so it was about four when I got to bed, ha! ha! But never mind, I thought it was a darned fine tribute.'[3]

Speaking in the House of Commons on March 28, Churchill said of Lloyd George: 'There was no man so gifted, so eloquent, so forceful, who knew the life of the people so well,' and he went on to tell the House, of the man whom he had first met at the turn of the century:

His warm heart was stirred by the many perils which beset the cottage homes: the health of the bread-winner, the fate of his widow, the nourishment and upbringing of his children, the meagre and haphazard provision of medical treatment and sanatoria, and the lack of any organized accessible medical service of a kind worthy of the age, from which the mass of the wage earners and the poor suffered.

All this excited his wrath. Pity and compassion lent their powerful wings. He knew the terror with which old age threatened the toiler—that after a life of exertion he could be no more than a burden at the fireside and in the family of a struggling son.

Churchill then turned to a personal memory. 'When I first became Lloyd George's friend and active associate, now more than forty years ago,' he said, 'this deep love of the people, the profound knowledge of their lives and of the undue and needless pressures under which they lived, impressed itself indelibly upon my mind.'

Churchill then recalled how, with the coming of war in 1914, Lloyd

[1] The Polish political parties who sent representatives to the Pruszkow meeting were the Polish Socialist Party, the National Party, the Populist Party, the Christian Labour Party and the Democratic Party. They were accompanied by an interpreter, who also failed to return (Clark Kerr's Moscow telegrams No. 1611 and 1612, 2 April 1945: Foreign Office papers, 954/20, folios 647–8).

[2] A prisoner in Tsarist Russia from 1911 to 1917, Kazimierz Puzak was now taken to Moscow and later tried, with the fifteen other Polish leaders, and sentenced to eighteen months' imprisonment. Released by Soviet amnesty at the end of 1945, he returned to Warsaw. Arrested in 1947, he was tried in Warsaw with five other Socialists, accused of resuscitating the activities of the Polish Socialist Party. Sentenced to ten years' imprisonment, subsequently reduced to five years by amnesty. He died in prison in Poland in 1950.

[3] Elizabeth Layton, letter of 27 March 1945: Nel papers.

George, although 'by public repute a pugnacious pacifist', rallied to the war effort 'and cast aside all other thoughts and aims'. On becoming Prime Minister in 1916, 'he imparted immediately a new surge of strength, of impulse, far stronger than anything that had been known up to that time, and extending over the whole field of wartime Government, every part of which was of equal interest to him'. Churchill's tribute continued, in words which many of those listening felt could apply equally to Churchill himself:

His long life was, from almost the beginning to almost the end, spent in political strife and controversy. He aroused intense and sometimes needless antagonisms. He had fierce and bitter quarrels at various times with all the parties. He faced undismayed the storms of criticism and hostility. In spite of all obstacles, including those he raised himself, he achieved his main purposes. As a man of action, resource and creative energy he stood, when at his zenith, without a rival.

'Much of his work abides,' Churchill ended, 'some of it will grow greatly in the future, and those who come after us will find the pillars of his life's toil upstanding, massive and indestructible; and we ourselves, gathered here today, may indeed be thankful that he voyaged with us through storm and tumult with so much help and guidance to bestow.' [1]

'I loved your speech about LG,' Clementine Churchill wrote from Cairo, where she was on her way to Moscow. 'It recalled forgotten blessings which he showered on the meek and lowly.' [2]

On March 29 Churchill went down to Chequers for the Easter weekend. 'After dinner and a film,' noted Marian Holmes, 'PM worked, after which he still didn't seem to want to retire. In merry reminiscent mood he recited poetry and sang the Glory Song.' [3]

On the morning of March 30, Good Friday, Marian Holmes was again on duty. 'PM worked from bed all morning,' she noted, 'and then decided to stay there for lunch. He was having sardines as an hors-d'oeuvre. On his tray was a small carafe of vinegar and another of whisky. Before I realised what was happening, he had poured whisky on to his sardines and vinegar into his glass. Quick decision. Tell him or risk the mix-up going unnoticed? Told him. Sawyers was summoned and we sorted it out. "I must be going dotty" the PM said.' [4]

---

[1] *Hansard*, 28 March 1945, columns 1377–80.
[2] Letter of 30 March 1945: Mary Soames, *Clementine Churchill, op. cit.*, page 367.
[3] Marian Holmes diary, 29 March 1945: Marian Walker Spicer papers.
[4] Marian Holmes diary, 30 March 1945: Marian Walker Spicer papers.

During the morning, Churchill had sent for his cousin Anita Leslie, who had just returned to England from France, having served overseas, mostly as an ambulance driver in the Middle East, for nearly five years. 'I believe she has done very good service,' Clementine Churchill explained. 'I think it would be rather nice if you asked her to luncheon.'[1] Churchill was in bed working when Anita Leslie arrived. 'I sat with him before and after lunch,' she later recalled. 'The bed was covered with papers, and secretaries kept coming in with telephone messages. I was in French Army uniform and Winston was intrigued by Croix de Guerre, newly won in the Alsace campaign.'[2] 'You ought to meet my cousin,' Churchill told Marian Holmes. 'She's a remarkable woman and has been under fire many times.'[3]

Churchill spoke to Anita Leslie of his recent visit to Germany. 'I hate to see brave men killed,' he told her, 'and the smoking planes fall out of the sky, but I am old and have to be near the fun.' As the afternoon wore on, Anita Leslie added, 'Winston grew ever more reflective.'[4]

Among the telegrams which Churchill dictated that day was a personal one to Roosevelt, from whom he had recently received four long telegrams. Each of them, as Churchill realised, was clearly the work of the State Department and Admiral Leahy. Indeed, on his way from Hyde Park to Warm Springs, Georgia, Roosevelt had only stopped briefly in Washington, for some luncheon meetings and to sign the telegrams.[5] To send Roosevelt some words of comfort, Churchill telegraphed:

I am delighted to see from the abundance of messages I have received from you this morning that you are back in Washington and in such vigour. I saw Bernie yesterday and he is coming tonight for the weekend. He seems in great form. As you know, I think he is a very wise man. Winant is coming tomorrow. Clemmie is in flight for Moscow and will be flying about there for at least a month, all of which hangs in my mind. By the way, did you ever receive a telegram from me of a purely private character, No. 914? It required no answer. But I should like to know that you received it. I will now address myself to our joint business.[6]

That evening, Churchill's American friend Bernard Baruch arrived

---

[1] Letter of 26 March 1945: Churchill papers, 20/198. Anita Leslie's father, Sir Shane Leslie, was Churchill's first cousin (the son of Lady Randolph Churchill's sister Leonie).

[2] Anita Leslie recollections: letter to the author, 11 February 1985.

[3] Marian Holmes diary, 30 March 1945: Marian Walker Spicer papers.

[4] Anita Leslie recollections: letter to the author, 11 February 1985.

[5] Warren F. Kimball (editor), *Churchill and Roosevelt: The Complete Correspondence*, volume 3, Princeton, New Jersey, 1984, page 597.

[6] Prime Minister's Personal Telegram, T.367/5, Prime Minister to President, No. 927, 'Personal and Top Secret', 30 March 1945: Churchill papers, 20/199.

for the weekend. The only other weekend visitors were Churchill's daughter Sarah, and his brother Jack.[1] That night Marian Holmes was again on duty. 'This is Miss Holmes,' Churchill explained to Bernard Baruch, 'she travels everywhere with me and has to put up with all kinds of conditions—even including bugs!'[2]

In Switzerland, SS General Wolff had continued his negotiations with British and American emissaries for the surrender of the German army in Italy. Churchill was concerned not to give Stalin any excuse to accuse Britain of seeking a separate peace with Germany. On March 30 he minuted to Eden:

> Have we not told the Russians that the only purpose of the contacts in Switzerland is to arrange a meeting at our military headquarters in Italy, where military questions will be discussed in the presence, if they wish, of a Russian representative, and that if at any moment political affairs are trenched upon the whole matter can be referred to the three Governments? It looks as if the Swiss conversations may go beyond that, if indeed they have not already gone beyond it. We have decided to ignore the insulting telegrams which Molotov has sent. This however does not relieve us from our obligation as Allies on any matter which might involve peace negotiations.[3]

Not Soviet protests however, but Allied strategic plans, disrupted the road to victory in the last days of March. On March 30 the Chiefs of Staff Committee discussed a telegram from Eisenhower to Montgomery, setting out his plan to advance, not to Berlin as previously agreed, but in a more southerly direction, through Leipzig to Dresden. Eisenhower having contacted Stalin about this on his own initiative, the British Chiefs of Staff were angered not to have been consulted beforehand, and protested to the United States Chiefs of Staff, as Cunningham noted on March 30, 'against this procedure and change of plan without any consultation with Combined Chiefs of Staff'.[4] Churchill supported his Chiefs of Staff, minuting to them on March 31:

> ... General Eisenhower may be wrong in supposing Berlin to be largely devoid of military and political importance. Even though German Government departments have to a great extent moved to the south, the dominating fact on German minds of the fall of Berlin should not be overlooked. The idea of neglecting Berlin and leaving it to the Russians to take at a later stage does not appear to me correct. As long as Berlin holds out and withstands a siege in the ruins, as it may easily do, German resistance

[1] Private Office diary, 30 March 1945.
[2] Marian Holmes diary, 30 March 1945: Marian Walker Spicer papers.
[3] Prime Minister's Personal Minute, M.273/5, 30 March 1945: Churchill papers, 20/209.
[4] Cunningham diary, 30 March 1945: Cunningham papers.

will be stimulated. The fall of Berlin might cause nearly all Germans to despair.

Under Eisenhower's plan, Churchill noted, 'we might be condemned to an almost static role in the North and virtually prevented from crossing the Elbe until an altogether later stage in the operations has been reached. All prospect also of the British entering Berlin with the Americans is ruled out.' Churchill added:

We weaken our case for a stronger concentration between the sea and the Hanover–Berlin flank by suggesting we should like to turn aside to clean up matters in Denmark, Norway and along the Baltic shore. It was only the other day that the CIGS was pointing out to me the impropriety of turning back or making a diversion to clean up Holland in spite of the shocking conditions prevailing in Western Holland. I accepted that view because I could not resist the argument that the speediest relief would come from the destruction of the main armed forces of the enemy and the advance towards Berlin. It seems to me to apply with much greater force against wasting time now with ferreting the Germans out of all the Baltic ports or going into Denmark. These views are contradictory.[1]

A telegram from Eisenhower had explained that the aim of the more southerly thrust was 'to join hands with the Russians or to attain general line of Elbe', and that the German Government ministries were believed to be 'moving' south, away from Berlin, whose importance was thus considerably reduced. He had no intention however, Eisenhower added, of crossing the Elbe.[2] To this, Churchill replied:

I do not know why it would be an advantage not to cross the Elbe. If the enemy's resistance should weaken, as you evidently expect and which may well be fulfilled, why should we not cross the Elbe and advance as far eastward as possible? This has an important political bearing, as the Russian armies of the South seem certain to enter Vienna and overrun Austria. If we deliberately leave Berlin to them, even if it should be in our grasp, the double event may strengthen their conviction, already apparent, that they have done everything.

Churchill still did not accept that Berlin should be by-passed. In this same telegram to Eisenhower he wrote:

. . . I do not consider myself that Berlin has yet lost its military and certainly not its political significance. The fall of Berlin would have a profound psychological effect on German resistance in every part of the Reich. While Berlin holds out great masses of Germans will feel it their duty to go down

[1] Prime Minister's Personal Minute, D.88/5, 31 March 1945: Premier papers, 3/398/5, folios 409–11.
[2] 'Forward' No. 18334, IZ 3172, 30 March 1945: Premier papers, 3/398/5.

fighting. The idea that the capture of Dresden and junction with the Russians there would be a superior gain does not commend itself to me. The parts of the German Government departments which have moved south can very quickly move northward again. But while Berlin remains under the German flag it cannot, in my opinion, fail to be the most decisive point in Germany.

Churchill went on to urge Eisenhower to persist in the plan 'on which we crossed the Rhine, namely that the 9th US Army should march with the 21st Army Group to the Elbe and beyond Berlin'. Churchill added:

This would not be in any way inconsistent with the great central thrust which you are now so rightly developing as the result of the brilliant operations of your Armies south of the Ruhr. It only shifts the weight of one army to the northern flank and this avoids the relegation of His Majesty's forces to an unexpectedly restricted sphere.[1]

On reading this last sentence, Eisenhower replied to Churchill at once:

I am disturbed, if not hurt, that you should suggest any thought on my part to 'relegate His Majesty's forces to an unexpectedly restricted sphere'. Nothing is further from my mind and I think my record of over two and a half years conduct commanding the Allied forces should eliminate any such idea. But further to this point I completely fail to see how the role, actions or prestige of the Second British and Canadian Armies are materially affected by the fact that the Ninth Army, advancing in its own zone, is controlled by Bradley, until I can be assured that our rear areas are substantially cleaned out and the thrust to Leipzig is successful. British and Canadian Armies execute work in exactly the same zone that Montgomery planned for them and he has even been given the opportunity to change that boundary if he so desires. The maximum extent to which his plans could be affected would be a possible short delay in making a power thrust across the Elbe but I repeat that if 'power' tactics are still necessary at that time then we must concentrate for each job, and must be in a satisfactory state.

If German resistance were to 'stiffen at all', Eisenhower warned, 'I can see that it is vitally necessary that I concentrate each for effort, and do not allow myself to be dispersed by attempting to do all these projects at once.'[2]

In urging Eisenhower to press forward towards Berlin, Churchill was vexed. There is only one thing worse than fighting with Allies, he commented to Brooke, 'and that is fighting without them'.[3] On the following day Churchill telegraphed to Eisenhower:

[1] Prime Minister's Personal Telegram, T.374/5, OZ 2072, 'Private, Confidential, Personal and Top Secret', 31 March 1945: Churchill papers, 20/213.
[2] 'Forward' No. 18428, IZ 3250, 'Personal', 2 p.m., 1 April 1945: Premier papers, 3/398/5, folio 415.
[3] Brooke diary, 1 April 1945: Bryant, *op. cit.*, volume 2, page 445.

It would be a grief to me if anything in my last disturbed or still more pained you. I only meant that the effect of the 21st Army Group arriving on the Elbe so spread out that it would be condemned to a static role would be a good deal less than what we hoped for, namely, to enter Berlin side by side with our American comrades. This impression arose in my mind because of what now turns out to be a misprint in your 'Forward' 18334, paragraph 4, which reached me in the following form: 'Montgomery will be responsible on patrol tasks and I propose to increase his forces &c.'

The expression 'on patrol tasks' disturbed me. It is now established that what you really said was 'for these tasks', namely, clearing the Northern ports and forcing the Elbe. The words 'on patrol tasks' were, in fact, substituted for 'for these tasks' by a clerical error. The exposure of this error will I am sure explain my phrase to you.

Returning to his 'main theme', Churchill wrote, 'I am, however, all the more impressed with the importance of entering Poland, which may well be open to us', especially in the light of a recent Soviet message to Eisenhower which had stated: 'Berlin has lost its former strategic importance'. This sentence, Churchill added, 'should be read in the light of what I mentioned of the political aspects. I deem it highly important that we should shake hands with the Russians as far to the East as possible.'[1]

Three days after sending this telegram to Eisenhower, Churchill telegraphed to Roosevelt: 'The changes in the main plan have now turned out to be very much less than we at first supposed. My personal relations with General Eisenhower are of the most friendly character. I regard the matter as closed, and to prove my sincerity I will use one of my very few Latin quotations: *Amantium irae amoris integratio est.*'[2]

'Worked for PM in the Cabinet Room at No. 10,' Marian Holmes noted in her diary on April 5. 'In dictating,' she added, 'he spelt out a Latin quotation for me and asked if I knew what it meant. "I'm afraid not." He said "It means the wrath of lovers hots up their love." '[3] The President's staff translated the quotation for him, rendering it more prosaically as 'Lover's quarrels always go with true love'.[4]

As relations with Russia worsened, Roosevelt agreed to telegraph

[1] Prime Minister's Personal Telegram, T.386/5, 'Private, Confidential, Personal and Top Secret', OZ 2096, 5.20 p.m., 2 April 1945: Premier papers, 3/398/5, folio 418.

[2] Prime Minister's Personal Telegram, T.405/4, Prime Minister to President, No. 933, 'Personal and Top Secret', 5 April 1945: Churchill papers, 20/214.

[3] Marian Holmes diary, 5 April 1945: Marian Walker Spicer papers.

[4] Warren J. Kimball (editor), *Churchill and Roosevelt: The Complete Correspondence*, Princeton 1984, volume 3, page 612.

direct to Stalin about Molotov's refusal to allow the British and American nominees to be considered for the Polish Provisional Government. In support of Roosevelt's protest, which was milder than he had wished, Churchill telegraphed to Stalin on March 31. Churchill wanted to know what Eden thought of his telegram. Eden 'likes it very much', John Peck reported back to Churchill.[1] In his telegram to Stalin, Churchill described the 'surprise and regret' with which he and Roosevelt had learned that Molotov's 'spontaneous offer' to allow observers or missions to enter Poland 'has now been withdrawn'. Churchill added:

We are therefore deprived of all means of checking for ourselves the information, often of a most painful character, which is sent us almost daily by the Polish Government in London. We do not understand why a veil of secrecy should thus be drawn over the Polish scene. We offer the fullest facilities to the Soviet Government to send Missions or individuals to visit any of the territories in our military occupation. In several cases this offer has been accepted by the Soviets and visits have taken place to mutual satisfaction. We ask that the principle of reciprocity shall be observed in these matters, which would help to make so good a foundation for our enduring partnership.

If their efforts to reach agreement about Poland were 'doomed to failure', Churchill told Stalin, he would be 'bound to confess the fact' to Parliament after the Easter Recess, and he reminded the Soviet leader:

No one has pleaded the cause of Russia with more fervour and conviction than I have tried to do. I was the first to raise my voice on 22nd June 1941. It is more than a year since I proclaimed to a startled world the justice of the Curzon Line for Russia's Western frontier, and this frontier has now been accepted by both the British Parliament and the President of the United States. It is as a sincere friend of Russia that I make my personal appeal to you and to your colleagues to come to a good understanding about Poland with the Western Democracies and not to smite down the hands of comradeship in the future guidance of the world which we now extend.[2]

'I doubt whether the Russians will give way enough,' Eden noted in his diary on April 1, the day this telegram was despatched to Moscow.[3] That same day, news began to reach London that the fifteen Polish leaders who had begun talks in Pruszkow with Colonel Pimenov on March 27 had disappeared.[4] To his wife, who had just reached

---

[1] John Peck, note for Churchill, 30 March 1945: Premier papers, 3/356/9, folio 548.

[2] Prime Minister's Personal Telegram, T.379/5, 'Personal and Top Secret', sent 1 April 1945 (sent on the previous day to Roosevelt as Prime Minister's Personal Telegram, T.371/5, Prime Minister to President, No. 929 of 31 March 1945: Churchill papers, 20/213.

[3] Eden diary, 1 April 1945: Eden memoirs, *The Reckoning, op. cit.*, page 526.

[4] Letter from Count Raczynski to Eden, and enclosure, 1 April 1945: Premier papers, 3/356/7.

Moscow from Cairo, Churchill telegraphed on the following day: 'At the moment you are the one bright spot in Anglo-Russian relations.'[1]

On April 3 the Anglo-American forces completed their encirclement of the Ruhr. Prisoners were being taken at the rate of between 15,000 to 20,000 a day.[2] The conquest of Germany could now be only a matter of two months at the outside.[3] But the political and ideological clash over Poland cast a dark cloud over the imminence of victory. 'The changes in the Russian attitude and atmosphere since Yalta are grave,' Churchill minuted to the Chiefs of Staff Committee on April 3, in suggesting a policy of closer cooperation with Turkey.[4] To the Dominion and Indian representatives who attended the War Cabinet on April 3, Churchill warned:

Relations with Russia, which had offered such fair promise at the Crimea Conference, had grown less cordial during the ensuing weeks. There had been grave difficulties over the Polish question; and it now seemed possible that Russia would not be willing to give full co-operation at the San Francisco Conference on the proposed new World Organization. It was by no means clear that we could count on Russia as a beneficent influence in Europe, or as a willing partner in maintaining the peace of the world. Yet, at the end of the war, Russia would be left in a position of preponderant power and influence throughout the whole of Europe.[5]

As to the United States, Churchill added, she had made 'enormous strides during the last two years, and had built up a military machine and supporting war production which was maintaining a vast military effort, not only in Europe but in the Pacific theatre'. The resources in men and material commanded by the United States 'were vastly superior to our own; and they had acquired during this war a new capacity and experience in marshalling these resources in war'. The British Commonwealth could only 'hold her own', Churchill added, 'by our superior statecraft and experience, and, above all, by the unity of the British Commonwealth of Nations'.

[1] 'Private', 2 April 1945: Churchill papers, 20/204.
[2] War Cabinet No. 39 of 1945, 3 April 1945: Cabinet papers, 65/50.
[3] On 3 April 1945 Churchill gave May 31 as the date 'towards which we should now work' but he added: 'it may well be that the end will come before this', possibly 'on 30th April'. (Prime Minister's Personal Minute, M.289/5, to the Ministry of Agriculture, Food, and War Transport, 3 April 1945: Churchill papers, 20/209.)
[4] Prime Minister's Personal Minute, D.94/5, 3 April 1945: Churchill papers, 20/209.
[5] War Cabinet No. 39 of 1945, 5.30 p.m., 3 April 1945, Confidential Annex: Cabinet papers, 65/52. The Dominion and Indian representatives present were Field Marshal Smuts (Prime Minister of South Africa), Peter Fraser (Prime Minister of New Zealand), F. M. Forde (Deputy Prime Minister of Australia), H. V. Evatt (Attorney General and Minister for External Affairs, Australia), Field Marshal Viscount Wavell (Viceroy of India) and Sir Firoz Khan Noon (Representative of the Government of India).

This 'superior statecraft' was even now facing its stiffest test of the war: the suggestion that Britain should refuse to send a delegation to San Francisco, as a 'possible stand', Churchill minuted to Lord Cranborne at the Dominions Office, 'against Russia's behaviour since Yalta about Poland'. Cranborne himself had proposed this course, writing to Churchill on April 3: 'It may not, of course, I fully recognize, be possible in any case to prevent Russia from doing what she wants in Eastern Europe. But we ought surely not to tie our hands before-hand, or present her with an umbrella of respectability for her misdeeds.' [1] Churchill replied to Cranborne that same day:

The picture of all the United Nations, with Britain and the United States at their head, being put off their stroke by a mere gesture of insolence from Stalin and Molotov is a bad one. The picture of the United States and Britain holding a Conference without Russia which all the United Nations attend is an immense rebuke to Russia. Moreover, the military power of Britain and the United States is at this moment greater than that of Russia and comprises practically the whole world outside Russian territory and the conquered Satellite Powers. There is no doubt on which side the hopes of humanity will rest.

Even if Russia herself did not come to San Francisco, and preferred to fight out the Polish question 'on the side of the Lublin Poles', Churchill felt that the Conference should go ahead. 'Les absents ont toujours tort', he told Cranborne. Churchill added: 'Nothing would show the Soviets where they get off more clearly.[2] Thus I consider that this is the best tactical path to follow, and also the rightful moral path for the great mass of the world to follow, headed by the English-speaking Armies and forces of all kinds.' [3]

The disputes with Russia were continuous: on April 3 Stalin had sent Roosevelt an abusive telegram, again claiming that the aim of the negotiations in Switzerland between the British and Americans, and SS General Wolff, for the surrender of all German forces in Italy, had 'permitted the Anglo-American troops to advance to the East and the Anglo-Americans promised in return to ease for the Germans the peace terms'. Roosevelt, in his reply, had told Stalin: 'Frankly I cannot avoid a feeling of bitter resentment toward your informers,

[1] 'Private and Personal', 3 April 1945: Foreign Office papers, 954/20, folios 529–30.

[2] Experts gathered at the International Court of Justice in the Hague in February 1985 confirmed privately that les absents on toujours tort 'has no roots in international law'. The practice of the International Court of Justice has indeed, in recent years, been the reverse. In the case of Iceland (fisheries), France (nuclear tests) and Iran (hostages) the Court has made persistent efforts to make allowances for the absentees' supposed position.

[3] Prime Minister's Personal Minute, M.291/5, 3 April 1945: Foreign Office papers, 954/20, folios 531–4.

whoever they are, for such vile misrepresentations of my actions or those of my trusted subordinates.'[1]

Churchill was much impressed by Roosevelt's protest. 'I am astounded,' he telegraphed to the President on April 5, 'that Stalin should have addressed to you a message so insulting to the honour of the United States and also of Great Britain.' Churchill added:

There is very little doubt in my mind that the Soviet leaders, whoever they may be, are surprised and disconcerted at the rapid advance of the Allied Armies in the west and the almost total defeat of the enemy on our front especially as they say they are themselves in no position to deliver a decisive attack before the middle of May. All this makes it the more important that we should join hands with the Russian armies as far to the east as possible and if circumstances allow, enter Berlin.

Now that the Russians were 'on the eve of taking Vienna', Churchill wrote, 'and very likely will occupy the whole of Austria, it may well be prudent for us to hold as much as possible in the north'.

The War Cabinet had instructed Churchill to send his own message of protest to Stalin. As Churchill told Roosevelt:

We must always be anxious lest the brutality of the Russian messages does not foreshadow some deep change of policy for which they are preparing. On the whole I incline to think it is no more than their natural expression when vexed or jealous.

For that very reason I deem it of the highest importance that a firm and blunt stand should be made at this juncture by our two countries in order that the air may be cleared and they realize that there is a point beyond which we will not tolerate insult. I believe this is the best chance of saving the future. If they are ever convinced that we are afraid of them and can be bullied into submission, then indeed I should despair of our future relations with them and much else.[2]

To Stalin, Churchill telegraphed that night, with the approval of the War Cabinet that, 'We consider that Field Marshal Alexander has full right to accept the surrender of the German army of 25 divisions on his front in Italy and to discuss such matters with German envoys who have the power to settle the terms of capitulation.' Nevertheless, Churchill added, 'we took especial care to invite your representatives to this purely military discussion at his headquarters should it take place. In fact however nothing resulted from any contacts in Switzerland. Our officers returned from Switzerland without having

[1] Text in President to Prime Minister, No. 734, 'Personal and Top Secret', 5 April 1945: Churchill papers, 20/214.

[2] Prime Minister's Personal Telegram, T.406/5, Prime Minister to President, No. 934, 'Personal and Top Secret', 5 April 1945: Churchill papers, 20/214.

succeeded in fixing a rendezvous in Italy for Kesselring's emissaries to come to.' Churchill's telegram continued:

There is no connexion whatever between any contacts at Berne or elsewhere with the total defeat of the German Armies on the Western Front. They have in fact fought with great obstinacy and inflicted upon us and the American Armies since the opening of our February offensive up to March 28 upwards of 87,000 casualties. However being outnumbered on the ground and literally overwhelmed in the Air by the vastly superior Anglo-American Air forces, which in the month of March alone dropped over 200,000 tons of bombs on Germany, the German Armies in the west have been decisively broken.

The fact that the German forces were outnumbered on the ground in the West, Churchill added, in what was intended as a conciliatory gesture, 'is due to the magnificent attacks and weight of the Soviet Armies'.[1]

It was to try to influence the line which would exist once those armies were to link up with the British and American forces that Churchill now directed his attention to the situation when the respective forces 'arrive in contact'. At that moment, he minuted to the Chiefs of Staff Committee, 'after the preliminary salutations have been exchanged', the armies should 'rest opposite each other' in the positions reached. His minute continued:

Thus, if we cross the Elbe and advance to Berlin, or on a line between Berlin and the Baltic which is all well within the Russian zone, we should not give this up as a military matter. It is a matter of State to be considered between the three Governments, and in relation to what the Russians do in the south where they will soon have occupied, not only Vienna, but all Austria. There cannot be such a hurry about our withdrawing from a place we have gained that the few days necessary for consulting the Governments in Washington and London cannot be found.

'I attach great importance to this,' Churchill added. Any decisions on holding the line or withdrawing could not be left to the Staff level. 'They must be referred to the President and me.'[2]

Before going to Chequers that Friday, Churchill sent his wife an account of his life since she had left for Moscow.

My darling Clemmie,

Since you were swirled away into the night, I have had the most exacting time. What with looking after Bernie Baruch and all the Dominion Premiers, as well as overwhelming toil, I have not found a minute to write. It is now

---

[1] Prime Minister's Personal Telegram, T.404/5, No. 1676 to Moscow, 'Top Secret', sent 12.40 a.m., 6 April 1945: Churchill papers, 20/214.

[2] Prime Minister's Personal Minute, D.99/5, 6 April 1945: Premier papers, 3/398/5, folio 395.

Friday, and I have just finished my sleep and am going down to Chequers, where Smuts is spending the weekend with me. Baruch and a very influential American called Flynn come tomorrow, and on Sunday Dr Evatt and Mr Forde (Deputy Prime Minister, Australia) arrive with their wives for luncheon. On Sunday also Mary Marlborough is coming over and bringing Blandford, now a Sandhurst cadet, to luncheon, and Mr Fraser (New Zealand) is spending the night. I arranged for Sarah to attend on me for weekends on duty while you are away, to help out with various official guests.

On Tuesday last Smuts dined with me alone at the Annexe. On Wednesday I gave a dinner at No. 10 to a lot of finance people, including the Chancellor of the Exchequer, the Governor of the Bank,[1] Lord Keynes, Max and Brendan, to hear Baruch talk, which he does to great purpose, being full of hope for the future of the world and declaring that we shall all be unable to do the work for the next seven years that will be clamoured for. All the stocks of the world will have to be replenished and all the houses and their fittings. There will be no unemployment, and international trade will flow again. Apparently we are to have all that the Huns and the Japs used to have, or most of it, and America is to help us in all suitable ways to get going.

A great deal of this 'pep' talk was agreed with by my friends above-mentioned. But I keep on asking myself all sorts of awkward questions. How are we to balance our Budget? How are we to place our exports where they are wanted; and how are we to make up across the exchange for all our losses of foreign investments; and how are we to buy the balance of our food, etc.?

Today I took Baruch to luncheon at New Court with Anthony de Rothschild. Jack[2] arranged this, and a number of important people, about ten, were brought in. All the windows have been blown out and patched with cardboard, so it was dark and cold. We had more 'pep' talk, which seemed to me to do good, especially with others there to put on the brake.

The President sent me several messages by Baruch, and now that Harry is ill and Byrnes has resigned, my poor friend is very much alone and, according to all accounts I receive, is bereft of much of his vigour. Many of the telegrams I get from him are clearly the work of others around him. However yesterday he came through with a telegraph, which perhaps Archie has shown you as I told him to do, which certainly ends up with a flash of his old fire, and is about the hottest thing I have seen so far in diplomatic intercourse.

Nine days later Hopkins told Halifax that Roosevelt was then so ill that 'hardly anything' of his recent telegrams 'had been his own—not even last sentence of his communication to UJ on "Crossword" '.[3]

---

[1] Lord Catto. The Chancellor of the Exchequer was Sir John Anderson.

[2] Churchill's brother.

[3] Telegram No. 2572 from Washington, 'Personal and Top Secret', 15 April 1945: Churchill papers, 20/214.

Churchill's letter to his wife continued:

I have told Archie to keep you well informed, but this will have to cease when you go away from Moscow. You will not have a cypher, and much of this stuff is dynamite. The same is true of letters. I do not feel able to write freely because I do not know how letters will be forwarded from Moscow. My telegrams also will be sent en clair from the Embassy. Well you know how great our difficulties are about Poland, Roumania, and this other row about alleged negotiations. I intend still to persevere, but it is very difficult.

What puzzles me is the inconsistency. There is no doubt that your visit is giving sincere pleasure. Gousev [1] called at the Foreign Office yesterday, as Anthony thought, to begin a long attack, but instead he spent a long time in conveying a message from his Government in praise of you and your work, and asking whether they might offer you the Order of the Red Banner of Labour, which was of course approved. I am hoping to find in my Box the full account of this interview, which Anthony promised to send me. If so I will enclose it.

I have also had a wrangle between our Staffs and the Americans, in which I participated with telegrams to the President, about a change of plan Eisenhower introduced on the Western Front, which has the effect among other things of taking away the 9th US Army from Montgomery's command and leaving him with a rough but considerably restricted and unspectacular task. The only times I ever quarrel with the Americans are when they fail to give us a fair share of opportunity to win glory.

Undoubtedly I feel much pain when I see our armies so much smaller than theirs. It has always been my wish to keep equal, but how can you do that against so mighty a nation and a population nearly three times your own?

The advances have been wonderful and, barring accidents, the end cannot be far off. Alex too is on the move, and Dicky, reinforced by General Oliver Leese, has done wonders in Burma. Our fleet also has fought by the side of the Americans in the great operations going on amid the Pacific islands. So one cannot doubt we are doing our bit, which must ever be the aim of the good and faithful ally.

I hope that Montgomery's advance will drain the Boche out of Holland, and that we shall soon begin to throw in food. At any rate for a whole week there have been no bombs or bangs. I have moved the Cabinets back to No. 10, and have also had one or two meals there. I am giving orders for the rehabilitation of that dwelling, otherwise we shall not be able to use it this year. If you have any strong views about this, pray write to me, so that I may have them carried out. The garden had become very nice now, the lawn is in good order, the herbaceous border is fully stocked and the little magnolia tree is at its best. We have had three or four sunny days during the week, but now it is cold and raining again.

One big goldfish was retrieved from the bottom of the pool at Chartwell. All the rest have been stolen or else eaten by an otter. I have put Scotland

---

[1] The Soviet Ambassador.

Yard on the work of finding the thief. I fear we shall never see our poor fish any more, and nothing is left but an unfruitful vengeance, and that about 1,000–1 against a thief and 20,000–1 against an otter.

The greater part of my Government have departed or about to depart to various countries on one excuse or another. Anthony continues to have a sore throat. I made him have a swab taken and, as I thought, a variety of streptos and staphylos[1] were found, for which he is now taking penicillin. I am myself in the best of health, but I have not found a minute to spare for the two or three interesting books I have at my bed-side. Indeed I am far behind this weekend in the ordinary Boxes.

I have had also to deal with Party matters. We have upwards of 540 candidates already chosen, and it is quite possible that the Election will take place at the end of June or July. Everyone is resigning himself to this unpleasant fact.

Last night I gave a dinner, through Crankie,[2] of thirty-five people in the big dining room of No. 10 to the Dominions representatives, War Cabinet, Chiefs of Staff and others. There was the greatest good temper and a brilliant speech was made by the Indian delegate, Sir Ramaswami Mudaliar. I told him that if he let it off at San Francisco in the same way, he would sweep the board for the British Empire. This he intends to do.

There is no doubt that Victory is an intoxicating draught. All these men from all over the Empire arrive with eyes glowing with admiration, and have nothing but praise for our conduct during these terrible years. The sense that the end may be near in Europe entrances all minds, and will give us, I trust, the impetus to overcome the many labours and uncertainties that lie ahead.

I have seen no one at all outside my official world, except that Anthony and I went to luncheon with the King of Norway, who is not at all well-disposed towards the Germans, nor is his son with the silly laugh. Certainly it is the silliest laugh I have ever heard. One of Hitler's punishments ought to be being tied up and made to listen to it for twelve hours a day.

Next Wednesday the King comes, and this will I expect be the last of the dinners of our war-time Cabinet, famous I think I may call it. The Wednesday following Mary Marlborough is to give me a dinner at Buck's Club, where gaiety will be the order of the night.

I fear this is a most aimless account of my doings. Like the entry in Mark Twain's diary: 'Got up, washed, went to bed.' Looking back on the days, they seem little more than that.

Then look at the questions looming ahead and the number of decisions which I shall have to take personally in the formation of a new Government,

[1] Dr Michael Dunnill writes: ' "Streptos" and "staphylos" refers to two groups of bacteria, known as streptococci and staphylococci, which commonly infect the upper respiratory tract resulting in sore throat, tonsilitis, etc. Before the advent of penicillin such infections often gave rise to unpleasant complications, and indeed do so today if not properly treated. Fortunately all streptococci are sensitive to penicillin, and in 1944 so were most staphylococci, though nowadays there are many resistant strains.' (Letter to the author, 30 June 1985.)

[2] 'Crankie': Sir Eric Crankshaw, secretary of the Government Hospitality Fund from 1929 to 1949. In 1920 he had been Churchill's Assistant Private Secretary at the War Office.

with all the personal pangs and pinches entailed. However so far everyone seems quite ready to be told where they get off or get in.

That business about the film rights of the *English-Speaking Peoples* is now settled, and the cheque is on its way to the Bank.

I am going to try to get to Chartwell on Monday if the weather is fine. The next day the Parl begins, and they will clamour for a statement about Poland. Our news from there is conflicting but, on the whole, not too discouraging. There is an intense desire for independence, and no particular admiration for either of the different Governments, or would-be Governments, which desire to be the saviours of the land on the cheap. I do not think there have been any serious troubles, but of course we are not allowed in to see.

I am sending out a call for MPs and candidates to come home from all fronts unless actually engaged in fighting. Randolph may be well enough to come home by the time you pass through Italy and, if so, you might give him a passage in Skymaster.

Bernie brought over a complete outfit of clothes and some chocolate for Winston, and the presentation took place this morning, but I did not hear about it until it was all over, so I have not seen the child.[1]

At dinner at Chequers that night, the talk, as Colville noted, 'was of the Americans, the PM saying that there was no greater exhibition of power in history than the American army fighting the battle of the Ardennes with its left hand and advancing from island to island towards Japan with its right'. After dinner, Churchill and his guests saw the Russian film *Kutusov*, which Stalin had sent him. 'The PM is greatly impressed,' Colville noted, 'by the unprejudiced attitude shewn in the film to the Tsarist régime.'[2] On the following night there was another Russian film, a documentary of the Yalta Conference.[3] After the film show, Churchill worked until 2 a.m., 'waxing very contemptuous of the FO', Colville noted, 'who, he said, always had to be active and never could see when it was wise to do nothing. "Mise en demeure" was a very good diplomatic phrase, but he never saw it used nowadays.'[4]

At midday on Monday April 9 Churchill drove from Chequers to Chartwell, with his daughter Sarah, for a picnic lunch. During the drive he dictated a further letter to his wife:

During the weekend I have had such good news about you from Moscow, and Clark Kerr telegraphs that your visit there did the utmost good at a most difficult time. I have telegraphed to M. Maisky, thanking them both, as

[1] Letter of 6 April 1945: Spencer-Churchill papers. As of 1986 no film had been made of Churchill's *History of the English Speaking Peoples* (first published in 1956).

[2] Colville diary, 6 April 1945: Colville papers.

[3] Private Office diary, 7 April 1945.

[4] Colville diary, 7 April 1945: Colville papers. 'Mise en demeure': a holding operation, to 'put on hold'.

you asked. I do hope you will be sensible and not overdo it. Insist upon days of leisure. They will understand. Otherwise you may be killed with kindness. The Soviet Press make a great fuss of your visit. I suppose you have been shown the extracts by the Embassy. Nevertheless I am enclosing a copy of what reached me.

I am longing to hear from you by secret channels about your interview with Stalin. Except any messages sent through the Embassy in the Embassy cipher, you should write only what you do not mind being read. I shall do the same in my telegrams.

We have had an important Chequers weekend, and it passed off very well. Mr Flynn could not come after all, but we had Judge Rosenman to stay last night. He has come over from the President, and has visited the liberated regions of Europe. I found him most interesting on the subjects of feeding the liberated peoples and the punishment of war criminals. I am now travelling from Chequers to Chartwell. It appears there are no bolts on the doors of the house, and some of them could be pushed open quite easily. I propose to take measures for the greater security of the valuables we have inside. Sarah comes with me. She was the mainstay of the weekend, and I was exceptionally punctual.[1]

Of the conversation with Judge Rosenman, Jock Colville had noted in his diary: 'the PM kept him up till 3 a.m. on the theme that Britain shall not starve or lower her exiguous rations still further to feed Axis satellites, while the American army and civil population live on their present gigantic diet'.[2]

To Roosevelt, Churchill telegraphed on the following day about the 'desperate' plight of the civil population of German-occupied Holland, where 'between two and three million people are facing starvation', and where 'large numbers' were already dying each day. Churchill asked Roosevelt to join him in arranging, through the Swiss government, for the despatch of food supplies through neutral Sweden. 'We invite the German Government,' Churchill added, 'to accord the facilities to enable this to be done.'[3] Before making any arrangements through the Red Cross with any German authority, Roosevelt replied, 'we should inform Stalin'.[4]

With Soviet approval, negotiations began with the German High Commissioner in Holland. It was agreed that in return for a halt to the westward advance of the Allied armies, the Germans would stop all repressive measures against the Dutch, and would help in the

---

[1] Letter of 9 April 1945: Spencer-Churchill papers. John Thomas Flynn, author and journalist, was a former Associate Editor of *Colliers* (1937 to 1942). Samuel Rosenman was a friend of Roosevelt from his pre-Presidential days, and for many years the President's chief speech writer.

[2] Colville diary, 8 April 1945: Colville papers.

[3] Prime Minister's Personal Telegram, T.426/5, Prime Minister to President, No. 938, 'Personal and Top Secret', 10 April 1945: Churchill papers, 20/214.

[4] President to Prime Minister, No. 740, 'Personal and Top Secret', 10 April 1945: Churchill papers, 20/214.

distribution of Allied relief supplies. 'The Dutch nation,' Churchill later wrote, 'has since most gratefully acknowledged by word and deed the help we were so proud to give them after their bravely borne afflictions.' [1]

At Chartwell, Churchill and his daughter had their picnic luncheon. They then returned to London, in time for Churchill to attend the evening War Cabinet, where much of the discussion was about the imminent end of the war in Europe. 'The Prime Minister,' as the minutes recorded, 'said that he hoped the day of the celebrations would be known as VE-day.' [2]

That night Churchill dined alone with Sarah. [3] Before dinner he wrote again to Clementine:

> I think there is very little doubt that the Government will break up shortly. Bevin has made a very hostile speech (answered today by Brendan) and it is clear he will not work with us. Generally the Party men are anxious to get at each other, and matters have gone so far that life inside the Cabinet will not be agreeable and might easily become inefficient. The prodigious advances we have made in Germany may easily bring matters to a close. [4]
>
> I expect the General Election about the middle of June, with the announcement of a dissolution in May. If we wait beyond June the holiday season will, with its irresistible lure, do harm to our interests. These dates seem to me to fit in very well with your plans. I will of course let you know about the President's moves. It would probably not be fitting that he should be here once the electoral fight was definitely begun.
>
> My darling one I think always of you & am so proud of you. Yr personality reaches the gt masses & touches their hearts. With all my love & constant kisses.
>
> I remain ever yr devoted husband
>
> W

Churchill ended his letter with his customary additional signature, a sketch of a pig, and also with a postscript: 'Sarah is dining with me alone *now* so I must cease.' [5]

That evening, in Italy, the Eighth Army launched its main assault northward, between Faenza and the southern shore of Lake Comacchio. Among the units participating in the attack, Alexander tele-

---

[1] Winston S. Churchill, *The Second World War*, volume 6, London 1954, page 411.

[2] War Cabinet No. 41 of 1945, 5.30 p.m., 9 April 1945: Cabinet papers, 65/50.

[3] Private Office diary, 9 April 1945.

[4] Commenting on Ernest Bevin's 'strong political attack' on the Conservatives, Jock Colville noted in his diary on 9 April 1945: 'The PM said to me while he was dressing at Chequers that if the Labour Party were going ahead on those lines, he thought the time had come for him to "brusquer les affaires"—i.e. to hasten the departure of the opposition groups from the Government.'

[5] Letter of 9 April 1945: Spencer-Churchill papers.

graphed to Churchill, were the 8th Indian Division, the 2nd New Zealand Division, the 6th South African Armoured Division, the 2nd Polish Corps, the Italian Cremona and Friuli Groups, and the Jewish Brigade. A diversionary attack was carried out by the 92nd United States Division.[1]

At noon on April 10 Churchill attended the Memorial Service for Lloyd George at Westminster Abbey. Among those present were Smuts, in his Field Marshal's uniform, and two of Lloyd George's grandsons, both in the uniforms of Army officers.[2]

That afternoon, in the House of Commons, Churchill presented a table of war casualties. There had been, between 3 September 1939 and 28 February 1945, a total of 216,287 British deaths on land, sea and in the air, 59,793 civilian casualties in Britain from German bombing raids and V bombs, and 30,179 merchant seamen killed as a result of enemy action.[3]

On April 10 Churchill received Stalin's answer to his strong rebuke of April 5. 'Neither I nor Molotov,' the Soviet leader declared, 'had any intention of "blackening" anyone.' But it was not a matter of 'wanting to "blacken", but of our having developed differing points of view as regards the rights and obligations of an ally'. Stalin added:

My messages are personal and strictly confidential. This makes it possible to speak one's mind clearly and frankly. This is the advantage of confidential communications. If, however, you are going to regard every frank statement of mine as offensive, it will make this kind of communication very difficult. I can assure you that I had and have no intention of offending anyone.[4]

'He has climbed down, ungraciously, in his way,' Colville noted, over the accusations of secret negotiations in Switzerland. 'It boiled down to this,' Colville added, 'the Russians are jealous of our rapid success

---

[1] F 61348, 'Top Secret', 17 April 1945: Churchill papers, 20/215.

[2] *The Times*, 11 April 1945 (there is a cutting of the Memorial Service report in Premier papers, 4/7/13, folio 1044).

[3] *Hansard*, 10 April 1945, columns 1689–90. In the First World War there had been 750,000 British military, air and naval deaths. Between the Normandy landings on 6 June 1944 and 9 April 1945 the battle deaths in the Allied ranks were: American, 82,020; British, 27,497; Canadian, 9,176; French, 8,981; Polish, 1,061; Czech, 113; Belgian 55 and Dutch 20, a total of 128,923. ('Top Secret', 'Notes for Prime Minister's Speech, 19 April 1945': Cabinet papers, 127/40.)

[4] Message sent 7 April 1945, received 10 April 1945, 'Premier J. V. Stalin to Prime Minister W. Churchill', 'Secret and Personal', sent by Churchill to Roosevelt as Prime Minister's Personal Telegram, T.434/5, Prime Minister to President, No. 941, 'Personal and Top Secret', 11 April 1945: Churchill papers, 20/214.

in the West, while, on the Oder at any rate, they are stuck.'[1] In answer to Churchill's complaint about no observers being allowed into Poland, Stalin wrote:

You wonder why the Polish theatre of military operations must be wrapped in mystery. In fact there is no mystery here. You ignore the fact that if British observers or other foreign observers were sent into Poland, the Poles would regard this as an insult to their national dignity, bearing in mind the fact, moreover, that the present attitude of the British Government to the Provisional Polish Government is regarded as unfriendly by the latter. So far as the Soviet Government is concerned, it cannot but take account of the negative attitude of the Provisional Government to the question of sending foreign observers into Poland.[2]

Stalin's answer effectively destroyed all hope of British or American observers being sent to Poland. 'I think the time has come,' Churchill minuted to Eden on April 8, 'for a show-down on these points, and the British and the United States are completely aligned. We may go far and long before finding an equally good occasion.'[3]

Four days later, however, Churchill received a telegram from Roosevelt, unwilling to make this an issue between the three leaders. 'I would minimize the general Soviet problem as much as possible,' Roosevelt wrote, 'because these problems, in one form or another, seem to arise every day and most of them straighten out as in the case of the Berne meeting.' Roosevelt added: 'We must be firm, however, and our course thus far is correct.'[4]

The difficulties of persuading the Americans to join with Britain in protest underlined the fact that, in the aftermath of Yalta, Britain, as Churchill later wrote, 'though still very powerful, could not act decisively alone'. Churchill added: 'I could at this stage only warn and plead. Thus this climax of apparently measureless success was to me a most unhappy time. I moved amid cheering crowds, or sat at a table adorned with congratulations and blessings from every part of the Grand Alliance, with an aching heart and a mind oppressed by forebodings.'[5]

On April 11, the Soviet Union signed a Treaty of friendship, mutual aid and post-war collaboration with Tito's Yugoslavia. That day, American forces reached the Elbe, and on April 12 they crossed it.

---

[1] Colville diary, 10 April 1945: Colville papers.

[2] 'Secret and Personal', sent 7 April 1945, received 10 April 1945: Churchill papers, 20/214.

[3] Prime Minister's Personal Minute, M.315/5, 8 April 1945: Foreign Office papers, 954/20, folio 548.

[4] President to Prime Minister, No. 742, 'Personal and Top Secret', 12 April 1945: Premier papers, 3/356/6.

[5] Winston S. Churchill, *The Second World War*, volume 6, London 1954, page 400.

Eisenhower's armies were now less than seventy miles from Berlin. The Thousand Year Reich, which had lasted for just twelve years, was almost at an end. The war with Japan, however, Churchill wrote to Herbert Morrison on April 11, 'still hangs over us like a vulture'.[1]

---

[1] Prime Minister's Personal Minute, M.329/5, 11 April 1945: Premier papers, 4/41/3, folio 234.

66

'An enviable death'

AT five o'clock on the afternoon of 12 April 1945, Churchill posed
for photographs with the Dominion representatives. He then
rested until nine in the evening, before going with Bernard Baruch to
a dinner of the Other Club, after which he returned to the Annexe.
That night Churchill telegraphed to his wife: 'I am very glad your
visit to Leningrad was so pleasant and interesting. Mary's MBE is
gazetted. You saw perhaps that poor Tom Mitford died of wounds,
and Basil Dufferin was killed. Here everything is quiet except politics.
Love.' [1]

It was midnight. As he worked, Churchill was brought the news
that Roosevelt was dead.

'I have just heard the grievous news of President Roosevelt's death,'
he added on his telegram to Clementine, and his distress was evident
to all those around him. 'I am much weakened in every way by his
loss,' he told Captain Pim early on the morning of April 13, as he set
about making arrangements for a possible flight to Hyde Park, for the
funeral on the following day. [2]

Churchill had already telegraphed to Lord Halifax in Washington, to ask if it would be all right if he came to the funeral. 'Have
spoken to Harry Hopkins and Stettinius,' Lord Halifax telegraphed
that same night, 'who are both much moved by your thought of
possibly coming over and who both warmly agree with my judgment
of the immense effect for good that would be produced. Nor do I
overlook the value if you came of your seeing Truman.'

The 'actual funeral at Hyde Park', Halifax added, 'would be private', except for Roosevelt's Cabinet, 'and of course you if you
came'. [3]

---

[1] Telegram of 13 April 1945 No. 1808, Foreign Office to Moscow, Spencer-Churchill papers.
[2] Pim recollections: Pim papers.
[3] Washington telegram No. 2484 of 12 April 1945, received 7.40 a.m., 13 April 1945, 'Top
Secret': Churchill papers, 20/214.

That Friday morning, Churchill sent his telegrams of condolence. The first was to Eleanor Roosevelt, to whom he wrote:

Accept my most profound sympathy in your grievous loss which is also the loss of the British nation and of the cause of freedom in every land. I feel so deeply for you all. As for myself, I have lost a dear and cherished friendship which was forged in the fire of war. I trust you may find consolation in the magnitude of his work and the glory of his name.[1]

A further telegram of condolence went that morning to Harry Hopkins:

I understand how deep your feelings of grief must be. I feel with you that we have lost one of our greatest friends and one of the most valiant champions of the causes for which we fight. I feel a very painful personal loss quite apart from the ties of public action which bound us so closely together. I had a true affection for Franklin.[2]

Churchill also telegraphed to Roosevelt's successor, Harry S. Truman, the former Vice President:

Pray accept from me the expression of my personal sympathy in the loss which you and the American nation have sustained in the death of our illustrious friend. I hope that I may be privileged to renew with you the intimate comradeship in the great cause we all serve that I enjoyed through these terrible years with him. I offer you my respectful good wishes as you step into the breach in the victorious lines of the United Nations.[3]

On April 13, as news of Roosevelt's death spread through the shocked ranks of the Allies, the Red Army entered Vienna. In Germany, the British army entered Belsen concentration camp, and the Americans entered Buchenwald. In London, Churchill told the War Cabinet of the representations which he and Roosevelt had made to Stalin 'for the reconstitution of the Polish Government'. Stalin's 'main reply' to these representations, Churchill explained, had been to Roosevelt. 'He thought,' the minutes recorded, 'that, in view of President Roosevelt's death, he must now take the lead in continuing this exchange with Marshal Stalin, but it was most important that the United Kingdom and United States Governments should continue to march in close accord in their handling of these representations to the Soviet Government in respect of Poland.' Churchill therefore

---

[1] Prime Minister's Personal Telegram, T.450/5, 13 April 1945: Churchill papers, 20/214. Later that day, John Martin minuted to Churchill: 'Mr Winant has telephoned to ask me to say that he thought your message to Mrs Roosevelt was the most beautiful he had ever read.' (Minute of 13 April 1945: Churchill papers, 20/199.)

[2] Prime Minister's Personal Telegram, T.454/5, 'Personal', 13 April 1945: Churchill papers, 20/199.

[3] Prime Minister's Personal Telegram, T.455/5, 'Personal' (seen by Eden, who agreed), 13 April 1945: Churchill papers, 20/199.

proposed 'to prepare a draft reply to Marshal Stalin, which he would send to the Foreign Secretary in Washington, so that the latter might take the opportunity of discussing its terms personally with President Truman and Mr Stettinius.' It was 'encouraging' Churchill added, 'that Marshal Stalin should have indicated readiness to use his influence with the Lublin Government to persuade them to withdraw their objections to M. Mikolajczyk's participation in the consultations about the reconstitution of the Polish Government, if the latter were willing to make a public statement accepting the decisions of the Crimea Conference on the Polish question and declaring that he favoured the establishment of friendly relations between Poland and the Soviet Union'. Churchill hoped that Mikolajczyk 'could be induced at least to declare himself in favour of friendly relations between Poland and the Soviet Union. If he were unwilling to go even so far as that, it would be impossible for us to continue to press the suggestion that he should participate in the consultations about the reconstitution of the Polish Government.'[1]

That afternoon Churchill went to the House of Commons, where he moved the adjournment of the House as a tribute to Roosevelt, 'whose friendship for the cause of freedom and for the causes of the weak and poor have won his immortal renown'.[2] 'I feel deeply for Winston,' Harold Nicolson noted in his diary, 'and this afternoon it was evident from his manner that it was a real body-blow.'[3]

From Buckingham Palace came a letter from the King:

My dear Winston,
I cannot tell you how sad I am at the sudden death of President Roosevelt. The news came as a great shock to me. I have lost a friend, but to you who have known him for so long & so intimately during this war, the sudden loss to yourself personally of a colleague & helpmate in the framing of far reaching decisions both for the prosecution of the war & for the future peace of the world must be overwhelming.
I send you all my sympathy at this moment.[4]

That afternoon, Churchill made plans to fly to the United States. The aeroplane would leave at 8.30 that night. By 7.45, however, as Cadogan noted in his diary, 'no decision reached—PM said he would decide at aerodrome'.[5] The new President, Harry S. Truman, was anxious to see Churchill, the two men never having met. 'Truman's

[1] War Cabinet No. 44 of 1915, 11.20 a.m., 13 April 1945, Confidential Annex: Cabinet papers, 65/52.
[2] *Hansard*, 13 April 1945, column 2116.
[3] Letter of 13 April 1945: Nigel Nicolson (editor), *op. cit.*, page 447.
[4] Letter of 13 April 1945: Churchill papers, 20/199.
[5] Cadogan diary, 13 April 1945: David Dilks (editor), *op. cit.*, page 727.

idea,' Halifax telegraphed to Churchill, 'was that after the funeral you might have two or three days' talk with him.'[1] Churchill decided, however, not to go. 'It would have been a solace to me to be present at Franklin's funeral,' Churchill telegraphed to Hopkins that night, 'but everyone here thought my duty next week lay at home, at a time when so many Ministers are out of the country.[2] How are you and when am I going to see you? I feel so much for you.'[3]

That evening, Churchill wrote to the King:

I am touched by the kindness of Your Majesty's letter. The sudden loss of this great friend and comrade in all our affairs is very hard for me. Ties have been shorn asunder which years had woven. We have to begin again in many ways.

I was tempted during the day to go over for the funeral and begin relations with the new man. However so many of Your Majesty's Ministers are out of the country, and the Foreign Secretary had arranged to go anyhow, and I felt the business next week in Parliament and also the ceremonies connected with the death of Mr Roosevelt are so important that I should be failing in my duty if I left the House of Commons without my close personal attention. I had to consider the tribute which should be paid to the late President, which clearly it is my business to deliver. The press of work is also very heavy. Therefore I thought it better that I should remain here in charge at this juncture.

Moreover I think that it would be a good thing that President Truman should come over here at about the same time as was proposed by his predecessor. He could visit his Armies in Germany, and he could be Your Majesty's guest. The actual ceremonial would have to be reconsidered but I am sure it would be a great advantage if he could come during the month of May, even if the clouds of May were likely to dissolve in rain. I am making this proposal to him and to Stettinius very strongly through Anthony, who has started and who I trust after 18 hours flying will arrive at American dawn.

All the news from the battlefronts is very encouraging. I should not be surprised if great events occurred within the next week or ten days.[4]

Truman was sorry to have lost the chance of an immediate meeting with Churchill. 'At no time in our respective histories,' he telegraphed to Churchill on April 13, 'has it been more important that the intimate, solid relations which you and the late President had forged between our countries be preserved and developed. It is my

[1] Washington telegram, No. 2487, 13 April 1945: Churchill papers, 20/199.

[2] Attlee, Lyttelton and Cranborne had left Britain for the United States, where they were to attend the San Francisco Conference.

[3] Prime Minister's Personal Telegram, T.459/5, 'Personal and Secret', 13 April 1945: Churchill papers, 20/199.

[4] Letter of 13 April 1945: Churchill papers, 20/193.

earnest hope that before too long, in the furtherance of this, we can arrange a personal meeting.' In the meantime, Truman continued, there were however, 'urgent problems requiring our immediate and joint consideration. I have in mind the pressing and dangerous problem of Poland and the Soviet attitude towards the Moscow negotiations. I am, of course, familiar with the exchanges which you and President Roosevelt have had between yourselves and with Marshal Stalin. I also know in general what President Roosevelt had in mind as the next step.'

Truman ended on a personal note. 'You can count on me,' he wrote, 'to continue the loyal and close collaboration which to the benefit of the entire world existed between you and our great President.'[1]

During April 13 Stettinius sent Truman a summary of United States relations 'with other countries'. It began with Britain, and it read:

Mr Churchill's policy is based fundamentally upon cooperation with the United States. It is based secondarily on maintaining the unity of the three great powers but the British Government has been showing increasing apprehension of Russia and her intentions. Churchill fully shares this Government's interpretation of the Yalta Agreements on Eastern Europe and liberated areas. He is inclined however to press this position with the Russians with what we consider unnecessary rigidity as to detail. The British long for security but are deeply conscious of their decline from a leading position to that of the junior partner of the Big Three and are anxious to buttress their position vis-a-vis United States and Russia both through exerting leadership over the countries of Western Europe and through knitting the Commonwealth more closely together.[2]

In his second telegram to Churchill, sent on April 14, Truman proposed a joint message to Stalin, requesting Truman's agreement to instructing Harriman and Clark Kerr 'to extend immediately' invitations to the Polish leaders, in London, including Mikolajczyk, Grabski and Stanczyk 'to come to Moscow to consult'.[3]

Churchill replied to Truman's telegram:

---

[1] President to Prime Minister, No. 1, 'Personal and Top Secret', 13 April 1945: Churchill papers, 20/214. 'I have had a very nice telegram from President Truman,' Churchill telegraphed to his wife on April 14, 'opening our relations on the best conditions.' ('Personal and Secret', 14 April 1945: Spencer-Churchill papers.)

[2] 'Special Information for the President', 13 April 1945: Harry S. Truman Papers (quoted in Warren F. Kimball, editor, *Churchill and Roosevelt, The Complete Correspondence*, volume 3, Princeton, New Jersey 1984, pages 633–7.

[3] President to Prime Minister, No. 2, 'Personal and Top Secret', 14 April 1945: Churchill papers, 20/214.

As I see it, the Lublin Government are feeling the strong sentiment of the Polish nation, which, though not unfriendly to Russia, is fiercely resolved on independence, and views with increasing disfavour a Polish Provisional Government which is in the main a Soviet puppet. They are endeavouring, in accord with the Soviet Government, to form a Government more broad-based than the present one by the addition of Polish personalities (including perhaps Witos) whom they have in their power, but whose aid they seek and need. This is a step in the right direction, but would not satisfy our requirements or the decisions of the Crimea Conference.[1]

On Saturday April 14 Churchill was at Chequers, where Smuts was among the weekend guests. 'Hectic day of work,' noted Marian Holmes. 'PM said "I hope you had a good rest last night because its going to be a helluva one tonight". When Field Marshal Smuts left the office to go to bed, he patted me on the shoulders and said "Goodnight to you young lady. You are the indispensable slave!" At 2.30 a.m., the PM said "I'm certainly working you hard tonight. If you die, I'll send a wreath of snowdrops".'[2]

Work continued unabated on Sunday April 15. Again Marian Holmes recorded in her diary the mood of the evening:

Film 'L'homme qui cherche la vérité'. Afterwards PM tried to dance a Viennese waltz in the Great Hall with Sarah Oliver. He got dizzy and cried 'Stop' and went staggering around closely followed by Cmdr. Thompson holding a chair in readiness for him to fall into.

PM was in a marvellous, ebullient mood. He came into the office where I was busy writing to a boyfriend overseas. He looked over my shoulder and read 'Hullo darling . . .' 'What is this vast opus you are engaged upon?' I replied 'It's a private letter' 'Oh, poor lamb. I am so sorry. Poor lamb, waiting up for me. I got quite carried away'.

He had an insatiable thirst for work. When Leslie Rowan gave him the last bit of work in the Box, he asked for more and said 'Come on—stop muckin' me about!' With Leslie Rowan, Commander Thompson and me beginning to wilt at 4 a.m. he said mischievously 'I don't know what you three are keeping each other up for!'[3]

Churchill remained at Chequers on Monday April 16, working from

[1] Prime Minister's Personal Telegram, T.473/5, Prime Minister to President, No. 3, 'Personal and Top Secret', 15 April 1945: Churchill papers, 20/214.

[2] Marian Holmes diary, 14 April 1945: Marian Walker Spicer papers.

[3] Marian Holmes diary, 15 April 1945: 'PM in most amiable mood', Marian Holmes noted four days later, on April 19. 'He dined in bed and worked from there from 9 till 1.45 a.m. He said if he could spend a month in bed he could really get some work done. Lunches or dinners wasted two hours "in chatter".' Marian Holmes diary, 19 April 1945: Marian Walker Spicer papers.

bed throughout the morning. 'He was oblivious of the time,' noted Marian Holmes. 'Reminded him that it was getting late and that he had a Bishop coming to lunch at No. 10 at 1.30. "I don't care a bloody damn for bishops!" he said and went on reading his papers. Leslie Rowan and Sawyers combined had better luck and we then tore back to London at high speed.'[1]

Following Roosevelt's death, and in deference to it, Stalin agreed to send Molotov to the San Francisco conference, instead of a less senior Soviet delegate.[2] This meant that all three Foreign Ministers would meet in San Francisco. On April 15 Eden, who was in Washington for Roosevelt's funeral, telegraphed to Churchill about the forthcoming debate on Poland in the House of Commons. Stettinius, who had mentioned the debate, 'said that he hoped that you would be able to indicate that events have taken a new turn in the light of the meeting of the three Foreign Secretaries'. Eden added:

I agreed, but told him that it was my view that it would do the Russians no harm to know how deep was our concern at the failure of the Moscow Commission thus far to make progress on the basis of Yalta decisions. I feel strongly that we must keep a steady pressure on the Russians. There is no justification yet for optimism, and our best chance of success in any of the conversations here is that the Russians should understand to the full the seriousness for us all of failure.[3]

Churchill shared Eden's caution, having already decided not to hold back his next two telegrams to Truman, about the invitations to Poles in London to join the Moscow discussions. 'The surprising gesture of Stalin's in sending Molotov at the last moment is all to the good,' he minuted to Cadogan, 'but should not interfere with the delivery to President Truman of the aforesaid telegrams.'[4] If a Polish Government were produced 'behind our backs which we cannot recognize', Cadogan minuted to Churchill, 'we shall be completely cut off from Poland as well as being placed in a very ignominious posi-

---

[1] Marian Holmes diary, 16 April 1945: Marian Walker Spicer papers. The Bishop who came to luncheon was Dr Lloyd, Bishop of St Albans. (Private Office diary, 16 April 1945.)

[2] The delegate originally chosen was Andrei Gromyko, Molotov's deputy, who had been present throughout the Foreign Ministers' discussions at Yalta. Gromyko was Soviet Foreign Minister from 1957 to 1985, when he became President of the USSR.

[3] No. 2557 from Washington to the Foreign Office, 15 April 1945: Premier papers, 3/356/6, folio 350.

[4] Minutes sent at 11.30 p.m., 14 April 1945: Premier papers, 3/356/5, folio 917.

tion'.[1] This was also Churchill's view. As he telegraphed to Eden on April 15: 'I consider you should deliver my message as drafted in spite of the effects of the Russian gesture sending Molotov.' The sending of Molotov, he wrote, 'may probably soften very much the Americans, both the President and the State Department, and may lead to a general enfeeblement of the front we make'. Churchill's telegram continued:

What have the Russians given up in now sending Molotov? They never ought to have withdrawn him from the delegation. All they do is to put themselves back in a position of greater advantage in the discussions and make themselves more right with the world. For this we ought not to lose the joint message to Stalin which defines our position in regard to Poland. In my opinion therefore you should not sacrifice this message either by undue insistence on improvements or by sob stuff about the noble Russian gesture.

'I should regret very much any weakening of the President's message about Poland,' Churchill ended, 'although no doubt he may wish to send agreeable acknowledgement of the tardy Russian despatch of Molotov.'[2] Neither should the 'gesture of Molotov's tardy mission', Churchill added in a second telegram, 'which cost the Russians less than nothing, in any way weaken our united pressure for a clearing up of the Polish situation'.[3]

That same day, April 15, Churchill and Truman sent their first joint telegram to Stalin, urging that the Moscow Commission should invite three Poles from London, Mikolajczyk, Grabski and Stanczyk, to participate in the discussions about the composition of a Polish Government of National Unity'.[4]

Churchill lunched on April 15 with Mikolajczyk, at Chequers. Smuts was also present, and after some discussion, Mikolajczyk agreed to issue a public declaration, drafted by Smuts, accepting 'the Crimea decision in regard to the future of Poland, its sovereign independent position and the formation of a provisional government representative of national unity'. The statement also declared that 'close and lasting friendship with Russia' was the 'keystone' of future Polish policy 'within the wider friendship of the United Nations'.[5] Churchill immedi-

[1] Minute of 14 April 1945: Premier papers, 3/356/5, folios 218–23.

[2] 'Personal and Top Secret', 15 April 1945: Premier papers, 3/356/5, folios 228–9.

[3] Telegram No. 3692 to Washington, 'Personal and Top Secret', scrambled to Resident Clerk, Foreign Office, 1.45 a.m., 15 April 1945: Premier papers, 3/356/5, folio 207.

[4] Prime Minister's Personal Telegram, T.490A/5, 'Personal and Top Secret', sent 15 April 1945, delivered 18 April 1945: Churchill papers, 20/214.

[5] 'Statement by Monsieur Mikolajczyk on Polish Question', 15 April 1945: Premier papers, 3/356/5, folio 194, included in Prime Minister's Personal Telegram, T.490/5 (to Halifax and Eden), No. 3724 to Washington, 16 April 1945: Churchill papers, 20/214.

ately sent this declaration to Stalin, with the covering note, 'I hope you will find this helpful.' [1]

During April 15, as he studied almost hourly reports of the renewed Soviet advances in the east, Churchill felt the need to send a message of caution to Truman. The first, which concerned Austria, had been drafted by Eden and sent to Churchill for approval. [2] Churchill approved the message, and it was sent to Truman under his name, without amendment. It read:

I am much concerned at the likelihood of Russian armies occupying large parts of Austria before any decisions are agreed for Allied action in that country. I fear that this may have incalculable effects if we do not at once make clear to the Russians our very real interest in what happens in Austria in the interim period before the establishment of full inter-Allied control. Would you be willing to join me in an approach to Marshal Stalin on the lines of the draft message contained in my immediately following telegram? [3]

The 'Churchill' message to Stalin, which had also been drafted by the Foreign Office, contained the sentence:

I would beg to impress upon you that our common purpose might well be prejudiced if far-reaching unilateral steps (e.g. the wholesale removal of industrial plant and equipment, regardless of whether or not it is German owned, or the elimination, without regard to their attitude towards the Nazis, of Austrians who might prove useful in re-establishing Austrian administration and economy) are taken by the Soviet Commanders on the spot before the four Powers have arrived at an agreed policy regarding the treatment of the many political and economic problems which will arise in Austria. [4]

Also on April 15, Churchill read two Joint Staff Mission reports, about military liaison with the Russians in the event of a Russian advance into Denmark, which was still under German control. [5] He at once minuted for the Chiefs of Staff Committee:

What is the proposal for the Russians to advance into Denmark? They have no land connection. Do they propose to make a disembarkation, and if so why? This has never been considered by His Majesty's Government or, so far as I am aware, by the United States Government. What is the point of it? What issue can arise in Denmark that cannot be settled at the peace table or armistice table? [6]

[1] Prime Minister's Personal Telegram, T.488/5, No. 1870 to Moscow, 16 April 1945: Premier papers, 3/356/5, folio 198.
[2] Foreign Secretary's Minute, PM/45/166.
[3] 'Draft Message to President', Prime Minister's Personal Telegram (to Anthony Eden), T.484/5, 15 April 1945: Churchill papers, 20/225.
[4] 'Draft Message to Marshal Stalin from the Prime Minister', Prime Minister's Personal Telegram (to Anthony Eden), T.484/5, 15 April 1945: Churchill papers, 20/225.
[5] Joint Staff Mission telegrams, JSM 693 and 694.
[6] Prime Minister's Personal Minute, D.110/5, 15 April 1945: Churchill papers, 20/209.

In Czechoslovakia, it was American forces which seemed likely to reach the capital before the Red Army. Bitterly, Churchill minuted to the Foreign Office: 'What happens if the Americans get to Prague first, as they seem very likely to do? Will the Russians then tell them whether the American Ambassador may take a tooth brush with him or not, or will it be the western Allies who will determine the character of the United Nations representation in the delivered capital?'[1]

It was clear that the Allied armies would soon meet. On April 15 Churchill prepared the text of a broadcast which he, Truman and Stalin could make simultaneously when the moment came. 'After long journeys and toils and victories across the land and oceans,' Churchill's draft began, 'the Armies of the great Allies have traversed Germany and joined hands in Berlin.'[2] No such Berlin link was to occur, however.

In Russia itself, Clementine Churchill was continuing her Red Cross tour. After a visit to the ballet in Leningrad on April 14, she wrote to her husband: 'The audience received me rapturously which touched me more than I can say,' and she added: 'I should like to be able to spend the whole summer here with you and Mary, boating up and down the Neva and swimming in the Baltic.'[3] Three days later Clementine Churchill telegraphed again: 'I think Leningrad is the most beautiful city I have ever seen. We are installed in a lovely villa in the suburbs and are about to start our tour.' Clementine added: 'I miss my quiet evenings with you.'[4] 'The weather here is bright and delightful,' Churchill replied. 'Everyone is as much astonished by it as by the rapidity with which Germany has been overrun. My work has been heavy, but the House of Commons is very kind to me.'[5]

On April 16 the United States 7th Army reached Nuremberg. Everywhere in Germany the fighting was severe. On April 17 Montgomery reported to Churchill that since February 8, 5,180 of his troops had been killed, and more than 21,000 injured.[6]

---

[1] Prime Minister's Personal Minute, M.344/5, 16 April 1945: Churchill papers, 20/209.

[2] 'Prime Minister to President Truman', 'Personal and Top Secret', 'Hold', 15 April 1945: Premier papers, 3/398/4, folio 309.

[3] Telegram of 15 April 1945: Spencer-Churchill papers.

[4] Cable and Wireless Telegram, 'Passed by Censor', 18 April 1945: Spencer-Churchill papers.

[5] 'Personal and Secret', 18 April 1945, No. 1935 to Moscow: Spencer-Churchill papers.

[6] M/572, 'Top Secret', 17 April 1945: Churchill papers, 20/215.

On the morning of April 17, Churchill was present in St Paul's Cathedral at the memorial service for President Roosevelt. Five sovereigns were present: George VI, King Olaf of Norway, King Peter of Yugoslavia, King George of Greece and Queen Wilhelmina of Holland. After the service, as Henry Channon noted in his diary, 'Winant, dark and romantically handsome, escorted Winston, who was in tears, to the door.' A few minutes later Channon and his son left the Cathedral, and, he wrote, 'turning back towards St Paul's we saw Winston standing bare-headed, framed between two columns of the portico, and he was sobbing as the shaft of sunlight fell on his face and the cameras clicked'.[1]

Churchill returned to the Annexe, where he lunched alone.[2] He then went to the House of Commons to make his tribute to Roosevelt, telling the House of their exchange of 'over 1,700 messages',[3] and their nine war-time meetings:

I conceived an admiration for him as a statesman, a man of affairs, and a war leader. I felt the utmost confidence in his upright, inspiring character and outlook, and a personal regard—affection I must say—for him beyond my power to express today. His love of his own country, his respect for its constitution, his power of gauging the tides and currents of its mobile public opinion, were always evident, but added to these were the beatings of that generous heart which was always stirred to anger and to action by spectacles of aggression and oppression by the strong against the weak. It is, indeed, a loss, a bitter loss to humanity that those heart-beats are stilled for ever.

It was Roosevelt, Churchill recalled, who had devised Lend Lease, 'which will stand forth as the most unselfish and unsordid financial act of any country in all history'. Even in his last months he faced his innumerable tasks 'unflinching', and Churchill added:

When death came suddenly upon him 'he had finished his mail'. That portion of his day's work was done. As the saying goes, he died in harness, and we may well say in battle harness, like his soldiers, sailors, and airmen, who side by side with ours are carrying on their task to the end all over the world. What an enviable death was his. He had brought his country through the worst of its perils and the heaviest of its toils. Victory had cast its sure and steady beam upon him.

In President Roosevelt, Churchill ended, 'there died the greatest American friend we have ever known, and the greatest champion of freedom who has ever brought help and comfort from the new world to the old'.[4]

[1] Channon diary, 17 April 1945: Robert James (editor), *Chips, op. cit.*, page 402.
[2] Private Office diary, 17 April 1945.
[3] *Hansard*, 17 April 1945, column 40.
[4] *Hansard*, 17 April 1945, columns 73–7.

67

'Intense horror'

THE third week of April 1945 saw the Anglo-American and Soviet armies drawing closer together in both northern and central Germany. 'It would seem,' Churchill telegraphed to Eden on April 18, 'that the Western Allies are not (repeat not) immediately in a position to force their way into Berlin.' The Americans had 'only their spear-heads', which were covering 'an immense front' and at the same time were engaged in battle with the Germans 'at many points'. The Russians had two and a half million troops on the section of the front opposite Berlin.

The move which Churchill now favoured was an advance by Montgomery to the Baltic, aimed at the port of Lübeck. 'Our arrival at Lübeck,' he told Eden, 'before our Russian friends from Stettin, would save a lot of argument later on. There is no reason why the Russians should occupy Denmark, which is a country to be liberated and to have its sovereignty restored. Our position at Lübeck, if we get it, would be decisive in this matter.'

On the same theme, Churchill told Eden that it would be 'well' for the western Allies to 'push on to Linz to meet the Russians there'. He also suggested 'an American circling movement to gain the region south of Stuttgart before it is occupied by the French'. In this region, Churchill pointed out, were the main German installations connected with 'their research into TA'—'Tube Alloys' the atomic bomb—'and we had better get hold of these in the interests of the special secrecy attaching to this topic'. These suggestions, Churchill added, 'are for your own information and as background in deep shadow'.[1]

Eden approved Churchill's suggestions. 'A Russian occupation of Denmark would cause us much embarrassment,' he replied. As to Prague, Eden commented: 'It might do the Russians much good if the Americans were to occupy the Czech capital, when no doubt, they

---

[1] Prime Minister's Personal Telegram, T.519/5, No. 3861 to Washington, 18 April 1945: Churchill papers, 28/215.

would be willing to invite Soviet Ambassador to join the United States and ourselves, in contrast to the behaviour the Russians have shown to us.'[1]

He was 'not prepared', Churchill told a Staff Conference on the morning of April 18, 'to give up such territorial advantage as we had obtained by the vigour of the British/American advance into Germany, until it had been agreed with the Russians that the feeding of the German population should be treated as a whole, and that the available supplies would be divided pro rata between the occupational zones'. Eisenhower, who was present, expressed his worry that, as a result of 'a Russian breakthrough on the northern front', the Russians would arrive at Lübeck, and 'advance into Denmark', ahead of Montgomery.[2]

As to the Russian zone in eastern Germany, Churchill assured Truman on April 18, he had no intention of trying to keep British or American troops further east of the line agreed upon 'rather hastily' at Quebec the previous September, at a time when, Churchill pointed out, 'it was not foreseen that General Eisenhower's armies would make such a mighty inroad into Germany'. All he now asked was that neither the British nor American troops who were east of the line should be 'hustled back at any point by some crude assertion of a local Russian General'.[3]

In Italy however, Churchill continued with his policy of active support for the Italians as against Tito's Yugoslavs. On April 18, as a direct result of the Soviet-Yugoslav Treaty of April 11, he agreed with a suggestion by Eden that, as Churchill expressed it, 'all supplies to Tito should be shut down on the best pretext that can be found'. The 'only way', he wrote, to 'split' the Communist Party in Italy was on Tito's claims to Istria and Trieste. Churchill added:

It is in our interests to prevent the Russian submergence of Central and Western Europe as far as possible. The Italians would certainly form on this front. The United States Government are very fond of Italy and would, I should say, certainly support them, especially on account of the strong Italian vote which the new President would surely be glad of. We should therefore be drawn into joint action with the United States and smooth out our affairs with Italy and win ardent support from the majority of Italians. This is a fairly good line-up.[4]

[1] Washington Telegram No. 2751, 'Personal and Top Secret', 20 April 1945: Churchill papers, 20/215.
[2] Staff Conference, Chiefs of Staff Committee No. 102 of 1945, 18 April 1945: Cabinet papers, 79/32.
[3] Prime Minister's Personal Telegram, T.515/5, Prime Minister to President, No. 7, 'Personal and Top Secret', 18 April 1945: Premier papers, 3/398/5, folio 340.
[4] Prime Minister's Personal Telegram, T.516/5, 18 April 1945: Churchill papers, 20/225

It was 'vain', Churchill telegraphed to Eden two days later, 'to throw away our substance in a losing game with Soviet Russia in Titoland. The harmony of Britain, United States and Italian interests about the Adriatic should henceforth be one of our main themes.' [1] When a request from Belgrade for British material to be sent to air training schools in Yugoslavia reached Churchill, he turned it down, minuting to Sir Orme Sargent at the Foreign Office:

If the Russians are willing to aid the Yugoslav Air Force, why have we got to divert from our scanty store the valuable material in officers and men? The great changes which have taken place in the connections and centre of gravity of the Yugoslav Government since we talked about providing them with an Air Force must not fall unnoticed. They have thrown themselves wholeheartedly into the hands of Russia. In these circumstances, I should deprecate our making any serious sacrifices for the right to play a losing game.

As you know, my view is that a diplomatic and even perhaps a military front can be made between Britain, the United States and Italy in the disputed Adriatic territory. Nothing will wrest Yugoslavia from the Russian grip. In this particular theatre the policy is 'disengage'. On the contrary in Greece it is 'hold fast'. [2]

A few moments later Churchill read another telegram from Belgrade, reporting Tito's remarks that 'We count primarily on the Soviet Union.' [3] These 'kind remarks', Churchill minuted to Sargent, 'should encourage the fading away of British arms and, so far as possible supplies of food', and he added: 'It is no use our running a race with Russia in bringing utmost help to Marshal Tito. Let him count primarily on the Soviet Union.' [4]

On April 18 General Eisenhower had telephoned Churchill about the entry of his troops into a number of concentration camps in western and central Germany. The first of these camps to be entered was Ohrdruf, near Gotha. The sight which had met the American troops as they entered this camp had been overwhelming in its horror: four thousand emaciated bodies dumped in ditches: Russian prisoners-of-war, Polish slave labourers, and Jews who had died of starvation and disease, or been cruelly murdered. On the following morning, General

[1] Prime Minister's Personal Minute, M.369/5, sent to Eden as Prime Minister's Personal Telegram, T.556/5, No. 3942 to Washington, 20 April 1945: Churchill papers, 20/215.
[2] Prime Minister's Personal Minute, M.372/5, 20 April 1945: Churchill papers, 20/209. The Yugoslav request was in Belgrade Telegram No. 486.
[3] Belgrade Telegram No. 484.
[4] Prime Minister's Personal Minute, M.376/5, 20 April 1945: Churchill papers, 20/209.

Bedell Smith telephoned Ismay with a further message for Churchill. 'The German concentration camps which have recently been overrun by the Allied armies,' Bedell Smith reported, 'are even indescribably more horrible than those about which General Eisenhower spoke to you yesterday and of which photographs have appeared in the press today.'

Among the newly liberated camps was Buchenwald, which Bedell Smith spoke of to Ismay as 'the acme of atrocity'.

Eisenhower suggested, as Ismay told Churchill, 'that you might care to arrange for a party of Members of Parliament, say half a dozen, together with some journalists, to go over at once': Eisenhower would 'gladly make all the arrangements for sending them forward'. An American delegation, Eisenhower told Churchill, 'might be too late to see the full horrors, whereas an English delegation, being so much closer, could get there in time'.[1]

Churchill at once agreed to Eisenhower's request, telling Eden that Eisenhower's hope was that the Members of Parliament and journalists 'should be sent out at the earliest possible moment to inspect the indescribable horrors, far beyond any hitherto exposed, which are coming to light as the various torture camps are examined'. Especially in the neighbourhood of Weimar, Churchill explained, 'the atrocities have surpassed all example or indeed imagination'.[2]

That afternoon Churchill told the House of Commons of the 'horror' felt by the Government at 'the proofs of these frightful crimes now coming into view', and he added:

I have this morning received an informal message from General Eisenhower saying that the new discoveries, particularly at Weimar, far surpass anything previously exposed. He invited me to send a body of Members of Parliament at once to his Headquarters in order that they may themselves have ocular and first-hand proof of these atrocities.

The matter is of urgency, as of course it is not possible to arrest the processes of decay in many cases. In view of this urgency, I have come to the conclusion that eight Members of this House and two Members of the House of Lords should form a Parliamentary Delegation, and should travel out at once to the Supreme Headquarters, where General Eisenhower will make all the necessary arrangements for their inspection of the scenes, whether in American or British sectors.

Members who volunteer for this extremely unpleasant but none the less necessary duty, should give their names to their Party Whips, in order that a body representative of all Parties may be selected by the usual methods during this afternoon. I should propose that they start tomorrow.

[1] 'Top Secret', 19 April 1945: Premier papers, 4/100/11, folios 769–70.
[2] Prime Minister's Personal Telegram, T.530/5, No. 3888 to Washington, 'Personal and Top Secret', 19 April 1945: Churchill papers, 20/215.

'I hope,' Churchill added, 'the House will approve of the somewhat rapid decision I have taken.'[1]

The House of Commons did approve. 'People are profoundly shocked here,' Churchill telegraphed to Eisenhower that same evening.[2] And on the following morning he telegraphed to his wife, who was then at Kislovodsk, in the Caucasus:

Delighted to get your telegram from Kislovodsk and to learn of all the kindness which has been shown you by the Russian people. In this friendship of our two peoples the greatest hope for the world resides. Here we are all shocked by the most horrible revelations of German cruelty in the concentration camps. General Eisenhower has invited me to send Parliamentary Delegation. I accepted at once and it will start tomorrow. They will go to the spot and see the horrors for themselves—a gruesome duty.[3]

The Parliamentary delegation reached Buchenwald on April 27. 'One half-naked skeleton,' they wrote in their report, 'tottering painfully along the passage as though on stilts, drew himself up when he saw our party, smiled, and saluted.' Ten days had passed since liberation. The number of daily deaths in the first days of liberation had been a hundred or more. Even on the day before their visit, thirty-five inmates had died, 'being already beyond the power of medicine to save'.[4]

After a week of Truman's Presidency, Churchill had formed a clear opinion of his Washington partner. 'My appreciation is,' he telegraphed to Eden on April 20, 'that the new man is not to be bullied by the Soviets. Seeking as I do a lasting friendship with the Russian people, I am sure this can only be founded on the recognition of Anglo-American strength.'[5] With President Truman, Churchill telegraphed to Reginald Leeper, 'we have a man in good health who advances with a firm step and is, I believe, extremely friendly to

[1] *Hansard*, 19 April 1945, column 390.
[2] Prime Minister's Personal Telegram, T.528/5, OZ 2490, 'Personal and Top Secret', 19 April 1945: Premier papers, 4/100/11, folio 767.
[3] 'Personal', No. 1956 to Moscow, 20 April 1945: Spencer-Churchill papers.
[4] 'Buchenwald Camp, The Report of a Parliamentary Delegation': Premier papers, 4/100/11. The members of the delegation were Earl Stanhope and Lord Addison (House of Lords), Colonel Tom Wickham, Sir Archibald Southby and Mrs Mavis Tate (Conservative), Ness Edwards and Alexander Sloan (Labour), Graham White (Liberal), Sir Henry Morris-Jones (Liberal National) and Tom Driberg (Independent). Their report was published as a Parliamentary Paper, Command No. 6626, *Buchenwald Camp: The Report of a Parliamentary Delegation*.
[5] Prime Minister's Personal Telegram, T.556/5, No. 3942 to Washington, 'Top Secret', 20 April 1945: Churchill papers, 20/215.

Britain'. Leeper should therefore work, in Greece, 'for our simple policy of the full, free, unfettered secret ballot, universal suffrage, and the expression of the will of the people in three or four months at the most'.[1]

On April 21 the Soviet Government signed a Treaty of Mutual Assistance with the Lublin Government. That same day, Soviet troops reached the suburbs of Berlin. In Italy, Alexander's forces entered Bologna, far south of the targets that had once been set for moving through northern Italy to the Ljubljana gap and Vienna.

In Germany itself, it was the sight of the corpses and survivors of the concentration camps that continued to shock the western world. 'I am sure Parliament would like you to receive another atrocity inspection team,' Churchill telegraphed to Eisenhower on April 21, 'if this is not too great a burden upon you, as soon as the present one returns.'[2] To his wife, Churchill telegraphed that same day: 'Intense horror has been caused by the revelations of German brutalities in the concentration camps. They did not have time to cover up their traces.' Churchill also sent his wife some personal news, and reflections:

Have just spent day in Bristol giving Degrees to Bevin and A. V. Alexander. Terrific crowd and joyous reception. I was also made a Freeman of the City. Many enquiries were made about your tour. The German war is moving very quickly but it is for the Commanders in the field to let us know when they consider the effective resisting power of the enemy is broken and when the period of mopping-up war criminals has begun. All three Great Powers are keeping in touch about this. We do not want to have premature rejoicings and we must always remember the struggle with Japan that lies ahead.[3]

On April 22 the Americans captured Cebu Island, ending the campaign in the Central Philippines. But it was clear that a prolonged struggle lay ahead to ensure the defeat of Japan. In Europe, as the British, American and Russian armies penetrated deeper and deeper into the German heartland, and as Alexander's multi-national forces crossed the river Po, driving the Germans northward, it was the political future of Europe which seemed ever more ominous. Learning from Lord Halifax that the Americans were opposed to setting up an Italian National Army, Churchill dictated an angry reply:

[1] Prime Minister's Personal Telegram, T.539/5, No. 971 to Athens, 'Important', 'Personal', 20 April 1945: Churchill papers, 20/215.
[2] Prime Minister's Personal Telegram, T.560/5, 21 April 1945: Premier papers, 4/100/11, folio 762. On April 24 Churchill instructed Colville to arrange for the circulation of the concentration camp photographs to the Cabinet. (Minute of 24 April 1945, Colville to Armstrong, Premier papers, 4/100/11, folio 707.)
[3] 'Personal and Secret', No. 1005 to Moscow, 21 April 1945: Spencer-Churchill papers

It would be well to find out what the American attitude actually is about Italy. Do they want her to recover her strength and play a part in resisting the westward trend of Communism and Sovietism, or do they want her to fall into Communist-fomented confusion? In the latter case we also should have to detach ourselves from the course of events.[1]

On reflection, Churchill did not send these bitter words, but they reflected his inner fears.

From Moscow, Stalin sought an assurance from Churchill that Mikolajczyk's statement of April 15 included acceptance of Lvov as an integral part of the Soviet Union. 'Since receiving your message,' Churchill had intended to telegraph to Stalin on April 18, 'I have made quite certain by explicit inquiry that Mikolajczyk accepts the Crimea decisions as a whole, including that part which deals with the Eastern frontiers of Poland. I should not indeed have thought it worth while to have forwarded his statement unless I had been sure this was the fact.'[2]

Churchill did not send this telegram. But on April 22, in answer to another request from Stalin as to whether Mikolajczyk agreed that Lvov should be incorporated in the Soviet Union, Mikolajczyk himself issued a further public statement, the draft of which he had shown Churchill at their meeting at Chequers on April 15. The new statement referred to 'the Soviet demand' for the Curzon Line, and specifically to Lvov. The Poles, Mikolajczyk wrote, 'are obliged to ask ourselves whether in the name of the so-called integrity of our republic we are to reject it and thereby jeopardize the whole body of our country's interests. The answer to this question must be "No".'

In telegraphing this statement to Stalin on April 22, Churchill commented: 'There is no doubt about the answer which he gives in his last sentence to the question you put to me, namely, that he accepts the Curzon Line including the Lvov cession to the Soviets. I hope this will be satisfactory to you.'[3]

From Washington, on the following day, Eden sent Churchill details of his discussion about Poland with Molotov and Stettinius. 'We made no progress whatever,' Eden telegraphed.[4] There seemed no prospect of the Russians allowing a National Unity Government to come into being. The Soviet Government, Eden added within the hour, 'were

[1] Prime Minister's Personal Telegram, T.584/5, 'Personal and Top Secret', 22 April 1945: Churchill papers, 20/215.

[2] 'Personal and Top Secret', 18 April 1945: Premier papers, 3/356/5, folio 151.

[3] Prime Minister's Personal Telegram, T.582/5, No. 2007 to Moscow, 'Personal and Top Secret', 22 April 1945: Premier papers, 3/356/5, folio 139.

[4] Washington Telegram, No. 2809, 'Top Secret and Personal', 23 April 1945: Premier papers, 3/356/6.

quite unrepentant about their treaty with the Warsaw Poles'.[1] That night Jock Colville noted in his diary:

The PM's box is in a ghastly state. He does little work and talks far too long, as he did last December before his Greek adventures refreshed him. This time, I think, it is the Polish question and the unsatisfactory conversations proceeding on that subject at Washington between Eden, Stettinius and Molotov that are weighing him down.[2]

'I am in full accord with all you are doing to stiffen the Americans and back them up to the hilt,' Churchill telegraphed to Eden. 'Especially should they not be sensitive to a charge of "ganging up" with us. Of course we shall work together and assist each other when we are in close agreement on large moral issues like this.'[3]

After talking to Eden and Stettinius on April 23, Molotov had gone to see Truman, who pointed out unequivocally that the American Government 'cannot agree to be a party to the formation of a Polish Government which is not representative of all Polish democratic elements'. Truman added, with equal toughness, that the American Government was 'deeply disappointed that the Soviet Government had not found it possible to carry out consultations with a representative group of Polish leaders, other than those new officials of the Warsaw régime'.[4] Churchill now had an ally in firmness. But the Russians were determined not to widen the Polish Government along the lines agreed at Yalta. 'I earnestly hope that means will be found to compose these serious difficulties,' Churchill telegraphed to Stalin on April 24, 'which if they continue will darken the hour of victory.'[5]

The 'hour of victory' was indeed getting close, and with it the political divisions of post-war Europe emerged as an imminent dilemma. Churchill, speaking on the morning of April 24 to Eisenhower, had in mind a possible American military drive to Prague. 'I asked him,' Churchill minuted for the Chiefs of Staff, 'whether he had deflected his troops from Prague to the south-east, to which he replied that he had never meant to go to Prague as there were two or three good divisions in the very west of Czechoslovakia, and it would

[1] Washington Telegram, No. 2810, 'Top Secret and Personal', 23 April 1945: Premier papers, 3/356/6.
[2] Colville diary, 23 April 1945: Colville papers.
[3] Prime Minister's Personal Telegram, T.616/5, No. 4098 to Washington, 'Personal and Top Secret', 24 April 1945: Churchill papers, 20/216.
[4] Washington Telegram, No. 2842, 'Most Immediate', 'Secret', 23 April 1945: Churchill papers, 20/216.
[5] Prime Minister's Personal Telegram, T.624/5, 'Personal and Top Secret', 24 April 1945: Churchill papers, 20/216 (sent to Truman as Prime Minister's Personal Telegram, T.623/5, Prime Minister to President No 15)

mean a serious alteration in the long-laid-down plans.' Resigned to watch a Soviet occupation of Prague, Churchill added: 'I thought it was too late now to bring the political aspect before him.'[1]

On the morning of April 25 Churchill learned from the British Ambassador in Sweden, Sir Victor Mallet, that the head of the SS, Heinrich Himmler, had offered to open negotiations with the western Allies, 'to capitulate on the whole Western front', while continuing the war against Russia on the eastern front. According to Himmler, 'Hitler was so desperately ill that he might be dead already and in any case would be so in two days' time.'

Churchill immediately summoned the War Cabinet to discuss this message. Himmler's 'reluctance to surrender on the Eastern front', the War Cabinet minutes noted, 'looked like a last attempt to sow discord between the Western Allies and Russia'. The British and American diplomats in Sweden who had been given this message by a Swedish intermediary had both replied to the intermediary 'that the Nazis would have to surrender to all the Allies simultaneously'.

This reply was approved, as was Churchill's suggestion that he should at once inform Stalin of the episode, and of the British response.[2] 'There can be no question,' Churchill telegraphed to Stalin, 'as far as His Majesty's Government is concerned of anything less than unconditional surrender simultaneously to the three major Powers. We consider Himmler should be told that German forces, either as individuals or in units, should everywhere surrender themselves to the Allied troops or representatives on the spot.' Until this happened, Churchill added, 'the attack of the Allies upon them on all sides and in all theatres where resistance continues will be prosecuted with the utmost vigour'.[3]

Half an hour after sending this telegram to Stalin, Churchill telephoned Truman with details of the Himmler offer. Truman took the call at the communications centre in the Pentagon Building. Marshall, King and Leahy were also present. It was the first time that Churchill and Truman had spoken to each other. The conversation, recorded by the Americans, began as follows:

'Churchill: Is that you, Mr President?
'Truman: This is the President, Mr Prime Minister.
'Churchill: How glad I am to hear your voice.
'Truman: Thank you very much, I am glad to hear yours.
'Churchill: I have several times talked to Franklin, but ... Have you

---

[1] Prime Minister's Personal Minute, D.121/5, 24 April 1945: Premier papers, 3/139/11A, folio 704.
[2] War Cabinet No. 52 of 1945, 25 April 1945, Confidential Annex: Cabinet papers, 65/52.
[3] Prime Minister's Personal Telegram, T.629/5, 'Personal and Top Secret', 25 April 1945: Churchill papers, 20/216.

received the report from Stockholm by your Ambassador?

'Truman: Yes, I have.

'Churchill: On that proposal?

'Truman: Yes. I have just a short message saying that there was such a proposal in existence.'

The two men then discussed what it was that Himmler was apparently able to surrender. 'Does that mean everything,' Truman asked, 'Norway, Denmark, Italy and Holland,' to which Churchill replied: 'They mentioned Italy, and Yugoslavia. We mentioned everything and have included that to take in Denmark and Norway. Everything on the Western Front, but he hasn't proposed to surrender on the Eastern Front. So we thought perhaps it would be necessary to report it to Stalin; that is, of course, to say that in our view the surrender must be simultaneous to agree to our terms.' The conversation continued:

'Truman: I think he should be forced to surrender to all three governments, Russia, you and the United States. I don't think we ought to even consider a piecemeal surrender.

'Churchill: No, no, no. Not a piecemeal surrender to a man like Himmler. Himmler will be speaking for the German state as much as anybody can. And therefore we thought that his negotiations must be carried on with the three governments.

'Truman: That's right, that's the way I feel exactly.'

Britain had already made it clear, Churchill told Truman, 'that there could be no question as far as His Majesty's Government is concerned of anything less than unconditional surrender simultaneously to the three major powers'. 'Alright,' Truman replied, 'I agree to that.'[1]

Before ending their telephone conversation, Churchill and Truman turned briefly to the Polish question, and to the possibility of a conference between them in little more than a month's time:

'Churchill: Good. I rejoice that our first conversation will be about the first of June. It's very good news.

'Truman: I hope to see you someday soon.

'Churchill: I am planning to. I'll be sending you some telegrams about that quite soon. I entirely agree with all that you've done on the Polish situation. We are walking hand in hand together.

'Truman: Well, I want to continue just that.

'Churchill: In fact, I am following your lead, backing up whatever you do on the matter.

'Truman: Thank you. Good night.'[2]

[1] Prime Minister's Personal Telegram, T.629/5, 'Personal and Top Secret', 25 April 1945: Churchill papers, 20/216.

[2] Transcript of a telephone conversation: Harry S. Truman, *Memoirs*, volume one, 'Year of Decisions', New York 1955, pages 88–94.

The Himmler proposal, Churchill commented to Colville, shows at any rate that 'they are done'.[1] Churchill, however, was weary. When Oswald Birley asked that day if the Prime Minister could sit for his portrait, Churchill minuted to Colville: 'You know as well as anybody whether there is any life left in me.'[2]

At 4.40 on the afternoon of April 25, near Torgau, on the river Elbe, a First Lieutenant and three men of a United States Intelligence and Reconnaissance Platoon found themselves face to face with men of the Red Army. Twenty-four hours later, at four in the afternoon on April 26, their divisional commanders, the Commander of the United States 69th Division and the Commander of the Russian 58th Guards Division, met in Torgau. A note in Churchill's papers reports: 'The mutual exchange of Allied prisoners-of-war was discussed.'[3] That evening, Churchill's voice was heard over the wireless, his actual words recorded six days earlier:

After long journeys, toils and victories across the land and oceans, across so many deadly battlefields, the Armies of the great Allies have traversed Germany and have joined hands together. Now their task will be the destruction of all remnants of German military resistance, the rooting out of the Nazi power and the subjugation of Hitler's Reich. For these purposes ample forces are available and we meet in true and victorious comradeship and with inflexible resolve to fulfil our purpose and our duty. Let all march forward upon the foe.[4]

The issuing of this message had been co-ordinated between Churchill, Stalin and Truman. 'If Stalin agrees,' Truman had informed Churchill twelve days earlier, 'I would be pleased to receive from you for consideration your draft of these messages.'[5] As to the actual broadcast, for which Churchill's draft was accepted, 'The timing will have to be worked out,' Churchill had intended to reply to Truman, 'on account of our living on a globe.'[6]

That same day, April 26, the Red Army entered Stettin, on the Baltic, and the French entered Ulm, on the Danube. To de Gaulle,

[1] Colville diary, 25 April 1945: Colville papers.

[2] Minute No. 15, 25 April 1945: Churchill papers, 20/196.

[3] 'Draft Announcement', 10 Downing Street, 27 April 1945: Premier papers, 3/398/4, folio 246.

[4] 'Recorded Message for Prime Minister on Link-up of Allied Forces in Germany', 'Recorded by the Prime Minister 8 p.m., 20 April 1945': Premier papers, 3/398/4, folio 276.

[5] 'Personal and Top Secret', President to Prime Minister, No. 3, 14 April 1945: Premier papers, 3/398/4, folio 310.

[6] 'Personal and Top Secret', 'Hold', 15 April 1940: Premier papers, 3/398/4, folio 309.

Churchill telegraphed his congratulations and praise for the 'prowess and achievement' of the French soldiers.[1] 'All of us here,' de Gaulle replied, 'are full of admiration for the long victorious struggle of the British army, navy and air force.' The French soldiers, de Gaulle added, were 'very grateful' to Churchill for the words 'of the fighter and leader that you are'.[2]

Although Himmler's offer to negotiate a surrender in the west had been rejected, it gave all those who knew of it a sense that the days of the Third Reich were strictly numbered. Jock Colville noted in his diary on April 26:

> At No. 10 there is a feeling of expectancy, based on yesterday's telegram but damped by the continued impasse over Poland (Stalin, by telegram, and Molotov in the US, keep on insisting that the reorganization of the Polish Government should be on the Yugoslav model—which has in fact been a complete victory for Russia in that benighted land). We are also damped by the amount of work pouring in and the failure of the PM to deal with it.[3]

In Switzerland, negotiations began again on April 26 for the surrender of the German army in Italy, operation 'Crossword' about which Stalin had earlier written so abusively to Roosevelt. Churchill now sent Stalin a full account of the new talks:

> The German envoys, with whom all contact was broken by us some days ago, have now arrived again on the Lake of Lucerne. They claim to have full powers to surrender the Army in Italy. Field-Marshal Alexander is therefore being told that he is free to permit these envoys to come to AFHQ in Italy. This they can easily do by going into France and being picked up by our aircraft from there. Will you please send Russian representatives forthwith to Field-Marshal Alexander's headquarters.
>
> Field-Marshal Alexander is free to accept the unconditional surrender of the considerable enemy army on his front, but all political issues are reserved to the three Governments.

Churchill pointed out to Stalin that Himmler's offer had not mentioned the armies in Italy, which were a purely military and local matter. 'We have spent a lot of blood in Italy,' Churchill added, 'and the capture of the German armies south of the Alps is a prize dear to the hearts of the British nation, with whom in this matter the United States have shared the costs and perils.'[4]

[1] Prime Minister's Personal Telegram, T.637/5, No. 788 to Paris, 'Personal', 26 April 1945: Churchill papers, 20/216.
[2] Telegram of 26 April 1945: Churchill papers, 20/216.
[3] Colville diary, 26 April 1945: Colville papers.
[4] Prime Minister's Personal Telegram, T.638/5, No. 2176 to Moscow, 'Most Immediate', 'Top Secret', 26 April 1945: Churchill papers, 20/216.

As Germany's Nazi empire collapsed, Churchill's thoughts went back to the empires which had collapsed, with equal completeness, in 1918. Reading a telegram from the British Ambassador in Brussels, Sir Hughe Knatchbull-Hugessen, of efforts being made to capture or at least to detain the heir to the Hapsburgs, Archduke Otto, Churchill telegraphed at once to the Ambassador that it was no part of British policy 'to hunt down' the Archduke, or to treat the loyalty which many Austrians friendly to Britain felt for their 'ancient monarchy' as if that monarchy was 'a criminal organization'. Wherever Britain was forced to depart from the 'ideal' of non-intervention, Churchill added, 'our guide is the will of the people, expressed by the vote of a free, unfettered, secret ballot, universal suffrage election'. The principal of constitutional monarchy, Churchill commented, 'is not, oddly enough, abhorrent to the British mind'. His telegram continued:

Personally, having lived through all these European disturbances and studied carefully their causes, I am of opinion that if the Allies at the peace table at Versailles had not imagined that the sweeping away of long-established dynasties was a form of progress, and if they had allowed a Hohenzollern, a Wittelsbach, and a Habsburg to return to their thrones, there would have been no Hitler. To Germany a symbolic point on which the loyalties of the military classes could centre would have been found, and a democratic basis of society might have been preserved by a crowned Weimar in contact with the victorious Allies.

'This is a personal view,' Churchill ended, 'but perhaps you would meditate upon it.' [1]

In his diary, Colville noted that Churchill 'instructed me to see that this telegram was given wide distribution inside the FO, which he accuses of republicanism'. That evening, after dining with the French Ambassador, René Massigli, Churchill returned to the Annexe to find Stalin's answer to his telegram about the Himmler peace offer. Churchill's answer, said Stalin, was 'the only correct one', and he added: 'Knowing you, I had no doubt that you would act just in this way.' Meanwhile, Stalin wrote, the Red Army 'will maintain its pressure on Berlin, in the interests of our common cause'. [2]

This telegram, Colville noted as 'the most friendly UJ has ever sent'. Its effect on Churchill was, momentarily, remarkable, as Colville recorded:

---

[1] Prime Minister's Personal Telegram, T.642/5, No. 224 to Brussels, 'Personal and Secret', 26 April 1945: Churchill papers, 20/225.
[2] 'Personal and Top Secret', 25 April 1945: Churchill papers, 20/216.

This quite fascinated him (he was not altogether sober to begin with) and I sat beside him in his room at the Annexe while he talked of nothing else, first of all to Brendan for $1\frac{1}{2}$ hours and then to me for another $1\frac{1}{2}$. His vanity was astonishing and I am glad UJ does not know what effect a few kind words, after so many harsh ones, might well have on our policy towards Russia. My suggestion that this telegram—thanking the PM for his attitude and frankness over the Himmler–Bernadotte business—might be prompted by a certain shame over the unworthy suspicions entertained over the earlier German approach to us (operation 'Crossword') was impatiently swept aside. Further joy was caused by a generous message from de Gaulle. But no work was done and I felt both irritated and slightly disgusted by this exhibition of susceptibility to flattery. It was nearly 5.0 a.m. when I got to bed.[1]

Churchill slept until after ten in the morning on April 27. During the day, reading of Alexander's plans to follow up his successes in the Po Valley by an advance on Trieste, Churchill telegraphed to Truman: 'It seems to me vital to get Trieste if we can do so in the easy manner proposed, and to run the risks inherent in these kinds of political–military operations. The late President always attached great importance to Trieste, which he thought should be an international port forming an outlet into the Adriatic from all the regions of the Danube basin.' There were many points to consider about this, Churchill added, 'but that there should be an outlet to the south seems of great interest to the trade of many states involved. The great thing is to be there before Tito's guerillas are in occupation. Therefore it does not seem to me there is a minute to wait.' The 'actual status' of Trieste, Churchill wrote, could be 'determined at leisure' and he continued: 'Possession is nine points of the law. I beg you for an early decision.'

Alexander and Mark Clark were in the process, Churchill noted, of gaining 'quite soon an overwhelming and timely victory' in North Italy. 'This is the time to back our successful generals, as we are doing on the North-West front.' The plan for the Anglo-American occupation of Venezia Giulia, Churchill pointed out to the President, 'has been hanging fire in Washington for a considerable time, with the result that Field Marshal Alexander is still without orders. I should therefore be most grateful if you would give your personal attention to this.'[2]

During the morning of April 27, Colville noted, Churchill was in 'benign mood'. But after luncheon 'the clouds descended' with the news of a victory by the Commonwealth Party candidate over the Conservative at Chelmsford, 'a Conservative seat'. Beaverbrook,

[1] Colville diary, 26 April 1945: Colville papers.

[2] Prime Minister's Personal Telegram, T.662/5, Prime Minister to President, No. 19, 'Personal and Top Secret', 27 April 1945: Churchill papers, 20/216.

Bracken, the Chief Whip, James Stuart and the Chairman of the Conservative Party Organization, Ralph Assheton, 'were at once summoned', Colville wrote, 'for a lengthy conclave'.[1] That night, Assheton dined with Churchill in London, drove in the car with him to Chequers, and, after watching newsreels, stayed up talking with him until three in the morning.[2]

A month earlier Churchill had read in the newspapers that Conservative Central Office had issued instructions that no one over seventy should be tolerated as a candidate at the forthcoming election. 'I naturally wish to know at the earliest moment whether this ban applies to me,' he had minuted to Ralph Assheton.[3] The newspapers, Assheton replied, had been misinformed about the age limit, 'though hints have been dropped in one or two cases'. The Conservative Association in Epping, however, was, according to reports, 'very satisfied with its Member. . . .'[4]

On Sunday April 29, while still at Chequers, Churchill and those with him awaited the news from Italy. 'During the after-dinner film,' noted Marian Holmes, 'I took down on the phone the exciting news from Field Marshal Alexander.'[5] At Caserta, two German officers from the German armies in Italy had signed the instrument of surrender. The war in Italy was over. 'It looks therefore,' Churchill telegraphed to Stalin, 'as if the entire German forces south of the Alps will almost immediately surrender.'[6]

In a telegram that night to Alexander, Churchill referred to the earlier, lost hopes for the Italian campaign:

That you and General Mark Clark should have been able to accomplish these tremendous and decisive results against a superior number of enemy divisions, after you have made great sacrifices of whole armies for the Western Front, is indeed another proof of your genius for war and of the intimate

---

[1] Colville diary, 27 April 1945: Colville papers.

[2] Private Office diary, 27 April 1945. The duty secretary, Marian Holmes, noted in her diary: 'They talked for at least two hours while Tommy Thompson, John Peck and I waited in the Great Hall. We had a drink and then played a vigorous game of "Pig in the Middle" with a pincushion. We wound up flinging cushions at each other and trying to suppress our laughter during these frolics. I finally went to bed at 2.45 a.m. & left them all to it.' (Marian Holmes diary, 27 April 1945: Marian Walker Spicer papers.)

[3] Minute of 19 March 1945: Percy Cohen papers (copy sent by Percy Cohen to the author, 21 November 1969).

[4] Minute of 20 March 1945: Percy Cohen papers. Ralph Assheton remained at Chequers on Saturday April 28. After dinner that night, the film was *The Mikado*, 'yet again', as Marian Holmes noted, 'with PM accompaniment singing all the songs'. (Marian Holmes diary, 28 April 1945: Marian Walker Spicer papers.)

[5] Marian Holmes diary, 29 April 1945: Marian Walker Spicer papers.

[6] Prime Minister's Personal Telegram, T.680/5, No. 2265 to Moscow, 'Personal and Top Secret', 29 April 1945: Churchill papers, 20/216.

brotherhood in arms between the British Commonwealth and Imperial forces and those of the United States.

Churchill's telegram to Alexander continued:

Never, I suppose, have so many nations advanced and manoeuvred in one line victoriously. The British, Americans, New Zealanders, South Africans, British-Indians, Poles, Jews, Brazilians, and strong forces of liberated Italians have all marched together in that high comradeship and unity of men fighting for freedom and for the deliverance of mankind. This great final battle in Italy will long stand out in history as one of the most famous episodes in the Second World War. Pray give my heartfelt congratulations to all your commanders and principal officers of all Services, and above all to the valiant and ardent troops whom they have led with so much skill.[1]

'I long to be with you during these tremendous days,' Clementine Churchill telegraphed to her husband from the Crimea on April 29, 'and I think of you constantly.'[2]

[1] Prime Minister's Personal Telegram, T.682/5, OZ 2731, 29 April 1945: Churchill papers, 20/216.

[2] Telegram of 29 April 1945 (from Simferopol, Crimea), 29 April 1945: Spencer-Churchill papers.

68

'Beneath these triumphs'

ON 29 April 1945, Churchill sent Stalin a final appeal about Poland. 'I have been much distressed,' he began, 'at the misunderstanding that has grown up between us on the Crimean Agreement about Poland.' Britain and America had agreed to allow the Lublin Government to become a 'new' Government, 'recognized on a broader democratic basis with the inclusion of democratic leaders from Poland itself and from Poles abroad'. For this purpose, the Moscow Commission had been set up 'to select the Poles who were to come for consultations'. Britain and America had excluded from their nominees those who they thought 'were extreme people unfriendly to Russia'. They had not selected anyone 'at present in the London Government', but chose instead 'three good men, Mikolajczyk, Grabski and Stanczyk who had earlier gone into opposition to the London Government of Arciczewski 'because they did not like its attitude towards Russia, and in particular its refusal to accept the eastern frontier', the Curzon Line 'which you and I agreed upon, now so long ago, and which I was the first man outside the Soviet Government to proclaim to the world as just and fair', together with the compensations for Poland in the West and North.

Not one of the three British and American nominees, Churchill pointed out, had been invited to Moscow to come before the Commission, however. Of the plan, at Yalta, to establish a Government based on 'universal suffrage and secret ballot', with all the democratic and anti-Nazi parties having the right to take part and put forward candidates, 'none of this has been allowed to move forward'. The Soviet Government has signed a Twenty Years Treaty with Bierut's Government 'although it remains neither new nor reorganized'. 'We have the feeling,' Churchill added, 'that it is we who have been dictated to and brought up against a stone wall upon matters which we sincerely believed were settled in a spirit of friendly comradeship in the Crimea.'

Stalin, in his most recent message to Churchill, on April 24, had suggested 'the Yugoslav precedent as a model for Poland'. Churchill commented:

... the way things have worked out in Yugoslavia certainly does not give me the feeling of a fifty-fifty interest and influence as between our two countries. Marshal Tito has become a complete dictator. He has proclaimed that his prime loyalties are to Soviet Russia. Although he allowed members of the Royal Yugoslav Government to enter his Government, they only number six as against 25 of his own nominees. We have the impression that they are not taken into consultation on matters of high policy and that it is becoming a one-party régime. However I have not made any complaint or comment about all this, and both at Yalta and at other times have acquiesced in the settlement which has been reached in Yugoslavia. I do not complain of any action you have taken there in spite of my misgivings and I hope it will all work out smoothly and make the Yugoslavs a prosperous and free people, friendly to both Russia and ourselves.

We could not, however, accept the (quote) Yugoslav model (unquote) as a guide to what should happen in Poland.

Churchill then told Stalin of the 'British flame' which still burned for Poland 'among the classes and parties in this Island', as a result of Britain having gone to war with Hitler, 'unprepared as we were', when Germany invaded Poland in September 1939. The British people, he declared, 'can never feel this war will have ended rightly unless Poland has a fair deal in the full sense of sovereignty, independence and freedom on the basis of friendship with Russia'. It was this, Churchill wrote, 'that I thought we had agreed at Yalta'.

There were now, Churchill said, 'all sorts of stories' being brought out of Poland, and 'eagerly listened to' by many Members of Parliament, and which 'at any time may be violently raised in Parliament or the Press in spite of my deprecating such action and on which M. Molotov will vouchsafe us no information at all in spite of repeated requests'.

Churchill then gave, as an example of these stories, the 'talk of the fifteen Poles who were said to have met the Russian Authorities for discussion over four weeks ago, and of M. Witos about whom there has been a similar but more recent report; and there are many other statements of deportations etc.', and he went on to ask Stalin:

How can I contradict such complaints when you give me no information whatever and when neither I nor the Americans are allowed to send anyone into Poland to find out for themselves the true state of affairs? There is no part of our occupied or liberated territory into which you are not free to send delegations, and people do not see why you should have any reasons against similar visits by British delegations to foreign countries liberated by you.

Churchill ended his telegram of April 29 with an appeal to Stalin which struck at the root of the widening conflict, and warned, not in anger but in near despair, of the dangers which that conflict posed:

There is not much comfort in looking into a future where you and the countries you dominate, plus the Communist Parties in many other States, are all drawn up on one side, and those who rally to the English-speaking nations and their associates or Dominions are on the other. It is quite obvious that their quarrel would tear the world to pieces and that all of us leading men on either side who had anything to do with that would be shamed before history. Even embarking on a long period of suspicions, of abuse and counter-abuse and of opposing policies would be a disaster hampering the great developments of world prosperity for the masses which are attainable only by our trinity. I hope there is no word or phrase in this outpouring of my heart to you which unwittingly gives offence. If so, let me know. But do not, I beg you, my friend Stalin, under-rate the divergencies which are opening about matters which you may think are small to us but which are symbolic of the way the English-speaking democracies look at life.[1]

This 'long and masterly telegram', Colville noted, was a 'final appeal to resolve the Polish impasse'.[2] 'Our Ambassador will show you my telegram to Stalin,' Churchill telegraphed to his wife, who had just returned to Moscow from south Russia. 'Our personal relations are very good at present,' he noted, no doubt with the 'Crossword' telegram still much in his mind, 'but there are many difficulties as you will see'. Churchill's telegram ended: 'You should express to Stalin personally my cordial feelings and my resolve and confidence that a complete understanding between the English-speaking world and Russia will be achieved and maintained for many years, as this is the only hope of the world.'[3]

The disputes with Stalin widened further on April 29, when the Soviet authorities who had established control in Vienna not only

[1] Prime Minister's Personal Telegram, T.675/5, No. 2255 to Moscow, 'Personal and Top Secret', 29 April 1945: Premier papers, 3/356/6. This telegram to Stalin was scrutinized and approved in the Foreign Office by Richard Law and Orme Sargent, to whom Churchill had written, in sending them the draft: 'Pray consider this very carefully with your experts in the Russian section and make me any suggestions you like. But do not try to mar the symmetry and coherence of the message'. (Prime Minister's Personal Minute, M.404/5, 27 April 1945: Foreign Office papers, 954/20, folio 664.)

[2] Colville diary, 1 May 1945: Colville papers.

[3] 'Personal and Secret', 2 May 1945: Spencer-Churchill papers.

announced over Moscow Radio the formation of a Provisional Austrian Government, but at the same time refused permission to both a British and an American Mission to fly to the former Austrian capital.

In a note to Churchill that day, Sir Orme Sargent pointed out that although Dr Karl Renner, the Chancellor and also Minister for Foreign Affairs of the new government, was an 'elderly social democrat of 74 summers' about whom Britain had 'no reason to take particular objection', nevertheless, 'the very fact that the Soviet Government have set up a Government in Austria without giving us any time to express our views, seems to indicate that they intend to take advantage of being alone on the spot in order to set up a puppet Government of their own making in the same way as they have in Roumania, Hungary and Bulgaria'.[1]

Sargent included with his minute a draft telegram from Churchill to Truman, which Churchill accepted unaltered, stating that the Soviet action over Austria 'makes me fear that the Russians are deliberately exploiting their arrival first into Austria to "organize" the country before we get there'.

'It seems to me,' the telegram continued, 'that unless we both take a strong stand now, we shall find it very difficult to exercise any influence in Austria during the period of her liberation from the Nazis. Would you be willing to join me in sending Marshal Stalin a message in the terms of my immediately following telegram?'[2]

The telegram to Stalin, also prepared by the Foreign Office, stressed that 'the treatment of Austria, as of Germany', was a matter of 'common concern' to all Four Powers who were 'to occupy and control those countries', and asking Stalin to issue the necessary instructions 'in order that the Allied missions may fly in at once from Italy'.[3]

Truman agreed with Churchill's request, replying that the Department of State had transmitted a protest to the American Embassy in Moscow 'which I believe to be in general agreement with your protest on the same subject'.[4]

Not only in Austria, Poland, and Yugoslavia, but also in Czecho-

---

[1] Permanent Under Secretary of State's Minute, PM/05/45/41, 29 April 1945: Premier papers, 4/33/6, folios 716–18.

[2] Prime Minister's Personal Telegram, T.701/5, Prime Minister to President, No. 25, 'Personal and Top Secret', 30 April 1945: Premier papers, 4/33/6.

[3] Prime Minister's Personal Telegram, T.702/5, 'Personal and Top Secret', 30 April 1945 (sent to Truman as Prime Minister to President, No. 26): Premier papers, 4/33/6. Like the telegram to Truman, this telegram was submitted to Churchill in draft by Orme Sargent, and accepted by Churchill in its entirety.

[4] President to Prime Minister, No. 19, 'Personal and Top Secret', 30 April 1945: Premier papers, 4/33/6, folio 704.

slovakia, Churchill saw danger in the imposition of Soviet control, so much so that in an earlier telegram to Truman on April 30 he had suggested that Eisenhower's forces should take advantage of 'any suitable opportunity that may arise' to advance into Czechoslovakia. As Churchill explained:

There can be little doubt that the liberation of Prague and as much as possible of the territory of Western Czechoslovakia by your forces might make the whole difference to the post-war situation in Czechoslovakia and might well influence that in nearby countries. On the other hand, if the Western Allies play no significant part in Czechoslovakia's liberation, that country will go the way of Yugoslavia.[1]

Even as Churchill's telegram was on its way to Truman, any chance of an American thrust to Prague was lost; on the following day, May 1, the Foreign Office received a telegram from Eisenhower, to the effect that he would not advance further into Austria than 'general area of Linz', and the River Enns. On the evening of April 30 Eisenhower had informed General Antonov of this self-denying ordnance.[2] 'From the political point of view,' Orme Sargent minuted to Churchill on May 1, 'It would have been better if he had said nothing and advanced as far as he could until he met the Russian forces to the West of Vienna.'[3] Churchill commented: 'I agree.'[4]

On the last day of April, a Monday, Churchill remained at Chequers for most of the day. 'PM working from bed,' Marian Holmes noted in her diary. 'John Peck came in just as I smelt burning and pointed frantically at the PM. Great puffs of smoke were rising from the collar of his bedjacket. He was so completely absorbed in the papers he was reading that he was completely oblivious both of the smoke and the large hole he had burned in his bedjacket by dropping lighted cigar ash. John Peck said "You're on fire, Sir. May I put you out?" "Yes, do" replied the PM nonchalantly.'[5]

During April 30, the Combined Anglo-American Chiefs of Staff put forward a plan to take over the Istrian Peninsula, the port of Fiume and the hinterland of Trieste as the German army in Italy surrendered: the date of the end of hostilities having been fixed for

[1] Prime Minister's Personal Telegram, T.687/5, Prime Minister to President, No. 24, 'Personal and Top Secret', 30 April 1945: Churchill papers, 20/216.
[2] SCAF 323, IZ 4390, 8.30 p.m., 30 April 1945: Premier papers, 3/398/5, folio 320.
[3] Foreign Office Minute PM/05/45/55, 1 May 1945: Premier papers, 3/398/5, folio 319.
[4] Note of 2 May 1945: Premier papers, 3/398/5, folio 319.
[5] Marian Holmes diary, 30 April 1945: Marian Walker Spicer papers.

May 2 at noon. Their plan was to seek Tito's agreement.[1] 'But it is surely a delusion,' Churchill telegraphed to Truman, 'to suppose the Yugoslav Government, with the Soviet Government behind them, would agree to our entering or taking control of Venezia Giulia including Fiume etc. They will undoubtedly try to overrun all this territory and will claim and occupy the ports of Trieste, Pola and Fiume, and once they get there I do not think they will go.' Churchill's telegram continued:

No one is more keen than I to play absolutely fair with the Soviet on matters of the surrender of the German armies, and as you see the messages we have both sent to Stalin have completely restored his confidence in this respect. On the other hand we have never undertaken to be limited in our advance to clear Italy, including these Adriatic Provinces, of the Germans by the approval either of the Yugoslavs or of the Russians, nor to report to them the military movements our Commanders think it right to make.

The Combined Chiefs of Staff had put great stress on the need for Anglo-American forces to occupy Trieste. But Churchill feared 'a stubborn refusal', coupled 'with a renewed effort of the Yugoslav partisans to arrive at Trieste before us'. Britain and America were 'as much entitled to move freely into Trieste', if they could get there, as the Russians had been 'to win their way into Vienna'. Churchill's advice to Truman was: 'We ought if possible to get there first and then talk about the rest of the Province.'

Churchill then set out what he saw as the political benefit of an allied presence in Trieste and Venezia Giulia. Some 'defence of Italian rights at the head of the Adriatic', he told Truman, 'might be the means of harmonious combination between the United States, the British and the Italian Governments and would split or render ineffective the Communist movement in Italy and especially in Northern Italy'.

In northern Europe, where the zones of occupation of Germany had been agreed, but where the American armies had already crossed further eastward, it was also agreed that, after a short period of time, the line of the original zones would be restored. Linking this eventual withdrawal with the situation in Venezia Giulia, Churchill told Truman:

There will be a great shock to public opinion in many countries when the American Armies of the North withdraw, as they have to do under the occupational zone scheme, on a front of several hundred miles to a distance of upwards of 120 miles to the West, and when the Soviet advance overflows all those vast areas of central Germany which the Americans had conquered.

[1] Combined Chiefs of Staff Telegram, FAN, 536: Cabinet papers, 105/147.

If at the same time the whole of the Northern Adriatic is occupied by Yugoslavs, who are the Russian tools and beneficiaries, this shock will be emphasized in a most intense degree.

'I beg you will consider these matters,' Churchill added, 'before allowing any disclosure of plans. . . .'[1]

In his reply, sent that same day, Truman agreed that when Alexander was 'endeavouring to establish his lines of communication to Austria and to establish his control over Trieste and Pola, there is no need for obtaining prior Russian consent'.[2] To Alexander, Churchill stressed his feeling that it would be 'highly important' that Britain and the Americans should 'get control' of Fiume, Trieste, Pola and the Istrian peninsula, 'and that your communications into Austria should be safeguarded'. There was of course going to be 'a frightful outcry' about these territories between the Italians and the Yugoslavs, and he added:

I am in favour of backing up the Italians because that will split their Communist forces and will also fit in with the very friendly interest the Americans have in Italy and which I should like also to share. I imagine the Italians care more about Trieste and Istria than about Communism, and it would be a good thing to have a settled Government in Italy which was united to the two western democracies. I doubt very much whether Tito will agree, if he got there, to you turning him out. He is claiming all sorts of territories.[3]

On the afternoon of May 1 Churchill went to the House of Commons for question time, where, as Colville noted in his diary, he told 'a House full to overflowing with people expecting a victory announcement that he had no statement to make about the war situation except that it was much better than it was five years ago'.[4]

'Generally he is good at making this sort of joke,' Harold Nicolson wrote to his son Nigel. 'But he was feeling ill or something—his manner was languid and his face puckered and creased—and it did not go down well. There was a perfunctory laugh, and then a feeling that we wished he hadn't said it.'[5]

---

[1] Prime Minister's Personal Telegram, T.685/2, Prime Minister to President, No. 22, 'Personal and Top Secret', 30 April 1945: Churchill papers, 20/216.

[2] President to Prime Minister, No. 18, 'Personal and Top Secret', 30 April 1945: Premier papers, 3/495/1.

[3] Prime Minister's Personal Telegram, T.707/5, OZ 2765, 'Guard', 'Personal and Top Secret', 1 May 1945: Churchill papers, 20/217.

[4] Colville diary, 1 May 1945: Colville papers. Churchill's actual words were: 'I have no special statement to make about the war position in Europe, except that it is definitely more satisfactory than it was this time five years ago.' (*Hansard*, 1 May 1945, column 1239.)

[5] Letter of 1 May 1945: Nigel Nicolson (editor), *op. cit.*, page 453.

One of the questions on May 1 was from Aneurin Bevan who, speaking of the plans for VE Day, felt that the fact that 'a very large number of our troops' would still be engaged in the Far East and the Middle East 'will exercise a very sobering restraint'. 'I hope,' Churchill replied, 'that soberness and restraint, for which my hon. Friend is renowned, will always be imitated with propriety in all parts of the country; but soberness and restraint do not necessarily prevent the joyous expression of the human heart.'[1]

That evening Churchill dined with Beaverbrook, Lyttelton, James Stuart and Ralph Assheton, for a discussion of election propaganda. In the middle of dinner, Jock Colville came in with a 'sensational announcement'. Hamburg radio had just announced the death of Hitler. He had died, according to the German broadcast, 'fighting with his last breath against Bolshevism'. 'Well,' commented Churchill, 'I must say I think he was perfectly right to die like that.' But Beaverbrook answered that he 'obviously did not'.[2] Beaverbrook was right. Hitler had committed suicide.

Churchill and his guests continued their discussion of electoral politics until three o'clock in the morning, 'and the PM then dawdled over a few telegrams', Colville noted, 'until after 4 a.m.'.[3]

Hitler was dead; two days earlier, Mussolini had been killed by Italian partisans in northern Italy. 'Several crises are coming to a head,' Churchill telegraphed to his wife, 'and as you see both our great enemies are dead.'

On May 2, Berlin surrendered to the 1st White Russian and 1st Ukrainian Armies. That same day, the city of Hamburg opened negotiations for its surrender. In Italy, nearly a million German soldiers laid down their arms. This surrender, Churchill told the House of Commons at 7.29 that evening, included the Austrian provinces of Salzburg, Vorarlberg and the Tyrol, as well as portions of Carinthia and Styria.

Churchill then spoke of how it had been 'particularly difficult and depressing' for the Army in Italy to have had 'tremendous inroads' made upon it for 'other great operations'. Yet, 'so weakened' as it was, it had made a decisive attack, and now the number of Germans who had surrendered to it 'constitutes, I believe, a record in the whole of this war, and cannot fail to be helpful to the further events, to which we are all looking forward'.

In a final tribute to the Army in Italy, Churchill told the House of Commons, of the British, Polish, New Zealand and American forces,

---

[1] *Hansard*, 1 May 1945, column 1242.
[2] Colville diary, 1 May 1945: Colville papers.
[3] Colville diary, 'that unseemly hour', 4 a.m., 2 May 1945: Colville papers.

of the Free Italian forces, of the South Africans and Brazilians, of the Negro Division of United States troops, the Jewish Brigade and the Japanese of American birth who were in action at Turin:[1]

Divided, as they were, by racial differences they were united and resolved upon their purpose, and now their reward has come. I am very glad that it has come at a time when it can be singled out. It stands out and brings to a conclusion the work of as gallant an Army as has ever marched, and brings to a pitch of fame and military reputation a Commander who, I may say, has always enjoyed the fullest confidence of the House of Commons.[2]

The work of that Commander, Alexander, was not yet over. Although his troops had entered Trieste, it was at once clear that Tito's Partisans had got there first. 'Should uncooperative contact be made,' Churchill telegraphed on May 2, 'no violence should occur except in self-defence.' A quarrel with the Yugoslavs 'would be a matter for the Peace Table and not for the field'. Churchill added: 'I have the greatest confidence in the way you will judge the difficult situation into which Victory is leading us.'[3]

British military supplies to Tito were still in transit. 'They should dwindle and die without another moment's delay,' Churchill minuted to Orme Sargent, and to the Chiefs of Staff Committee on May 2. 'No new shipment of any sort or kind is to start. Those ships that are on the seas may deliver their burdens.' This instruction, Churchill added, 'must be taken as a decision.'[4] The Chiefs of Staff were not too happy about this. Any 'sudden cessation of supplies', Cunningham remarked two days later, 'might result in throwing the Yugoslavs into the arms of the Russians'.[5] 'You have no doubt read the telegram,' Churchill telegraphed to Eden, 'showing Tito's breach of faith with Alexander, and that Freyberg's New Zealanders only just got into Trieste, Monfalcone and Gorizia ahead of the Tito-ite patrols. The awkward moment was avoided by the fact that we were in heavy strength and they were no more than patrols pegging out claims.'[6]

[1] 'Conduct of South African troops has been magnificent and I rejoice to think that they were in at the death,' Churchill had telegraphed to the acting Prime Minister of South Africa on April 30 (Prime Minister's Personal Telegram, T.718/5, No. 28 to South Africa, 'Top Secret and Personal', 30 April 1945: Churchill papers, 20/217). To the New Zealand acting Prime Minister he had telegraphed that same day: 'New Zealand troops were in at the death and have fought with splendid tenacity throughout' (Prime Minister's Personal Telegram, T.720/5, No. 86 to New Zealand, 'Top Secret and Personal', 30 April 1945: Churchill papers, 20/217).

[2] *Hansard*, 2 May 1945, column 1509.

[3] Prime Minister's Personal Telegram, T.723/5, OZ 2799, 'Guard', 2 May 1945: Churchill papers, 20/217.

[4] Prime Minister's Personal Minute, M.443/5, 2 May 1945: Churchill papers, 20/209.

[5] Chiefs of Staff Committee No. 117 of 1945, 4 May 1945: Cabinet papers, 79/33.

[6] Prime Minister's Personal Telegram, T.771/5, No. 363 to San Francisco, 'Top Secret', 5 May 1945: Churchill papers, 20/217.

On the evening of May 2, Churchill went out to dine with Noël Coward and with two friends of the inter-war years, Lady Juliet Duff and Venetia Montagu. Returning to the Annexe at 1.30 in the morning, he 'did a little work', as his Private Office diary recorded, 'and read newspapers until 3.30 a.m., when he went to bed'.[1]

One of Churchill's minutes on May 2 reflected his sense of imminent victory. 'Can anything be done,' he asked Sir James Grigg, 'with military bands during the celebrations, when they occur, in London and the country?'[2] Orders were 'being given', Grigg replied, 'for military bands to play in public places to the maximum extent possible on VE day and the following day. . . .'[3]

On the morning of May 3, Elizabeth Layton was taking dictation from Churchill when, as she noted in her diary, Captain Pim came in 'to announce the fall of Rangoon'.[4] That same day, in Germany, the United States 3rd Army entered Bavaria, while in Austria, the 7th Army captured Innsbruck. On the Baltic, British troops reached Lübeck. 'I am so glad you have got Lübeck,' Churchill telegraphed to Montgomery.[5] The reasons for Churchill's pleasure were not only military. 'Our troops in Lübeck,' Cunningham noted in his diary, 'and so have cut off the Russians from Denmark. Minute from the PM asking if we can get into Copenhagen.'[6] Two days later, Churchill explained to Eden how:

In the north, Eisenhower threw in an American corps with great dexterity to help Montgomery in his advance on Lübeck. He got there with twelve hours to spare. There were reports from the British Naval Attaché at Stockholm, which we are testing, that according to Swedish information, the Russians have dropped parachutists a few miles south of Copenhagen and

---

[1] Private Office diary, 2 May 1945. 'The Prime Minister was at his most benign,' Noël Coward later recalled, 'and suddenly, towards the end of dinner, looking across the table at the man who had carried England through her dark years, I felt an upsurge of gratitude that melted into hero worship. This was a profoundly significant moment in the history of our country; the long, long hoped-for victory was so very near, and the fact that we were in the presence of the man who had contributed so much foresight, courage and genius to winning it struck Juliet and Venetia at the same instant that it struck me. Emotion submerged us and without exchanging a word, as simultaneously as though we had carefully rehearsed it, the three of us rose to our feet and drank Mr Churchill's health.' (Noël Coward, *Future Indefinite*, London 1954, pages 327–8.)

[2] Prime Minister's Personal Minute, M.442/5, Premier papers, 4/41/8, folio 568.

[3] Minute dated 2 May 1945: Premier papers, 4/41/8, folio 567.

[4] Elizabeth Layton, diary entry for 3 May 1945: Nel papers.

[5] Prime Minister's Personal Telegram, T.742/5, 'Personal and Secret, also Private', 'Top Secret', 3 May 1945: Churchill papers, 20/217.

[6] Cunningham diary, 3 May 1945: Cunningham papers.

that Communist activities have appeared there. It now appears there were only two parachutists. We are sending in a moderate holding force to Copenhagen by air, and the rest of Denmark is being rapidly occupied from henceforward by our fast-moving armoured columns. I think therefore, having regard to the joyous feeling of the Danes and the abject submission and would-be partisanship of the surrendered Huns, we shall head our Soviet friends off at this point too.[1]

During May 3, German envoys, sent by Hitler's successor, Admiral Doenitz, arrived at Montgomery's headquarters on Luneburg heath. 'A very high power delegation,' Montgomery telegraphed to Churchill, 'and I hope to get from it the unconditional surrender of all German forces in Holland and Friesland including the islands and Heligoland and Schleswig-Holstein and Denmark.'[2]

Churchill had spent all of May 3 in bed, working in the morning, lunching alone, then having his afternoon sleep. He got up only at six in the evening for a meeting of the War Cabinet. He then went to University College Hospital, where he saw his brother Jack, who was recovering from a heart attack.[3] That evening, Churchill dined at the Other Club. He then returned to the Annexe, where he worked until shortly before three in the morning.[4] The secretary on duty that night, Marian Holmes, noted in her diary: 'PM very tired, v busy, but in marvellous good-humoured form. Jock Colville borrowed his stylo and forgot to return it. PM said "That's most immoral—in fact lousy and unethical". When saying goodnight to me, he grinned and said "It's nice to be winning, isn't it?" Got to bed at 4.30 a.m.'[5]

On May 4, in San Francisco, Molotov revealed to a startled Stettinius that the sixteen Polish negotiators who had met with Colonel

---

[1] Prime Minister's Personal Telegram, T.771/5, No. 363 to San Francisco, 'Top Secret', 5 May 1945: Churchill papers, 20/217.

[2] 'Top Secret', 'Special, unnumbered signal', 'Personal and Private', 3 May 1945: Churchill papers, 20/217.

[3] Jack Churchill had been taken ill in the last week of April at the Royal Dorset Yacht Club, Weymouth. A week later he had recovered sufficiently to be taken to London. Dr Adam Gray, who accompanied him to London, later recalled how, when he and the stretcher bearers were loading Jack Churchill into the ambulance, 'he decided to take a pinch of snuff and insisted on it!' Dr Gray added: 'During the time that Major Churchill was under my care, I was in daily communication by phone with the Prime Minister, who required full details personally. On one occasion I was in contact by telephone with the PM who was then travelling by train from Bristol to London about 60 miles per hour; he mentioned that he had not realized till then that such means of communication was possible.' (Dr Adam Gray, recollections: letter to the author, 14 February 1969.) Jack Churchill died on 23 February 1947.

[4] Private Office diary, 3 May 1945.

[5] Marian Holmes diary, 3 May 1945: Marian Walker Spicer papers.

Pimenov at Pruszkow on March 27 had 'been arrested by the Red Army' on charges of having earlier caused 'the death of 200 Red Army officers', a figure, Eden telegraphed to Churchill from San Francisco, 'I seem to remember was the same figure Stalin quoted at Yalta'. The effects on American opinion, Eden added, 'are likely to be serious, and I have no doubt that they will be so at home'.[1]

The Polish 'deadlock', Churchill replied, could now 'probably only be resolved at a conference between the three Heads of Governments'. The location, he felt, should be 'some unshattered town in Germany, if such can be found'. The conference should take place 'at latest at the beginning of July'. Meanwhile, 'I think it would be a mistake', Churchill wrote, for Britain and America to announce, as Eden has suggested, that they would be content with one-third, or even forty per cent, Polish non-Communist representation in a National Unity Government. The Polish problem, Churchill added, 'may be easier to settle when set in relation to the now numerous outstanding questions of the utmost gravity which acquire urgent settlement with the Russians'. Churchill now set out his deepest worries of what had come to pass since Yalta, telling Eden:

I fear terrible things have happened during the Russian advance through Germany to the Elbe. The proposed withdrawal of the United States Army to the occupational lines which were arranged with the Russians and Americans in Quebec and which were marked in yellow on the maps we studied there, would mean the tide of Russian domination sweeping forward 120 miles on a front of 300 or 400 miles. This would be an event which, if it occurred, would be one of the most melancholy in history.

After it was over and the territory occupied by the Russians, Poland would be completely engulfed and buried deep in Russian-occupied lands. What would in fact be the Russian frontier would run from the North Cape in Norway, along the Finnish–Swedish frontier, across the Baltic to a point just east of Lübeck along the at present agreed line of occupation and along the frontier between Bavaria to Czechoslovakia to the frontiers of Austria which is nominally to be in quadruple occupation, and half-way across that country to the Isonzo River behind which Tito and Russia will claim everything to the east.

Thus the territories under Russian control would include the Baltic Provinces, all of Germany to the occupational line, all Czechoslovakia, a large part of Austria, the whole of Yugoslavia, Hungary, Roumania, Bulgaria, until Greece in her present tottering condition is reached. It would include all the great capitals of middle Europe including Berlin, Vienna, Budapest, Belgrade, Bucharest and Sofia. The position of Turkey and Constantinople will certainly come immediately into discussion.

This constitutes an event in the history of Europe to which there has been

---

[1] No. 132 from San Francisco, 'Most Immediate', 'Secret', 4 May 1945: Churchill papers, 20/217.

no parallel, and which has not been faced by the Allies in their long and hazardous struggle. The Russian demands on Germany for reparations alone will be such as to enable her to prolong the occupation almost indefinitely, at any rate for many years, during which time Poland will sink with many other States into the vast zone of Russian-controlled Europe, not necessarily economically Sovietised but police-governed.

It was 'just about time', Churchill told Eden, that these formidable issues 'were examined between the principal Powers as a whole'. Nor did he see the situation as yet hopeless. As he told Eden:

We have several powerful bargaining counters on our side, the use of which might make for a peaceful agreement.

First, the Allies ought not to retreat from their present positions to the occupational line until we are satisfied about Poland and also about the temporary character of the Russian occupation of Germany, and the conditions to be established in the Russianized or Russian-controlled countries in the Danube Valley particularly Austria and Czechoslovakia, and the Balkans.

Secondly, we may be able to please them about the exits from the Black Sea and the Baltic as part of a general settlement.

All these matters can only be settled before the United States Armies in Europe are weakened. If they are not settled before the United States Armies withdraw from Europe and the Western World folds up its war machines, there are no prospects of a satisfactory solution and very little of preventing a third World War. It is to this early and speedy showdown and settlement with Russia that we must now turn our hopes.

'Meanwhile,' Churchill ended, 'I am against weakening our claim against Russia on behalf of Poland in any way.'[1]

While Churchill was at Downing Street on the afternoon of May 4, he put through a telephone call to Eisenhower, telling the Supreme Commander, as the note of the conversation recorded, 'that he was somewhat concerned at the reports that Russian parachutists had landed in Copenhagen, and emphasised the importance of our getting there first'. The conversation continued:

General Eisenhower said that 21st Army Group had armoured columns ready to push into Denmark, and were also prepared to drop a small airborne force into Copenhagen.

The Prime Minister then drew attention to the importance of getting to Prague first if it could be done.

General Eisenhower said that he had this point uppermost in his mind.

This conversation took place at 6.45 p.m. Ten minutes later, Field Marshal Montgomery was on the line. He had just 'concluded an

---

[1] Prime Minister's Personal Telegram, T.754/5, No. 321 to San Francisco, 'Personal and Top Secret', 4 May 1945: Foreign Office papers, 954/20 (Eden papers), folios 710–13.

interview', he said, with German representations, headed by Admiral von Friedeburg and including General Kinzl. 'The Germans had signed an instrument of surrender,' Montgomery told Churchill, 'by which all German forces, naval, army and air in Denmark, Holland, Schleswig Holstein, the Frisian Islands and Heligoland would lay down their arms at 8 a.m. double British summer time, on the 5th May.' Montgomery added: 'that he fully appreciated the necessity of our getting to Copenhagen before the Russians and that a party of about 100 airborne troops were being despatched at once'.

The German surrender to Montgomery would take place in less than twenty-five hours' time. Churchill at once telephoned Eisen-hower—it was now 7.15 p.m. according to the note of their conversation:

> The Prime Minister had a further private talk with General Eisenhower. He said that he assumed that General Eisenhower would issue a communiqué setting out the terms of the surrender which had been signed. He hoped that General Eisenhower would say that this message had just been received from Field Marshal Montgomery and that the Germans had surrendered to the 21st Army Group.
>
> General Eisenhower confirmed this and added that the German representatives were now on the way to his, General Eisenhower's Headquarters in order to discuss terms for the surrender of Norway and the remaining German forces. He, General Eisenhower, had told the Russians that he proposed to tell the German representatives that the German Armies opposite the Anglo-American Armies should surrender to them, and the German Armies opposite the Russian Armies should surrender to the Soviet.[1]

'My dear Prime Minister,' wrote General Ismay as soon as he was told the news of the imminent German surrender. 'Your Defence Office, with intense pride and—if we may be so bold—with deep affection offer their most grateful congratulations to the Chief, whose superb leadership has today been crowned with a triumph which only History will be able to measure.'[2]

Churchill at once summoned the Chiefs of Staff to the Cabinet Room at 10 Downing Street. 'We found him on the telephone,' Brooke noted in his diary, 'busy telling the King about his conversation with Ike and Monty. He then told us all about it, and he was evidently seriously affected by the fact that the war was to all intents and purposes over as far as Germany was concerned. He thanked us all very nicely and with tears in his eyes for all we had done in the war

---

[1] 'Record of Telephone Conversations held on the afternoon of 4th May 1945', Chiefs of Staff Committee No. 118 of 1945, 7.15 p.m., 4 May 1945, Annex: Cabinet papers, 79/33.

[2] Brooke diary, 4 May 1945: Bryant, *op. cit.*, volume 2, page 454.

and all the endless work we had put in "from El Alamein to where we are now". He then shook hands with all of us.'[1]

In the presence of the Chiefs of Staff, Churchill then made his fifth telephone call of the hour, once more to Eisenhower, to ask about the surrender of the Channel Islands. 'Everything was laid on,' Eisenhower assured him. Arrangements were in the hands of the Commander-in-Chief, Plymouth. Churchill ended this call by telling Eisenhower, as the note of the conversation recorded, 'that the Channel Islands had been in British possession for many centuries, and that he hoped that the surrender would be made to a British Officer'.[2]

Churchill and the Chiefs of Staff now turned to the question of the areas occupied by the British and American armies east of the Elbe. British and American forces, Churchill commented, 'had penetrated deep into Germany and occupied territory which fell within the zone which it had been agreed should be occupied by the Russians. This was a valuable bargaining counter and we should not move out of territory which we had occupied until after the Conference between Heads of States had been held'.

The question then arose as to where such a conference could be held, with Churchill asking Portal 'if he could say what towns in Germany had escaped damage, and were, therefore, suitable for the venue of such a conference'.[3]

To Clementine Churchill, who had arrived in Moscow on May 4 from southern Russia, Churchill telegraphed that night, with Poland still weighing on his mind: 'You seem to have had a triumphant tour, and I only wish matters could be settled between you and the Russian common people.' His telegram continued:

It is astonishing one is not in a more buoyant frame of mind in public matters. During the last three days we have heard of the death of Mussolini and Hitler; Alexander has taken a million prisoners of war; Montgomery took 500,000 additional yesterday and far more than a million today; all north-west Germany, Holland and Denmark are to be surrendered early tomorrow morning with all troops and ships, etc.; the next day Norway and the U-boats will, I believe, give in; and we are all occupied here with preparations for Victory-Europe Day.

Meanwhile I need scarcely tell you that beneath these triumphs lie poisonous politics and deadly international rivalries.

---

[1] Letter of 4 May 1945: Churchill papers, 20/201.

[2] 'Record of Telephone Conversations held on the afternoon of 4th May 1945', Chiefs of Staff Committee No. 118 of 1945, 7.15 p.m., 4 May 1945, Annex: Cabinet papers, 79/33.

[3] Staff Conference, Chiefs of Staff Committee No. 118 of 1945, 7.15 p.m., 4 May 1945: Cabinet papers, 79/33.

Churchill advised his wife to 'come home', after 'rendering the fullest compliments to your hospitable hosts'.[1] 'In the midst of all this military glory,' Clementine Churchill replied, 'I know that you are having harrassing and sometimes sad experiences.'[2]

That night, the United States 7th Army captured Berchtesgaden, Hitler's former mountain home. On the following day the United States 3rd Army entered Linz, the first city to be entered by the German army at the time of the annexation of Austria in 1938. To Eden, Churchill telegraphed on May 5:

You will by now have heard the news of the tremendous surrender that has been made to Montgomery of all North-West Germany, Holland, and Denmark, both as regards men and ships. The men alone must be more than a million. Thus in three successive days 2,500,000 Huns have surrendered to our two British commanders. This is quite a satisfactory incident in our military history. Ike has been splendid throughout. We must vie with him in sportsmanship.

Events in Poland, however, continued to cast their shadow and their curse. Churchill ended his telegram to Eden:

The case about the fifteen Poles, as admitted by Molotov to the Americans, is one on which we must soon tell Stalin quite plainly what the consequences will be. The perfidy by which these Poles were enticed into a Russian conference and then held fast in the Russian grip is one which will emerge in great detail from the stories which have reached us, and there is no doubt that the publication in detail of this event upon the authority of the great western Allies, would produce a primary change in the entire structure of world forces.

'We must make sure our Russian Allies understand what is at stake', Churchill warned, 'but also', he cautioned, 'we must make sure that the United States are with us'.[3]

To Truman, Churchill telegraphed that same day:

I am most concerned about the fate of the fifteen Polish representatives, in view of the statement made by Molotov to Stettinius at San Francisco that they had been arrested by the Red Army, and I think you and I should consult together very carefully upon this matter. If these Poles were enticed

---

[1] 'Not Registered', 'Top Secret', No. 2419 to Moscow, 4 May 1945: Churchill papers, 20/204.
[2] Moscow telegram, No. 1714, 'Personal', 'Immediate', 5 May 1945: Churchill papers, 20/204.
[3] Prime Minister's Personal Telegram, T.771/5, No. 363 to San Francisco, 'Top Secret', 5 May 1945: Foreign Office papers, 954/20 (Eden papers), folios 718–21.

into Russian hands and are now no longer alive, one cannot quite tell how far such a crime would influence the future.[1]

Churchill was convinced, as he had telegraphed to Eden on May 5, that 'nothing can save us all from a great catastrophe but a meeting and a showdown as early as possible at some point in Germany which is under American and British control and affords reasonable accommodation'.[2] But the immediate dangers as he saw them, in Denmark and Istria, had to be dealt with at once. He therefore telegraphed to Montgomery in the early hours of May 6:

I am concerned to hear of the delay of twenty-four hours in the passing of your armour into Denmark. We attribute the greatest importance to forestalling the Russians either in Copenhagen or in any part of Denmark. I hope you will be able to reassure me that all is well. I am very glad to hear that General Dewing and an airborne company was flying into Copenhagen yesterday. The reported Russian parachutists seem only to have amounted to two. However, it is better in these matters to be sure than sorry.[3]

Five minutes later Churchill telegraphed to Alexander:

I am very glad you got into Trieste, Gorizia and Monfalcone in time to put your foot in the door. Tito, backed by Russia, will push hard, but I do not think that they will dare attack you in your present position. Unless you can make a satisfactory working arrangement with Tito, the argument must be taken up by the Governments. There is no question of your making any agreement with him about incorporating Istria, or any part of the pre-war Italy, in 'his new Yugoslavia'. The destiny of this part of the world is reserved for the Peace table, and you should certainly make him aware of this.

In order to avoid leading Tito or the Yugoslav Commanders into any temptation, it would be wise to have a solid mass of troops in this area and with a great superiority of modern weapons and frequent demonstrations of the Air Force, as far as possible without hurting your advance in the direction of Vienna, which I am sure you are pressing with all possible speed.

'You are clearly entitled,' Churchill added, 'to advance as far and as fast as you can into former enemy territory, until you form contact with the Russian or Yugoslav forces.'[4]

The political aspects of these forward moves in Denmark and in

[1] Prime Minister's Personal Telegram, T.778/5, Prime Minister to President, No. 33, No. 4460 to Washington (repeated as No. 2454 to Moscow and No. 412 to San Francisco, Personal for Secretary of State), 'Personal and Top Secret', 5 May 1945: Foreign Office papers, 954/20 (Eden papers), folios 722.

[2] Prime Minister's Personal Telegram, T.771/5, No. 363 to San Francisco, 'Top Secret', 5 May 1945: Foreign Office papers, 954/20 (Eden papers), folios 718–21.

[3] Prime Minister's Personal Telegram, T.788/5, OZ 2904, 'Personal and Top Secret', 2.05 a.m., 6 May 1945: Churchill papers, 20/217.

[4] Prime Minister's Personal Telegram, T.791/5, 'Guard', 'Through Special Channel', 'Personal and Top Secret', 2.10 a.m., 6 May 1945: Churchill papers, 20/217.

Istria were potentially explosive. Yet it was the Victory in Europe celebrations which had now to be planned, as General Jodl, the German Chief of Staff, and General Eisenhower, began on May 6 the long drawn out but definite process towards the unconditional surrender of the remaining German fighting troops. The issues in political contention would have in any case to wait for the next meeting of the Big Three, which would clearly take place only after the now imminent end to the war in Europe. On May 6, Churchill received a telegram from Stalin, justifying the arrest of the sixteen Polish negotiators, who were, he said, 'undergoing investigation in Moscow' as 'diversionists and disturbers of order' in the rear of the Red Army.[1] Churchill at once telegraphed to Truman:

It seems to me that matters can hardly be carried farther by correspondence and that, as soon as possible, there should be a meeting of the three heads of Governments.

Meanwhile we should hold firmly to the existing position obtained or being obtained by our armies in Yugoslavia, in Austria, in Czechoslovakia, on the main central United States front and on the British front reaching up to Lübeck including Denmark.

There will be plenty to occupy both Armies in collecting the prisoners during the next few days, and we may hope that the VE celebration will also occupy the public mind at home. Thereafter I feel that we must earnestly consider our attitude towards the Soviets and show them how much we have to offer or withhold.

Churchill added that he was as anxious as Truman 'to avoid giving the impression of "ganging up" ' against Stalin, while at the same time maintaining Anglo-American 'essential unity of action on matters affecting good faith and international morality'.[2]

On May 6, Churchill lunched with two of his daughters, Sarah and Diana, as well as with Brendan Bracken and Stanislaw Mikolajczyk. In the afternoon he went to visit his brother, who was still in hospital. That night he dined with his daughter Sarah, Ambassador Winant, and a friend, Johnny Dodge, who had just been released from four years in German captivity.[3] After dinner he discussed arrangements for VE-

---

[1] 'Personal and Top Secret', 5 May 1945: Churchill papers, 20/217. Sent to Truman as Prime Minister to President, No. 35, 6 May 1945: Churchill papers, 20/217.

[2] Prime Minister's Personal Telegram, T.793/5, Prime Minister to President, No. 34, No. 4670 to Washington (repeated as No. 2456 to Moscow), 'Personal and Top Secret', 6 May 1945: Foreign Office papers, 954/20 (Eden papers), folio 723.

[3] Born in New York, and a friend of Lady Randolph Churchill, Dodge had been given a Commission by Churchill in October 1914, in the Royal Naval Division. He had been wounded twice during the Gallipoli landings. In 1920 he had been imprisoned by the Bolsheviks at Batum. After his capture by the Germans in June 1940, he had escaped four times, but been recaptured each time.

Day with Herbert Morrison, James Stuart and Sir Edward Bridges.[1]

At 2.41 a.m., in the early hours of May 7, as Churchill slept, General Jodl signed the instrument of surrender at Eisenhower's headquarters, Bedell Smith signing for the Allied Supreme Command, General Suslaparov for Russia and General Sevez for France. All fighting was to cease one minute after midnight on May 8th/9th.

The first member of Churchill's circle to receive the news, and to do so by telephone from Eisenhower, was Ismay, who, as John Martin noted, 'rang me up in the small hours, but we decided not to waken PM'.[2] It was Captain Pim who, when Churchill awoke on the morning of May 7, took him the news. 'For five years,' Churchill told Pim, 'you've brought me bad news, sometimes worse than others. Now you've redeemed yourself.'[3]

On the morning of May 7, Churchill was concerned at the pressure of Tito's partisans to take over as much of Istria as possible.[4] A 'steady gathering of British or British-controlled forces on this front', Churchill telegraphed to Alexander, 'if you can spare them, is most likely to maintain peace and most convenient if unpleasantness arises'. Churchill added: 'Let me know what you are doing in massing forces against this Muscovite tentacle, of which Tito is the crook.'[5] To Eisenhower, Churchill telegraphed a few moments later that he hoped his most recent move 'does not inhibit you to advance to Prague if you have the troops and do not meet the Russians earlier'. Churchill continued: 'I thought you did not mean to tie yourself down if you had the troops and the country was empty'.[6]

Eisenhower had originally suggested that the surrender should be announced by the Governments of the three Great Powers simultaneously, on Tuesday May 8. Churchill had then suggested to Truman and Stalin that the announcement should be made at 3 p.m. London time, 4 p.m. in Moscow and 9 a.m. in Washington. But Eisenhower then asked for the announcement to be moved forward to 6 p.m. London time that same day, May 7, as the orders to lay down their arms would be broadcast en clair to the German troops during May 7, and could not then be kept secret.

Churchill therefore proposed 6 p.m., May 7, as the moment for the

---

[1] Private Office diary, 6 May 1945.

[2] Martin diary, 7 May 1945: Martin papers.

[3] Pim memoirs, typescript: Pim papers.

[4] Telegram NAF 949: Cabinet papers, 105/143.

[5] Prime Minister's Personal Telegram, T.806/5, 'Personal and Secret', 'Guard', 7 May 1945: Churchill papers, 20/218.

[6] Prime Minister's Personal Telegram, T.807/5, 'Top Secret', 'Private and Confidential', OZ 2920, 'Most Immediate', 7 May 1945: Churchill papers, 20/218. Eisenhower's most recent report was in SCAF 349. (Cabinet papers, 105/159.)

announcement, this being noon in Washington and 7 p.m. in Moscow. Assuming that this timing would be accepted by Truman and Stalin, he alerted his Chiefs of Staff and War Cabinet to be ready to go together with him to Buckingham Palace at 6.30 that evening, when the announcement of victory would be made. By midday on May 7, however, it became clear that this plan was impossible. Stalin, as Admiral Cunningham noted in his diary, was 'refusing to recognize the signatures at Eisenhower's headquarters, and wanting it done in Berlin and by Zhukov'. Cunningham was one of the five guests invited to lunch that day at Downing Street with Churchill. 'He is in great form,' Cunningham noted, 'but much annoyed with Russians.'[1] Brooke, who was also present at the luncheon, noted in his diary:

It was a disturbed lunch. Winston was expecting a telephone call from the President which only came through after lunch. Meanwhile he received a telegram from Ike stating that it was likely he would have to fly to Berlin for the required Russian final negotiations. This necessitated a call being put through to Ike, which got through during the pudding period! In the intervals Winston discussed the pros and cons of elections in June. We stressed the cons from the military point of view, stating that it could lead only to dispersal of effort which would be better devoted to the war.[2]

Stalin was insistent that no arrangements had yet been made to receive the surrender of German forces on the eastern front, where, as he telegraphed to Churchill, German resistance 'is not slackening and, to judge from radio intercepts, an appreciable group of German forces is openly declaring its intention to continue resistance and not to obey Doenitz's order for surrender'. The Soviet High Command, Stalin added, would therefore like to hold up the announcement of the end of the war until the time when the instrument of surrender signed at Eisenhower's headquarters 'enters into force', a minute after midnight on May 8, the first minute of May 9. Stalin therefore proposed making the announcement at seven in the morning, Moscow time, on May 9.[3] President Truman's first reaction was that he too would have to wait before making an official announcement 'unless Stalin approves an earlier release'.[4]

At midday, as confusion grew over the timing of the announcement, Churchill telegraphed to Truman, asking him to telephone him 'on the open line as soon as you get this, asking for Colonel Warden,

---

[1] Cunningham diary, 7 May 1945: Cunningham papers. The other guests were Brooke, Portal, Ismay and Hollis.

[2] Brooke diary, 7 May 1945: Bryant, op. cit., volume 2, pages 455-6.

[3] 'Personal and Secret', 7 May 1945: Churchill papers, 20/218.

[4] Telephone message, received by telephone from Washington, 7 May 1945: Churchill papers, 20/218.

Whitehall 4433'. In speaking back, Churchill added 'I will address you as Admiral. We can then both tell UJ what we are going to do.'[1]

The telephone call took place at 4.10 p.m. London time, less than two hours before Churchill wanted to make the historic announcement. He spoke to Admiral Leahy, whose Secretary noted down the conversation:

LEAHY: Admiral Leahy speaking.
CHURCHILL: It is me, the Prime Minister.
LEAHY: Colonel Warden, yes, sir.
CHURCHILL: You've got my telegram?
LEAHY: I have your telegram, sir. This is a message which the other Admiral asked me to convey to Colonel Warden.
CHURCHILL: We are on the 'Secret' now, so we can talk quite freely. A message that he asked you to convey to me was what?
LEAHY: I convey the following message to you. In view of agreements already made, my Chief asks me to tell you that he cannot act without approval of Uncle Joe. Did you understand, sir?
CHURCHILL: Will you let somebody with a younger ear listen to it? I am not quite sure I got it all down I have got my secretary here. My ears are a bit deaf, you know . . .

Through the 'younger ear'—John Peck—and then again directly to Leahy, Churchill asked for an announcement that evening. But Leahy said, on Truman's behalf, that it must wait until May 9, as requested by Stalin. An hour later Churchill telephoned the White House again. 'Mr Churchill called me from London on the open telephone,' Leahy noted in his diary, 'telling me that crowds celebrating in the streets of London were beyond control and that he must make an announcement of the victory at noon.'[2]

To the last moment, Churchill had hoped that his announcement of victory could be made that evening. At half past five he summoned Elizabeth Layton, and dictated to her three hundred words for a short broadcast. 'They were stirring and purposeful to a degree,' she wrote home that day. 'At 5.55 we finished,' she added, 'then suddenly a phone call came through and it was decided not to broadcast.'[3] 'It was an anti-climax to us,' Marian Holmes noted, 'especially with the crowds thronging the streets and Whitehall and already celebrating Victory.'[4]

[1] Prime Minister's Personal Telegram, T.811/5, Prime Minister to President, No. 36, 'Personal and Top Secret', 7 May 1945: Churchill papers, 20/218.
[2] Transcript of a telephone conversation: Fleet Admiral William D. Leahy, *I Was There*, New York 1950, pages 359–63.
[3] Elizabeth Layton, letter of 7 May 1945: Nel papers.
[4] Marian Holmes diary, 7 May 1945: Marian Walker Spicer papers.

Churchill had lost May 7. He now insisted upon May 8. Tuesday May 8, he telegraphed to Truman that evening, 'will be treated as Victory in Europe Day and will be regarded as a holiday. This was necessary on account of the masses of work people who have to be considered. I have informed Marshal Stalin.'[1]

To Stalin, Churchill telegraphed that he had decided 'with much regret', in view of the 'difficulty in concerting an earlier release', to postpone his broadcast announcement of victory from that evening, May 7, to the following day, May 8, at 3 p.m. British Double Summer Time, 4 p.m. Moscow time. A statement had already been issued to the Press, he added, that May 8 'will be treated as Victory in Europe Day and will be regarded as a holiday'.[2]

That afternoon, as the Chiefs of Staff were ready to leave No. 10, Churchill led them into the garden for a photograph. 'Churchill toasted the triumvirate as "the architects of victory", Ismay later recalled.' Ismay added: 'I hoped that they would raise their glasses to the chief who had been the master-planner, but perhaps they were too moved to trust their voices.'[3] Later that day, Ismay told Joan Bright that Churchill had himself put out the tray of glasses and drinks, so that Brooke, Portal, Cunningham and Ismay could celebrate this first news with him. 'It was a sad example of human imperceptiveness,' she noted in later years, 'that neither the Chief of the Imperial General Staff, nor the First Sea Lord, nor the Chief of the Air Staff saluted him in a toast. General Ismay, in his modesty, in their presence would never have done so. Mr Churchill drank to them, each one in turn.' It was possible, Joan Bright added, 'that they were shy, it is certain that they were British, it is probable that they reacted as a committee, a body without a heart, and that each waited for the other to take the initiative. Whatever the reason it was an opportunity missed that the Grand Old Man, who had been the architect of the victory they were marking, did not receive a tribute from his three closest military advisers.'[4]

At 6.30 that evening, the War Cabinet heard an account of the day's exchanges, and endorsed Churchill's decision.[5] Churchill then rested for two hours, before dining with Brendan Bracken. He afterwards visited the Private Secretaries' Mess 'and stayed there for half an hour', as his Private Office diary recorded.[6]

---

[1] Prime Minister's Personal Telegram, T.814/5, Prime Minister to President No. 37, 'Personal and Top Secret', 7 May 1945: Churchill papers, 20/218.

[2] Prime Minister's Personal Telegram, T.815/5, No. 2483 to Moscow, 'Most Immediate', 'Personal and Top Secret', sent at 9.10 p.m., 7 May 1945: Churchill papers, 20/218.

[3] Ismay memoirs, *op. cit.*, page 394.

[4] Joan Bright Astley, *The Inner Circle, a view of war at the top*, London 1971, page 206.

[5] War Cabinet No. 59 of 1945, 6.30 p.m., 7 May 1945: Cabinet papers, 65/50.

[6] Private Office diary, 7 May 1945.

At midnight, Churchill began his evening's work. Elizabeth Layton was the secretary on late duty that night. As she came into his room for that final night's dictation of the war in Europe, Churchill looked up with the words: 'Hullo, Miss Layton. Well, the war's over, you've played your part.' Then, as she wrote home, 'an enormous thunderstorm broke—claps, bangs and crashes. He kept saying "What was that?—oh, thunder", because it *sounded* like rockets, not because he thought it might be! Then he'd say "Might as well have another war—what was that? oh, thunder".' [1]

It was 3.45 on the morning of May 8 when Churchill went to bed.

---

[1] Elizabeth Layton, letter of 7 May 1945: Nel papers.

69
VE Day

ON Tuesday, 8 May 1945, Churchill stayed in bed all morning, working on his Victory broadcast. During the morning, following enquiries which he had made, he received assurances from Scotland Yard and the Ministry of Food that there was no shortage of beer in the capital, 'though of course', as John Martin pointed out, 'individual public houses here and there may run dry'.[1] At one moment Churchill left his bedroom to walk along the corridor to the Map Room, carrying with him, as Captain Pim later recalled, 'a gift of bottles of champagne and a large Gruyere cheese' together with a note 'For Captain Pim and his officers with the Prime Minister's compliments on Victory Day in Europe'.[2]

While working on his own broadcast, Churchill also received a request from the King, who would, as John Peck noted, 'be grateful if you would suggest an alternate ending to his broadcast, as you offered'.[3] Churchill at once dictated a final paragraph for the King's broadcast, which read, to take into account that there were still small pockets of German resistance on what was left of the eastern front:

All organized resistance by Germany is at an end. The German High Command has ordered that firing shall cease on all fronts at midnight tonight; and even though some fanatical groups should seek to prolong for a time the struggle in the South and East of Europe, they will soon be overcome. The power and might of Germany is finally broken.[4]

Shortly after one o'clock, Churchill drove to Buckingham Palace for lunch with the King, who noted in his diary: 'We congratulated each other on the end of the European War. The day we have been

---

[1] Note by John Martin for the Prime Minister, 8 May 1945: Premier papers, 4/41/8, folio 564.
[2] Sir Richard Pim recollections: letter to the author, 21 June 1985.
[3] Notes by John Peck: Premier papers, 4/41/2, folio 134.
[4] 'Amendment suggested': Premier papers, 4/41/2, folio 124.

longing for has arrived at last and we can look back with thankfulness to God that our tribulation is over.' [1]

Leaving Buckingham Palace, Churchill returned to Downing Street to put the finishing touches to his broadcast.

'All my thoughts are with you on this supreme day my darling,' Clementine Churchill telegraphed from Moscow that morning. 'It could not have happened without you.' [2] 'Please be sure,' she telegraphed again an hour later, 'and keep official and popular rejoicings going tomorrow at the same pitch as today with special reference to Russia. This is important.' [3] 'We shall certainly keep rejoicings going,' was Churchill's reply. [4]

Both Churchill and his wife were distressed not to be together on Victory-in-Europe Day. As the British Chargé d'Affaires in Moscow, Frank Roberts, wrote to John Martin two days later: 'it was with the greatest reluctance that Mrs Churchill and I both felt it our duty to advise against cutting short her stay here, but on her return Mrs Churchill will, I think, be able to persuade the Prime Minister that this was the only possible course to take'. Clementine Churchill's presence in Russia 'at this particular moment', Roberts added, 'has symbolized more than anything else could have done the friendship between the peoples of the two countries and also the personal ties between the leaders of the two countries which, despite all causes of friction, are a very genuine source of pride and satisfaction to this country'. [5]

Stalin made one last effort to postpone the announcement of the Allied victory until May 9, on the grounds, as Admiral Cunningham noted, 'that there was still fighting going on on the Russian front'. 'This,' Cunningham added, 'will be resisted.' [6] 'I shall make it clear in my announcement,' Churchill telegraphed to Stalin that morning, 'that there is still resistance in some places.' But this was 'not surprising,' he added, 'considering the immense length of the front and the disorganized condition of the German Government.' [7]

At midday came a message from Washington, from President

---

[1] King George VI, diary, 8 May 1945: John W. Wheeler-Bennett, *King George VI, op. cit.*, page 625.

[2] Moscow Telegram, No. 1767, 'Most Immediate', sent 8.10 a.m., received 10.55 a.m., 8 May 1945: Churchill papers, 20/204.

[3] Moscow Telegram, No. 1768, 'Most Immediate', sent 9.34 a.m., received 11.58 a.m., 8 May 1945: Churchill papers, 20/204.

[4] Manuscript note (taken down by Leslie Rowan): Spencer-Churchill papers.

[5] British Embassy, Moscow, 10 May 1945: Cabinet papers, 20/204.

[6] Cunningham diary, 8 May 1945: Cunningham papers.

[7] Prime Minister's Personal Telegram, T.823/5, 'Personal and Top Secret', 8 May 1945: Churchill papers, 20/218.

Truman: 'With warm affection, we hail our comrades-in-arms across the Atlantic.'[1]

Churchill now prepared to broadcast to the British people, and to the world, from the Cabinet Room at 10 Downing Street. Elizabeth Layton retyped the undelivered broadcast of the previous evening, and then joined 'a huge body' of Private Secretaries and typists who had come to No. 10 from the Annexe, and stood waiting outside the Cabinet Room door.[2] 'The PM had a trial run,' noted Marian Holmes, 'and we heard through the loudspeaker "What you doing?" (PM) "They are just fixing the microphone, sir" (John Martin). Then a terrific trumpet from the PM as he vigorously blew his nose. "Pull those blinds down. Can't see what I'm doing" (PM).'[3]

'Of course,' Elizabeth Layton wrote home, 'it was only coming out to us, not all over the place.'[4]

At three o'clock Churchill began his broadcast. 'Yesterday morning,' he told his millions of listeners, 'at 2.41 a.m. at Headquarters, General Jodl, the representative of the German High Command, and Grand Admiral Doenitz, the designated head of the German State, signed the act of unconditional surrender of all German land, sea, and air forces in Europe to the Allied Expeditionary Force, and simultaneously to the Soviet High Command.' This agreement would be ratified 'today' in Berlin, where Air Chief Marshal Tedder and General de Lattre de Tassigny would sign it on behalf of Eisenhower, and Marshal Zhukov on behalf of the Soviet High Command. The four German signatories would be Field Marshal Keitel and the Commanders-in-Chief of the German Army, Navy and Air Force. Hostilities would end officially 'at one minute after midnight tonight', but 'in the interests of saving lives' the Cease Fire 'began yesterday to be sounded all along the front, and our dear Channel Islands are also to be freed today'. Churchill then spoke of the eastern front:

The Germans are still in places resisting the Russian troops, but should they continue to do so after midnight they will, of course, deprive themselves of the protection of the laws of war, and will be attacked from all quarters by the Allied troops. It is not surprising that on such long fronts and in the existing disorder of the enemy the orders of the German High Command should not in every case be obeyed immediately. This does not, in our opinion, with the best military advice at our disposal, constitute any reason for withholding from the nation the facts communicated to us by General Eisenhower of the unconditional surrender already signed at Rheims, nor should

---

[1] Telegram of 8 May 1945, unnumbered: Churchill papers, 20/218.
[2] Elizabeth Layton, letter of 8 May 1945: Nel papers.
[3] Marian Holmes diary, 8 May 1945: Marian Walker Spicer papers.
[4] Elizabeth Layton, letter of 8 May 1945: Nel papers.

it prevent us from celebrating today and tomorrow (Wednesday) as Victory in Europe days.

'Today, perhaps,' Churchill added, 'we shall think mostly of ourselves. Tomorrow we shall pay a particular tribute to our Russian comrades, whose prowess in the field has been one of the grand contributions to the general victory.' Churchill's broadcast continued:

The German war is therefore at an end. After years of intense preparation, Germany hurled herself on Poland at the beginning of September, 1939; and, in pursuance of our guarantee to Poland and in agreement with the French Republic, Great Britain, the British Empire and Commonwealth of Nations, declared war upon this foul aggressor. After gallant France had been struck down we, from this Island and from our united Empire, maintained the struggle single-handed for a whole year until we were joined by the military might of Soviet Russia, and later by the overwhelming power and resources of the United States of America.

Finally almost the whole world was combined against the evil-doers, who are now prostrate before us.

At this phrase, 'the evil doers, who are now prostrate before us', Harold Nicolson, who was among the crowd listening to the speech being relayed through loudspeakers in Parliament Square, noted: 'The crowd gasped.' [1] Churchill continued:

We may allow ourselves a brief period of rejoicing; but let us not forget for a moment the toil and efforts that lie ahead. Japan, with all her treachery and greed, remains unsubdued. The injury she has inflicted on Great Britain, the United States, and other countries, and her detestable cruelties, call for justice and retribution. We must now devote all our strength and resources to the completion of our task, both at home and abroad. Advance, Britannia! Long live the cause of freedom! God save the King. [2]

'The PM's voice broke,' noted Marian Holmes, 'as he said "Advance, Britannia!"' [3]

'My darling,' Clementine Churchill telegraphed from Moscow, 'Here we in the British Embassy have all been listening to your solemn words. God bless you. M. Herriot is here and sends you his devoted greetings. Alleluia. All my love. Clemmie.' [4]

Herriot, a former French Prime Minister and President of the Chamber of Deputies, had been interned near Berlin in 1944, and liberated by Soviet troops a few days before VE Day. Listening to Churchill's broadcast, he wept, then told Clementine:

[1] Letter of 8 May 1945 (to Nigel Nicolson): Nigel Nicolson (editor), *op. cit.*, page 456.
[2] Broadcast of 8 May 1945: Churchill papers, 9/169
[3] Marian Holmes diary, 8 May 1945: Marian Walker Spicer papers.
[4] Moscow Telegram No. 1773, sent at 4 p.m., received 6.50 p.m., 8 May 1945: Churchill papers, 20/204.

I am afraid you may think it unmanly of me to weep, but I have just heard Mr Churchill's voice. The last time I heard his voice was on the day in Tours in 1940 when he implored the French Government to hold firm and continue the struggle. His noble words of leadership that day were unavailing. When we heard the French Government's answer, and knew that they meant to give up the fight, tears streamed down Mr Churchill's face. So you will understand if I weep today, I do not feel unmanned.[1]

Another of those who heard Churchill speak was his son. 'Was greatly moved by your splendid speech,' he telegraphed, 'which I heard 8,000 feet above Dinaric Alps en route from Belgrade to Caserta. . . .'[2]

His broadcast over, Churchill left 10 Downing Street by the garden gate, passing in the garden through a line of his secretaries who 'clapped and cheered like anything', as Elizabeth Layton wrote home, 'and he grinned and seemed quite pleased and said: "Thank you so much, thank you *so* much." '

Churchill then drove in an open car across the Horse Guards Parade and on to the House of Commons. 'We followed as far as we could,' Elizabeth Layton noted, 'but were soon jammed, and the noise and cheering was deafening. I think he was very touched.'[3] 'The vast crowds of cheering people in Parliament Square,' noted Churchill's Private Office diary, 'made it almost impossible for the cars to get through, and he did not reach the Chamber until almost 3.30 p.m.'[4] Harold Nicolson, who had entered the Chamber to be there to greet him, wrote in his letter of how 'a slight stir was observed behind the Speaker's chair, and Winston, looking coy and cheerful, came in. The house rose as a man, and yelled and yelled and waved their Order Papers. He responded, not with a bow exactly, but with an odd shy jerk of the head and with a wide grin. Then he started to read to us the statement that he had just made on the wireless.'[5]

After Churchill had finished, 'he put his manuscript aside', Nicolson noted, and with 'wide gestures' thanked the House of Commons for its 'noble support' of him throughout the war years.[6] During his words

[1] Clementine Spencer Churchill, *My Visit to Russia*, London 1945, pages 56–7 Twenty years earlier, in January 1925, when Churchill met Herriot in Paris, he wrote to Clementine: 'I had an interview with Herriot in his sick room. Poor man—he seemed vy seedy & worn with worry & phlebitis. We got on well' (Letter of 10 January 1925). From 1947 to 1954 Herriot was President of the National Assembly. He died in 1957, aged 85.
[2] Caserta Telegram, F/72752, 'Personal', received 11.35 p.m., 8 May 1945: Churchill papers, 20/205.
[3] Elizabeth Layton, letter of 8 May 1945: Nel papers.
[4] Private Office diary, 8 May 1945.
[5] Harold Nicolson, letter of 8 May 1945 (to Nigel Nicolson): Nigel Nicolson (editor), *op. cit.*, page 457.
[6] Harold Nicolson, letter of 8 May 1945 (to Nigel Nicolson): Nigel Nicolson (editor), *op. cit.*, page 457.

of thanks, Churchill spoke of his 'deep gratitude' to the House of Commons, which had proved itself 'the strongest foundation for waging war that has ever been seen in the whole of our long history'. Churchill added:

We have all of us made our mistakes, but the strength of the Parliamentary institution has been shown to enable it at the same moment to preserve all the title-deeds of democracy while waging war in the most stern and protracted form. I wish to give my hearty thanks to men of all Parties, to everyone in every part of the House wherever they sit, for the way in which the liveliness of Parliamentary institutions has been maintained under the fire of the enemy, and for the way in which we have been able to persevere—and we could have persevered much longer if need had been—till all the objectives which we set before us for the procuring of the unlimited and unconditional surrender of the enemy had been achieved.

Churchill had been in the House of Commons twenty-six years earlier when Lloyd George had announced the Unconditional Surrender of Germany. 'I recollect well,' he said, 'at the end of the last war, more than a quarter of a century ago, that the House, when it heard the long list of the surrender terms, the armistice terms, which had been imposed upon the Germans, did not feel inclined for debate or business, but desired to offer thanks to Almighty God, to the Great Power which seems to shape and design the fortunes of nations and the destiny of man: and I therefore beg, Sir, with your permission to move: "That this House do now attend at the Church of St Margaret, Westminster, to give humble and reverent thanks to Almighty God for our deliverance from the threat of German domination." This is the identical Motion which was moved in former times.' [1]

The House of Commons then adjourned, Members walking across Old Palace Yard to St Margaret's for a service of Thanksgiving. The service began with the singing of the National Anthem, followed by words of thanksgiving and dedication, read by the Speaker's Chaplain, Canon Don. The congregation then sang 'The Old Hundredth', 'All people that on earth do dwell, sing to the Lord with cheerful voice. . . .' followed by the singing of Psalm 124 by the Choir, 'Our soul set free'. The Speaker then read out the names of the twenty-one Members of Parliament who had been killed during the war, among them two of Churchill's younger friends, Ronald Cartland and Victor Cazalet. [2]

Returning to the House of Commons, Churchill moved 'That this House do now adjourn'. It was 4.31 p.m. Churchill, as Nicolson noted, 'made a dash for the Smoking Room', and he added:

[1] *Hansard*, 8 May 1945, columns 1867–9.
[2] 'Service of Thanksgiving': *Hansard*, columns 1870–4. Cartland had been killed during the retreat from Dunkirk, Cazalet in the air crash in which General Sikorski had been killed.

When he was passing through Central Hall the crowd there broke into loud clapping. He hesitated and then hurried on. A little boy dashed out: 'Please, sir, may I have your autograph?' Winston took a long time getting out his glasses and wiping them. Then he ruffled the little boy's hair and gave him back his beastly little album. 'That will remind you of a glorious day,' he said, and the crowd clapped louder than before.[1]

Churchill then returned through milling, excited crowds to the Annexe. After a short while, he then drove to Buckingham Palace, for the previous day's postponed meeting of the King with the War Cabinet and Chiefs of Staff. Returning to the Annexe, his Private Office diary noted, Churchill then went on to the Ministry of Health balcony overlooking Whitehall, 'where vast crowds had assembled in the hope of seeing him'.[2] 'God bless you all,' he told them, 'This is your victory!' at which the crowd roared back, 'No—it is yours,' and he went on: 'It is the victory of the cause of freedom in every land In all our long history we have never seen a greater day than this. Everyone, man or woman, has done their best. Everyone has tried. Neither the long years, nor the dangers, nor the fierce attacks of the enemy, have in any way weakened the independent resolve of the British nation. God bless you all.'[3]

Churchill returned to the Annexe, where Gilbert Winant introduced him to his son, who had just returned after being a prisoner-of-war in Germany. Churchill then dined with his daughters Sarah and Diana, Diana's husband Duncan Sandys, and Lord Camrose, who noted how, at the end of dinner, 'Winston was informed by Commander Thompson and Desmond Morton that there was a tremendous crowd in Parliament Street and that they were calling for a speech. Winston said simply "I will go up in five minutes". He was wearing his "boiler" suit, and when asked by Morton if he would change he replied emphatically that he would go as he was.' Camrose's account continued:

I accompanied him on the long walk from the Annexe through the various Government buildings, and the roar of enthusiasm which came up from the crowd at the sight of him and his grandson, Julian Sandys, was deafening. I went on to one of the adjoining balconies. Not only was the space immediately in front of the building packed, but there was a sea of faces stretching far up Whitehall and right down to Parliament Square.

It was half past ten. As Churchill spoke, Camrose noted, 'the crowd roared and roared again'.[4] 'The roaring and cheering,' wrote Elizabeth Layton, who was on the adjoining balcony, 'exceeded by

[1] Letter of 8 May 1945 (to Nigel Nicolson): Nigel Nicolson (editor), *op. cit.*, page 458.
[2] Private Office diary, 8 May 1945.
[3] Speech of 8 May 1945.
[4] 'VE Night, 8th May, 1945', notes written on 9 May 1945: Camrose papers.

double anything I can remember at the Coronation.'[1] Churchill told the thousands assembled below him:

My dear friends, this is your hour. This is not victory of a party or of any class. It's a victory of the great British nation as a whole. We were the first, in this ancient island, to draw the sword against tyranny. After a while we were left all alone against the most tremendous military power that has been seen. We were all alone for a whole year.

There we stood, alone. Did anyone want to give in?

'No,' shouted the crowd.
'Were we downhearted?'
'No!'

Churchill continued:

The lights went out and the bombs came down. But every man, woman and child in the country had no thought of quitting the struggle. London can take it. So we came back after long months from the jaws of death, out of the mouth of hell, while all the world wondered. When shall the reputation and faith of this generation of English men and women fail? I say that in the long years to come not only will the people of this island but of the world, wherever the bird of freedom chirps in human hearts, look back to what we've done and they will say 'do not despair, do not yield to violence and tyranny, march straight forward and die if need be—unconquered'. Now we have emerged from one deadly struggle—a terrible foe has been cast on the ground and awaits our judgment and our mercy.

Churchill then spoke of the war in the Far East, telling the crowd:

But there is another foe who occupies large portions of the British Empire, a foe stained with cruelty and greed—the Japanese. I rejoice we can all take a night off today and another day tomorrow. Tomorrow our great Russian allies will also be celebrating victory and after that we must begin the task of rebuilding our hearth and homes, doing our utmost to make this country a land in which all have a chance, in which all have a duty, and we must turn ourselves to fulfill our duty to our own countrymen, and to our gallant allies of the United States who were so foully and treacherously attacked by Japan. We will go hand and hand with them. Even if it is a hard struggle we will not be the ones who will fail.[2]

The crowd replied by singing 'Land of Hope and Glory' and 'For He's a Jolly Good Fellow'. Churchill then returned to the Annexe, where he spent the rest of the evening with Lord Camrose.[3] The Americans, Churchill told his guest, had advanced '120 miles farther

---

[1] Elizabeth Layton, letter of 8 May 1945: Nel papers.
[2] Speech of 8 May 1945.
[3] Private Office diary, 8 May 1945.

than was expected and, in accordance with the arrangement made with Stalin, would have to come back that distance'. Stalin would have 'eight capitals in his control'.[1] Churchill 'was making sure of Italy and the Istrian Province and, of course, Greece'. Churchill also told Camrose 'that he had agreed the European line with Stalin; while it was not all he could wish, it gave some guarantee for the future'. That Camrose added, 'was very secret indeed'.

Camrose's account continued:

In the middle of our conversation he called in Rowan, one of his secretaries, to ask if there were any telegrams for his attention, whereupon Rowan brought in a pile of files 6 inches high. From these he passed to me to read (1) telegram from the Italian Prime Minister in very effusive terms (2) copy of telegram sent to Clemmie giving her material for a broadcast in Russia today (Wednesday) and (3) copy of a telegram from Truman, for which he desired immediate publication. Rowan, who had been in and out of the room five or six times, said he thought this had already been done.

Then he called for the newspapers, Was very annoyed with a cartoon in the *Daily Mail*, praised the *Daily Telegraph* pictures and proceeded to read *Times* leader.[2] This led him to recall a *Daily Telegraph* leader in his favour in regard to the air programme in 1934 and to say that Baldwin lunching with him two years ago had admitted how great a mistake he had made on the question of air preparedness.

Camrose's account ended:

I left him at 1.15 with the pile of files before him, all of which he said would be dealt with before he went to bed. On the point of my leaving he had Rowan in again and said he had found some request in the files that he should visit the City today (Wednesday). Asked Rowan whether the Lord Mayor was very anxious for the visit. On the latter saying he thought so he replied 'Very well, I shall go to Mansion House at 4 o'clock tomorrow to take a glass of wine with his lordship.'

He also had an idea of calling on the Russian Ambassador and perhaps the American.[3]

Among the telegrams in the files which Rowan had brought in was one announcing the liberation from German captivity of three former

---

[1] Warsaw, Prague, Budapest, Bucharest, Sofia, Belgrade, Berlin and Vienna.

[2] The *Daily Mail* cartoon showed Churchill, sitting in an armchair, his feet up on his desk, drink held high, with the caption 'The same to you!' 'What amuses me about this cartoon,' Churchill wrote to Viscount Rothermere, the paper's owner, 'is that it was no doubt intended to be friendly in character, and I am sorry that the *Daily Mail* should have such a cartoonist to carry out its policy.' The letter was never sent. (Churchill papers, 20/199.)

[3] 'VE Night, 8th May 1945', notes written on 9 May 1945: Camrose papers. On 9 May 1945, accompanied by his daughter Mary, Churchill drove through the streets of London in an open car, visiting the American, Soviet, and French embassies, and making short speeches in each.

French Prime Ministers, Paul Reynaud, Edouard Daladier and Léon Blum. 'I send you my warmest congratulations on your liberation,' Churchill telegraphed. 'I need not tell you how often my thoughts were with you during the long years of captivity nor how glad I am to be able to rejoice with you on this day of victory.'[1]

One of the telegrams which Churchill sent that evening was to his wife, in Moscow. 'It would be a good thing,' he told her, 'if you broadcast to the Russian people tomorrow Wednesday, provided that were agreeable to the Kremlin.' He then sent the text of his own message to the Russian people, which Clementine Churchill did indeed broadcast. 'It is my firm belief,' he declared, 'that on the friendship and understanding between the British and Russian peoples depends the future of mankind. Here in our island home we are thinking today very often about you all, and we send you from the bottom of our hearts our wishes for your happiness and well being and that, after all the sacrifices and sufferings of the Dark Valley through which we have marched together, we may also in loyal comradeship and sympathy walk in the sunshine of victorious peace. I have asked my Wife to speak these few words of friendship and admiration to you all.'[2]

The Soviet Union was also in Churchill's mind that evening as he read a telegram from the British Chargé d'Affaires in Moscow, Frank Roberts. It concerned a complaint from the Soviet Government about the way in which the British Government was protesting about the sixteen Polish emissaries who had been seized outside Warsaw, and were now being held in prison in Moscow.[3] 'We are utterly indifferent,' Churchill told Roberts, 'to anything that the Soviets may say by way of propaganda. No one here believes a single word.' When it becomes 'worthwhile', Churchill added, 'devastating replies can be made in Parliament'. At present, however, the British Government was endeavouring 'to shield the Soviets'.

As the German war came to an end, the breach with the Soviet Union was almost complete. 'It is no longer desired by us,' Churchill told Roberts, 'to maintain detailed arguments with the Soviet Government about their views and actions.'[4]

An hour after sending this telegram to Moscow, Churchill received a telegram from San Francisco. It was from Anthony Eden. 'All my

---

[1] Prime Minister's Personal Telegram, T.836/5: Churchill papers, 20/218.
[2] Foreign Office Telegram No. 2504 to Moscow, 'Top Secret', sent at 9.45 p.m., 8 May 1945: Churchill papers, 20/205.
[3] Moscow Telegram No. 1747.
[4] Prime Minister's Personal Telegram, T.828/5, No. 2505 to Moscow, 'Personal and Top Secret', despatched at 10.05 p.m., 8 May 1945: Churchill papers, 20/218.

thoughts are with you,' he telegraphed, 'on this day which is so essentially your day. It is you who have led, uplifted and inspired us
through the worst days. Without you this day could not have been.'[1]

[1] San Francisco Telegram, No. 195, 'Immediate', 'Personal', sent 1.40 p.m., received 11.10
p.m., 8 May 1945: Churchill papers, 20/218.

Maps

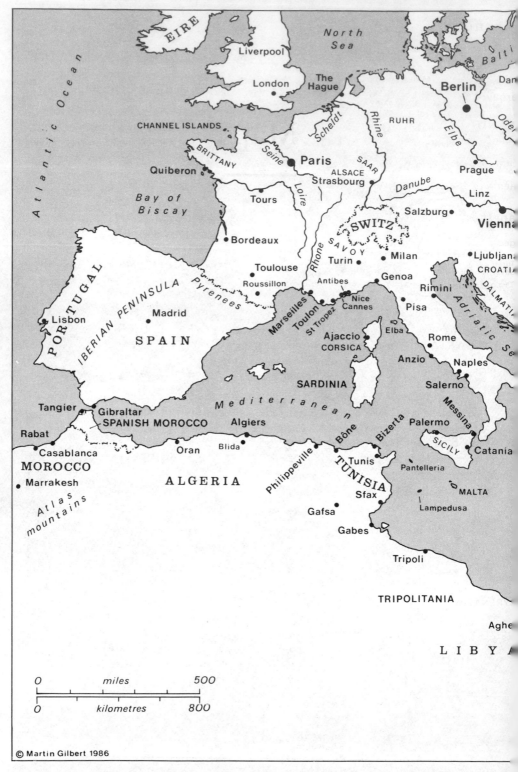

1 The Mediterranean and Europe

2 Greece and the Aegean Sea

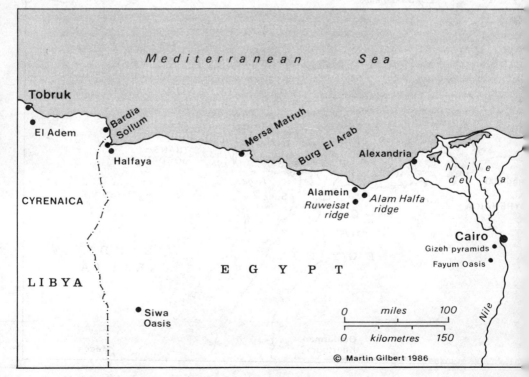

© Martin Gilbert 1986

3 The Western Desert

Tunisia

5   Southern Italy and the Adriatic

Munich•

B A V A R I A

Linz•   *Danube*   **Vienna** •

SALZBURG
Salzburg
Berchtesgaden

Enns

A U S T R I A

VORARLBERG

T Y R O L
Innsbruck•

SWITZ

Brenner
Pass

C A R I N T H I A

STYRIA

Maribor•
S L O V E N I A

Julian Alps

VENEZIA-GIULIA

Udine•

Ljubljana•

L O M B A R D Y

Lake
Garda

Verona•

Piave

Isonzo

Gorizia•
Monfalcone•
Trieste•

I S T R I A

Fiume•

Zagreb•

Sava

Y U G O S L A V I A

C R O A T I A

Po   *Adige*

Venice•

Pola•

D A L M A T I A

Lake
Comacchio

Bologna•

Monte
Battaglia

Faenza•

▽ ☀ GOTHIC LINE ▽ ▽ ▽ ▽ ▽ ▽ ▽

Pisa•
Leghorn•

Florence•
San
Casciano•

Croce•

Metauro

Ancona•

A
d
r
i
a
t
i
c

Zadar•

Sibenik•

Cecina•

Siena•

A
p
e
n
n
i
n
e
s

I T A L Y

S e a

ELBA

Pescaro•

0   *miles*   70
0   *kilometres*   120

© Martin Gilbert 1986

Rome •

Liri   *Rapido*

Campoleone•

Anzio•
Cisterna•

Sonnino•

Cassino•
Ausonia
Spigno•

Foggia•

Capua•
Caserta•

Garigliano

5   Northern Italy, Istria and Austria

7 Europe from the Atlantic to the Volga

© Martin Gilbert 1986

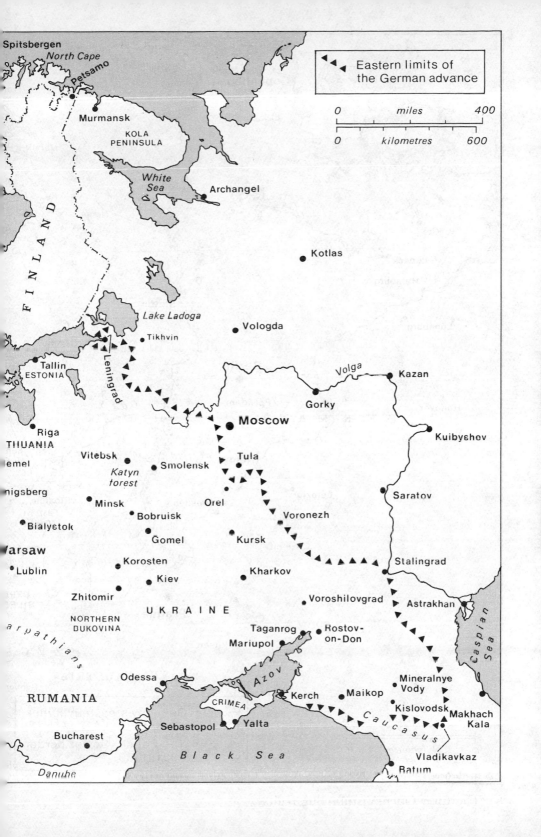

Spitsbergen

North Cape

Petsamo

• Murmansk

KOLA
PENINSULA

*White
Sea*

• Archangel

FINLAND

Lake Ladoga

• Tikhvin

• Kotlas

• Vologda

• Tallin
ESTONIA

Volga

• Kazan

Leningrad

• Gorky

Moscow

• Kuibyshev

• Riga

THUANIA

• Vitebsk

*Katyn
forest*

• Smolensk

• Tula

• Saratov

emel

nigsberg

• Minsk

• Bobruisk

• Orel

• Voronezh

• Bialystok

• Gomel

• Kursk

Varsaw

• Lublin

• Korosten

• Kiev

• Kharkov

• Stalingrad

• Zhitomir

U K R A I N E

• Voroshilovgrad

• Astrakhan

NORTHERN
BUKOVINA

• Taganrog

• Rostov-
on-Don

*Caspian
Sea*

arpathians

Mariupol

Azov

• Odessa

CRIMEA

• Kerch

• Maikop

• Mineralnye
Vody

RUMANIA

• Sebastopol

• Yalta

Caucasus

• Kislovodsk

• Makhach
Kala

• Bucharest

Black   Sea

Danube

Vladikavkaz

• Batum

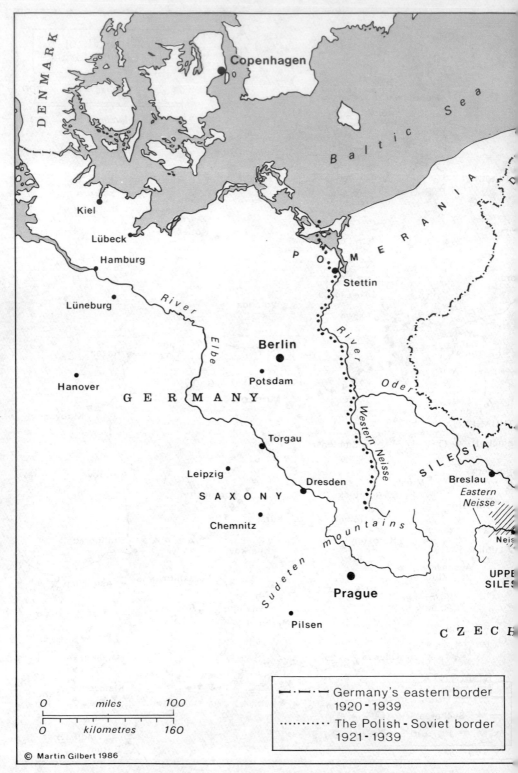

8 The Elbe–Oder–Vistula–Bug region

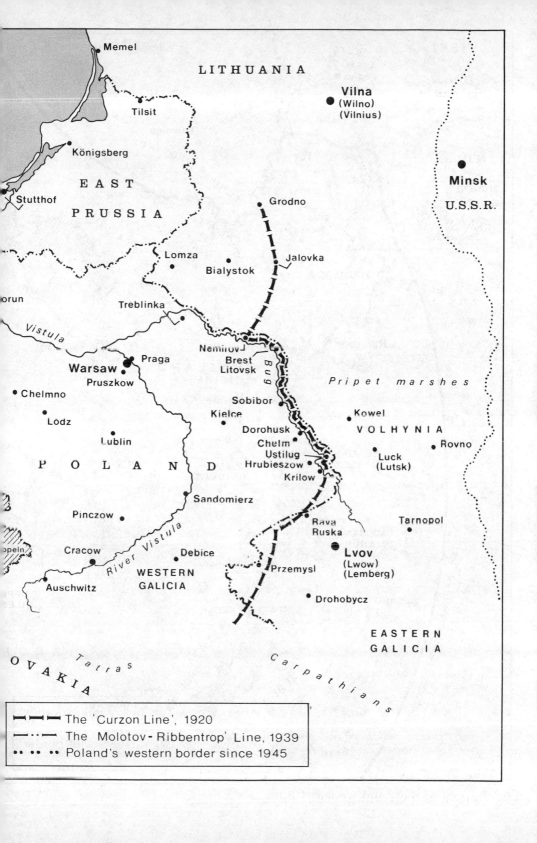

Memel

LITHUANIA

Tilsit

Königsberg

EAST

PRUSSIA

Stutthof

Vilna
(Wilno)
(Vilnius)

Minsk

U.S.S.R.

Grodno

Lomza

Bialystok

Jalovka

Treblinka

Vistula

Nemirov

Brest
Litovsk

Warsaw

Praga

Pruszkow

Chelmno

Pripet marshes

Kowel

Sobibor

Lodz

Kielce

Dorohusk

VOLHYNIA

Lublin

Chelm

Ustilug

Hrubieszow

Luck
(Lutsk)

Rovno

POLAND

Krilow

Sandomierz

Pinczow

Rava
Ruska

Tarnopol

Cracow

Debice

Przemysl

Lvov
(Lwow)
(Lemberg)

Auschwitz

WESTERN
GALICIA

River Vistula

Drohobycz

OVAKIA

Tatras

Carpathians

EASTERN
GALICIA

▬▬▬▬	The 'Curzon Line', 1920
—·—·—	The 'Molotov-Ribbentrop' Line, 1939
• • • •	Poland's western border since 1945

orun

opeln

Bug

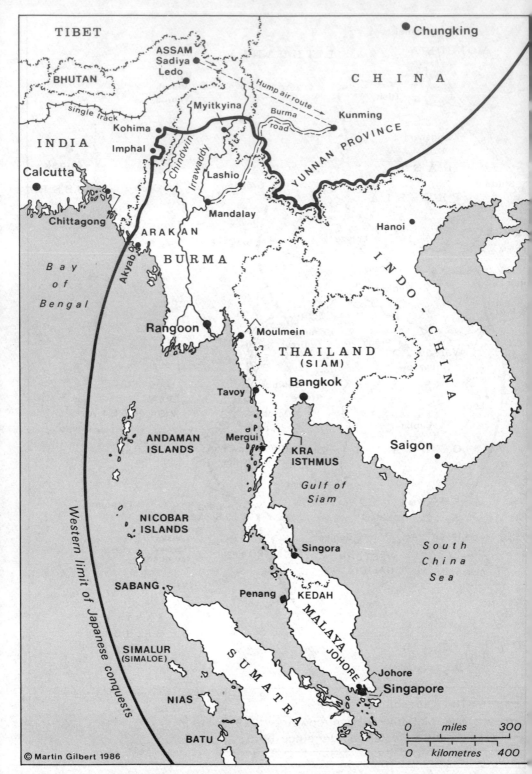

9 Burma, Malaya and western China

MONGOLIA

U.S.S.R.

SAKHALIN

MANCHUKUO

Port Arthur

Sea of Japan

JAPAN

Tokyo

KOREA

Yokohama
Nagoya
Kobe
Hiroshima

Nagasaki

CHINA

TIBET
Himalayas

Chungking

Shanghai

INDIA

FUKIEN

FORMOSA

BURMA

Canton

Hong Kong

Pacific

Ocean

under Japanese occupation

Rangoon

SIAM

Bangkok

INDO-CHINA

Saigon

Lingayen
CORREGIDOR
Bataan

LUZON

Manila

PHILIPPINE
ISLANDS

CAROLINE
ISLANDS

Kra

South
China
Sea

CEBU

Leyte Gulf

TRUK

MALAYA

Singapore

MINDANAO

SUMATRA

BORNEO

NEW GUINEA

Bismarck
Sea

Rabaul

Java
Sea

DUTCH EAST INDIES

AMBOINA

Dutch

British

Limit of Japanese conquests

JAVA

TIMOR

Indian

Ocean

Darwin

Coral
Sea

0   miles   1000

0   kilometres   1500

© Martin Gilbert 1986

AUSTRALIA

10   The Western Pacific

11   Great Britain

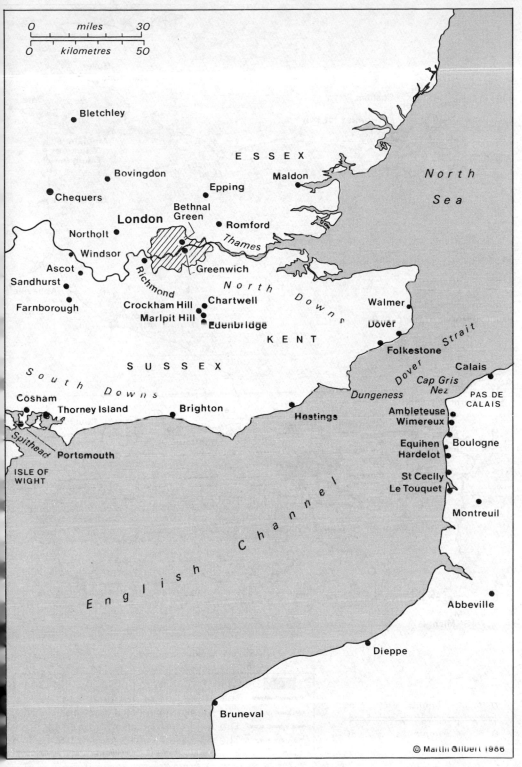

Scale: miles 0 — 30, kilometres 0 — 50

Bletchley

ESSEX

Bovingdon

Chequers

Epping

Maldon

North Sea

London

Bethnal Green

Northolt

Romford

Thames

Windsor

Greenwich

Ascot

Richmond

North Downs

Sandhurst

Crockham Hill

Chartwell

Walmer

Farnborough

Marlpit Hill

Edenbridge

Dover

KENT

Folkestone

Dover Strait

South Downs

SUSSEX

Cosham

Thorney Island

Brighton

Hastings

Dungeness

Cap Gris Nez

Calais

PAS DE CALAIS

Spithead

Portsmouth

Ambleteuse

Wimereux

ISLE OF WIGHT

Equihen

Hardelot

Boulogne

St Cecily

Le Touquet

English Channel

Montreuil

Abbeville

Dieppe

Bruneval

© Martin Gilbert 1986

Map Labels

Dover
Folkestone
Strait of Dover
Calais
Cap Gris Nez
Dungeness
Ambleteuse
Wimereux
Boulogne

Southampton
Cosham
THORNEY ISLAND
Portsmouth

Beachy
Head

Le Touquet

Abbeville

English Channel

Dieppe

Cherbourg
COTENTIN PENINSULA
UTAH
OMAHA
Arromanches
Courseulles
Canal de Caen
Le Havre
Rouen
Honfleur
Hamel
Blay
Bayeux
Caen
Tilly
Villers Bocage
Falaise
Orne
Seine

N O R M A N D Y

Mont
St Michel

	Allied forces by midnight, 6 June 1944
	The Allied line on 18 June 1944
	The Allied line on 18 July 1944
	The Allied line on 13 August 1944
	The Allied line on 16 August 1944

0 miles 50

0 kilometres 80

© Martin Gilbert 1986

13   The English Channel from Cherbourg to Calais

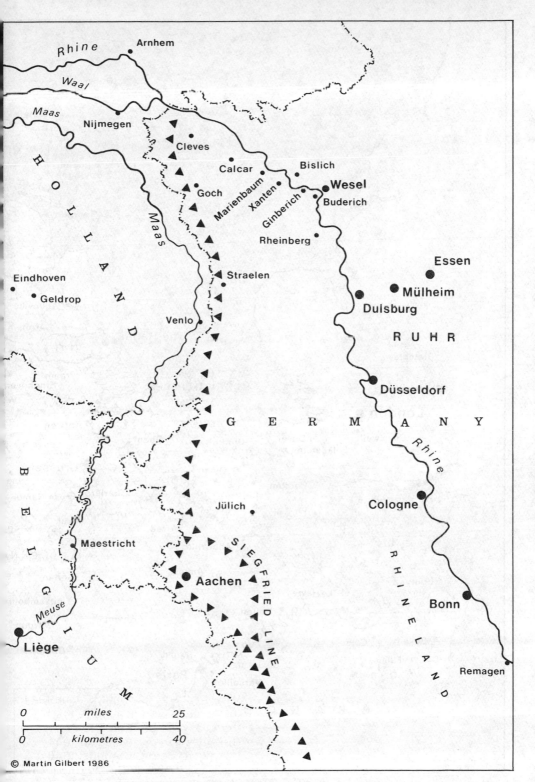

14 The Rhine from Arnhem to Remagen

© Martin Gilbert 1986

North Sea

FRISIAN ISLANDS

FRIESLAND

Rhine Arnhem

The Hague HOLLAN

Rotterdam

Eindhoven

WALCHEREN

Flushing Ve

Ostend Antwerp

Bletchley

Chequers

London

Chartwell

Dover Dunkirk Ghent Louvain

Folkestone Calais Brussels

St Omer Scheldt B Liè

E

Boulogne Ploegsteert L Charleroi Namur

Armentieres Lille G

Portsmouth I

Arras Givet U Bastog

English Channel Abbeville M

A R D E N N E

Dieppe Amiens

Cherbourg Sedan

Arromanches Le Havre Luxembourg

COTENTIN Rouen Verdun

Bayeux Caen Rheims

Falaise Châlons

NORMANDY Neuilly

St.Germain Paris

Versailles Seine

F R A N C E

Sens

© Martin Gilbert 1986

15   From Normandy to the Baltic

Index

Index

Compiled by the author